AVENGERS VS. X-MEN. Contains material originally published in magazine form as AVENGERS VS. X-MEN #0-12; POINT ONE #1; AVX: VS #1-6; AVENGERS VS. X-MEN: INFINITE #1, #6 and #10. First printing 2012. ISBN# 978-0-7851-6317-6. Published by MARVEL WORLDWIDE, INC., a subsidiary of MARVEL ENTERTAINMENT, LLC. OFFICE OF PUBLICATION: 135 West 50th Street, New York, NY 10020. Copyright © 2012 Marvel Characters, Inc. All rights reserved. $75.00 per copy in the U.S. and $85.00 in Canada (GST #R127032852); Canadian Agreement #40668537. All characters featured in this issue and the distinctive names and likenesses thereof, and all related indicia are trademarks of Marvel Characters, Inc. No similarity between any of the names, characters, persons, and/or institutions in this magazine with those of any living or dead person or institution is intended, and any such similarity which may exist is purely coincidental. **Printed in the U.S.A.** ALAN FINE, EVP - Office of the President, Marvel Worldwide, Inc. and EVP & CMO Marvel Characters B.V.; DAN BUCKLEY, Publisher & President - Print, Animation & Digital Divisions; JOE QUESADA, Chief Creative Officer; TOM BREVOORT, SVP of Publishing; DAVID BOGART, SVP of Operations & Procurement, Publishing; RUWAN JAYATILLEKE, SVP & Associate Publisher, Publishing; C.B. CEBULSKI, SVP of Creator & Content Development; DAVID GABRIEL, SVP of Publishing Sales & Circulation; MICHAEL PASCIULLO, SVP of Brand Planning & Communications; JIM O'KEEFE, VP of Operations & Logistics; DAN CARR, Executive Director of Publishing Technology; SUSAN CRESPI, Editorial Operations Manager; ALEX MORALES, Publishing Operations Manager; STAN LEE, Chairman Emeritus. For information regarding advertising in Marvel Comics or on Marvel.com, please contact Niza Disla, Director of Marvel Partnerships, at ndisla@marvel.com. For Marvel subscription inquiries, please call 800-217-9158. **Manufactured between 9/10/2012 and 10/22/2012 by R.R. DONNELLEY, INC., SALEM, VA, USA.**

0 9 8 7 6 5 4 3 2 1

STORY

JASON AARON, BRIAN MICHAEL BENDIS, ED BRUBAKER, MATT FRACTION & JONATHAN HICKMAN

POINT ONE #1
WRITER: JEPH LOEB
PENCILER: ED MCGUINNESS
INKER: DEXTER VINES
COLORS: MORRY HOLLOWELL
COVER ART: ADAM KUBERT &
MORRY HOLLOWELL

AVENGERS VS. X-MEN #0
WRITERS: BRIAN MICHAEL BENDIS
(SCARLET WITCH)
& JASON AARON (HOPE)
ARTIST: FRANK CHO
COLOR ART: JASON KEITH
COVER ART: FRANK CHO & JASON KEITH

AVENGERS VS. X-MEN #1
SCRIPT: BRIAN MICHAEL BENDIS
PENCILS: JOHN ROMITA, JR.
INKS: SCOTT HANNA
COLORS: LAURA MARTIN
COVER ART: JIM CHEUNG & JUSTIN PONSOR

AVENGERS VS. X-MEN #2
SCRIPT: JASON AARON
PENCILS: JOHN ROMITA, JR.
INKS: SCOTT HANNA
COLORS: LAURA MARTIN
COVER ART: JIM CHEUNG & LAURA MARTIN

AVENGERS VS. X-MEN #3
SCRIPT: ED BRUBAKER
PENCILS: JOHN ROMITA, JR.
INKS: SCOTT HANNA
COLORS: LAURA MARTIN
COVER ART: JIM CHEUNG & LAURA MARTIN

AVENGERS VS. X-MEN #4
SCRIPT: JONATHAN HICKMAN
PENCILS: JOHN ROMITA, JR.
INKS: SCOTT HANNA
COLORS: LAURA MARTIN
COVER ART: JIM CHEUNG & LAURA MARTIN

AVENGERS VS. X-MEN #5
SCRIPT: MATT FRACTION
PENCILS: JOHN ROMITA, JR.
INKS: SCOTT HANNA
COLORS: LAURA MARTIN
COVER ART: JIM CHEUNG & JUSTIN PONSOR

AVENGERS VS. X-MEN #6
SCRIPT: JONATHAN HICKMAN
PENCILS: OLIVIER COIPEL
INKS: MARK MORALES
COLORS: LAURA MARTIN
COVER ART: JIM CHEUNG & JUSTIN PONSOR

AVENGERS VS. X-MEN #7
SCRIPT: MATT FRACTION
PENCILS: OLIVIER COIPEL
INKS: MARK MORALES
COLORS: LAURA MARTIN
COVER ART: JIM CHEUNG & JUSTIN PONSOR

AVENGERS VS. X-MEN #8
SCRIPT: BRIAN MICHAEL BENDIS
PENCILS: ADAM KUBERT
INKS: JOHN DELL
COLORS: LAURA MARTIN
WITH LARRY MOLINAR
COVER ART: JIM CHEUNG & JUSTIN PONSOR

AVENGERS VS. X-MEN #9
SCRIPT: JASON AARON
PENCILS: ADAM KUBERT
INKS: JOHN DELL
COLORS: LAURA MARTIN
WITH LARRY MOLINAR
COVER ART: JIM CHEUNG,
MARK MORALES & JUSTIN PONSOR

AVENGERS VS. X-MEN #10
SCRIPT: ED BRUBAKER
PENCILS: ADAM KUBERT
INKS: JOHN DELL
COLORS: LAURA MARTIN
WITH LARRY MOLINAR
COVER ART: JIM CHEUNG & JUSTIN PONSOR

AVENGERS VS. X-MEN #11
SCRIPT: BRIAN MICHAEL BENDIS
PENCILS: OLIVIER COIPEL
INKS: MARK MORALES
COLORS: LAURA MARTIN
COVER ART: JIM CHEUNG & JUSTIN PONSOR

AVENGERS VS. X-MEN #12
SCRIPT: JASON AARON
PENCILS: ADAM KUBERT
INKS: JOHN DELL WITH MARK
MORALES & ADAM KUBERT
COLORS: LAURA MARTIN
WITH JUSTIN PONSOR
COVER ART: JIM CHEUNG & JUSTIN PONSOR

LETTERS: CHRIS ELIOPOULOS WITH COMICRAFT'S ALBERT DESCHESNE (POINT ONE)
ASSISTANT EDITORS: JOHN DENNING & JAKE THOMAS
ASSOCIATE EDITOR: LAUREN SANKOVITCH
CONSULTING EDITOR: NICK LOWE   EDITOR: TOM BREVOORT

AVX: VS #1

IRON MAN VS. MAGNETO
WRITER: JASON AARON
ARTIST: ADAM KUBERT
COLOR ARTIST: MORRY HOLLOWELL

THING VS. NAMOR
WRITER: KATHRYN IMMONEN
PENCILS: STUART IMMONEN
INKS: WADE VON GRAWBADGER
COLORS: JIM CHARALAMPIDIS
COVER ART: ADAM KUBERT & LAURA MARTIN

AVX: VS #2

CAPTAIN AMERICA VS. GAMBIT
WRITER/PENCILS: STEVE McNIVEN
INKS: JOHN DELL
COLORS: MORRY HOLLOWELL

SPIDER-MAN VS. COLOSSUS
WRITER: KIERON GILLEN
ARTIST: SALVADOR LARROCA
COLOR ARTIST: JIM CHARALAMPIDIS
COVER ART: SALVADOR LARROCA & ROCHELLE ROSENBERG

AVX: VS #3

THING VS. COLOSSUS
WRITER: JEPH LOEB
PENCILS: ED McGUINNESS
INKS: DEXTER VINES
COLORS: MORRY HOLLOWELL

BLACK WIDOW VS. MAGIK
WRITER: CHRISTOPHER YOST
PENCILS: TERRY DODSON
INKS: RACHEL DODSON
COLORS: GURU EFX
COVER ART: ED McGUINNESS & CHRIS SOTOMAYOR

AVX: VS #4

DAREDEVIL VS. PSYLOCKE
WRITER: RICK REMENDER
ARTIST: BRANDON PETERSON

THOR VS. EMMA FROST
WRITER/ARTIST: KAARE ANDREWS
COVER ART: BRANDON PETERSON

AVX: VS #5

HAWKEYE VS. ANGEL
WRITER: MATT FRACTION
PENCILS: LEINIL FRANCIS YU
INKS: GERRY ALANGUILAN
COLORS: SUNNY GHO

BLACK PANTHER VS. STORM
WRITER: JASON AARON
ARTIST: TOM RANEY
COLOR ARTIST: JIM CHARALAMPIDIS
COVER ART: LEINIL FRANCIS YU & MARTE GRACIA

AVX: VS #6

HOPE VS. SCARLET WITCH
WRITER: KIERON GILLEN
PENCILS: JIM CHEUNG
INKS: MARK MORALES, JIM CHEUNG & MARK ROSLYN
COLORS: DAVID CURIEL

CYCLOPS VS. CAPTAIN AMERICA
WRITER: BRIAN MICHAEL BENDIS
ARTIST: JIM MAHFOOD

AVX: SCIENCE BATTLE!
WRITER: KATHERYN IMMONEN
PENCILS: STUART IMMONEN
INKS: WADE VON GRAWBADGER
COLORS: MARTE GRACIA

CAPTAIN AMERICA VS. HAVOK
ARTIST: MIKE DEODATO
COLOR ARTIST: RAIN BEREDO

RED HULK VS. DOMINO
WRITER/PENCILS: ED McGUINNESS
INKS: MARK MORALES
COLORS: BRIAN REBER

TOAD VS. JARVIS
WRITER: CHRISTOPHER HASTINGS
ARTIST: JACOB CHABOT

SPIDER-WOMAN VS. X-WOMEN (KINDA)
WRITER: JEPH LOEB
ARTIST: ART ADAMS
COLOR ARTIST: MARTE GRACIA

IRON FIST VS. ICEMAN
WRITER: JASON AARON
ARTIST: RAMÓN PÉREZ
COLOR ARTIST: JORDIE BELLAIRE

SQUIRREL GIRL VS. PIXIE
WRITER: DAN SLOTT
ARTIST: KATIE COOK
COVER ART: JIM CHEUNG & JUSTIN PONSOR

LETTERS: VC'S JOE CARAMAGNA WITH COMICRAFT'S ALBERT DESCHESNE (THING VS. COLOSSUS)
ASSISTANT EDITOR: JORDAN D. WHITE
EDITOR: NICK LOWE

INFINITE COMICS #1
WRITER: MARK WAID
ARTIST: STUART IMMONEN
COLOR ARTIST: MARTE GRACIA

INFINITE COMICS #6 & #10
CO-PLOT & SCRIPT: MARK WAID
CO-PLOT & BREAKDOWNS: YVES BIGEREL
PENCILS & INKS: CARLO BARBERI (#6) & REILLY BROWN (#10)
COLORS: MARTE GRACIA WITH CHRIS SOTOMAYOR (#10)

LETTERER: CHRIS ELIOPOULOS
COVER: JOE QUESADA & RICHARD ISANOVE
ASSISTANT EDITOR: JORDAN D. WHITE
CONSULTING EDITOR: TOM BREVOORT
EDITOR: NICK LOWE

SPECIAL THANKS TO TIM SMITH III & MANNY MEDEROS

COLLECTION EDITOR: JENNIFER GRÜNWALD ASSISTANT EDITORS: ALEX STARBUCK & NELSON RIBEIRO
EDITOR, SPECIAL PROJECTS: MARK D. BEAZLEY SENIOR EDITOR, SPECIAL PROJECTS: JEFF YOUNGQUIST
SENIOR VICE PRESIDENT OF SALES: DAVID GABRIEL SVP OF BRAND PLANNING & COMMUNICATIONS: MICHAEL PASCIULLO
BOOK DESIGN: JEFF POWELL

EDITOR IN CHIEF: AXEL ALONSO CHIEF CREATIVE OFFICER: JOE QUESADA
PUBLISHER: DAN BUCKLEY EXECUTIVE PRODUCER: ALAN FINE

INTRODUCTION

A bit of a confession. Or perhaps a case of full disclosure: I haven't the slightest idea what I'm doing. Not in the figurative sense, at least. In the literal sense, sure. I'm writing a forward for a comic-book crossover of gigantic proportions. But really, what the hell am I doing? I've never done this before (that's a total lie. I've written one previous forward for Ed Brubaker, he just doesn't know it, nor has he asked me to do so — but it's ready when you are, Ed!). So why me? What qualifies yours truly to write the lead-in to Marvel's biggest story of the year? For one, I think traveling the globe engaging in the age-old battle of good vs. evil while wearing what ultimately boils down to little underwear is a pretty big qualifier. And as long as we're being honest with each other, who else was going to write this, Kevin Smith?

Back before I stepped in the ring for a living, I would spend most of my time crank-calling my local comic shops and asking them who would win in a fight: the Hulk or the Thing? This would get the biggest reactions out of All American Comics store manager Kevin O'Brien — which is doubly hilarious since I worked there at the time — and it became a running gag. There was just something about the famous throwdown that drew me to the idea of two good guys slugging it out. Shades of gray are just that much more interesting. That's what makes this book for me. You have the two biggest and most powerful teams in the Marvel Universe going to war with each other. This isn't good guy vs. bad guy. This is shades of gray at its finest. What happens when two powerhouse teams believe so strongly in their cause? Who's in the right? They're all good guys, right? Is it possible for heroes to act like villains and vice versa?

This is fantasy warfare at its finest, but don't just take my word for it. The creative team assembled to handle the monumental task of taking you on this ride is chock-full of heavy hitters just like the two teams pitted against each other. Arguably, we have gathered the best writers in the current comic-book landscape — Brian Bendis, Jonathan Hickman, Matt Fraction — plus Ed Brubaker and Jason Aaron's beard. Writers who have time and again caused me to scream out loud on airplanes and in public places with their masterful storytelling. Artists — like John Romita Jr., Olivier Coipel and Adam Kubert — who frequently get me to do double and triple takes at breathtaking splash pages and beautifully drawn panels of characters I feel like I've known since childhood. Hell, we even have the best colorist — Laura Martin — and letterer — Chris Eliopoulos — for your reading enjoyment.

Something the masses never thought they would have seen lies within these pages. Marvel's biggest heroes at each other's throats brought to you by an assembly of Marvel's greatest creative team. This is Abe Lincoln vs. George Washington. Muhammad Ali in his prime vs. a young Mike Tyson. CM Punk vs. Stone Cold Steve Austin (sorry, I had to). This is everything that's cool about comics. If you're a diehard fan, or you're reading for the first time: Get lost in this once-in-a-lifetime story, you won't be disappointed. Get to reading...

Phil Brooks
AKA CM Punk
WWE Champion

It's not surprising that CM Punk cites the radical "Rowdy" Roddy Piper as a childhood influence. After all, Punk is the embodiment of the anti-establishment, whose skill at igniting verbal "pipe bombs" is rivaled only by Hot Rod himself.

Punk even looks the part of rebel with his too-numerous-to-count tattoos and body piercings. Yet he waxes way more philosophical than his exterior might suggest, and has shown a diverse set of interests that include ghost hunting, G.I. Joe and the "Straight Edge" movement — a subculture that rejects the use of drugs, alcohol and a dependency lifestyle. Punk's only bad habit: his addiction to competition.

His in-ring repertoire is an assimilation of fighting styles, all of which were put on full display during his debut in The Land of the Extreme in 2006. Since then, Punk has added many accomplishments to his considerable résumé — including the ECW, WWE, World Heavyweight, World Tag Team and Intercontinental Championships.

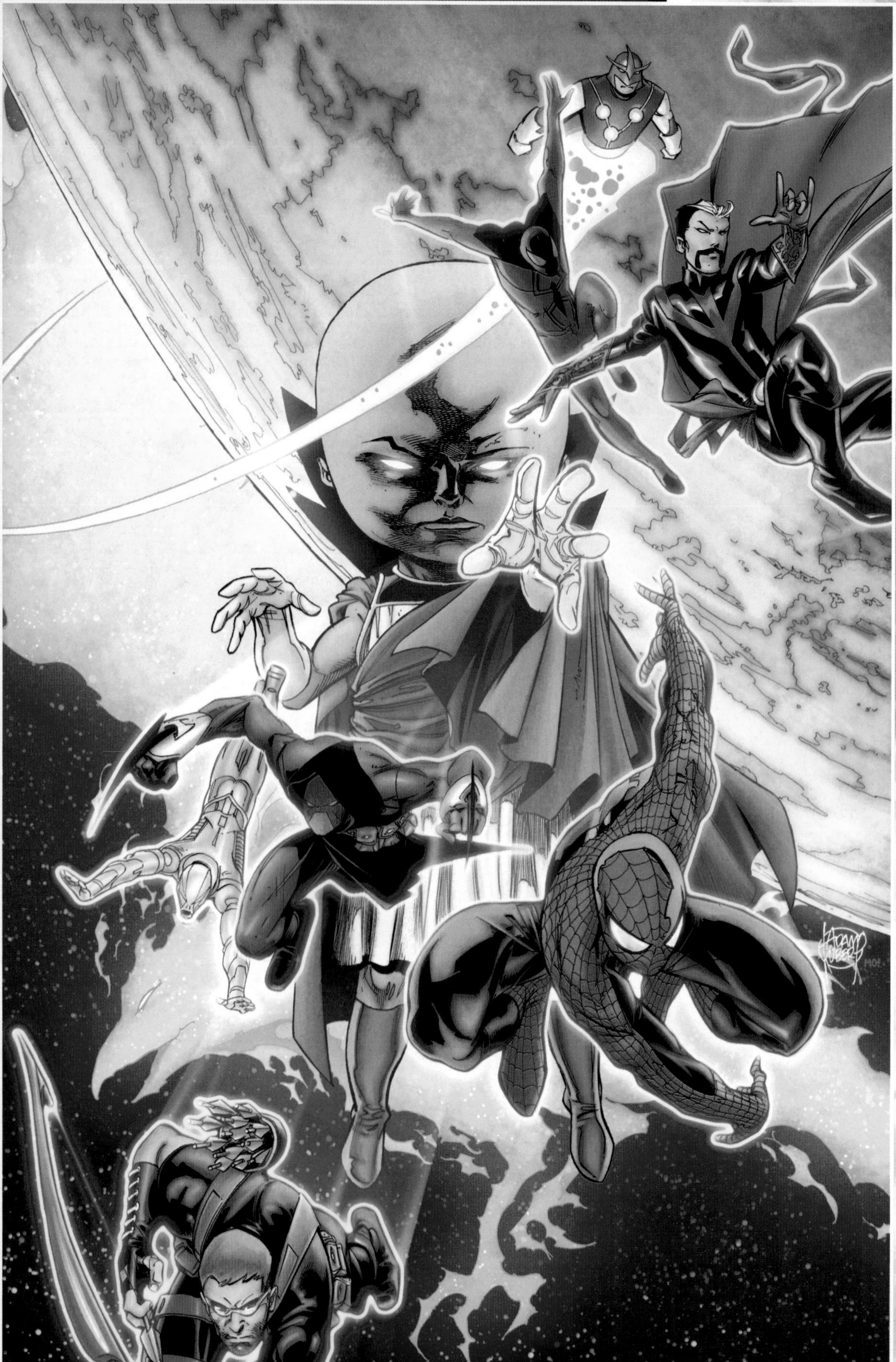

POINT ONE #1

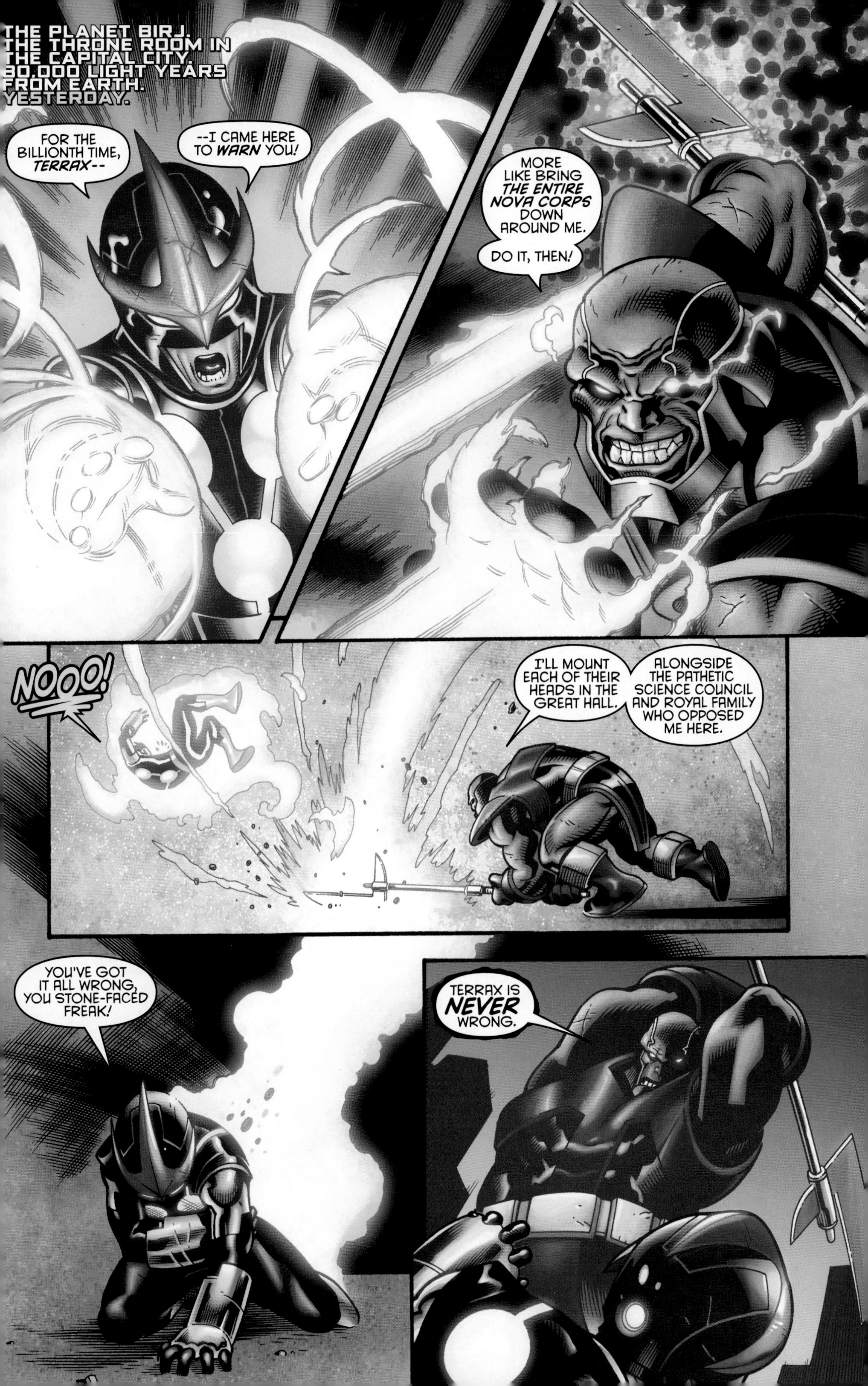
THE PLANET BIRJ. THE THRONE ROOM IN THE CAPITAL CITY. 30,000 LIGHT YEARS FROM EARTH. YESTERDAY.
FOR THE BILLIONTH TIME, TERRAX--
--I CAME HERE TO WARN YOU!
MORE LIKE BRING THE ENTIRE NOVA CORPS DOWN AROUND ME.
DO IT, THEN!
NOOO!
I'LL MOUNT EACH OF THEIR HEADS IN THE GREAT HALL.
ALONGSIDE THE PATHETIC SCIENCE COUNCIL AND ROYAL FAMILY WHO OPPOSED ME HERE.
YOU'VE GOT IT ALL WRONG, YOU STONE-FACED FREAK!
TERRAX IS NEVER WRONG.

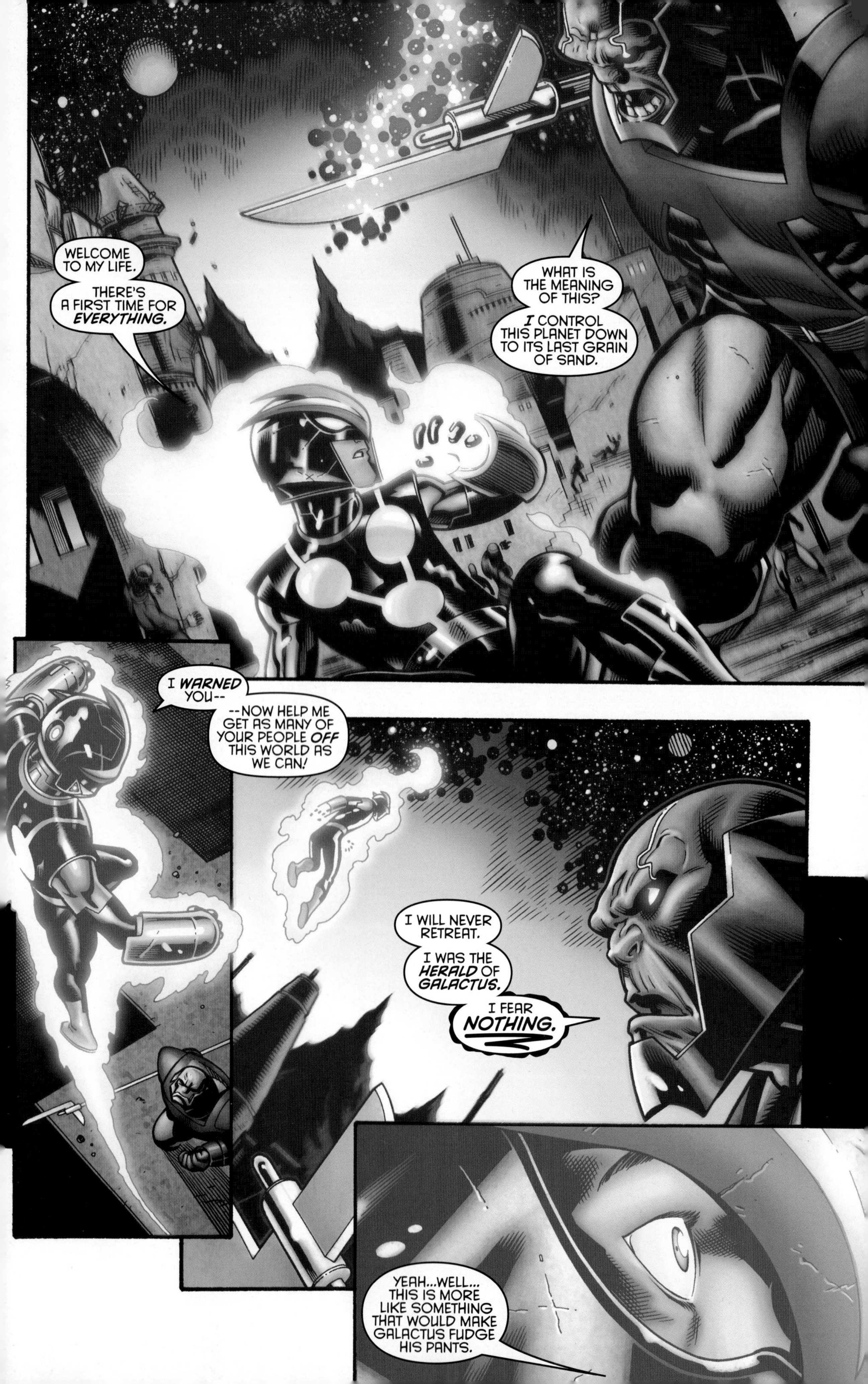
WELCOME TO MY LIFE.
THERE'S A FIRST TIME FOR *EVERYTHING.*
WHAT IS THE MEANING OF THIS?
I CONTROL THIS PLANET DOWN TO ITS LAST GRAIN OF SAND.
I *WARNED* YOU--
--NOW HELP ME GET AS MANY OF YOUR PEOPLE *OFF* THIS WORLD AS WE CAN!
I WILL NEVER RETREAT.
I WAS THE *HERALD* OF *GALACTUS.*
I FEAR *NOTHING.*
YEAH...WELL... THIS IS MORE LIKE SOMETHING THAT WOULD MAKE GALACTUS FUDGE HIS PANTS.

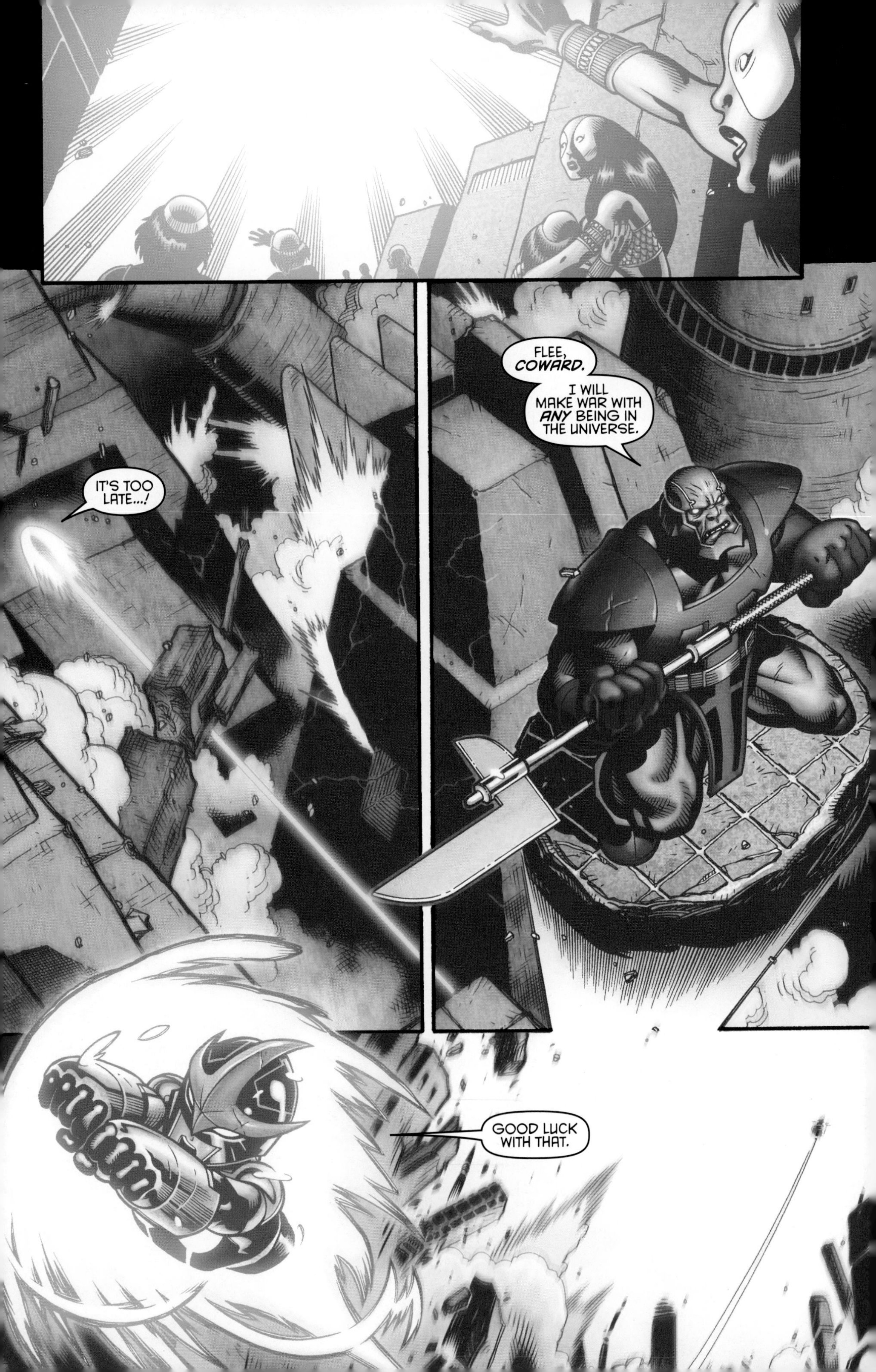
IT'S TOO LATE...!
FLEE, COWARD.
I WILL MAKE WAR WITH ANY BEING IN THE UNIVERSE.
GOOD LUCK WITH THAT.

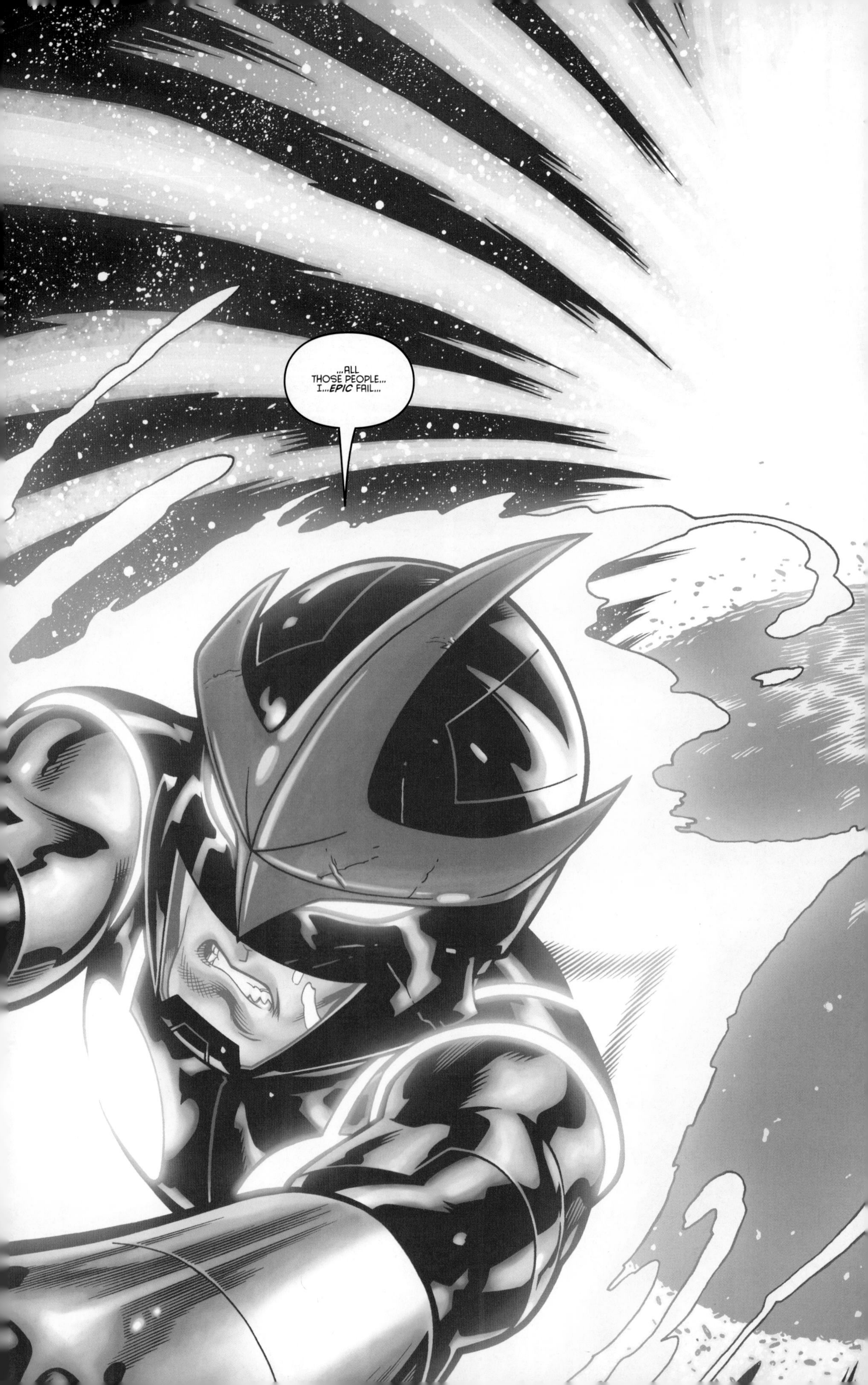
...ALL THOSE PEOPLE... I...*EPIC* FAIL...

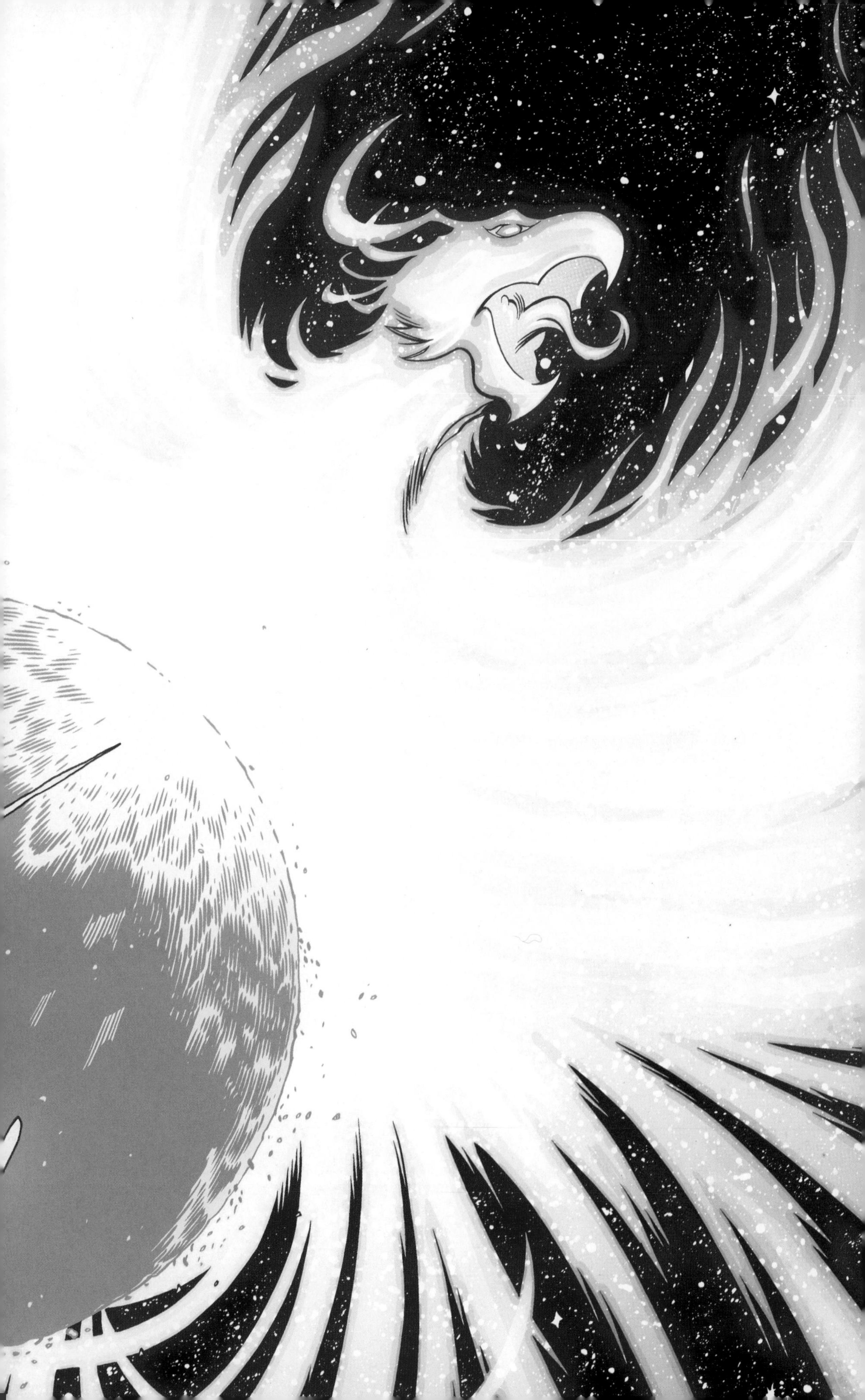

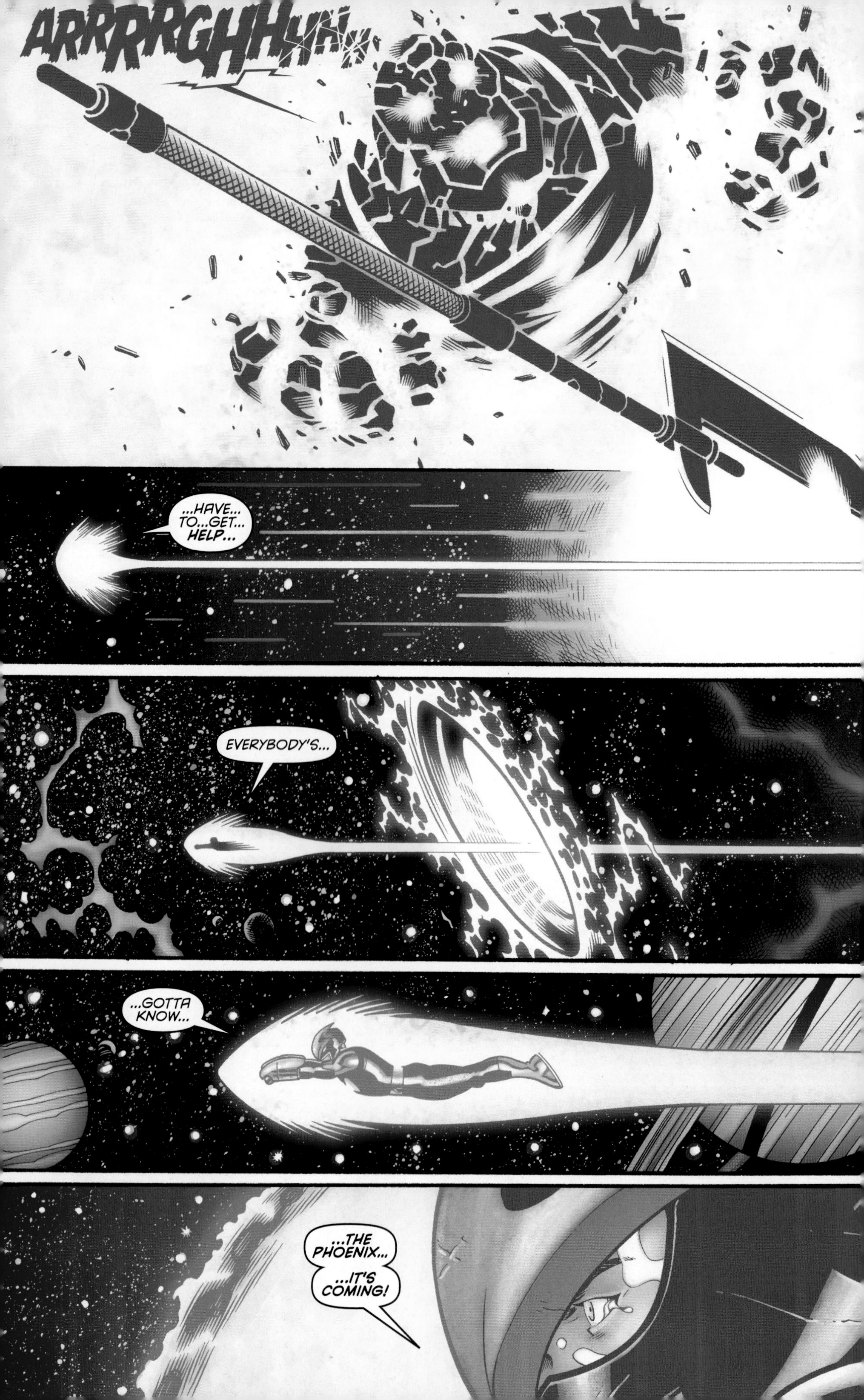
ARRRRGHH
...HAVE... TO...GET... HELP...
EVERYBODY'S...
...GOTTA KNOW...
...THE PHOENIX...
...IT'S COMING!

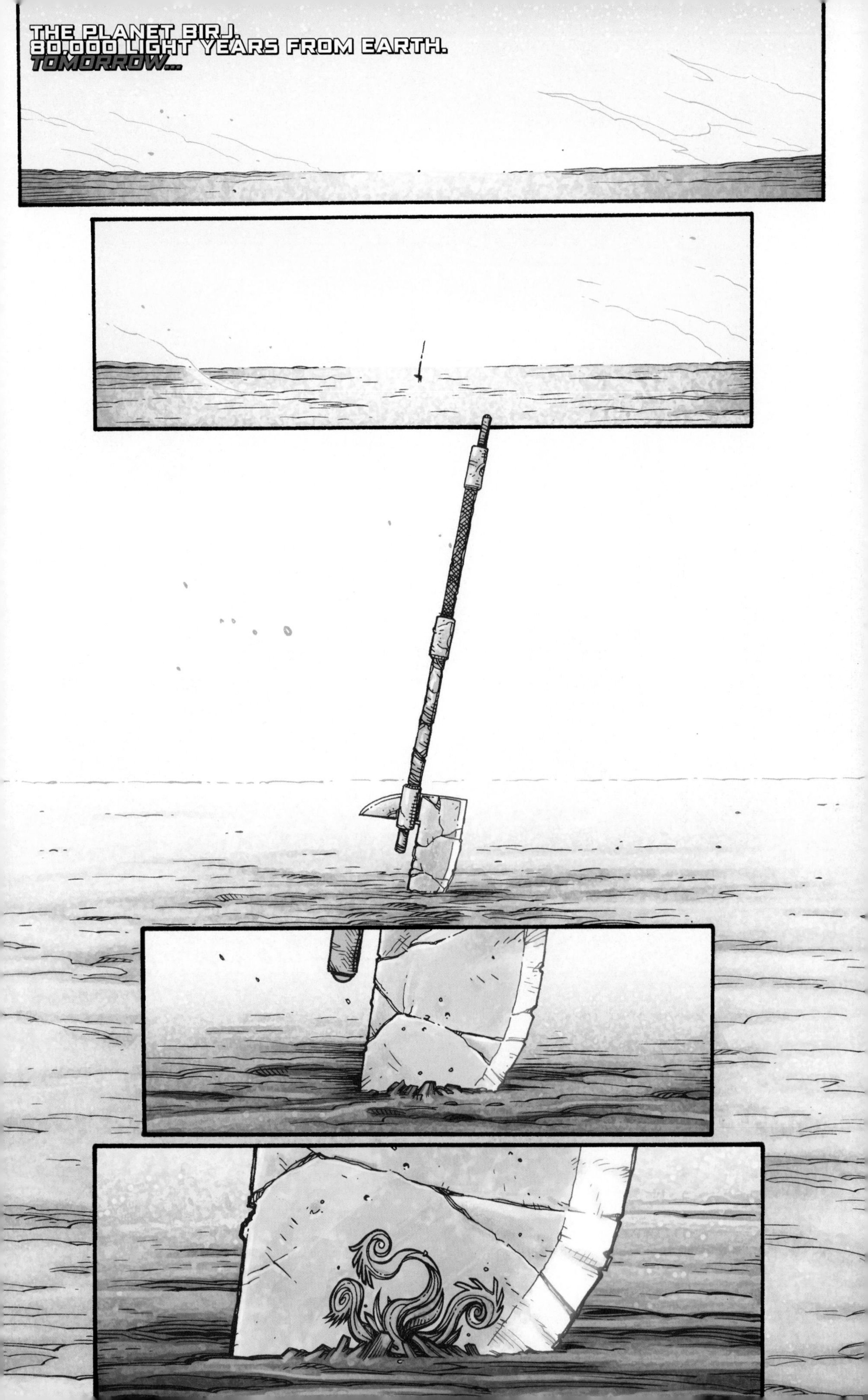
THE PLANET BIRJ.
80,000 LIGHT YEARS FROM EARTH.
TOMORROW...

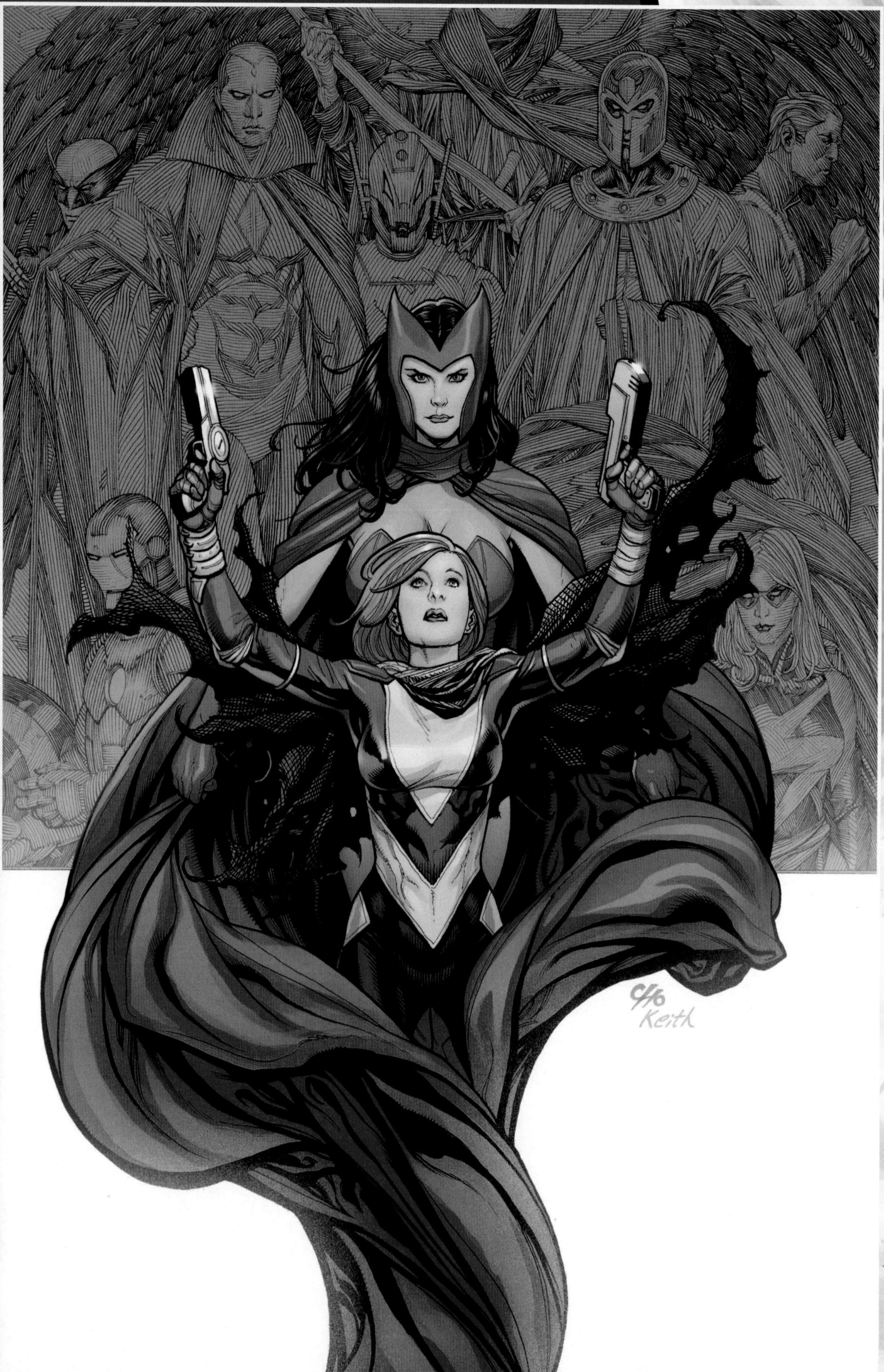

AVENGERS VS. X-MEN #0

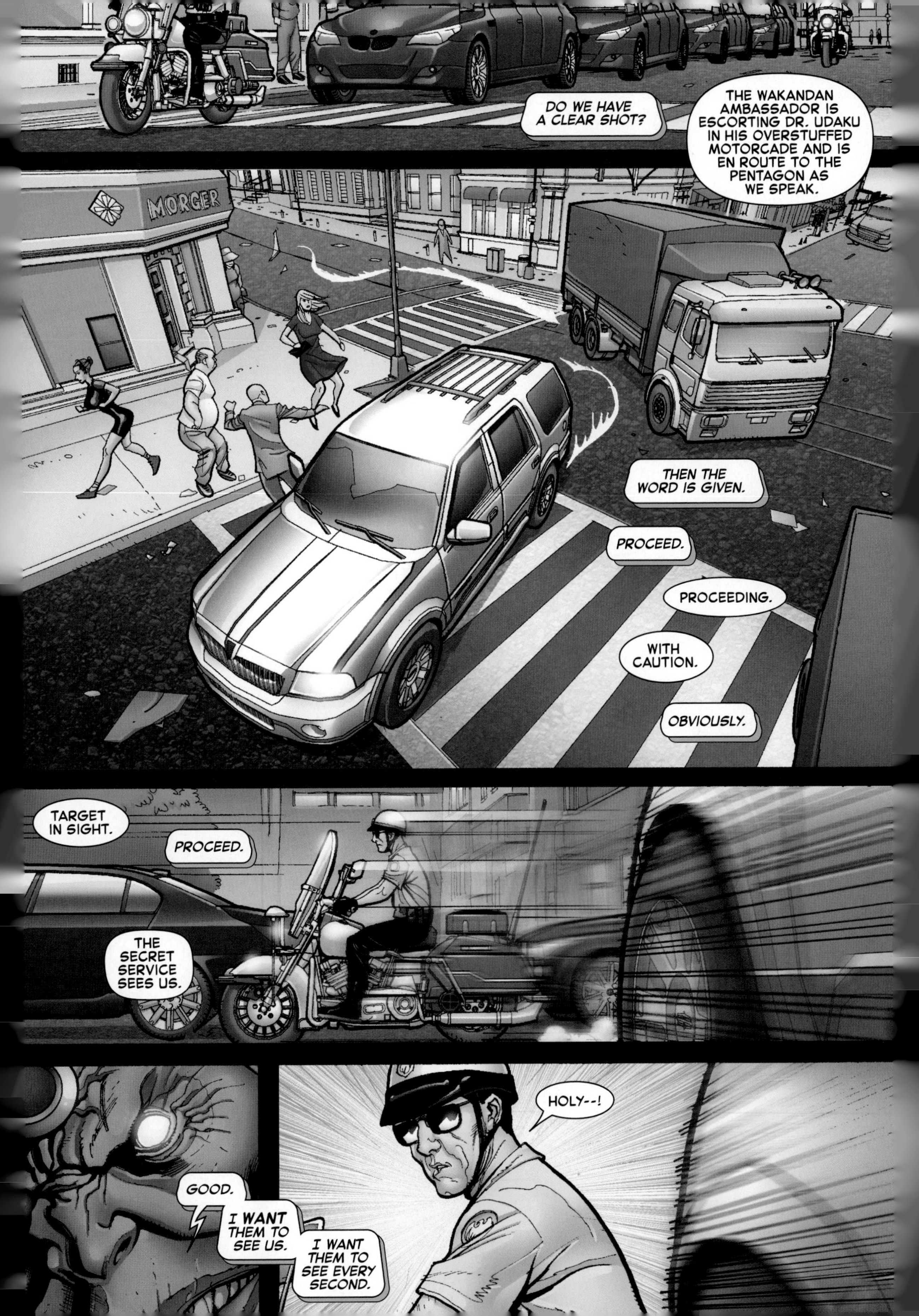
DO WE HAVE A CLEAR SHOT?
THE WAKANDAN AMBASSADOR IS ESCORTING DR. UDAKU IN HIS OVERSTUFFED MOTORCADE AND IS EN ROUTE TO THE PENTAGON AS WE SPEAK.
MORGER
THEN THE WORD IS GIVEN.
PROCEED.
PROCEEDING.
WITH CAUTION.
OBVIOUSLY.
TARGET IN SIGHT.
PROCEED.
THE SECRET SERVICE SEES US.
HOLY--!
GOOD.
I WANT THEM TO SEE US.
I WANT THEM TO SEE EVERY SECOND.

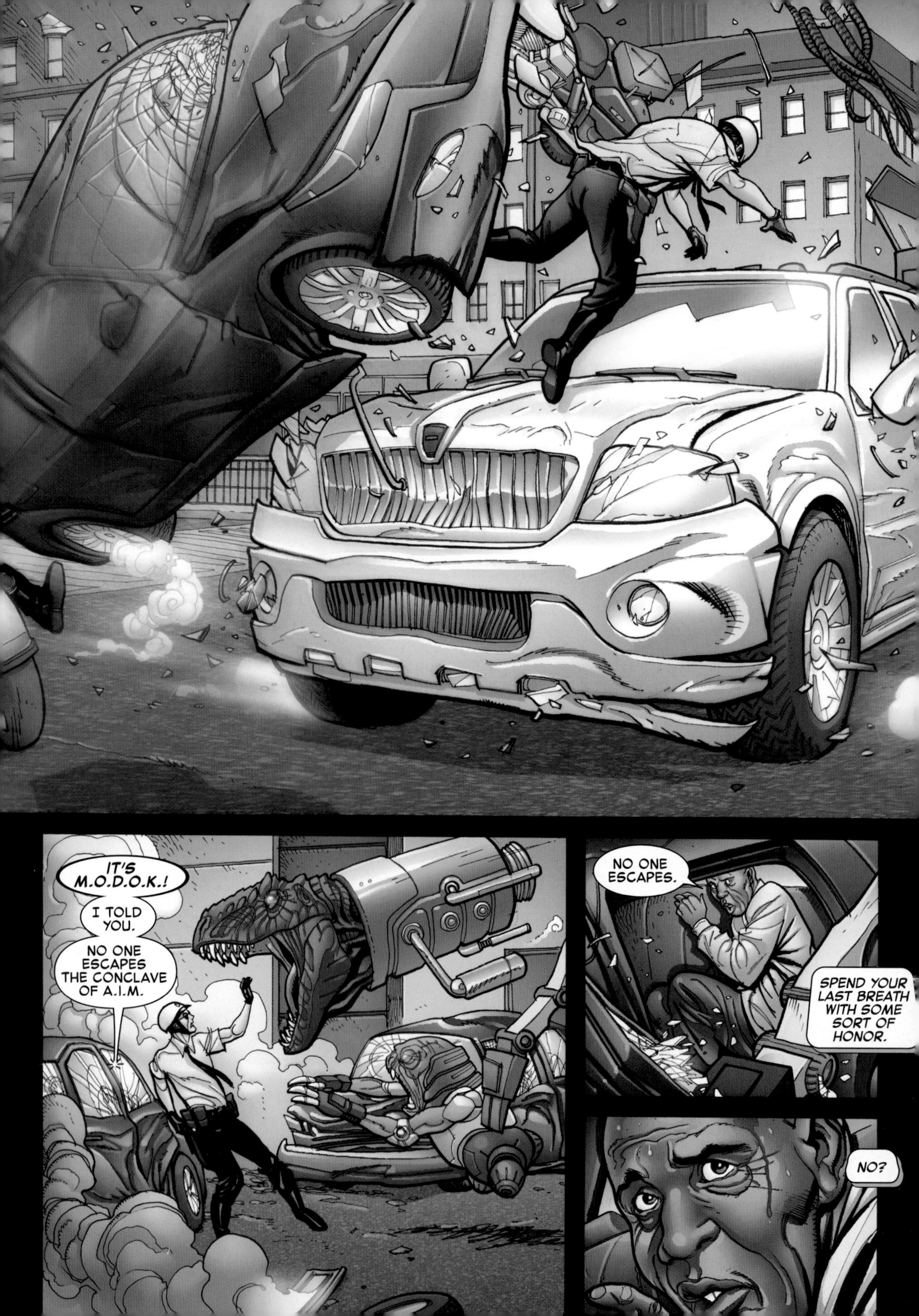
IT'S M.O.D.O.K.!
I TOLD YOU.
NO ONE ESCAPES THE CONCLAVE OF A.I.M.
NO ONE ESCAPES.
SPEND YOUR LAST BREATH WITH SOME SORT OF HONOR.
NO?

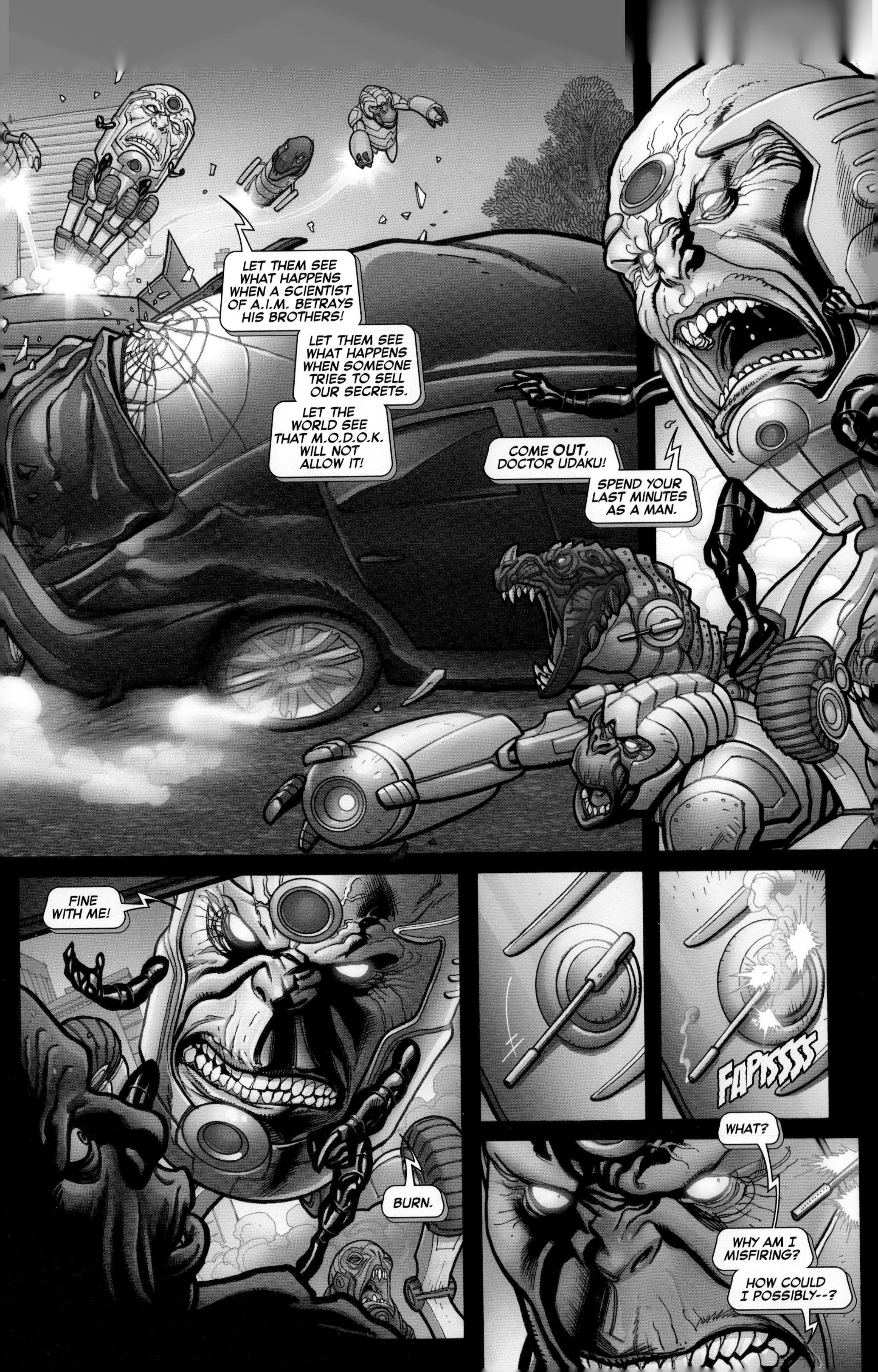
LET THEM SEE WHAT HAPPENS WHEN A SCIENTIST OF A.I.M. BETRAYS HIS BROTHERS!
LET THEM SEE WHAT HAPPENS WHEN SOMEONE TRIES TO SELL OUR SECRETS.
LET THE WORLD SEE THAT M.O.D.O.K. WILL NOT ALLOW IT!
COME OUT, DOCTOR UDAKU!
SPEND YOUR LAST MINUTES AS A MAN.
FINE WITH ME!
BURN.
FAPSSSS
WHAT?
WHY AM I MISFIRING?
HOW COULD I POSSIBLY--?

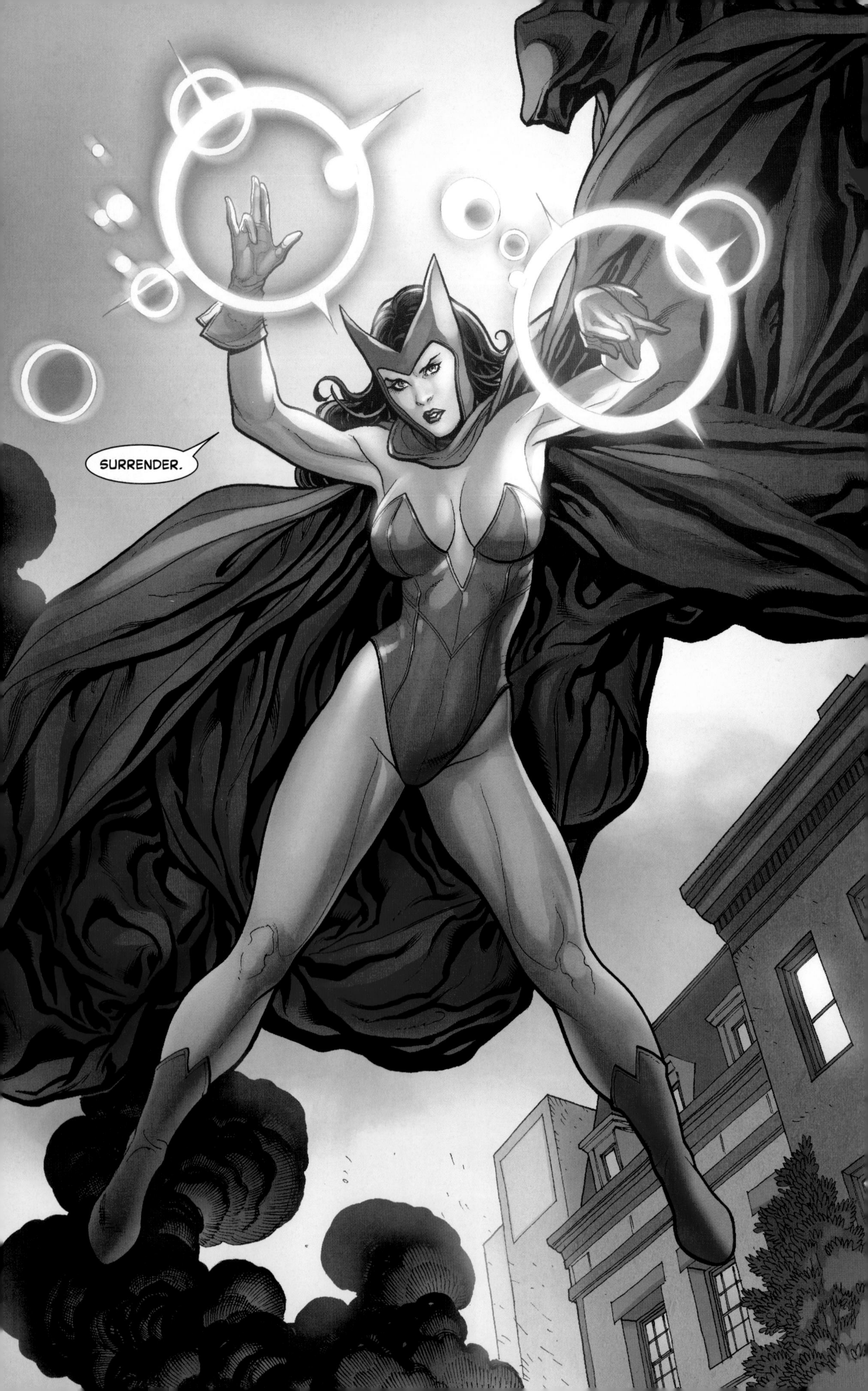
SURRENDER.

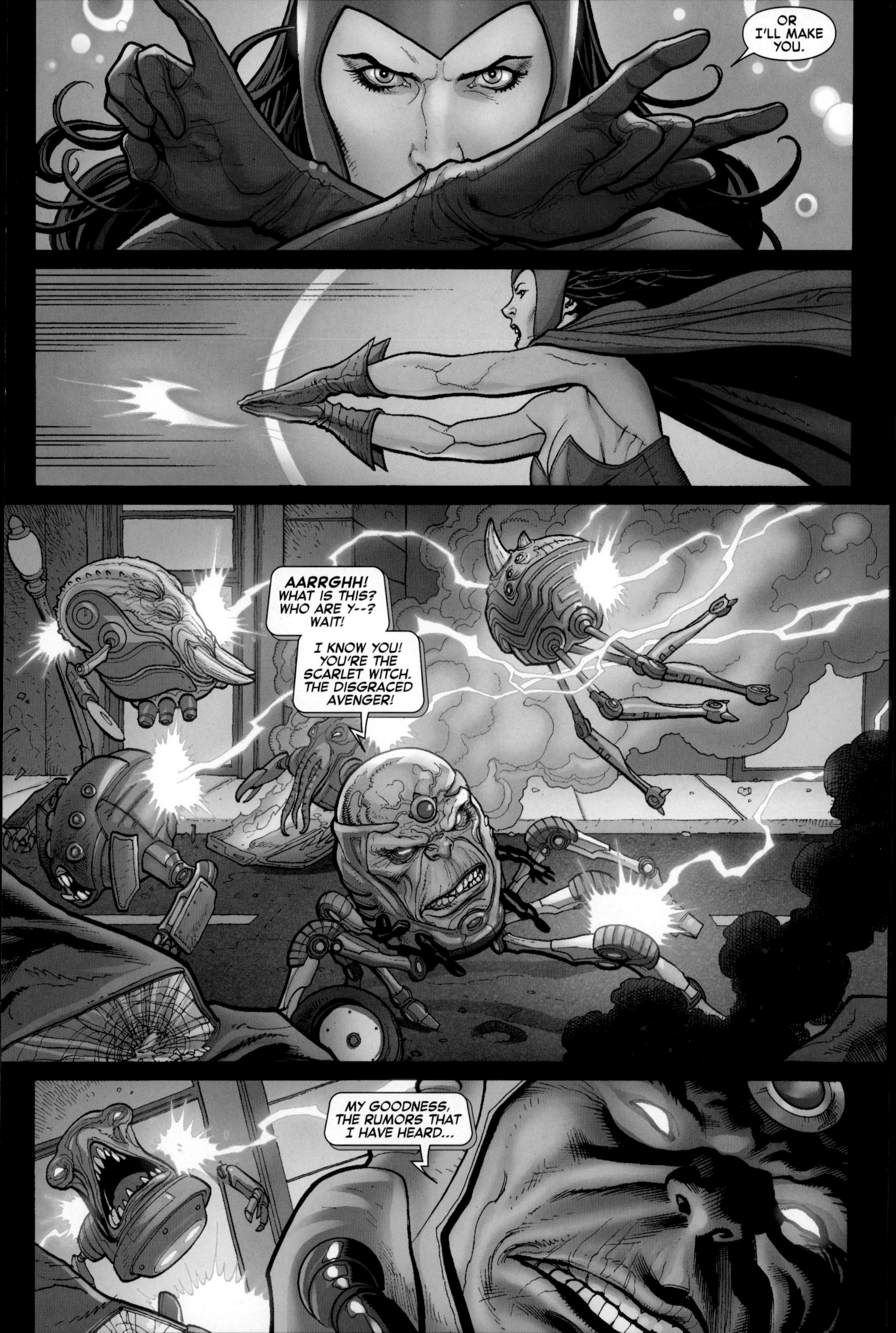
OR I'LL MAKE YOU.
AARRGHH! WHAT IS THIS? WHO ARE Y--? WAIT!
I KNOW YOU! YOU'RE THE SCARLET WITCH. THE DISGRACED AVENGER!
MY GOODNESS, THE RUMORS THAT I HAVE HEARD...

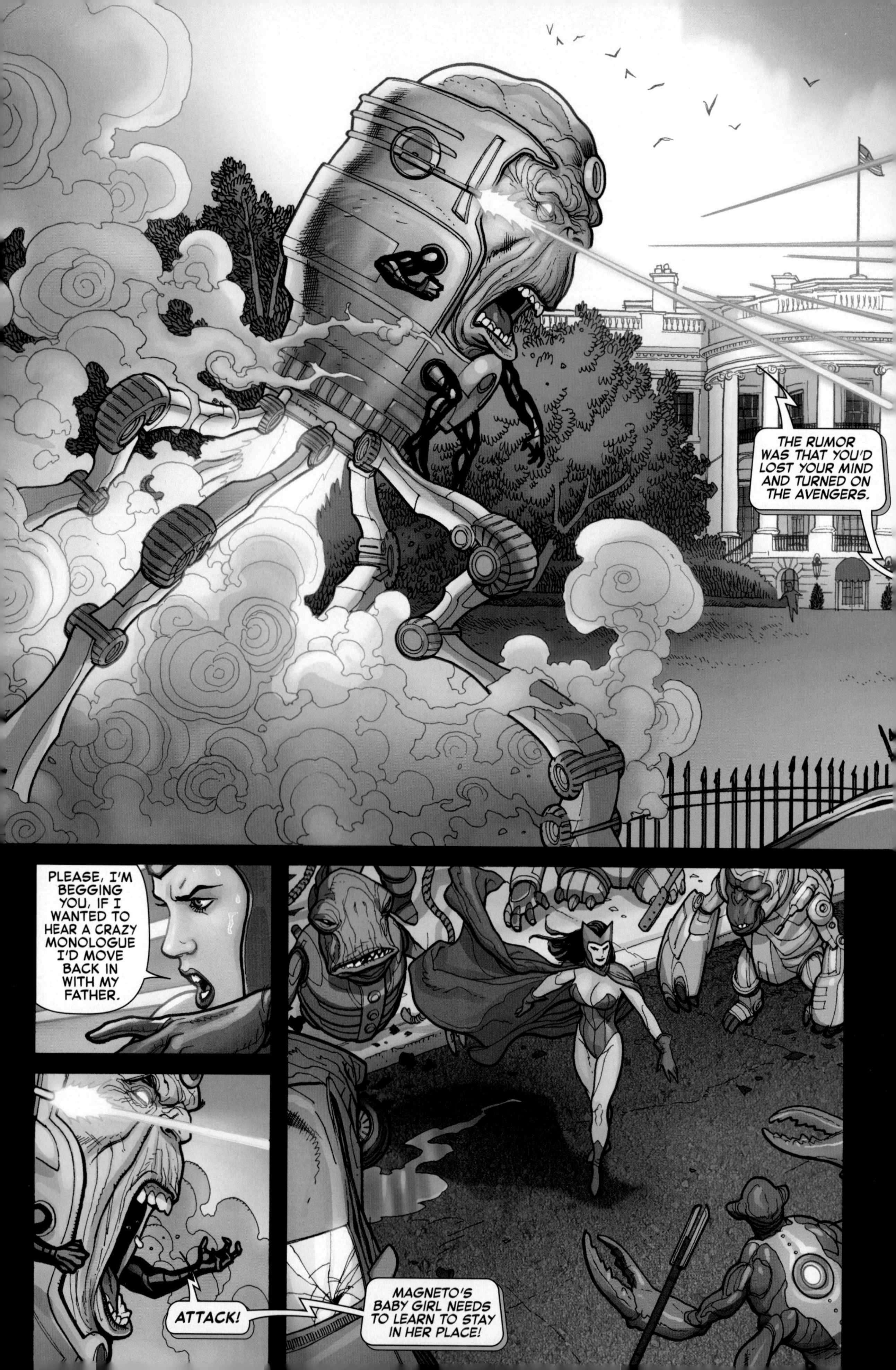

THE RUMOR WAS THAT YOU'D LOST YOUR MIND AND TURNED ON THE AVENGERS.
PLEASE, I'M BEGGING YOU, IF I WANTED TO HEAR A CRAZY MONOLOGUE I'D MOVE BACK IN WITH MY FATHER.
ATTACK!
MAGNETO'S BABY GIRL NEEDS TO LEARN TO STAY IN HER PLACE!

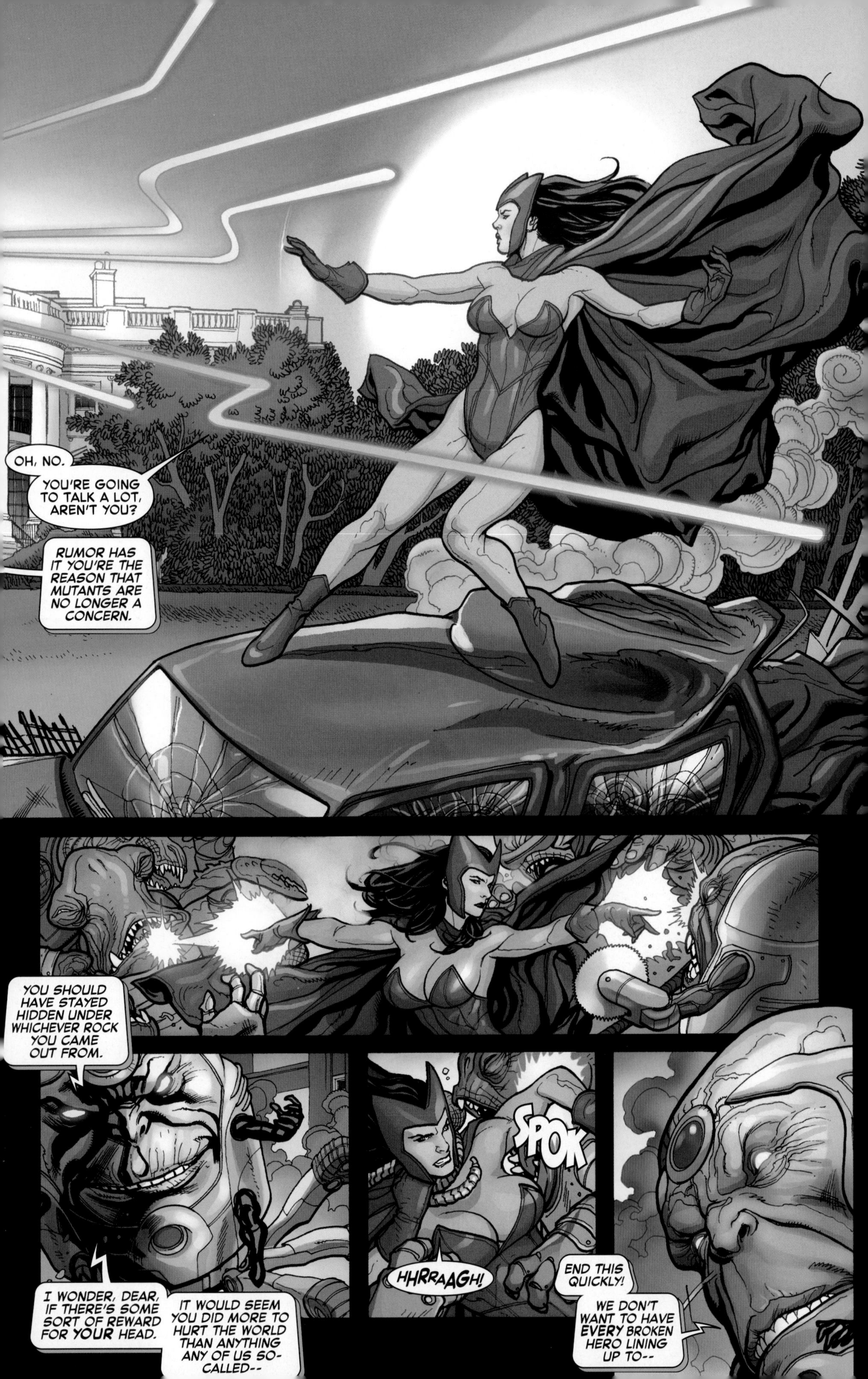
OH, NO.
YOU'RE GOING TO TALK A LOT, AREN'T YOU?
RUMOR HAS IT YOU'RE THE REASON THAT MUTANTS ARE NO LONGER A CONCERN.
YOU SHOULD HAVE STAYED HIDDEN UNDER WHICHEVER ROCK YOU CAME OUT FROM.
I WONDER, DEAR, IF THERE'S SOME SORT OF REWARD FOR YOUR HEAD.
IT WOULD SEEM YOU DID MORE TO HURT THE WORLD THAN ANYTHING ANY OF US SO-CALLED--
SPOK
HHRRAAGH!
END THIS QUICKLY!
WE DON'T WANT TO HAVE EVERY BROKEN HERO LINING UP TO--

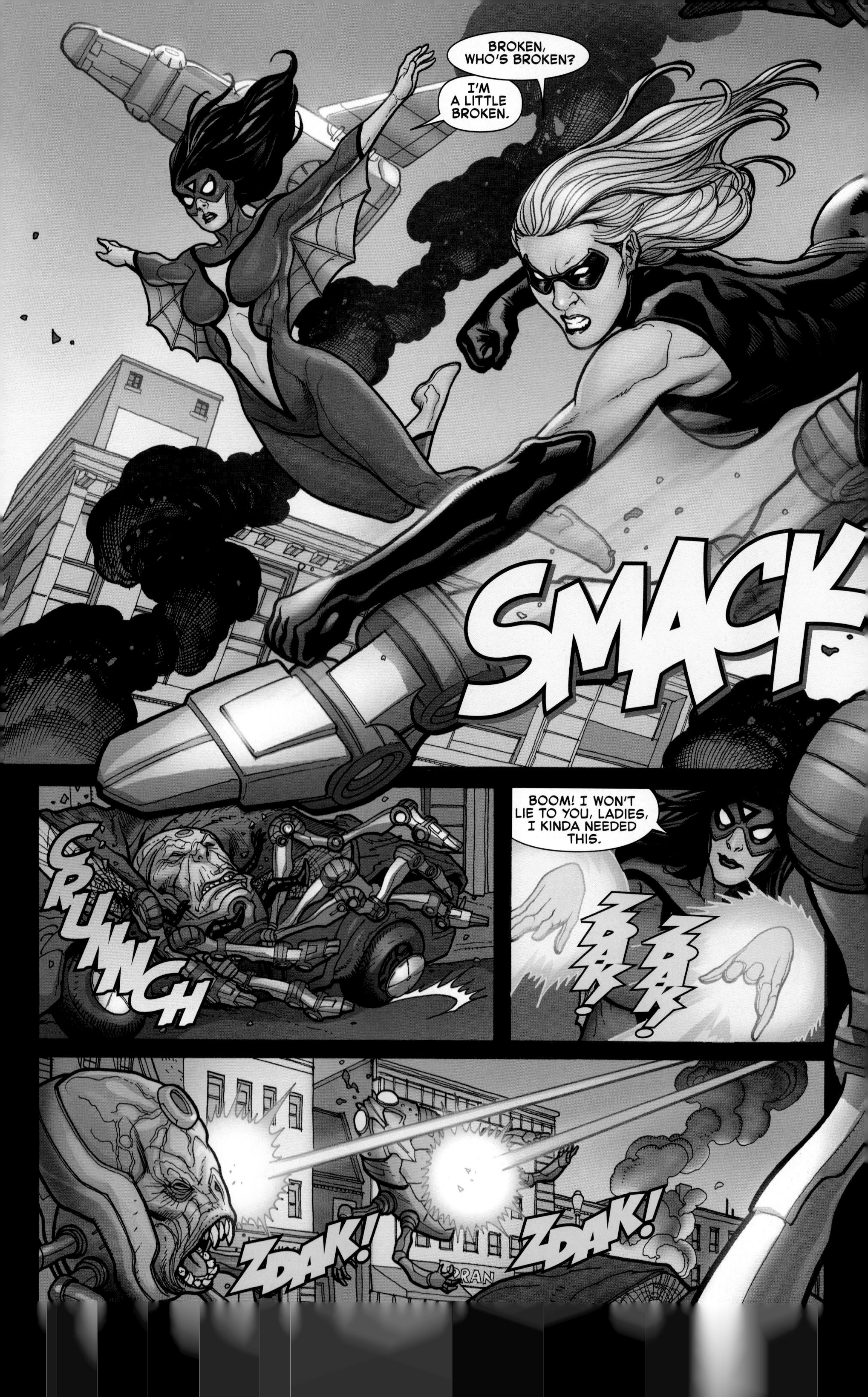
BROKEN, WHO'S BROKEN?
I'M A LITTLE BROKEN.
SMACK
CRUNNCH
BOOM! I WON'T LIE TO YOU, LADIES, I KINDA NEEDED THIS.
ZAK!
ZAK!
ZDAK!
ZDAK!

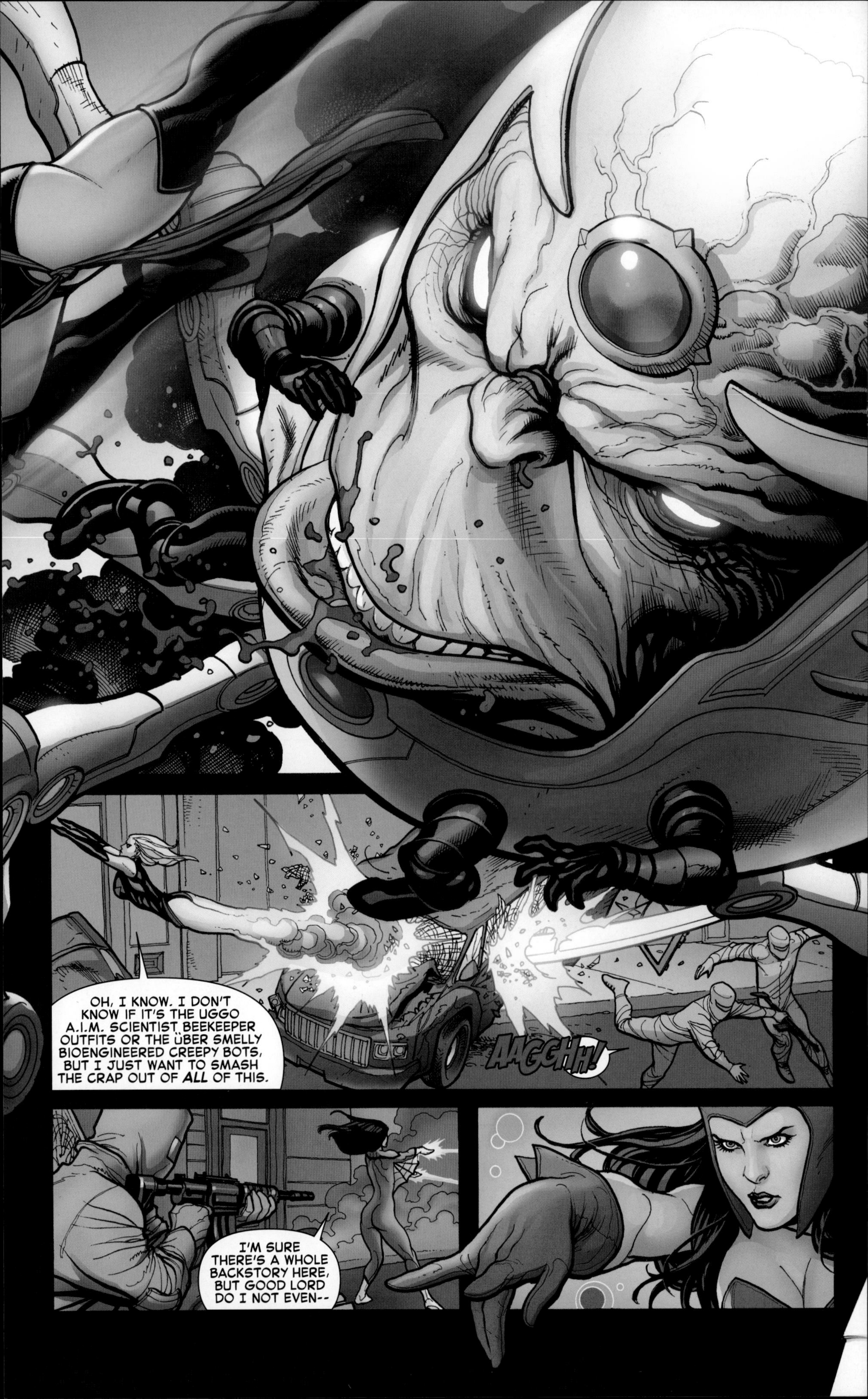
OH, I KNOW. I DON'T KNOW IF IT'S THE UGGO A.I.M. SCIENTIST BEEKEEPER OUTFITS OR THE ÜBER SMELLY BIOENGINEERED CREEPY BOTS, BUT I JUST WANT TO SMASH THE CRAP OUT OF ALL OF THIS.
AAGGHH!
I'M SURE THERE'S A WHOLE BACKSTORY HERE, BUT GOOD LORD DO I NOT EVEN--

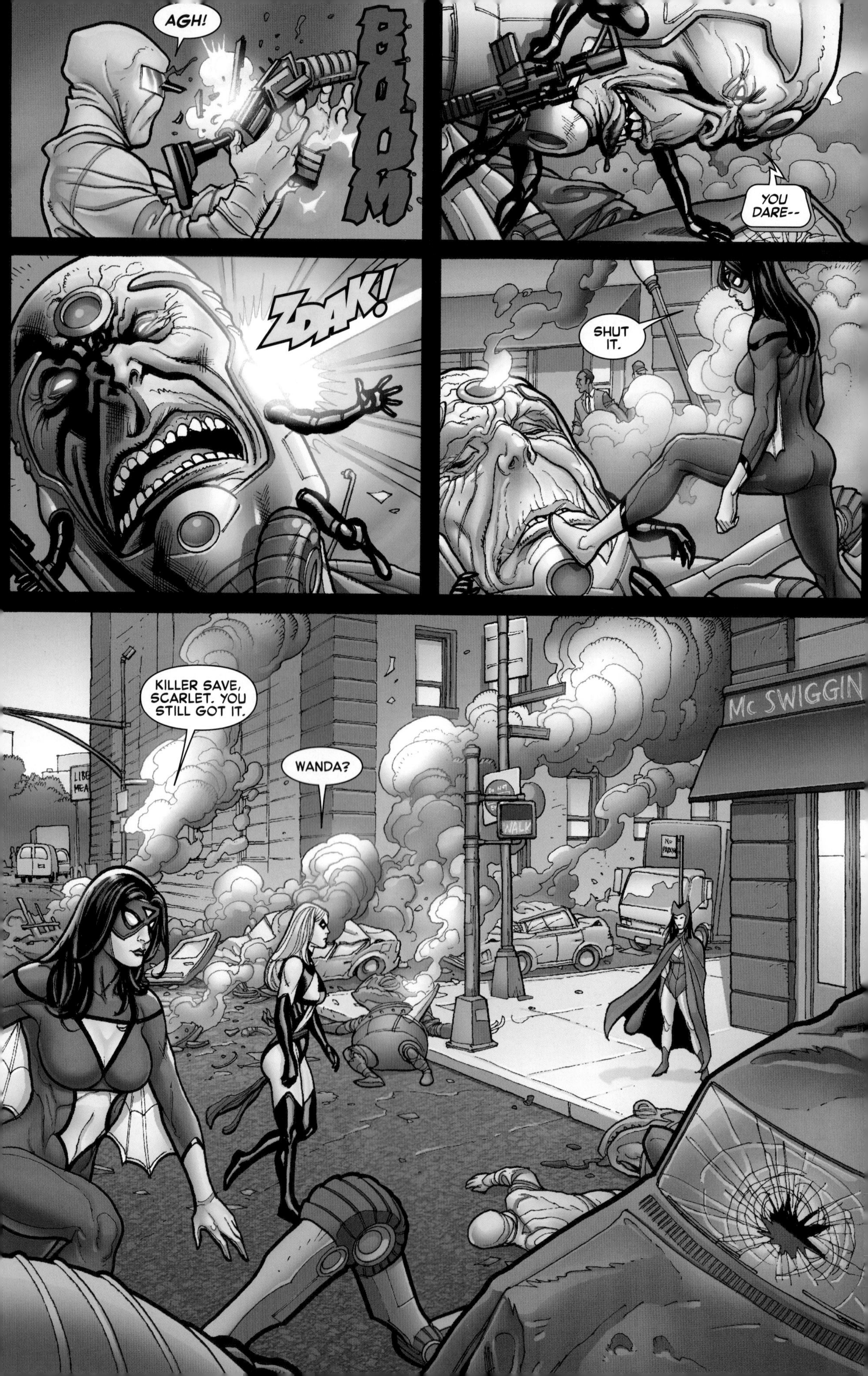
AGH!
BOOM
YOU DARE--
ZDAK!
SHUT IT.
KILLER SAVE, SCARLET. YOU STILL GOT IT.
WANDA?
McSWIGGIN
WALK

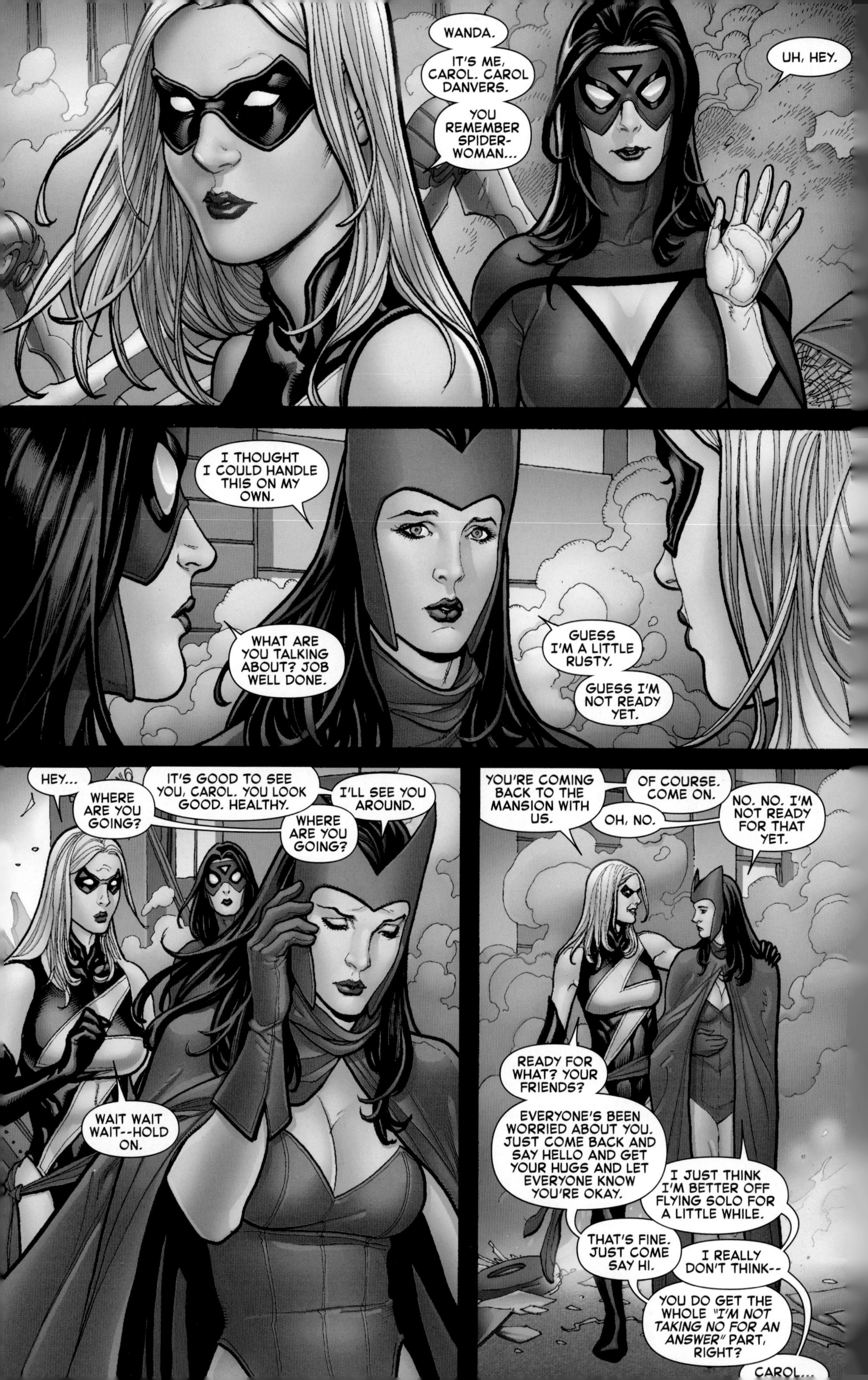
WANDA.
IT'S ME, CAROL. CAROL DANVERS.
YOU REMEMBER SPIDER-WOMAN...
UH, HEY.
I THOUGHT I COULD HANDLE THIS ON MY OWN.
WHAT ARE YOU TALKING ABOUT? JOB WELL DONE.
GUESS I'M A LITTLE RUSTY.
GUESS I'M NOT READY YET.
HEY...
IT'S GOOD TO SEE YOU, CAROL. YOU LOOK GOOD. HEALTHY.
I'LL SEE YOU AROUND.
WHERE ARE YOU GOING?
WHERE ARE YOU GOING?
WAIT WAIT WAIT--HOLD ON.
YOU'RE COMING BACK TO THE MANSION WITH US.
OF COURSE. COME ON.
OH, NO.
NO. NO. I'M NOT READY FOR THAT YET.
READY FOR WHAT? YOUR FRIENDS?
EVERYONE'S BEEN WORRIED ABOUT YOU. JUST COME BACK AND SAY HELLO AND GET YOUR HUGS AND LET EVERYONE KNOW YOU'RE OKAY.
I JUST THINK I'M BETTER OFF FLYING SOLO FOR A LITTLE WHILE.
THAT'S FINE. JUST COME SAY HI.
I REALLY DON'T THINK--
YOU DO GET THE WHOLE *"I'M NOT TAKING NO FOR AN ANSWER"* PART, RIGHT?
CAROL...

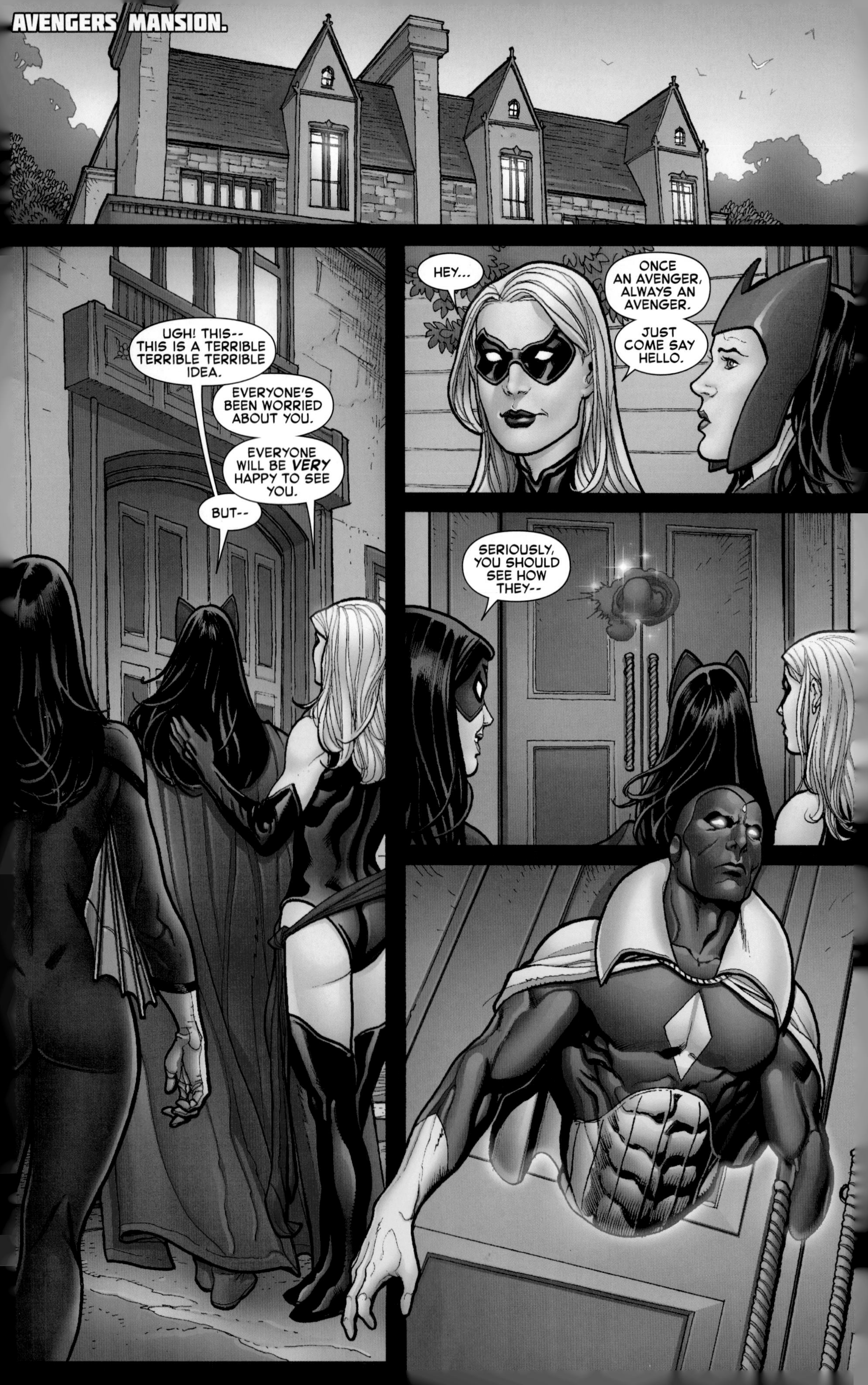
AVENGERS MANSION.
UGH! THIS-- THIS IS A TERRIBLE TERRIBLE TERRIBLE IDEA.
EVERYONE'S BEEN WORRIED ABOUT YOU.
EVERYONE WILL BE *VERY* HAPPY TO SEE YOU.
BUT--
HEY...
ONCE AN AVENGER, ALWAYS AN AVENGER.
JUST COME SAY HELLO.
SERIOUSLY, YOU SHOULD SEE HOW THEY--

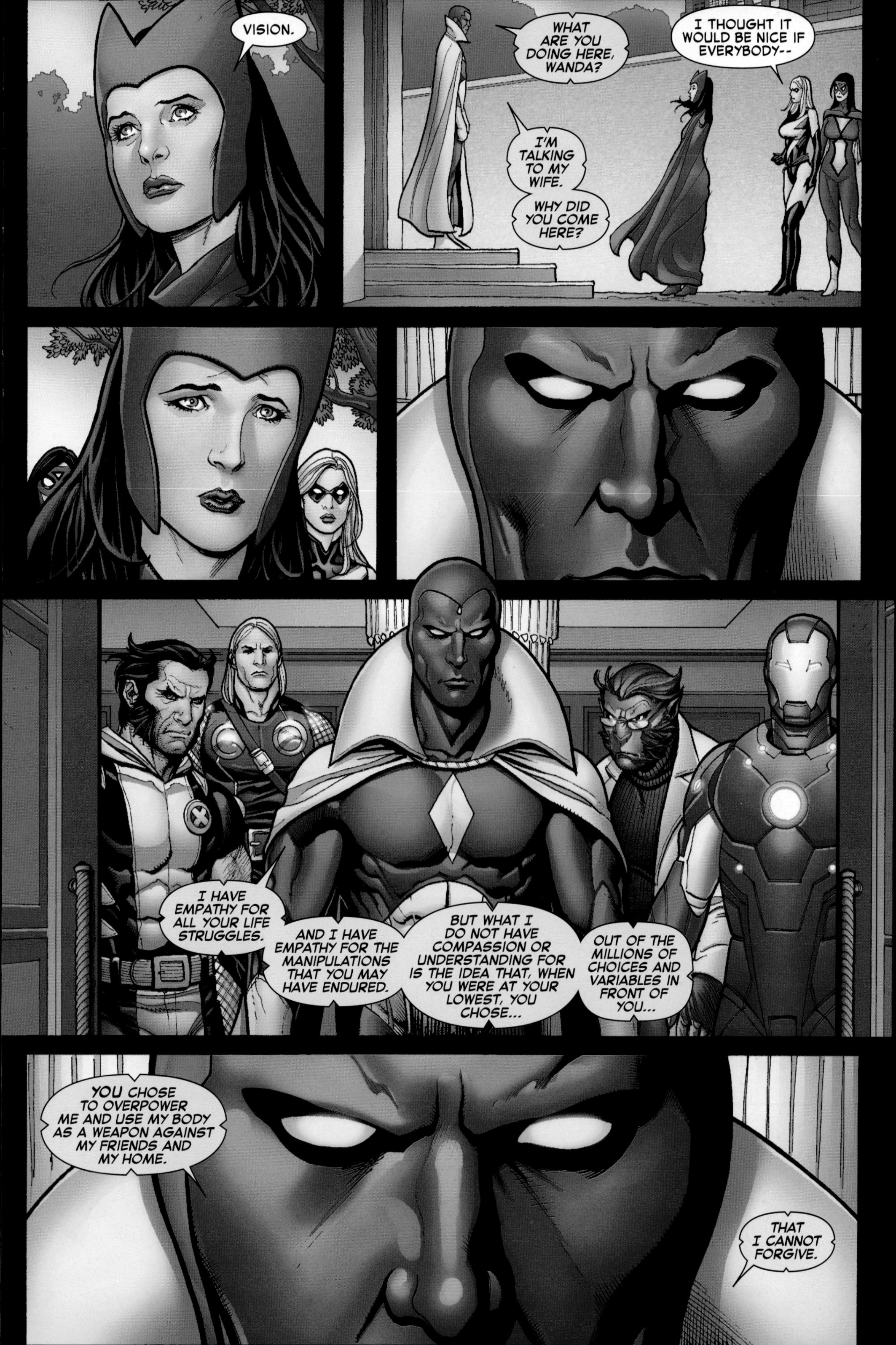
VISION.
WHAT ARE YOU DOING HERE, WANDA?
I'M TALKING TO MY WIFE.
WHY DID YOU COME HERE?
I THOUGHT IT WOULD BE NICE IF EVERYBODY--
I HAVE EMPATHY FOR ALL YOUR LIFE STRUGGLES.
AND I HAVE EMPATHY FOR THE MANIPULATIONS THAT YOU MAY HAVE ENDURED.
BUT WHAT I DO NOT HAVE COMPASSION OR UNDERSTANDING FOR IS THE IDEA THAT, WHEN YOU WERE AT YOUR LOWEST, YOU CHOSE...
OUT OF THE MILLIONS OF CHOICES AND VARIABLES IN FRONT OF YOU...
YOU CHOSE TO OVERPOWER ME AND USE MY BODY AS A WEAPON AGAINST MY FRIENDS AND MY HOME.
THAT I CANNOT FORGIVE.

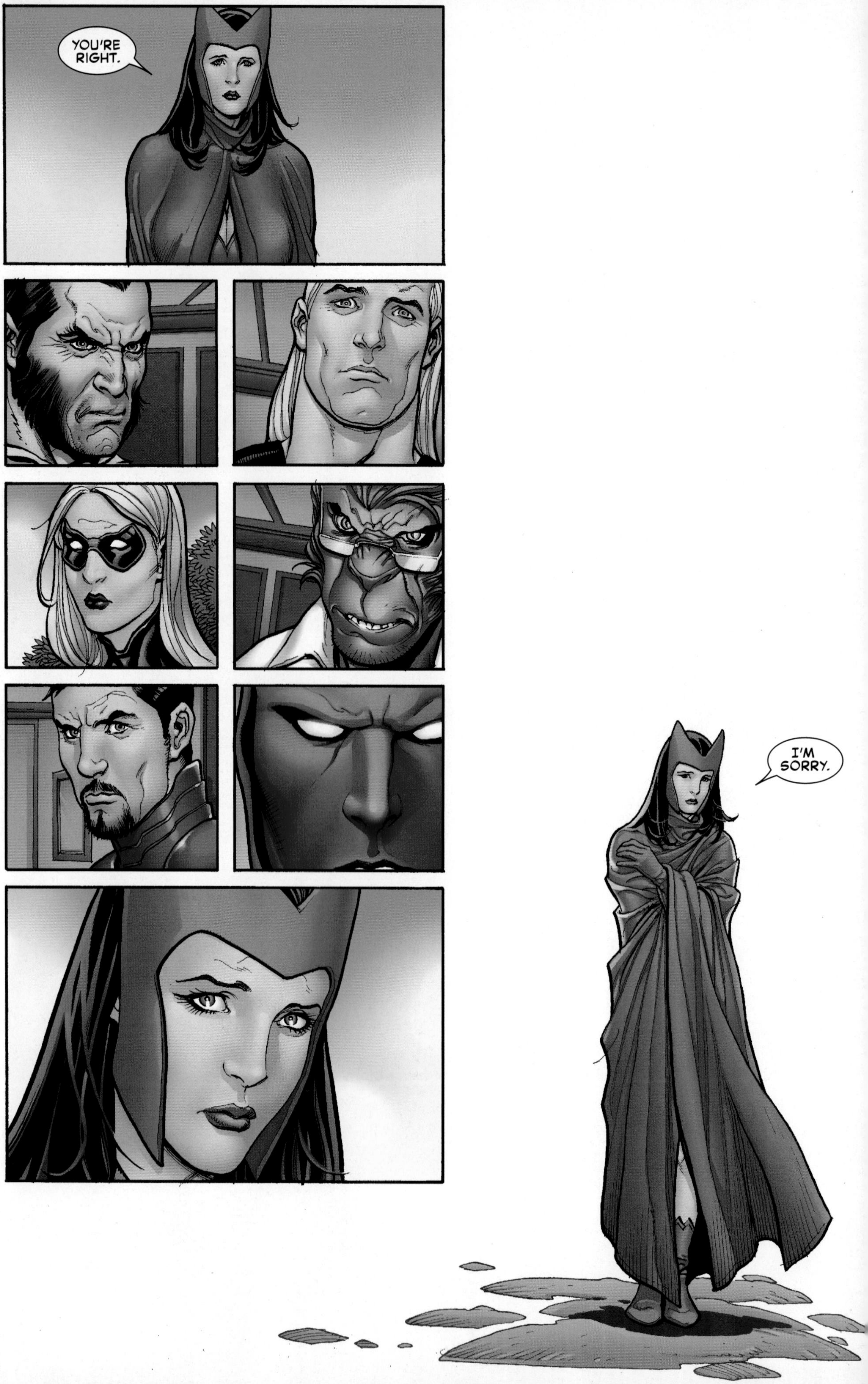
YOU'RE RIGHT.
I'M SORRY.

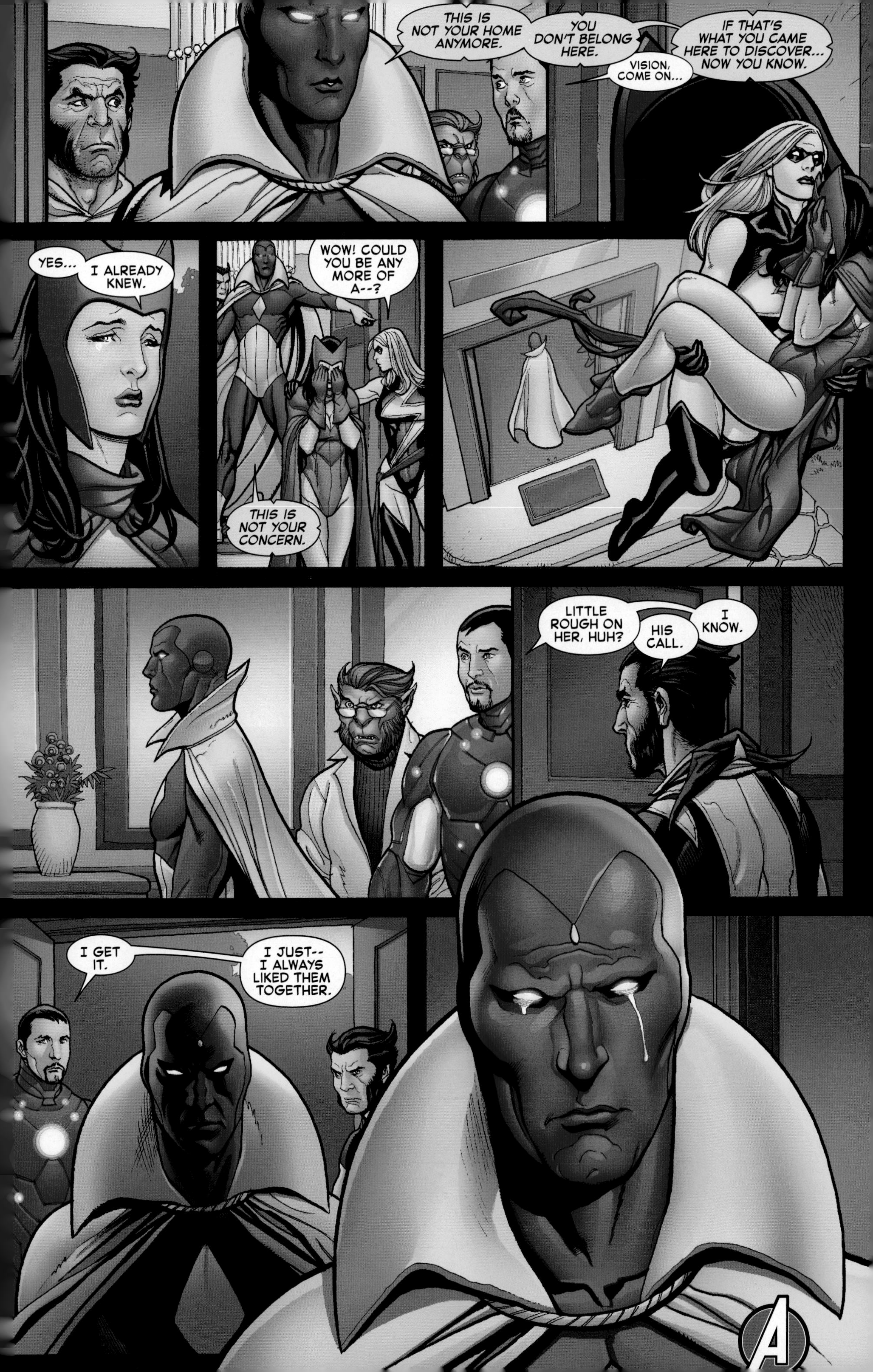
THIS IS NOT YOUR HOME ANYMORE.
YOU DON'T BELONG HERE.
IF THAT'S WHAT YOU CAME HERE TO DISCOVER... NOW YOU KNOW.
VISION, COME ON...
YES...
I ALREADY KNEW.
WOW! COULD YOU BE ANY MORE OF A--?
THIS IS NOT YOUR CONCERN.
LITTLE ROUGH ON HER, HUH?
HIS CALL.
I KNOW.
I GET IT.
I JUST-- I ALWAYS LIKED THEM TOGETHER.

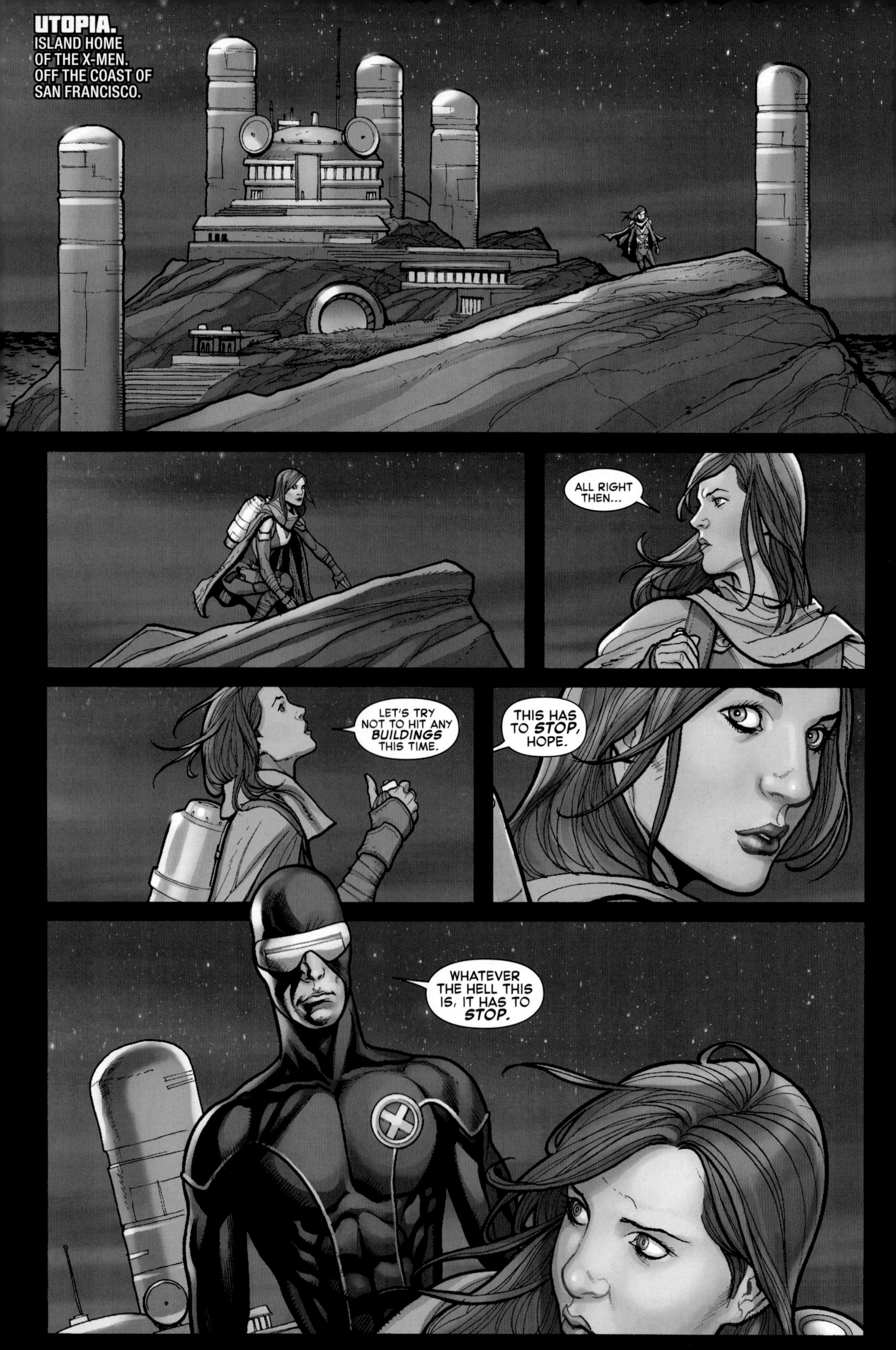
UTOPIA.
ISLAND HOME OF THE X-MEN. OFF THE COAST OF SAN FRANCISCO.
ALL RIGHT THEN...
LET'S TRY NOT TO HIT ANY BUILDINGS THIS TIME.
THIS HAS TO STOP, HOPE.
WHATEVER THE HELL THIS IS, IT HAS TO STOP.

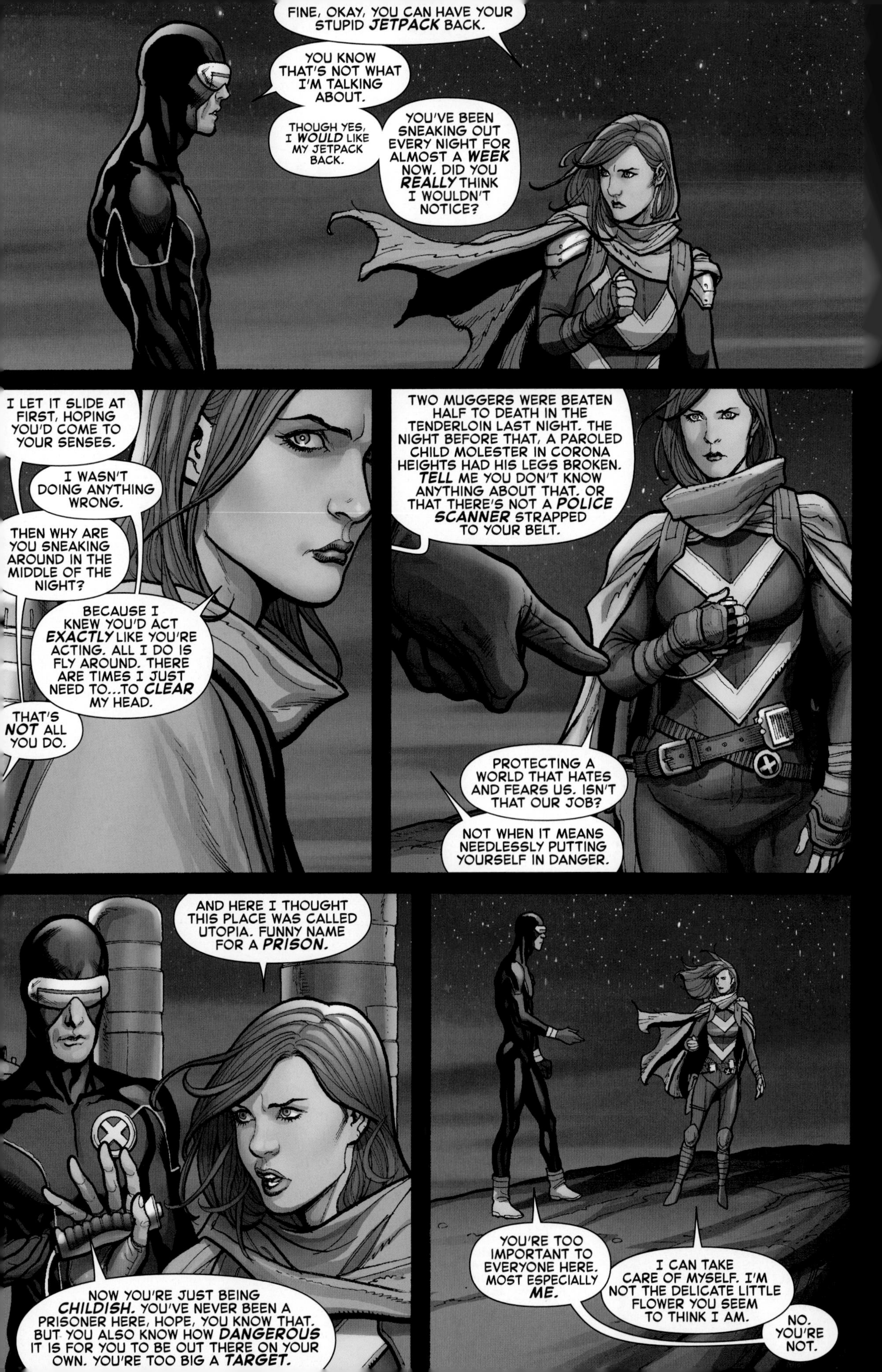
FINE, OKAY, YOU CAN HAVE YOUR STUPID JETPACK BACK.
YOU KNOW THAT'S NOT WHAT I'M TALKING ABOUT.
THOUGH YES, I WOULD LIKE MY JETPACK BACK.
YOU'VE BEEN SNEAKING OUT EVERY NIGHT FOR ALMOST A WEEK NOW. DID YOU REALLY THINK I WOULDN'T NOTICE?
I LET IT SLIDE AT FIRST, HOPING YOU'D COME TO YOUR SENSES.
I WASN'T DOING ANYTHING WRONG.
THEN WHY ARE YOU SNEAKING AROUND IN THE MIDDLE OF THE NIGHT?
BECAUSE I KNEW YOU'D ACT EXACTLY LIKE YOU'RE ACTING. ALL I DO IS FLY AROUND. THERE ARE TIMES I JUST NEED TO...TO CLEAR MY HEAD.
THAT'S NOT ALL YOU DO.
TWO MUGGERS WERE BEATEN HALF TO DEATH IN THE TENDERLOIN LAST NIGHT. THE NIGHT BEFORE THAT, A PAROLED CHILD MOLESTER IN CORONA HEIGHTS HAD HIS LEGS BROKEN. TELL ME YOU DON'T KNOW ANYTHING ABOUT THAT. OR THAT THERE'S NOT A POLICE SCANNER STRAPPED TO YOUR BELT.
PROTECTING A WORLD THAT HATES AND FEARS US. ISN'T THAT OUR JOB?
NOT WHEN IT MEANS NEEDLESSLY PUTTING YOURSELF IN DANGER.
AND HERE I THOUGHT THIS PLACE WAS CALLED UTOPIA. FUNNY NAME FOR A PRISON.
NOW YOU'RE JUST BEING CHILDISH. YOU'VE NEVER BEEN A PRISONER HERE, HOPE, YOU KNOW THAT. BUT YOU ALSO KNOW HOW DANGEROUS IT IS FOR YOU TO BE OUT THERE ON YOUR OWN. YOU'RE TOO BIG A TARGET.
YOU'RE TOO IMPORTANT TO EVERYONE HERE. MOST ESPECIALLY ME.
I CAN TAKE CARE OF MYSELF. I'M NOT THE DELICATE LITTLE FLOWER YOU SEEM TO THINK I AM.
NO. YOU'RE NOT.

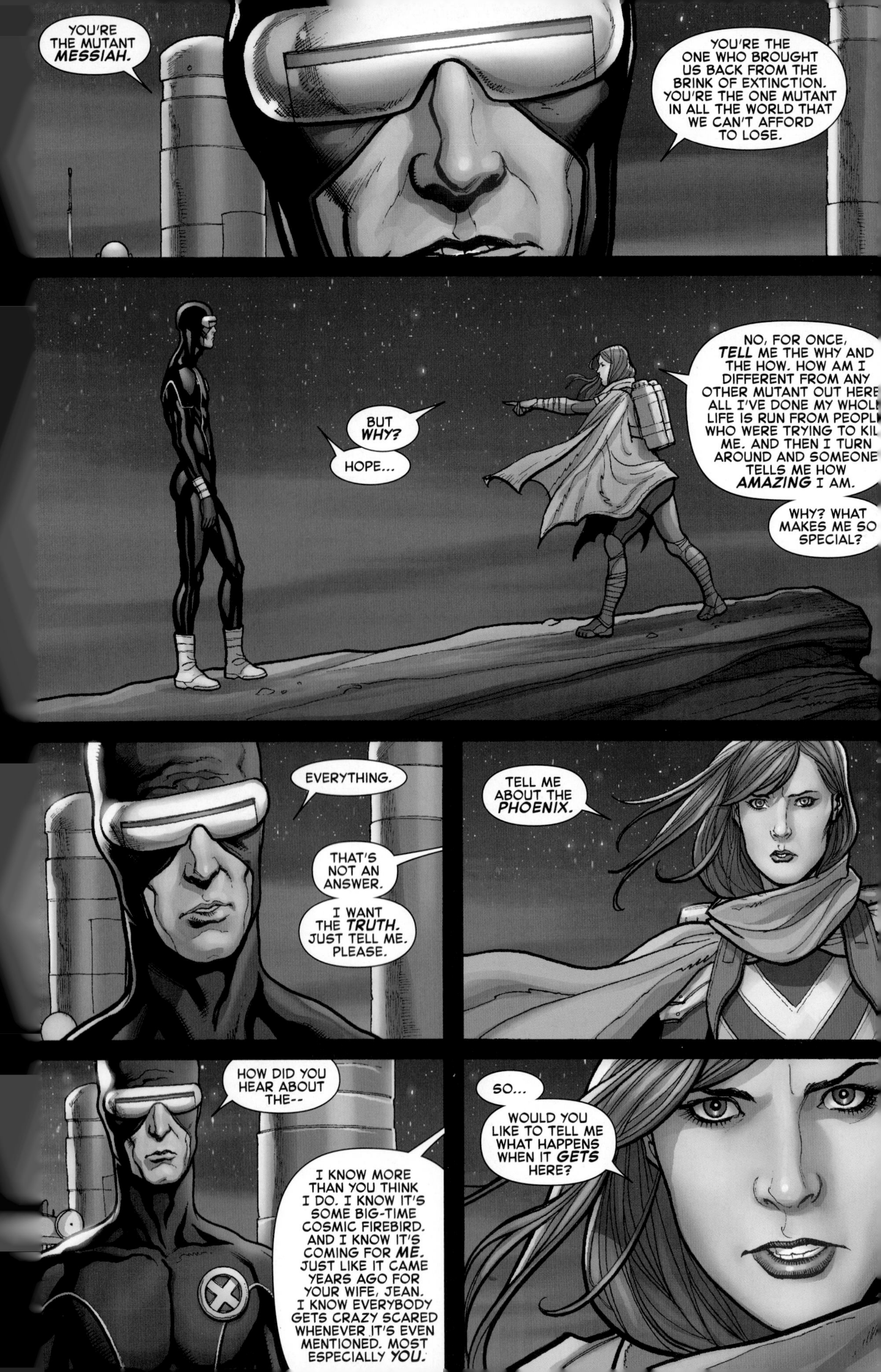
YOU'RE THE MUTANT MESSIAH.
YOU'RE THE ONE WHO BROUGHT US BACK FROM THE BRINK OF EXTINCTION. YOU'RE THE ONE MUTANT IN ALL THE WORLD THAT WE CAN'T AFFORD TO LOSE.
BUT WHY?
HOPE...
NO, FOR ONCE, TELL ME THE WHY AND THE HOW. HOW AM I DIFFERENT FROM ANY OTHER MUTANT OUT HERE ALL I'VE DONE MY WHOL LIFE IS RUN FROM PEOPL WHO WERE TRYING TO KIL ME. AND THEN I TURN AROUND AND SOMEONE TELLS ME HOW AMAZING I AM.
WHY? WHAT MAKES ME SO SPECIAL?
EVERYTHING.
THAT'S NOT AN ANSWER.
I WANT THE TRUTH. JUST TELL ME. PLEASE.
TELL ME ABOUT THE PHOENIX.
HOW DID YOU HEAR ABOUT THE--
I KNOW MORE THAN YOU THINK I DO. I KNOW IT'S SOME BIG-TIME COSMIC FIREBIRD. AND I KNOW IT'S COMING FOR ME. JUST LIKE IT CAME YEARS AGO FOR YOUR WIFE, JEAN. I KNOW EVERYBODY GETS CRAZY SCARED WHENEVER IT'S EVEN MENTIONED. MOST ESPECIALLY YOU.
SO...
WOULD YOU LIKE TO TELL ME WHAT HAPPENS WHEN IT GETS HERE?

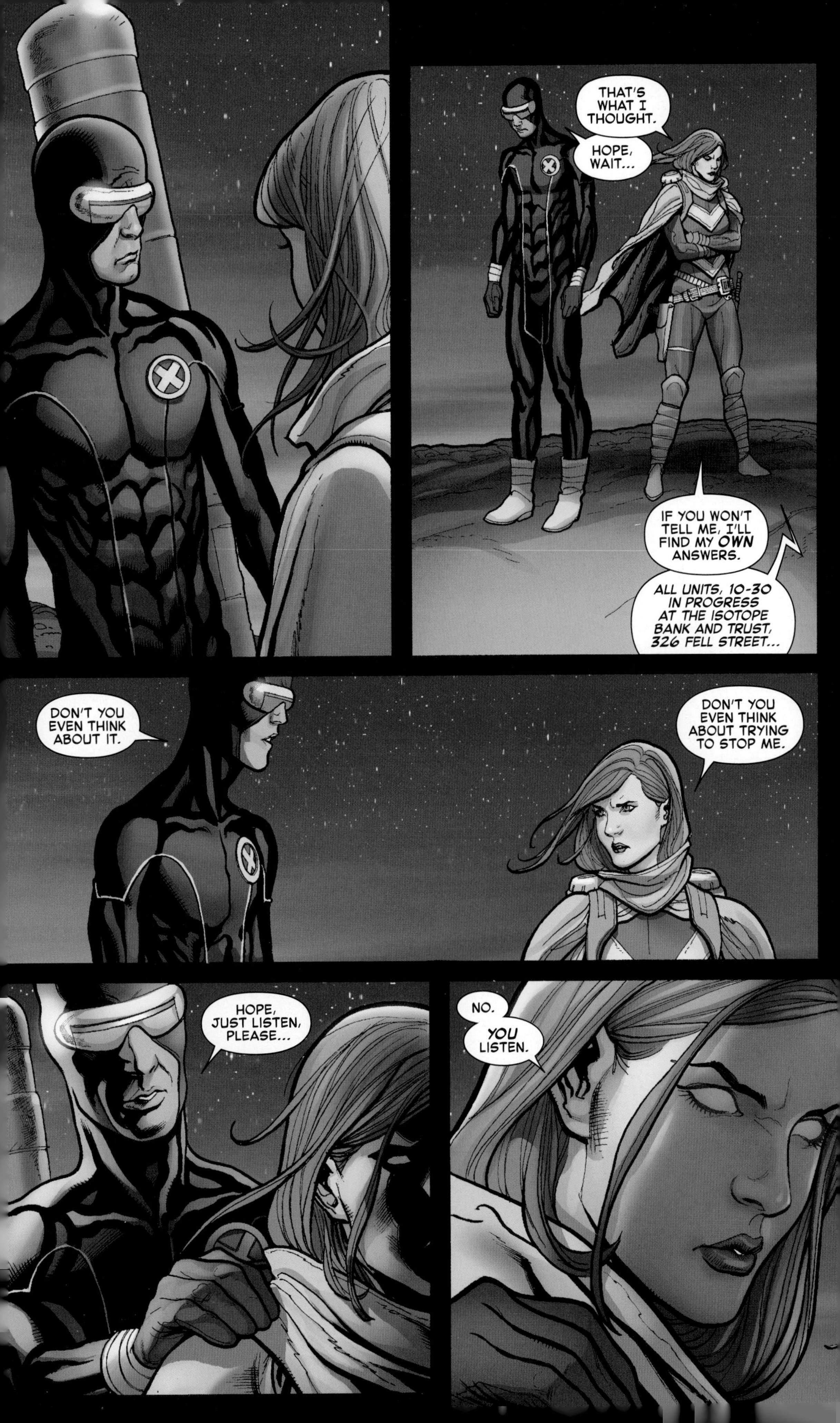
THAT'S WHAT I THOUGHT.
HOPE, WAIT...
IF YOU WON'T TELL ME, I'LL FIND MY OWN ANSWERS.
ALL UNITS, 10-30 IN PROGRESS AT THE ISOTOPE BANK AND TRUST, 326 FELL STREET...
DON'T YOU EVEN THINK ABOUT IT.
DON'T YOU EVEN THINK ABOUT TRYING TO STOP ME.
HOPE, JUST LISTEN, PLEASE...
NO.
YOU LISTEN.

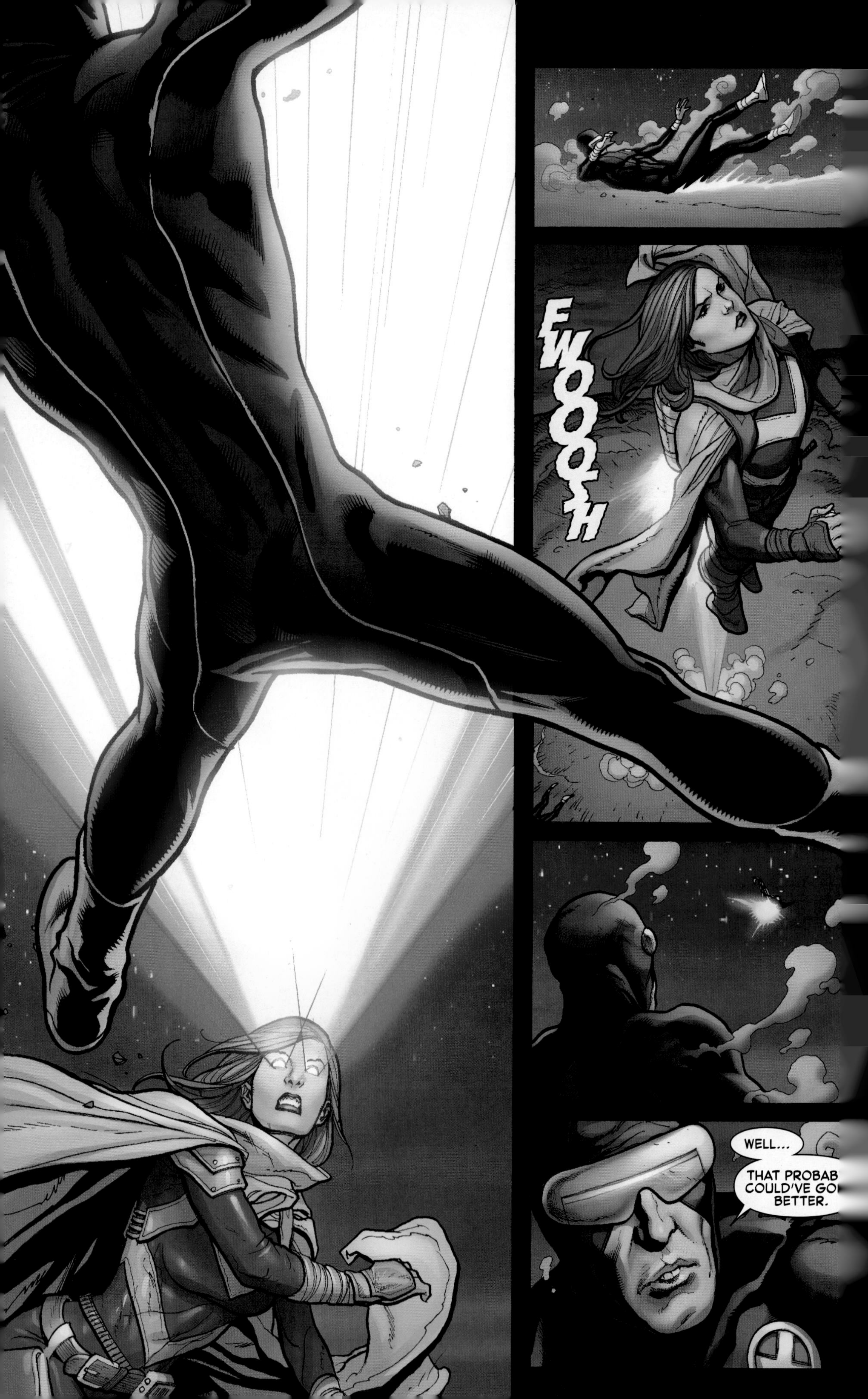
EWOOOH
WELL...
THAT PROBAB
COULD'VE GO
BETTER.

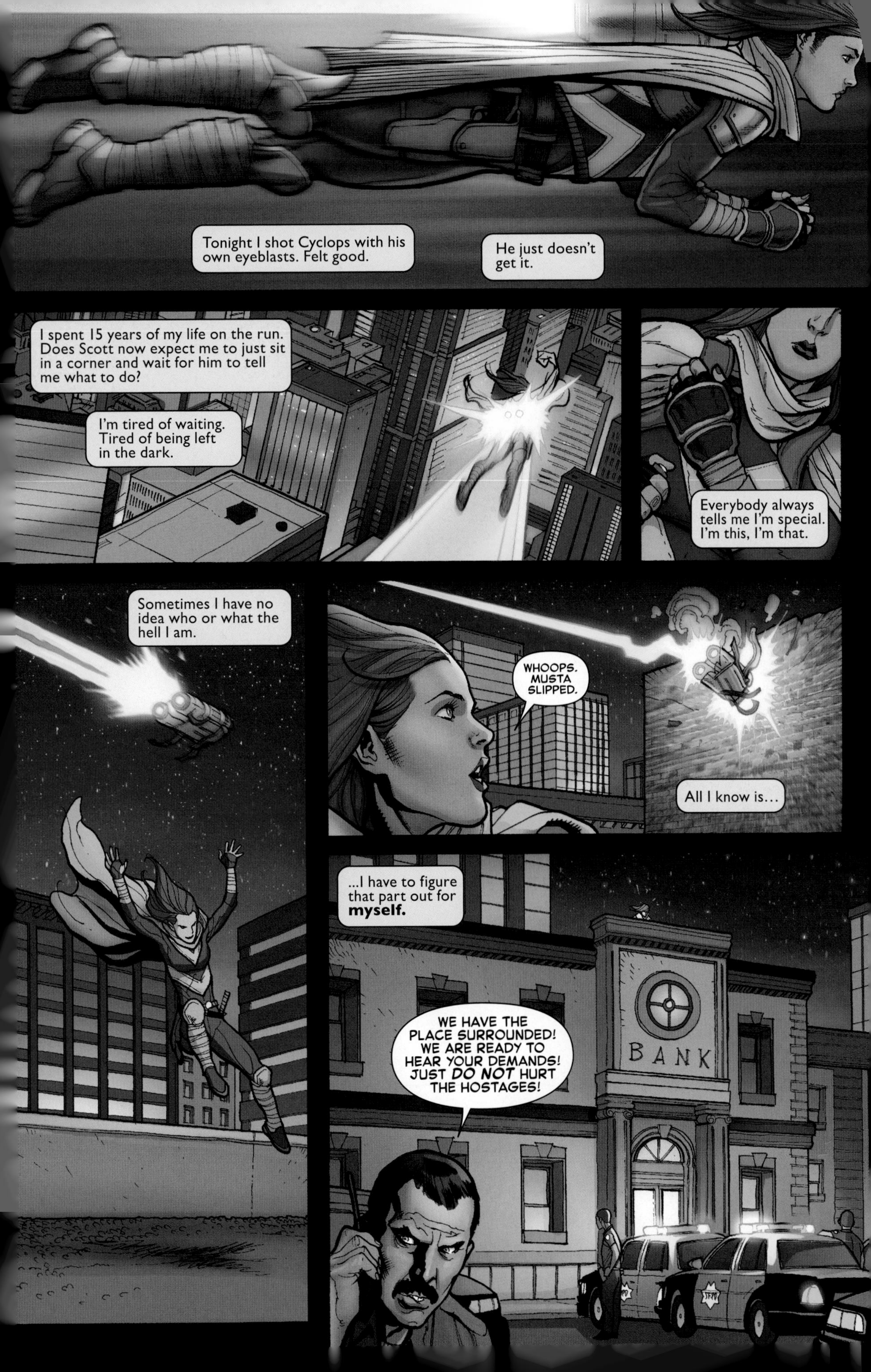

Tonight I shot Cyclops with his own eyeblasts. Felt good.
He just doesn't get it.
I spent 15 years of my life on the run. Does Scott now expect me to just sit in a corner and wait for him to tell me what to do?
I'm tired of waiting. Tired of being left in the dark.
Everybody always tells me I'm special. I'm this, I'm that.
Sometimes I have no idea who or what the hell I am.
WHOOPS. MUSTA SLIPPED.
All I know is…
...I have to figure that part out for **myself.**
BANK
WE HAVE THE PLACE SURROUNDED! WE ARE READY TO HEAR YOUR DEMANDS! JUST ***DO NOT*** HURT THE HOSTAGES!

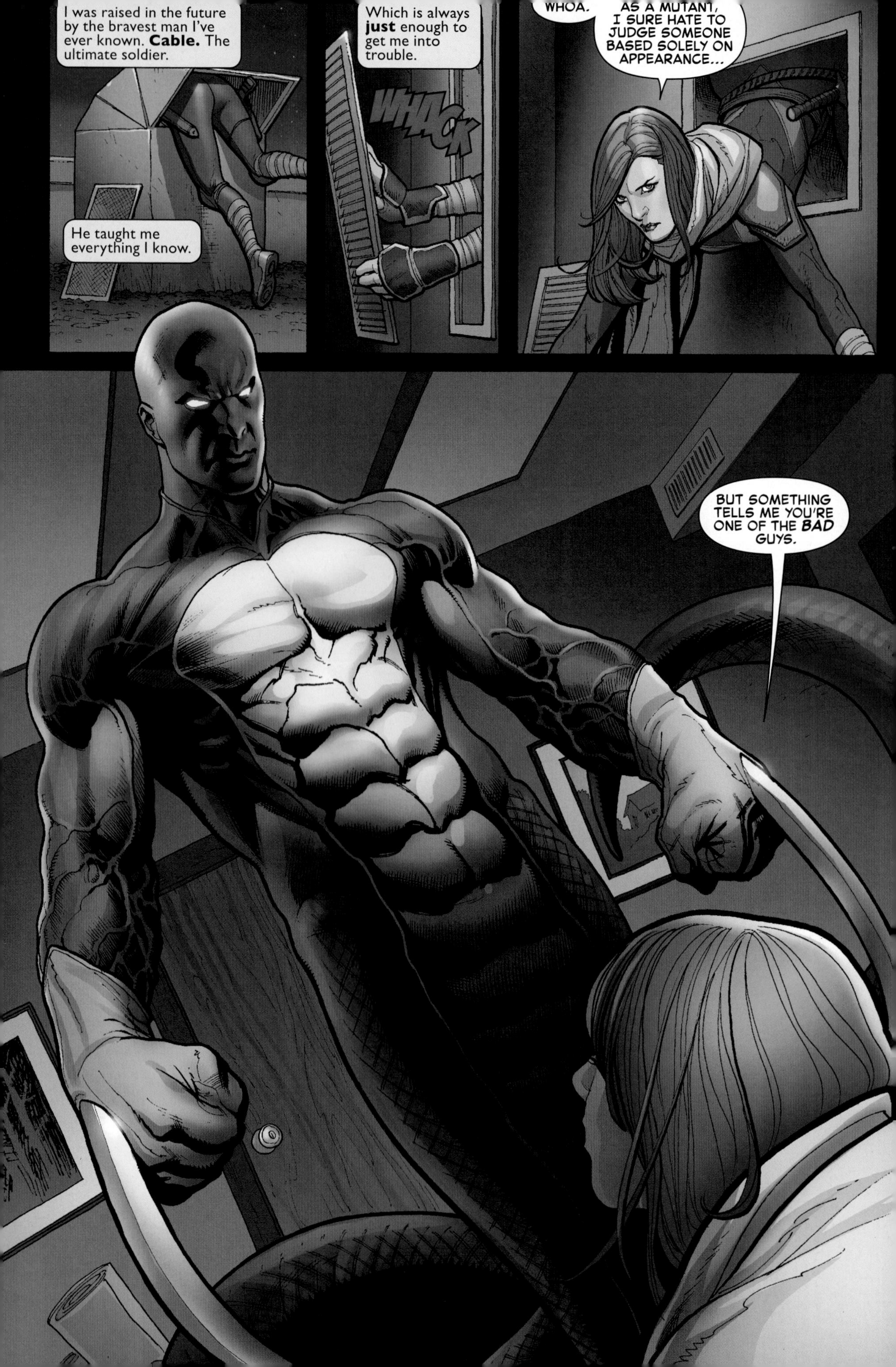
I was raised in the future by the bravest man I've ever known. **Cable.** The ultimate soldier.
He taught me everything I know.
Which is always **just** enough to get me into trouble.
WHACK
WHOA.
AS A MUTANT, I SURE HATE TO JUDGE SOMEONE BASED SOLELY ON APPEARANCE...
BUT SOMETHING TELLS ME YOU'RE ONE OF THE *BAD* GUYS.

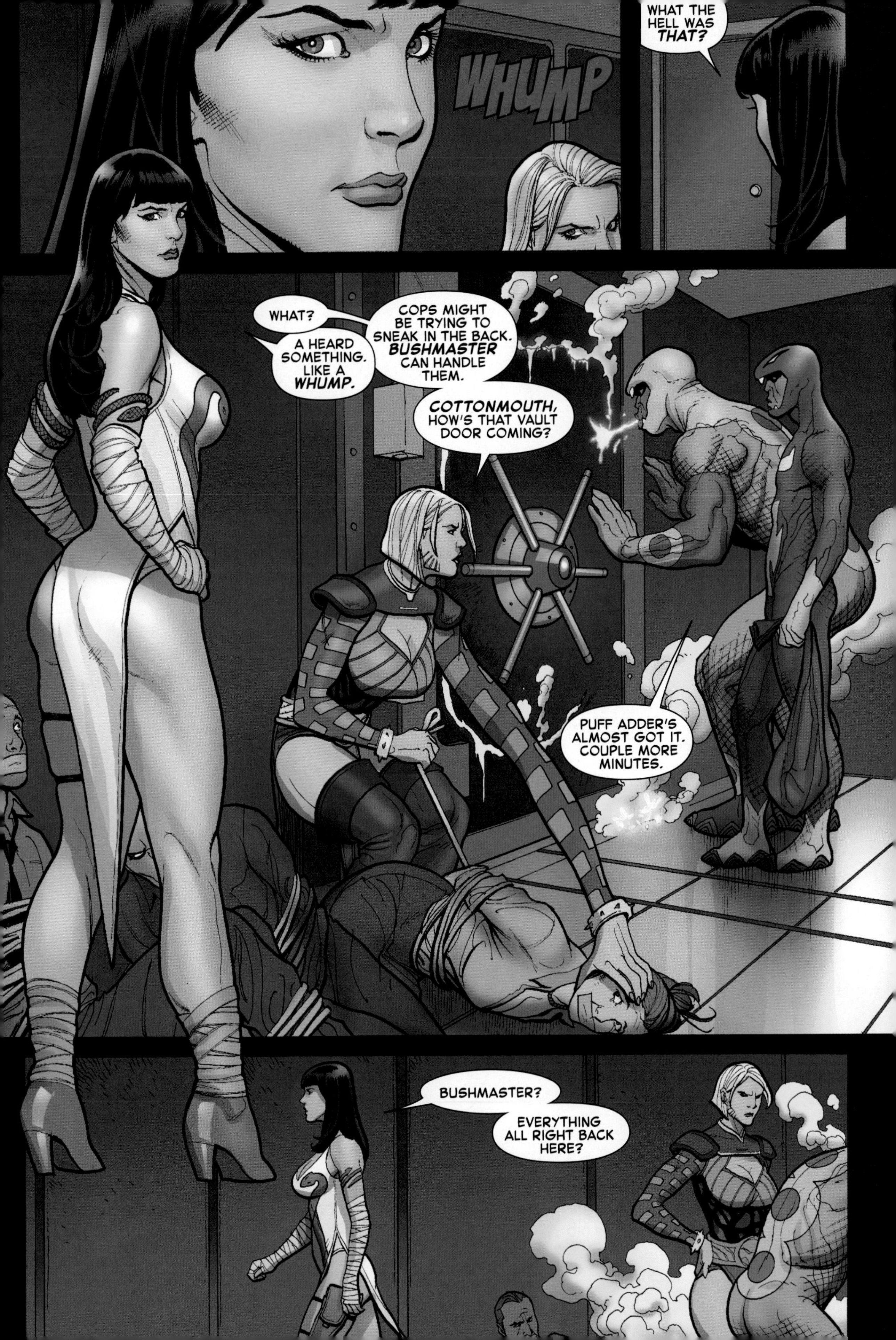
WHUMP
WHAT THE HELL WAS THAT?
WHAT?
A HEARD SOMETHING. LIKE A WHUMP.
COPS MIGHT BE TRYING TO SNEAK IN THE BACK. BUSHMASTER CAN HANDLE THEM.
COTTONMOUTH, HOW'S THAT VAULT DOOR COMING?
PUFF ADDER'S ALMOST GOT IT. COUPLE MORE MINUTES.
BUSHMASTER?
EVERYTHING ALL RIGHT BACK HERE?

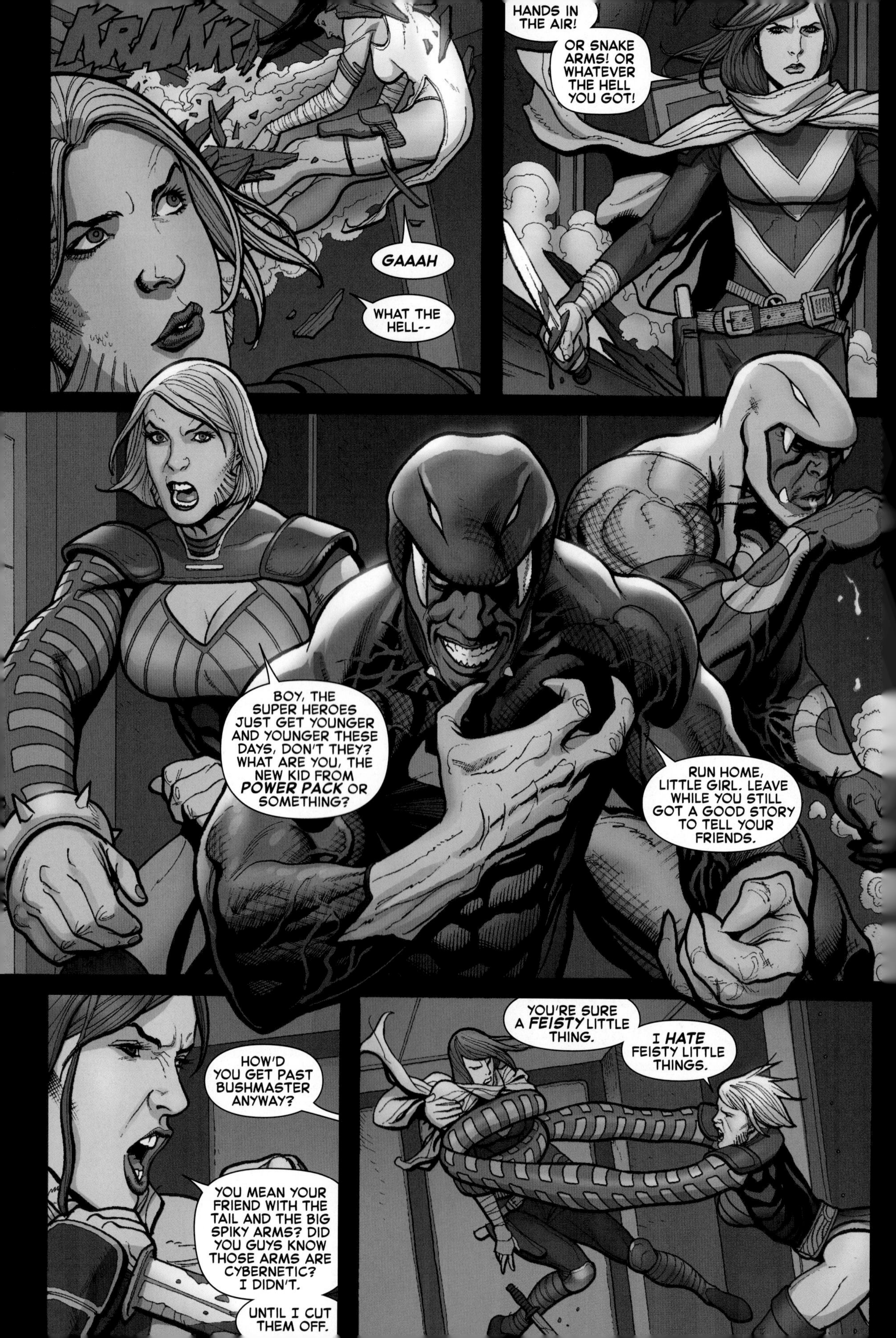
KRANK
GAAAH
WHAT THE HELL--
HANDS IN THE AIR!
OR SNAKE ARMS! OR WHATEVER THE HELL YOU GOT!
BOY, THE SUPER HEROES JUST GET YOUNGER AND YOUNGER THESE DAYS, DON'T THEY? WHAT ARE YOU, THE NEW KID FROM POWER PACK OR SOMETHING?
RUN HOME, LITTLE GIRL. LEAVE WHILE YOU STILL GOT A GOOD STORY TO TELL YOUR FRIENDS.
HOW'D YOU GET PAST BUSHMASTER ANYWAY?
YOU MEAN YOUR FRIEND WITH THE TAIL AND THE BIG SPIKY ARMS? DID YOU GUYS KNOW THOSE ARMS ARE CYBERNETIC? I DIDN'T.
UNTIL I CUT THEM OFF.
YOU'RE SURE A FEISTY LITTLE THING.
I HATE FEISTY LITTLE THINGS.

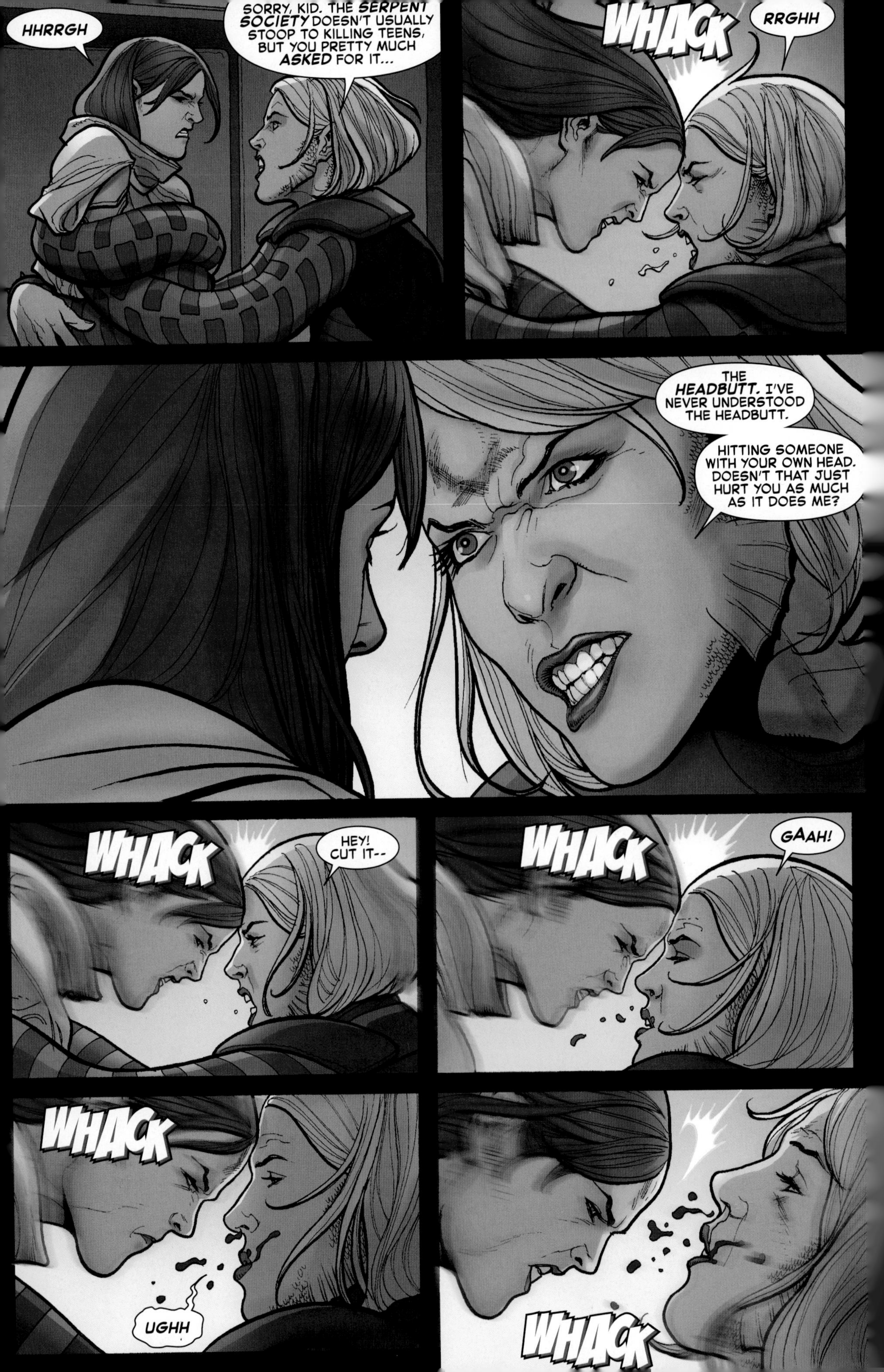
HHRRGH
SORRY, KID. THE SERPENT SOCIETY DOESN'T USUALLY STOOP TO KILLING TEENS, BUT YOU PRETTY MUCH ASKED FOR IT...
WHACK
RRGHH
THE HEADBUTT. I'VE NEVER UNDERSTOOD THE HEADBUTT.
HITTING SOMEONE WITH YOUR OWN HEAD. DOESN'T THAT JUST HURT YOU AS MUCH AS IT DOES ME?
WHACK
HEY! CUT IT--
WHACK
GAAH!
WHACK
UGHH
WHACK

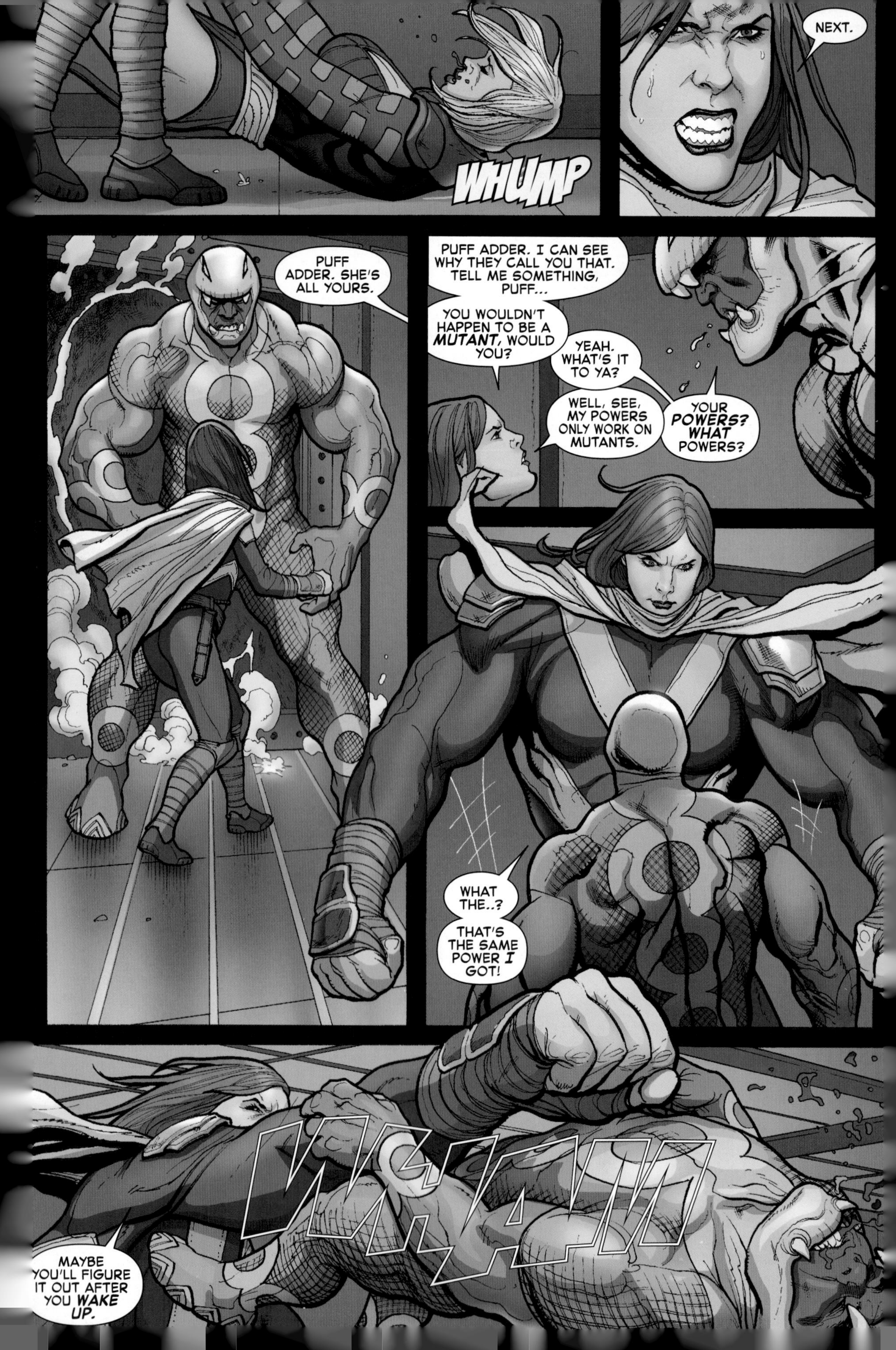
WHUMP
NEXT.
PUFF ADDER. SHE'S ALL YOURS.
PUFF ADDER. I CAN SEE WHY THEY CALL YOU THAT. TELL ME SOMETHING, PUFF...
YOU WOULDN'T HAPPEN TO BE A MUTANT, WOULD YOU?
YEAH. WHAT'S IT TO YA?
WELL, SEE, MY POWERS ONLY WORK ON MUTANTS.
YOUR POWERS? WHAT POWERS?
WHAT THE..?
THAT'S THE SAME POWER I GOT!
MAYBE YOU'LL FIGURE IT OUT AFTER YOU WAKE UP.

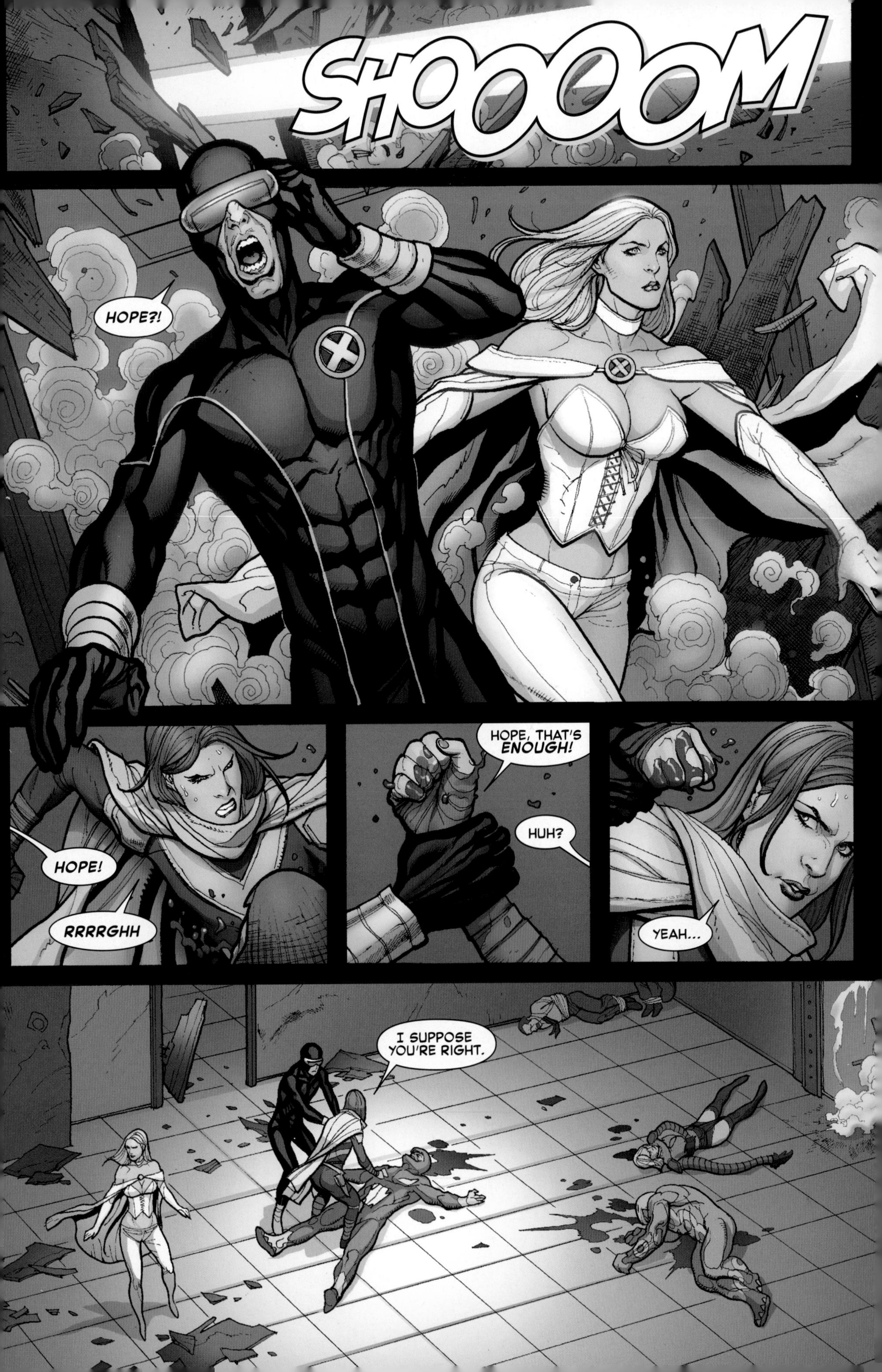
SHOOOOM
HOPE?!
HOPE!
RRRRGHH
HOPE, THAT'S ENOUGH!
HUH?
YEAH...
I SUPPOSE YOU'RE RIGHT.

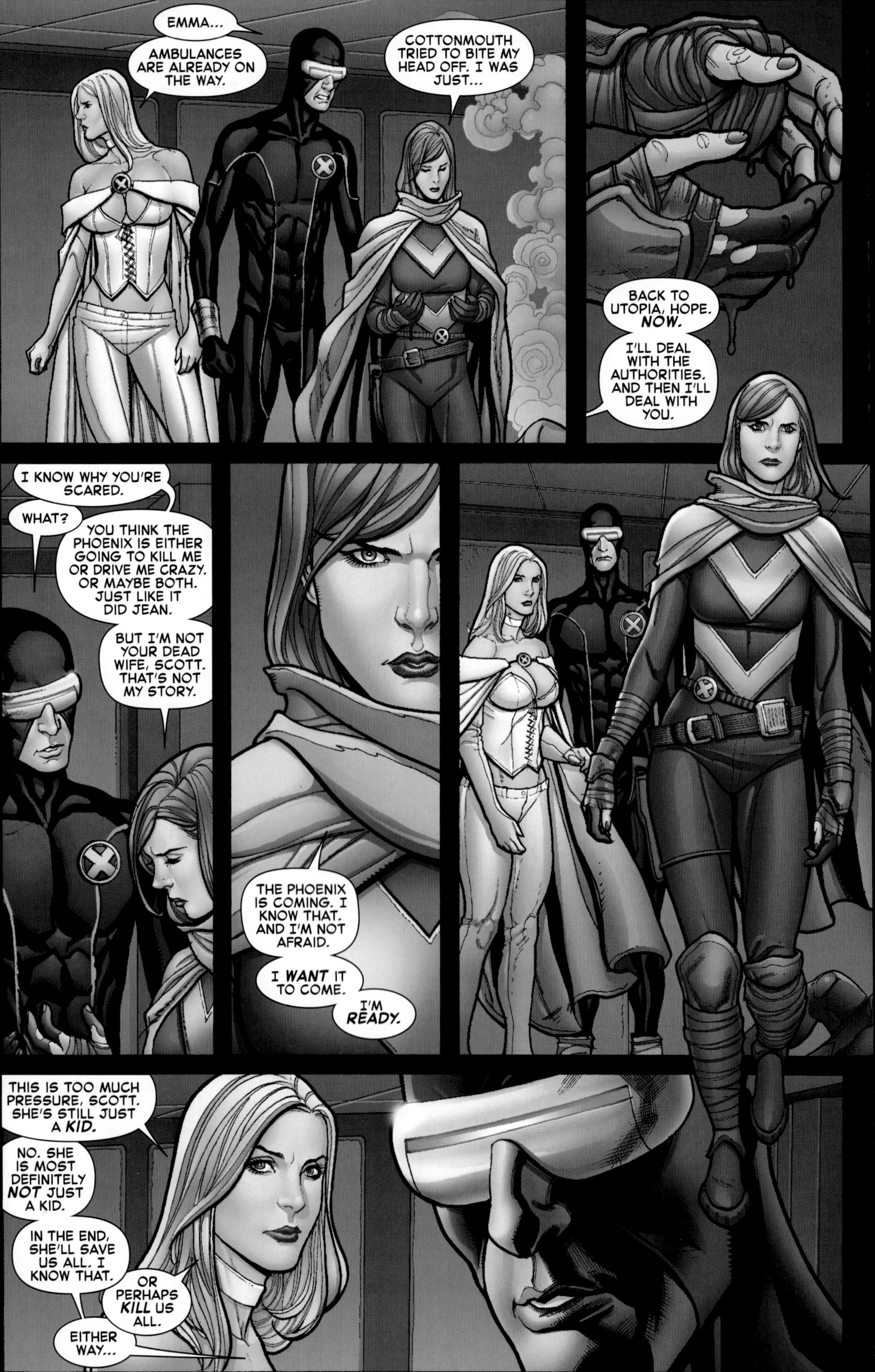
EMMA...
AMBULANCES ARE ALREADY ON THE WAY.
COTTONMOUTH TRIED TO BITE MY HEAD OFF. I WAS JUST...
BACK TO UTOPIA, HOPE. NOW.
I'LL DEAL WITH THE AUTHORITIES. AND THEN I'LL DEAL WITH YOU.
I KNOW WHY YOU'RE SCARED.
WHAT?
YOU THINK THE PHOENIX IS EITHER GOING TO KILL ME OR DRIVE ME CRAZY. OR MAYBE BOTH. JUST LIKE IT DID JEAN.
BUT I'M NOT YOUR DEAD WIFE, SCOTT. THAT'S NOT MY STORY.
THE PHOENIX IS COMING. I KNOW THAT. AND I'M NOT AFRAID.
I WANT IT TO COME.
I'M READY.
THIS IS TOO MUCH PRESSURE, SCOTT. SHE'S STILL JUST A KID.
NO. SHE IS MOST DEFINITELY NOT JUST A KID.
IN THE END, SHE'LL SAVE US ALL. I KNOW THAT.
OR PERHAPS KILL US ALL.
EITHER WAY...

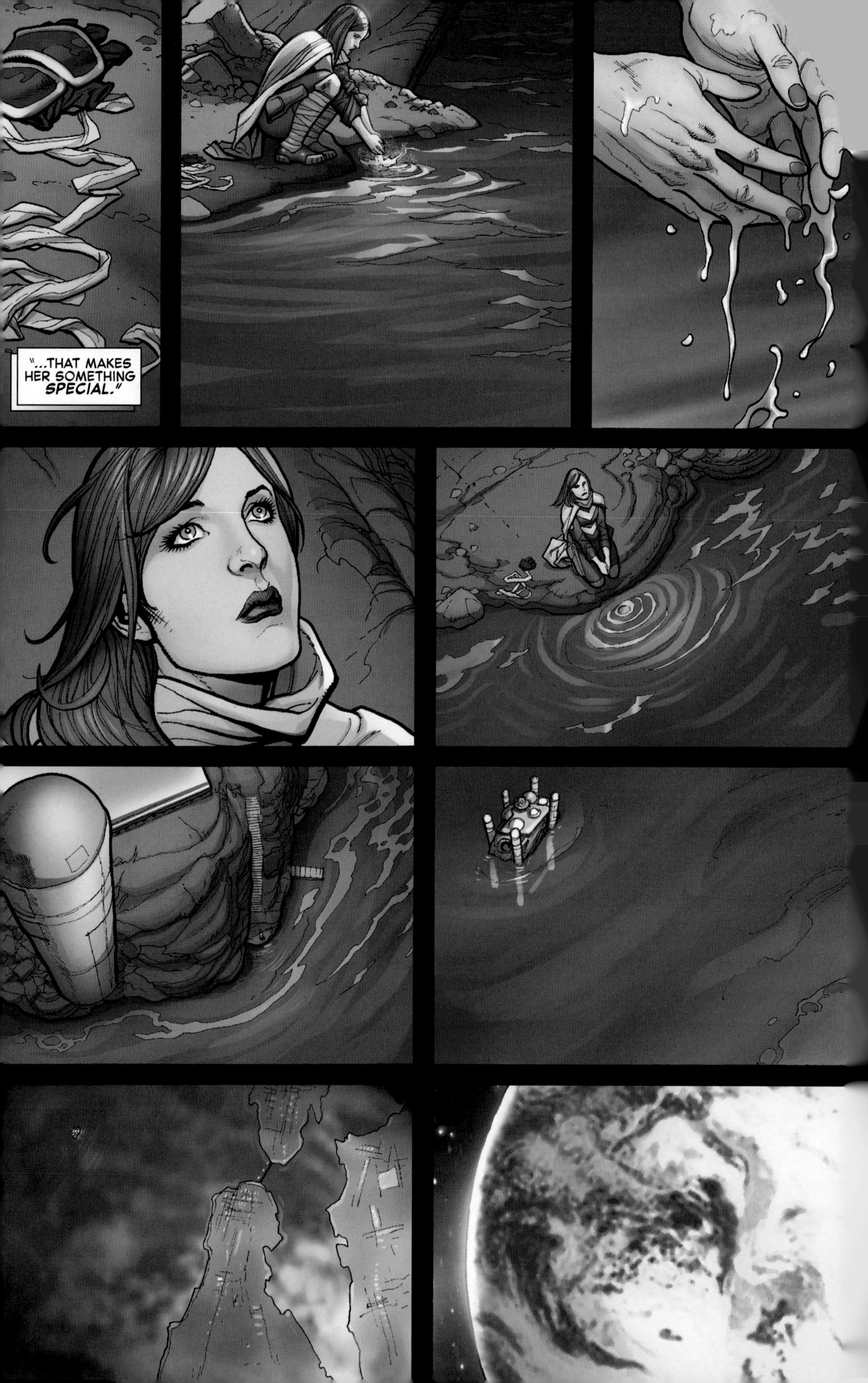
"...THAT MAKES HER SOMETHING SPECIAL."

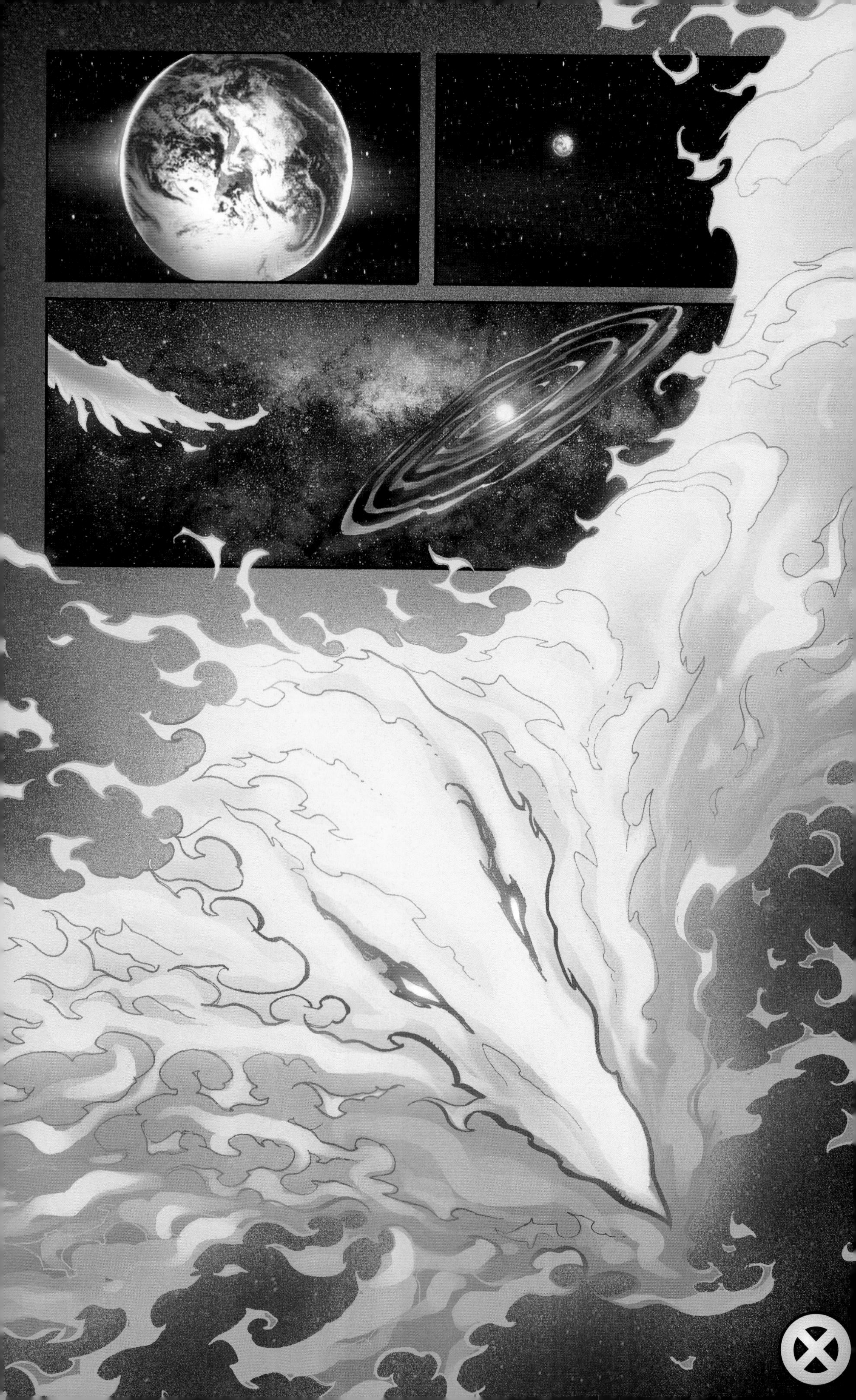

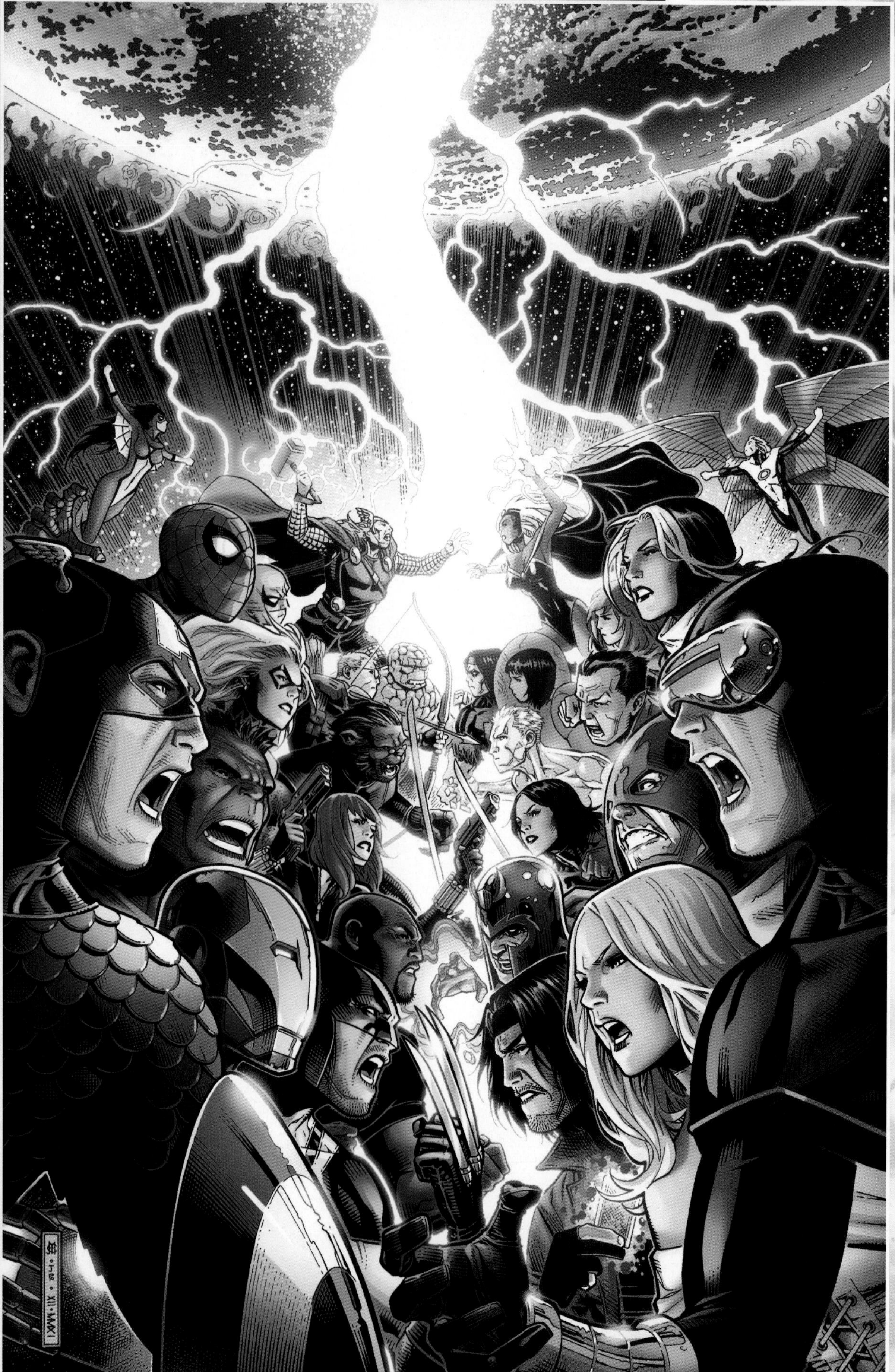

ROUND 1

AND THERE CAME A DAY, A DAY UNLIKE ANY OTHER, WHEN EARTH'S MIGHTIEST HEROES FOUND THEMSELVES UNITED AGAINST A COMMON THREAT! ON THAT DAY THE AVENGERS WERE BORN, TO FIGHT THE FOES NO SINGLE SUPER HERO COULD WITHSTAND!

AVENGERS
VS.
X-MEN

CHILDREN OF THE ATOM. MUTANTS — FEARED AND HATED BY THE WORLD THEY HAVE SWORN TO PROTECT. THESE ARE THE STRANGEST HEROES OF ALL!

AVENGERS

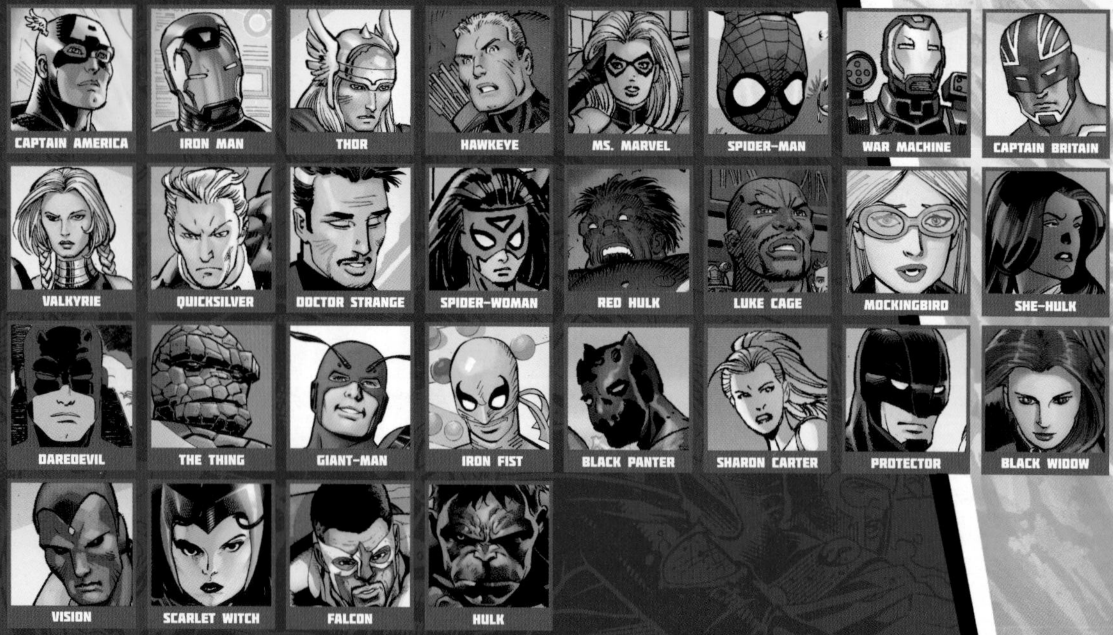
CAPTAIN AMERICA
IRON MAN
THOR
HAWKEYE
MS. MARVEL
SPIDER-MAN
WAR MACHINE
CAPTAIN BRITAIN
VALKYRIE
QUICKSILVER
DOCTOR STRANGE
SPIDER-WOMAN
RED HULK
LUKE CAGE
MOCKINGBIRD
SHE-HULK
DAREDEVIL
THE THING
GIANT-MAN
IRON FIST
BLACK PANTER
SHARON CARTER
PROTECTOR
BLACK WIDOW
VISION
SCARLET WITCH
FALCON
HULK

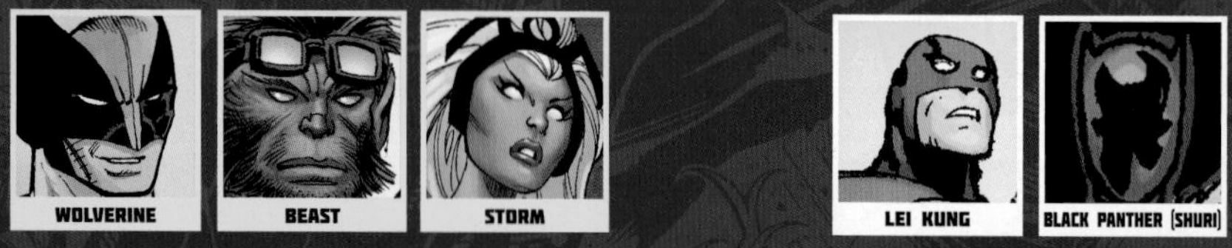
WOLVERINE
BEAST
STORM
LEI KUNG
BLACK PANTHER (SHURI)

X-MEN

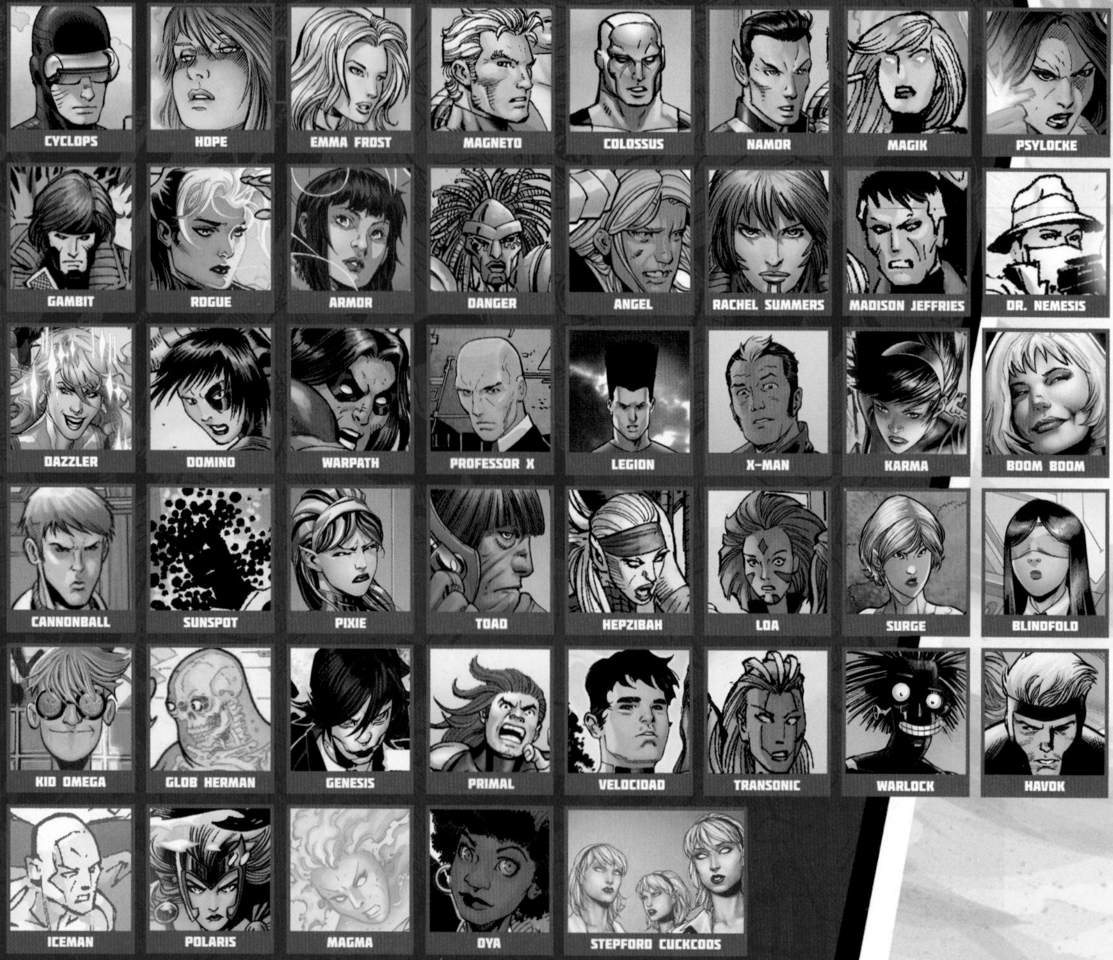
CYCLOPS
HOPE
EMMA FROST
MAGNETO
COLOSSUS
NAMOR
MAGIK
PSYLOCKE
GAMBIT
ROGUE
ARMOR
DANGER
ANGEL
RACHEL SUMMERS
MADISON JEFFRIES
DR. NEMESIS
DAZZLER
DOMINO
WARPATH
PROFESSOR X
LEGION
X-MAN
KARMA
BOOM BOOM
CANNONBALL
SUNSPOT
PIXIE
TOAD
HEPZIBAH
LOA
SURGE
BLINDFOLD
KID OMEGA
GLOB HERMAN
GENESIS
PRIMAL
VELOCIDAD
TRANSONIC
WARLOCK
HAVOK
ICEMAN
POLARIS
MAGMA
OYA
STEPFORD CUCKOOS

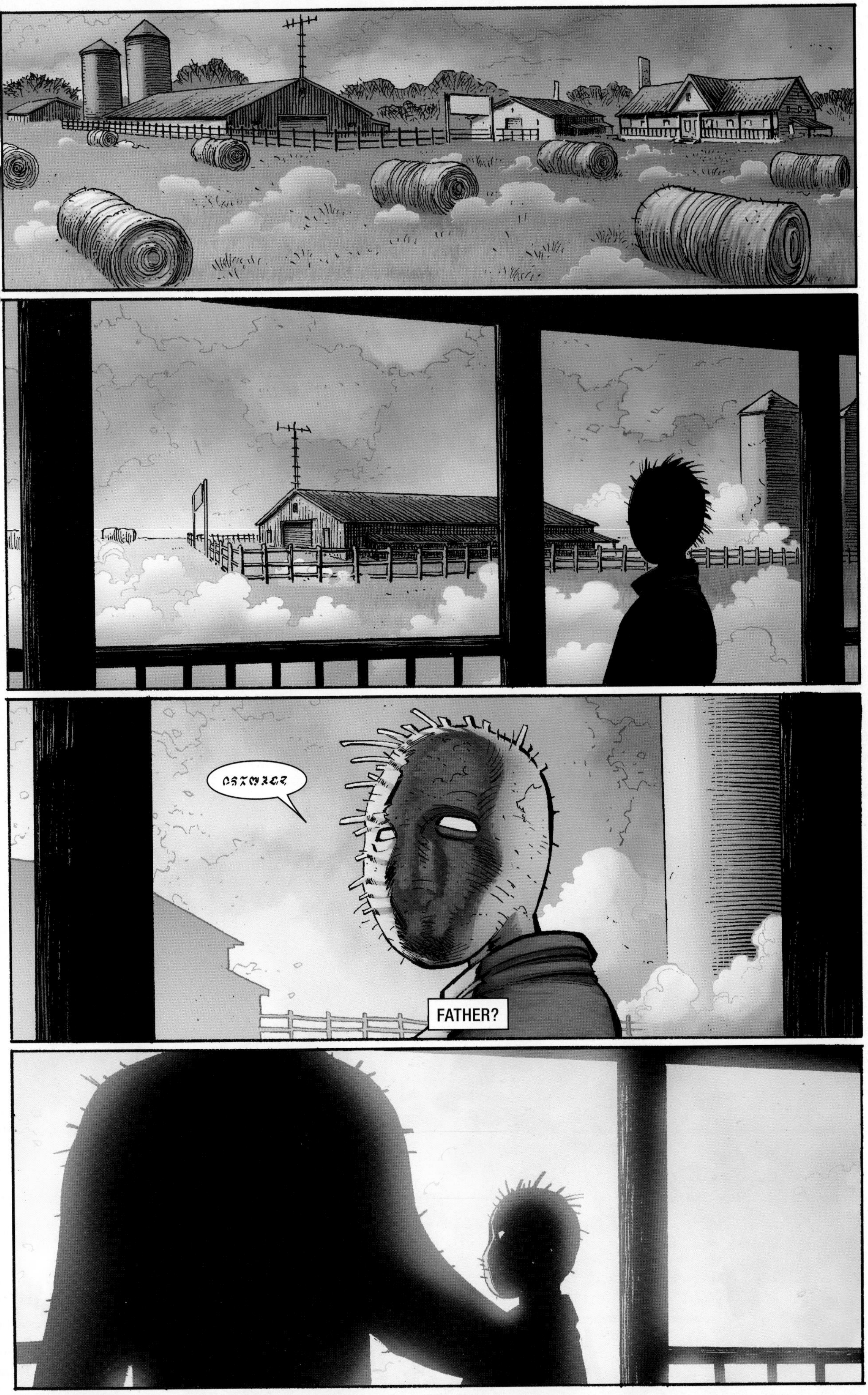
FATHER?

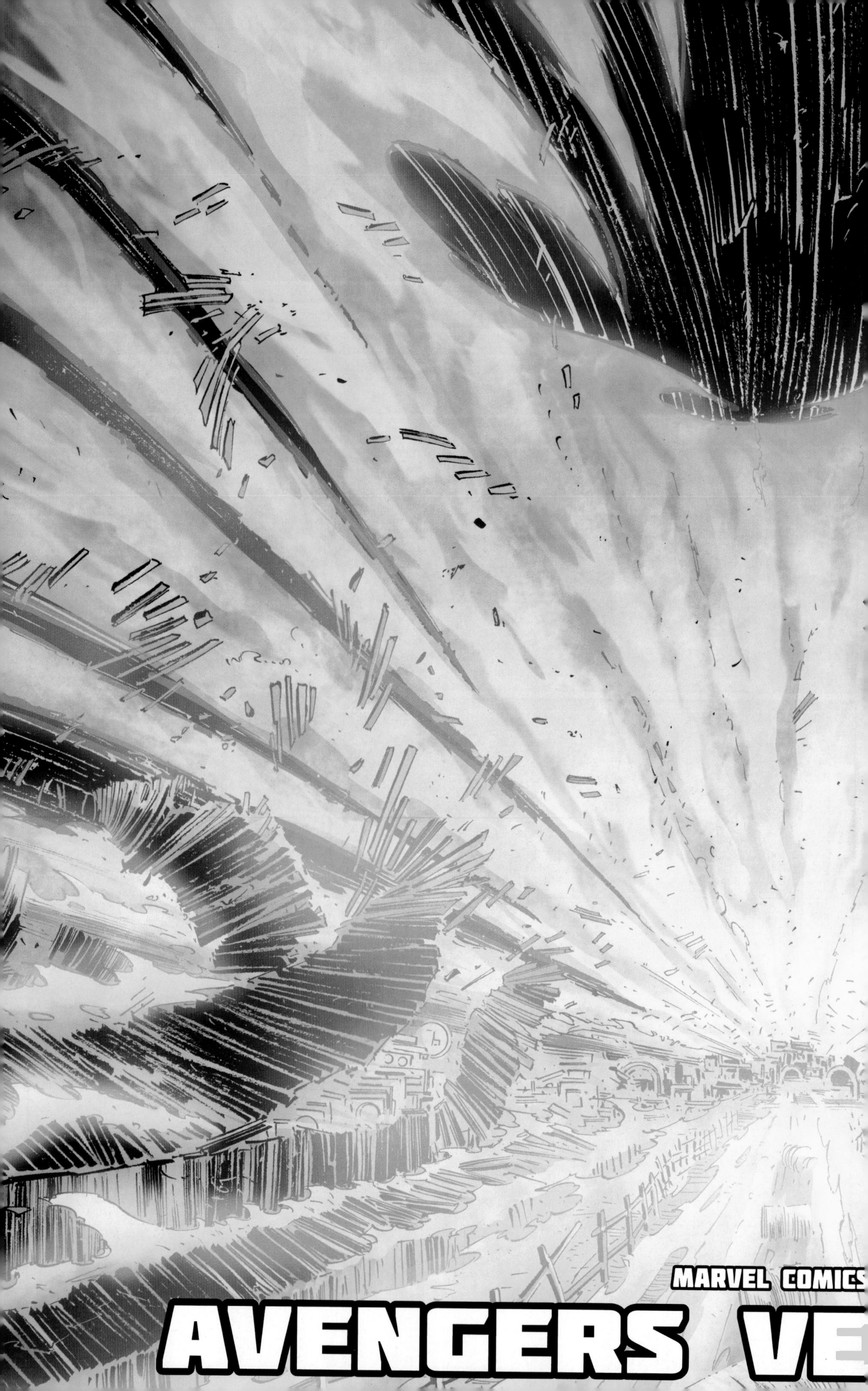
MARVEL COMICS
AVENGERS VE

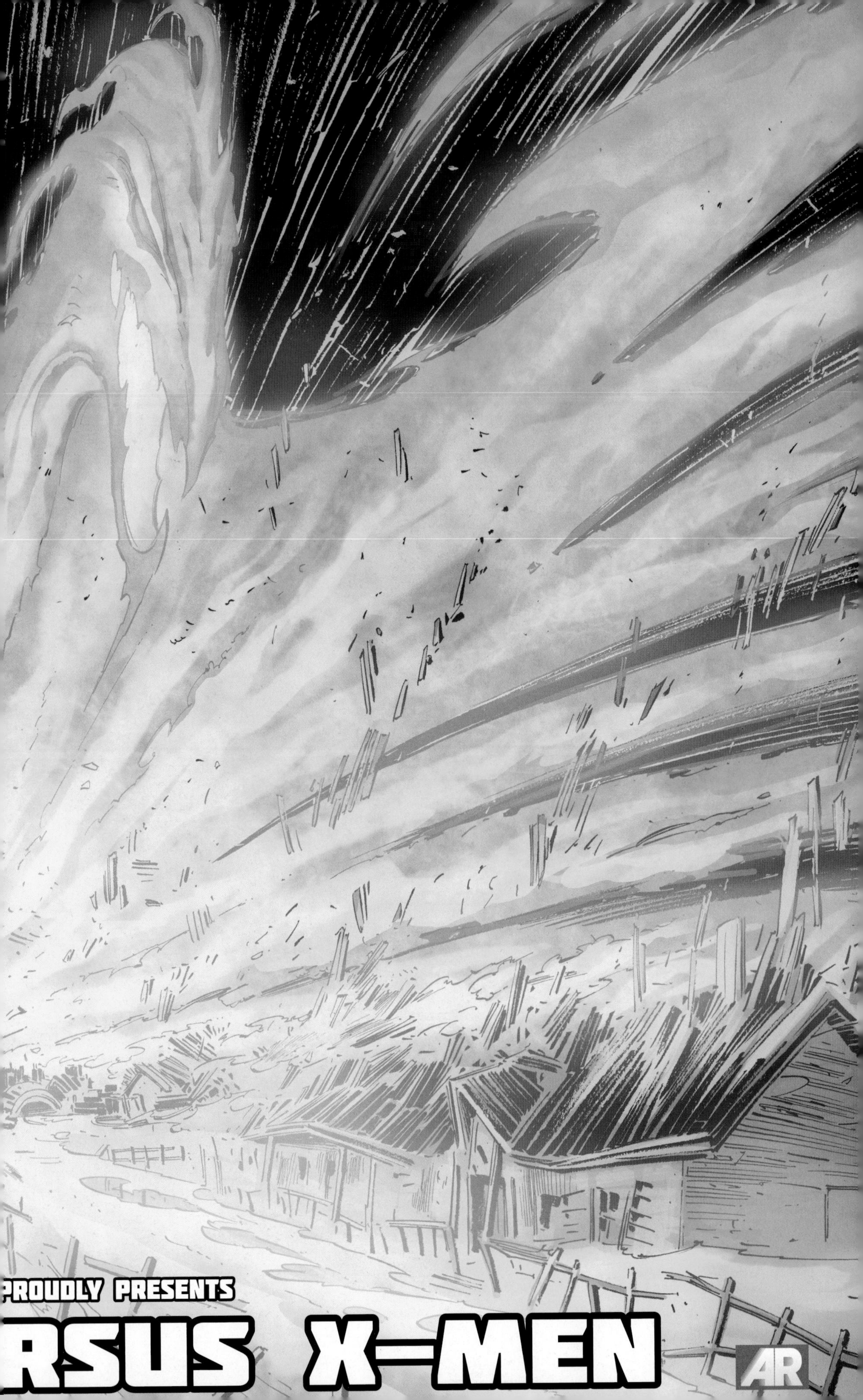
PROUDLY PRESENTS
RSUS X-MEN
AR

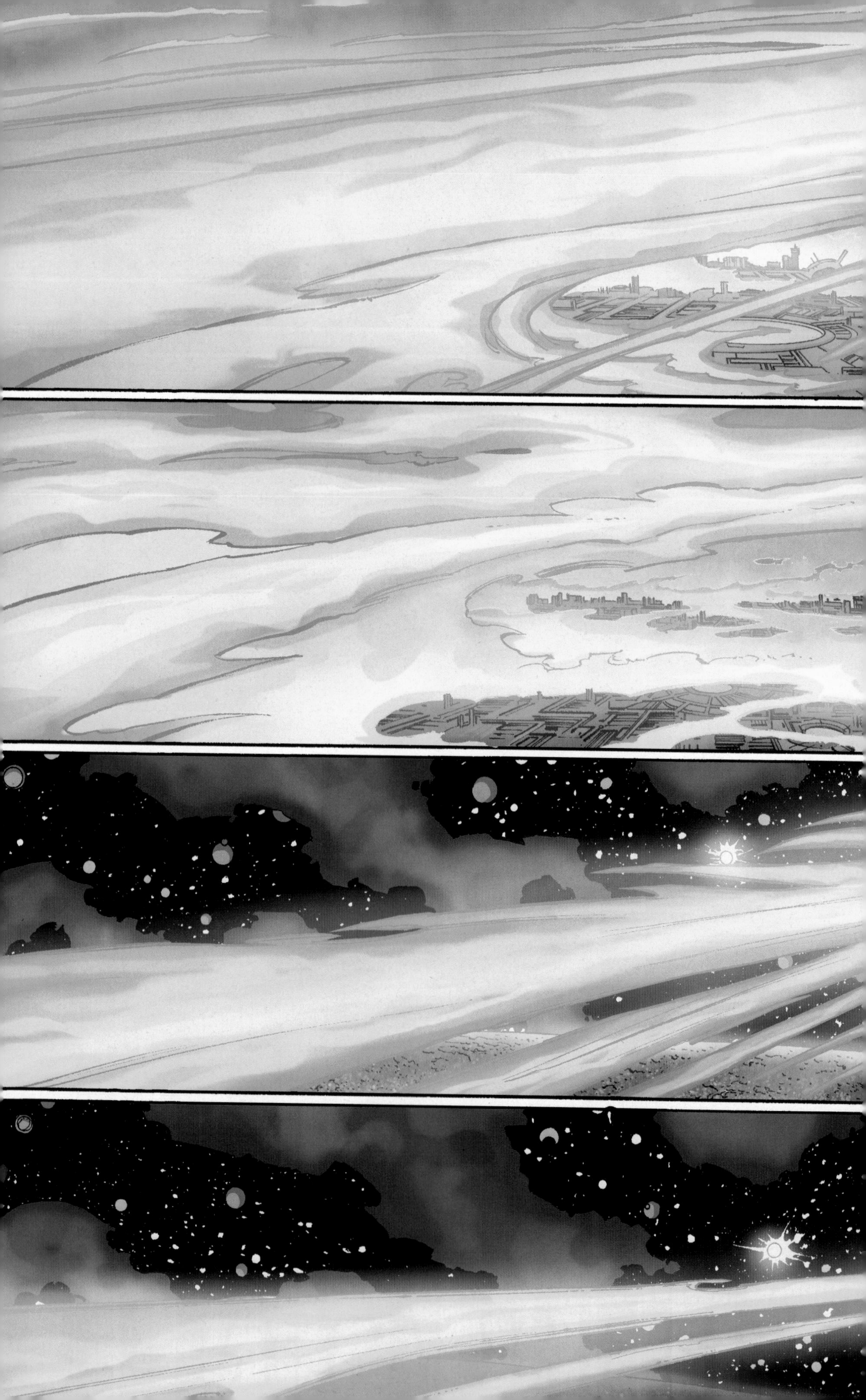

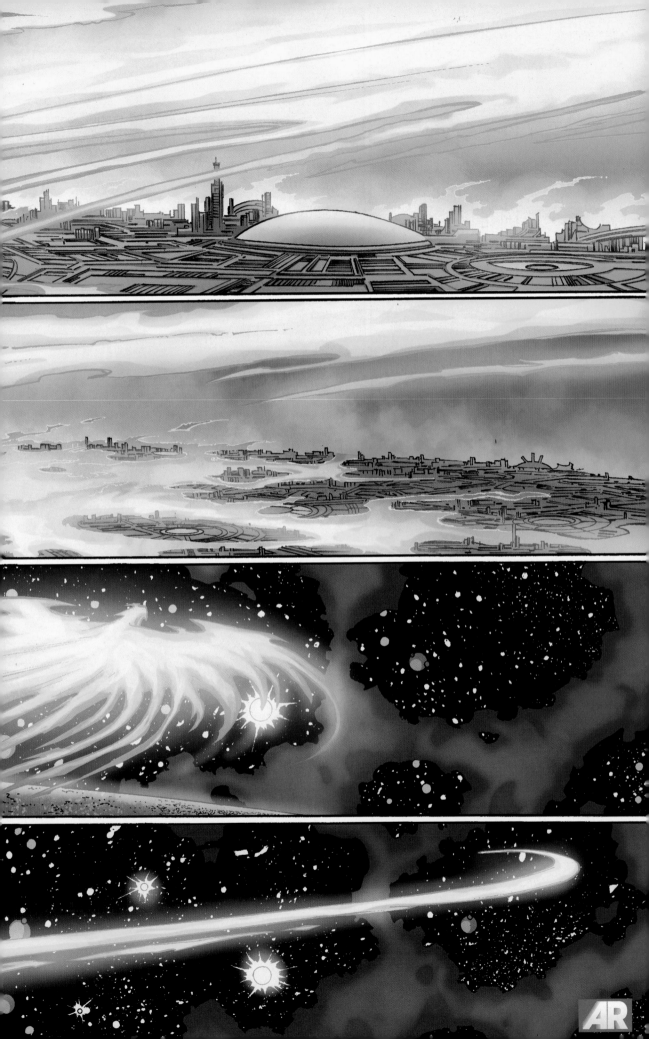

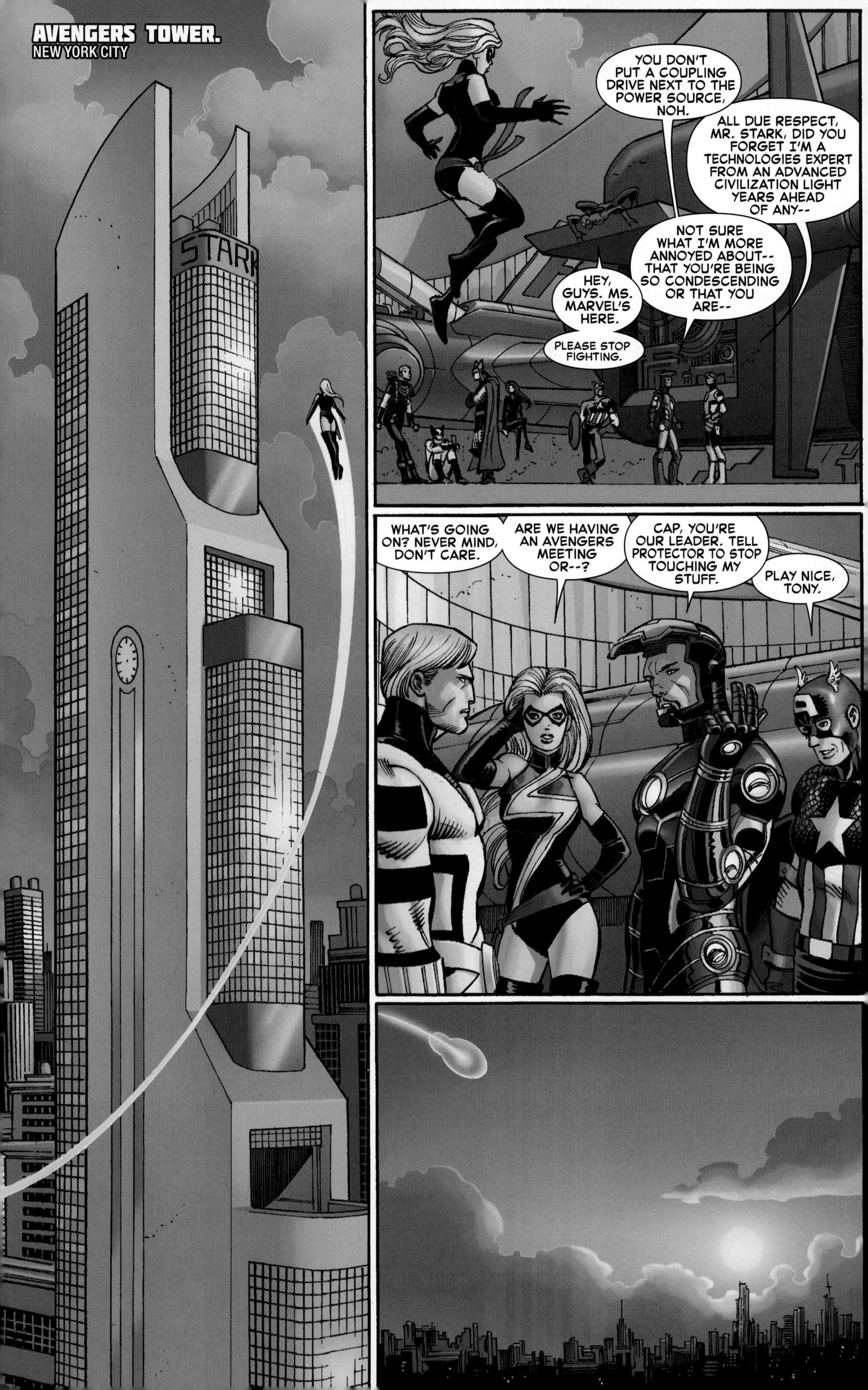
AVENGERS TOWER.
NEW YORK CITY
STARK
YOU DON'T PUT A COUPLING DRIVE NEXT TO THE POWER SOURCE, NOH.
ALL DUE RESPECT, MR. STARK, DID YOU FORGET I'M A TECHNOLOGIES EXPERT FROM AN ADVANCED CIVILIZATION LIGHT YEARS AHEAD OF ANY--
NOT SURE WHAT I'M MORE ANNOYED ABOUT-- THAT YOU'RE BEING SO CONDESCENDING OR THAT YOU ARE--
HEY, GUYS. MS. MARVEL'S HERE.
PLEASE STOP FIGHTING.
WHAT'S GOING ON? NEVER MIND, DON'T CARE.
ARE WE HAVING AN AVENGERS MEETING OR--?
CAP, YOU'RE OUR LEADER. TELL PROTECTOR TO STOP TOUCHING MY STUFF.
PLAY NICE, TONY.

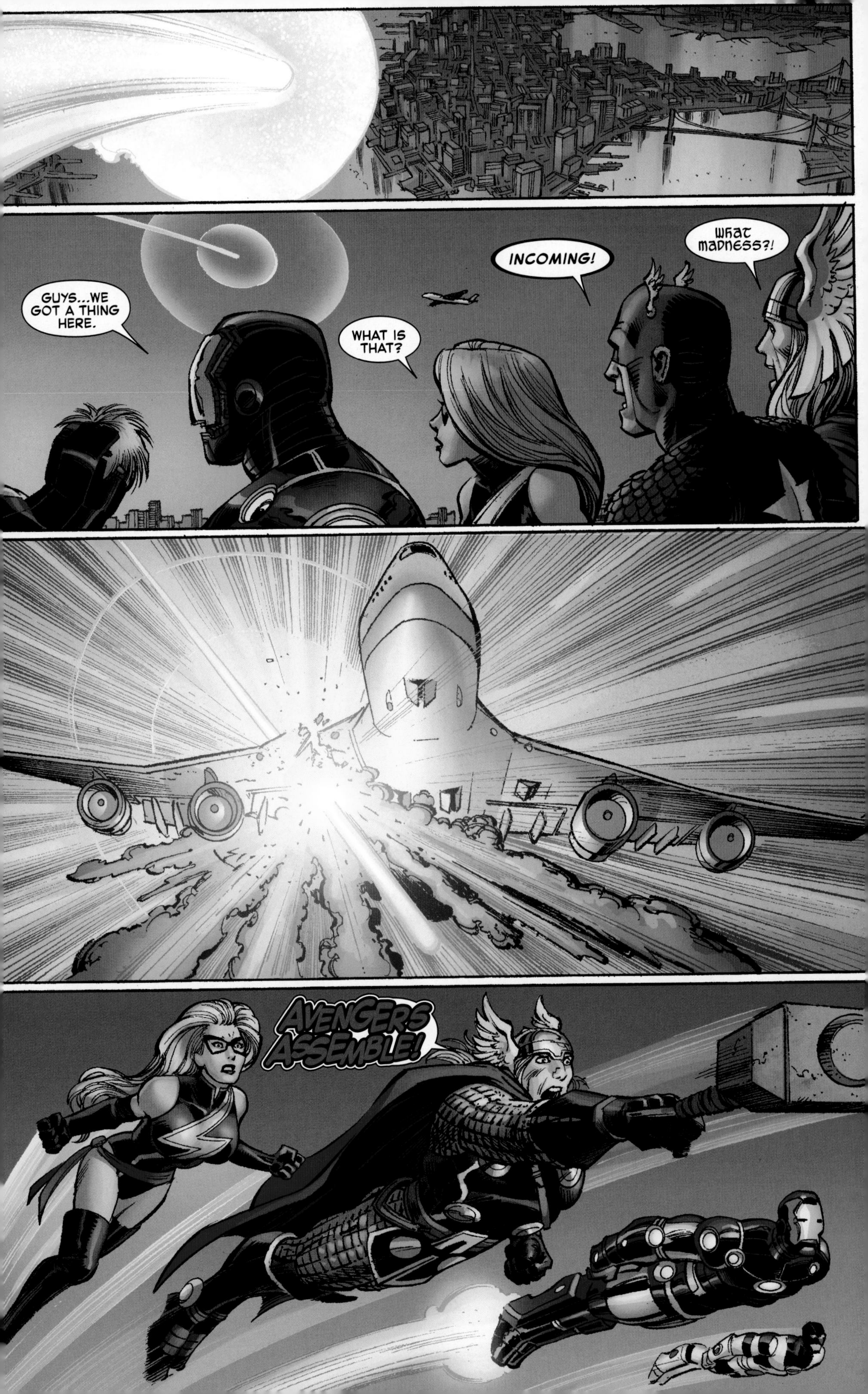
GUYS...WE GOT A THING HERE.
WHAT IS THAT?
INCOMING!
WHAT MADNESS?!
AVENGERS ASSEMBLE!

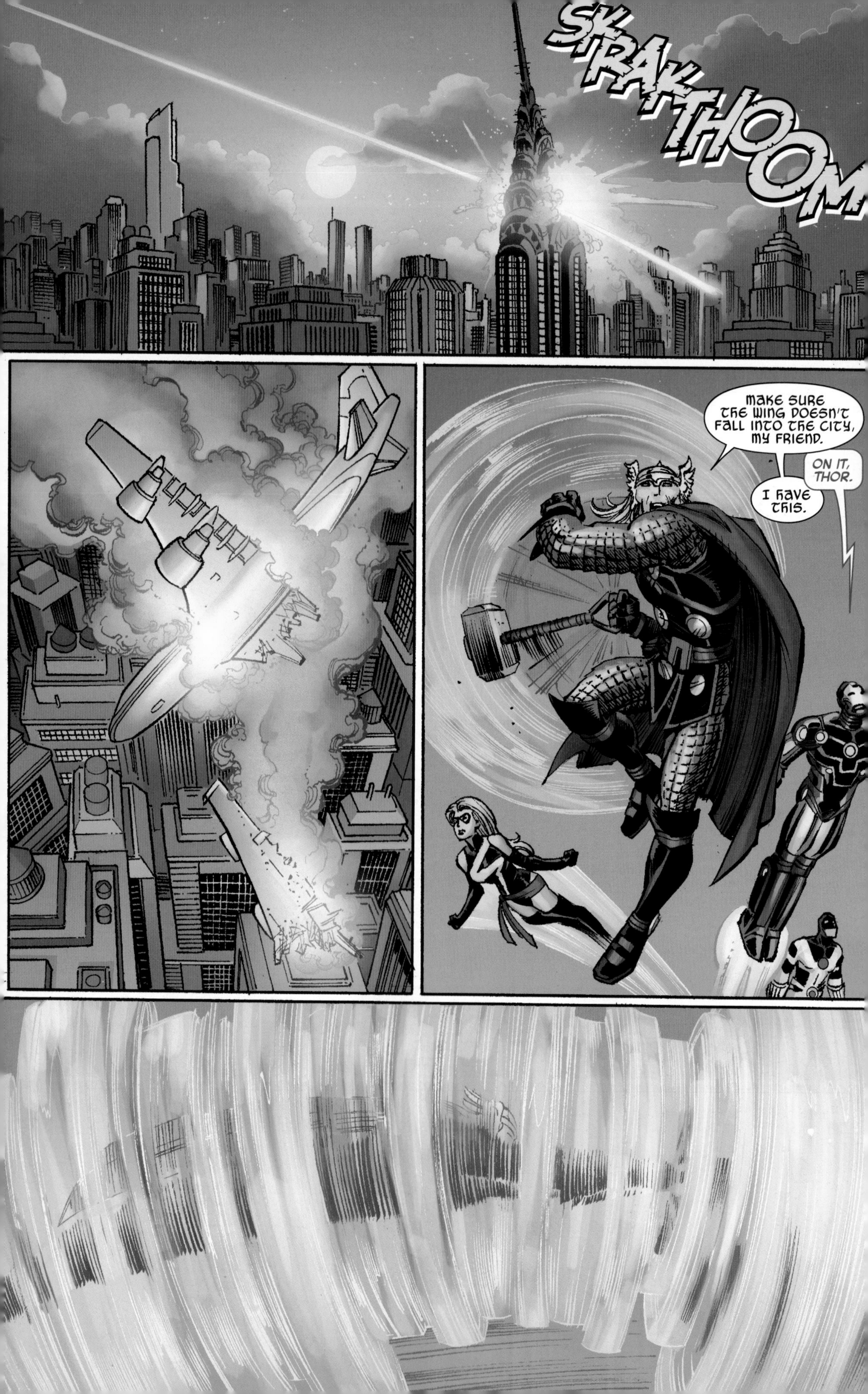
SKRAKTHOOM
MAKE SURE THE WING DOESN'T FALL INTO THE CITY, MY FRIEND.
I HAVE THIS.
ON IT, THOR.

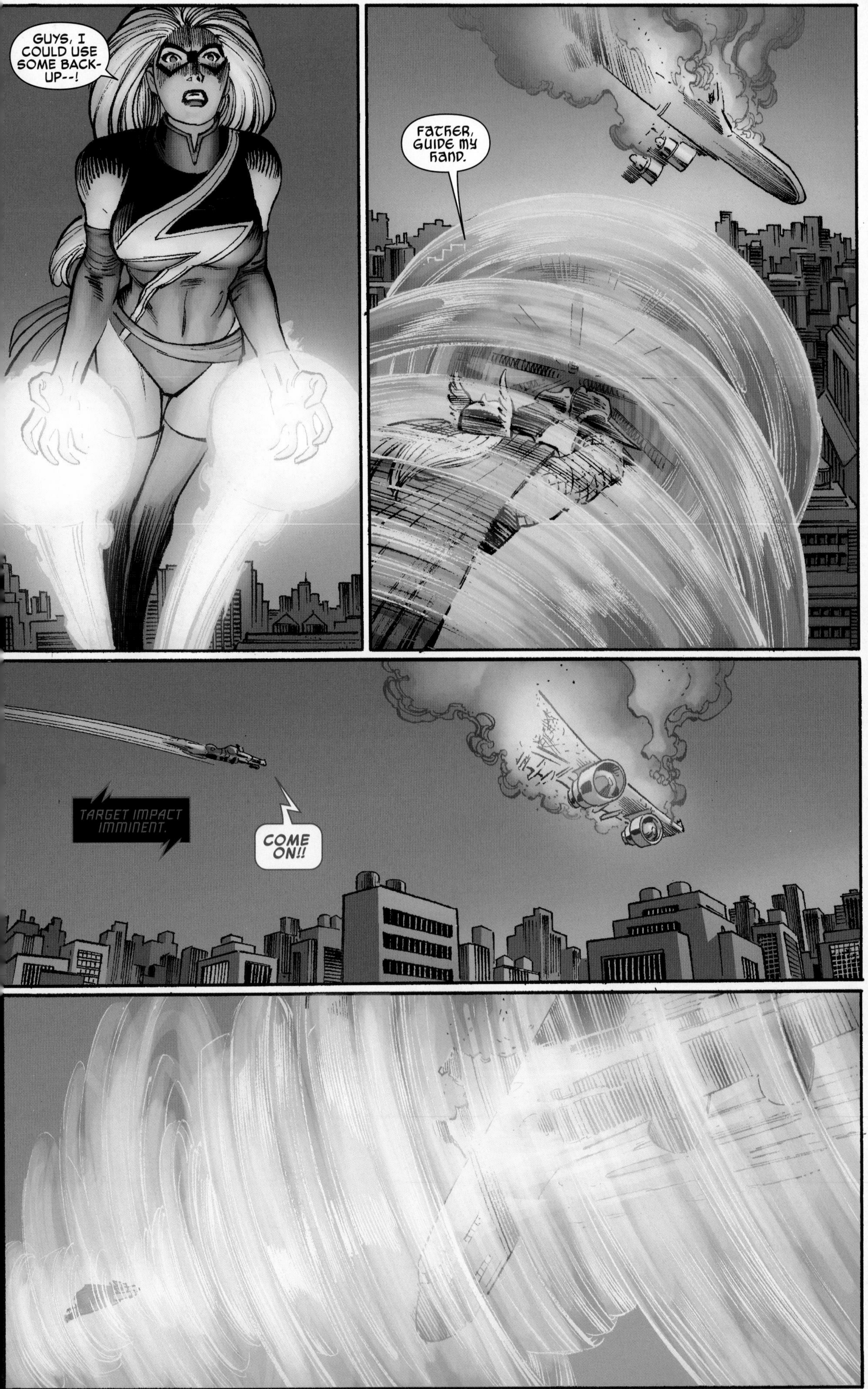
GUYS, I COULD USE SOME BACK-UP--!
FATHER, GUIDE MY HAND.
TARGET IMPACT IMMINENT.
COME ON!!

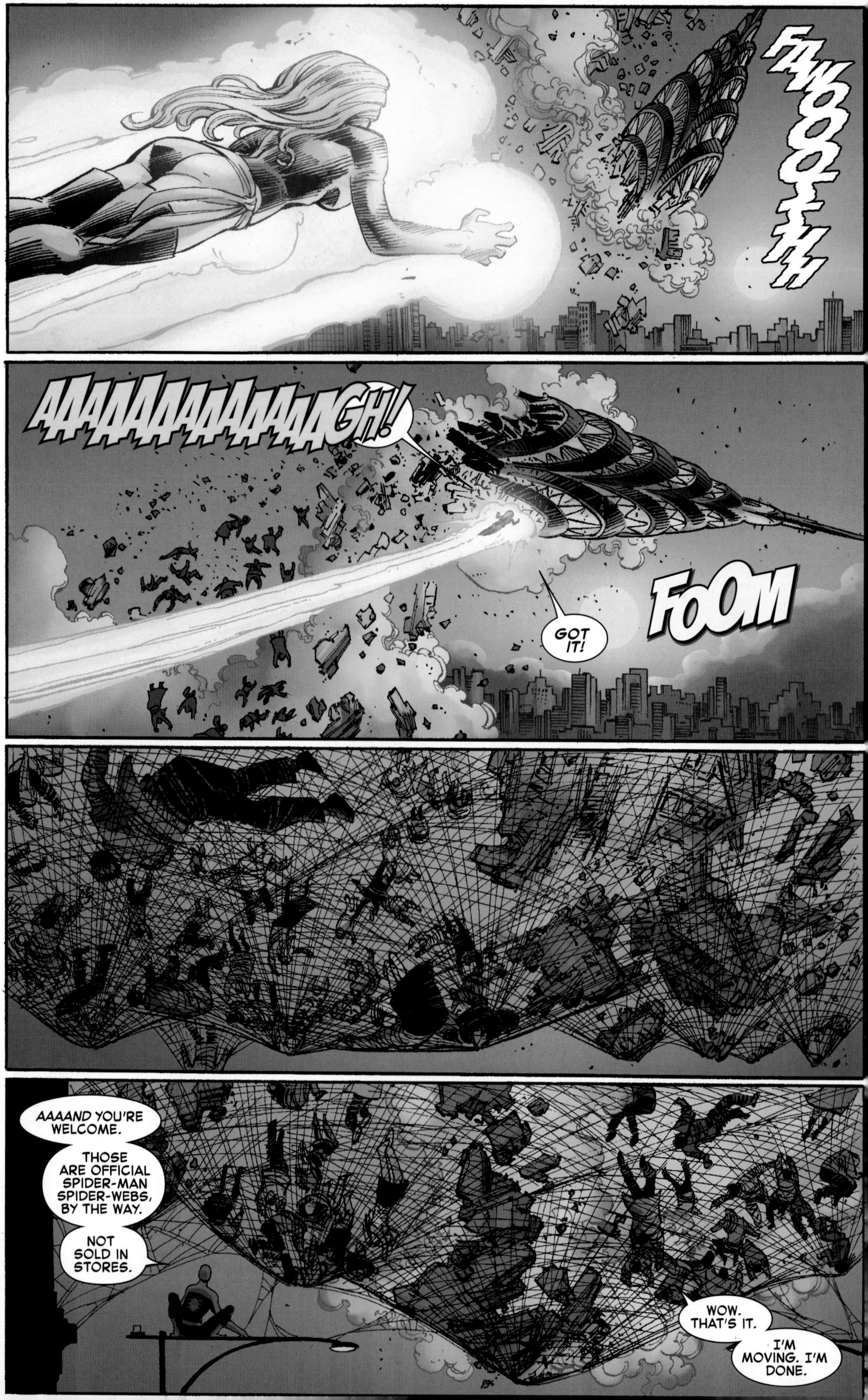
FWOOOOSHH
AAAAAAAAAAAAAAGH!
GOT IT!
FOOM
AAAAND YOU'RE WELCOME.
THOSE ARE OFFICIAL SPIDER-MAN SPIDER-WEBS, BY THE WAY.
NOT SOLD IN STORES.
WOW. THAT'S IT.
I'M MOVING. I'M DONE.

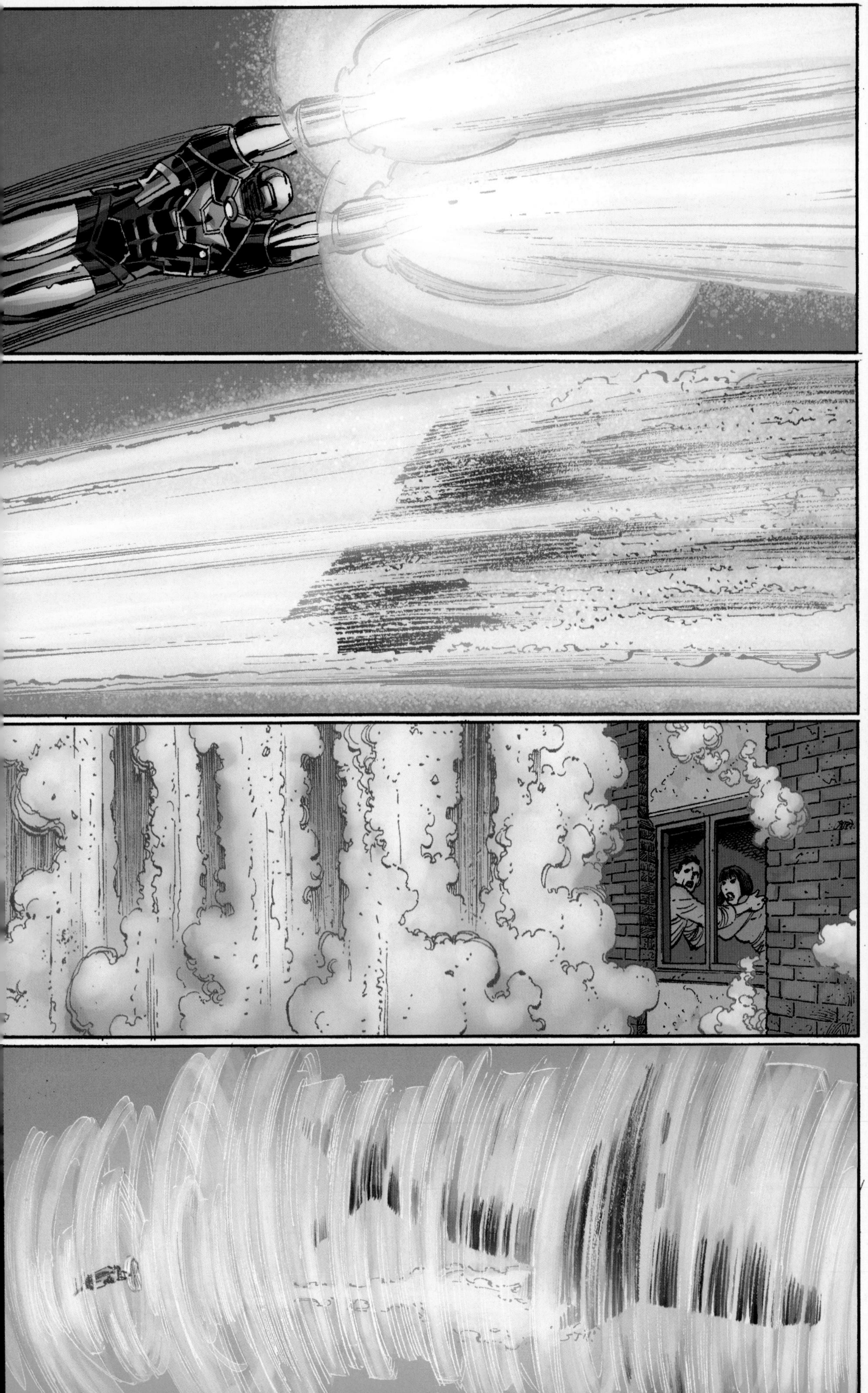

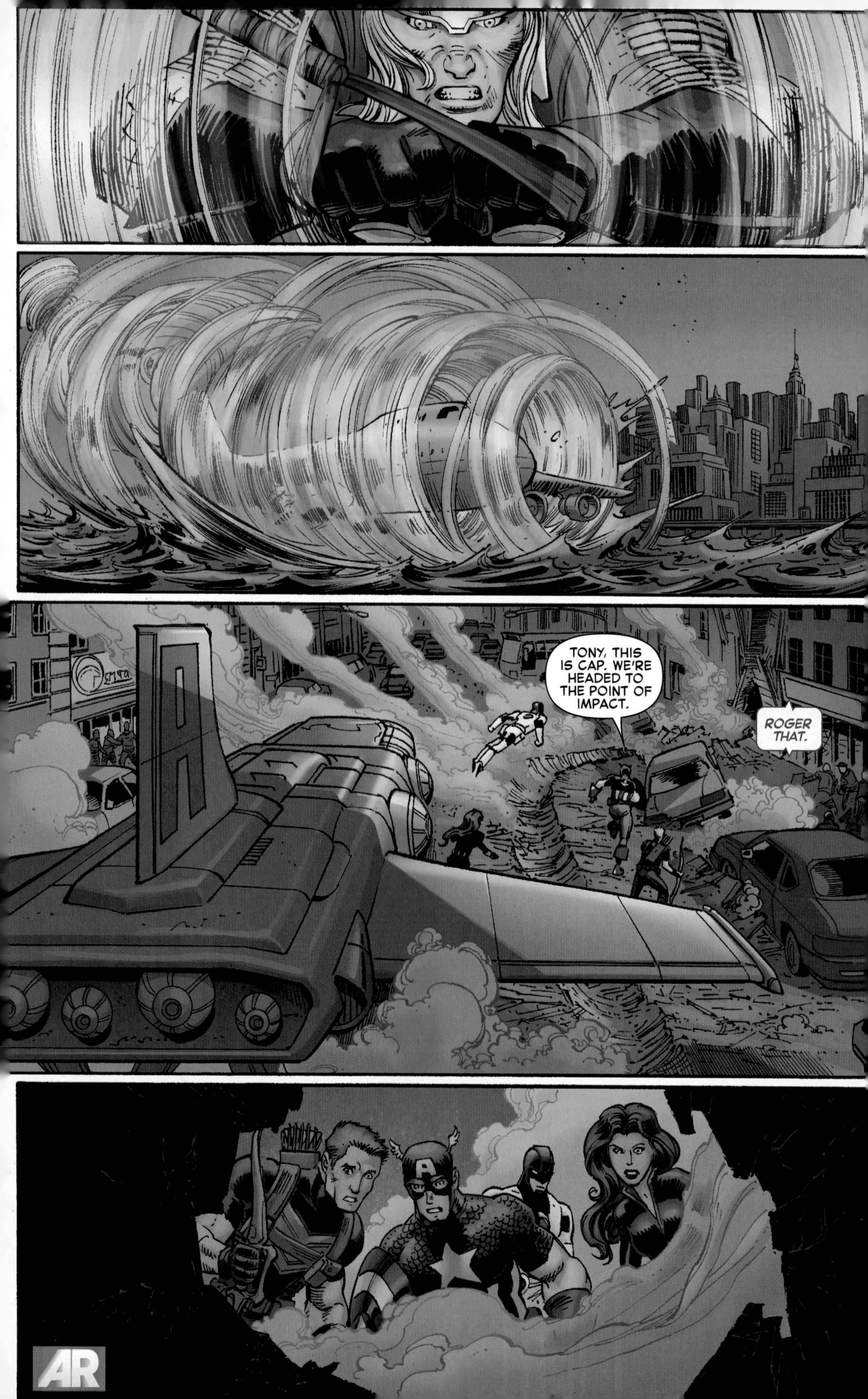
TONY, THIS IS CAP. WE'RE HEADED TO THE POINT OF IMPACT.
ROGER THAT.

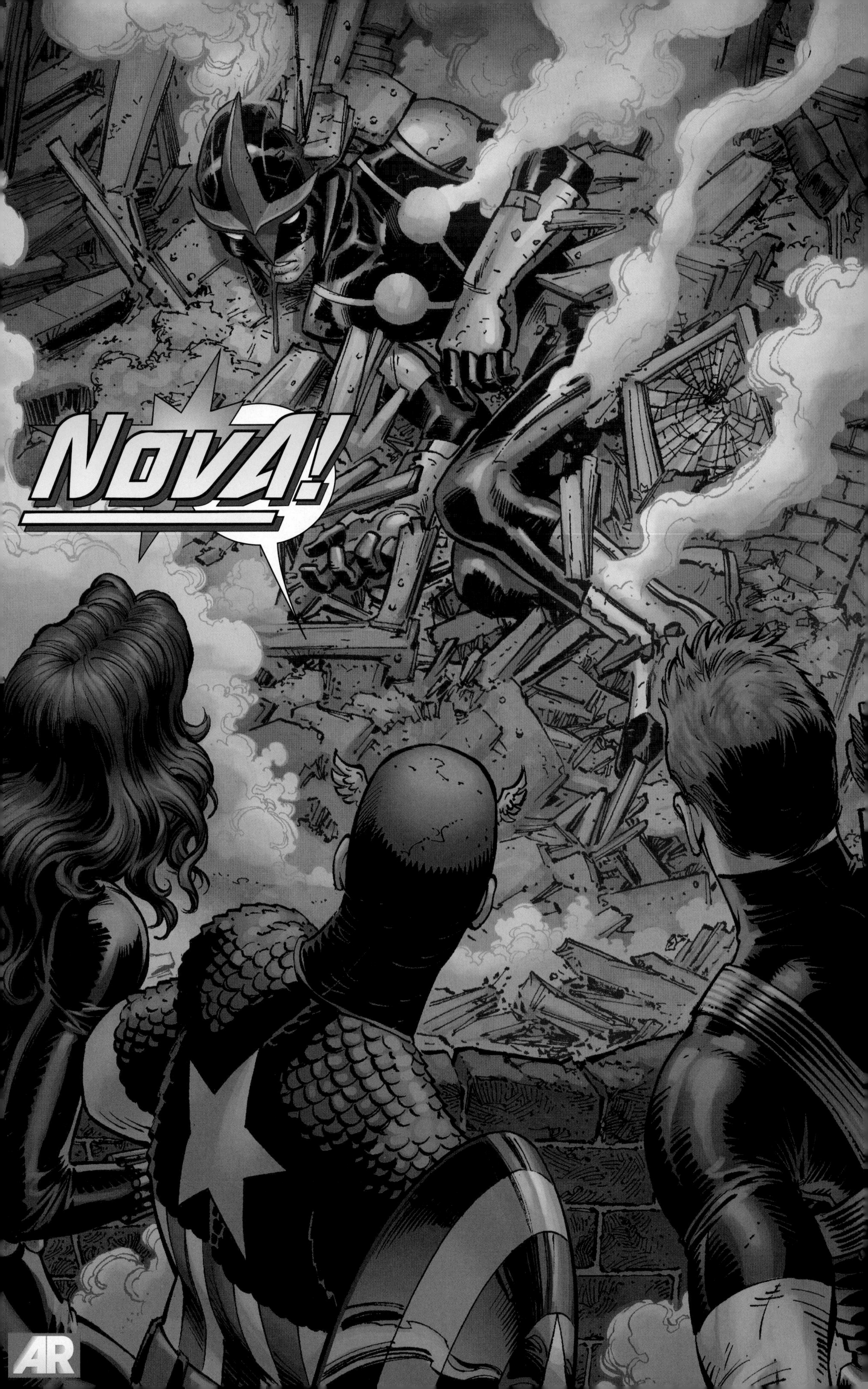
NOVA!

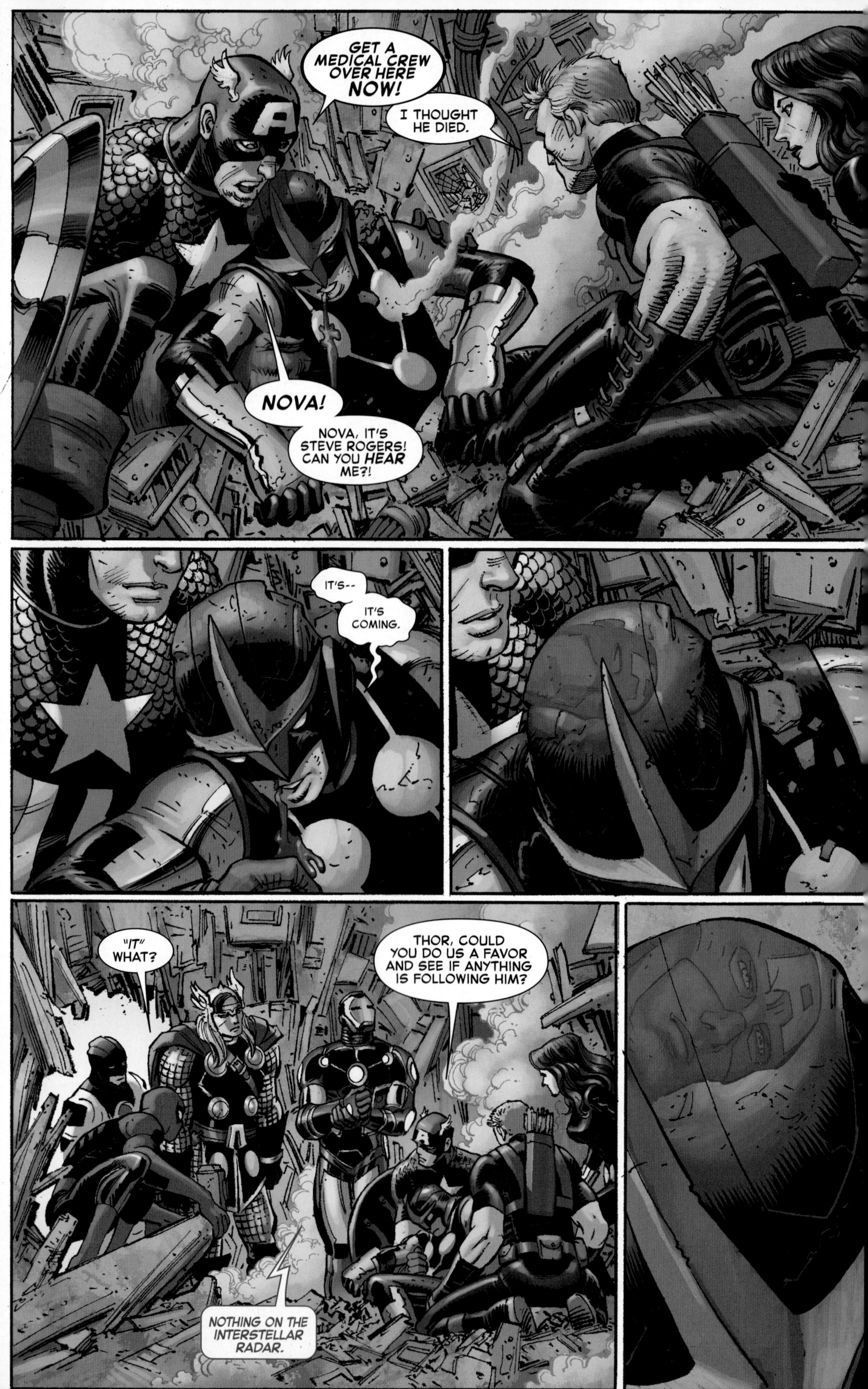
GET A MEDICAL CREW OVER HERE NOW!
I THOUGHT HE DIED.
NOVA!
NOVA, IT'S STEVE ROGERS! CAN YOU HEAR ME?!
IT'S--
IT'S COMING.
"IT" WHAT?
THOR, COULD YOU DO US A FAVOR AND SEE IF ANYTHING IS FOLLOWING HIM?
NOTHING ON THE INTERSTELLAR RADAR.

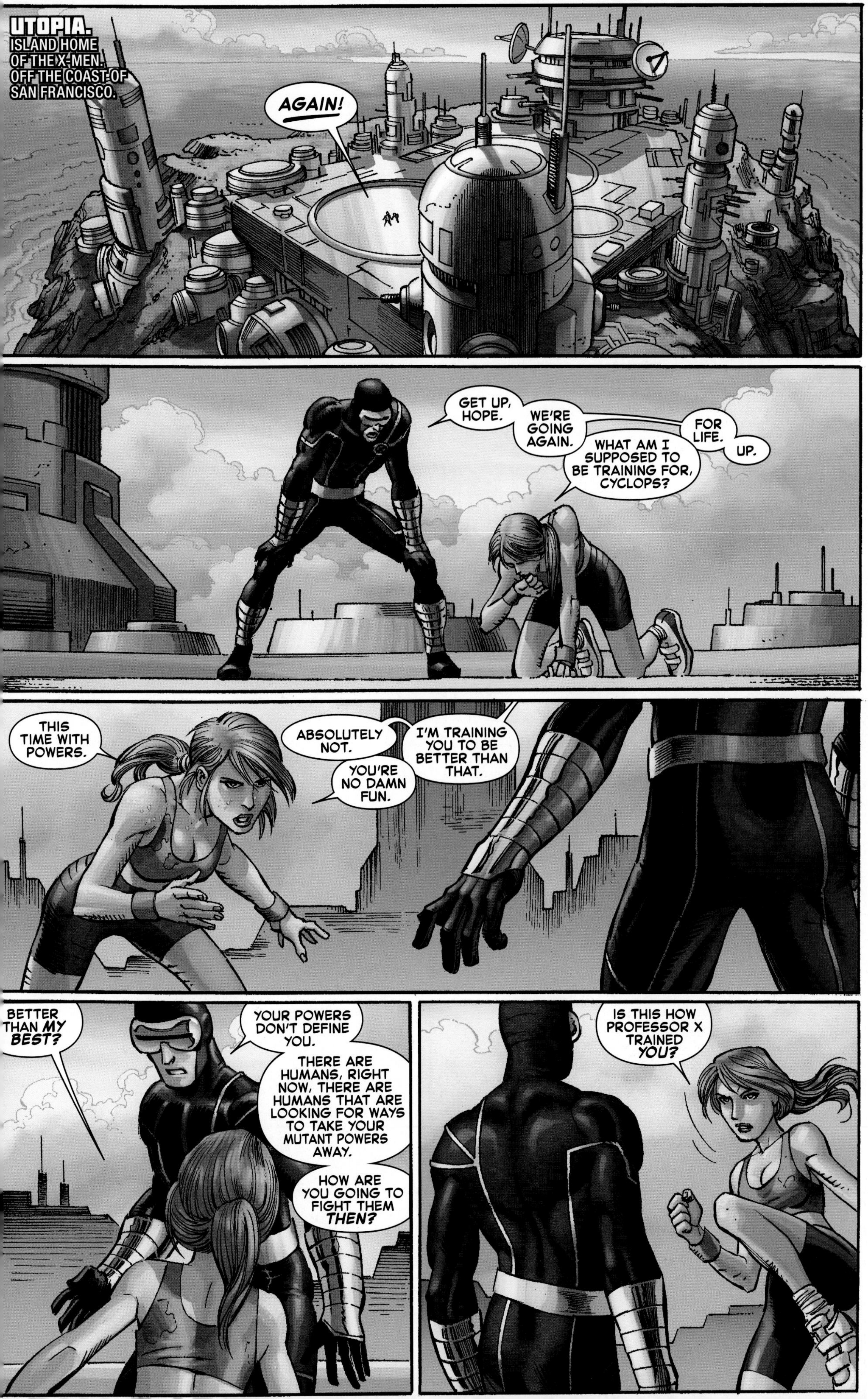
UTOPIA.
ISLAND HOME OF THE X-MEN. OFF THE COAST OF SAN FRANCISCO.
AGAIN!
GET UP, HOPE.
WE'RE GOING AGAIN.
WHAT AM I SUPPOSED TO BE TRAINING FOR, CYCLOPS?
FOR LIFE.
UP.
THIS TIME WITH POWERS.
ABSOLUTELY NOT.
YOU'RE NO DAMN FUN.
I'M TRAINING YOU TO BE BETTER THAN THAT.
BETTER THAN MY BEST?
YOUR POWERS DON'T DEFINE YOU.
THERE ARE HUMANS, RIGHT NOW, THERE ARE HUMANS THAT ARE LOOKING FOR WAYS TO TAKE YOUR MUTANT POWERS AWAY.
HOW ARE YOU GOING TO FIGHT THEM THEN?
IS THIS HOW PROFESSOR X TRAINED YOU?

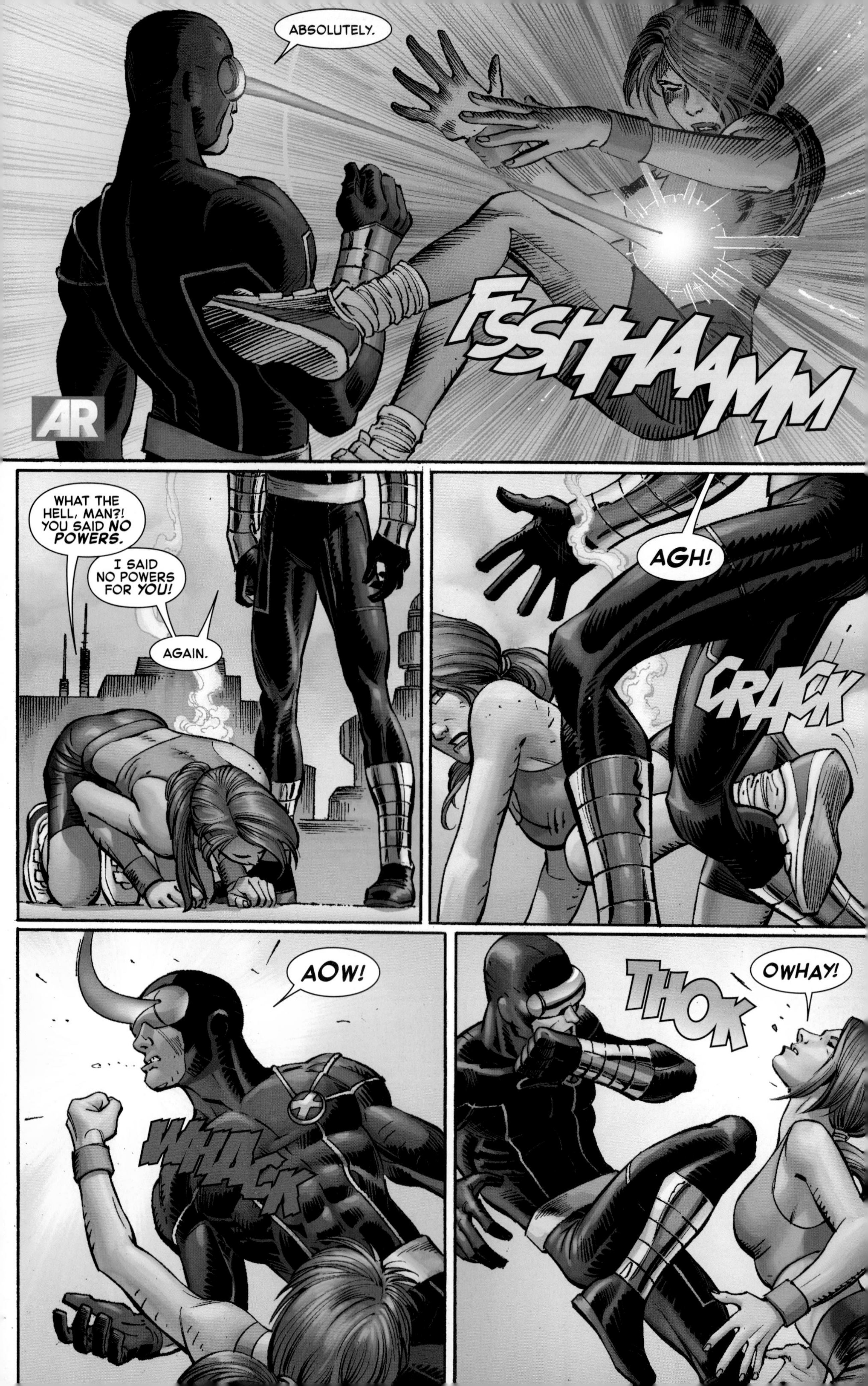

ABSOLUTELY.
FSSHHAAMM
WHAT THE HELL, MAN?! YOU SAID NO POWERS.
I SAID NO POWERS FOR YOU!
AGAIN.
AGH!
CRACK
AOW!
WHACK
THOK
OWHAY!

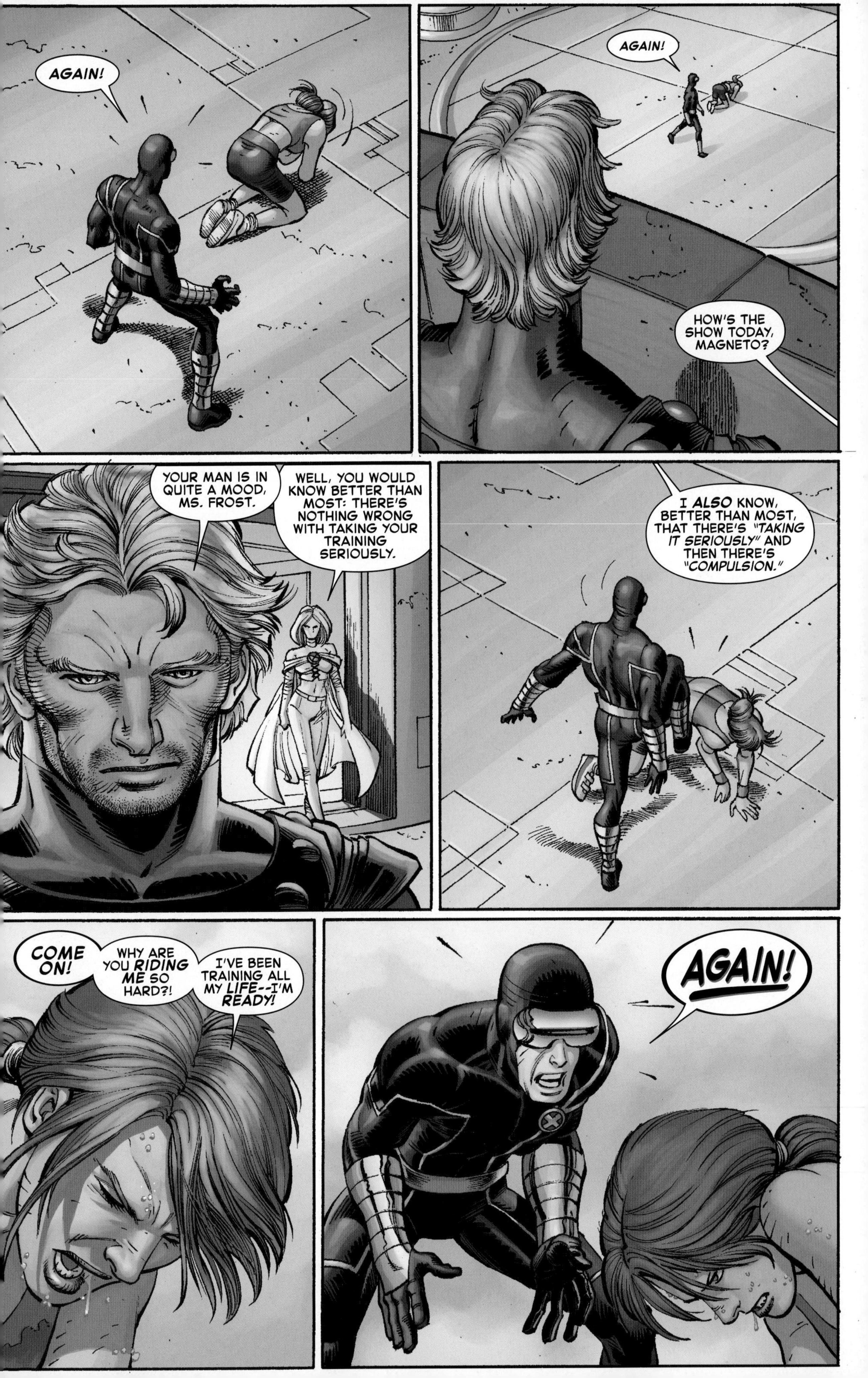
AGAIN!
AGAIN!
HOW'S THE SHOW TODAY, MAGNETO?
YOUR MAN IS IN QUITE A MOOD, MS. FROST.
WELL, YOU WOULD KNOW BETTER THAN MOST: THERE'S NOTHING WRONG WITH TAKING YOUR TRAINING SERIOUSLY.
I ALSO KNOW, BETTER THAN MOST, THAT THERE'S "TAKING IT SERIOUSLY" AND THEN THERE'S "COMPULSION."
COME ON!
WHY ARE YOU RIDING ME SO HARD?!
I'VE BEEN TRAINING ALL MY LIFE--I'M READY!
AGAIN!

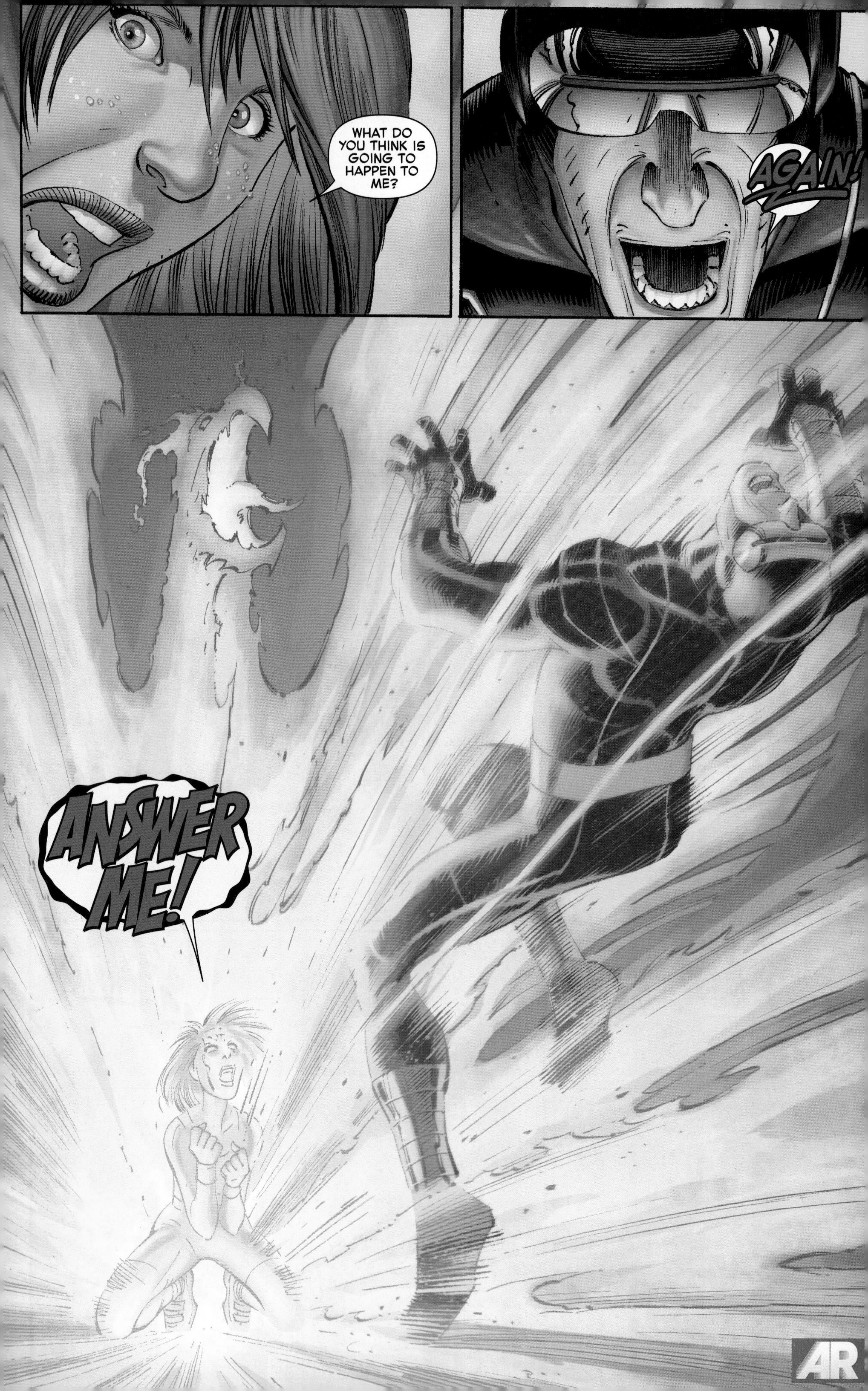
WHAT DO YOU THINK IS GOING TO HAPPEN TO ME?
AGAIN!
ANSWER ME!

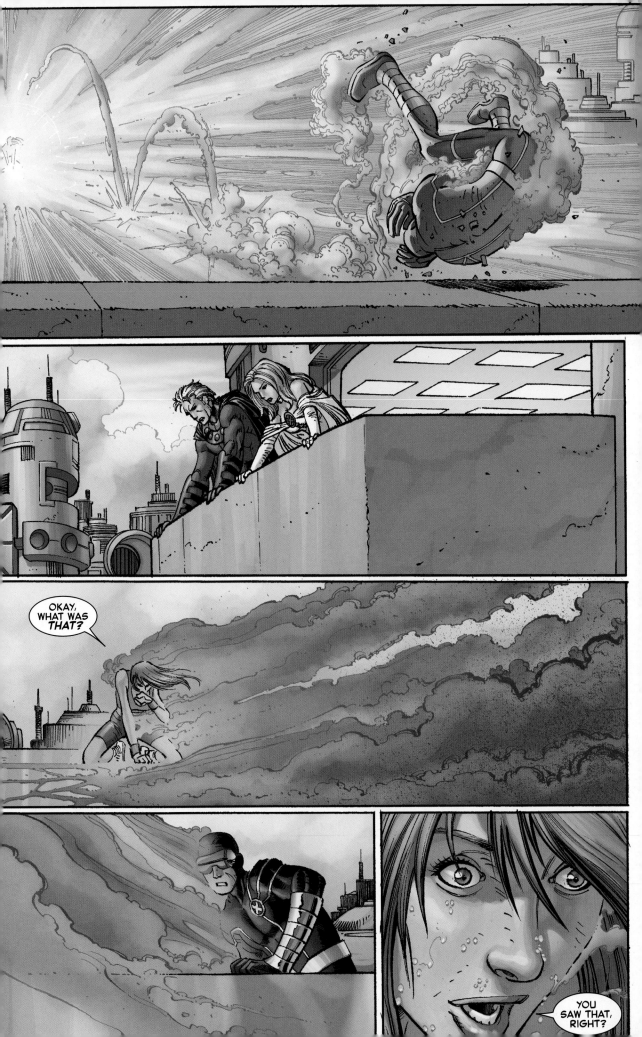

OKAY, WHAT WAS *THAT*?

YOU SAW THAT, RIGHT?

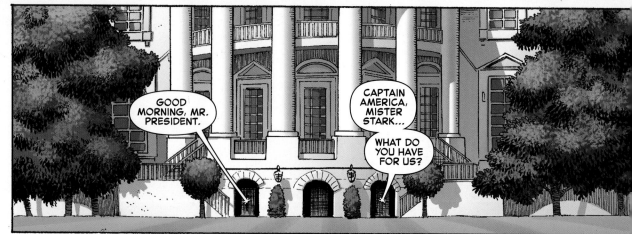

GOOD MORNING, MR. PRESIDENT.

CAPTAIN AMERICA, MISTER STARK...

WHAT DO YOU HAVE FOR US?

SINCE THE SKRULL INVASION YOU'VE ASKED TO BE KEPT ABREAST OF ANY INTERSTELLAR SITUATIONS THAT WE COME ACROSS.

LAST NIGHT, WE INTERCEPTED THE ARRIVAL OF A MEMBER OF THE INTERGALACTIC NOVA CORPS.

HE CAME WITH A RATHER VAGUE, YET ALARMING, WARNING AND THEN LAPSED INTO A COMA.

THE SCORCH MARKS AND WEAR AND TEAR ON HIS UNIFORM LEAD US TO BELIEVE HE SURVIVED A CONFLICT WITH AN IMMENSE ENERGY SOURCE.

WE HAD BOTH THOR AND TONY HERE DO PERSONAL AND SATELLITE INTERSTELLAR RECON--

WHAT WE FOUND WAS, WELL, DISTURBING.

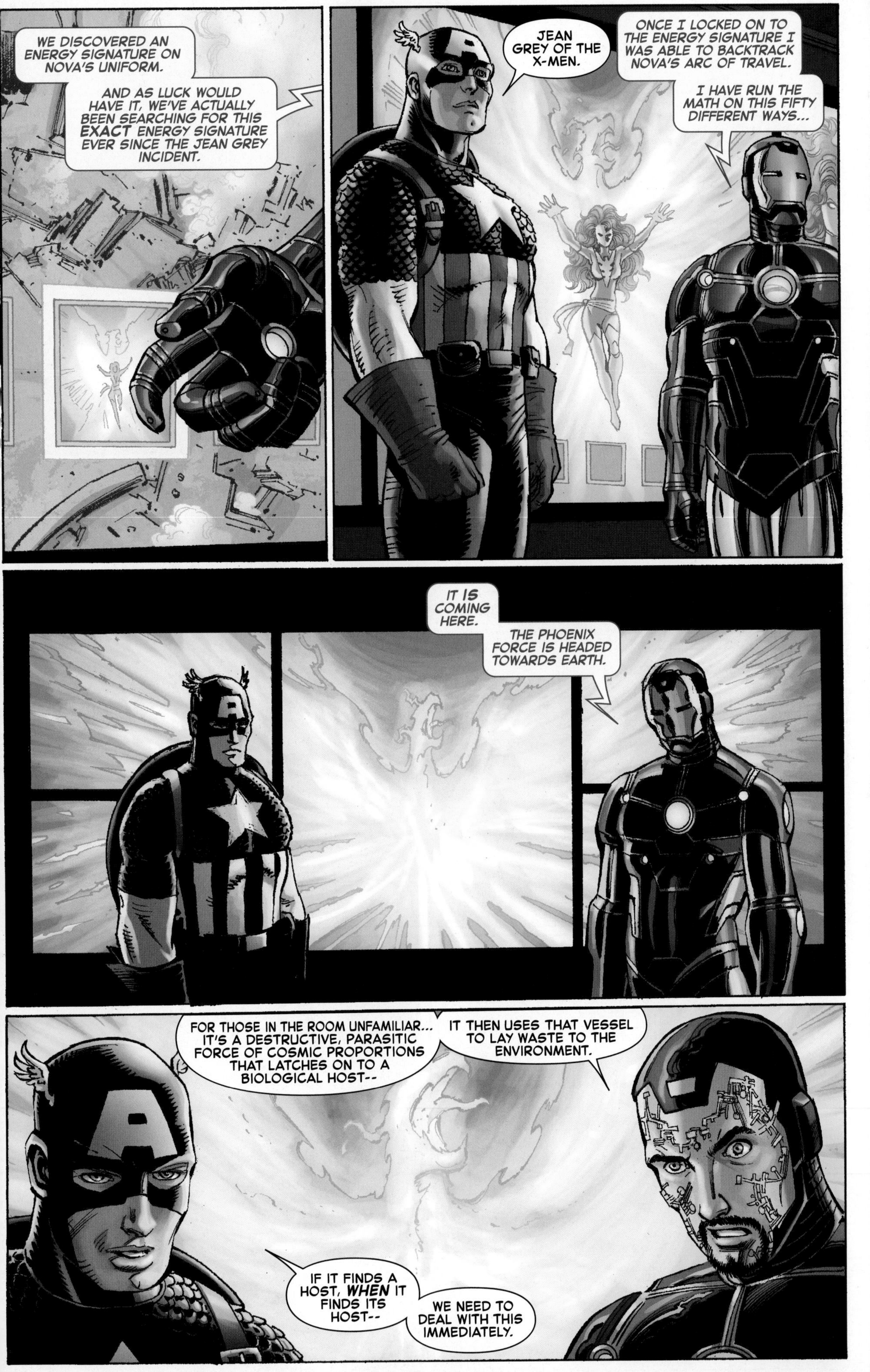
WE DISCOVERED AN ENERGY SIGNATURE ON NOVA'S UNIFORM.
AND AS LUCK WOULD HAVE IT, WE'VE ACTUALLY BEEN SEARCHING FOR THIS EXACT ENERGY SIGNATURE EVER SINCE THE JEAN GREY INCIDENT.
JEAN GREY OF THE X-MEN.
ONCE I LOCKED ON TO THE ENERGY SIGNATURE I WAS ABLE TO BACKTRACK NOVA'S ARC OF TRAVEL.
I HAVE RUN THE MATH ON THIS FIFTY DIFFERENT WAYS...
IT IS COMING HERE.
THE PHOENIX FORCE IS HEADED TOWARDS EARTH.
FOR THOSE IN THE ROOM UNFAMILIAR... IT'S A DESTRUCTIVE, PARASITIC FORCE OF COSMIC PROPORTIONS THAT LATCHES ON TO A BIOLOGICAL HOST--
IT THEN USES THAT VESSEL TO LAY WASTE TO THE ENVIRONMENT.
IF IT FINDS A HOST, WHEN IT FINDS ITS HOST--
WE NEED TO DEAL WITH THIS IMMEDIATELY.

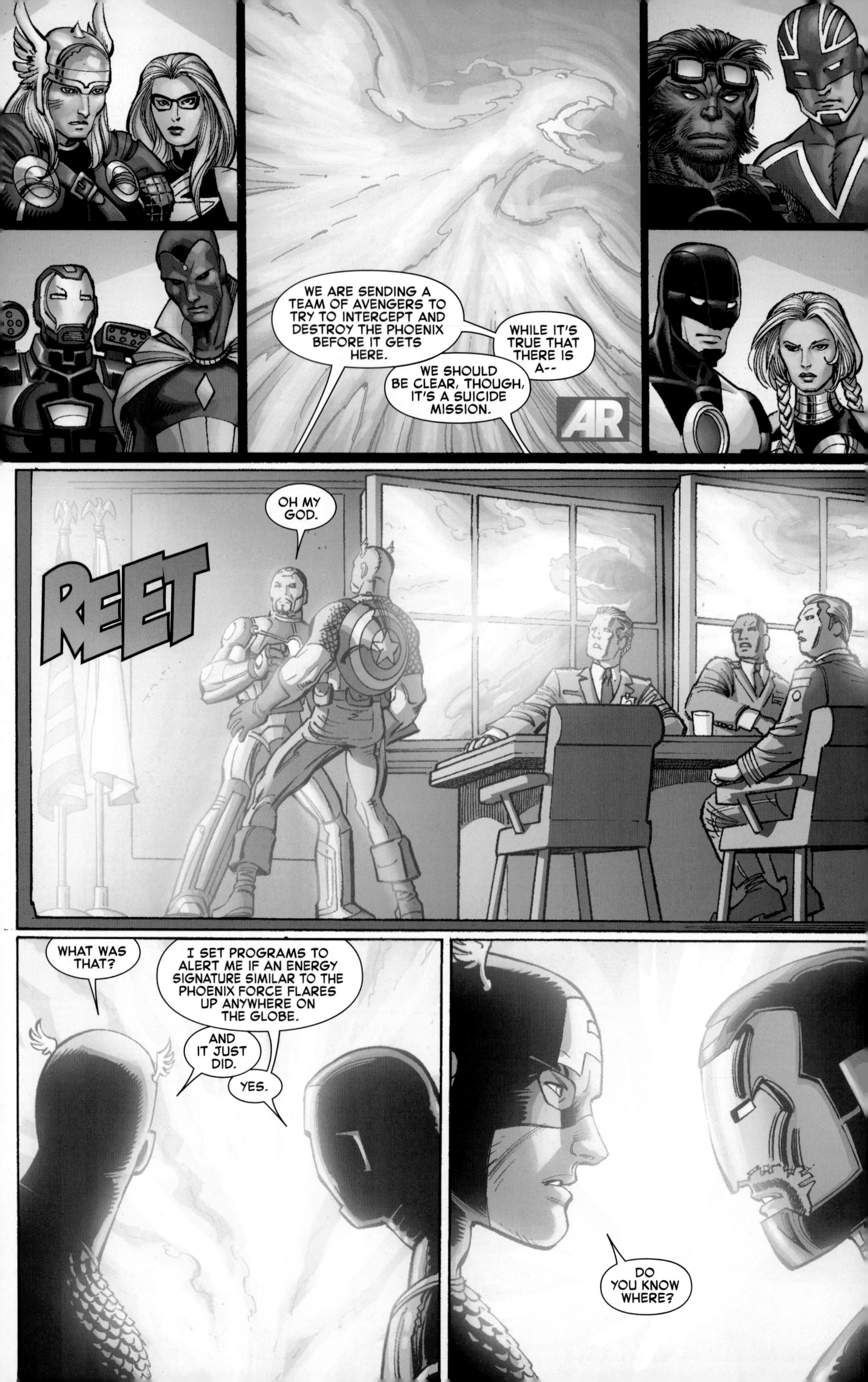
WE ARE SENDING A TEAM OF AVENGERS TO TRY TO INTERCEPT AND DESTROY THE PHOENIX BEFORE IT GETS HERE.
WHILE IT'S TRUE THAT THERE IS A--
WE SHOULD BE CLEAR, THOUGH, IT'S A SUICIDE MISSION.
AR
OH MY GOD.
REEET
WHAT WAS THAT?
I SET PROGRAMS TO ALERT ME IF AN ENERGY SIGNATURE SIMILAR TO THE PHOENIX FORCE FLARES UP ANYWHERE ON THE GLOBE.
AND IT JUST DID.
YES.
DO YOU KNOW WHERE?

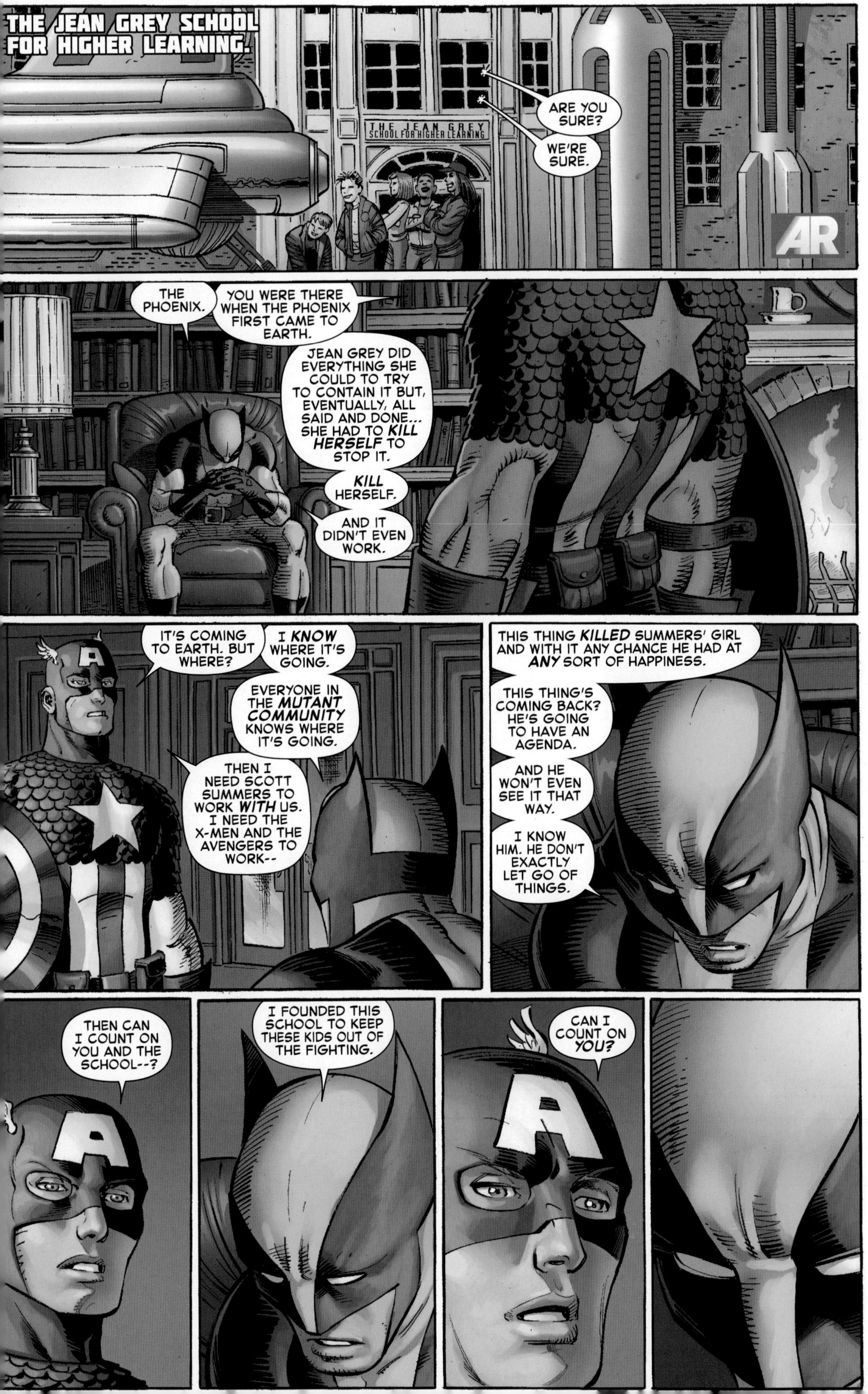
THE JEAN GREY SCHOOL FOR HIGHER LEARNING.
THE JEAN GREY SCHOOL FOR HIGHER LEARNING
ARE YOU SURE?
WE'RE SURE.
AR
THE PHOENIX.
YOU WERE THERE WHEN THE PHOENIX FIRST CAME TO EARTH.
JEAN GREY DID EVERYTHING SHE COULD TO TRY TO CONTAIN IT BUT, EVENTUALLY, ALL SAID AND DONE... SHE HAD TO KILL HERSELF TO STOP IT.
KILL HERSELF.
AND IT DIDN'T EVEN WORK.
IT'S COMING TO EARTH. BUT WHERE?
I KNOW WHERE IT'S GOING.
EVERYONE IN THE MUTANT COMMUNITY KNOWS WHERE IT'S GOING.
THEN I NEED SCOTT SUMMERS TO WORK WITH US. I NEED THE X-MEN AND THE AVENGERS TO WORK--
THIS THING KILLED SUMMERS' GIRL AND WITH IT ANY CHANCE HE HAD AT ANY SORT OF HAPPINESS.
THIS THING'S COMING BACK? HE'S GOING TO HAVE AN AGENDA.
AND HE WON'T EVEN SEE IT THAT WAY.
I KNOW HIM. HE DON'T EXACTLY LET GO OF THINGS.
THEN CAN I COUNT ON YOU AND THE SCHOOL--?
I FOUNDED THIS SCHOOL TO KEEP THESE KIDS OUT OF THE FIGHTING.
CAN I COUNT ON YOU?

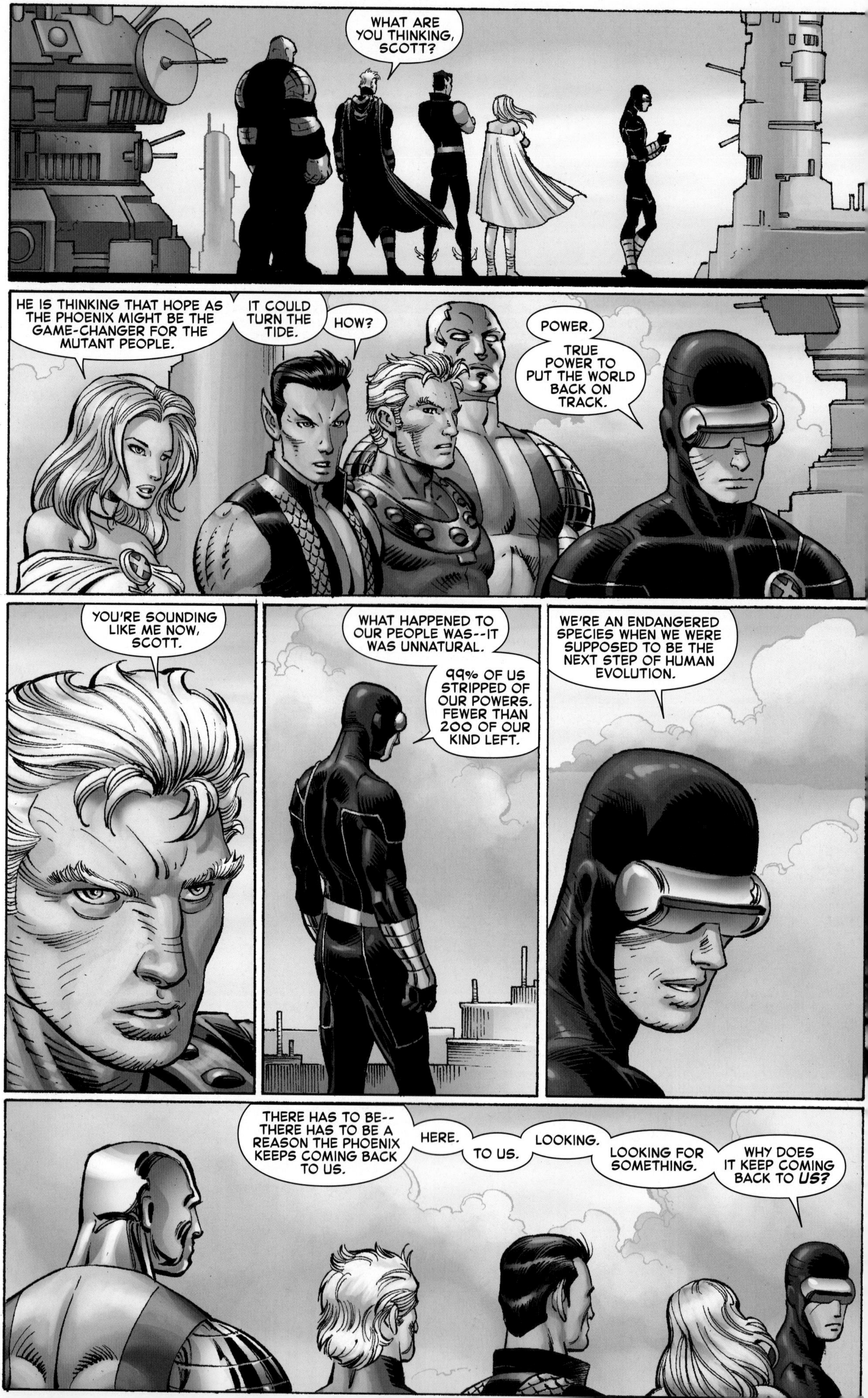
WHAT ARE YOU THINKING, SCOTT?
HE IS THINKING THAT HOPE AS THE PHOENIX MIGHT BE THE GAME-CHANGER FOR THE MUTANT PEOPLE.
IT COULD TURN THE TIDE.
HOW?
POWER.
TRUE POWER TO PUT THE WORLD BACK ON TRACK.
YOU'RE SOUNDING LIKE ME NOW, SCOTT.
WHAT HAPPENED TO OUR PEOPLE WAS--IT WAS UNNATURAL.
99% OF US STRIPPED OF OUR POWERS. FEWER THAN 200 OF OUR KIND LEFT.
WE'RE AN ENDANGERED SPECIES WHEN WE WERE SUPPOSED TO BE THE NEXT STEP OF HUMAN EVOLUTION.
THERE HAS TO BE-- THERE HAS TO BE A REASON THE PHOENIX KEEPS COMING BACK TO US.
HERE.
TO US.
LOOKING.
LOOKING FOR SOMETHING.
WHY DOES IT KEEP COMING BACK TO US?

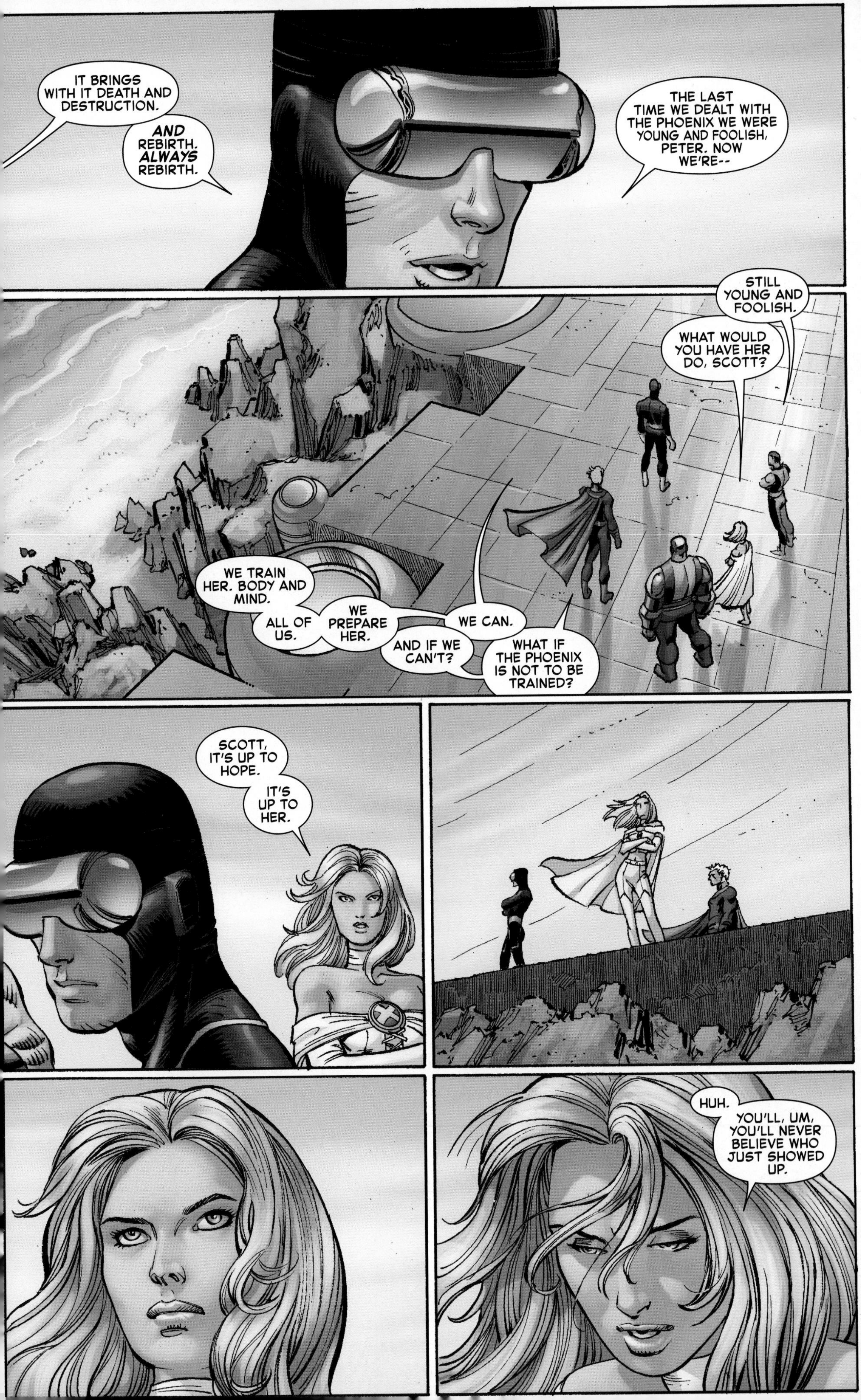
IT BRINGS WITH IT DEATH AND DESTRUCTION.
AND REBIRTH. ALWAYS REBIRTH.
THE LAST TIME WE DEALT WITH THE PHOENIX WE WERE YOUNG AND FOOLISH, PETER. NOW WE'RE--
STILL YOUNG AND FOOLISH.
WHAT WOULD YOU HAVE HER DO, SCOTT?
WE TRAIN HER. BODY AND MIND.
ALL OF US.
WE PREPARE HER.
WE CAN.
AND IF WE CAN'T?
WHAT IF THE PHOENIX IS NOT TO BE TRAINED?
SCOTT, IT'S UP TO HOPE.
IT'S UP TO HER.
HUH.
YOU'LL, UM, YOU'LL NEVER BELIEVE WHO JUST SHOWED UP.

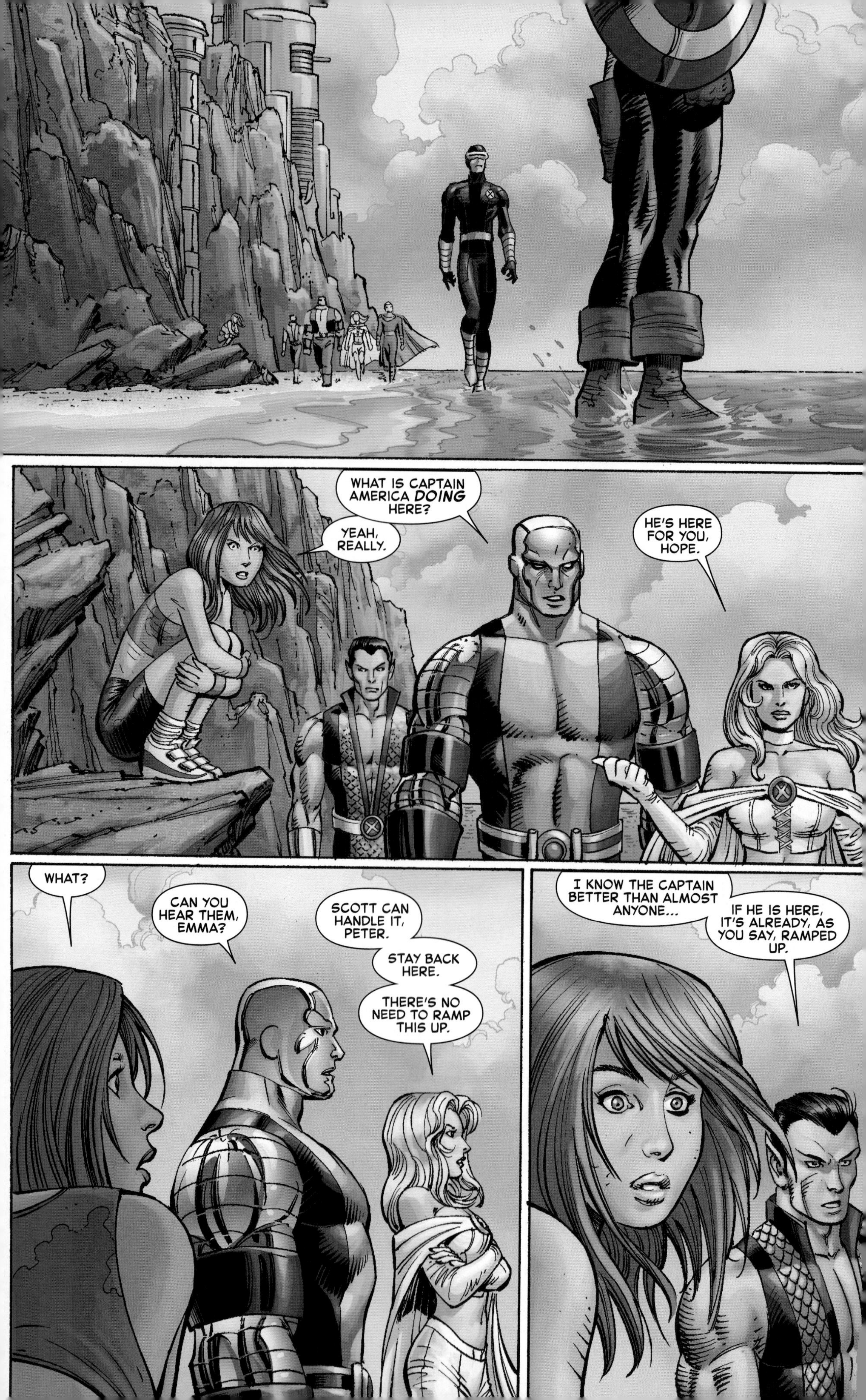
WHAT IS CAPTAIN AMERICA DOING HERE?
YEAH, REALLY.
HE'S HERE FOR YOU, HOPE.
WHAT?
CAN YOU HEAR THEM, EMMA?
SCOTT CAN HANDLE IT, PETER.
STAY BACK HERE.
THERE'S NO NEED TO RAMP THIS UP.
I KNOW THE CAPTAIN BETTER THAN ALMOST ANYONE...
IF HE IS HERE, IT'S ALREADY, AS YOU SAY, RAMPED UP.

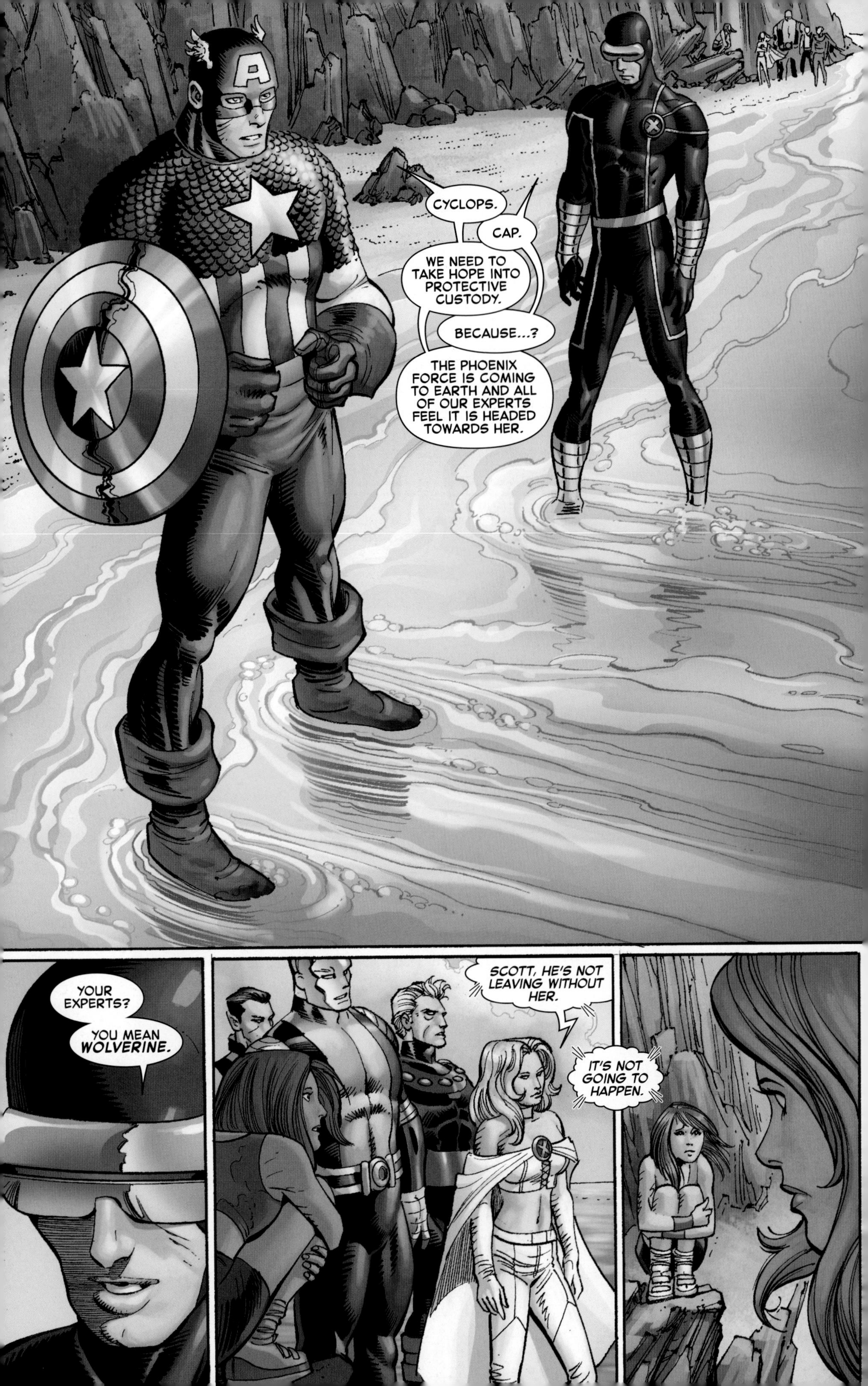
CYCLOPS.
CAP.
WE NEED TO TAKE HOPE INTO PROTECTIVE CUSTODY.
BECAUSE...?
THE PHOENIX FORCE IS COMING TO EARTH AND ALL OF OUR EXPERTS FEEL IT IS HEADED TOWARDS HER.
YOUR EXPERTS?
YOU MEAN *WOLVERINE.*
SCOTT, HE'S NOT LEAVING WITHOUT HER.
IT'S NOT GOING TO HAPPEN.

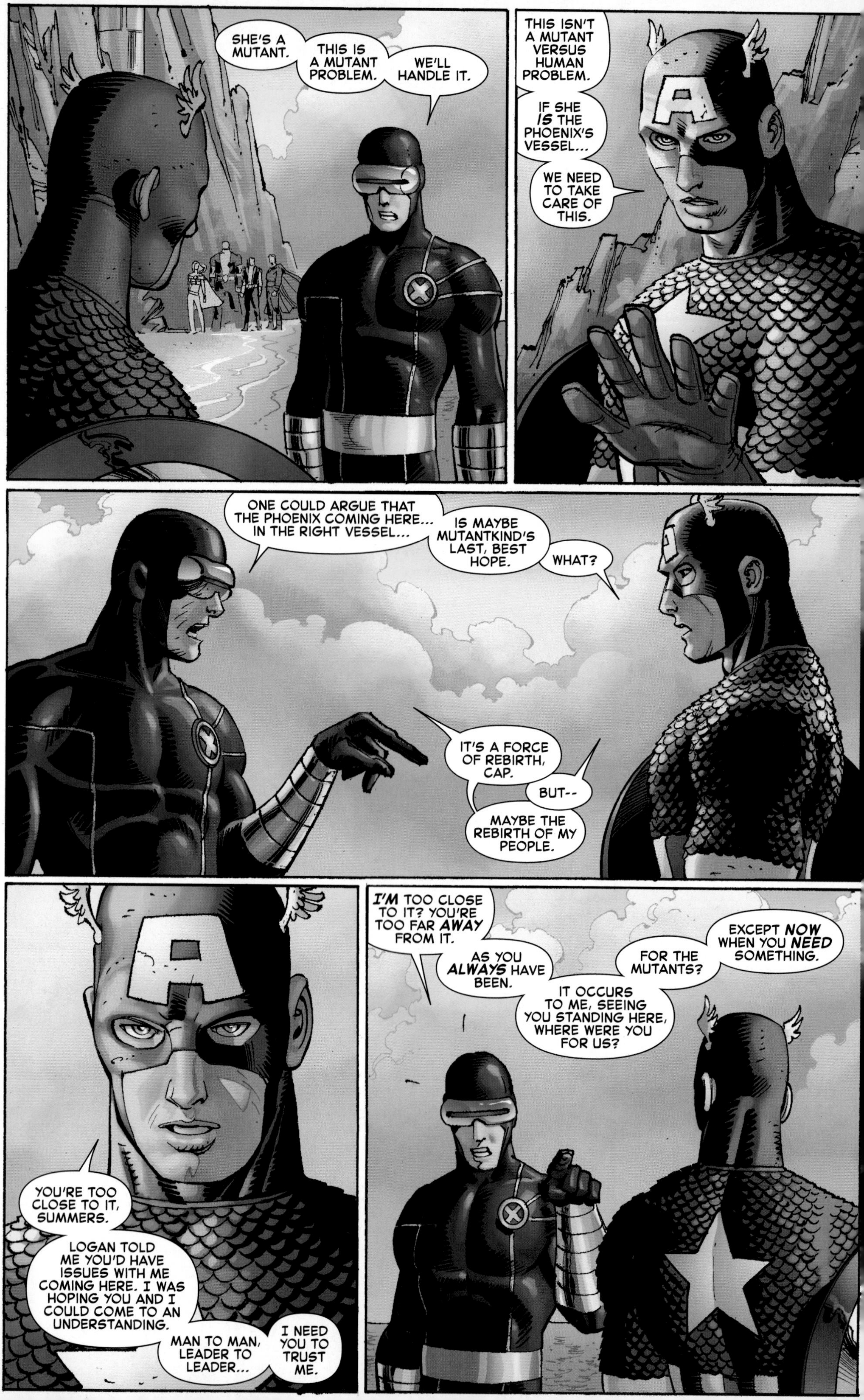
SHE'S A MUTANT.
THIS IS A MUTANT PROBLEM.
WE'LL HANDLE IT.
THIS ISN'T A MUTANT VERSUS HUMAN PROBLEM.
IF SHE *IS* THE PHOENIX'S VESSEL...
WE NEED TO TAKE CARE OF THIS.
ONE COULD ARGUE THAT THE PHOENIX COMING HERE... IN THE RIGHT VESSEL...
IS MAYBE MUTANTKIND'S LAST, BEST HOPE.
WHAT?
IT'S A FORCE OF REBIRTH, CAP.
BUT--
MAYBE THE REBIRTH OF MY PEOPLE.
YOU'RE TOO CLOSE TO IT, SUMMERS.
LOGAN TOLD ME YOU'D HAVE ISSUES WITH ME COMING HERE. I WAS HOPING YOU AND I COULD COME TO AN UNDERSTANDING.
MAN TO MAN, LEADER TO LEADER...
I NEED YOU TO TRUST ME.
I'M TOO CLOSE TO IT? YOU'RE TOO FAR *AWAY* FROM IT.
AS YOU *ALWAYS* HAVE BEEN.
FOR THE MUTANTS?
EXCEPT *NOW* WHEN YOU *NEED* SOMETHING.
IT OCCURS TO ME, SEEING YOU STANDING HERE, WHERE WERE YOU FOR US?

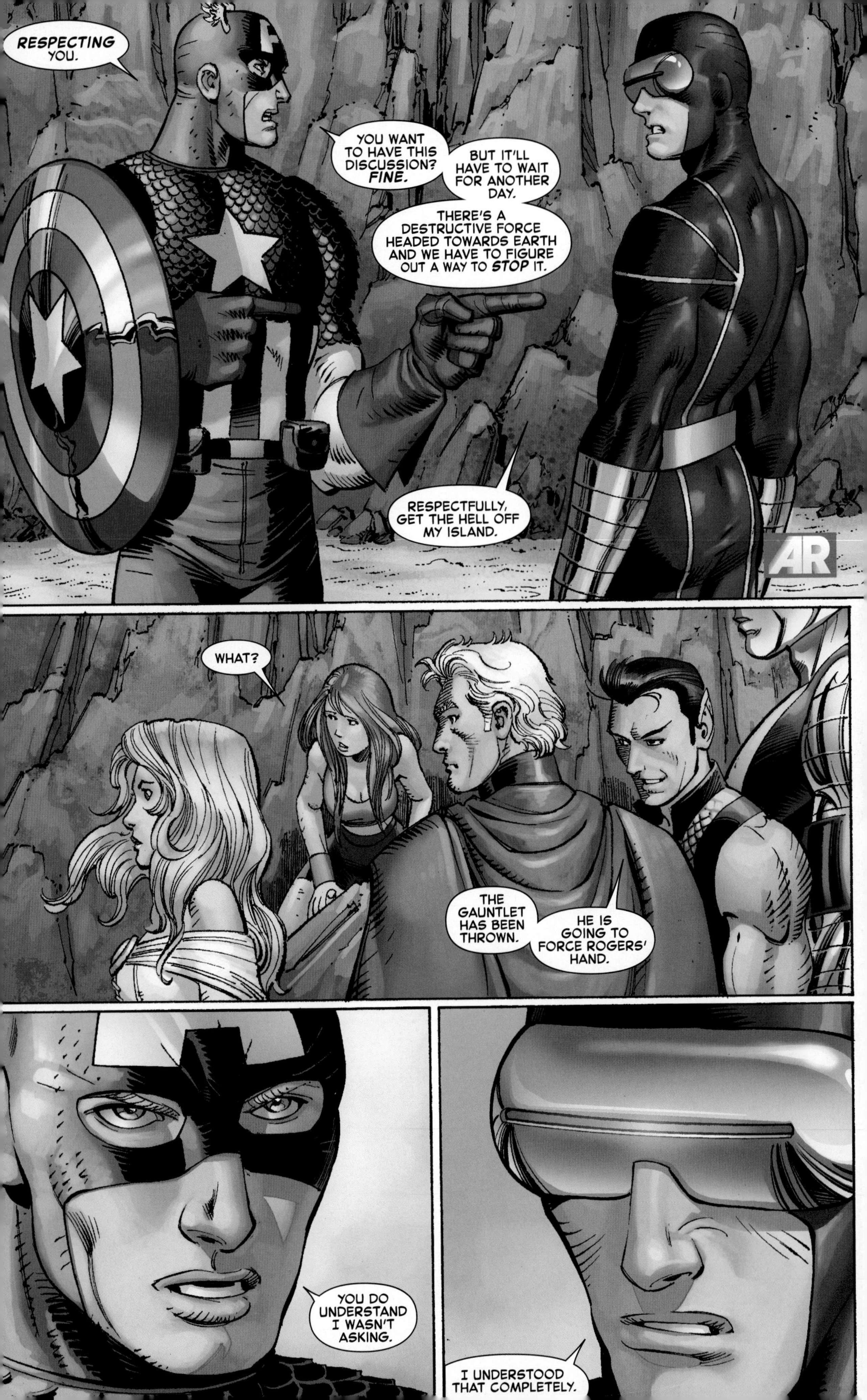
RESPECTING YOU.
YOU WANT TO HAVE THIS DISCUSSION? FINE.
BUT IT'LL HAVE TO WAIT FOR ANOTHER DAY.
THERE'S A DESTRUCTIVE FORCE HEADED TOWARDS EARTH AND WE HAVE TO FIGURE OUT A WAY TO STOP IT.
RESPECTFULLY, GET THE HELL OFF MY ISLAND.
WHAT?
THE GAUNTLET HAS BEEN THROWN.
HE IS GOING TO FORCE ROGERS' HAND.
YOU DO UNDERSTAND I WASN'T ASKING.
I UNDERSTOOD THAT COMPLETELY.

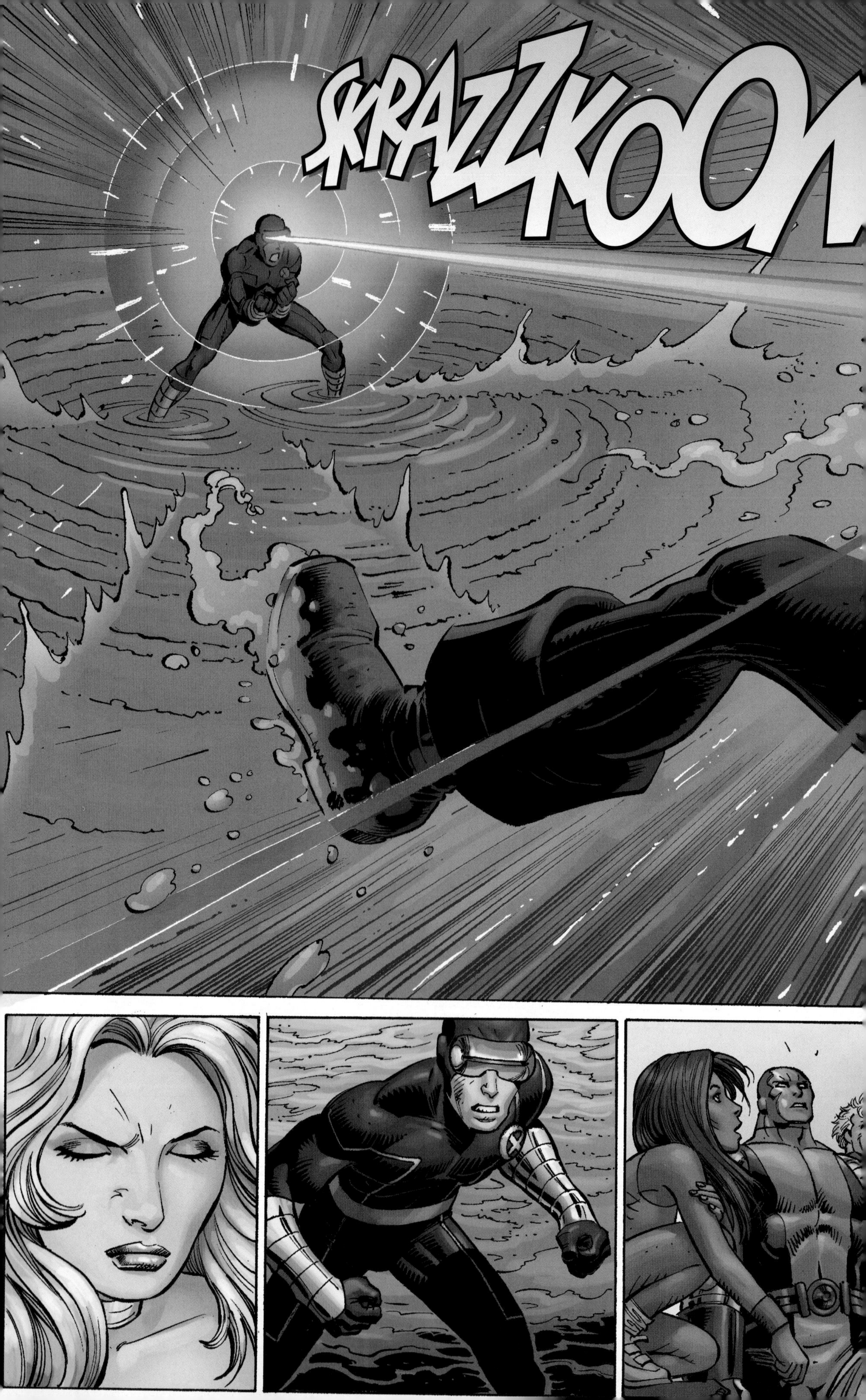
SKRAZZKOOM

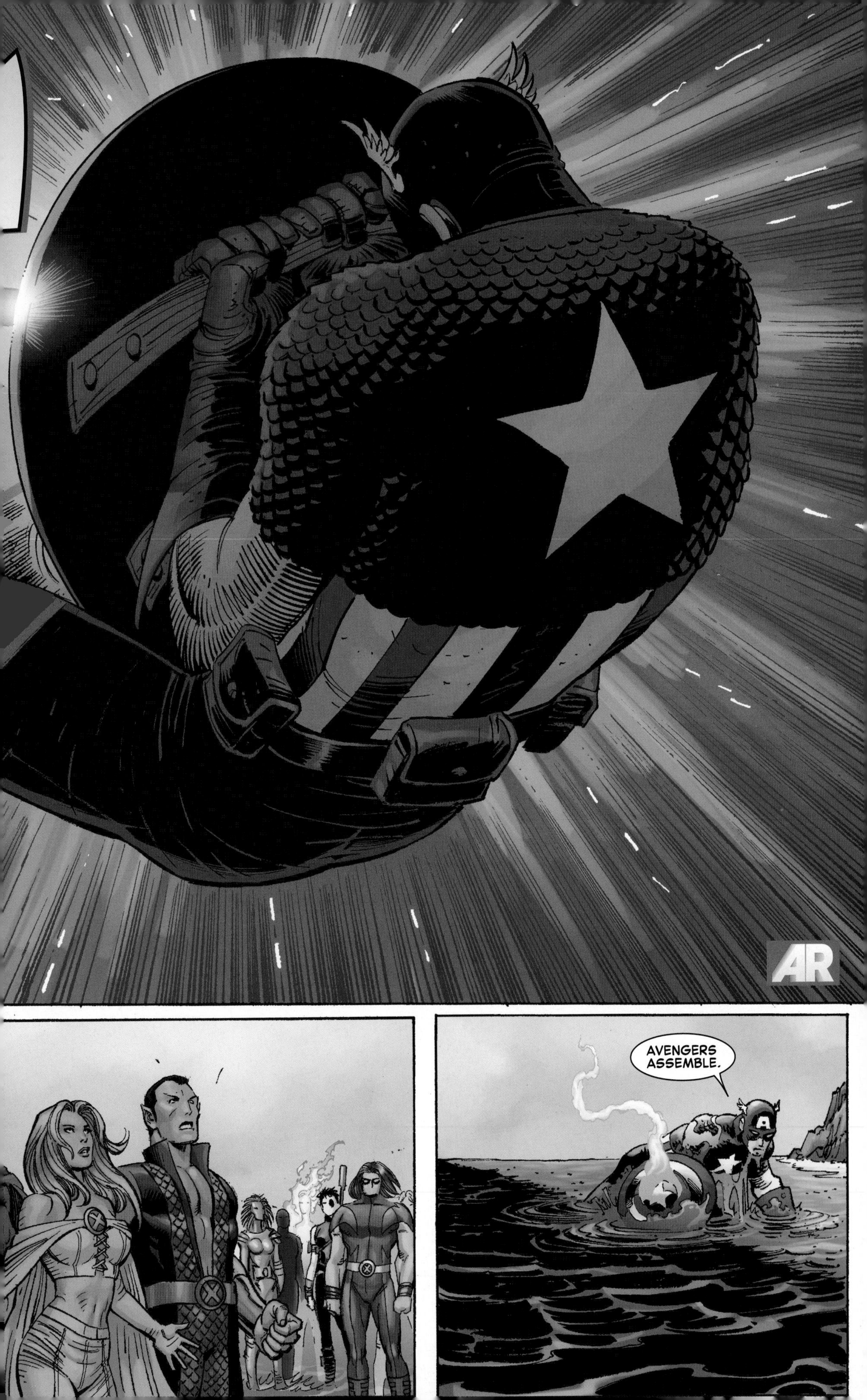
AVENGERS ASSEMBLE.

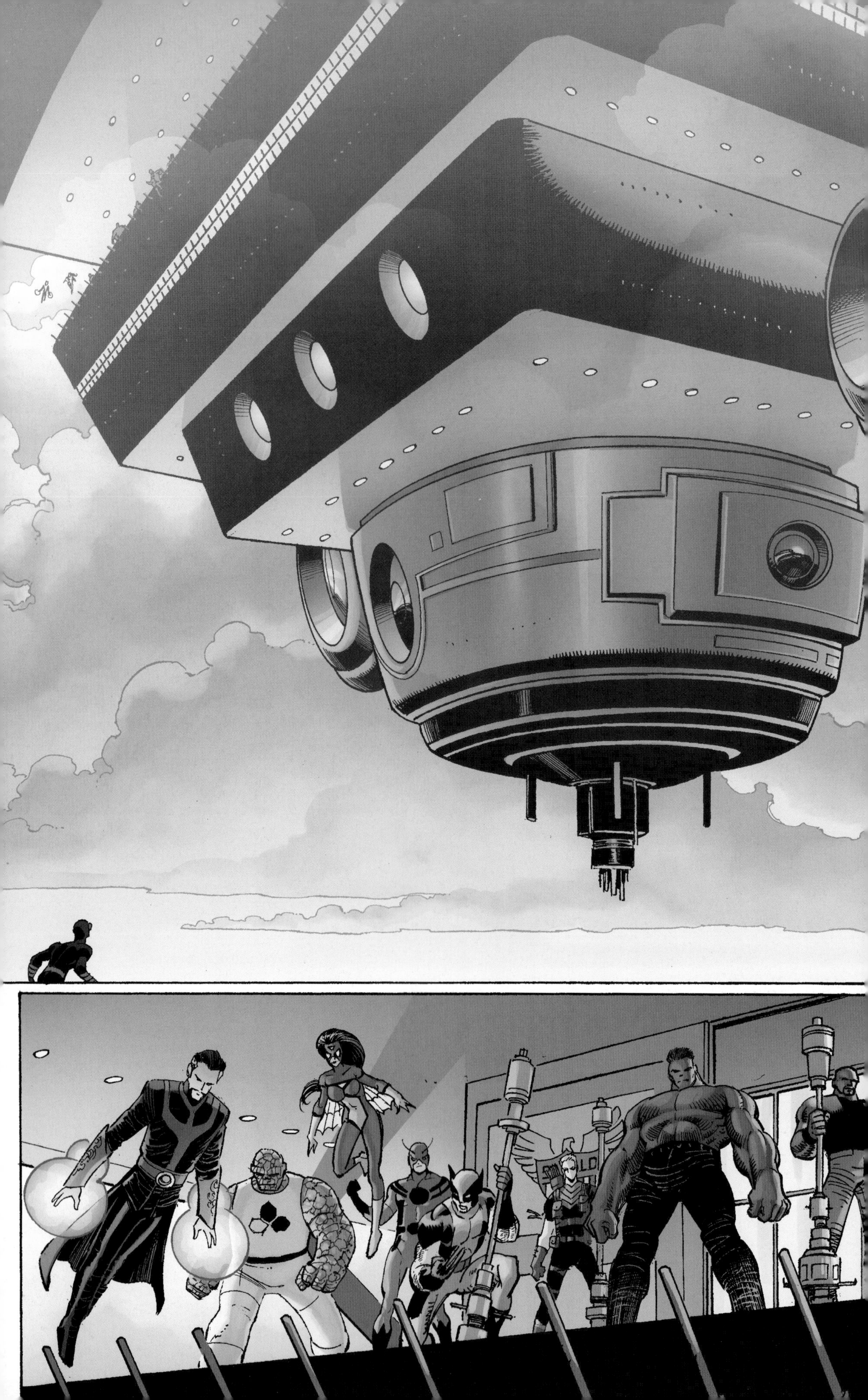

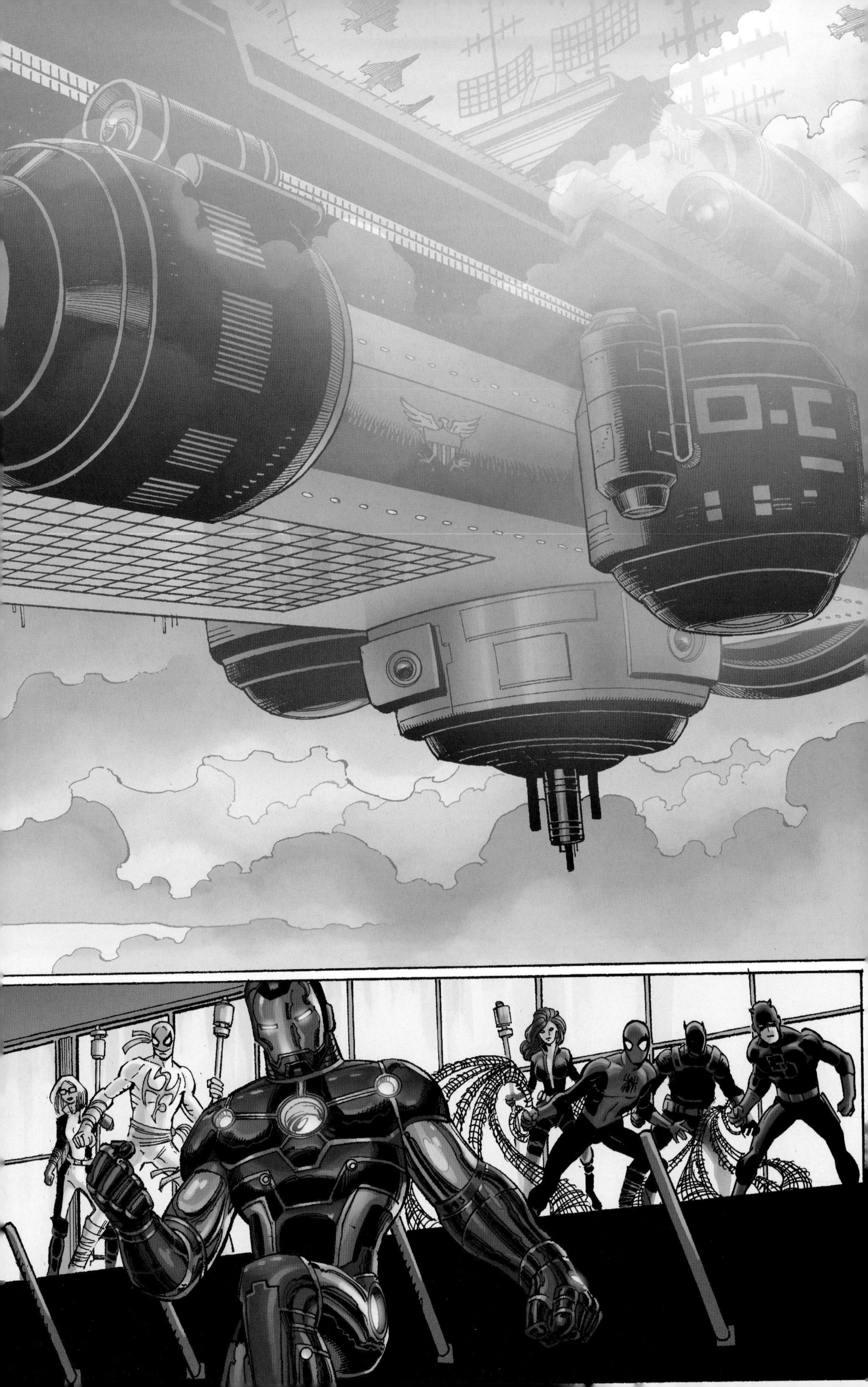

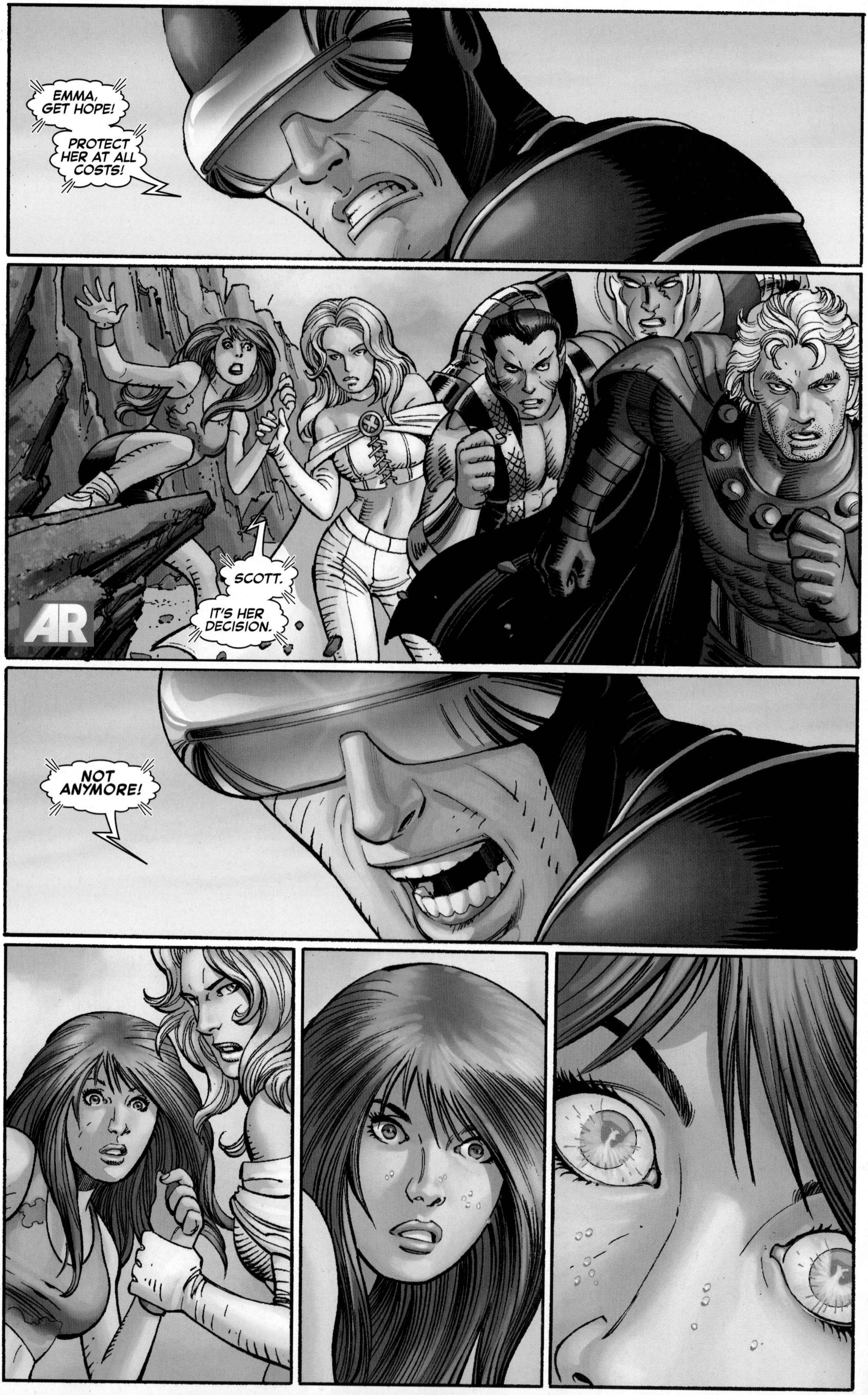
EMMA, GET HOPE!
PROTECT HER AT ALL COSTS!
SCOTT.
IT'S HER DECISION.
NOT ANYMORE!

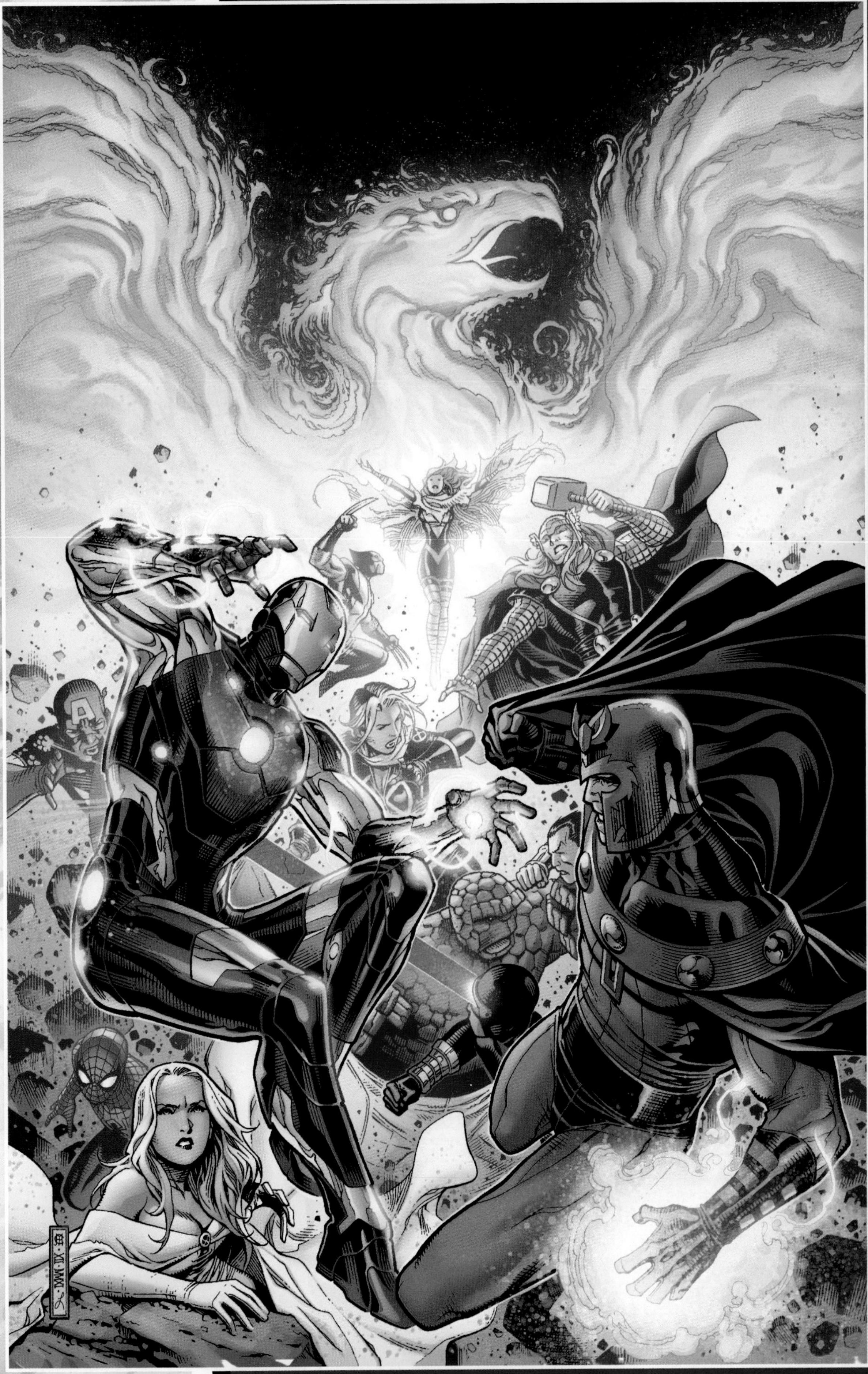

ROUND 2

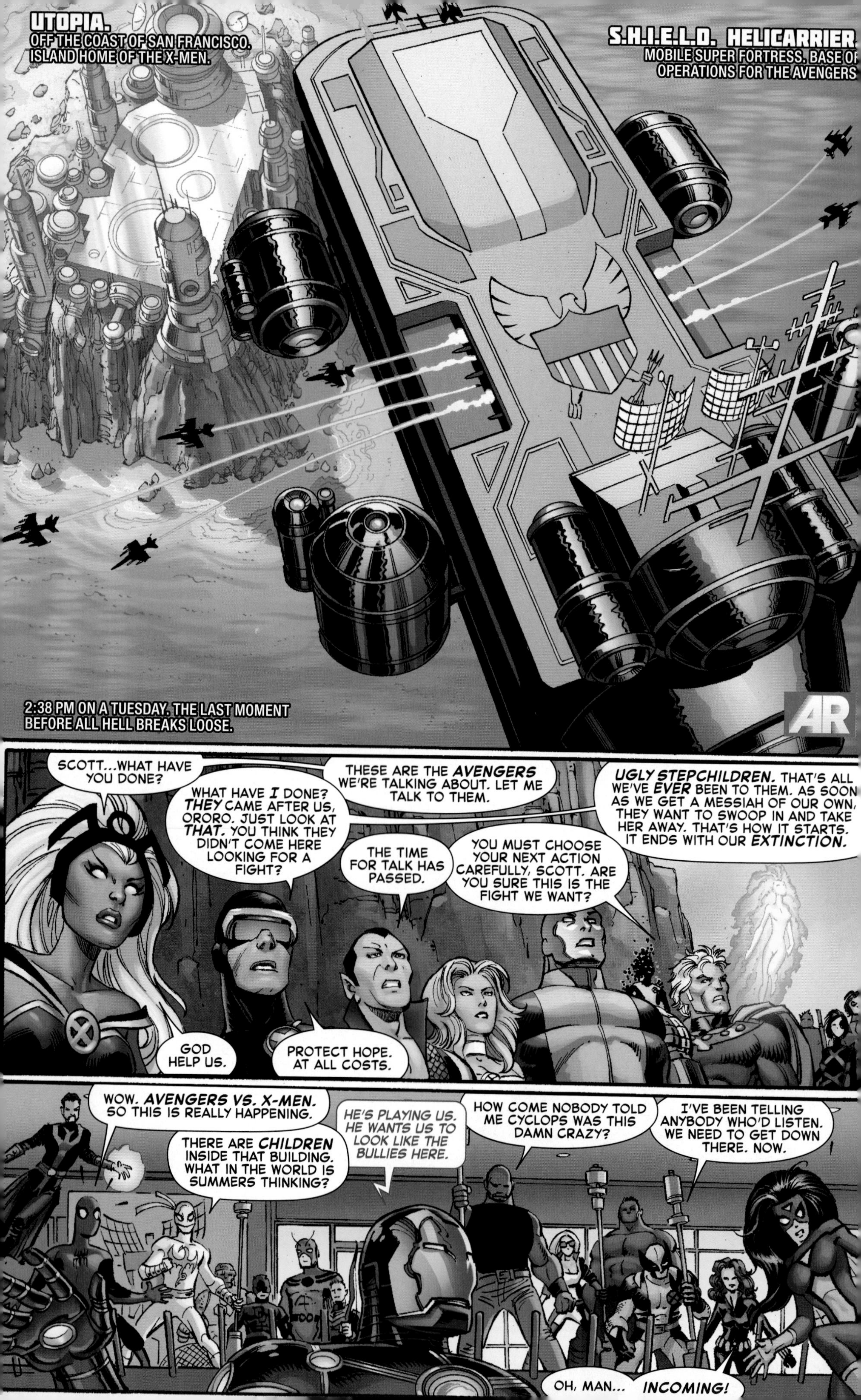
UTOPIA.
OFF THE COAST OF SAN FRANCISCO. ISLAND HOME OF THE X-MEN.
S.H.I.E.L.D. HELICARRIER.
MOBILE SUPER FORTRESS. BASE OF OPERATIONS FOR THE AVENGERS.
2:38 PM ON A TUESDAY. THE LAST MOMENT BEFORE ALL HELL BREAKS LOOSE.
SCOTT...WHAT HAVE YOU DONE?
WHAT HAVE I DONE? THEY CAME AFTER US, ORORO. JUST LOOK AT THAT. YOU THINK THEY DIDN'T COME HERE LOOKING FOR A FIGHT?
THESE ARE THE AVENGERS WE'RE TALKING ABOUT. LET ME TALK TO THEM.
UGLY STEPCHILDREN. THAT'S ALL WE'VE EVER BEEN TO THEM. AS SOON AS WE GET A MESSIAH OF OUR OWN, THEY WANT TO SWOOP IN AND TAKE HER AWAY. THAT'S HOW IT STARTS. IT ENDS WITH OUR EXTINCTION.
THE TIME FOR TALK HAS PASSED.
YOU MUST CHOOSE YOUR NEXT ACTION CAREFULLY, SCOTT. ARE YOU SURE THIS IS THE FIGHT WE WANT?
GOD HELP US.
PROTECT HOPE. AT ALL COSTS.
WOW. AVENGERS VS. X-MEN. SO THIS IS REALLY HAPPENING.
THERE ARE CHILDREN INSIDE THAT BUILDING. WHAT IN THE WORLD IS SUMMERS THINKING?
HE'S PLAYING US. HE WANTS US TO LOOK LIKE THE BULLIES HERE.
HOW COME NOBODY TOLD ME CYCLOPS WAS THIS DAMN CRAZY?
I'VE BEEN TELLING ANYBODY WHO'D LISTEN. WE NEED TO GET DOWN THERE. NOW.
OH, MAN... INCOMING!

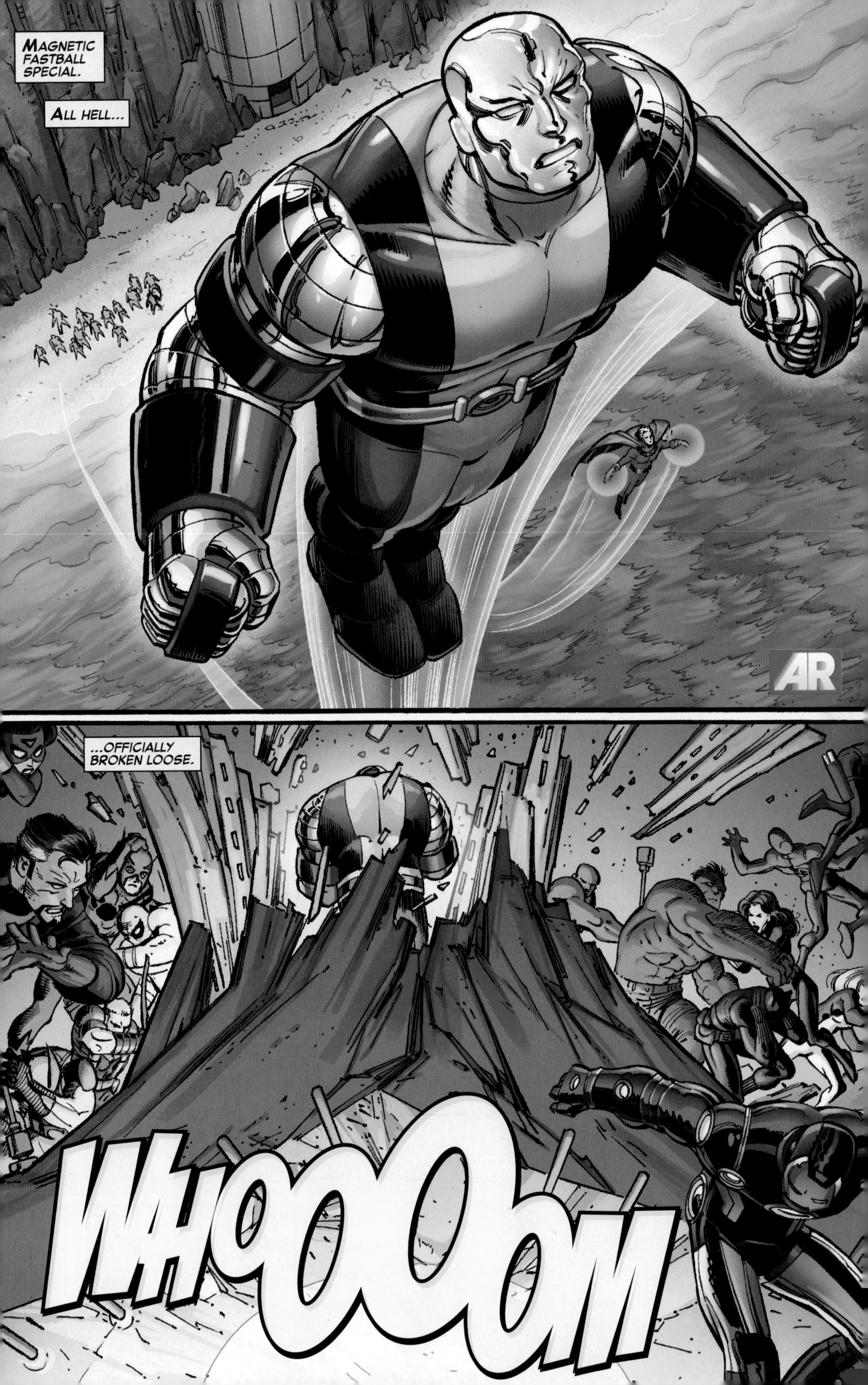
Magnetic fastball special.
All hell...
...officially broken loose.
WHOOOOM

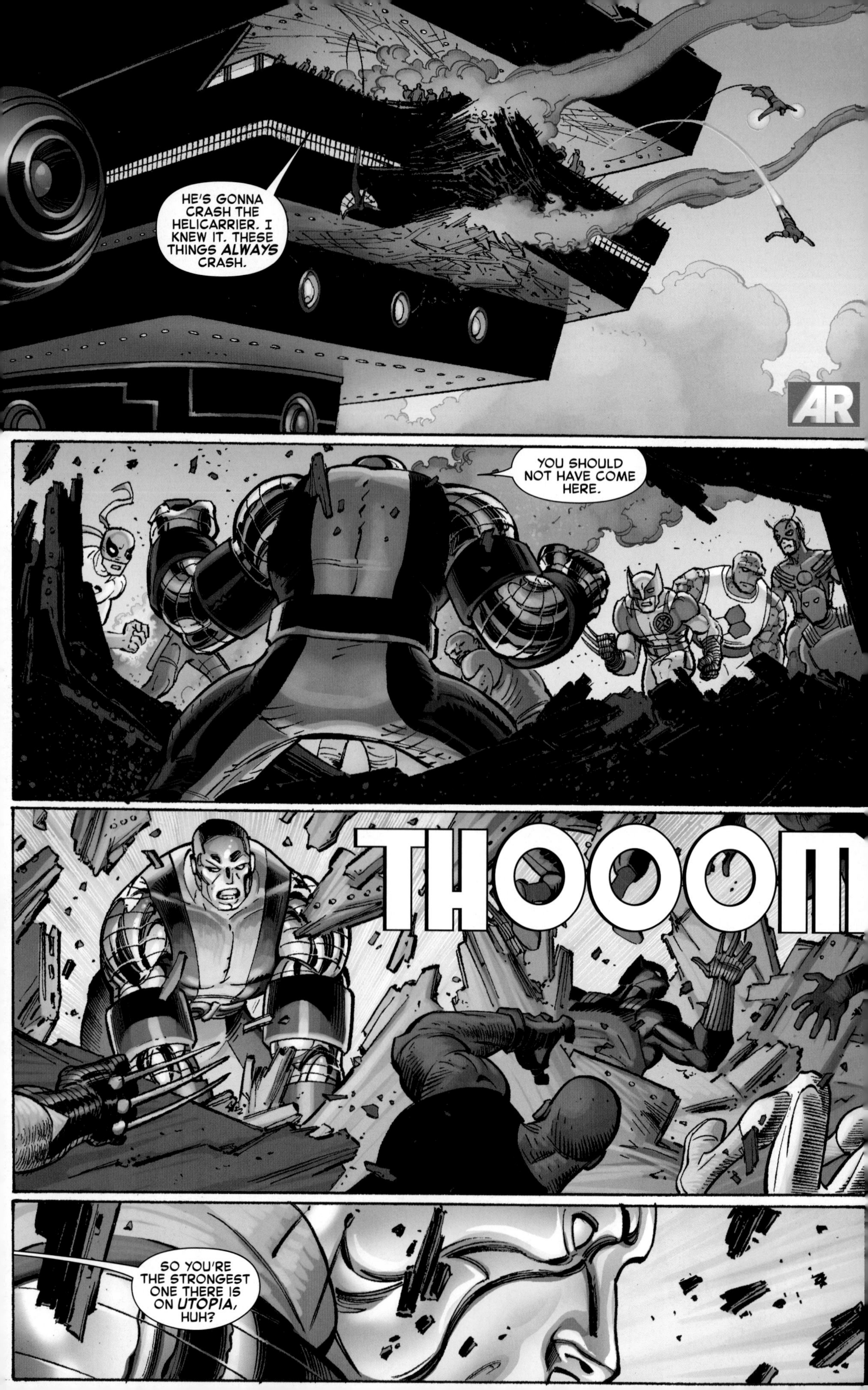
HE'S GONNA CRASH THE HELICARRIER. I KNEW IT. THESE THINGS ALWAYS CRASH.
AR
YOU SHOULD NOT HAVE COME HERE.
THOOOM
SO YOU'RE THE STRONGEST ONE THERE IS ON UTOPIA, HUH?

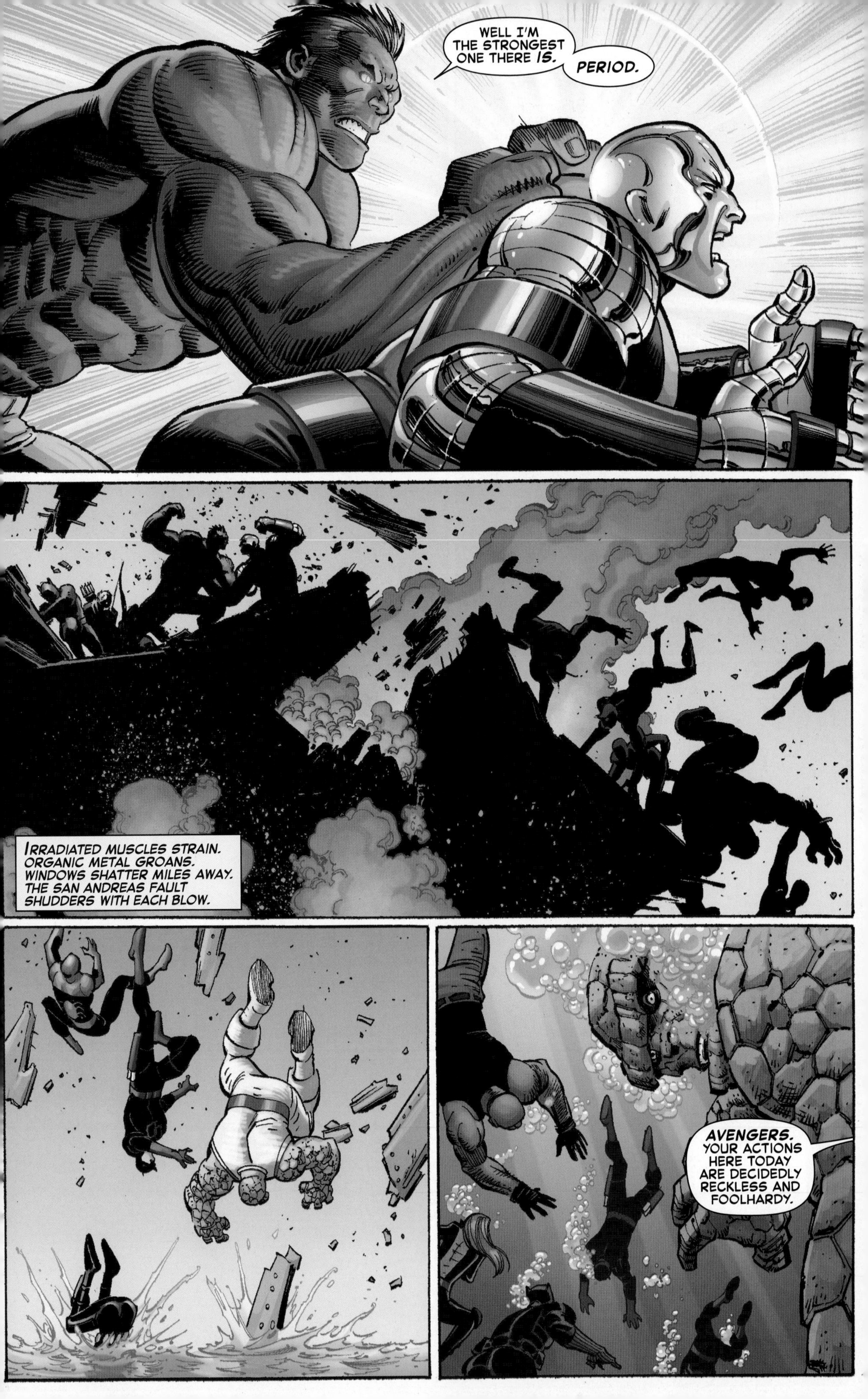
WELL I'M THE STRONGEST ONE THERE IS.
PERIOD.
IRRADIATED MUSCLES STRAIN. ORGANIC METAL GROANS. WINDOWS SHATTER MILES AWAY. THE SAN ANDREAS FAULT SHUDDERS WITH EACH BLOW.
AVENGERS. YOUR ACTIONS HERE TODAY ARE DECIDEDLY RECKLESS AND FOOLHARDY.

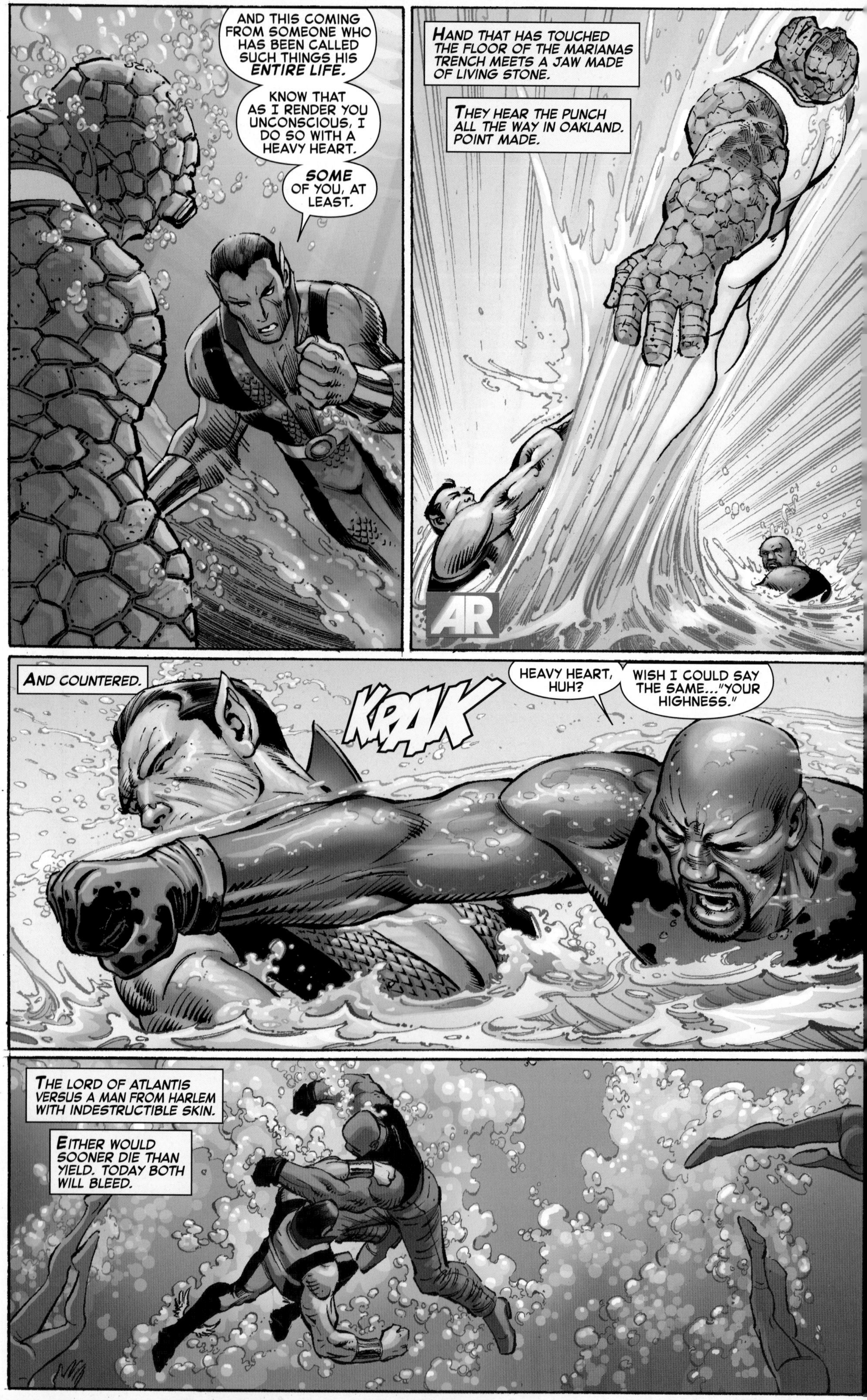

AND THIS COMING FROM SOMEONE WHO HAS BEEN CALLED SUCH THINGS HIS ENTIRE LIFE.
KNOW THAT AS I RENDER YOU UNCONSCIOUS, I DO SO WITH A HEAVY HEART.
SOME OF YOU, AT LEAST.
HAND THAT HAS TOUCHED THE FLOOR OF THE MARIANAS TRENCH MEETS A JAW MADE OF LIVING STONE.
THEY HEAR THE PUNCH ALL THE WAY IN OAKLAND. POINT MADE.
AND COUNTERED.
KRAK
HEAVY HEART, HUH?
WISH I COULD SAY THE SAME..."YOUR HIGHNESS."
THE LORD OF ATLANTIS VERSUS A MAN FROM HARLEM WITH INDESTRUCTIBLE SKIN.
EITHER WOULD SOONER DIE THAN YIELD. TODAY BOTH WILL BLEED.

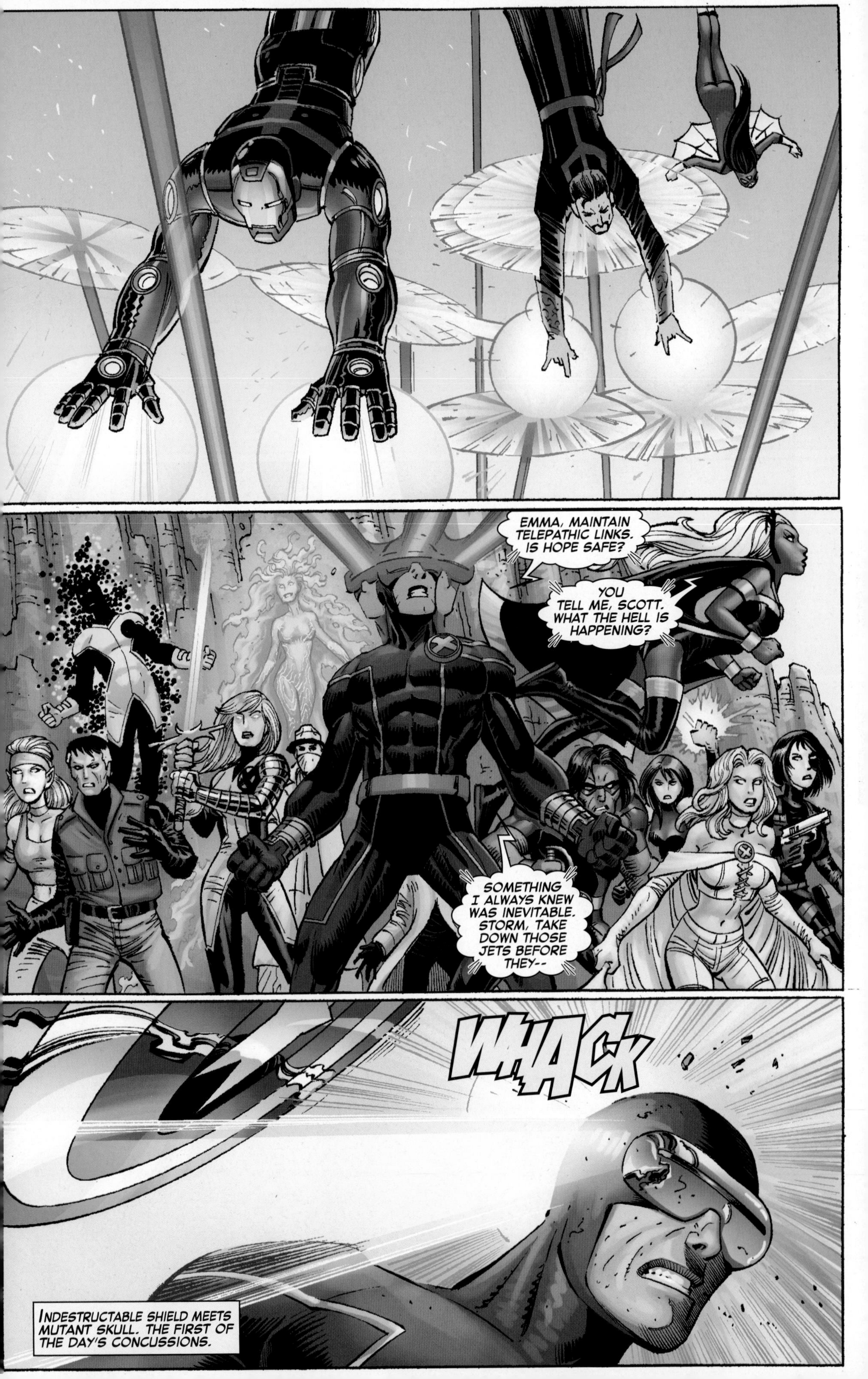

EMMA, MAINTAIN TELEPATHIC LINKS. IS HOPE SAFE?
YOU TELL ME, SCOTT. WHAT THE HELL IS HAPPENING?
SOMETHING I ALWAYS KNEW WAS INEVITABLE. STORM, TAKE DOWN THOSE JETS BEFORE THEY--
WHACK
INDESTRUCTABLE SHIELD MEETS MUTANT SKULL. THE FIRST OF THE DAY'S CONCUSSIONS.

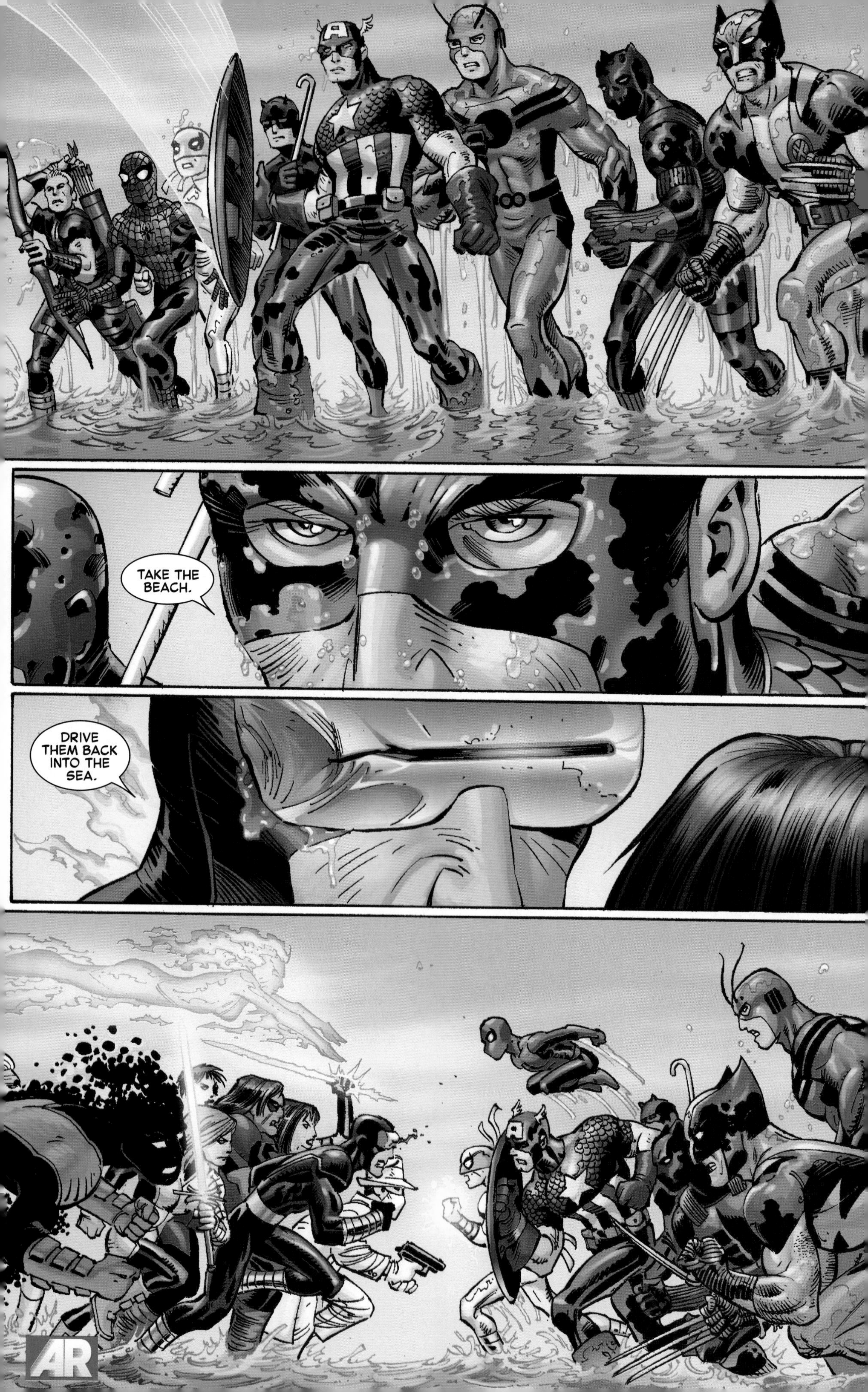
TAKE THE BEACH.
DRIVE THEM BACK INTO THE SEA.
AR

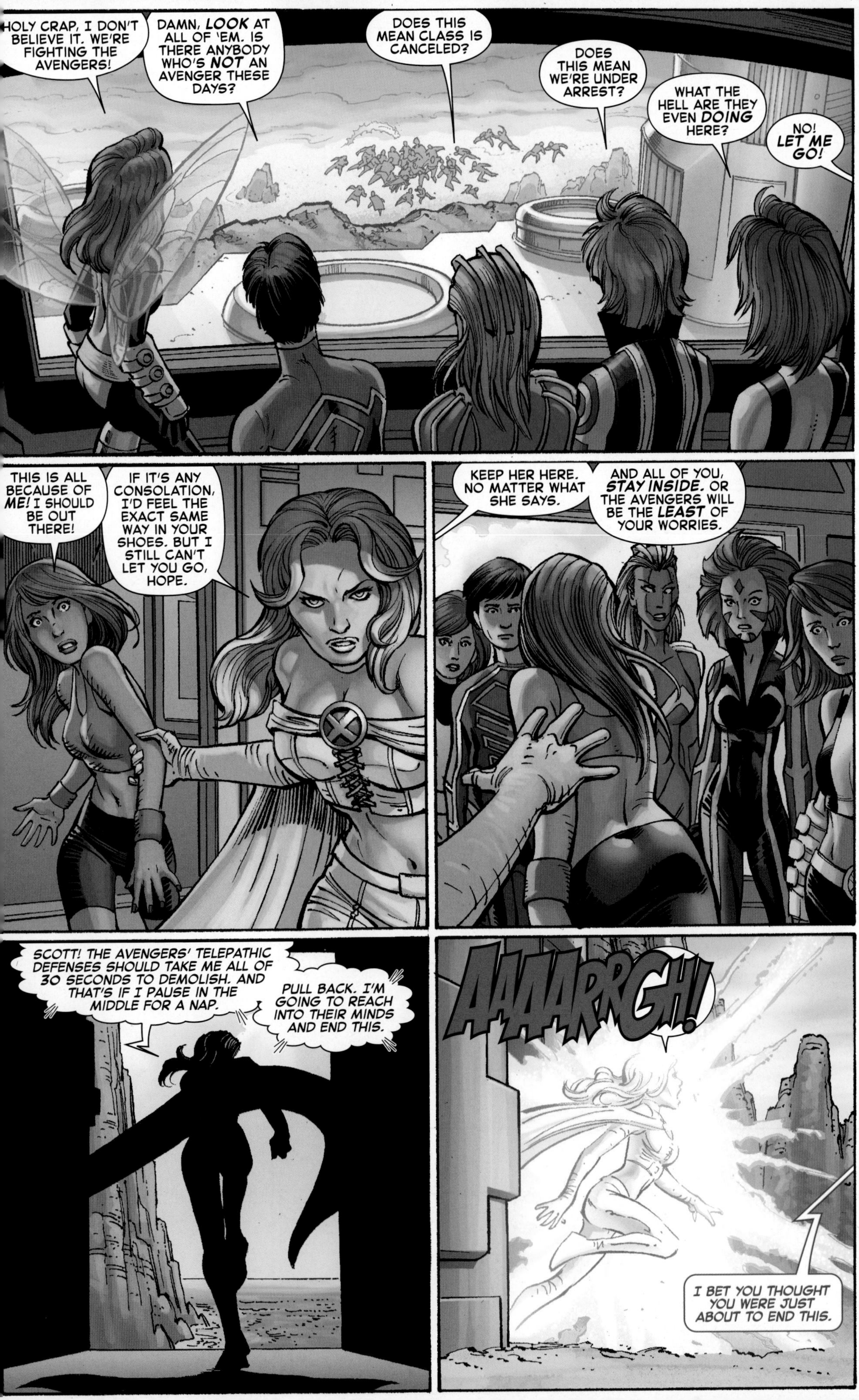
HOLY CRAP, I DON'T BELIEVE IT. WE'RE FIGHTING THE AVENGERS!
DAMN, LOOK AT ALL OF 'EM. IS THERE ANYBODY WHO'S NOT AN AVENGER THESE DAYS?
DOES THIS MEAN CLASS IS CANCELED?
DOES THIS MEAN WE'RE UNDER ARREST?
WHAT THE HELL ARE THEY EVEN DOING HERE?
NO! LET ME GO!
THIS IS ALL BECAUSE OF ME! I SHOULD BE OUT THERE!
IF IT'S ANY CONSOLATION, I'D FEEL THE EXACT SAME WAY IN YOUR SHOES. BUT I STILL CAN'T LET YOU GO, HOPE.
KEEP HER HERE. NO MATTER WHAT SHE SAYS.
AND ALL OF YOU, STAY INSIDE. OR THE AVENGERS WILL BE THE LEAST OF YOUR WORRIES.
SCOTT! THE AVENGERS' TELEPATHIC DEFENSES SHOULD TAKE ME ALL OF 30 SECONDS TO DEMOLISH. AND THAT'S IF I PAUSE IN THE MIDDLE FOR A NAP.
PULL BACK. I'M GOING TO REACH INTO THEIR MINDS AND END THIS.
AAAARRGH!
I BET YOU THOUGHT YOU WERE JUST ABOUT TO END THIS.

MICROSCOPIC TELEPATHIC TASERS. YOU JUST BREATHED IN ROUGHLY 17,000 OF THEM. THE HARDER YOU THINK, THE MORE THEY SHOCK YOU.

SO SORRY, EMMA, MY SWEET. I DO HOPE YOU'LL LET ME MAKE THIS UP TO YOU OVER DINNER SOMETIME.

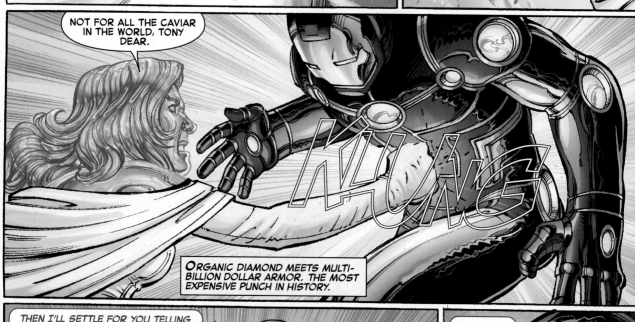

NOT FOR ALL THE CAVIAR IN THE WORLD, TONY DEAR.

KUNG

ORGANIC DIAMOND MEETS MULTI-BILLION DOLLAR ARMOR. THE MOST EXPENSIVE PUNCH IN HISTORY.

THEN I'LL SETTLE FOR YOU TELLING YOUR BOYFRIEND TO STOP BEING SUCH A DANGEROUS LUNATIC. WE'RE NOT HERE TO ARREST THE GIRL OR ANYONE ELSE. WE'RE HERE TO HELP.

THEN LEARN THE GIRL'S NAME. IT'S HOPE. AND WE DON'T REMEMBER ASKING FOR YOUR HELP.

WARNING: EXTREME MAGNETIC FIELD DETECTED. IMPLEMENTING ANTI-MAGNETISM SAFEGUARDS.

OH, FOR THE LOVE OF...WHAT NOW?

OH. RIGHT.

THAT.

HI THERE.

MAN IN A METAL SUIT VERSUS THE MUTANT MASTER OF MAGNETISM.

IF YOU THINK THIS IS NO CONTEST, YOU'VE NEVER MET TONY STARK.

ELSEWHERE.

LIVE

...LIVE FOOTAGE NOW FROM A TRAFFIC COPTER IN SAN FRANCISCO WHERE THERE APPEARS TO BE AN EPIC BATTLE TAKING PLACE...

CCN

AVENGERS, X-MEN ENGAGED IN FREE-FOR-ALL MELEE

WE SHOULD BE THERE.

THIS IS *OUR* FIGHT. WE HAVE TO GO. I AM GOING.

LIVE

CCN

AVENGERS, X-MEN ENGAGED IN FREE-FOR-ALL MELEE

PLEASE...

COME WITH ME.

CCN

AVENGERS, X-MEN ENGAG

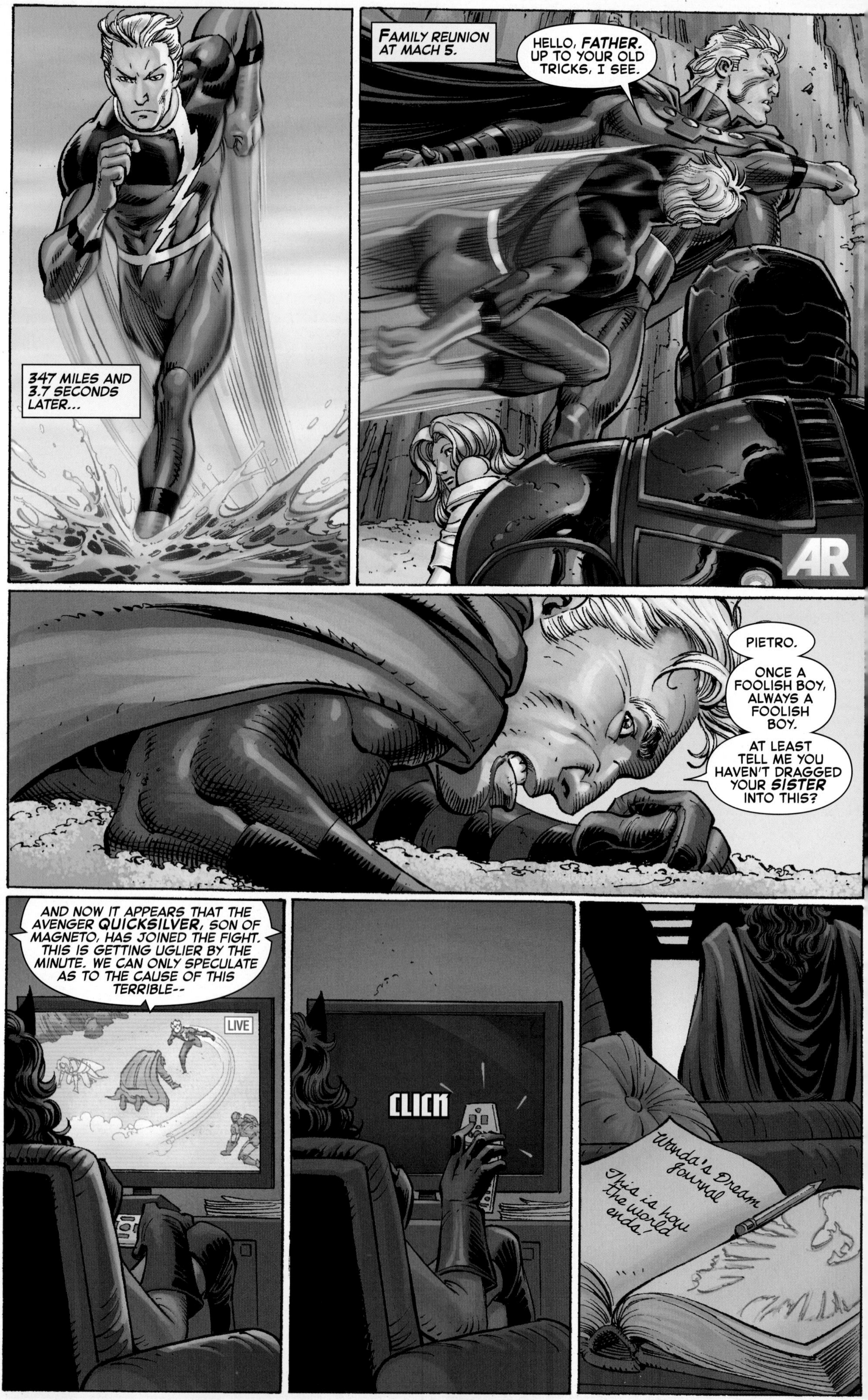
347 MILES AND 3.7 SECONDS LATER...
FAMILY REUNION AT MACH 5.
HELLO, FATHER. UP TO YOUR OLD TRICKS, I SEE.
AR
PIETRO.
ONCE A FOOLISH BOY, ALWAYS A FOOLISH BOY.
AT LEAST TELL ME YOU HAVEN'T DRAGGED YOUR SISTER INTO THIS?
AND NOW IT APPEARS THAT THE AVENGER QUICKSILVER, SON OF MAGNETO, HAS JOINED THE FIGHT. THIS IS GETTING UGLIER BY THE MINUTE. WE CAN ONLY SPECULATE AS TO THE CAUSE OF THIS TERRIBLE--
LIVE
CLICK
Wanda's Dream Journal
This is how the world ends!

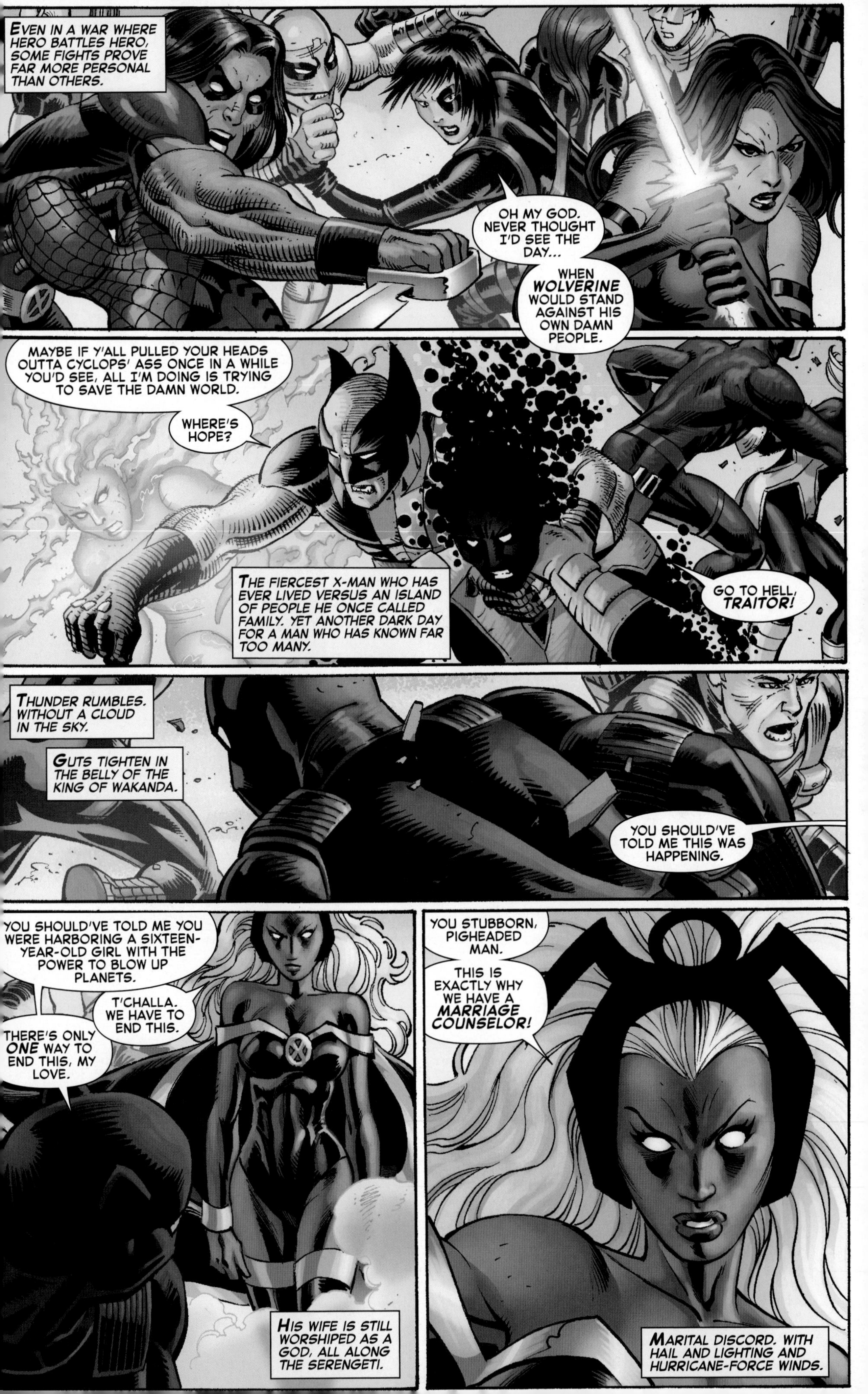
EVEN IN A WAR WHERE HERO BATTLES HERO, SOME FIGHTS PROVE FAR MORE PERSONAL THAN OTHERS.
OH MY GOD. NEVER THOUGHT I'D SEE THE DAY...
WHEN WOLVERINE WOULD STAND AGAINST HIS OWN DAMN PEOPLE.
MAYBE IF Y'ALL PULLED YOUR HEADS OUTTA CYCLOPS' ASS ONCE IN A WHILE YOU'D SEE, ALL I'M DOING IS TRYING TO SAVE THE DAMN WORLD.
WHERE'S HOPE?
THE FIERCEST X-MAN WHO HAS EVER LIVED VERSUS AN ISLAND OF PEOPLE HE ONCE CALLED FAMILY. YET ANOTHER DARK DAY FOR A MAN WHO HAS KNOWN FAR TOO MANY.
GO TO HELL, TRAITOR!
THUNDER RUMBLES. WITHOUT A CLOUD IN THE SKY.
GUTS TIGHTEN IN THE BELLY OF THE KING OF WAKANDA.
YOU SHOULD'VE TOLD ME THIS WAS HAPPENING.
YOU SHOULD'VE TOLD ME YOU WERE HARBORING A SIXTEEN-YEAR-OLD GIRL WITH THE POWER TO BLOW UP PLANETS.
T'CHALLA. WE HAVE TO END THIS.
THERE'S ONLY ONE WAY TO END THIS, MY LOVE.
HIS WIFE IS STILL WORSHIPED AS A GOD, ALL ALONG THE SERENGETI.
YOU STUBBORN, PIGHEADED MAN.
THIS IS EXACTLY WHY WE HAVE A MARRIAGE COUNSELOR!
MARITAL DISCORD. WITH HAIL AND LIGHTING AND HURRICANE-FORCE WINDS.

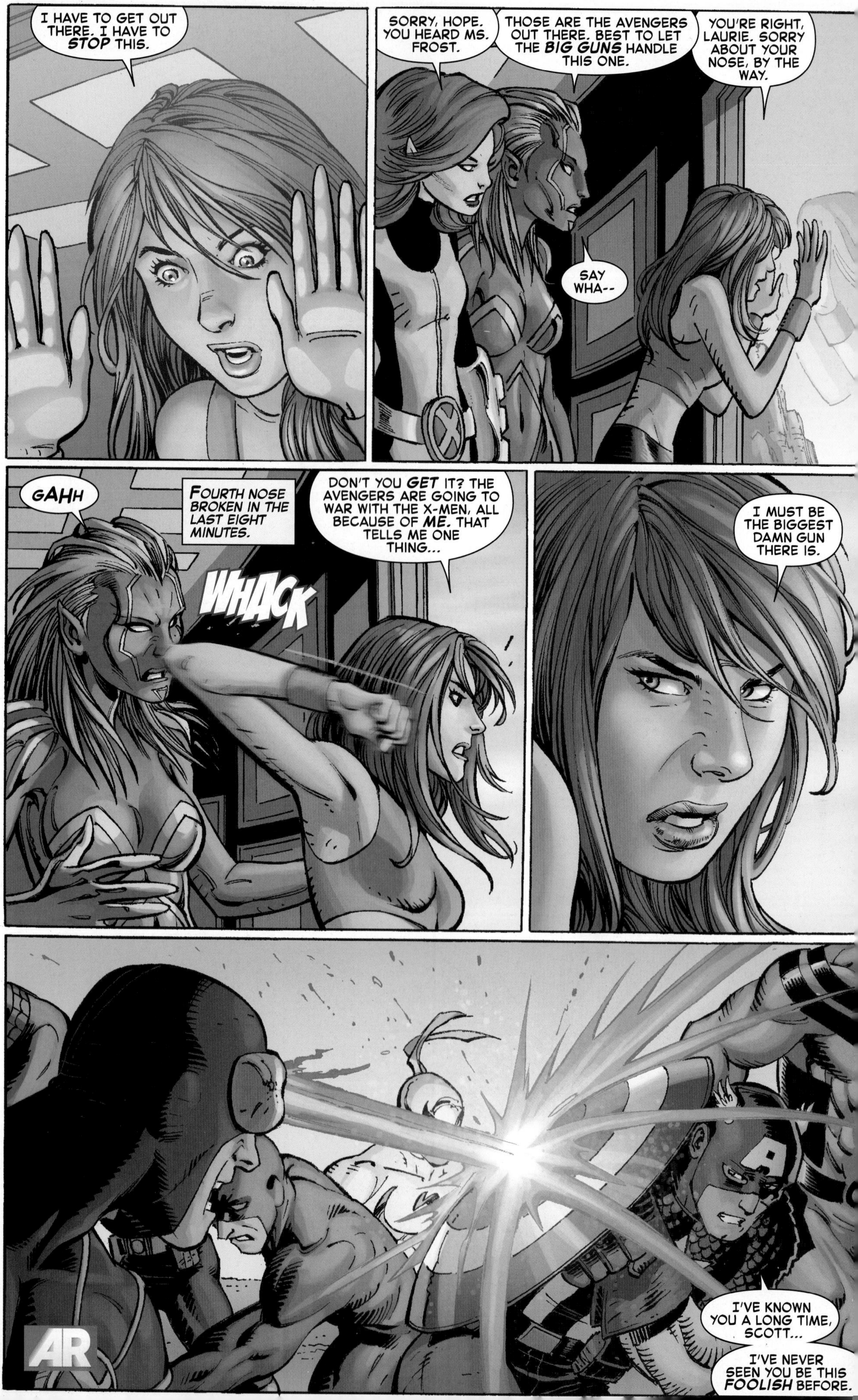

I HAVE TO GET OUT THERE. I HAVE TO STOP THIS.
SORRY, HOPE. YOU HEARD MS. FROST.
THOSE ARE THE AVENGERS OUT THERE. BEST TO LET THE BIG GUNS HANDLE THIS ONE.
YOU'RE RIGHT, LAURIE. SORRY ABOUT YOUR NOSE, BY THE WAY.
SAY WHA--
GAHH
FOURTH NOSE BROKEN IN THE LAST EIGHT MINUTES.
DON'T YOU GET IT? THE AVENGERS ARE GOING TO WAR WITH THE X-MEN, ALL BECAUSE OF ME. THAT TELLS ME ONE THING...
WHACK
I MUST BE THE BIGGEST DAMN GUN THERE IS.
I'VE KNOWN YOU A LONG TIME, SCOTT...
I'VE NEVER SEEN YOU BE THIS FOOLISH BEFORE.

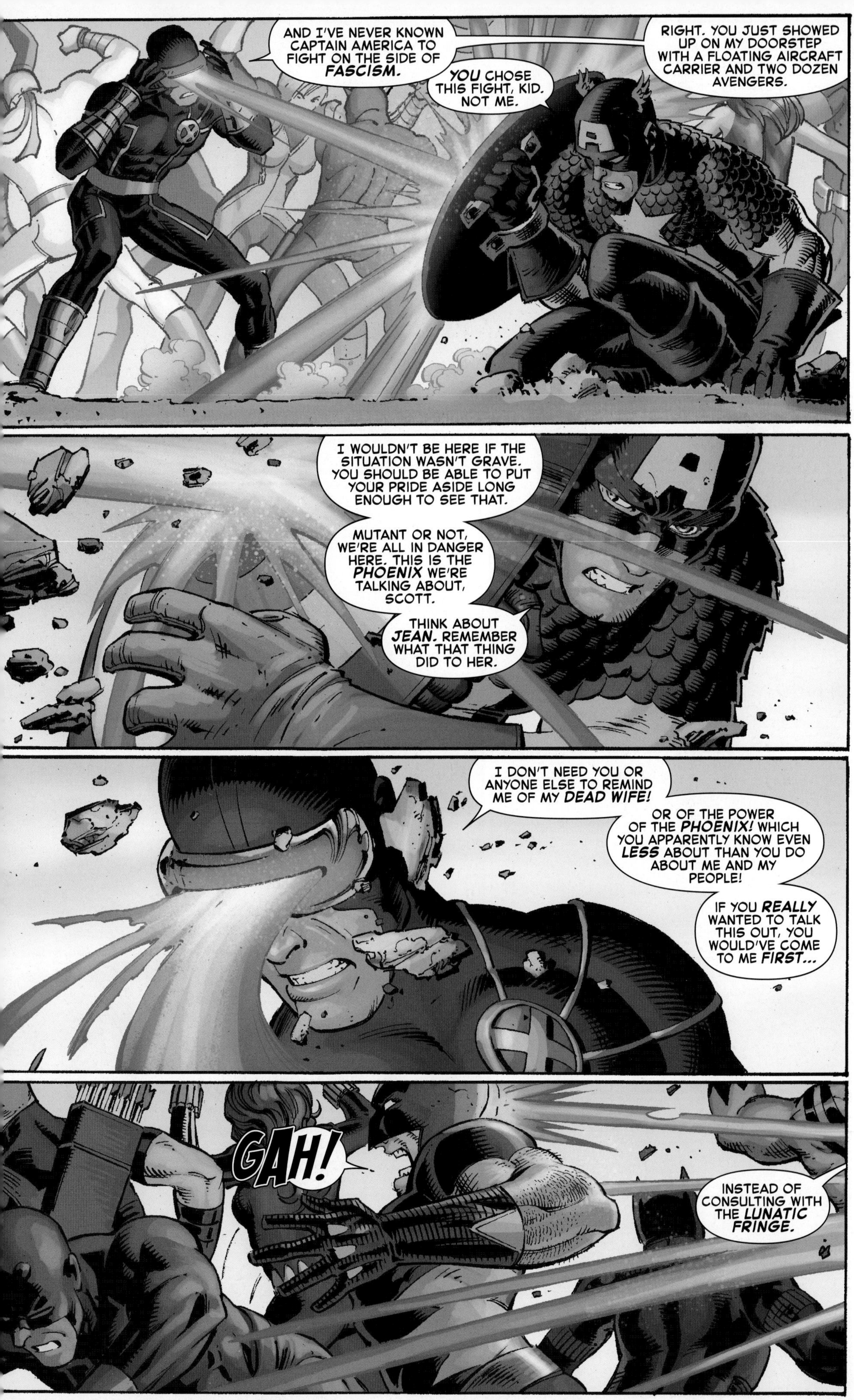
AND I'VE NEVER KNOWN CAPTAIN AMERICA TO FIGHT ON THE SIDE OF FASCISM.
YOU CHOSE THIS FIGHT, KID. NOT ME.
RIGHT. YOU JUST SHOWED UP ON MY DOORSTEP WITH A FLOATING AIRCRAFT CARRIER AND TWO DOZEN AVENGERS.
I WOULDN'T BE HERE IF THE SITUATION WASN'T GRAVE. YOU SHOULD BE ABLE TO PUT YOUR PRIDE ASIDE LONG ENOUGH TO SEE THAT.
MUTANT OR NOT, WE'RE ALL IN DANGER HERE. THIS IS THE PHOENIX WE'RE TALKING ABOUT, SCOTT.
THINK ABOUT JEAN. REMEMBER WHAT THAT THING DID TO HER.
I DON'T NEED YOU OR ANYONE ELSE TO REMIND ME OF MY DEAD WIFE!
OR OF THE POWER OF THE PHOENIX! WHICH YOU APPARENTLY KNOW EVEN LESS ABOUT THAN YOU DO ABOUT ME AND MY PEOPLE!
IF YOU REALLY WANTED TO TALK THIS OUT, YOU WOULD'VE COME TO ME FIRST...
GAH!
INSTEAD OF CONSULTING WITH THE LUNATIC FRINGE.

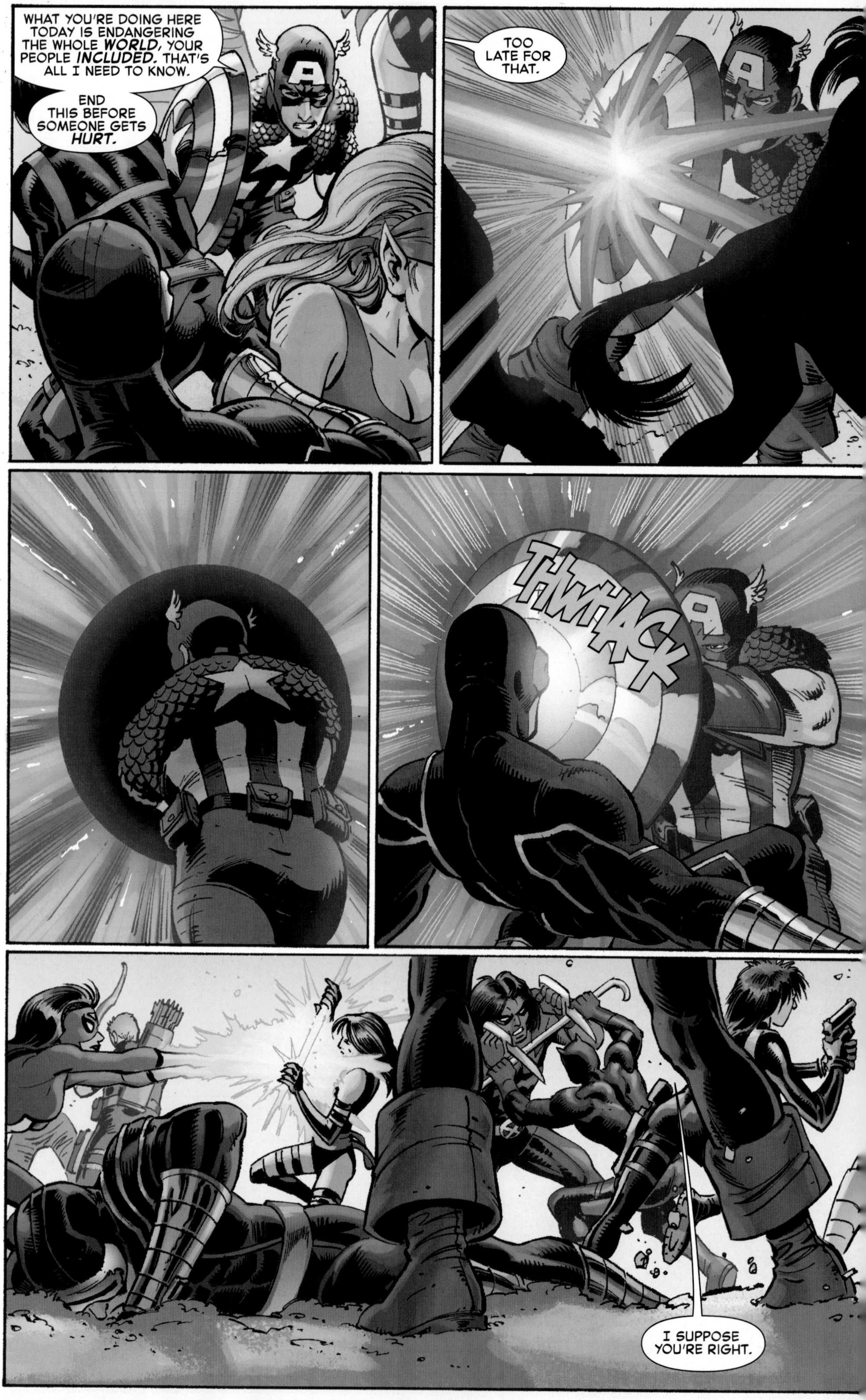
WHAT YOU'RE DOING HERE TODAY IS ENDANGERING THE WHOLE **WORLD**, YOUR PEOPLE **INCLUDED.** THAT'S ALL I NEED TO KNOW.
END THIS BEFORE SOMEONE GETS **HURT.**
TOO LATE FOR THAT.
THWHACK
I SUPPOSE YOU'RE RIGHT.

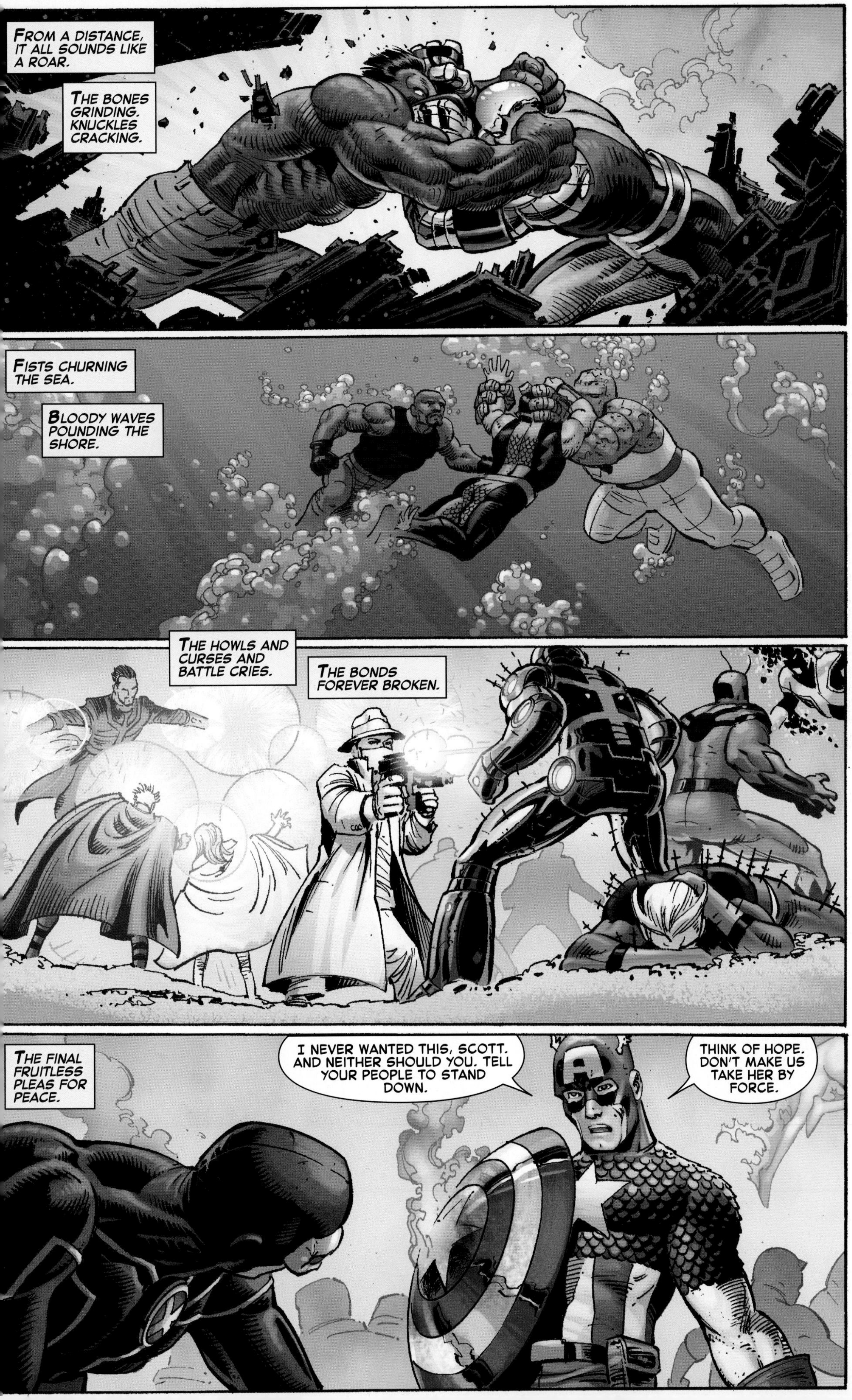
FROM A DISTANCE, IT ALL SOUNDS LIKE A ROAR.
THE BONES GRINDING. KNUCKLES CRACKING.
FISTS CHURNING THE SEA.
BLOODY WAVES POUNDING THE SHORE.
THE HOWLS AND CURSES AND BATTLE CRIES.
THE BONDS FOREVER BROKEN.
THE FINAL FRUITLESS PLEAS FOR PEACE.
I NEVER WANTED THIS, SCOTT. AND NEITHER SHOULD YOU. TELL YOUR PEOPLE TO STAND DOWN.
THINK OF HOPE. DON'T MAKE US TAKE HER BY FORCE.

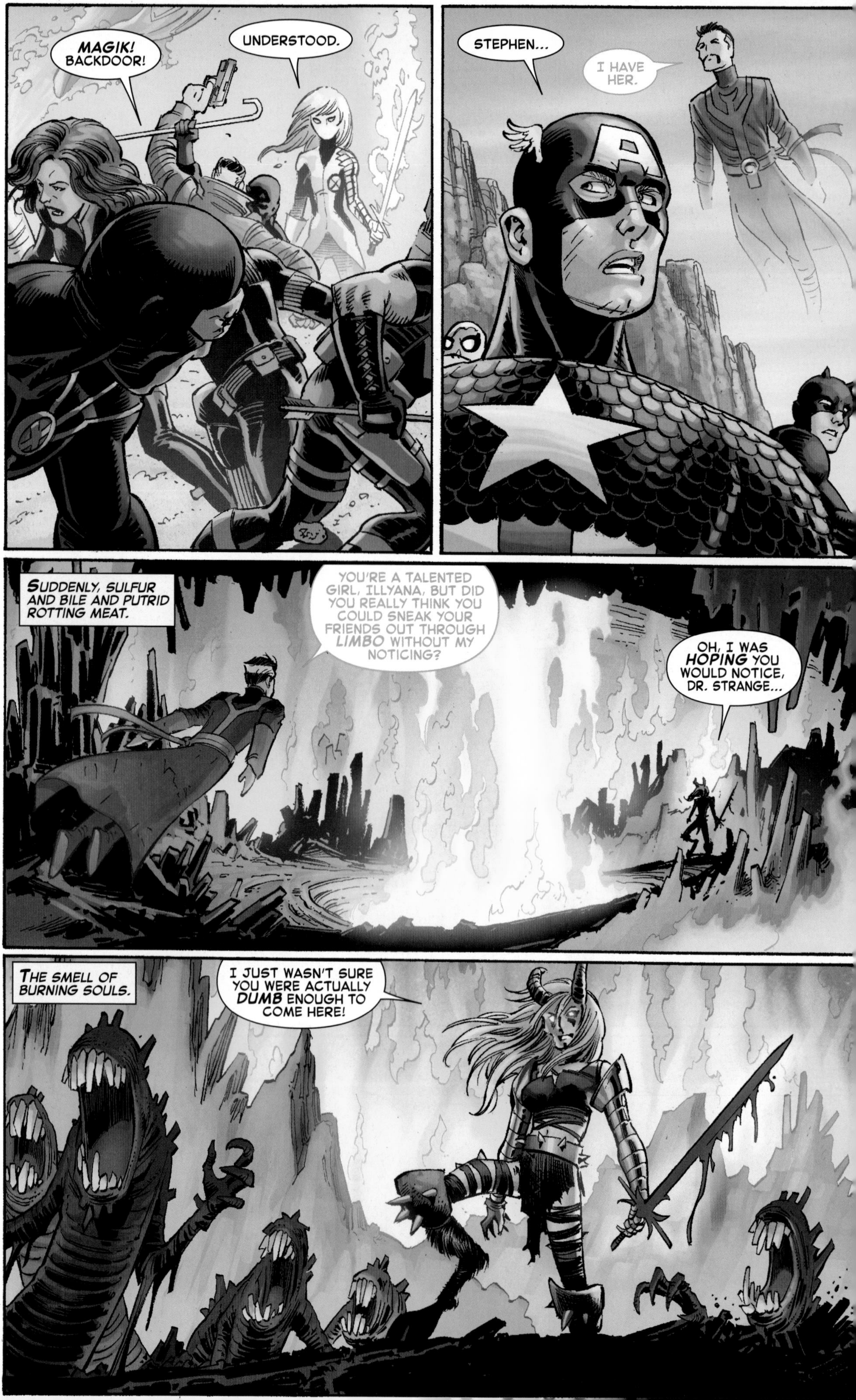
MAGIK! BACKDOOR!
UNDERSTOOD.
STEPHEN...
I HAVE HER.
SUDDENLY, SULFUR AND BILE AND PUTRID ROTTING MEAT.
YOU'RE A TALENTED GIRL, ILLYANA, BUT DID YOU REALLY THINK YOU COULD SNEAK YOUR FRIENDS OUT THROUGH LIMBO WITHOUT MY NOTICING?
OH, I WAS HOPING YOU WOULD NOTICE, DR. STRANGE...
THE SMELL OF BURNING SOULS.
I JUST WASN'T SURE YOU WERE ACTUALLY DUMB ENOUGH TO COME HERE!

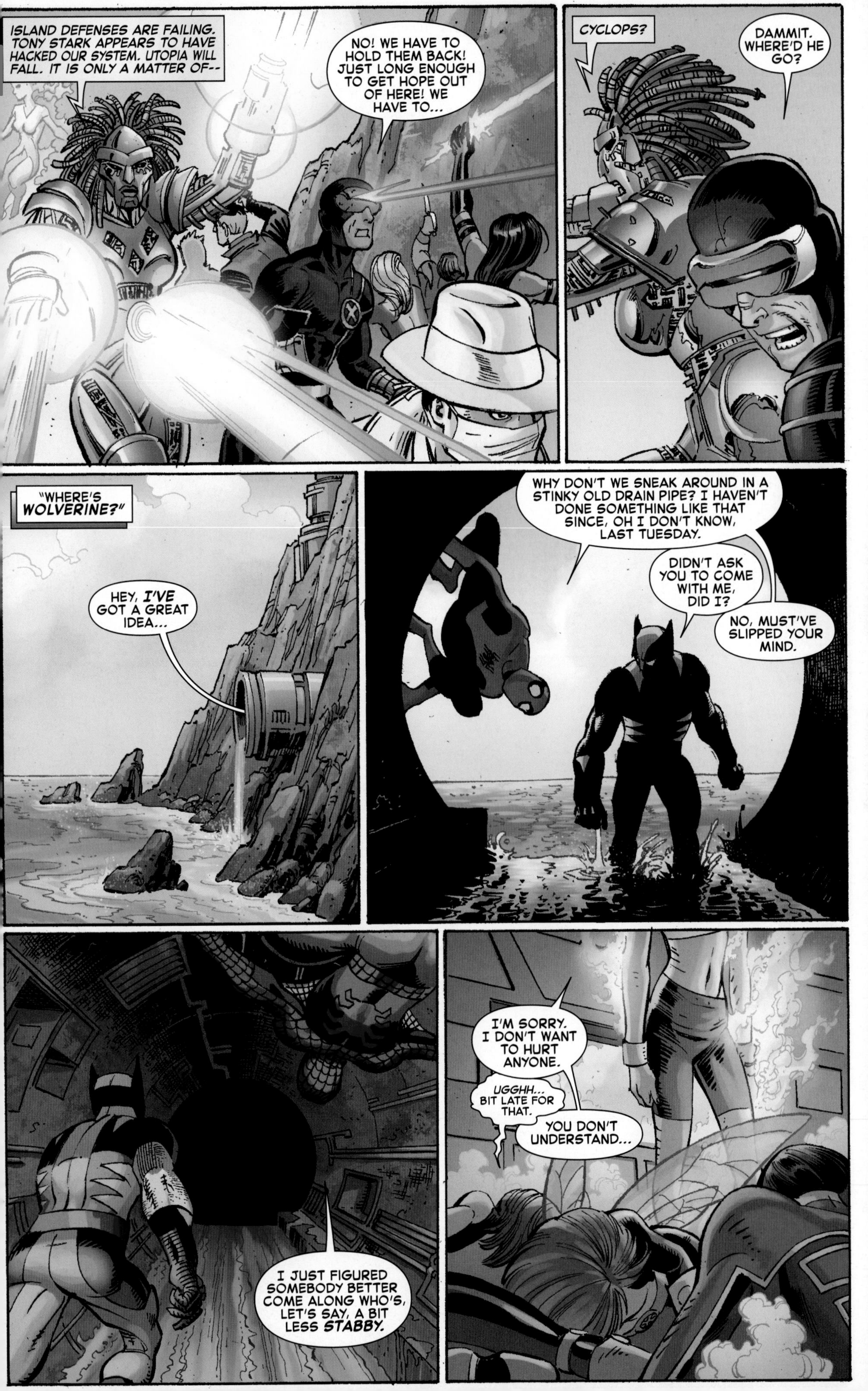
ISLAND DEFENSES ARE FAILING. TONY STARK APPEARS TO HAVE HACKED OUR SYSTEM. UTOPIA WILL FALL. IT IS ONLY A MATTER OF--
NO! WE HAVE TO HOLD THEM BACK! JUST LONG ENOUGH TO GET HOPE OUT OF HERE! WE HAVE TO...
CYCLOPS?
DAMMIT. WHERE'D HE GO?
"WHERE'S WOLVERINE?"
HEY, I'VE GOT A GREAT IDEA...
WHY DON'T WE SNEAK AROUND IN A STINKY OLD DRAIN PIPE? I HAVEN'T DONE SOMETHING LIKE THAT SINCE, OH I DON'T KNOW, LAST TUESDAY.
DIDN'T ASK YOU TO COME WITH ME, DID I?
NO, MUST'VE SLIPPED YOUR MIND.
I JUST FIGURED SOMEBODY BETTER COME ALONG WHO'S, LET'S SAY, A BIT LESS STABBY.
I'M SORRY. I DON'T WANT TO HURT ANYONE.
UGGHH... BIT LATE FOR THAT.
YOU DON'T UNDERSTAND...

THE CLOSER IT GETS, THE MORE I FEEL IT.

THE MORE THE POWER GROWS INSIDE ME.

WHOA. IS SHE, UH, SUPPOSED TO BE ON *FIRE* LIKE THAT?

OUTTA THE WAY.

HEY, NO, WHAT ARE YOU DOING?

SNIKT

WHAT HAS TO BE DONE.

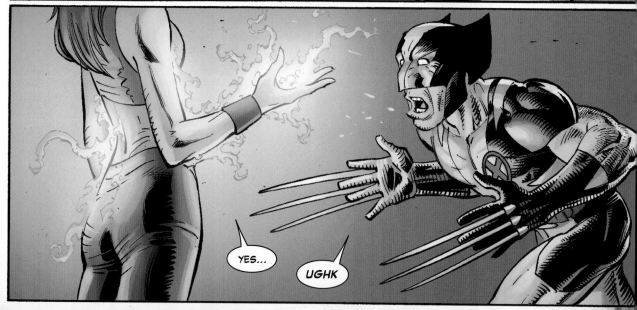

YES...

UGHK

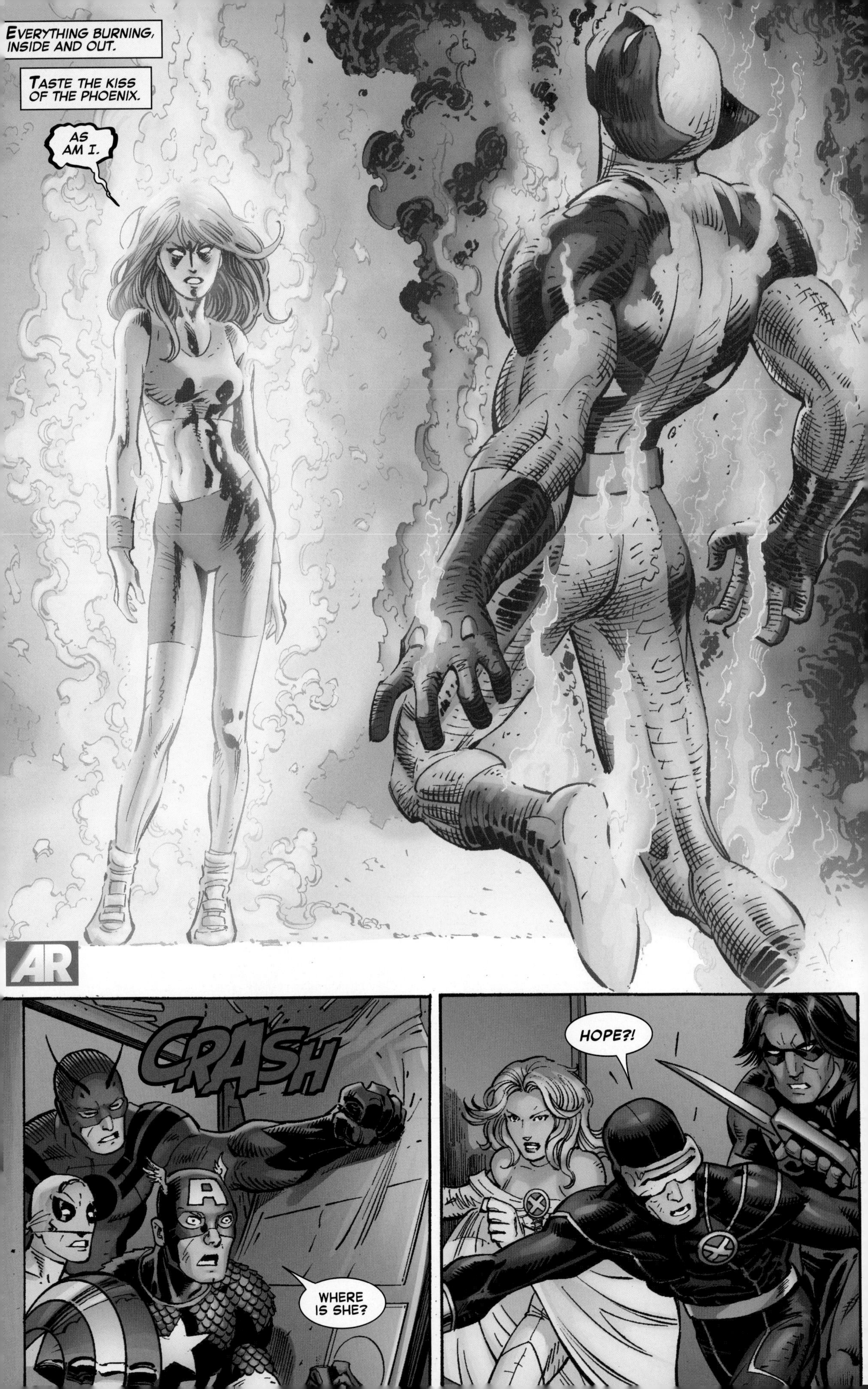
EVERYTHING BURNING, INSIDE AND OUT.
TASTE THE KISS OF THE PHOENIX.
AS AM I.
CRASH
WHERE IS SHE?
HOPE?!

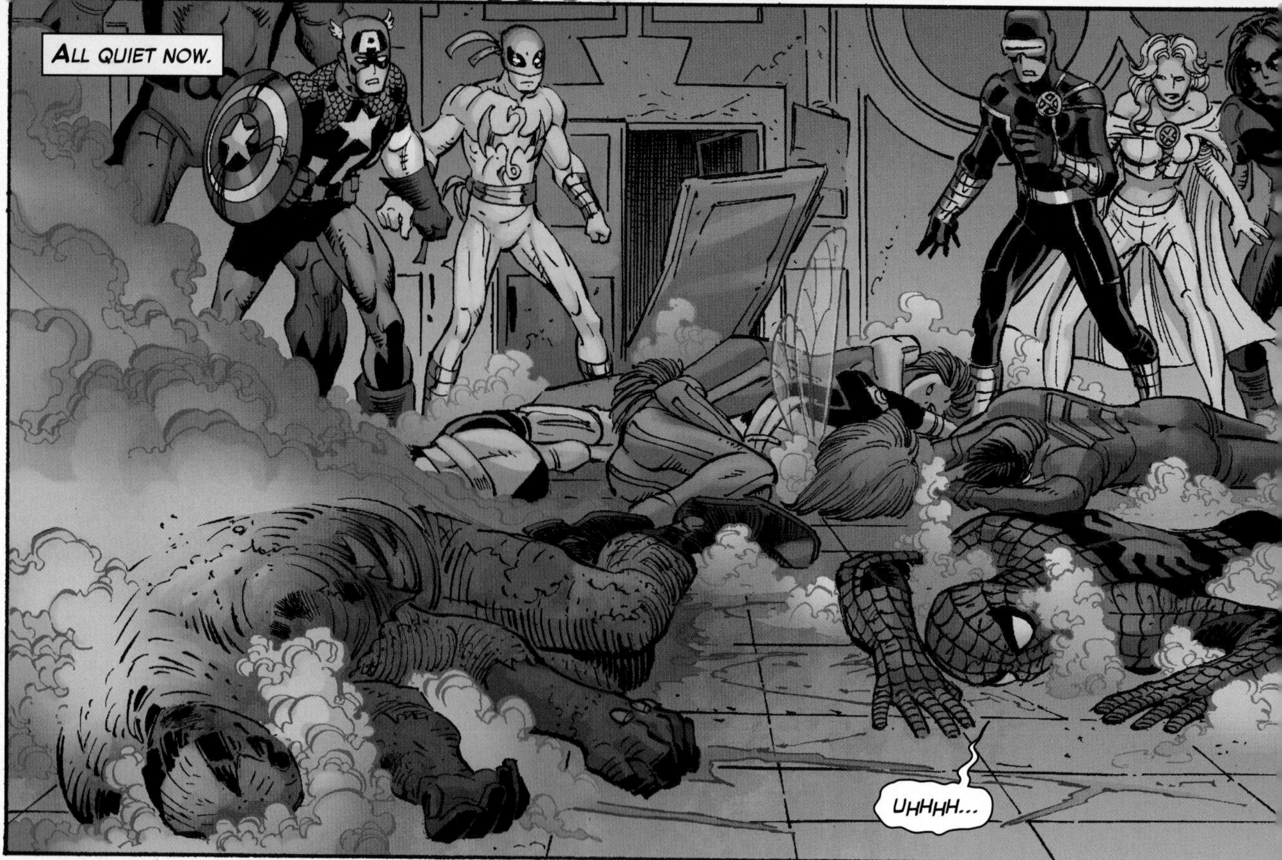

ALL QUIET NOW.
UHHHH...

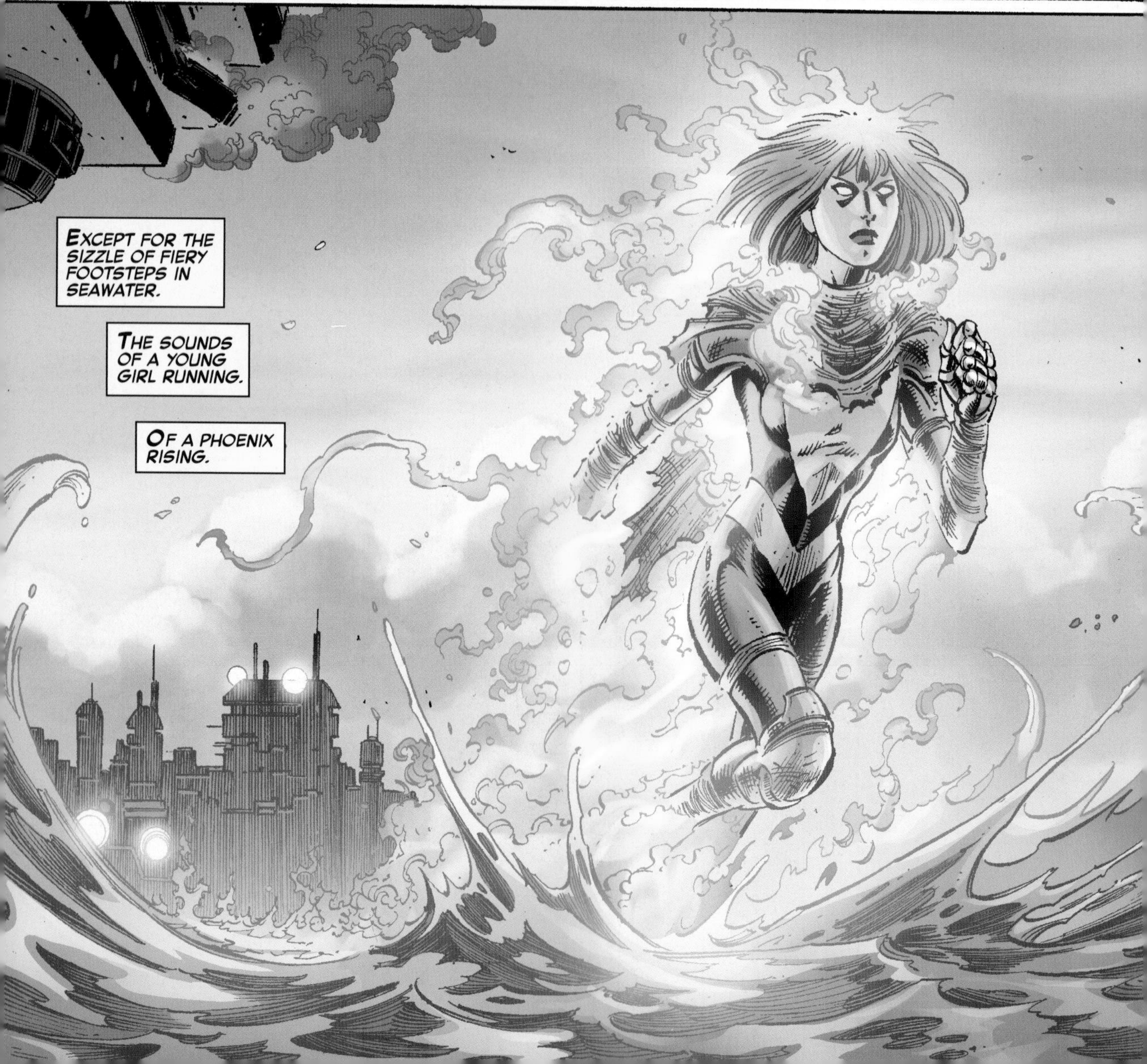

EXCEPT FOR THE SIZZLE OF FIERY FOOTSTEPS IN SEAWATER.
THE SOUNDS OF A YOUNG GIRL RUNNING.
OF A PHOENIX RISING.

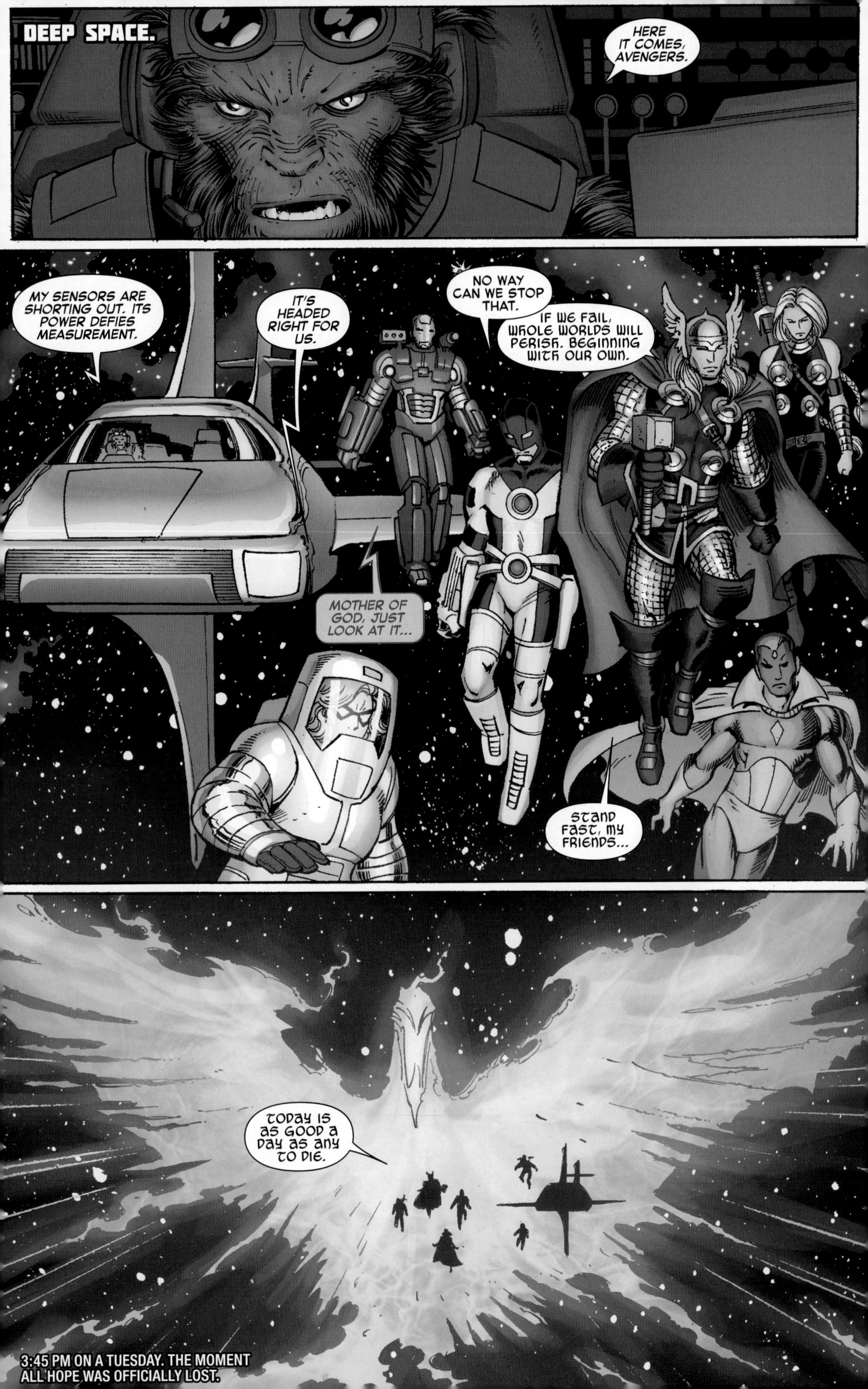
DEEP SPACE.
HERE IT COMES, AVENGERS.
MY SENSORS ARE SHORTING OUT. ITS POWER DEFIES MEASUREMENT.
IT'S HEADED RIGHT FOR US.
NO WAY CAN WE STOP THAT.
IF WE FAIL, WHOLE WORLDS WILL PERISH. BEGINNING WITH OUR OWN.
MOTHER OF GOD, JUST LOOK AT IT...
STAND FAST, MY FRIENDS...
TODAY IS AS GOOD A DAY AS ANY TO DIE.
3:45 PM ON A TUESDAY. THE MOMENT ALL HOPE WAS OFFICIALLY LOST.

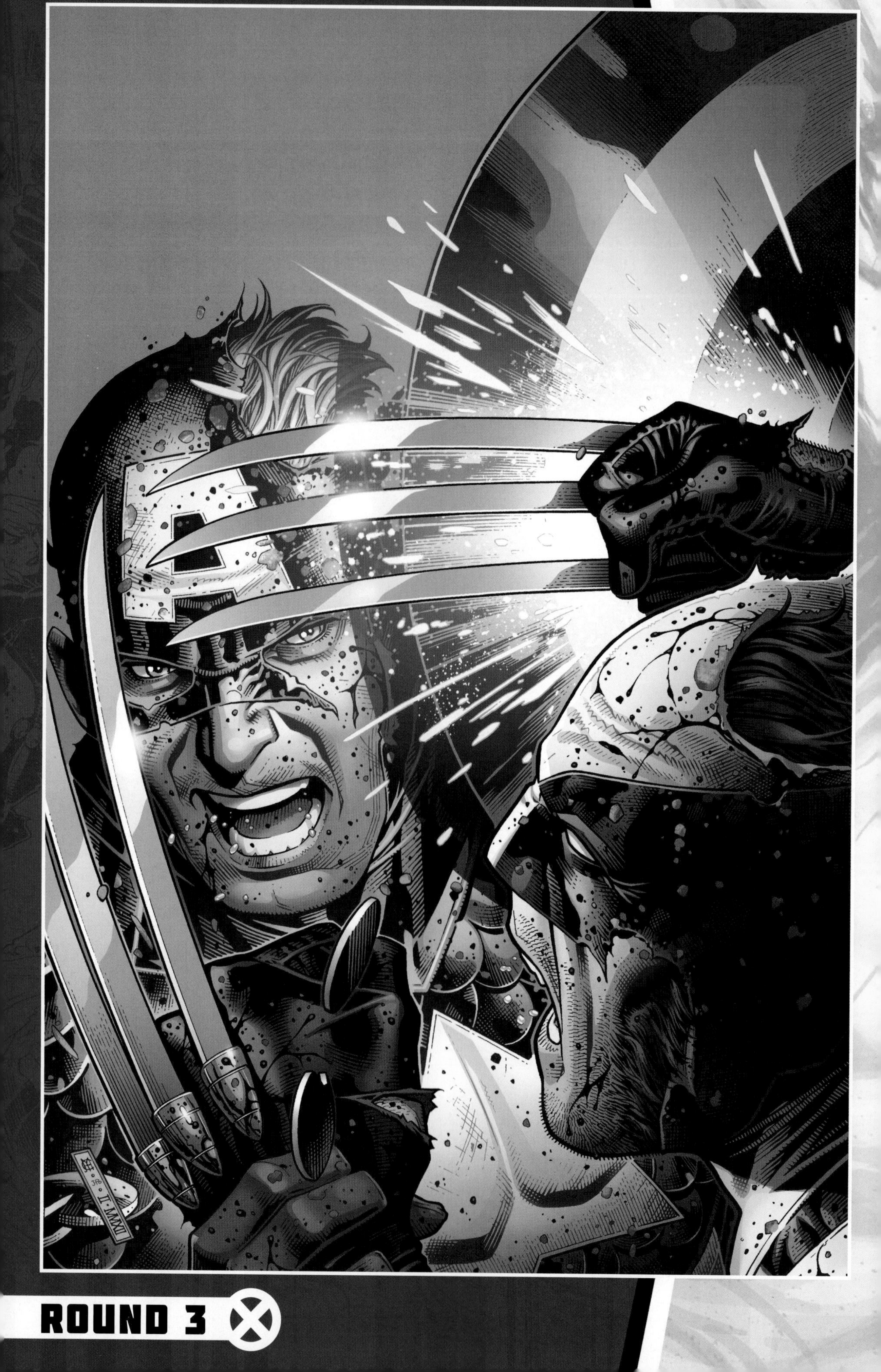

ROUND 3

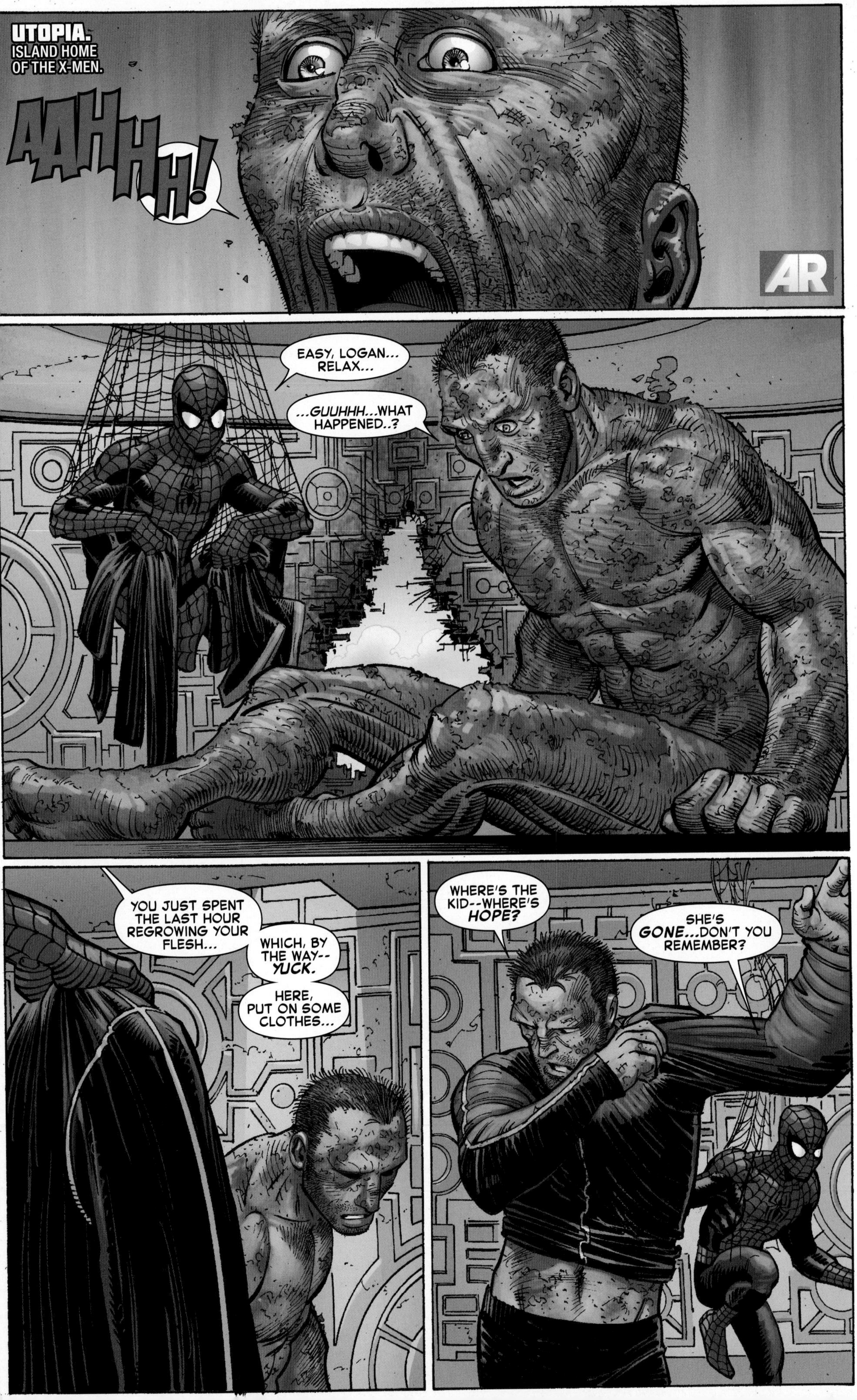
UTOPIA.
ISLAND HOME OF THE X-MEN.
AAHHHH!
EASY, LOGAN... RELAX...
...GUUHHH...WHAT HAPPENED..?
YOU JUST SPENT THE LAST HOUR REGROWING YOUR FLESH...
WHICH, BY THE WAY-- YUCK.
HERE, PUT ON SOME CLOTHES...
WHERE'S THE KID--WHERE'S HOPE?
SHE'S GONE...DON'T YOU REMEMBER?

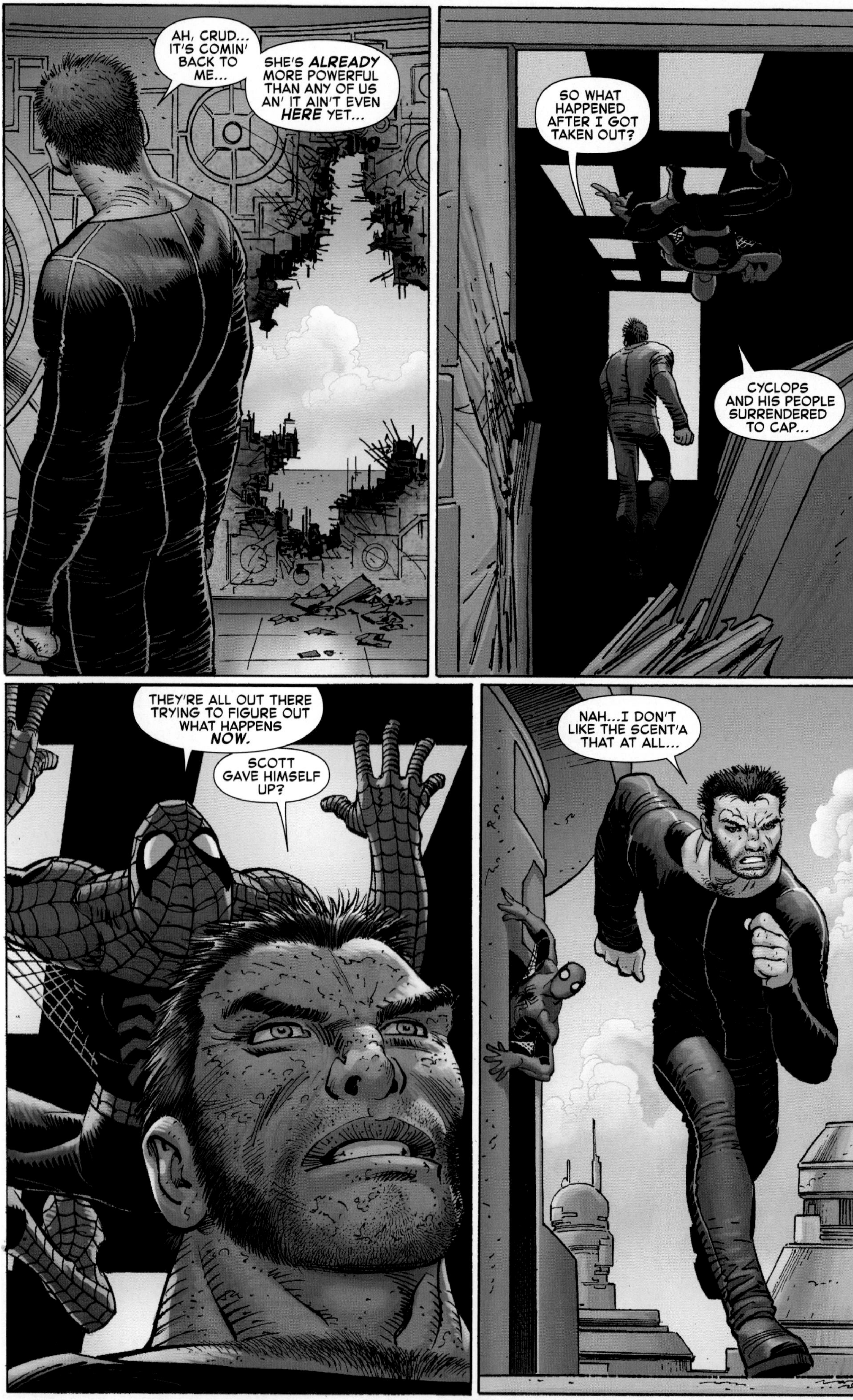
AH, CRUD... IT'S COMIN' BACK TO ME...
SHE'S ALREADY MORE POWERFUL THAN ANY OF US AN' IT AIN'T EVEN HERE YET...
SO WHAT HAPPENED AFTER I GOT TAKEN OUT?
CYCLOPS AND HIS PEOPLE SURRENDERED TO CAP...
THEY'RE ALL OUT THERE TRYING TO FIGURE OUT WHAT HAPPENS NOW.
SCOTT GAVE HIMSELF UP?
NAH...I DON'T LIKE THE SCENT'A THAT AT ALL...

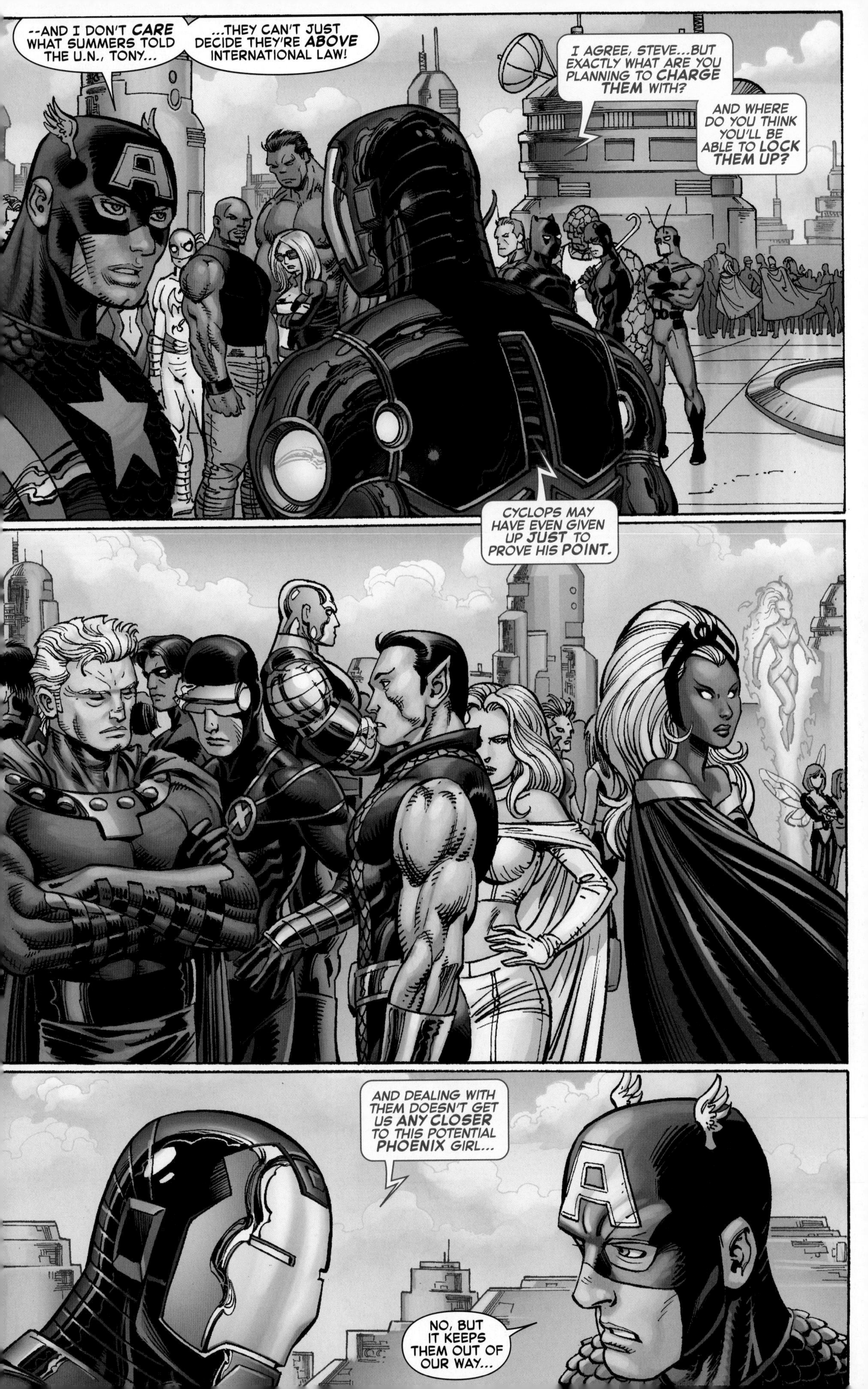
--AND I DON'T CARE WHAT SUMMERS TOLD THE U.N., TONY...
...THEY CAN'T JUST DECIDE THEY'RE ABOVE INTERNATIONAL LAW!
I AGREE, STEVE...BUT EXACTLY WHAT ARE YOU PLANNING TO CHARGE THEM WITH?
AND WHERE DO YOU THINK YOU'LL BE ABLE TO LOCK THEM UP?
CYCLOPS MAY HAVE EVEN GIVEN UP JUST TO PROVE HIS POINT.
AND DEALING WITH THEM DOESN'T GET US ANY CLOSER TO THIS POTENTIAL PHOENIX GIRL...
NO, BUT IT KEEPS THEM OUT OF OUR WAY...

AGAIN, *WHERE?* ARE YOU GOING TO EMPTY THE ENTIRE *RAFT* TO PUT THE X-MEN IN THERE? BECAUSE THAT DOESN'T SOUND LIKE YOUR STYLE AT ALL.

I'M TRYING TO *SAVE* THAT GIRL...

I'M TRYING TO SAVE OUR *WHOLE* WORLD...

I KNOW, BUT IT WASN'T TOO LONG AGO I WAS SAYING THINGS *JUST* LIKE THAT...

AND YOU WERE ON THE *OTHER* SIDE, THEN.

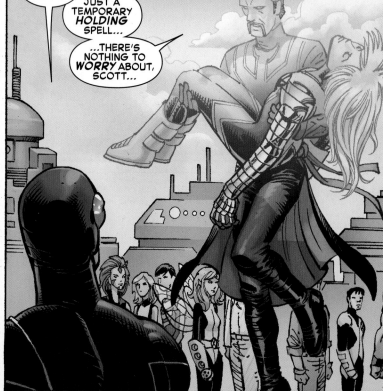

IS *SHE* HURT?

JUST A TEMPORARY *HOLDING* SPELL...

...THERE'S NOTHING TO *WORRY* ABOUT, SCOTT...

GOOD, WE DON'T NEED ANY MORE--

HEY!

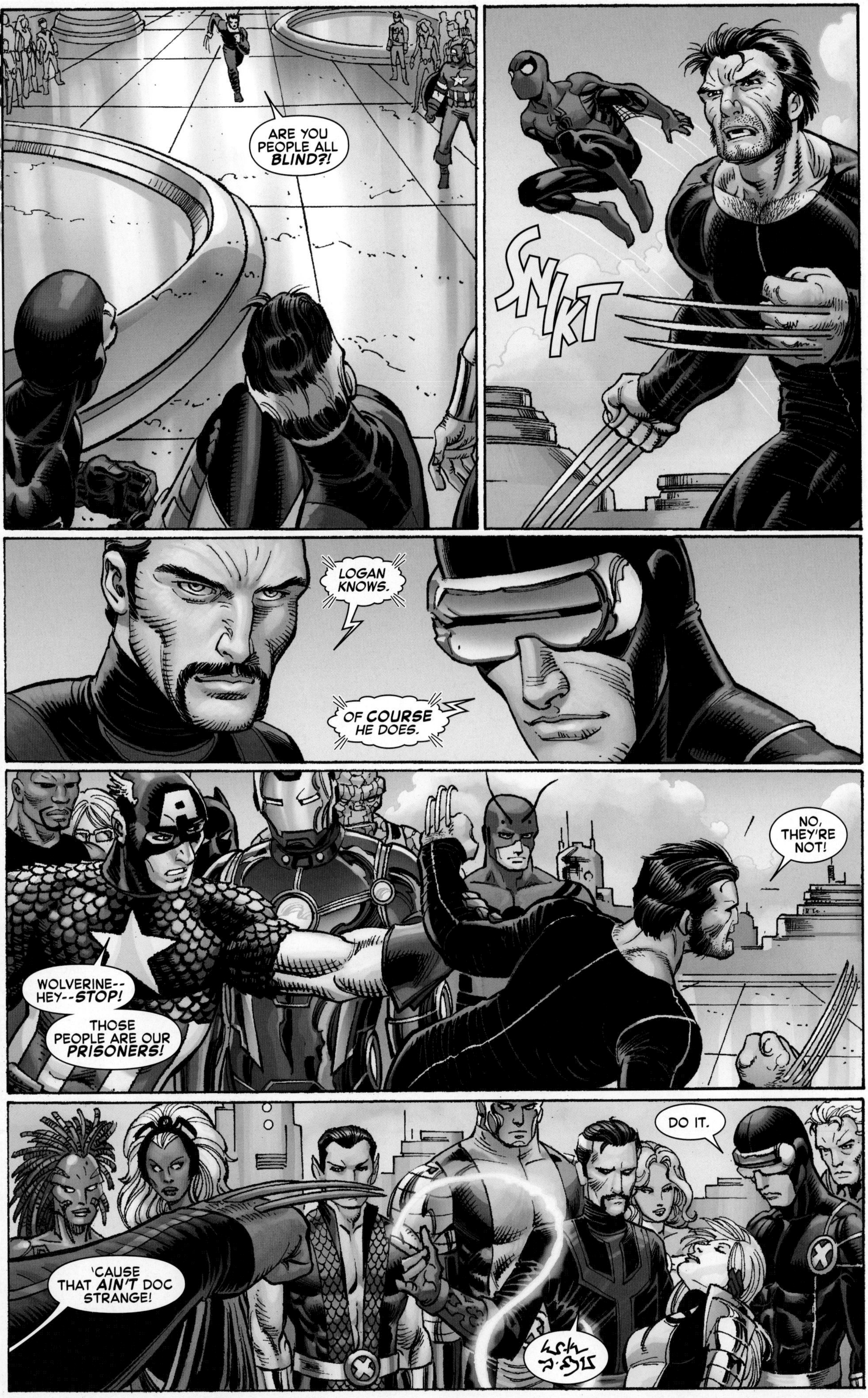
ARE YOU PEOPLE ALL BLIND?!
SNIKT
LOGAN KNOWS.
OF COURSE HE DOES.
NO, THEY'RE NOT!
WOLVERINE-- HEY--STOP!
THOSE PEOPLE ARE OUR PRISONERS!
DO IT.
'CAUSE THAT AIN'T DOC STRANGE!

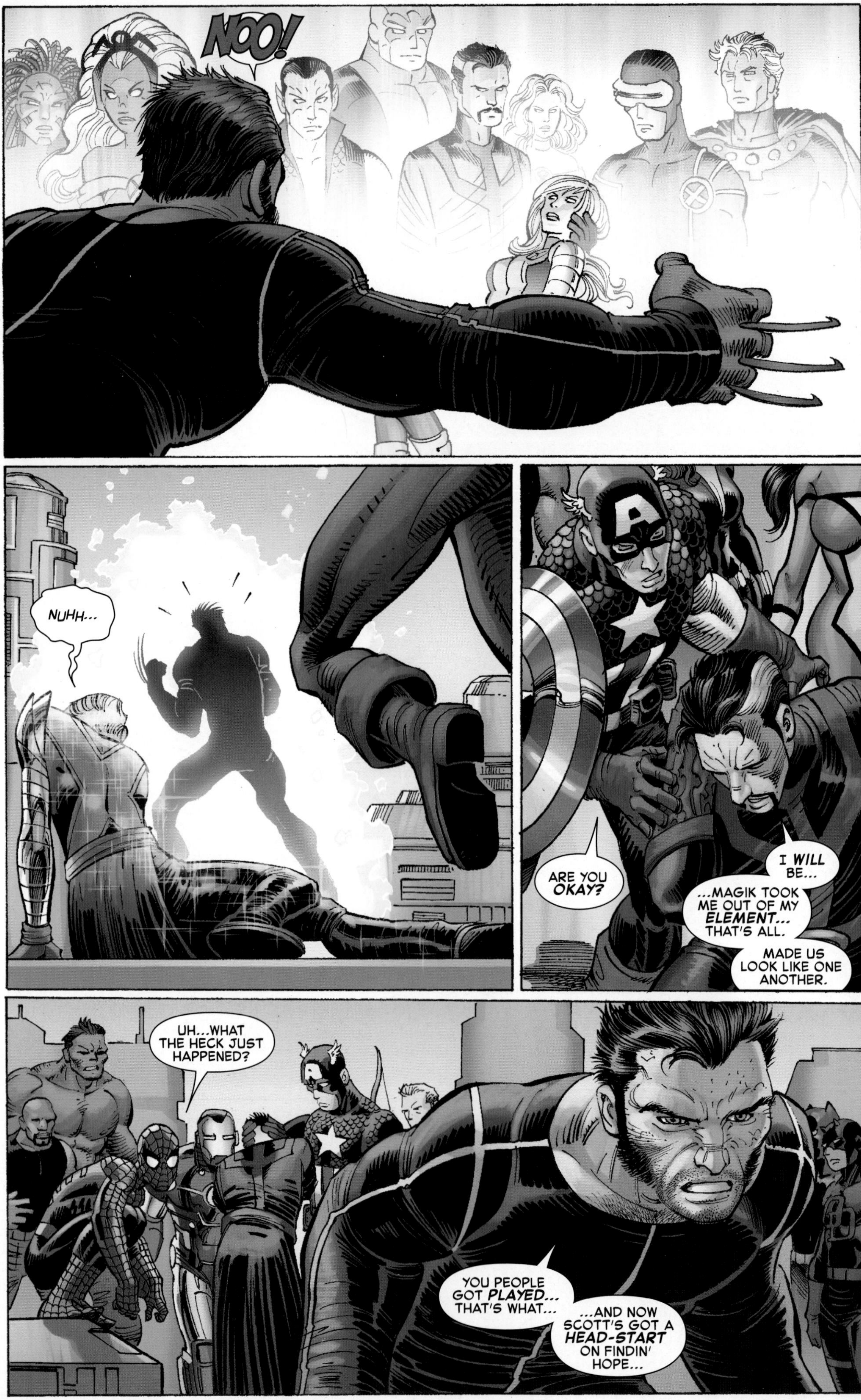
NOO!
NUHH...
ARE YOU OKAY?
I WILL BE...
...MAGIK TOOK ME OUT OF MY ELEMENT... THAT'S ALL.
MADE US LOOK LIKE ONE ANOTHER.
UH...WHAT THE HECK JUST HAPPENED?
YOU PEOPLE GOT PLAYED... THAT'S WHAT...
...AND NOW SCOTT'S GOT A HEAD-START ON FINDIN' HOPE...

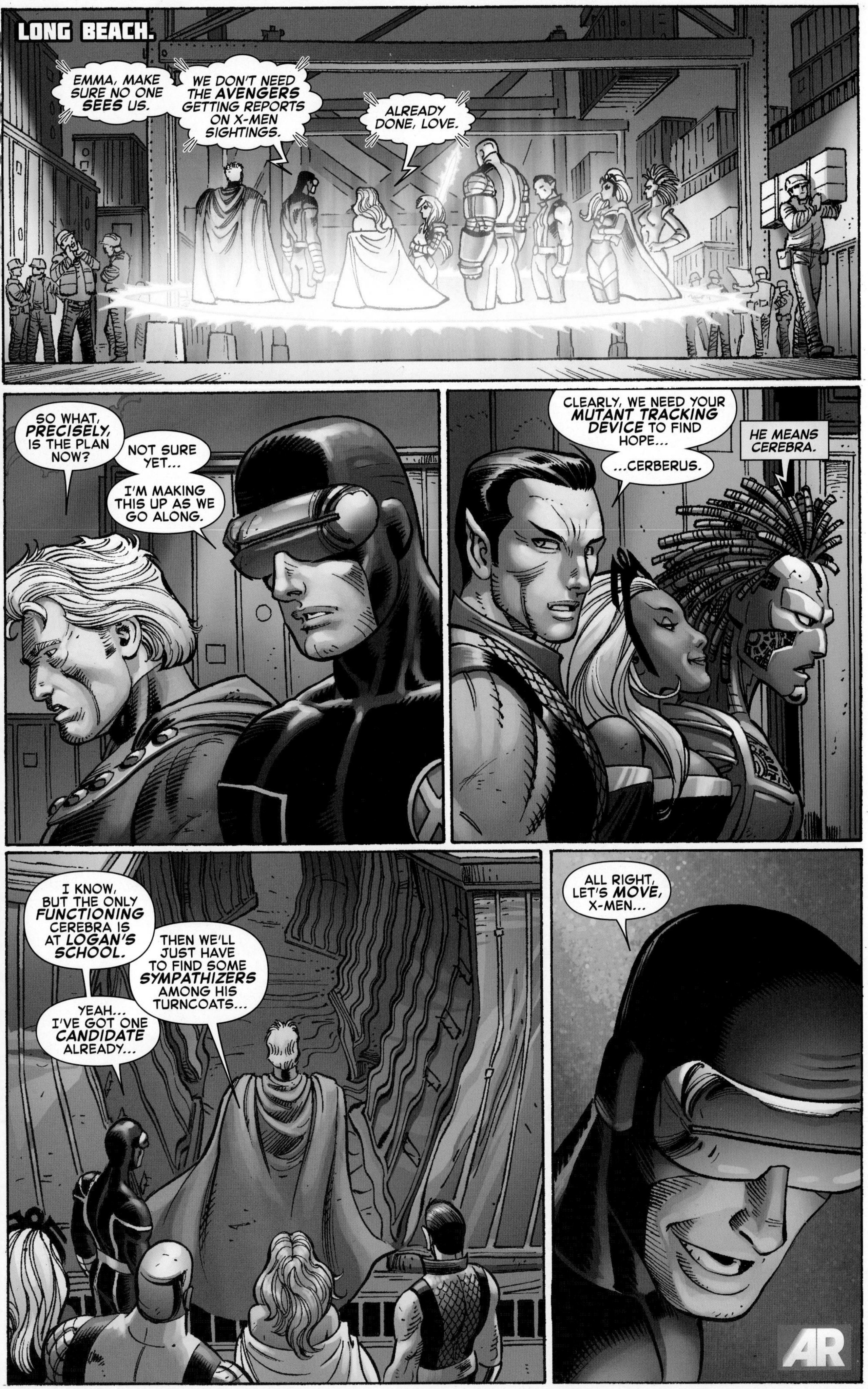
LONG BEACH.
EMMA, MAKE SURE NO ONE SEES US.
WE DON'T NEED THE AVENGERS GETTING REPORTS ON X-MEN SIGHTINGS.
ALREADY DONE, LOVE.
SO WHAT, PRECISELY, IS THE PLAN NOW?
NOT SURE YET...
I'M MAKING THIS UP AS WE GO ALONG.
CLEARLY, WE NEED YOUR MUTANT TRACKING DEVICE TO FIND HOPE...
...CERBERUS.
HE MEANS CEREBRA.
I KNOW, BUT THE ONLY FUNCTIONING CEREBRA IS AT LOGAN'S SCHOOL.
THEN WE'LL JUST HAVE TO FIND SOME SYMPATHIZERS AMONG HIS TURNCOATS...
YEAH... I'VE GOT ONE CANDIDATE ALREADY...
ALL RIGHT, LET'S MOVE, X-MEN...

"...HOPE *NEEDS* US, EVEN IF SHE DOESN'T *THINK* SHE DOES."

SAN FRANCISCO.

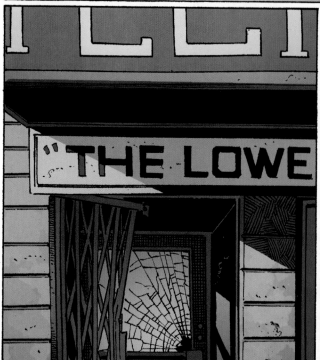

"THE LOWE

OKAY, HOPE... LET'S SEE IF YOU WERE PAYING ATTENTION WHEN CABLE WAS TEACHING...

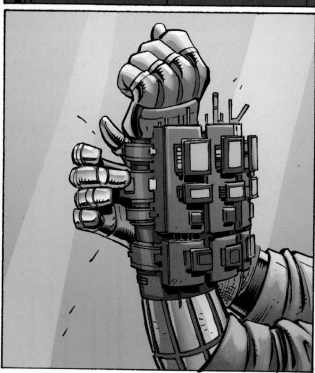

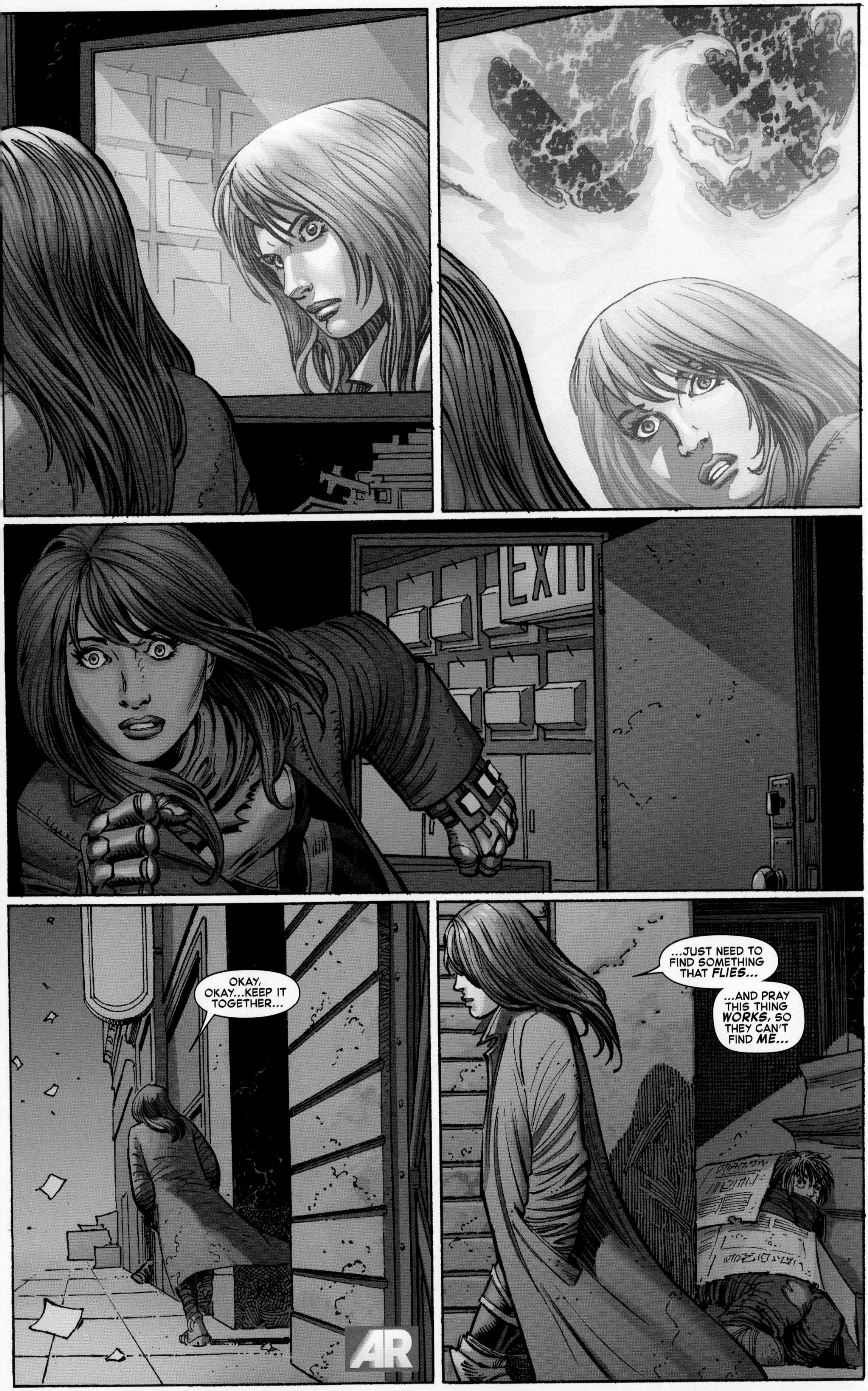
EXIT
OKAY, OKAY...KEEP IT TOGETHER...
...JUST NEED TO FIND SOMETHING THAT *FLIES*...
...AND PRAY THIS THING *WORKS*, SO THEY CAN'T FIND *ME*...
AR

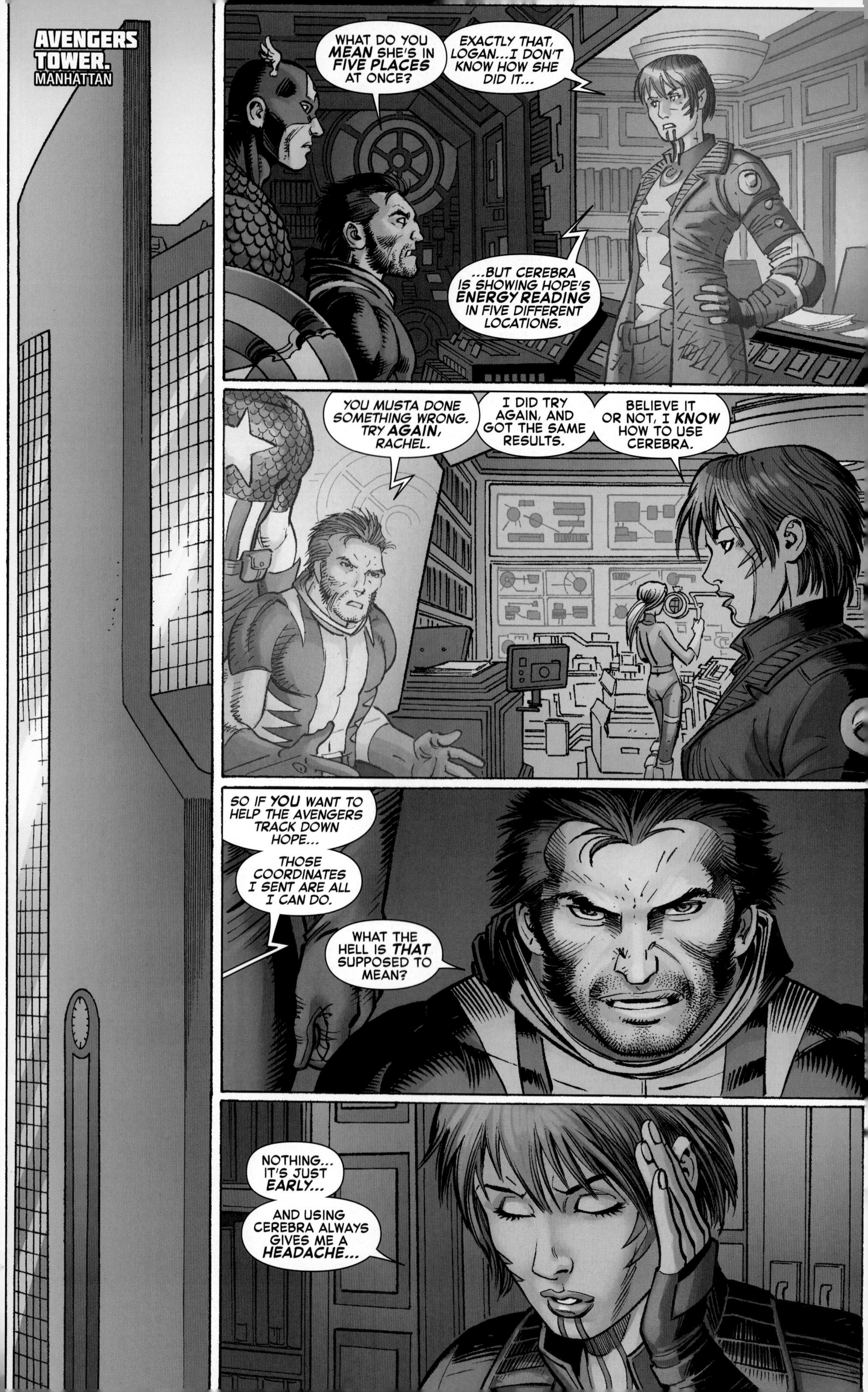
AVENGERS TOWER. MANHATTAN
WHAT DO YOU MEAN SHE'S IN FIVE PLACES AT ONCE?
EXACTLY THAT, LOGAN...I DON'T KNOW HOW SHE DID IT...
...BUT CEREBRA IS SHOWING HOPE'S ENERGY READING IN FIVE DIFFERENT LOCATIONS.
YOU MUSTA DONE SOMETHING WRONG. TRY AGAIN, RACHEL.
I DID TRY AGAIN, AND GOT THE SAME RESULTS.
BELIEVE IT OR NOT, I KNOW HOW TO USE CEREBRA.
SO IF YOU WANT TO HELP THE AVENGERS TRACK DOWN HOPE...
THOSE COORDINATES I SENT ARE ALL I CAN DO.
WHAT THE HELL IS THAT SUPPOSED TO MEAN?
NOTHING... IT'S JUST EARLY...
AND USING CEREBRA ALWAYS GIVES ME A HEADACHE...

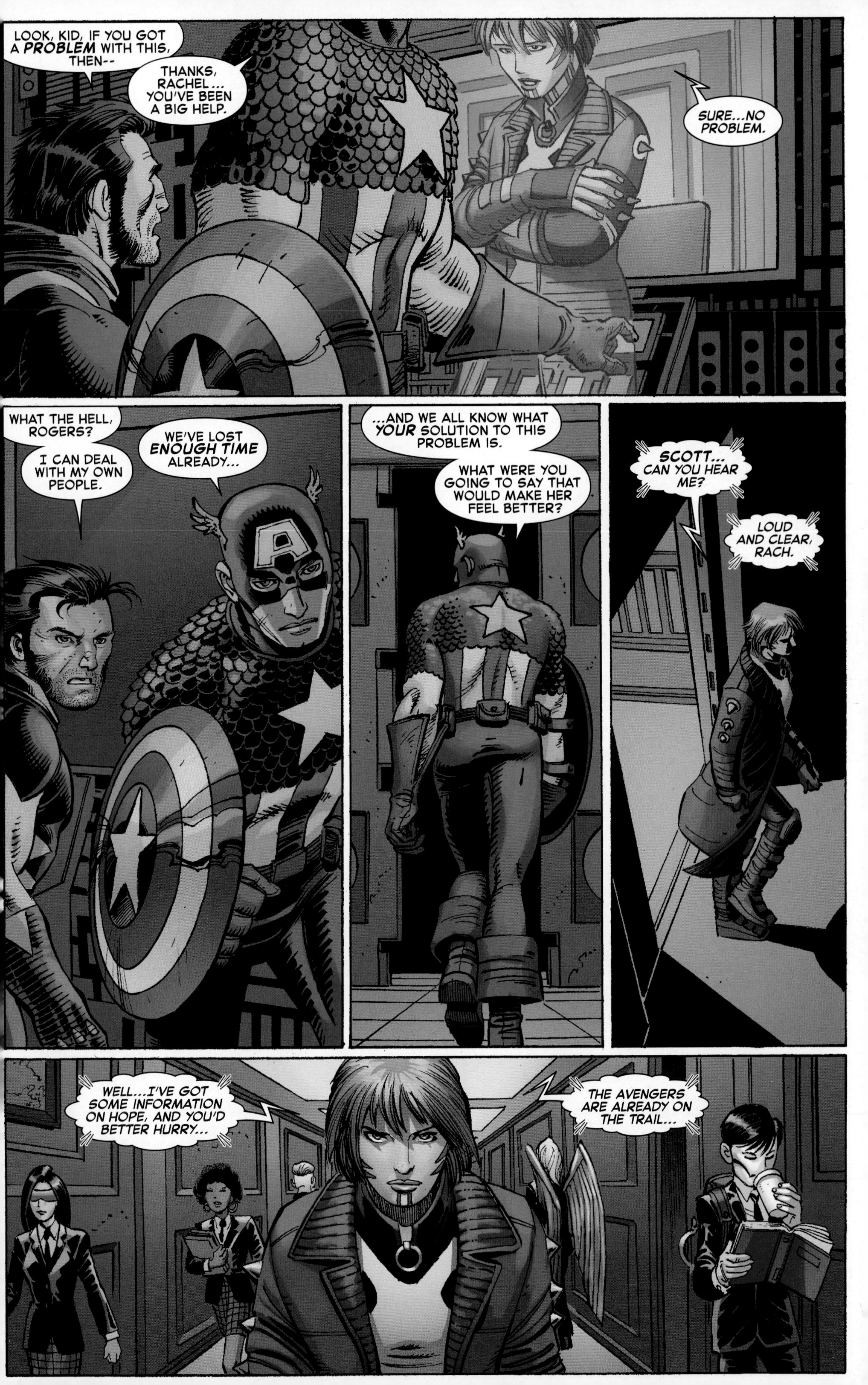
LOOK, KID, IF YOU GOT A PROBLEM WITH THIS, THEN--
THANKS, RACHEL... YOU'VE BEEN A BIG HELP.
SURE...NO PROBLEM.
WHAT THE HELL, ROGERS?
I CAN DEAL WITH MY OWN PEOPLE.
WE'VE LOST ENOUGH TIME ALREADY...
...AND WE ALL KNOW WHAT YOUR SOLUTION TO THIS PROBLEM IS.
WHAT WERE YOU GOING TO SAY THAT WOULD MAKE HER FEEL BETTER?
SCOTT... CAN YOU HEAR ME?
LOUD AND CLEAR, RACH.
WELL...I'VE GOT SOME INFORMATION ON HOPE, AND YOU'D BETTER HURRY...
THE AVENGERS ARE ALREADY ON THE TRAIL...

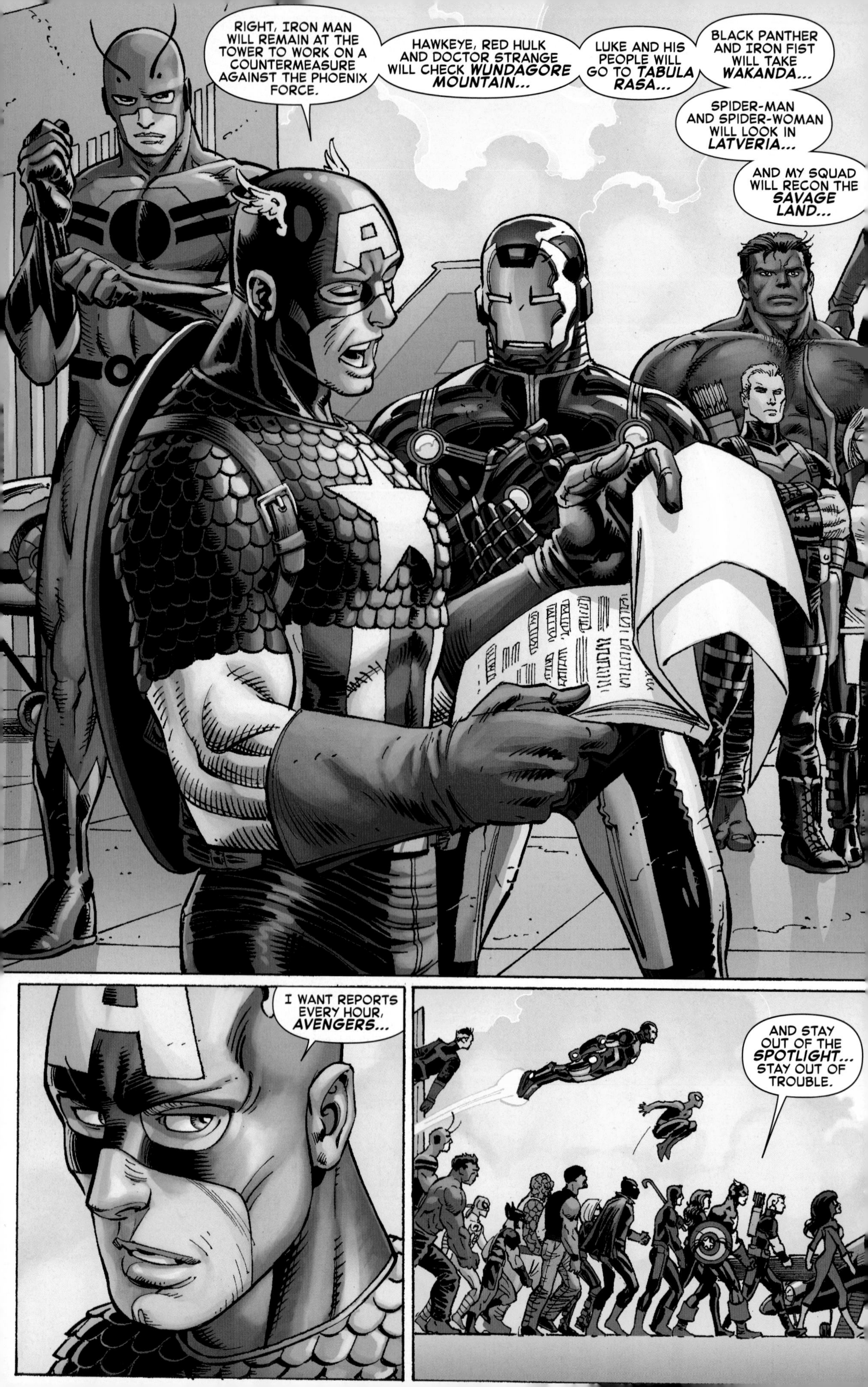
RIGHT, IRON MAN WILL REMAIN AT THE TOWER TO WORK ON A COUNTERMEASURE AGAINST THE PHOENIX FORCE.
HAWKEYE, RED HULK AND DOCTOR STRANGE WILL CHECK WUNDAGORE MOUNTAIN...
LUKE AND HIS PEOPLE WILL GO TO TABULA RASA...
BLACK PANTHER AND IRON FIST WILL TAKE WAKANDA...
SPIDER-MAN AND SPIDER-WOMAN WILL LOOK IN LATVERIA...
AND MY SQUAD WILL RECON THE SAVAGE LAND...
I WANT REPORTS EVERY HOUR, AVENGERS...
AND STAY OUT OF THE SPOTLIGHT... STAY OUT OF TROUBLE.

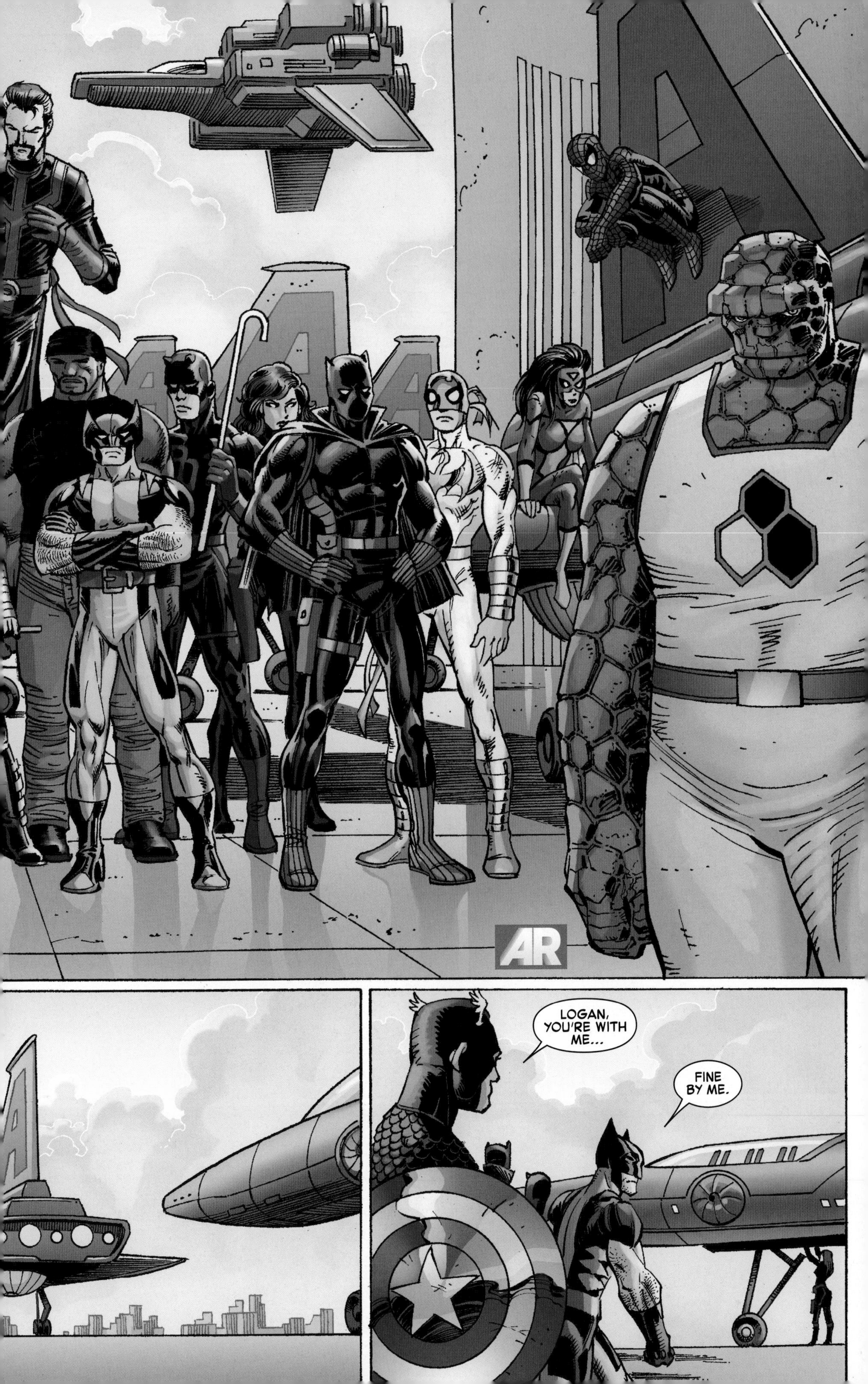
LOGAN, YOU'RE WITH ME...
FINE BY ME.

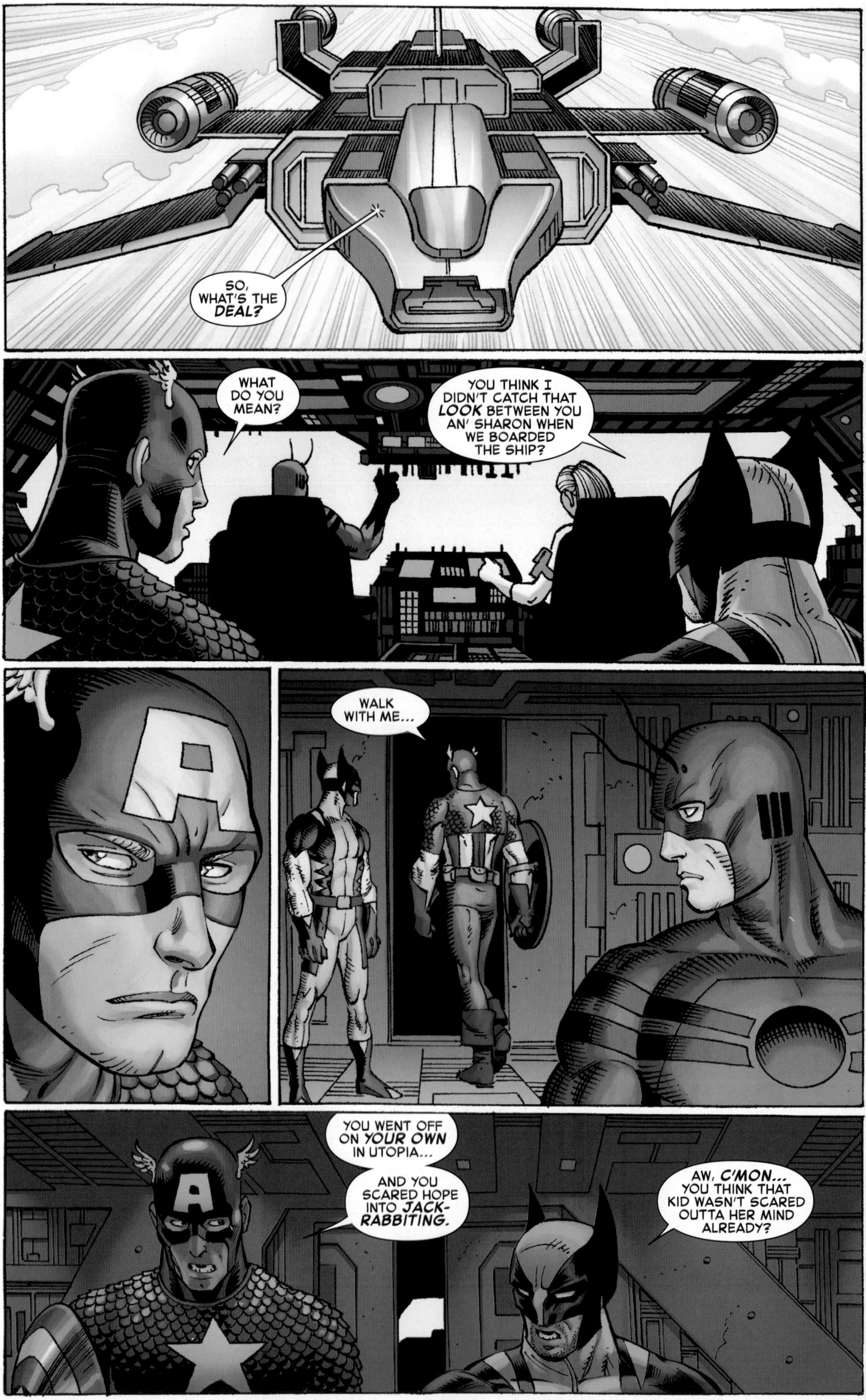
SO, WHAT'S THE *DEAL?*
WHAT DO YOU MEAN?
YOU THINK I DIDN'T CATCH THAT *LOOK* BETWEEN YOU AN' SHARON WHEN WE BOARDED THE SHIP?
WALK WITH ME...
YOU WENT OFF ON *YOUR OWN* IN UTOPIA...
AND YOU SCARED HOPE INTO *JACK-RABBITING.*
AW, *C'MON...* YOU THINK THAT KID WASN'T SCARED OUTTA HER MIND ALREADY?

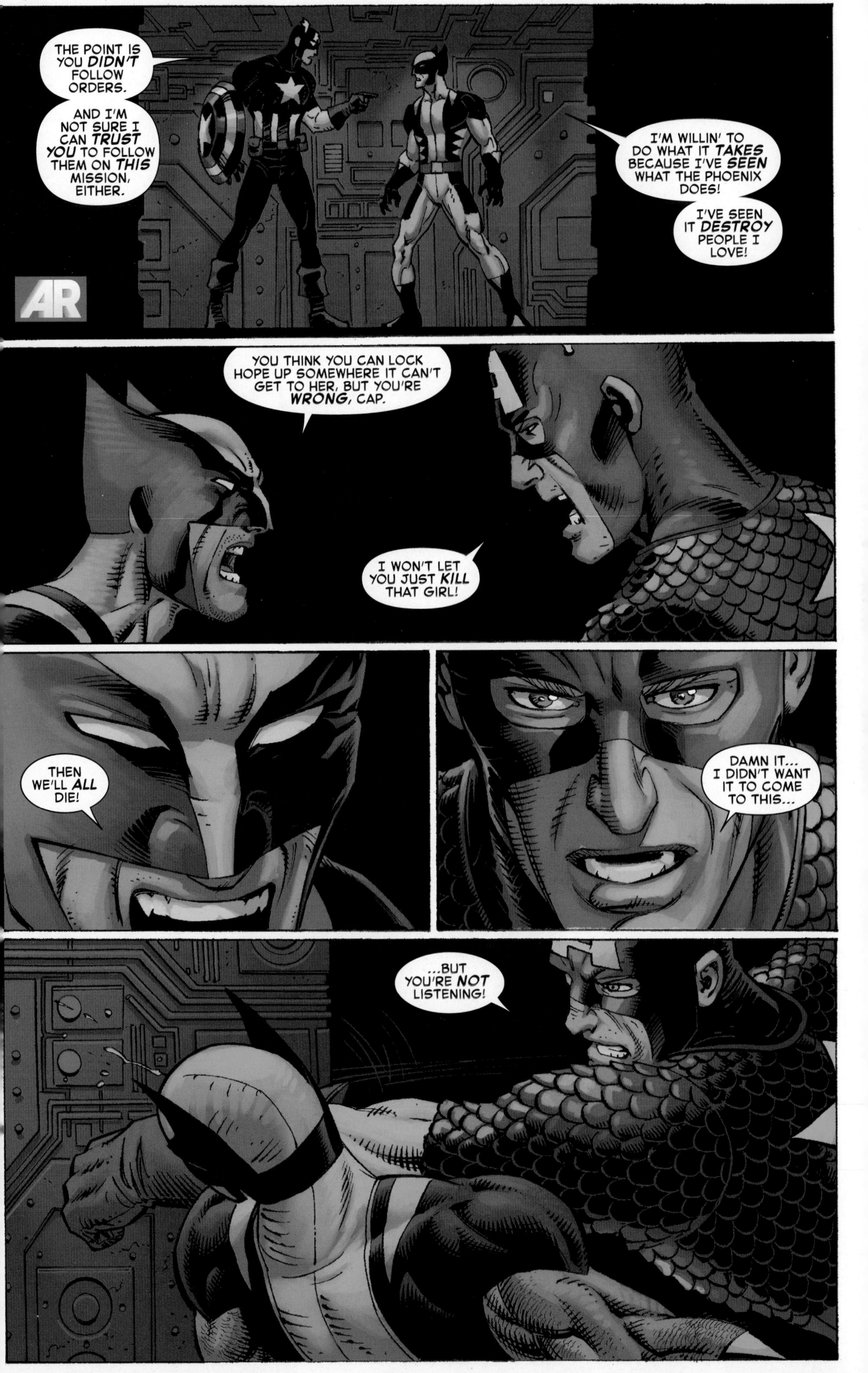
THE POINT IS YOU DIDN'T FOLLOW ORDERS.
AND I'M NOT SURE I CAN TRUST YOU TO FOLLOW THEM ON THIS MISSION, EITHER.
I'M WILLIN' TO DO WHAT IT TAKES BECAUSE I'VE SEEN WHAT THE PHOENIX DOES!
I'VE SEEN IT DESTROY PEOPLE I LOVE!
YOU THINK YOU CAN LOCK HOPE UP SOMEWHERE IT CAN'T GET TO HER, BUT YOU'RE WRONG, CAP.
I WON'T LET YOU JUST KILL THAT GIRL!
THEN WE'LL ALL DIE!
DAMN IT... I DIDN'T WANT IT TO COME TO THIS...
...BUT YOU'RE NOT LISTENING!

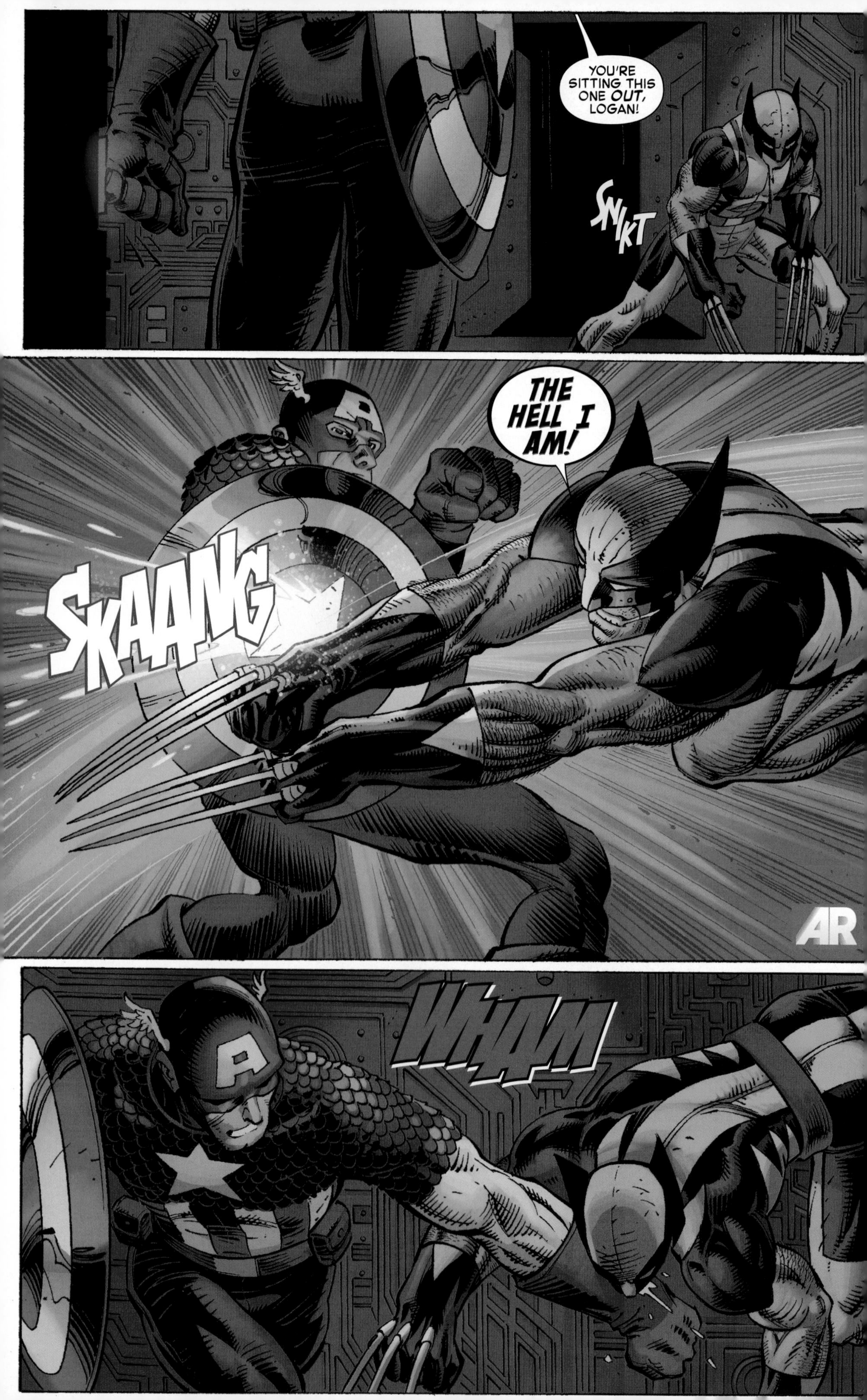
YOU'RE SITTING THIS ONE OUT, LOGAN!
SNIKT
THE HELL I AM!
SKAANG
AR
WHAM

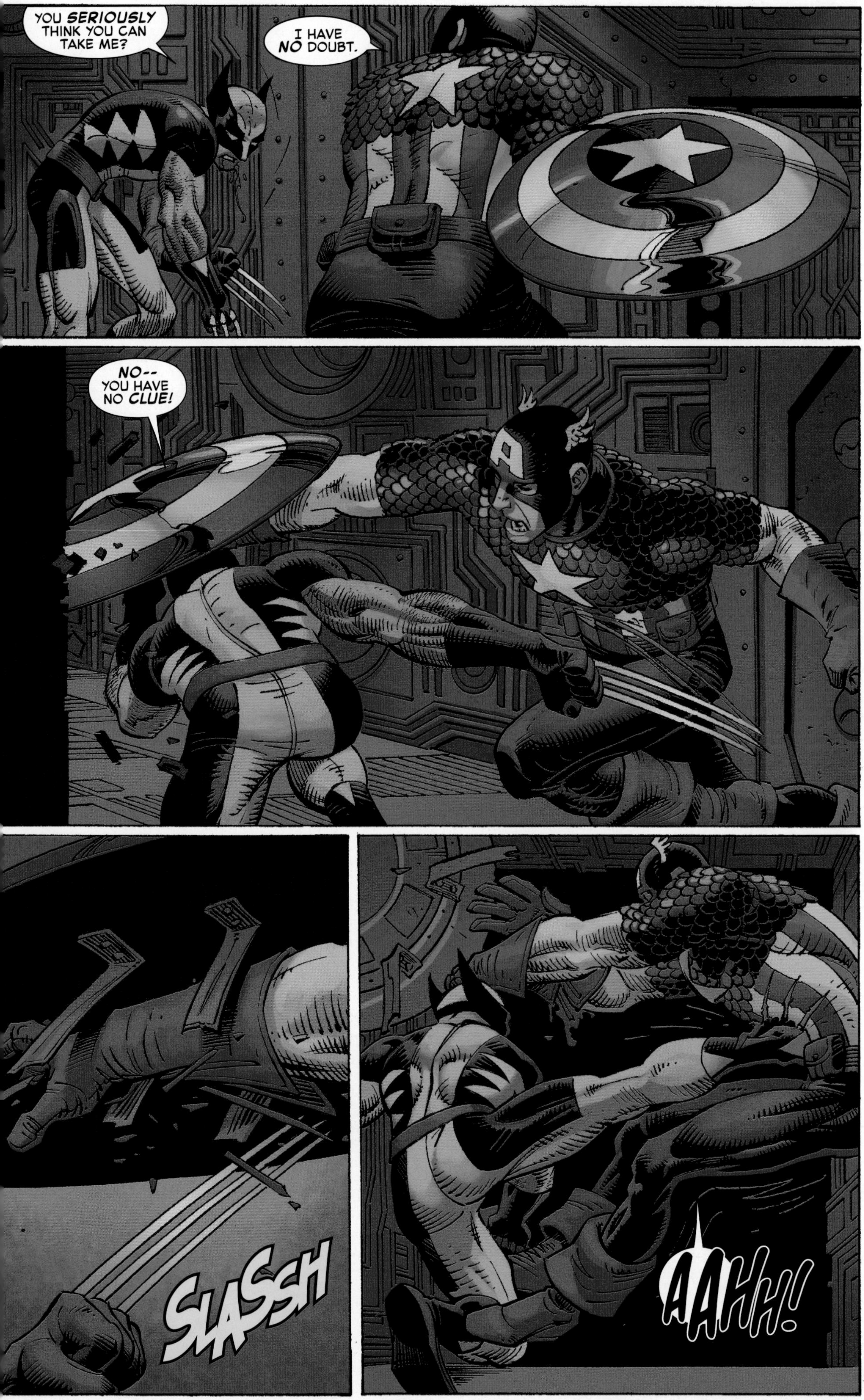
YOU SERIOUSLY THINK YOU CAN TAKE ME?
I HAVE NO DOUBT.
NO-- YOU HAVE NO CLUE!
SLASSH
AAHH!

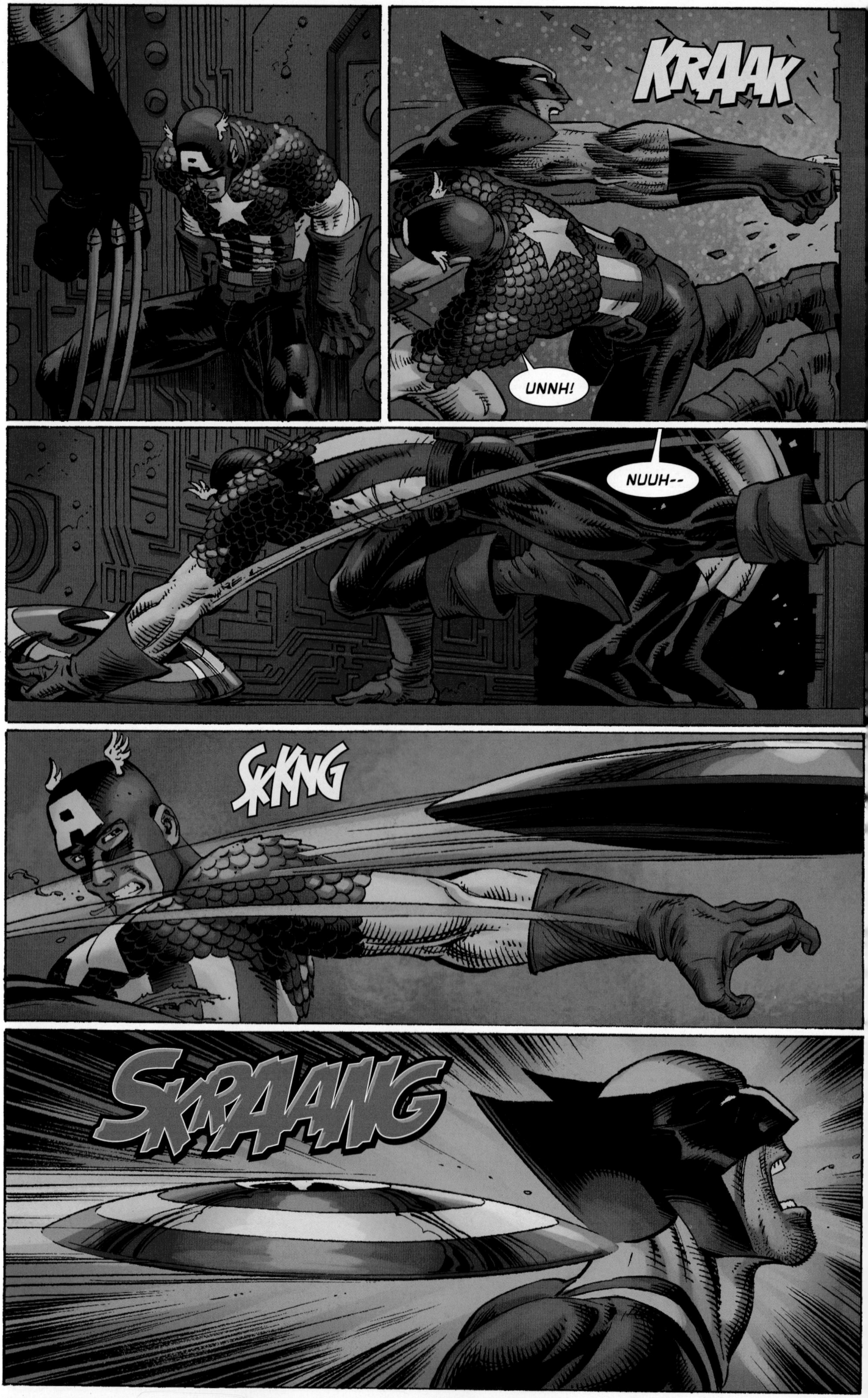
KRAAK
UNNH!
NUUH--
SKKNG
SKRAAANG

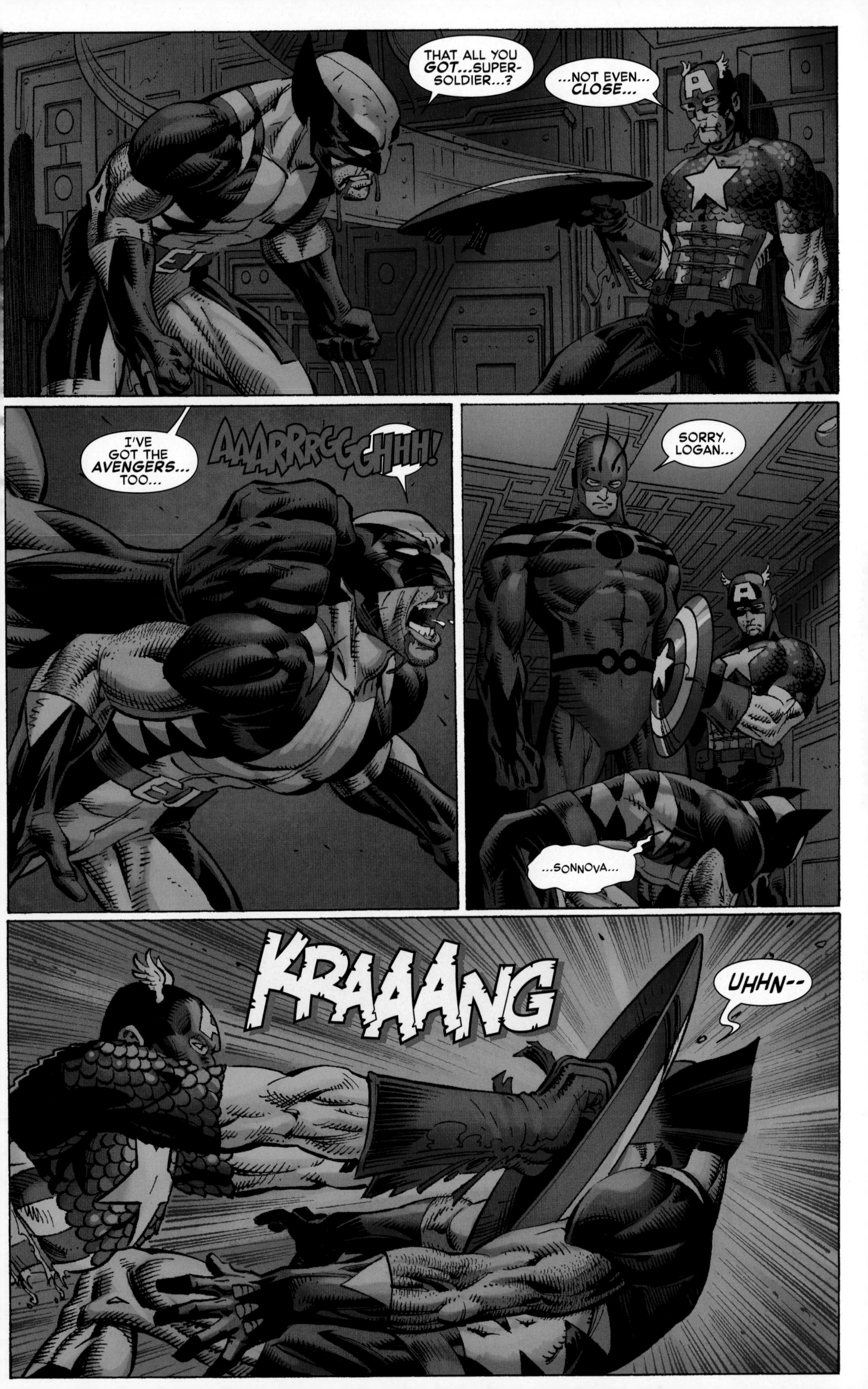
THAT ALL YOU GOT...SUPER-SOLDIER...?
...NOT EVEN... CLOSE...
I'VE GOT THE AVENGERS... TOO...
AAARRRGGGHHH!
SORRY, LOGAN...
...SONNOVA...
KRAAANG
UHHN--

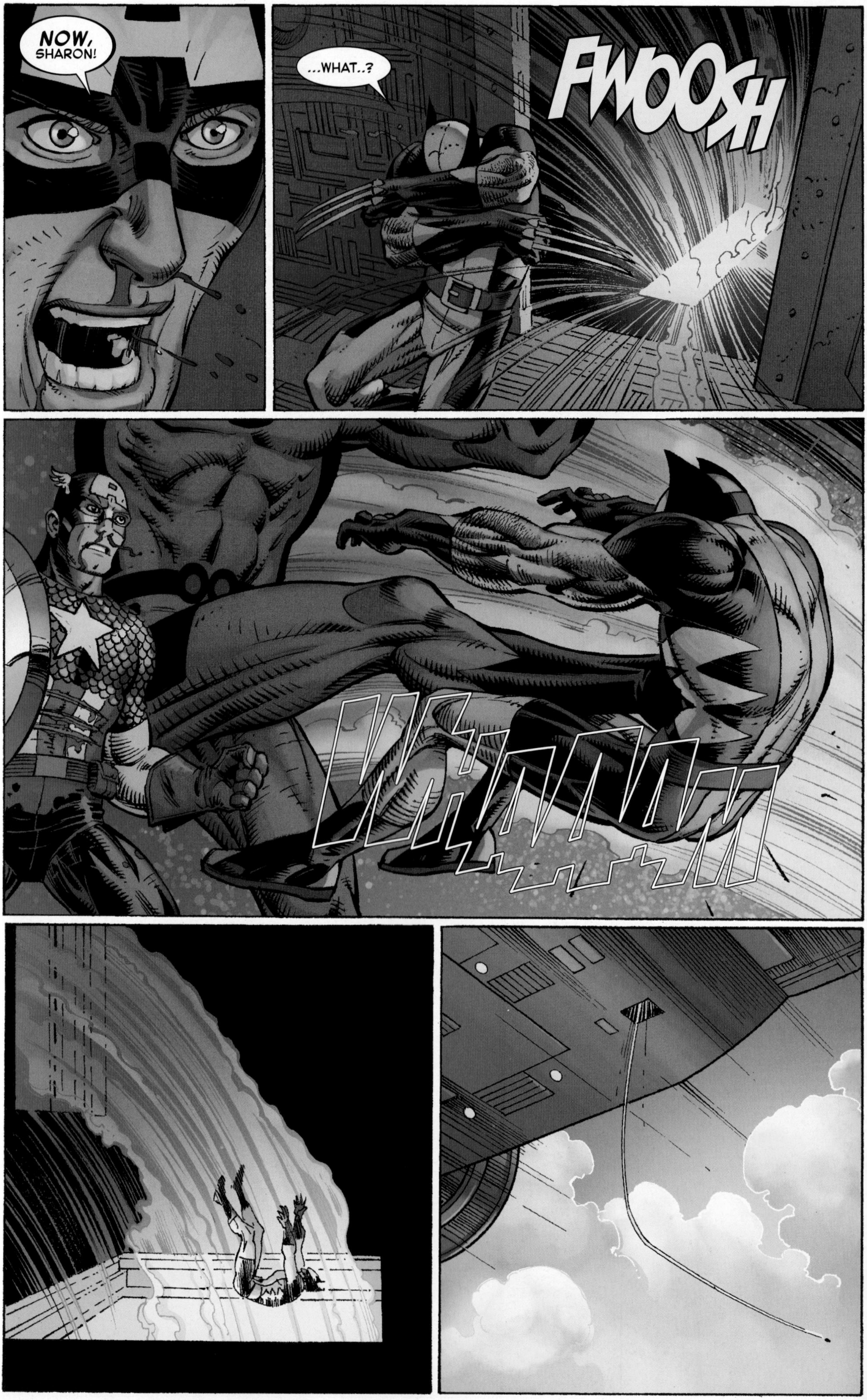
NOW, SHARON!
...WHAT..?
FWOOSH
WHAAM

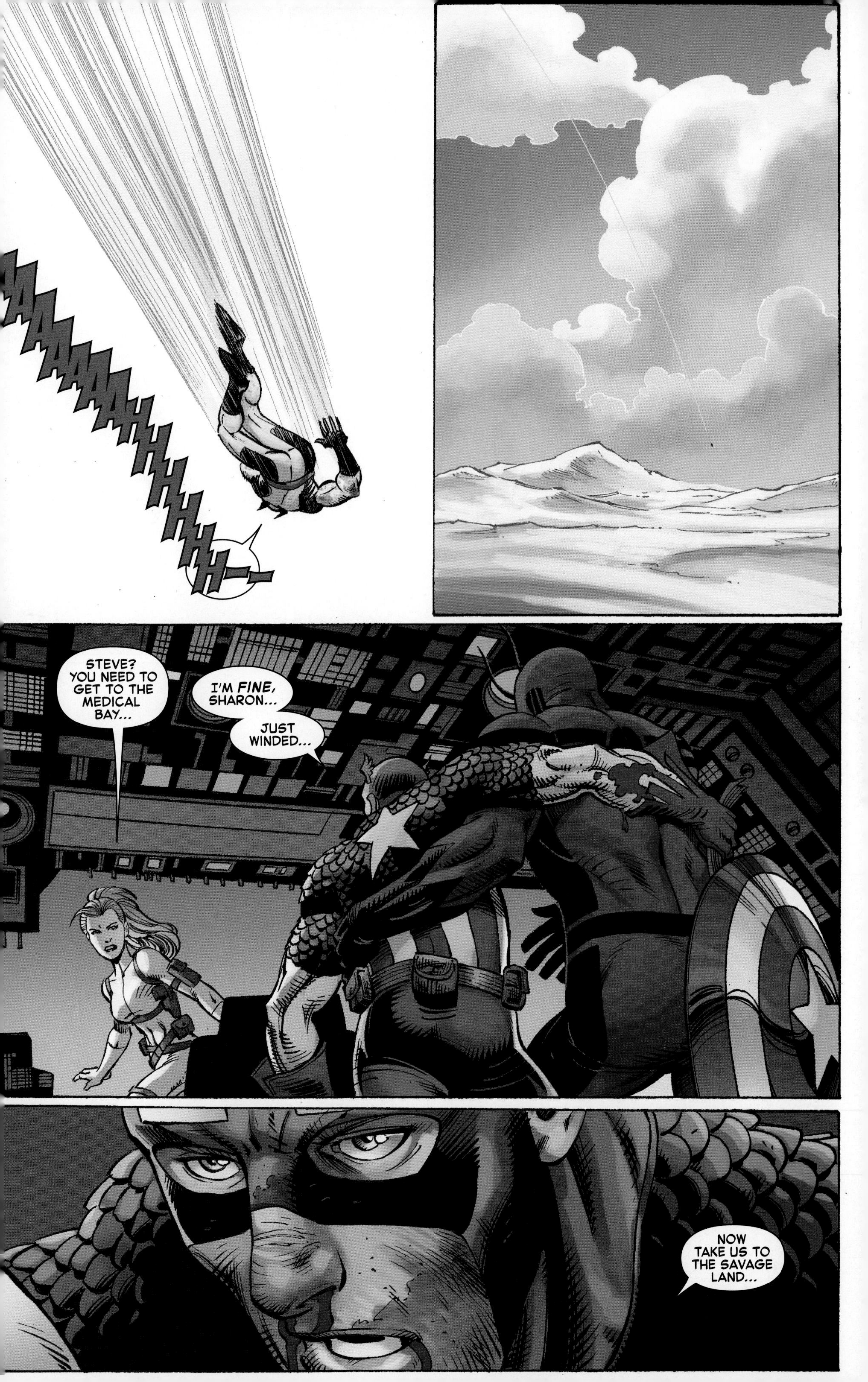
AAAAAAAAHHHHHH--
STEVE? YOU NEED TO GET TO THE MEDICAL BAY...
I'M *FINE*, SHARON...
JUST WINDED...
NOW TAKE US TO THE SAVAGE LAND...

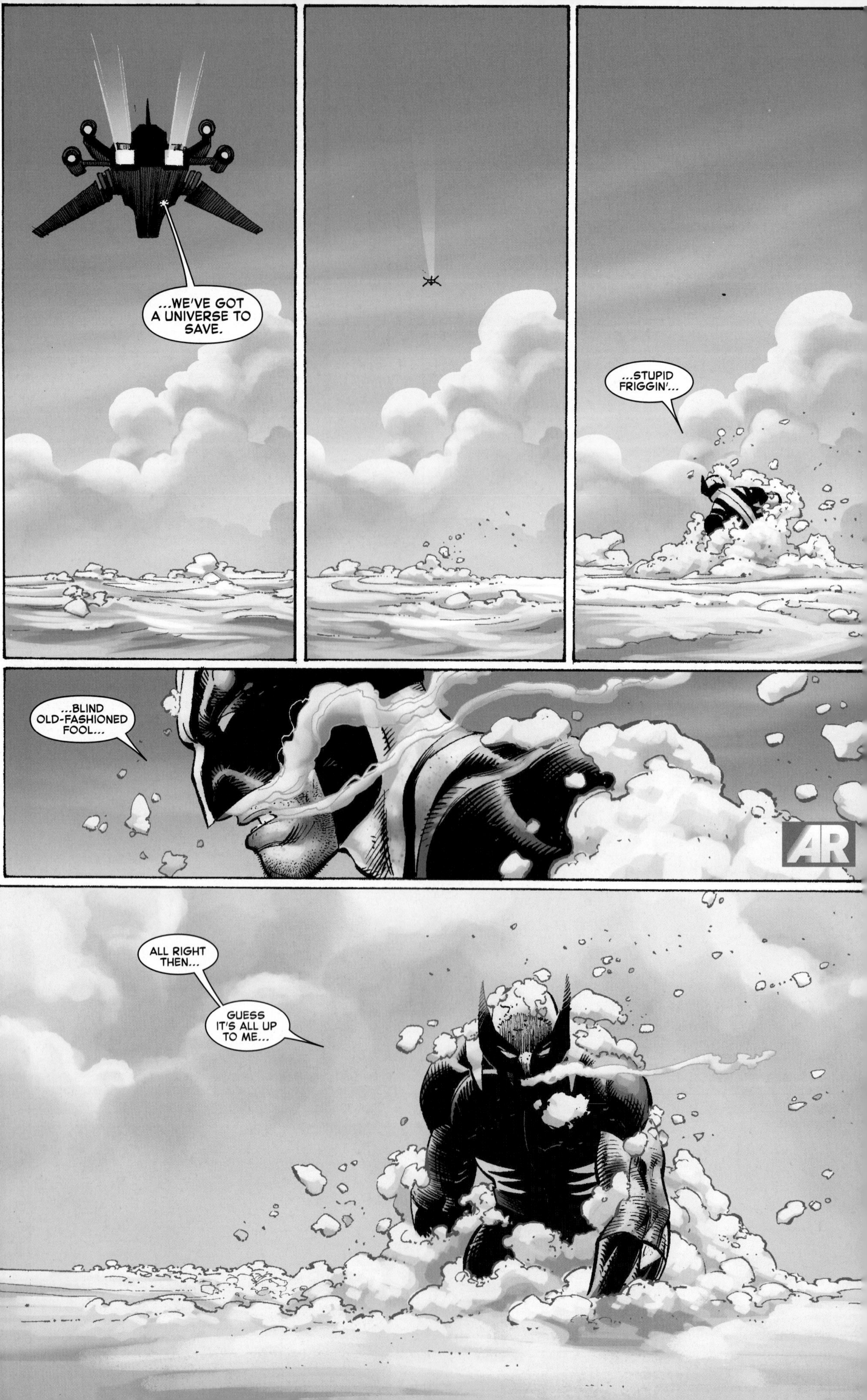
...WE'VE GOT A UNIVERSE TO SAVE.
...STUPID FRIGGIN'...
...BLIND OLD-FASHIONED FOOL...
ALL RIGHT THEN...
GUESS IT'S ALL UP TO ME...

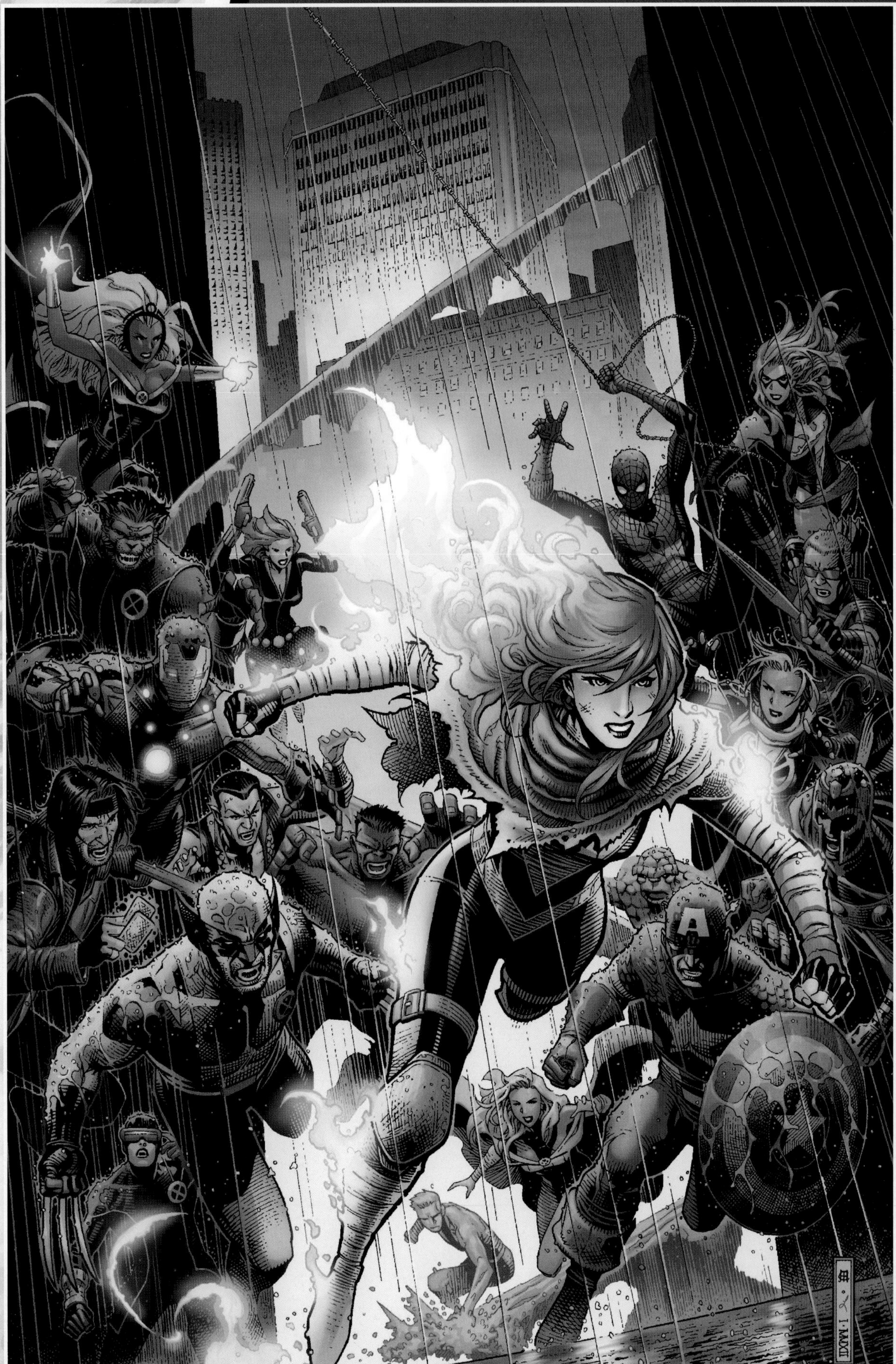

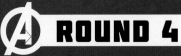

ROUND 4

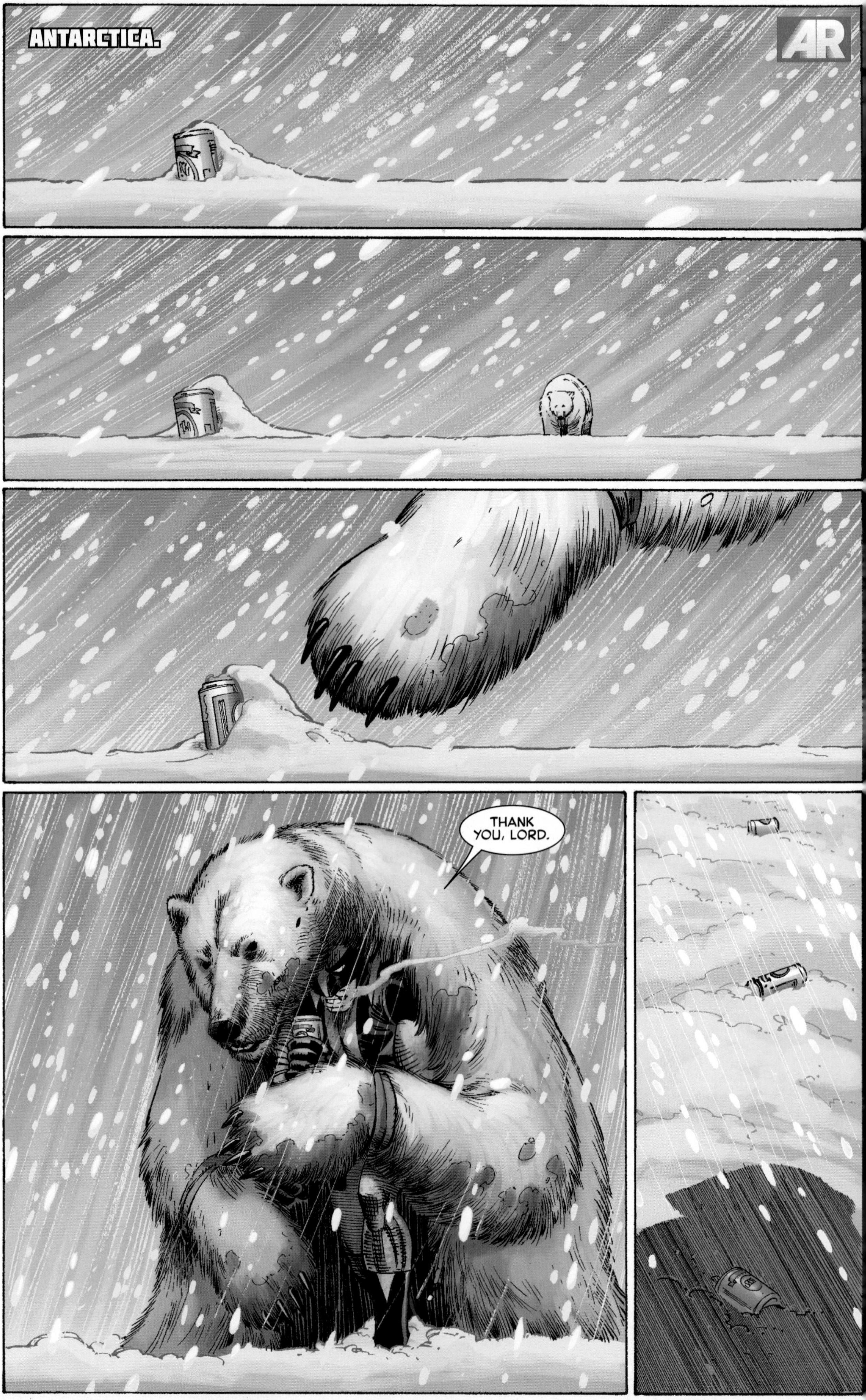
ANTARCTICA.
THANK YOU, LORD.

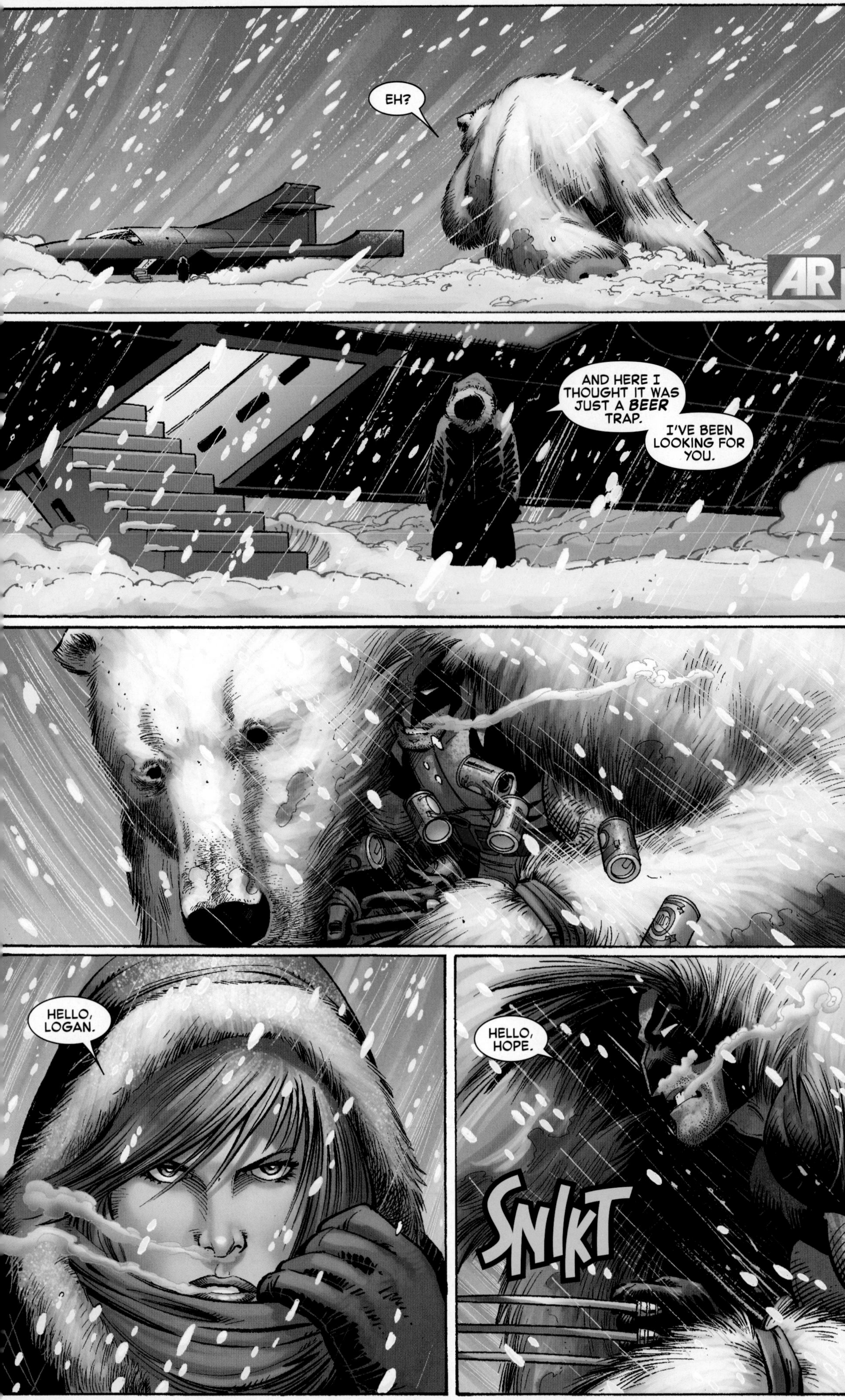
EH?
AR
AND HERE I THOUGHT IT WAS JUST A BEER TRAP.
I'VE BEEN LOOKING FOR YOU.
HELLO, LOGAN.
HELLO, HOPE.
SNIKT

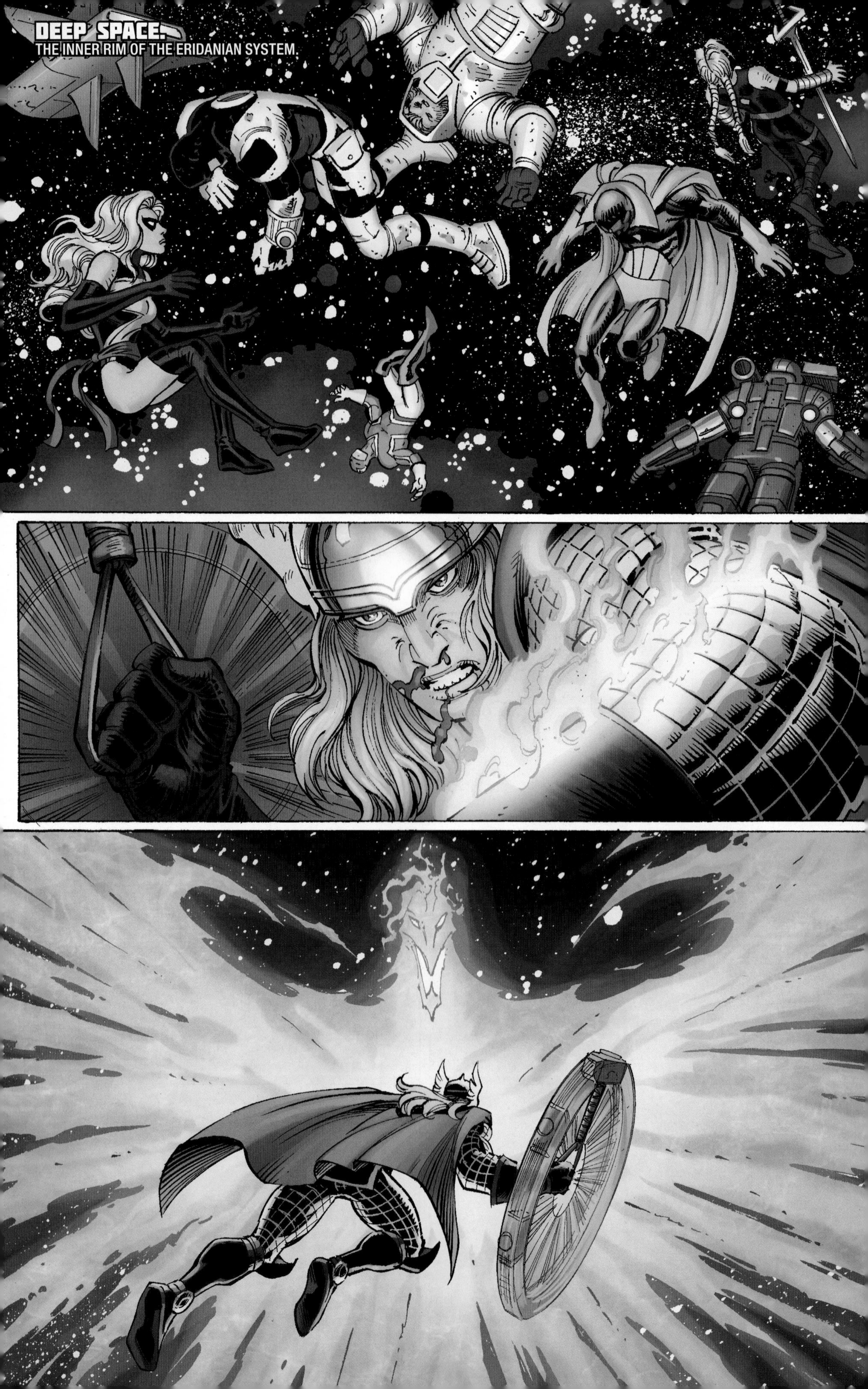
DEEP SPACE.
THE INNER RIM OF THE ERIDANIAN SYSTEM.

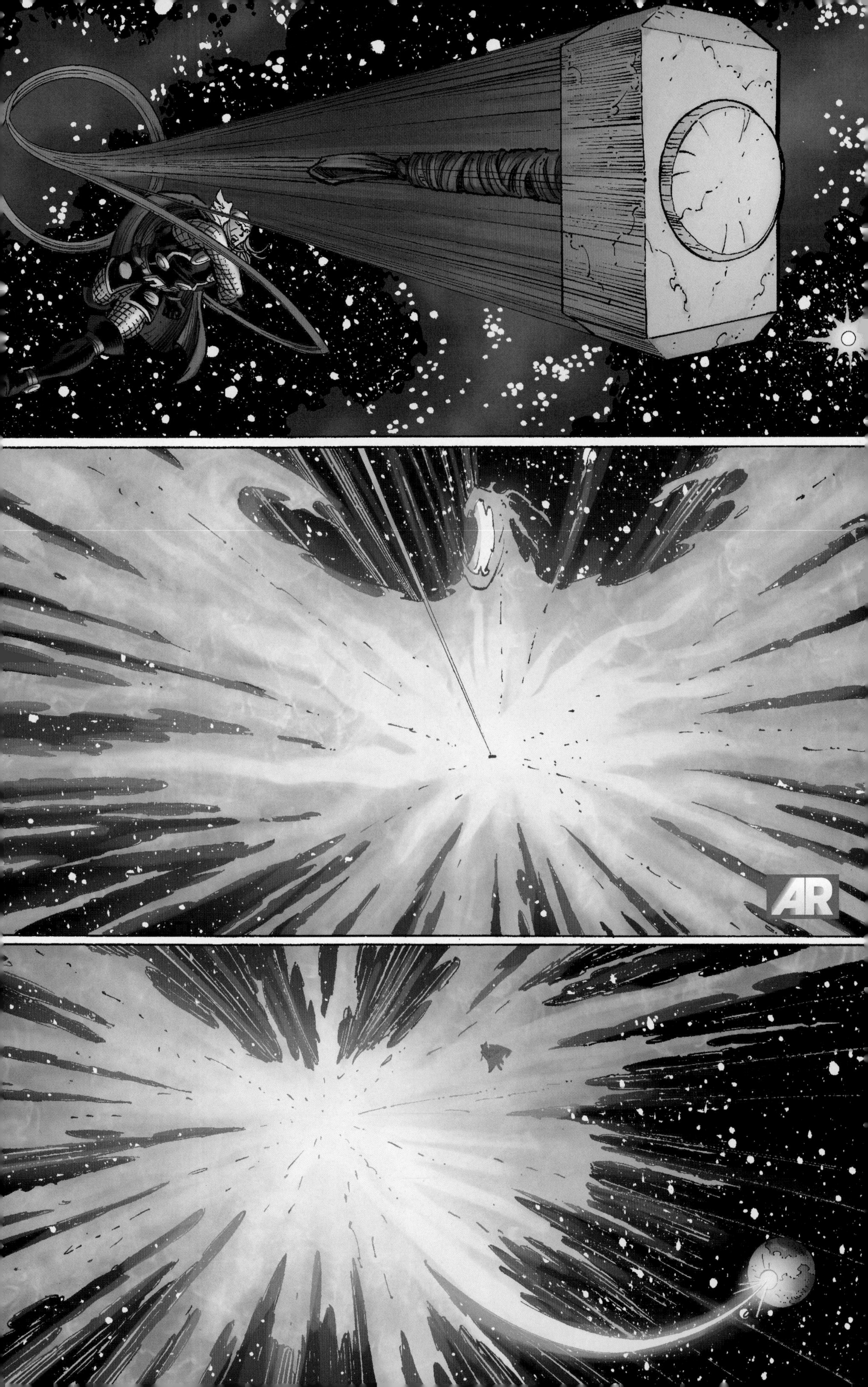

AR

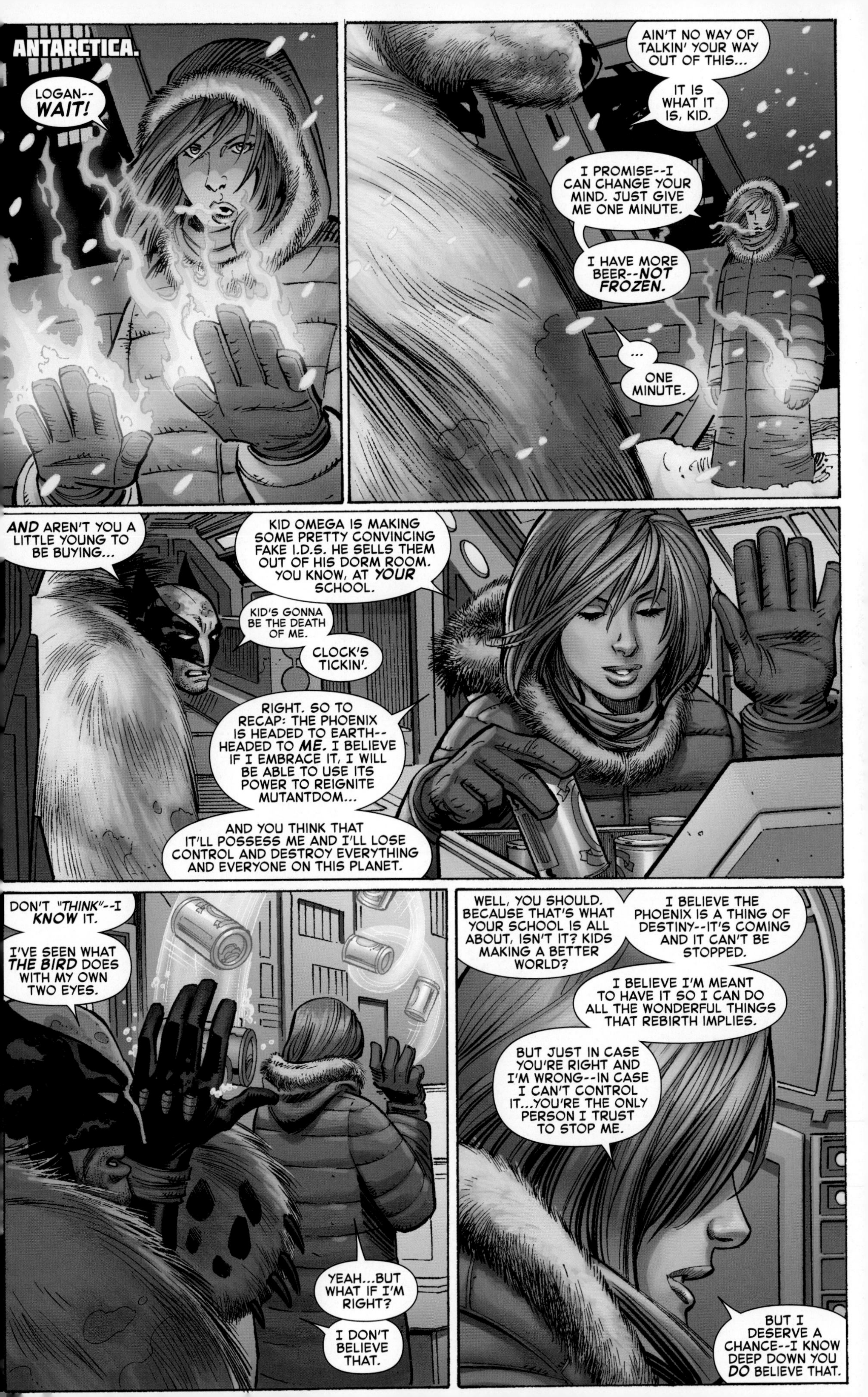

ANTARCTICA.
LOGAN-- WAIT!
AIN'T NO WAY OF TALKIN' YOUR WAY OUT OF THIS...
IT IS WHAT IT IS, KID.
I PROMISE--I CAN CHANGE YOUR MIND. JUST GIVE ME ONE MINUTE.
I HAVE MORE BEER--NOT FROZEN.
...
ONE MINUTE.
AND AREN'T YOU A LITTLE YOUNG TO BE BUYING...
KID OMEGA IS MAKING SOME PRETTY CONVINCING FAKE I.D.S. HE SELLS THEM OUT OF HIS DORM ROOM. YOU KNOW, AT YOUR SCHOOL.
KID'S GONNA BE THE DEATH OF ME.
CLOCK'S TICKIN'.
RIGHT. SO TO RECAP: THE PHOENIX IS HEADED TO EARTH--HEADED TO ME. I BELIEVE IF I EMBRACE IT, I WILL BE ABLE TO USE ITS POWER TO REIGNITE MUTANTDOM...
AND YOU THINK THAT IT'LL POSSESS ME AND I'LL LOSE CONTROL AND DESTROY EVERYTHING AND EVERYONE ON THIS PLANET.
DON'T "THINK"--I KNOW IT.
I'VE SEEN WHAT THE BIRD DOES WITH MY OWN TWO EYES.
YEAH...BUT WHAT IF I'M RIGHT?
I DON'T BELIEVE THAT.
WELL, YOU SHOULD. BECAUSE THAT'S WHAT YOUR SCHOOL IS ALL ABOUT, ISN'T IT? KIDS MAKING A BETTER WORLD?
I BELIEVE THE PHOENIX IS A THING OF DESTINY--IT'S COMING AND IT CAN'T BE STOPPED.
I BELIEVE I'M MEANT TO HAVE IT SO I CAN DO ALL THE WONDERFUL THINGS THAT REBIRTH IMPLIES.
BUT JUST IN CASE YOU'RE RIGHT AND I'M WRONG--IN CASE I CAN'T CONTROL IT...YOU'RE THE ONLY PERSON I TRUST TO STOP ME.
BUT I DESERVE A CHANCE--I KNOW DEEP DOWN YOU DO BELIEVE THAT.

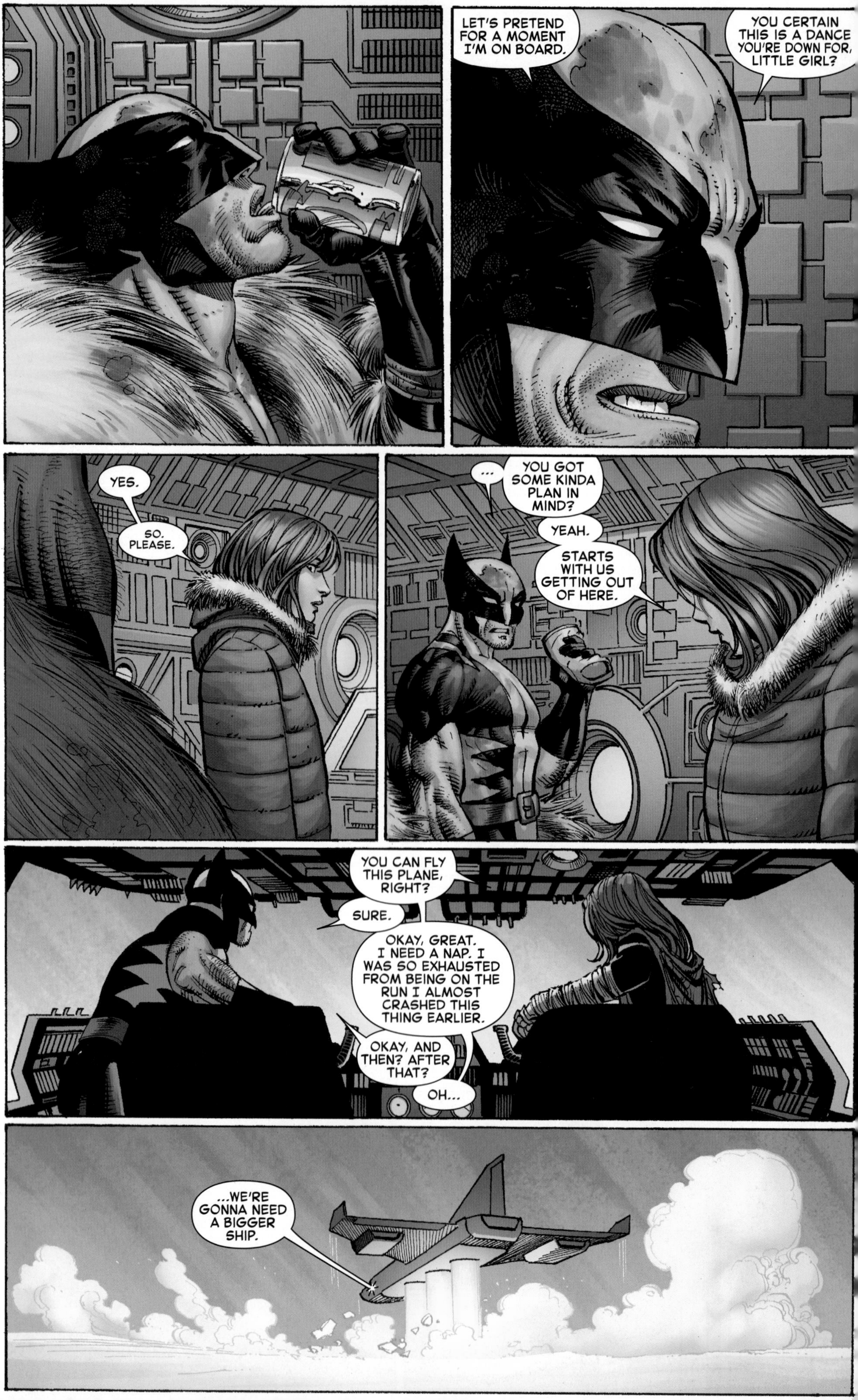
LET'S PRETEND FOR A MOMENT I'M ON BOARD.
YOU CERTAIN THIS IS A DANCE YOU'RE DOWN FOR, LITTLE GIRL?
YES.
SO. PLEASE.
...
YOU GOT SOME KINDA PLAN IN MIND?
YEAH.
STARTS WITH US GETTING OUT OF HERE.
YOU CAN FLY THIS PLANE, RIGHT?
SURE.
OKAY, GREAT. I NEED A NAP. I WAS SO EXHAUSTED FROM BEING ON THE RUN I ALMOST CRASHED THIS THING EARLIER.
OKAY, AND THEN? AFTER THAT?
OH...
...WE'RE GONNA NEED A BIGGER SHIP.

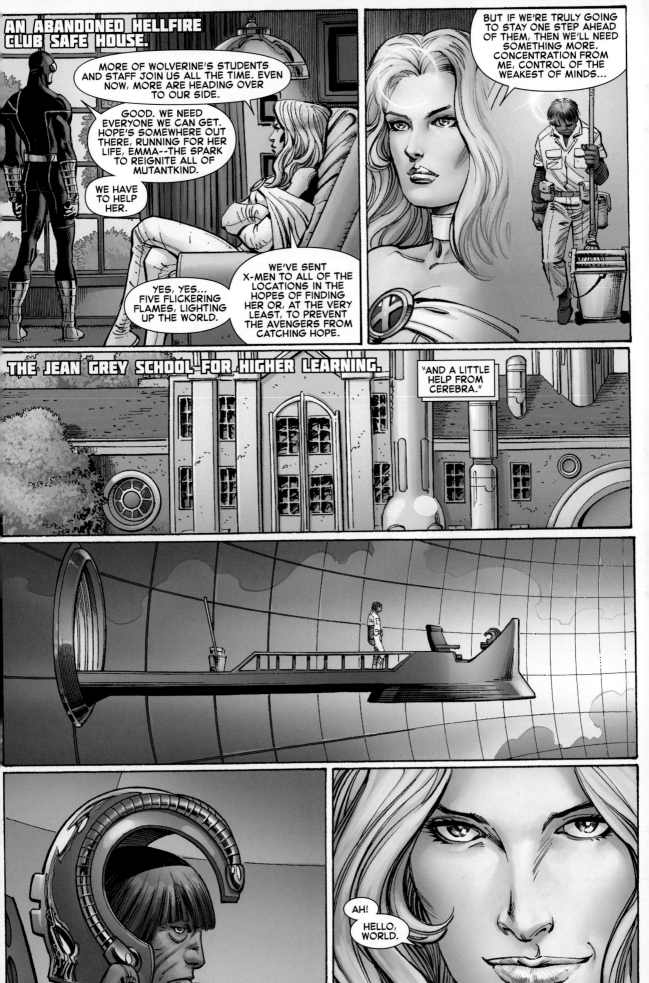

AN ABANDONED HELLFIRE CLUB SAFE HOUSE.

MORE OF WOLVERINE'S STUDENTS AND STAFF JOIN US ALL THE TIME. EVEN NOW, MORE ARE HEADING OVER TO OUR SIDE.

GOOD. WE NEED EVERYONE WE CAN GET. HOPE'S SOMEWHERE OUT THERE, RUNNING FOR HER LIFE, EMMA--THE SPARK TO REIGNITE ALL OF MUTANTKIND.

WE HAVE TO HELP HER.

YES, YES... FIVE FLICKERING FLAMES, LIGHTING UP THE WORLD.

WE'VE SENT X-MEN TO ALL OF THE LOCATIONS IN THE HOPES OF FINDING HER OR, AT THE VERY LEAST, TO PREVENT THE AVENGERS FROM CATCHING HOPE.

BUT IF WE'RE TRULY GOING TO STAY ONE STEP AHEAD OF THEM, THEN WE'LL NEED SOMETHING MORE. CONCENTRATION FROM ME, CONTROL OF THE WEAKEST OF MINDS...

THE JEAN GREY SCHOOL FOR HIGHER LEARNING.

"AND A LITTLE HELP FROM CEREBRA."

AH! HELLO, WORLD.

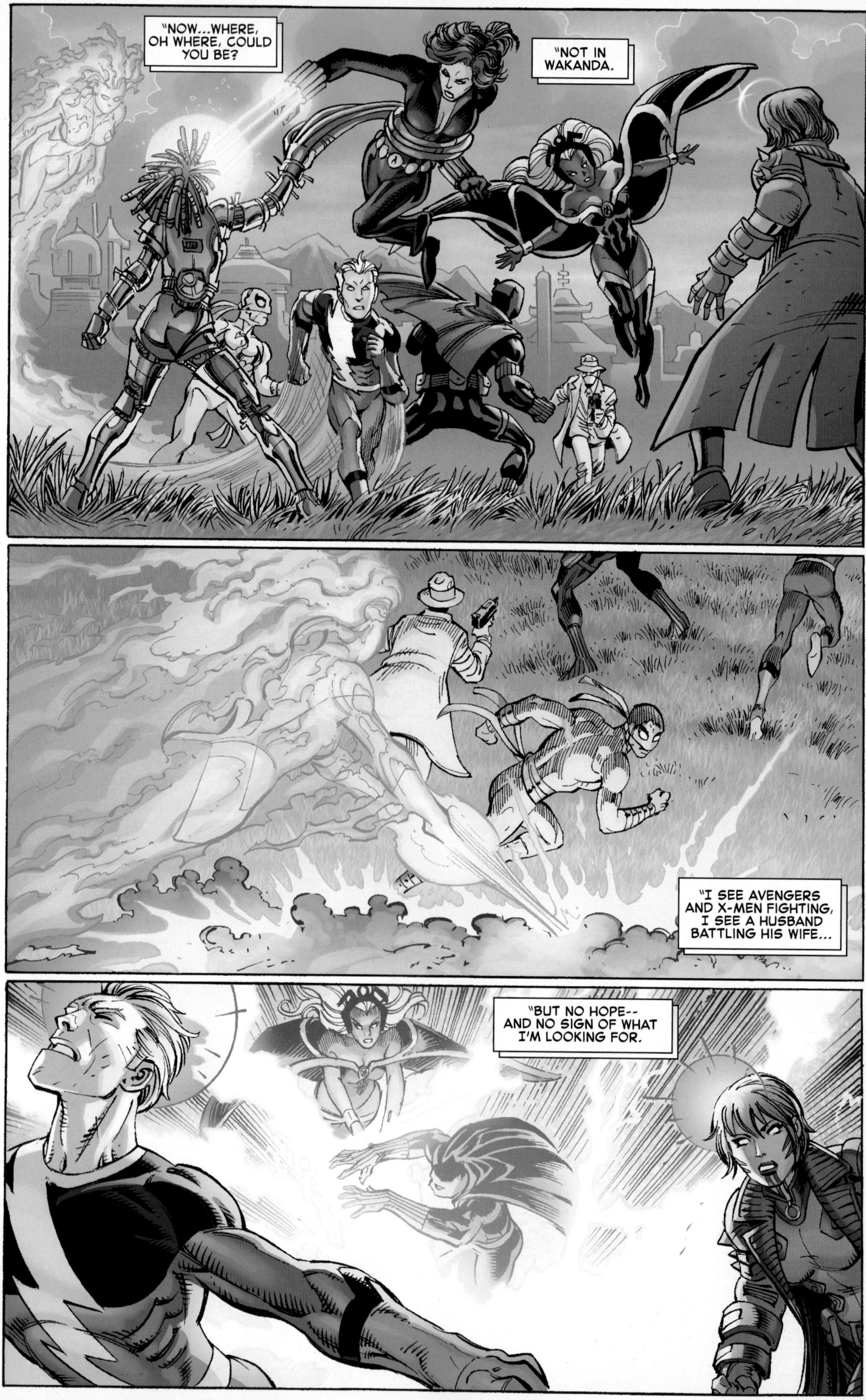
"NOW...WHERE, OH WHERE, COULD YOU BE?
"NOT IN WAKANDA.
"I SEE AVENGERS AND X-MEN FIGHTING, I SEE A HUSBAND BATTLING HIS WIFE...
"BUT NO HOPE-- AND NO SIGN OF WHAT I'M LOOKING FOR.

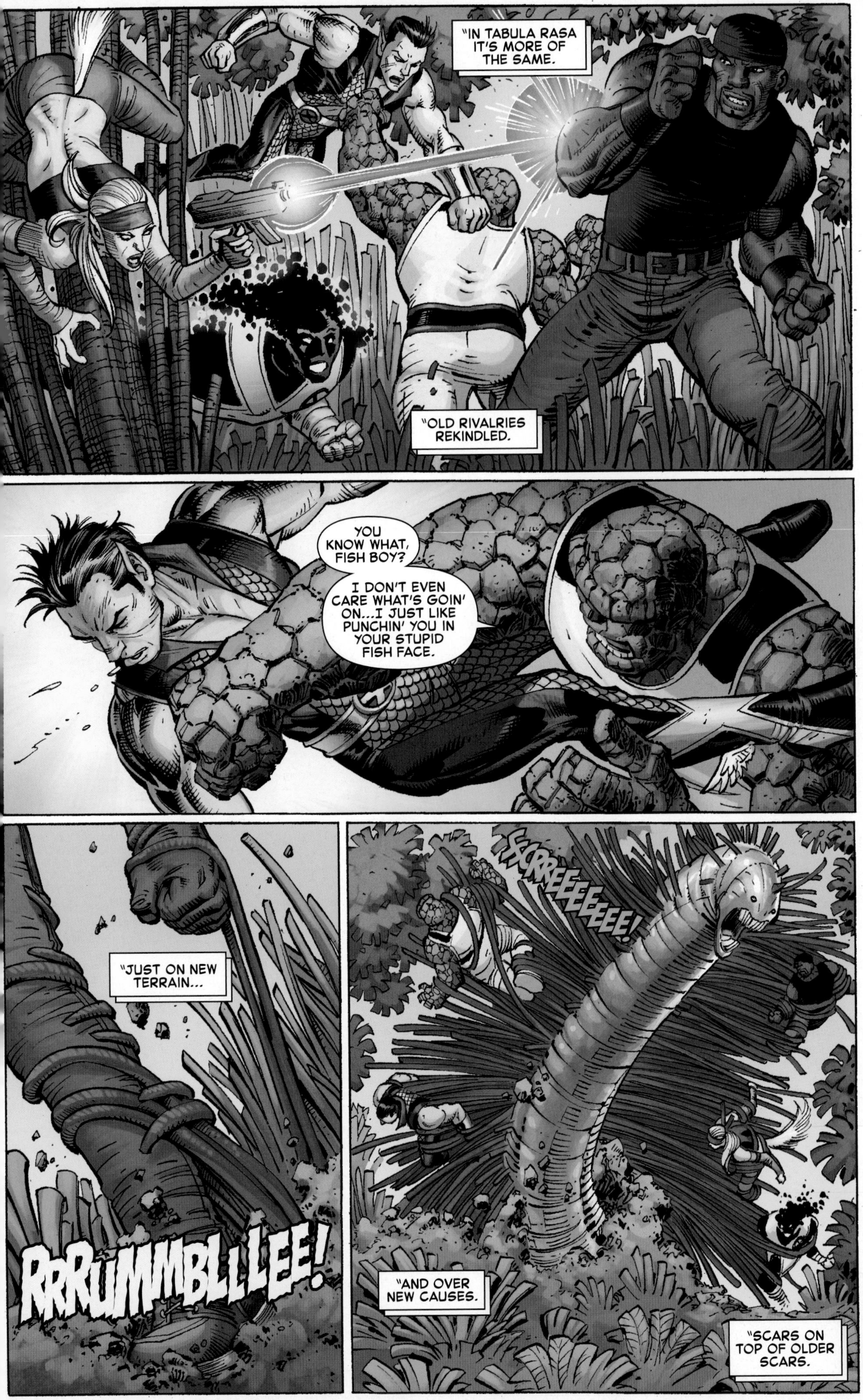
"IN TABULA RASA IT'S MORE OF THE SAME.
"OLD RIVALRIES REKINDLED.
YOU KNOW WHAT, FISH BOY?
I DON'T EVEN CARE WHAT'S GOIN' ON...I JUST LIKE PUNCHIN' YOU IN YOUR STUPID FISH FACE.
"JUST ON NEW TERRAIN...
RRRUMMBLLLEE!
SCRREEEEEEEE!
"AND OVER NEW CAUSES.
"SCARS ON TOP OF OLDER SCARS.

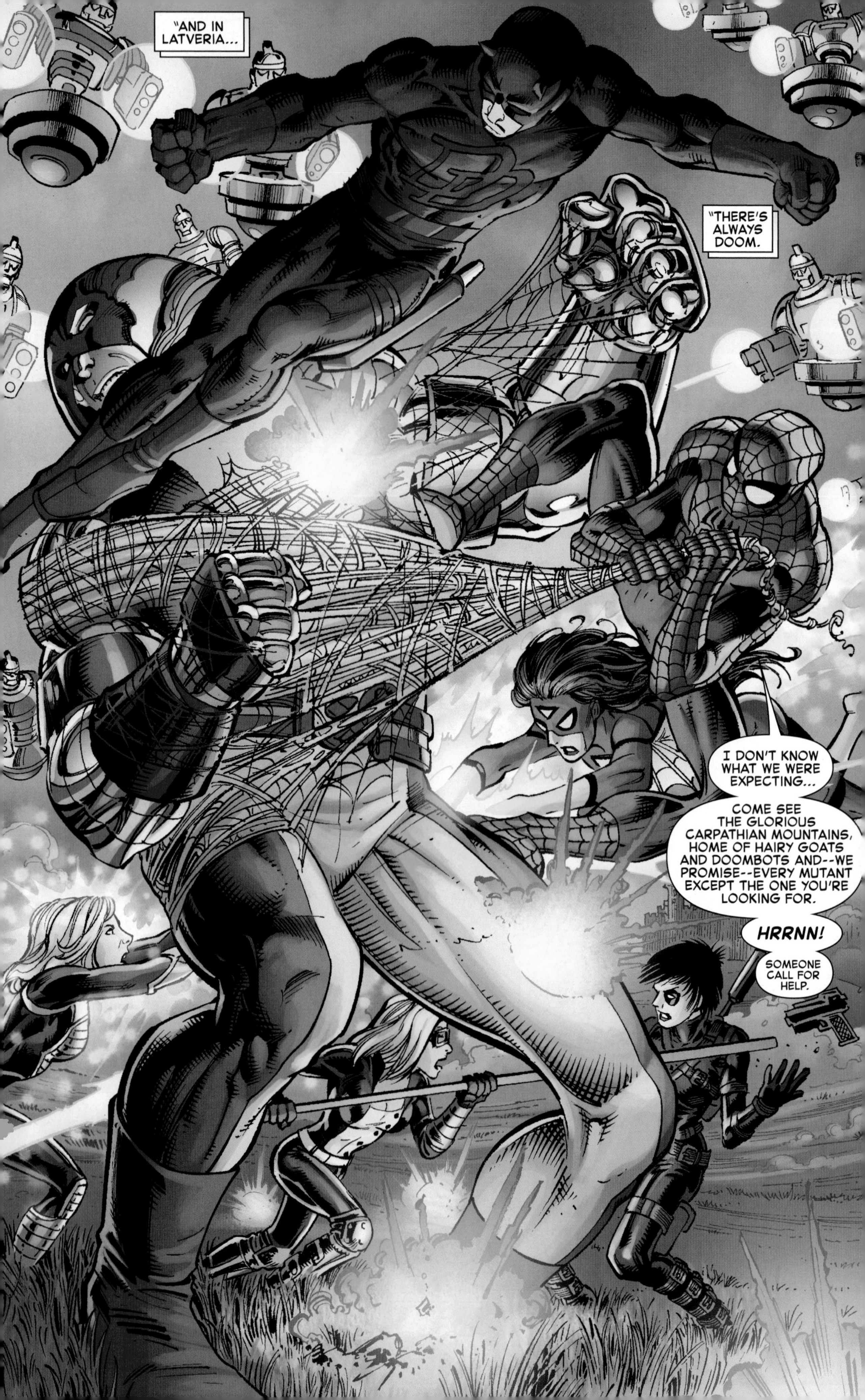
"AND IN LATVERIA...
"THERE'S ALWAYS DOOM.
I DON'T KNOW WHAT WE WERE EXPECTING...
COME SEE THE GLORIOUS CARPATHIAN MOUNTAINS, HOME OF HAIRY GOATS AND DOOMBOTS AND--WE PROMISE--EVERY MUTANT EXCEPT THE ONE YOU'RE LOOKING FOR.
HRRNN!
SOMEONE CALL FOR HELP.

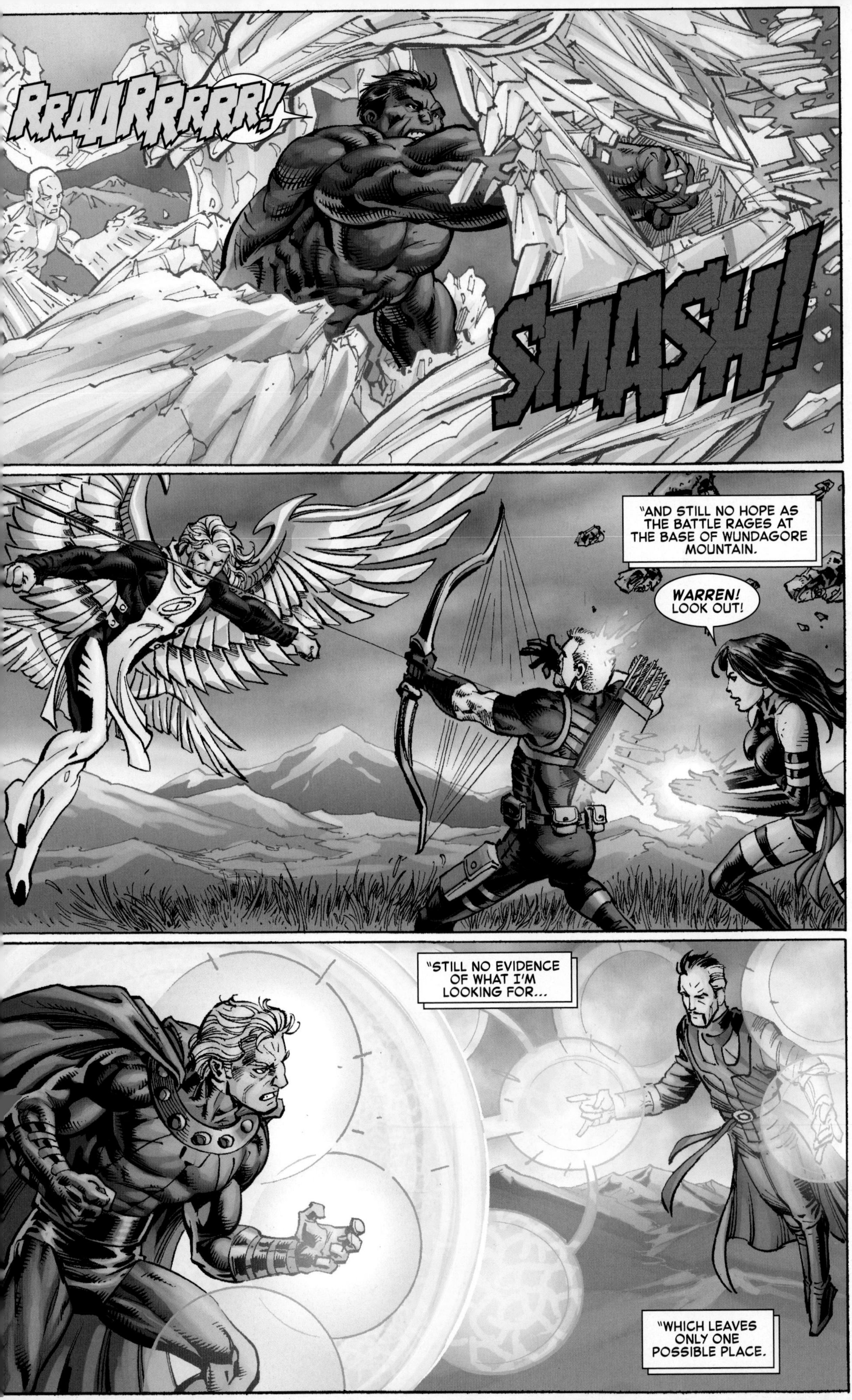
RRAAARRRRR!
SMASH!
"AND STILL NO HOPE AS THE BATTLE RAGES AT THE BASE OF WUNDAGORE MOUNTAIN.
WARREN! LOOK OUT!
"STILL NO EVIDENCE OF WHAT I'M LOOKING FOR...
"WHICH LEAVES ONLY ONE POSSIBLE PLACE.

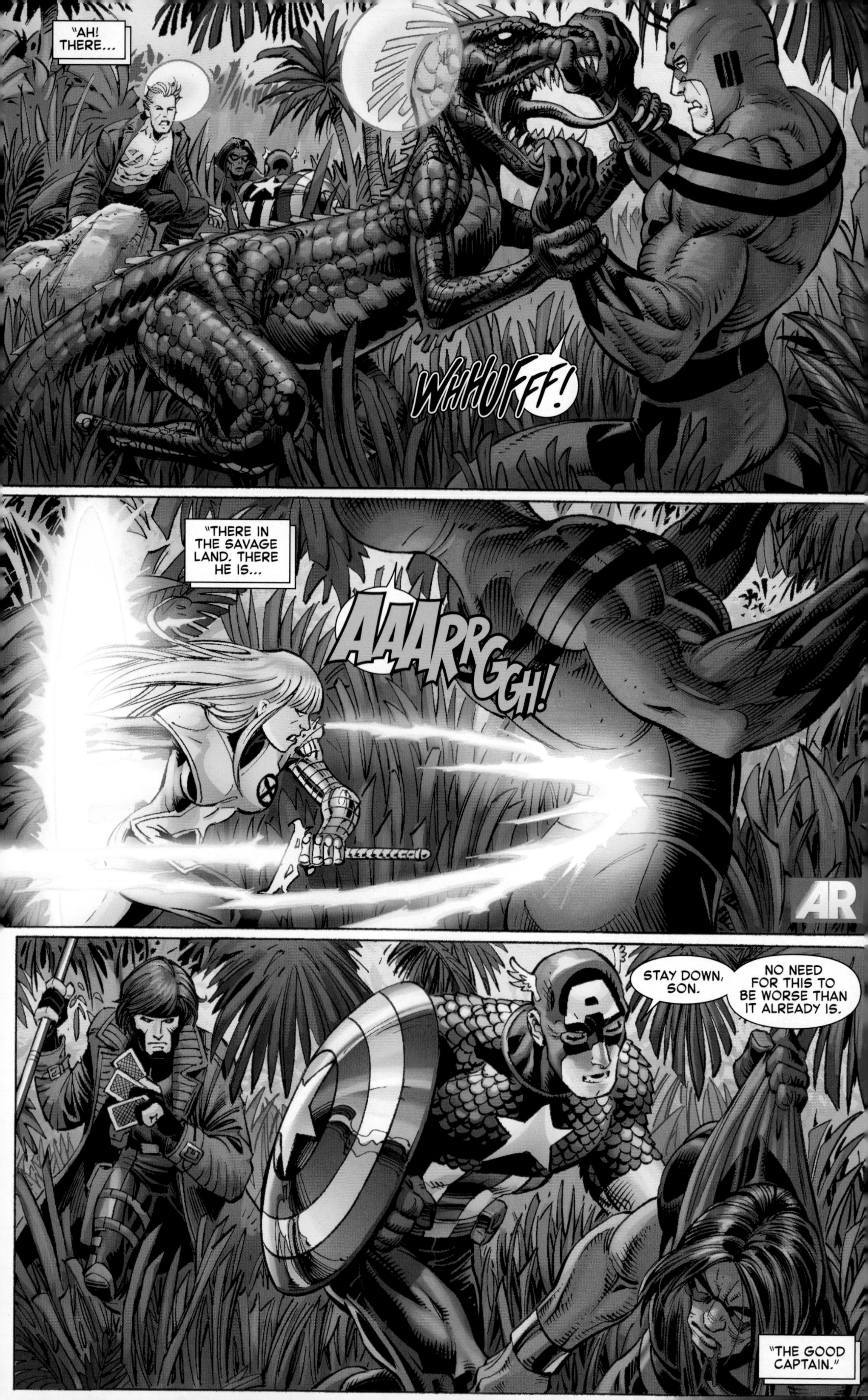
"AH! THERE...
WHHUFFF!
"THERE IN THE SAVAGE LAND. THERE HE IS...
AAARRGGH!
STAY DOWN, SON.
NO NEED FOR THIS TO BE WORSE THAN IT ALREADY IS.
"THE GOOD CAPTAIN."

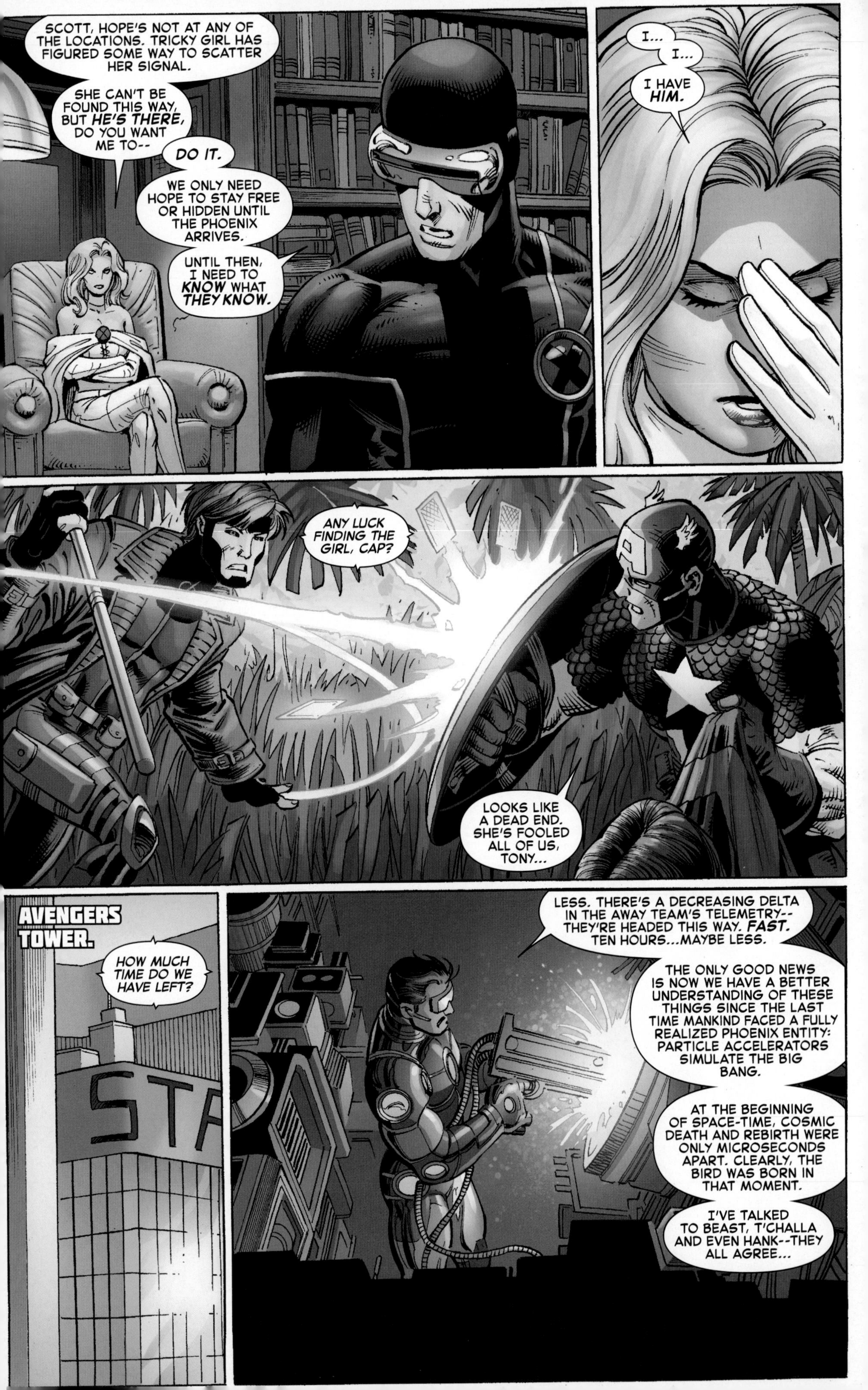
SCOTT, HOPE'S NOT AT ANY OF THE LOCATIONS. TRICKY GIRL HAS FIGURED SOME WAY TO SCATTER HER SIGNAL.
SHE CAN'T BE FOUND THIS WAY, BUT HE'S THERE, DO YOU WANT ME TO--
DO IT.
WE ONLY NEED HOPE TO STAY FREE OR HIDDEN UNTIL THE PHOENIX ARRIVES.
UNTIL THEN, I NEED TO KNOW WHAT THEY KNOW.
I...
I...
I HAVE HIM.
ANY LUCK FINDING THE GIRL, CAP?
LOOKS LIKE A DEAD END. SHE'S FOOLED ALL OF US, TONY...
AVENGERS TOWER.
HOW MUCH TIME DO WE HAVE LEFT?
LESS. THERE'S A DECREASING DELTA IN THE AWAY TEAM'S TELEMETRY-- THEY'RE HEADED THIS WAY. FAST. TEN HOURS...MAYBE LESS.
THE ONLY GOOD NEWS IS NOW WE HAVE A BETTER UNDERSTANDING OF THESE THINGS SINCE THE LAST TIME MANKIND FACED A FULLY REALIZED PHOENIX ENTITY: PARTICLE ACCELERATORS SIMULATE THE BIG BANG.
AT THE BEGINNING OF SPACE-TIME, COSMIC DEATH AND REBIRTH WERE ONLY MICROSECONDS APART. CLEARLY, THE BIRD WAS BORN IN THAT MOMENT.
I'VE TALKED TO BEAST, T'CHALLA AND EVEN HANK--THEY ALL AGREE...
STA

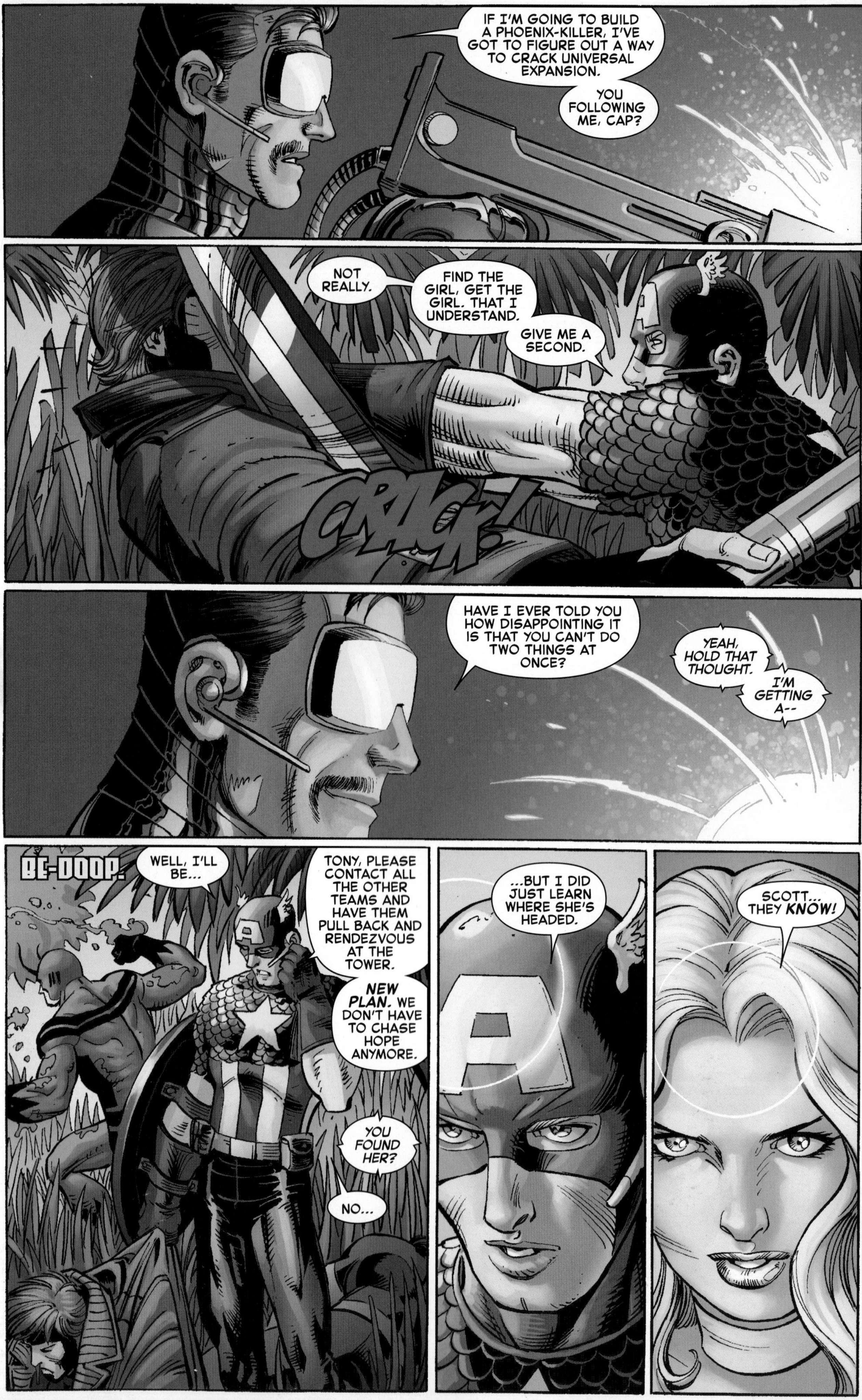
IF I'M GOING TO BUILD A PHOENIX-KILLER, I'VE GOT TO FIGURE OUT A WAY TO CRACK UNIVERSAL EXPANSION.
YOU FOLLOWING ME, CAP?
NOT REALLY.
FIND THE GIRL, GET THE GIRL. THAT I UNDERSTAND.
GIVE ME A SECOND.
CRACK!
HAVE I EVER TOLD YOU HOW DISAPPOINTING IT IS THAT YOU CAN'T DO TWO THINGS AT ONCE?
YEAH, HOLD THAT THOUGHT.
I'M GETTING A--
BE-DOOP.
WELL, I'LL BE...
TONY, PLEASE CONTACT ALL THE OTHER TEAMS AND HAVE THEM PULL BACK AND RENDEZVOUS AT THE TOWER.
NEW PLAN. WE DON'T HAVE TO CHASE HOPE ANYMORE.
YOU FOUND HER?
NO...
...BUT I DID JUST LEARN WHERE SHE'S HEADED.
SCOTT... THEY KNOW!

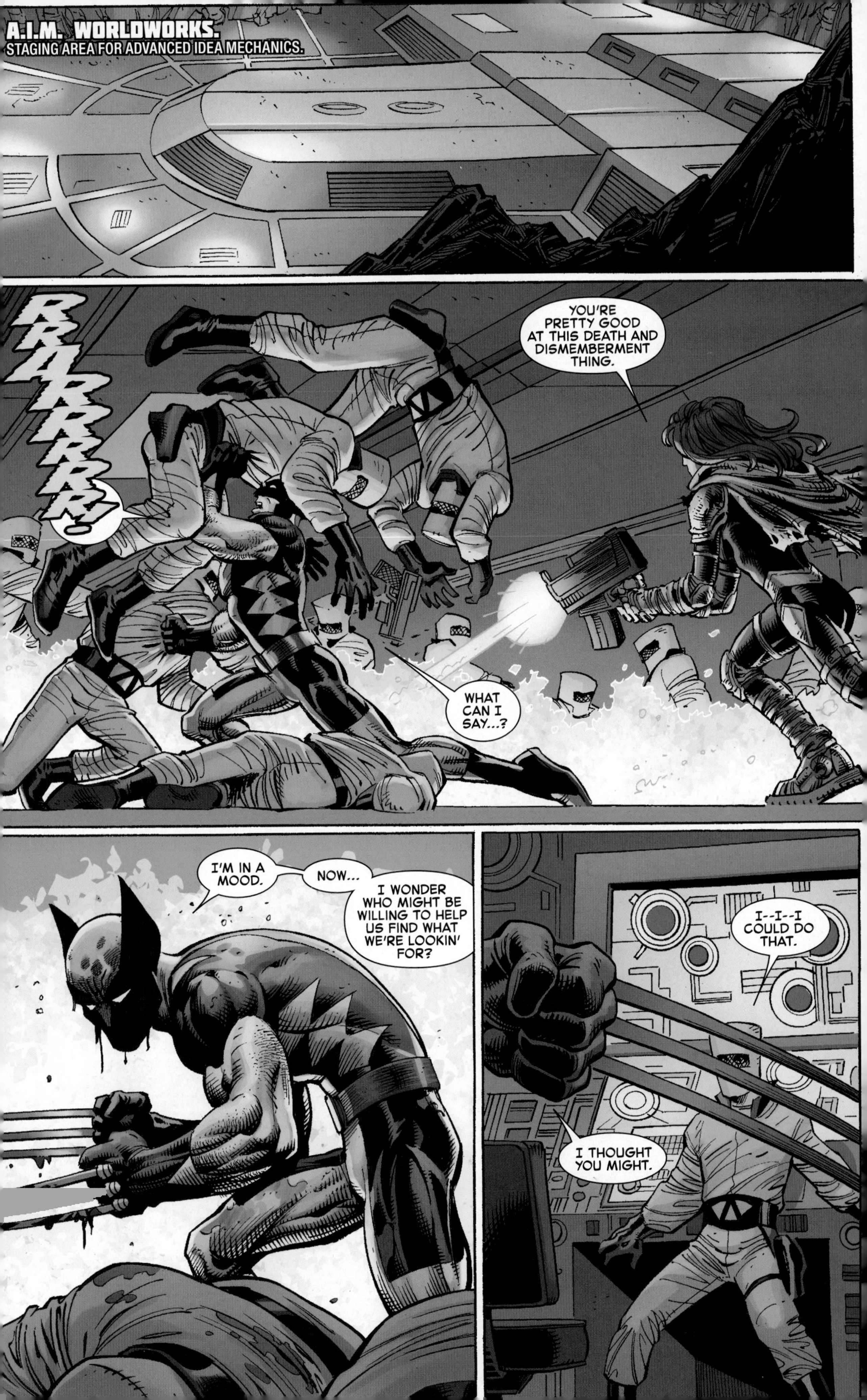
A.I.M. WORLDWORKS.
STAGING AREA FOR ADVANCED IDEA MECHANICS.
RRARRRR!
YOU'RE PRETTY GOOD AT THIS DEATH AND DISMEMBERMENT THING.
WHAT CAN I SAY...?
I'M IN A MOOD.
NOW...
I WONDER WHO MIGHT BE WILLING TO HELP US FIND WHAT WE'RE LOOKIN' FOR?
I--I--I COULD DO THAT.
I THOUGHT YOU MIGHT.

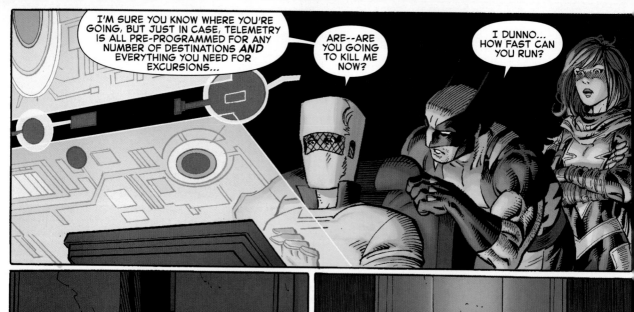

I'M SURE YOU KNOW WHERE YOU'RE GOING, BUT JUST IN CASE, TELEMETRY IS ALL PRE-PROGRAMMED FOR ANY NUMBER OF DESTINATIONS *AND* EVERYTHING YOU NEED FOR EXCURSIONS...

ARE--ARE YOU GOING TO KILL ME NOW?

I DUNNO... HOW FAST CAN YOU RUN?

WHOA.

I DID SAY BIGGER, DIDN'T I?

HEY...

A REDHEADED GIRL SAYS SHE WANTS TO GO TO THE MOON...

I GOTTA TAKE HER.

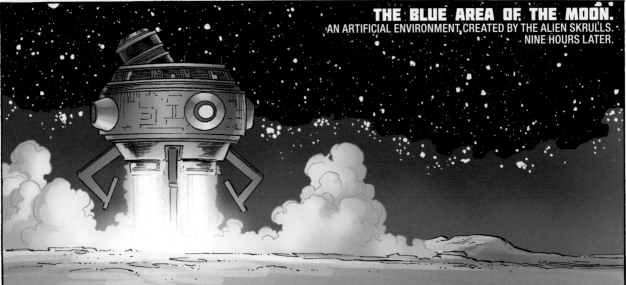

THE BLUE AREA OF THE MOON.
AN ARTIFICIAL ENVIRONMENT, CREATED BY THE ALIEN SKRULLS.
NINE HOURS LATER.

IT'S SO CLOSE NOW.

I CAN FEEL IT.

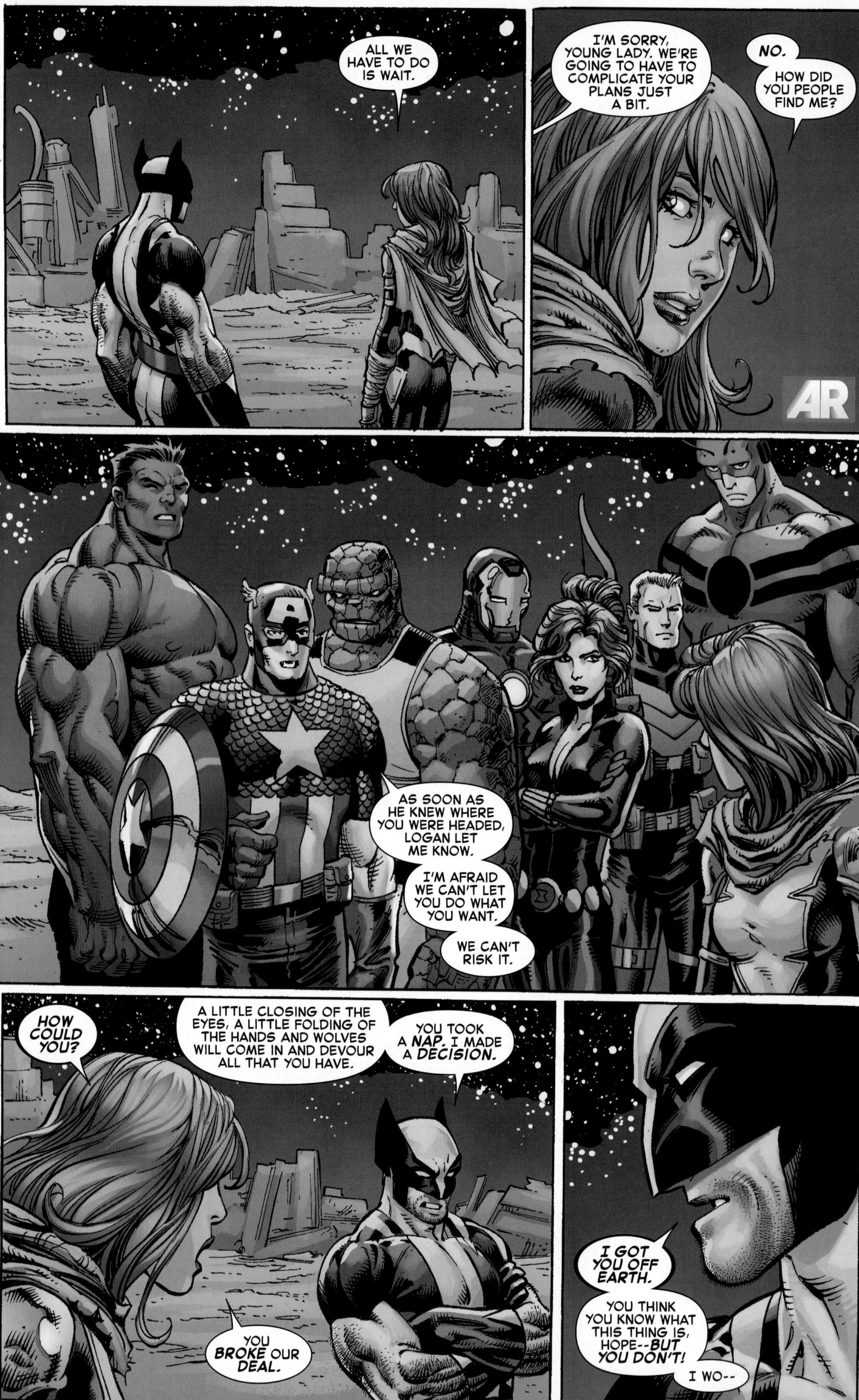
ALL WE HAVE TO DO IS WAIT.
I'M SORRY, YOUNG LADY. WE'RE GOING TO HAVE TO COMPLICATE YOUR PLANS JUST A BIT.
NO.
HOW DID YOU PEOPLE FIND ME?
AS SOON AS HE KNEW WHERE YOU WERE HEADED, LOGAN LET ME KNOW.
I'M AFRAID WE CAN'T LET YOU DO WHAT YOU WANT.
WE CAN'T RISK IT.
HOW COULD YOU?
A LITTLE CLOSING OF THE EYES, A LITTLE FOLDING OF THE HANDS AND WOLVES WILL COME IN AND DEVOUR ALL THAT YOU HAVE.
YOU TOOK A NAP. I MADE A DECISION.
YOU BROKE OUR DEAL.
I GOT YOU OFF EARTH.
YOU THINK YOU KNOW WHAT THIS THING IS, HOPE--BUT YOU DON'T!
I WO--

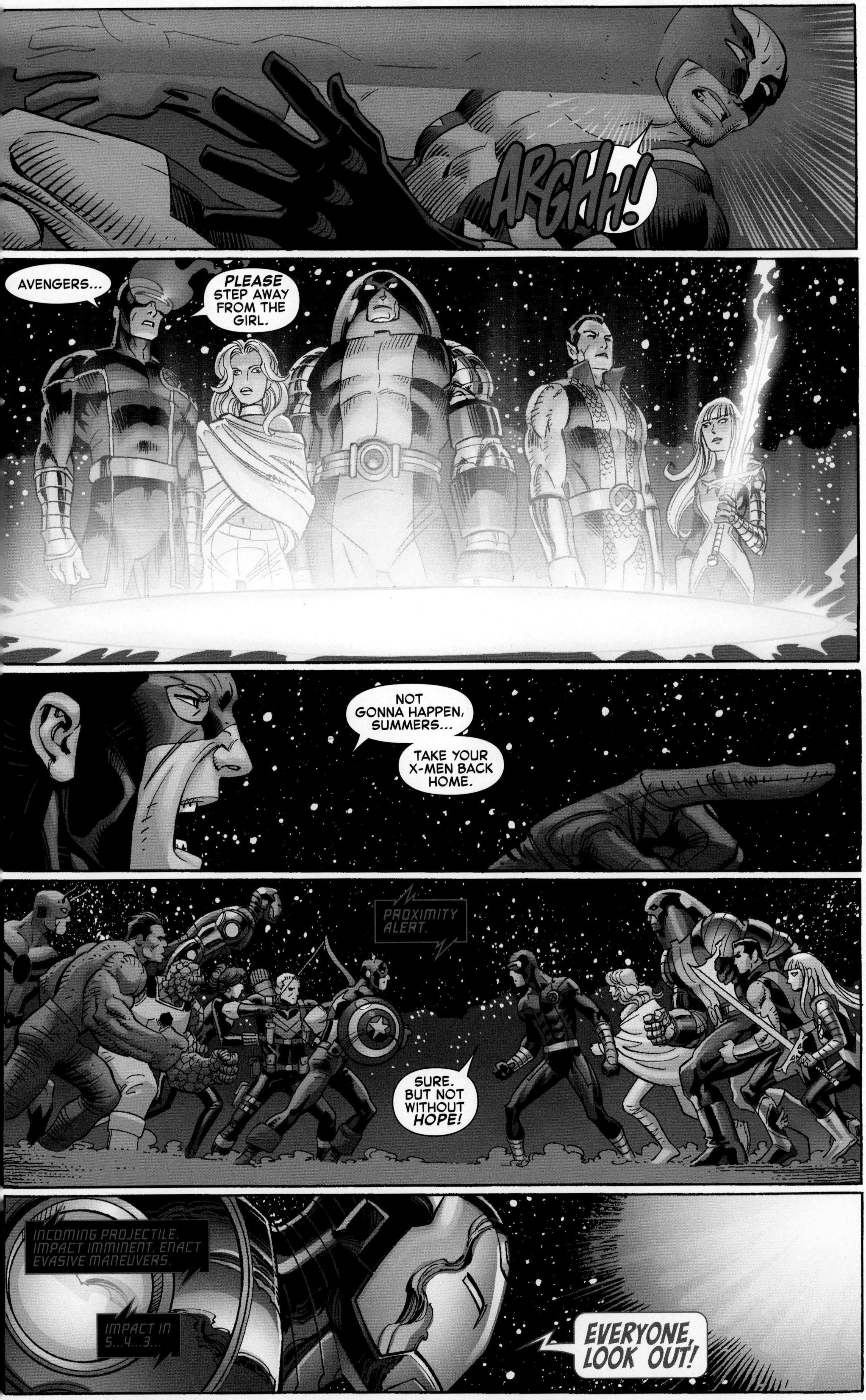
ARGHH!
AVENGERS...
PLEASE STEP AWAY FROM THE GIRL.
NOT GONNA HAPPEN, SUMMERS...
TAKE YOUR X-MEN BACK HOME.
PROXIMITY ALERT.
SURE. BUT NOT WITHOUT HOPE!
INCOMING PROJECTILE. IMPACT IMMINENT. ENACT EVASIVE MANEUVERS.
IMPACT IN 5...4...3...
EVERYONE, LOOK OUT!

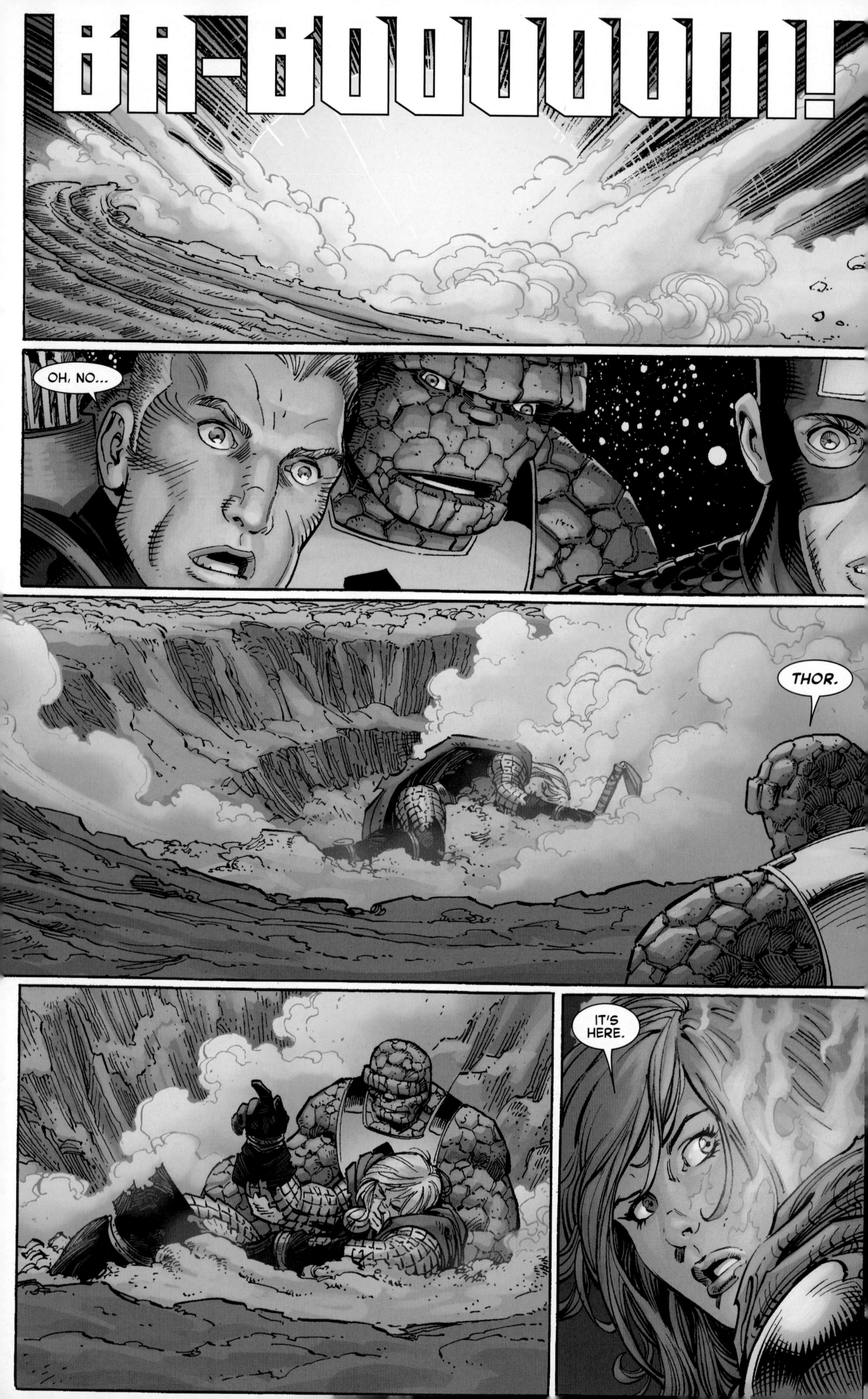
BA-BOOOOOM!
OH, NO...
THOR.
IT'S HERE.

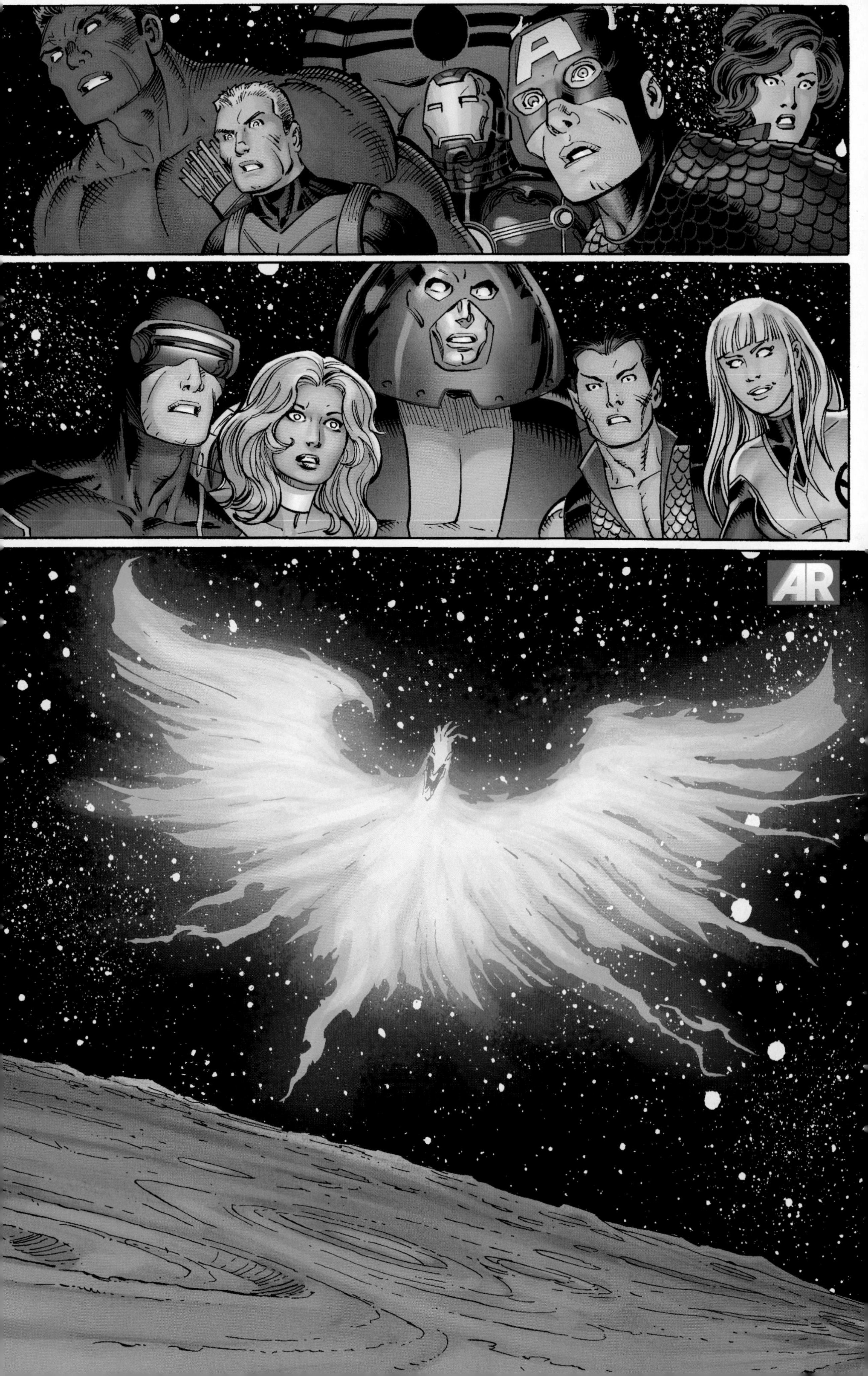

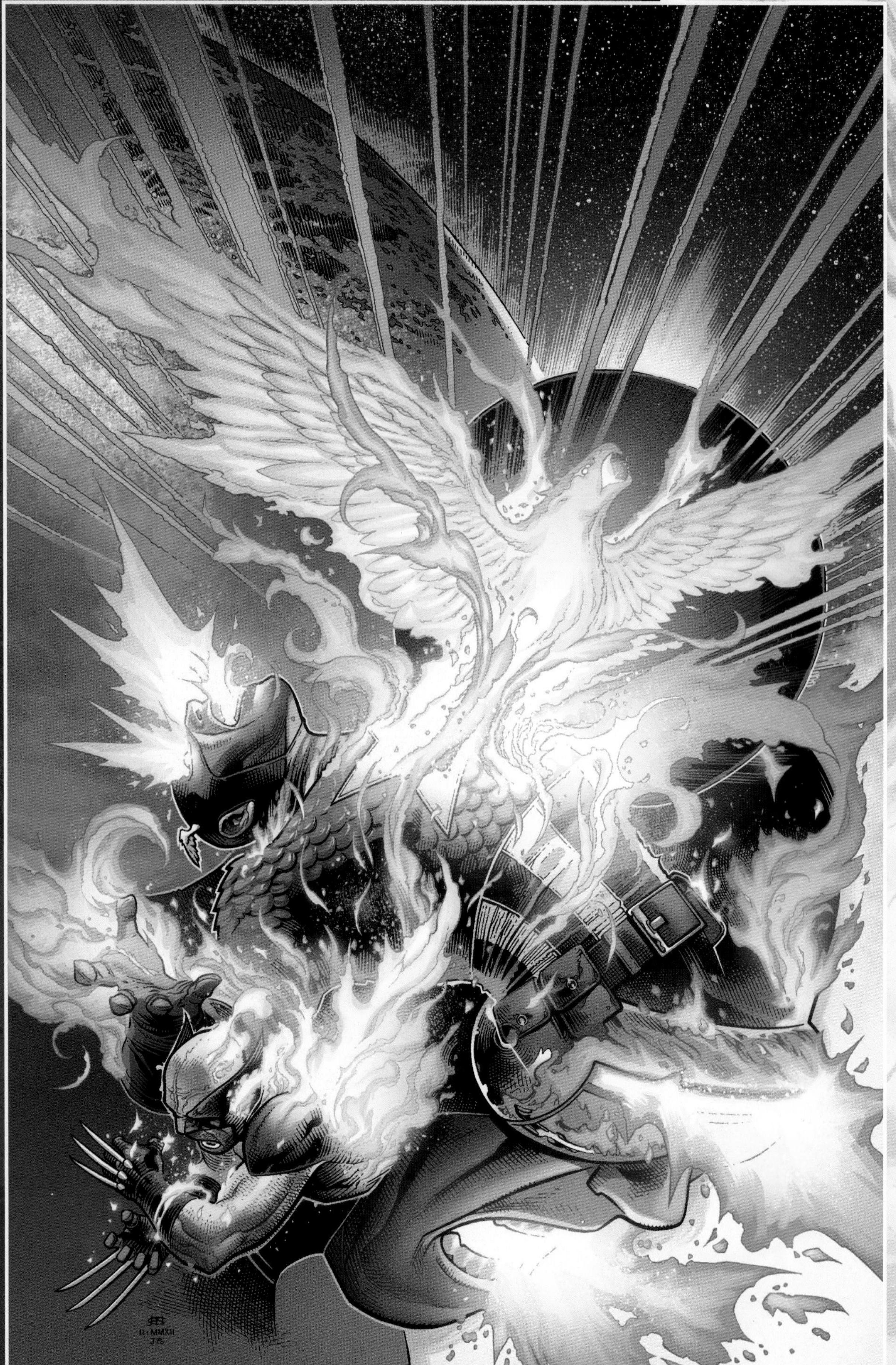

ROUND 5

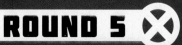

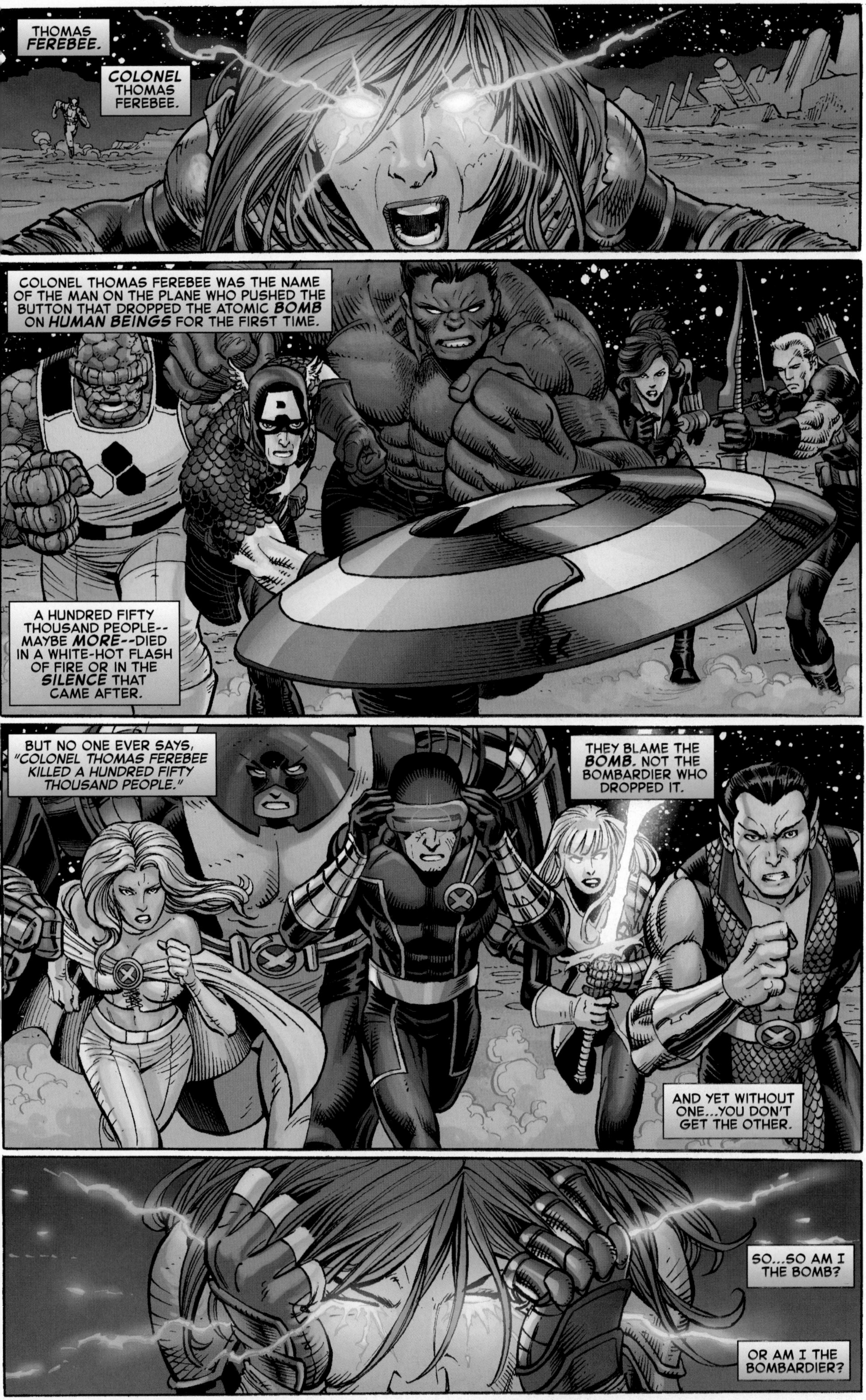
THOMAS FEREBEE.
COLONEL THOMAS FEREBEE.
COLONEL THOMAS FEREBEE WAS THE NAME OF THE MAN ON THE PLANE WHO PUSHED THE BUTTON THAT DROPPED THE ATOMIC BOMB ON HUMAN BEINGS FOR THE FIRST TIME.
A HUNDRED FIFTY THOUSAND PEOPLE--MAYBE MORE--DIED IN A WHITE-HOT FLASH OF FIRE OR IN THE SILENCE THAT CAME AFTER.
BUT NO ONE EVER SAYS, "COLONEL THOMAS FEREBEE KILLED A HUNDRED FIFTY THOUSAND PEOPLE."
THEY BLAME THE BOMB. NOT THE BOMBARDIER WHO DROPPED IT.
AND YET WITHOUT ONE...YOU DON'T GET THE OTHER.
SO...SO AM I THE BOMB?
OR AM I THE BOMBARDIER?

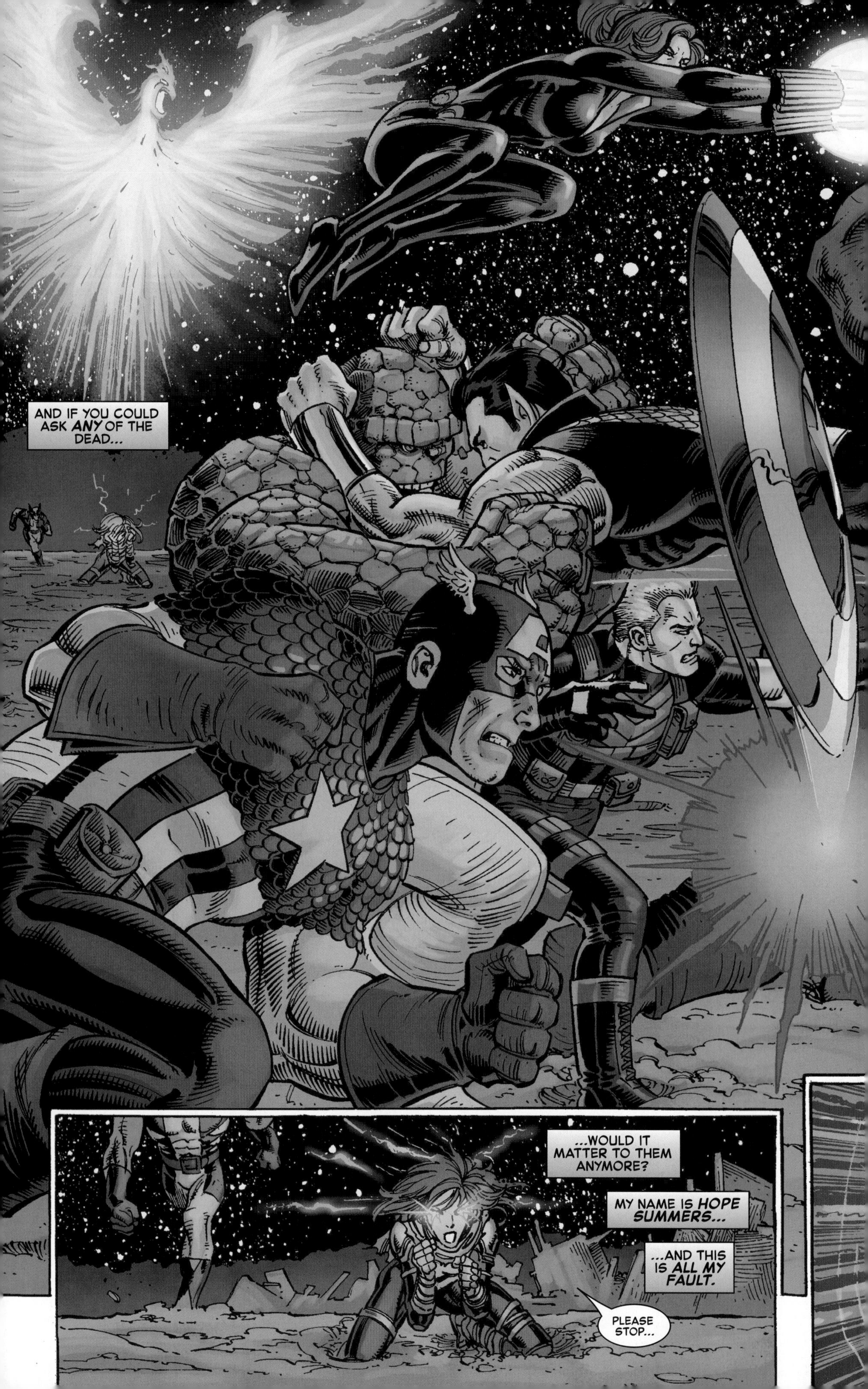
AND IF YOU COULD ASK ANY OF THE DEAD...
...WOULD IT MATTER TO THEM ANYMORE?
MY NAME IS HOPE SUMMERS...
...AND THIS IS ALL MY FAULT.
PLEASE STOP...

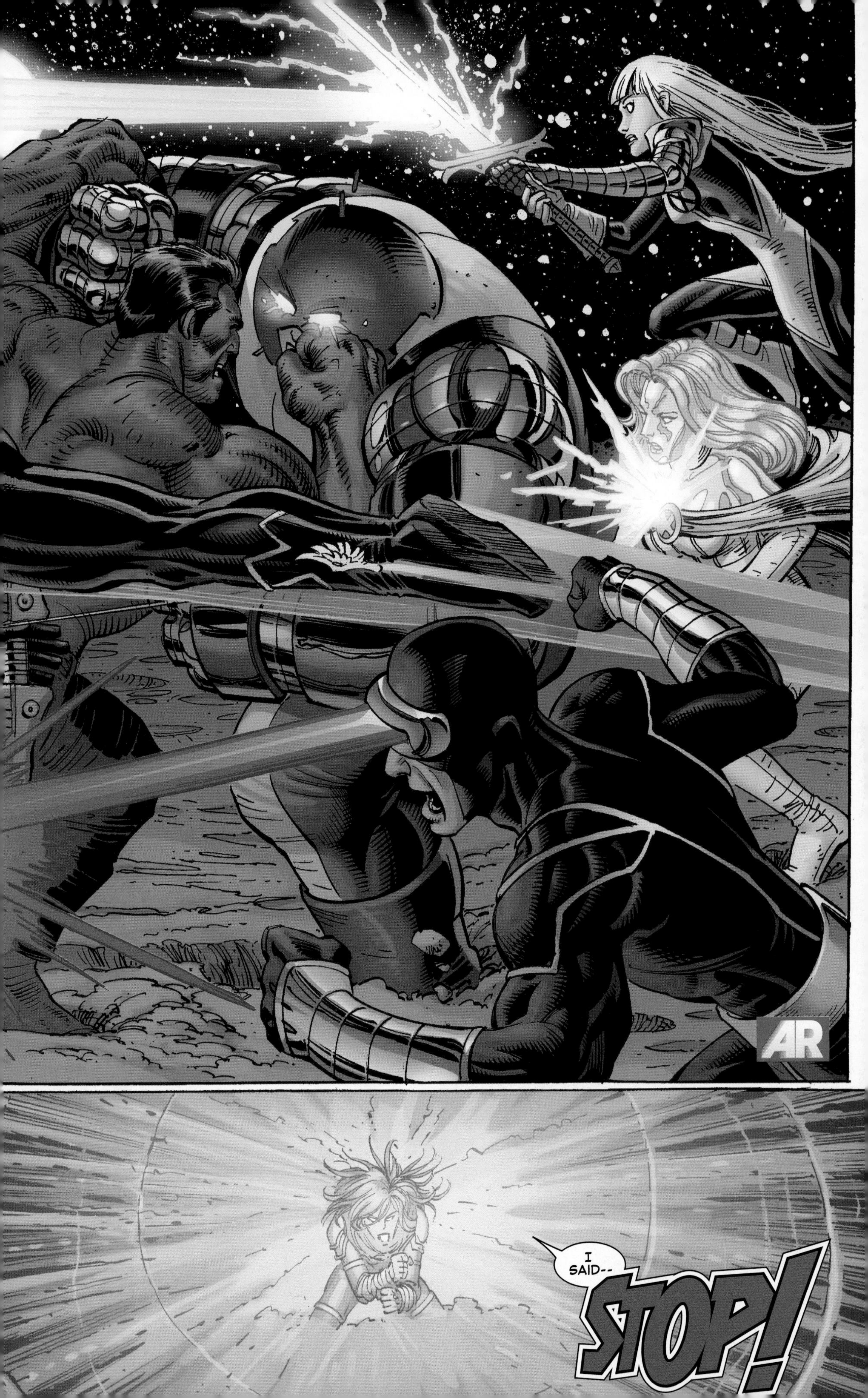
I SAID--
STOP!

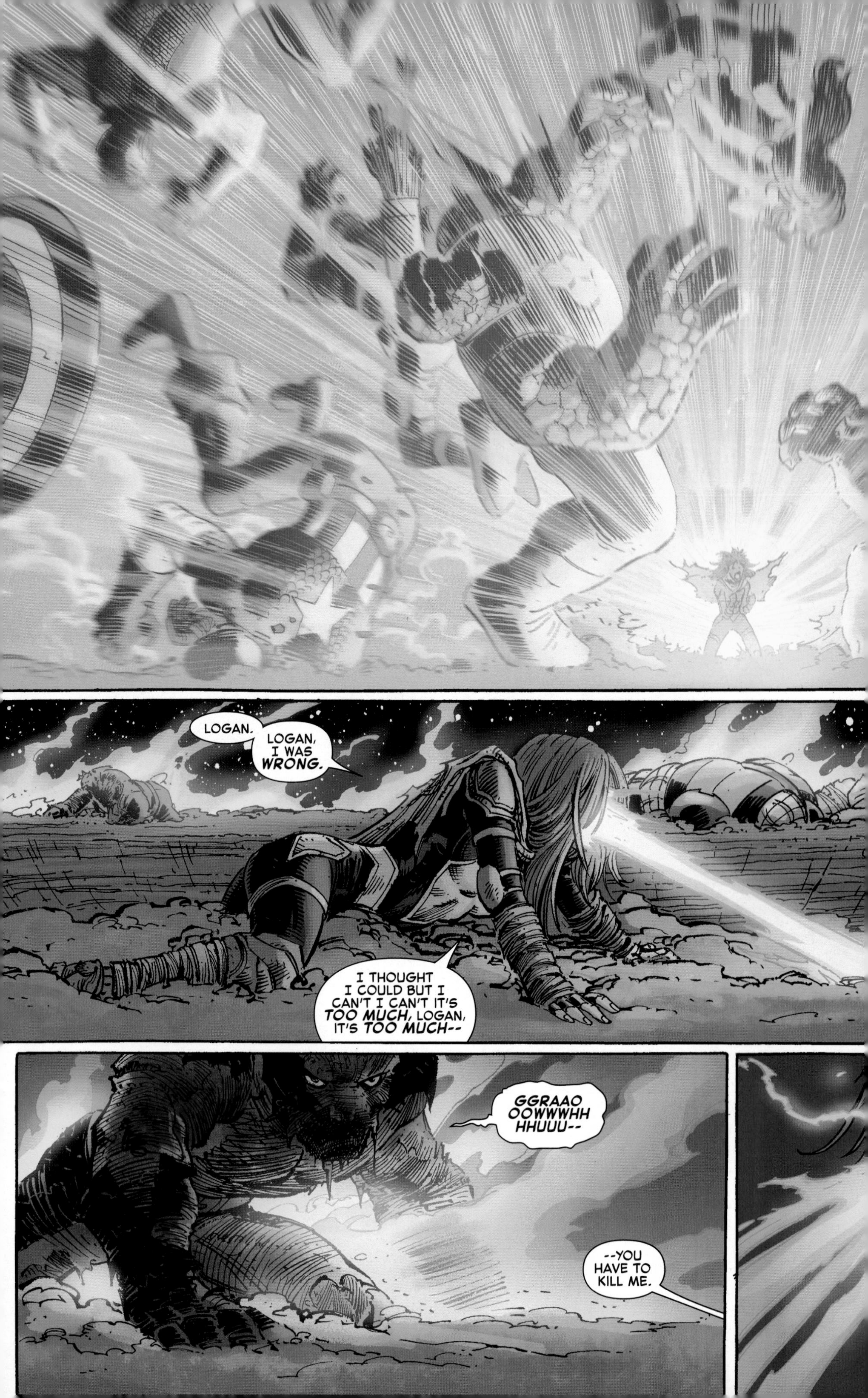
LOGAN.
LOGAN, I WAS WRONG.
I THOUGHT I COULD BUT I CAN'T I CAN'T IT'S TOO MUCH, LOGAN, IT'S TOO MUCH--
GGRAAO OOWWWHH HHUUU--
--YOU HAVE TO KILL ME.

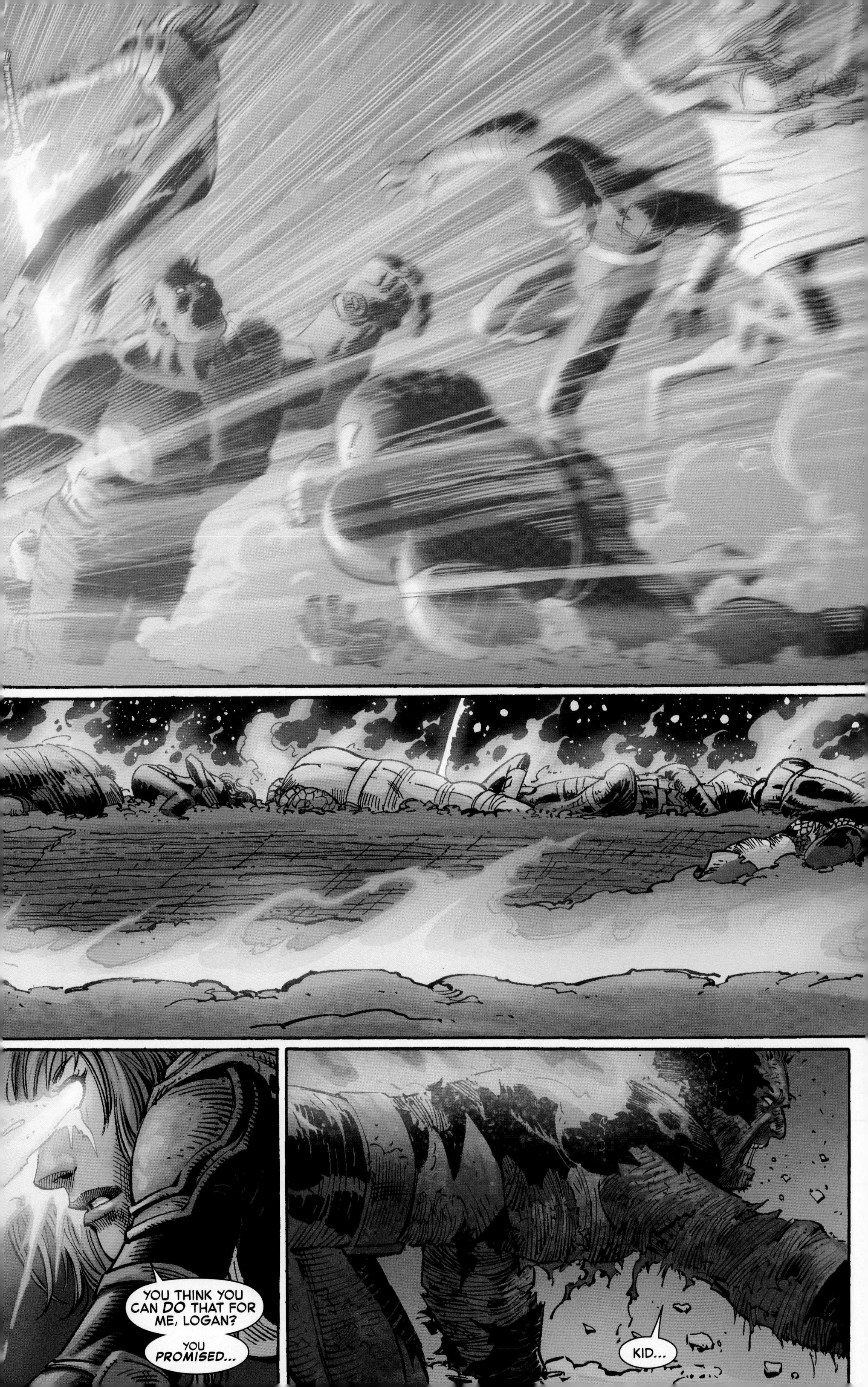
YOU THINK YOU CAN DO THAT FOR ME, LOGAN?
YOU PROMISED...
KID...

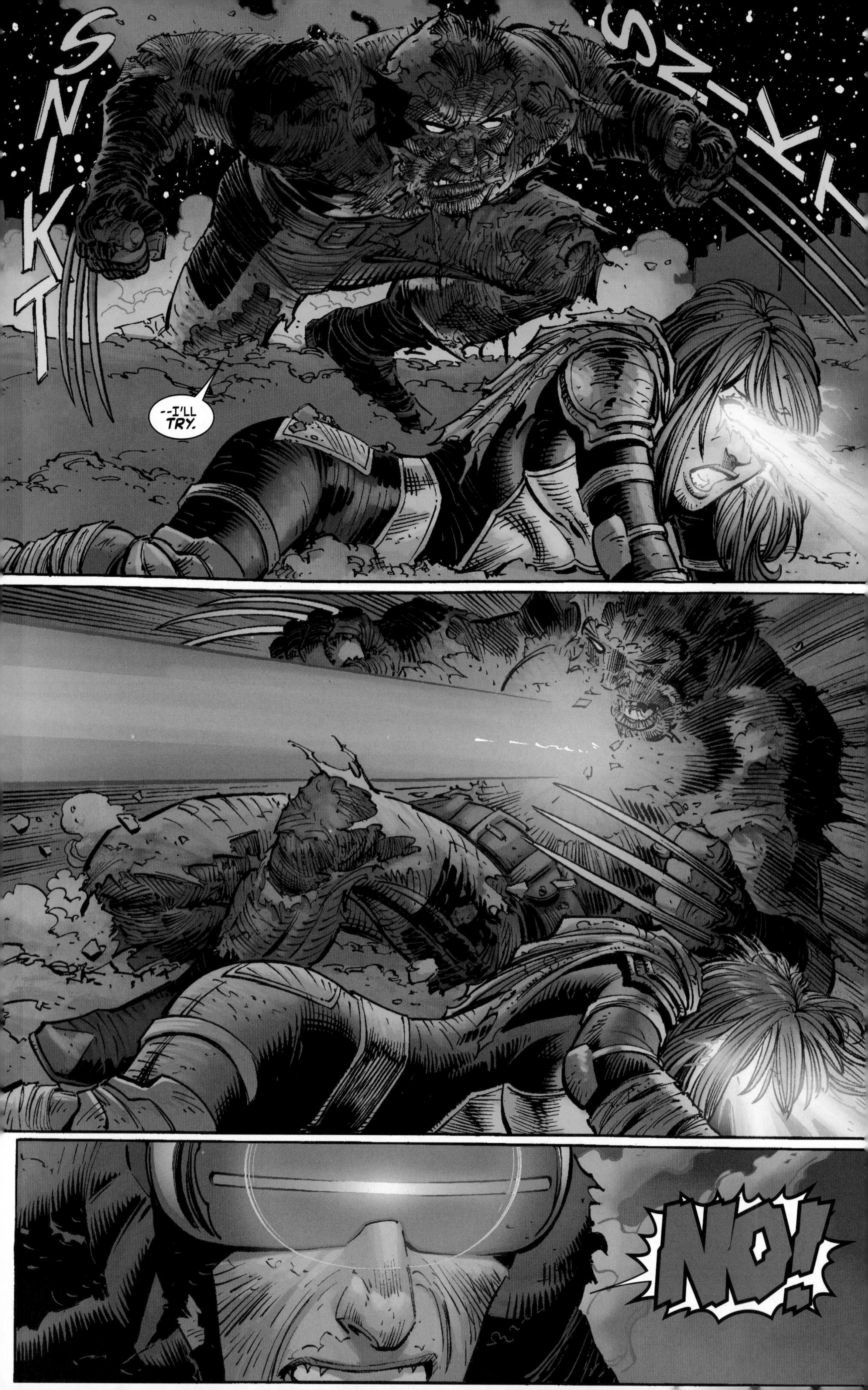
SNIKT
SNIKT
--I'LL TRY.
NO!

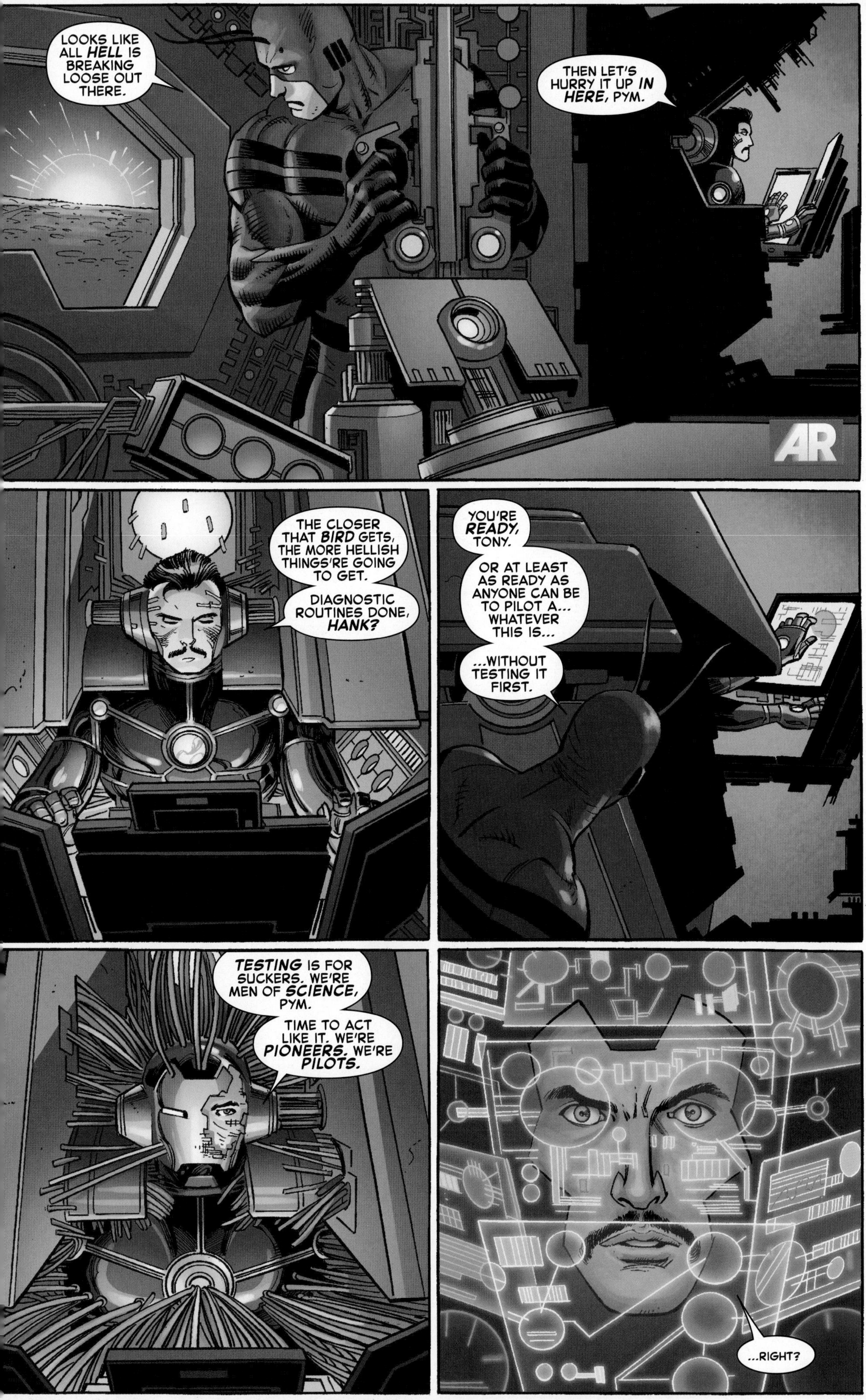
LOOKS LIKE ALL HELL IS BREAKING LOOSE OUT THERE.
THEN LET'S HURRY IT UP IN HERE, PYM.
THE CLOSER THAT BIRD GETS, THE MORE HELLISH THINGS'RE GOING TO GET.
DIAGNOSTIC ROUTINES DONE, HANK?
YOU'RE READY, TONY.
OR AT LEAST AS READY AS ANYONE CAN BE TO PILOT A... WHATEVER THIS IS...
...WITHOUT TESTING IT FIRST.
TESTING IS FOR SUCKERS. WE'RE MEN OF SCIENCE, PYM.
TIME TO ACT LIKE IT. WE'RE PIONEERS. WE'RE PILOTS.
...RIGHT?

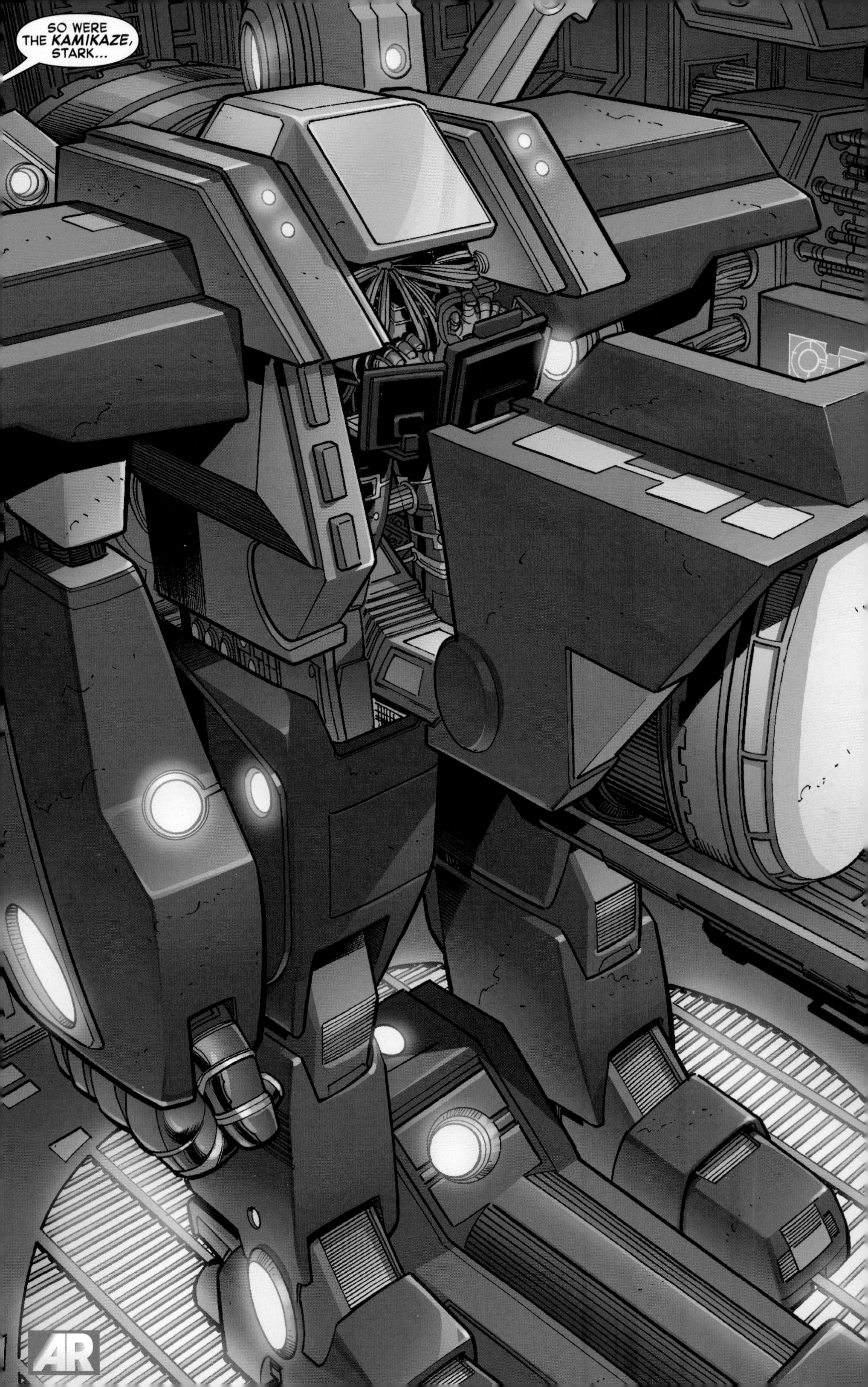
SO WERE THE KAMIKAZE, STARK...
AR

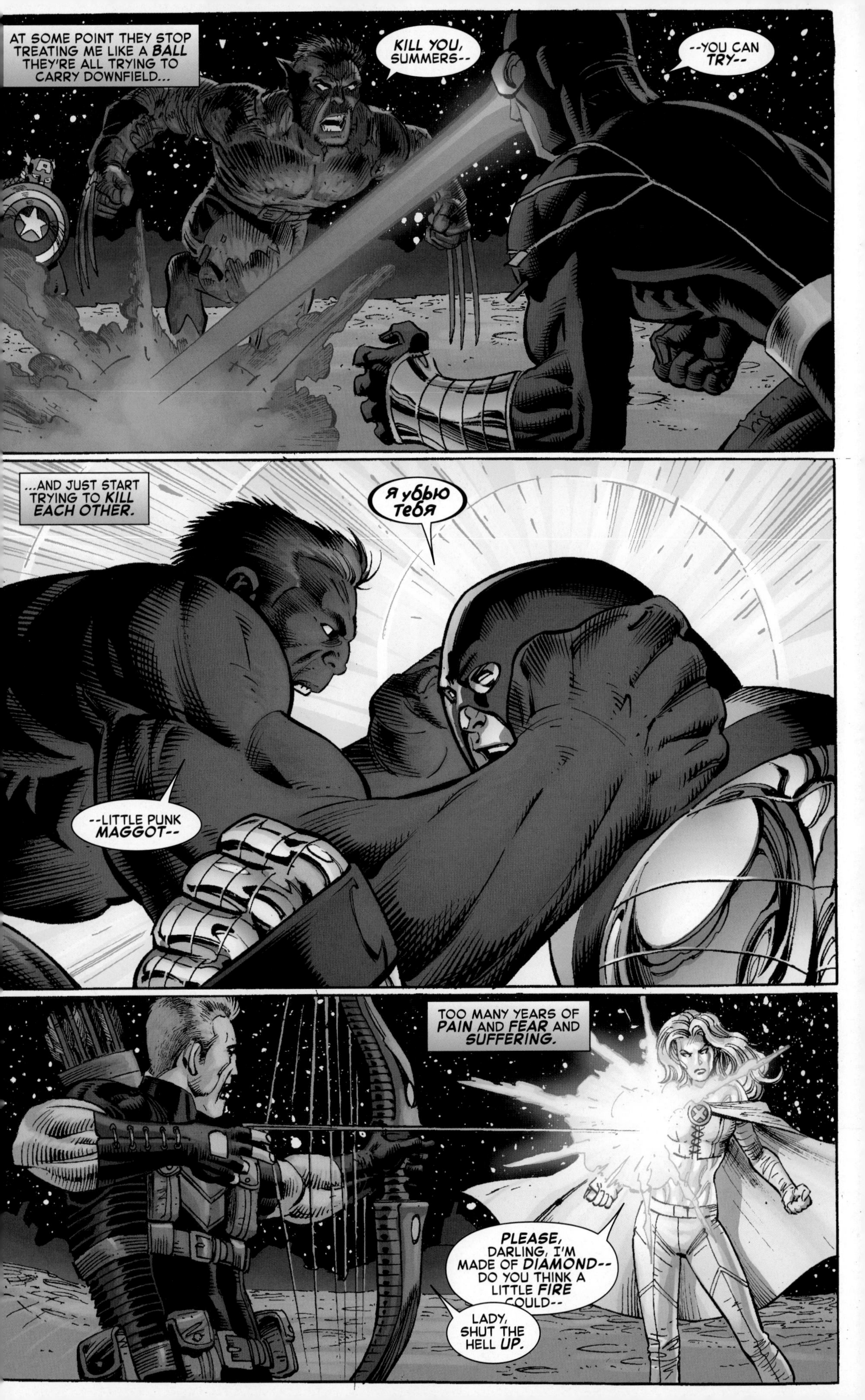
AT SOME POINT THEY STOP TREATING ME LIKE A BALL THEY'RE ALL TRYING TO CARRY DOWNFIELD...
KILL YOU, SUMMERS--
--YOU CAN TRY--
...AND JUST START TRYING TO KILL EACH OTHER.
Я убью тебя
--LITTLE PUNK MAGGOT--
TOO MANY YEARS OF PAIN AND FEAR AND SUFFERING.
PLEASE, DARLING, I'M MADE OF DIAMOND-- DO YOU THINK A LITTLE FIRE COULD--
LADY, SHUT THE HELL UP.

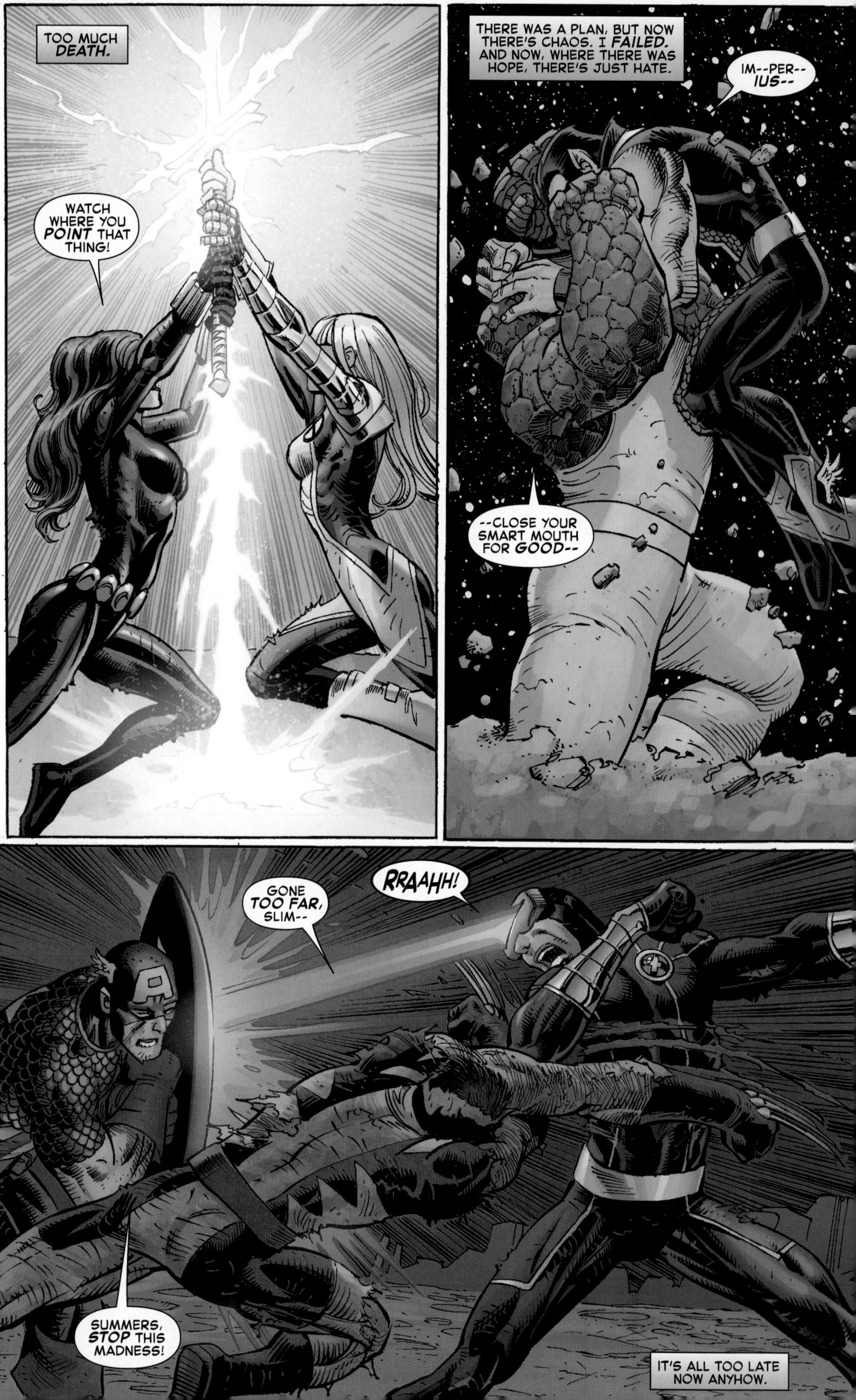
TOO MUCH DEATH.
WATCH WHERE YOU POINT THAT THING!
THERE WAS A PLAN, BUT NOW THERE'S CHAOS. I FAILED. AND NOW, WHERE THERE WAS HOPE, THERE'S JUST HATE.
IM--PER--IUS--
--CLOSE YOUR SMART MOUTH FOR GOOD--
GONE TOO FAR, SLIM--
RRAAHH!
SUMMERS, STOP THIS MADNESS!
IT'S ALL TOO LATE NOW ANYHOW.

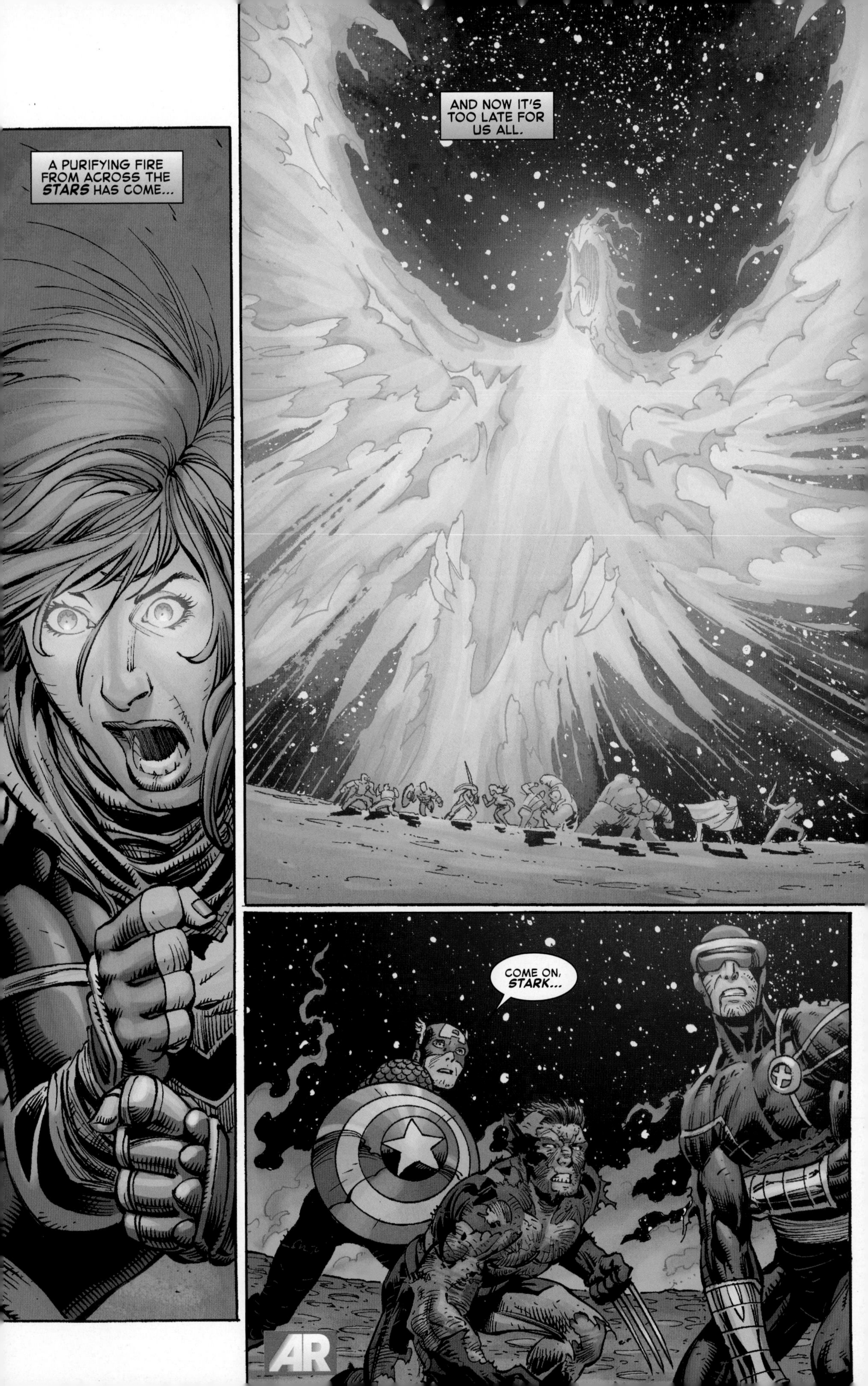
A PURIFYING FIRE FROM ACROSS THE STARS HAS COME...
AND NOW IT'S TOO LATE FOR US ALL.
COME ON, STARK...

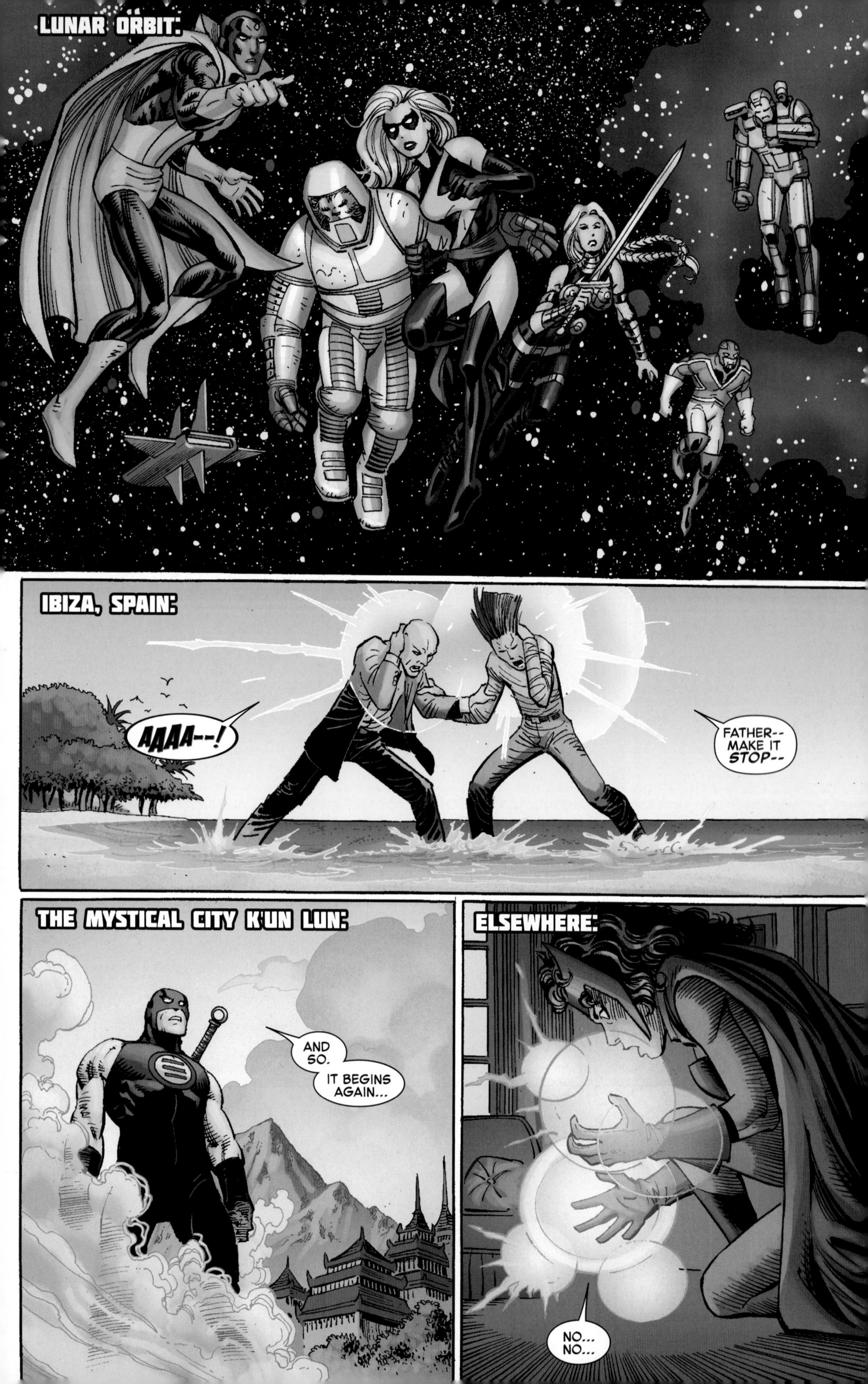
LUNAR ORBIT:
IBIZA, SPAIN:
AAAA--!
FATHER-- MAKE IT STOP--
THE MYSTICAL CITY K'UN LUN:
AND SO.
IT BEGINS AGAIN...
ELSEWHERE:
NO... NO...

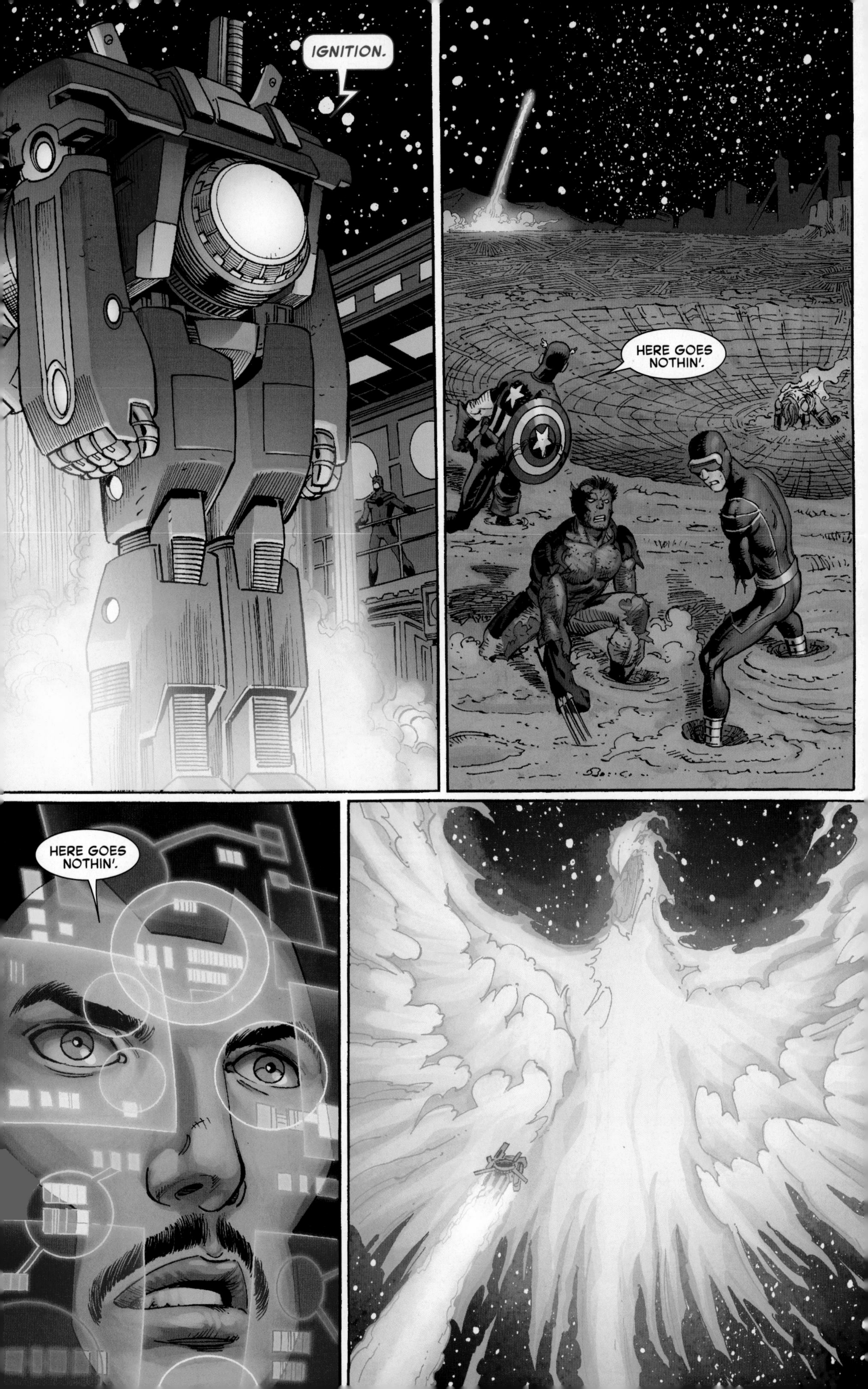
IGNITION.
HERE GOES NOTHIN'.
HERE GOES NOTHIN'.

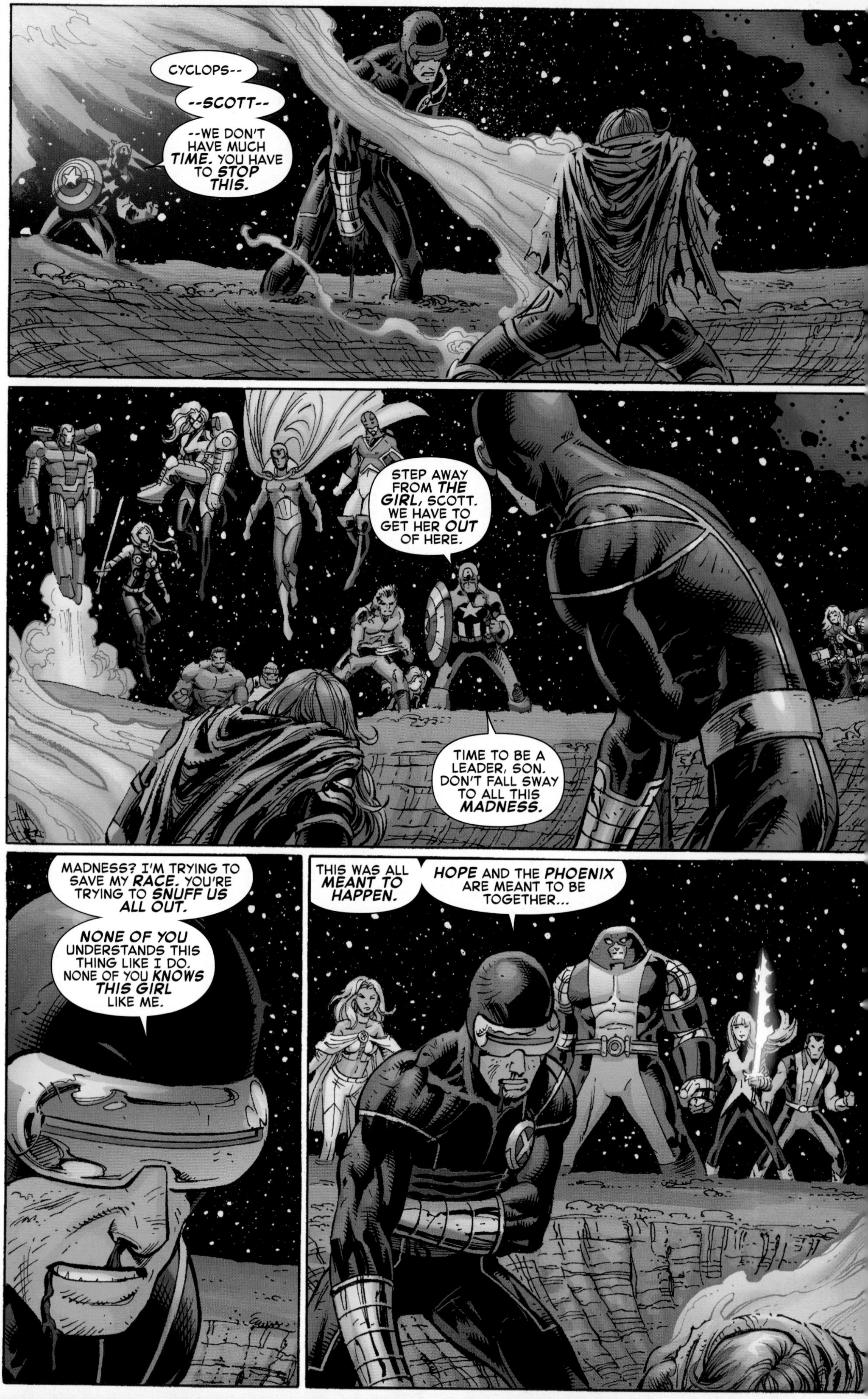
CYCLOPS--
--SCOTT--
--WE DON'T HAVE MUCH TIME. YOU HAVE TO STOP THIS.
STEP AWAY FROM THE GIRL, SCOTT. WE HAVE TO GET HER OUT OF HERE.
TIME TO BE A LEADER, SON. DON'T FALL SWAY TO ALL THIS MADNESS.
MADNESS? I'M TRYING TO SAVE MY RACE. YOU'RE TRYING TO SNUFF US ALL OUT.
NONE OF YOU UNDERSTANDS THIS THING LIKE I DO. NONE OF YOU KNOWS THIS GIRL LIKE ME.
THIS WAS ALL MEANT TO HAPPEN.
HOPE AND THE PHOENIX ARE MEANT TO BE TOGETHER...

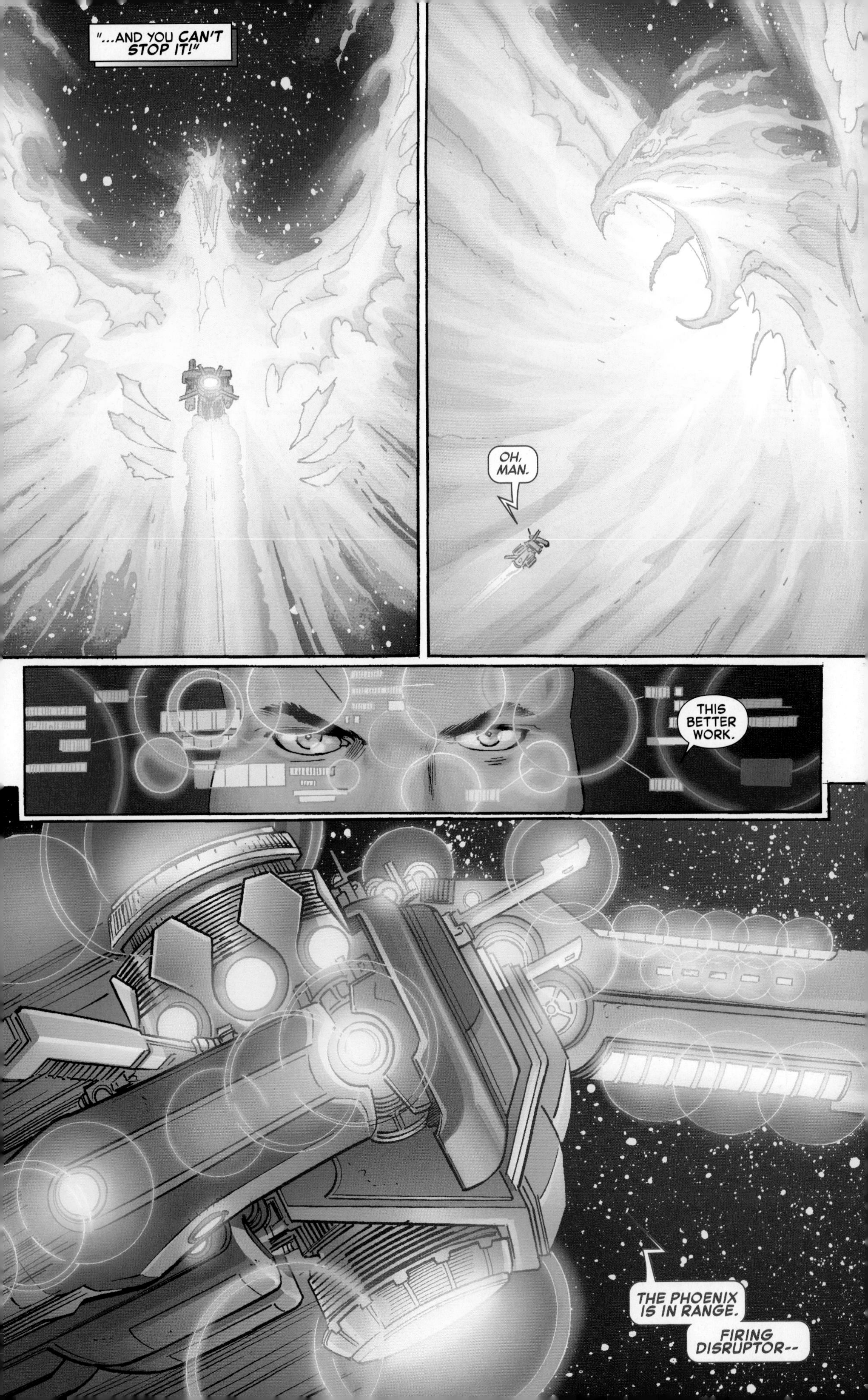
"...AND YOU CAN'T STOP IT!"
OH, MAN.
THIS BETTER WORK.
THE PHOENIX IS IN RANGE.
FIRING DISRUPTOR--

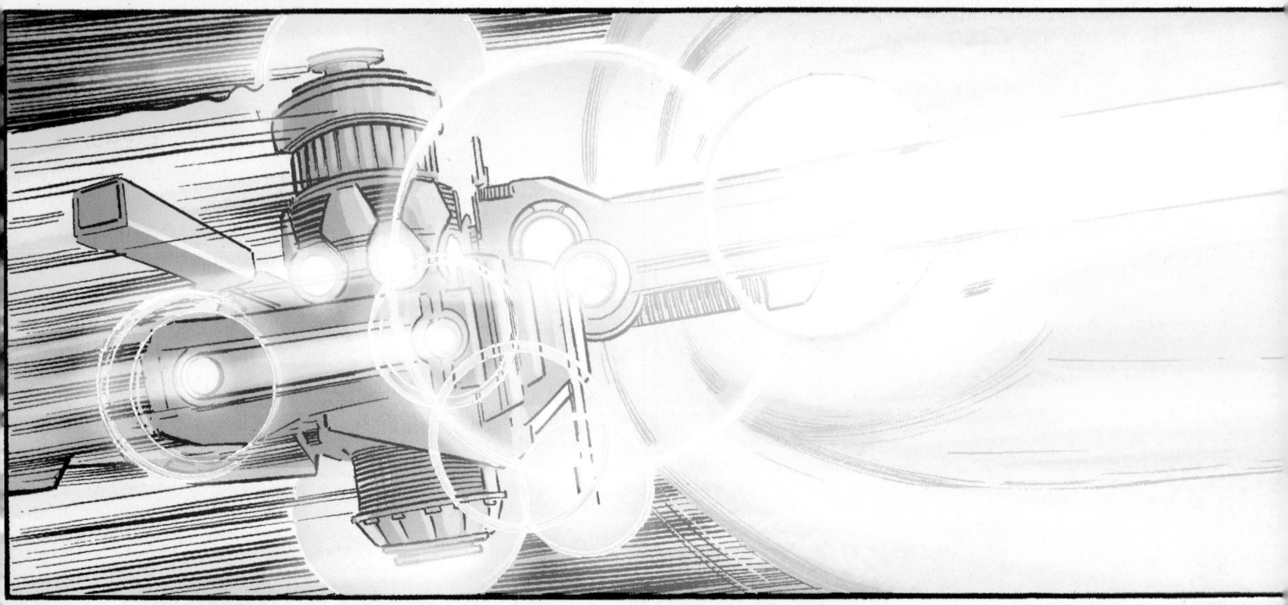
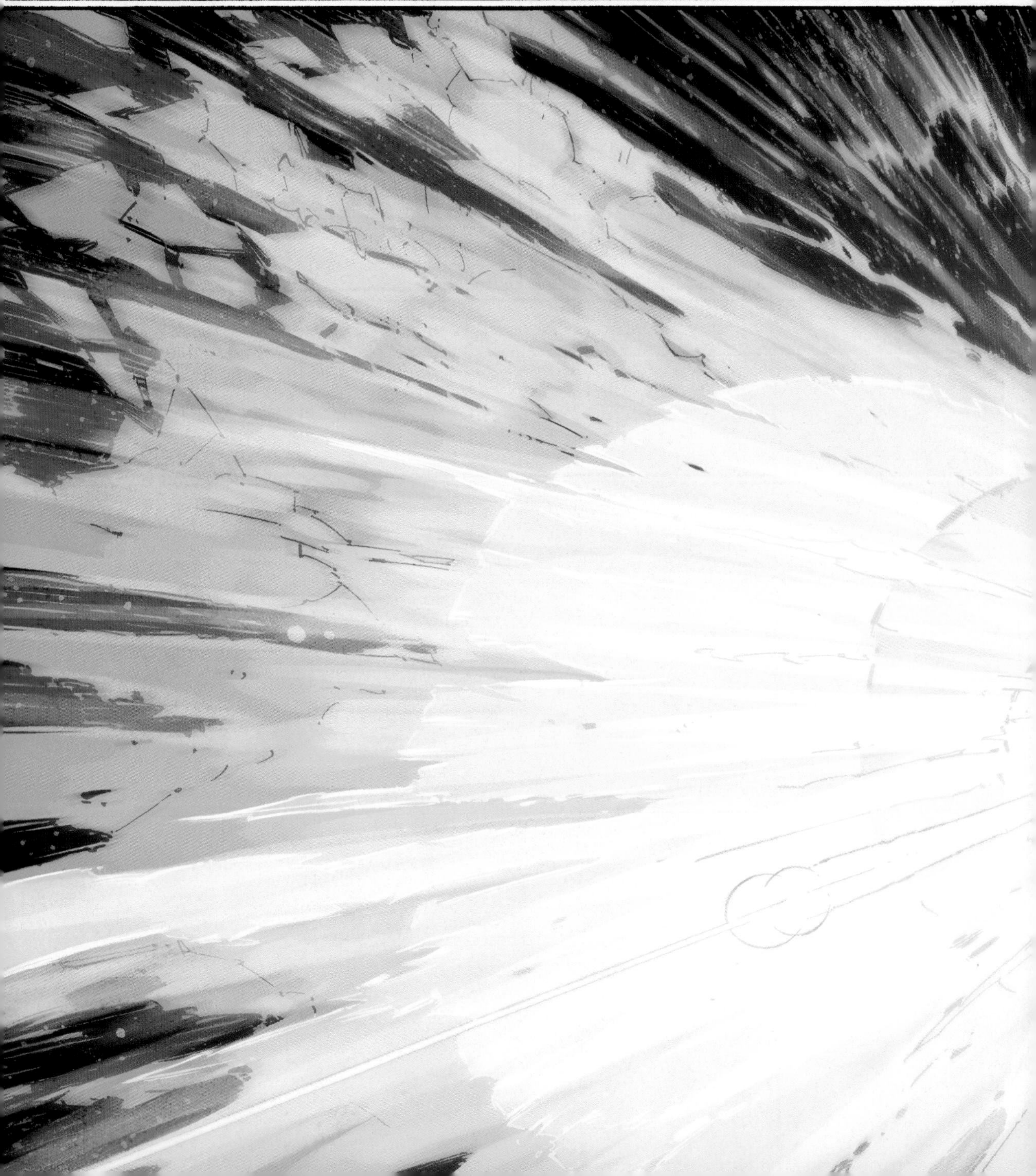

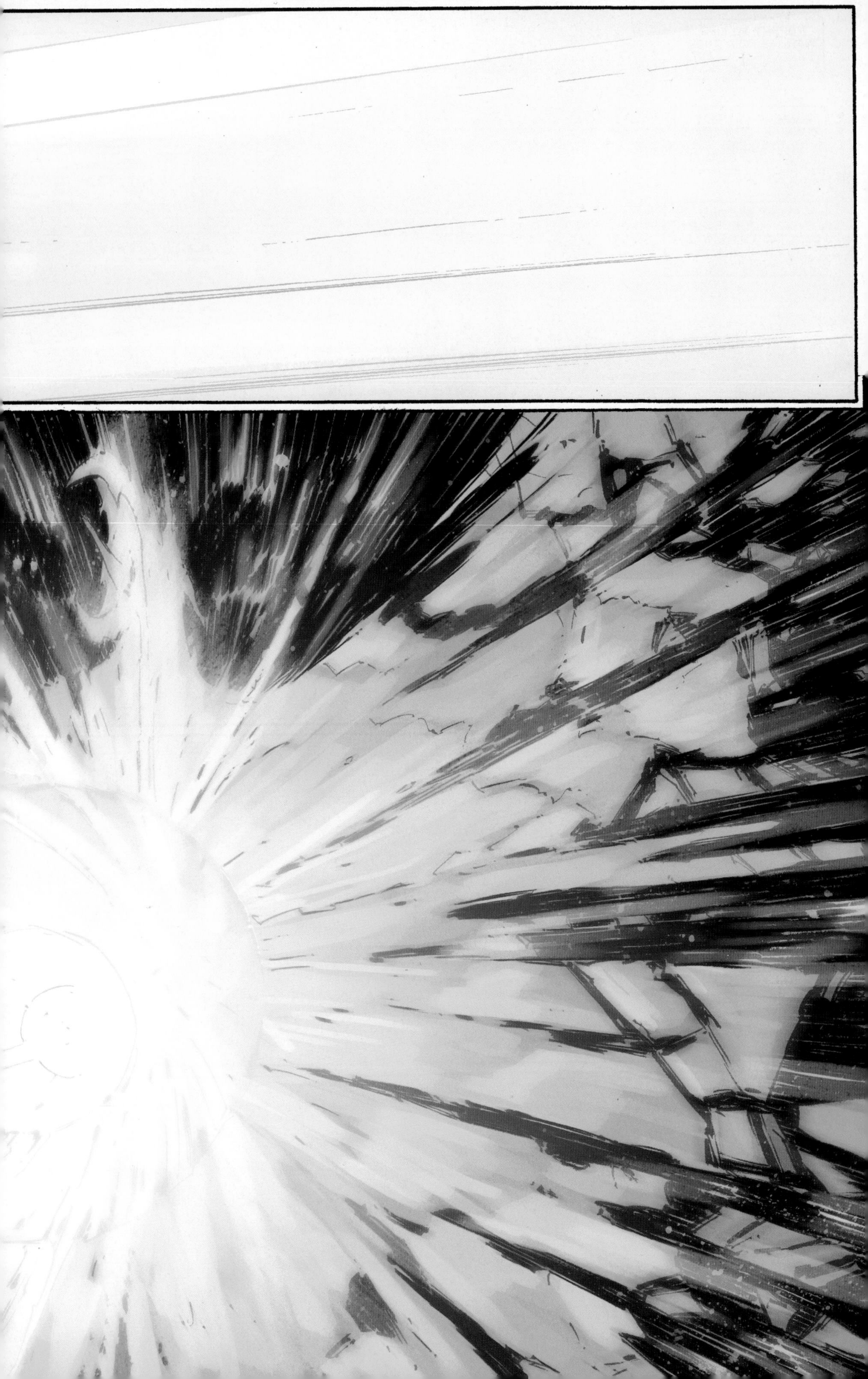

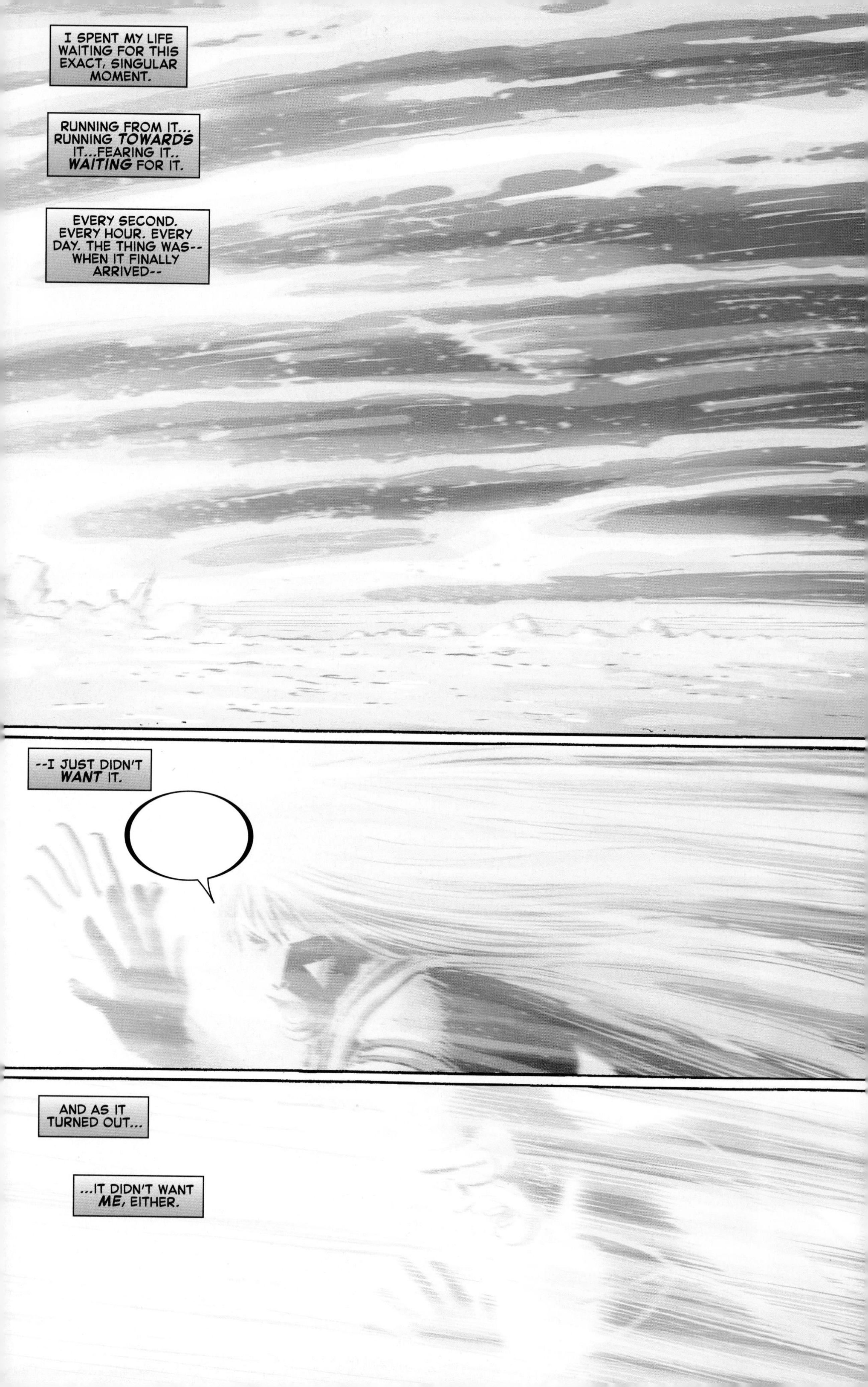
I SPENT MY LIFE WAITING FOR THIS EXACT, SINGULAR MOMENT.
RUNNING FROM IT... RUNNING *TOWARDS* IT...FEARING IT.. *WAITING* FOR IT.
EVERY SECOND. EVERY HOUR. EVERY DAY. THE THING WAS-- WHEN IT FINALLY ARRIVED--
--I JUST DIDN'T *WANT* IT.
AND AS IT TURNED OUT...
...IT DIDN'T WANT *ME,* EITHER.

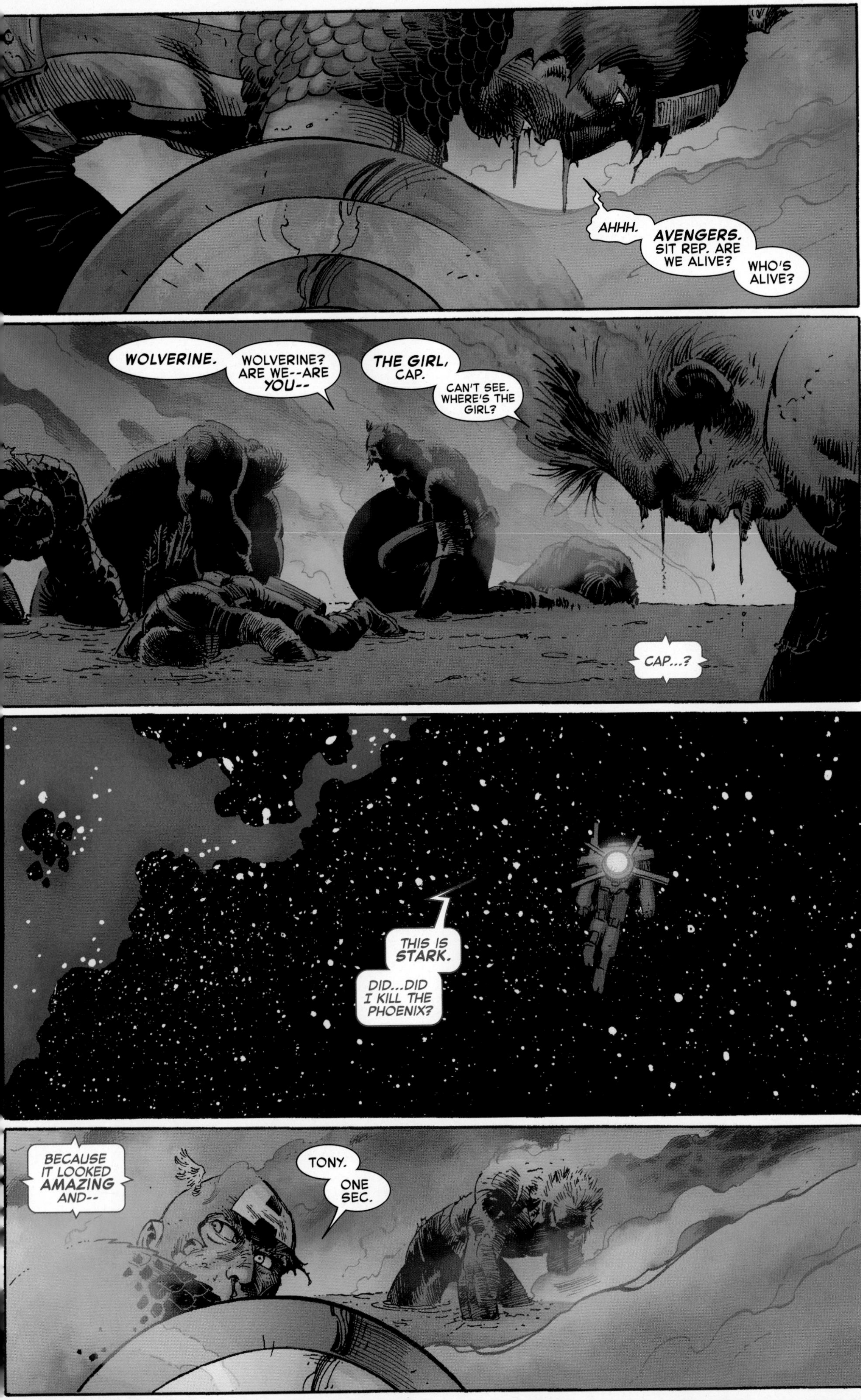
AHHH.
AVENGERS. SIT REP. ARE WE ALIVE?
WHO'S ALIVE?
WOLVERINE.
WOLVERINE? ARE WE--ARE YOU--
THE GIRL, CAP.
CAN'T SEE. WHERE'S THE GIRL?
CAP...?
THIS IS STARK.
DID...DID I KILL THE PHOENIX?
BECAUSE IT LOOKED AMAZING AND--
TONY.
ONE SEC.

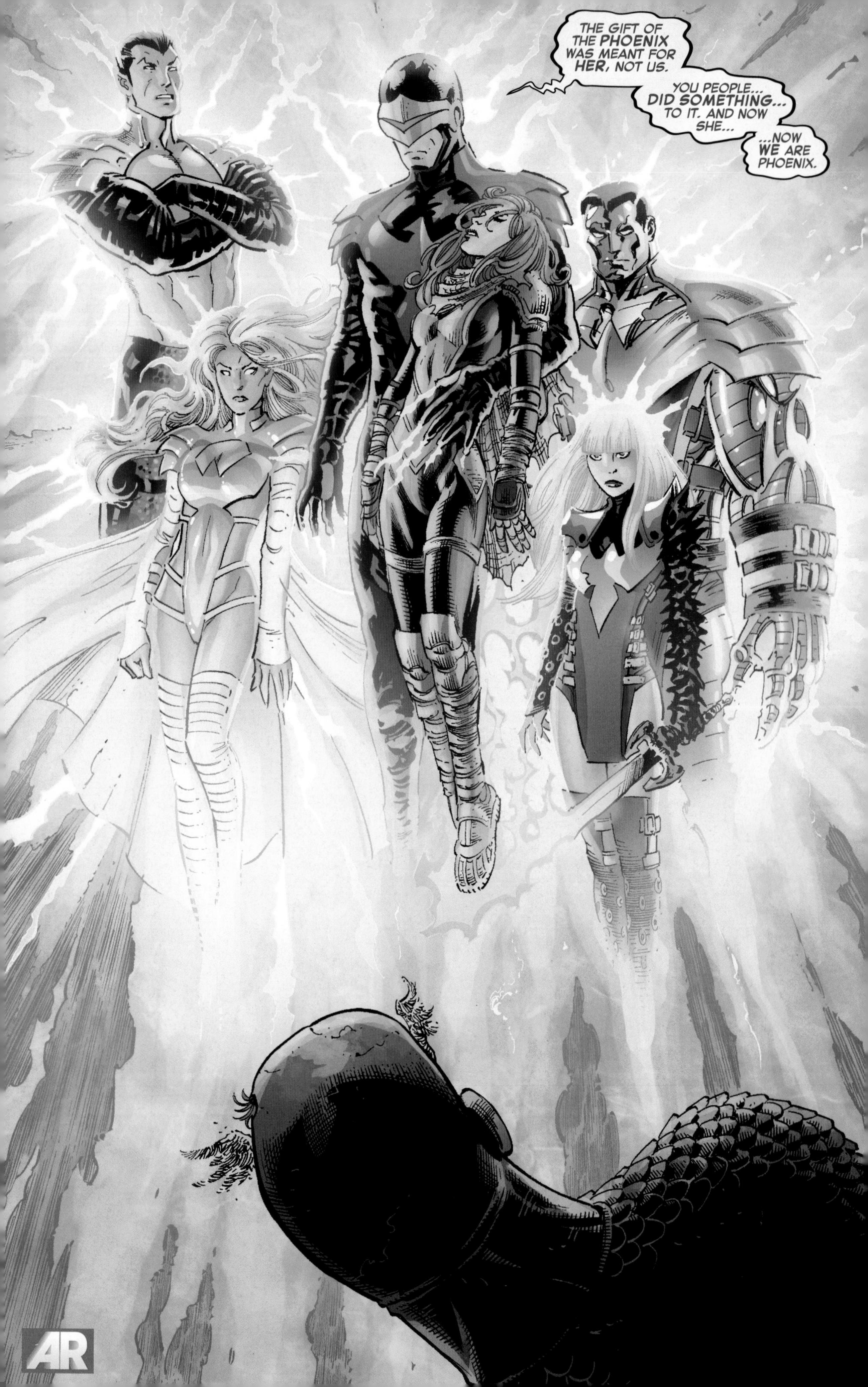
THE GIFT OF THE PHOENIX WAS MEANT FOR HER, NOT US.
YOU PEOPLE... DID SOMETHING... TO IT. AND NOW SHE...
...NOW WE ARE PHOENIX.

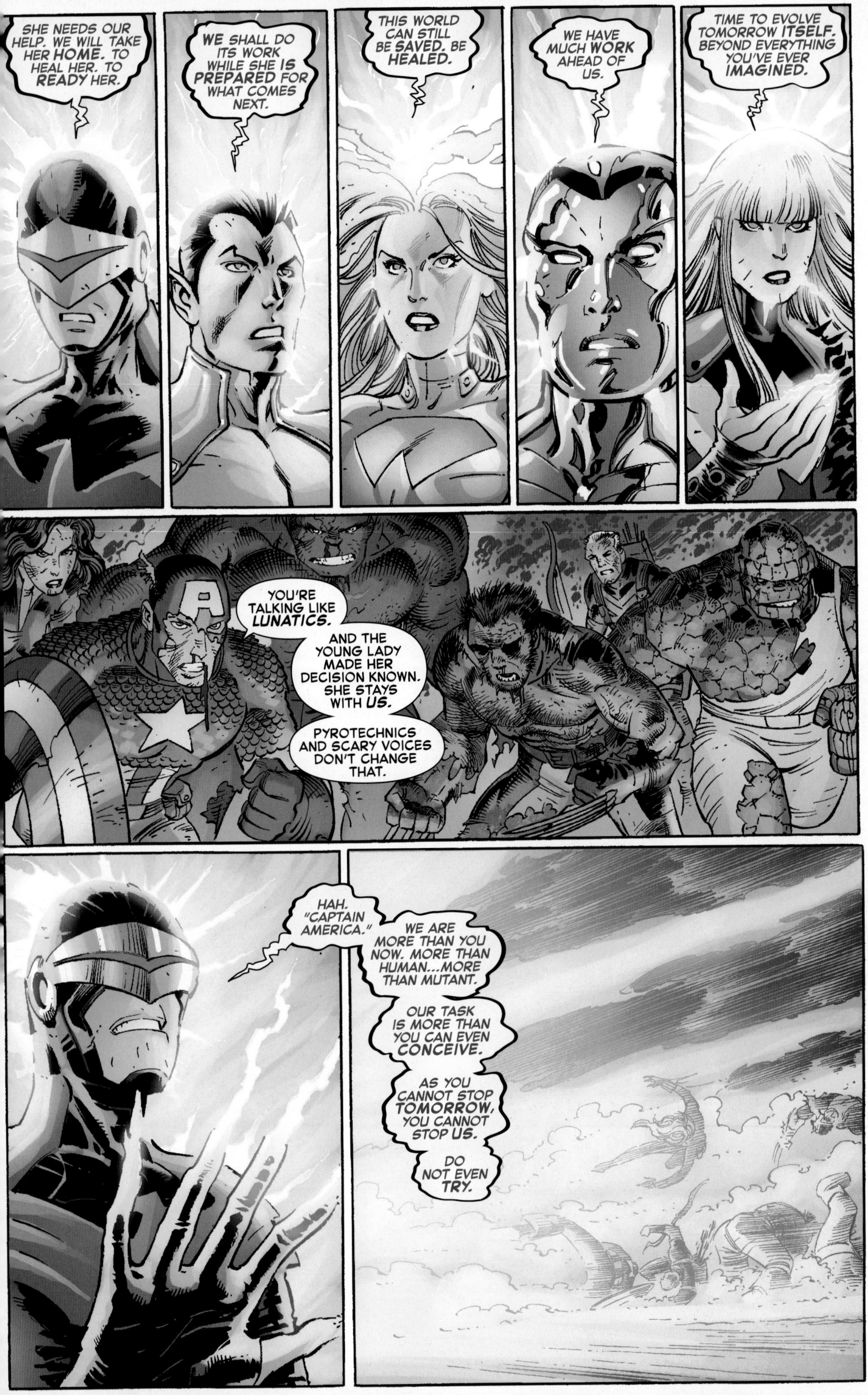
SHE NEEDS OUR HELP. WE WILL TAKE HER HOME. TO HEAL HER. TO READY HER.
WE SHALL DO ITS WORK WHILE SHE IS PREPARED FOR WHAT COMES NEXT.
THIS WORLD CAN STILL BE SAVED. BE HEALED.
WE HAVE MUCH WORK AHEAD OF US.
TIME TO EVOLVE TOMORROW ITSELF. BEYOND EVERYTHING YOU'VE EVER IMAGINED.
YOU'RE TALKING LIKE LUNATICS.
AND THE YOUNG LADY MADE HER DECISION KNOWN. SHE STAYS WITH US.
PYROTECHNICS AND SCARY VOICES DON'T CHANGE THAT.
HAH. "CAPTAIN AMERICA."
WE ARE MORE THAN YOU NOW. MORE THAN HUMAN...MORE THAN MUTANT.
OUR TASK IS MORE THAN YOU CAN EVEN CONCEIVE.
AS YOU CANNOT STOP TOMORROW, YOU CANNOT STOP US.
DO NOT EVEN TRY.

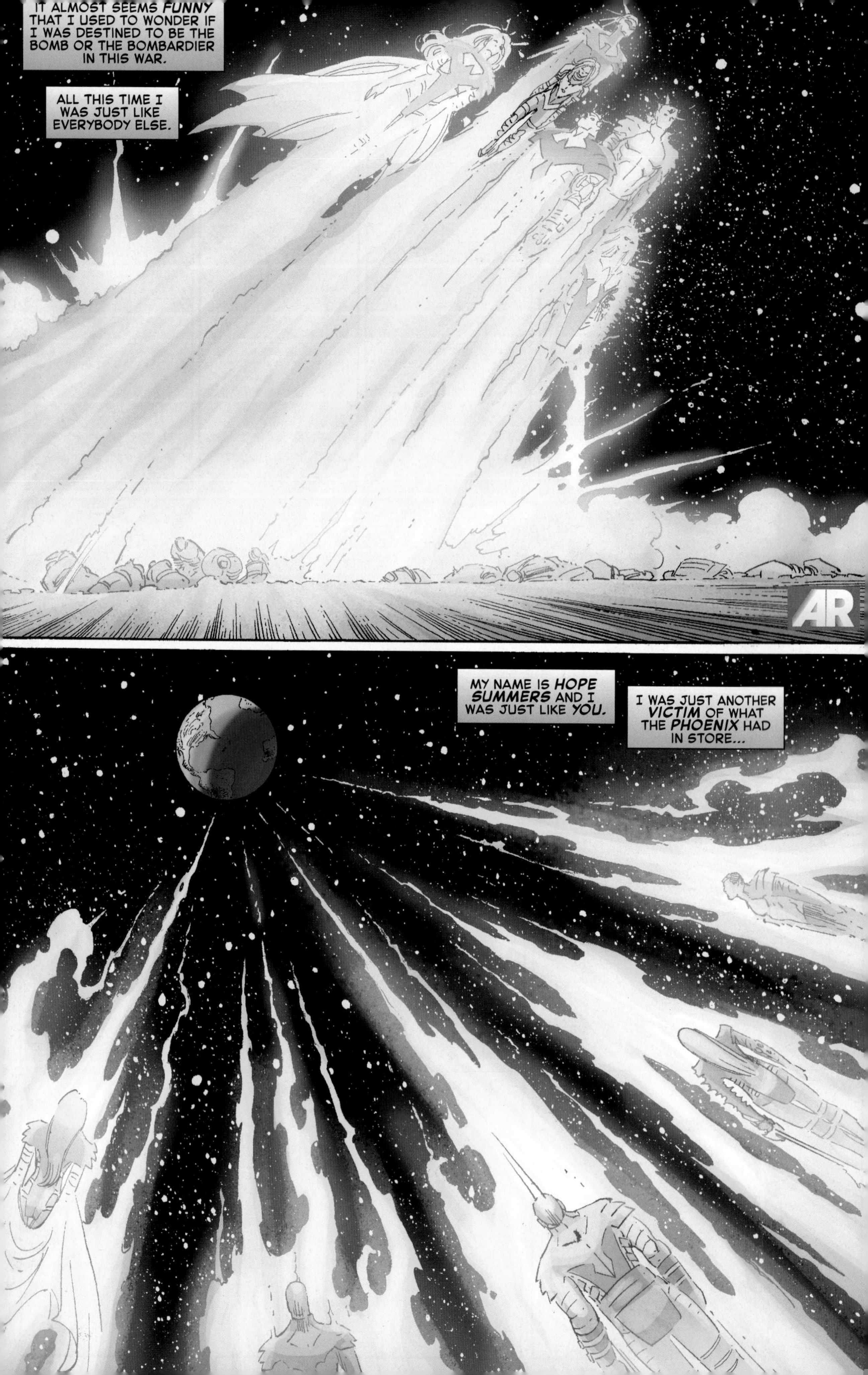
IT ALMOST SEEMS FUNNY THAT I USED TO WONDER IF I WAS DESTINED TO BE THE BOMB OR THE BOMBARDIER IN THIS WAR.
ALL THIS TIME I WAS JUST LIKE EVERYBODY ELSE.
MY NAME IS HOPE SUMMERS AND I WAS JUST LIKE YOU.
I WAS JUST ANOTHER VICTIM OF WHAT THE PHOENIX HAD IN STORE...

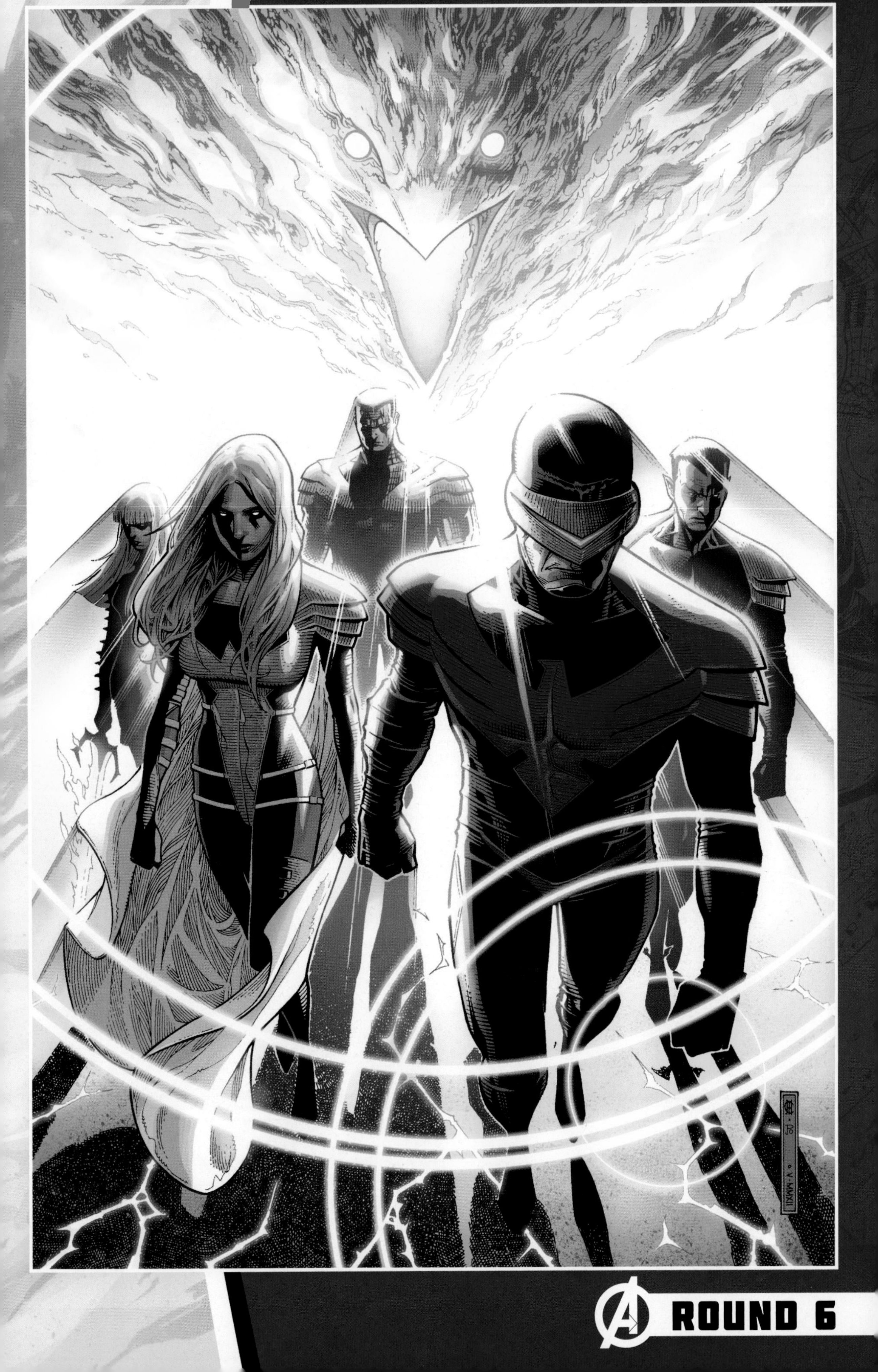

ROUND 6

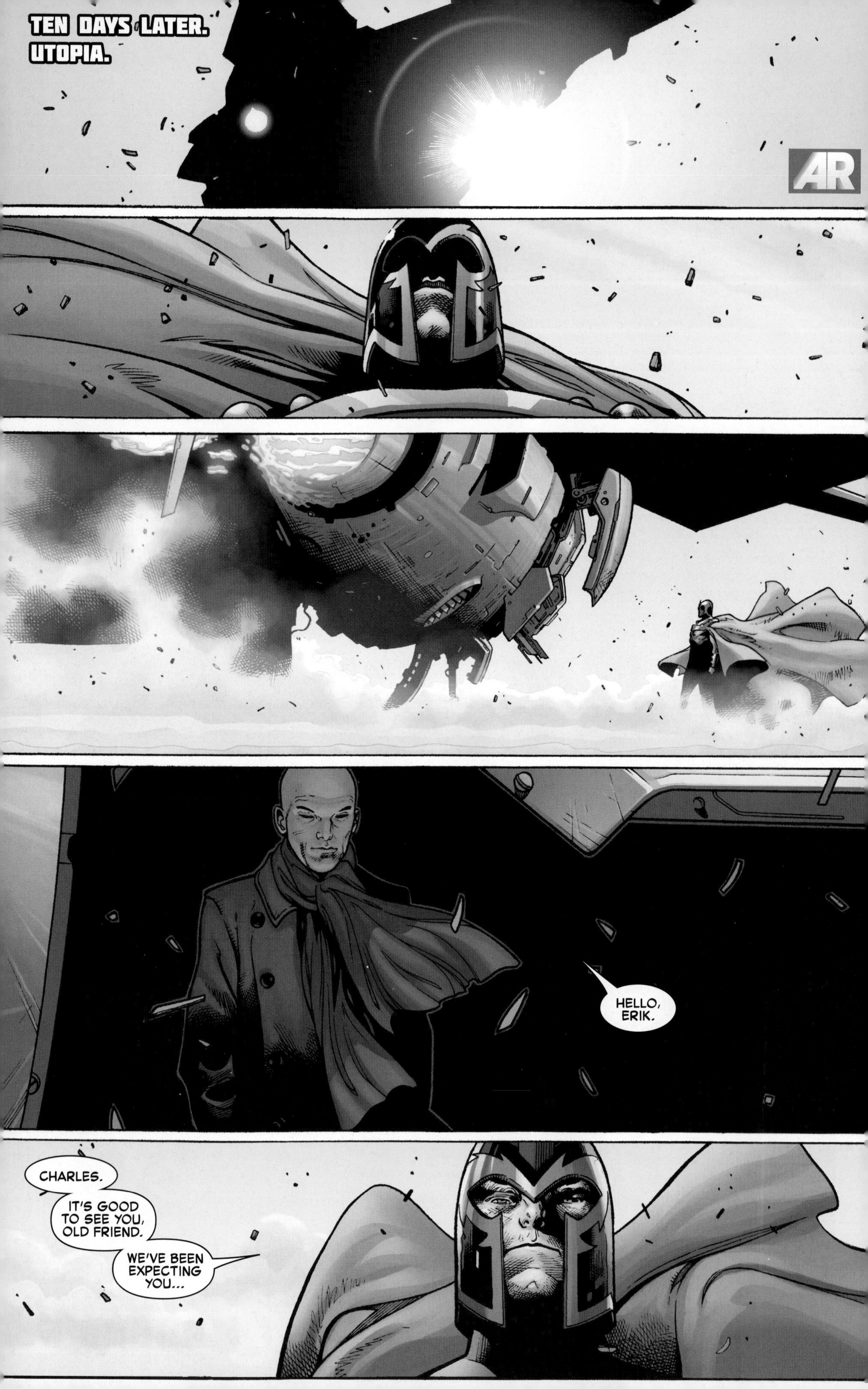
TEN DAYS LATER.
UTOPIA.
AR
HELLO, ERIK.
CHARLES.
IT'S GOOD TO SEE YOU, OLD FRIEND.
WE'VE BEEN EXPECTING YOU...

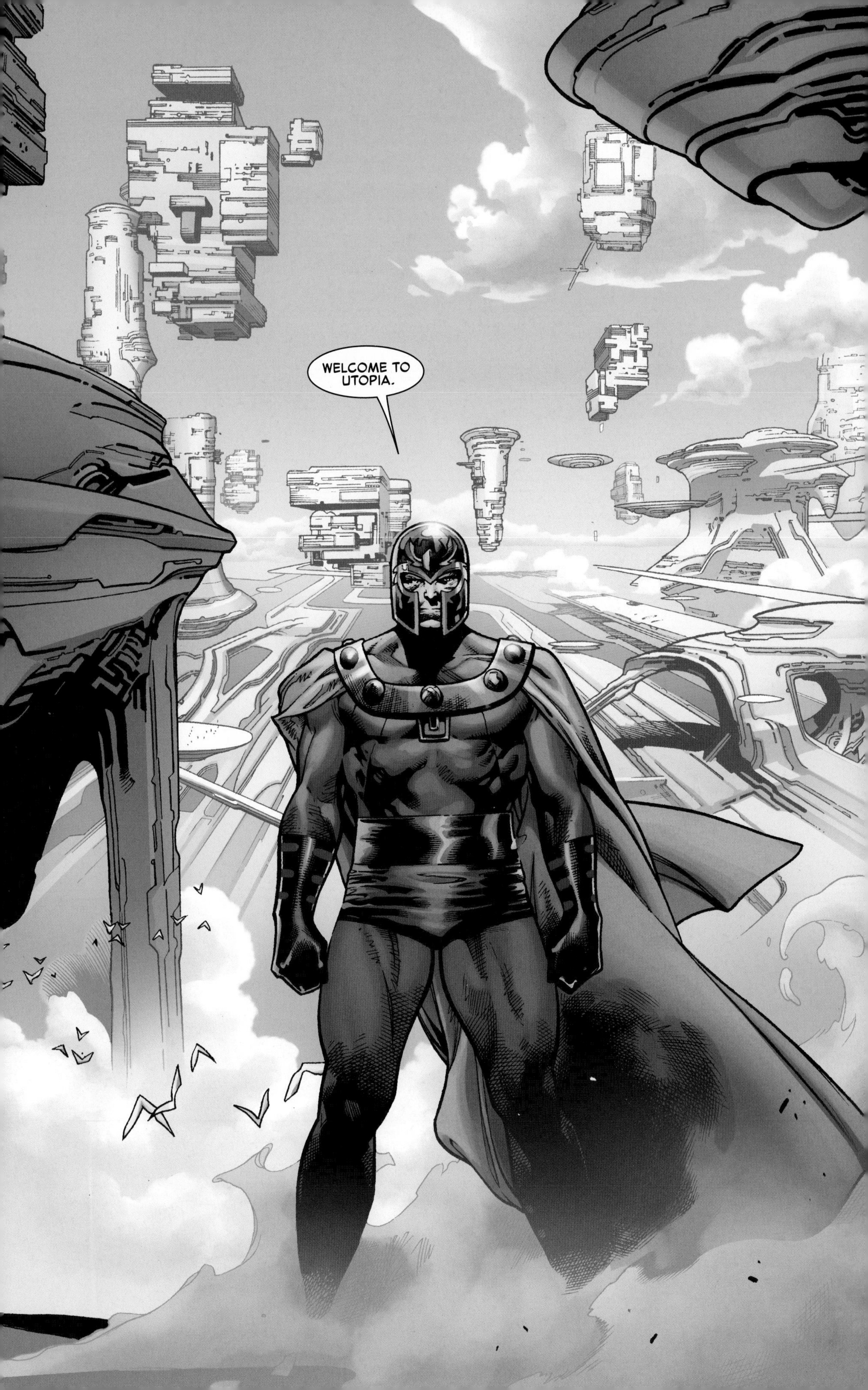
WELCOME TO UTOPIA.

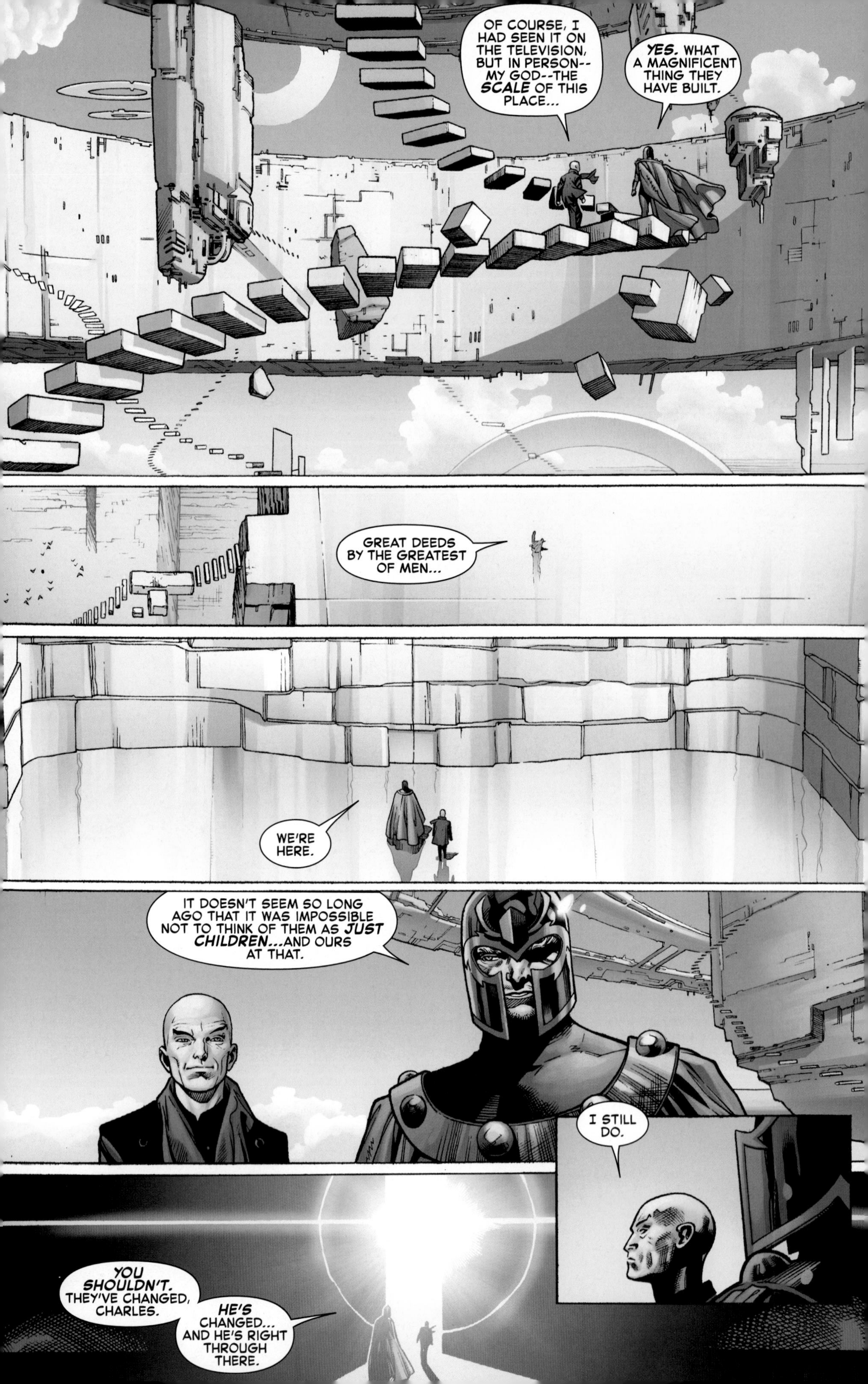
OF COURSE, I HAD SEEN IT ON THE TELEVISION, BUT IN PERSON-- MY GOD--THE SCALE OF THIS PLACE...
YES. WHAT A MAGNIFICENT THING THEY HAVE BUILT.
GREAT DEEDS BY THE GREATEST OF MEN...
WE'RE HERE.
IT DOESN'T SEEM SO LONG AGO THAT IT WAS IMPOSSIBLE NOT TO THINK OF THEM AS JUST CHILDREN...AND OURS AT THAT.
I STILL DO.
YOU SHOULDN'T. THEY'VE CHANGED, CHARLES.
HE'S CHANGED... AND HE'S RIGHT THROUGH THERE.

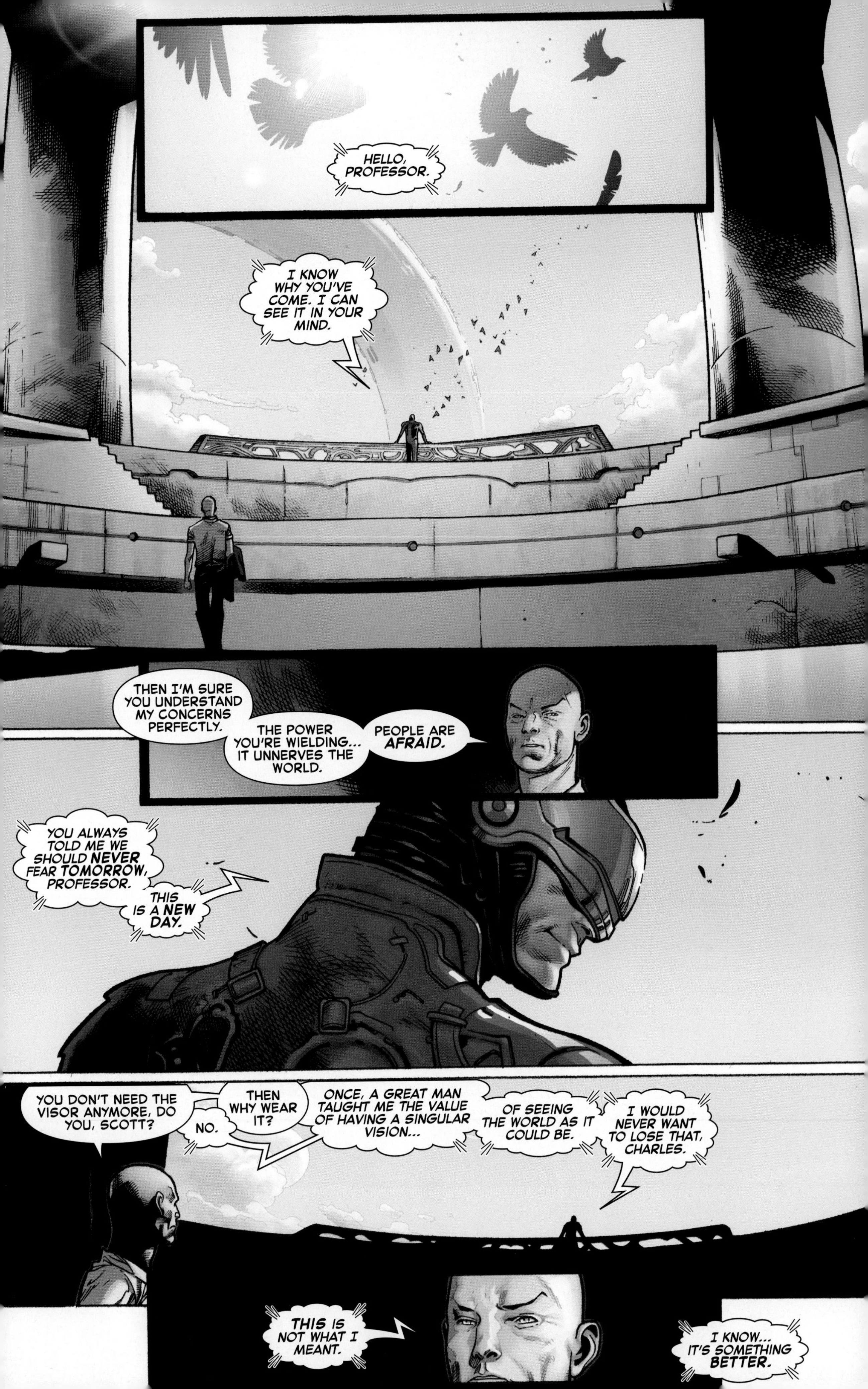
HELLO, PROFESSOR.
I KNOW WHY YOU'VE COME. I CAN SEE IT IN YOUR MIND.
THEN I'M SURE YOU UNDERSTAND MY CONCERNS PERFECTLY.
THE POWER YOU'RE WIELDING... IT UNNERVES THE WORLD.
PEOPLE ARE AFRAID.
YOU ALWAYS TOLD ME WE SHOULD NEVER FEAR TOMORROW, PROFESSOR.
THIS IS A NEW DAY.
YOU DON'T NEED THE VISOR ANYMORE, DO YOU, SCOTT?
NO.
THEN WHY WEAR IT?
ONCE, A GREAT MAN TAUGHT ME THE VALUE OF HAVING A SINGULAR VISION...
OF SEEING THE WORLD AS IT COULD BE.
I WOULD NEVER WANT TO LOSE THAT, CHARLES.
THIS IS NOT WHAT I MEANT.
I KNOW... IT'S SOMETHING BETTER.

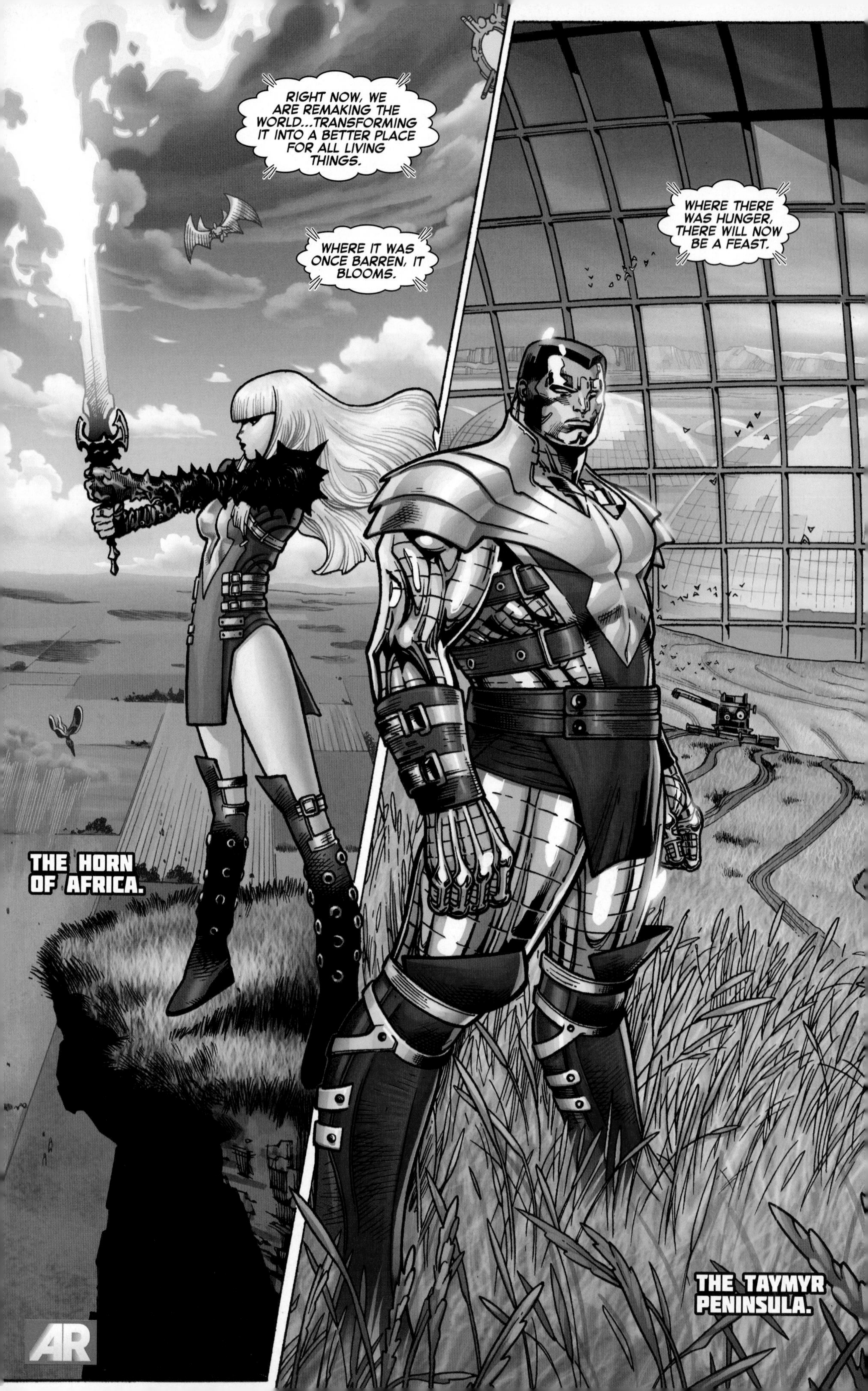
RIGHT NOW, WE ARE REMAKING THE WORLD...TRANSFORMING IT INTO A BETTER PLACE FOR ALL LIVING THINGS.
WHERE IT WAS ONCE BARREN, IT BLOOMS.
WHERE THERE WAS HUNGER, THERE WILL NOW BE A FEAST.
THE HORN OF AFRICA.
THE TAYMYR PENINSULA.
AR

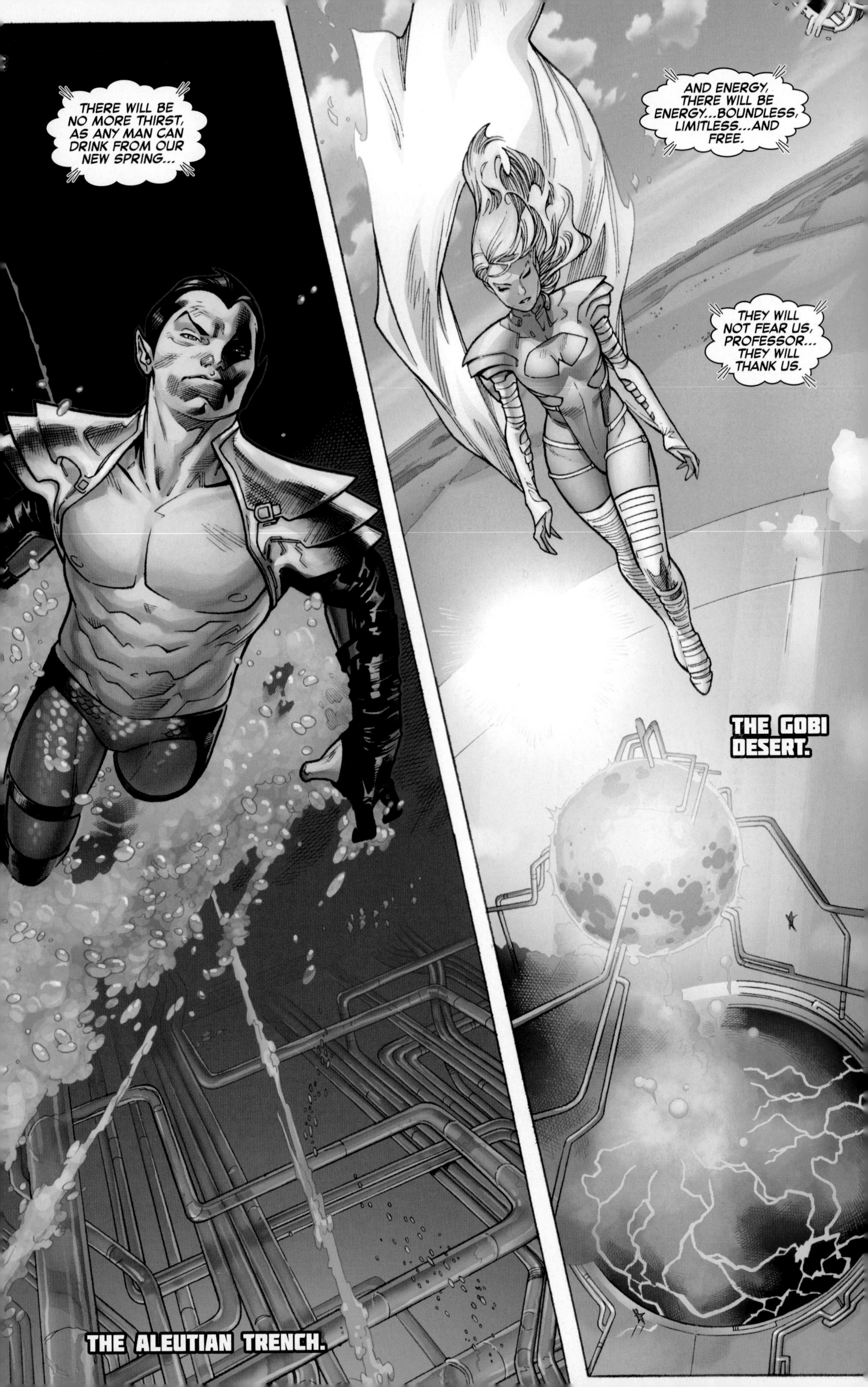
THE ALEUTIAN TRENCH.
THERE WILL BE NO MORE THIRST, AS ANY MAN CAN DRINK FROM OUR NEW SPRING...
THE GOBI DESERT.
AND ENERGY, THERE WILL BE ENERGY...BOUNDLESS, LIMITLESS...AND FREE.
THEY WILL NOT FEAR US, PROFESSOR... THEY WILL THANK US.

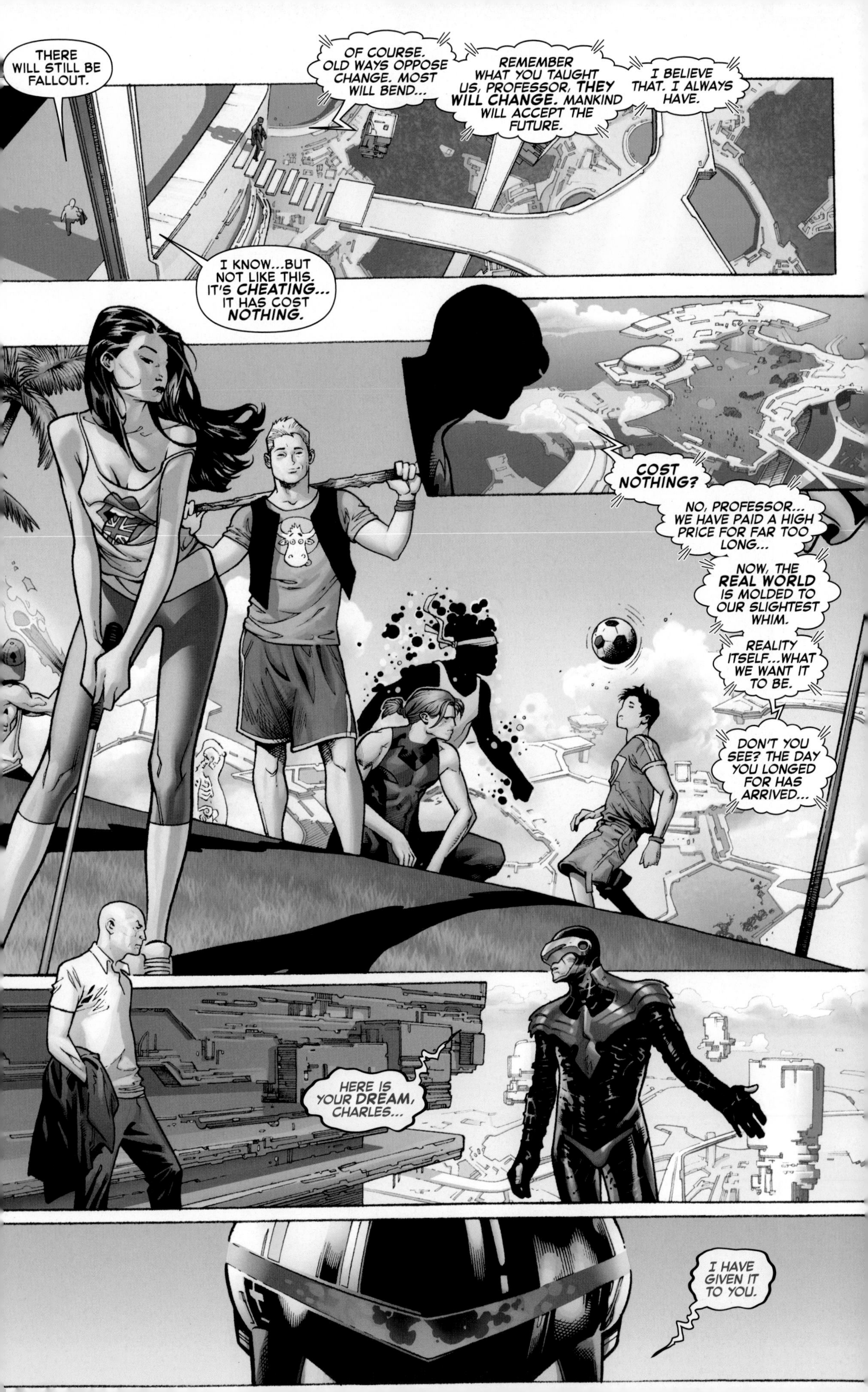
THERE WILL STILL BE FALLOUT.
OF COURSE. OLD WAYS OPPOSE CHANGE. MOST WILL BEND...
REMEMBER WHAT YOU TAUGHT US, PROFESSOR, THEY WILL CHANGE. MANKIND WILL ACCEPT THE FUTURE.
I BELIEVE THAT. I ALWAYS HAVE.
I KNOW...BUT NOT LIKE THIS. IT'S CHEATING... IT HAS COST NOTHING.
COST NOTHING?
NO, PROFESSOR... WE HAVE PAID A HIGH PRICE FOR FAR TOO LONG...
NOW, THE REAL WORLD IS MOLDED TO OUR SLIGHTEST WHIM.
REALITY ITSELF...WHAT WE WANT IT TO BE.
DON'T YOU SEE? THE DAY YOU LONGED FOR HAS ARRIVED...
HERE IS YOUR DREAM, CHARLES...
I HAVE GIVEN IT TO YOU.

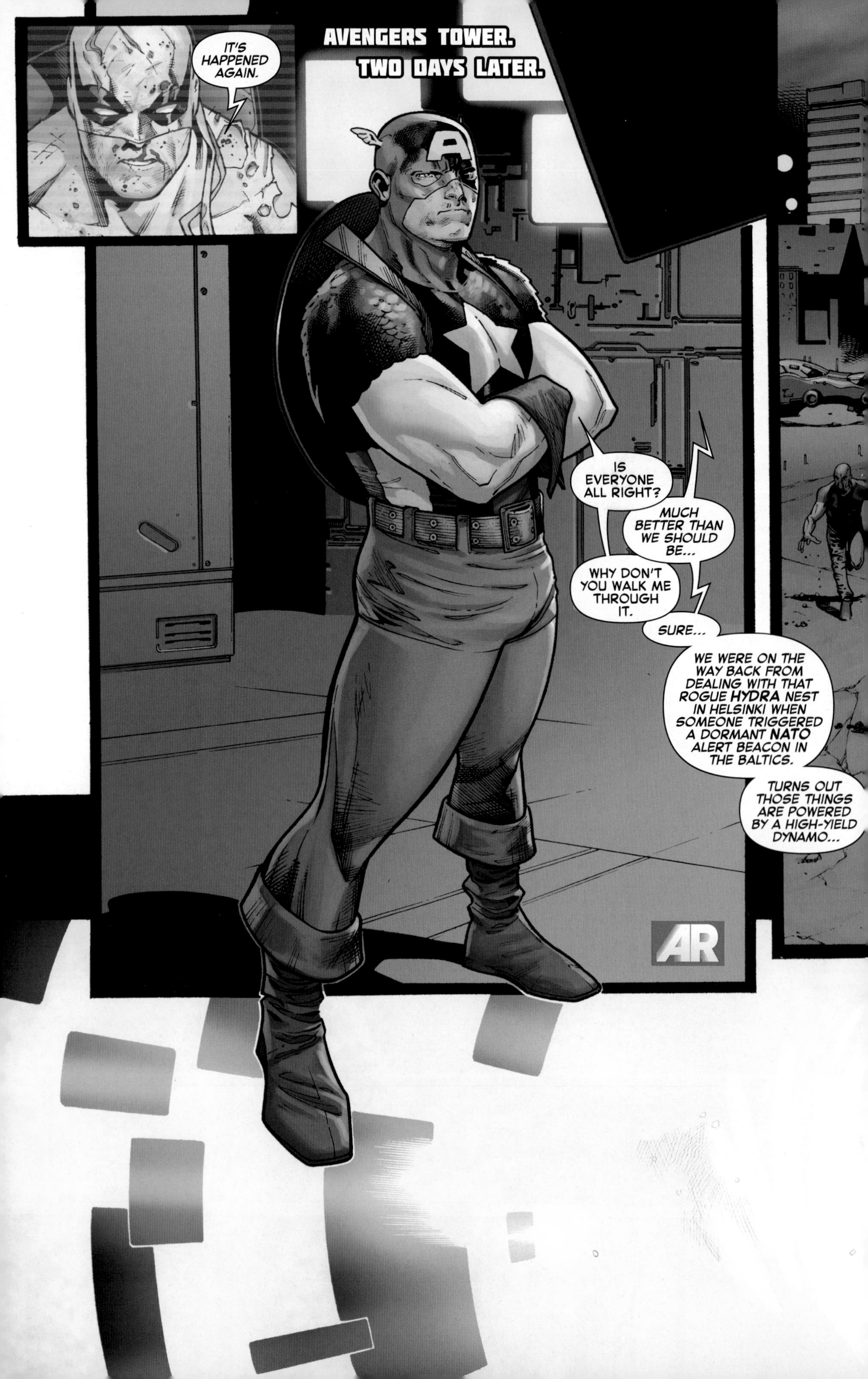
AVENGERS TOWER.
TWO DAYS LATER.
IT'S HAPPENED AGAIN.
IS EVERYONE ALL RIGHT?
MUCH BETTER THAN WE SHOULD BE...
WHY DON'T YOU WALK ME THROUGH IT.
SURE...
WE WERE ON THE WAY BACK FROM DEALING WITH THAT ROGUE HYDRA NEST IN HELSINKI WHEN SOMEONE TRIGGERED A DORMANT NATO ALERT BEACON IN THE BALTICS.
TURNS OUT THOSE THINGS ARE POWERED BY A HIGH-YIELD DYNAMO...

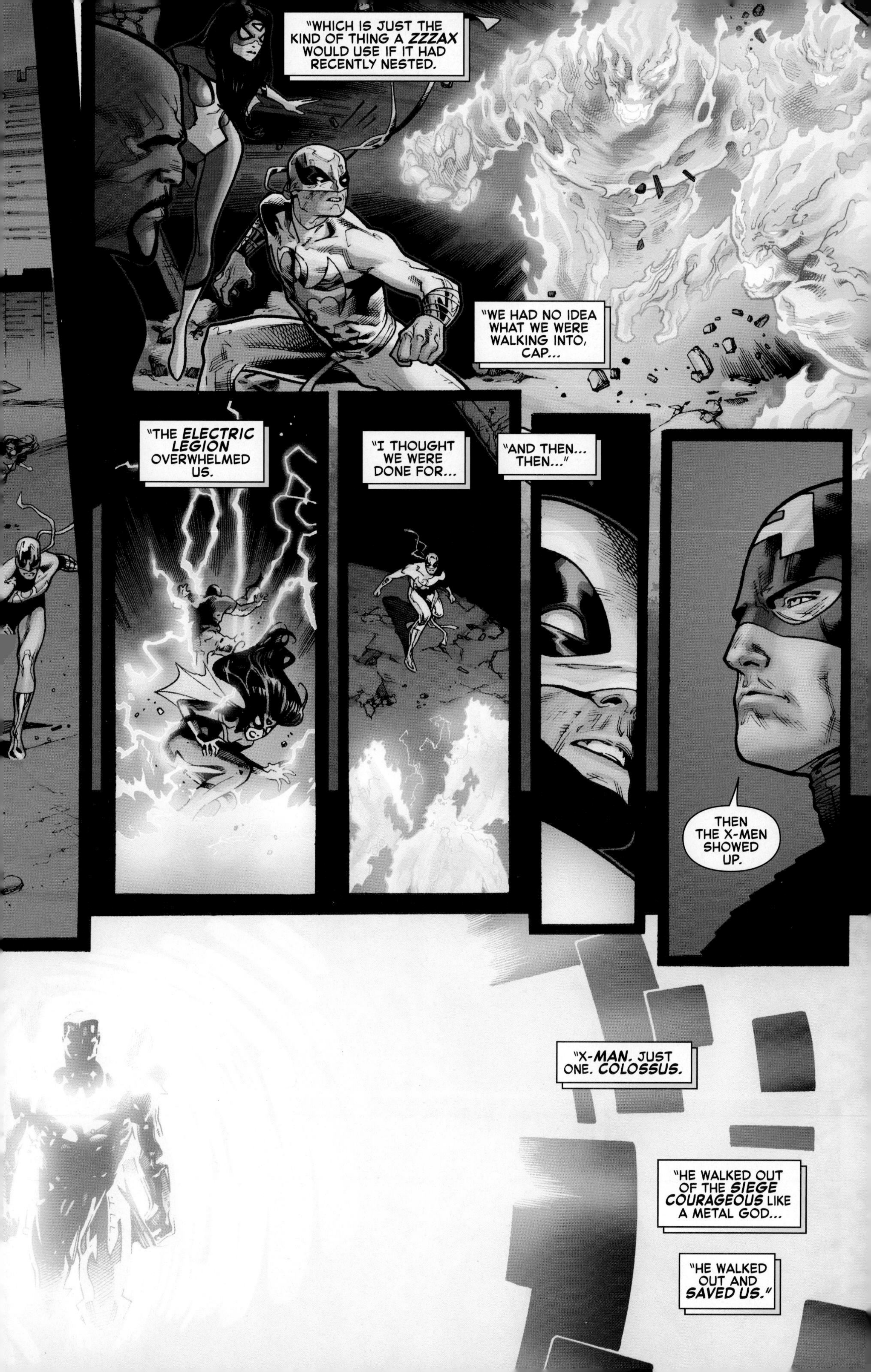

"WHICH IS JUST THE KIND OF THING A ZZZAX WOULD USE IF IT HAD RECENTLY NESTED.
"WE HAD NO IDEA WHAT WE WERE WALKING INTO, CAP...
"THE ELECTRIC LEGION OVERWHELMED US.
"I THOUGHT WE WERE DONE FOR...
"AND THEN... THEN..."
THEN THE X-MEN SHOWED UP.
"X-MAN. JUST ONE. COLOSSUS.
"HE WALKED OUT OF THE SIEGE COURAGEOUS LIKE A METAL GOD...
"HE WALKED OUT AND SAVED US."

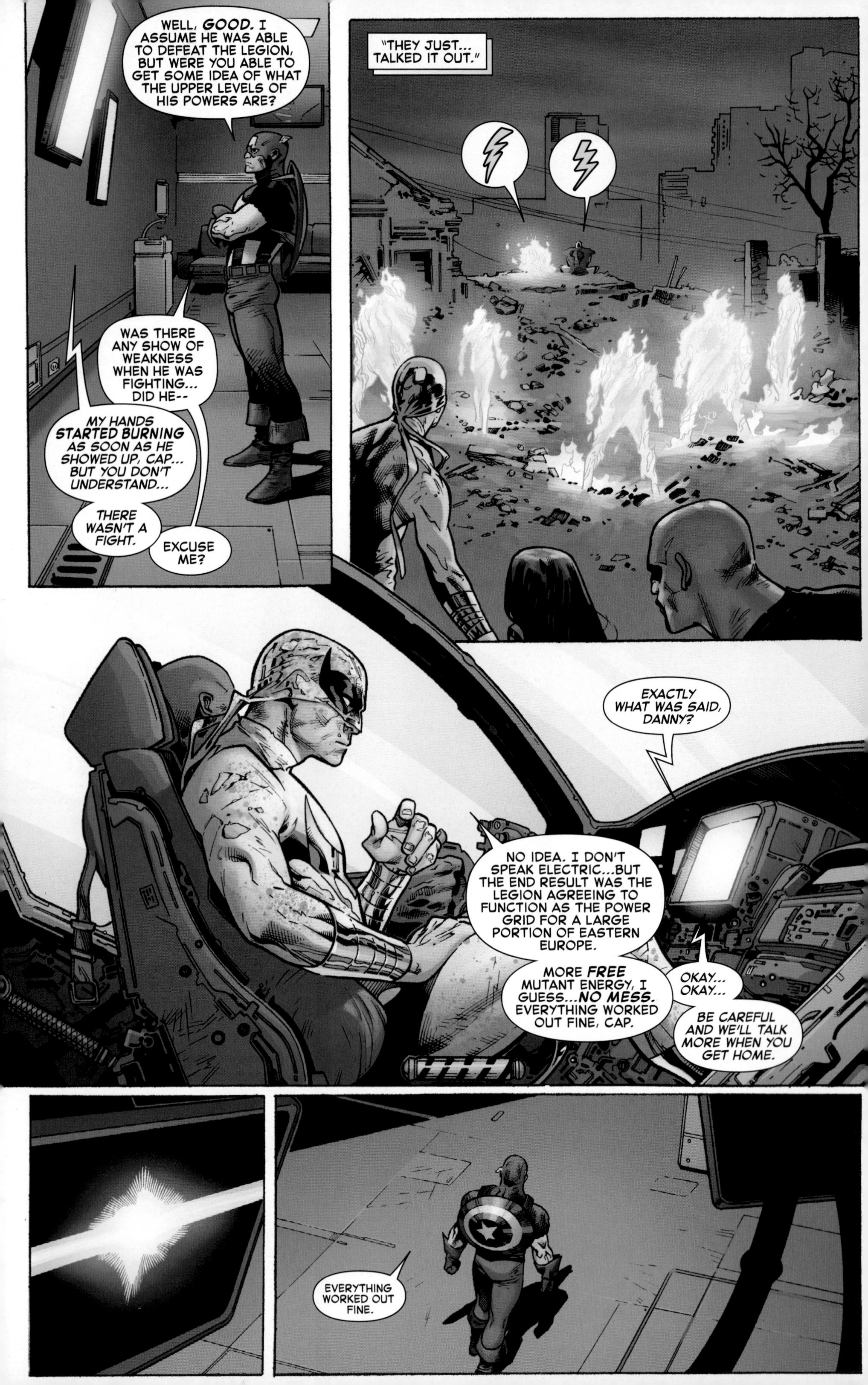
WELL, GOOD. I ASSUME HE WAS ABLE TO DEFEAT THE LEGION, BUT WERE YOU ABLE TO GET SOME IDEA OF WHAT THE UPPER LEVELS OF HIS POWERS ARE?
WAS THERE ANY SHOW OF WEAKNESS WHEN HE WAS FIGHTING... DID HE--
MY HANDS STARTED BURNING AS SOON AS HE SHOWED UP, CAP... BUT YOU DON'T UNDERSTAND...
THERE WASN'T A FIGHT.
EXCUSE ME?
"THEY JUST... TALKED IT OUT."
EXACTLY WHAT WAS SAID, DANNY?
NO IDEA. I DON'T SPEAK ELECTRIC...BUT THE END RESULT WAS THE LEGION AGREEING TO FUNCTION AS THE POWER GRID FOR A LARGE PORTION OF EASTERN EUROPE.
MORE FREE MUTANT ENERGY, I GUESS...NO MESS. EVERYTHING WORKED OUT FINE, CAP.
OKAY... OKAY...
BE CAREFUL AND WE'LL TALK MORE WHEN YOU GET HOME.
EVERYTHING WORKED OUT FINE.

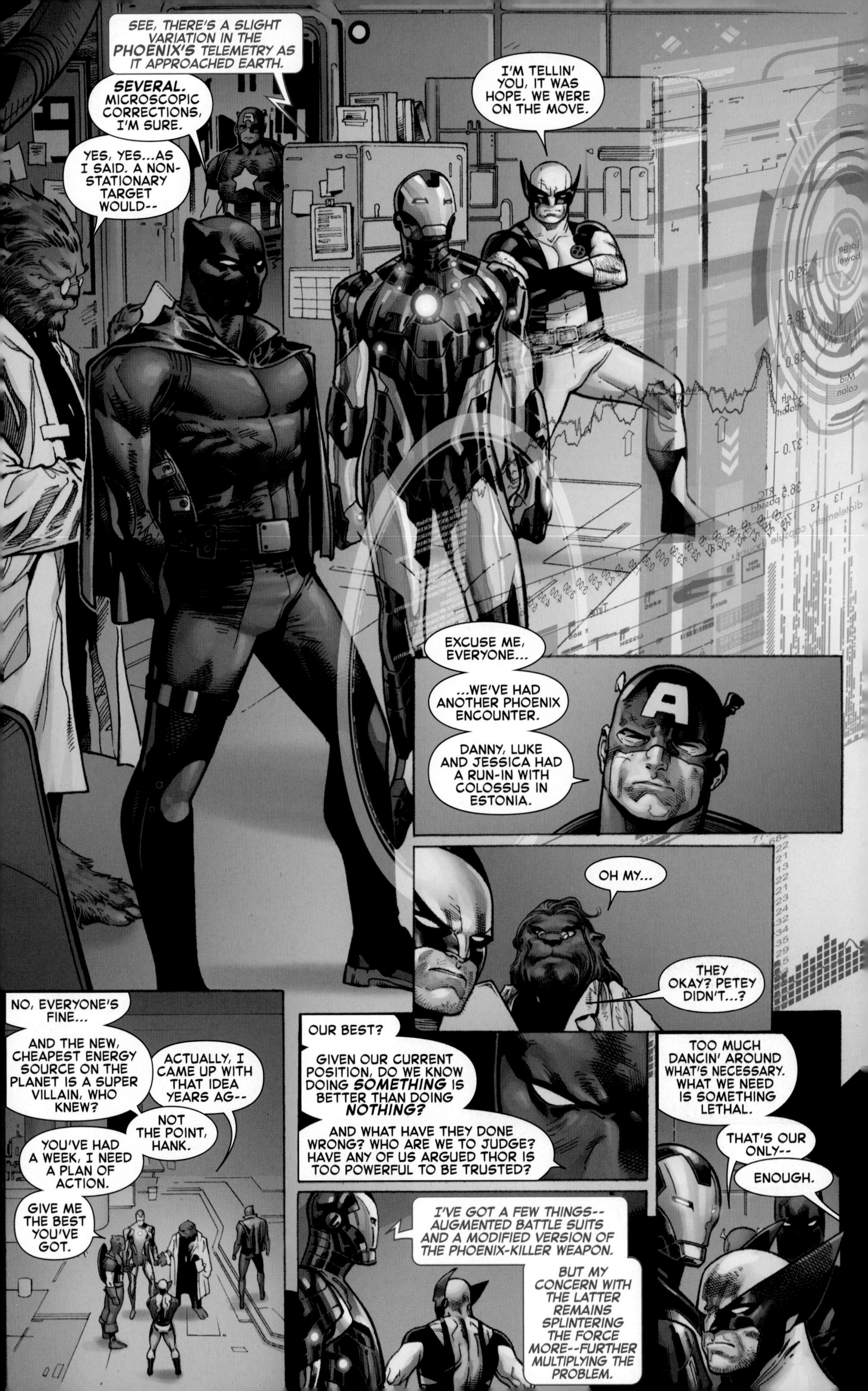
SEE, THERE'S A SLIGHT VARIATION IN THE PHOENIX'S TELEMETRY AS IT APPROACHED EARTH.
SEVERAL. MICROSCOPIC CORRECTIONS, I'M SURE.
YES, YES...AS I SAID. A NON-STATIONARY TARGET WOULD--
I'M TELLIN' YOU, IT WAS HOPE. WE WERE ON THE MOVE.
EXCUSE ME, EVERYONE...
...WE'VE HAD ANOTHER PHOENIX ENCOUNTER.
DANNY, LUKE AND JESSICA HAD A RUN-IN WITH COLOSSUS IN ESTONIA.
OH MY...
THEY OKAY? PETEY DIDN'T...?
NO, EVERYONE'S FINE...
AND THE NEW, CHEAPEST ENERGY SOURCE ON THE PLANET IS A SUPER VILLAIN, WHO KNEW?
ACTUALLY, I CAME UP WITH THAT IDEA YEARS AG--
NOT THE POINT, HANK.
YOU'VE HAD A WEEK, I NEED A PLAN OF ACTION.
GIVE ME THE BEST YOU'VE GOT.
OUR BEST?
GIVEN OUR CURRENT POSITION, DO WE KNOW DOING SOMETHING IS BETTER THAN DOING NOTHING?
AND WHAT HAVE THEY DONE WRONG? WHO ARE WE TO JUDGE? HAVE ANY OF US ARGUED THOR IS TOO POWERFUL TO BE TRUSTED?
TOO MUCH DANCIN' AROUND WHAT'S NECESSARY. WHAT WE NEED IS SOMETHING LETHAL.
THAT'S OUR ONLY--
ENOUGH.
I'VE GOT A FEW THINGS--AUGMENTED BATTLE SUITS AND A MODIFIED VERSION OF THE PHOENIX-KILLER WEAPON.
BUT MY CONCERN WITH THE LATTER REMAINS SPLINTERING THE FORCE MORE--FURTHER MULTIPLYING THE PROBLEM.

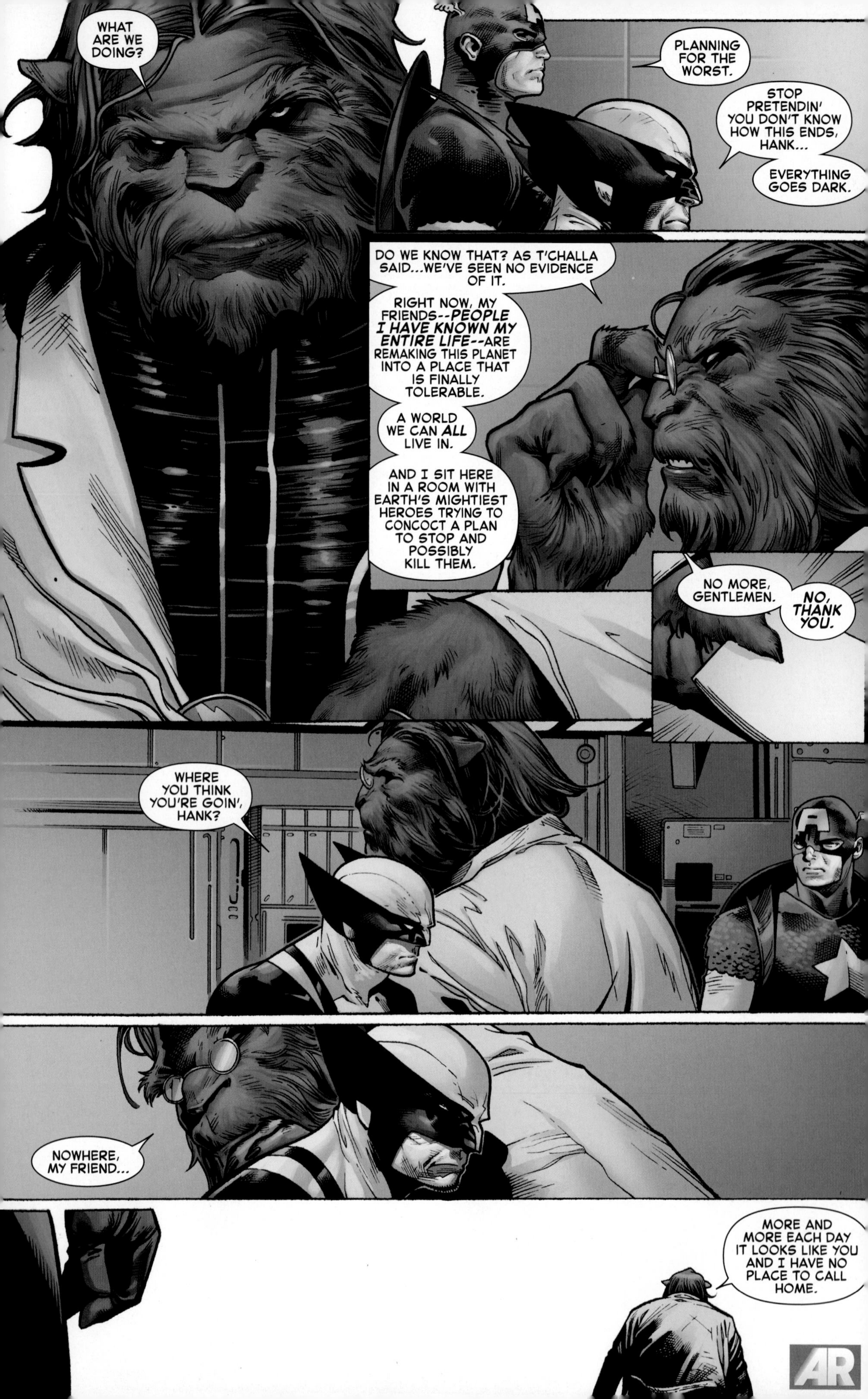
WHAT ARE WE DOING?
PLANNING FOR THE WORST.
STOP PRETENDIN' YOU DON'T KNOW HOW THIS ENDS, HANK...
EVERYTHING GOES DARK.
DO WE KNOW THAT? AS T'CHALLA SAID...WE'VE SEEN NO EVIDENCE OF IT.
RIGHT NOW, MY FRIENDS--PEOPLE I HAVE KNOWN MY ENTIRE LIFE--ARE REMAKING THIS PLANET INTO A PLACE THAT IS FINALLY TOLERABLE.
A WORLD WE CAN ALL LIVE IN.
AND I SIT HERE IN A ROOM WITH EARTH'S MIGHTIEST HEROES TRYING TO CONCOCT A PLAN TO STOP AND POSSIBLY KILL THEM.
NO MORE, GENTLEMEN.
NO, THANK YOU.
WHERE YOU THINK YOU'RE GOIN', HANK?
NOWHERE, MY FRIEND...
MORE AND MORE EACH DAY IT LOOKS LIKE YOU AND I HAVE NO PLACE TO CALL HOME.

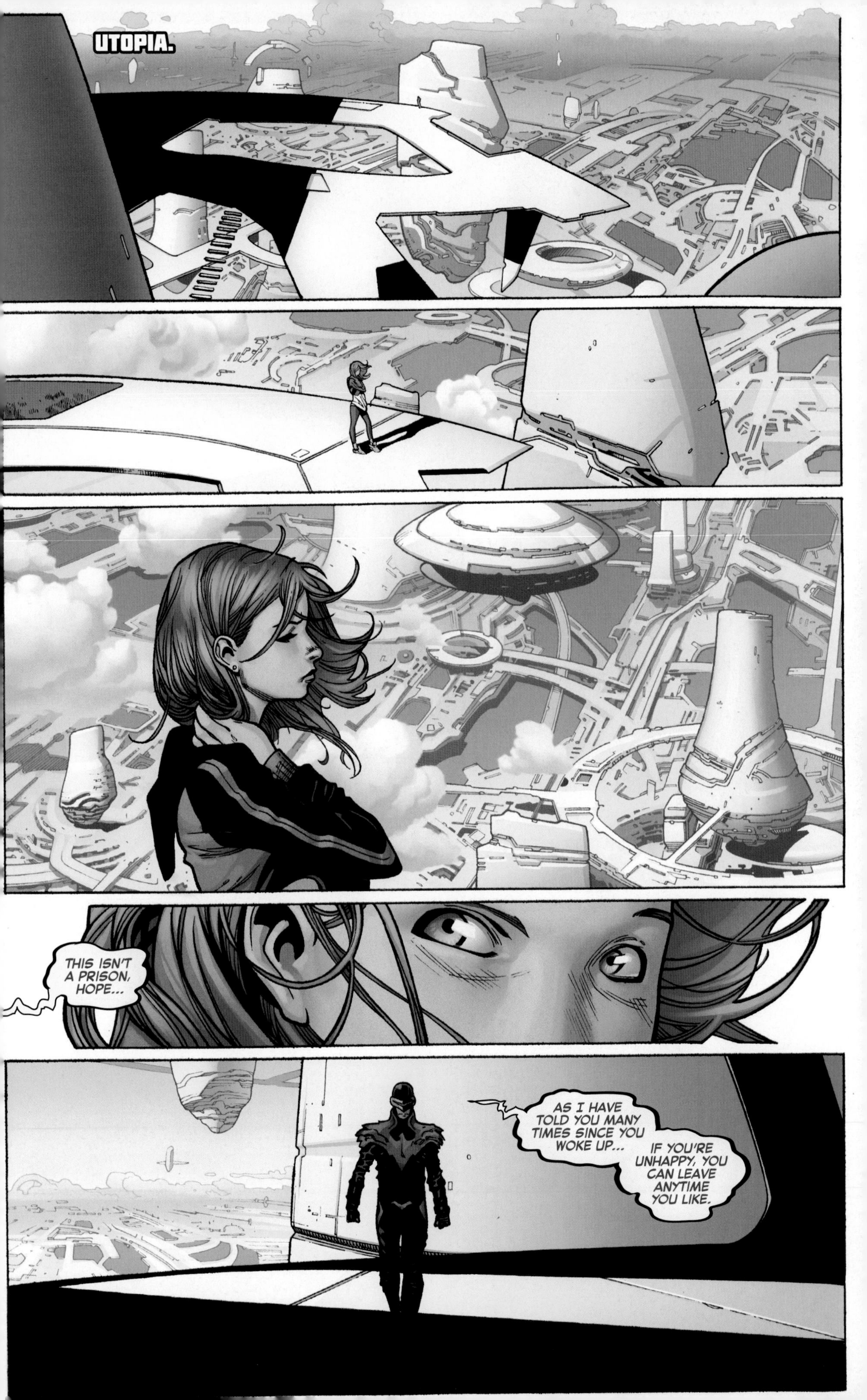
UTOPIA.
THIS ISN'T A PRISON, HOPE...
AS I HAVE TOLD YOU MANY TIMES SINCE YOU WOKE UP...
IF YOU'RE UNHAPPY, YOU CAN LEAVE ANYTIME YOU LIKE.

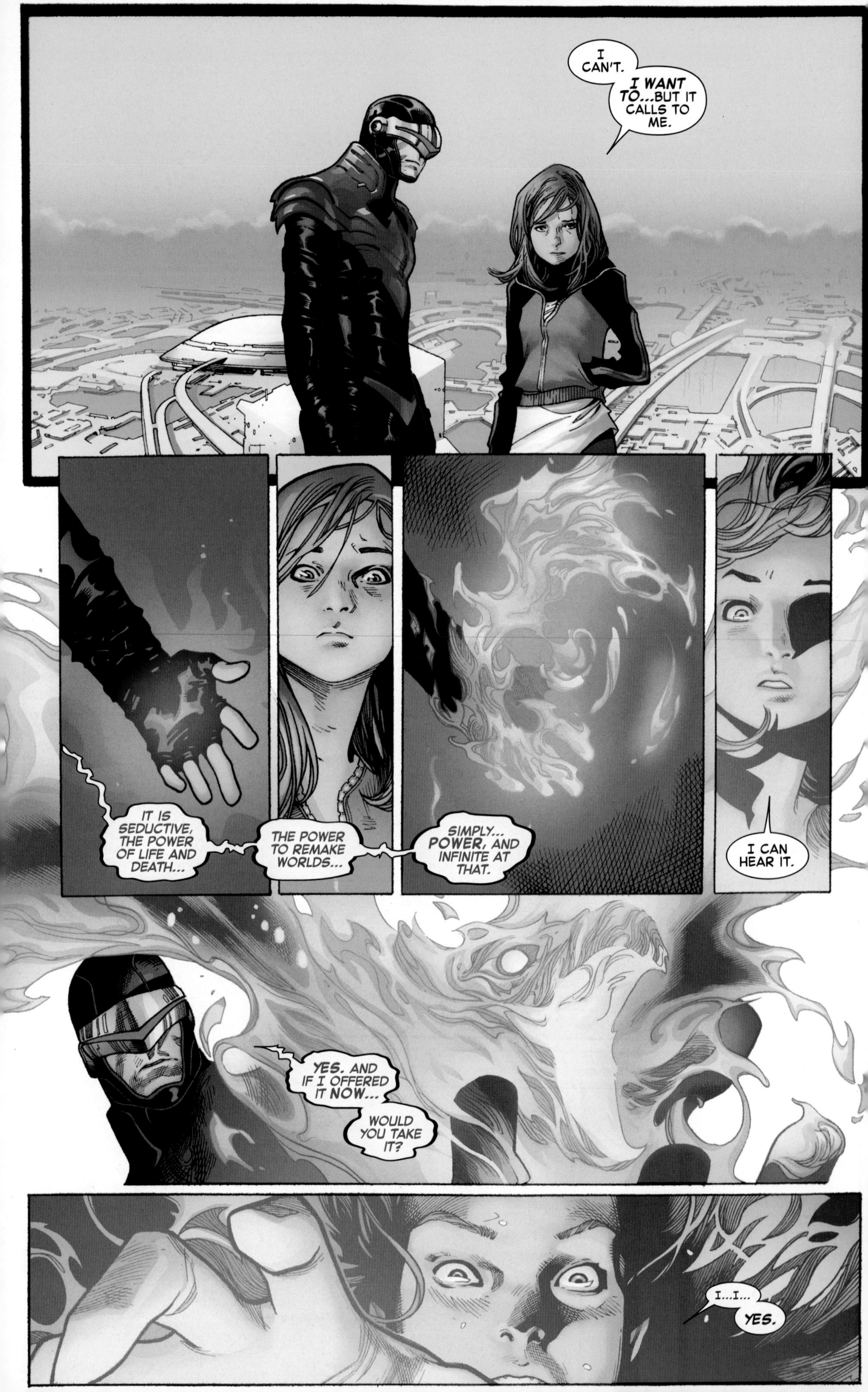
I CAN'T. I WANT TO...BUT IT CALLS TO ME.
IT IS SEDUCTIVE, THE POWER OF LIFE AND DEATH...
THE POWER TO REMAKE WORLDS...
SIMPLY... POWER, AND INFINITE AT THAT.
I CAN HEAR IT.
YES. AND IF I OFFERED IT NOW...
WOULD YOU TAKE IT?
I...I...
YES.

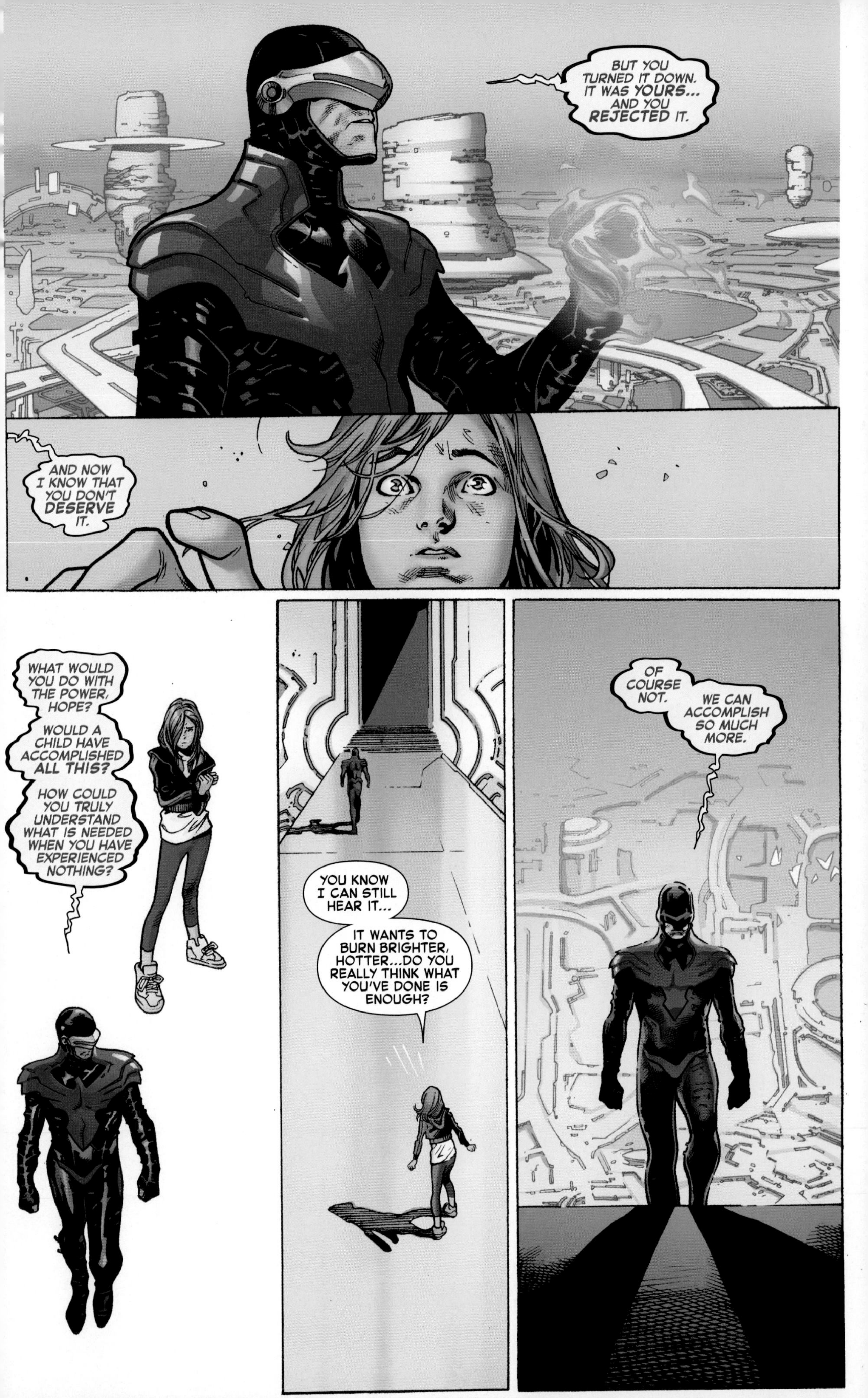
BUT YOU TURNED IT DOWN. IT WAS YOURS... AND YOU REJECTED IT.
AND NOW I KNOW THAT YOU DON'T DESERVE IT.
WHAT WOULD YOU DO WITH THE POWER, HOPE?
WOULD A CHILD HAVE ACCOMPLISHED ALL THIS?
HOW COULD YOU TRULY UNDERSTAND WHAT IS NEEDED WHEN YOU HAVE EXPERIENCED NOTHING?
YOU KNOW I CAN STILL HEAR IT...
IT WANTS TO BURN BRIGHTER, HOTTER...DO YOU REALLY THINK WHAT YOU'VE DONE IS ENOUGH?
OF COURSE NOT.
WE CAN ACCOMPLISH SO MUCH MORE.

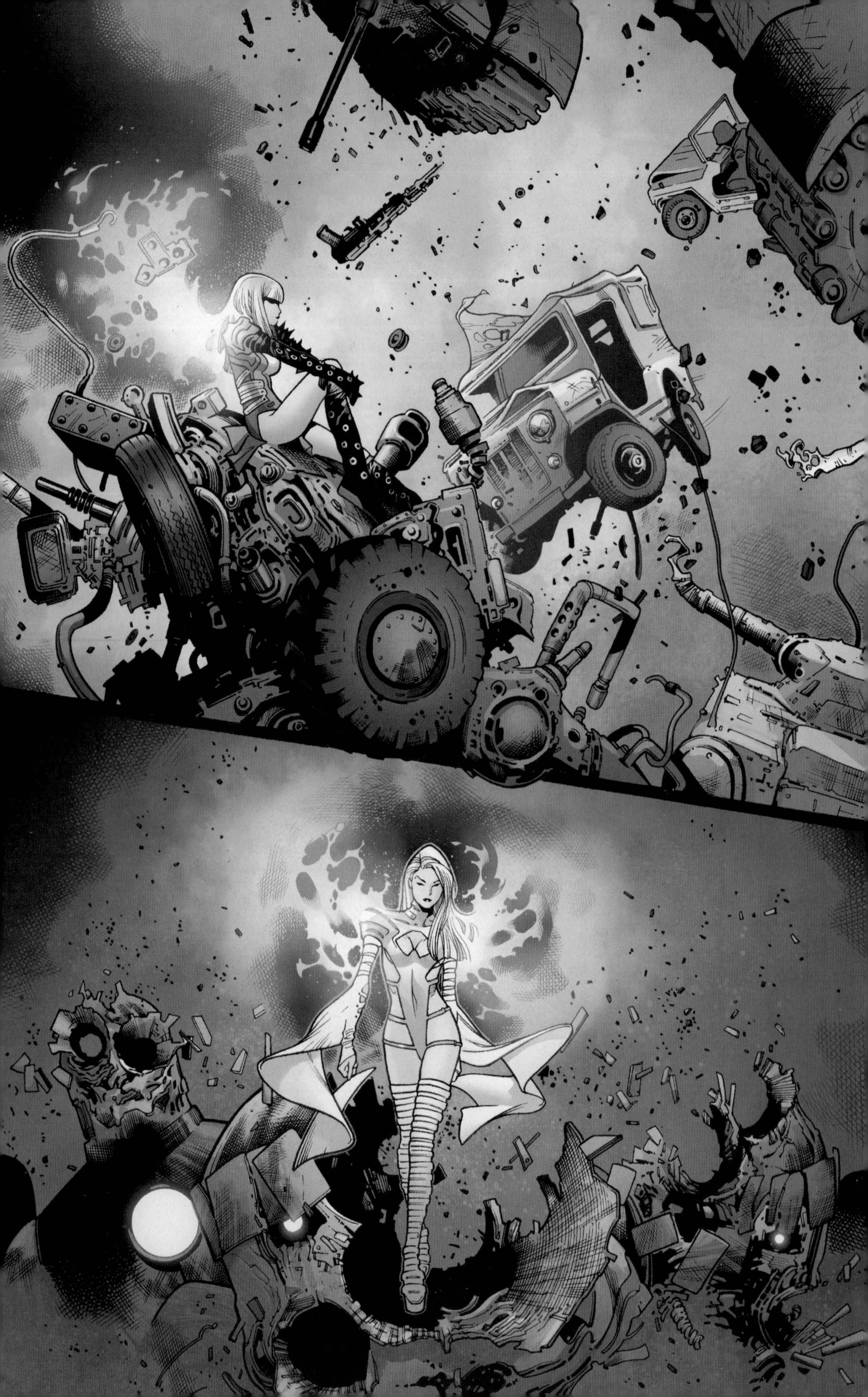

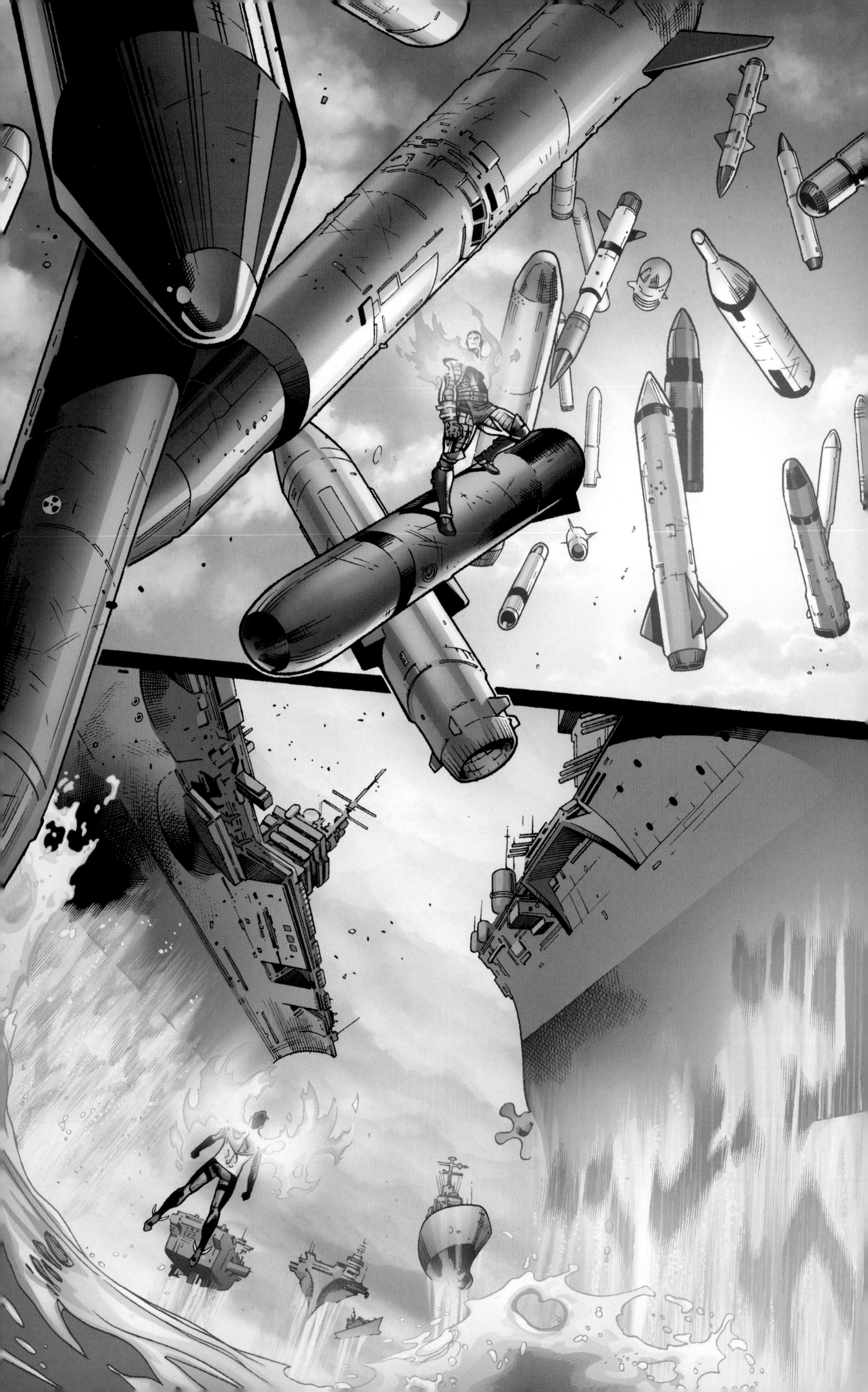

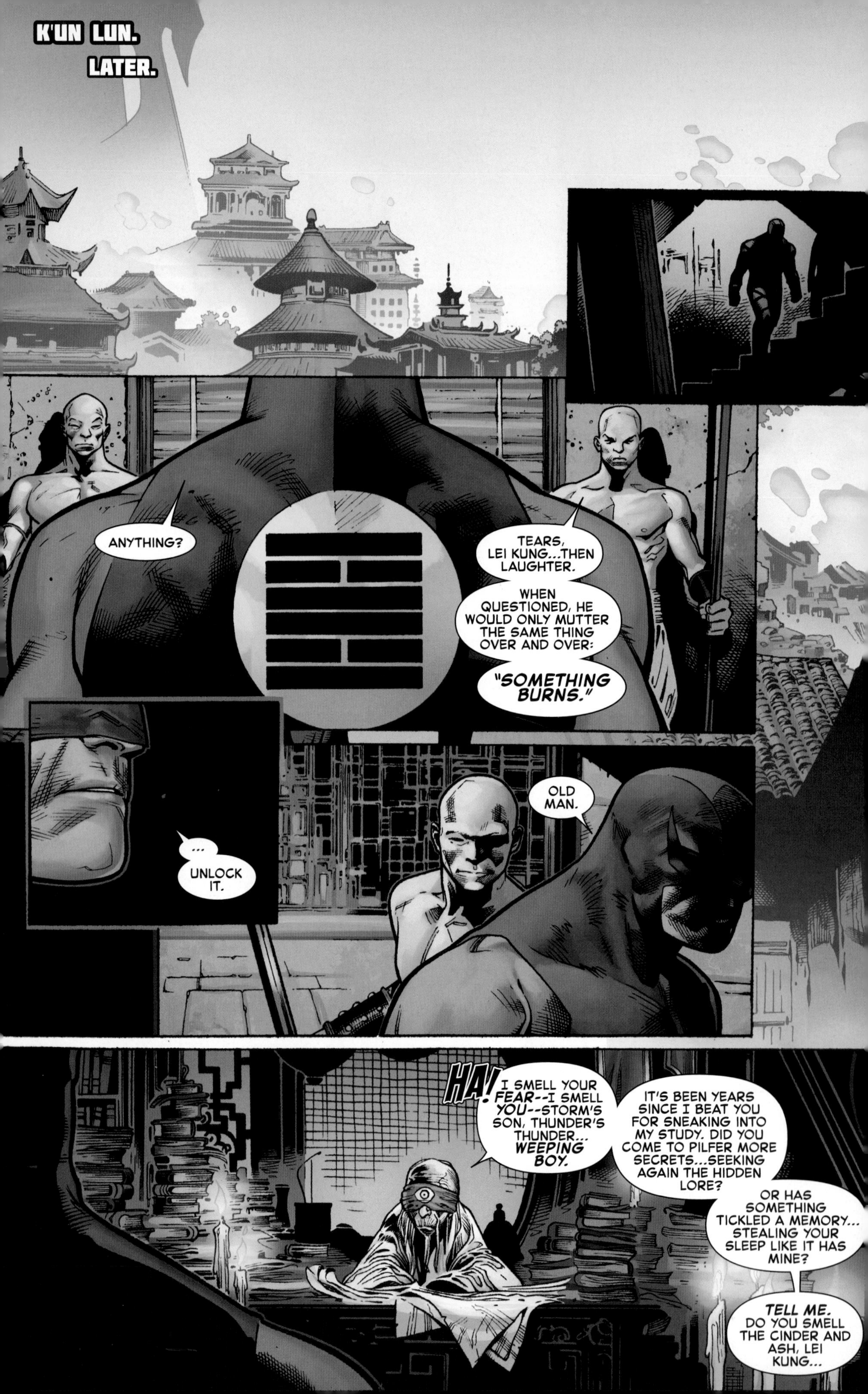
K'UN LUN.
LATER.
ANYTHING?
TEARS, LEI KUNG...THEN LAUGHTER.
WHEN QUESTIONED, HE WOULD ONLY MUTTER THE SAME THING OVER AND OVER:
"SOMETHING BURNS."
... UNLOCK IT.
OLD MAN.
HA!
I SMELL YOUR FEAR--I SMELL YOU--STORM'S SON, THUNDER'S THUNDER... WEEPING BOY.
IT'S BEEN YEARS SINCE I BEAT YOU FOR SNEAKING INTO MY STUDY. DID YOU COME TO PILFER MORE SECRETS...SEEKING AGAIN THE HIDDEN LORE?
OR HAS SOMETHING TICKLED A MEMORY... STEALING YOUR SLEEP LIKE IT HAS MINE?
TELL ME. DO YOU SMELL THE CINDER AND ASH, LEI KUNG...

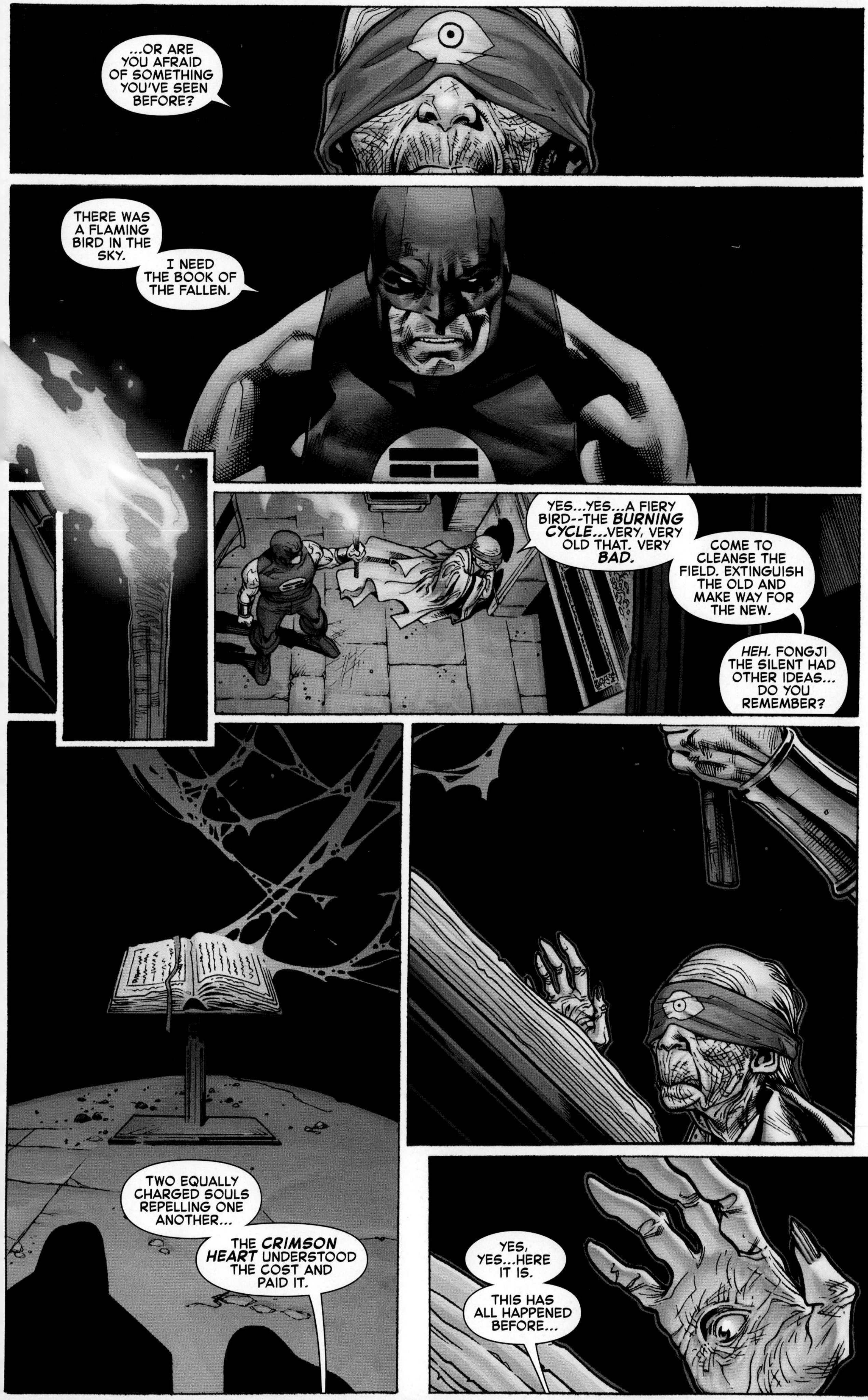
...OR ARE YOU AFRAID OF SOMETHING YOU'VE SEEN BEFORE?
THERE WAS A FLAMING BIRD IN THE SKY.
I NEED THE BOOK OF THE FALLEN.
YES...YES...A FIERY BIRD--THE BURNING CYCLE...VERY, VERY OLD THAT. VERY BAD.
COME TO CLEANSE THE FIELD. EXTINGUISH THE OLD AND MAKE WAY FOR THE NEW.
HEH. FONGJI THE SILENT HAD OTHER IDEAS... DO YOU REMEMBER?
TWO EQUALLY CHARGED SOULS REPELLING ONE ANOTHER...
THE CRIMSON HEART UNDERSTOOD THE COST AND PAID IT.
YES, YES...HERE IT IS.
THIS HAS ALL HAPPENED BEFORE...

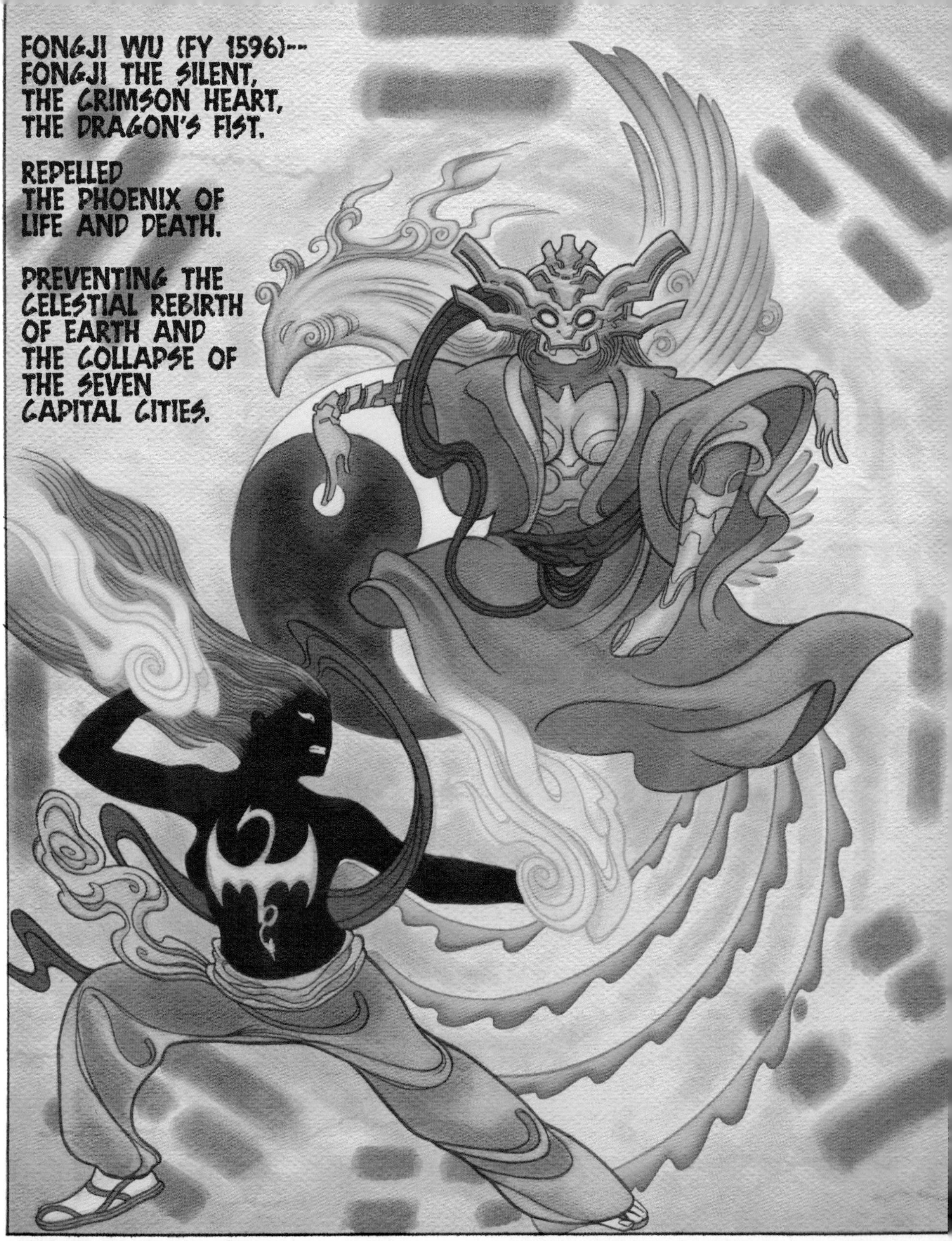
FONGJI WU (FY 1596)--
FONGJI THE SILENT,
THE CRIMSON HEART,
THE DRAGON'S FIST.
REPELLED
THE PHOENIX OF
LIFE AND DEATH.
PREVENTING THE
CELESTIAL REBIRTH
OF EARTH AND
THE COLLAPSE OF
THE SEVEN
CAPITAL CITIES.
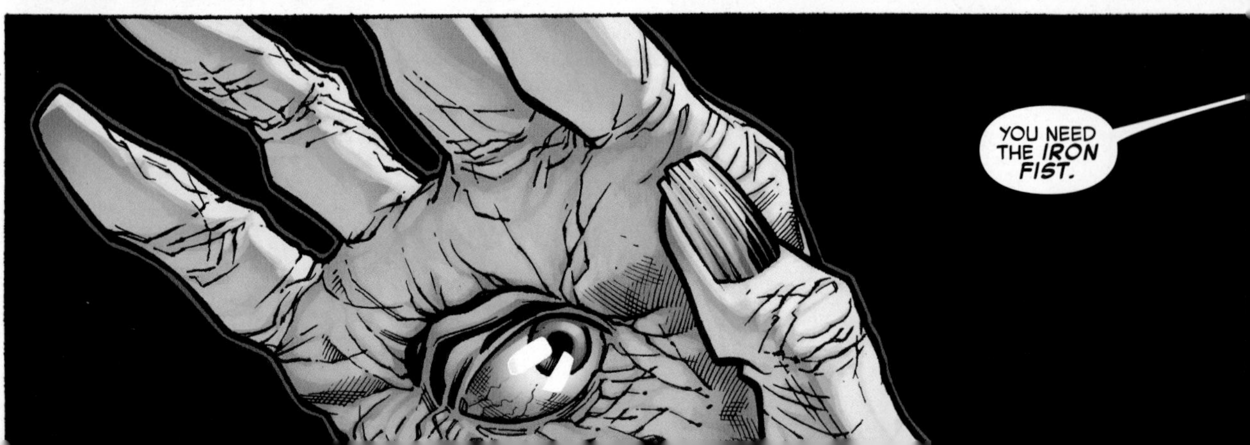
YOU NEED THE *IRON FIST*.

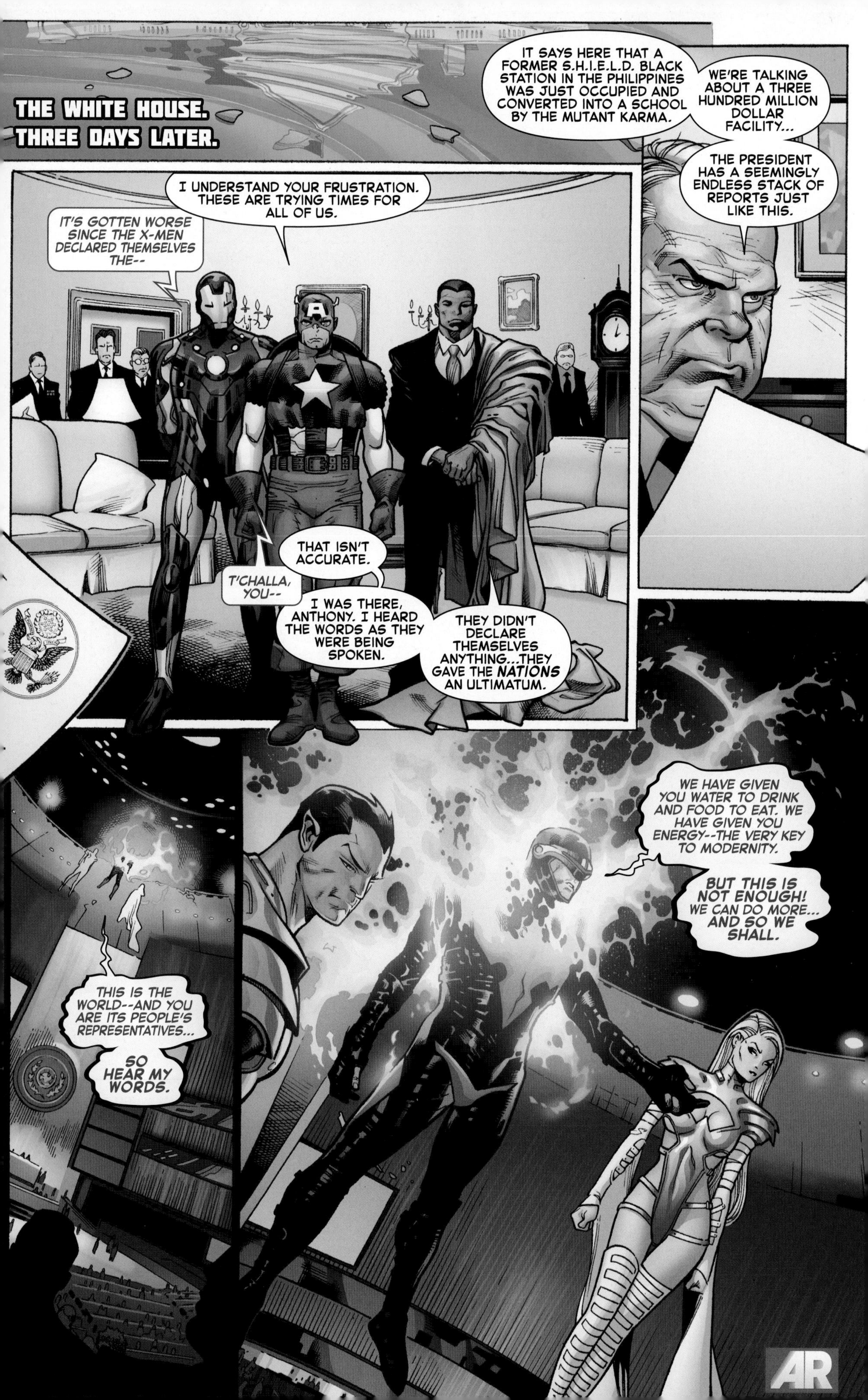
THE WHITE HOUSE.
THREE DAYS LATER.
IT SAYS HERE THAT A FORMER S.H.I.E.L.D. BLACK STATION IN THE PHILIPPINES WAS JUST OCCUPIED AND CONVERTED INTO A SCHOOL BY THE MUTANT KARMA.
WE'RE TALKING ABOUT A THREE HUNDRED MILLION DOLLAR FACILITY...
THE PRESIDENT HAS A SEEMINGLY ENDLESS STACK OF REPORTS JUST LIKE THIS.
I UNDERSTAND YOUR FRUSTRATION. THESE ARE TRYING TIMES FOR ALL OF US.
IT'S GOTTEN WORSE SINCE THE X-MEN DECLARED THEMSELVES THE--
THAT ISN'T ACCURATE.
T'CHALLA, YOU--
I WAS THERE, ANTHONY. I HEARD THE WORDS AS THEY WERE BEING SPOKEN.
THEY DIDN'T DECLARE THEMSELVES ANYTHING...THEY GAVE THE NATIONS AN ULTIMATUM.
THIS IS THE WORLD--AND YOU ARE ITS PEOPLE'S REPRESENTATIVES...
SO HEAR MY WORDS.
WE HAVE GIVEN YOU WATER TO DRINK AND FOOD TO EAT. WE HAVE GIVEN YOU ENERGY--THE VERY KEY TO MODERNITY.
BUT THIS IS NOT ENOUGH! WE CAN DO MORE... AND SO WE SHALL.
AR

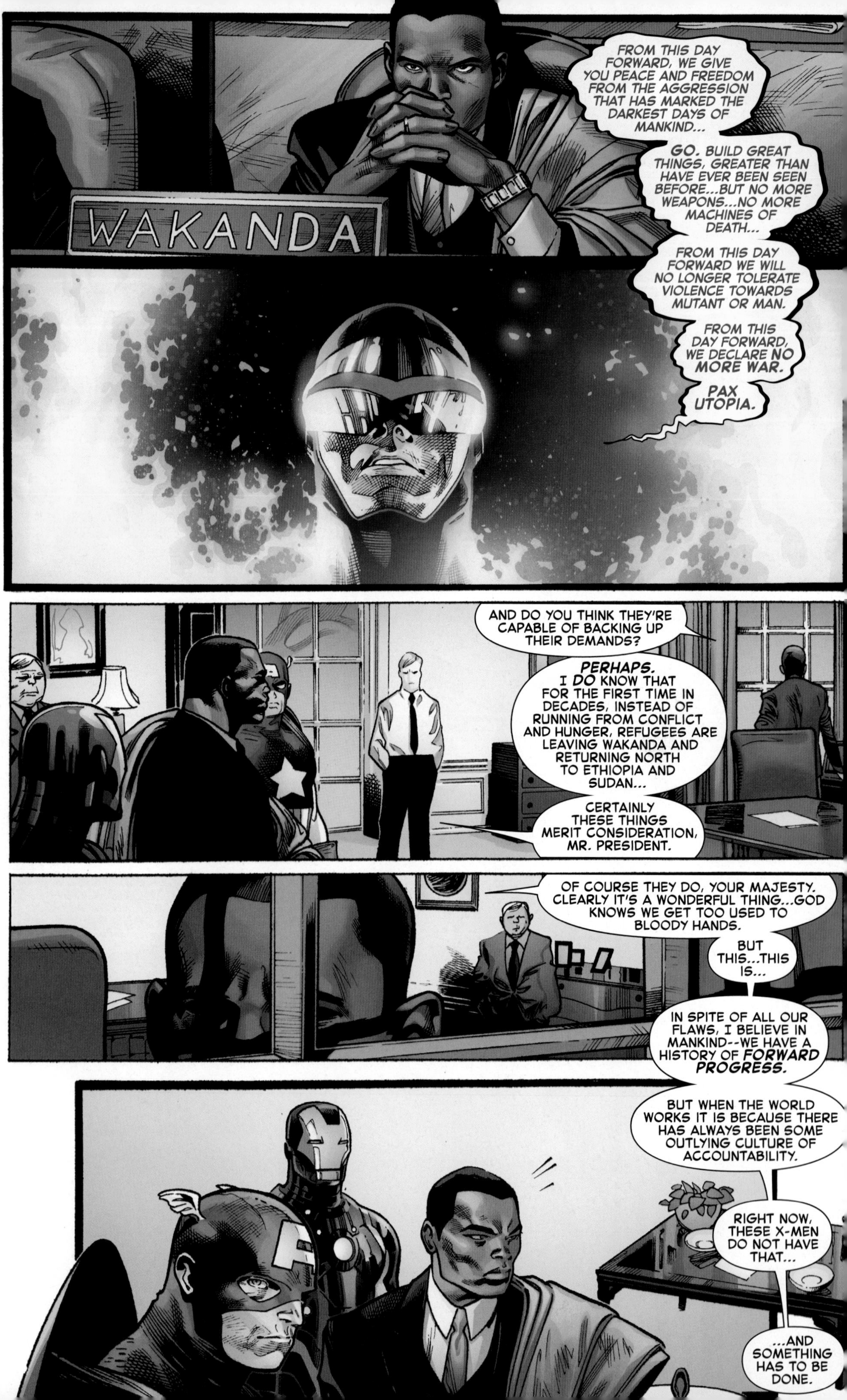
WAKANDA
FROM THIS DAY FORWARD, WE GIVE YOU PEACE AND FREEDOM FROM THE AGGRESSION THAT HAS MARKED THE DARKEST DAYS OF MANKIND...
GO. BUILD GREAT THINGS, GREATER THAN HAVE EVER BEEN SEEN BEFORE...BUT NO MORE WEAPONS...NO MORE MACHINES OF DEATH...
FROM THIS DAY FORWARD WE WILL NO LONGER TOLERATE VIOLENCE TOWARDS MUTANT OR MAN.
FROM THIS DAY FORWARD, WE DECLARE NO MORE WAR.
PAX UTOPIA.
AND DO YOU THINK THEY'RE CAPABLE OF BACKING UP THEIR DEMANDS?
PERHAPS. I DO KNOW THAT FOR THE FIRST TIME IN DECADES, INSTEAD OF RUNNING FROM CONFLICT AND HUNGER, REFUGEES ARE LEAVING WAKANDA AND RETURNING NORTH TO ETHIOPIA AND SUDAN...
CERTAINLY THESE THINGS MERIT CONSIDERATION, MR. PRESIDENT.
OF COURSE THEY DO, YOUR MAJESTY. CLEARLY IT'S A WONDERFUL THING...GOD KNOWS WE GET TOO USED TO BLOODY HANDS.
BUT THIS...THIS IS...
IN SPITE OF ALL OUR FLAWS, I BELIEVE IN MANKIND--WE HAVE A HISTORY OF FORWARD PROGRESS.
BUT WHEN THE WORLD WORKS IT IS BECAUSE THERE HAS ALWAYS BEEN SOME OUTLYING CULTURE OF ACCOUNTABILITY.
RIGHT NOW, THESE X-MEN DO NOT HAVE THAT...
...AND SOMETHING HAS TO BE DONE.

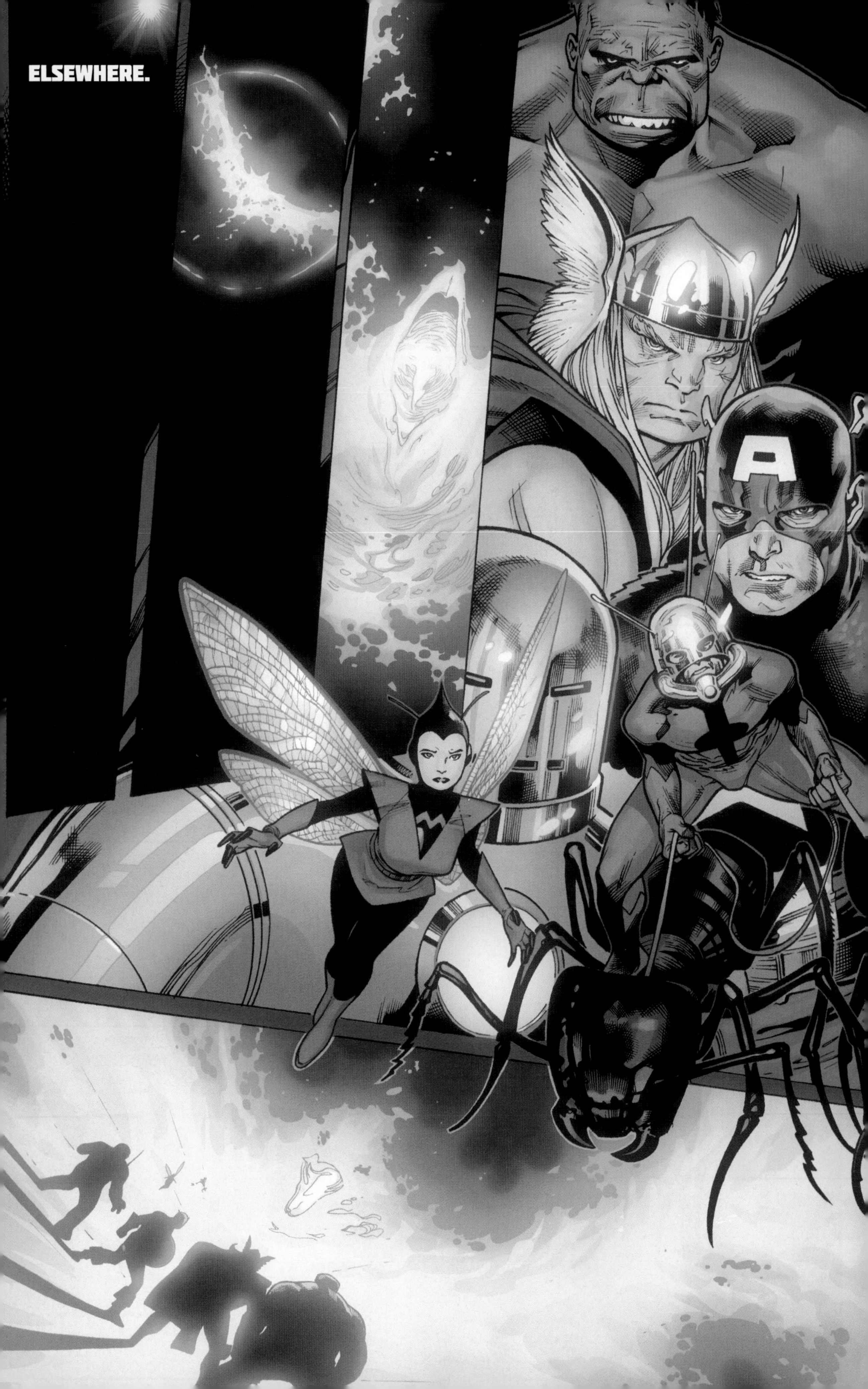
ELSEWHERE.

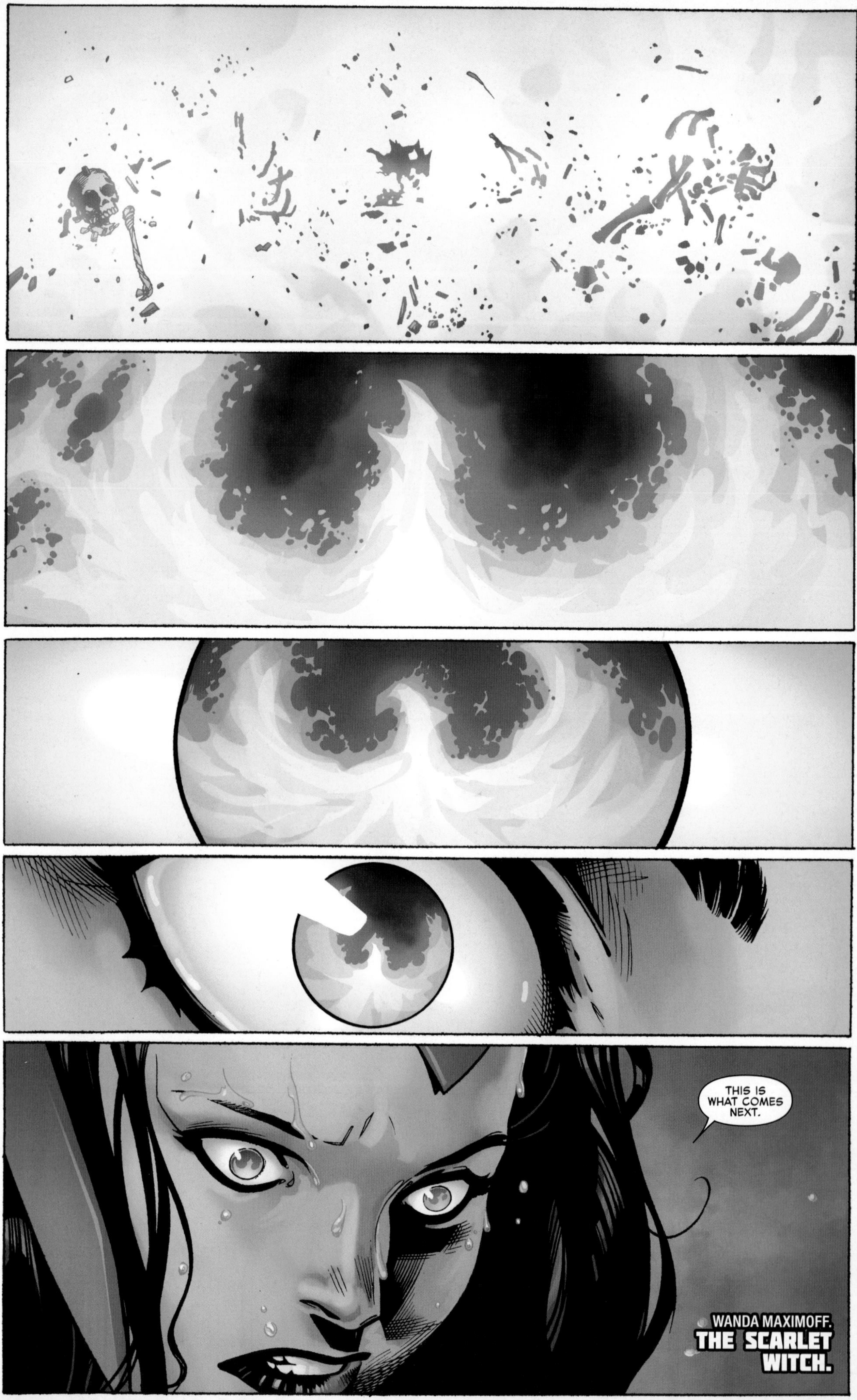
THIS IS WHAT COMES NEXT.
WANDA MAXIMOFF.
THE SCARLET WITCH.

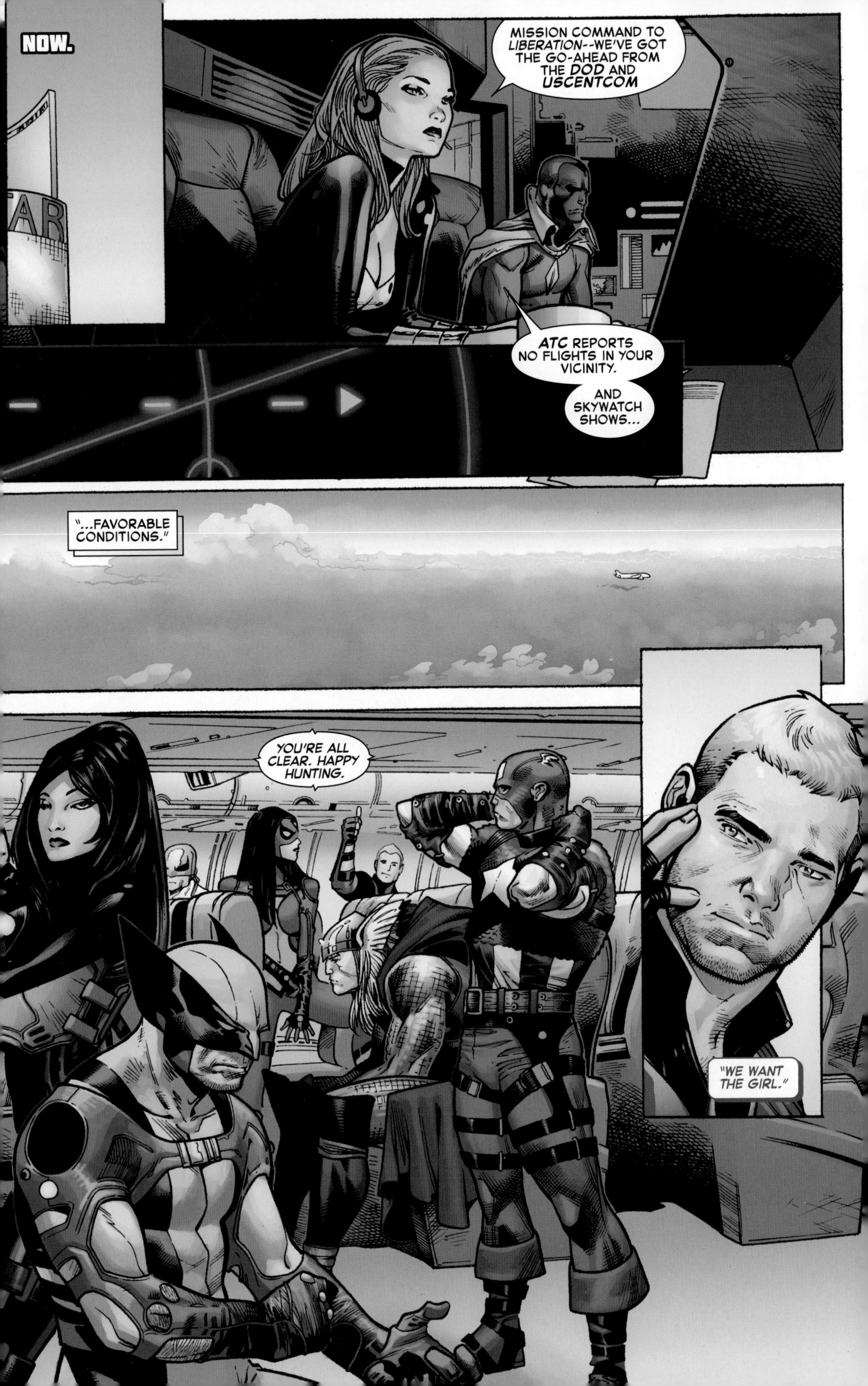
NOW.
MISSION COMMAND TO LIBERATION--WE'VE GOT THE GO-AHEAD FROM THE DOD AND USCENTCOM
ATC REPORTS NO FLIGHTS IN YOUR VICINITY.
AND SKYWATCH SHOWS...
"...FAVORABLE CONDITIONS."
YOU'RE ALL CLEAR. HAPPY HUNTING.
"WE WANT THE GIRL."

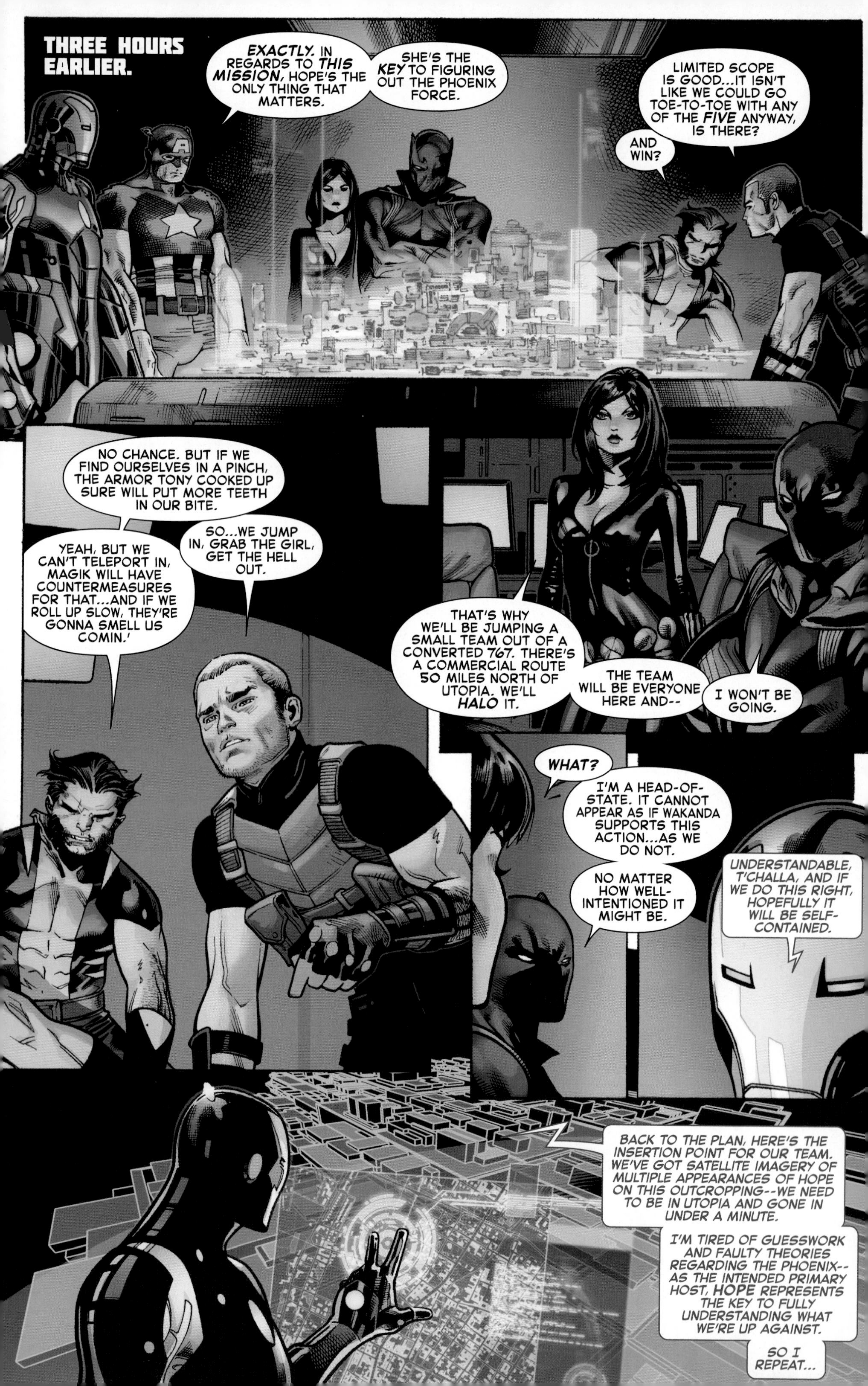
THREE HOURS EARLIER.
EXACTLY. IN REGARDS TO THIS MISSION, HOPE'S THE ONLY THING THAT MATTERS.
SHE'S THE KEY TO FIGURING OUT THE PHOENIX FORCE.
LIMITED SCOPE IS GOOD...IT ISN'T LIKE WE COULD GO TOE-TO-TOE WITH ANY OF THE FIVE ANYWAY, IS THERE?
AND WIN?
NO CHANCE. BUT IF WE FIND OURSELVES IN A PINCH, THE ARMOR TONY COOKED UP SURE WILL PUT MORE TEETH IN OUR BITE.
SO...WE JUMP IN, GRAB THE GIRL, GET THE HELL OUT.
YEAH, BUT WE CAN'T TELEPORT IN, MAGIK WILL HAVE COUNTERMEASURES FOR THAT...AND IF WE ROLL UP SLOW, THEY'RE GONNA SMELL US COMIN.'
THAT'S WHY WE'LL BE JUMPING A SMALL TEAM OUT OF A CONVERTED 767. THERE'S A COMMERCIAL ROUTE 50 MILES NORTH OF UTOPIA. WE'LL HALO IT.
THE TEAM WILL BE EVERYONE HERE AND--
I WON'T BE GOING.
WHAT?
I'M A HEAD-OF-STATE. IT CANNOT APPEAR AS IF WAKANDA SUPPORTS THIS ACTION...AS WE DO NOT.
NO MATTER HOW WELL-INTENTIONED IT MIGHT BE.
UNDERSTANDABLE, T'CHALLA, AND IF WE DO THIS RIGHT, HOPEFULLY IT WILL BE SELF-CONTAINED.
BACK TO THE PLAN, HERE'S THE INSERTION POINT FOR OUR TEAM. WE'VE GOT SATELLITE IMAGERY OF MULTIPLE APPEARANCES OF HOPE ON THIS OUTCROPPING--WE NEED TO BE IN UTOPIA AND GONE IN UNDER A MINUTE.
I'M TIRED OF GUESSWORK AND FAULTY THEORIES REGARDING THE PHOENIX--AS THE INTENDED PRIMARY HOST, HOPE REPRESENTS THE KEY TO FULLY UNDERSTANDING WHAT WE'RE UP AGAINST.
SO I REPEAT...

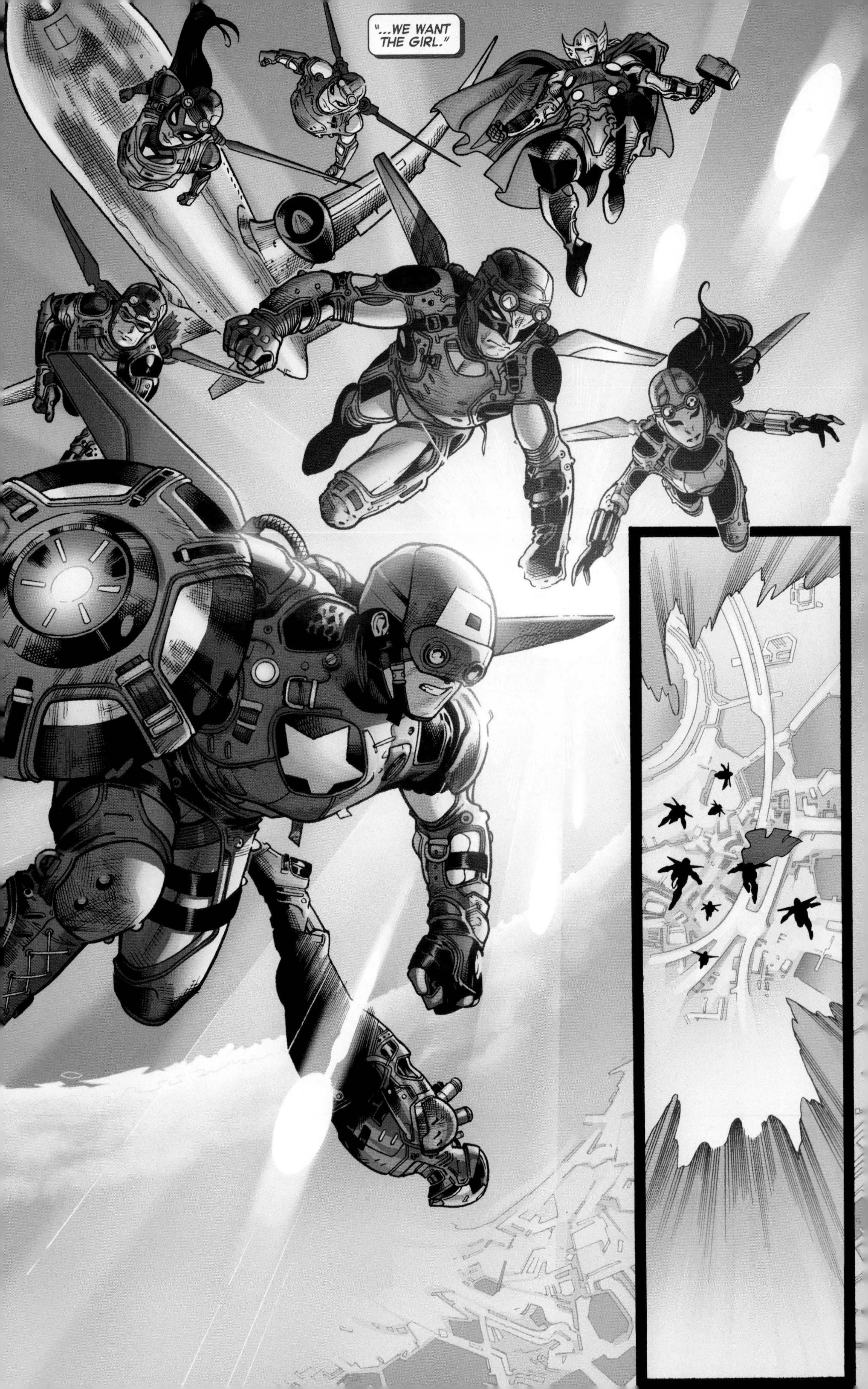
"...WE WANT THE GIRL."

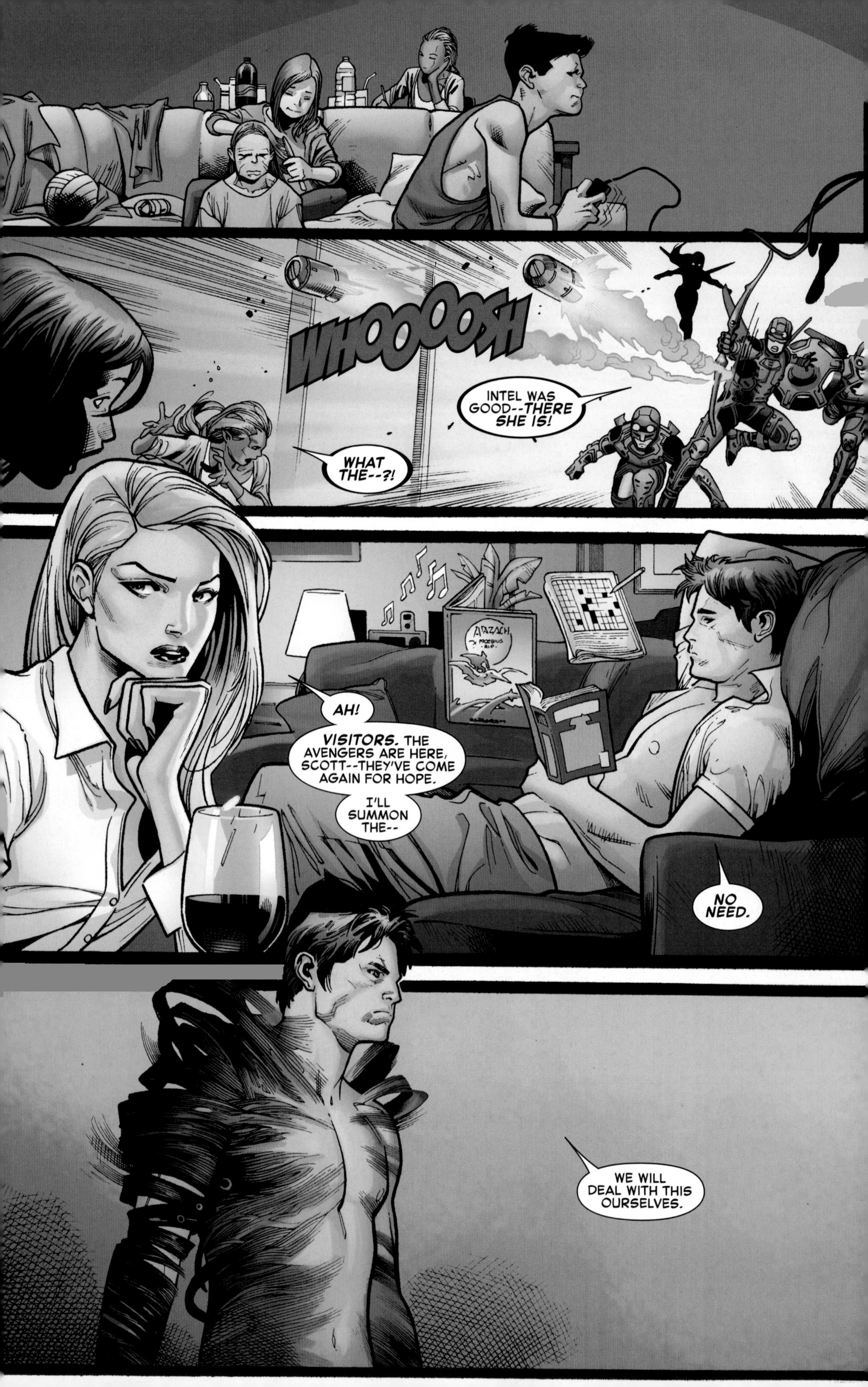
WHOOOOOSH
INTEL WAS GOOD--THERE SHE IS!
WHAT THE--?!
AH!
VISITORS. THE AVENGERS ARE HERE, SCOTT--THEY'VE COME AGAIN FOR HOPE.
I'LL SUMMON THE--
NO NEED.
WE WILL DEAL WITH THIS OURSELVES.

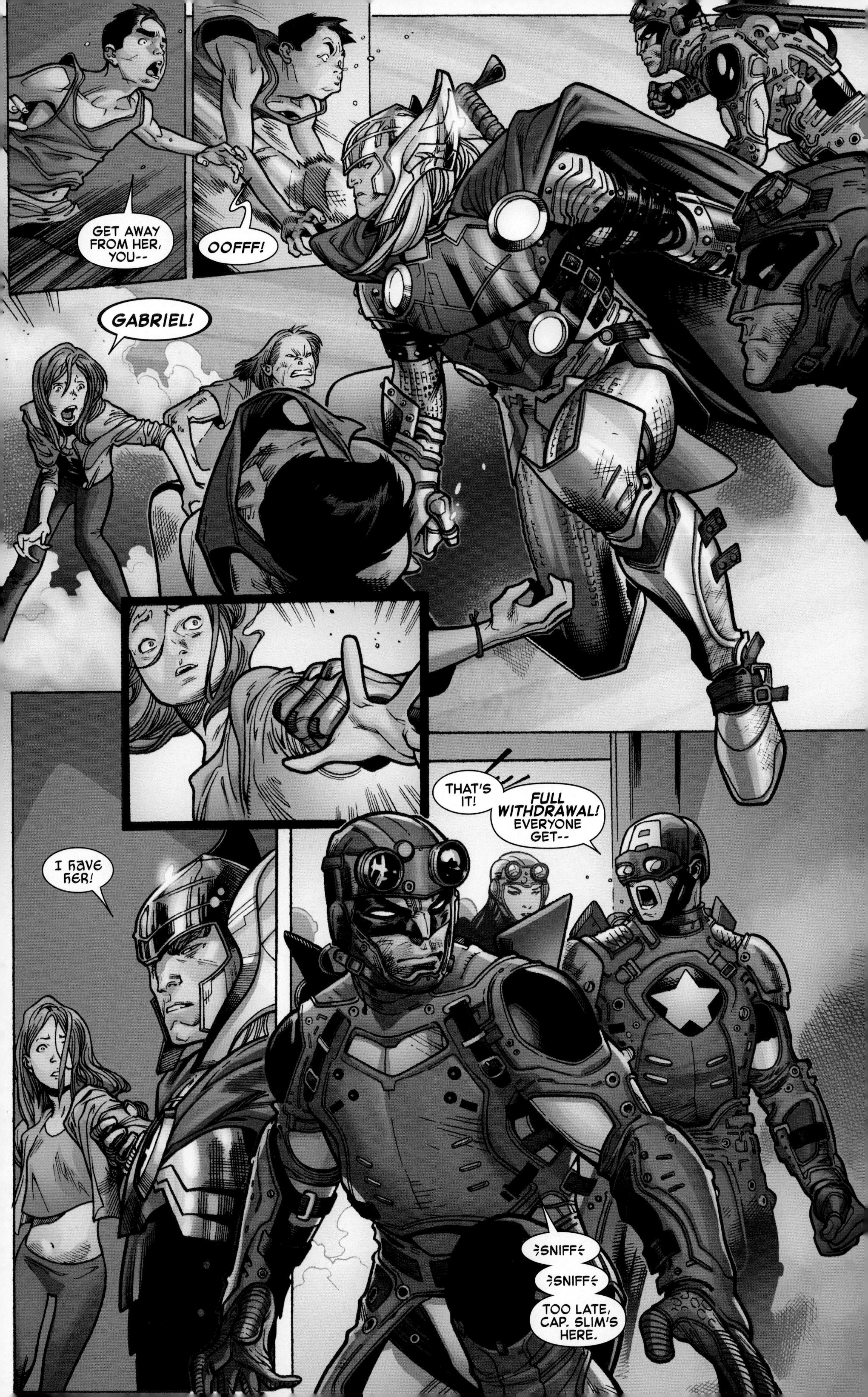
GET AWAY FROM HER, YOU--
OOFFF!
GABRIEL!
THAT'S IT!
FULL WITHDRAWAL! EVERYONE GET--
I HAVE HER!
⊰SNIFF⊱
⊰SNIFF⊱
TOO LATE, CAP. SLIM'S HERE.

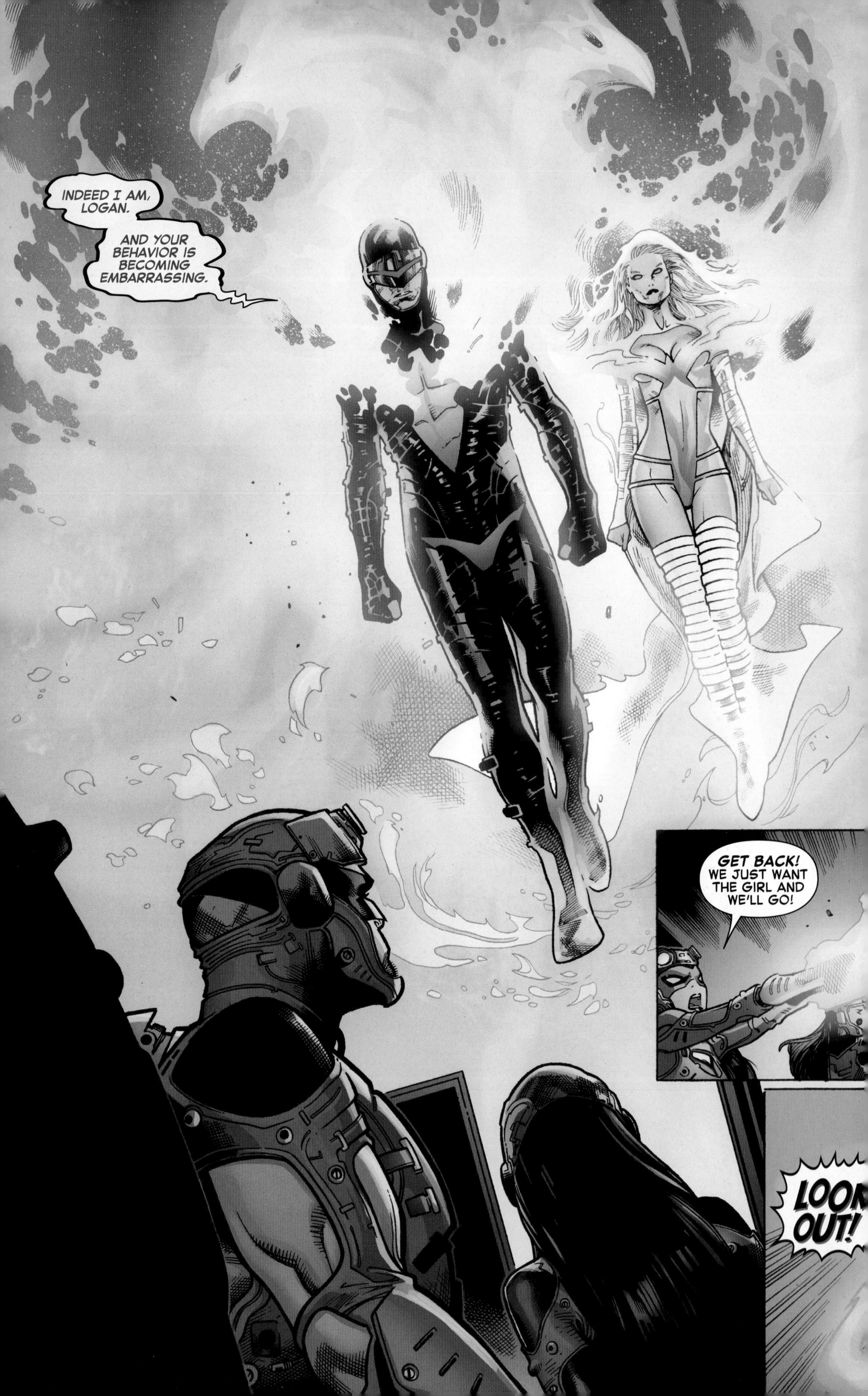
INDEED I AM, LOGAN.
AND YOUR BEHAVIOR IS BECOMING EMBARRASSING.
GET BACK! WE JUST WANT THE GIRL AND WE'LL GO!
LOOK OUT!

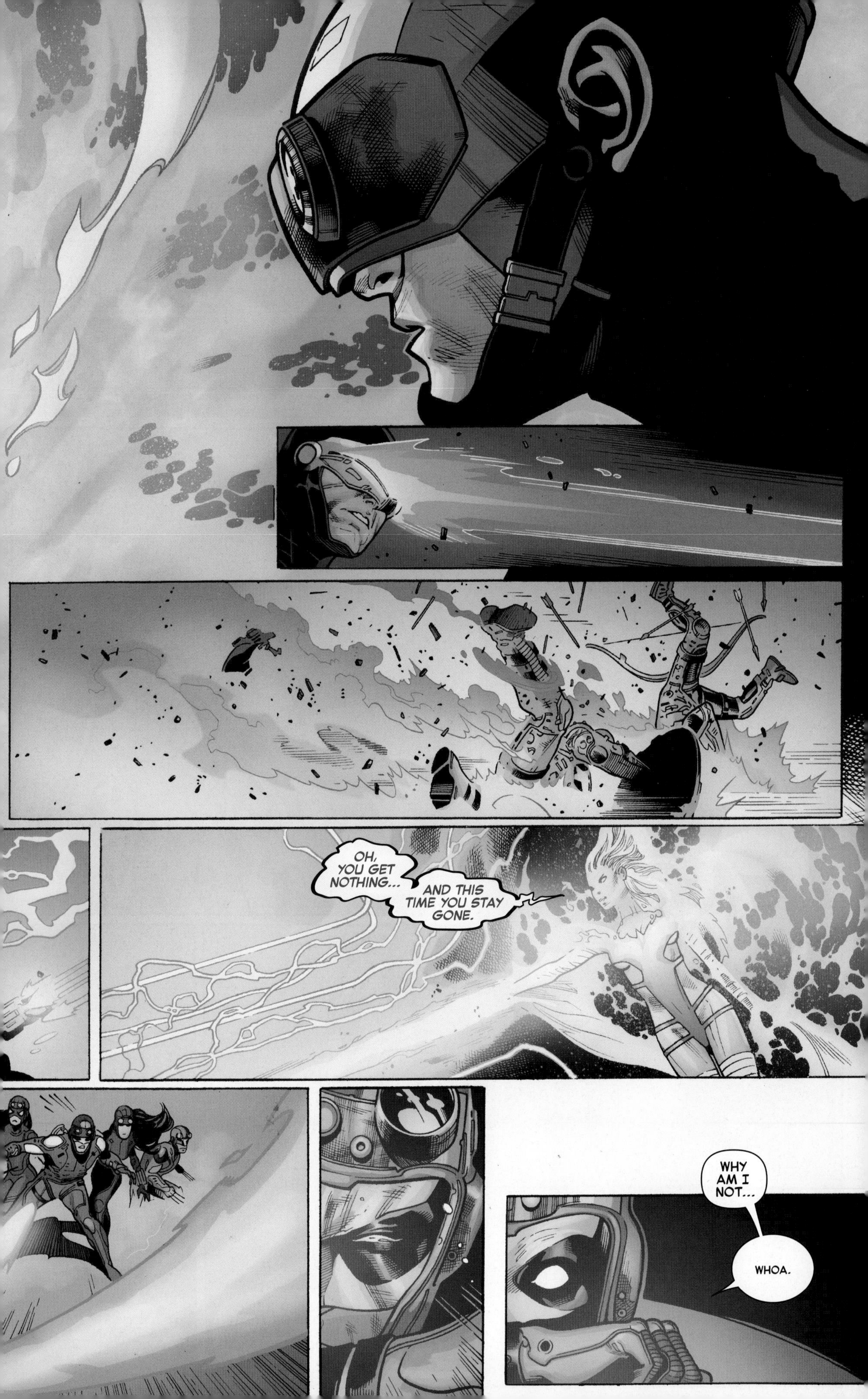
OH, YOU GET NOTHING...
AND THIS TIME YOU STAY GONE.
WHY AM I NOT...
WHOA.

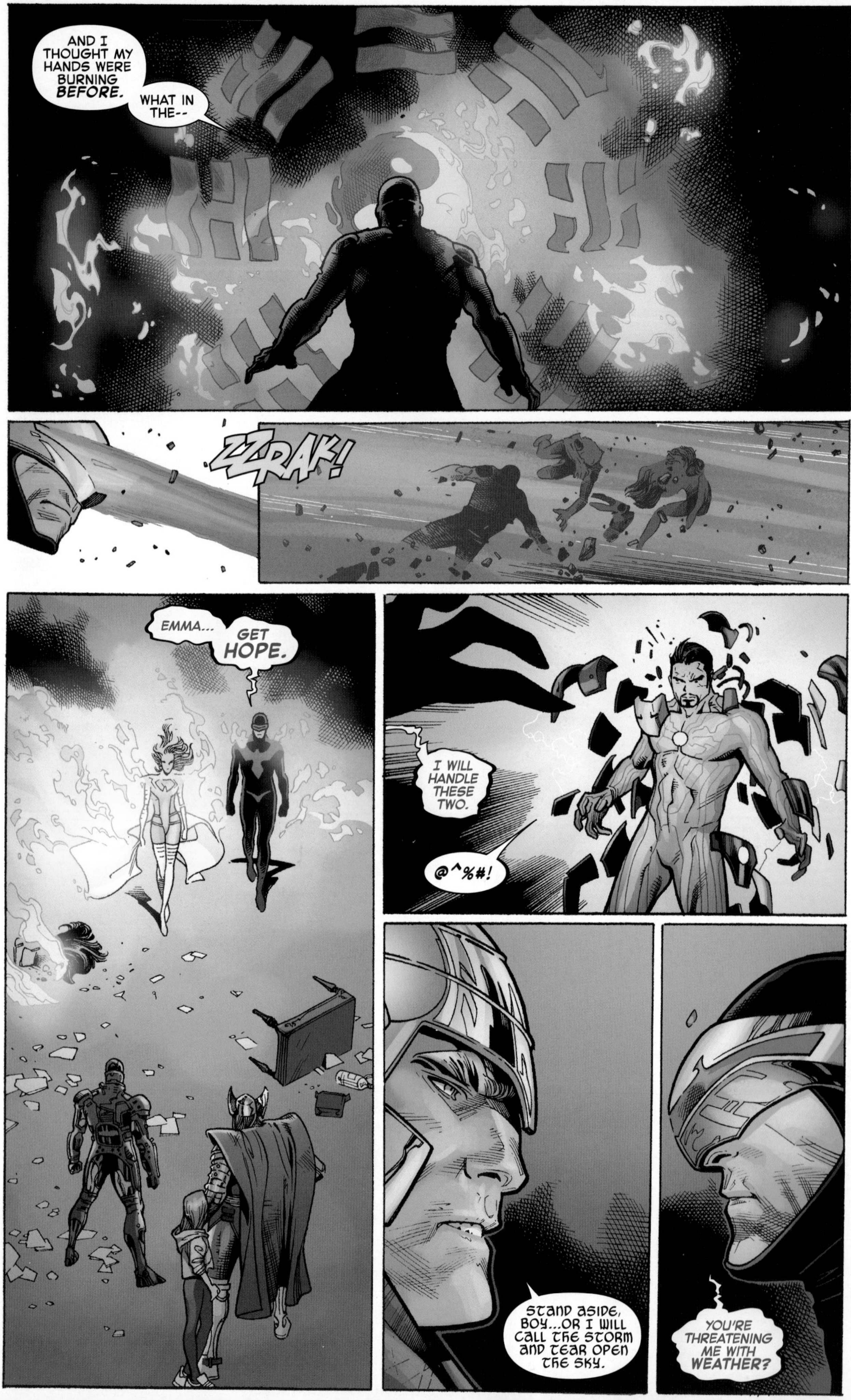

AND I THOUGHT MY HANDS WERE BURNING BEFORE.
WHAT IN THE--
ZZRAK!
EMMA... GET HOPE.
I WILL HANDLE THESE TWO.
@^%#!
STAND ASIDE, BOY...OR I WILL CALL THE STORM AND TEAR OPEN THE SKY.
YOU'RE THREATENING ME WITH WEATHER?

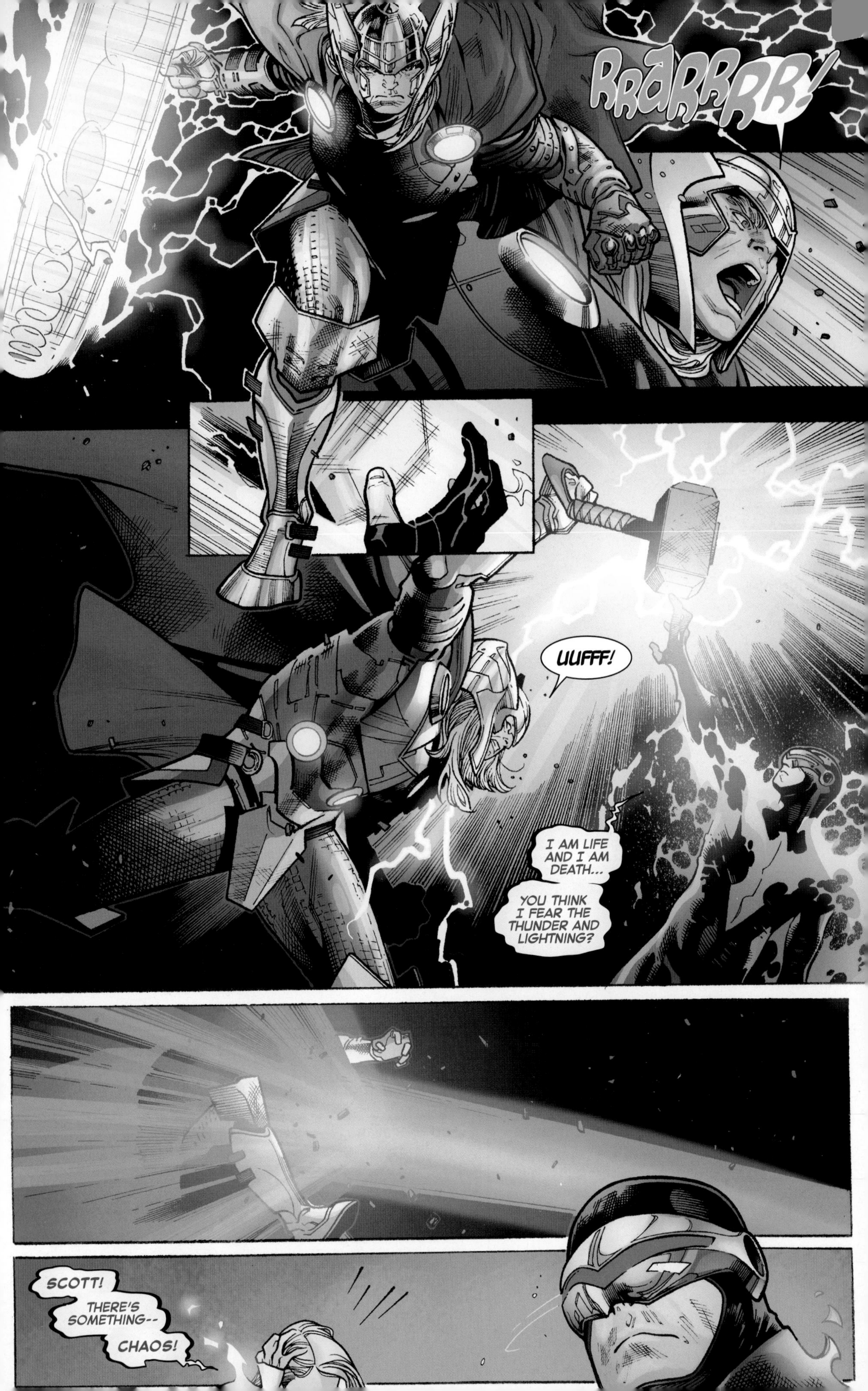
RRARRRR!
UUFFF!
I AM LIFE AND I AM DEATH...
YOU THINK I FEAR THE THUNDER AND LIGHTNING?
SCOTT!
THERE'S SOMETHING--
CHAOS!

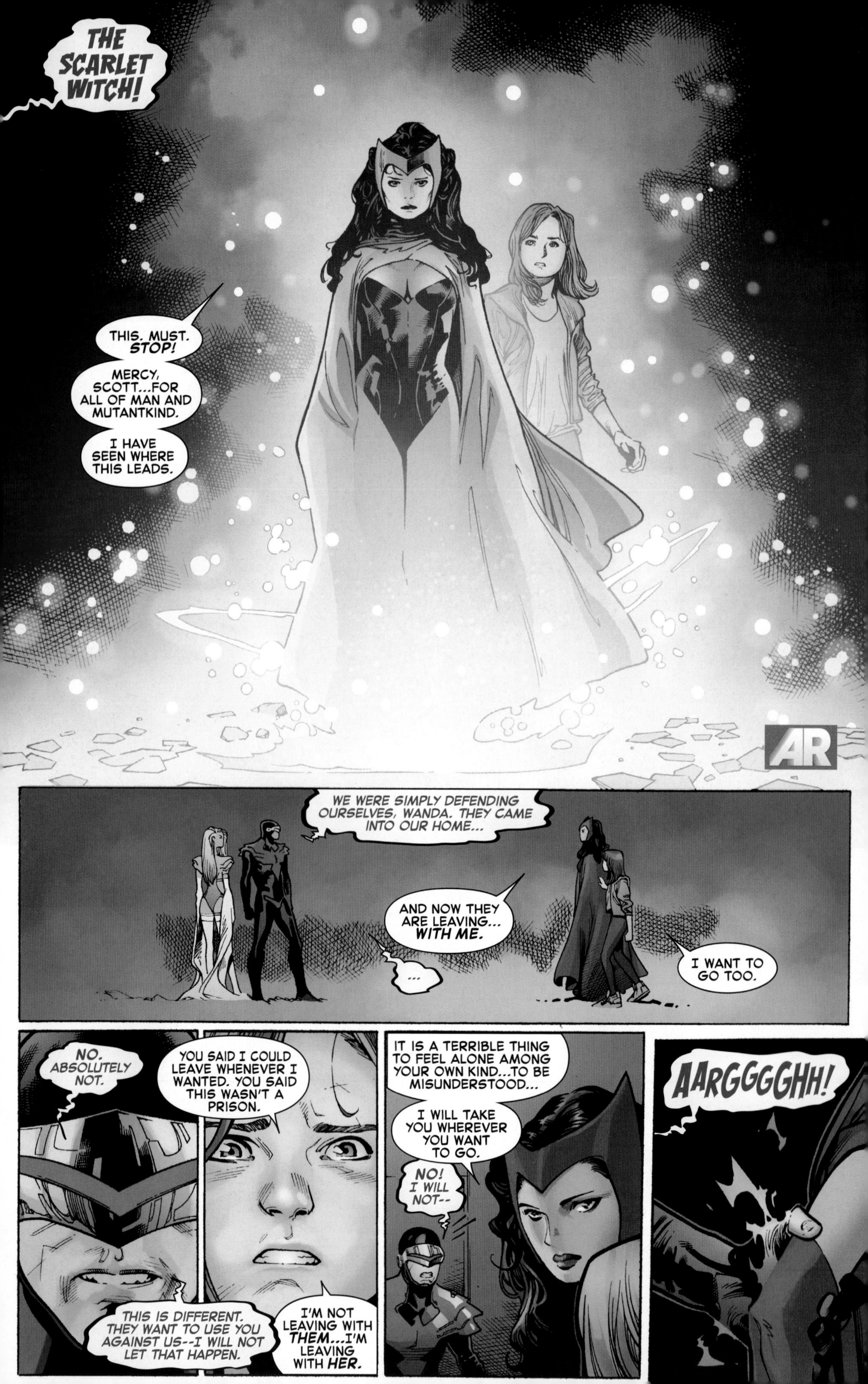
THE SCARLET WITCH!
THIS. MUST. STOP!
MERCY, SCOTT...FOR ALL OF MAN AND MUTANTKIND.
I HAVE SEEN WHERE THIS LEADS.
AR
WE WERE SIMPLY DEFENDING OURSELVES, WANDA. THEY CAME INTO OUR HOME...
AND NOW THEY ARE LEAVING... WITH ME.
...
I WANT TO GO TOO.
NO. ABSOLUTELY NOT.
YOU SAID I COULD LEAVE WHENEVER I WANTED. YOU SAID THIS WASN'T A PRISON.
THIS IS DIFFERENT. THEY WANT TO USE YOU AGAINST US--I WILL NOT LET THAT HAPPEN.
I'M NOT LEAVING WITH THEM...I'M LEAVING WITH HER.
IT IS A TERRIBLE THING TO FEEL ALONE AMONG YOUR OWN KIND...TO BE MISUNDERSTOOD...
I WILL TAKE YOU WHEREVER YOU WANT TO GO.
NO! I WILL NOT--
AARGGGGHH!

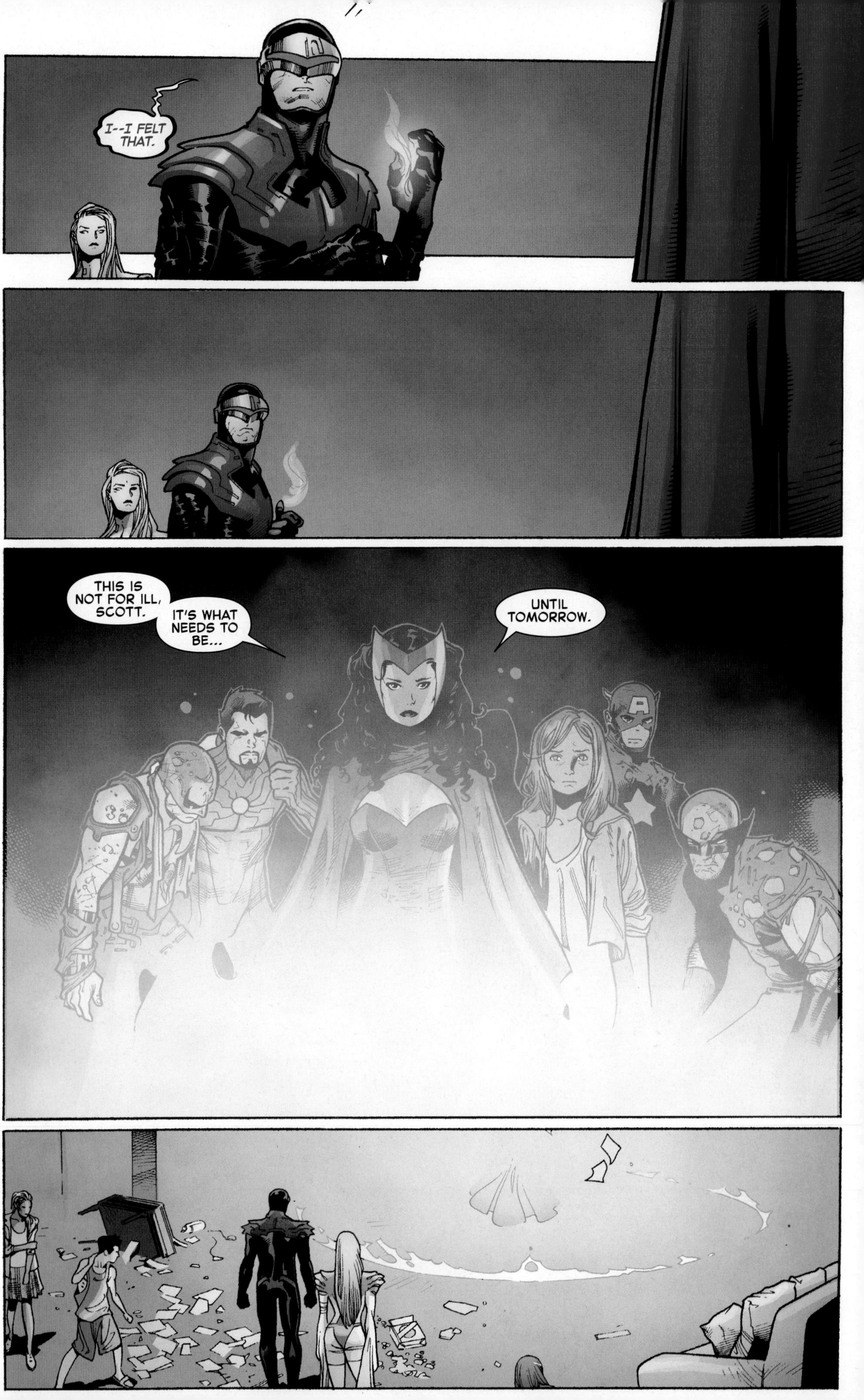
I--I FELT THAT.
THIS IS NOT FOR ILL, SCOTT.
IT'S WHAT NEEDS TO BE...
UNTIL TOMORROW.

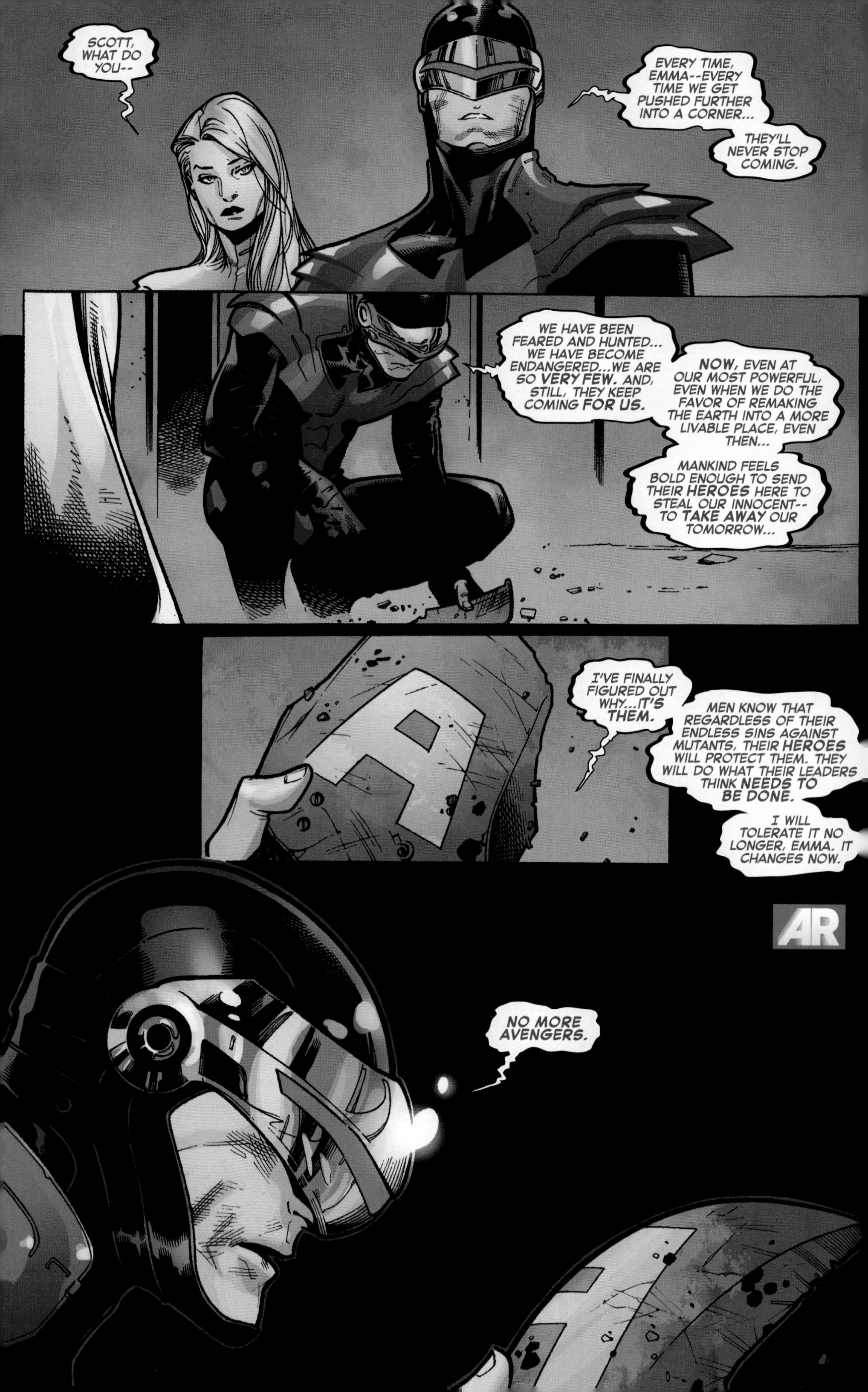
SCOTT, WHAT DO YOU--
EVERY TIME, EMMA--EVERY TIME WE GET PUSHED FURTHER INTO A CORNER...
THEY'LL NEVER STOP COMING.
WE HAVE BEEN FEARED AND HUNTED... WE HAVE BECOME ENDANGERED...WE ARE SO VERY FEW. AND, STILL, THEY KEEP COMING FOR US.
NOW, EVEN AT OUR MOST POWERFUL, EVEN WHEN WE DO THE FAVOR OF REMAKING THE EARTH INTO A MORE LIVABLE PLACE, EVEN THEN...
MANKIND FEELS BOLD ENOUGH TO SEND THEIR HEROES HERE TO STEAL OUR INNOCENT--TO TAKE AWAY OUR TOMORROW...
I'VE FINALLY FIGURED OUT WHY...IT'S THEM.
MEN KNOW THAT REGARDLESS OF THEIR ENDLESS SINS AGAINST MUTANTS, THEIR HEROES WILL PROTECT THEM. THEY WILL DO WHAT THEIR LEADERS THINK NEEDS TO BE DONE.
I WILL TOLERATE IT NO LONGER, EMMA. IT CHANGES NOW.
AR
NO MORE AVENGERS.

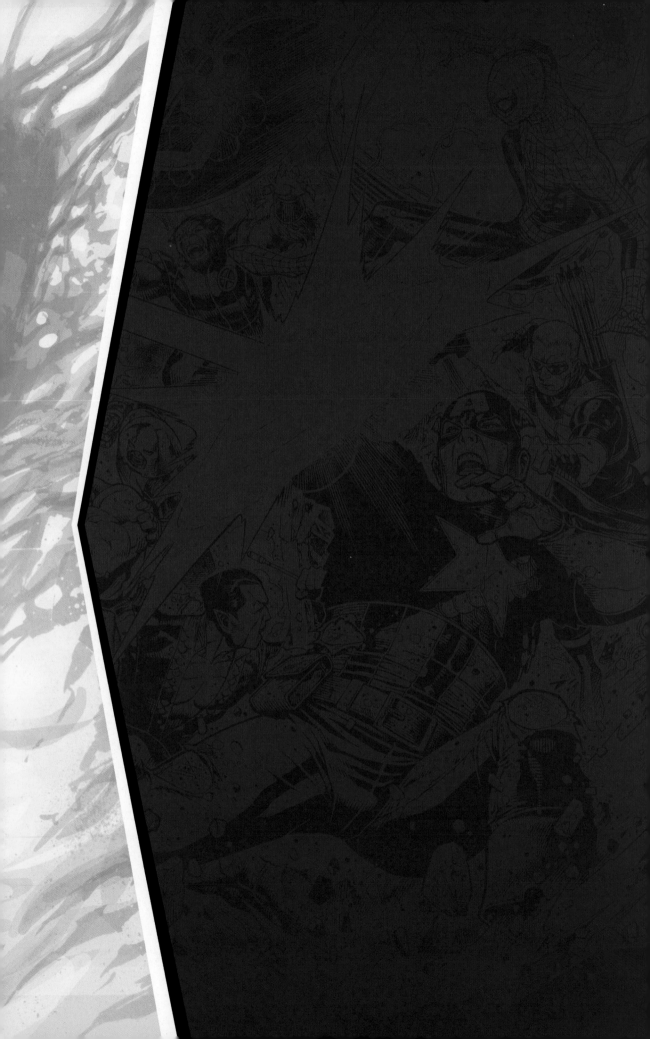

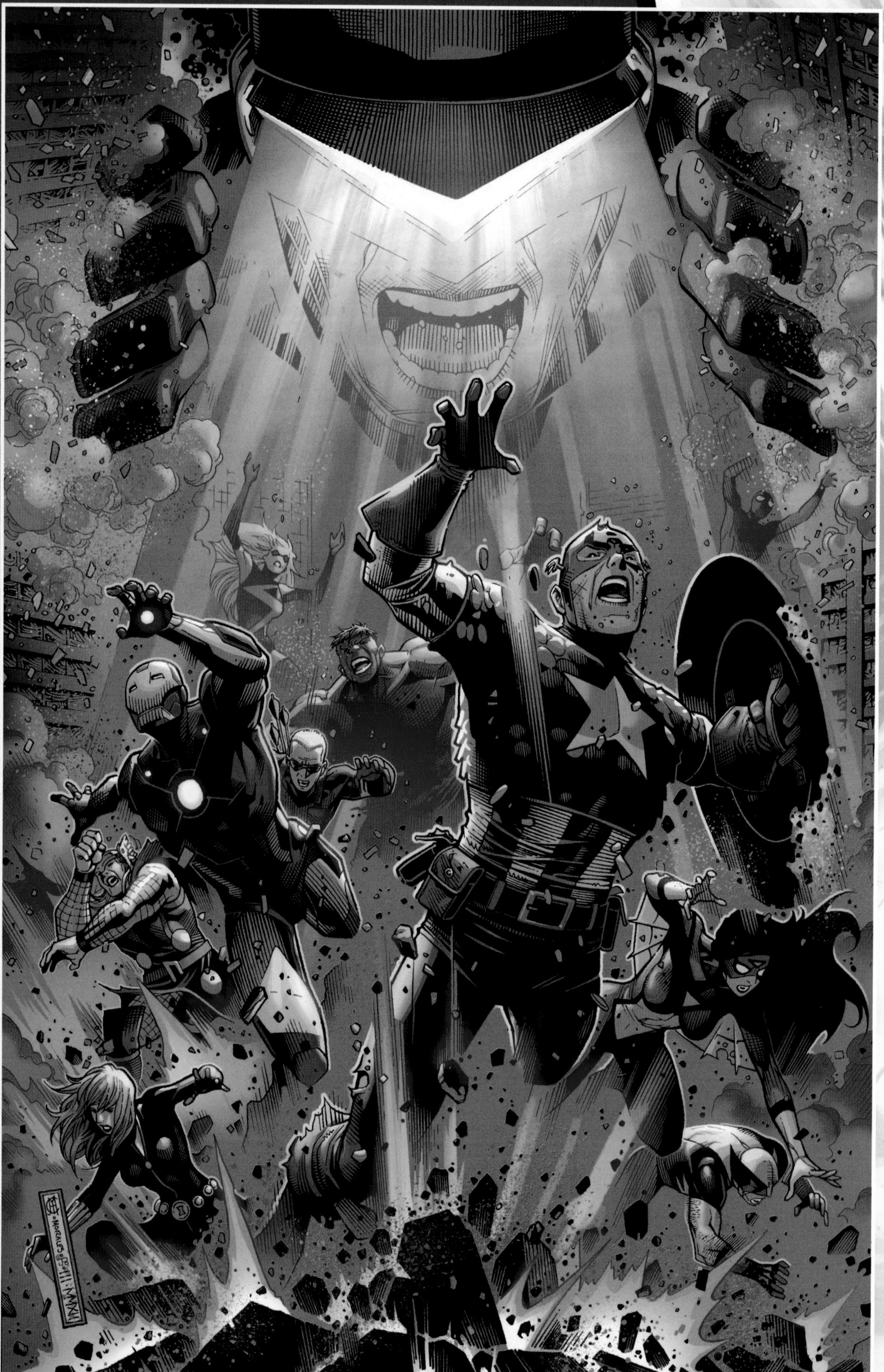

ROUND 7

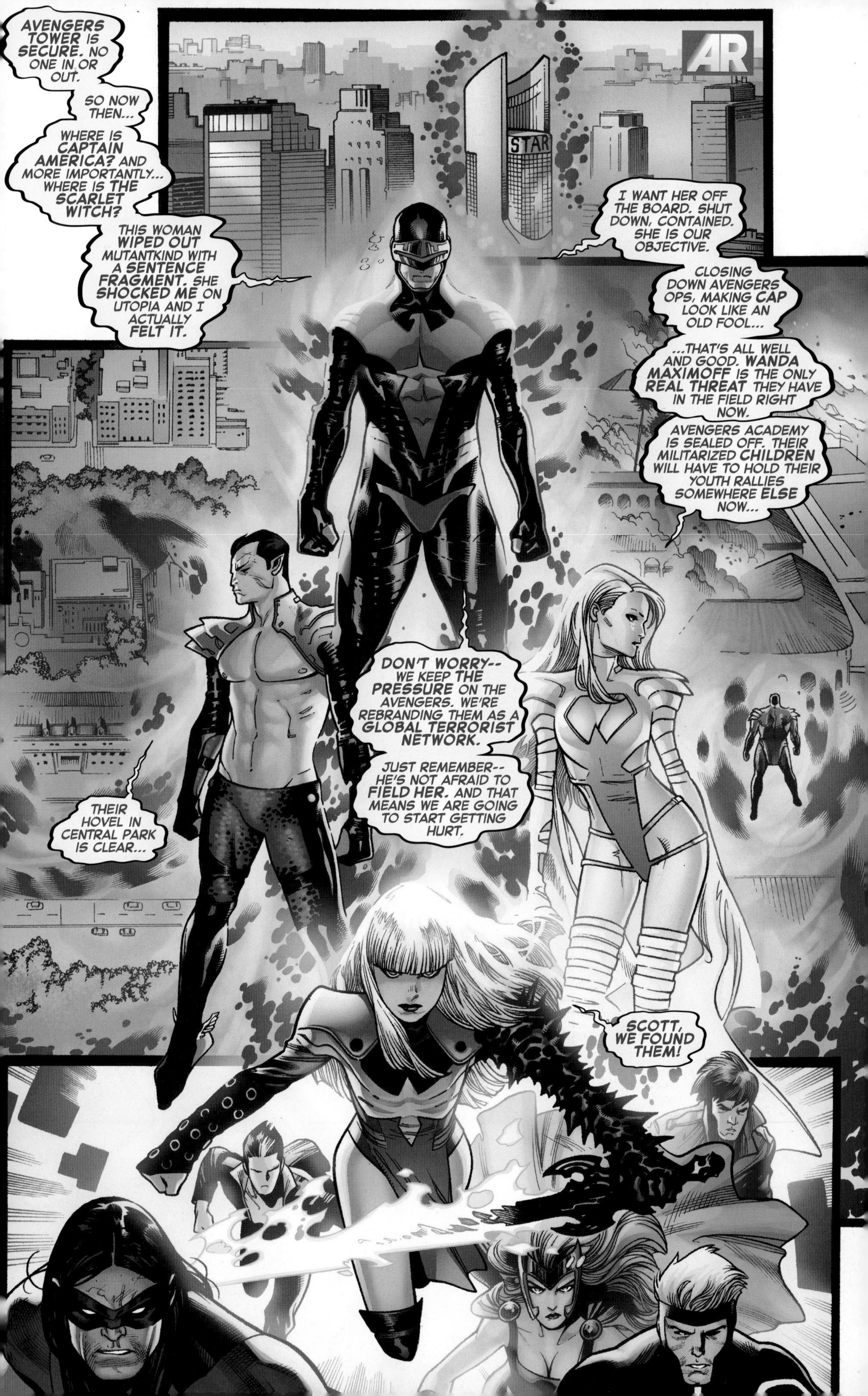
AR
AVENGERS TOWER IS SECURE. NO ONE IN OR OUT.
SO NOW THEN...
WHERE IS CAPTAIN AMERICA? AND MORE IMPORTANTLY... WHERE IS THE SCARLET WITCH?
THIS WOMAN WIPED OUT MUTANTKIND WITH A SENTENCE FRAGMENT. SHE SHOCKED ME ON UTOPIA AND I ACTUALLY FELT IT.
STAR
I WANT HER OFF THE BOARD. SHUT DOWN, CONTAINED. SHE IS OUR OBJECTIVE.
CLOSING DOWN AVENGERS OPS, MAKING CAP LOOK LIKE AN OLD FOOL...
...THAT'S ALL WELL AND GOOD. WANDA MAXIMOFF IS THE ONLY REAL THREAT THEY HAVE IN THE FIELD RIGHT NOW.
AVENGERS ACADEMY IS SEALED OFF. THEIR MILITARIZED CHILDREN WILL HAVE TO HOLD THEIR YOUTH RALLIES SOMEWHERE ELSE NOW...
THEIR HOVEL IN CENTRAL PARK IS CLEAR...
DON'T WORRY-- WE KEEP THE PRESSURE ON THE AVENGERS. WE'RE REBRANDING THEM AS A GLOBAL TERRORIST NETWORK.
JUST REMEMBER-- HE'S NOT AFRAID TO FIELD HER. AND THAT MEANS WE ARE GOING TO START GETTING HURT.
SCOTT, WE FOUND THEM!

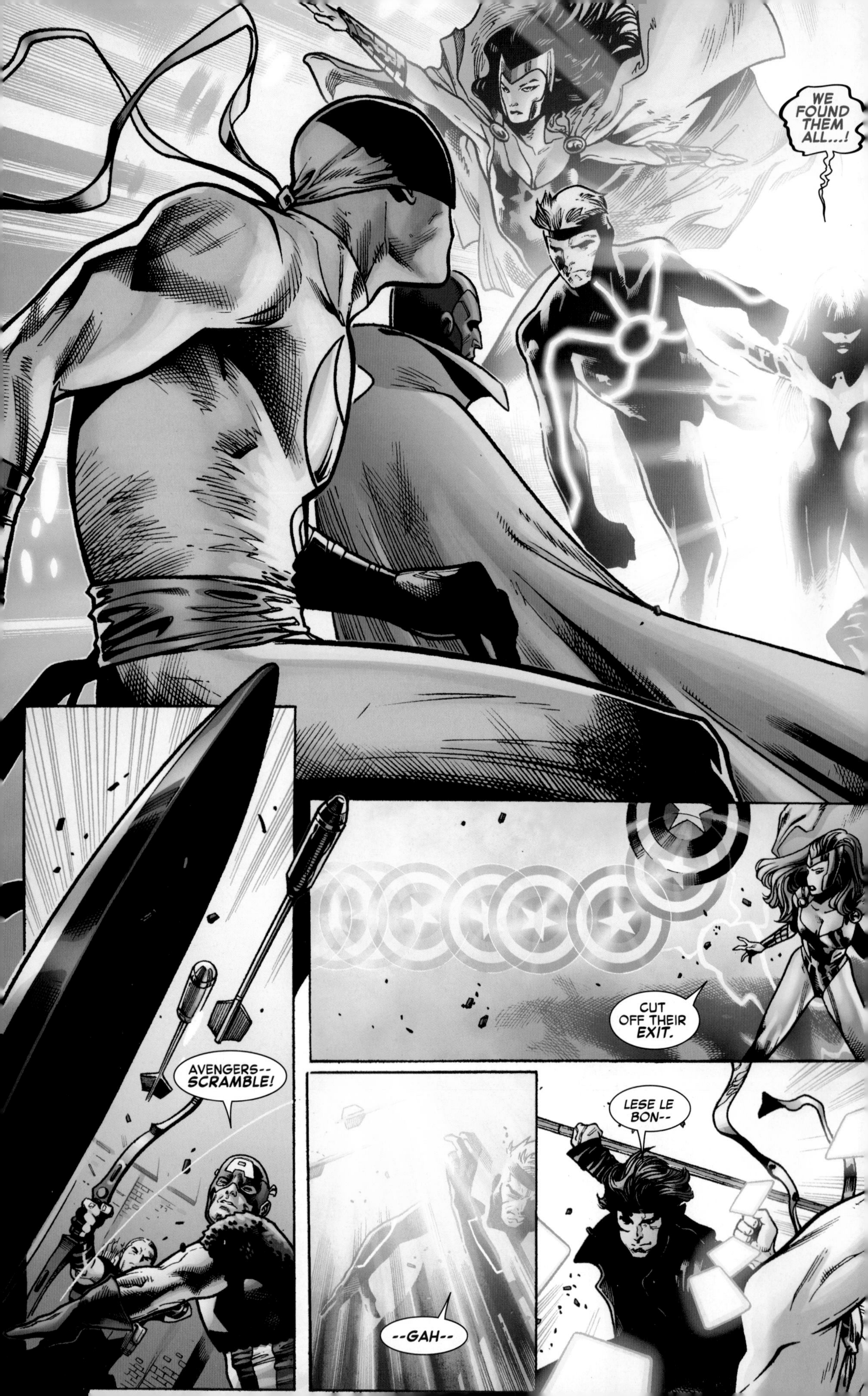
WE FOUND THEM ALL...!
CUT OFF THEIR EXIT.
AVENGERS-- SCRAMBLE!
--GAH--
LESE LE BON--

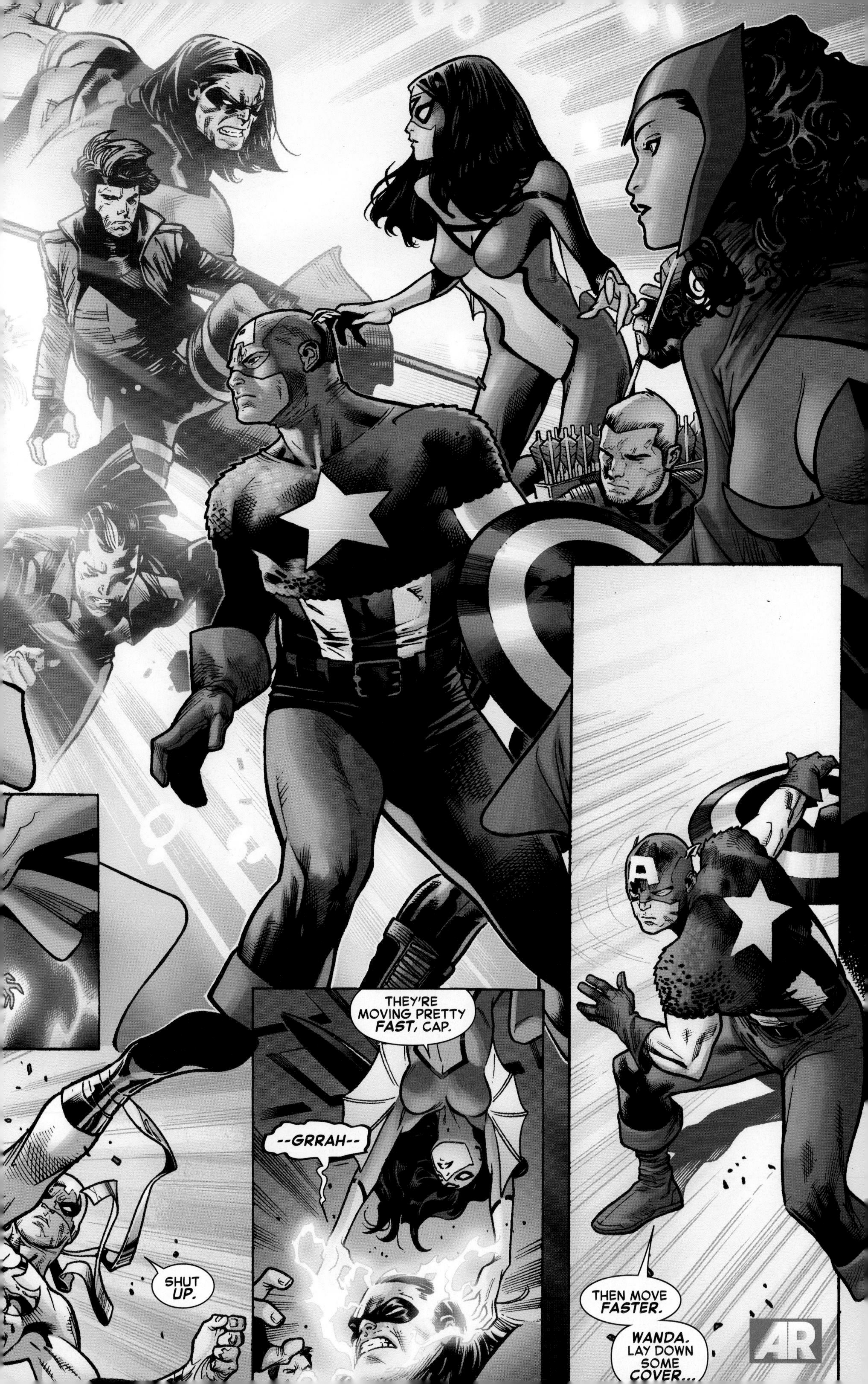
SHUT UP.
THEY'RE MOVING PRETTY FAST, CAP.
--GRRAH--
THEN MOVE FASTER.
WANDA. LAY DOWN SOME COVER...
AR

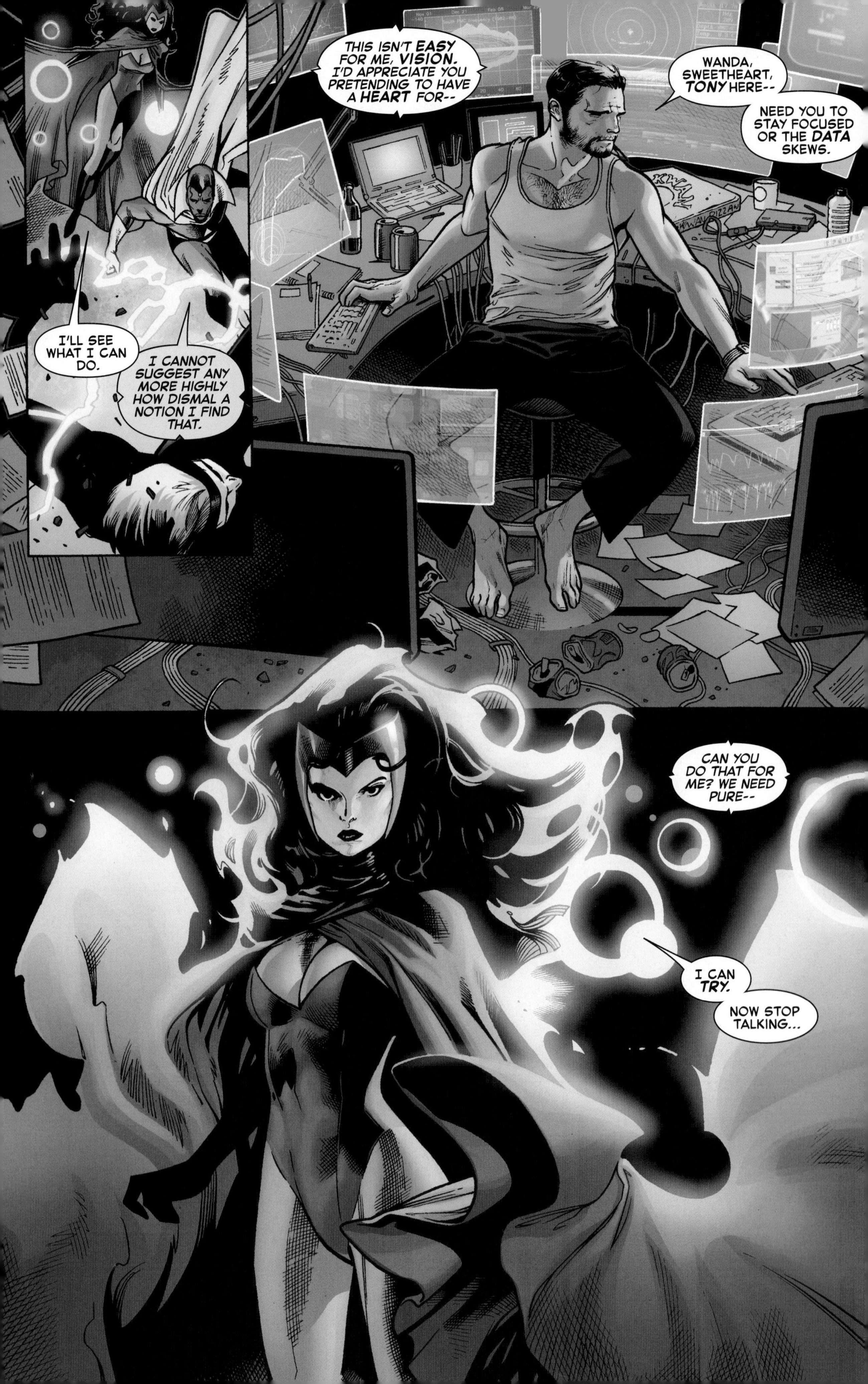
I'LL SEE WHAT I CAN DO.
I CANNOT SUGGEST ANY MORE HIGHLY HOW DISMAL A NOTION I FIND THAT.
THIS ISN'T EASY FOR ME, VISION. I'D APPRECIATE YOU PRETENDING TO HAVE A HEART FOR--
WANDA, SWEETHEART, TONY HERE--
NEED YOU TO STAY FOCUSED OR THE DATA SKEWS.
CAN YOU DO THAT FOR ME? WE NEED PURE--
I CAN TRY.
NOW STOP TALKING...

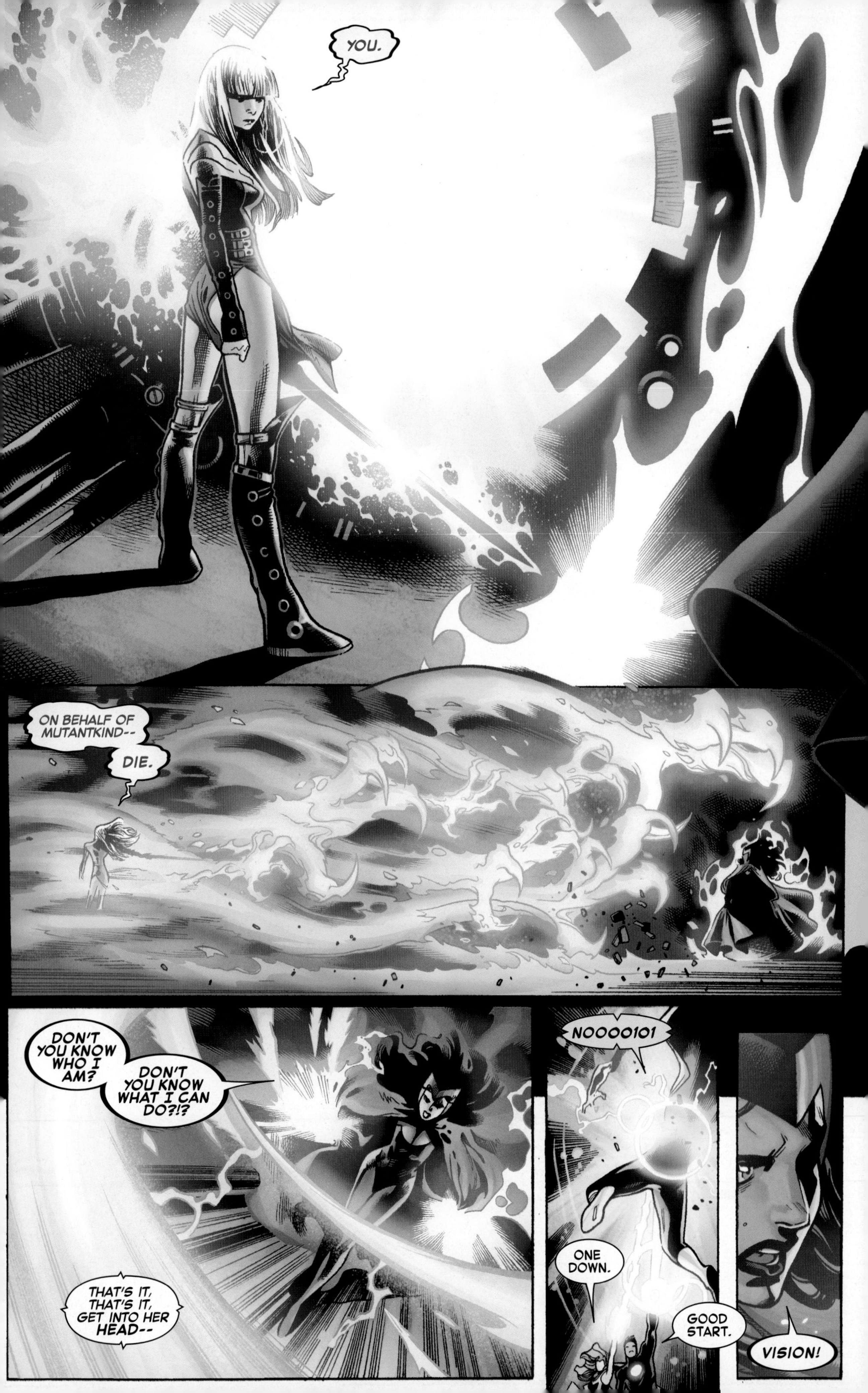
YOU.
ON BEHALF OF MUTANTKIND--
DIE.
DON'T YOU KNOW WHO I AM?
DON'T YOU KNOW WHAT I CAN DO?!?
THAT'S IT, THAT'S IT, GET INTO HER HEAD--
NOOOO101
ONE DOWN.
GOOD START.
VISION!

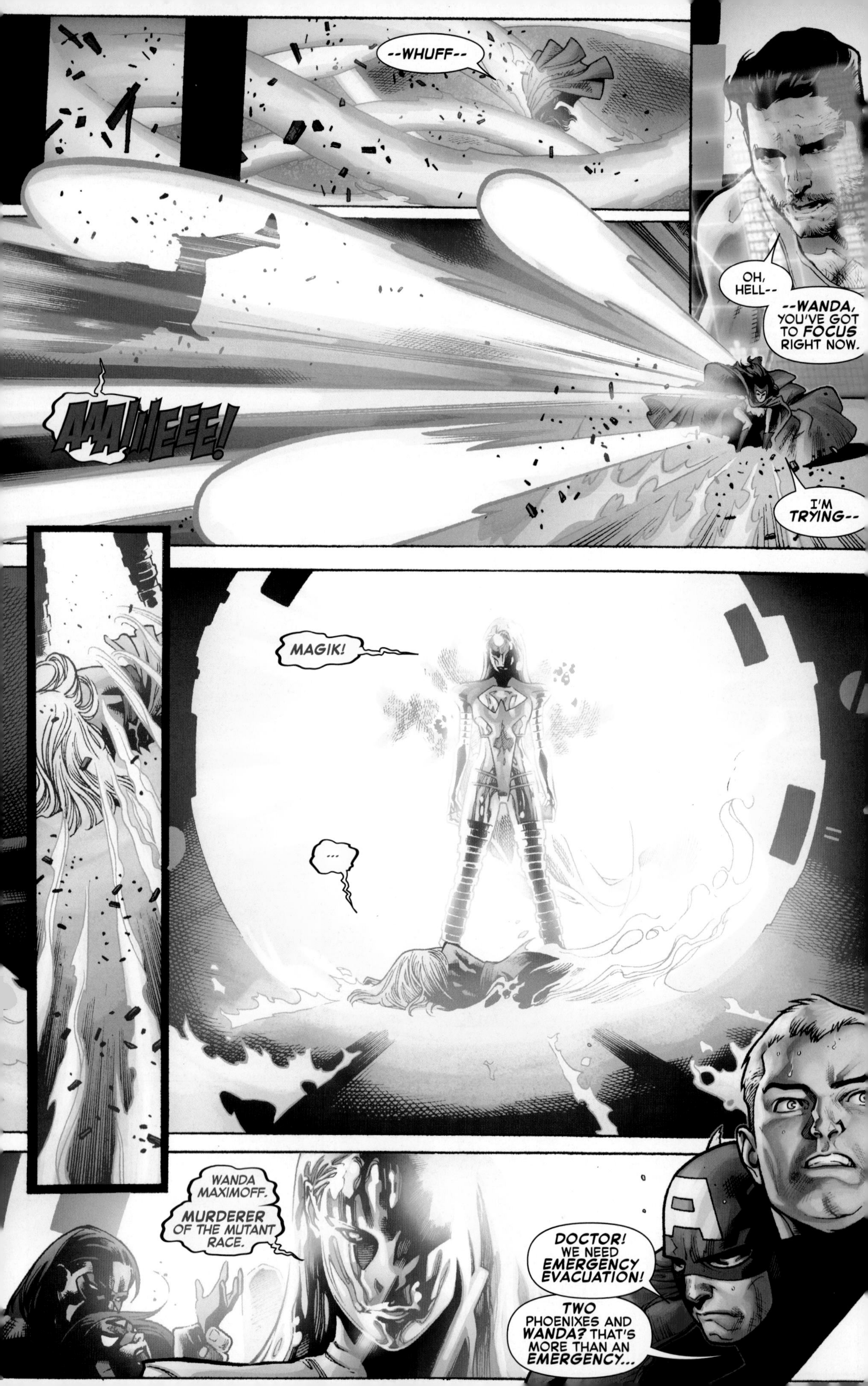
--WHUFF--
OH, HELL--
--WANDA, YOU'VE GOT TO FOCUS RIGHT NOW.
AAAIIIEEE!
I'M TRYING--
MAGIK!
...
WANDA MAXIMOFF.
MURDERER OF THE MUTANT RACE.
DOCTOR! WE NEED EMERGENCY EVACUATION!
TWO PHOENIXES AND WANDA? THAT'S MORE THAN AN EMERGENCY...

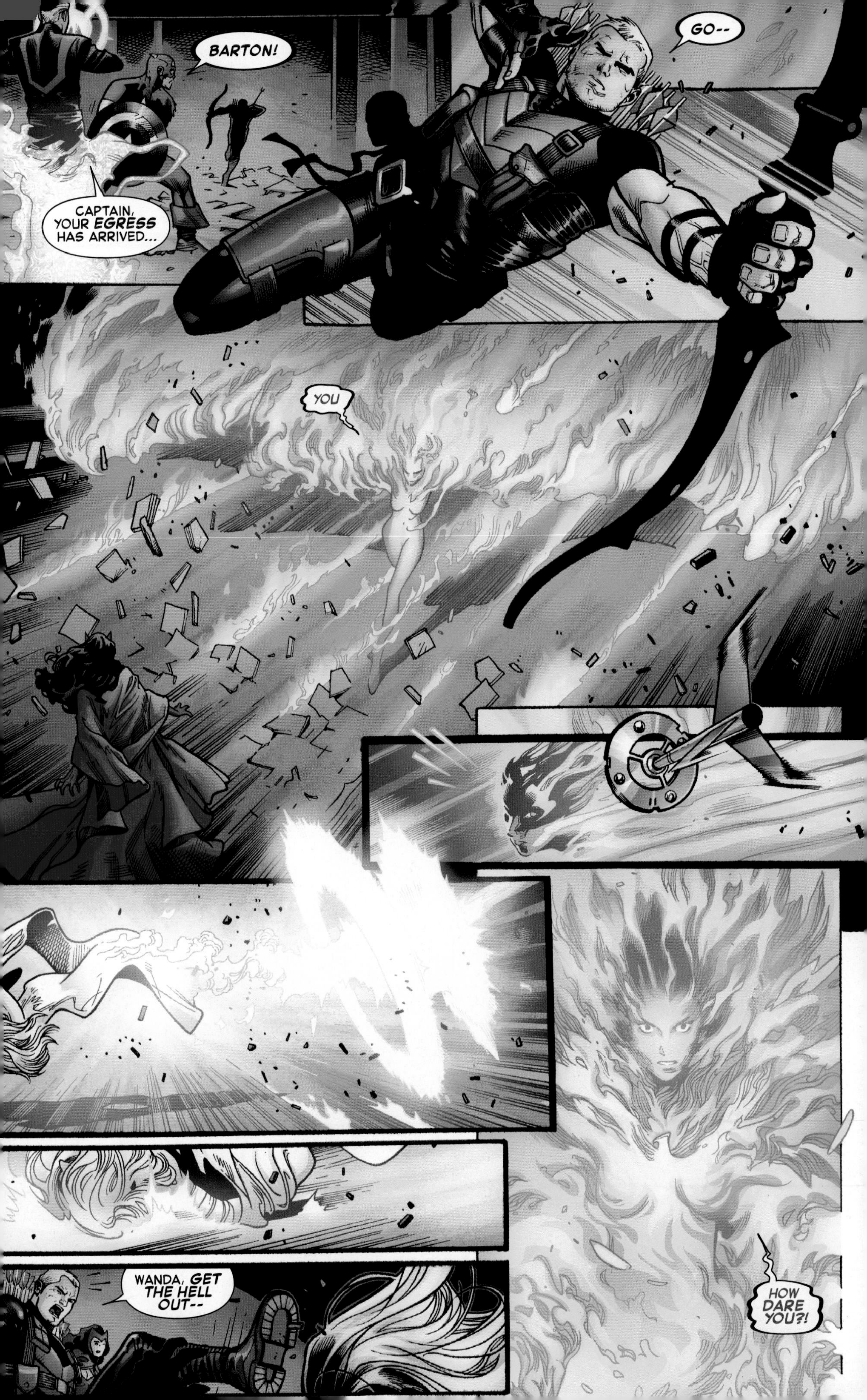
BARTON!
GO--
CAPTAIN, YOUR EGRESS HAS ARRIVED...
YOU
WANDA, GET THE HELL OUT--
HOW DARE YOU?!

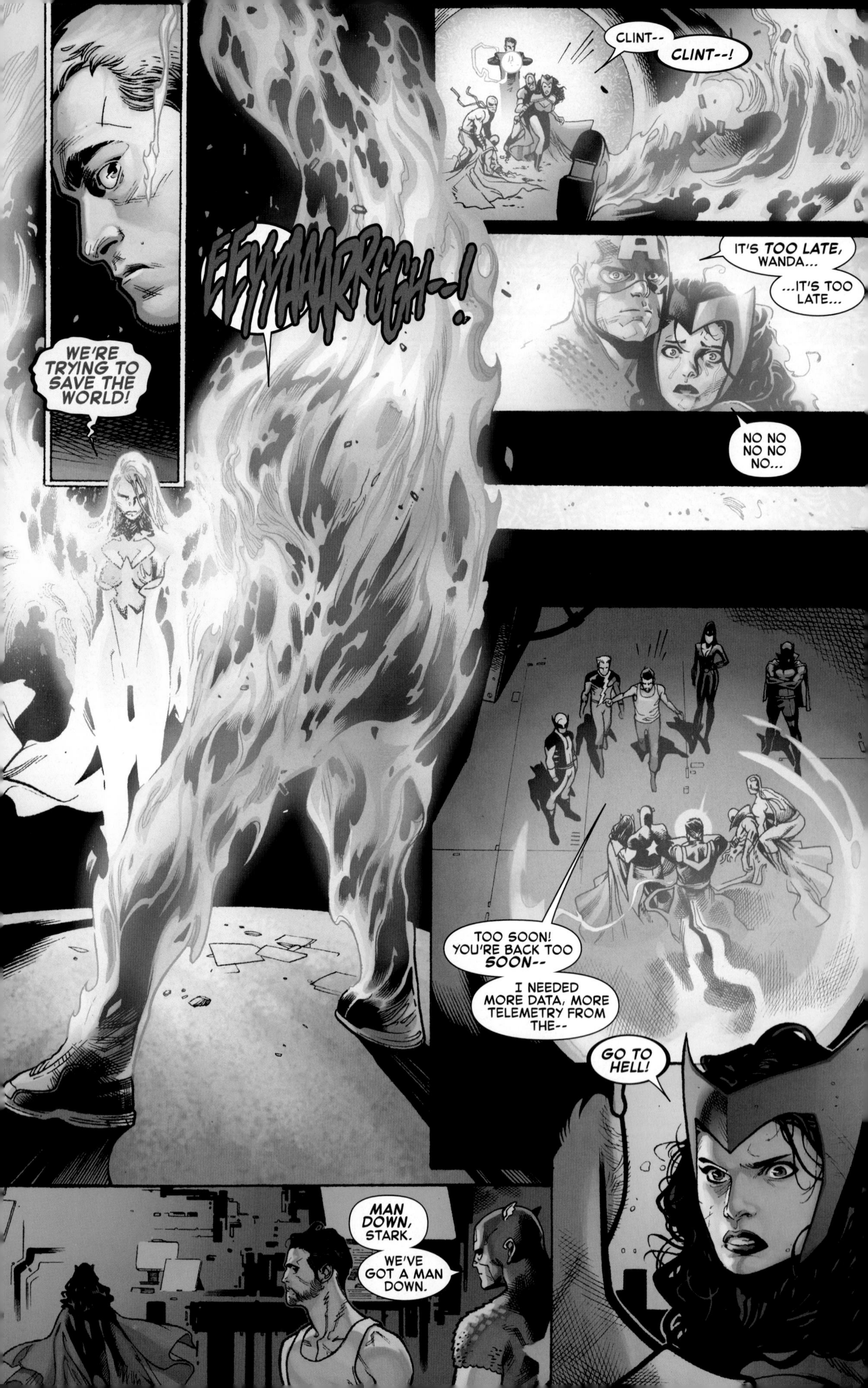

CLINT--
CLINT--!
IT'S TOO LATE, WANDA...
...IT'S TOO LATE...
NO NO NO NO NO...
WE'RE TRYING TO SAVE THE WORLD!
EEYYAAARRGGH--!
TOO SOON! YOU'RE BACK TOO SOON--
I NEEDED MORE DATA, MORE TELEMETRY FROM THE--
GO TO HELL!
MAN DOWN, STARK.
WE'VE GOT A MAN DOWN.

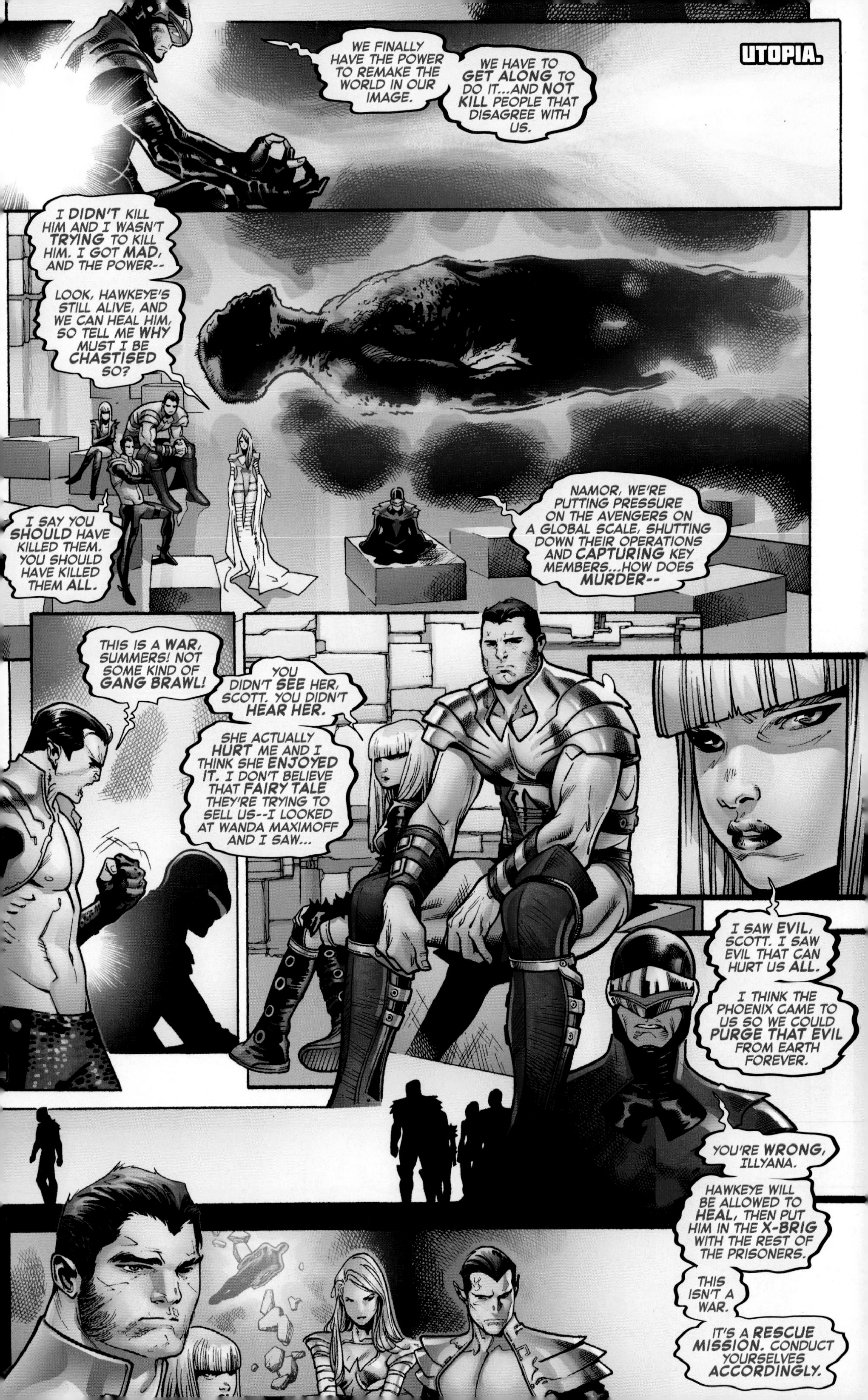
UTOPIA.
WE FINALLY HAVE THE POWER TO REMAKE THE WORLD IN OUR IMAGE.
WE HAVE TO GET ALONG TO DO IT...AND NOT KILL PEOPLE THAT DISAGREE WITH US.
I DIDN'T KILL HIM AND I WASN'T TRYING TO KILL HIM. I GOT MAD, AND THE POWER--
LOOK, HAWKEYE'S STILL ALIVE, AND WE CAN HEAL HIM, SO TELL ME WHY MUST I BE CHASTISED SO?
I SAY YOU SHOULD HAVE KILLED THEM. YOU SHOULD HAVE KILLED THEM ALL.
NAMOR, WE'RE PUTTING PRESSURE ON THE AVENGERS ON A GLOBAL SCALE, SHUTTING DOWN THEIR OPERATIONS AND CAPTURING KEY MEMBERS...HOW DOES MURDER--
THIS IS A WAR, SUMMERS! NOT SOME KIND OF GANG BRAWL!
YOU DIDN'T SEE HER, SCOTT. YOU DIDN'T HEAR HER.
SHE ACTUALLY HURT ME AND I THINK SHE ENJOYED IT. I DON'T BELIEVE THAT FAIRY TALE THEY'RE TRYING TO SELL US--I LOOKED AT WANDA MAXIMOFF AND I SAW...
I SAW EVIL, SCOTT. I SAW EVIL THAT CAN HURT US ALL.
I THINK THE PHOENIX CAME TO US SO WE COULD PURGE THAT EVIL FROM EARTH FOREVER.
YOU'RE WRONG, ILLYANA.
HAWKEYE WILL BE ALLOWED TO HEAL, THEN PUT HIM IN THE X-BRIG WITH THE REST OF THE PRISONERS.
THIS ISN'T A WAR.
IT'S A RESCUE MISSION. CONDUCT YOURSELVES ACCORDINGLY.

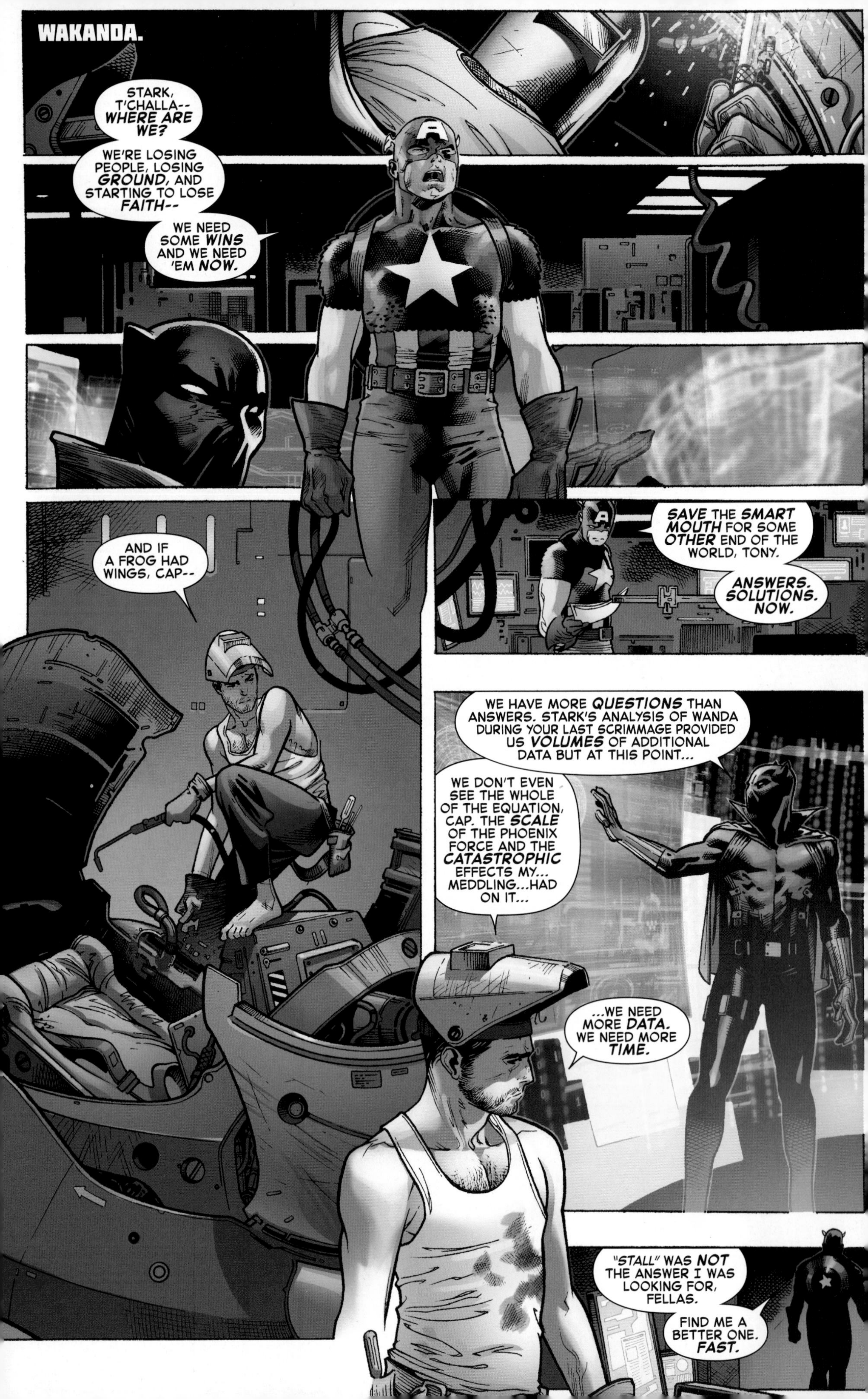
WAKANDA.
STARK, T'CHALLA-- WHERE ARE WE?
WE'RE LOSING PEOPLE, LOSING GROUND, AND STARTING TO LOSE FAITH--
WE NEED SOME WINS AND WE NEED 'EM NOW.
AND IF A FROG HAD WINGS, CAP--
SAVE THE SMART MOUTH FOR SOME OTHER END OF THE WORLD, TONY.
ANSWERS. SOLUTIONS. NOW.
WE HAVE MORE QUESTIONS THAN ANSWERS. STARK'S ANALYSIS OF WANDA DURING YOUR LAST SCRIMMAGE PROVIDED US VOLUMES OF ADDITIONAL DATA BUT AT THIS POINT...
WE DON'T EVEN SEE THE WHOLE OF THE EQUATION, CAP. THE SCALE OF THE PHOENIX FORCE AND THE CATASTROPHIC EFFECTS MY... MEDDLING...HAD ON IT...
...WE NEED MORE DATA. WE NEED MORE TIME.
"STALL" WAS NOT THE ANSWER I WAS LOOKING FOR, FELLAS.
FIND ME A BETTER ONE. FAST.

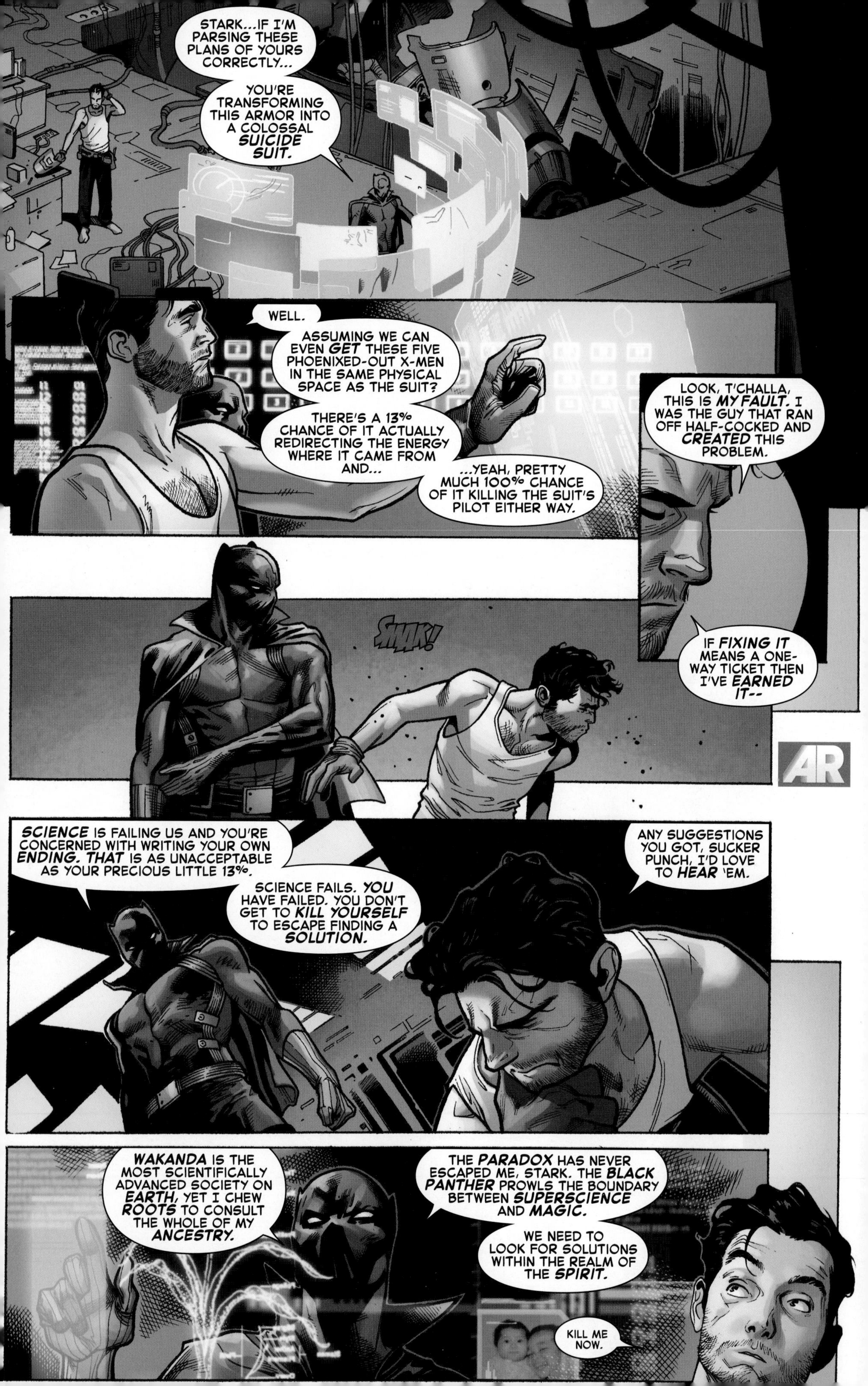
STARK...IF I'M PARSING THESE PLANS OF YOURS CORRECTLY...
YOU'RE TRANSFORMING THIS ARMOR INTO A COLOSSAL SUICIDE SUIT.
WELL.
ASSUMING WE CAN EVEN GET THESE FIVE PHOENIXED-OUT X-MEN IN THE SAME PHYSICAL SPACE AS THE SUIT?
THERE'S A 13% CHANCE OF IT ACTUALLY REDIRECTING THE ENERGY WHERE IT CAME FROM AND...
...YEAH, PRETTY MUCH 100% CHANCE OF IT KILLING THE SUIT'S PILOT EITHER WAY.
LOOK, T'CHALLA, THIS IS MY FAULT. I WAS THE GUY THAT RAN OFF HALF-COCKED AND CREATED THIS PROBLEM.
IF FIXING IT MEANS A ONE-WAY TICKET THEN I'VE EARNED IT--
SMAK!
SCIENCE IS FAILING US AND YOU'RE CONCERNED WITH WRITING YOUR OWN ENDING. THAT IS AS UNACCEPTABLE AS YOUR PRECIOUS LITTLE 13%.
SCIENCE FAILS. YOU HAVE FAILED. YOU DON'T GET TO KILL YOURSELF TO ESCAPE FINDING A SOLUTION.
ANY SUGGESTIONS YOU GOT, SUCKER PUNCH, I'D LOVE TO HEAR 'EM.
WAKANDA IS THE MOST SCIENTIFICALLY ADVANCED SOCIETY ON EARTH, YET I CHEW ROOTS TO CONSULT THE WHOLE OF MY ANCESTRY.
THE PARADOX HAS NEVER ESCAPED ME, STARK. THE BLACK PANTHER PROWLS THE BOUNDARY BETWEEN SUPERSCIENCE AND MAGIC.
WE NEED TO LOOK FOR SOLUTIONS WITHIN THE REALM OF THE SPIRIT.
KILL ME NOW.

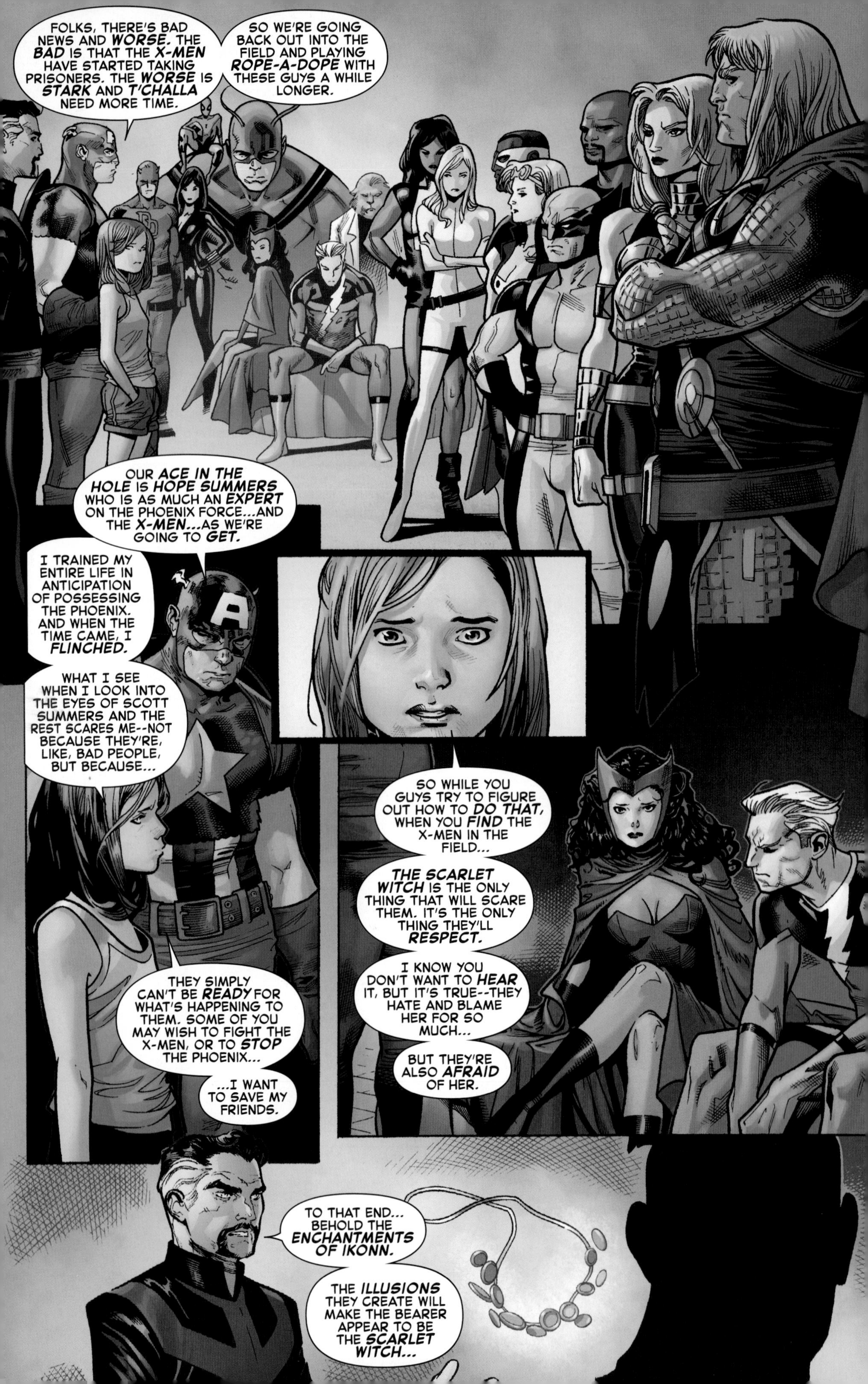
FOLKS, THERE'S BAD NEWS AND WORSE. THE BAD IS THAT THE X-MEN HAVE STARTED TAKING PRISONERS. THE WORSE IS STARK AND T'CHALLA NEED MORE TIME.
SO WE'RE GOING BACK OUT INTO THE FIELD AND PLAYING ROPE-A-DOPE WITH THESE GUYS A WHILE LONGER.
OUR ACE IN THE HOLE IS HOPE SUMMERS WHO IS AS MUCH AN EXPERT ON THE PHOENIX FORCE...AND THE X-MEN...AS WE'RE GOING TO GET.
I TRAINED MY ENTIRE LIFE IN ANTICIPATION OF POSSESSING THE PHOENIX. AND WHEN THE TIME CAME, I FLINCHED.
WHAT I SEE WHEN I LOOK INTO THE EYES OF SCOTT SUMMERS AND THE REST SCARES ME--NOT BECAUSE THEY'RE, LIKE, BAD PEOPLE, BUT BECAUSE...
THEY SIMPLY CAN'T BE READY FOR WHAT'S HAPPENING TO THEM. SOME OF YOU MAY WISH TO FIGHT THE X-MEN, OR TO STOP THE PHOENIX...
...I WANT TO SAVE MY FRIENDS.
SO WHILE YOU GUYS TRY TO FIGURE OUT HOW TO DO THAT, WHEN YOU FIND THE X-MEN IN THE FIELD...
THE SCARLET WITCH IS THE ONLY THING THAT WILL SCARE THEM. IT'S THE ONLY THING THEY'LL RESPECT.
I KNOW YOU DON'T WANT TO HEAR IT, BUT IT'S TRUE--THEY HATE AND BLAME HER FOR SO MUCH...
BUT THEY'RE ALSO AFRAID OF HER.
TO THAT END... BEHOLD THE ENCHANTMENTS OF IKONN.
THE ILLUSIONS THEY CREATE WILL MAKE THE BEARER APPEAR TO BE THE SCARLET WITCH...

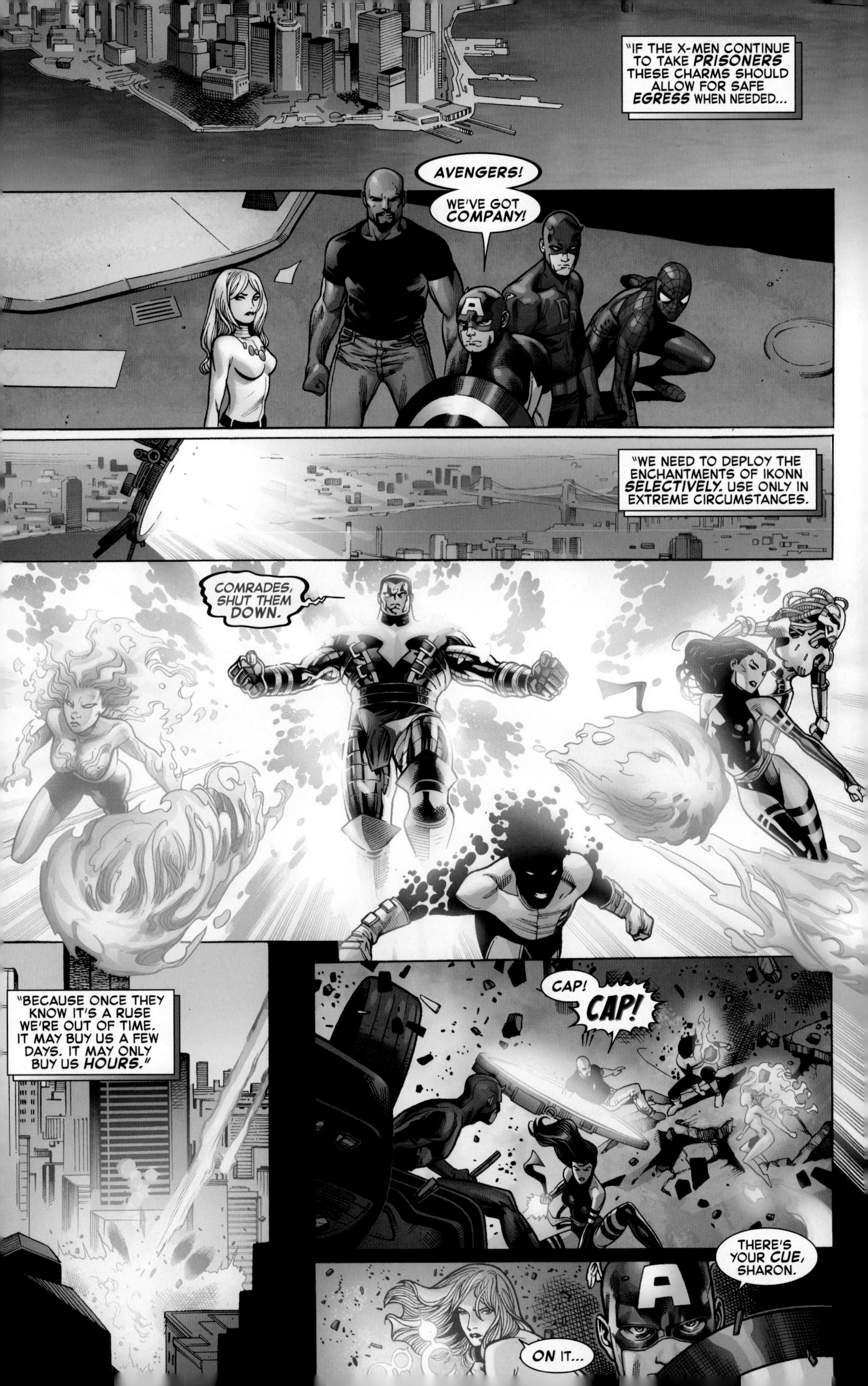
"IF THE X-MEN CONTINUE TO TAKE PRISONERS THESE CHARMS SHOULD ALLOW FOR SAFE EGRESS WHEN NEEDED...
AVENGERS!
WE'VE GOT COMPANY!
"WE NEED TO DEPLOY THE ENCHANTMENTS OF IKONN SELECTIVELY. USE ONLY IN EXTREME CIRCUMSTANCES.
COMRADES, SHUT THEM DOWN.
"BECAUSE ONCE THEY KNOW IT'S A RUSE WE'RE OUT OF TIME. IT MAY BUY US A FEW DAYS. IT MAY ONLY BUY US HOURS."
CAP! CAP!
THERE'S YOUR CUE, SHARON.
ON IT...

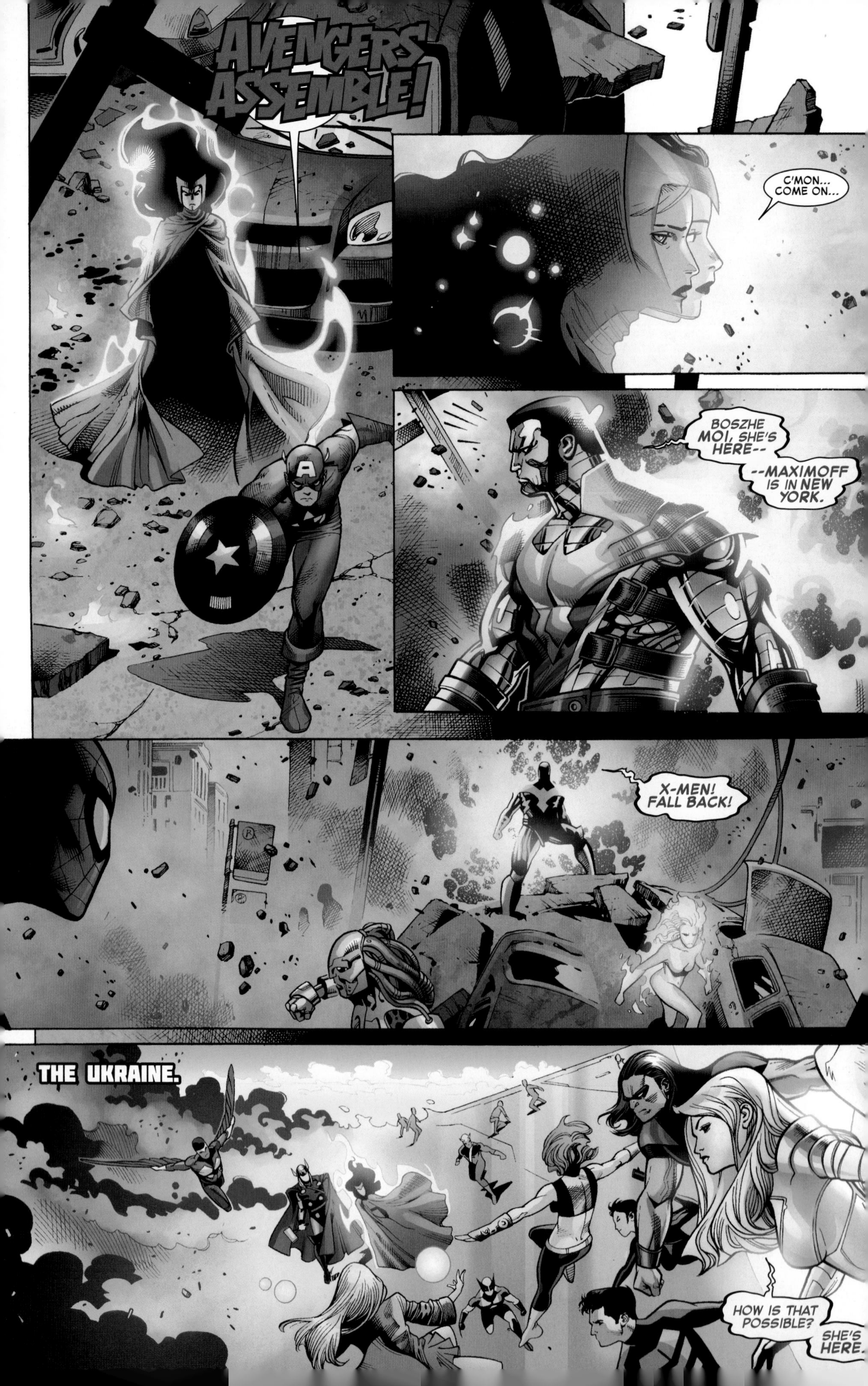
AVENGERS ASSEMBLE!
C'MON... COME ON...
BOSZHE MOI, SHE'S HERE--
--MAXIMOFF IS IN NEW YORK.
X-MEN! FALL BACK!
THE UKRAINE.
HOW IS THAT POSSIBLE?
SHE'S HERE.

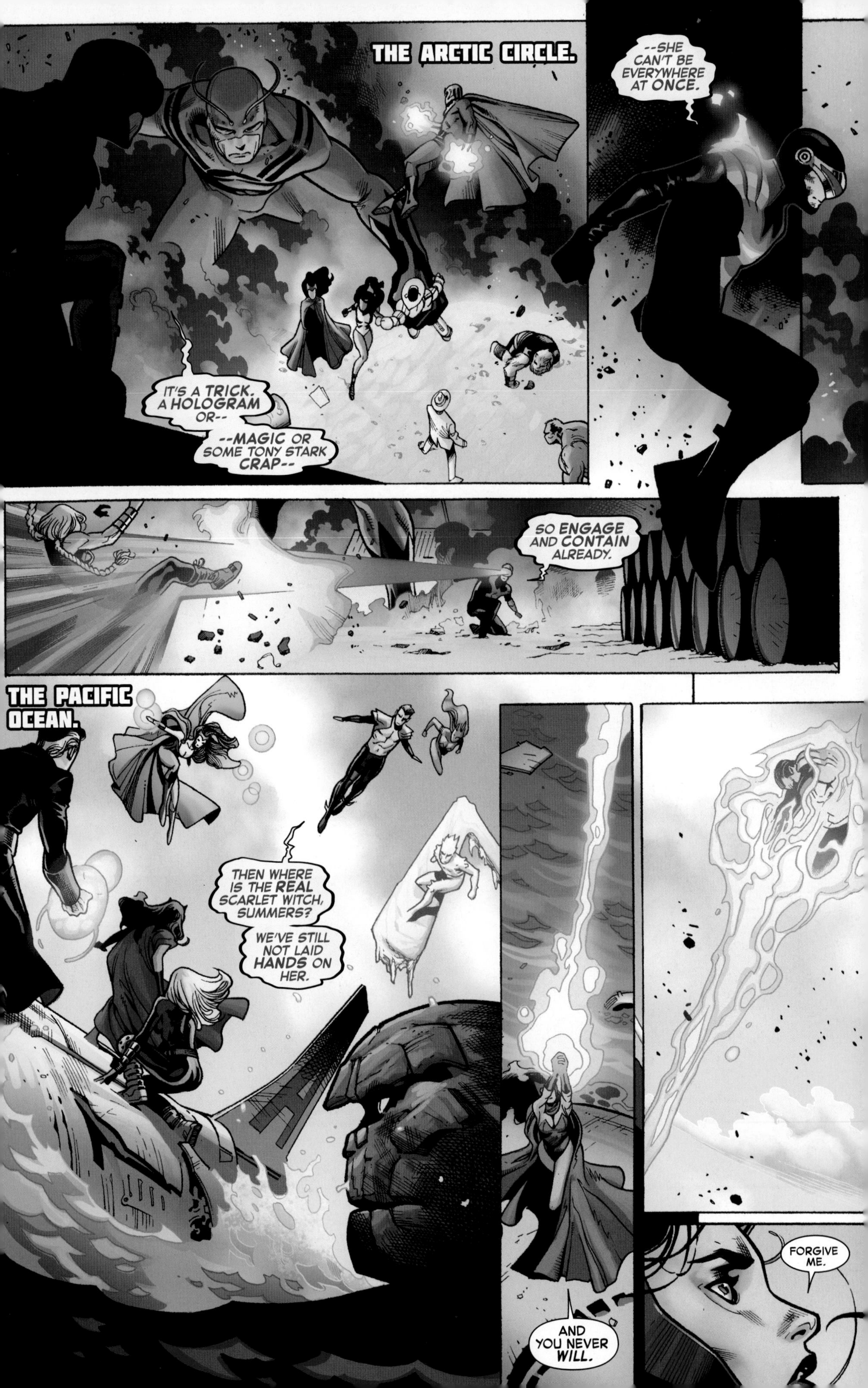
THE ARCTIC CIRCLE.
--SHE CAN'T BE EVERYWHERE AT ONCE.
IT'S A TRICK. A HOLOGRAM OR--
--MAGIC OR SOME TONY STARK CRAP--
SO ENGAGE AND CONTAIN ALREADY.
THE PACIFIC OCEAN.
THEN WHERE IS THE REAL SCARLET WITCH, SUMMERS?
WE'VE STILL NOT LAID HANDS ON HER.
FORGIVE ME.
AND YOU NEVER WILL.

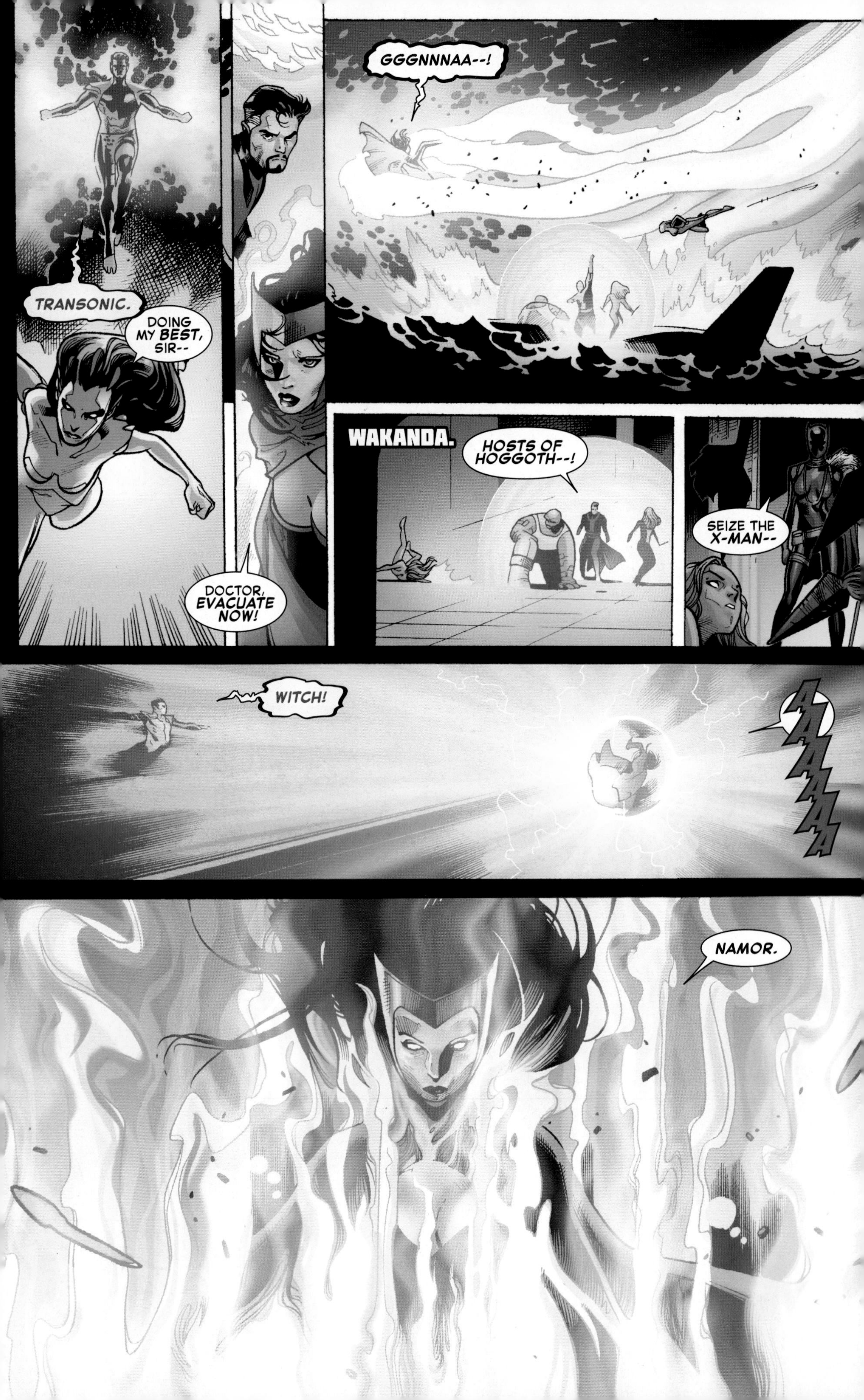

TRANSONIC.
DOING MY BEST, SIR--
DOCTOR, EVACUATE NOW!
GGGNNNAA--!
WAKANDA.
HOSTS OF HOGGOTH--!
SEIZE THE X-MAN--
WITCH!
AAAAAAA
NAMOR.

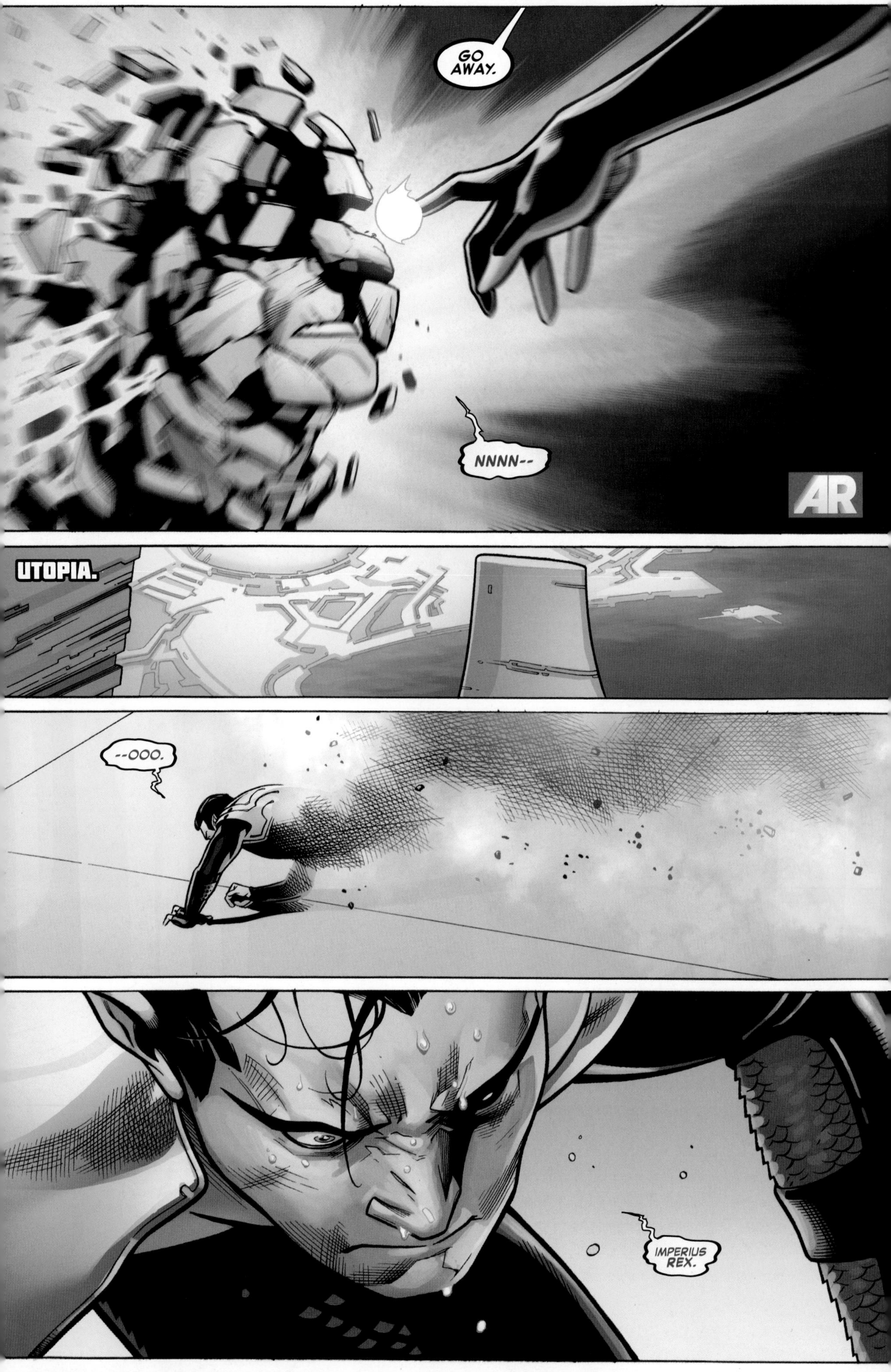
GO AWAY.
NNNN--
UTOPIA.
--OOO.
IMPERIUS REX.

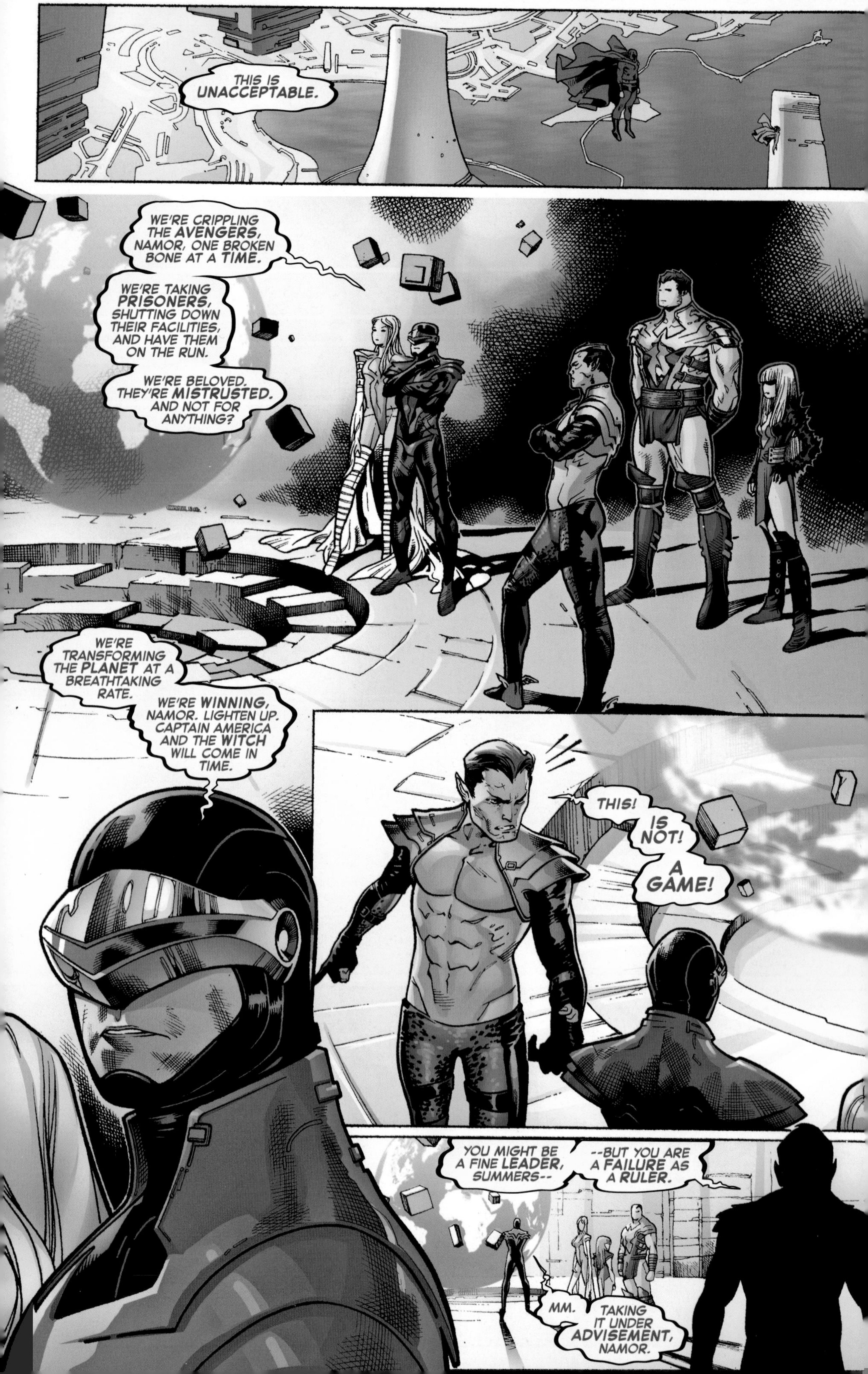
THIS IS UNACCEPTABLE.
WE'RE CRIPPLING THE AVENGERS, NAMOR, ONE BROKEN BONE AT A TIME.
WE'RE TAKING PRISONERS, SHUTTING DOWN THEIR FACILITIES, AND HAVE THEM ON THE RUN.
WE'RE BELOVED. THEY'RE MISTRUSTED. AND NOT FOR ANYTHING?
WE'RE TRANSFORMING THE PLANET AT A BREATHTAKING RATE.
WE'RE WINNING, NAMOR. LIGHTEN UP. CAPTAIN AMERICA AND THE WITCH WILL COME IN TIME.
THIS!
IS NOT!
A GAME!
YOU MIGHT BE A FINE LEADER, SUMMERS--
--BUT YOU ARE A FAILURE AS A RULER.
MM.
TAKING IT UNDER ADVISEMENT, NAMOR.

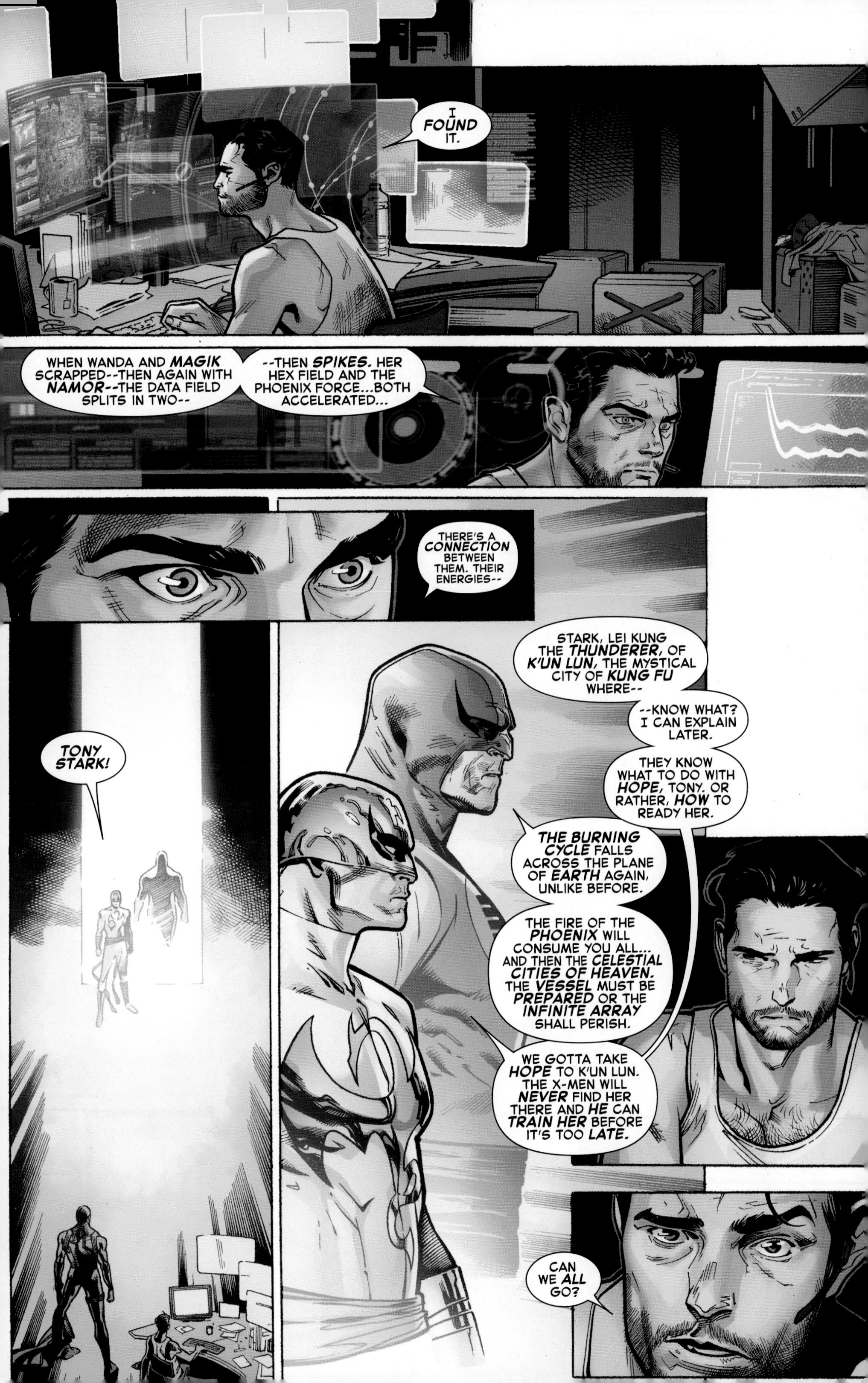
I FOUND IT.
WHEN WANDA AND MAGIK SCRAPPED--THEN AGAIN WITH NAMOR--THE DATA FIELD SPLITS IN TWO--
--THEN SPIKES. HER HEX FIELD AND THE PHOENIX FORCE...BOTH ACCELERATED...
THERE'S A CONNECTION BETWEEN THEM. THEIR ENERGIES--
TONY STARK!
STARK, LEI KUNG THE THUNDERER, OF K'UN LUN, THE MYSTICAL CITY OF KUNG FU WHERE--
--KNOW WHAT? I CAN EXPLAIN LATER.
THEY KNOW WHAT TO DO WITH HOPE, TONY. OR RATHER, HOW TO READY HER.
THE BURNING CYCLE FALLS ACROSS THE PLANE OF EARTH AGAIN, UNLIKE BEFORE.
THE FIRE OF THE PHOENIX WILL CONSUME YOU ALL... AND THEN THE CELESTIAL CITIES OF HEAVEN. THE VESSEL MUST BE PREPARED OR THE INFINITE ARRAY SHALL PERISH.
WE GOTTA TAKE HOPE TO K'UN LUN. THE X-MEN WILL NEVER FIND HER THERE AND HE CAN TRAIN HER BEFORE IT'S TOO LATE.
CAN WE ALL GO?

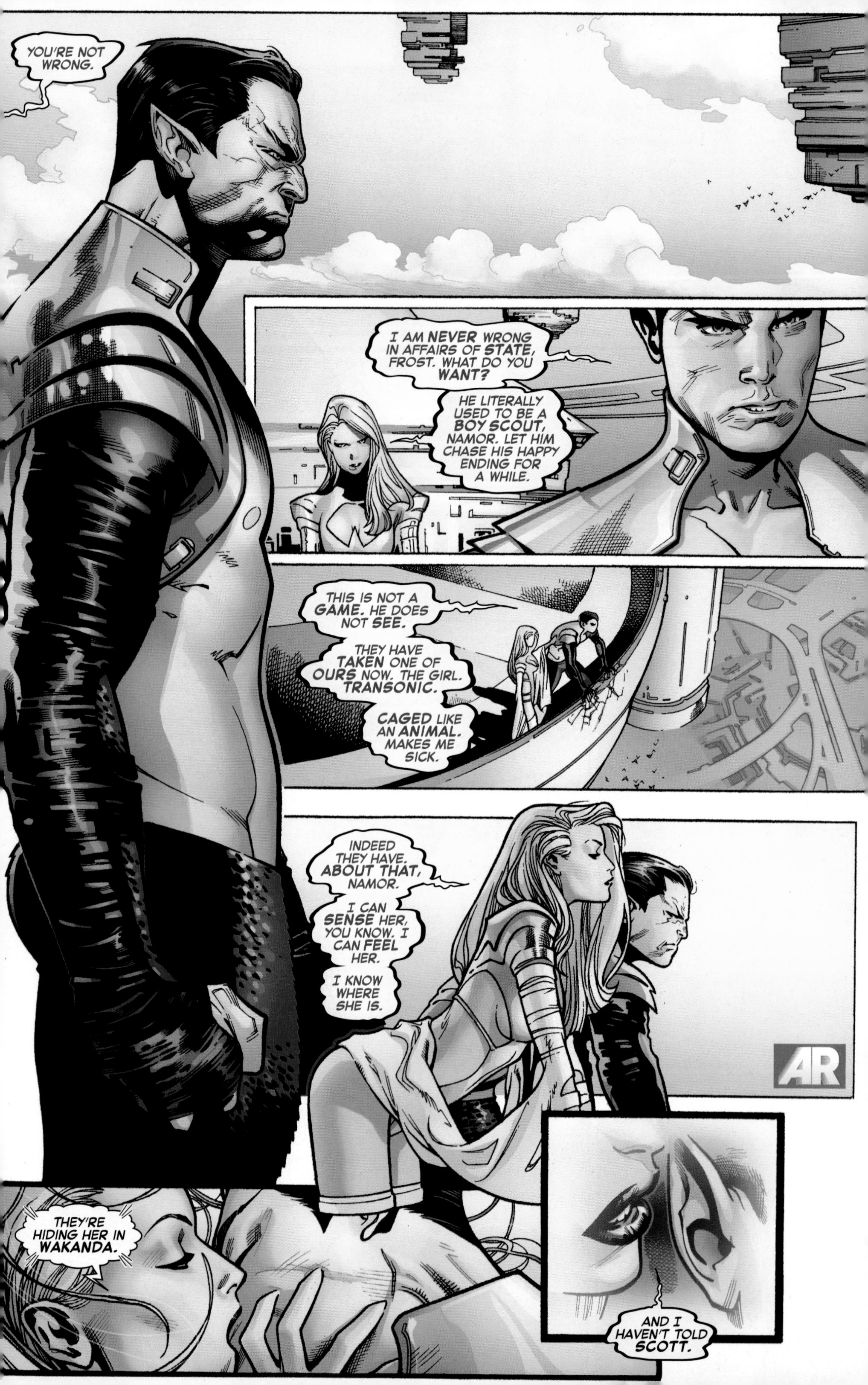
YOU'RE NOT WRONG.
I AM NEVER WRONG IN AFFAIRS OF STATE, FROST. WHAT DO YOU WANT?
HE LITERALLY USED TO BE A BOY SCOUT, NAMOR. LET HIM CHASE HIS HAPPY ENDING FOR A WHILE.
THIS IS NOT A GAME. HE DOES NOT SEE.
THEY HAVE TAKEN ONE OF OURS NOW. THE GIRL. TRANSONIC.
CAGED LIKE AN ANIMAL. MAKES ME SICK.
INDEED THEY HAVE. ABOUT THAT, NAMOR.
I CAN SENSE HER, YOU KNOW. I CAN FEEL HER.
I KNOW WHERE SHE IS.
THEY'RE HIDING HER IN WAKANDA.
AND I HAVEN'T TOLD SCOTT.

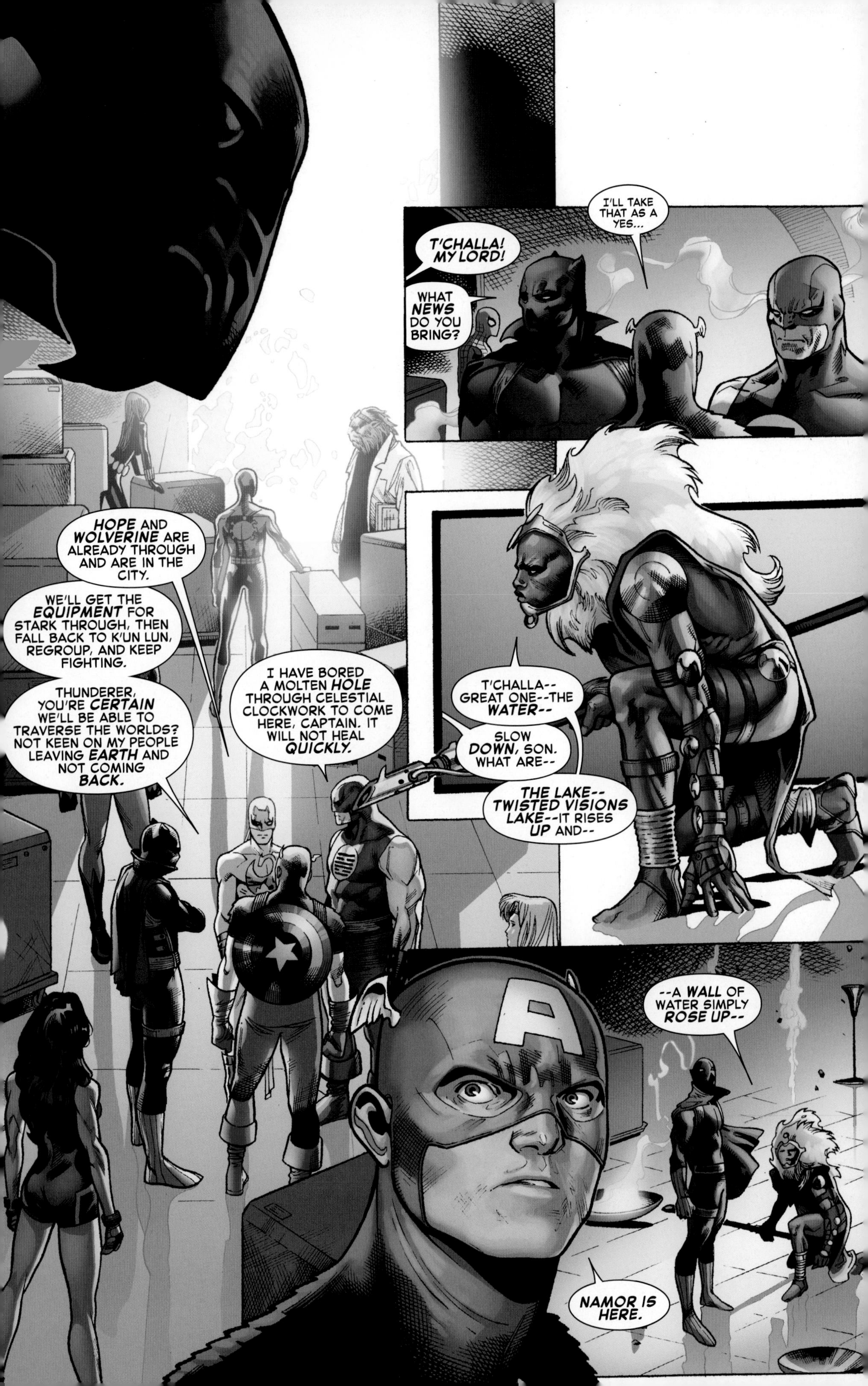
T'CHALLA! MY LORD!
WHAT NEWS DO YOU BRING?
I'LL TAKE THAT AS A YES...
HOPE AND WOLVERINE ARE ALREADY THROUGH AND ARE IN THE CITY.
WE'LL GET THE EQUIPMENT FOR STARK THROUGH, THEN FALL BACK TO K'UN LUN, REGROUP, AND KEEP FIGHTING.
THUNDERER, YOU'RE CERTAIN WE'LL BE ABLE TO TRAVERSE THE WORLDS? NOT KEEN ON MY PEOPLE LEAVING EARTH AND NOT COMING BACK.
I HAVE BORED A MOLTEN HOLE THROUGH CELESTIAL CLOCKWORK TO COME HERE, CAPTAIN. IT WILL NOT HEAL QUICKLY.
T'CHALLA-- GREAT ONE--THE WATER--
SLOW DOWN, SON. WHAT ARE--
THE LAKE-- TWISTED VISIONS LAKE--IT RISES UP AND--
--A WALL OF WATER SIMPLY ROSE UP--
NAMOR IS HERE.

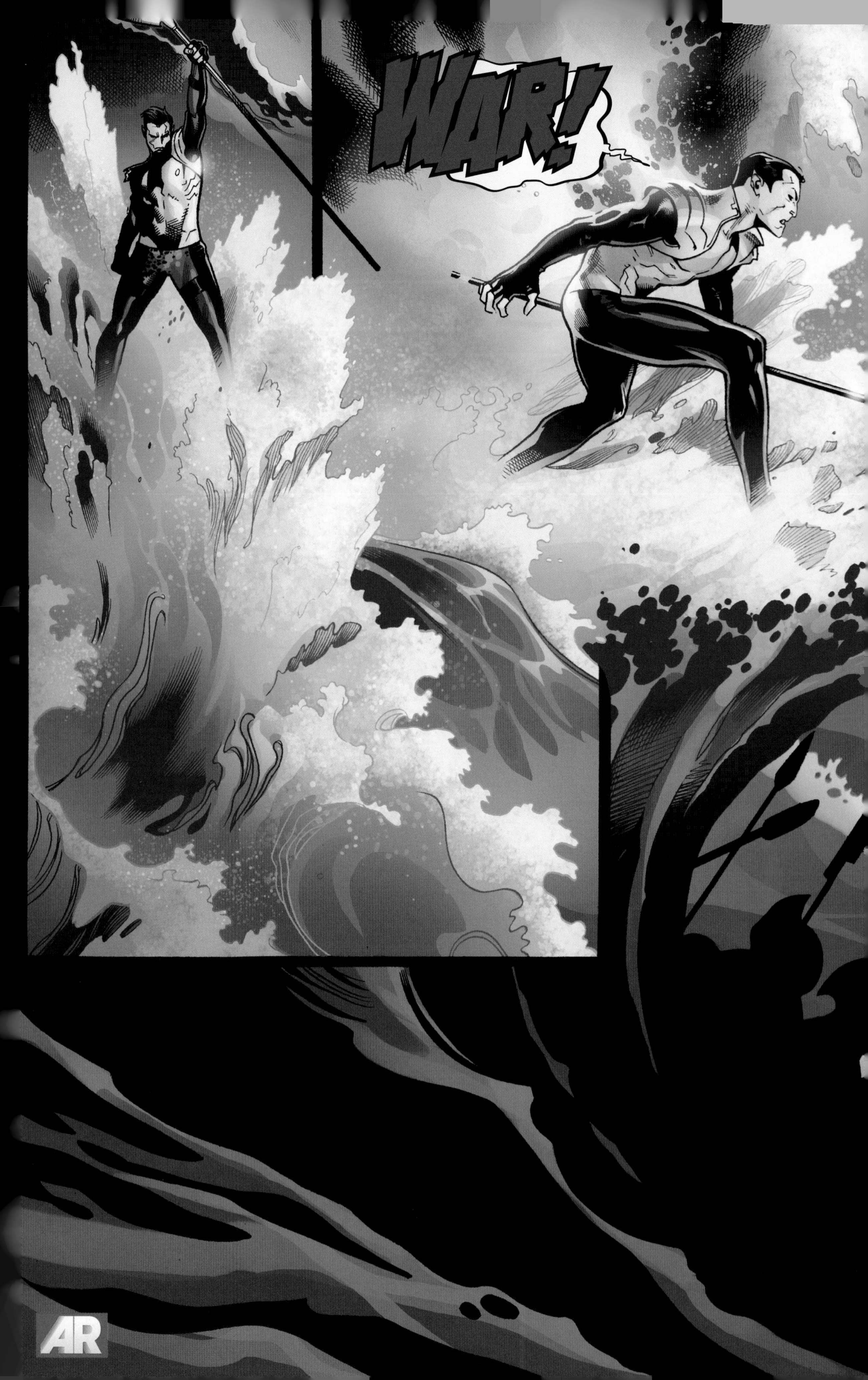
WAR!

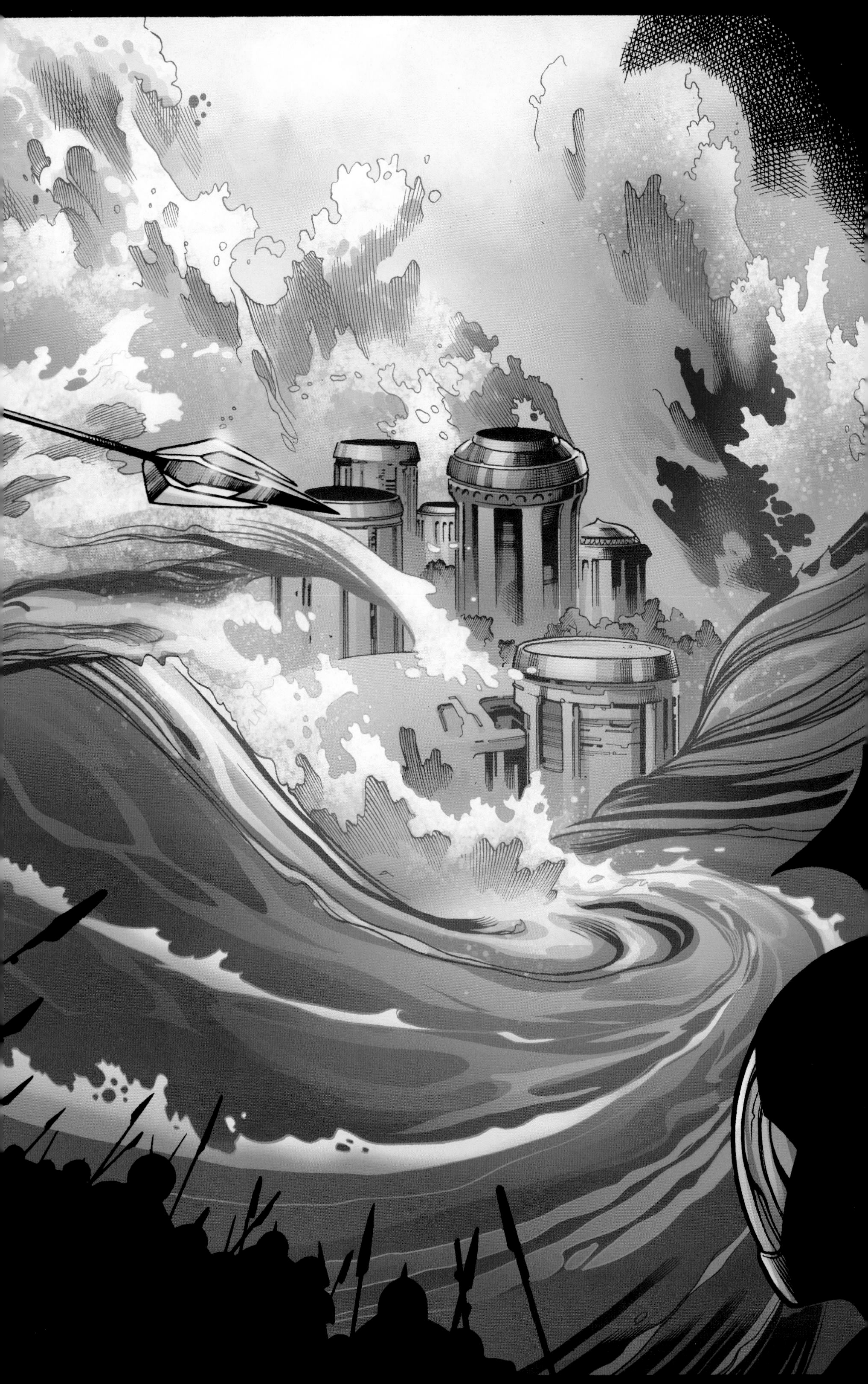

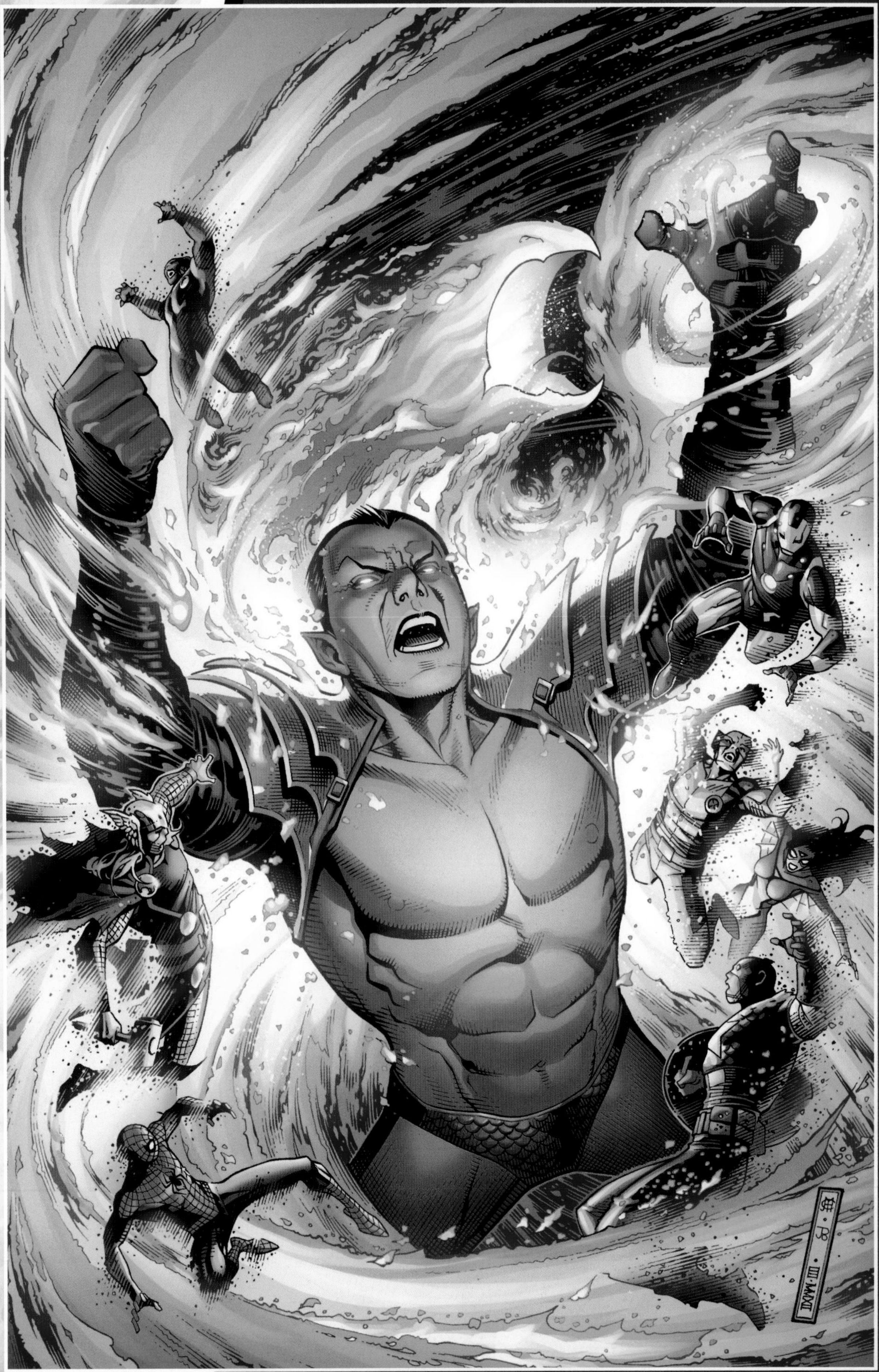

ROUND 8

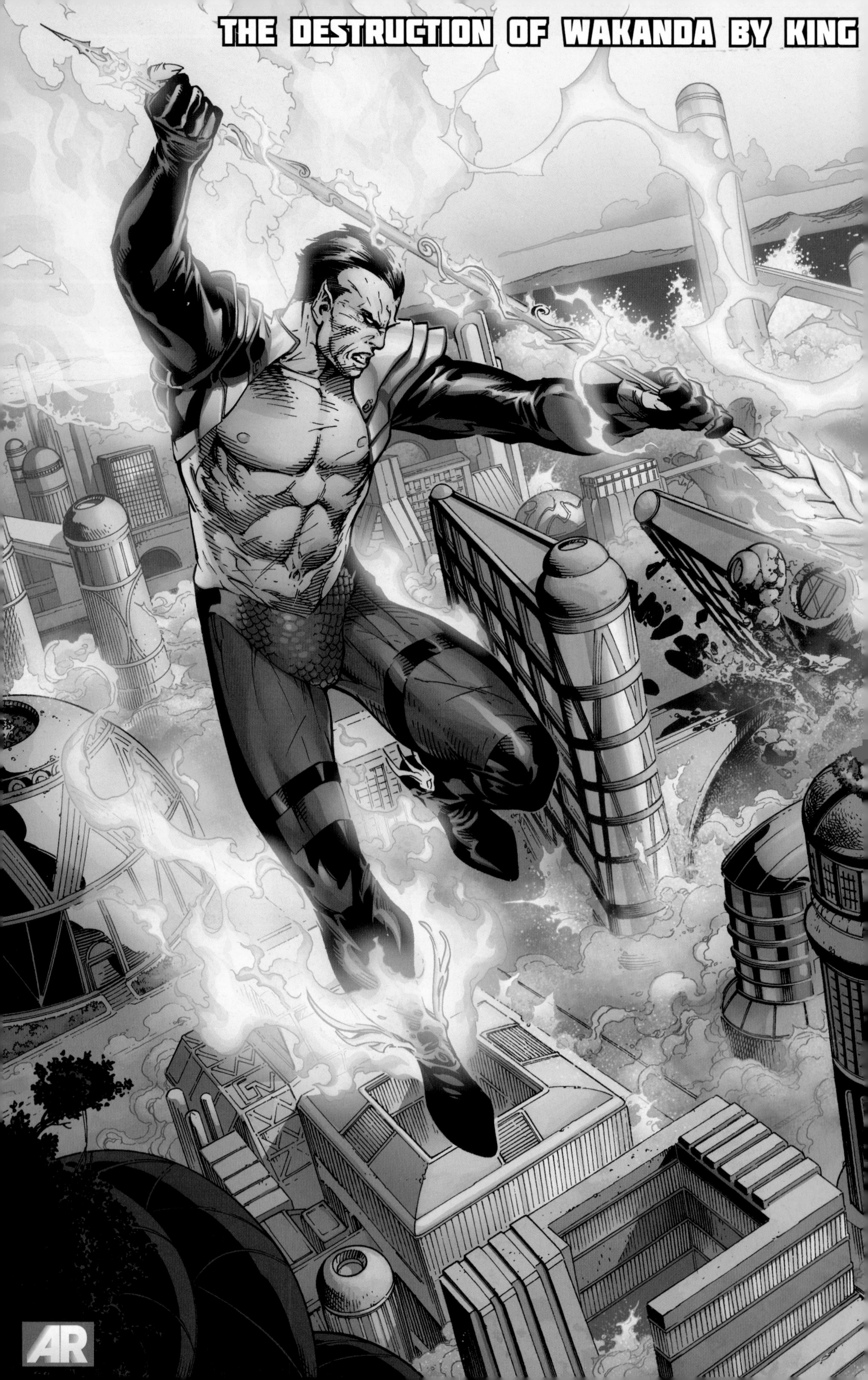
THE DESTRUCTION OF WAKANDA BY KING
AR

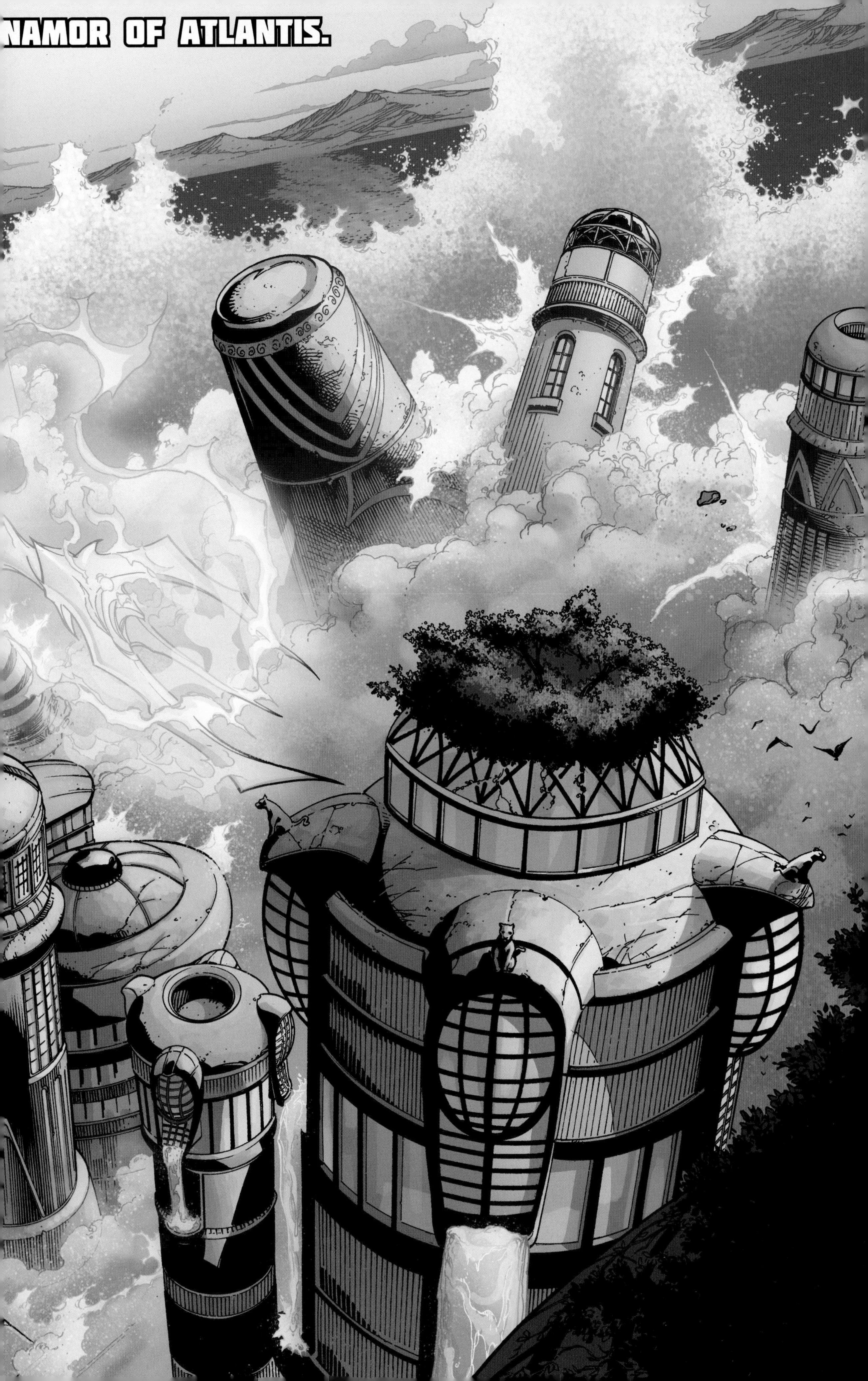
NAMOR OF ATLANTIS.

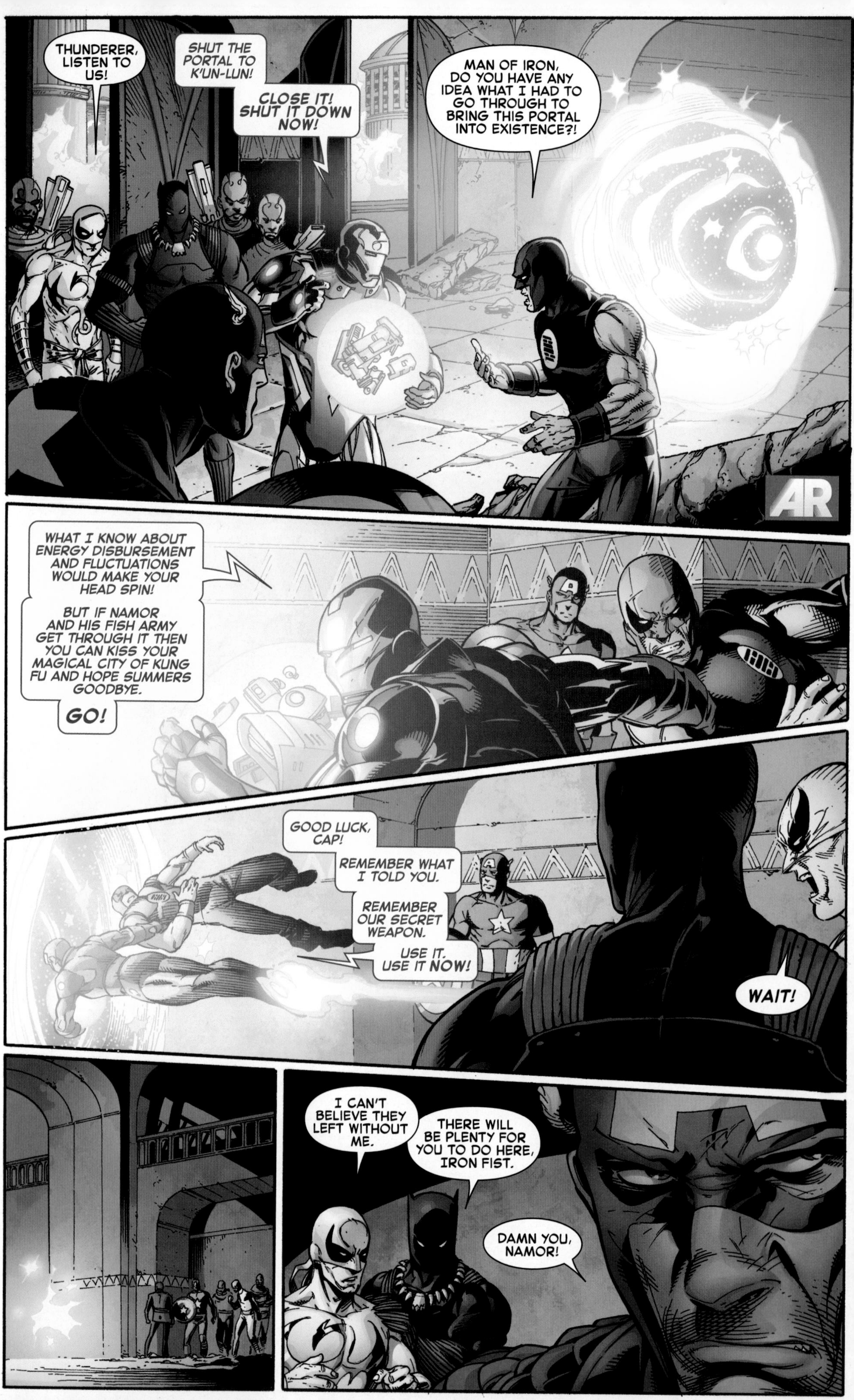
THUNDERER, LISTEN TO US!
SHUT THE PORTAL TO K'UN-LUN!
CLOSE IT! SHUT IT DOWN NOW!
MAN OF IRON, DO YOU HAVE ANY IDEA WHAT I HAD TO GO THROUGH TO BRING THIS PORTAL INTO EXISTENCE?!
AR
WHAT I KNOW ABOUT ENERGY DISBURSEMENT AND FLUCTUATIONS WOULD MAKE YOUR HEAD SPIN!
BUT IF NAMOR AND HIS FISH ARMY GET THROUGH IT THEN YOU CAN KISS YOUR MAGICAL CITY OF KUNG FU AND HOPE SUMMERS GOODBYE.
GO!
GOOD LUCK, CAP!
REMEMBER WHAT I TOLD YOU.
REMEMBER OUR SECRET WEAPON.
USE IT. USE IT NOW!
WAIT!
I CAN'T BELIEVE THEY LEFT WITHOUT ME.
THERE WILL BE PLENTY FOR YOU TO DO HERE, IRON FIST.
DAMN YOU, NAMOR!

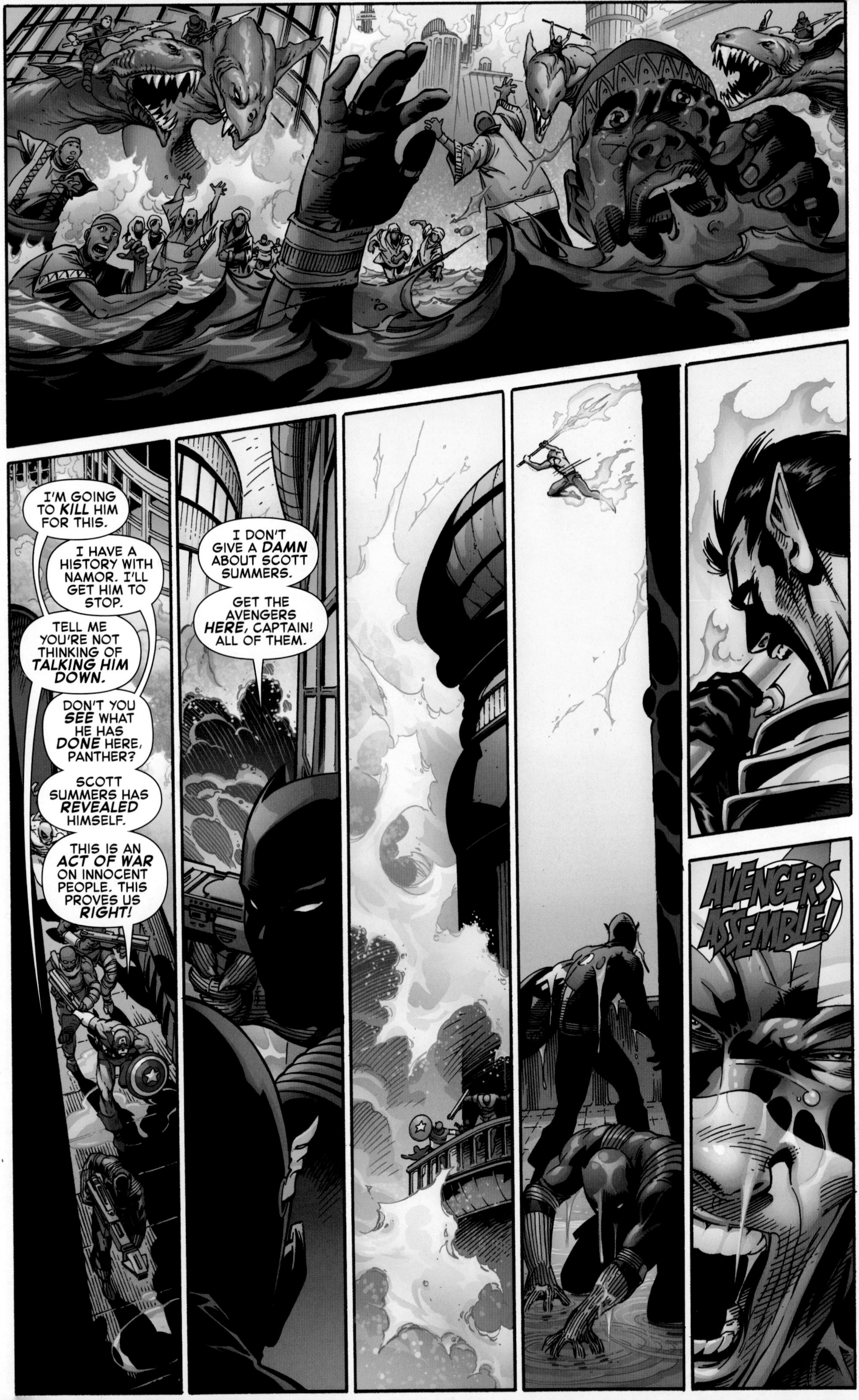

I'M GOING TO KILL HIM FOR THIS.
I HAVE A HISTORY WITH NAMOR. I'LL GET HIM TO STOP.
TELL ME YOU'RE NOT THINKING OF TALKING HIM DOWN.
DON'T YOU SEE WHAT HE HAS DONE HERE, PANTHER?
SCOTT SUMMERS HAS REVEALED HIMSELF.
THIS IS AN ACT OF WAR ON INNOCENT PEOPLE. THIS PROVES US RIGHT!
I DON'T GIVE A DAMN ABOUT SCOTT SUMMERS.
GET THE AVENGERS HERE, CAPTAIN! ALL OF THEM.
AVENGERS ASSEMBLE!

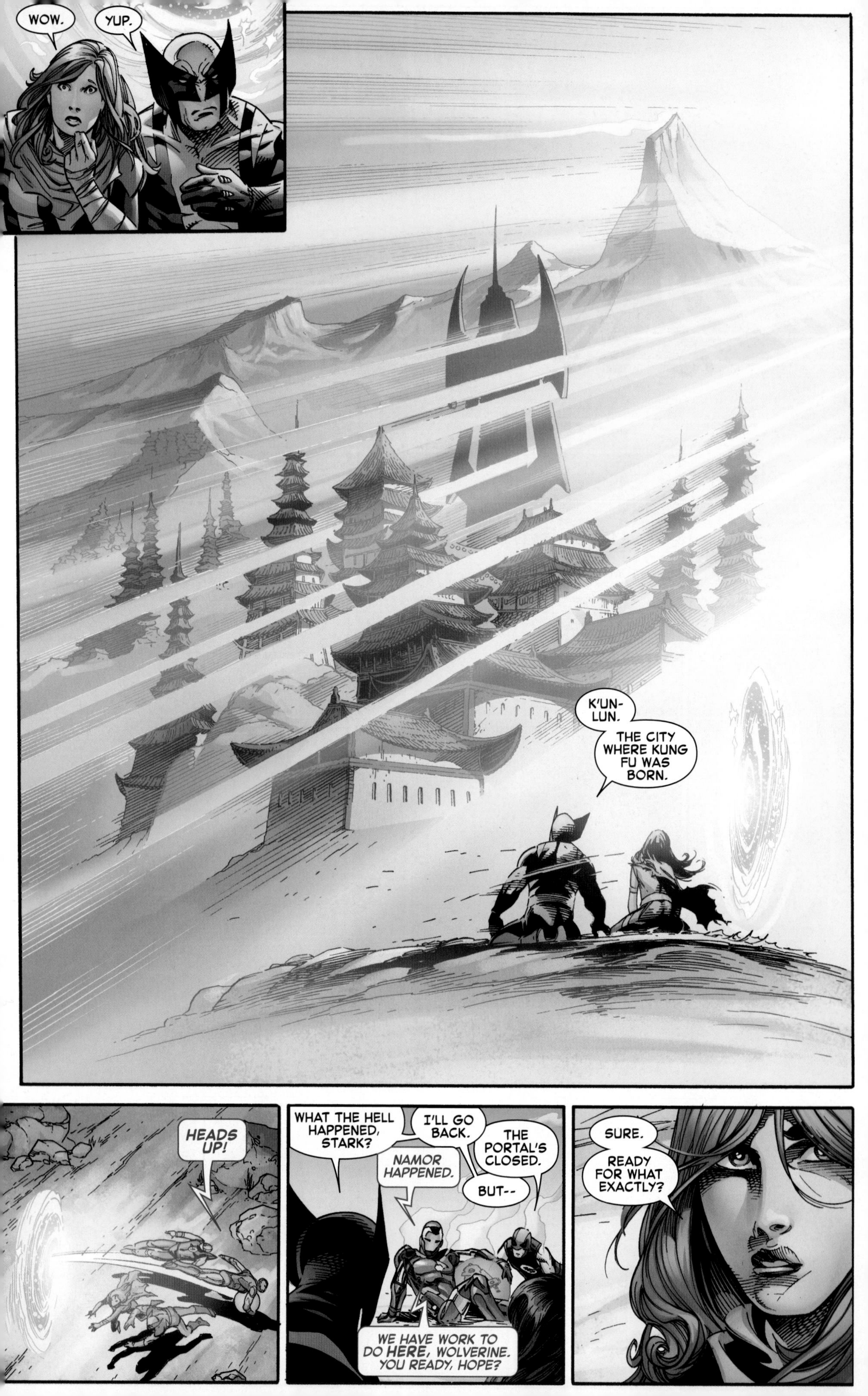
WOW.
YUP.
K'UN-LUN.
THE CITY WHERE KUNG FU WAS BORN.
HEADS UP!
WHAT THE HELL HAPPENED, STARK?
I'LL GO BACK.
THE PORTAL'S CLOSED.
NAMOR HAPPENED.
BUT--
WE HAVE WORK TO DO HERE, WOLVERINE. YOU READY, HOPE?
SURE.
READY FOR WHAT EXACTLY?

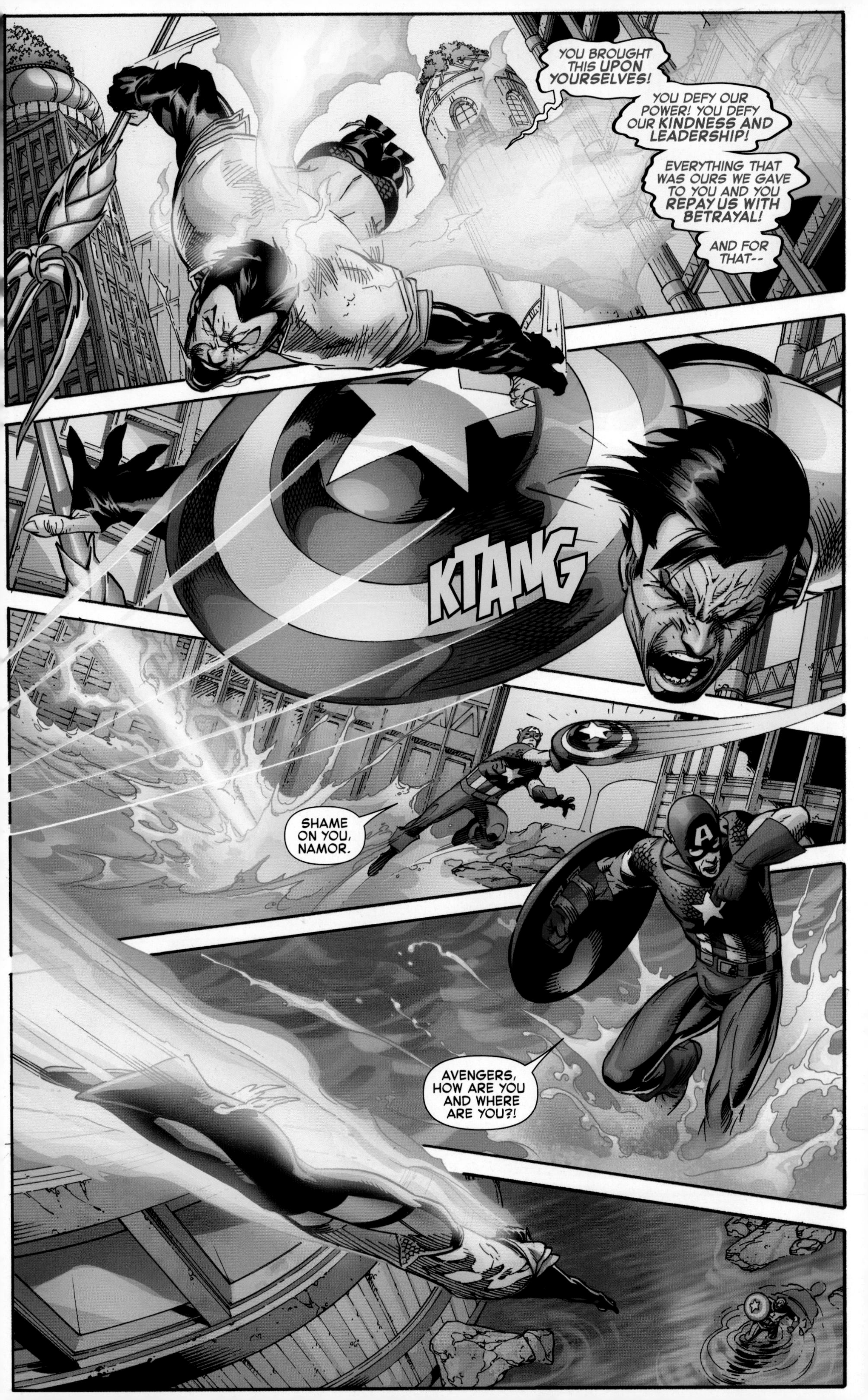
YOU BROUGHT THIS UPON YOURSELVES!
YOU DEFY OUR POWER! YOU DEFY OUR KINDNESS AND LEADERSHIP!
EVERYTHING THAT WAS OURS WE GAVE TO YOU AND YOU REPAY US WITH BETRAYAL!
AND FOR THAT--
KTANG
SHAME ON YOU, NAMOR.
AVENGERS, HOW ARE YOU AND WHERE ARE YOU?!

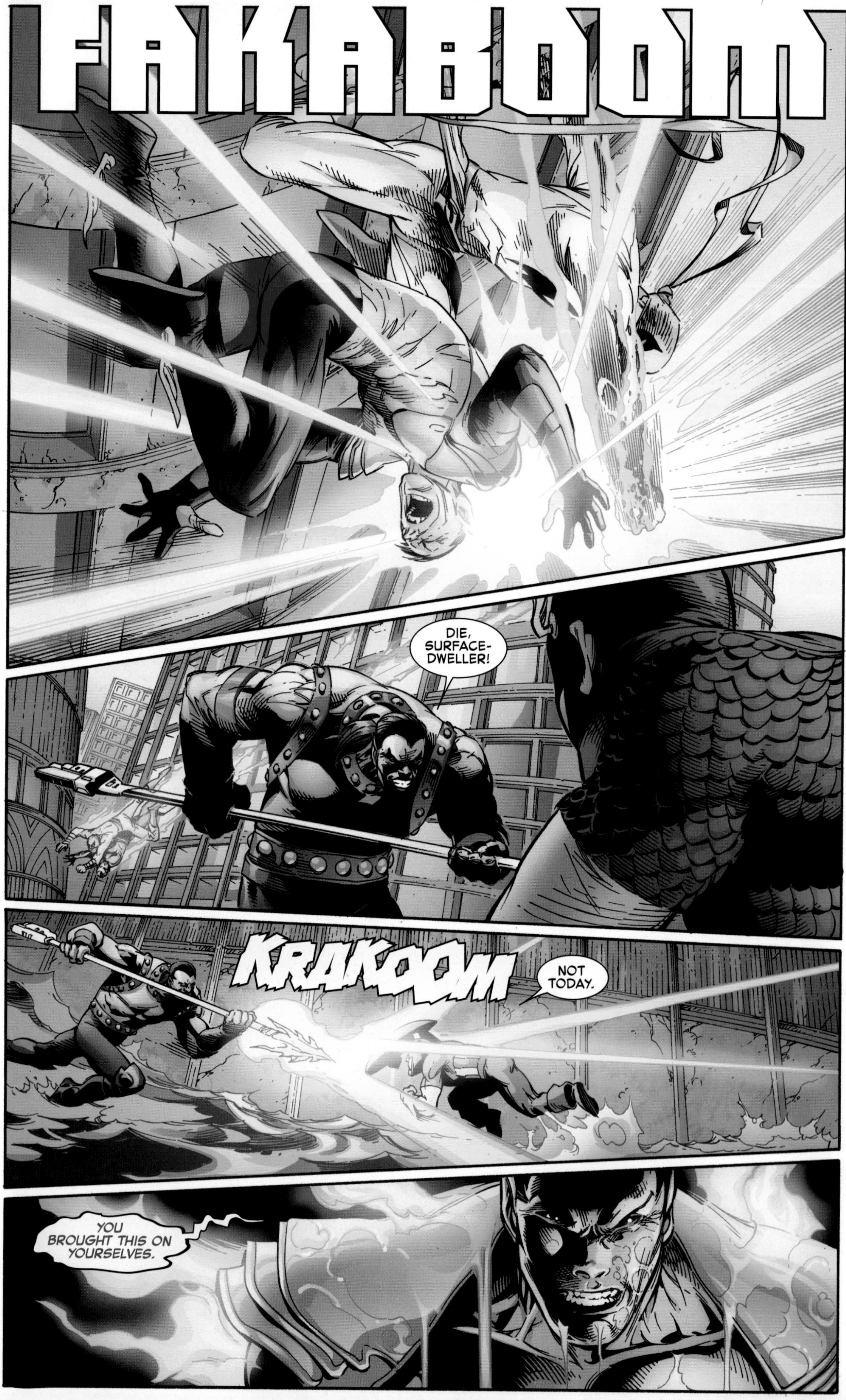
FAKABOOM
DIE, SURFACE-DWELLER!
KRAKOOM
NOT TODAY.
YOU BROUGHT THIS ON YOURSELVES.

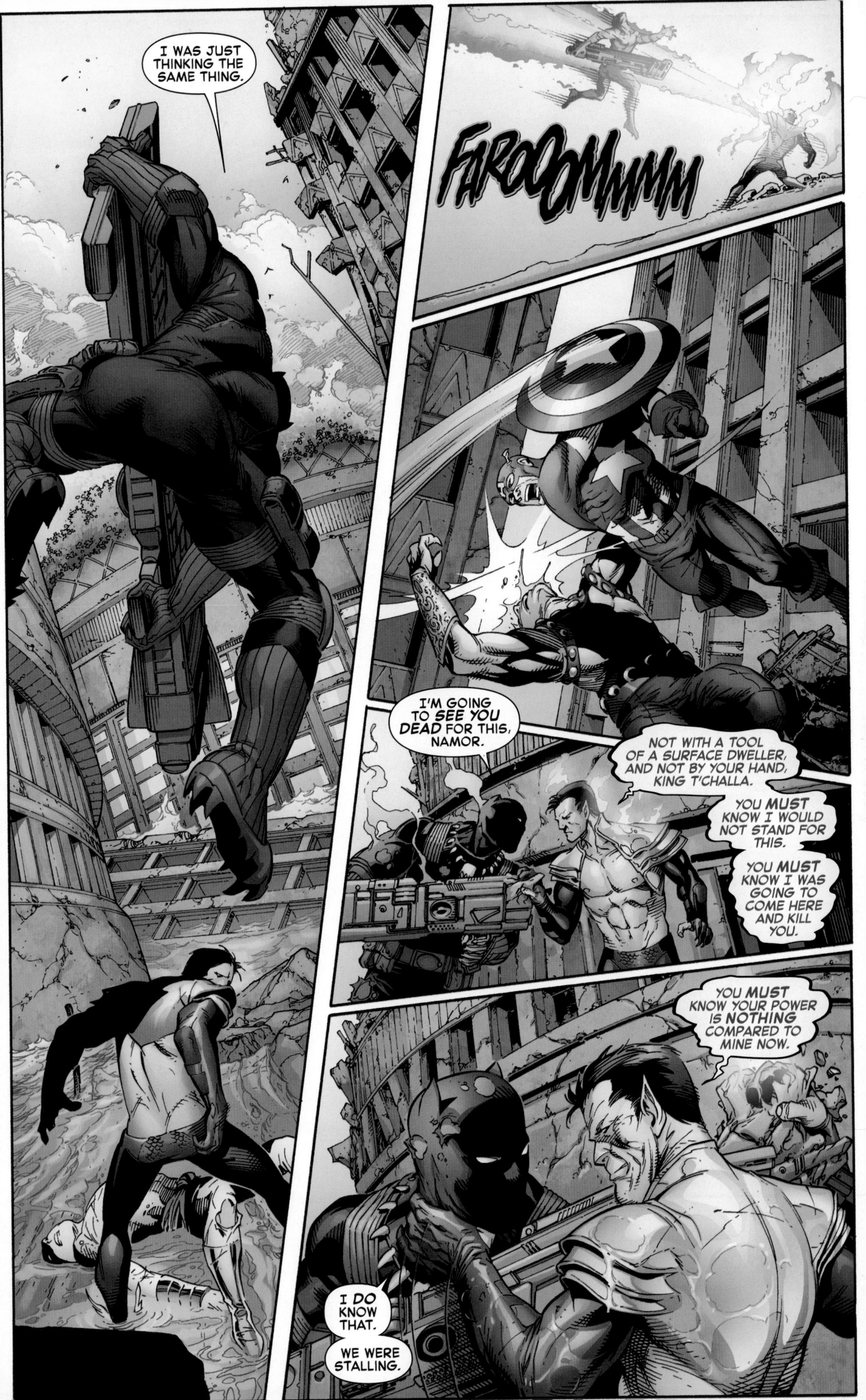
I WAS JUST THINKING THE SAME THING.
FAROOOMMMM
I'M GOING TO SEE YOU DEAD FOR THIS, NAMOR.
NOT WITH A TOOL OF A SURFACE DWELLER, AND NOT BY YOUR HAND, KING T'CHALLA.
YOU MUST KNOW I WOULD NOT STAND FOR THIS.
YOU MUST KNOW I WAS GOING TO COME HERE AND KILL YOU.
YOU MUST KNOW YOUR POWER IS NOTHING COMPARED TO MINE NOW.
I DO KNOW THAT.
WE WERE STALLING.

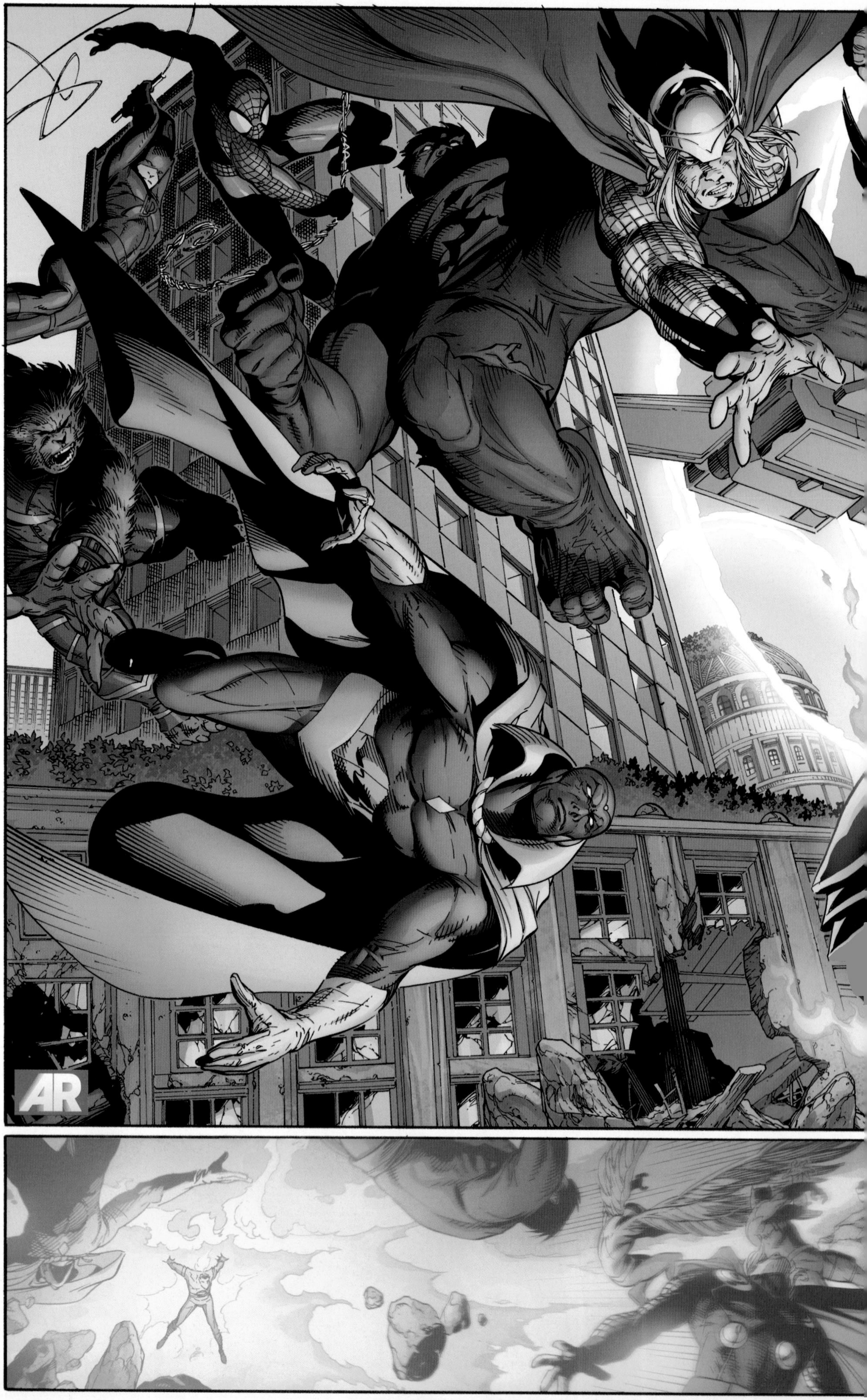

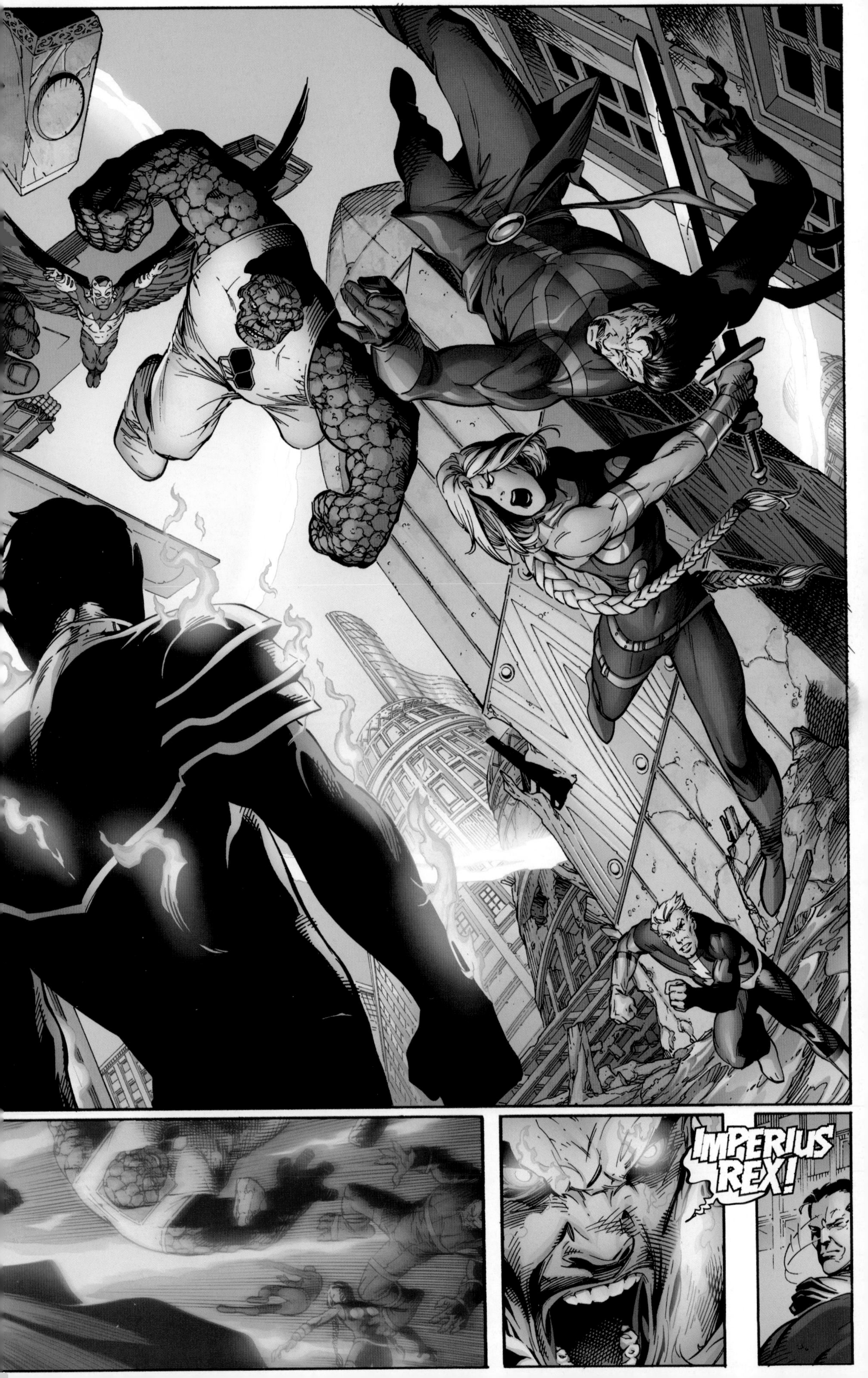
IMPERIUS REX!

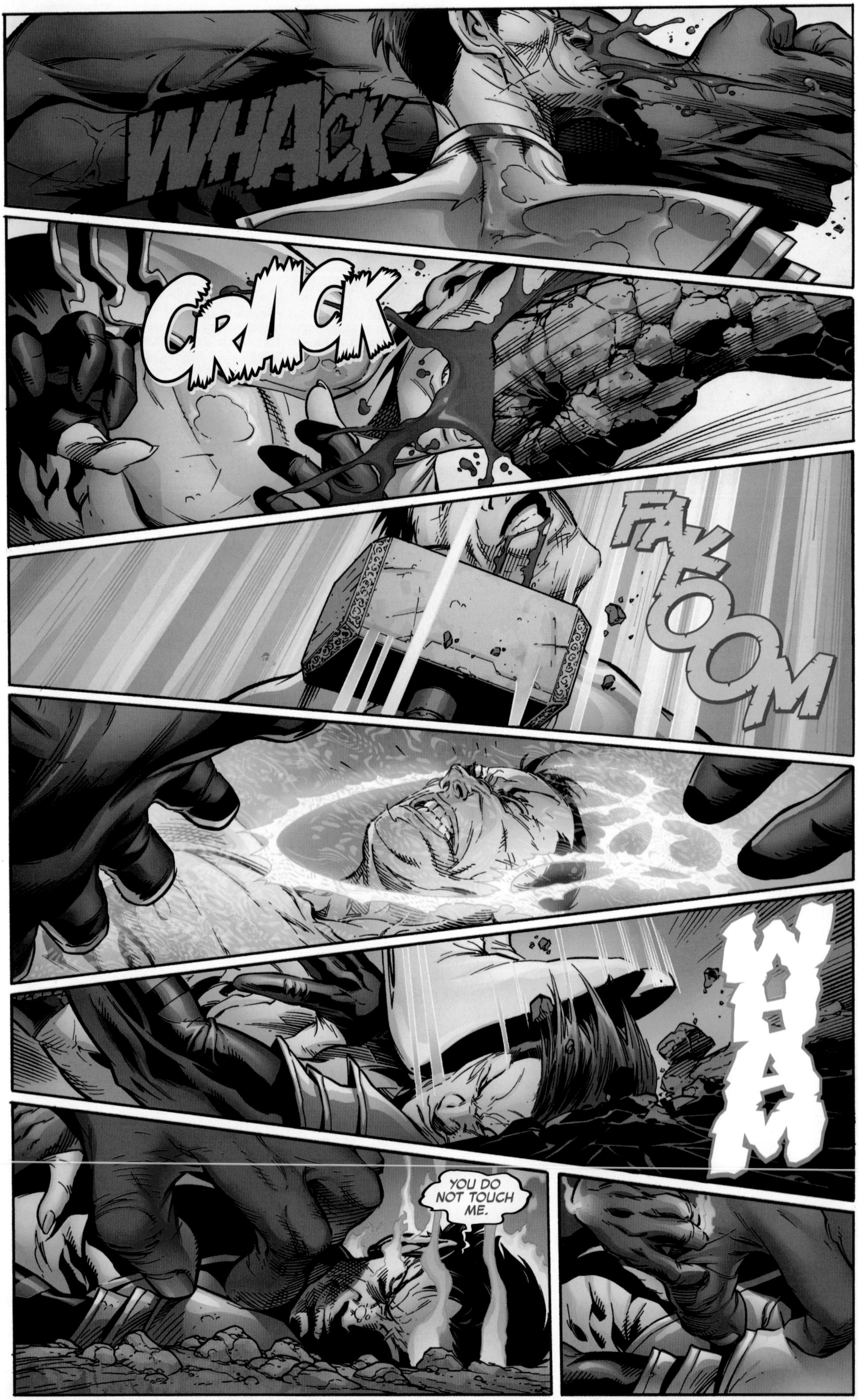
WHACK
CRACK
FAKOOOM
WHAM
YOU DO NOT TOUCH ME.

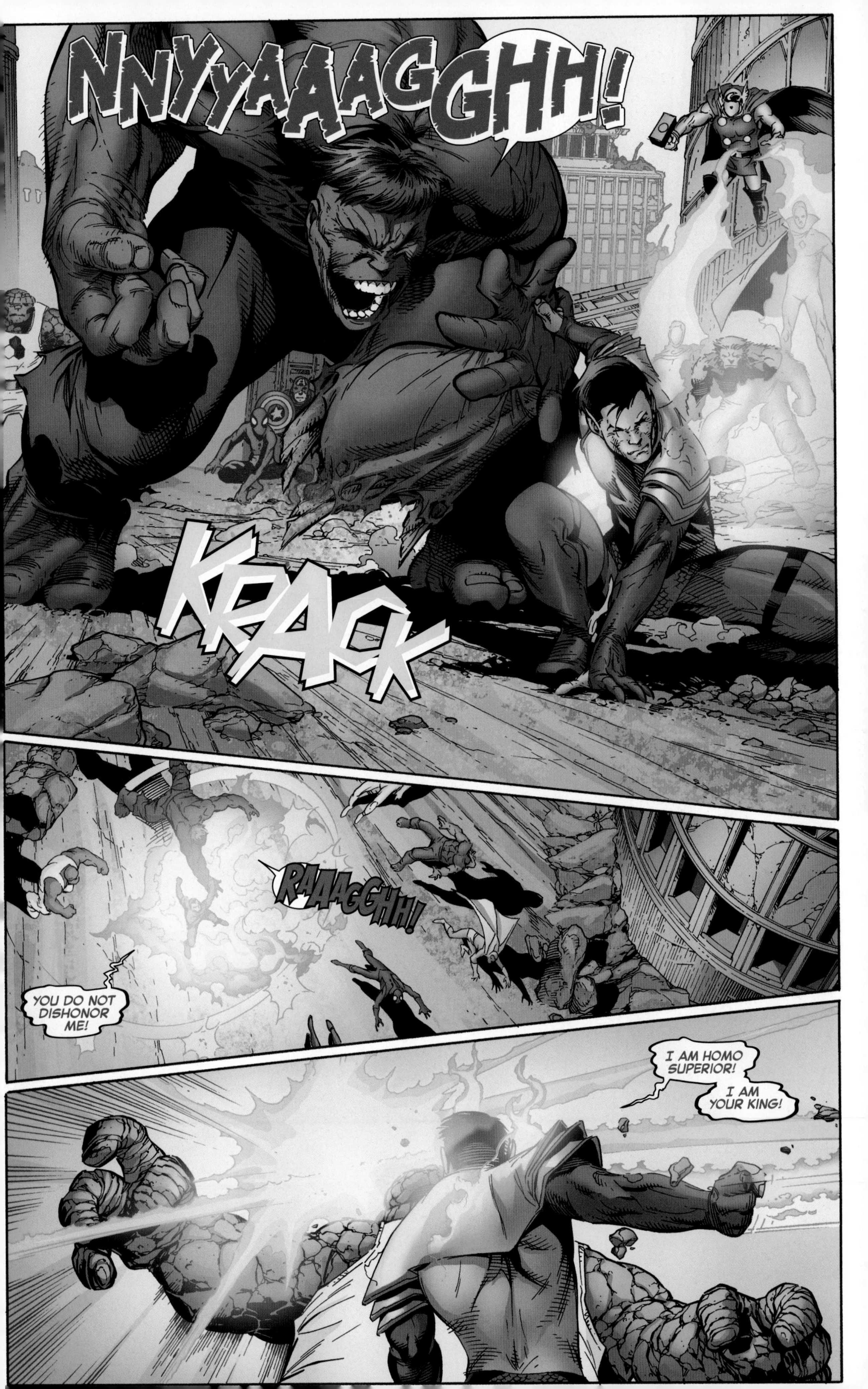
NNYYAAAGGHH!
KRAACK
RAAAGGHH!
YOU DO NOT DISHONOR ME!
I AM HOMO SUPERIOR!
I AM YOUR KING!

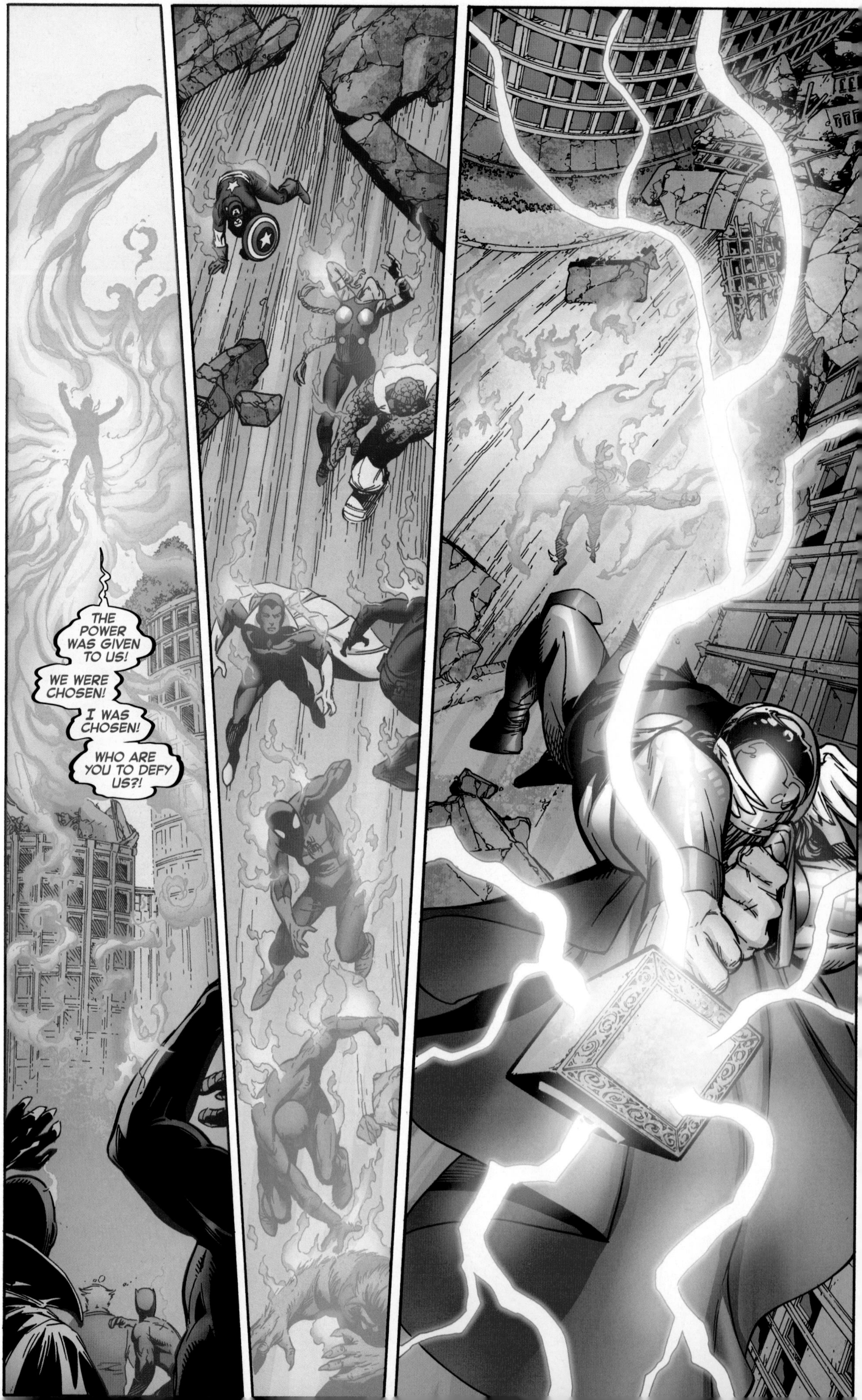
THE POWER WAS GIVEN TO US!
WE WERE CHOSEN!
I WAS CHOSEN!
WHO ARE YOU TO DEFY US?!

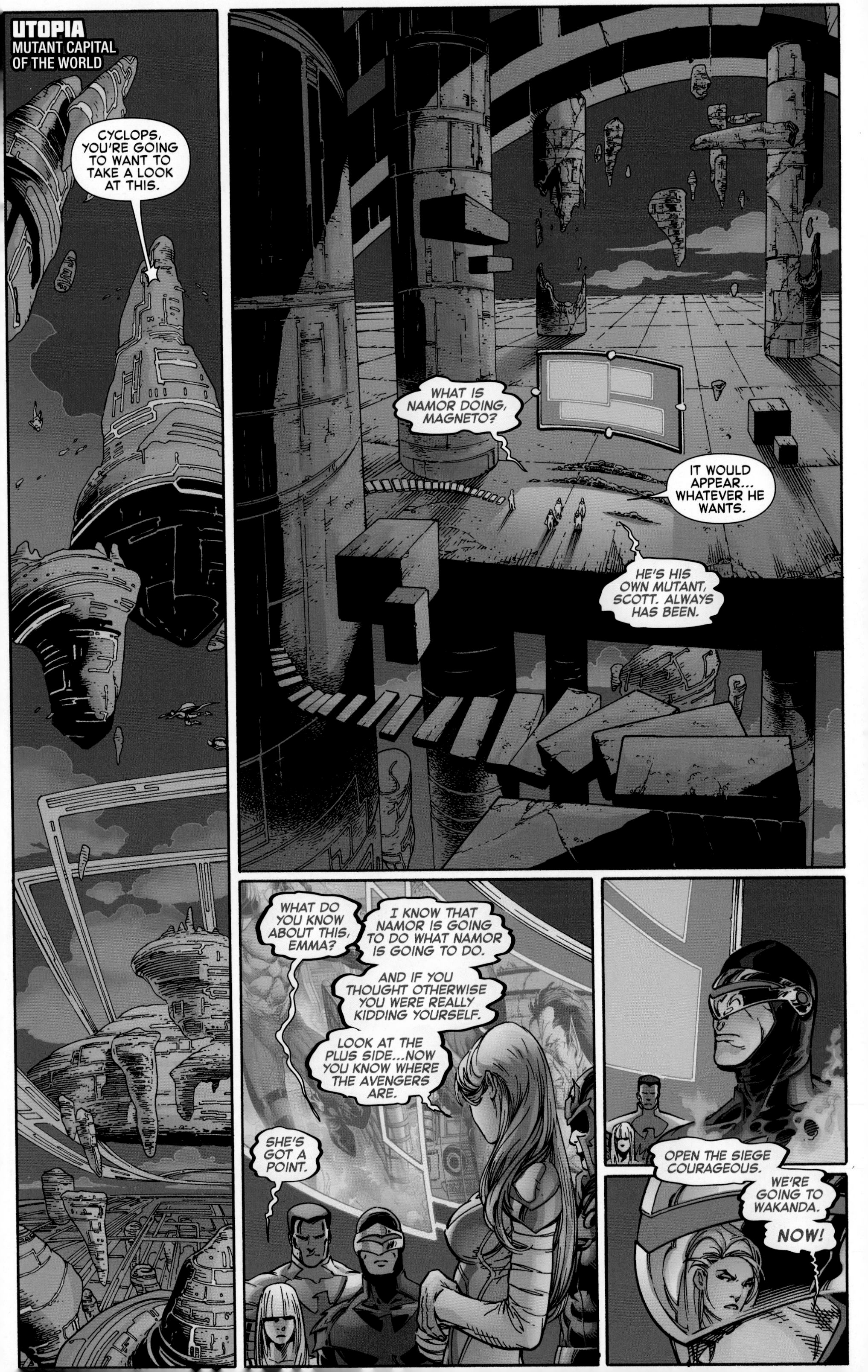
UTOPIA
MUTANT CAPITAL OF THE WORLD
CYCLOPS, YOU'RE GOING TO WANT TO TAKE A LOOK AT THIS.
WHAT IS NAMOR DOING, MAGNETO?
IT WOULD APPEAR... WHATEVER HE WANTS.
HE'S HIS OWN MUTANT, SCOTT. ALWAYS HAS BEEN.
WHAT DO YOU KNOW ABOUT THIS, EMMA?
I KNOW THAT NAMOR IS GOING TO DO WHAT NAMOR IS GOING TO DO.
AND IF YOU THOUGHT OTHERWISE YOU WERE REALLY KIDDING YOURSELF.
LOOK AT THE PLUS SIDE...NOW YOU KNOW WHERE THE AVENGERS ARE.
SHE'S GOT A POINT.
OPEN THE SIEGE COURAGEOUS.
WE'RE GOING TO WAKANDA.
NOW!

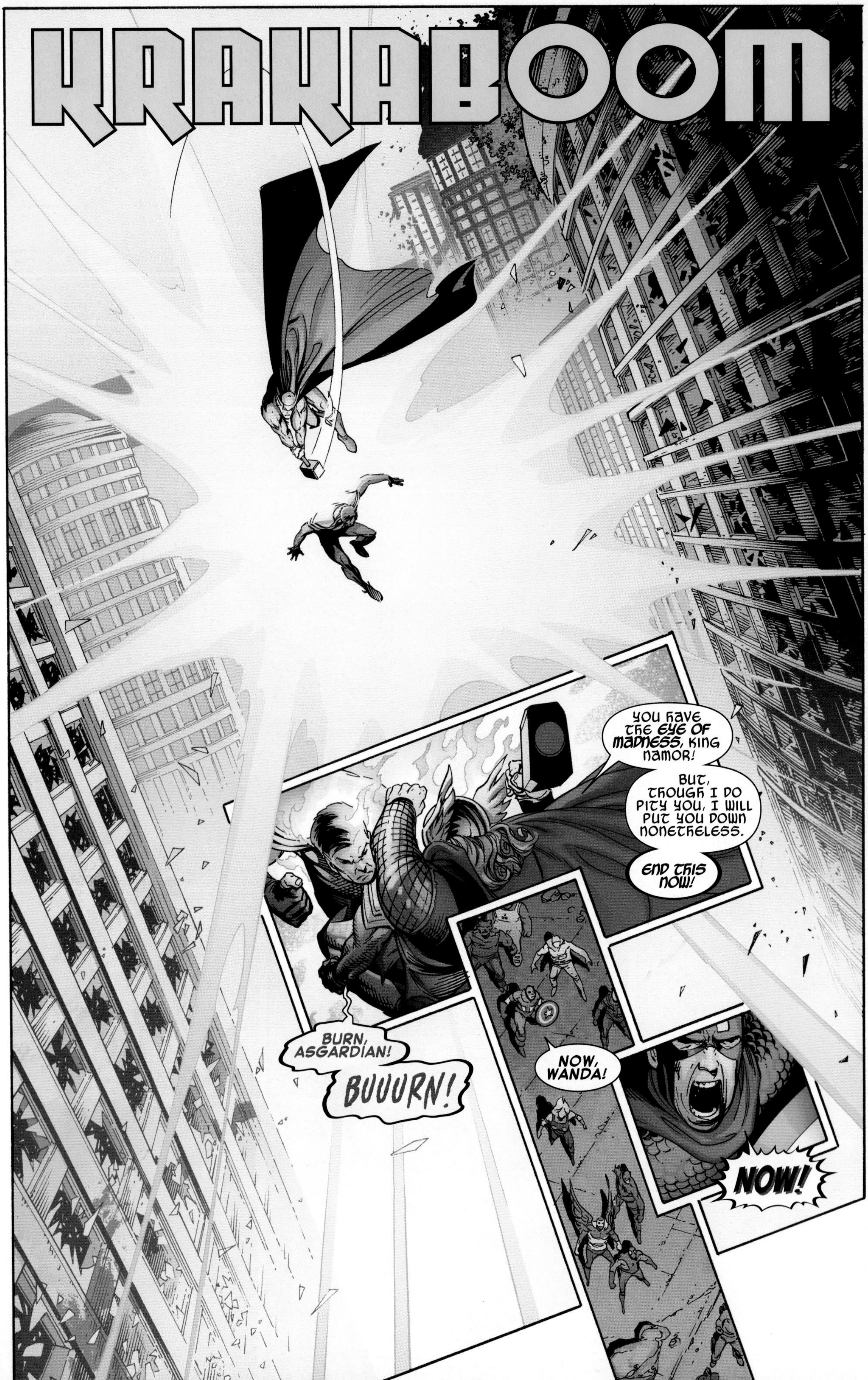
KRAKABOOM
YOU HAVE THE EYE OF MADNESS, KING NAMOR!
BUT, THOUGH I DO PITY YOU, I WILL PUT YOU DOWN NONETHELESS.
END THIS NOW!
BURN, ASGARDIAN!
BUUURN!
NOW, WANDA!
NOW!

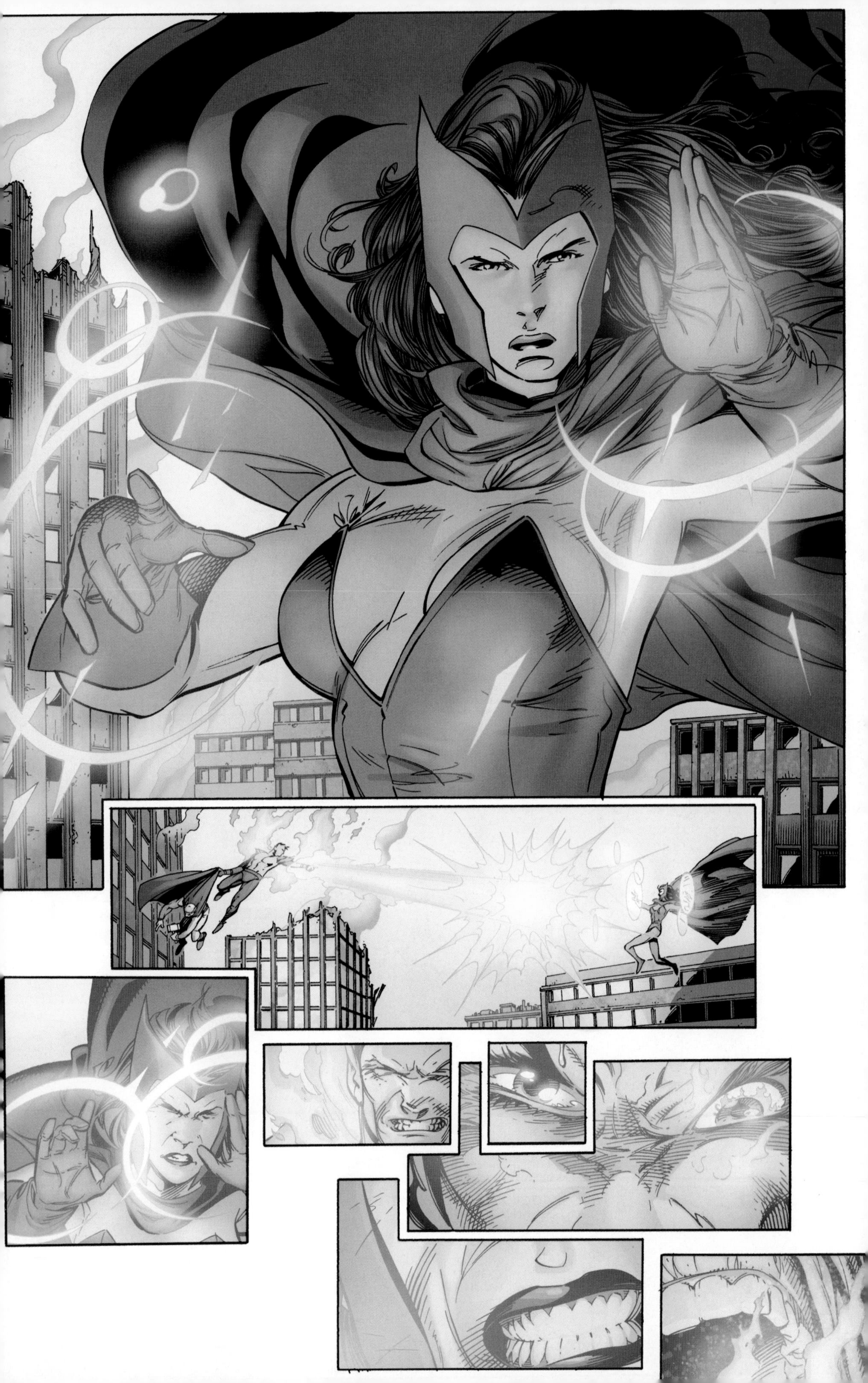

MYYAAAGGH!

WHAT'S HAPPENING?!

RRRRGH!

KRAFOOM

AND *THAT'S* JUST 'CAUSE YOU'RE YOU.

DID WE WIN?

WIN?

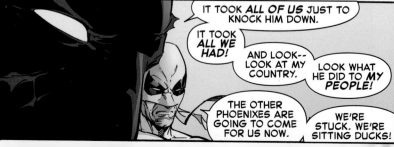

IT TOOK *ALL OF US* JUST TO KNOCK HIM DOWN.

IT TOOK *ALL WE HAD!*

AND LOOK-- LOOK AT MY COUNTRY.

LOOK WHAT HE DID TO *MY PEOPLE!*

THE OTHER PHOENIXES ARE GOING TO COME FOR US NOW.

WE'RE STUCK. WE'RE SITTING DUCKS!

UM...

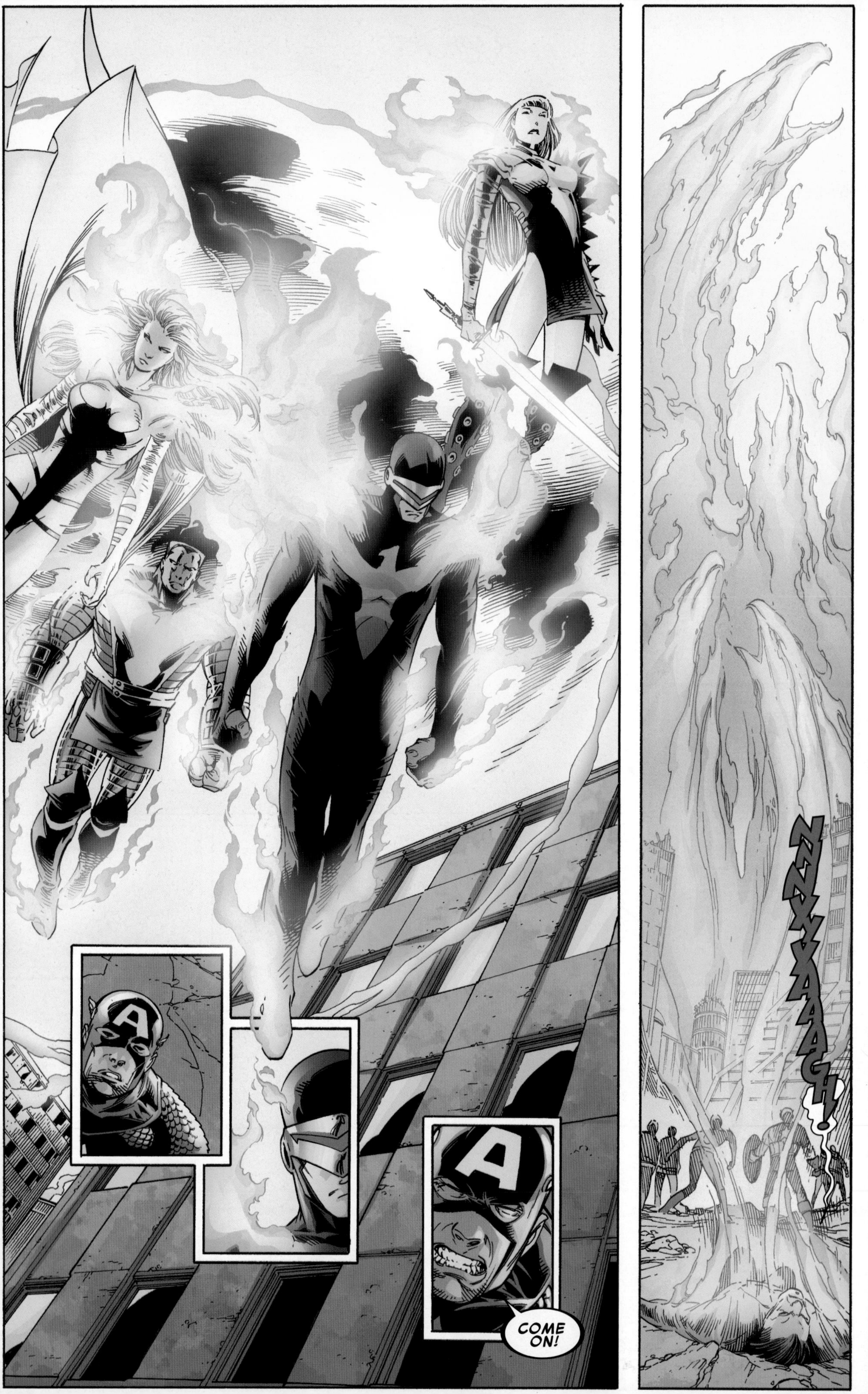
COME ON!
NNNYAAAGH!

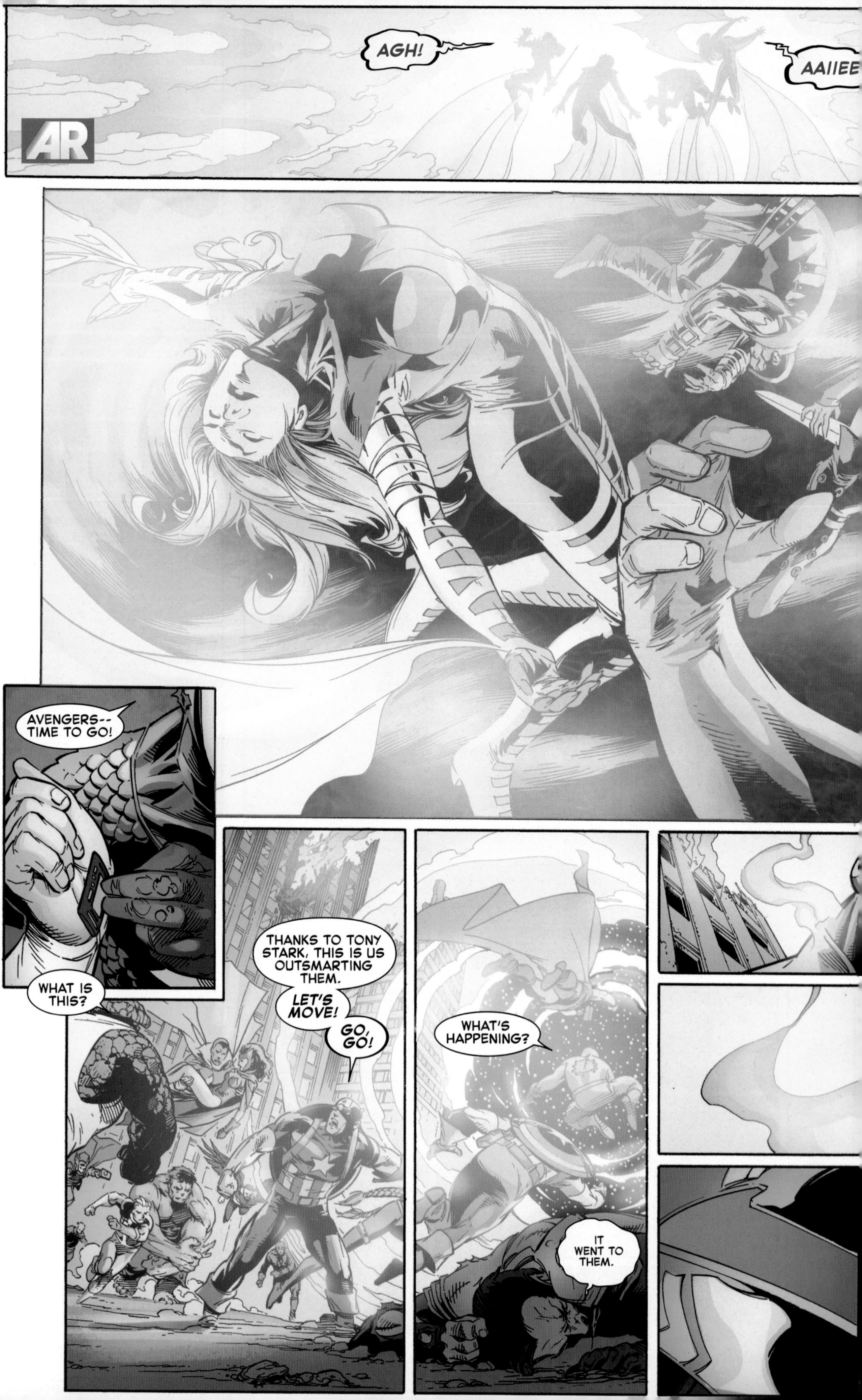
AGH!
AAIIEE
AR
AVENGERS-- TIME TO GO!
WHAT IS THIS?
THANKS TO TONY STARK, THIS IS US OUTSMARTING THEM.
LET'S MOVE!
GO, GO!
WHAT'S HAPPENING?
IT WENT TO THEM.

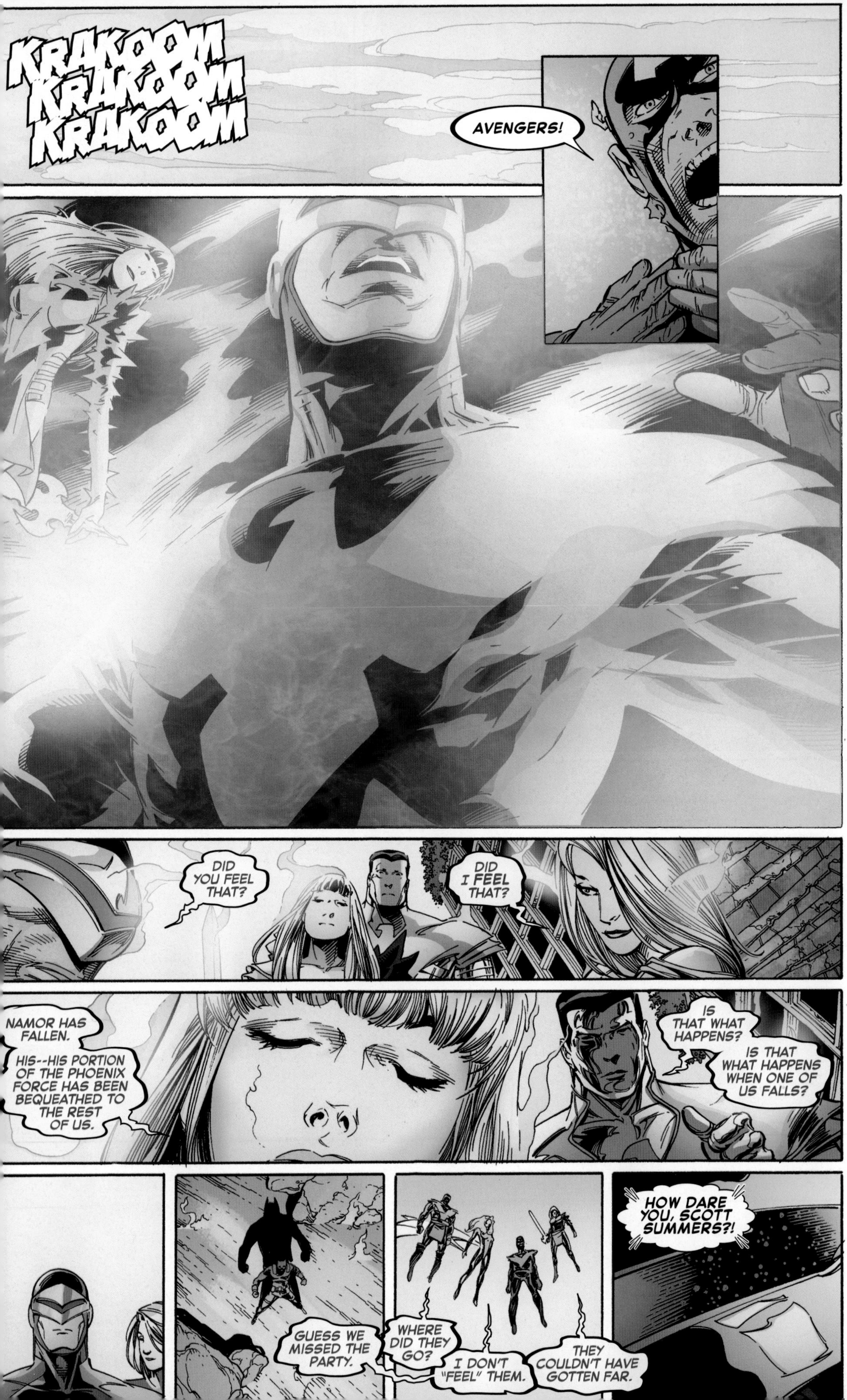
KRAKOOM KRAKOOM KRAKOOM
AVENGERS!
DID YOU FEEL THAT?
DID I FEEL THAT?
NAMOR HAS FALLEN.
HIS--HIS PORTION OF THE PHOENIX FORCE HAS BEEN BEQUEATHED TO THE REST OF US.
IS THAT WHAT HAPPENS?
IS THAT WHAT HAPPENS WHEN ONE OF US FALLS?
GUESS WE MISSED THE PARTY.
WHERE DID THEY GO?
I DON'T "FEEL" THEM.
THEY COULDN'T HAVE GOTTEN FAR.
HOW DARE YOU, SCOTT SUMMERS?!

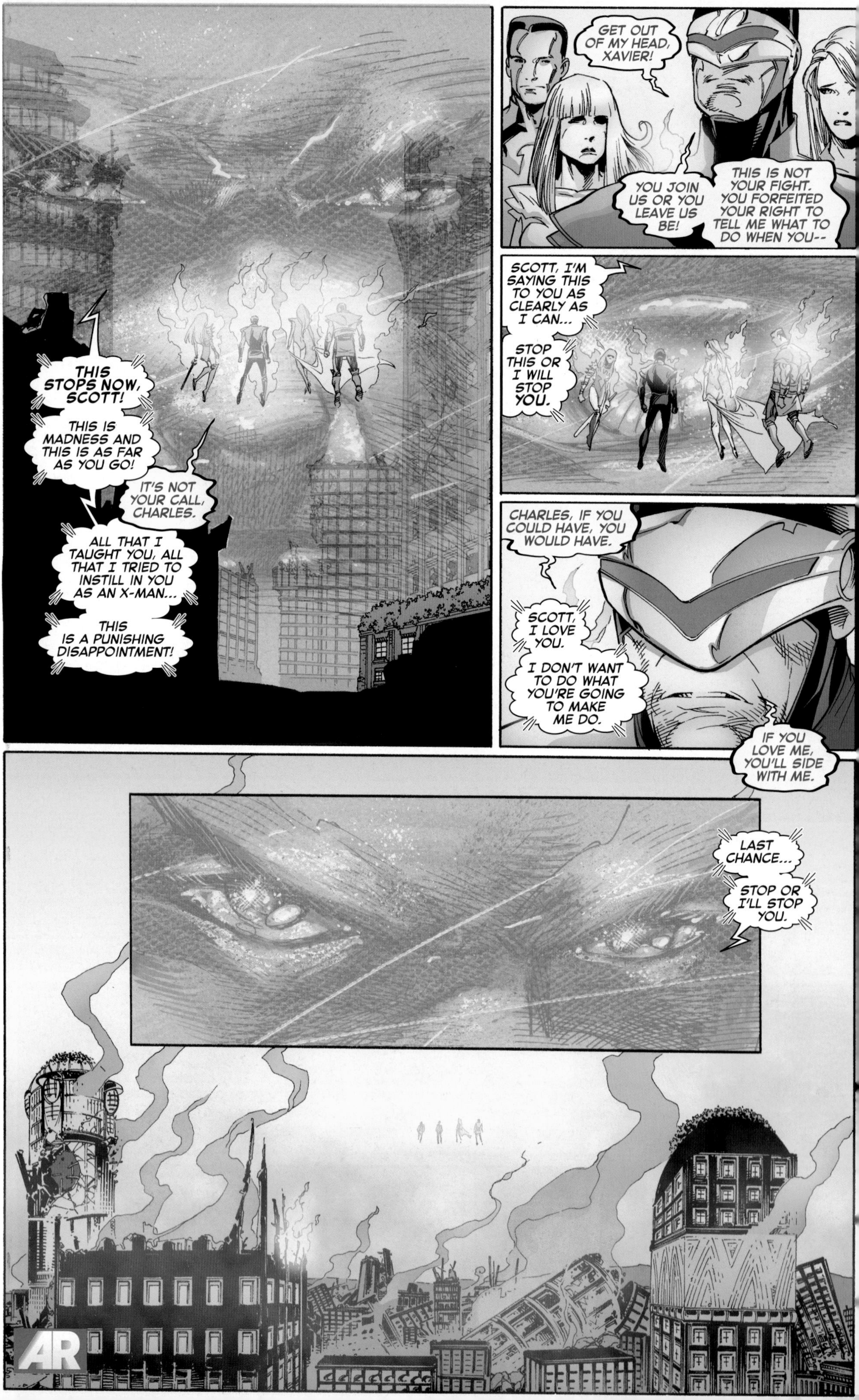
THIS STOPS NOW, SCOTT!
THIS IS MADNESS AND THIS IS AS FAR AS YOU GO!
IT'S NOT YOUR CALL, CHARLES.
ALL THAT I TAUGHT YOU, ALL THAT I TRIED TO INSTILL IN YOU AS AN X-MAN...
THIS IS A PUNISHING DISAPPOINTMENT!
GET OUT OF MY HEAD, XAVIER!
YOU JOIN US OR YOU LEAVE US BE!
THIS IS NOT YOUR FIGHT. YOU FORFEITED YOUR RIGHT TO TELL ME WHAT TO DO WHEN YOU--
SCOTT, I'M SAYING THIS TO YOU AS CLEARLY AS I CAN...
STOP THIS OR I WILL STOP YOU.
CHARLES, IF YOU COULD HAVE, YOU WOULD HAVE.
SCOTT, I LOVE YOU.
I DON'T WANT TO DO WHAT YOU'RE GOING TO MAKE ME DO.
IF YOU LOVE ME, YOU'LL SIDE WITH ME.
LAST CHANCE...
STOP OR I'LL STOP YOU.

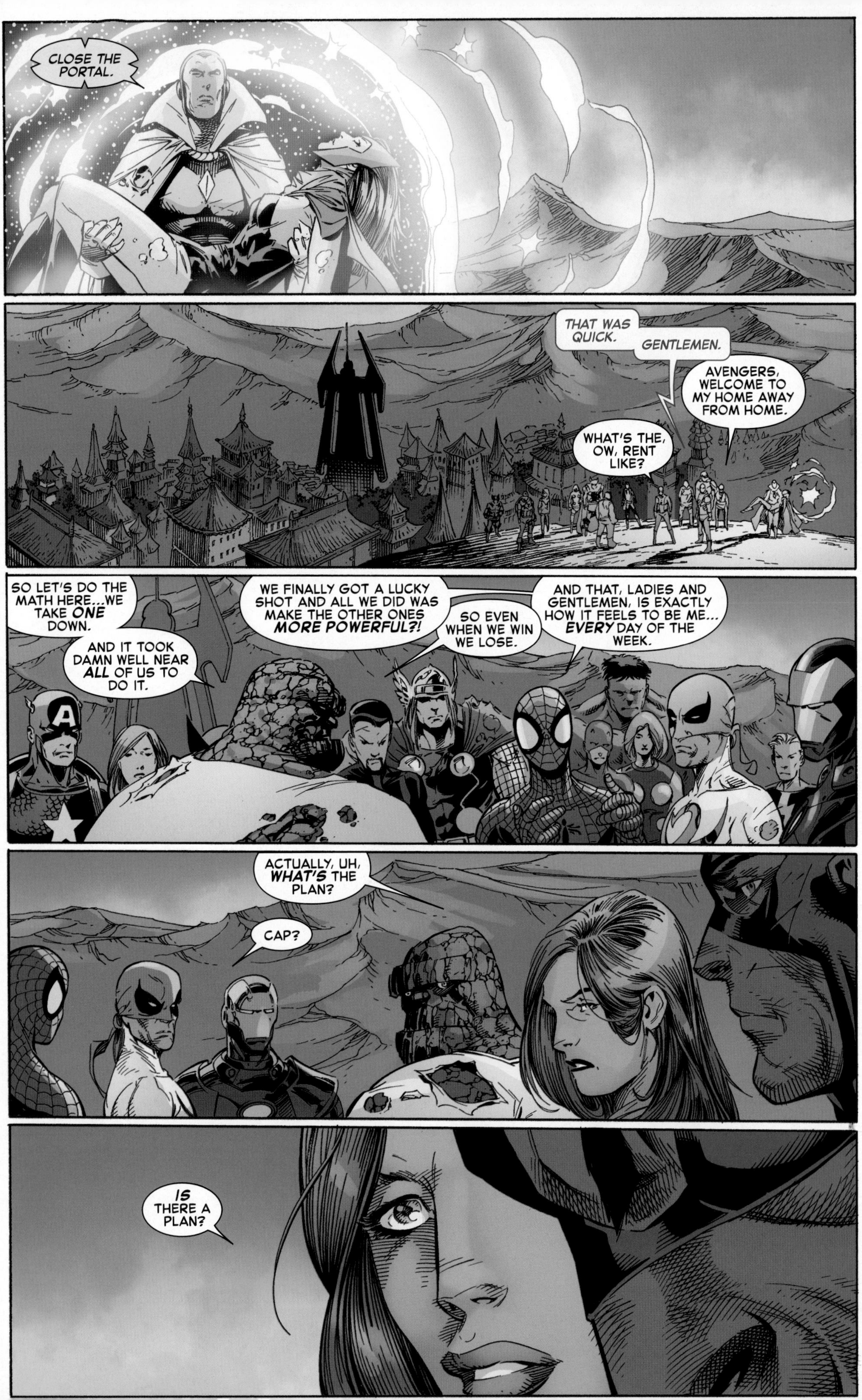
CLOSE THE PORTAL.
THAT WAS QUICK.
GENTLEMEN.
AVENGERS, WELCOME TO MY HOME AWAY FROM HOME.
WHAT'S THE, OW, RENT LIKE?
SO LET'S DO THE MATH HERE...WE TAKE ONE DOWN.
AND IT TOOK DAMN WELL NEAR ALL OF US TO DO IT.
WE FINALLY GOT A LUCKY SHOT AND ALL WE DID WAS MAKE THE OTHER ONES MORE POWERFUL?!
SO EVEN WHEN WE WIN WE LOSE.
AND THAT, LADIES AND GENTLEMEN, IS EXACTLY HOW IT FEELS TO BE ME... EVERY DAY OF THE WEEK.
ACTUALLY, UH, WHAT'S THE PLAN?
CAP?
IS THERE A PLAN?

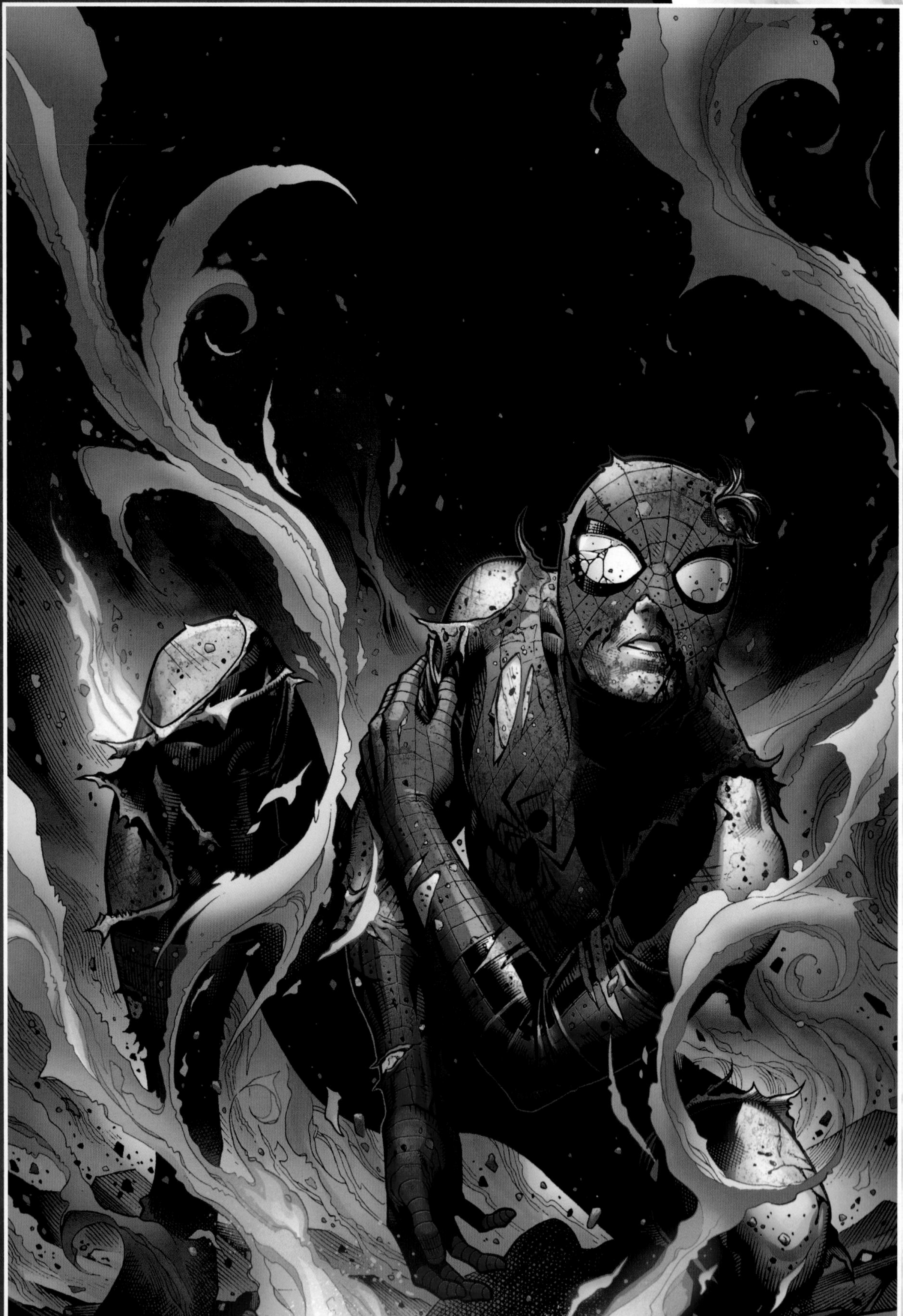
MORALES · JB · III · MMXII

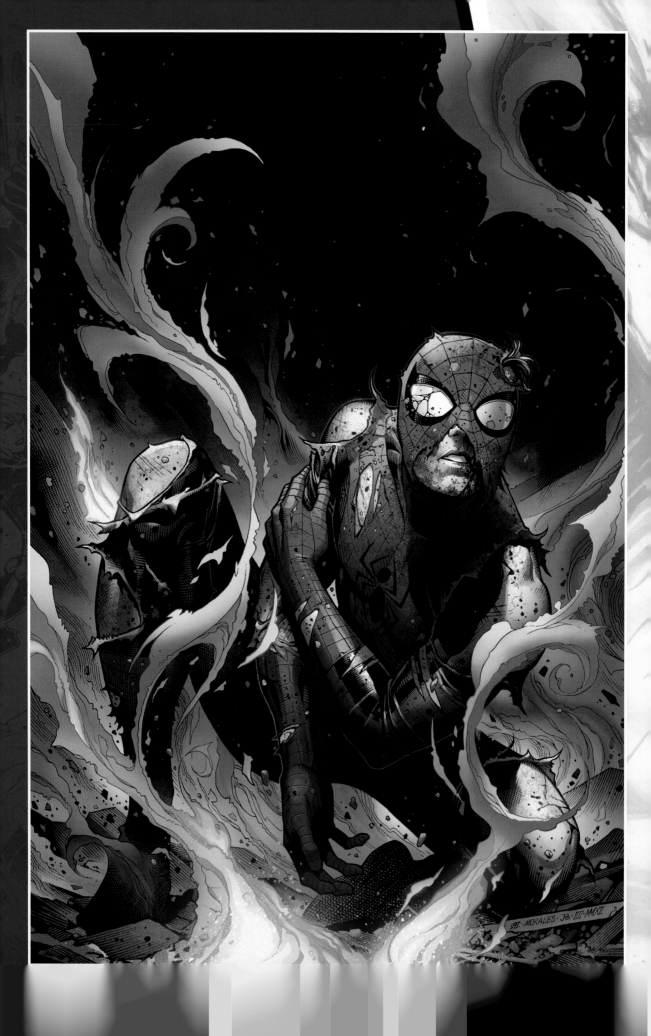

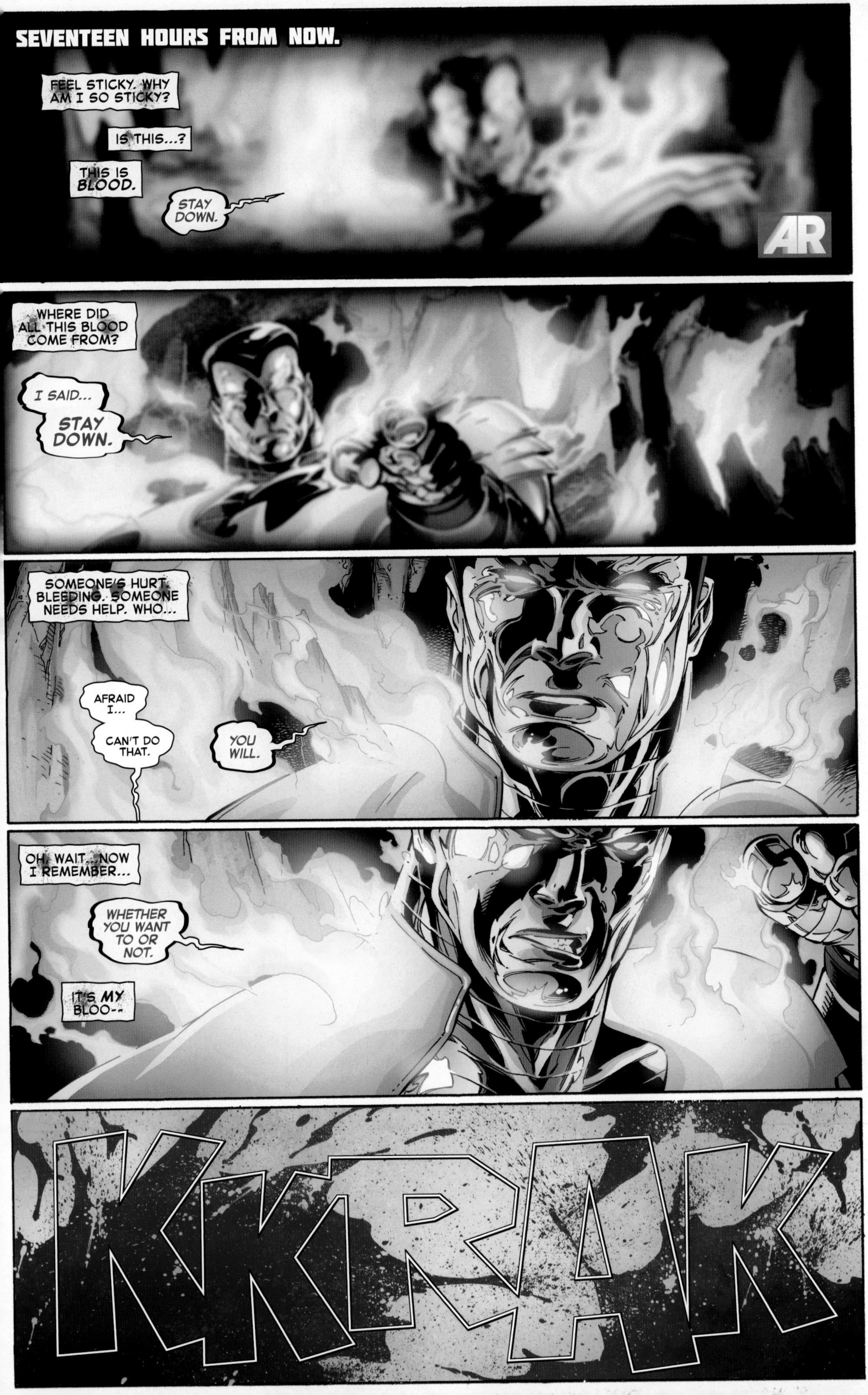
SEVENTEEN HOURS FROM NOW.
FEEL STICKY. WHY AM I SO STICKY?
IS THIS...?
THIS IS BLOOD.
STAY DOWN.
AR
WHERE DID ALL THIS BLOOD COME FROM?
I SAID...
STAY DOWN.
SOMEONE'S HURT. BLEEDING. SOMEONE NEEDS HELP. WHO...
AFRAID I...
CAN'T DO THAT.
YOU WILL.
OH, WAIT...NOW I REMEMBER...
WHETHER YOU WANT TO OR NOT.
IT'S MY BLOO--
KKRAK

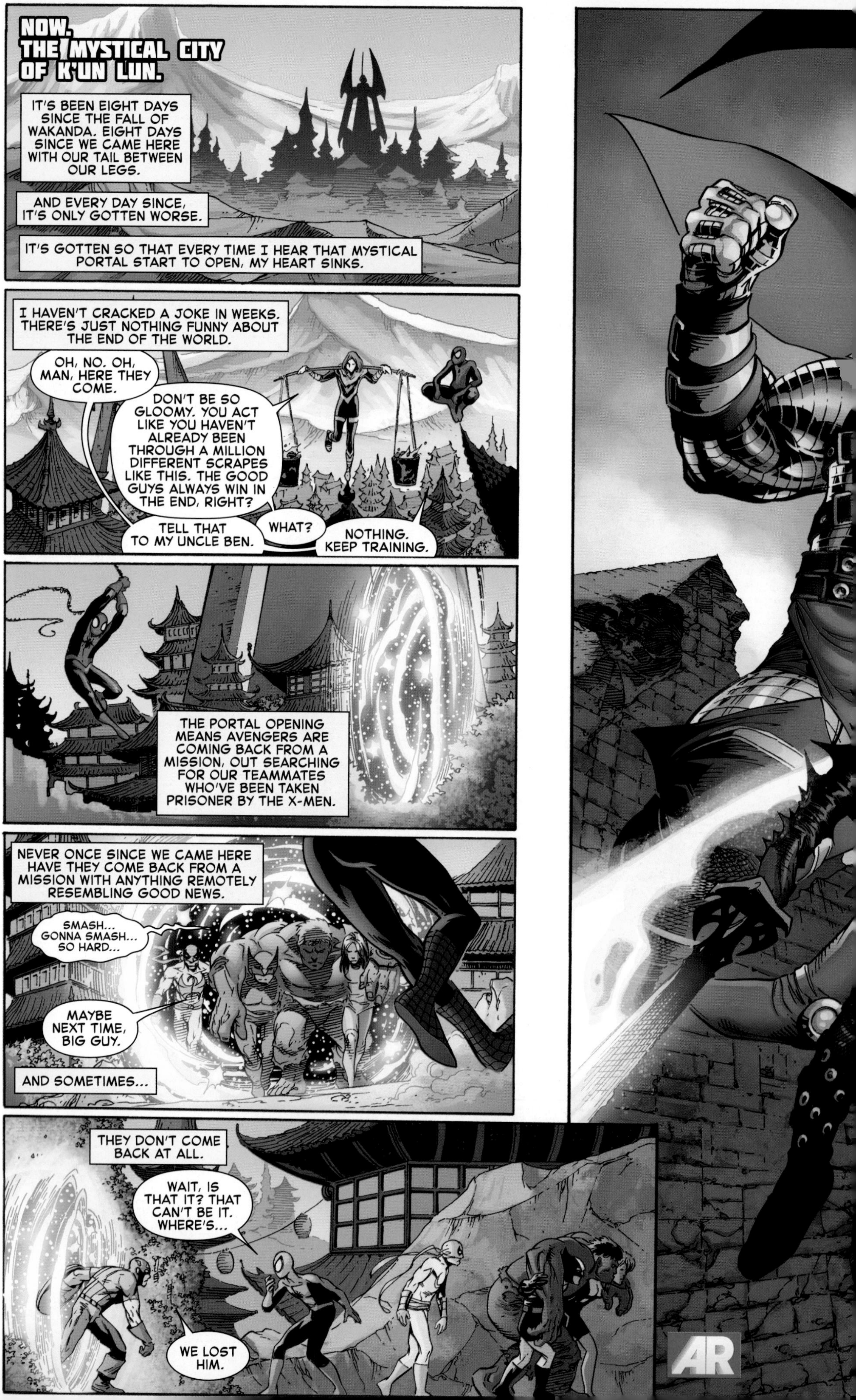
NOW. THE MYSTICAL CITY OF K'UN LUN.
IT'S BEEN EIGHT DAYS SINCE THE FALL OF WAKANDA. EIGHT DAYS SINCE WE CAME HERE WITH OUR TAIL BETWEEN OUR LEGS.
AND EVERY DAY SINCE, IT'S ONLY GOTTEN WORSE.
IT'S GOTTEN SO THAT EVERY TIME I HEAR THAT MYSTICAL PORTAL START TO OPEN, MY HEART SINKS.
I HAVEN'T CRACKED A JOKE IN WEEKS. THERE'S JUST NOTHING FUNNY ABOUT THE END OF THE WORLD.
OH, NO. OH, MAN, HERE THEY COME.
DON'T BE SO GLOOMY. YOU ACT LIKE YOU HAVEN'T ALREADY BEEN THROUGH A MILLION DIFFERENT SCRAPES LIKE THIS. THE GOOD GUYS ALWAYS WIN IN THE END, RIGHT?
TELL THAT TO MY UNCLE BEN.
WHAT?
NOTHING. KEEP TRAINING.
THE PORTAL OPENING MEANS AVENGERS ARE COMING BACK FROM A MISSION, OUT SEARCHING FOR OUR TEAMMATES WHO'VE BEEN TAKEN PRISONER BY THE X-MEN.
NEVER ONCE SINCE WE CAME HERE HAVE THEY COME BACK FROM A MISSION WITH ANYTHING REMOTELY RESEMBLING GOOD NEWS.
SMASH... GONNA SMASH... SO HARD...
MAYBE NEXT TIME, BIG GUY.
AND SOMETIMES...
THEY DON'T COME BACK AT ALL.
WAIT, IS THAT IT? THAT CAN'T BE IT. WHERE'S...
WE LOST HIM.

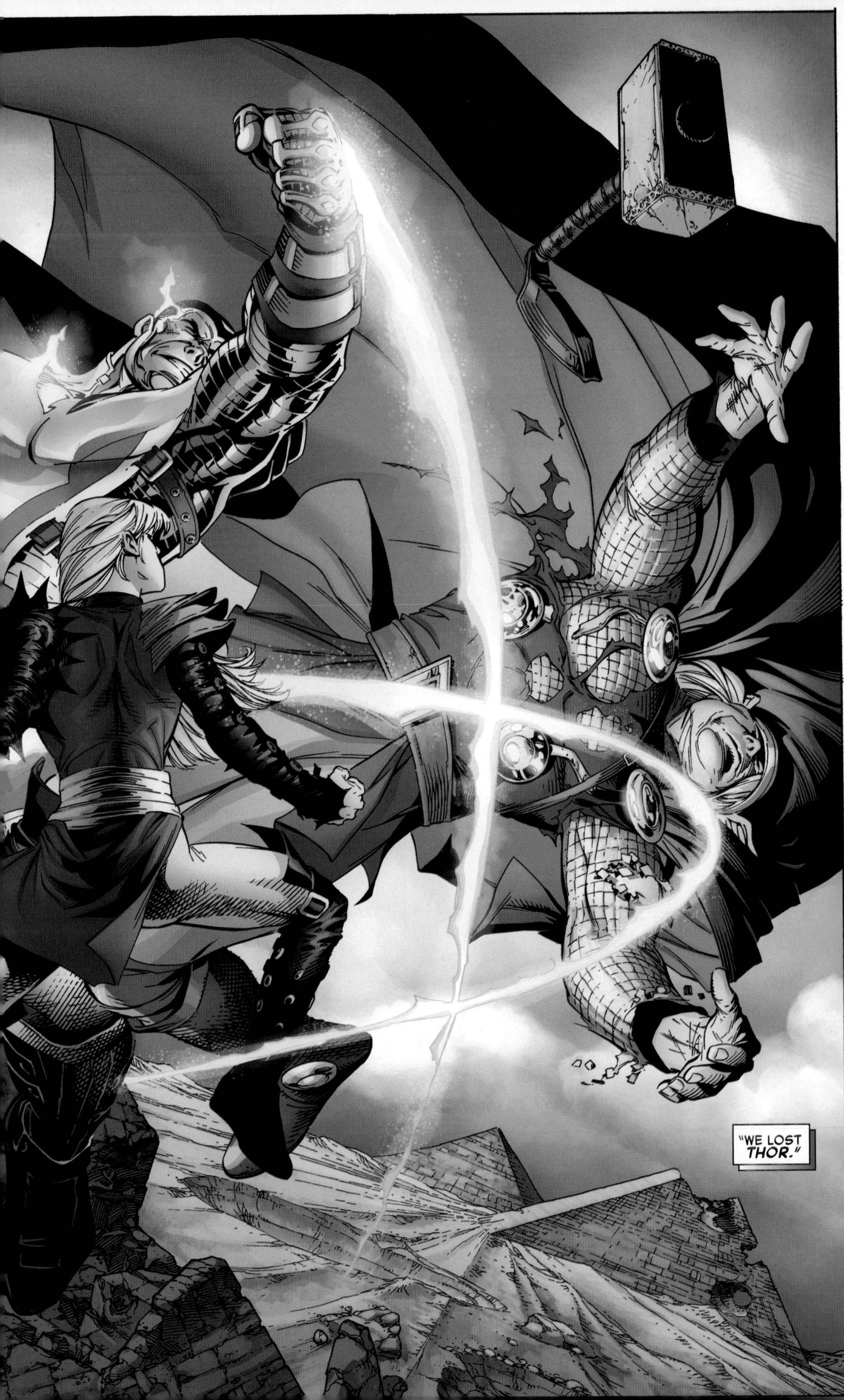
"WE LOST THOR."

YOU LOST... THOR? HOW DO YOU LOSE THOR?

YOU KNOW WE ONLY HAD *ONE* OF HIM, RIGHT?

A JOKE. THERE YOU GO. I'M SO DARNED PROUD OF MYSELF.

THE PHOENIX. WANDA'S HEX MAGIC HOPE. THE IRON FIST SOMEHOW IT ALL FIT TOGETHER...

IS THAT *ALL* THAT CAME BACK? WHERE'S THE BIG GUY WITH THE HAMMER?

GET BACK TO YOUR TRAINING.

I'M SICK OF BALANCING WITH BUCKETS AND DOING ONE-HANDED PUSH-UPS AND HEARING ALL ABOUT THE 36 CHAMBERS OF WHAT-THE-HELL-EVER. ALL ANYBODY EVER WANTS ME TO DO IS TRAIN. I'M READY TO HIT SOMETHING REAL FOR A CHANGE.

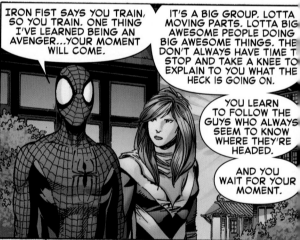

IRON FIST SAYS YOU TRAIN, SO YOU TRAIN. ONE THING I'VE LEARNED BEING AN AVENGER...YOUR MOMENT WILL COME.

IT'S A BIG GROUP. LOTTA MOVING PARTS. LOTTA BIG AWESOME PEOPLE DOING BIG AWESOME THINGS. THE DON'T ALWAYS HAVE TIME T STOP AND TAKE A KNEE TO EXPLAIN TO YOU WHAT THE HECK IS GOING ON.

YOU LEARN TO FOLLOW THE GUYS WHO ALWAYS SEEM TO KNOW WHERE THEY'RE HEADED.

AND YOU WAIT FOR YOUR MOMENT.

WE'RE GETTING KILLED OUT THERE. THE PHOENIX HOSTS ARE MORE POWERFUL THAN EVER. AND HALF OUR PEOPLE ARE EITHER LAID UP OR MISSING.

WHERE THE HELL IS TONY?

SOMEHOW...

DOESN'T MATTER HOW MANY GODS OR SUPER-SOLDIERS OR HULKS THEY GOT ON THE PAYROLL. ONCE YOU'RE AN AVENGER, IT NEVER FAILS...

SOONER OR LATER THE TIME COMES WHEN IT'S YOUR TURN TO STEP UP TO THE PLATE.

YOU JUST GOTTA MAKE SURE YOU'RE READY.

I AM READY. I DON'T KNOW WHAT HAPPENED ON THE MOON, BUT I KNOW I'M READY TO PROVE MY--

NO MORE QUESTIONS, DANIEL-SAN. WAX ON, WAX OFF. PAINT THE FENCE. SAND THE FLOOR. DON'T LET JOHNNY SWEEP THE LEG.

GOD HELP US ALL.

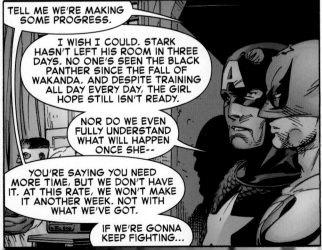

WE CAN'T GO ON LIKE THIS.

TELL ME WE'RE MAKING SOME PROGRESS.

I WISH I COULD. STARK HASN'T LEFT HIS ROOM IN THREE DAYS. NO ONE'S SEEN THE BLACK PANTHER SINCE THE FALL OF WAKANDA. AND DESPITE TRAINING ALL DAY EVERY DAY, THE GIRL HOPE STILL ISN'T READY.

NOR DO WE EVEN FULLY UNDERSTAND WHAT WILL HAPPEN ONCE SHE--

YOU'RE SAYING YOU NEED MORE TIME, BUT WE DON'T HAVE IT. AT THIS RATE, WE WON'T MAKE IT ANOTHER WEEK. NOT WITH WHAT WE'VE GOT.

IF WE'RE GONNA KEEP FIGHTING...

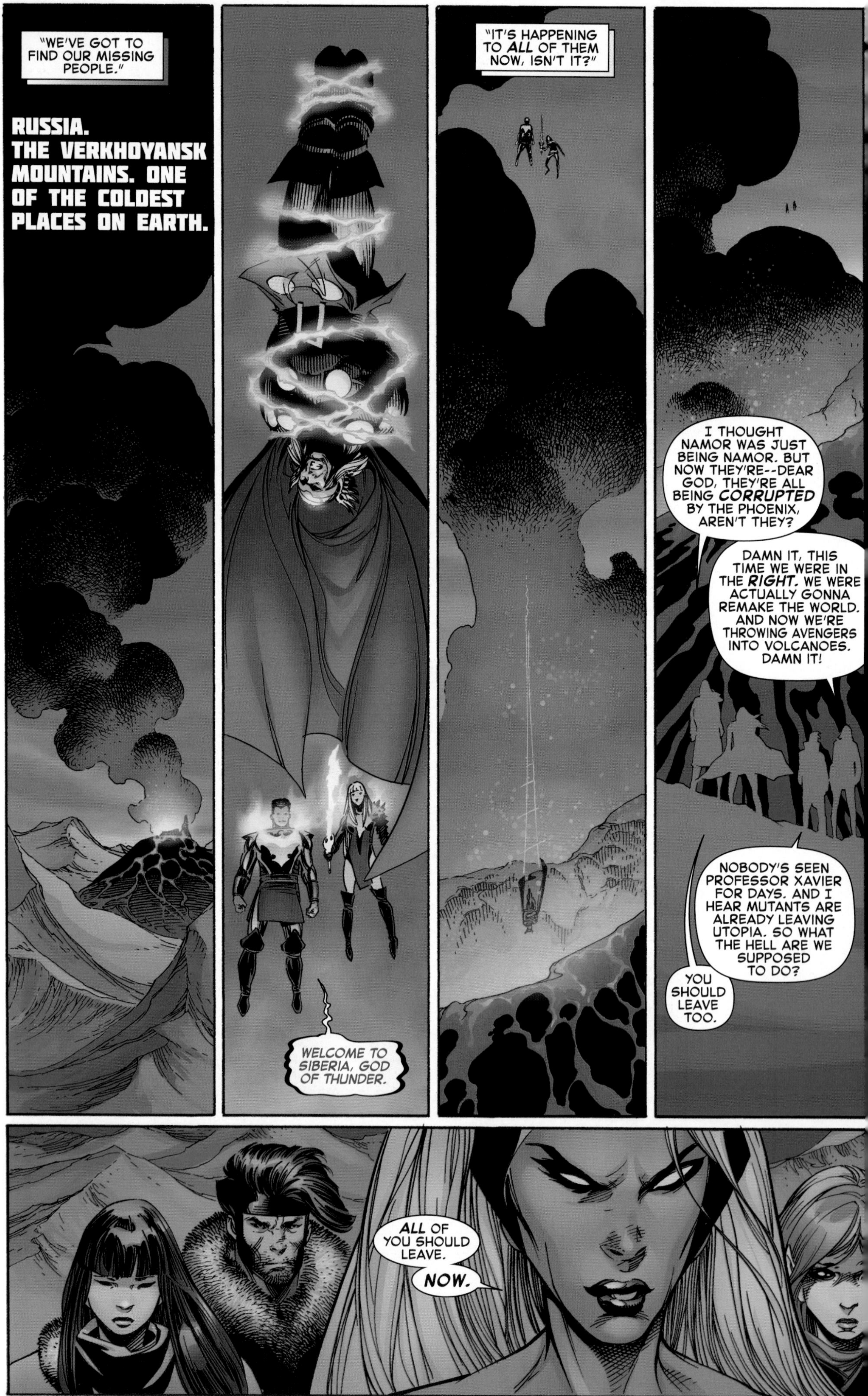
"WE'VE GOT TO FIND OUR MISSING PEOPLE."
RUSSIA. THE VERKHOYANSK MOUNTAINS. ONE OF THE COLDEST PLACES ON EARTH.
WELCOME TO SIBERIA, GOD OF THUNDER.
"IT'S HAPPENING TO ALL OF THEM NOW, ISN'T IT?"
I THOUGHT NAMOR WAS JUST BEING NAMOR. BUT NOW THEY'RE--DEAR GOD, THEY'RE ALL BEING CORRUPTED BY THE PHOENIX, AREN'T THEY?
DAMN IT, THIS TIME WE WERE IN THE RIGHT. WE WERE ACTUALLY GONNA REMAKE THE WORLD. AND NOW WE'RE THROWING AVENGERS INTO VOLCANOES. DAMN IT!
NOBODY'S SEEN PROFESSOR XAVIER FOR DAYS. AND I HEAR MUTANTS ARE ALREADY LEAVING UTOPIA. SO WHAT THE HELL ARE WE SUPPOSED TO DO?
YOU SHOULD LEAVE TOO.
ALL OF YOU SHOULD LEAVE.
NOW.

ETHIOPIA.
THE DANAKIL DESERT.
THE HOTTEST PLACE
ON EARTH.

LOVELY SPOT YOU PICKED FOR A MEETING, EMMA.

IT'S THE MOST INHOSPITABLE LAND I COULD FIND. NO OTHER MINDS AROUND FOR MILES. I ENJOY...THE QUIET.

WHY ARE WE HERE? SINCE NAMOR WENT ROGUE, EVERYTHING IS ON THE VERGE OF GOING TO HELL. I NEED YOU BACK AT UTOPIA, WITH ME.

I COULD END THIS ALL IN THE BLINK OF AN EYE, SCOTT.

SINCE NAMOR FELL, SINCE WE RECEIVED HIS PORTION OF THE POWER, I'VE BEEN REACHING OUT, TOUCHING EVERY MIND ON THE FACE OF THE EARTH. INCLUDING THE AVENGERS.

I COULD REACH INSIDE THEIR HEADS RIGHT NOW AND SIMPLY TURN THEM OFF. JUST LIKE FLICKING A SWITCH. I THINK...

I THINK PART OF ME WANTS TO DO IT.

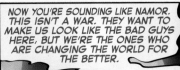

NOW YOU'RE SOUNDING LIKE NAMOR. THIS ISN'T A WAR. THEY WANT TO MAKE US LOOK LIKE THE BAD GUYS HERE, BUT WE'RE THE ONES WHO ARE CHANGING THE WORLD FOR THE BETTER.

THE AVENGERS WILL COME AROUND. WE WON'T GIVE THEM ANY OTHER CHOICE.

GET IT TOGETHER AND COME HOME, EMMA, AND LET'S FINISH WHAT WE STARTED.

I KNOW WHERE THEY'RE KEEPING HOPE.

WHAT DID YOU SAY?

I'VE BEEN PEEKING INSIDE SO MANY MINDS. AND SOME OF THE THINGS I'VE FOUND...

EMMA, FOCUS. WHERE IS SHE? WHERE'S HOPE?

IT SOUNDS MADE UP, BUT APPARENTLY IT'S REAL. IT'S CALLED... K'UN LUN.

SCOTT, WAIT, DON'T GO... I'M WORRIED ABOUT...

ABOUT WHAT I MIGHT DO NEXT...

PLEASE...

STOP ME.

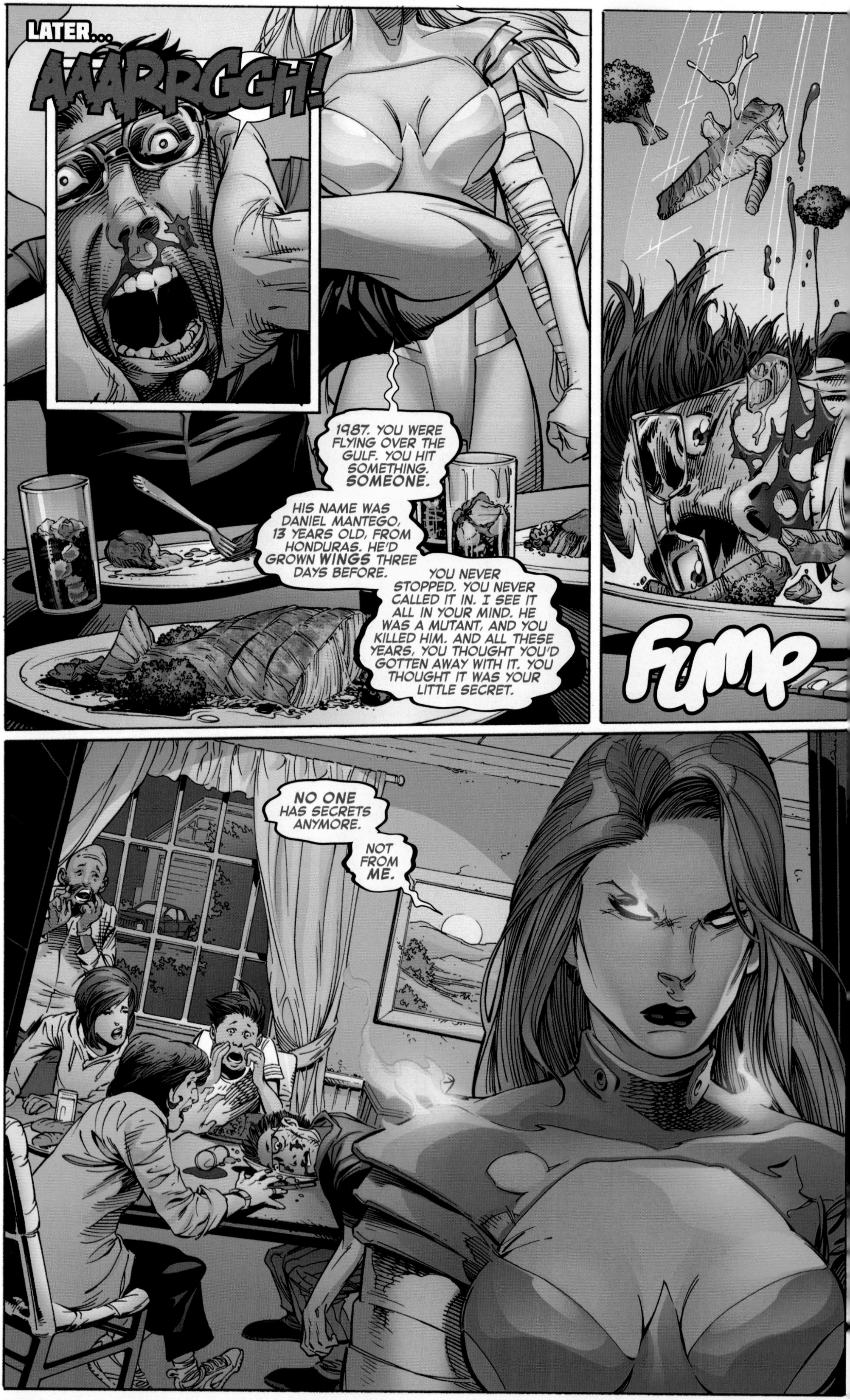
LATER...
AAARRGGH!
1987. YOU WERE FLYING OVER THE GULF. YOU HIT SOMETHING. SOMEONE.
HIS NAME WAS DANIEL MANTEGO, 13 YEARS OLD, FROM HONDURAS. HE'D GROWN WINGS THREE DAYS BEFORE.
YOU NEVER STOPPED. YOU NEVER CALLED IT IN. I SEE IT ALL IN YOUR MIND. HE WAS A MUTANT, AND YOU KILLED HIM. AND ALL THESE YEARS, YOU THOUGHT YOU'D GOTTEN AWAY WITH IT. YOU THOUGHT IT WAS YOUR LITTLE SECRET.
FUMP
NO ONE HAS SECRETS ANYMORE.
NOT FROM ME.

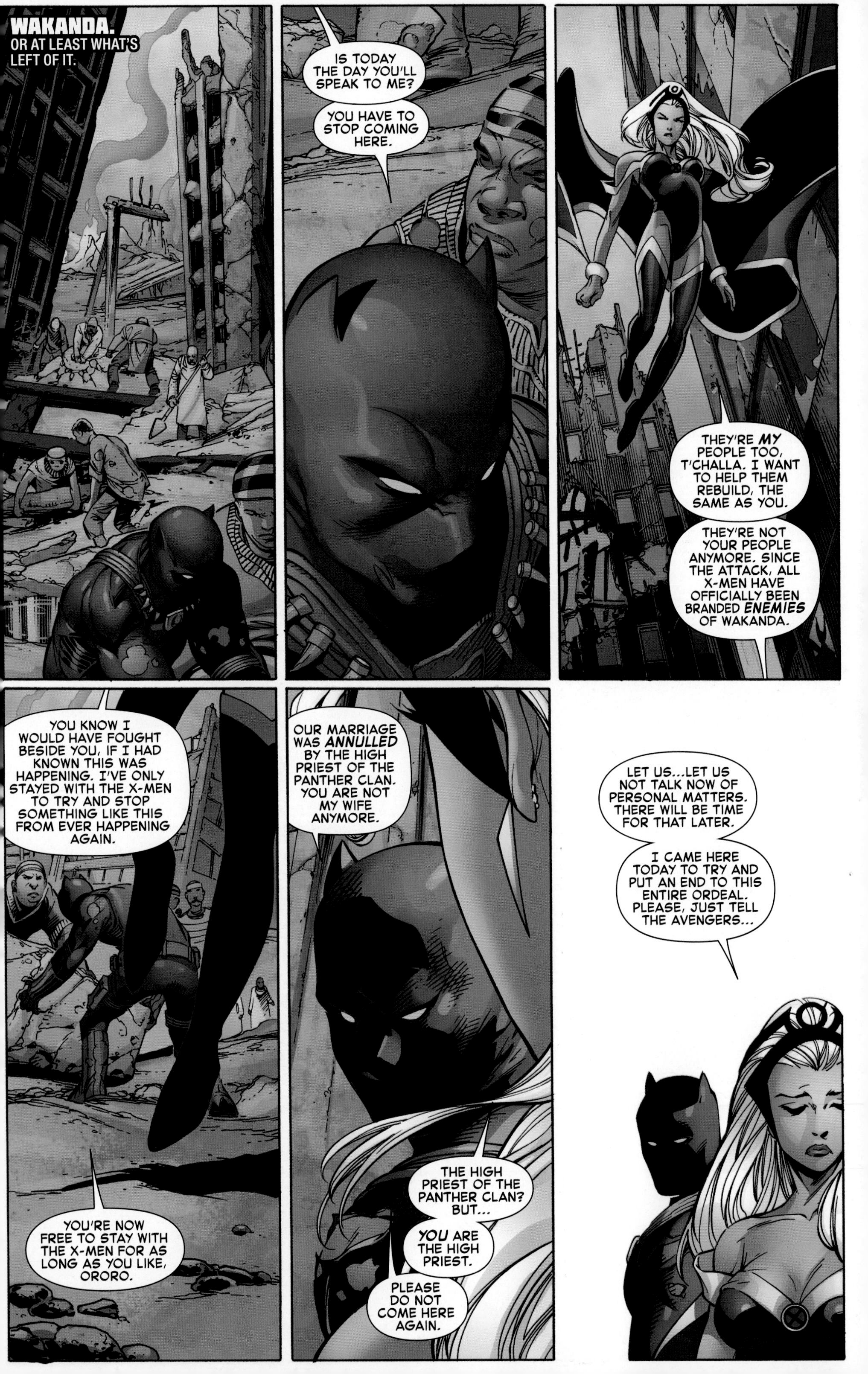
WAKANDA. OR AT LEAST WHAT'S LEFT OF IT.
IS TODAY THE DAY YOU'LL SPEAK TO ME?
YOU HAVE TO STOP COMING HERE.
THEY'RE MY PEOPLE TOO, T'CHALLA. I WANT TO HELP THEM REBUILD, THE SAME AS YOU.
THEY'RE NOT YOUR PEOPLE ANYMORE. SINCE THE ATTACK, ALL X-MEN HAVE OFFICIALLY BEEN BRANDED ENEMIES OF WAKANDA.
YOU KNOW I WOULD HAVE FOUGHT BESIDE YOU, IF I HAD KNOWN THIS WAS HAPPENING. I'VE ONLY STAYED WITH THE X-MEN TO TRY AND STOP SOMETHING LIKE THIS FROM EVER HAPPENING AGAIN.
YOU'RE NOW FREE TO STAY WITH THE X-MEN FOR AS LONG AS YOU LIKE, ORORO.
OUR MARRIAGE WAS ANNULLED BY THE HIGH PRIEST OF THE PANTHER CLAN. YOU ARE NOT MY WIFE ANYMORE.
THE HIGH PRIEST OF THE PANTHER CLAN? BUT...
YOU ARE THE HIGH PRIEST.
PLEASE DO NOT COME HERE AGAIN.
LET US...LET US NOT TALK NOW OF PERSONAL MATTERS. THERE WILL BE TIME FOR THAT LATER.
I CAME HERE TODAY TO TRY AND PUT AN END TO THIS ENTIRE ORDEAL. PLEASE, JUST TELL THE AVENGERS...

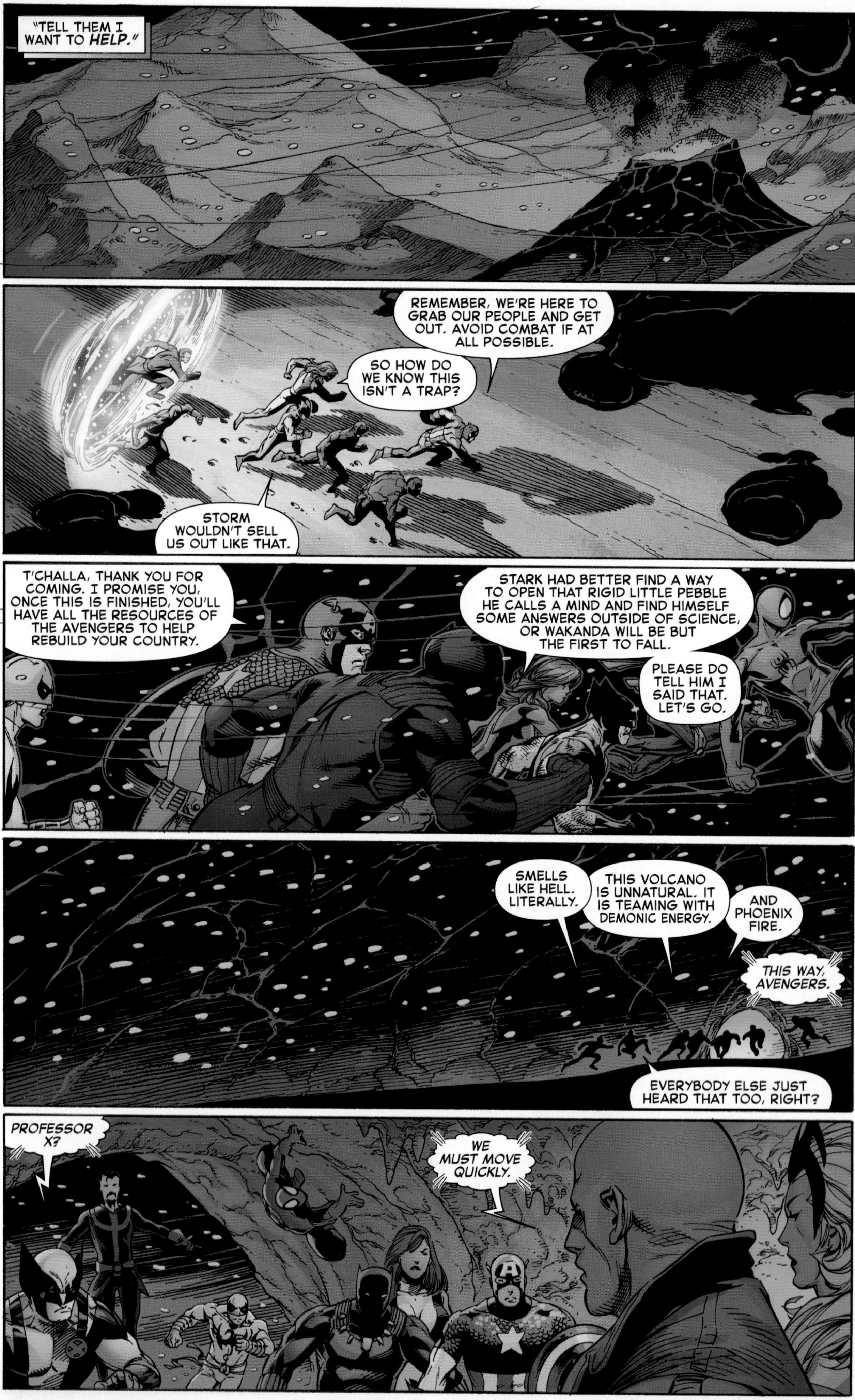
"TELL THEM I WANT TO HELP."
REMEMBER, WE'RE HERE TO GRAB OUR PEOPLE AND GET OUT. AVOID COMBAT IF AT ALL POSSIBLE.
SO HOW DO WE KNOW THIS ISN'T A TRAP?
STORM WOULDN'T SELL US OUT LIKE THAT.
T'CHALLA, THANK YOU FOR COMING. I PROMISE YOU, ONCE THIS IS FINISHED, YOU'LL HAVE ALL THE RESOURCES OF THE AVENGERS TO HELP REBUILD YOUR COUNTRY.
STARK HAD BETTER FIND A WAY TO OPEN THAT RIGID LITTLE PEBBLE HE CALLS A MIND AND FIND HIMSELF SOME ANSWERS OUTSIDE OF SCIENCE, OR WAKANDA WILL BE BUT THE FIRST TO FALL.
PLEASE DO TELL HIM I SAID THAT. LET'S GO.
SMELLS LIKE HELL. LITERALLY.
THIS VOLCANO IS UNNATURAL. IT IS TEAMING WITH DEMONIC ENERGY.
AND PHOENIX FIRE.
THIS WAY, AVENGERS.
EVERYBODY ELSE JUST HEARD THAT TOO, RIGHT?
PROFESSOR X?
WE MUST MOVE QUICKLY.

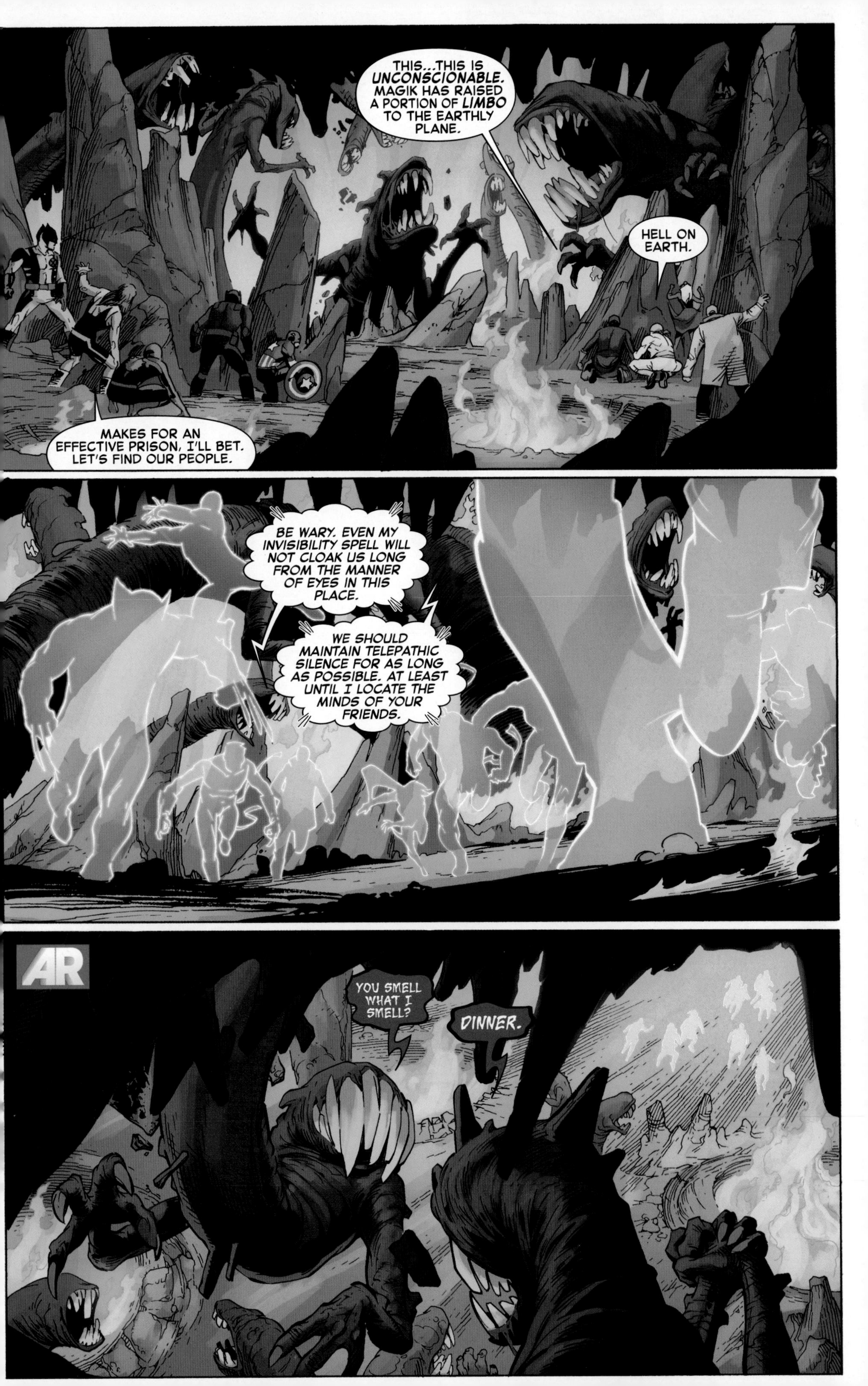
THIS...THIS IS UNCONSCIONABLE. MAGIK HAS RAISED A PORTION OF LIMBO TO THE EARTHLY PLANE.
HELL ON EARTH.
MAKES FOR AN EFFECTIVE PRISON, I'LL BET. LET'S FIND OUR PEOPLE.
BE WARY. EVEN MY INVISIBILITY SPELL WILL NOT CLOAK US LONG FROM THE MANNER OF EYES IN THIS PLACE.
WE SHOULD MAINTAIN TELEPATHIC SILENCE FOR AS LONG AS POSSIBLE. AT LEAST UNTIL I LOCATE THE MINDS OF YOUR FRIENDS.
YOU SMELL WHAT I SMELL?
DINNER.

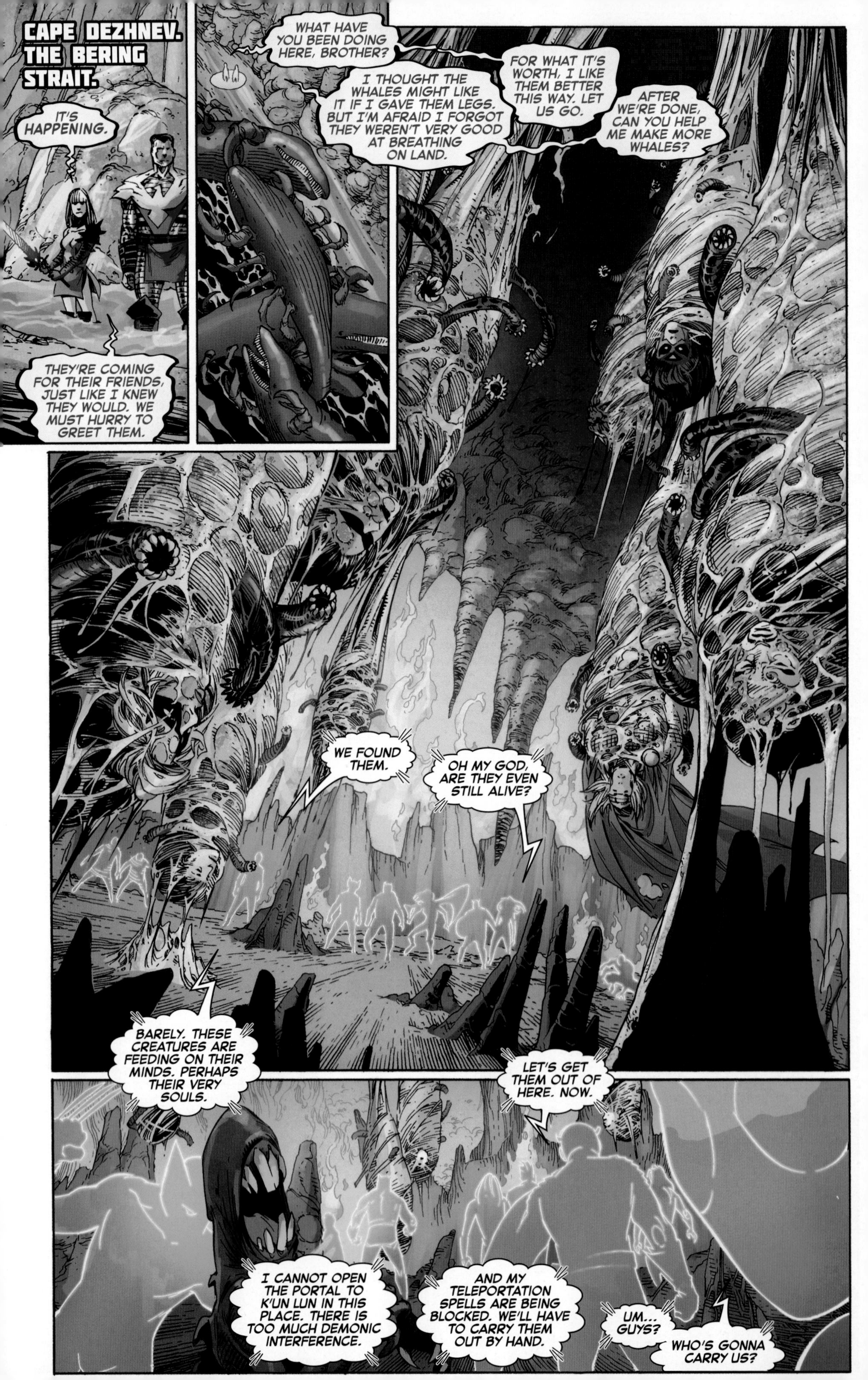
CAPE DEZHNEV. THE BERING STRAIT.
IT'S HAPPENING.
THEY'RE COMING FOR THEIR FRIENDS, JUST LIKE I KNEW THEY WOULD. WE MUST HURRY TO GREET THEM.
WHAT HAVE YOU BEEN DOING HERE, BROTHER?
I THOUGHT THE WHALES MIGHT LIKE IT IF I GAVE THEM LEGS. BUT I'M AFRAID I FORGOT THEY WEREN'T VERY GOOD AT BREATHING ON LAND.
FOR WHAT IT'S WORTH, I LIKE THEM BETTER THIS WAY. LET US GO.
AFTER WE'RE DONE, CAN YOU HELP ME MAKE MORE WHALES?
WE FOUND THEM.
OH MY GOD, ARE THEY EVEN STILL ALIVE?
BARELY. THESE CREATURES ARE FEEDING ON THEIR MINDS. PERHAPS THEIR VERY SOULS.
LET'S GET THEM OUT OF HERE. NOW.
I CANNOT OPEN THE PORTAL TO K'UN LUN IN THIS PLACE. THERE IS TOO MUCH DEMONIC INTERFERENCE.
AND MY TELEPORTATION SPELLS ARE BEING BLOCKED. WE'LL HAVE TO CARRY THEM OUT BY HAND.
UM... GUYS?
WHO'S GONNA CARRY US?

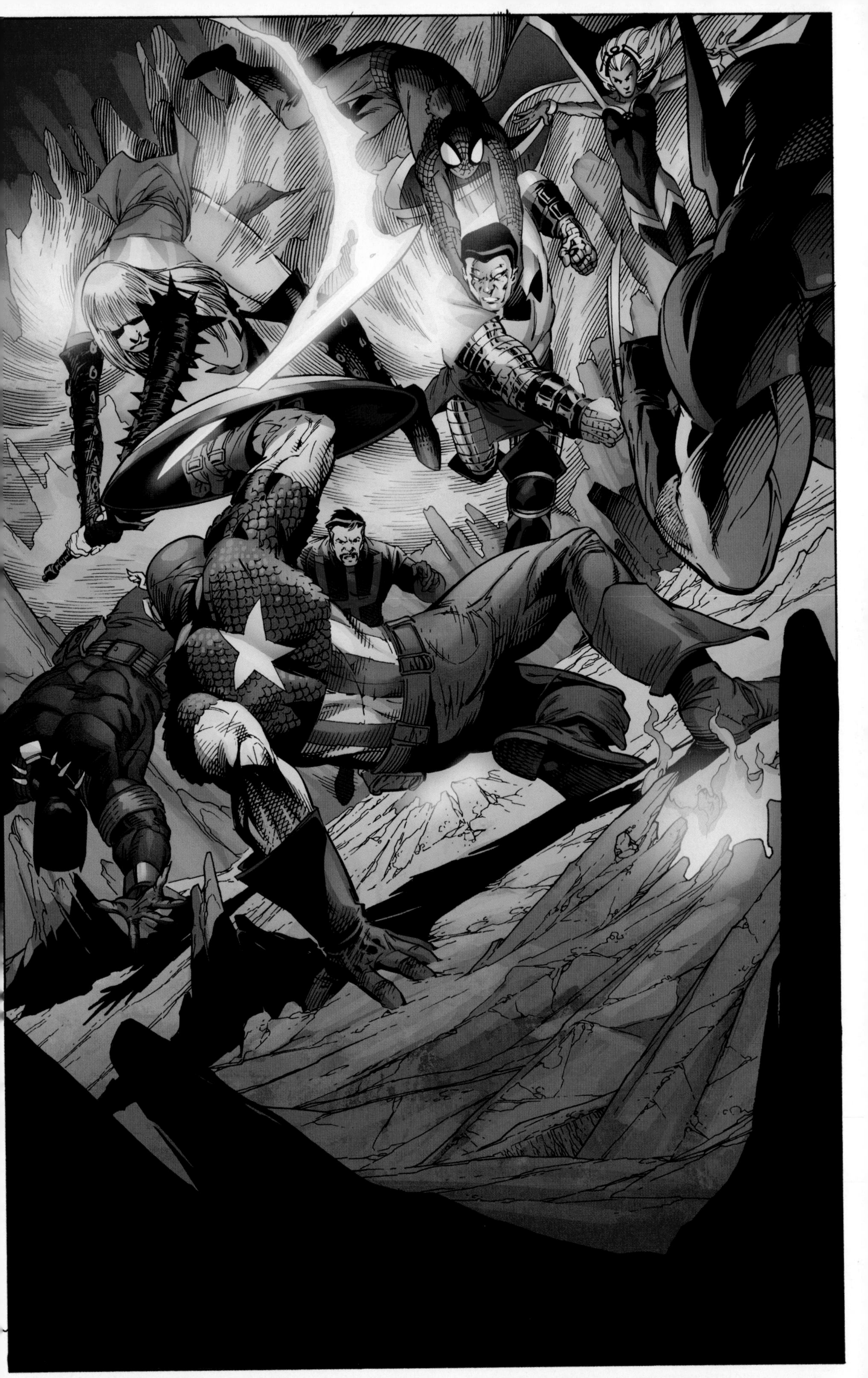

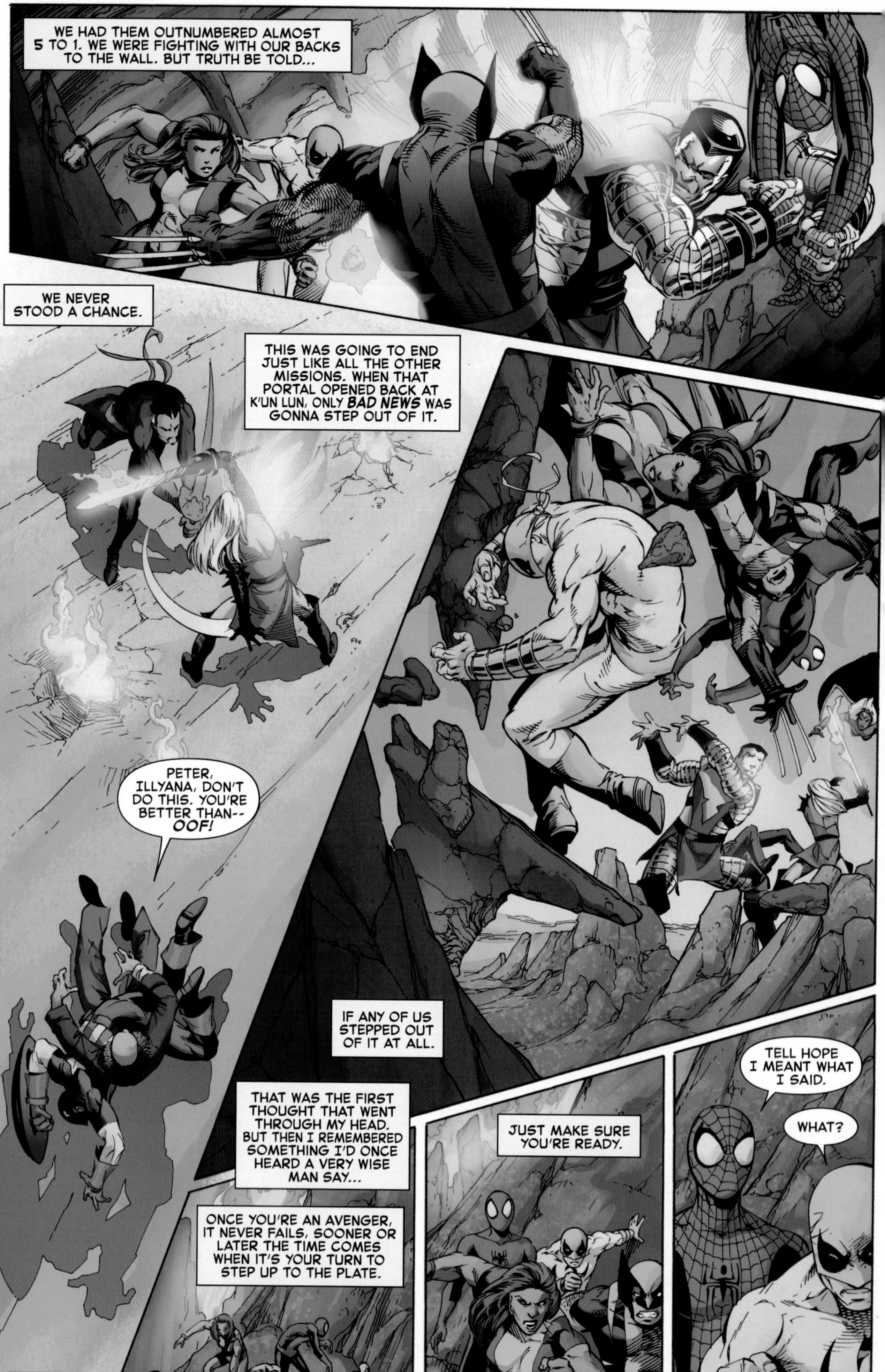

WE HAD THEM OUTNUMBERED ALMOST 5 TO 1. WE WERE FIGHTING WITH OUR BACKS TO THE WALL. BUT TRUTH BE TOLD...
WE NEVER STOOD A CHANCE.
THIS WAS GOING TO END JUST LIKE ALL THE OTHER MISSIONS. WHEN THAT PORTAL OPENED BACK AT K'UN LUN, ONLY BAD NEWS WAS GONNA STEP OUT OF IT.
PETER, ILLYANA, DON'T DO THIS. YOU'RE BETTER THAN-- OOF!
IF ANY OF US STEPPED OUT OF IT AT ALL.
THAT WAS THE FIRST THOUGHT THAT WENT THROUGH MY HEAD. BUT THEN I REMEMBERED SOMETHING I'D ONCE HEARD A VERY WISE MAN SAY...
ONCE YOU'RE AN AVENGER, IT NEVER FAILS, SOONER OR LATER THE TIME COMES WHEN IT'S YOUR TURN TO STEP UP TO THE PLATE.
JUST MAKE SURE YOU'RE READY.
TELL HOPE I MEANT WHAT I SAID.
WHAT?

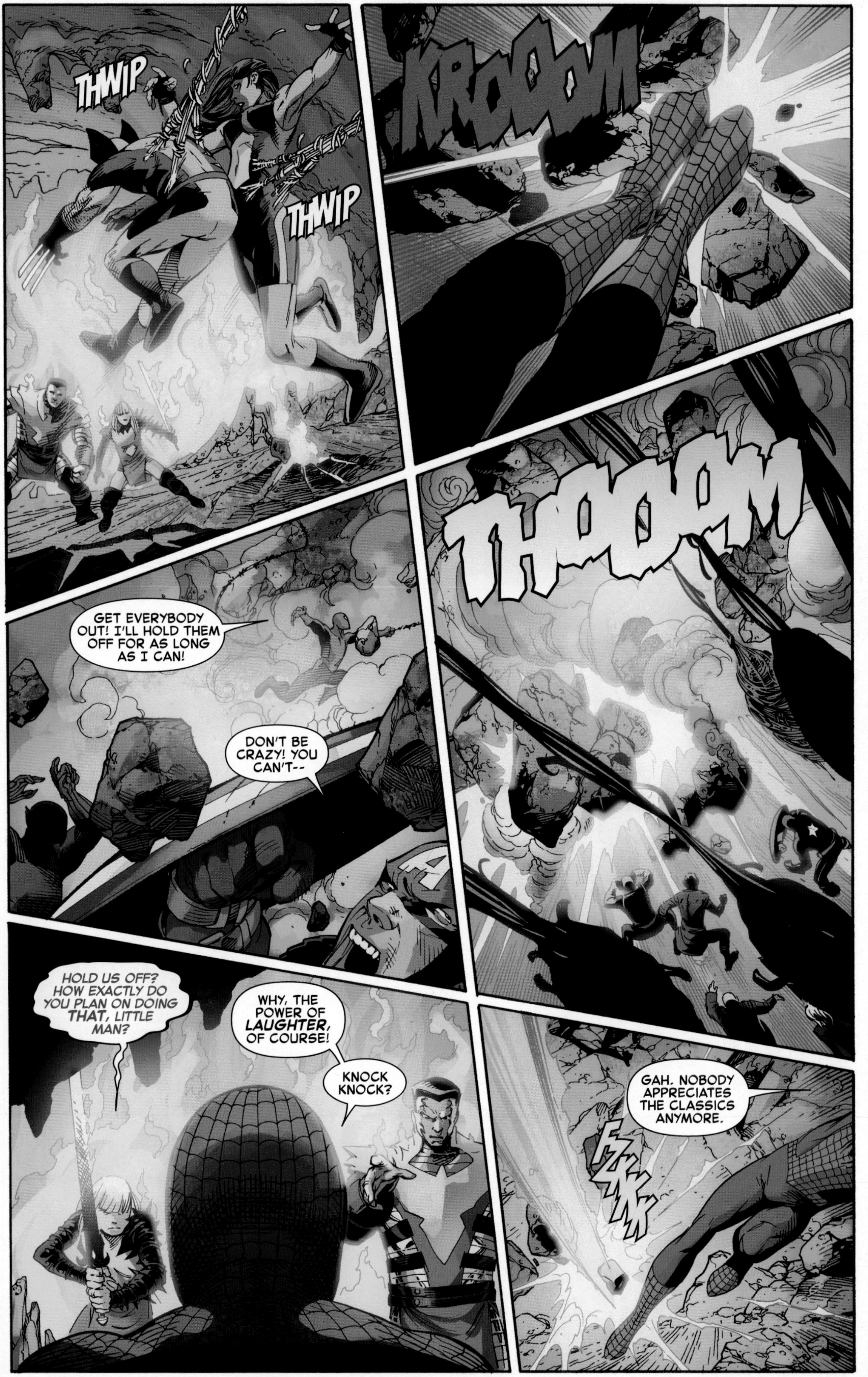
THWIP
THWIP
KROOOM
THOOOM
GET EVERYBODY OUT! I'LL HOLD THEM OFF FOR AS LONG AS I CAN!
DON'T BE CRAZY! YOU CAN'T--
HOLD US OFF? HOW EXACTLY DO YOU PLAN ON DOING THAT, LITTLE MAN?
WHY, THE POWER OF LAUGHTER, OF COURSE!
KNOCK KNOCK?
GAH. NOBODY APPRECIATES THE CLASSICS ANYMORE.

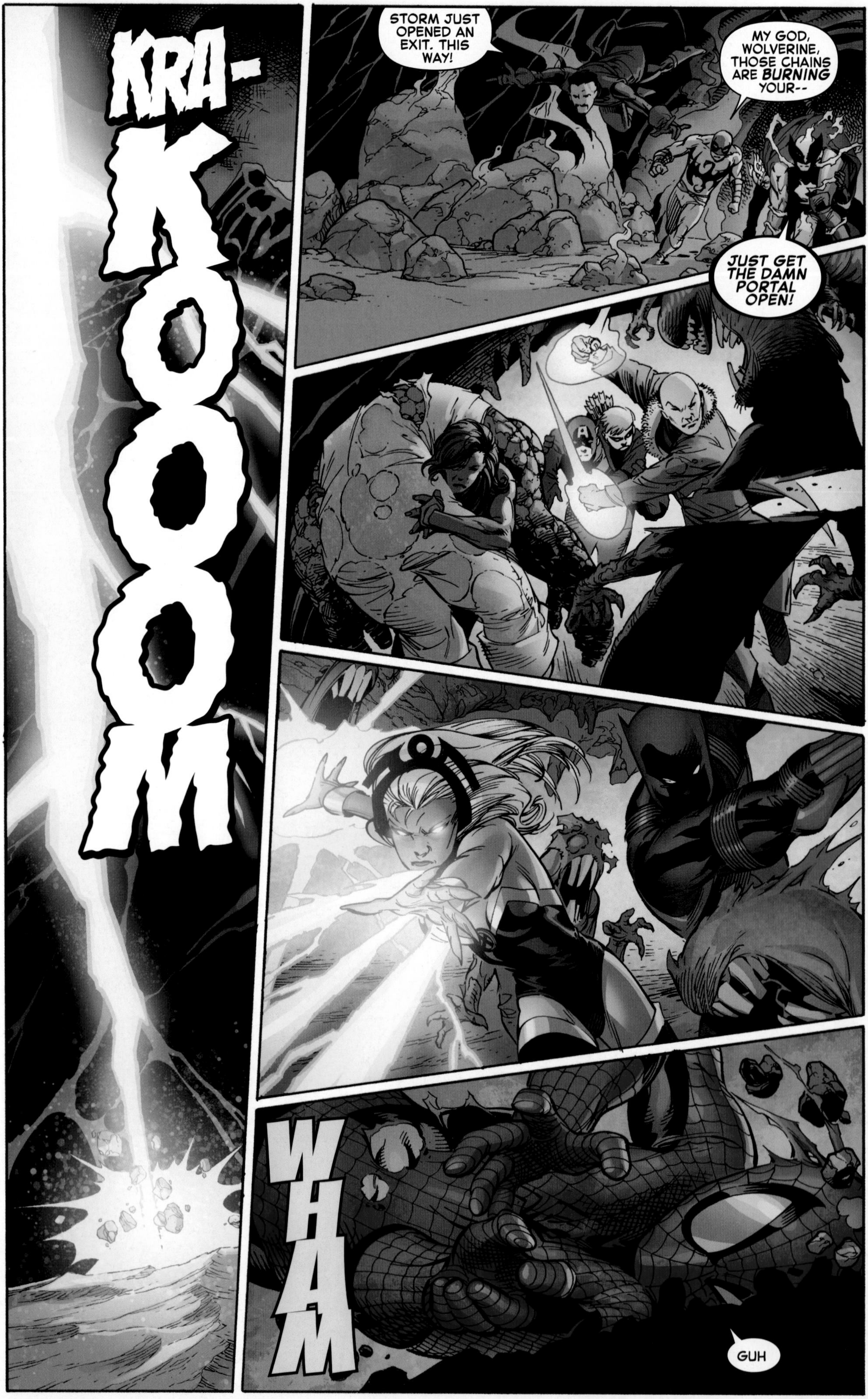
KRA-KOOOOM
STORM JUST OPENED AN EXIT. THIS WAY!
MY GOD, WOLVERINE, THOSE CHAINS ARE BURNING YOUR--
JUST GET THE DAMN PORTAL OPEN!
WHAM
GUH

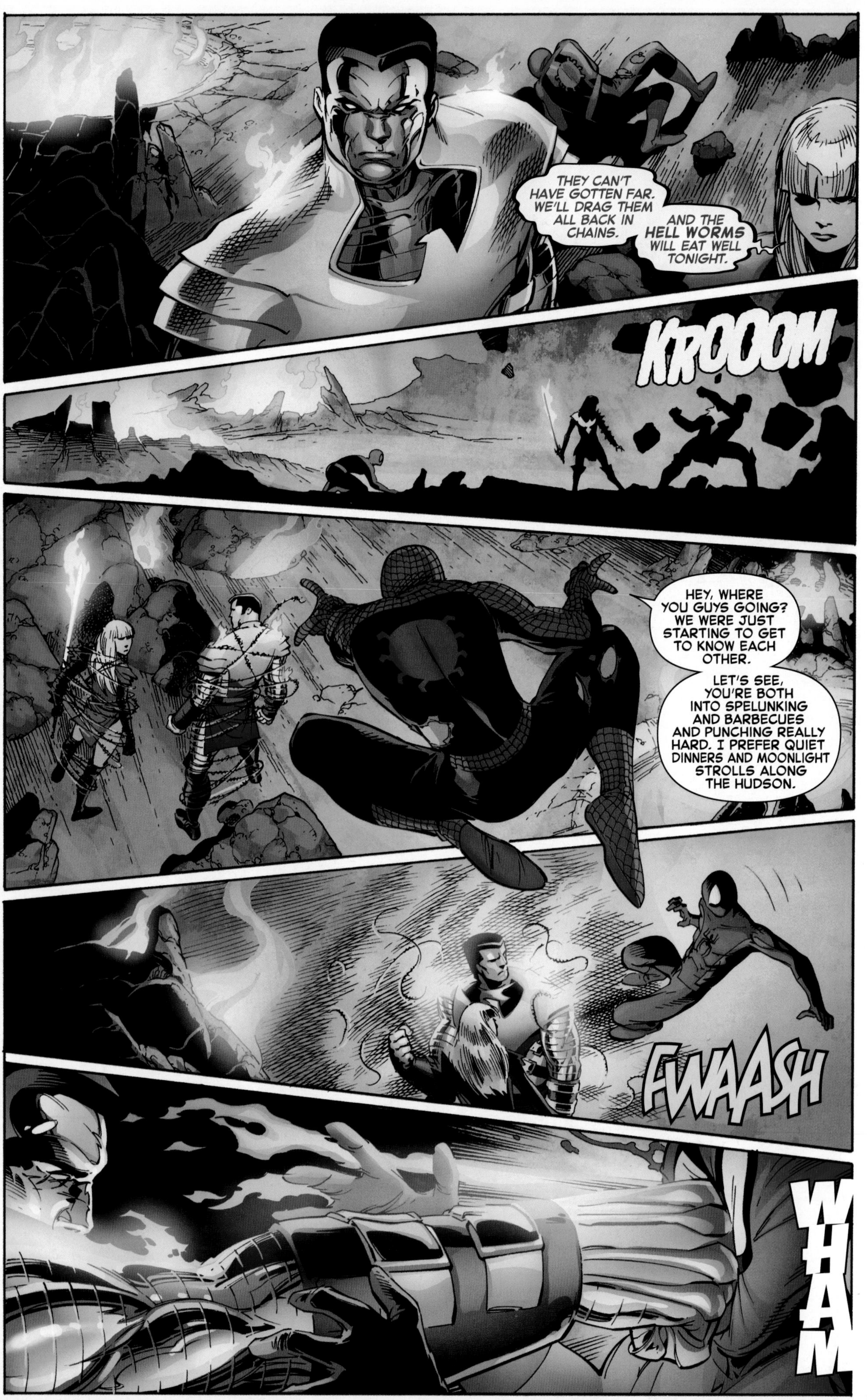

THEY CAN'T HAVE GOTTEN FAR. WE'LL DRAG THEM ALL BACK IN CHAINS.
AND THE HELL WORMS WILL EAT WELL TONIGHT.
KROOOM
HEY, WHERE YOU GUYS GOING? WE WERE JUST STARTING TO GET TO KNOW EACH OTHER.
LET'S SEE, YOU'RE BOTH INTO SPELUNKING AND BARBECUES AND PUNCHING REALLY HARD. I PREFER QUIET DINNERS AND MOONLIGHT STROLLS ALONG THE HUDSON.
FWAASH
WHAM

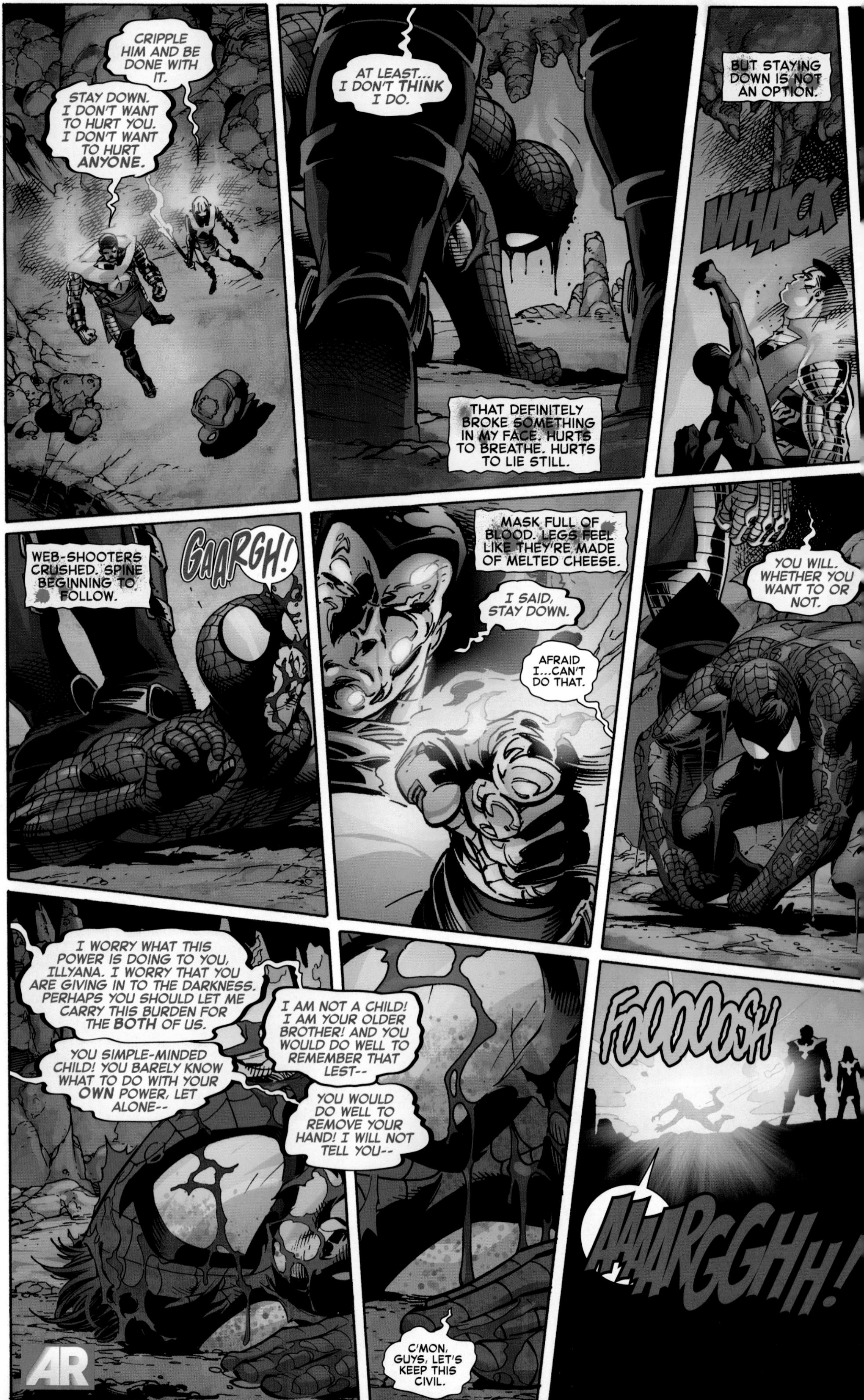

CRIPPLE HIM AND BE DONE WITH IT.
STAY DOWN. I DON'T WANT TO HURT YOU. I DON'T WANT TO HURT ANYONE.
AT LEAST... I DON'T THINK I DO.
THAT DEFINITELY BROKE SOMETHING IN MY FACE. HURTS TO BREATHE. HURTS TO LIE STILL.
BUT STAYING DOWN IS NOT AN OPTION.
WHACK
WEB-SHOOTERS CRUSHED. SPINE BEGINNING TO FOLLOW.
GAARGH!
MASK FULL OF BLOOD. LEGS FEEL LIKE THEY'RE MADE OF MELTED CHEESE.
I SAID, STAY DOWN.
AFRAID I...CAN'T DO THAT.
YOU WILL. WHETHER YOU WANT TO OR NOT.
I WORRY WHAT THIS POWER IS DOING TO YOU, ILLYANA. I WORRY THAT YOU ARE GIVING IN TO THE DARKNESS. PERHAPS YOU SHOULD LET ME CARRY THIS BURDEN FOR THE BOTH OF US.
YOU SIMPLE-MINDED CHILD! YOU BARELY KNOW WHAT TO DO WITH YOUR OWN POWER, LET ALONE--
I AM NOT A CHILD! I AM YOUR OLDER BROTHER! AND YOU WOULD DO WELL TO REMEMBER THAT LEST--
YOU WOULD DO WELL TO REMOVE YOUR HAND! I WILL NOT TELL YOU--
C'MON, GUYS, LET'S KEEP THIS CIVIL.
FOOOOOSH
AAAARGGHH!
AR

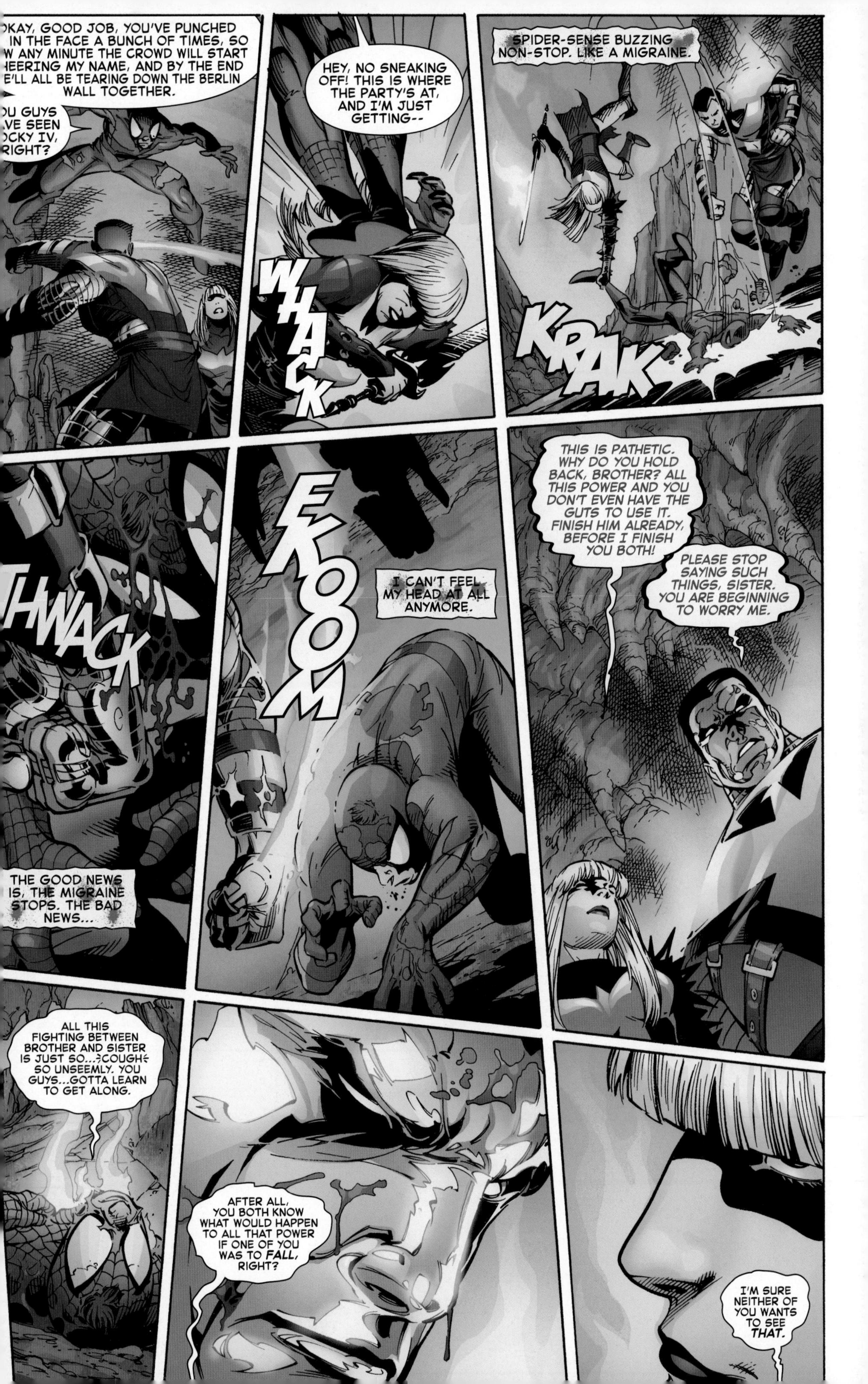
OKAY, GOOD JOB, YOU'VE PUNCHED IN THE FACE A BUNCH OF TIMES, SO ANY MINUTE THE CROWD WILL START CHEERING MY NAME, AND BY THE END WE'LL ALL BE TEARING DOWN THE BERLIN WALL TOGETHER.
YOU GUYS HAVE SEEN ROCKY IV, RIGHT?
HEY, NO SNEAKING OFF! THIS IS WHERE THE PARTY'S AT, AND I'M JUST GETTING--
WHACK
SPIDER-SENSE BUZZING NON-STOP. LIKE A MIGRAINE.
KRAK
THWACK
THE GOOD NEWS IS, THE MIGRAINE STOPS. THE BAD NEWS...
EKOOOM
I CAN'T FEEL MY HEAD AT ALL ANYMORE.
THIS IS PATHETIC. WHY DO YOU HOLD BACK, BROTHER? ALL THIS POWER AND YOU DON'T EVEN HAVE THE GUTS TO USE IT. FINISH HIM ALREADY, BEFORE I FINISH YOU BOTH!
PLEASE STOP SAYING SUCH THINGS, SISTER. YOU ARE BEGINNING TO WORRY ME.
ALL THIS FIGHTING BETWEEN BROTHER AND SISTER IS JUST SO...COUGH SO UNSEEMLY. YOU GUYS...GOTTA LEARN TO GET ALONG.
AFTER ALL, YOU BOTH KNOW WHAT WOULD HAPPEN TO ALL THAT POWER IF ONE OF YOU WAS TO FALL, RIGHT?
I'M SURE NEITHER OF YOU WANTS TO SEE THAT.

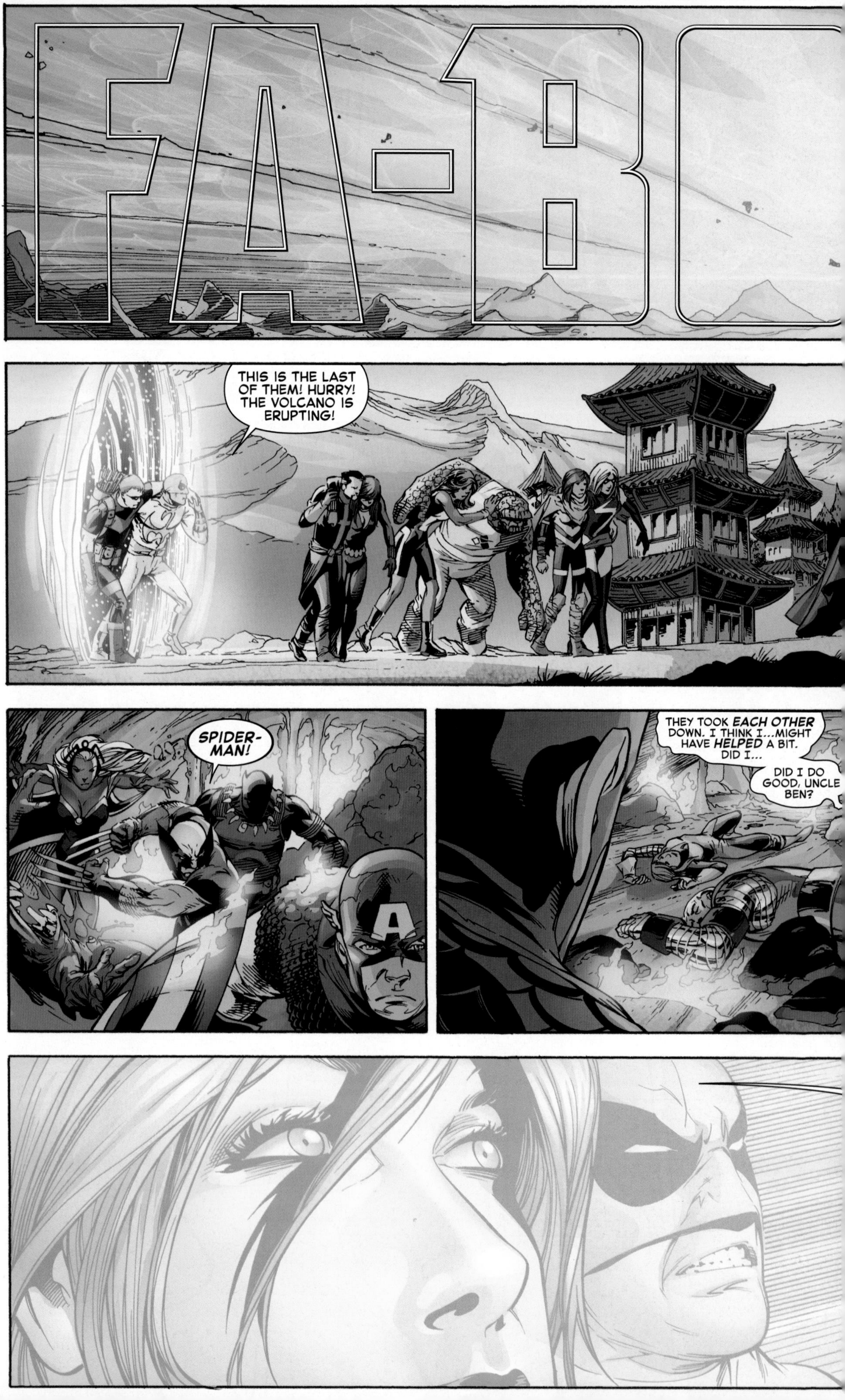
FA-BO
THIS IS THE LAST OF THEM! HURRY! THE VOLCANO IS ERUPTING!
SPIDER-MAN!
THEY TOOK EACH OTHER DOWN. I THINK I...MIGHT HAVE HELPED A BIT. DID I...
DID I DO GOOD, UNCLE BEN?

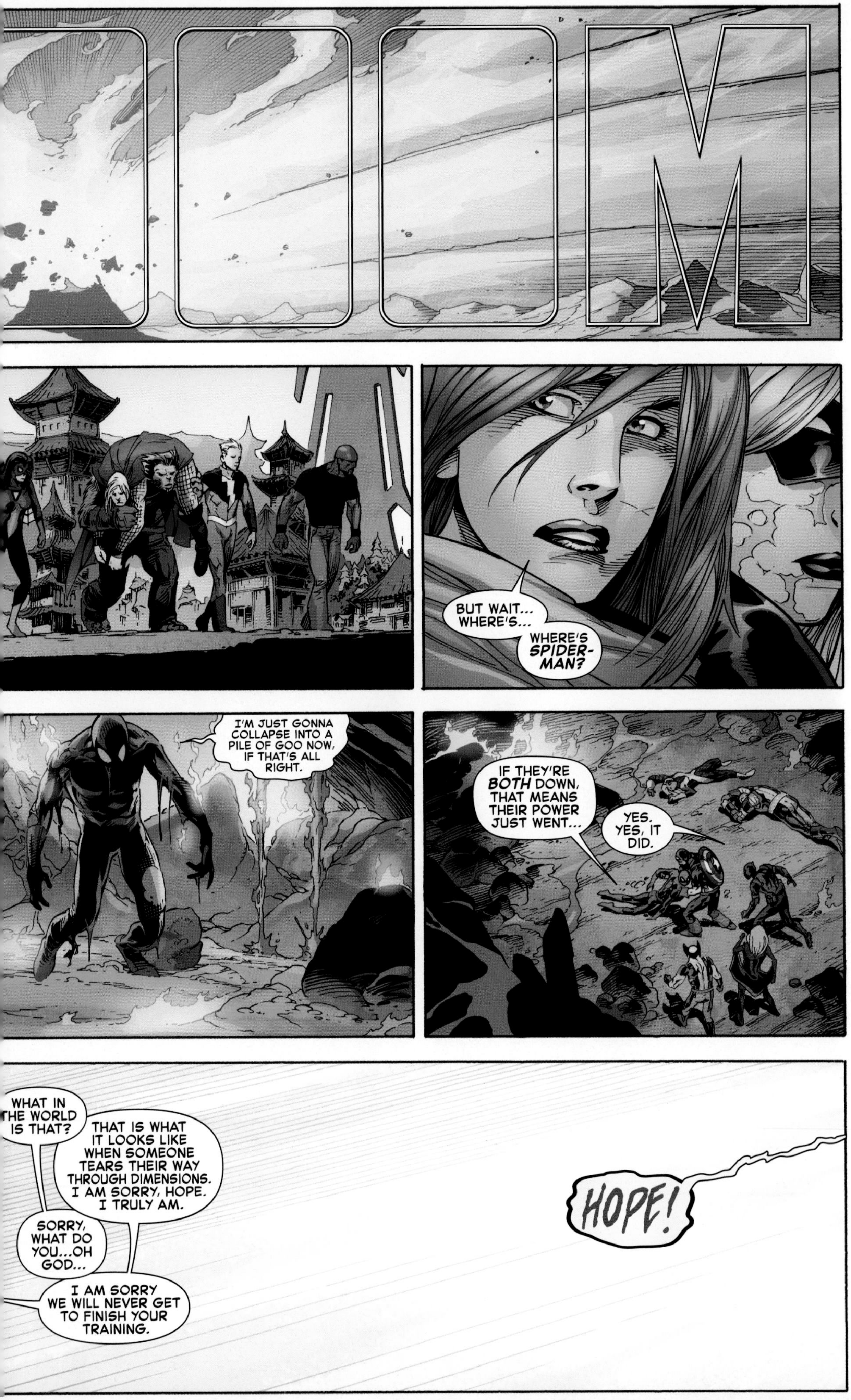
DOOM
BUT WAIT... WHERE'S...
WHERE'S SPIDER-MAN?
I'M JUST GONNA COLLAPSE INTO A PILE OF GOO NOW, IF THAT'S ALL RIGHT.
IF THEY'RE BOTH DOWN, THAT MEANS THEIR POWER JUST WENT...
YES. YES, IT DID.
WHAT IN THE WORLD IS THAT?
THAT IS WHAT IT LOOKS LIKE WHEN SOMEONE TEARS THEIR WAY THROUGH DIMENSIONS. I AM SORRY, HOPE. I TRULY AM.
SORRY, WHAT DO YOU...OH GOD...
I AM SORRY WE WILL NEVER GET TO FINISH YOUR TRAINING.
HOPE!

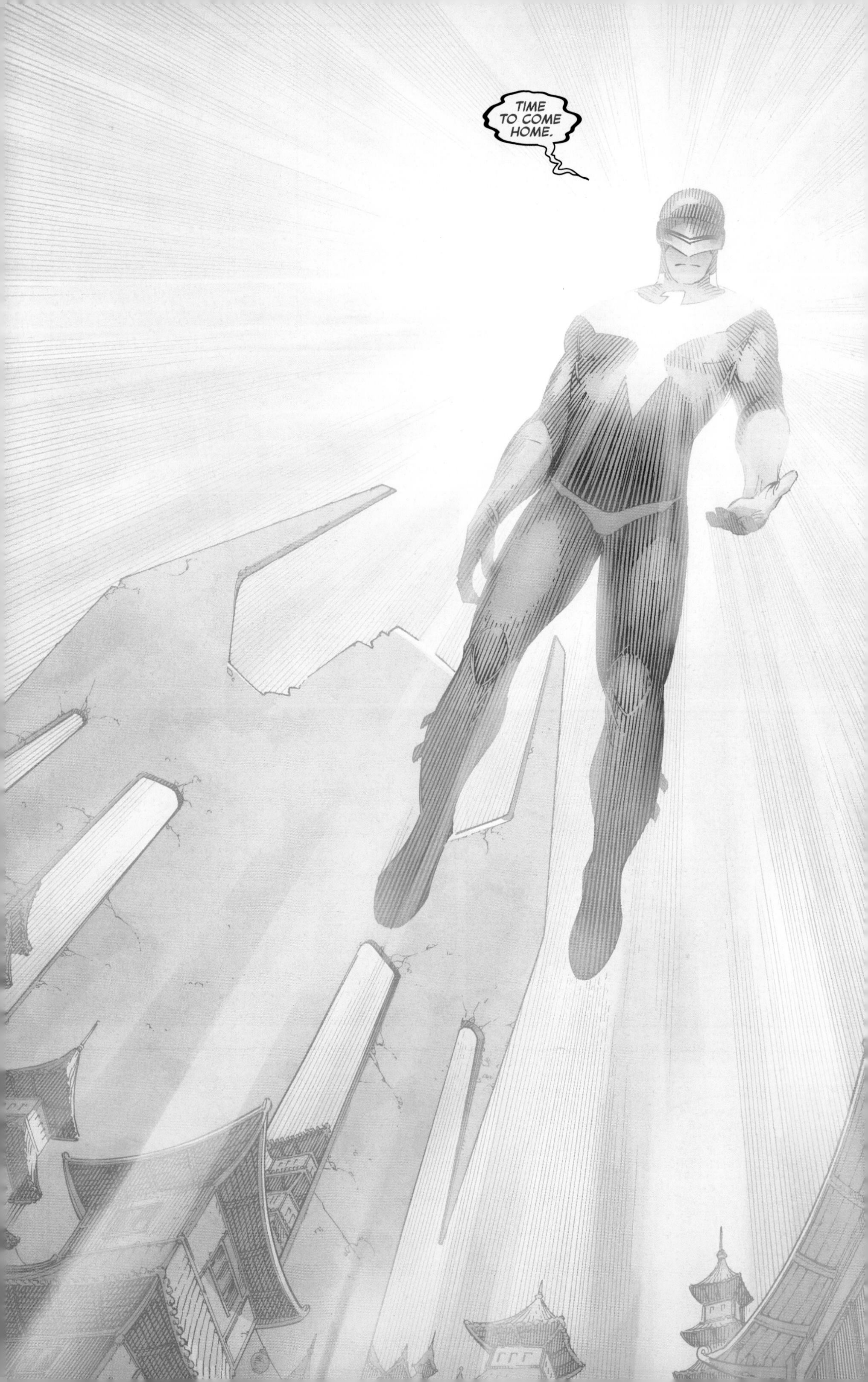
TIME TO COME HOME.

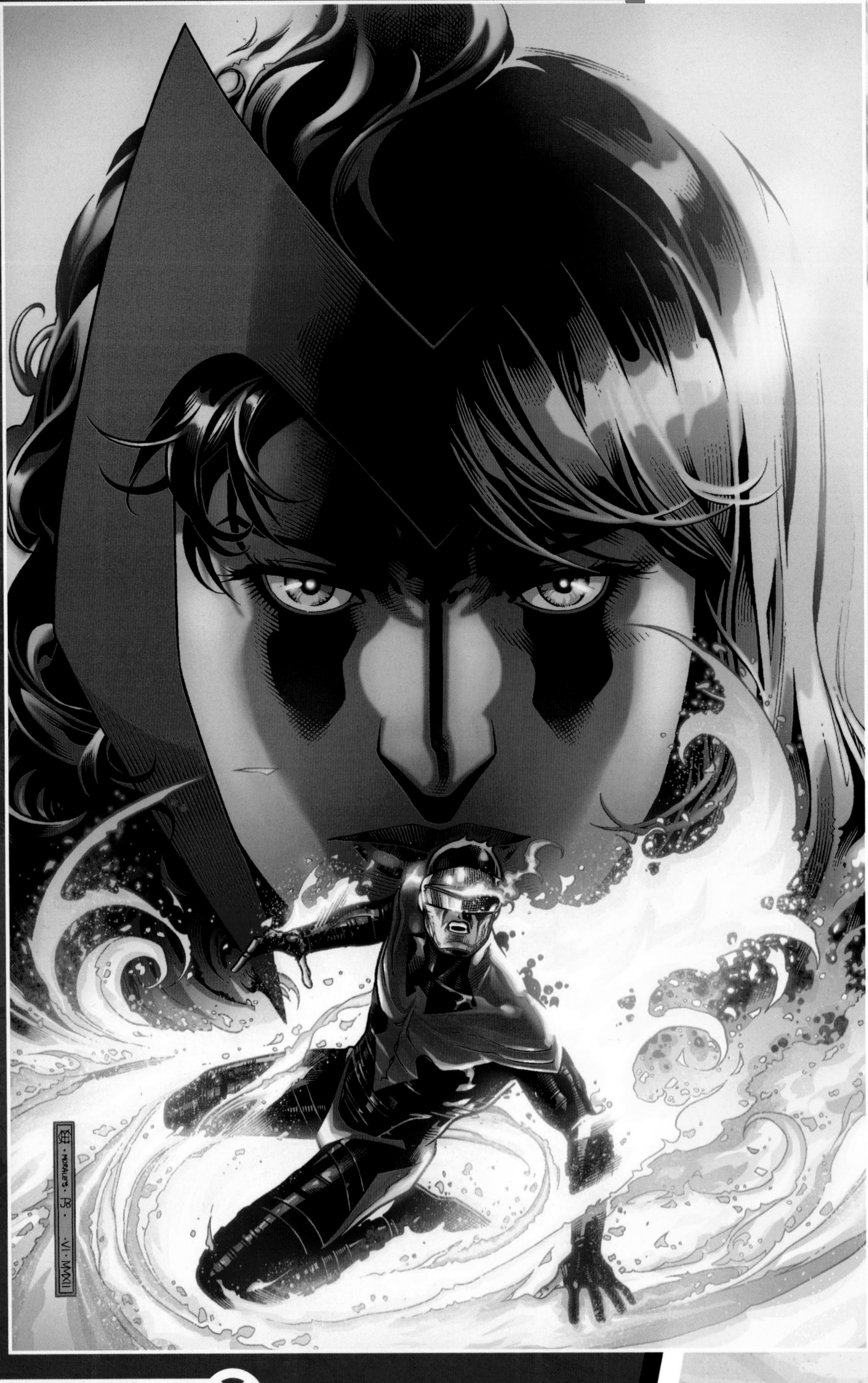

ROUND 10

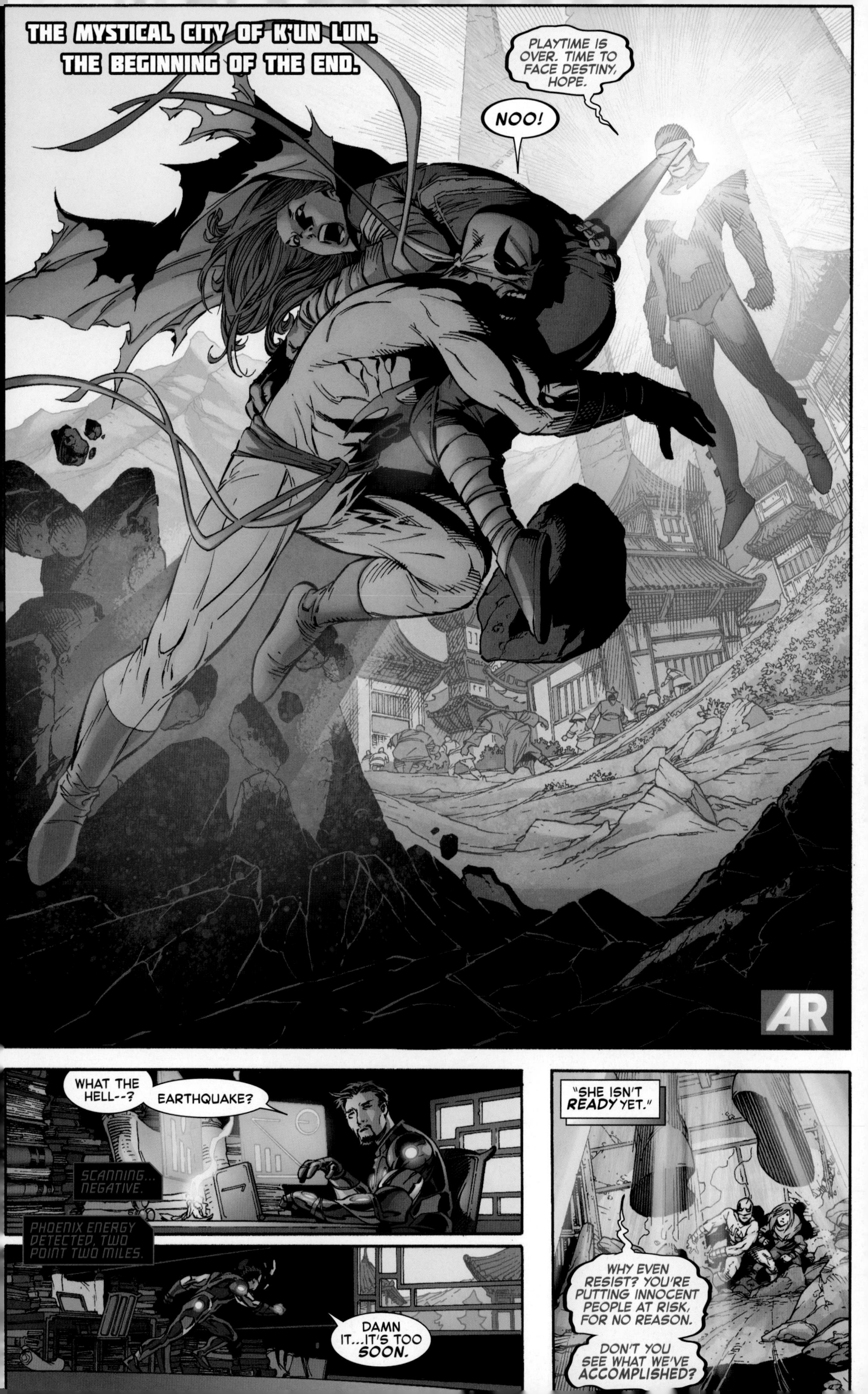
THE MYSTICAL CITY OF K'UN LUN.
THE BEGINNING OF THE END.
PLAYTIME IS OVER. TIME TO FACE DESTINY, HOPE.
NOO!
AR
WHAT THE HELL--?
EARTHQUAKE?
SCANNING... NEGATIVE.
PHOENIX ENERGY DETECTED, TWO POINT TWO MILES.
DAMN IT...IT'S TOO SOON.
"SHE ISN'T READY YET."
WHY EVEN RESIST? YOU'RE PUTTING INNOCENT PEOPLE AT RISK, FOR NO REASON.
DON'T YOU SEE WHAT WE'VE ACCOMPLISHED?

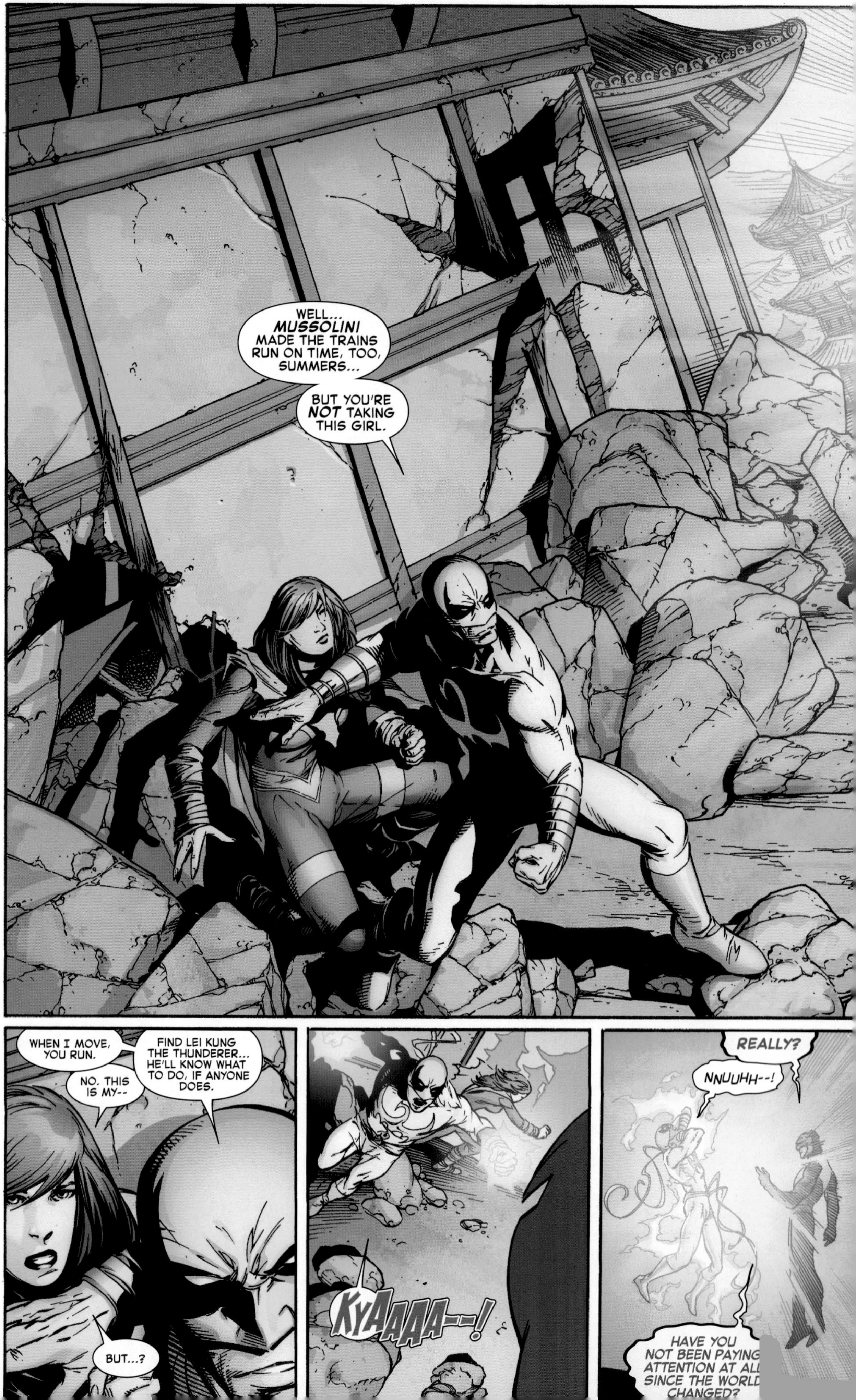
WELL... MUSSOLINI MADE THE TRAINS RUN ON TIME, TOO, SUMMERS...
BUT YOU'RE NOT TAKING THIS GIRL.
WHEN I MOVE, YOU RUN.
NO. THIS IS MY--
FIND LEI KUNG THE THUNDERER... HE'LL KNOW WHAT TO DO, IF ANYONE DOES.
BUT...?
KYAAAA--!
REALLY?
NNUUHH--!
HAVE YOU NOT BEEN PAYING ATTENTION AT ALL SINCE THE WORLD CHANGED?

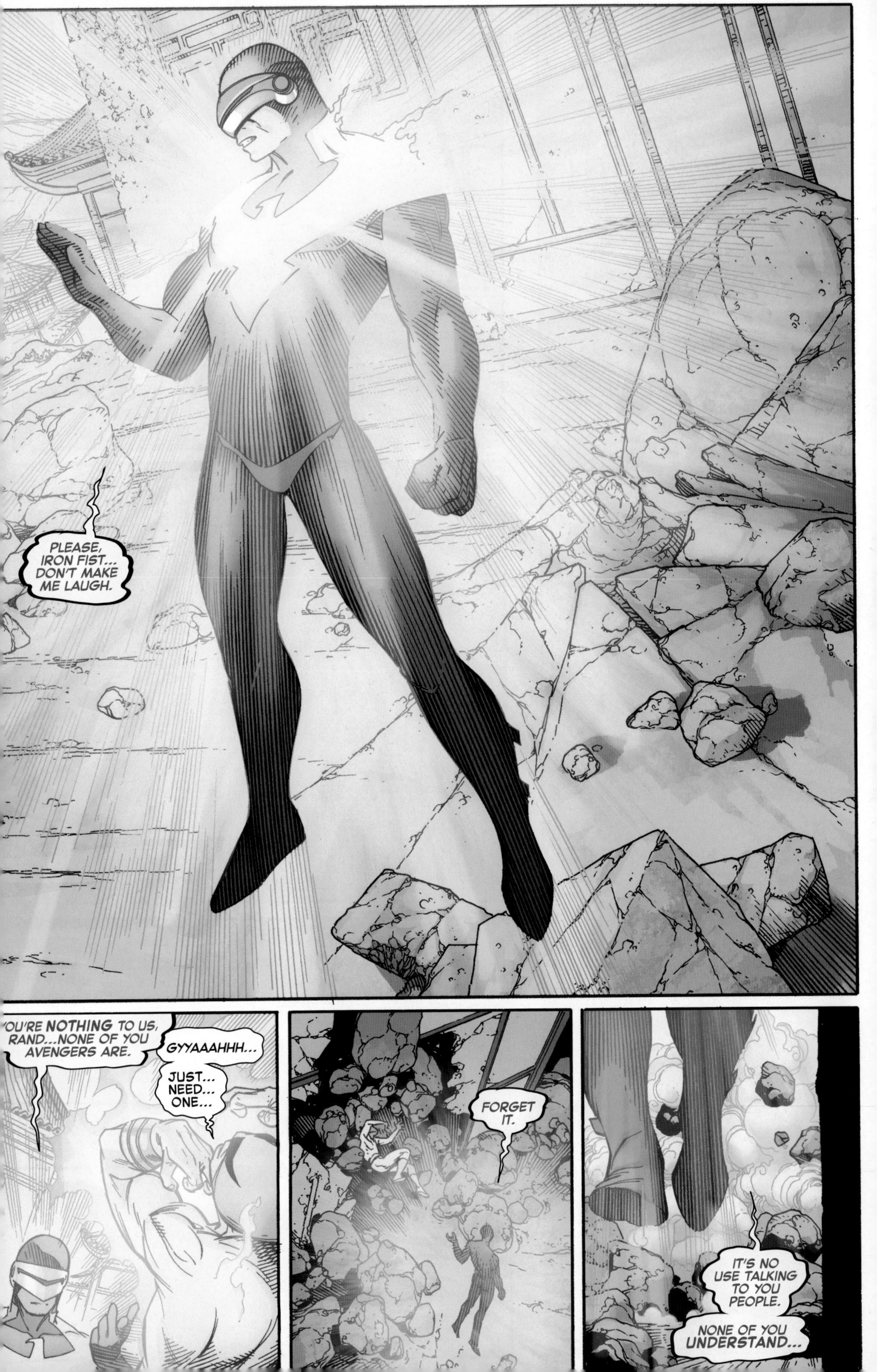
PLEASE, IRON FIST... DON'T MAKE ME LAUGH.
YOU'RE NOTHING TO US, RAND...NONE OF YOU AVENGERS ARE.
GYYAAAHHH...
JUST... NEED... ONE...
FORGET IT.
IT'S NO USE TALKING TO YOU PEOPLE.
NONE OF YOU UNDERSTAND...

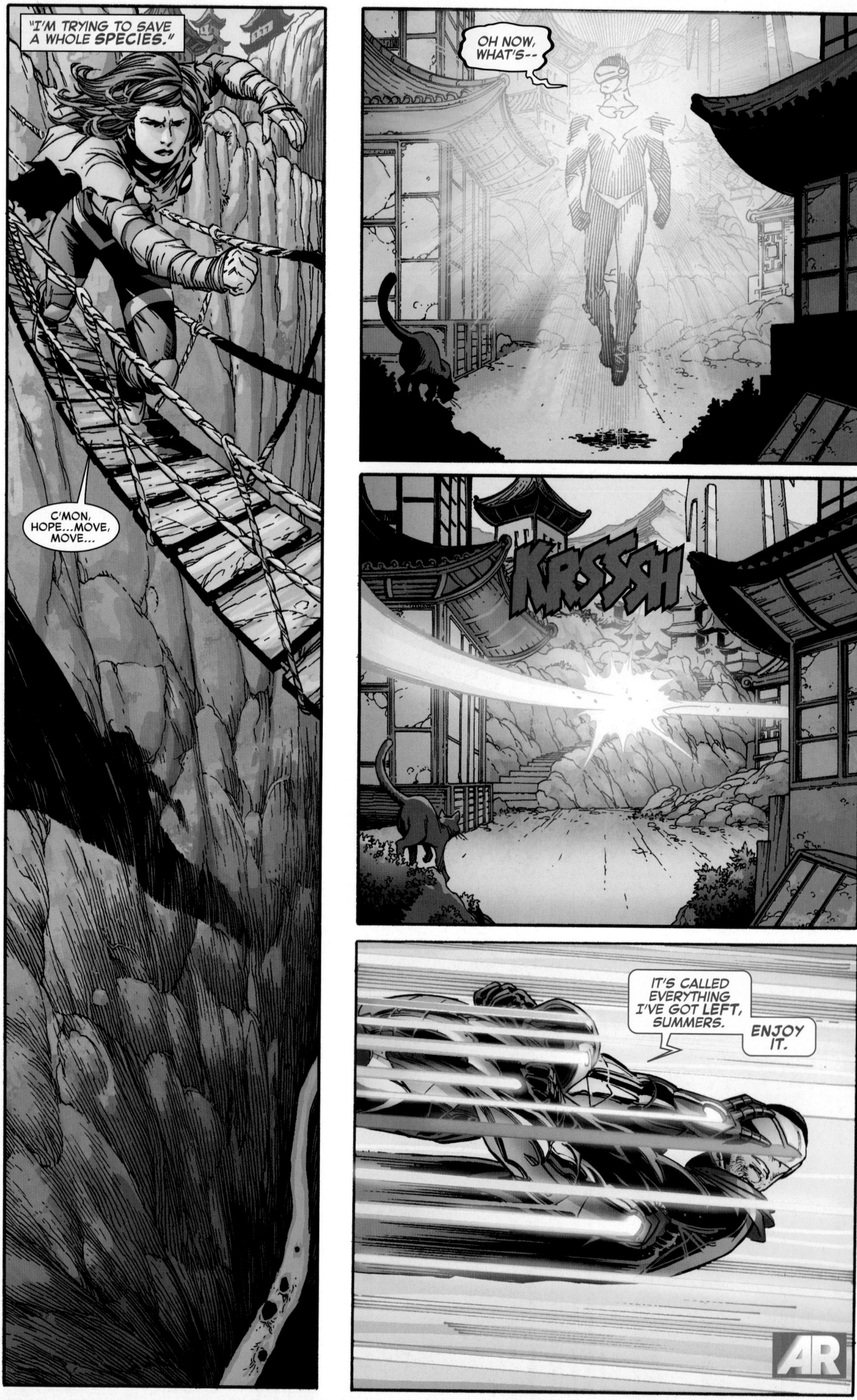
"I'M TRYING TO SAVE A WHOLE SPECIES."
C'MON, HOPE...MOVE, MOVE...
OH NOW, WHAT'S--
KRSSSH
IT'S CALLED EVERYTHING I'VE GOT LEFT, SUMMERS.
ENJOY IT.

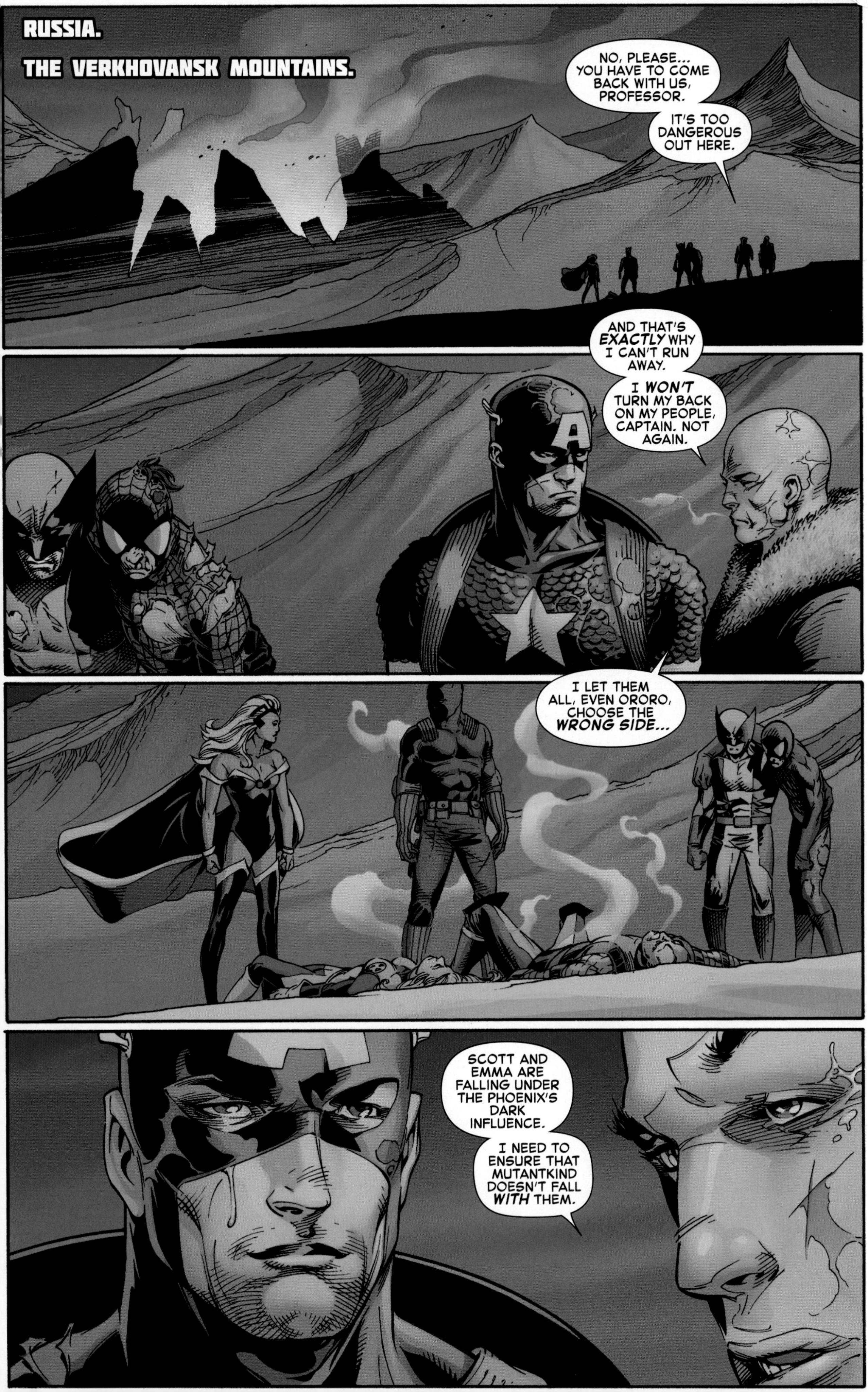
RUSSIA.
THE VERKHOVANSK MOUNTAINS.
NO, PLEASE... YOU HAVE TO COME BACK WITH US, PROFESSOR.
IT'S TOO DANGEROUS OUT HERE.
AND THAT'S EXACTLY WHY I CAN'T RUN AWAY.
I WON'T TURN MY BACK ON MY PEOPLE, CAPTAIN. NOT AGAIN.
I LET THEM ALL, EVEN ORORO, CHOOSE THE WRONG SIDE...
SCOTT AND EMMA ARE FALLING UNDER THE PHOENIX'S DARK INFLUENCE.
I NEED TO ENSURE THAT MUTANTKIND DOESN'T FALL WITH THEM.

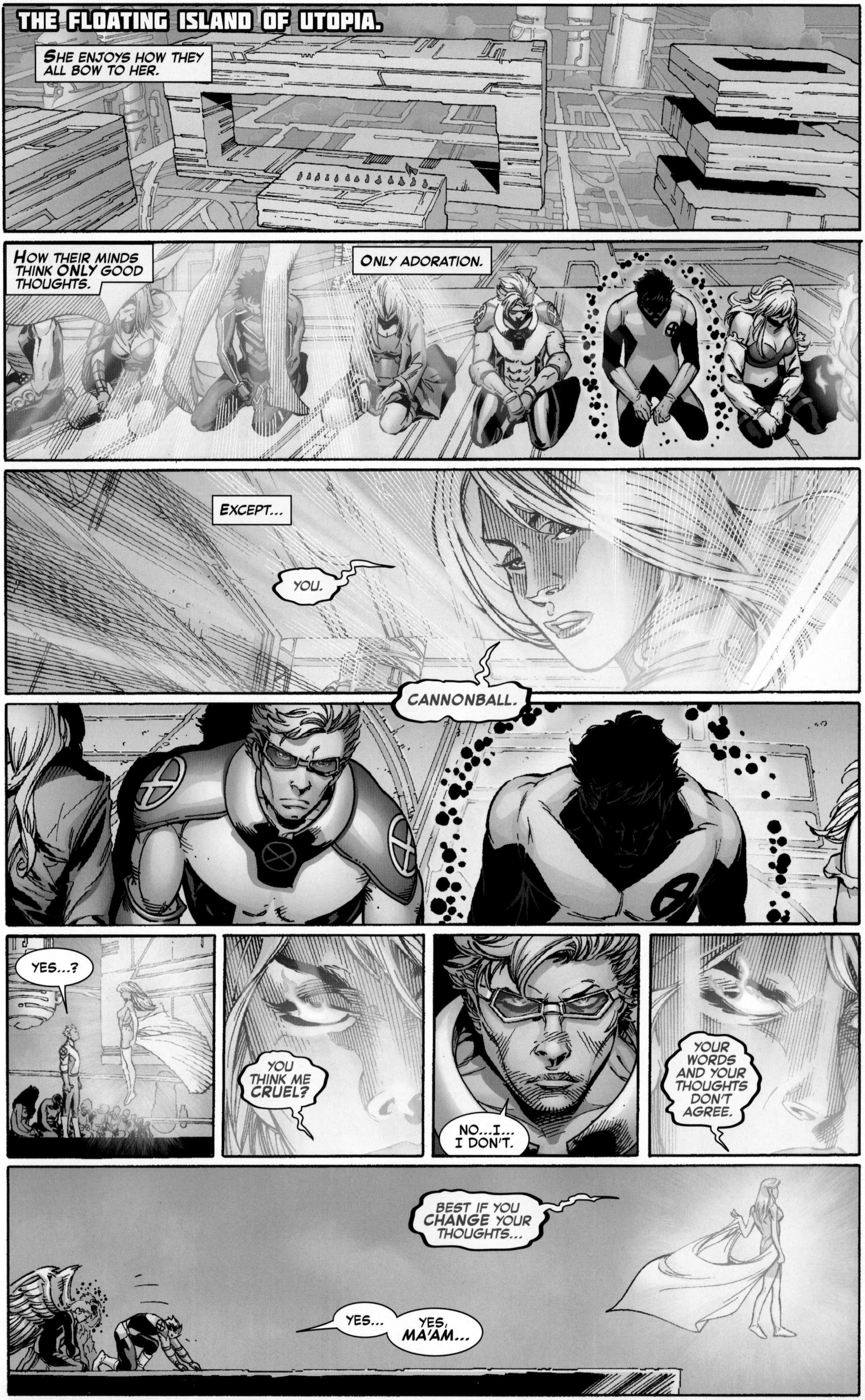
THE FLOATING ISLAND OF UTOPIA.
SHE ENJOYS HOW THEY ALL BOW TO HER.
HOW THEIR MINDS THINK ONLY GOOD THOUGHTS.
ONLY ADORATION.
EXCEPT...
YOU.
CANNONBALL.
YES...?
YOU THINK ME CRUEL?
NO...I... I DON'T.
YOUR WORDS AND YOUR THOUGHTS DON'T AGREE.
BEST IF YOU CHANGE YOUR THOUGHTS...
YES...
YES, MA'AM...

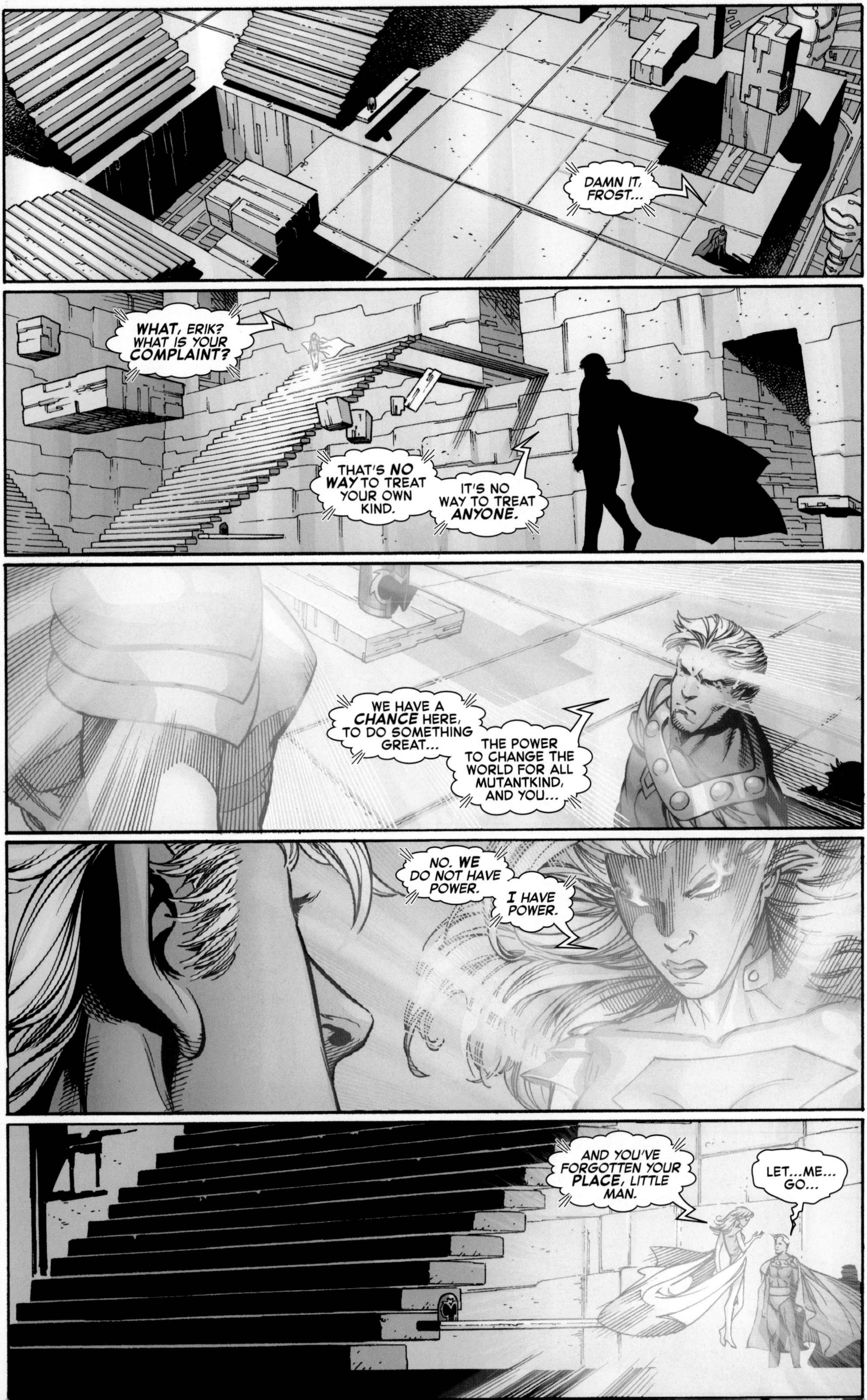
DAMN IT, FROST...
WHAT, ERIK? WHAT IS YOUR COMPLAINT?
THAT'S NO WAY TO TREAT YOUR OWN KIND.
IT'S NO WAY TO TREAT ANYONE.
WE HAVE A CHANCE HERE, TO DO SOMETHING GREAT...
THE POWER TO CHANGE THE WORLD FOR ALL MUTANTKIND, AND YOU...
NO. WE DO NOT HAVE POWER.
I HAVE POWER.
AND YOU'VE FORGOTTEN YOUR PLACE, LITTLE MAN.
LET...ME... GO...

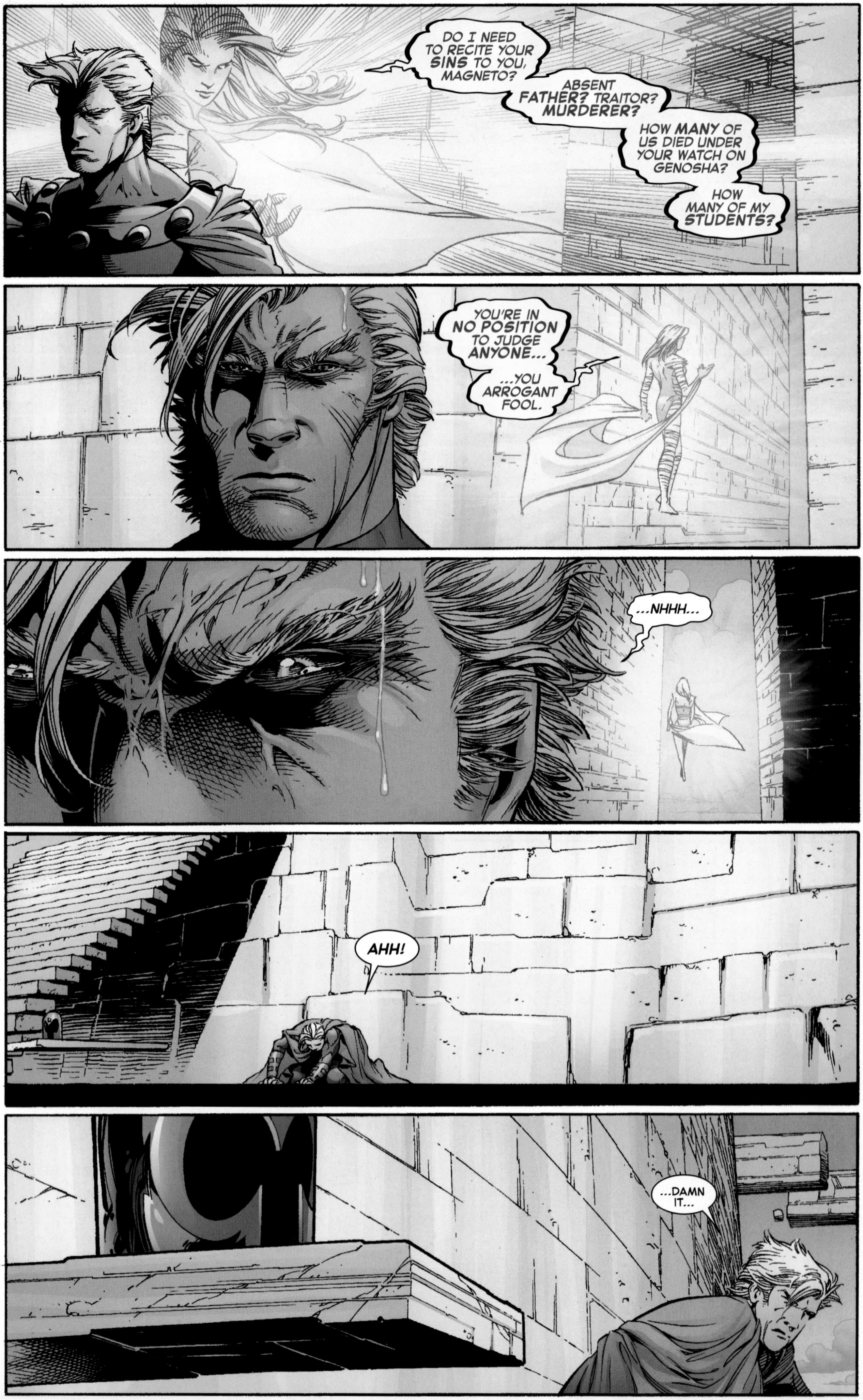
DO I NEED TO RECITE YOUR SINS TO YOU, MAGNETO?
ABSENT FATHER? TRAITOR? MURDERER?
HOW MANY OF US DIED UNDER YOUR WATCH ON GENOSHA?
HOW MANY OF MY STUDENTS?
YOU'RE IN NO POSITION TO JUDGE ANYONE...
...YOU ARROGANT FOOL.
...NHHH...
AHH!
...DAMN IT...

YOU'RE WASTING MY *TIME*, STARK... AND IT DOESN'T MATTER.

I'LL FIND THE GIRL. THIS WHOLE *CITY* CAN'T STOP ME.

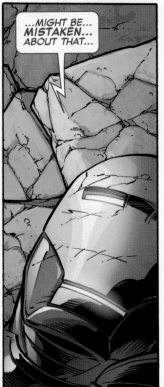

...MIGHT BE... MISTAKEN... ABOUT THAT...

I'M PRACTICALLY A GOD...MYSTICAL KUNG FU DOESN'T WORRY ME.

POWER LEVELS RECHARGING... 8 PERCENT...

OUTER HULL RESEALING IN FIVE POINT THREE MINUTES...

NOT FAST ENOUGH...

DON'T GET IN MY WAY AGAIN.

AR

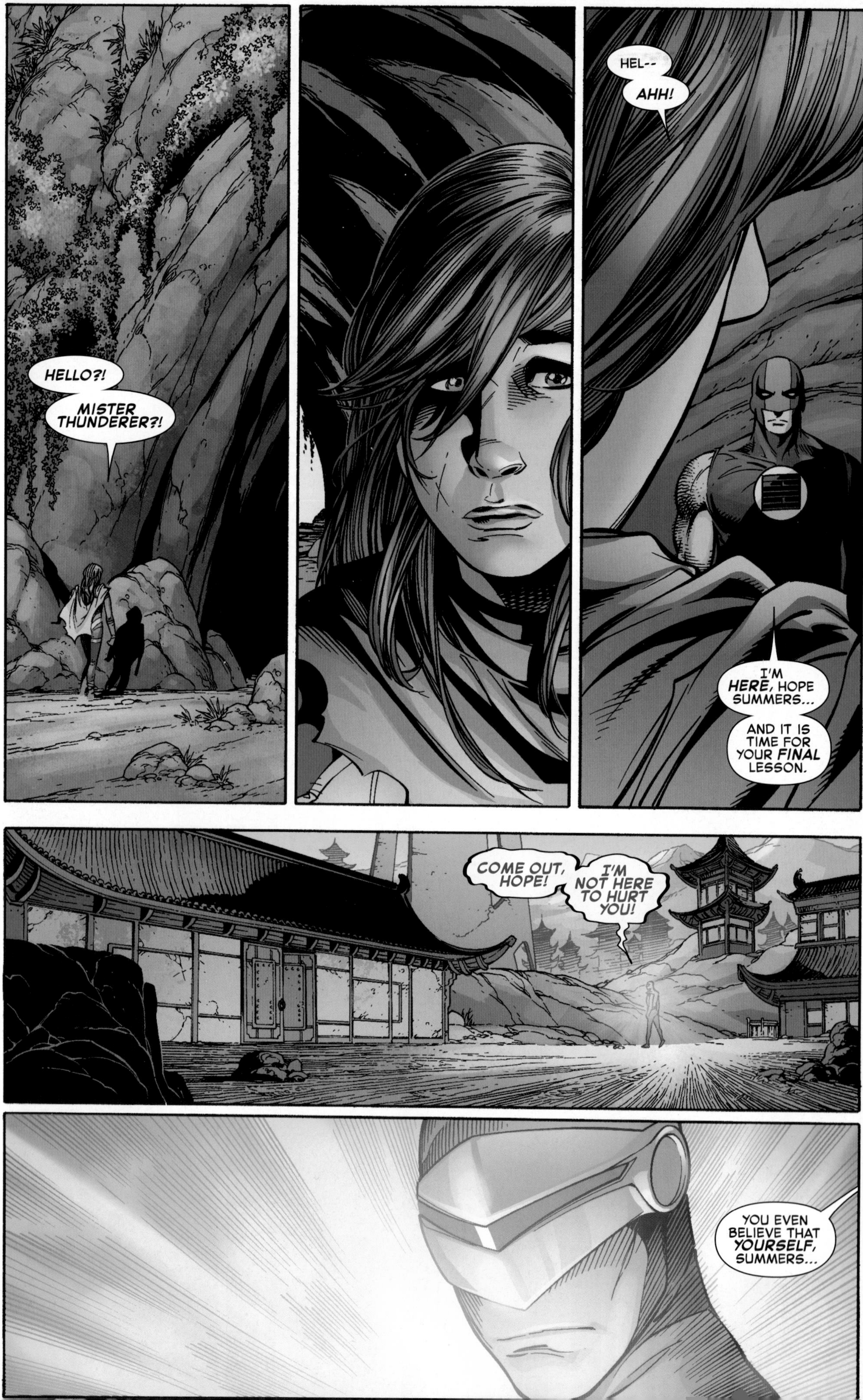
HELLO?!
MISTER THUNDERER?!
HEL--
AHH!
I'M HERE, HOPE SUMMERS...
AND IT IS TIME FOR YOUR FINAL LESSON.
COME OUT, HOPE!
I'M NOT HERE TO HURT YOU!
YOU EVEN BELIEVE THAT YOURSELF, SUMMERS...

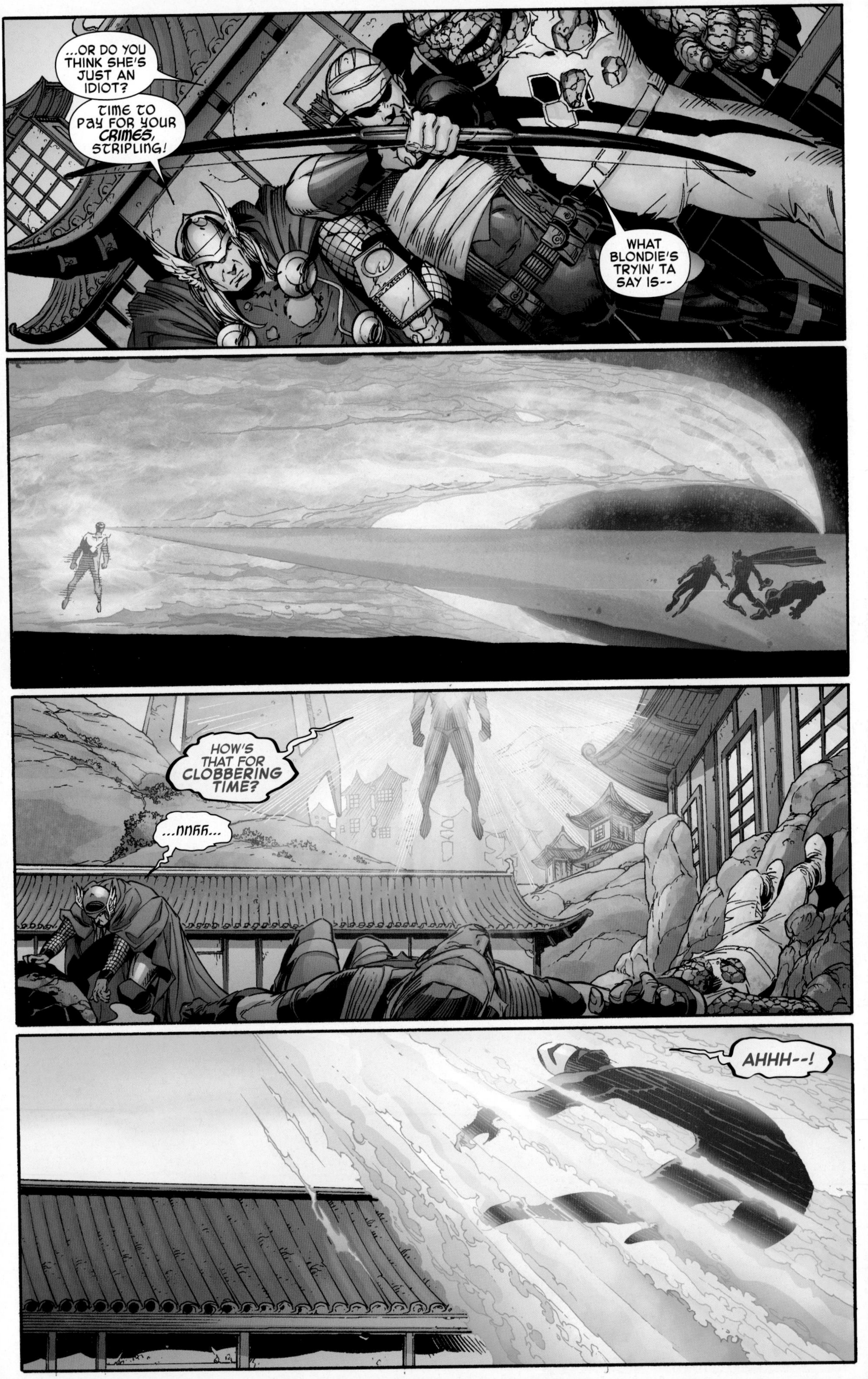
...OR DO YOU THINK SHE'S JUST AN IDIOT?
TIME TO PAY FOR YOUR CRIMES, STRIPLING!
WHAT BLONDIE'S TRYIN' TA SAY IS--
HOW'S THAT FOR CLOBBERING TIME?
...NNHH...
AHHH--!

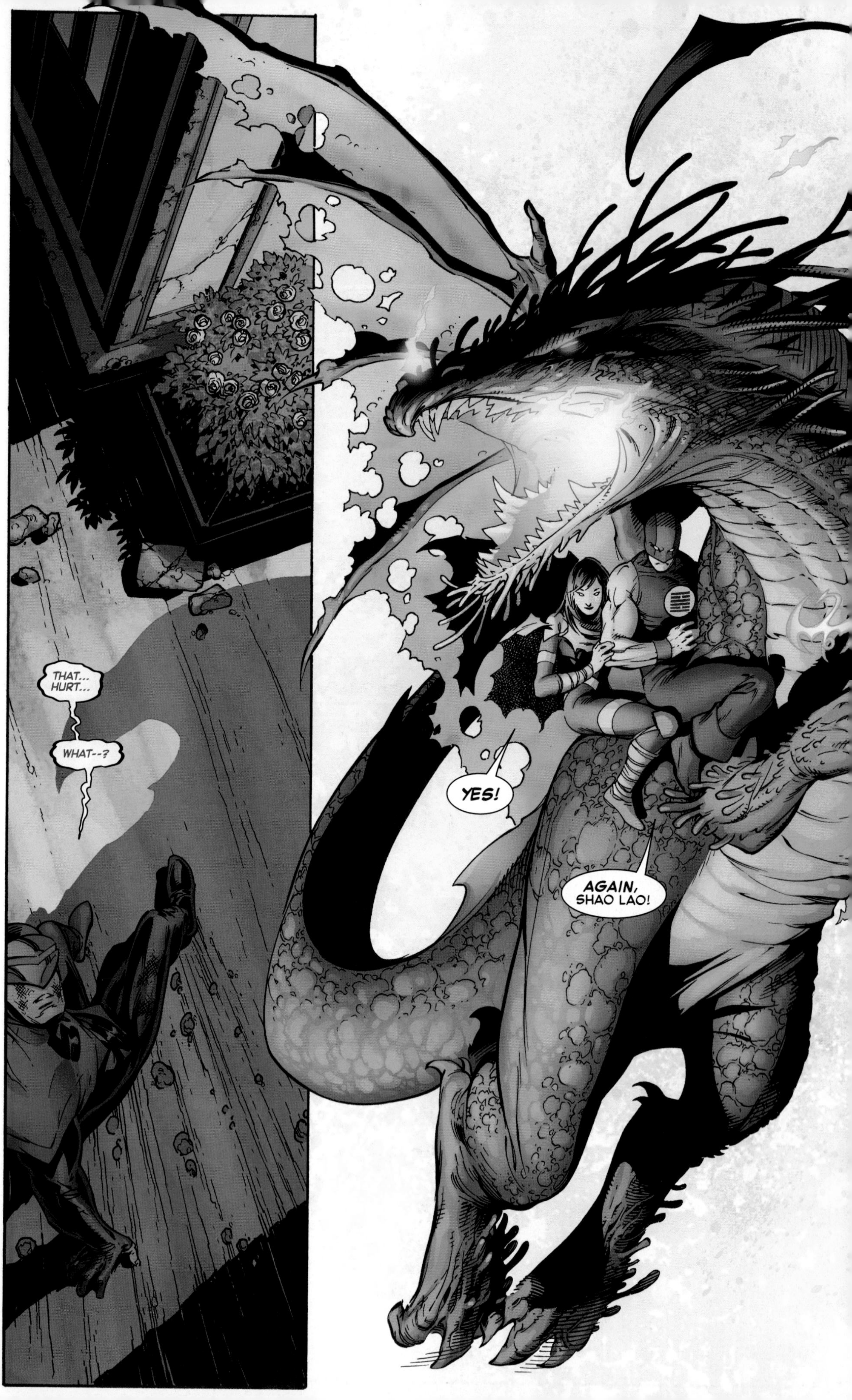
THAT... HURT...
WHAT--?
YES!
AGAIN, SHAO LAO!

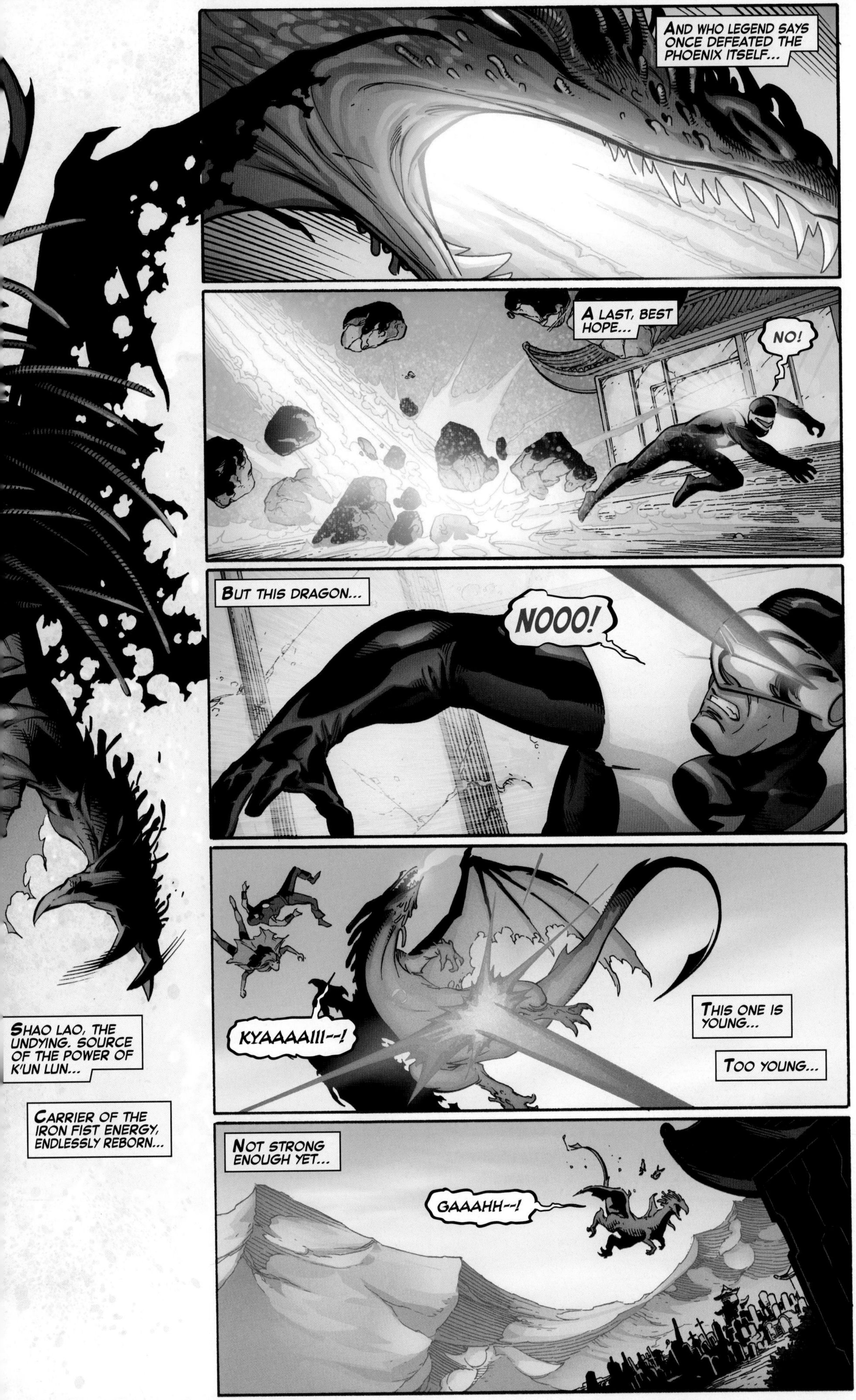
AND WHO LEGEND SAYS ONCE DEFEATED THE PHOENIX ITSELF...
A LAST, BEST HOPE...
NO!
BUT THIS DRAGON...
NOOO!
SHAO LAO, THE UNDYING. SOURCE OF THE POWER OF K'UN LUN...
CARRIER OF THE IRON FIST ENERGY, ENDLESSLY REBORN...
KYAAAAIII--!
THIS ONE IS YOUNG...
TOO YOUNG...
NOT STRONG ENOUGH YET...
GAAAHH--!

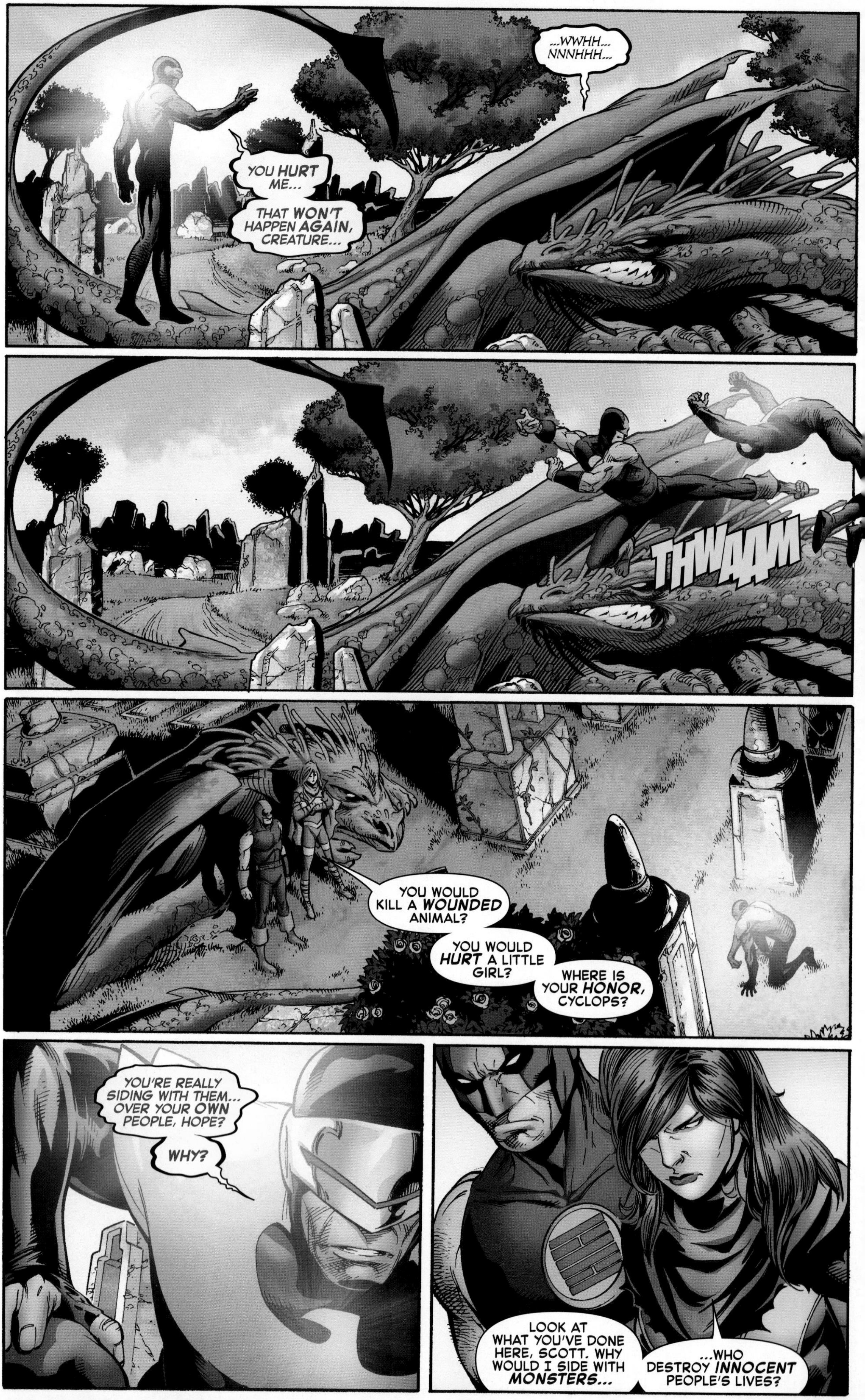
...WWHH... NNNHHH...
YOU HURT ME...
THAT WON'T HAPPEN AGAIN, CREATURE...
THWAAM
YOU WOULD KILL A WOUNDED ANIMAL?
YOU WOULD HURT A LITTLE GIRL?
WHERE IS YOUR HONOR, CYCLOPS?
YOU'RE REALLY SIDING WITH THEM... OVER YOUR OWN PEOPLE, HOPE?
WHY?
LOOK AT WHAT YOU'VE DONE HERE, SCOTT. WHY WOULD I SIDE WITH MONSTERS...
...WHO DESTROY INNOCENT PEOPLE'S LIVES?

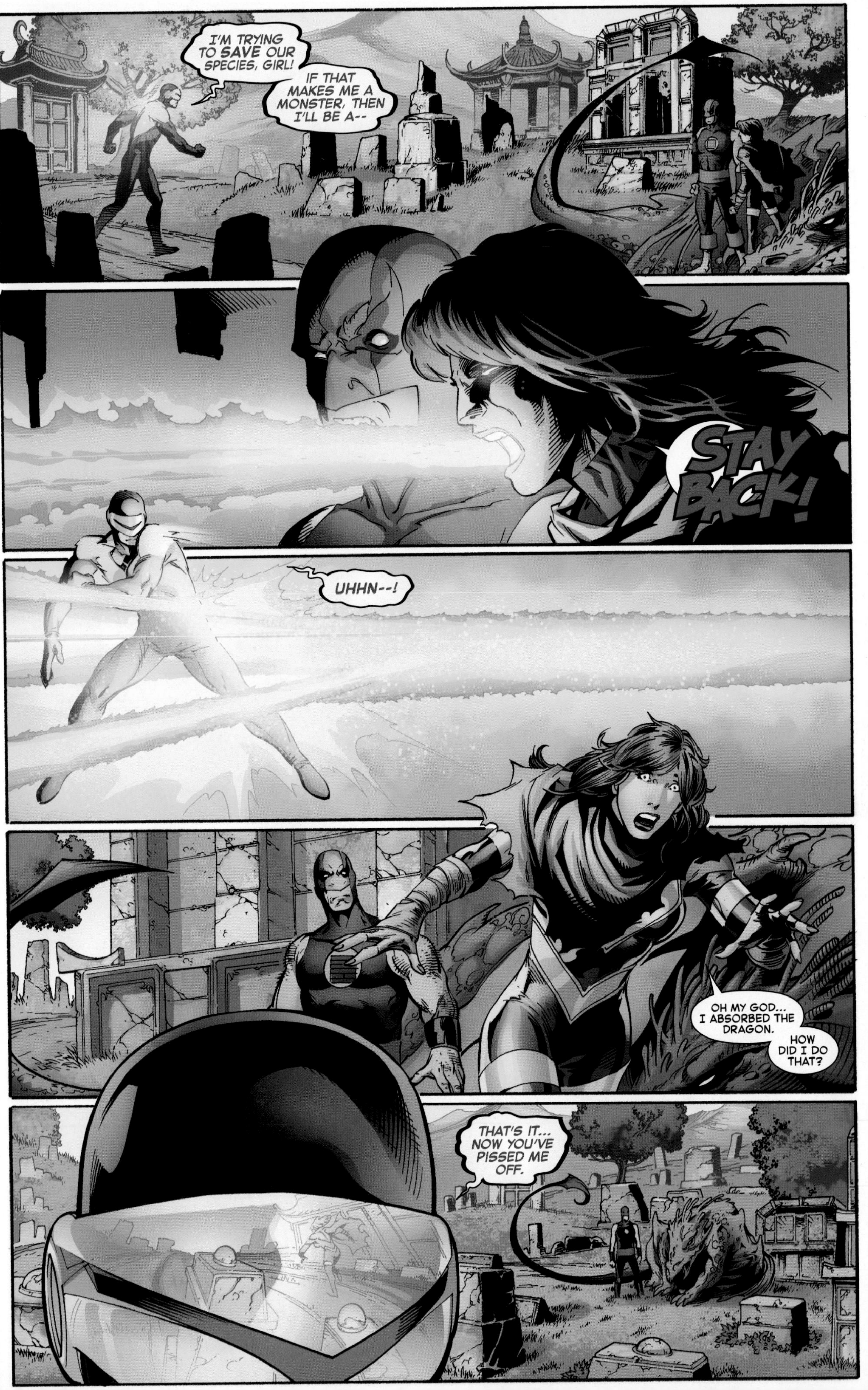
I'M TRYING TO SAVE OUR SPECIES, GIRL!
IF THAT MAKES ME A MONSTER, THEN I'LL BE A--
STAY BACK!
UHHN--!
OH MY GOD... I ABSORBED THE DRAGON.
HOW DID I DO THAT?
THAT'S IT... NOW YOU'VE PISSED ME OFF.

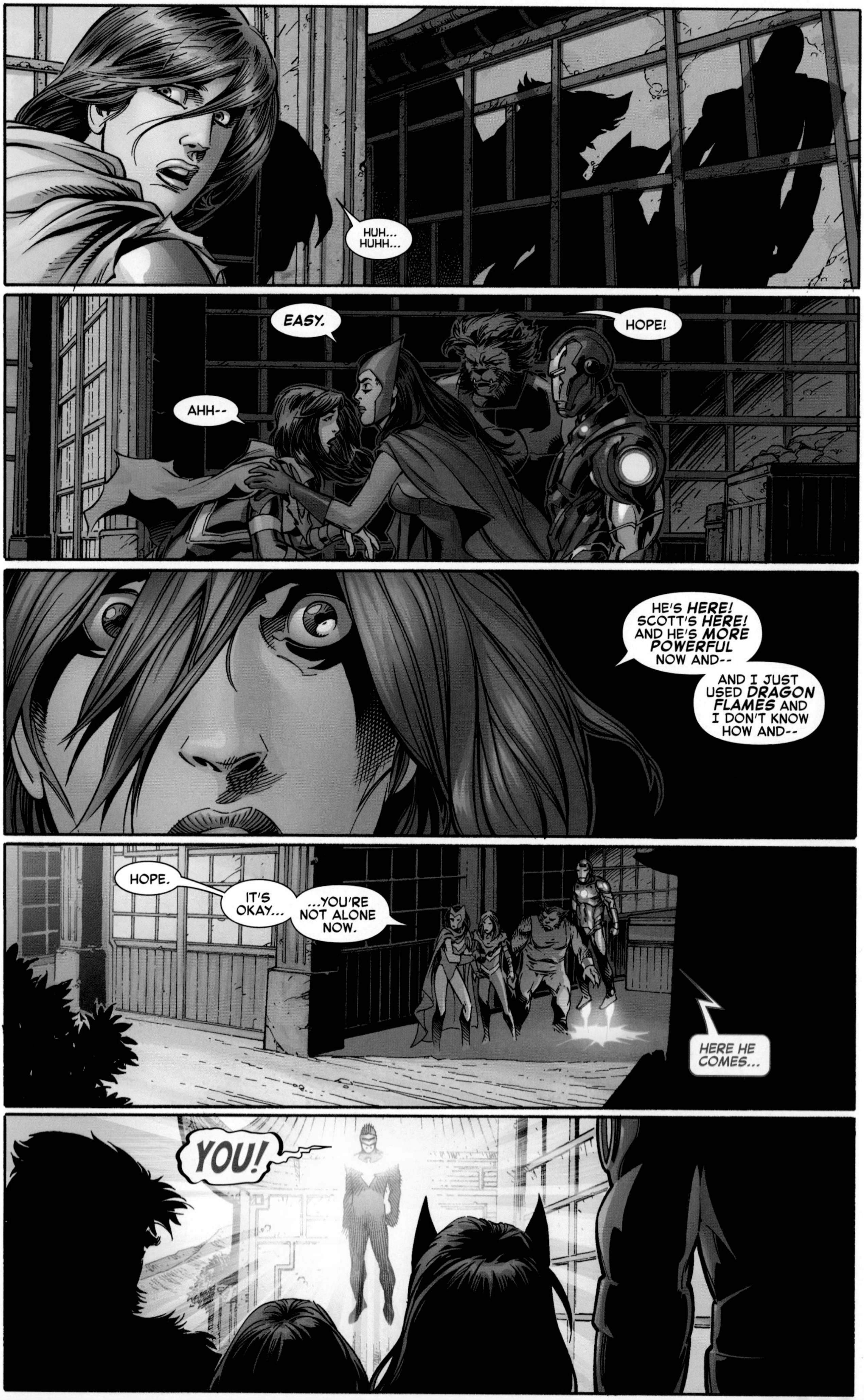
HUH... HUHH...
EASY.
HOPE!
AHH--
HE'S HERE! SCOTT'S HERE! AND HE'S MORE POWERFUL NOW AND--
AND I JUST USED DRAGON FLAMES AND I DON'T KNOW HOW AND--
HOPE.
IT'S OKAY...
...YOU'RE NOT ALONE NOW.
HERE HE COMES...
YOU!

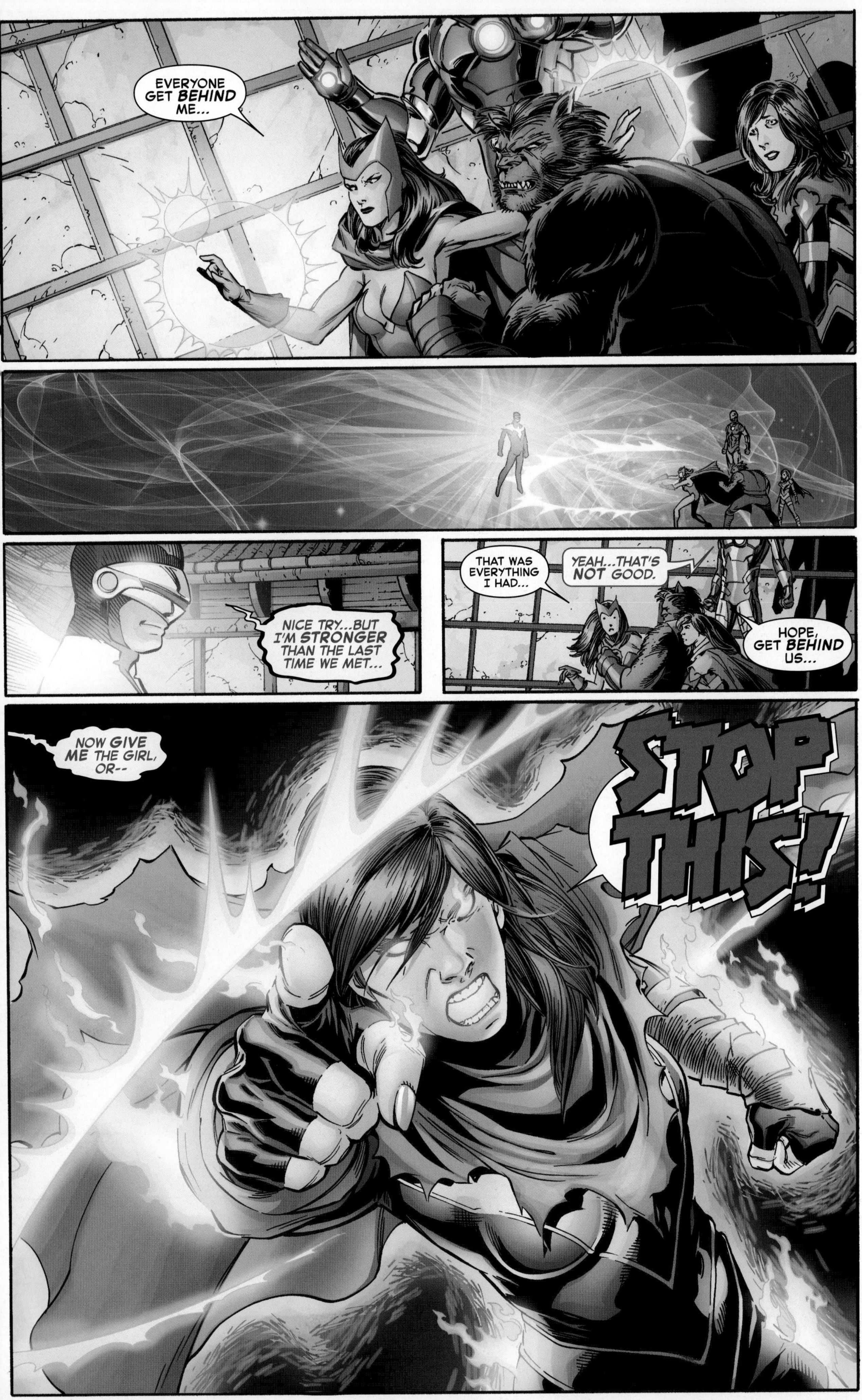
EVERYONE GET BEHIND ME...
NICE TRY...BUT I'M STRONGER THAN THE LAST TIME WE MET...
THAT WAS EVERYTHING I HAD...
YEAH...THAT'S NOT GOOD.
HOPE, GET BEHIND US...
NOW GIVE ME THE GIRL, OR--
STOP THIS!

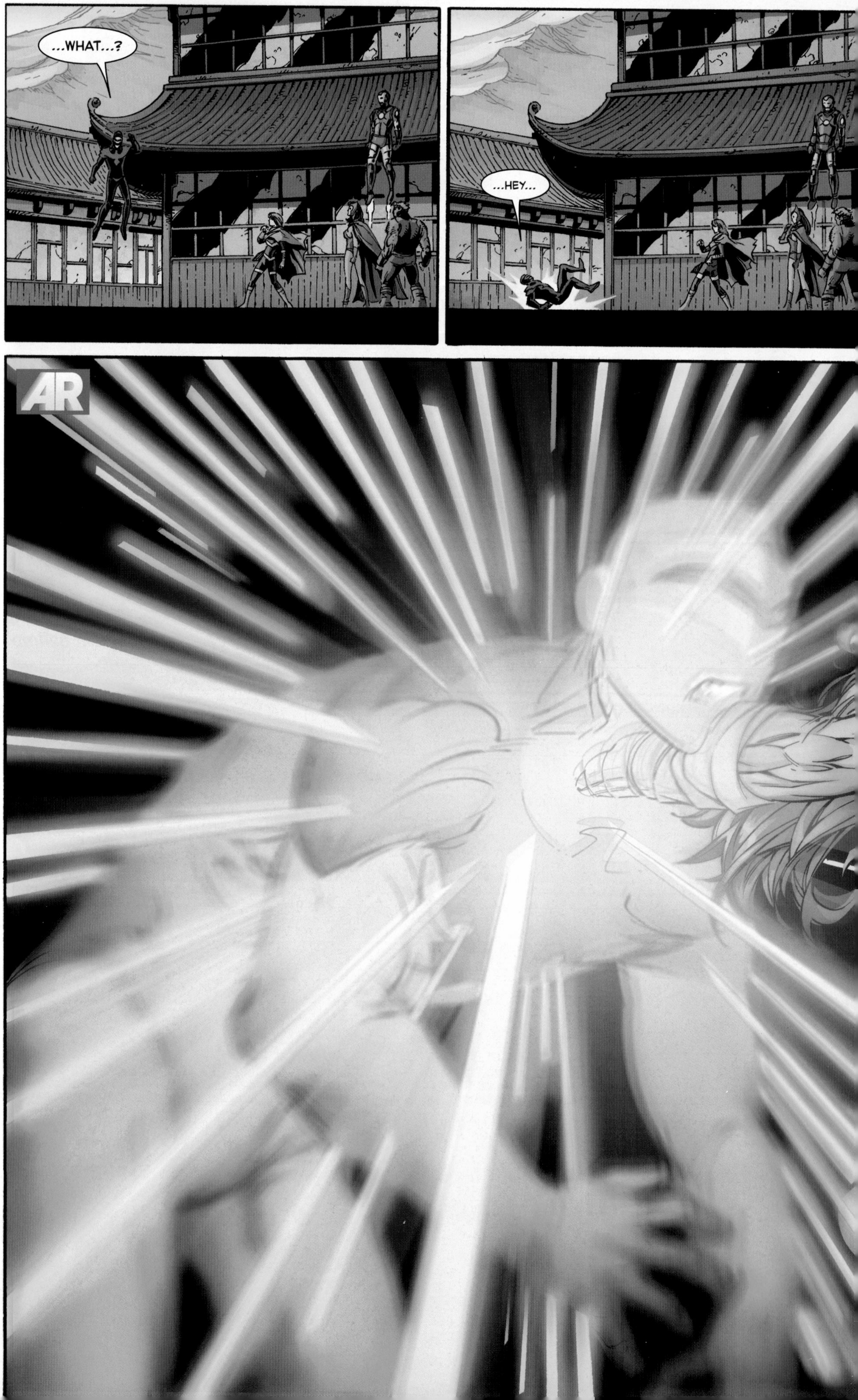
...WHAT...?
...HEY...

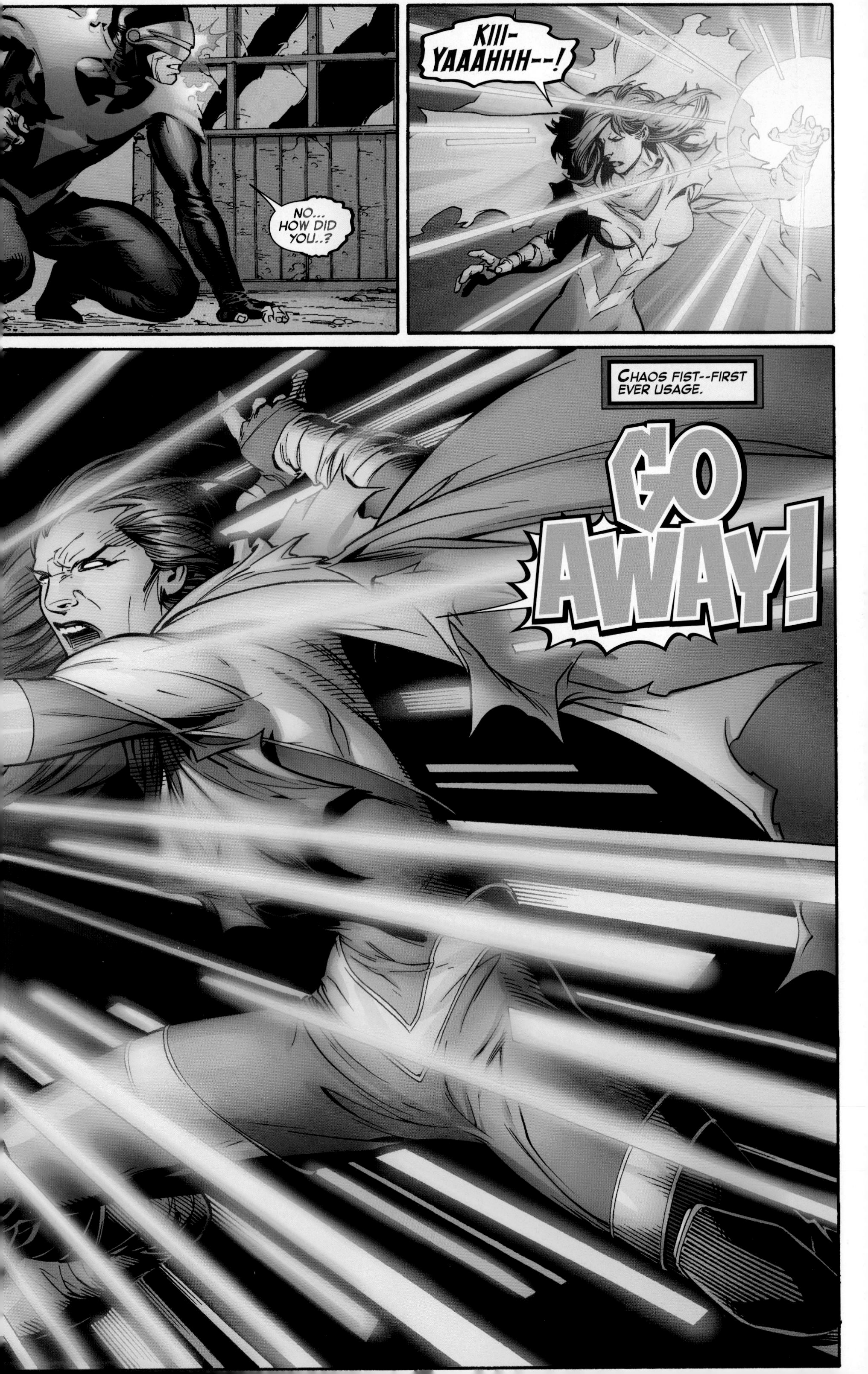
NO... HOW DID YOU..?
KIII-YAAAHHH--!
CHAOS FIST--FIRST EVER USAGE.
GO AWAY!

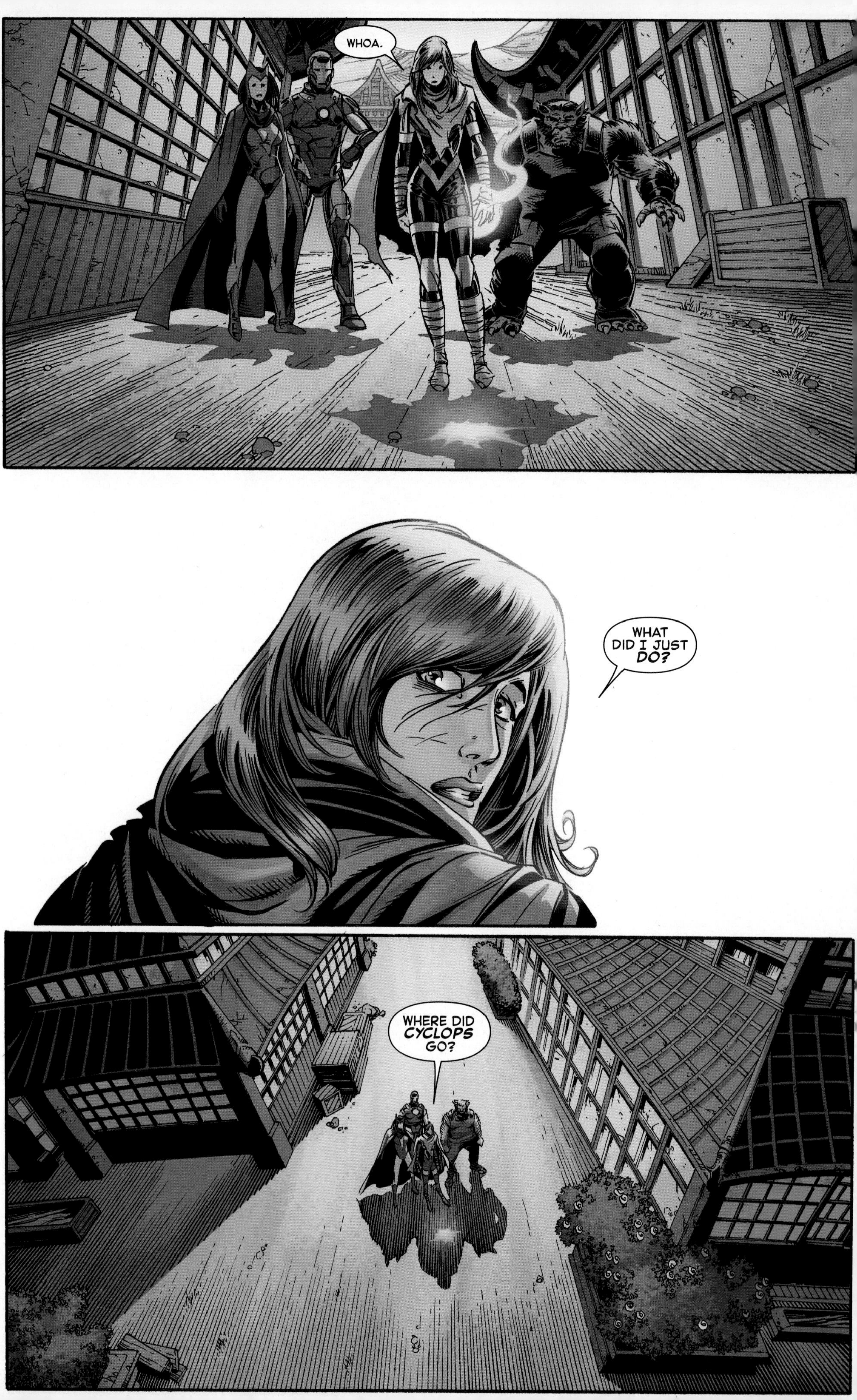
WHOA.
WHAT DID I JUST DO?
WHERE DID CYCLOPS GO?

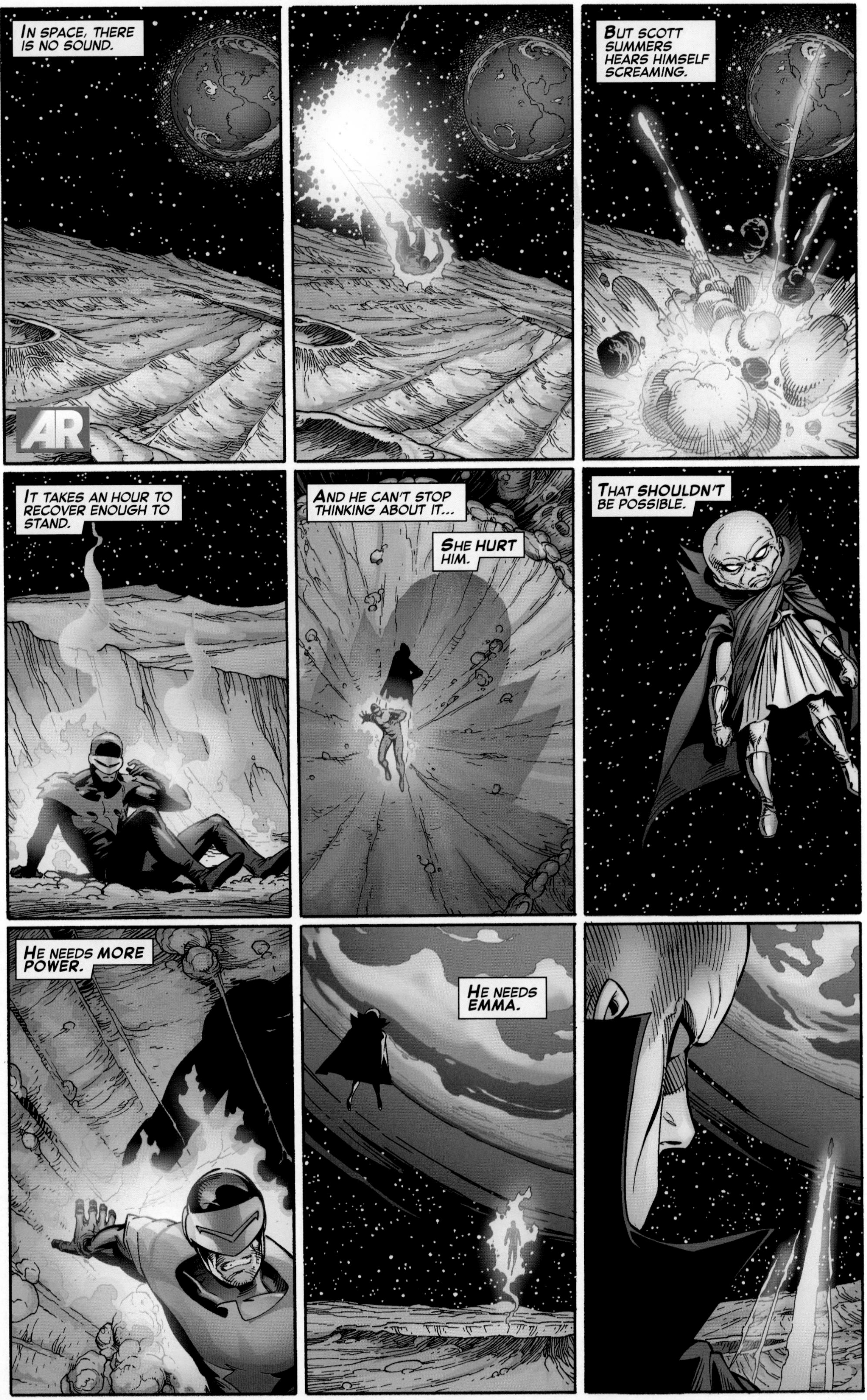
In space, there is no sound.
But Scott Summers hears himself screaming.
It takes an hour to recover enough to stand.
And he can't stop thinking about it...
She hurt him.
That shouldn't be possible.
He needs more power.
He needs Emma.

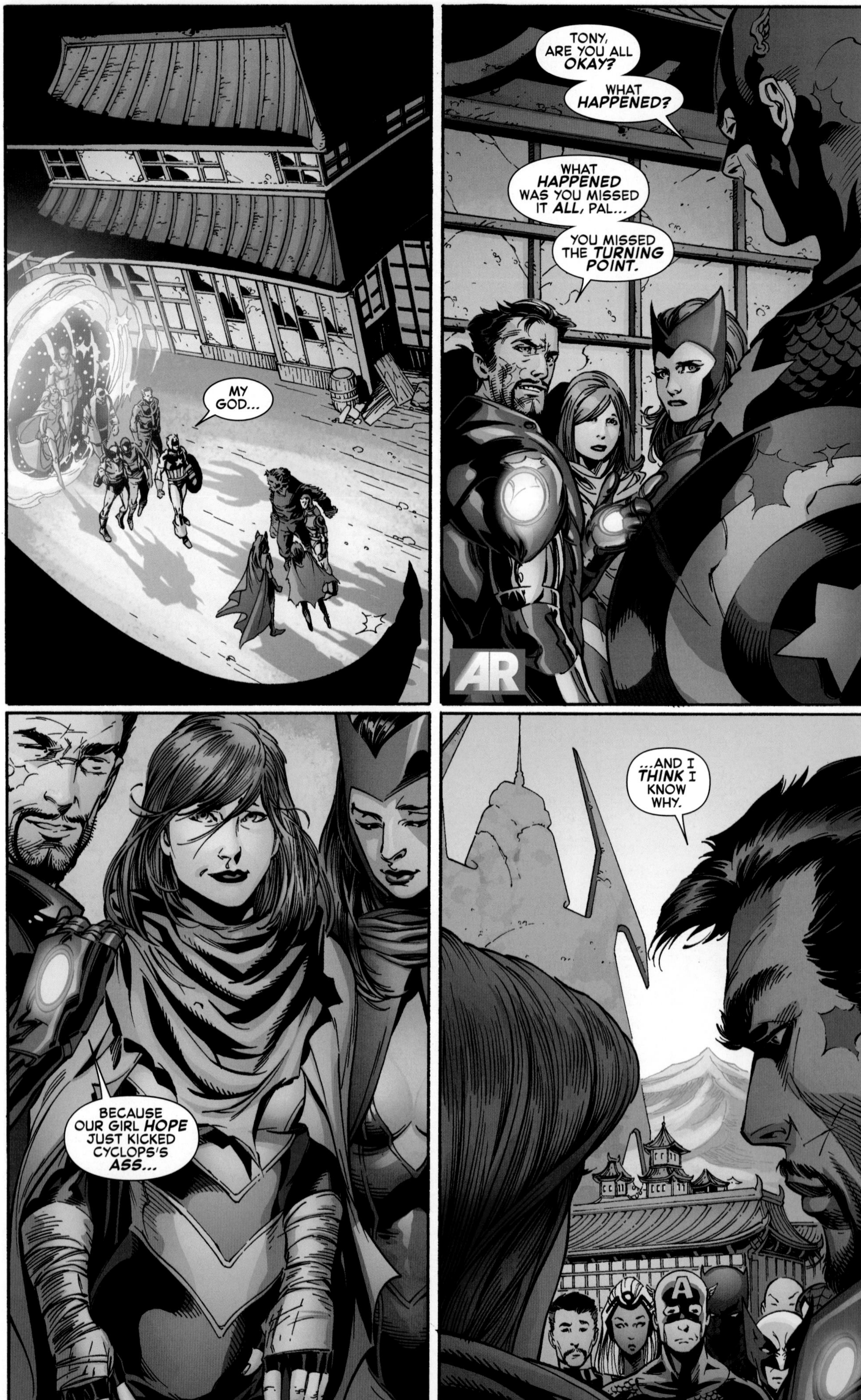

MY GOD...
TONY, ARE YOU ALL OKAY?
WHAT HAPPENED?
WHAT HAPPENED WAS YOU MISSED IT ALL, PAL...
YOU MISSED THE TURNING POINT.
BECAUSE OUR GIRL HOPE JUST KICKED CYCLOPS'S ASS...
...AND I THINK I KNOW WHY.

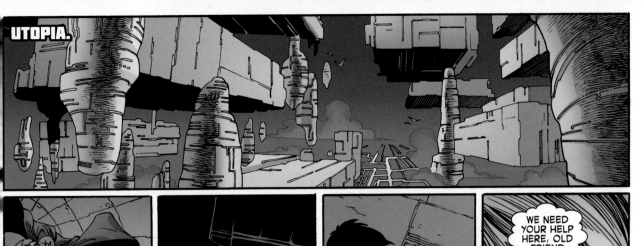

CHARLES XAVIER...PLEASE HEAR MY THOUGHTS...

WE NEED YOUR HELP HERE, OLD FRIEND.

SCOTT AND EMMA... THEY'RE LOSING CONTROL.

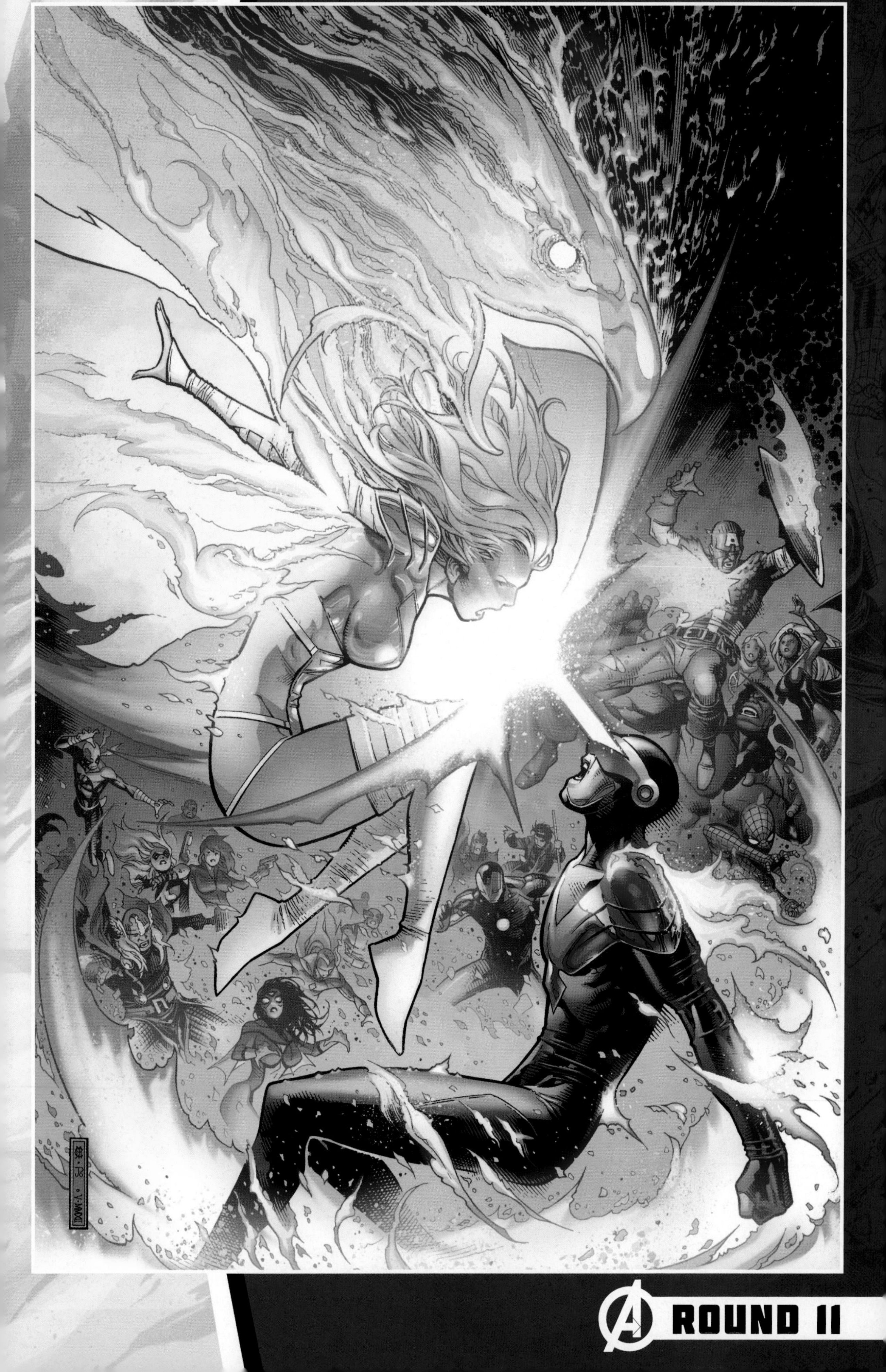

ROUND 11

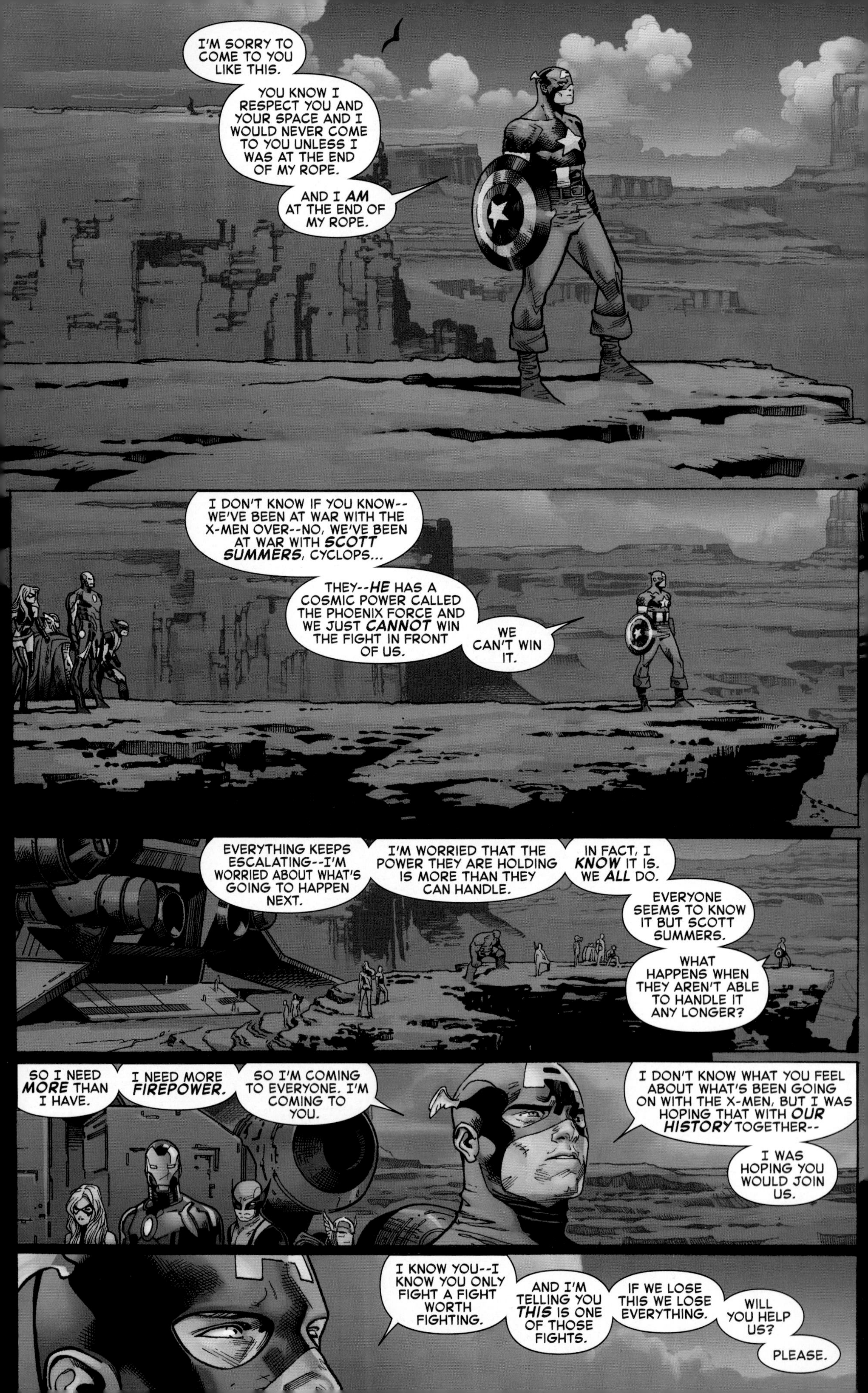
I'M SORRY TO COME TO YOU LIKE THIS.
YOU KNOW I RESPECT YOU AND YOUR SPACE AND I WOULD NEVER COME TO YOU UNLESS I WAS AT THE END OF MY ROPE.
AND I AM AT THE END OF MY ROPE.
I DON'T KNOW IF YOU KNOW-- WE'VE BEEN AT WAR WITH THE X-MEN OVER--NO, WE'VE BEEN AT WAR WITH SCOTT SUMMERS, CYCLOPS...
THEY--HE HAS A COSMIC POWER CALLED THE PHOENIX FORCE AND WE JUST CANNOT WIN THE FIGHT IN FRONT OF US.
WE CAN'T WIN IT.
EVERYTHING KEEPS ESCALATING--I'M WORRIED ABOUT WHAT'S GOING TO HAPPEN NEXT.
I'M WORRIED THAT THE POWER THEY ARE HOLDING IS MORE THAN THEY CAN HANDLE.
IN FACT, I KNOW IT IS. WE ALL DO.
EVERYONE SEEMS TO KNOW IT BUT SCOTT SUMMERS.
WHAT HAPPENS WHEN THEY AREN'T ABLE TO HANDLE IT ANY LONGER?
SO I NEED MORE THAN I HAVE.
I NEED MORE FIREPOWER.
SO I'M COMING TO EVERYONE. I'M COMING TO YOU.
I DON'T KNOW WHAT YOU FEEL ABOUT WHAT'S BEEN GOING ON WITH THE X-MEN, BUT I WAS HOPING THAT WITH OUR HISTORY TOGETHER--
I WAS HOPING YOU WOULD JOIN US.
I KNOW YOU--I KNOW YOU ONLY FIGHT A FIGHT WORTH FIGHTING.
AND I'M TELLING YOU THIS IS ONE OF THOSE FIGHTS.
IF WE LOSE THIS WE LOSE EVERYTHING.
WILL YOU HELP US?
PLEASE.

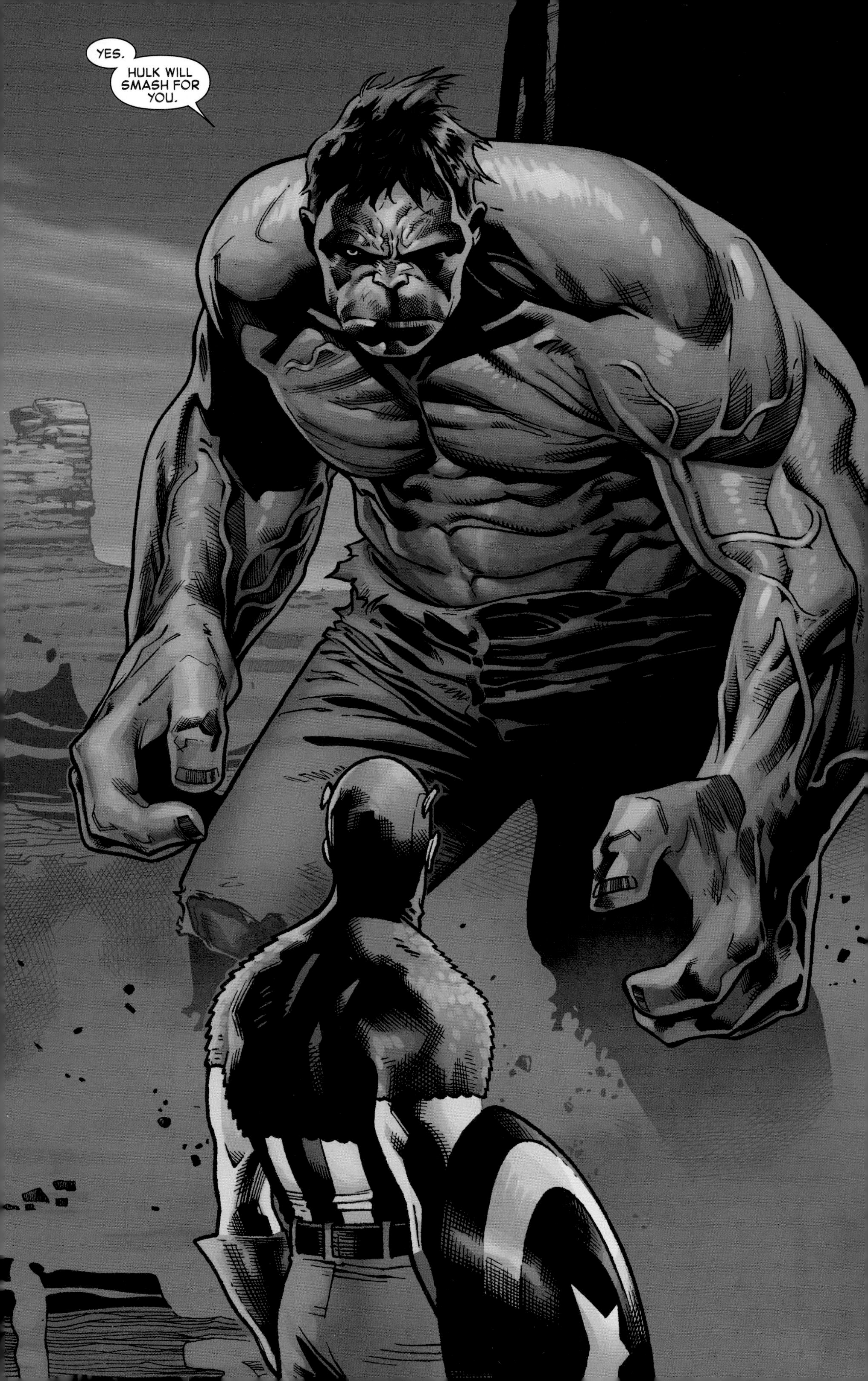
YES.
HULK WILL SMASH FOR YOU.

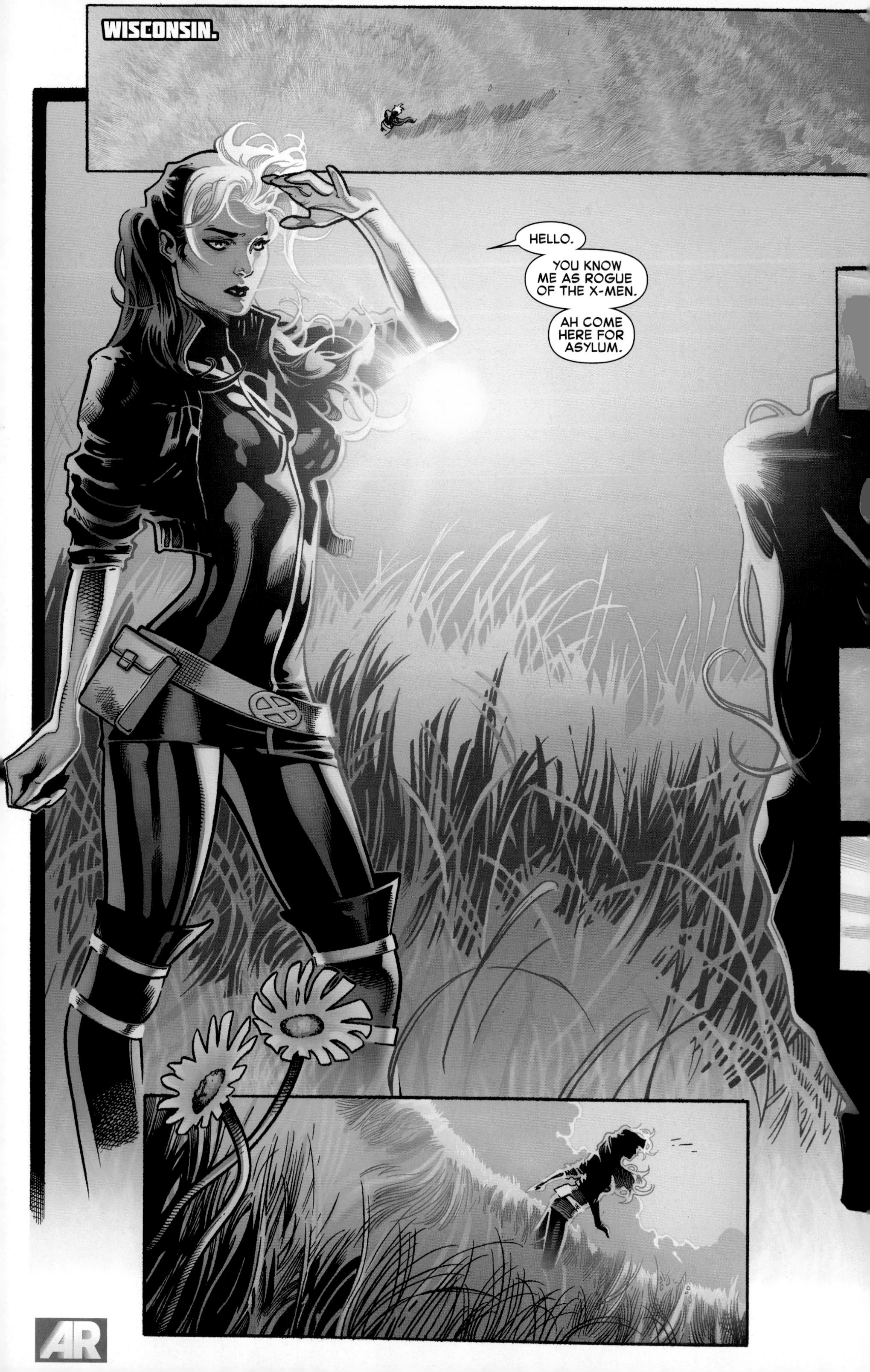
WISCONSIN.
HELLO.
YOU KNOW ME AS ROGUE OF THE X-MEN.
AH COME HERE FOR ASYLUM.

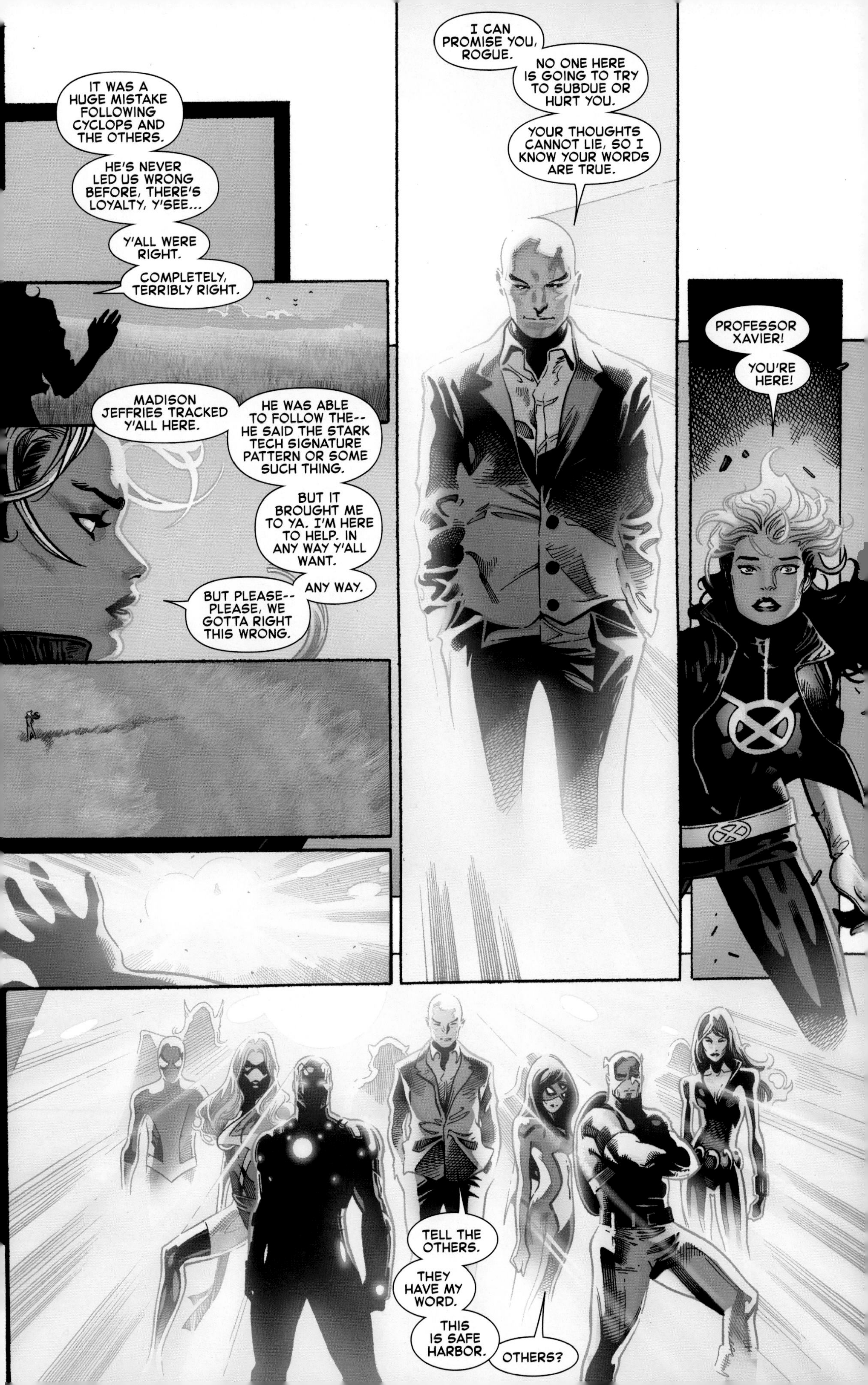
IT WAS A HUGE MISTAKE FOLLOWING CYCLOPS AND THE OTHERS.
HE'S NEVER LED US WRONG BEFORE, THERE'S LOYALTY, Y'SEE...
Y'ALL WERE RIGHT.
COMPLETELY, TERRIBLY RIGHT.
MADISON JEFFRIES TRACKED Y'ALL HERE.
HE WAS ABLE TO FOLLOW THE-- HE SAID THE STARK TECH SIGNATURE PATTERN OR SOME SUCH THING.
BUT IT BROUGHT ME TO YA. I'M HERE TO HELP. IN ANY WAY Y'ALL WANT.
ANY WAY.
BUT PLEASE-- PLEASE, WE GOTTA RIGHT THIS WRONG.
I CAN PROMISE YOU, ROGUE.
NO ONE HERE IS GOING TO TRY TO SUBDUE OR HURT YOU.
YOUR THOUGHTS CANNOT LIE, SO I KNOW YOUR WORDS ARE TRUE.
PROFESSOR XAVIER!
YOU'RE HERE!
TELL THE OTHERS.
THEY HAVE MY WORD.
THIS IS SAFE HARBOR.
OTHERS?

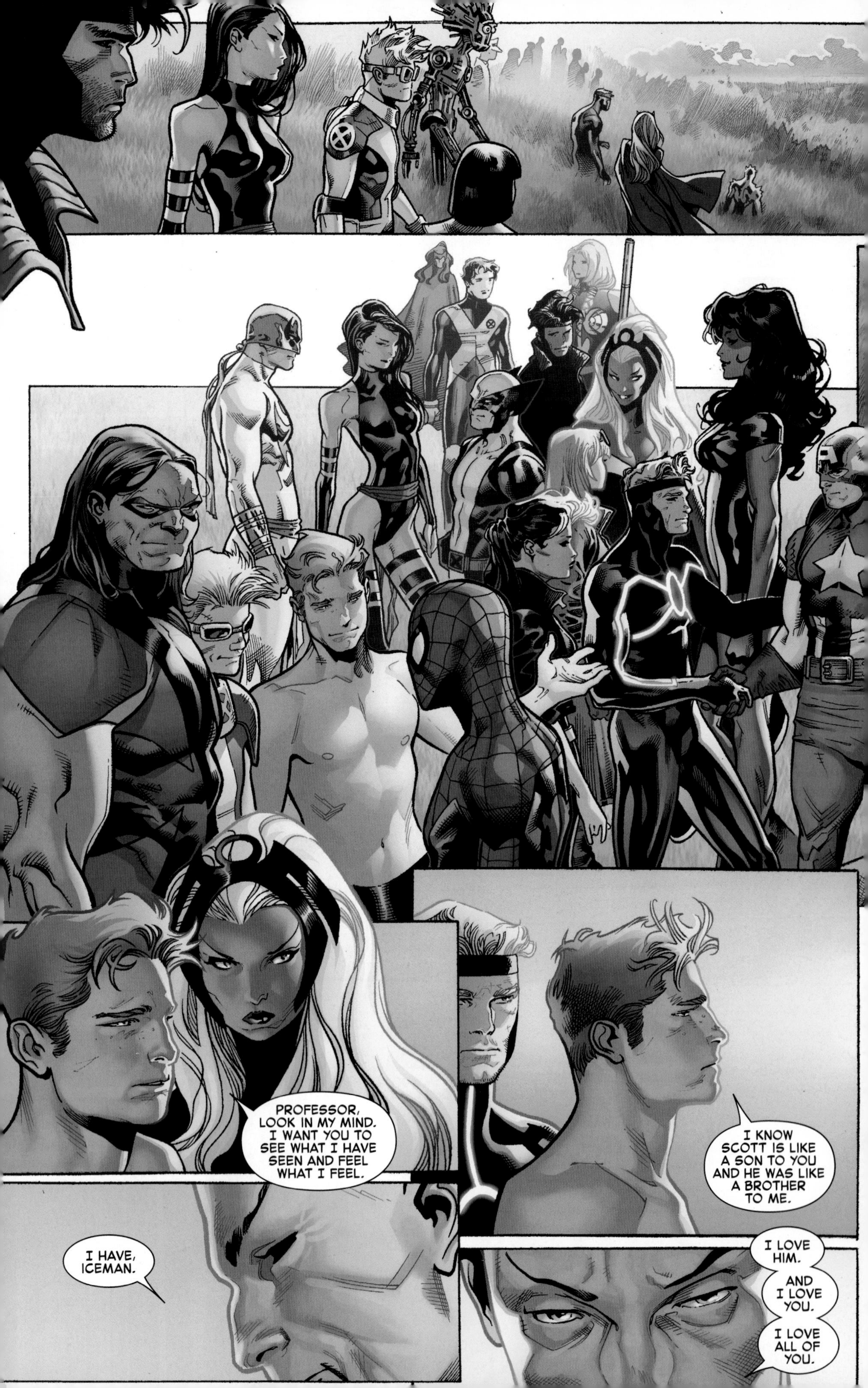
PROFESSOR, LOOK IN MY MIND. I WANT YOU TO SEE WHAT I HAVE SEEN AND FEEL WHAT I FEEL.
I KNOW SCOTT IS LIKE A SON TO YOU AND HE WAS LIKE A BROTHER TO ME.
I HAVE, ICEMAN.
I LOVE HIM.
AND I LOVE YOU.
I LOVE ALL OF YOU.

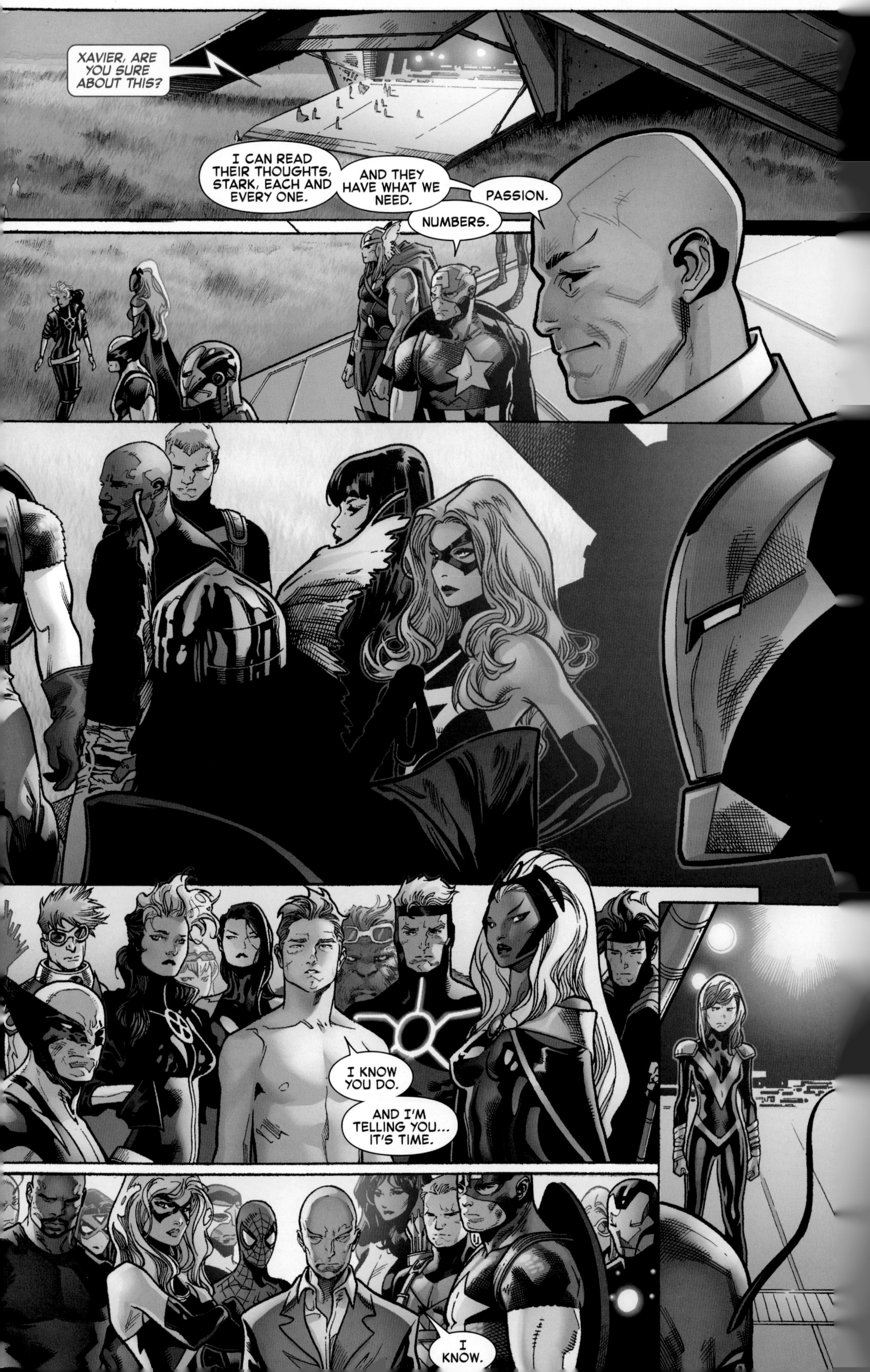
XAVIER, ARE YOU SURE ABOUT THIS?
I CAN READ THEIR THOUGHTS, STARK, EACH AND EVERY ONE.
AND THEY HAVE WHAT WE NEED.
PASSION.
NUMBERS.
I KNOW YOU DO.
AND I'M TELLING YOU... IT'S TIME.
I KNOW.

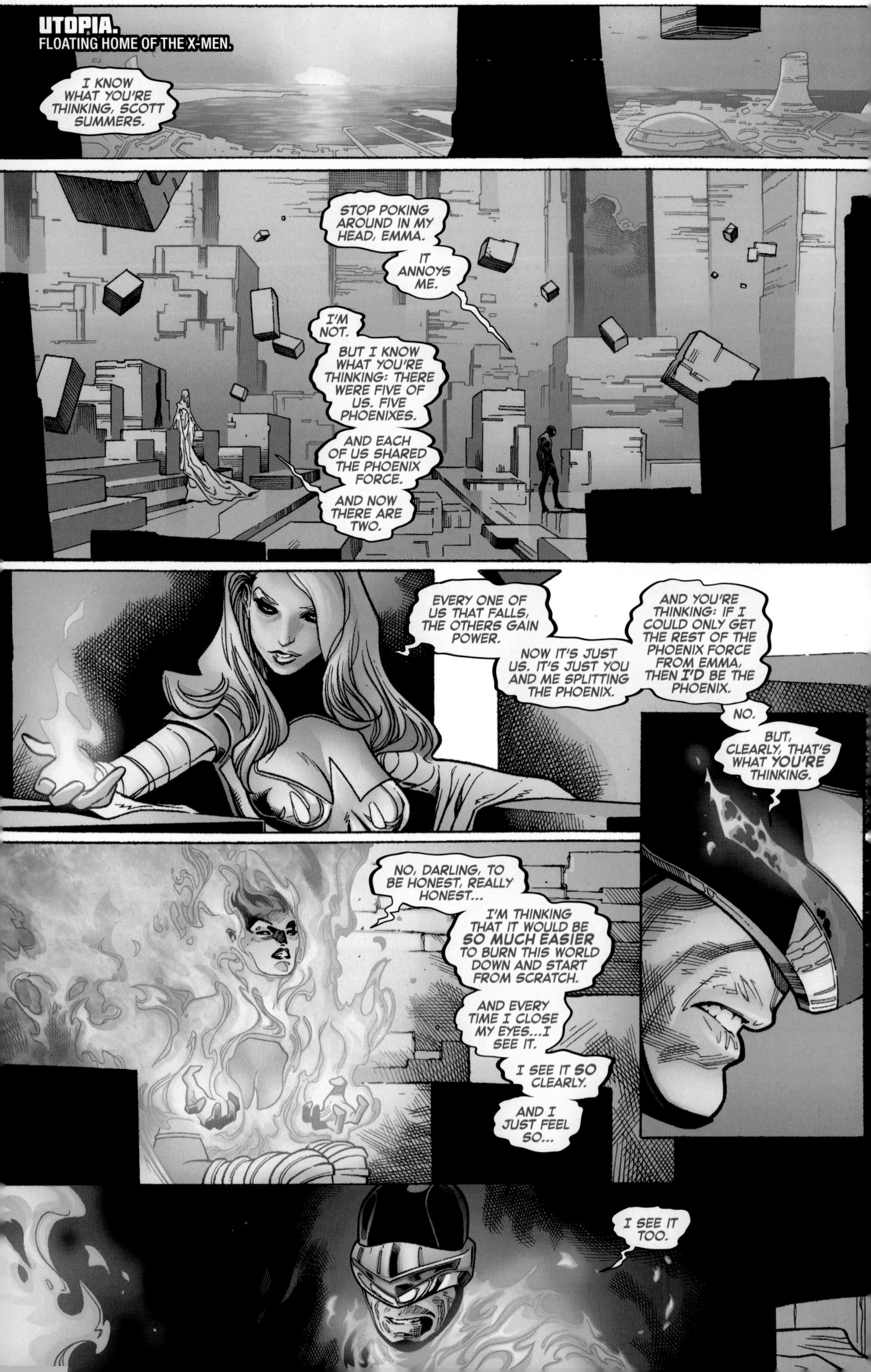
UTOPIA.
FLOATING HOME OF THE X-MEN.
I KNOW WHAT YOU'RE THINKING, SCOTT SUMMERS.
STOP POKING AROUND IN MY HEAD, EMMA.
IT ANNOYS ME.
I'M NOT.
BUT I KNOW WHAT YOU'RE THINKING: THERE WERE FIVE OF US. FIVE PHOENIXES.
AND EACH OF US SHARED THE PHOENIX FORCE.
AND NOW THERE ARE TWO.
EVERY ONE OF US THAT FALLS, THE OTHERS GAIN POWER.
NOW IT'S JUST US. IT'S JUST YOU AND ME SPLITTING THE PHOENIX.
AND YOU'RE THINKING: IF I COULD ONLY GET THE REST OF THE PHOENIX FORCE FROM EMMA, THEN I'D BE THE PHOENIX.
NO.
BUT, CLEARLY, THAT'S WHAT YOU'RE THINKING.
NO, DARLING, TO BE HONEST, REALLY HONEST...
I'M THINKING THAT IT WOULD BE SO MUCH EASIER TO BURN THIS WORLD DOWN AND START FROM SCRATCH.
AND EVERY TIME I CLOSE MY EYES...I SEE IT.
I SEE IT SO CLEARLY.
AND I JUST FEEL SO...
I SEE IT TOO.

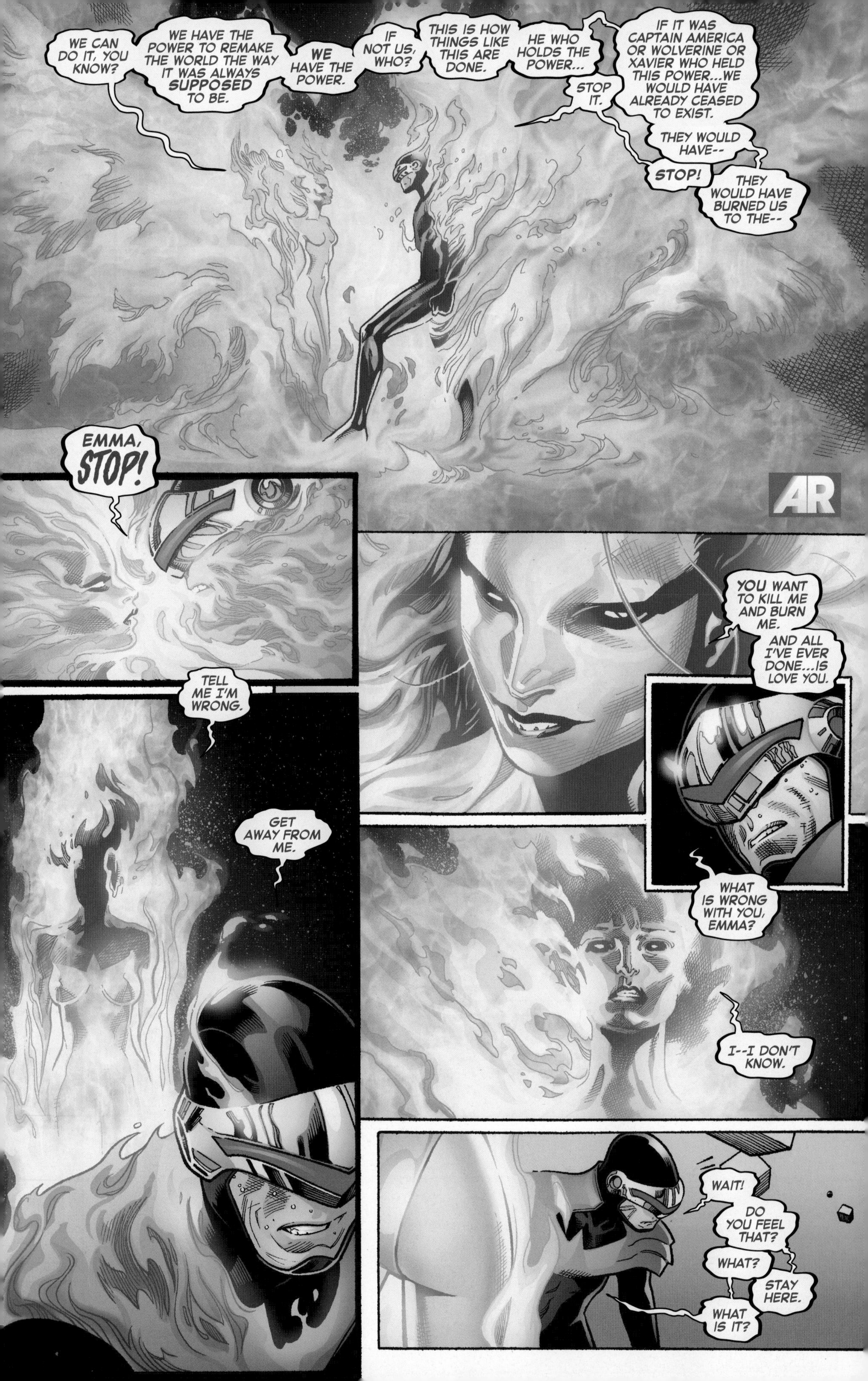

WE CAN DO IT, YOU KNOW?
WE HAVE THE POWER TO REMAKE THE WORLD THE WAY IT WAS ALWAYS SUPPOSED TO BE.
WE HAVE THE POWER.
IF NOT US, WHO?
THIS IS HOW THINGS LIKE THIS ARE DONE.
HE WHO HOLDS THE POWER...
STOP IT.
IF IT WAS CAPTAIN AMERICA OR WOLVERINE OR XAVIER WHO HELD THIS POWER...WE WOULD HAVE ALREADY CEASED TO EXIST.
THEY WOULD HAVE--
STOP!
THEY WOULD HAVE BURNED US TO THE--
EMMA, STOP!
YOU WANT TO KILL ME AND BURN ME.
AND ALL I'VE EVER DONE...IS LOVE YOU.
TELL ME I'M WRONG.
GET AWAY FROM ME.
WHAT IS WRONG WITH YOU, EMMA?
I--I DON'T KNOW.
WAIT!
DO YOU FEEL THAT?
WHAT?
STAY HERE.
WHAT IS IT?

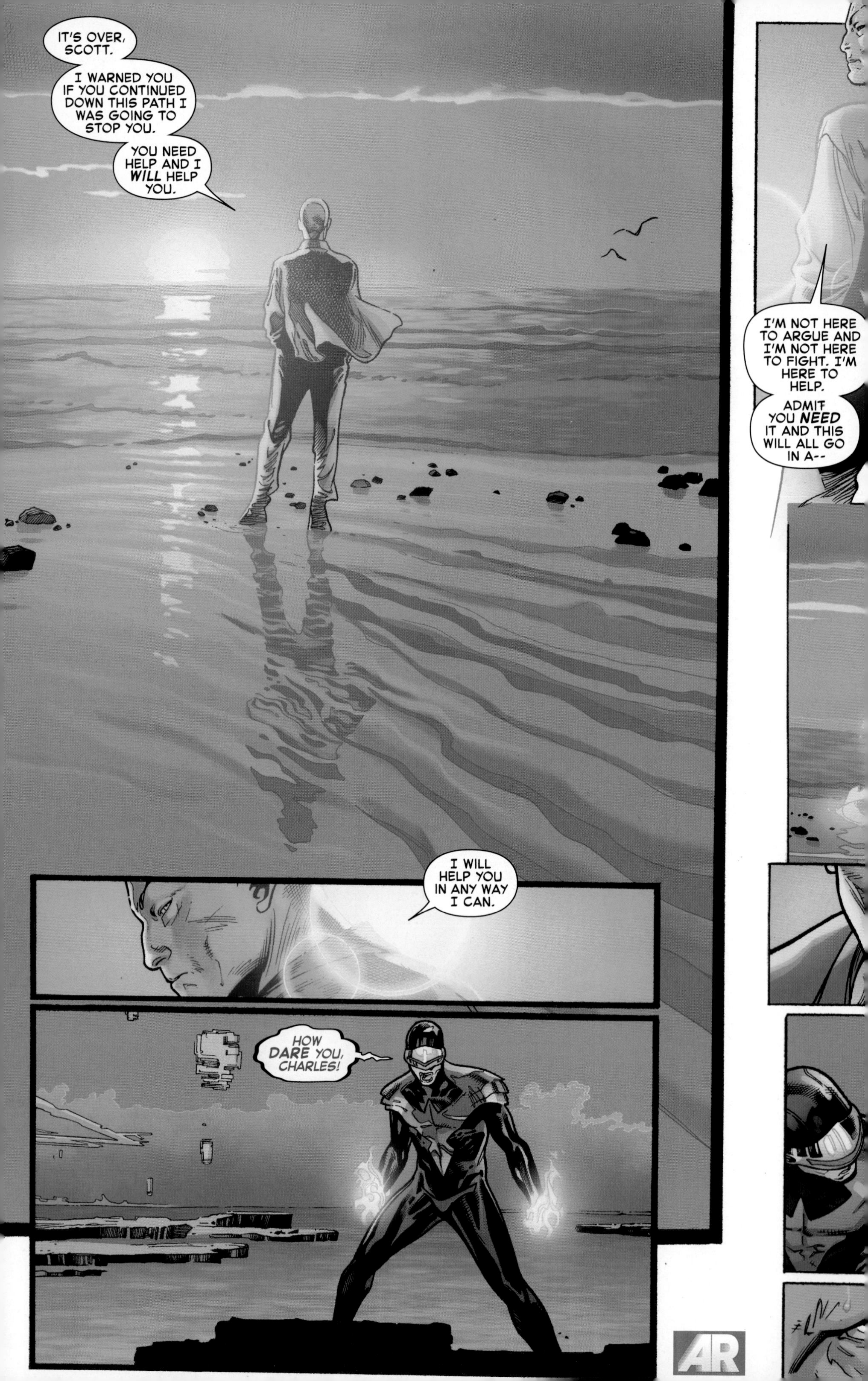
IT'S OVER, SCOTT.
I WARNED YOU IF YOU CONTINUED DOWN THIS PATH I WAS GOING TO STOP YOU.
YOU NEED HELP AND I WILL HELP YOU.
I WILL HELP YOU IN ANY WAY I CAN.
HOW DARE YOU, CHARLES!
I'M NOT HERE TO ARGUE AND I'M NOT HERE TO FIGHT. I'M HERE TO HELP.
ADMIT YOU NEED IT AND THIS WILL ALL GO IN A--
AR

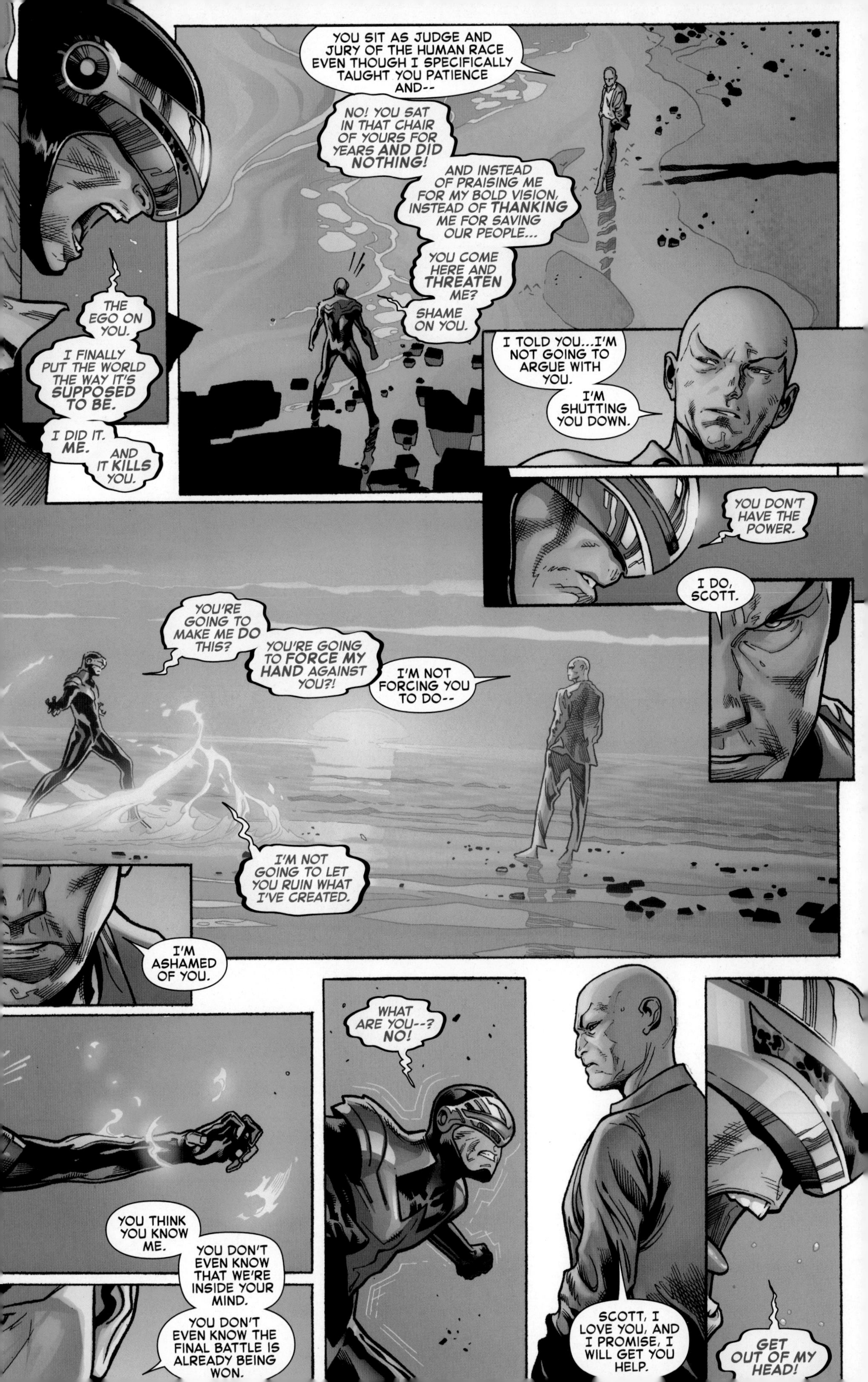

YOU SIT AS JUDGE AND JURY OF THE HUMAN RACE EVEN THOUGH I SPECIFICALLY TAUGHT YOU PATIENCE AND--
NO! YOU SAT IN THAT CHAIR OF YOURS FOR YEARS AND DID NOTHING!
AND INSTEAD OF PRAISING ME FOR MY BOLD VISION, INSTEAD OF THANKING ME FOR SAVING OUR PEOPLE...
YOU COME HERE AND THREATEN ME?
SHAME ON YOU.
THE EGO ON YOU.
I FINALLY PUT THE WORLD THE WAY IT'S SUPPOSED TO BE.
I DID IT. ME.
AND IT KILLS YOU.
I TOLD YOU...I'M NOT GOING TO ARGUE WITH YOU.
I'M SHUTTING YOU DOWN.
YOU DON'T HAVE THE POWER.
I DO, SCOTT.
YOU'RE GOING TO MAKE ME DO THIS?
YOU'RE GOING TO FORCE MY HAND AGAINST YOU?!
I'M NOT FORCING YOU TO DO--
I'M NOT GOING TO LET YOU RUIN WHAT I'VE CREATED.
I'M ASHAMED OF YOU.
WHAT ARE YOU--? NO!
YOU THINK YOU KNOW ME.
YOU DON'T EVEN KNOW THAT WE'RE INSIDE YOUR MIND.
YOU DON'T EVEN KNOW THE FINAL BATTLE IS ALREADY BEING WON.
SCOTT, I LOVE YOU, AND I PROMISE, I WILL GET YOU HELP.
GET OUT OF MY HEAD!

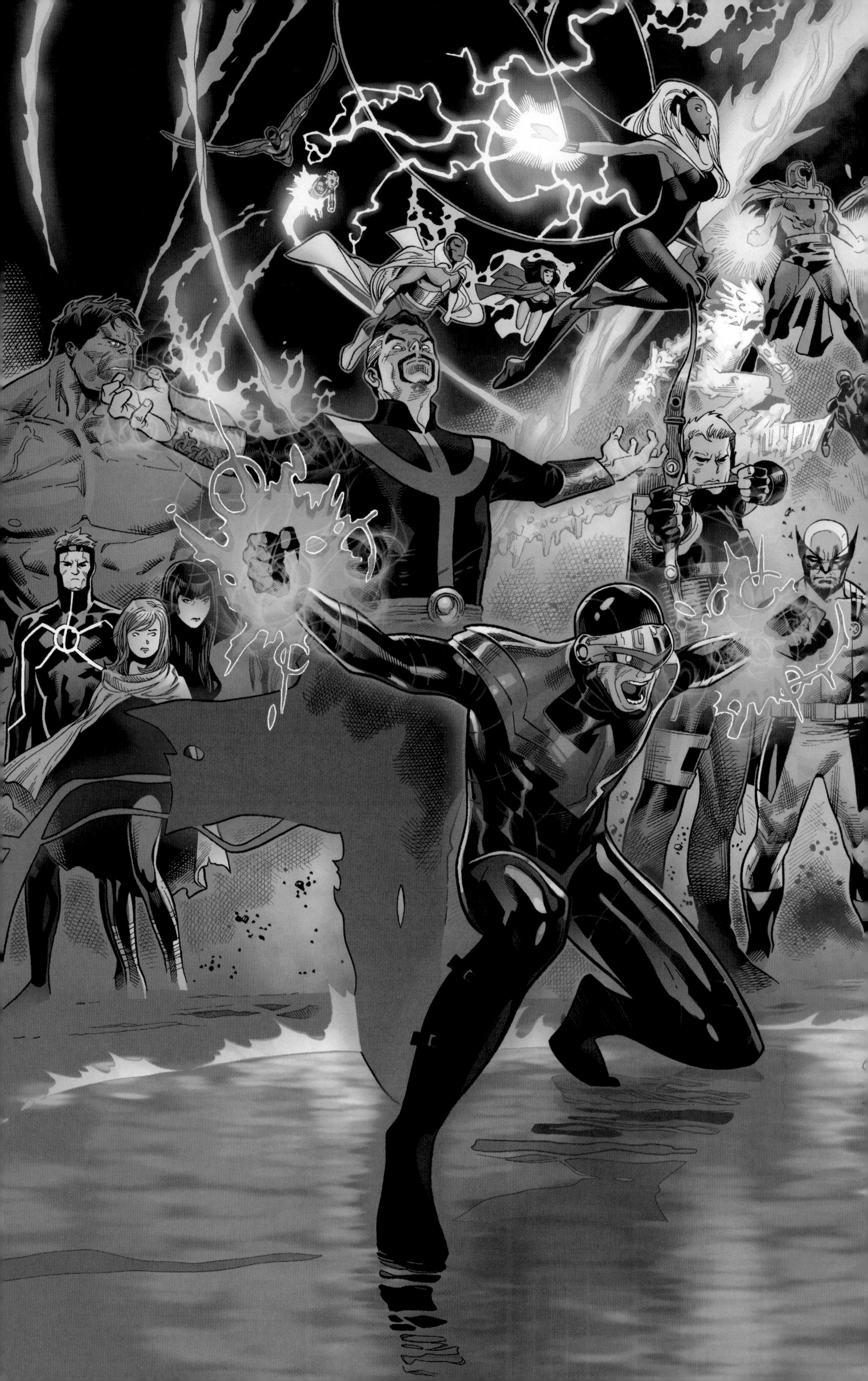

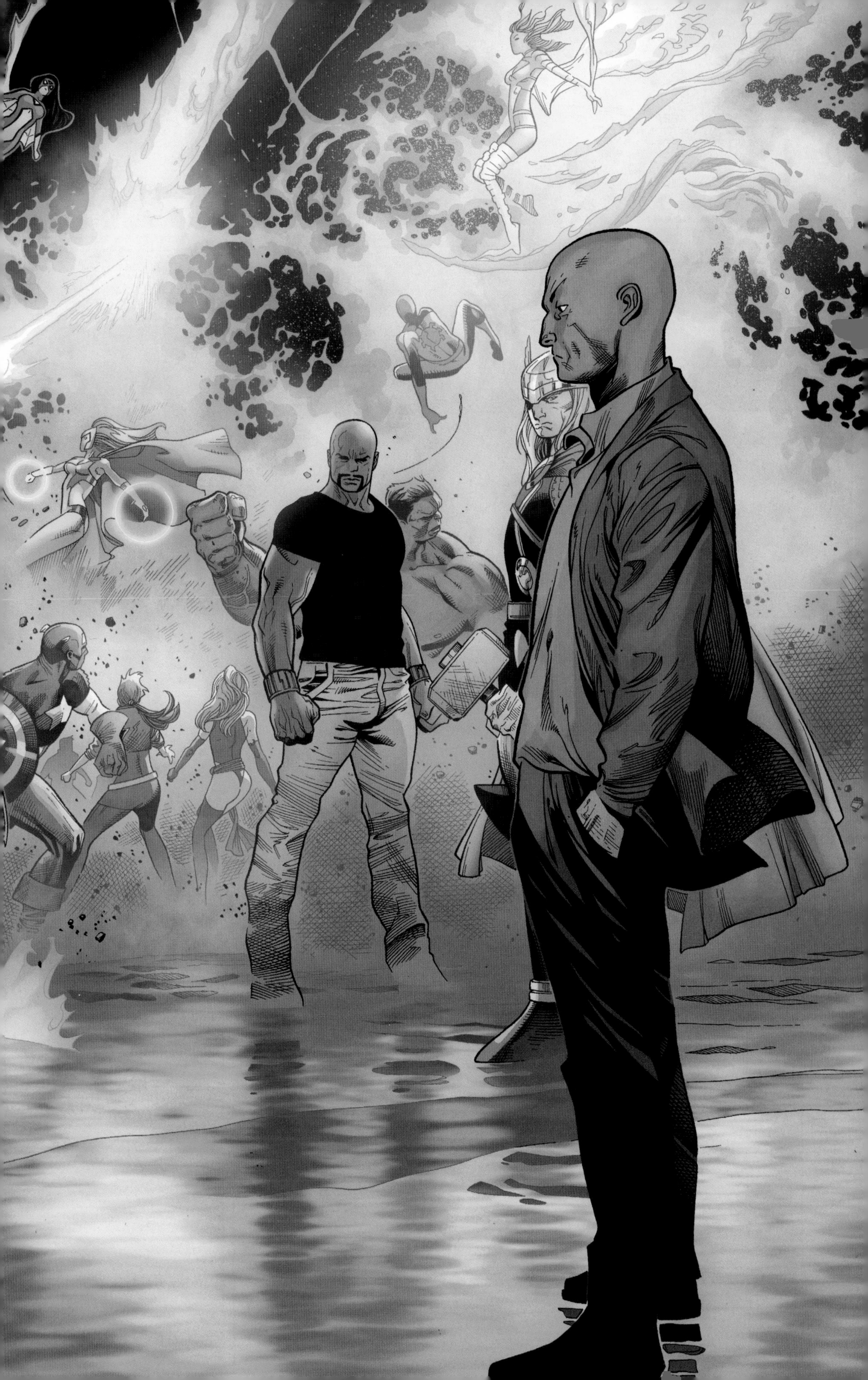

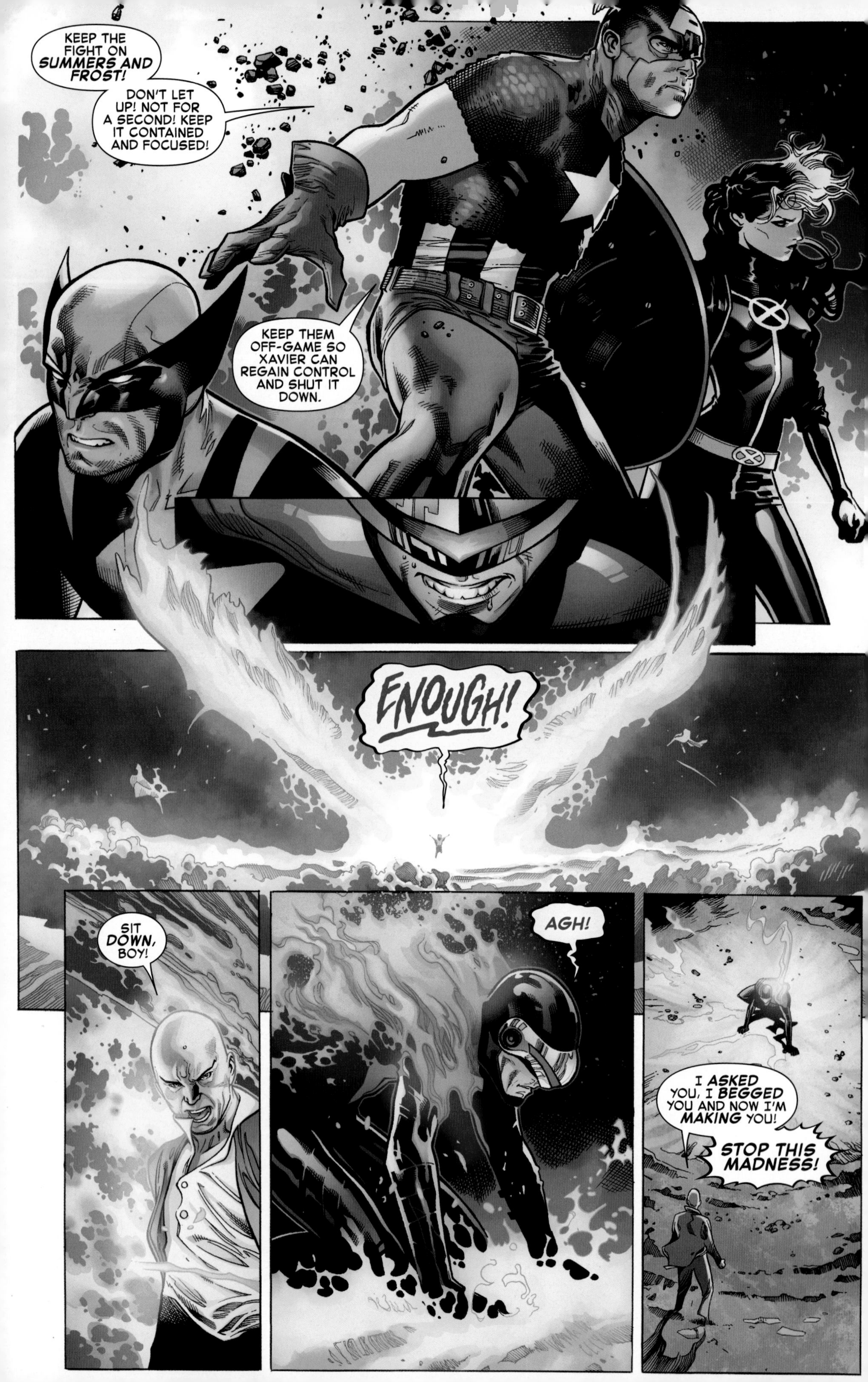
KEEP THE FIGHT ON SUMMERS AND FROST!
DON'T LET UP! NOT FOR A SECOND! KEEP IT CONTAINED AND FOCUSED!
KEEP THEM OFF-GAME SO XAVIER CAN REGAIN CONTROL AND SHUT IT DOWN.
ENOUGH!
SIT DOWN, BOY!
AGH!
I ASKED YOU, I BEGGED YOU AND NOW I'M MAKING YOU!
STOP THIS MADNESS!

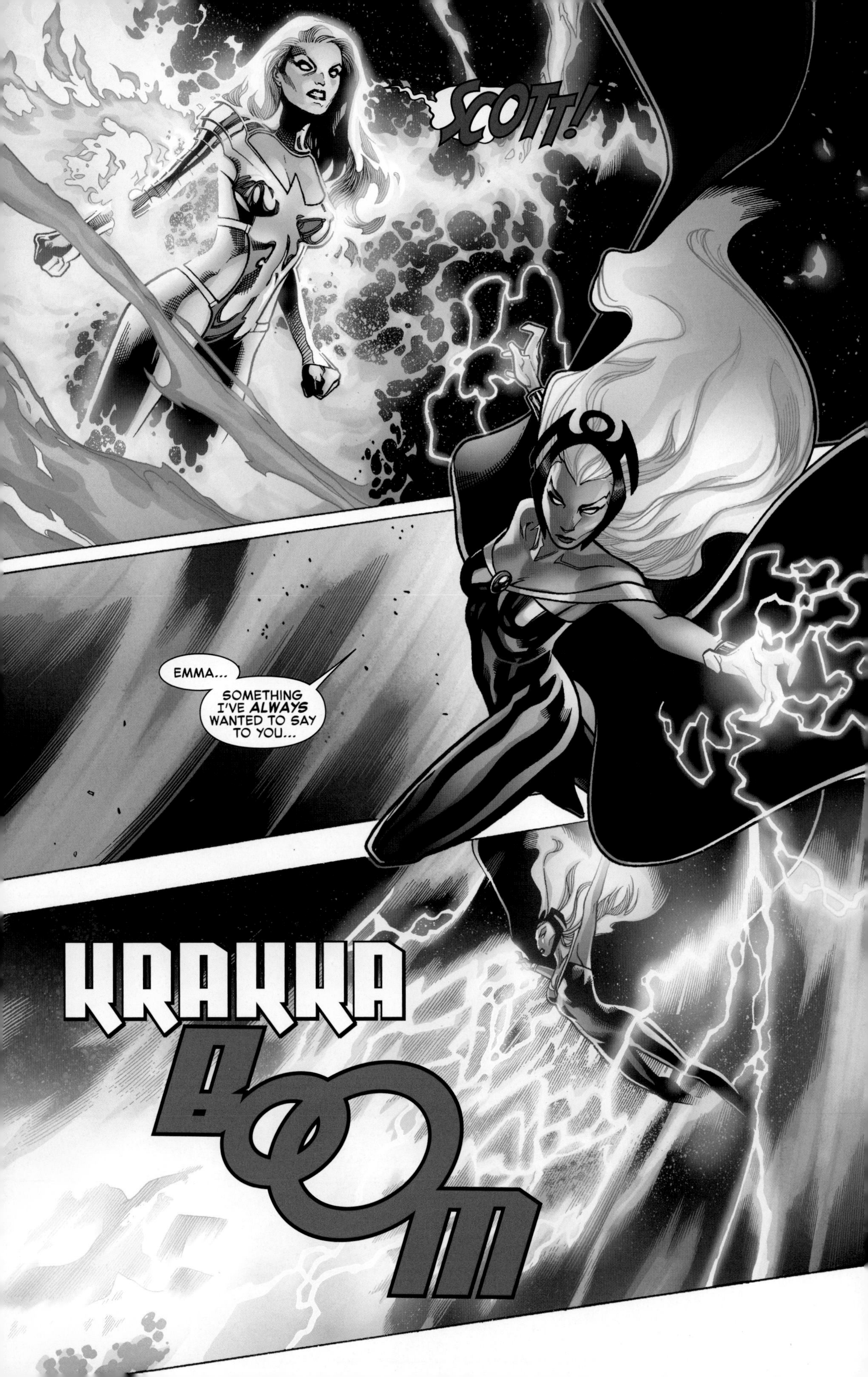
SCOTT!
EMMA...
SOMETHING I'VE ALWAYS WANTED TO SAY TO YOU...
KRAKKA
BOOM

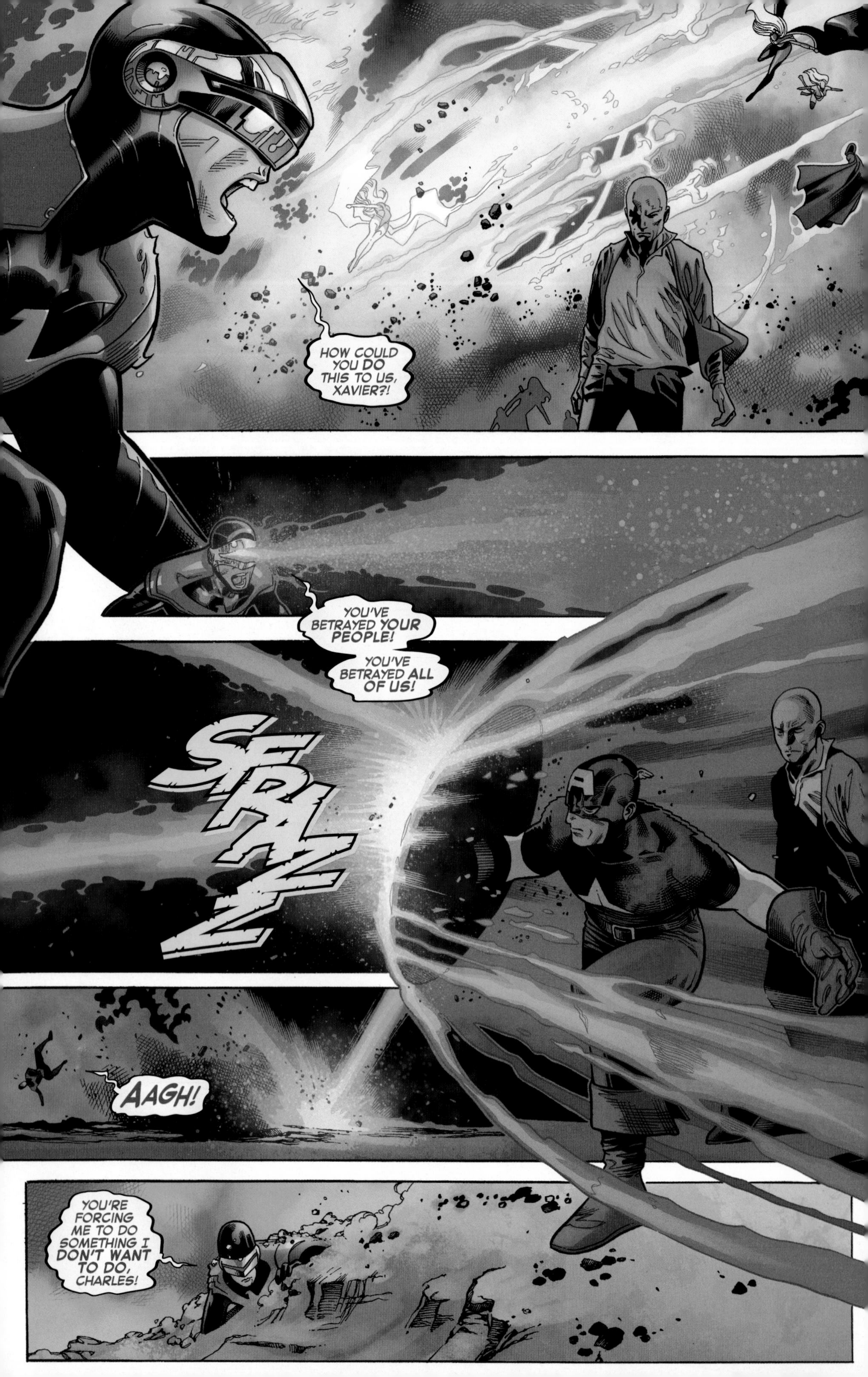
HOW COULD YOU DO THIS TO US, XAVIER?!
YOU'VE BETRAYED YOUR PEOPLE!
YOU'VE BETRAYED ALL OF US!
SFZZZ
AAGH!
YOU'RE FORCING ME TO DO SOMETHING I DON'T WANT TO DO, CHARLES!

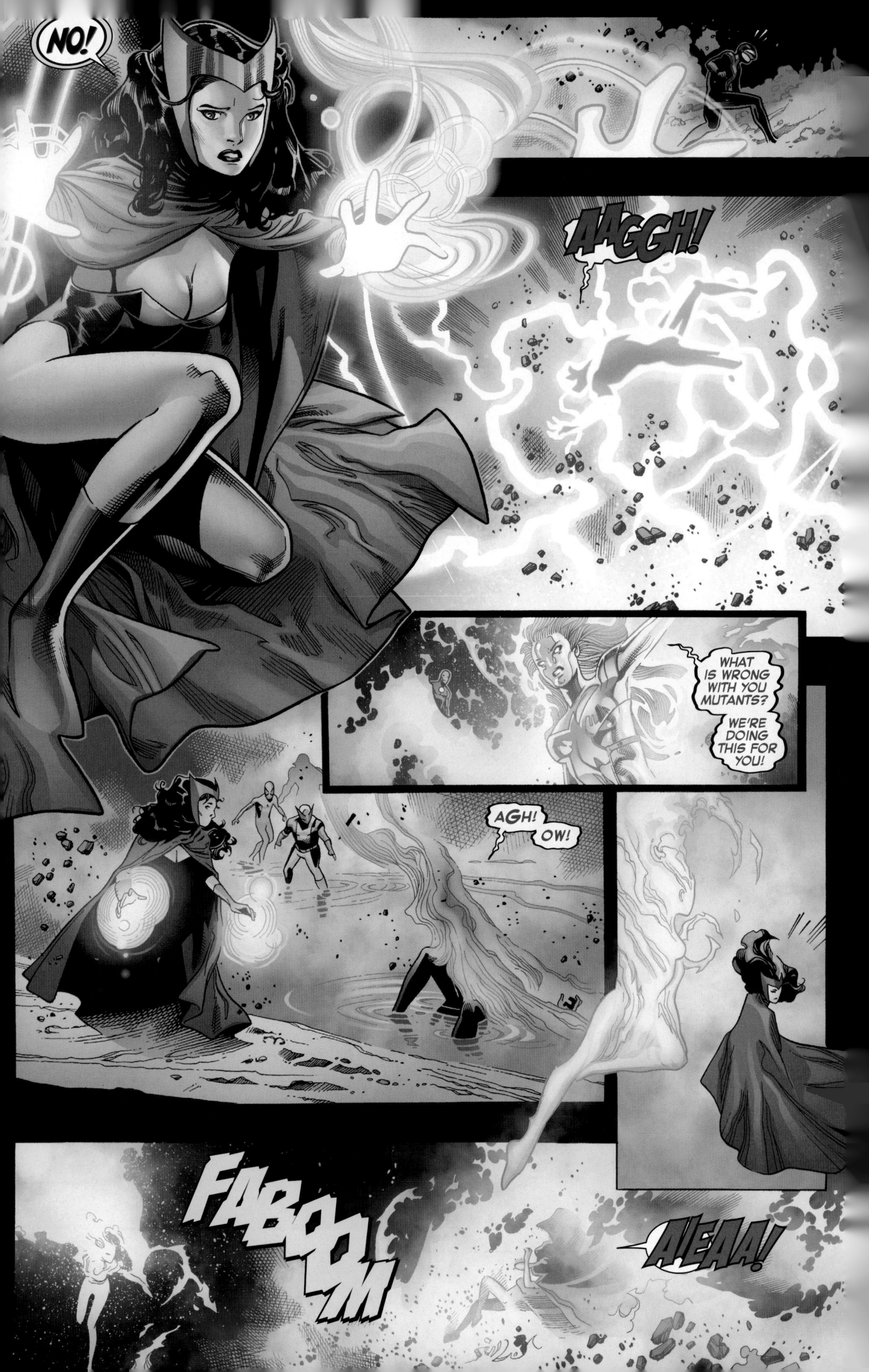

NO!
AAGGH!
WHAT IS WRONG WITH YOU MUTANTS?
WE'RE DOING THIS FOR YOU!
AGH!
OW!
FABOOM
AIEAA!

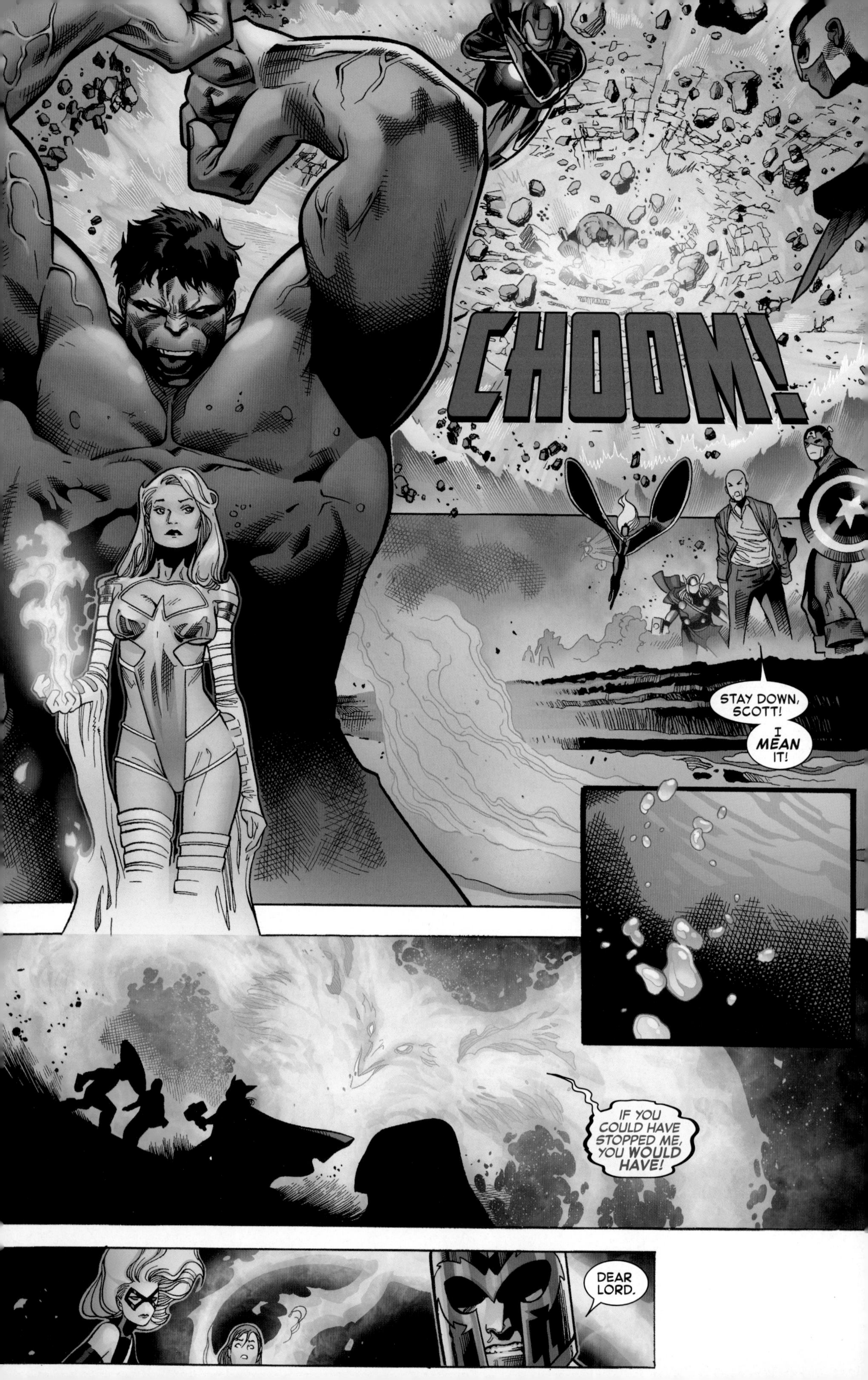
CHOOM!
STAY DOWN, SCOTT!
I MEAN IT!
IF YOU COULD HAVE STOPPED ME, YOU WOULD HAVE!
DEAR LORD.

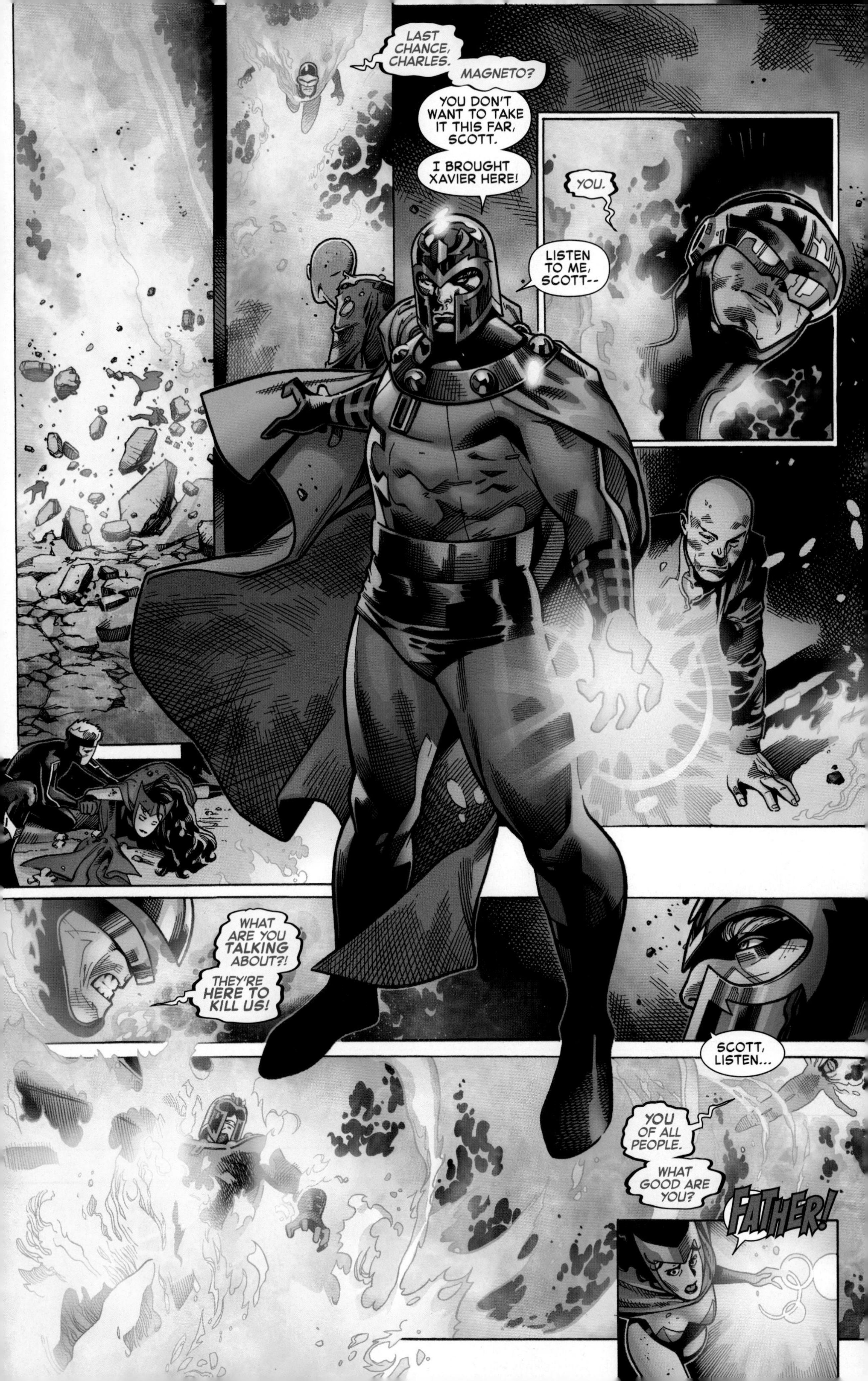
LAST CHANCE, CHARLES.
MAGNETO?
YOU DON'T WANT TO TAKE IT THIS FAR, SCOTT.
I BROUGHT XAVIER HERE!
YOU.
LISTEN TO ME, SCOTT--
WHAT ARE YOU TALKING ABOUT?!
THEY'RE HERE TO KILL US!
SCOTT, LISTEN...
YOU OF ALL PEOPLE.
WHAT GOOD ARE YOU?
FATHER!

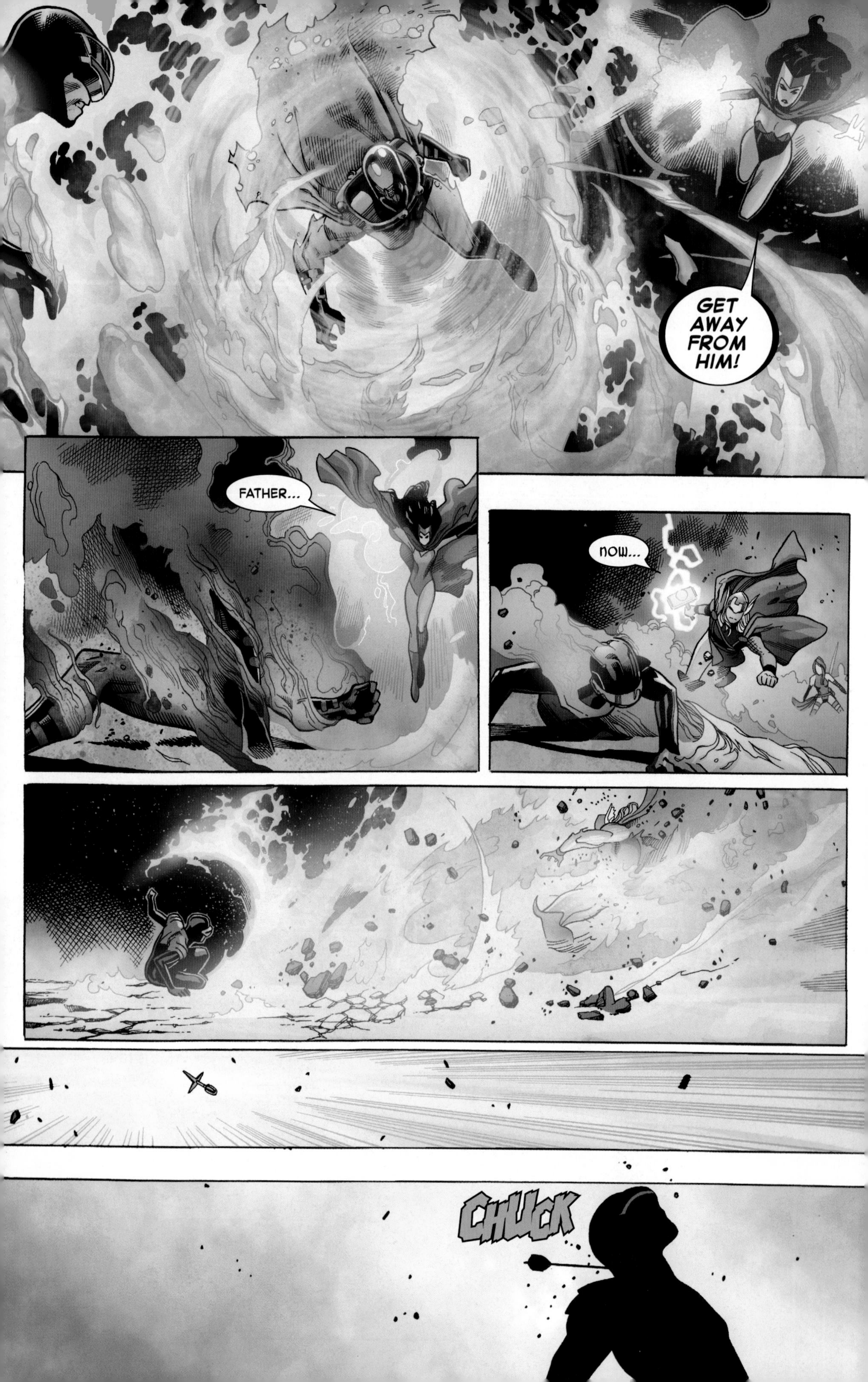
GET AWAY FROM HIM!
FATHER...
NOW...
CHUCK

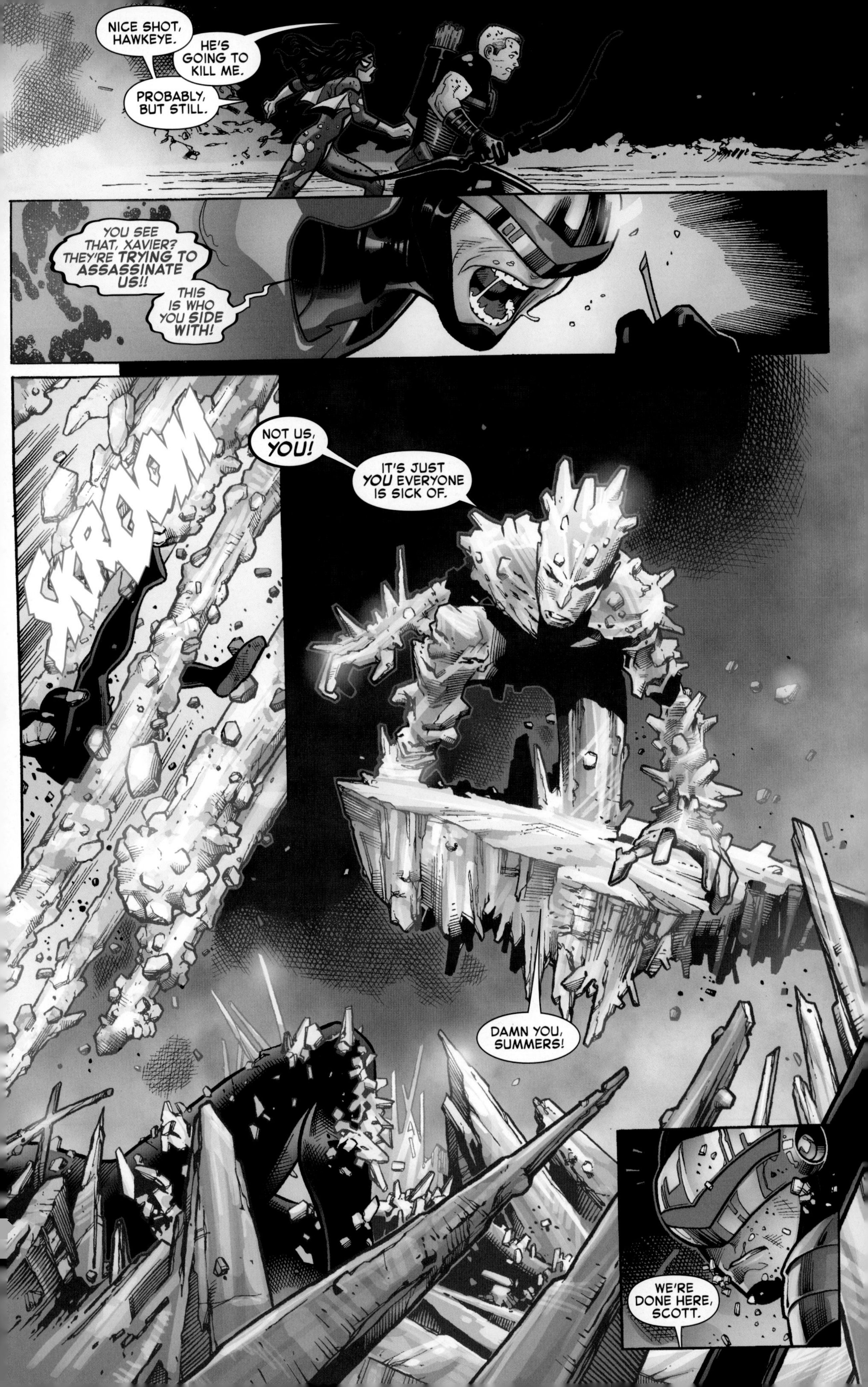
NICE SHOT, HAWKEYE.
HE'S GOING TO KILL ME.
PROBABLY, BUT STILL.
YOU SEE THAT, XAVIER? THEY'RE TRYING TO ASSASSINATE US!!
THIS IS WHO YOU SIDE WITH!
SKROOM
NOT US, YOU!
IT'S JUST YOU EVERYONE IS SICK OF.
DAMN YOU, SUMMERS!
WE'RE DONE HERE, SCOTT.

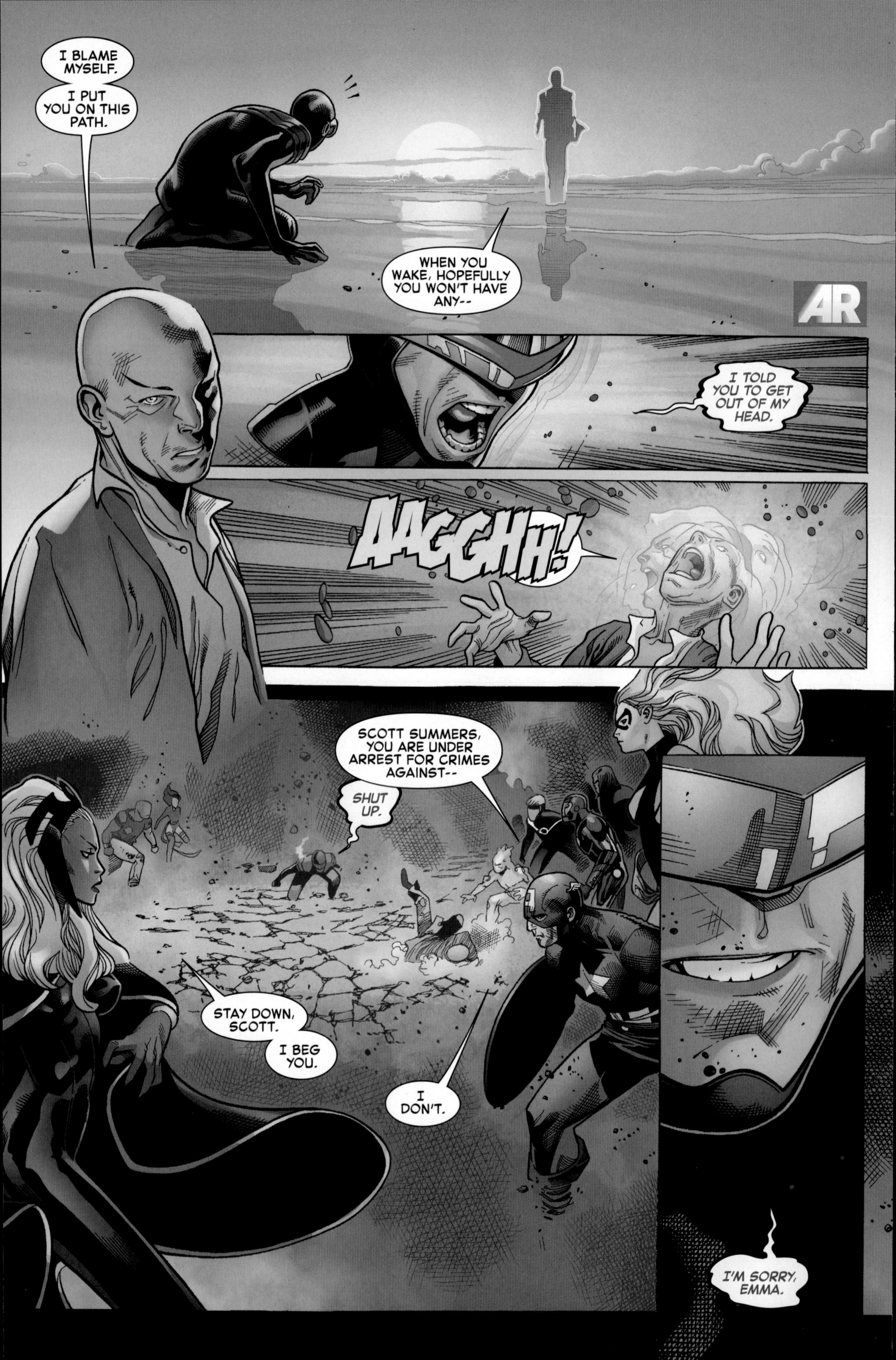

I BLAME MYSELF.
I PUT YOU ON THIS PATH.
WHEN YOU WAKE, HOPEFULLY YOU WON'T HAVE ANY--
AR
I TOLD YOU TO GET OUT OF MY HEAD.
AAGGHH!
SCOTT SUMMERS, YOU ARE UNDER ARREST FOR CRIMES AGAINST--
SHUT UP.
STAY DOWN, SCOTT.
I BEG YOU.
I DON'T.
I'M SORRY, EMMA.

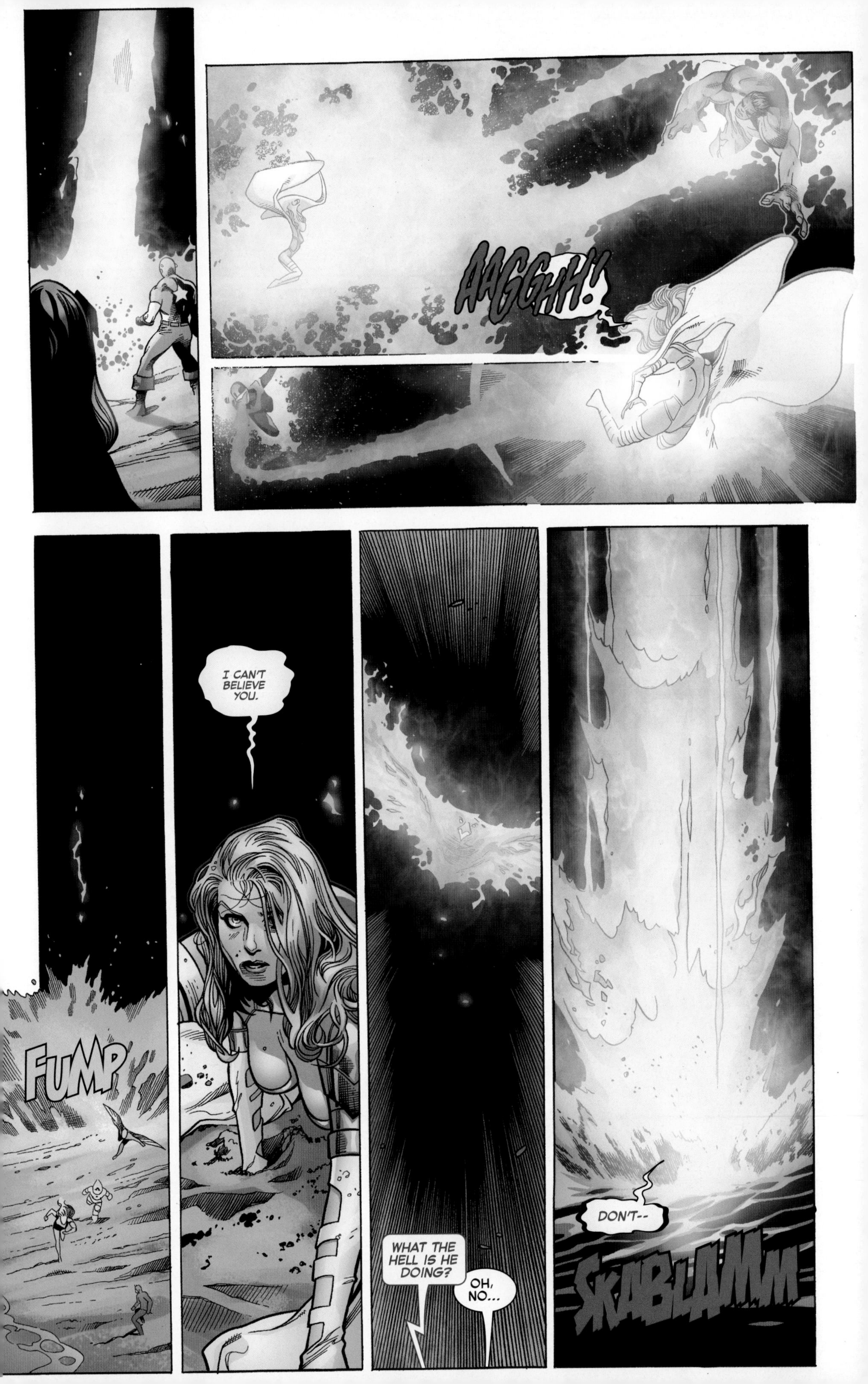
AAGGHH!
FUMP
I CAN'T BELIEVE YOU.
WHAT THE HELL IS HE DOING?
OH, NO...
DON'T--
SKABLAMM

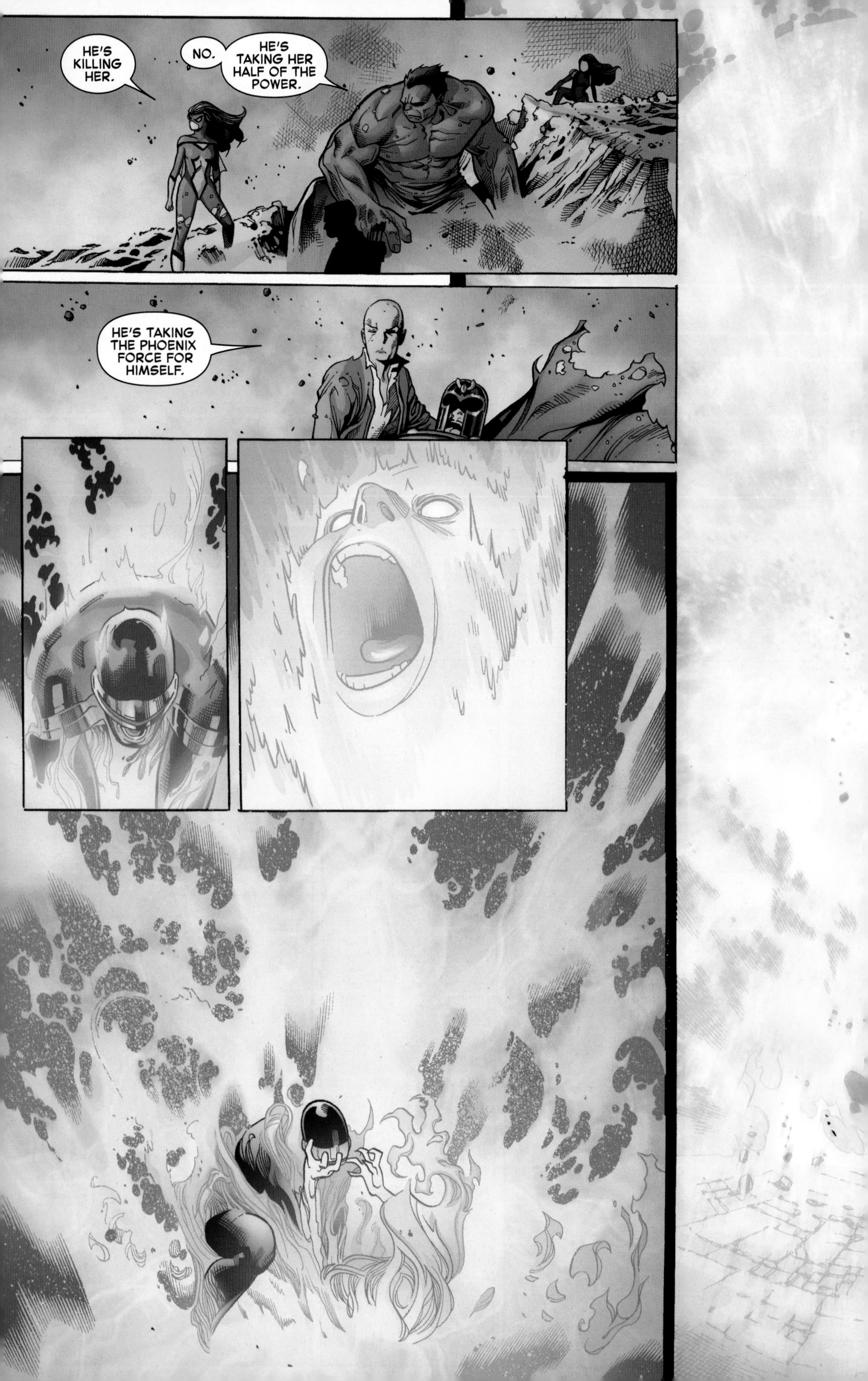
HE'S KILLING HER.
NO.
HE'S TAKING HER HALF OF THE POWER.
HE'S TAKING THE PHOENIX FORCE FOR HIMSELF.

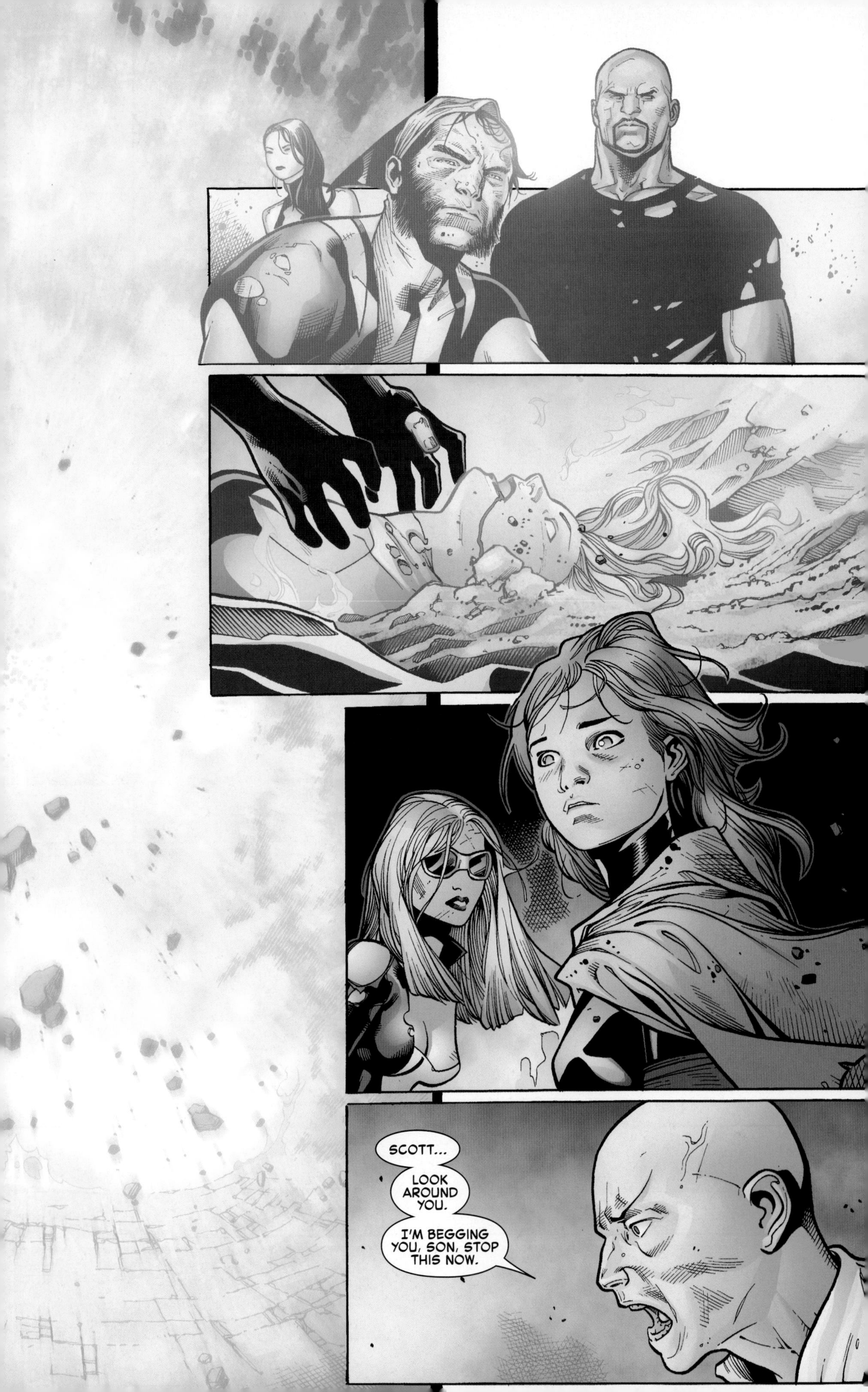
SCOTT...
LOOK AROUND YOU.
I'M BEGGING YOU, SON, STOP THIS NOW.

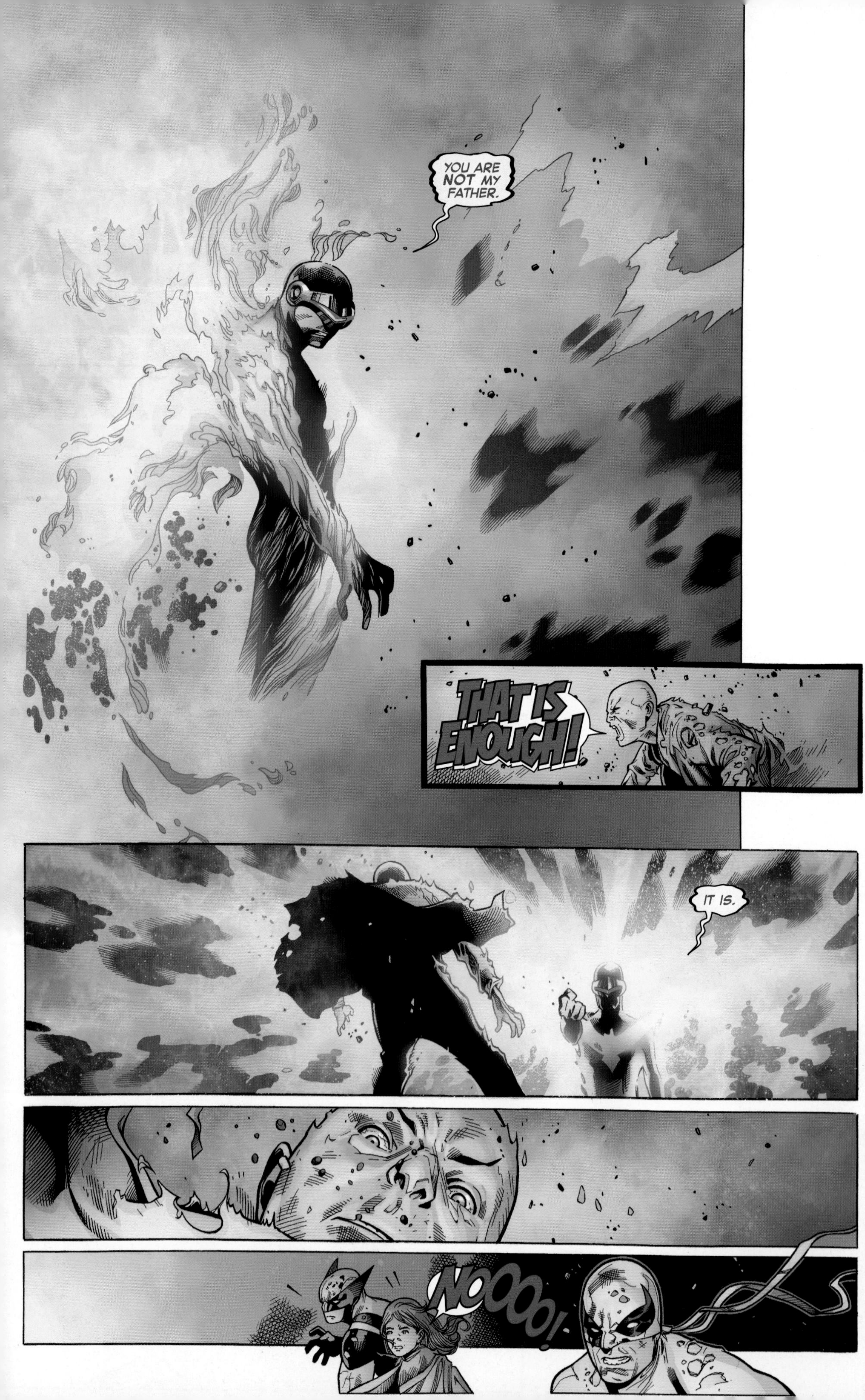
YOU ARE NOT MY FATHER.
THAT IS ENOUGH!
IT IS.
NOOOO!

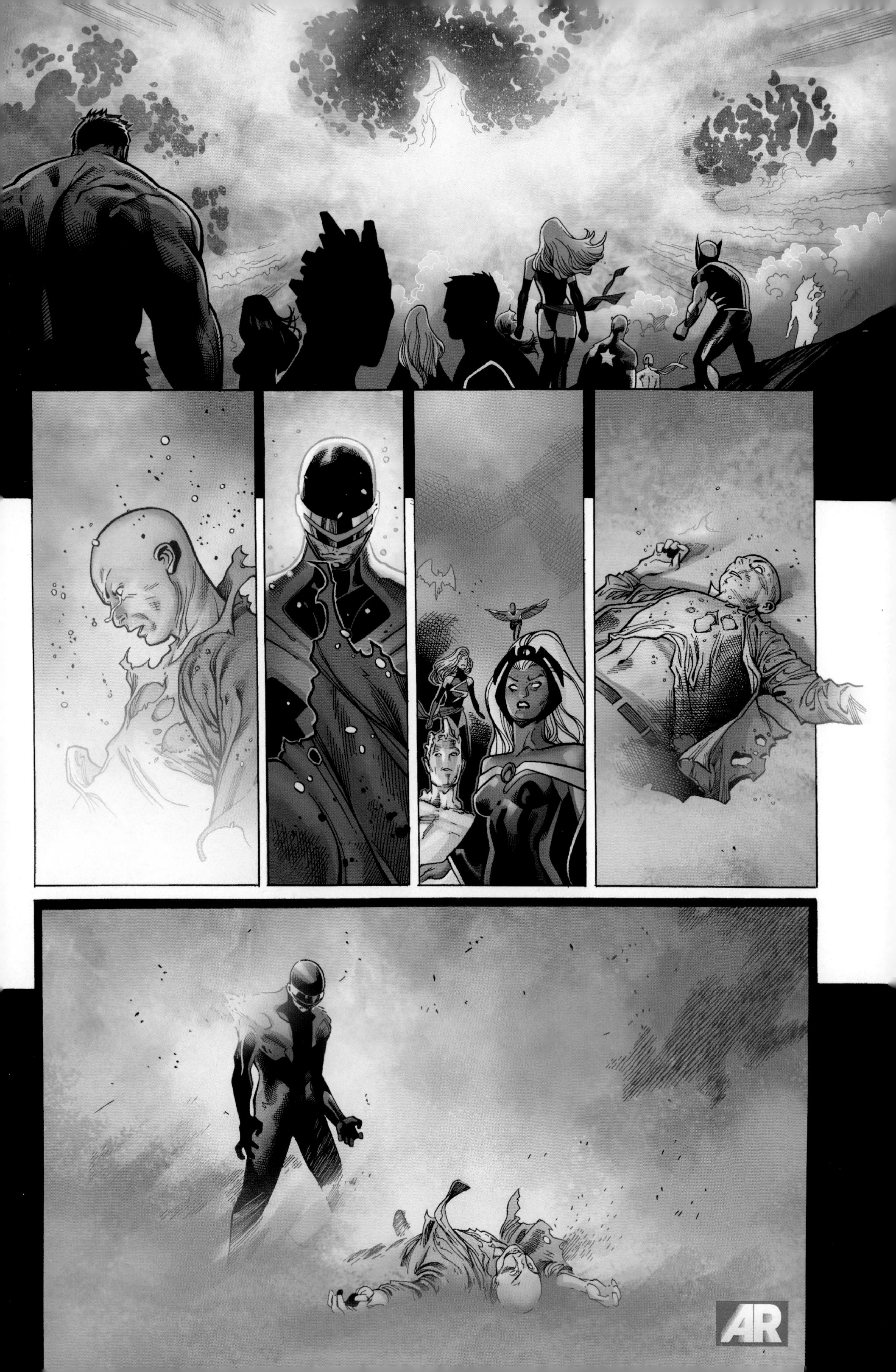

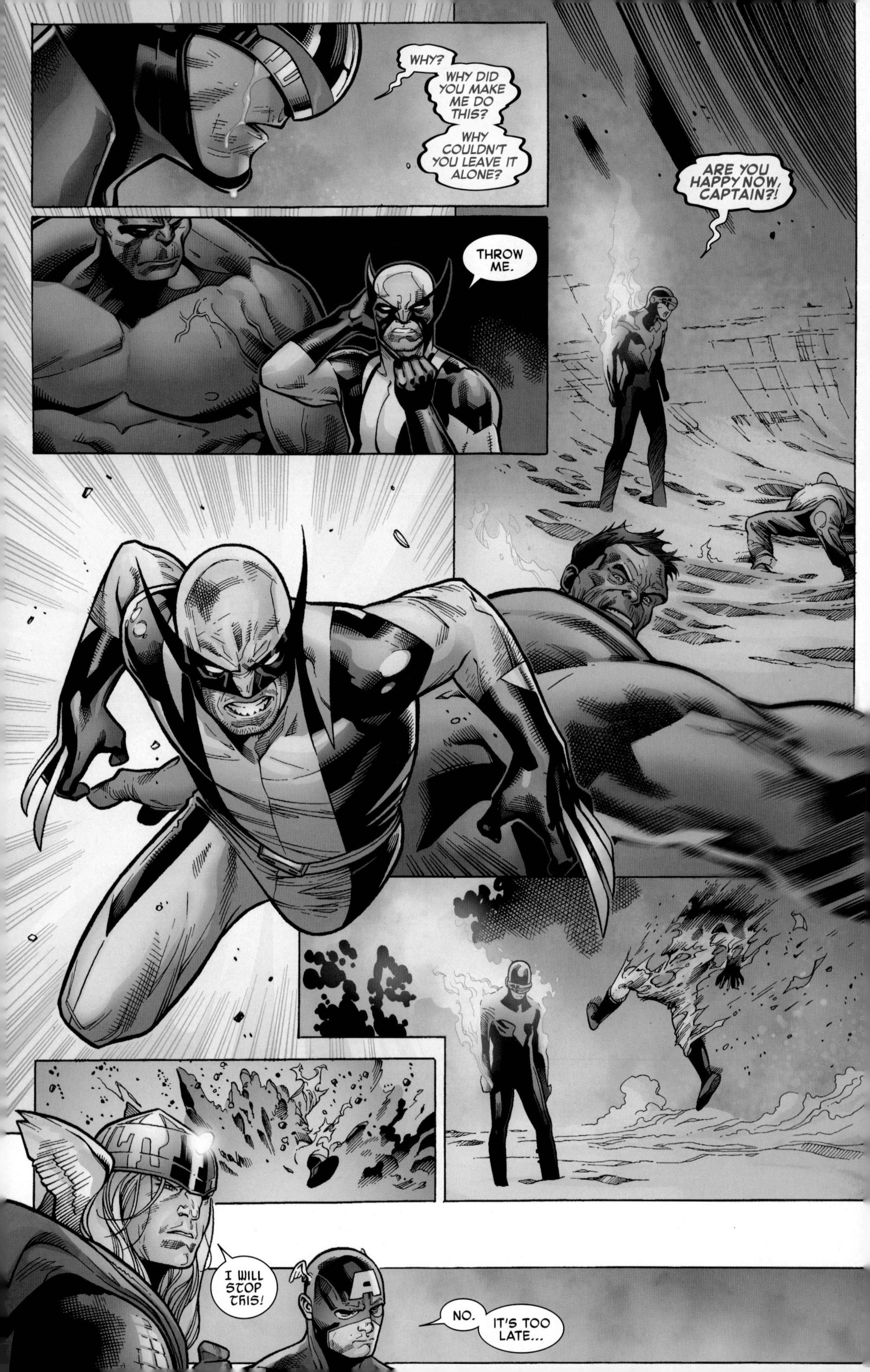
WHY?
WHY DID YOU MAKE ME DO THIS?
WHY COULDN'T YOU LEAVE IT ALONE?
ARE YOU HAPPY NOW, CAPTAIN?!
THROW ME.
I WILL STOP THIS!
NO.
IT'S TOO LATE...

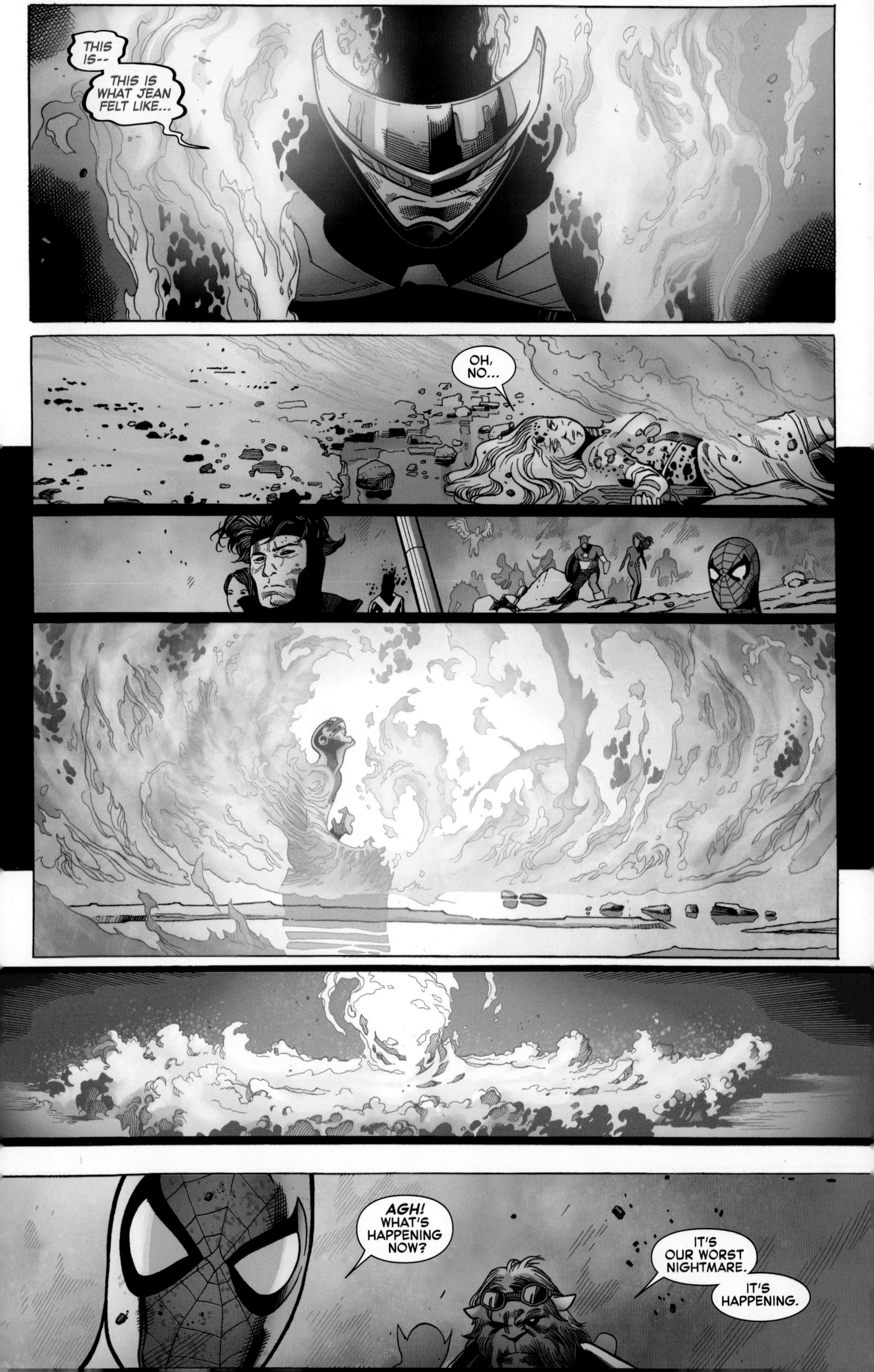
THIS IS--
THIS IS WHAT JEAN FELT LIKE...
OH, NO...
AGH! WHAT'S HAPPENING NOW?
IT'S OUR WORST NIGHTMARE.
IT'S HAPPENING.

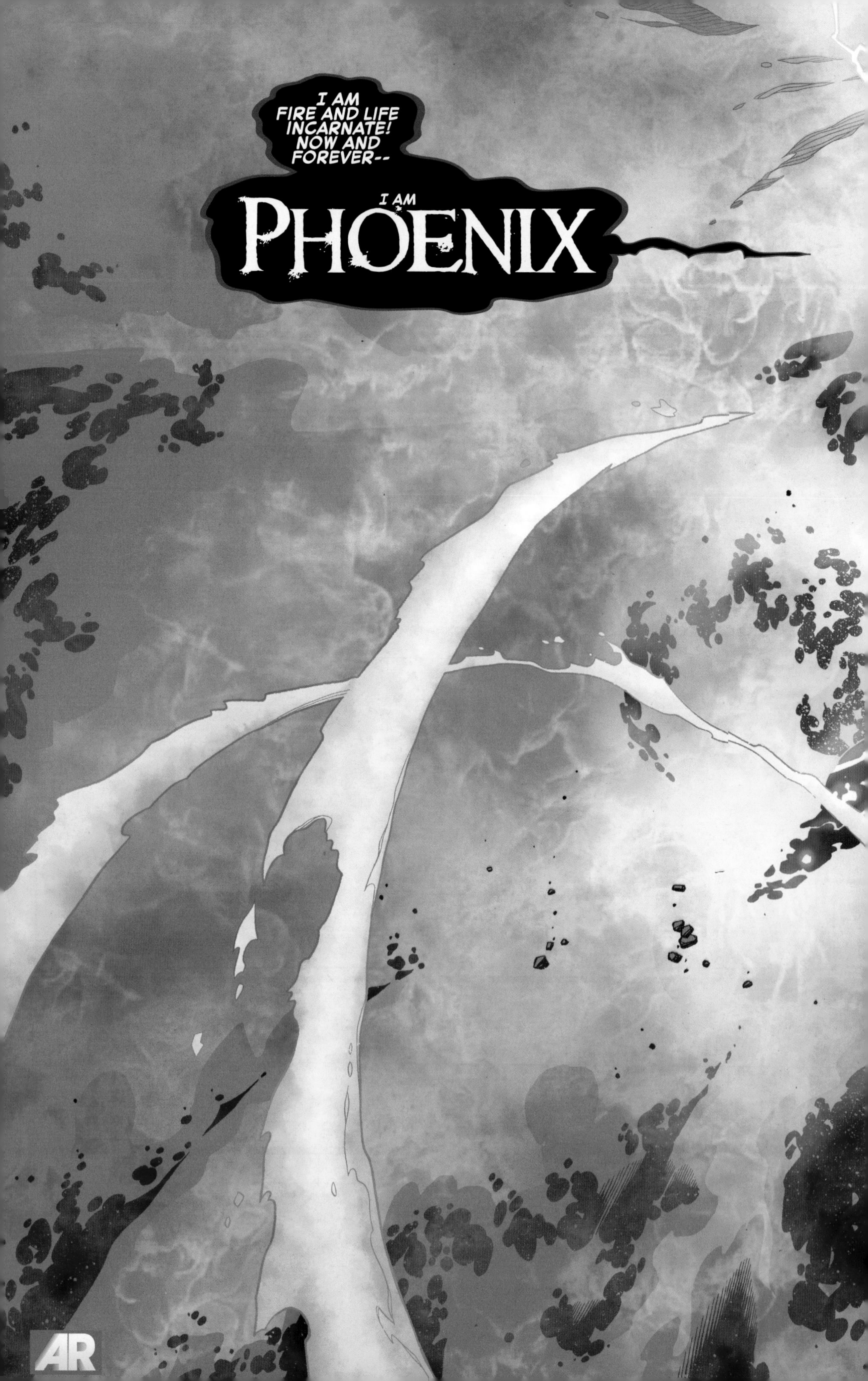
I AM FIRE AND LIFE INCARNATE! NOW AND FOREVER--
I AM PHOENIX

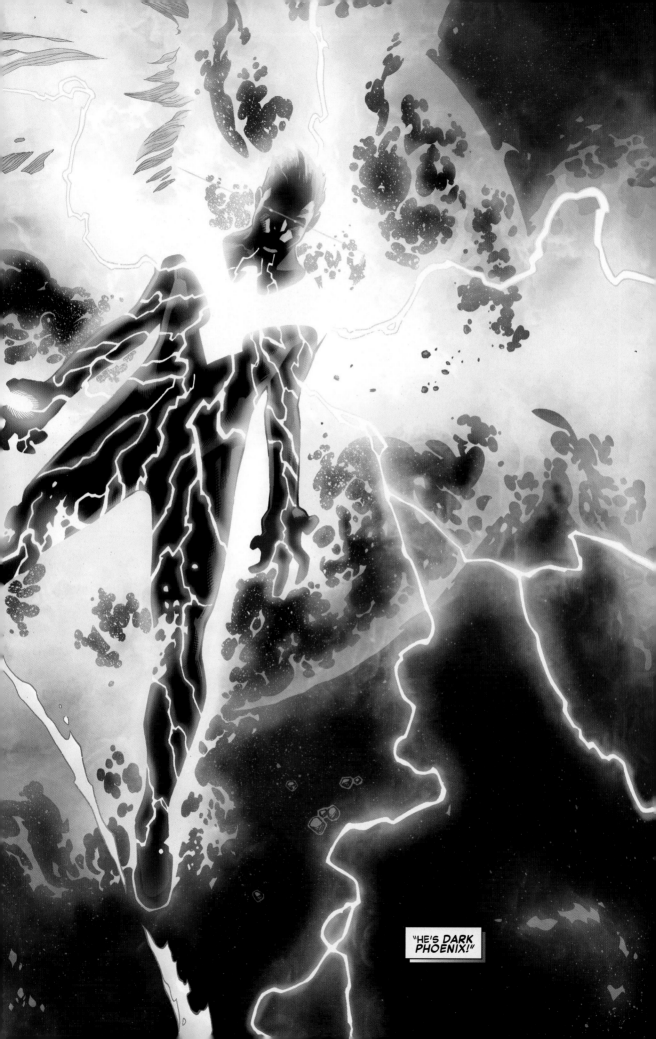

"HE'S DARK PHOENIX!"

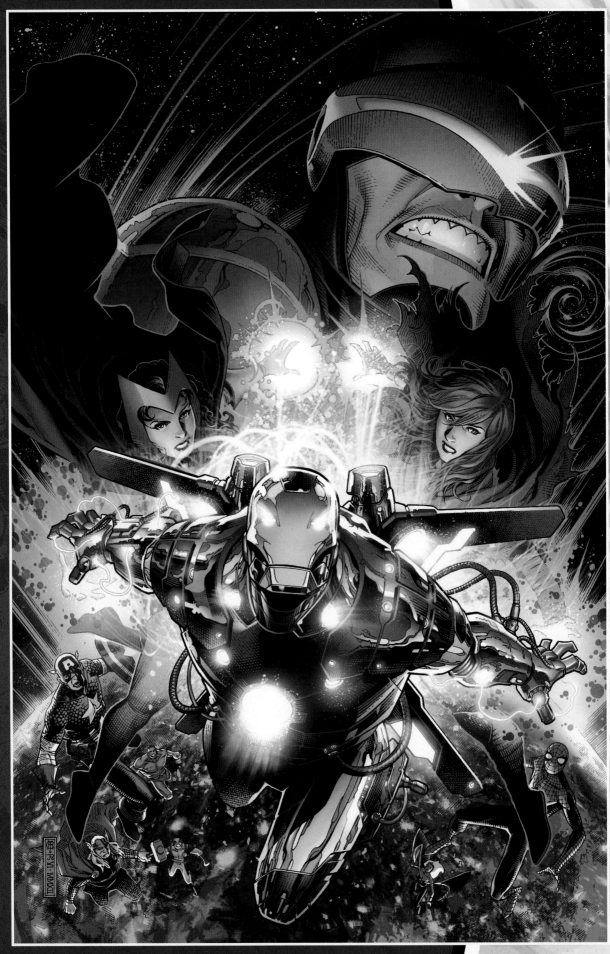

ROUND 12

"ONCE UPON A TIME, THE *SCARLET WITCH* SAID...

"'*NO MORE MUTANTS.*'

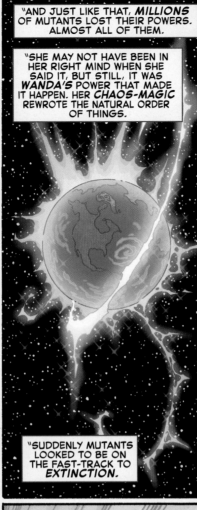

"AND JUST LIKE THAT, *MILLIONS* OF MUTANTS LOST THEIR POWERS. ALMOST ALL OF THEM.

"SHE MAY NOT HAVE BEEN IN HER RIGHT MIND WHEN SHE SAID IT, BUT STILL, IT WAS *WANDA'S* POWER THAT MADE IT HAPPEN. HER *CHAOS-MAGIC* REWROTE THE NATURAL ORDER OF THINGS.

"SUDDENLY MUTANTS LOOKED TO BE ON THE FAST-TRACK TO *EXTINCTION.*

"ENTER THEIR OLD FRIEND, THE *PHOENIX.*

"AN ANCIENT COSMIC ENTITY. A FORCE OF DESTRUCTION AND REBIRTH. ONE WE BARELY UNDERSTAND. ONE THAT HAS SHOWN A REPEATED INTEREST IN EARTH'S MUTANT POPULATION.

"NOW HERE'S WHERE WE'RE OPERATING SOLELY ON CONJECTURE. BUT IT'S MY BELIEF THAT WHEN WANDA MADE HER DECLARATION, THE PHOENIX TOOK NOTE.

"WHEN WANDA SAID, 'NO MORE MUTANTS,' THE PHOENIX SAID, 'SCREW THAT...'

"'*MORE MUTANTS.*'

"AND *HOPE* WAS BORN.

"HER COMING HERALDED WITH AN EXPLOSION OF POWER. A MESSIAH IN THE EYES OF HER PEOPLE. DESTINED, OR SO EVERYONE BELIEVES, TO SOMEDAY INHERIT THE FULL POWER OF THE PHOENIX.

AR

"THE PRIMAL CHAOS OF WANDA'S MUTANT MAGIC. THE FIERY ORDER OF THE PHOENIX. TWO COSMIC POWERS, CAUGHT IN SOME KIND OF CRAZY CYCLE, ACTING AS CONTRARY FORCES, AS *YIN AND YANG.*

"AND ALL OF IT EMBODIED IN TWO AMAZINGLY POWERFUL WOMEN."

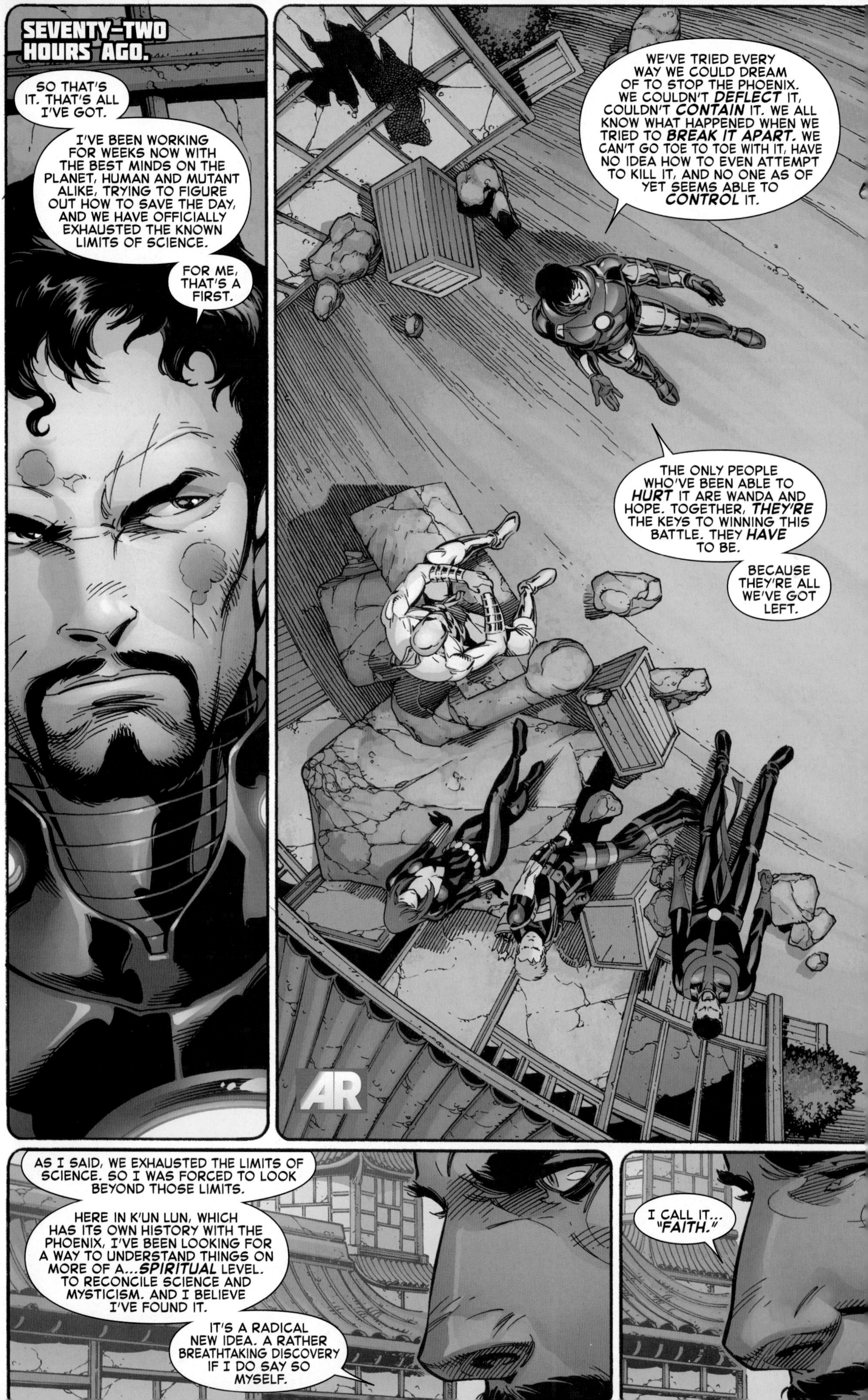
SEVENTY-TWO HOURS AGO.
SO THAT'S IT. THAT'S ALL I'VE GOT.
I'VE BEEN WORKING FOR WEEKS NOW WITH THE BEST MINDS ON THE PLANET, HUMAN AND MUTANT ALIKE, TRYING TO FIGURE OUT HOW TO SAVE THE DAY, AND WE HAVE OFFICIALLY EXHAUSTED THE KNOWN LIMITS OF SCIENCE.
FOR ME, THAT'S A FIRST.
WE'VE TRIED EVERY WAY WE COULD DREAM OF TO STOP THE PHOENIX. WE COULDN'T DEFLECT IT, COULDN'T CONTAIN IT. WE ALL KNOW WHAT HAPPENED WHEN WE TRIED TO BREAK IT APART. WE CAN'T GO TOE TO TOE WITH IT, HAVE NO IDEA HOW TO EVEN ATTEMPT TO KILL IT, AND NO ONE AS OF YET SEEMS ABLE TO CONTROL IT.
THE ONLY PEOPLE WHO'VE BEEN ABLE TO HURT IT ARE WANDA AND HOPE. TOGETHER, THEY'RE THE KEYS TO WINNING THIS BATTLE. THEY HAVE TO BE.
BECAUSE THEY'RE ALL WE'VE GOT LEFT.
AR
AS I SAID, WE EXHAUSTED THE LIMITS OF SCIENCE. SO I WAS FORCED TO LOOK BEYOND THOSE LIMITS.
HERE IN K'UN LUN, WHICH HAS ITS OWN HISTORY WITH THE PHOENIX, I'VE BEEN LOOKING FOR A WAY TO UNDERSTAND THINGS ON MORE OF A...SPIRITUAL LEVEL. TO RECONCILE SCIENCE AND MYSTICISM. AND I BELIEVE I'VE FOUND IT.
IT'S A RADICAL NEW IDEA. A RATHER BREATHTAKING DISCOVERY IF I DO SAY SO MYSELF.
I CALL IT... "FAITH."

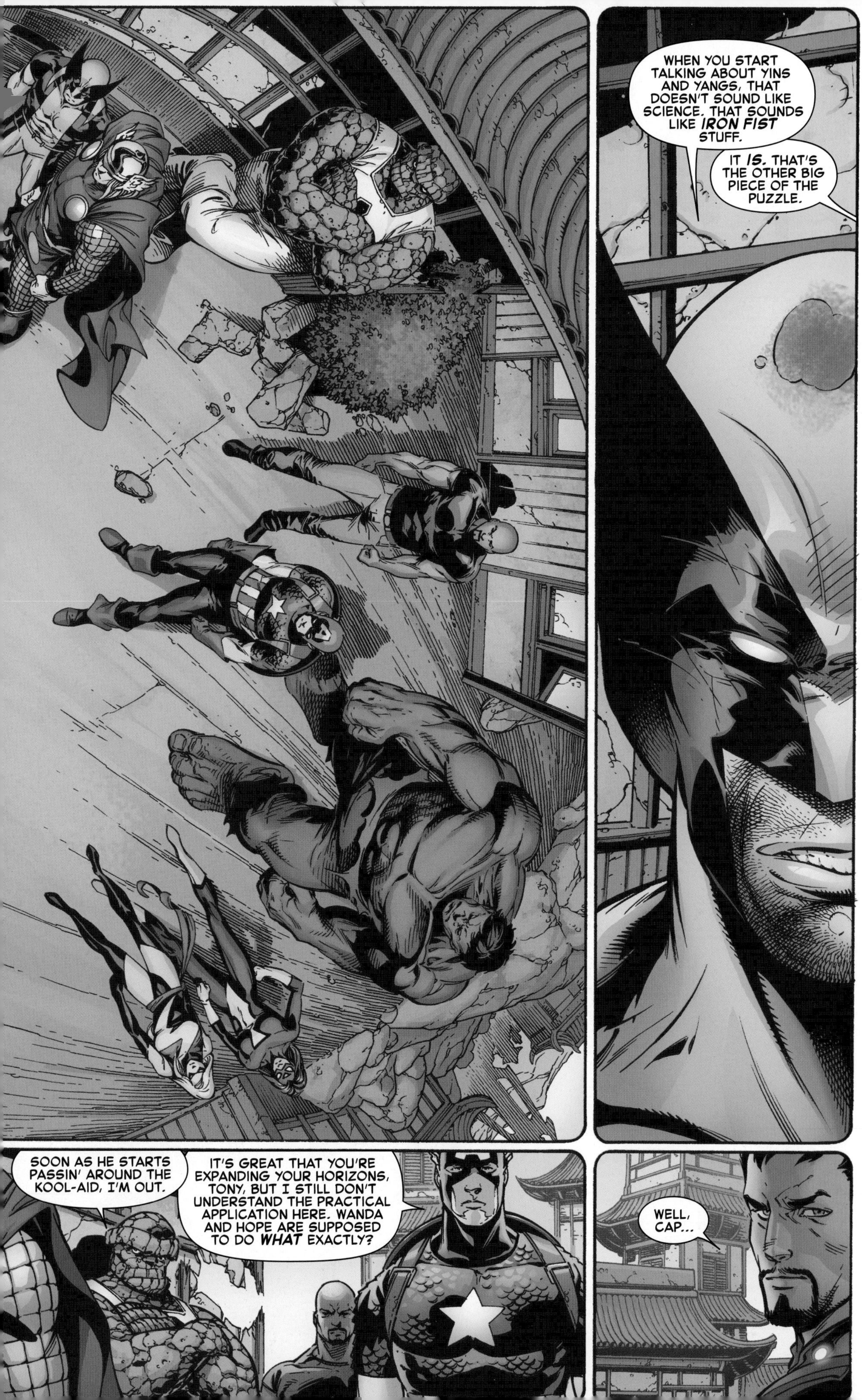
WHEN YOU START TALKING ABOUT YINS AND YANGS, THAT DOESN'T SOUND LIKE SCIENCE. THAT SOUNDS LIKE IRON FIST STUFF.
IT IS. THAT'S THE OTHER BIG PIECE OF THE PUZZLE.
SOON AS HE STARTS PASSIN' AROUND THE KOOL-AID, I'M OUT.
IT'S GREAT THAT YOU'RE EXPANDING YOUR HORIZONS, TONY, BUT I STILL DON'T UNDERSTAND THE PRACTICAL APPLICATION HERE. WANDA AND HOPE ARE SUPPOSED TO DO WHAT EXACTLY?
WELL, CAP...

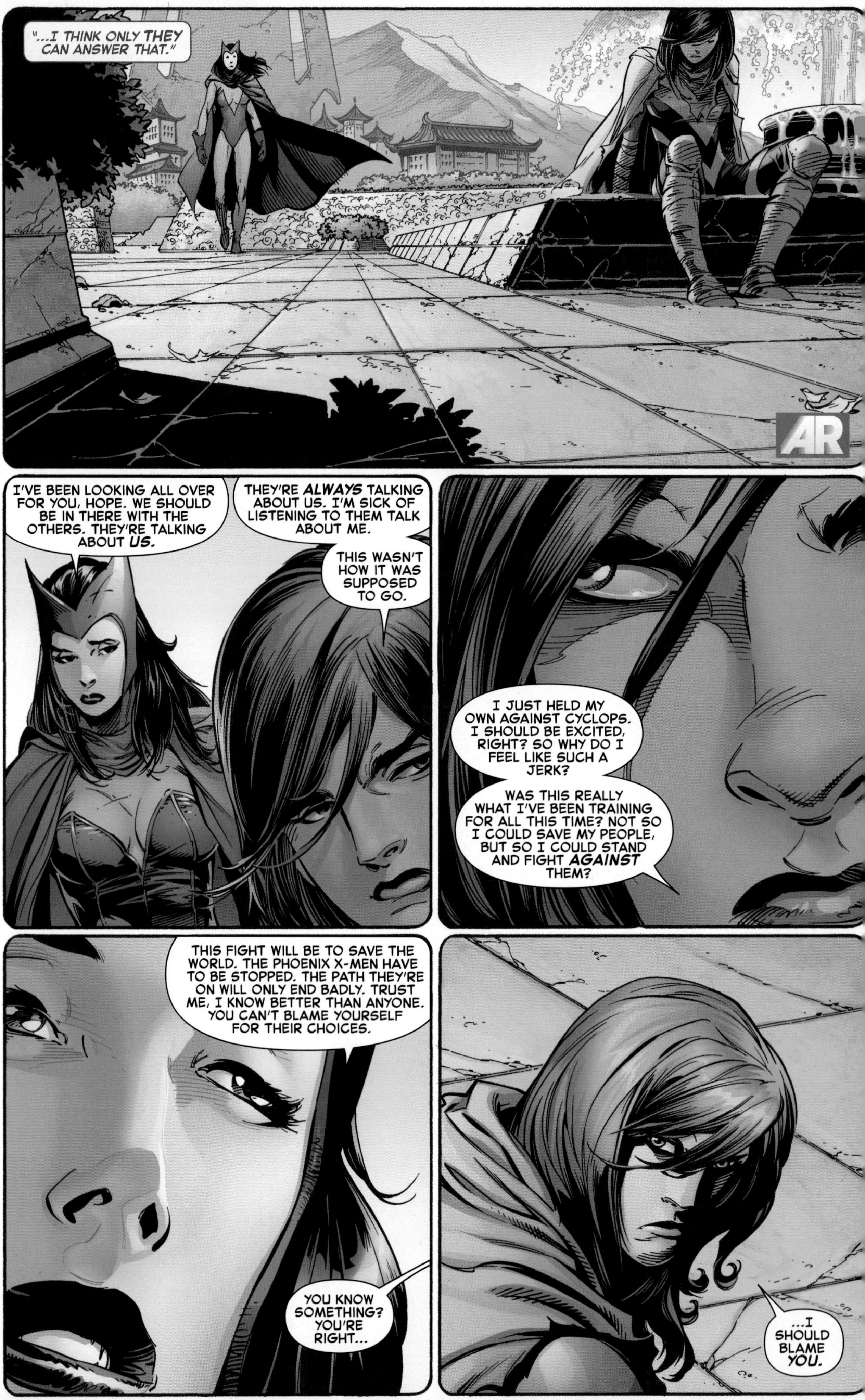
"...I THINK ONLY THEY CAN ANSWER THAT."
AR
I'VE BEEN LOOKING ALL OVER FOR YOU, HOPE. WE SHOULD BE IN THERE WITH THE OTHERS. THEY'RE TALKING ABOUT US.
THEY'RE ALWAYS TALKING ABOUT US. I'M SICK OF LISTENING TO THEM TALK ABOUT ME.
THIS WASN'T HOW IT WAS SUPPOSED TO GO.
I JUST HELD MY OWN AGAINST CYCLOPS. I SHOULD BE EXCITED, RIGHT? SO WHY DO I FEEL LIKE SUCH A JERK?
WAS THIS REALLY WHAT I'VE BEEN TRAINING FOR ALL THIS TIME? NOT SO I COULD SAVE MY PEOPLE, BUT SO I COULD STAND AND FIGHT AGAINST THEM?
THIS FIGHT WILL BE TO SAVE THE WORLD. THE PHOENIX X-MEN HAVE TO BE STOPPED. THE PATH THEY'RE ON WILL ONLY END BADLY. TRUST ME, I KNOW BETTER THAN ANYONE. YOU CAN'T BLAME YOURSELF FOR THEIR CHOICES.
YOU KNOW SOMETHING? YOU'RE RIGHT...
...I SHOULD BLAME YOU.

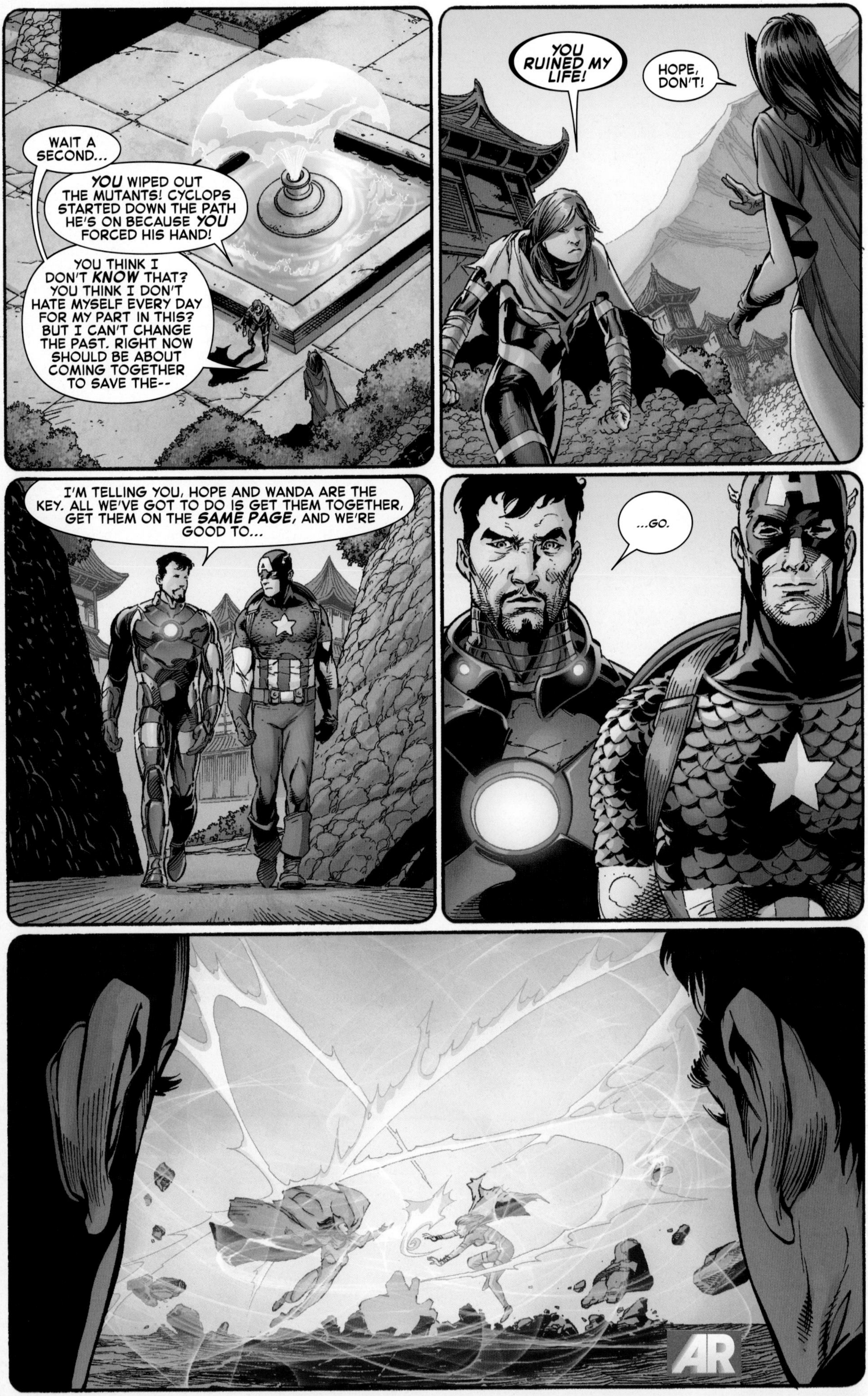
WAIT A SECOND...
YOU WIPED OUT THE MUTANTS! CYCLOPS STARTED DOWN THE PATH HE'S ON BECAUSE YOU FORCED HIS HAND!
YOU THINK I DON'T KNOW THAT? YOU THINK I DON'T HATE MYSELF EVERY DAY FOR MY PART IN THIS? BUT I CAN'T CHANGE THE PAST. RIGHT NOW SHOULD BE ABOUT COMING TOGETHER TO SAVE THE--
YOU RUINED MY LIFE!
HOPE, DON'T!
I'M TELLING YOU, HOPE AND WANDA ARE THE KEY. ALL WE'VE GOT TO DO IS GET THEM TOGETHER, GET THEM ON THE SAME PAGE, AND WE'RE GOOD TO...
...GO.
AR

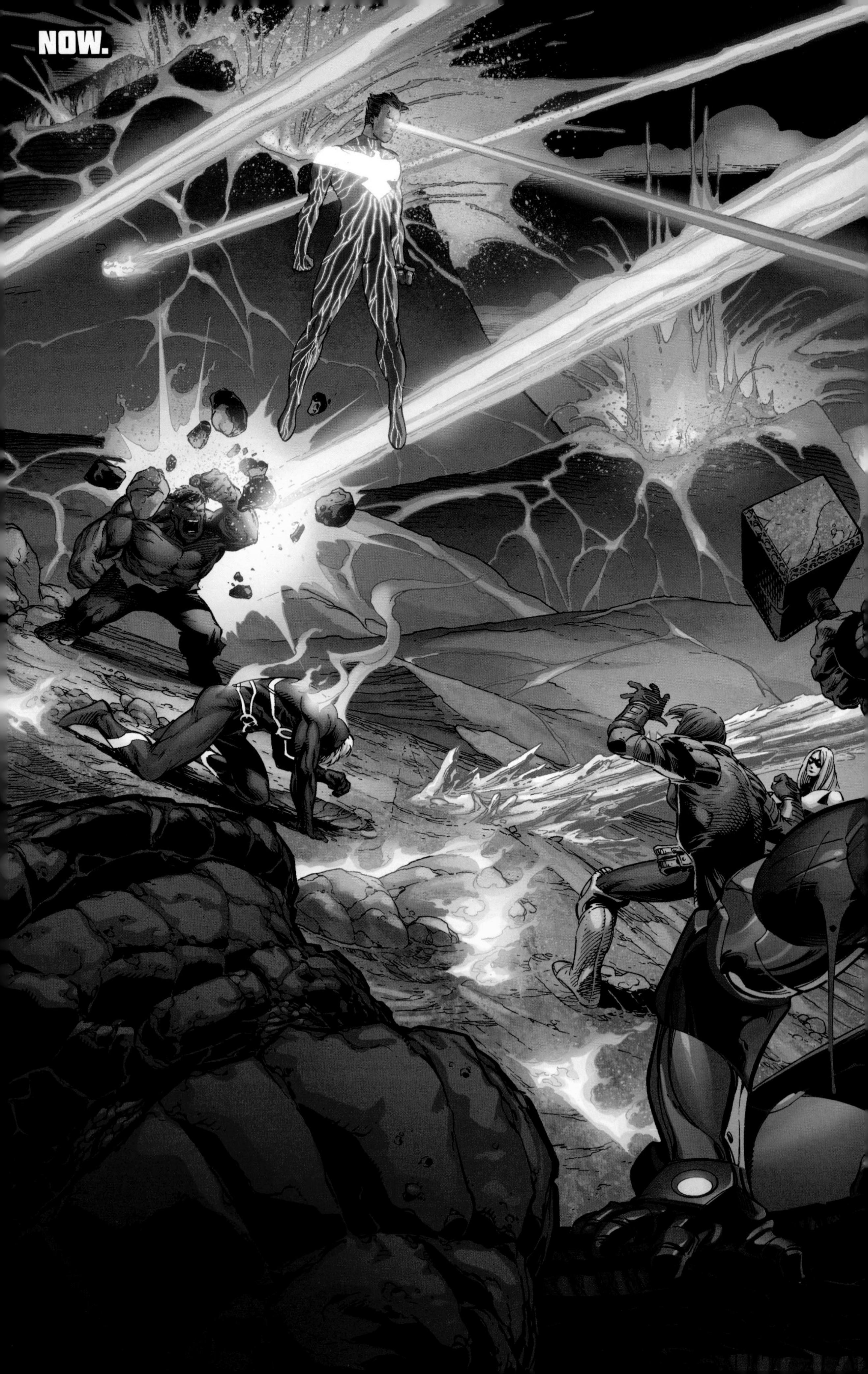
NOW.

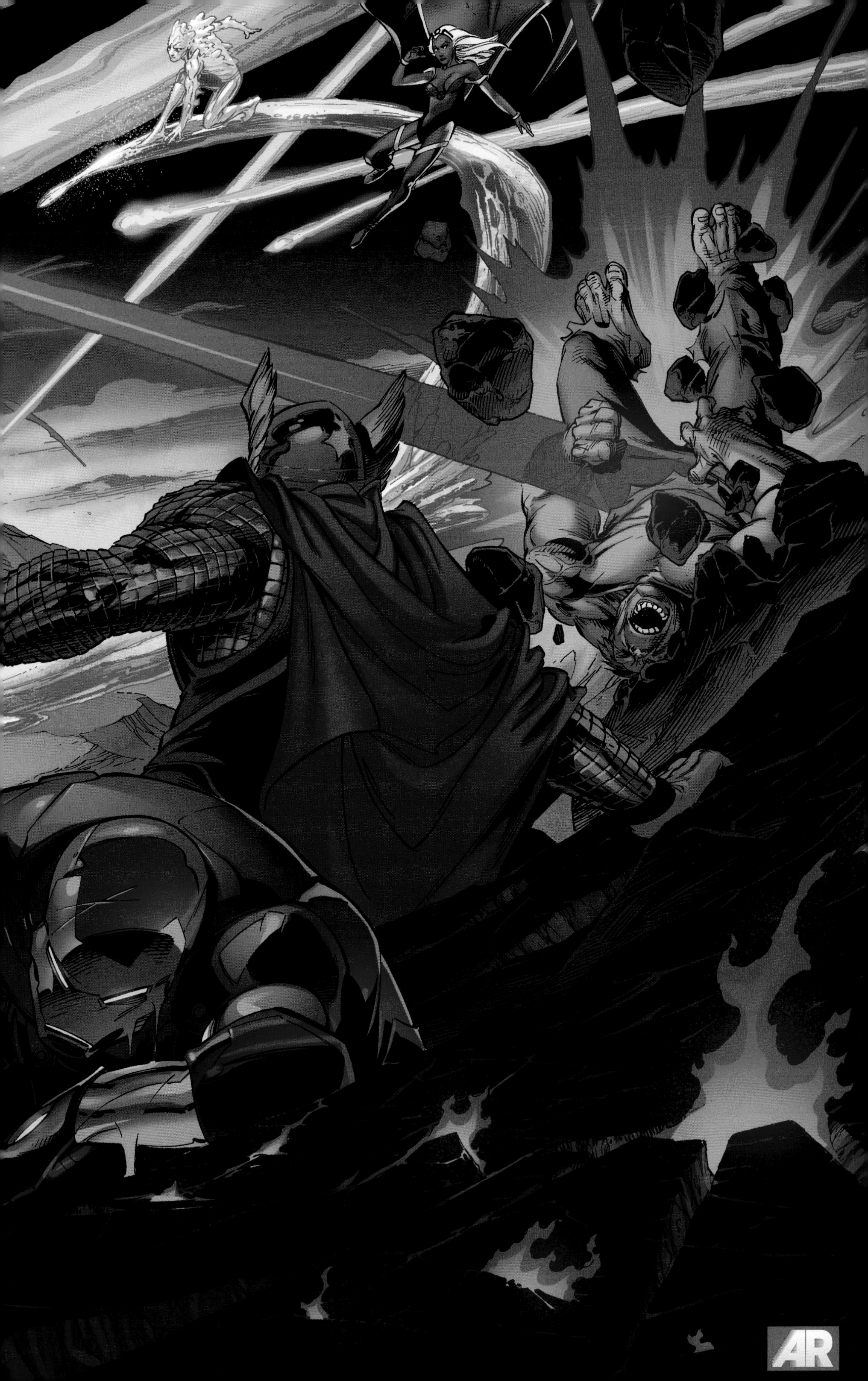

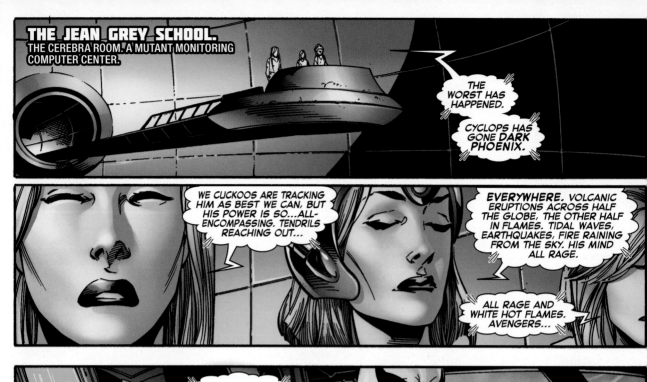

THE JEAN GREY SCHOOL.
THE CEREBRA ROOM. A MUTANT MONITORING COMPUTER CENTER.

THE WORST HAS HAPPENED.

CYCLOPS HAS GONE *DARK PHOENIX.*

WE CUCKOOS ARE TRACKING HIM AS BEST WE CAN, BUT HIS POWER IS SO...ALL-ENCOMPASSING. TENDRILS REACHING OUT...

EVERYWHERE. VOLCANIC ERUPTIONS ACROSS HALF THE GLOBE, THE OTHER HALF IN FLAMES. TIDAL WAVES, EARTHQUAKES, FIRE RAINING FROM THE SKY. HIS MIND ALL RAGE.

ALL RAGE AND WHITE HOT FLAMES. AVENGERS...

...HE'S TEARING THE ENTIRE *PLANET* APART.

WE'LL BE RIGHT ON TOP OF HIM IN A MATTER OF MINUTES. FOR WHATEVER GOOD THAT WILL DO US.

MY GOD. THE OCEAN IS *BURNING.*

KEEP YOUR HEAD IN THE GAME, ALL OF YOU.

THIS IS *CAPTAIN AMERICA* TO ALL TEAMS! I DON'T HAVE TIME FOR ANY LAST MINUTE SPEECHES AND NEITHER DO YOU! YOU ALL KNOW THE DRILL! IT'S THE END OF THE WORLD! *THIS* IS WHAT WE DO!

THE EARTH DOESN'T DIE ON OUR WATCH!

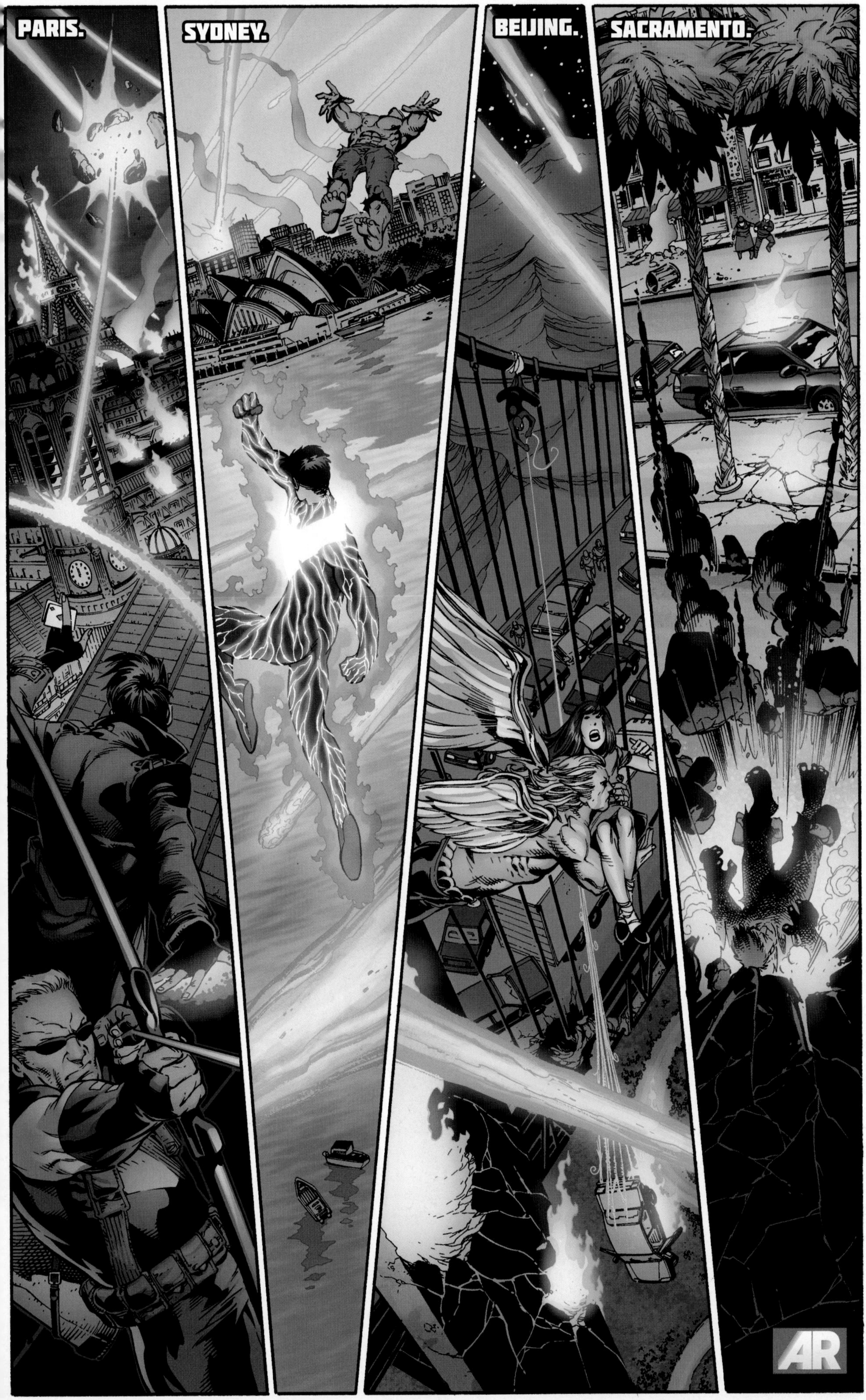
PARIS.
SYDNEY.
BEIJING.
SACRAMENTO.

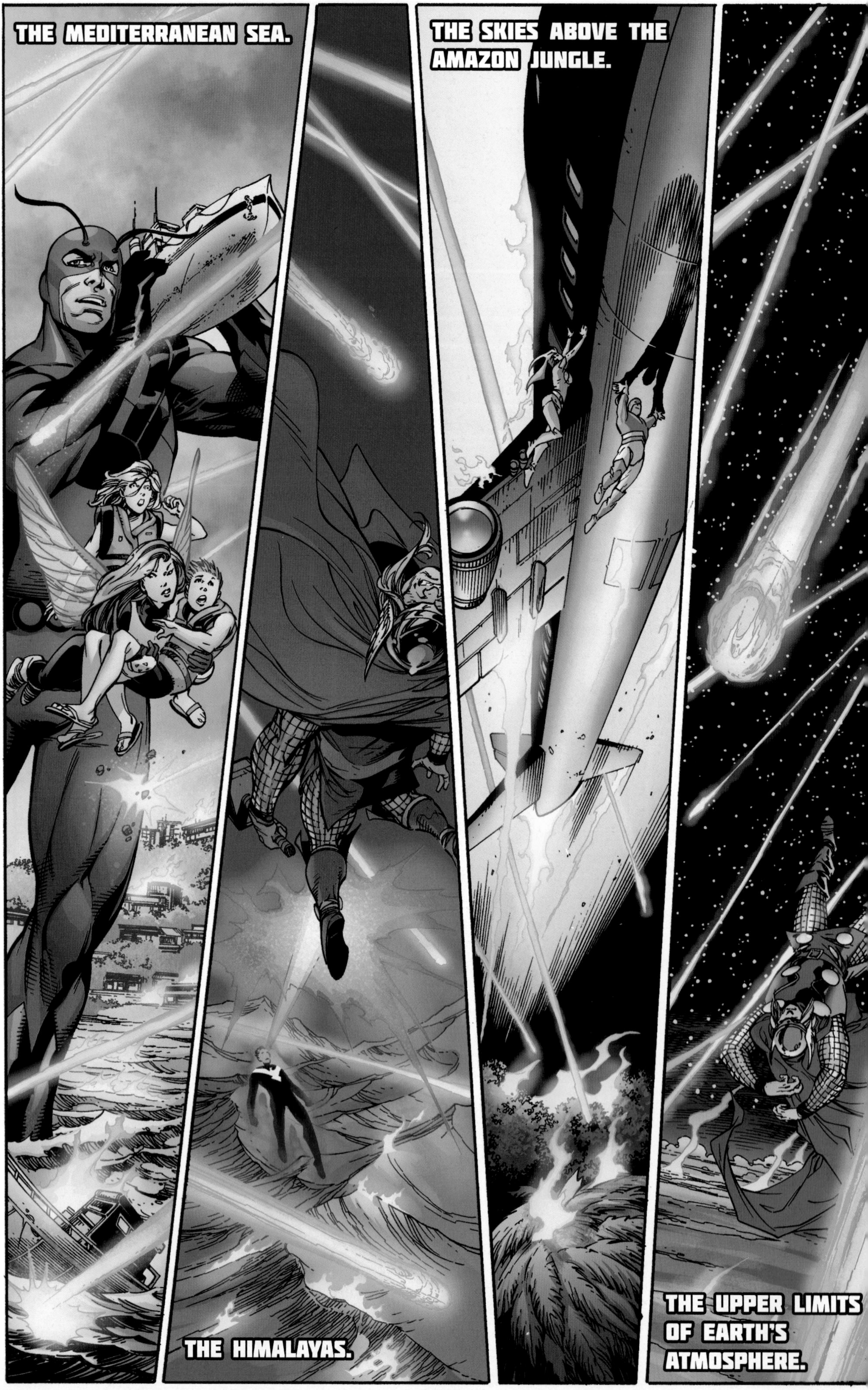
THE MEDITERRANEAN SEA.
THE HIMALAYAS.
THE SKIES ABOVE THE AMAZON JUNGLE.
THE UPPER LIMITS OF EARTH'S ATMOSPHERE.

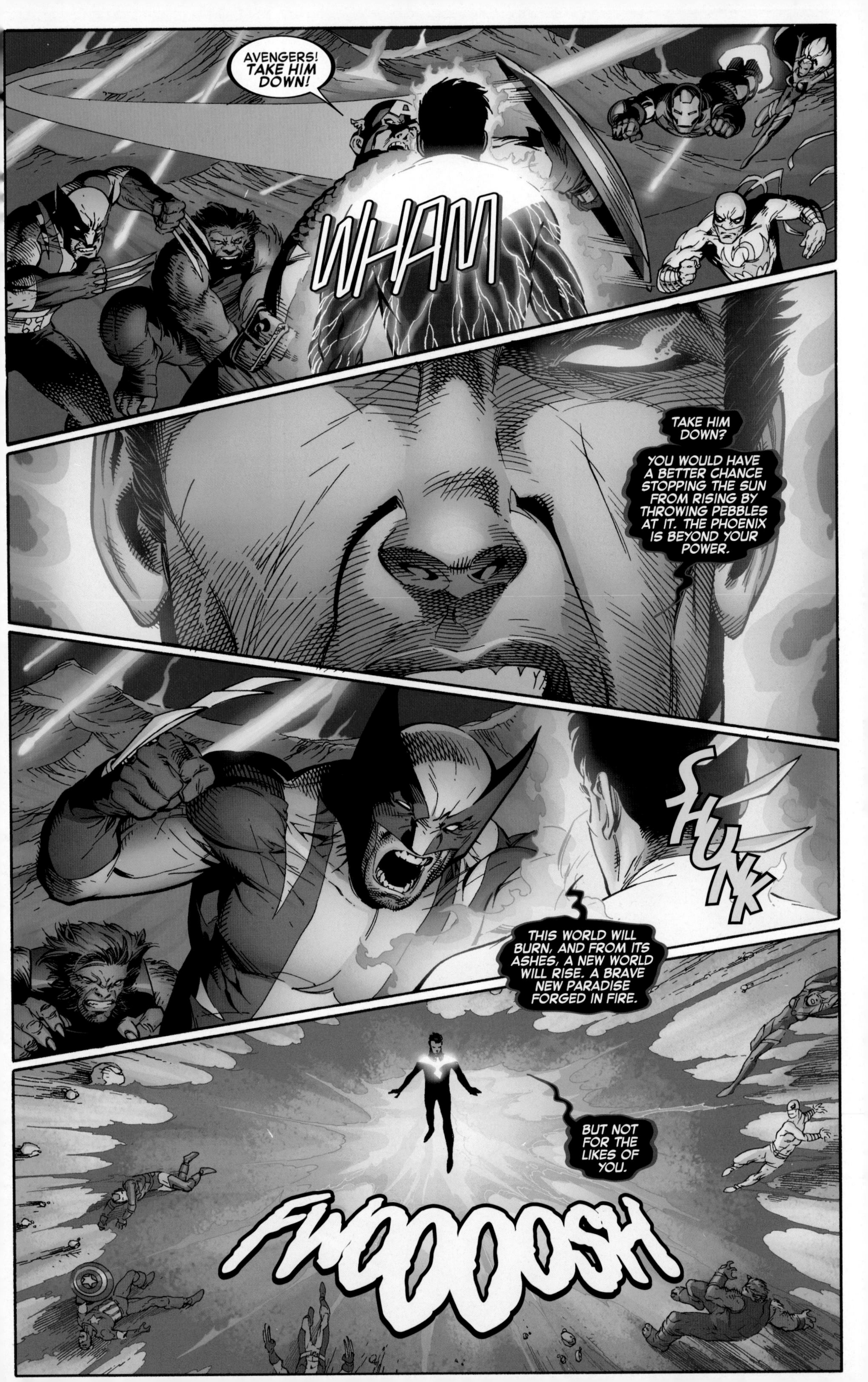
AVENGERS! TAKE HIM DOWN!
WHAM
TAKE HIM DOWN?
YOU WOULD HAVE A BETTER CHANCE STOPPING THE SUN FROM RISING BY THROWING PEBBLES AT IT. THE PHOENIX IS BEYOND YOUR POWER.
SHUNK
THIS WORLD WILL BURN, AND FROM ITS ASHES, A NEW WORLD WILL RISE. A BRAVE NEW PARADISE FORGED IN FIRE.
BUT NOT FOR THE LIKES OF YOU.
FWOOOOSH

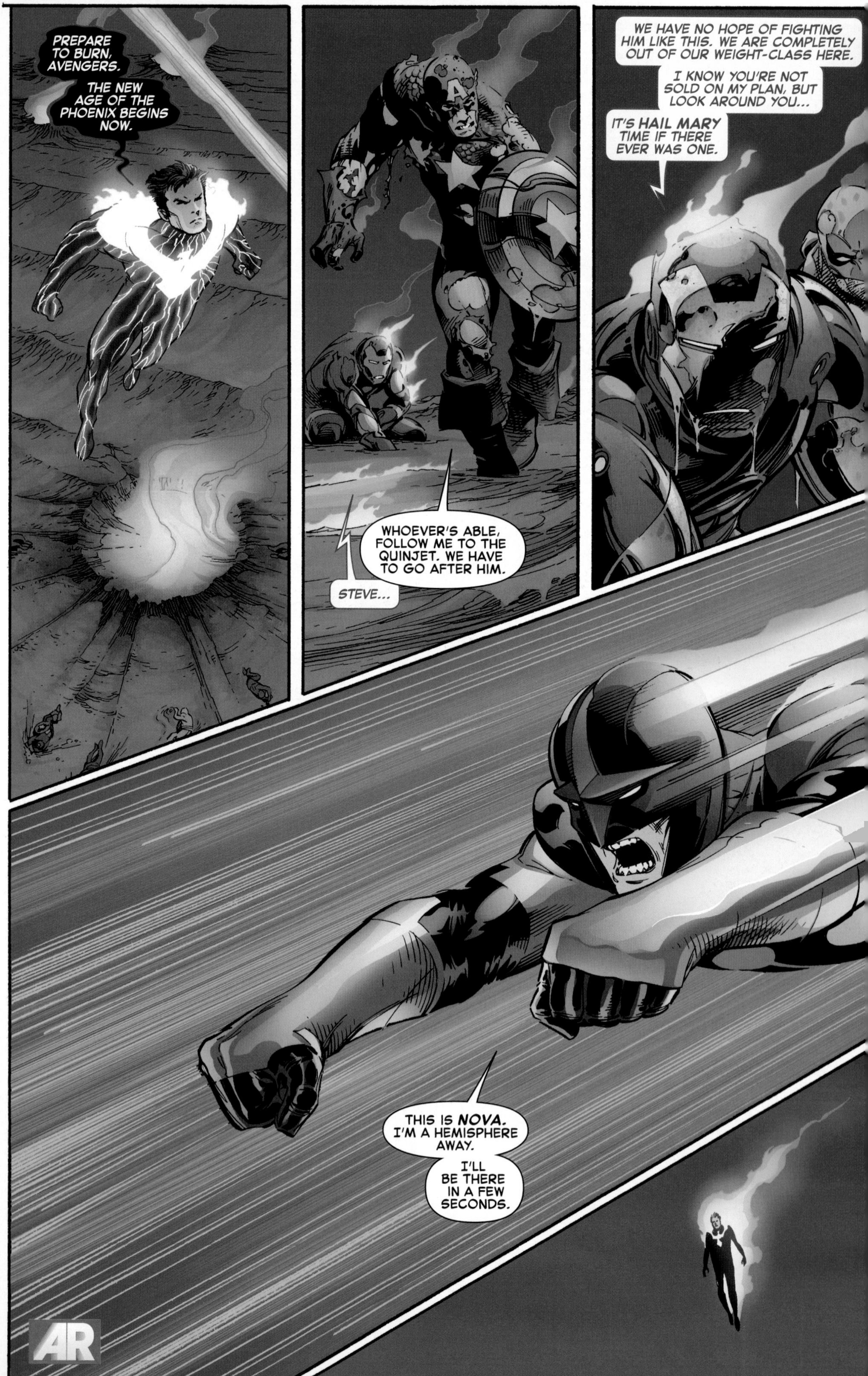
PREPARE TO BURN, AVENGERS.
THE NEW AGE OF THE PHOENIX BEGINS NOW.
WHOEVER'S ABLE, FOLLOW ME TO THE QUINJET. WE HAVE TO GO AFTER HIM.
STEVE...
WE HAVE NO HOPE OF FIGHTING HIM LIKE THIS. WE ARE COMPLETELY OUT OF OUR WEIGHT-CLASS HERE.
I KNOW YOU'RE NOT SOLD ON MY PLAN, BUT LOOK AROUND YOU...
IT'S HAIL MARY TIME IF THERE EVER WAS ONE.
THIS IS NOVA. I'M A HEMISPHERE AWAY.
I'LL BE THERE IN A FEW SECONDS.

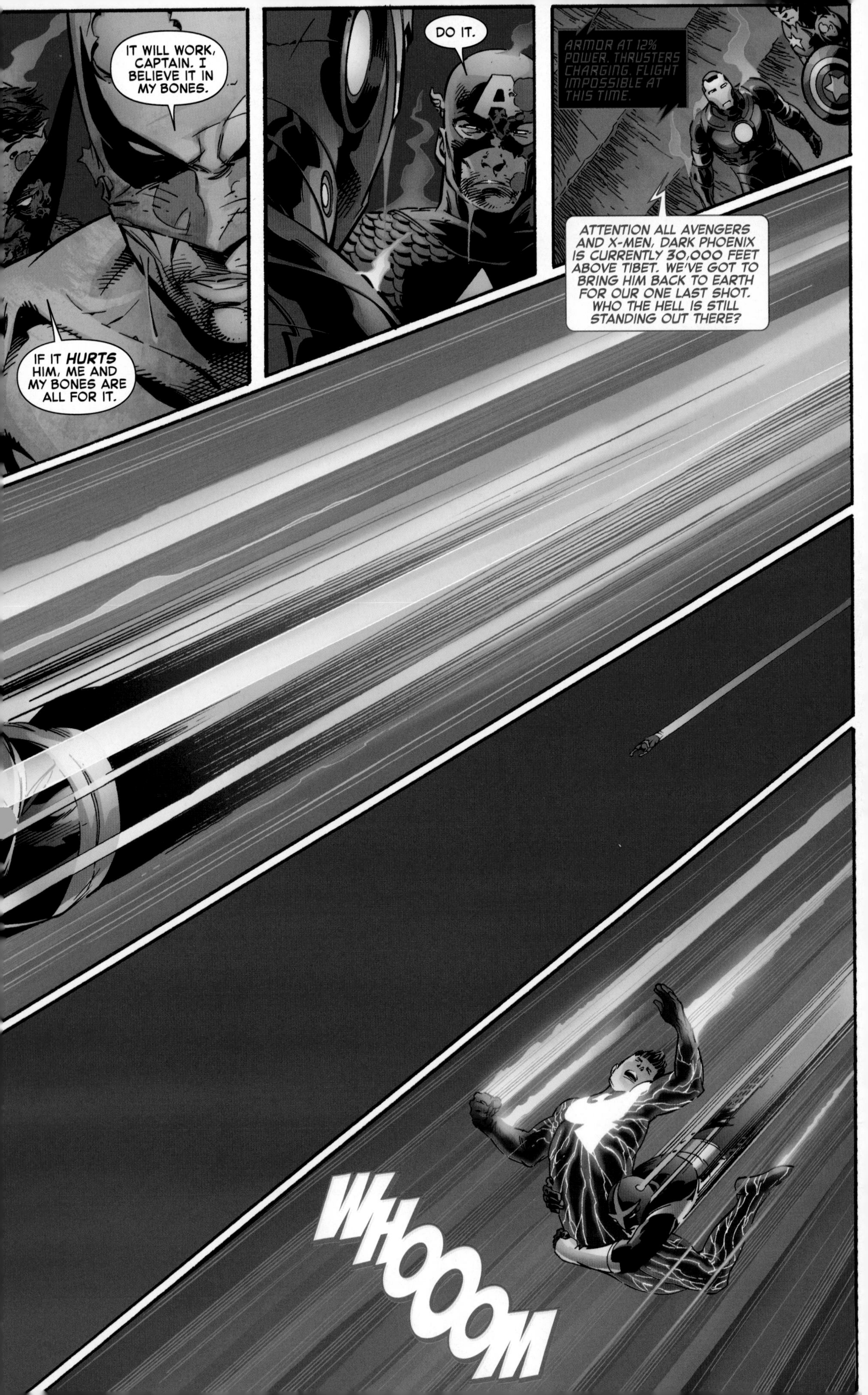
IT WILL WORK, CAPTAIN. I BELIEVE IT IN MY BONES.
IF IT HURTS HIM, ME AND MY BONES ARE ALL FOR IT.
DO IT.
ARMOR AT 12% POWER. THRUSTERS CHARGING. FLIGHT IMPOSSIBLE AT THIS TIME.
ATTENTION ALL AVENGERS AND X-MEN, DARK PHOENIX IS CURRENTLY 30,000 FEET ABOVE TIBET. WE'VE GOT TO BRING HIM BACK TO EARTH FOR OUR ONE LAST SHOT. WHO THE HELL IS STILL STANDING OUT THERE?
WHOOOOM

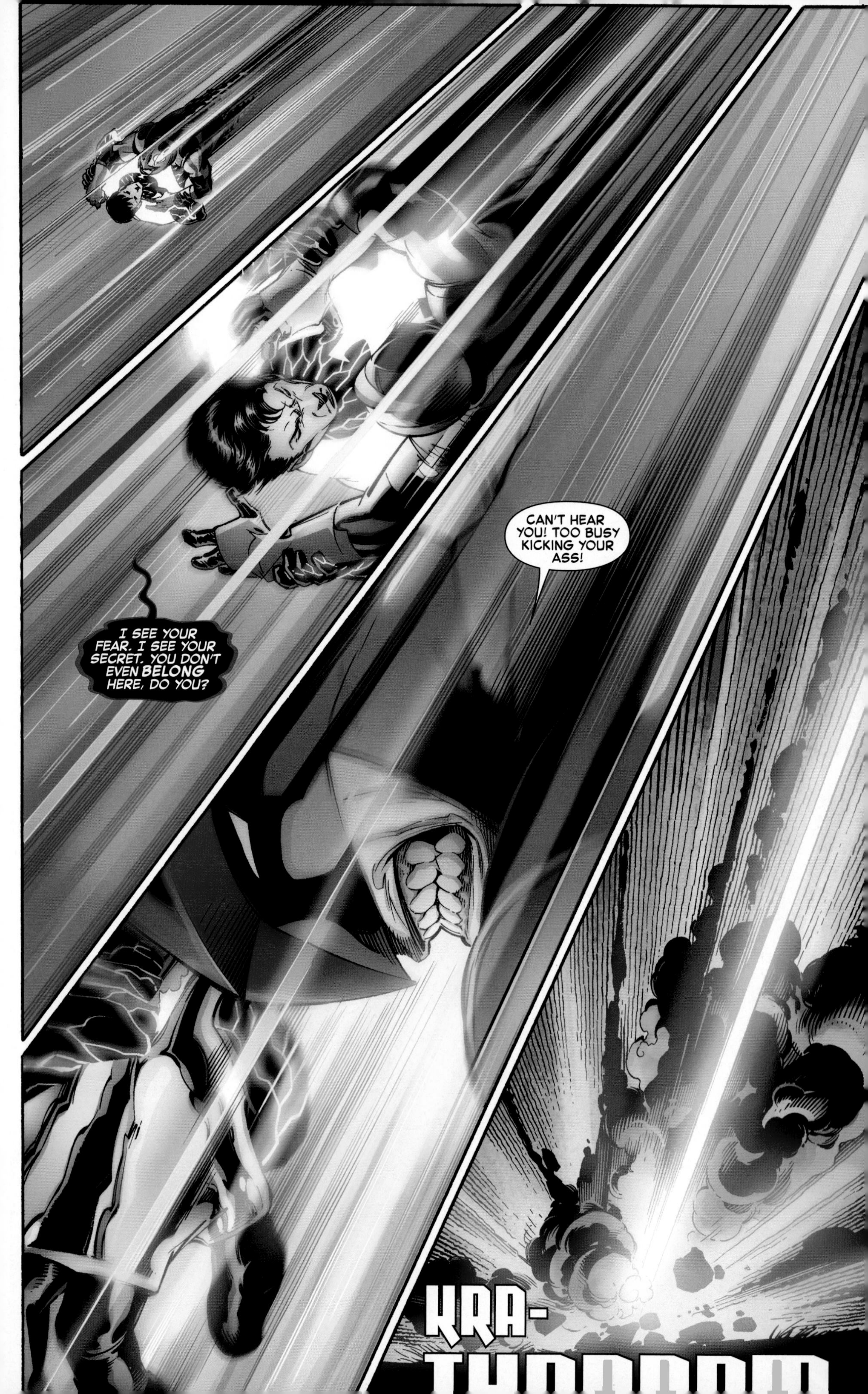
I SEE YOUR FEAR. I SEE YOUR SECRET. YOU DON'T EVEN BELONG HERE, DO YOU?
CAN'T HEAR YOU! TOO BUSY KICKING YOUR ASS!
KRA-

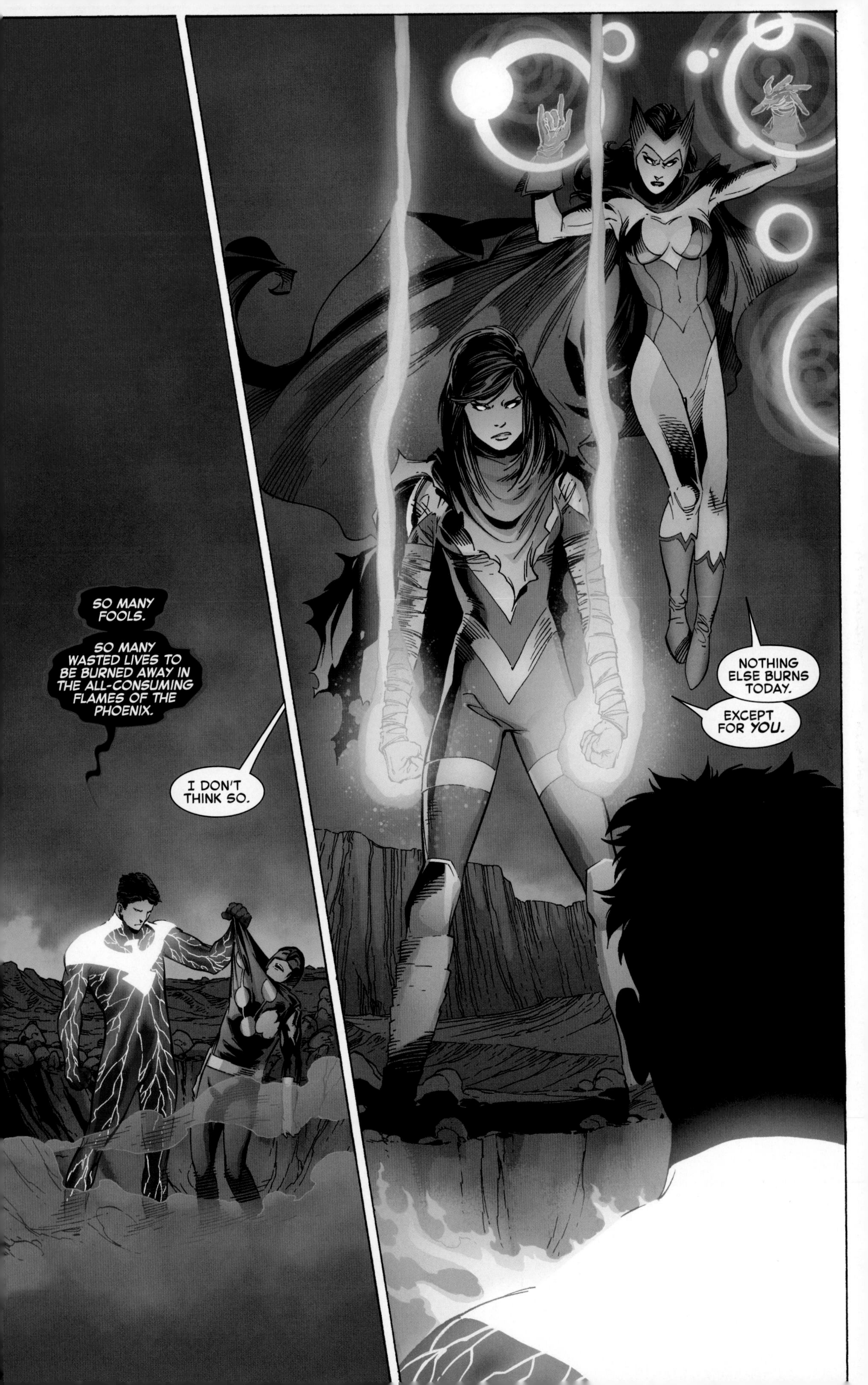
SO MANY FOOLS.
SO MANY WASTED LIVES TO BE BURNED AWAY IN THE ALL-CONSUMING FLAMES OF THE PHOENIX.
I DON'T THINK SO.
NOTHING ELSE BURNS TODAY.
EXCEPT FOR YOU.

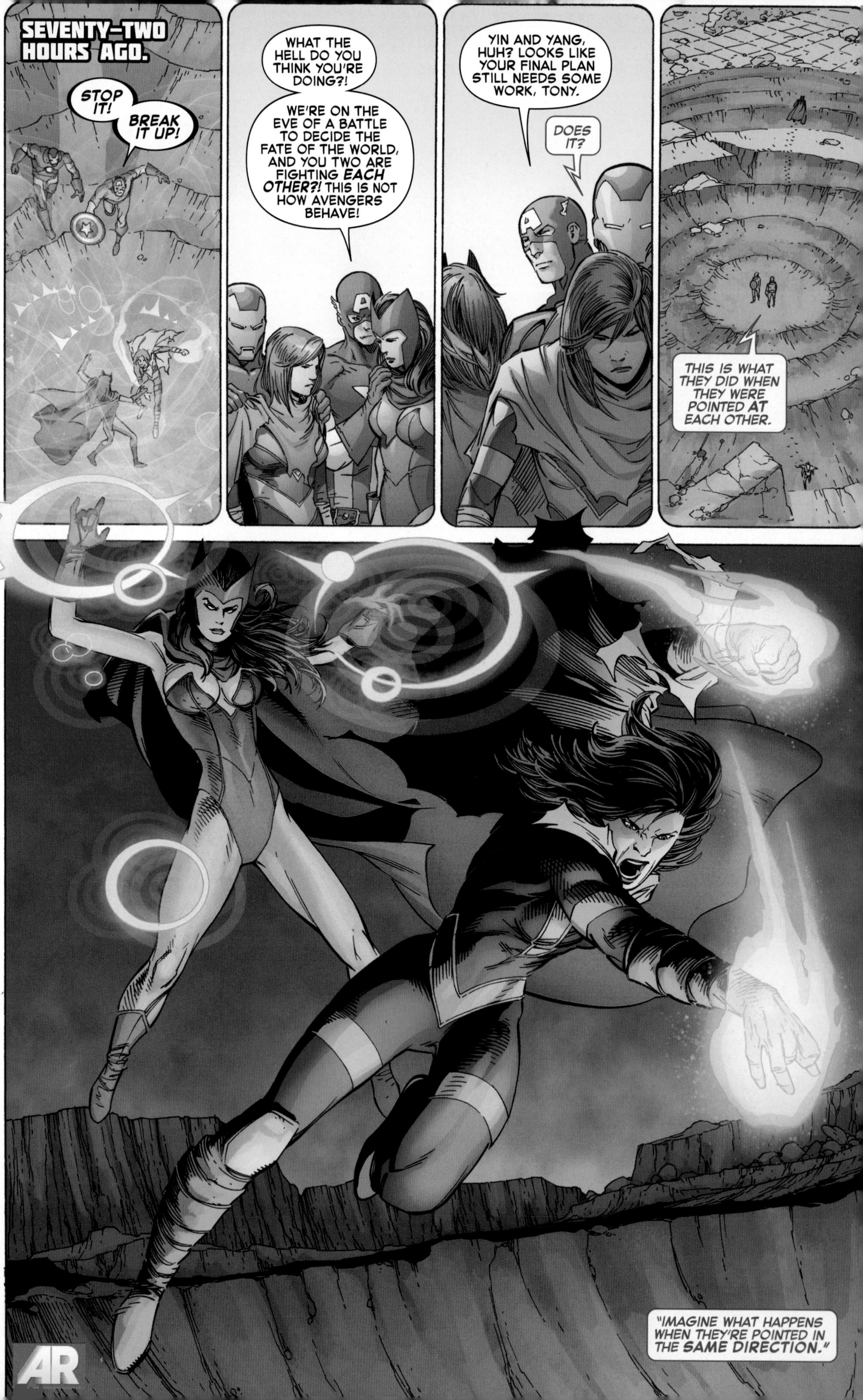
SEVENTY-TWO HOURS AGO.
STOP IT!
BREAK IT UP!
WHAT THE HELL DO YOU THINK YOU'RE DOING?!
WE'RE ON THE EVE OF A BATTLE TO DECIDE THE FATE OF THE WORLD, AND YOU TWO ARE FIGHTING EACH OTHER?! THIS IS NOT HOW AVENGERS BEHAVE!
YIN AND YANG, HUH? LOOKS LIKE YOUR FINAL PLAN STILL NEEDS SOME WORK, TONY.
DOES IT?
THIS IS WHAT THEY DID WHEN THEY WERE POINTED AT EACH OTHER.
"IMAGINE WHAT HAPPENS WHEN THEY'RE POINTED IN THE SAME DIRECTION."
AR

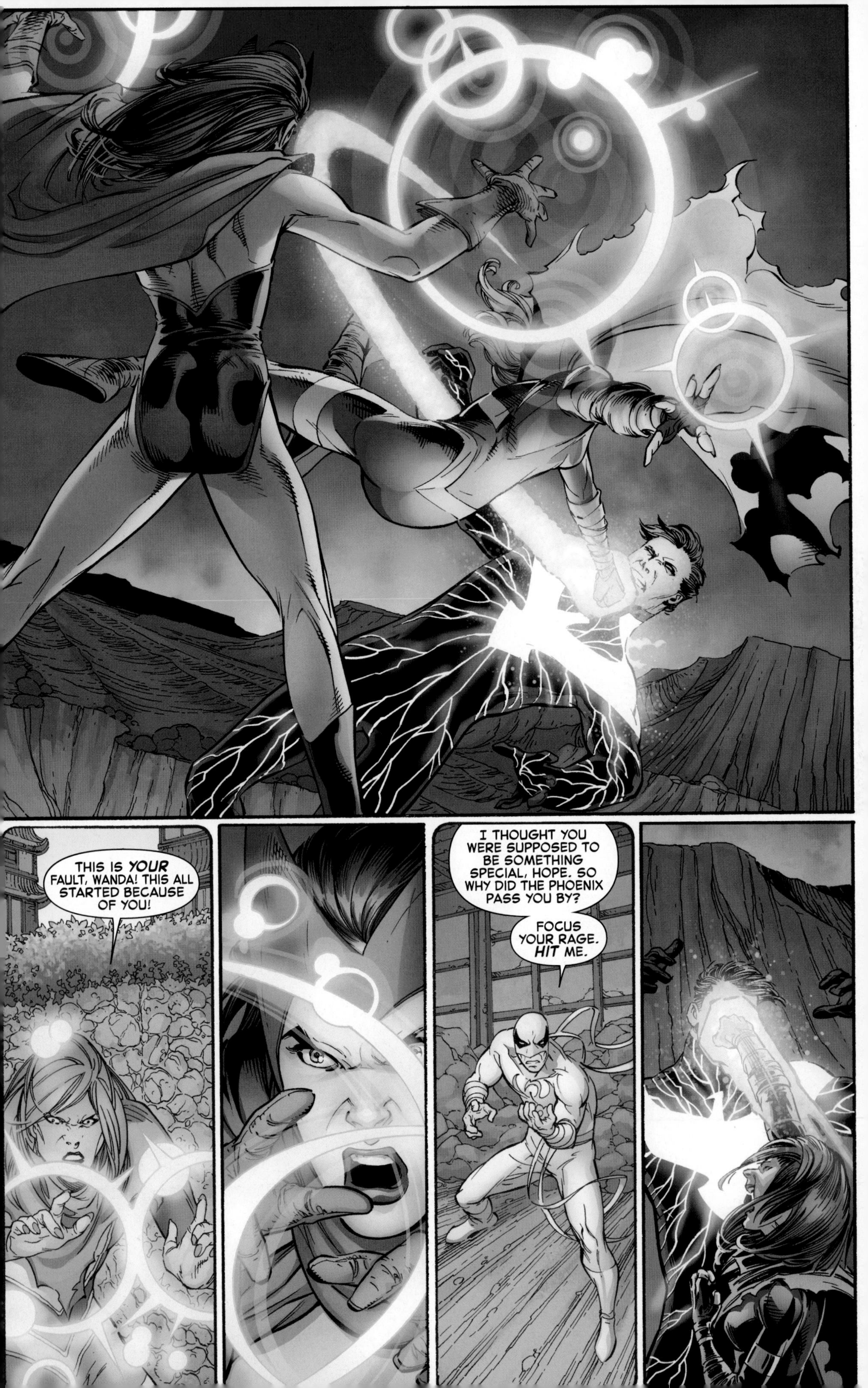
THIS IS *YOUR* FAULT, WANDA! THIS ALL STARTED BECAUSE OF YOU!
I THOUGHT YOU WERE SUPPOSED TO BE SOMETHING SPECIAL, HOPE. SO WHY DID THE PHOENIX PASS YOU BY?
FOCUS YOUR RAGE. *HIT* ME.

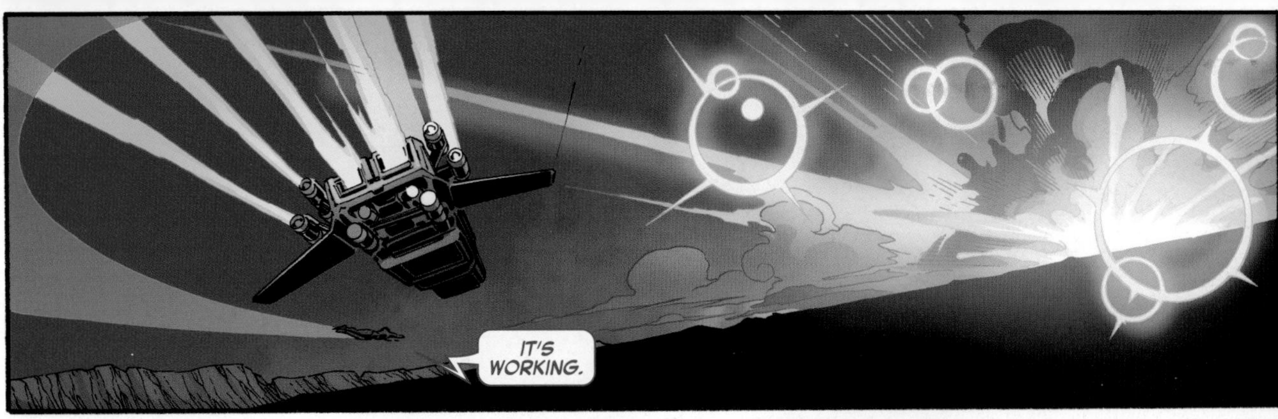
IT'S WORKING.
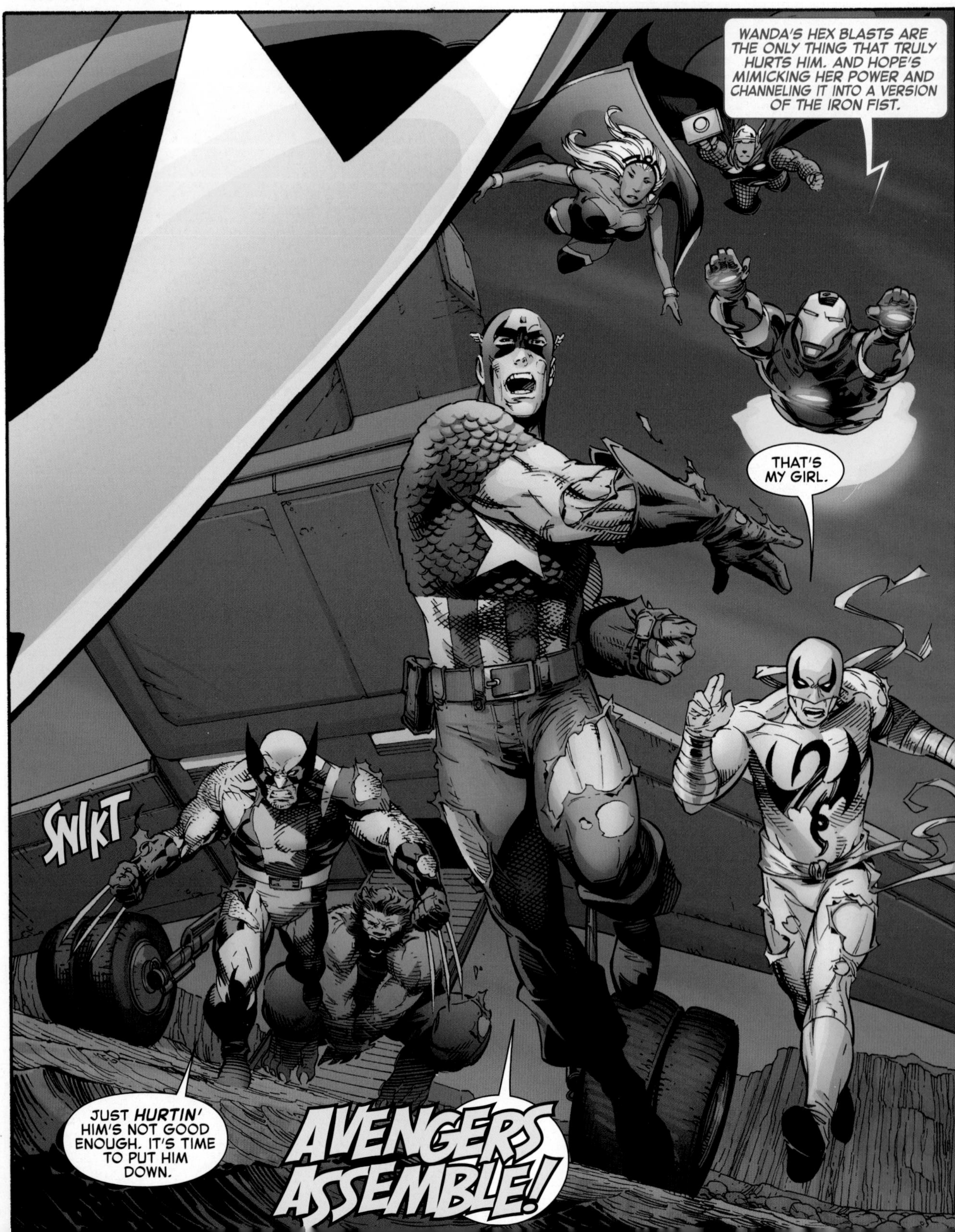
WANDA'S HEX BLASTS ARE THE ONLY THING THAT TRULY HURTS HIM. AND HOPE'S MIMICKING HER POWER AND CHANNELING IT INTO A VERSION OF THE IRON FIST.
THAT'S MY GIRL.
SNIKT
JUST HURTIN' HIM'S NOT GOOD ENOUGH. IT'S TIME TO PUT HIM DOWN.
AVENGERS ASSEMBLE!

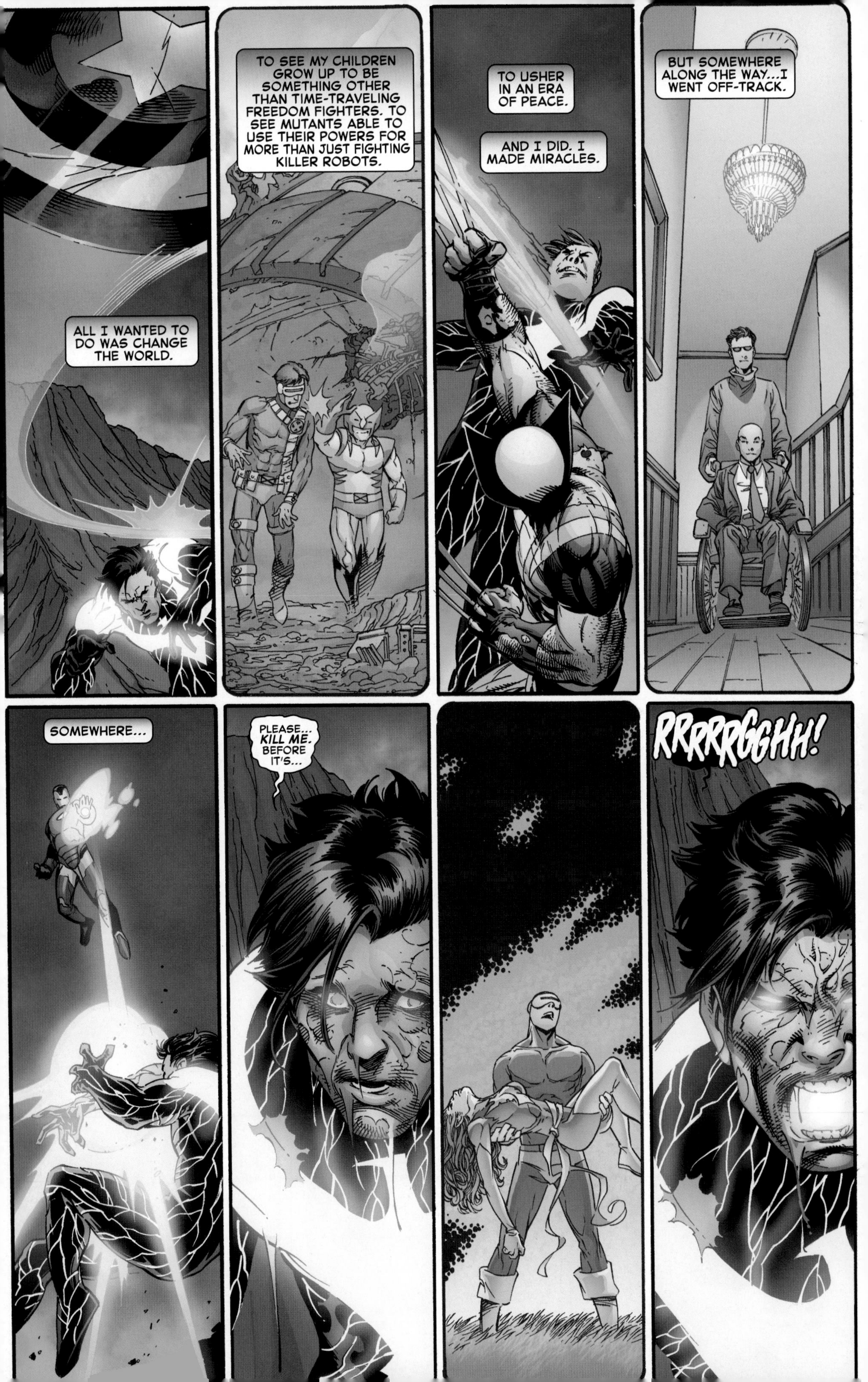

ALL I WANTED TO DO WAS CHANGE THE WORLD.
TO SEE MY CHILDREN GROW UP TO BE SOMETHING OTHER THAN TIME-TRAVELING FREEDOM FIGHTERS. TO SEE MUTANTS ABLE TO USE THEIR POWERS FOR MORE THAN JUST FIGHTING KILLER ROBOTS.
TO USHER IN AN ERA OF PEACE.
AND I DID. I MADE MIRACLES.
BUT SOMEWHERE ALONG THE WAY...I WENT OFF-TRACK.
SOMEWHERE...
PLEASE... KILL ME. BEFORE IT'S...
RRRRRGGHH!

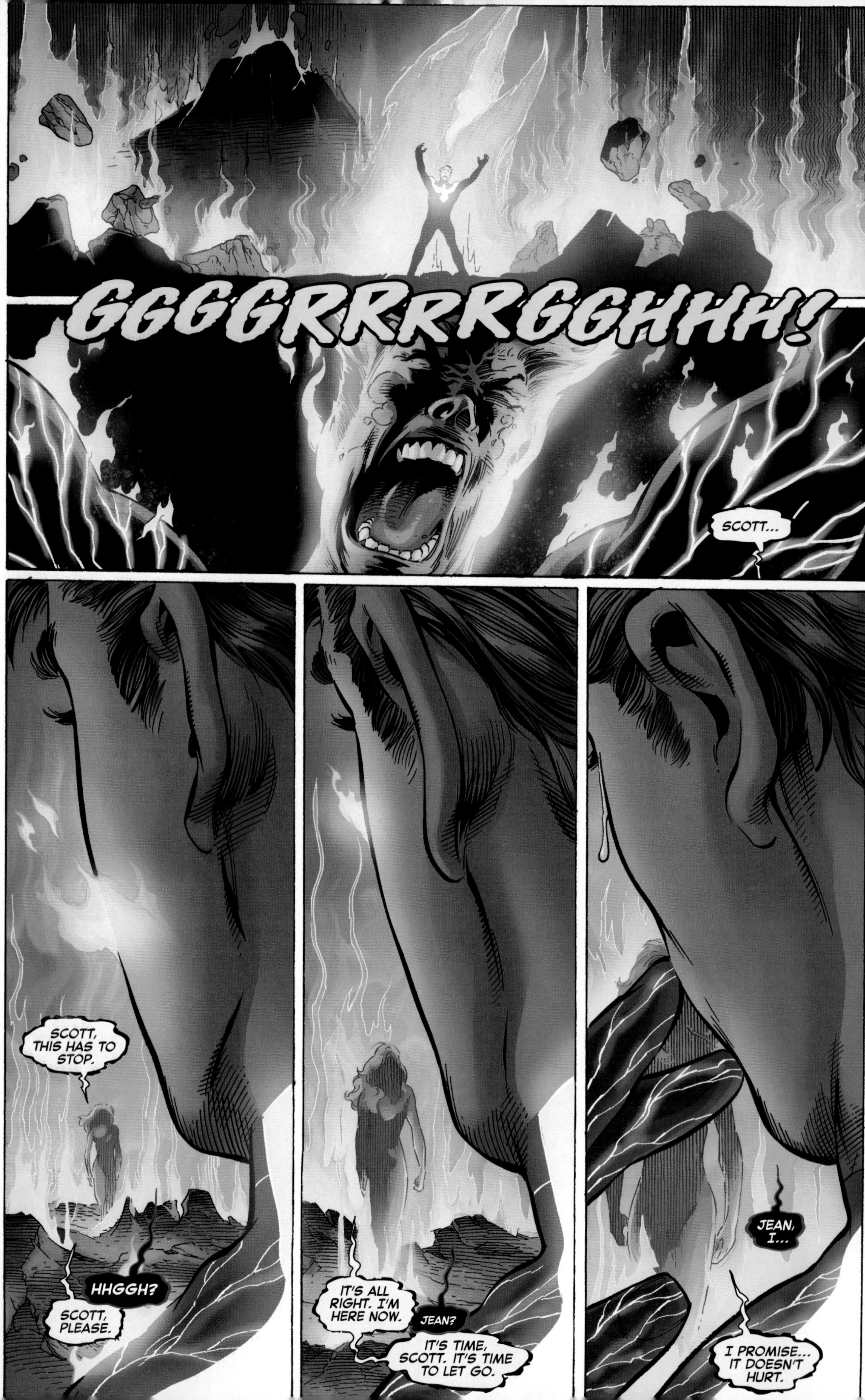
GGGGRRRRRGGHHH!
SCOTT...
SCOTT, THIS HAS TO STOP.
HHGGH?
SCOTT, PLEASE.
IT'S ALL RIGHT. I'M HERE NOW.
JEAN?
IT'S TIME, SCOTT. IT'S TIME TO LET GO.
JEAN, I...
I PROMISE... IT DOESN'T HURT.

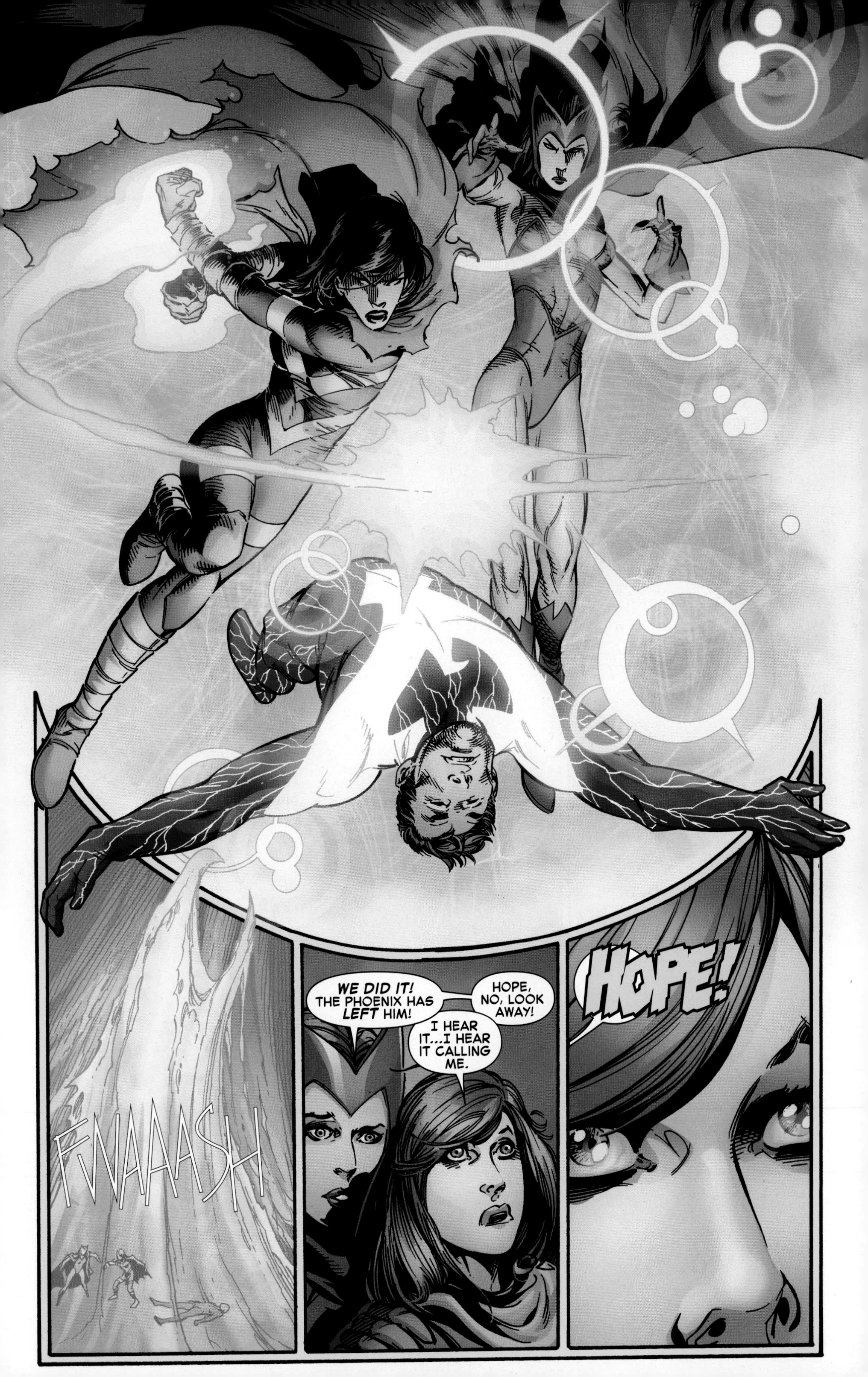
FWAAASH
WE DID IT! THE PHOENIX HAS LEFT HIM!
HOPE, NO, LOOK AWAY!
I HEAR IT...I HEAR IT CALLING ME.
HOPE!

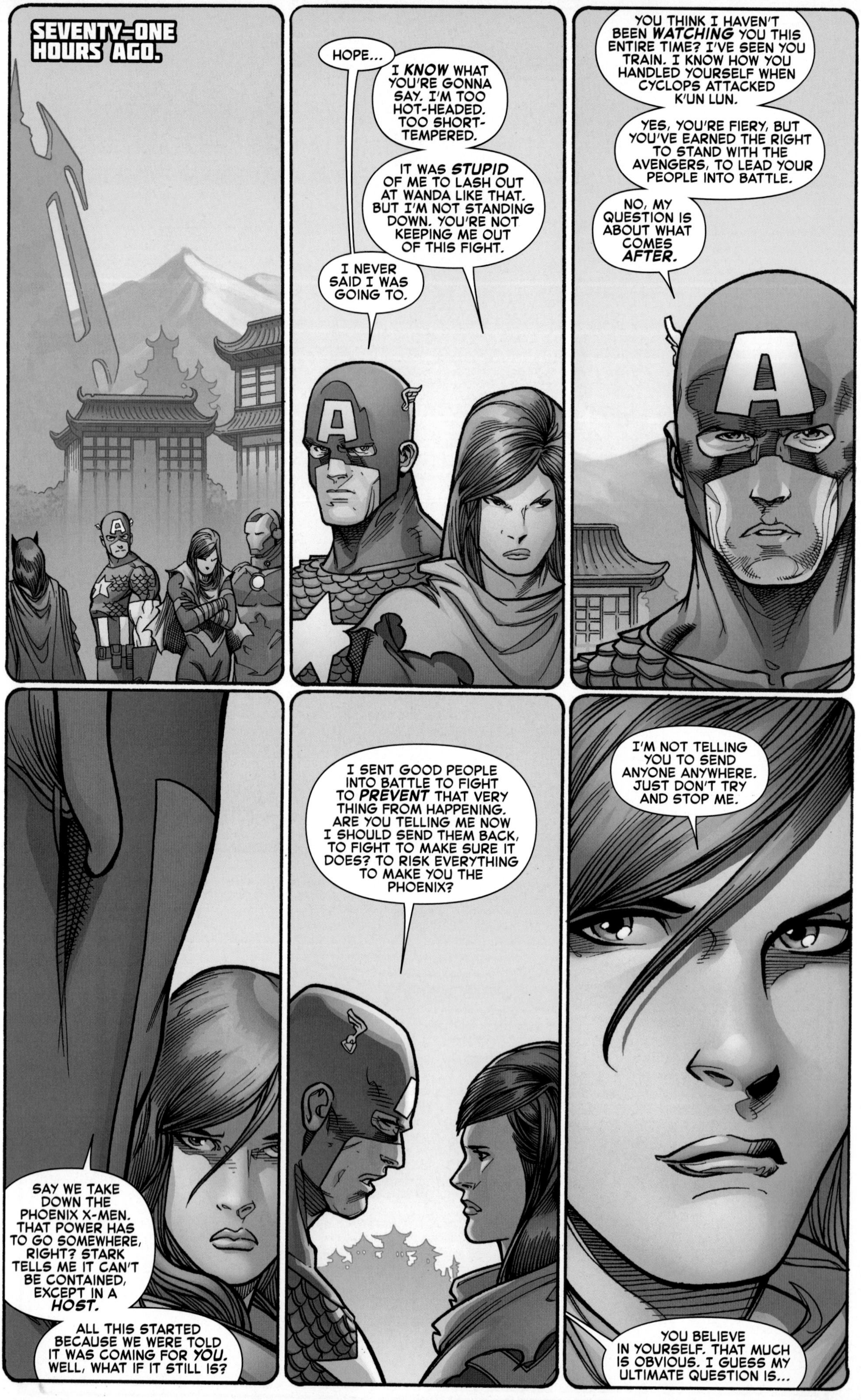
SEVENTY-ONE HOURS AGO.
HOPE...
I KNOW WHAT YOU'RE GONNA SAY. I'M TOO HOT-HEADED. TOO SHORT-TEMPERED.
IT WAS STUPID OF ME TO LASH OUT AT WANDA LIKE THAT. BUT I'M NOT STANDING DOWN. YOU'RE NOT KEEPING ME OUT OF THIS FIGHT.
I NEVER SAID I WAS GOING TO.
YOU THINK I HAVEN'T BEEN WATCHING YOU THIS ENTIRE TIME? I'VE SEEN YOU TRAIN. I KNOW HOW YOU HANDLED YOURSELF WHEN CYCLOPS ATTACKED K'UN LUN.
YES, YOU'RE FIERY, BUT YOU'VE EARNED THE RIGHT TO STAND WITH THE AVENGERS, TO LEAD YOUR PEOPLE INTO BATTLE.
NO, MY QUESTION IS ABOUT WHAT COMES AFTER.
SAY WE TAKE DOWN THE PHOENIX X-MEN. THAT POWER HAS TO GO SOMEWHERE, RIGHT? STARK TELLS ME IT CAN'T BE CONTAINED, EXCEPT IN A HOST.
ALL THIS STARTED BECAUSE WE WERE TOLD IT WAS COMING FOR YOU. WELL, WHAT IF IT STILL IS?
I SENT GOOD PEOPLE INTO BATTLE TO FIGHT TO PREVENT THAT VERY THING FROM HAPPENING. ARE YOU TELLING ME NOW I SHOULD SEND THEM BACK, TO FIGHT TO MAKE SURE IT DOES? TO RISK EVERYTHING TO MAKE YOU THE PHOENIX?
I'M NOT TELLING YOU TO SEND ANYONE ANYWHERE. JUST DON'T TRY AND STOP ME.
YOU BELIEVE IN YOURSELF. THAT MUCH IS OBVIOUS. I GUESS MY ULTIMATE QUESTION IS...

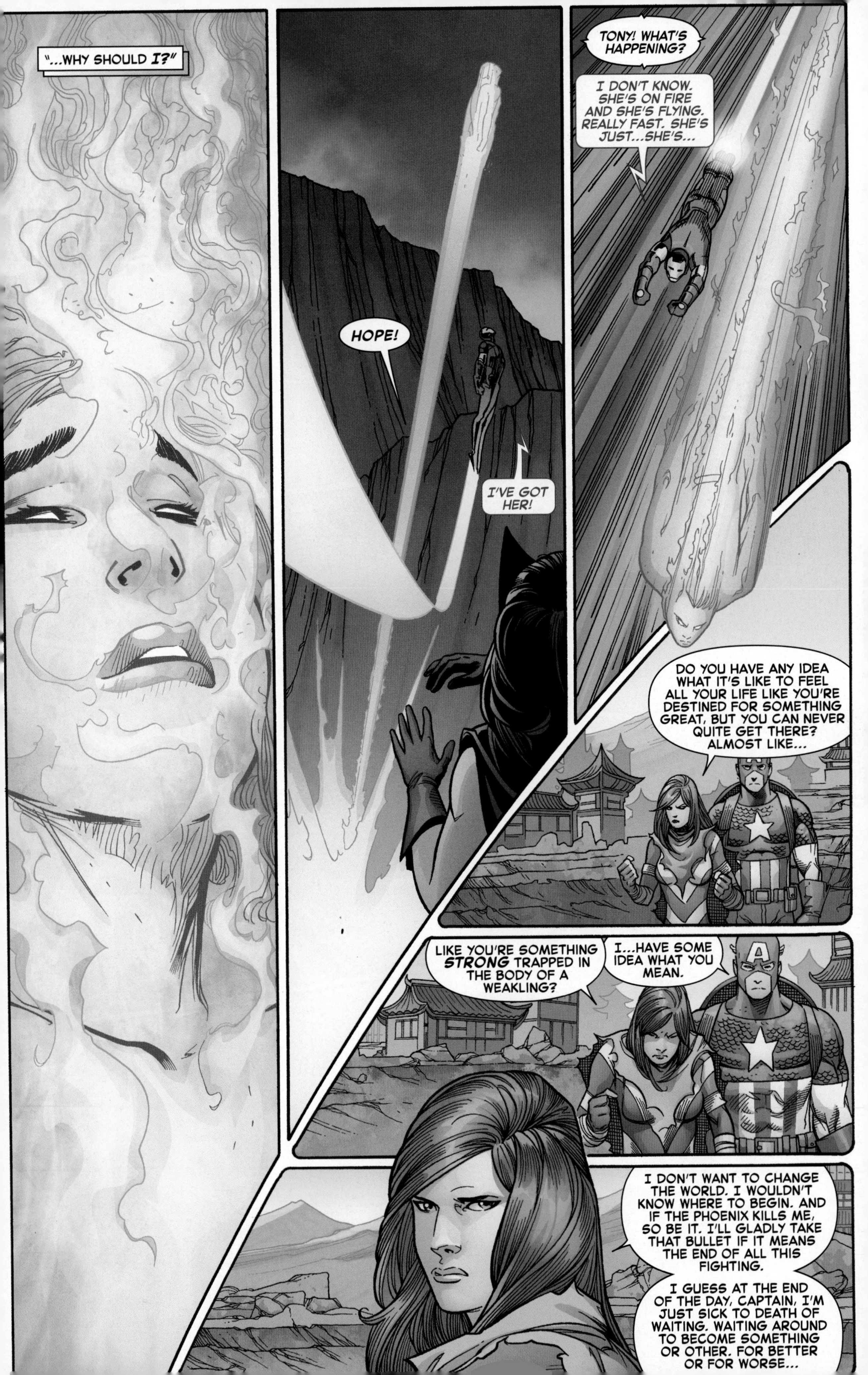
"...WHY SHOULD I?"
HOPE!
I'VE GOT HER!
TONY! WHAT'S HAPPENING?
I DON'T KNOW. SHE'S ON FIRE AND SHE'S FLYING. REALLY FAST. SHE'S JUST...SHE'S...
DO YOU HAVE ANY IDEA WHAT IT'S LIKE TO FEEL ALL YOUR LIFE LIKE YOU'RE DESTINED FOR SOMETHING GREAT, BUT YOU CAN NEVER QUITE GET THERE? ALMOST LIKE...
LIKE YOU'RE SOMETHING STRONG TRAPPED IN THE BODY OF A WEAKLING?
I...HAVE SOME IDEA WHAT YOU MEAN.
I DON'T WANT TO CHANGE THE WORLD. I WOULDN'T KNOW WHERE TO BEGIN. AND IF THE PHOENIX KILLS ME, SO BE IT. I'LL GLADLY TAKE THAT BULLET IF IT MEANS THE END OF ALL THIS FIGHTING.
I GUESS AT THE END OF THE DAY, CAPTAIN, I'M JUST SICK TO DEATH OF WAITING. WAITING AROUND TO BECOME SOMETHING OR OTHER. FOR BETTER OR FOR WORSE...

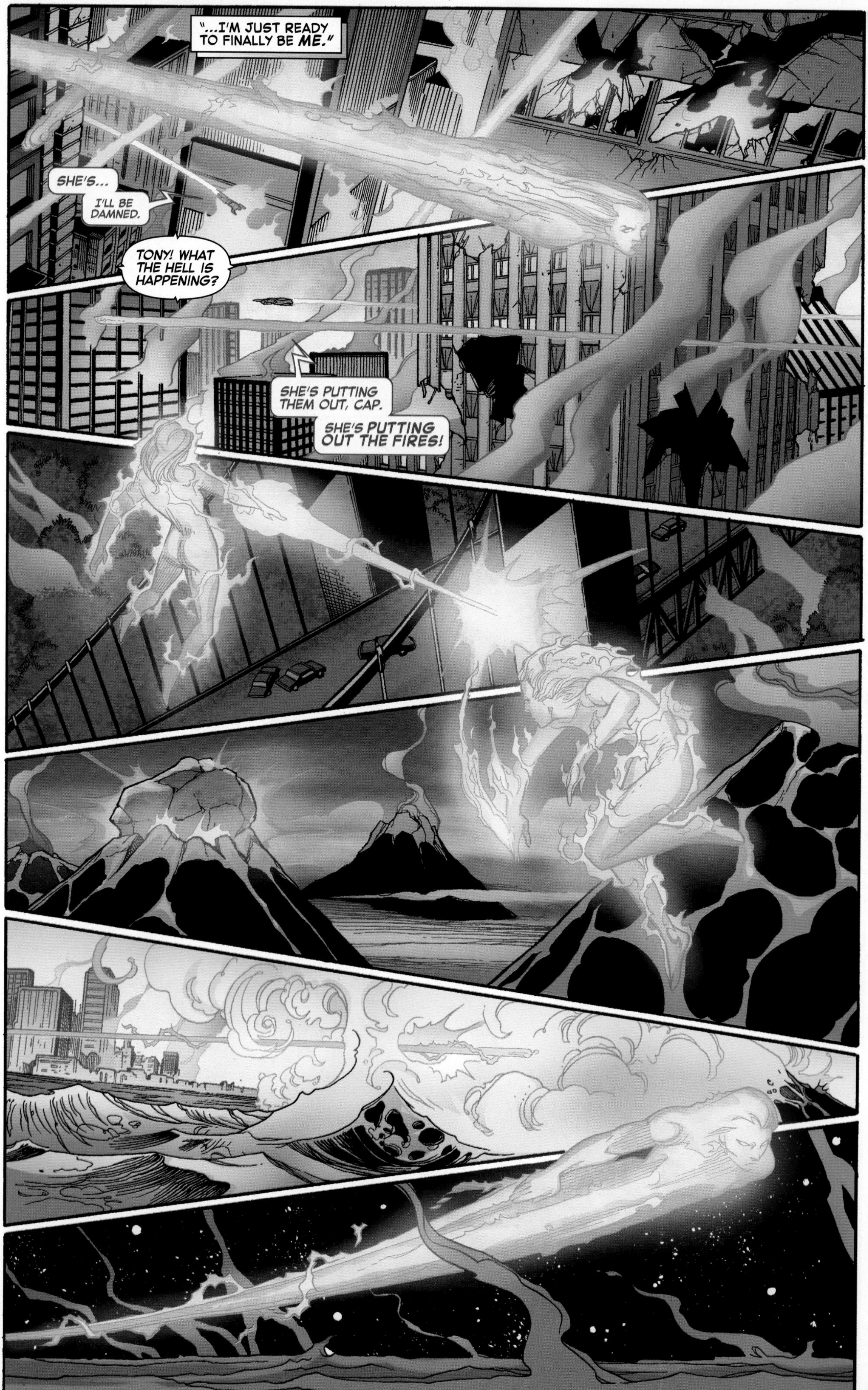
"...I'M JUST READY TO FINALLY BE ME."
SHE'S...
I'LL BE DAMNED.
TONY! WHAT THE HELL IS HAPPENING?
SHE'S PUTTING THEM OUT, CAP.
SHE'S PUTTING OUT THE FIRES!

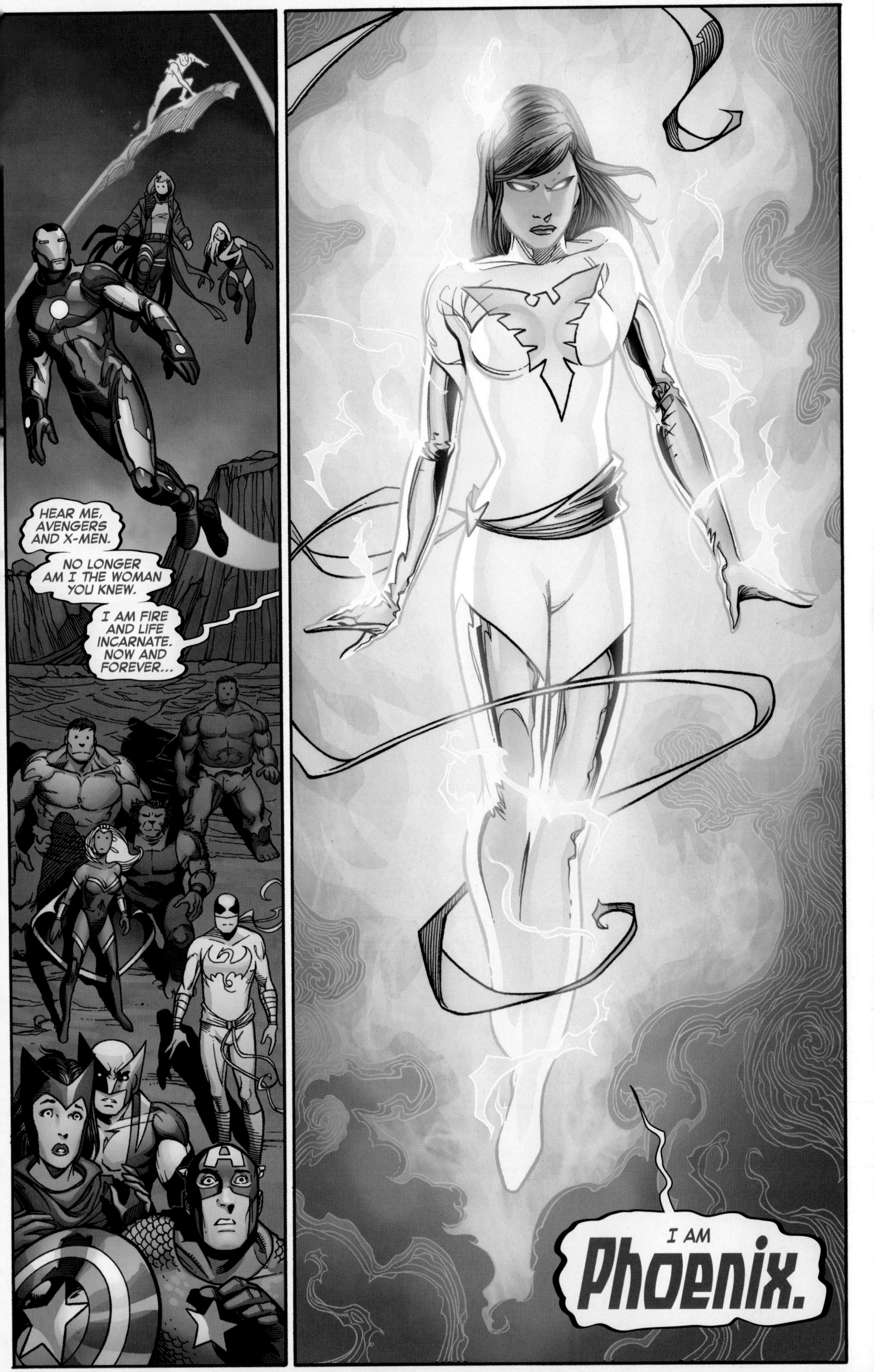
HEAR ME, AVENGERS AND X-MEN.
NO LONGER AM I THE WOMAN YOU KNEW.
I AM FIRE AND LIFE INCARNATE. NOW AND FOREVER...
I AM Phoenix.

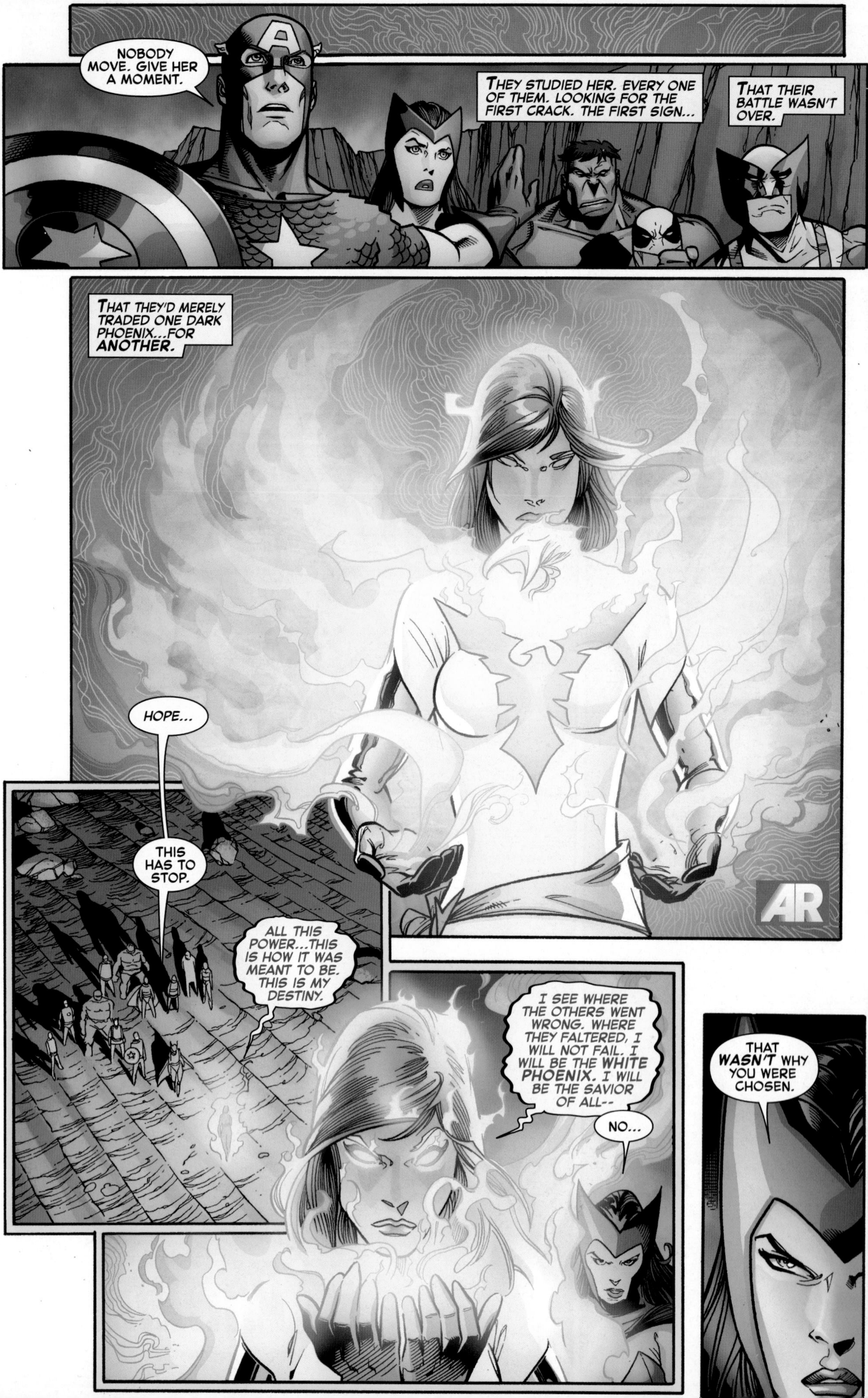
NOBODY MOVE. GIVE HER A MOMENT.
THEY STUDIED HER. EVERY ONE OF THEM. LOOKING FOR THE FIRST CRACK. THE FIRST SIGN...
THAT THEIR BATTLE WASN'T OVER.
THAT THEY'D MERELY TRADED ONE DARK PHOENIX...FOR ANOTHER.
HOPE...
THIS HAS TO STOP.
AR
ALL THIS POWER...THIS IS HOW IT WAS MEANT TO BE. THIS IS MY DESTINY.
I SEE WHERE THE OTHERS WENT WRONG. WHERE THEY FALTERED, I WILL NOT FAIL. I WILL BE THE WHITE PHOENIX. I WILL BE THE SAVIOR OF ALL--
NO...
THAT WASN'T WHY YOU WERE CHOSEN.

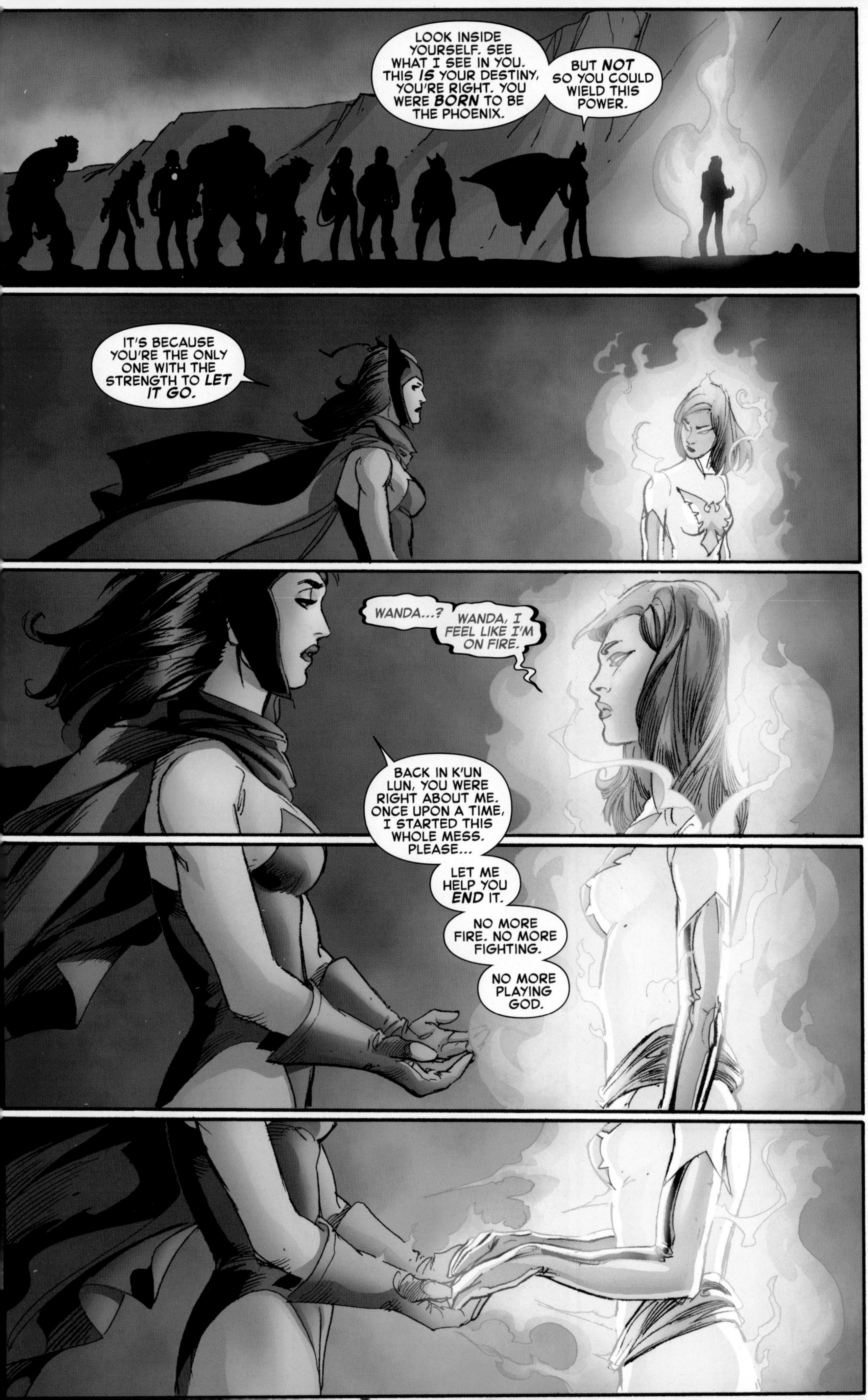
LOOK INSIDE YOURSELF. SEE WHAT I SEE IN YOU. THIS *IS* YOUR DESTINY, YOU'RE RIGHT. YOU WERE *BORN* TO BE THE PHOENIX.
BUT *NOT* SO YOU COULD WIELD THIS POWER.
IT'S BECAUSE YOU'RE THE ONLY ONE WITH THE STRENGTH TO *LET IT GO.*
WANDA...?
WANDA, I FEEL LIKE I'M ON FIRE.
BACK IN K'UN LUN, YOU WERE RIGHT ABOUT ME. ONCE UPON A TIME, I STARTED THIS WHOLE MESS. PLEASE...
LET ME HELP YOU *END* IT.
NO MORE FIRE. NO MORE FIGHTING.
NO MORE PLAYING GOD.

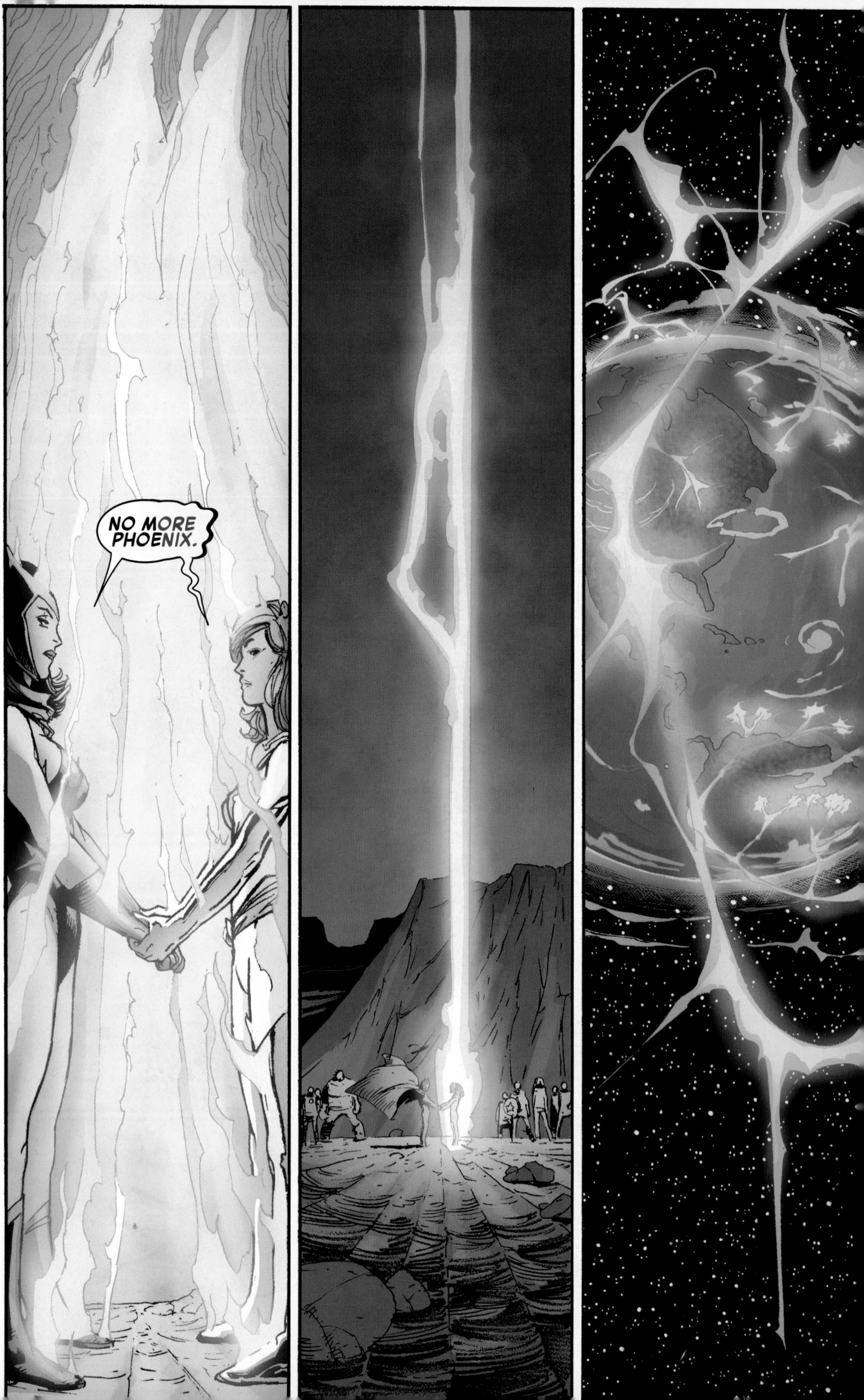
NO MORE PHOENIX.

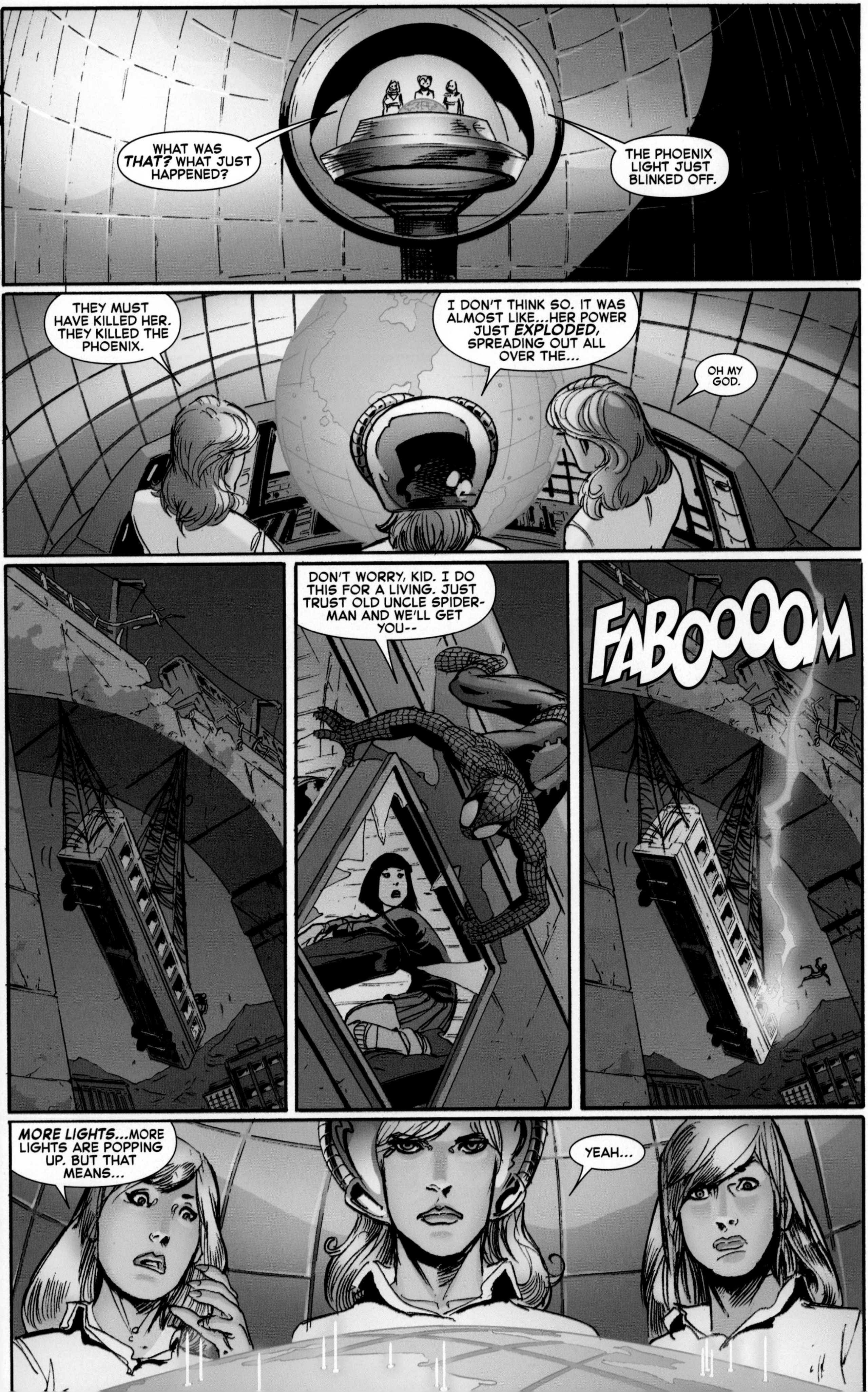
WHAT WAS THAT? WHAT JUST HAPPENED?
THE PHOENIX LIGHT JUST BLINKED OFF.
THEY MUST HAVE KILLED HER. THEY KILLED THE PHOENIX.
I DON'T THINK SO. IT WAS ALMOST LIKE...HER POWER JUST EXPLODED, SPREADING OUT ALL OVER THE...
OH MY GOD.
DON'T WORRY, KID. I DO THIS FOR A LIVING. JUST TRUST OLD UNCLE SPIDER-MAN AND WE'LL GET YOU--
FABOOOOM
MORE LIGHTS...MORE LIGHTS ARE POPPING UP. BUT THAT MEANS...
YEAH...

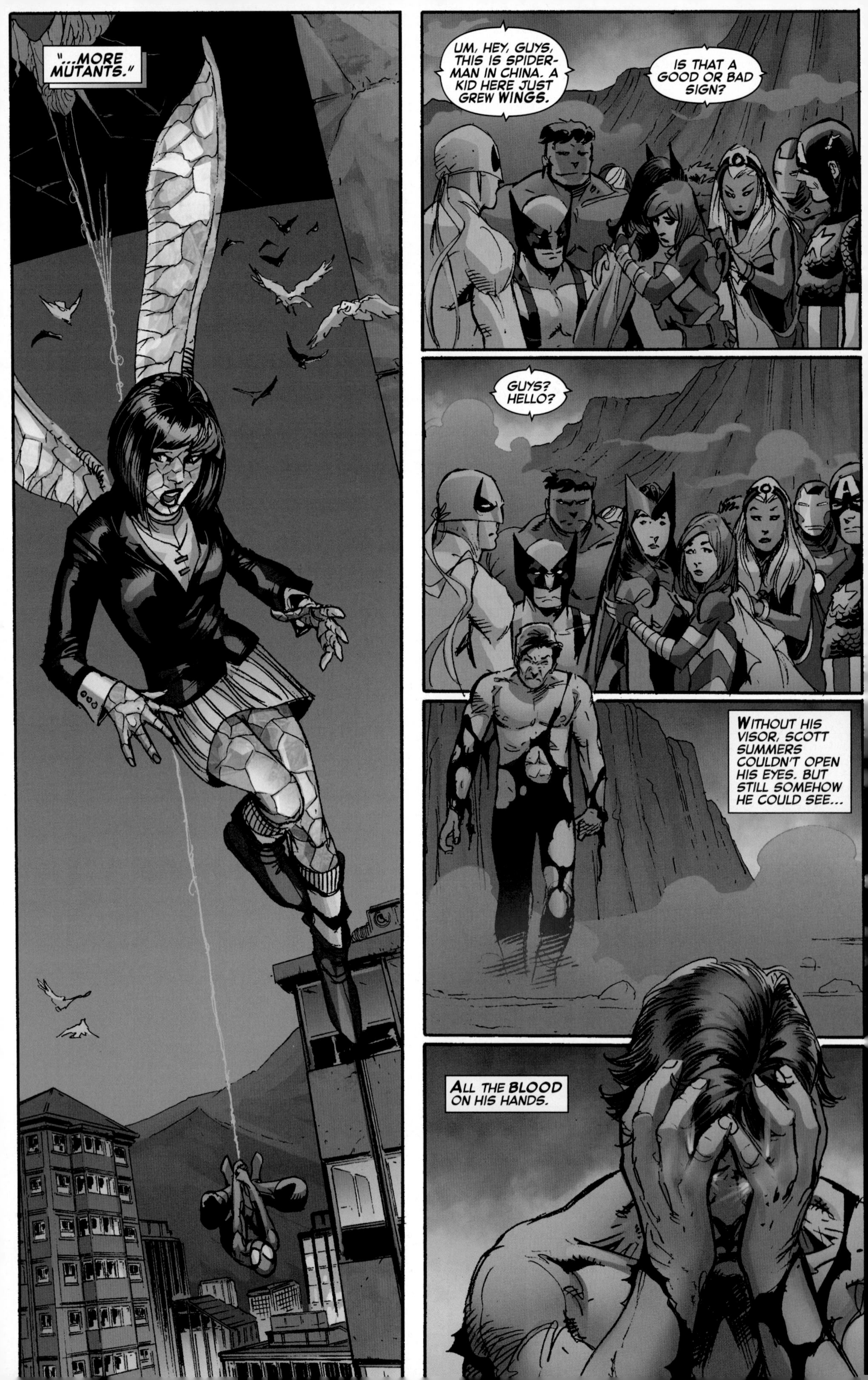
"...MORE MUTANTS."
UM, HEY, GUYS, THIS IS SPIDER-MAN IN CHINA. A KID HERE JUST GREW WINGS.
IS THAT A GOOD OR BAD SIGN?
GUYS? HELLO?
WITHOUT HIS VISOR, SCOTT SUMMERS COULDN'T OPEN HIS EYES. BUT STILL SOMEHOW HE COULD SEE...
ALL THE BLOOD ON HIS HANDS.

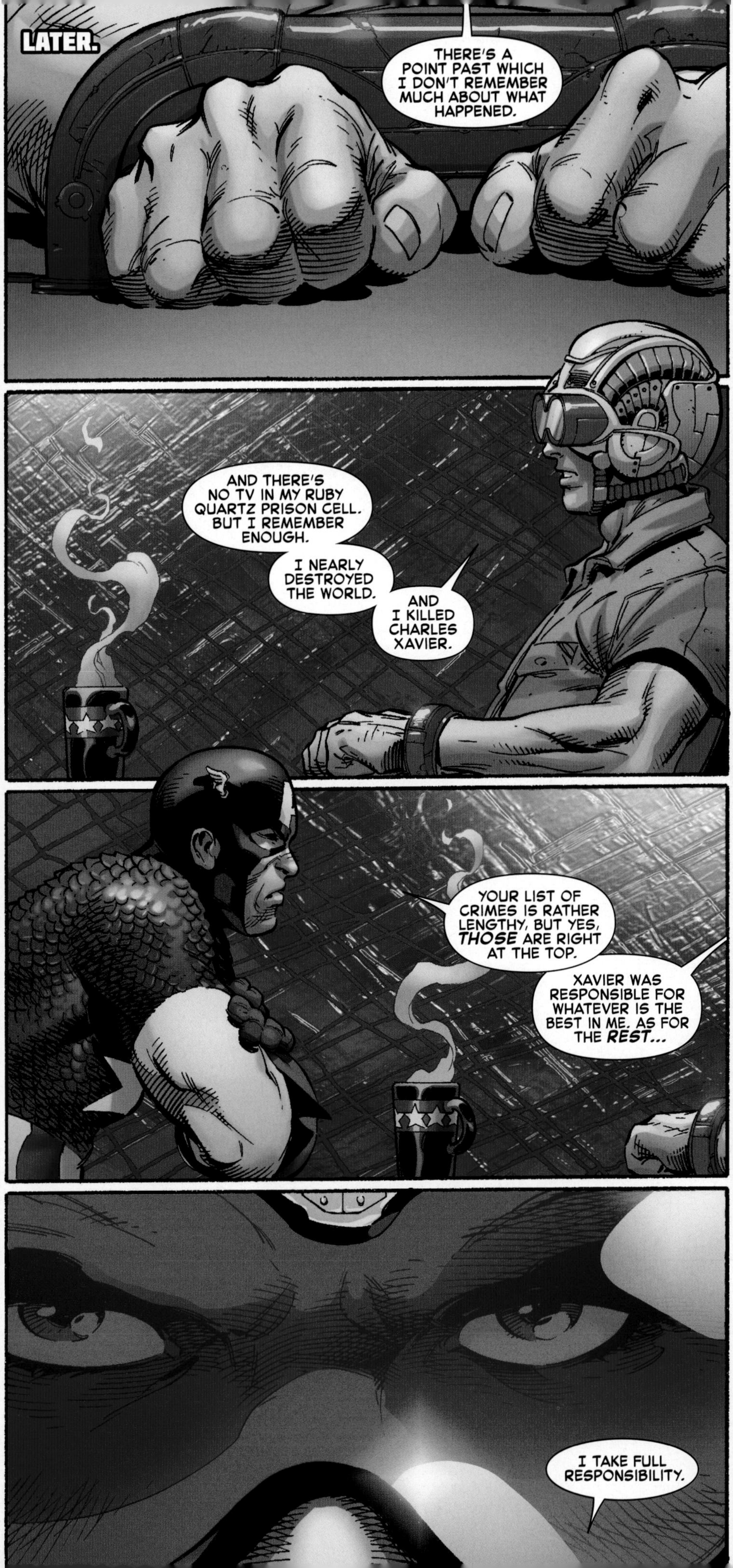
LATER.
THERE'S A POINT PAST WHICH I DON'T REMEMBER MUCH ABOUT WHAT HAPPENED.
AND THERE'S NO TV IN MY RUBY QUARTZ PRISON CELL. BUT I REMEMBER ENOUGH.
I NEARLY DESTROYED THE WORLD.
AND I KILLED CHARLES XAVIER.
YOUR LIST OF CRIMES IS RATHER LENGTHY, BUT YES, *THOSE* ARE RIGHT AT THE TOP.
XAVIER WAS RESPONSIBLE FOR WHATEVER IS THE BEST IN ME. AS FOR THE *REST*...
I TAKE FULL RESPONSIBILITY.

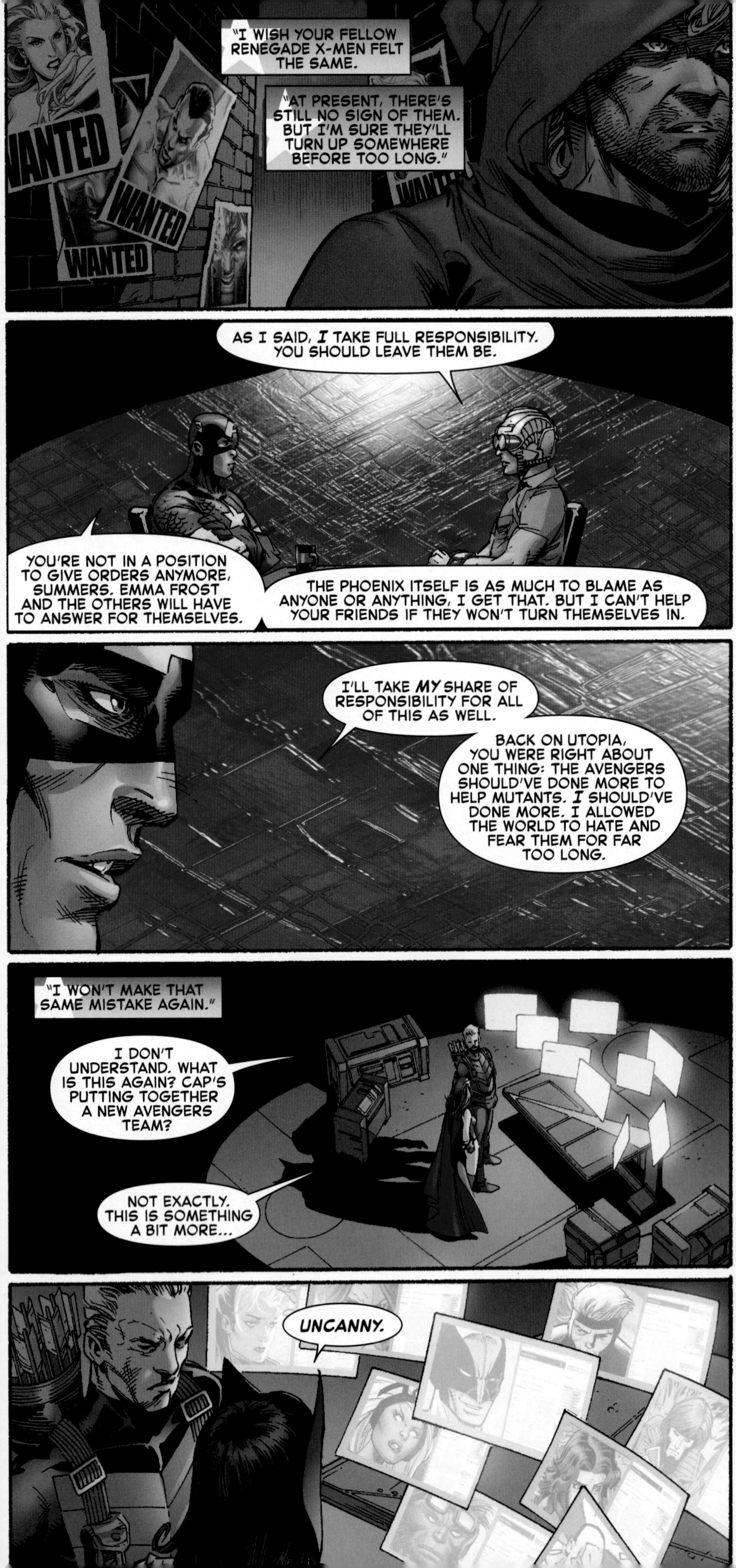
"I WISH YOUR FELLOW RENEGADE X-MEN FELT THE SAME.
"AT PRESENT, THERE'S STILL NO SIGN OF THEM. BUT I'M SURE THEY'LL TURN UP SOMEWHERE BEFORE TOO LONG."
WANTED
WANTED
WANTED
AS I SAID, *I* TAKE FULL RESPONSIBILITY. YOU SHOULD LEAVE THEM BE.
YOU'RE NOT IN A POSITION TO GIVE ORDERS ANYMORE, SUMMERS. EMMA FROST AND THE OTHERS WILL HAVE TO ANSWER FOR THEMSELVES.
THE PHOENIX ITSELF IS AS MUCH TO BLAME AS ANYONE OR ANYTHING, I GET THAT. BUT I CAN'T HELP YOUR FRIENDS IF THEY WON'T TURN THEMSELVES IN.
I'LL TAKE *MY* SHARE OF RESPONSIBILITY FOR ALL OF THIS AS WELL.
BACK ON UTOPIA, YOU WERE RIGHT ABOUT ONE THING: THE AVENGERS SHOULD'VE DONE MORE TO HELP MUTANTS. *I* SHOULD'VE DONE MORE. I ALLOWED THE WORLD TO HATE AND FEAR THEM FOR FAR TOO LONG.
"I WON'T MAKE THAT SAME MISTAKE AGAIN."
I DON'T UNDERSTAND. WHAT IS THIS AGAIN? CAP'S PUTTING TOGETHER A NEW AVENGERS TEAM?
NOT EXACTLY. THIS IS SOMETHING A BIT MORE...
UNCANNY.

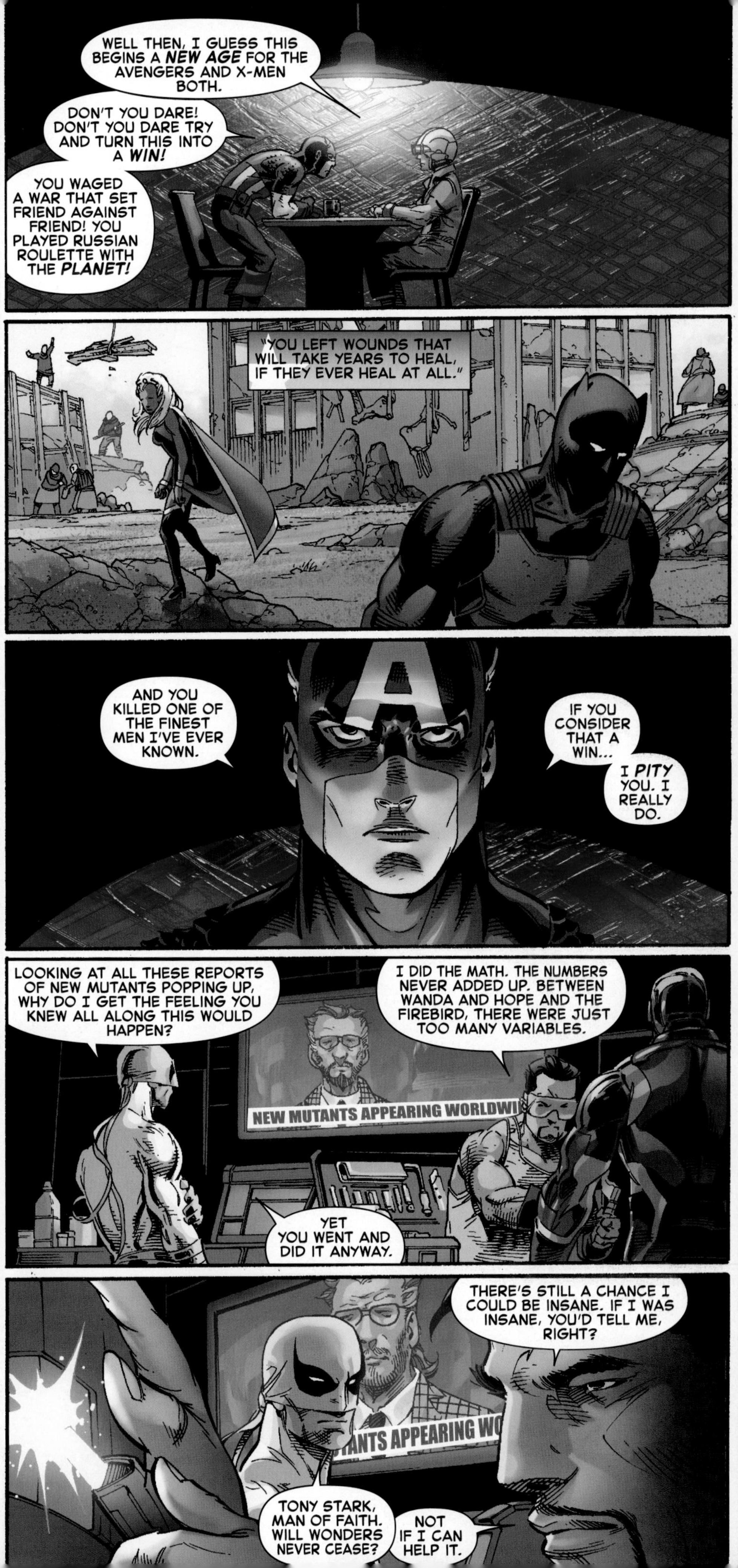
WELL THEN, I GUESS THIS BEGINS A NEW AGE FOR THE AVENGERS AND X-MEN BOTH.
DON'T YOU DARE! DON'T YOU DARE TRY AND TURN THIS INTO A WIN!
YOU WAGED A WAR THAT SET FRIEND AGAINST FRIEND! YOU PLAYED RUSSIAN ROULETTE WITH THE PLANET!
"YOU LEFT WOUNDS THAT WILL TAKE YEARS TO HEAL, IF THEY EVER HEAL AT ALL."
AND YOU KILLED ONE OF THE FINEST MEN I'VE EVER KNOWN.
IF YOU CONSIDER THAT A WIN...
I PITY YOU. I REALLY DO.
LOOKING AT ALL THESE REPORTS OF NEW MUTANTS POPPING UP, WHY DO I GET THE FEELING YOU KNEW ALL ALONG THIS WOULD HAPPEN?
I DID THE MATH. THE NUMBERS NEVER ADDED UP. BETWEEN WANDA AND HOPE AND THE FIREBIRD, THERE WERE JUST TOO MANY VARIABLES.
NEW MUTANTS APPEARING WORLDWI
YET YOU WENT AND DID IT ANYWAY.
THERE'S STILL A CHANCE I COULD BE INSANE. IF I WAS INSANE, YOU'D TELL ME, RIGHT?
TANTS APPEARING WO
TONY STARK, MAN OF FAITH. WILL WONDERS NEVER CEASE?
NOT IF I CAN HELP IT.

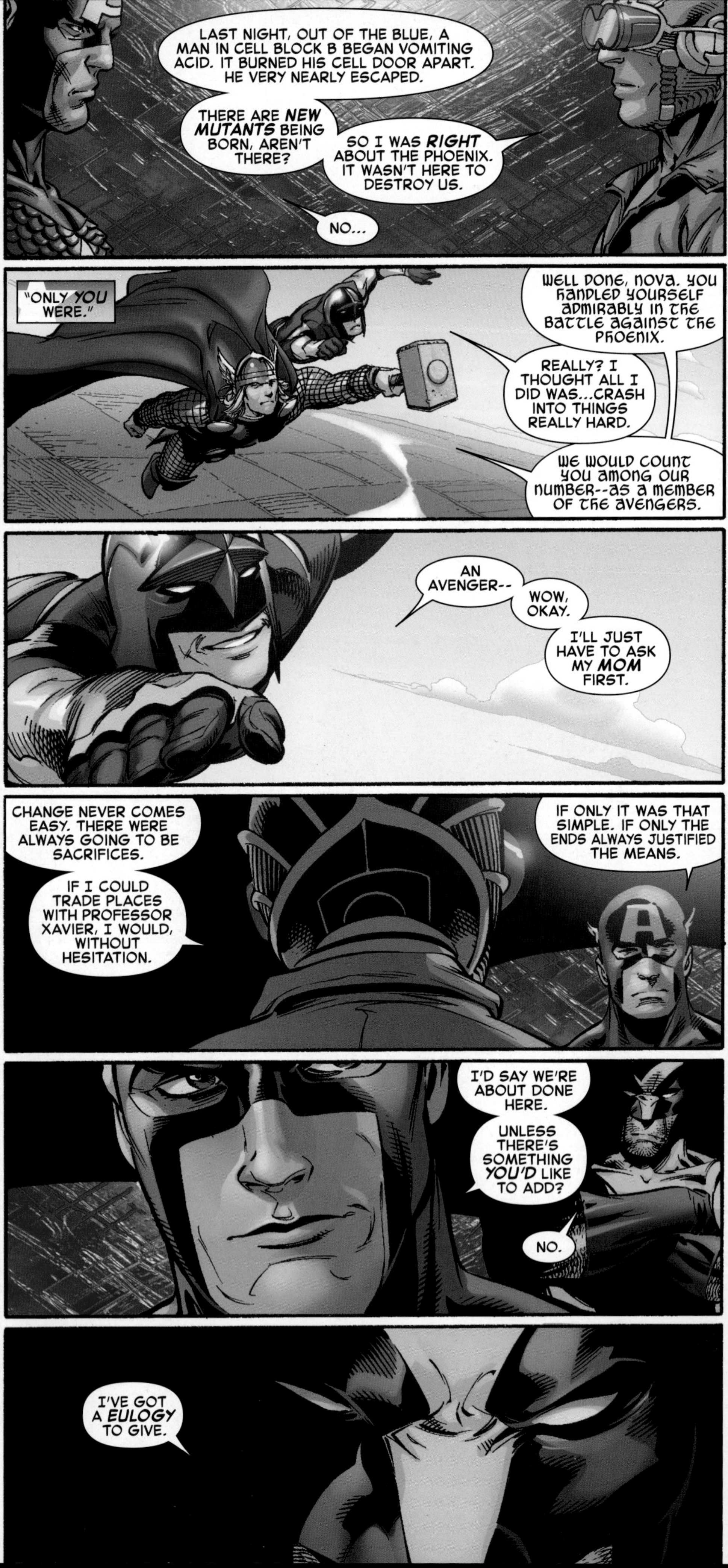
LAST NIGHT, OUT OF THE BLUE, A MAN IN CELL BLOCK B BEGAN VOMITING ACID. IT BURNED HIS CELL DOOR APART. HE VERY NEARLY ESCAPED.
THERE ARE NEW MUTANTS BEING BORN, AREN'T THERE?
SO I WAS RIGHT ABOUT THE PHOENIX. IT WASN'T HERE TO DESTROY US.
NO...
"ONLY YOU WERE."
WELL DONE, NOVA. YOU HANDLED YOURSELF ADMIRABLY IN THE BATTLE AGAINST THE PHOENIX.
REALLY? I THOUGHT ALL I DID WAS...CRASH INTO THINGS REALLY HARD.
WE WOULD COUNT YOU AMONG OUR NUMBER--AS A MEMBER OF THE AVENGERS.
AN AVENGER--
WOW, OKAY.
I'LL JUST HAVE TO ASK MY MOM FIRST.
CHANGE NEVER COMES EASY. THERE WERE ALWAYS GOING TO BE SACRIFICES.
IF I COULD TRADE PLACES WITH PROFESSOR XAVIER, I WOULD, WITHOUT HESITATION.
IF ONLY IT WAS THAT SIMPLE. IF ONLY THE ENDS ALWAYS JUSTIFIED THE MEANS.
I'D SAY WE'RE ABOUT DONE HERE.
UNLESS THERE'S SOMETHING YOU'D LIKE TO ADD?
NO.
I'VE GOT A EULOGY TO GIVE.

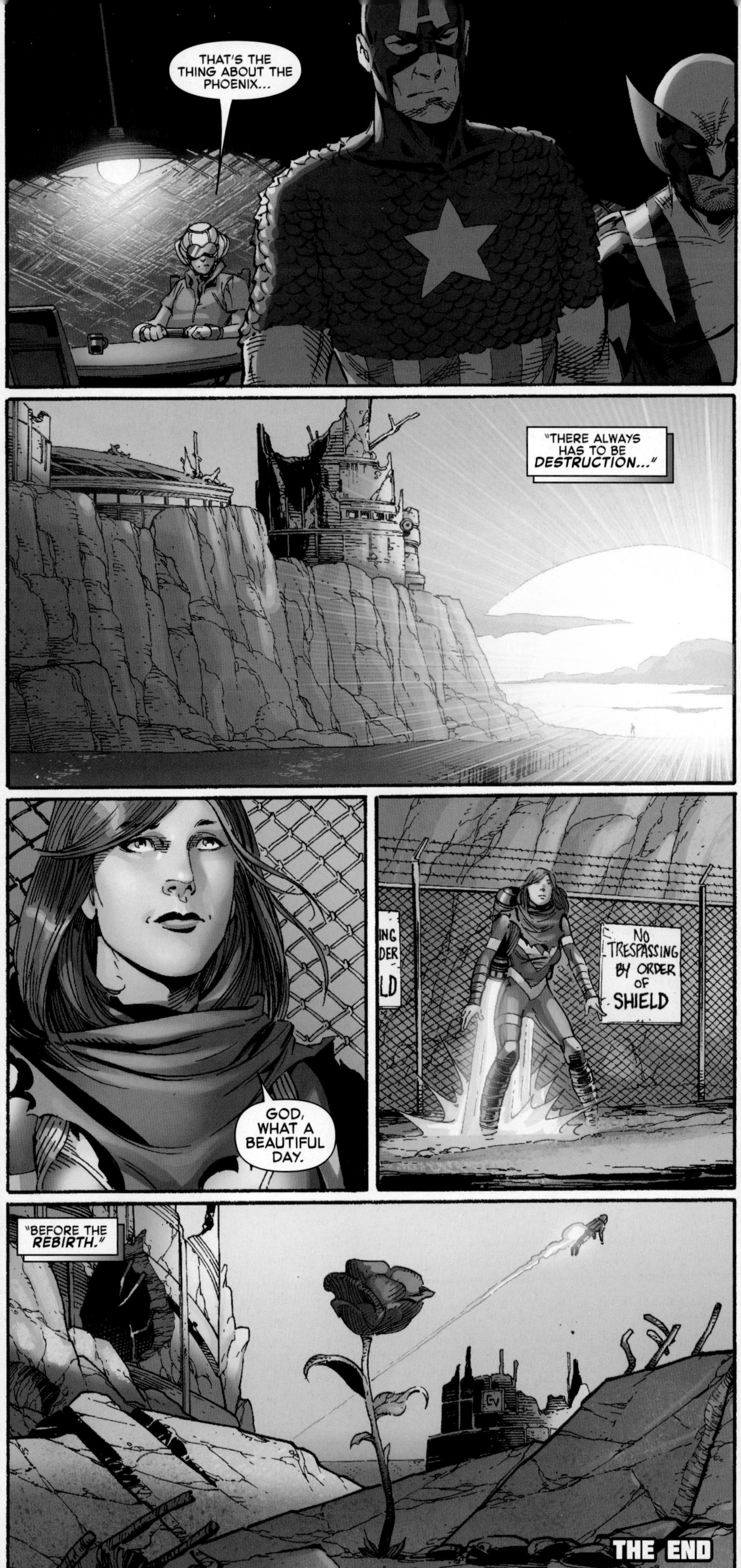
THAT'S THE THING ABOUT THE PHOENIX...
"THERE ALWAYS HAS TO BE DESTRUCTION..."
GOD, WHAT A BEAUTIFUL DAY.
NO TRESPASSING BY ORDER OF SHIELD
"BEFORE THE REBIRTH."
THE END

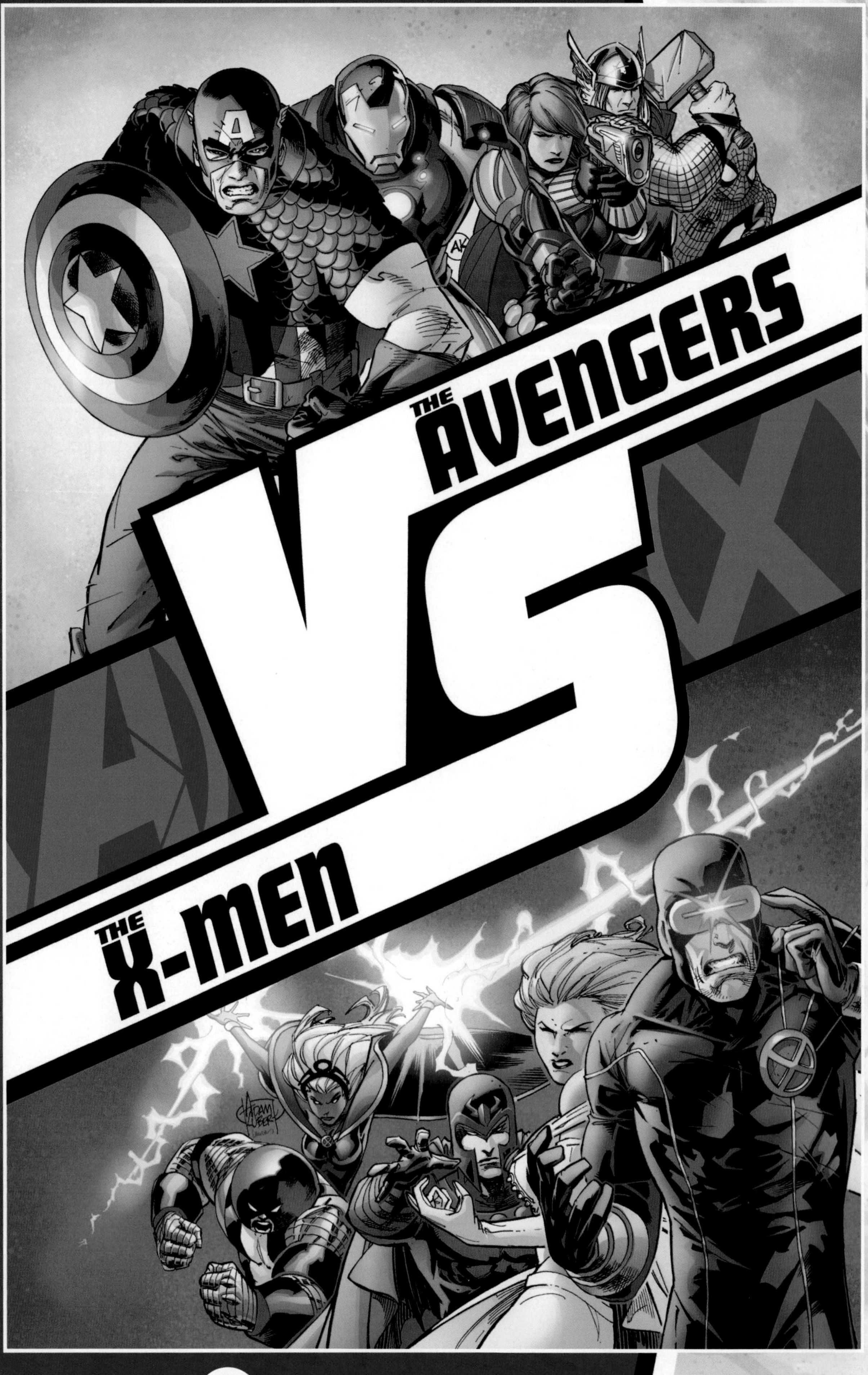
THE AVENGERS
VS
THE X-MEN

ISSUE #1

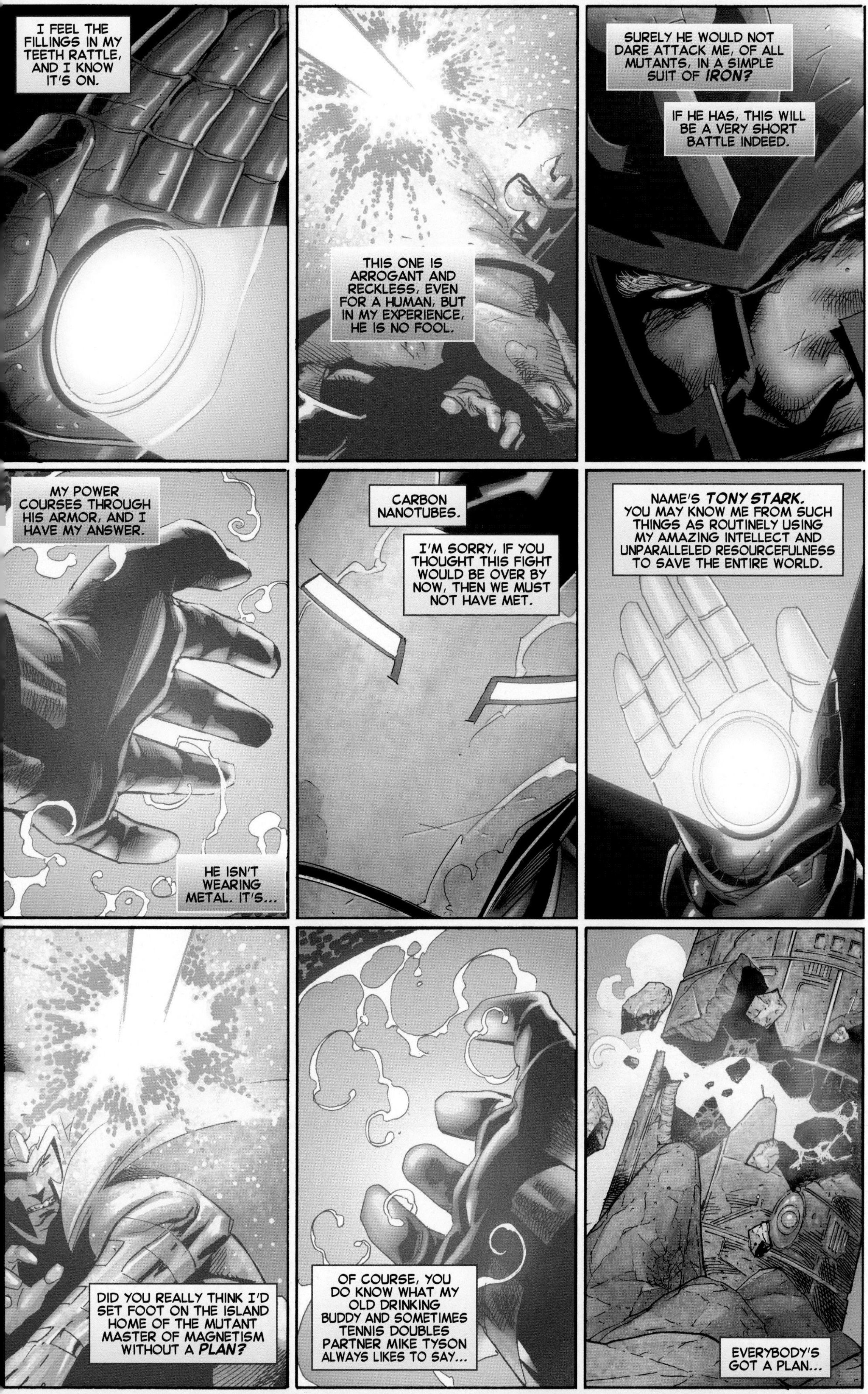

I FEEL THE FILLINGS IN MY TEETH RATTLE, AND I KNOW IT'S ON.
THIS ONE IS ARROGANT AND RECKLESS, EVEN FOR A HUMAN, BUT IN MY EXPERIENCE, HE IS NO FOOL.
SURELY HE WOULD NOT DARE ATTACK ME, OF ALL MUTANTS, IN A SIMPLE SUIT OF *IRON?*
IF HE HAS, THIS WILL BE A VERY SHORT BATTLE INDEED.
MY POWER COURSES THROUGH HIS ARMOR, AND I HAVE MY ANSWER.
HE ISN'T WEARING METAL. IT'S...
CARBON NANOTUBES.
I'M SORRY, IF YOU THOUGHT THIS FIGHT WOULD BE OVER BY NOW, THEN WE MUST NOT HAVE MET.
NAME'S *TONY STARK.* YOU MAY KNOW ME FROM SUCH THINGS AS ROUTINELY USING MY AMAZING INTELLECT AND UNPARALLELED RESOURCEFULNESS TO SAVE THE ENTIRE WORLD.
DID YOU REALLY THINK I'D SET FOOT ON THE ISLAND HOME OF THE MUTANT MASTER OF MAGNETISM WITHOUT A *PLAN?*
OF COURSE, YOU DO KNOW WHAT MY OLD DRINKING BUDDY AND SOMETIMES TENNIS DOUBLES PARTNER MIKE TYSON ALWAYS LIKES TO SAY...
EVERYBODY'S GOT A PLAN...

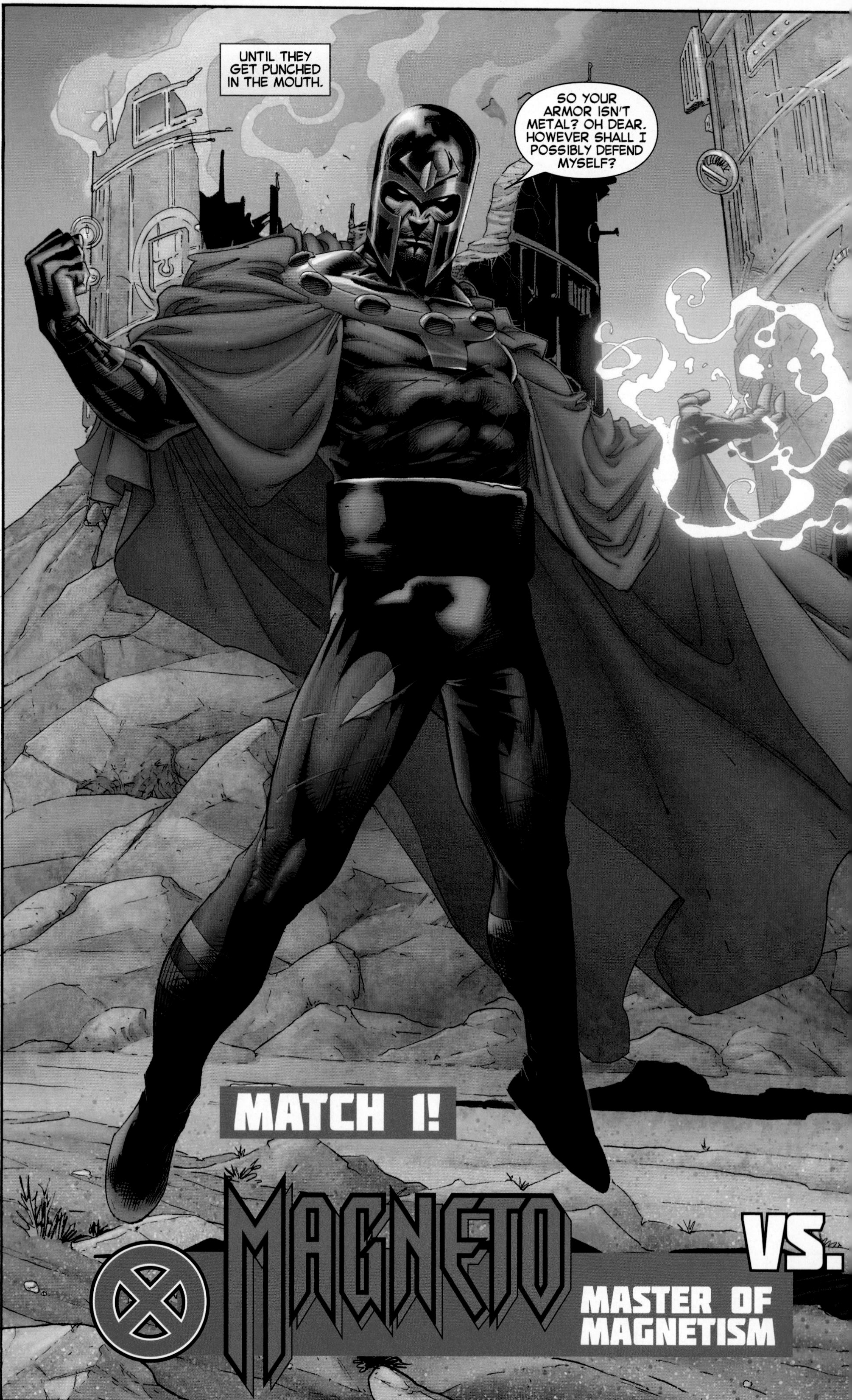
UNTIL THEY GET PUNCHED IN THE MOUTH.
SO YOUR ARMOR ISN'T METAL? OH DEAR. HOWEVER SHALL I POSSIBLY DEFEND MYSELF?
MATCH 1!
MAGNETO
VS.
MASTER OF MAGNETISM

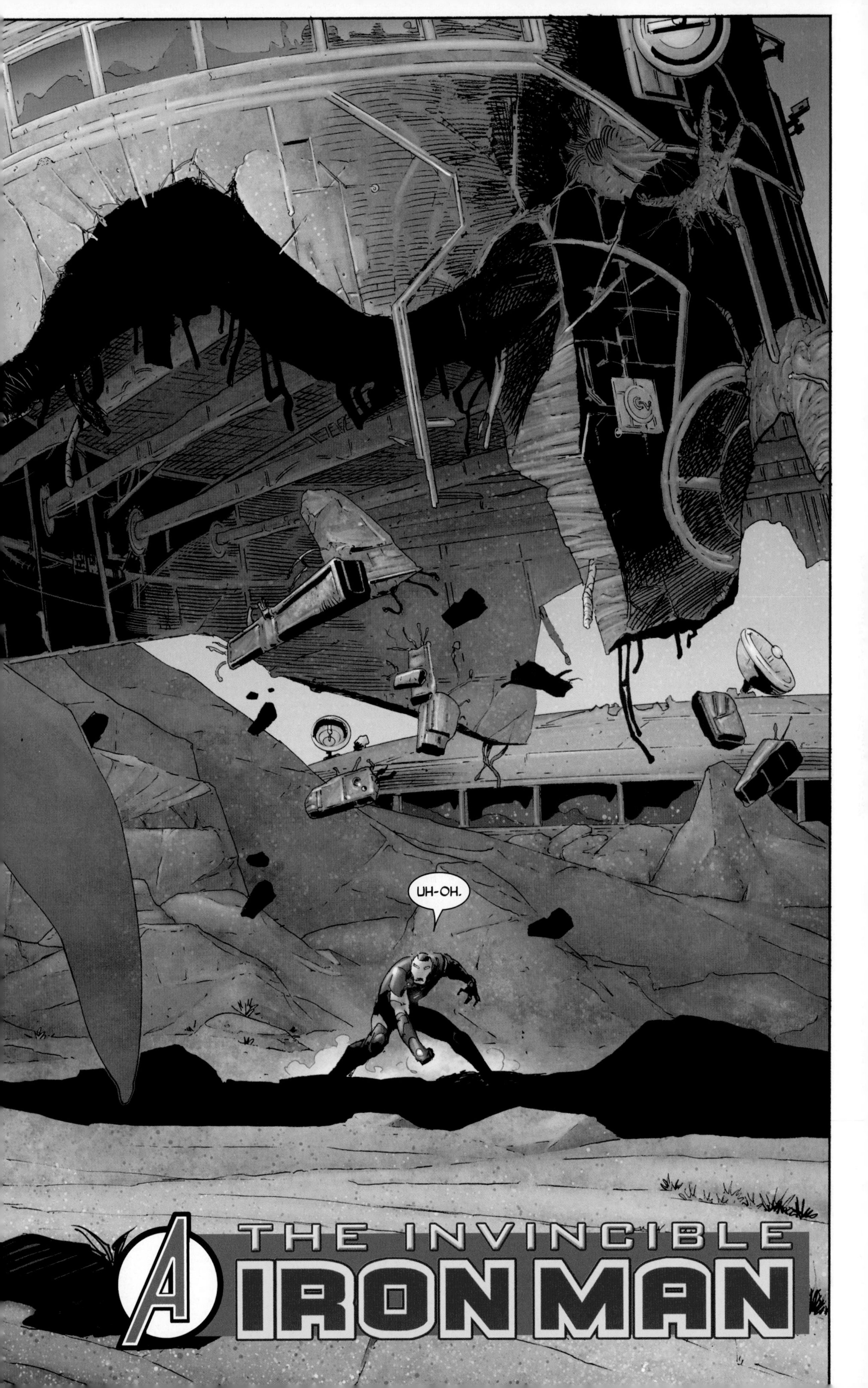
UH-OH.
THE INVINCIBLE
IRON MAN

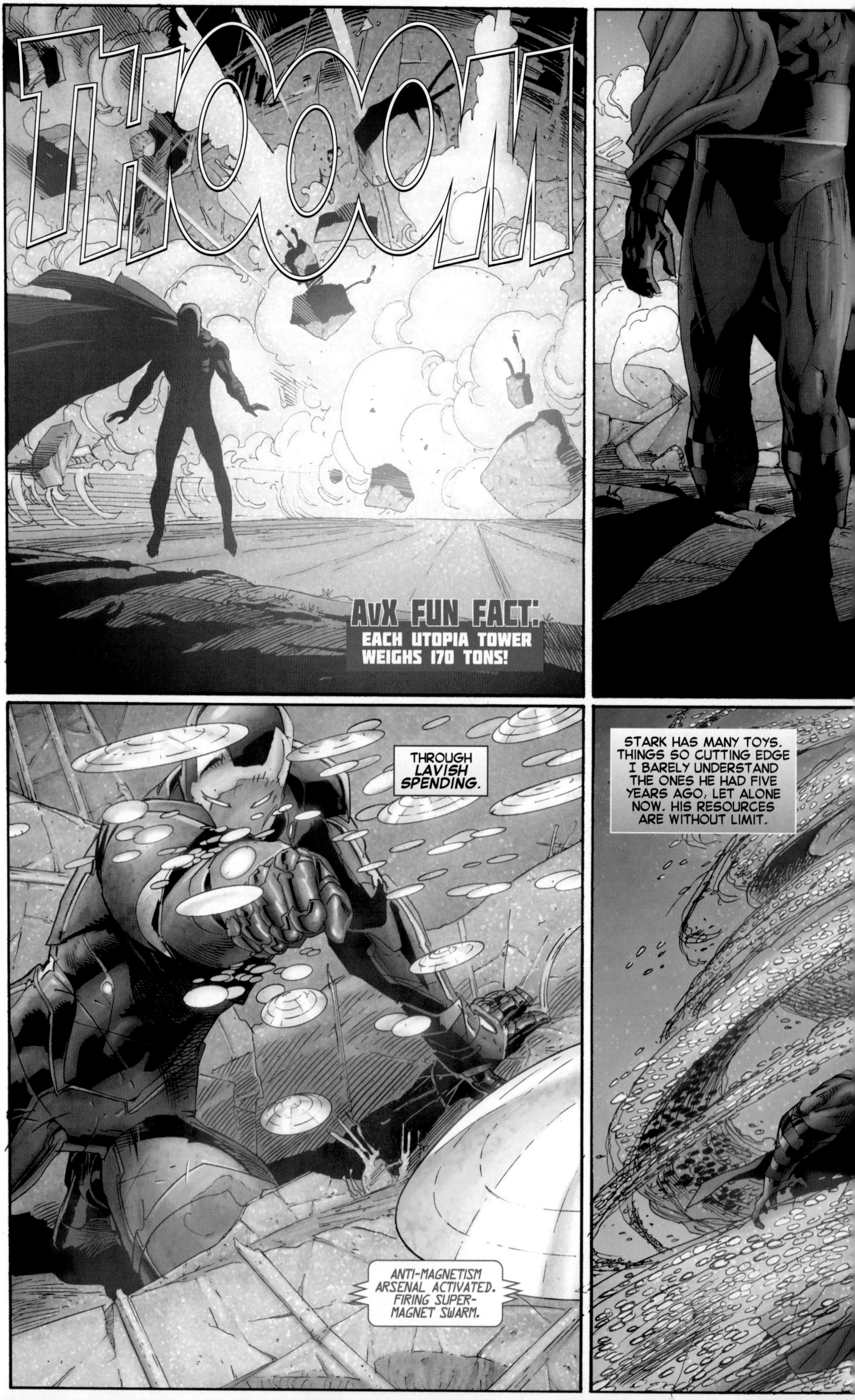
THOOOM
AvX FUN FACT:
EACH UTOPIA TOWER WEIGHS 170 TONS!
THROUGH LAVISH SPENDING.
ANTI-MAGNETISM ARSENAL ACTIVATED. FIRING SUPER-MAGNET SWARM.
STARK HAS MANY TOYS. THINGS SO CUTTING EDGE I BARELY UNDERSTAND THE ONES HE HAD FIVE YEARS AGO, LET ALONE NOW. HIS RESOURCES ARE WITHOUT LIMIT.

STAY DOWN, AVENGER. YOU ARE IN THE WRONG THIS DAY.

IN CASE YOU WERE WONDERING, YES, HAVING 200 TONS OF RUBBLE* DROPPED ON YOUR HEAD WHILE WEARING NANO-TECH ARMOR DOES INDEED HURT QUITE A LOT.

AvX FUN FACT:
*IRON MAN LIKES TO EXAGGERATE.

THANKFULLY SYSTEMS ARE STILL ONLINE. TIME TO SAVE THE DAY THE ONLY WAY I KNOW HOW.

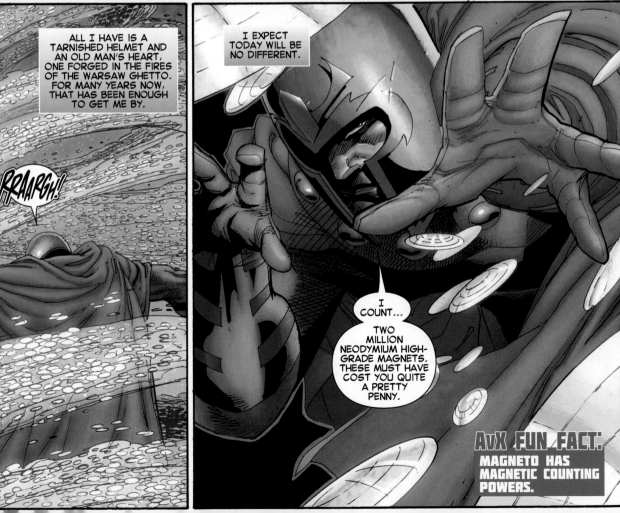

ALL I HAVE IS A TARNISHED HELMET AND AN OLD MAN'S HEART, ONE FORGED IN THE FIRES OF THE WARSAW GHETTO. FOR MANY YEARS NOW, THAT HAS BEEN ENOUGH TO GET ME BY.

RRAARGH!

I EXPECT TODAY WILL BE NO DIFFERENT.

I COUNT...

TWO MILLION NEODYMIUM HIGH-GRADE MAGNETS. THESE MUST HAVE COST YOU QUITE A PRETTY PENNY.

AvX FUN FACT:
MAGNETO HAS MAGNETIC COUNTING POWERS.

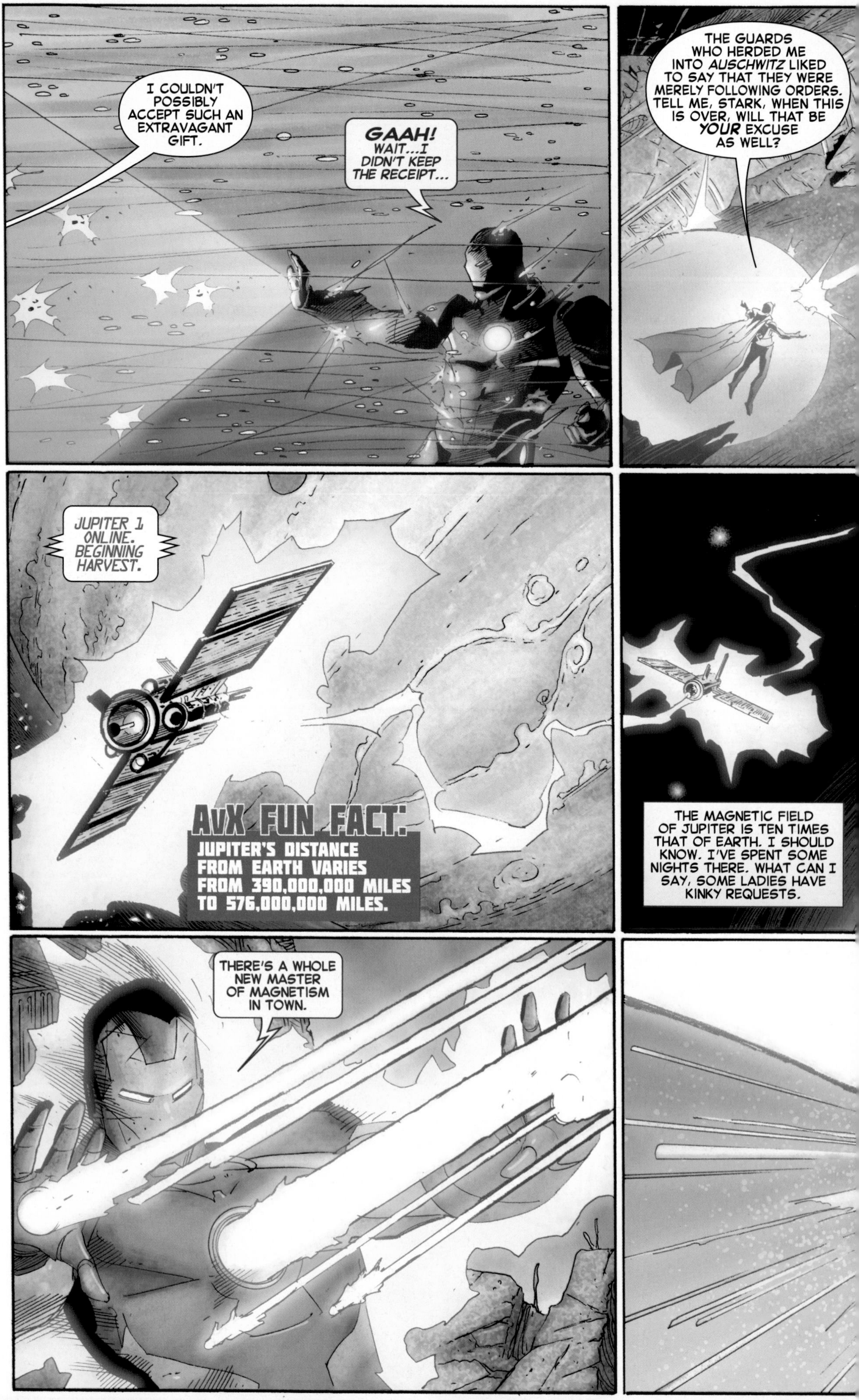
I COULDN'T POSSIBLY ACCEPT SUCH AN EXTRAVAGANT GIFT.
GAAH! WAIT...I DIDN'T KEEP THE RECEIPT...
THE GUARDS WHO HERDED ME INTO AUSCHWITZ LIKED TO SAY THAT THEY WERE MERELY FOLLOWING ORDERS. TELL ME, STARK, WHEN THIS IS OVER, WILL THAT BE YOUR EXCUSE AS WELL?
JUPITER 1 ONLINE. BEGINNING HARVEST.
AvX FUN FACT:
JUPITER'S DISTANCE FROM EARTH VARIES FROM 390,000,000 MILES TO 576,000,000 MILES.
THE MAGNETIC FIELD OF JUPITER IS TEN TIMES THAT OF EARTH. I SHOULD KNOW. I'VE SPENT SOME NIGHTS THERE. WHAT CAN I SAY, SOME LADIES HAVE KINKY REQUESTS.
THERE'S A WHOLE NEW MASTER OF MAGNETISM IN TOWN.

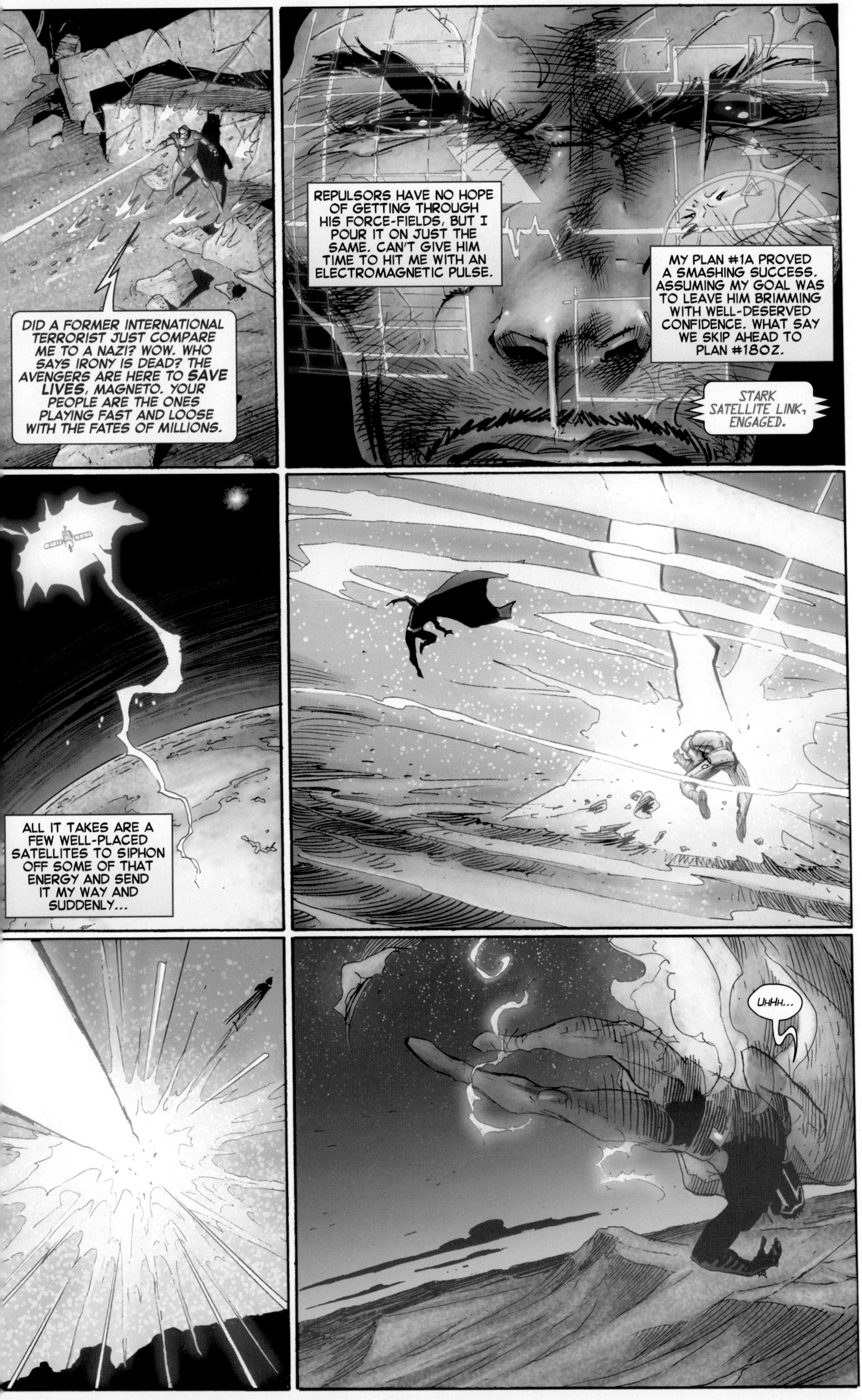
DID A FORMER INTERNATIONAL TERRORIST JUST COMPARE ME TO A NAZI? WOW. WHO SAYS IRONY IS DEAD? THE AVENGERS ARE HERE TO SAVE LIVES, MAGNETO. YOUR PEOPLE ARE THE ONES PLAYING FAST AND LOOSE WITH THE FATES OF MILLIONS.
REPULSORS HAVE NO HOPE OF GETTING THROUGH HIS FORCE-FIELDS, BUT I POUR IT ON JUST THE SAME. CAN'T GIVE HIM TIME TO HIT ME WITH AN ELECTROMAGNETIC PULSE.
MY PLAN #1A PROVED A SMASHING SUCCESS. ASSUMING MY GOAL WAS TO LEAVE HIM BRIMMING WITH WELL-DESERVED CONFIDENCE. WHAT SAY WE SKIP AHEAD TO PLAN #180Z.
STARK SATELLITE LINK, ENGAGED.
ALL IT TAKES ARE A FEW WELL-PLACED SATELLITES TO SIPHON OFF SOME OF THAT ENERGY AND SEND IT MY WAY AND SUDDENLY...
UHHH...

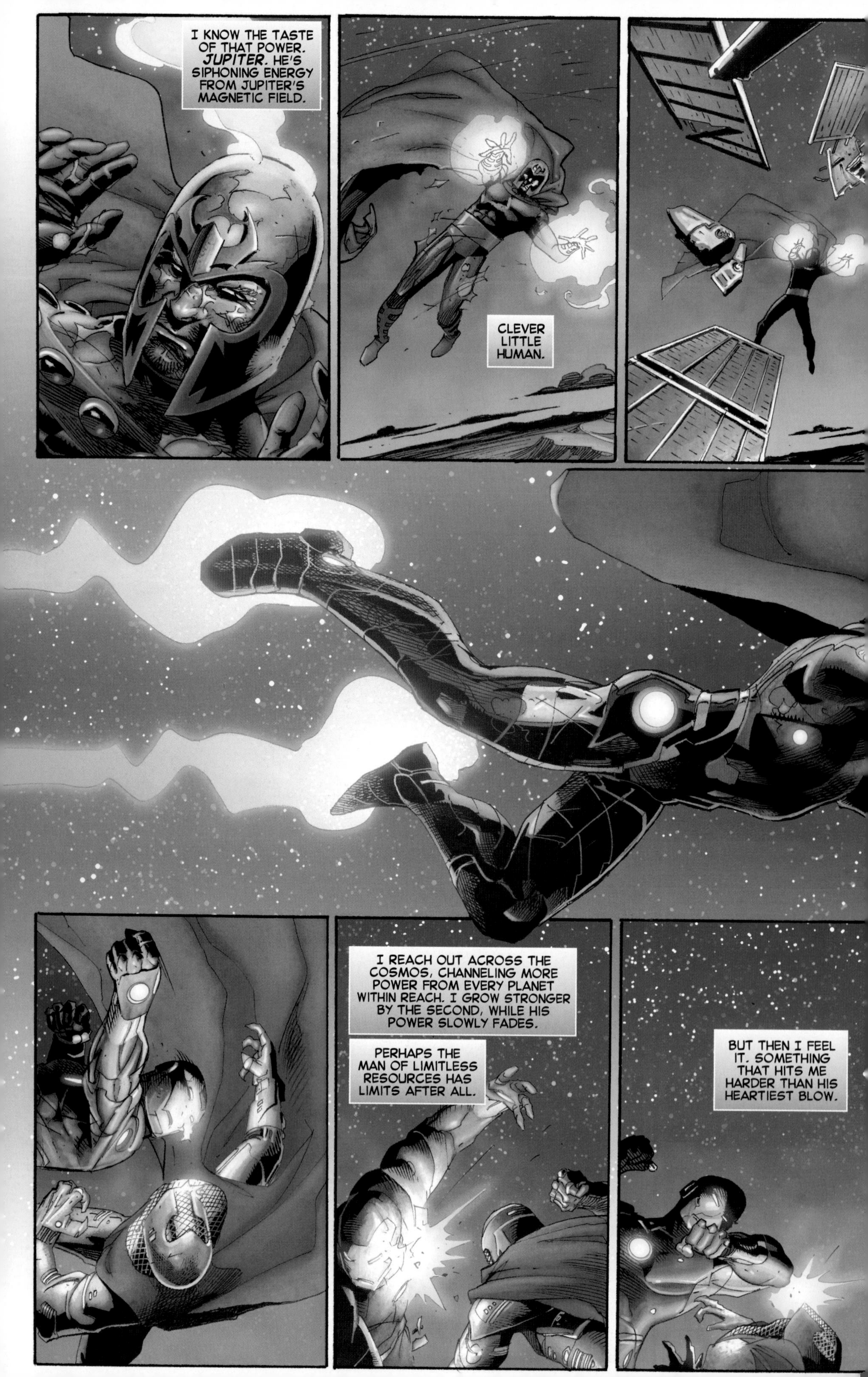
I KNOW THE TASTE OF THAT POWER. *JUPITER.* HE'S SIPHONING ENERGY FROM JUPITER'S MAGNETIC FIELD.
CLEVER LITTLE HUMAN.
I REACH OUT ACROSS THE COSMOS, CHANNELING MORE POWER FROM EVERY PLANET WITHIN REACH. I GROW STRONGER BY THE SECOND, WHILE HIS POWER SLOWLY FADES.
PERHAPS THE MAN OF LIMITLESS RESOURCES HAS LIMITS AFTER ALL.
BUT THEN I FEEL IT. SOMETHING THAT HITS ME HARDER THAN HIS HEARTIEST BLOW.

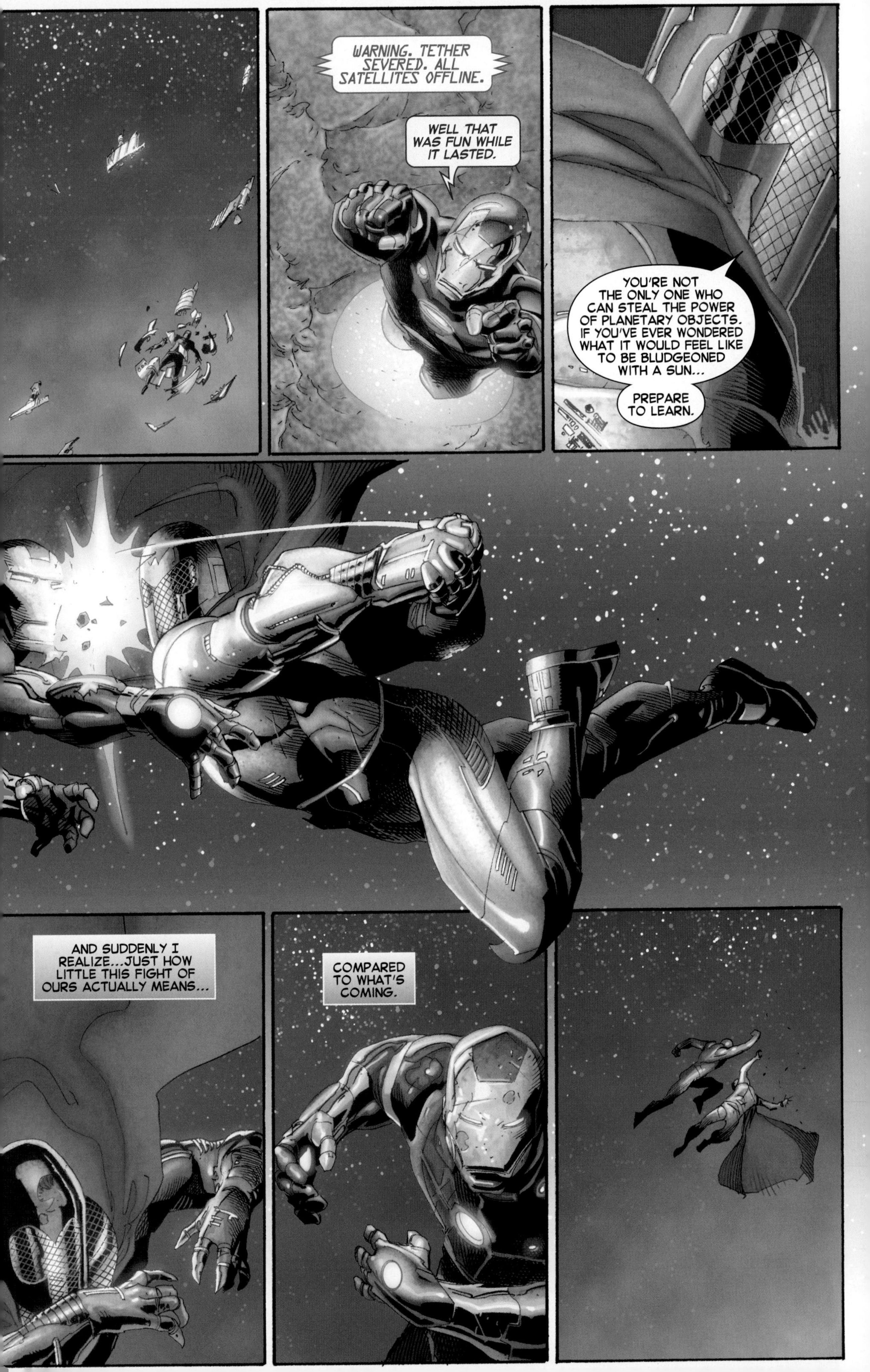
WARNING. TETHER SEVERED. ALL SATELLITES OFFLINE.
WELL THAT WAS FUN WHILE IT LASTED.
YOU'RE NOT THE ONLY ONE WHO CAN STEAL THE POWER OF PLANETARY OBJECTS. IF YOU'VE EVER WONDERED WHAT IT WOULD FEEL LIKE TO BE BLUDGEONED WITH A SUN...
PREPARE TO LEARN.
AND SUDDENLY I REALIZE...JUST HOW LITTLE THIS FIGHT OF OURS ACTUALLY MEANS...
COMPARED TO WHAT'S COMING.

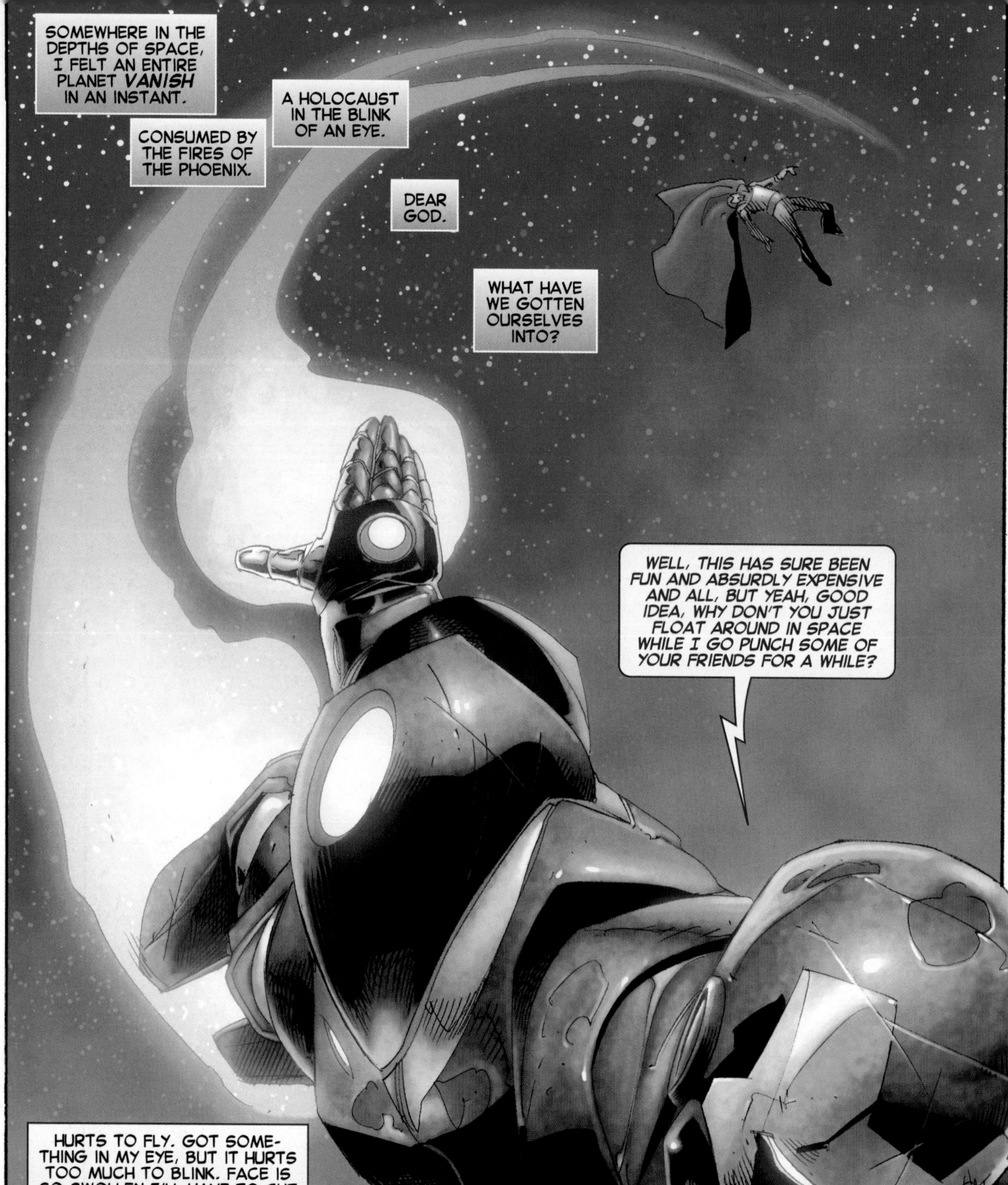
SOMEWHERE IN THE DEPTHS OF SPACE, I FELT AN ENTIRE PLANET VANISH IN AN INSTANT.
CONSUMED BY THE FIRES OF THE PHOENIX.
A HOLOCAUST IN THE BLINK OF AN EYE.
DEAR GOD.
WHAT HAVE WE GOTTEN OURSELVES INTO?
WELL, THIS HAS SURE BEEN FUN AND ABSURDLY EXPENSIVE AND ALL, BUT YEAH, GOOD IDEA, WHY DON'T YOU JUST FLOAT AROUND IN SPACE WHILE I GO PUNCH SOME OF YOUR FRIENDS FOR A WHILE?
HURTS TO FLY. GOT SOMETHING IN MY EYE, BUT IT HURTS TOO MUCH TO BLINK. FACE IS SO SWOLLEN I'LL HAVE TO CUT MY HELMET OFF WITH A BLOWTORCH. NOTE TO SELF: REMEMBER TO COME BACK HERE AND MAKE THAT OLD MAN EAT A NUKE.
A REALLY BIG ONE.
WINNER:
IRON MAN
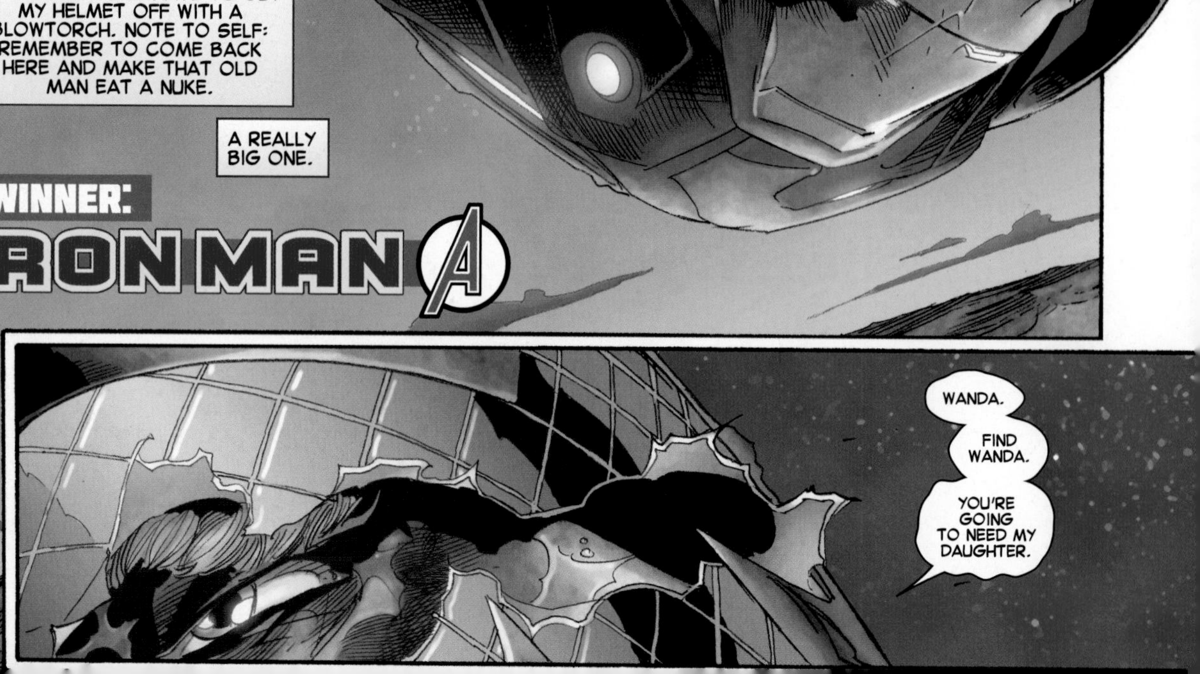
WANDA.
FIND WANDA.
YOU'RE GOING TO NEED MY DAUGHTER.

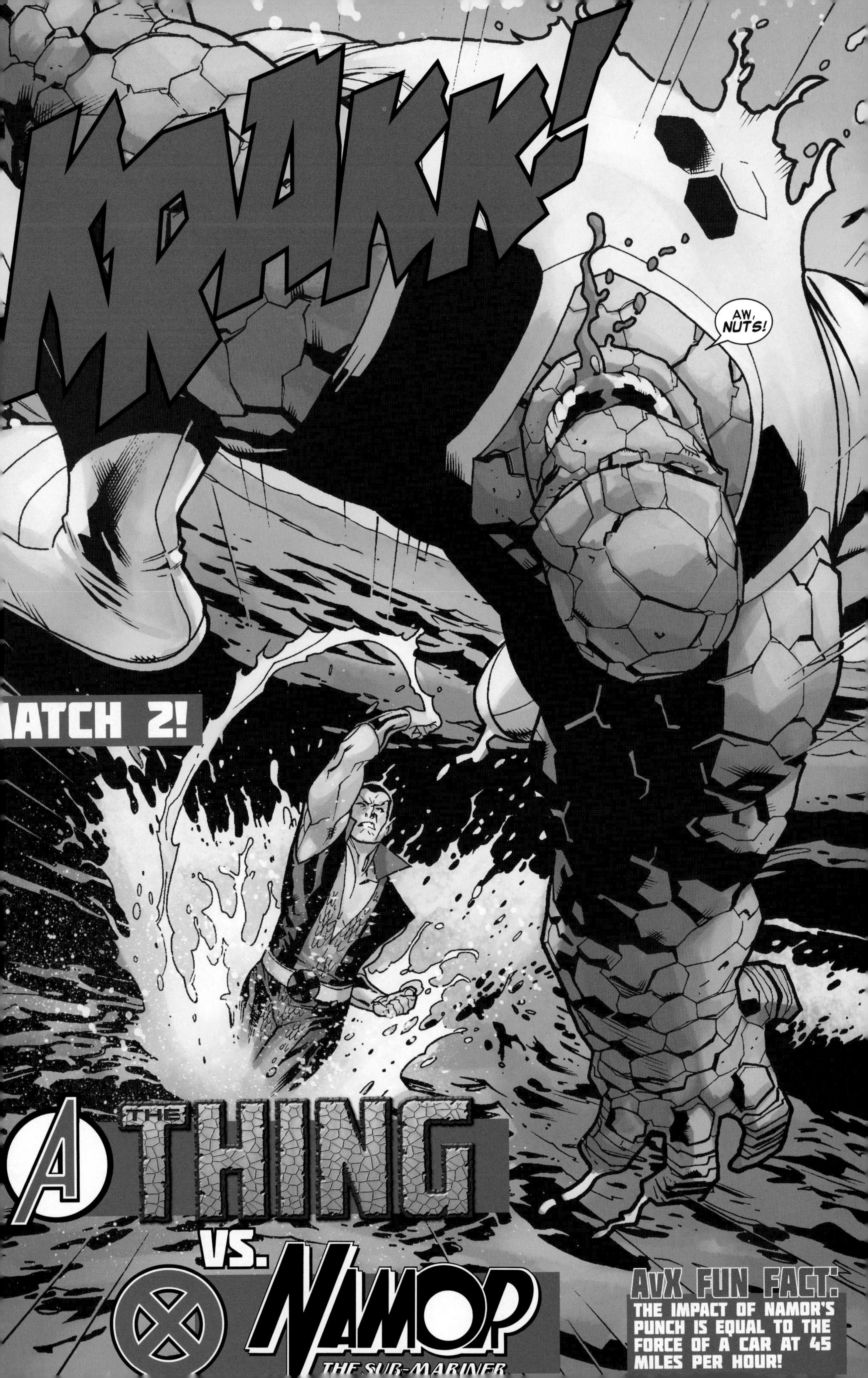
KRAKK!
AW, NUTS!
MATCH 2!
THE THING
VS.
NAMOR
THE SUB-MARINER
AvX FUN FACT:
THE IMPACT OF NAMOR'S PUNCH IS EQUAL TO THE FORCE OF A CAR AT 45 MILES PER HOUR!

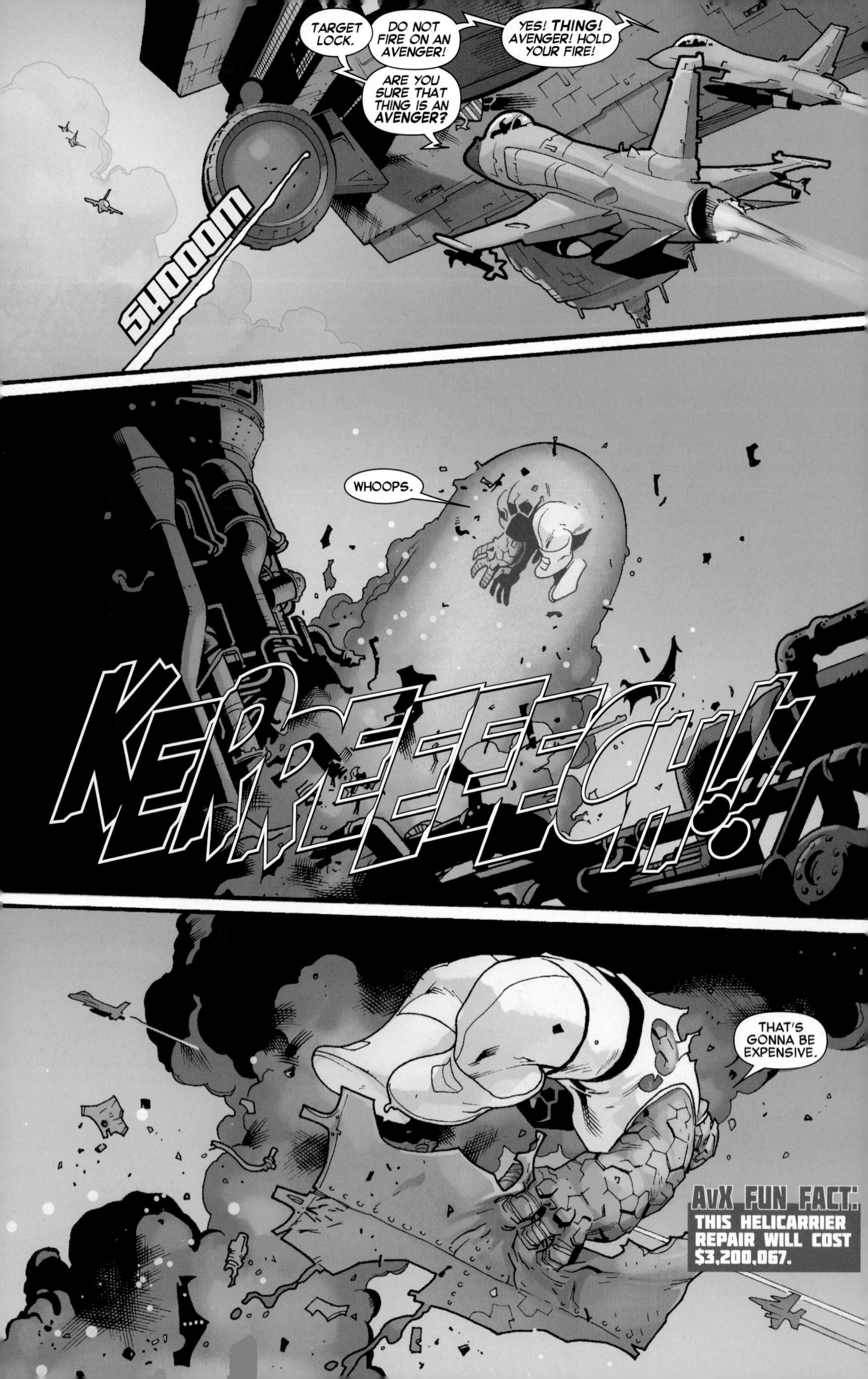
TARGET LOCK.
DO NOT FIRE ON AN AVENGER!
YES! THING! AVENGER! HOLD YOUR FIRE!
ARE YOU SURE THAT THING IS AN AVENGER?
SHOOOM
WHOOPS.
KERRRREEEECH!!
THAT'S GONNA BE EXPENSIVE.
AvX FUN FACT:
THIS HELICARRIER REPAIR WILL COST $3,200,067.

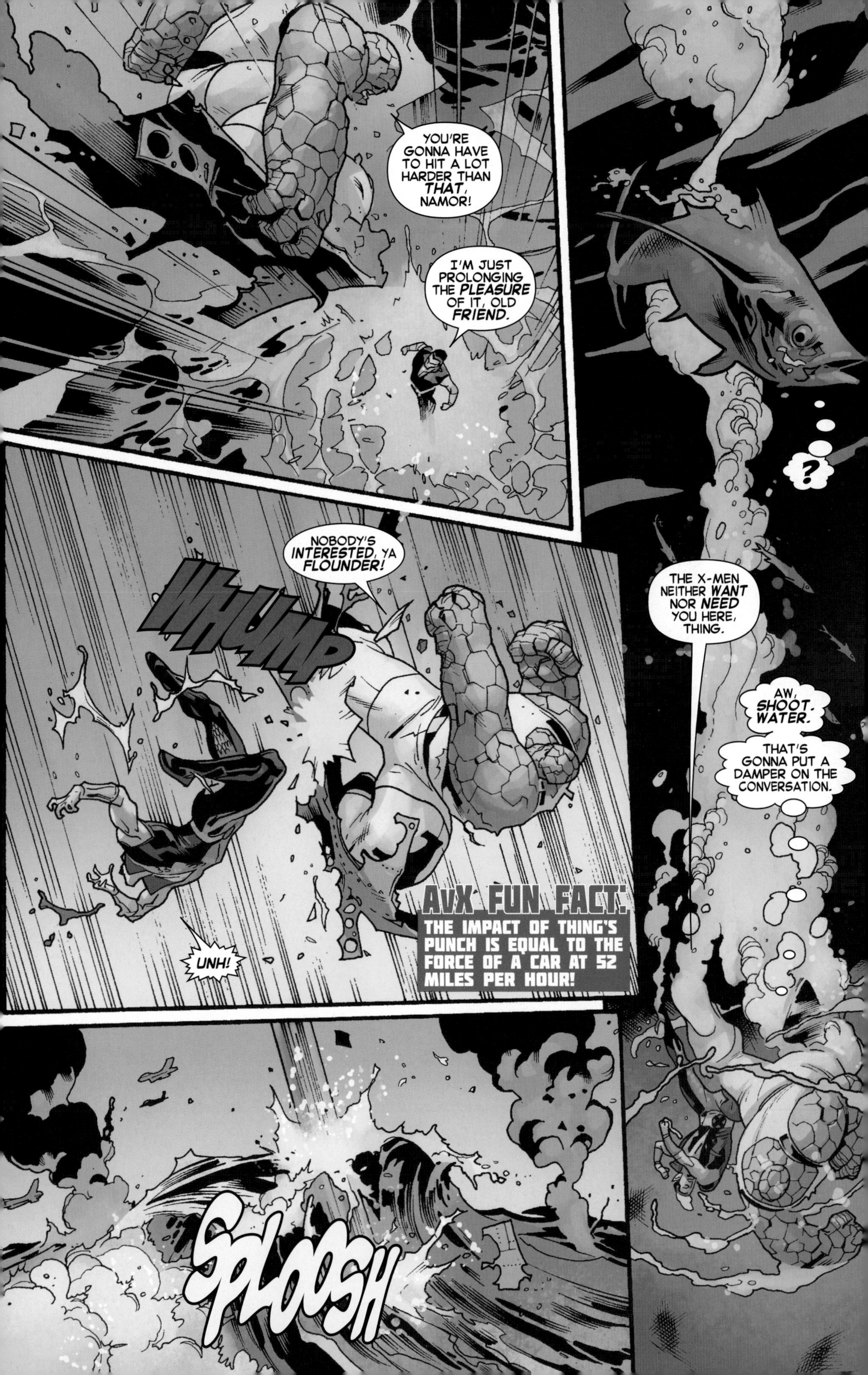
YOU'RE GONNA HAVE TO HIT A LOT HARDER THAN THAT, NAMOR!
I'M JUST PROLONGING THE PLEASURE OF IT, OLD FRIEND.
?
NOBODY'S INTERESTED, YA FLOUNDER!
WHUMP
UNH!
AvX FUN FACT:
THE IMPACT OF THING'S PUNCH IS EQUAL TO THE FORCE OF A CAR AT 52 MILES PER HOUR!
THE X-MEN NEITHER WANT NOR NEED YOU HERE, THING.
AW, SHOOT. WATER.
THAT'S GONNA PUT A DAMPER ON THE CONVERSATION.
SPLOOSH

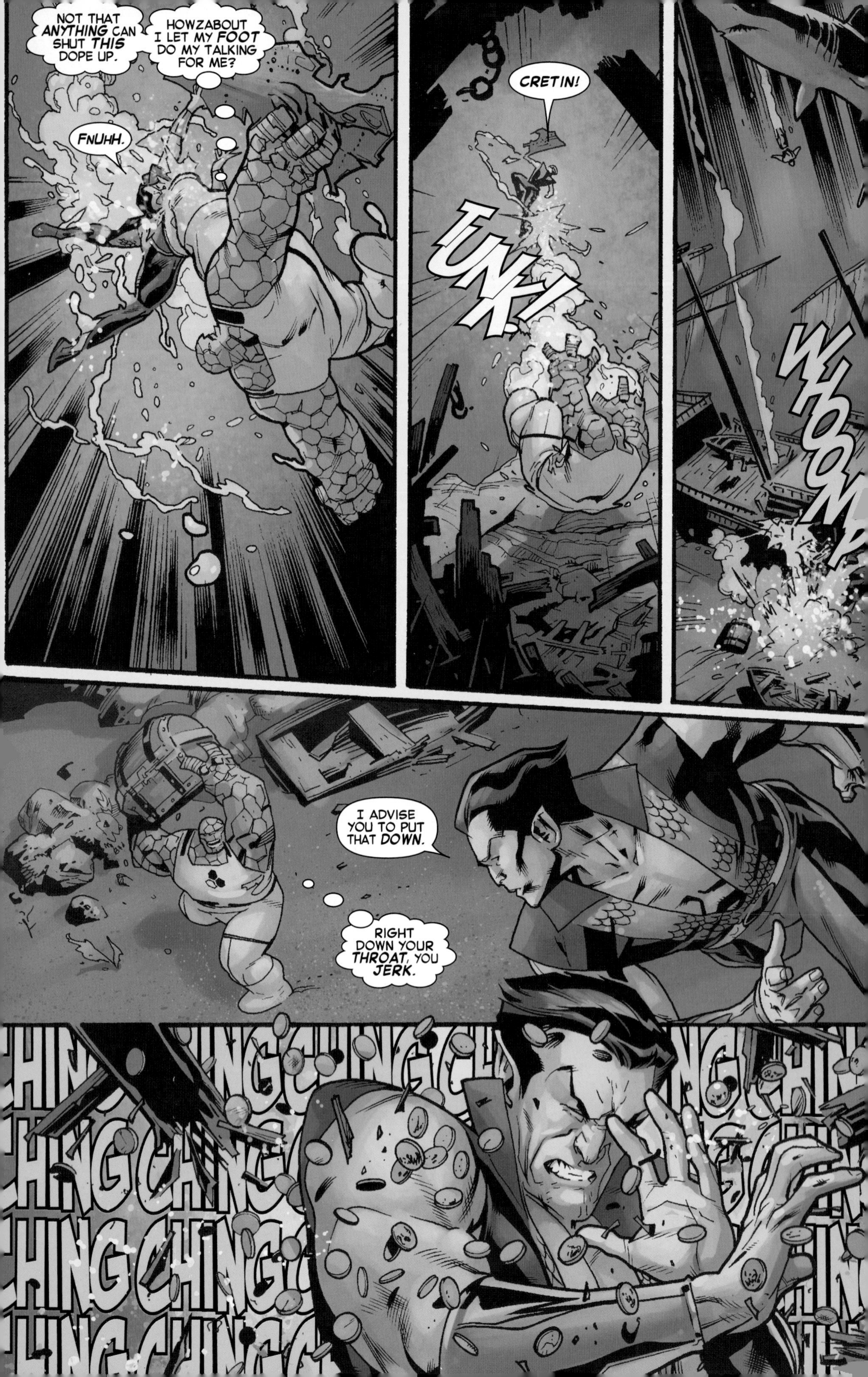
NOT THAT ANYTHING CAN SHUT THIS DOPE UP.
HOWZABOUT I LET MY FOOT DO MY TALKING FOR ME?
FNUHH.
CRETIN!
TUNK!
WHOOMP!
I ADVISE YOU TO PUT THAT DOWN.
RIGHT DOWN YOUR THROAT, YOU JERK.
CHING CHING CHING CHING

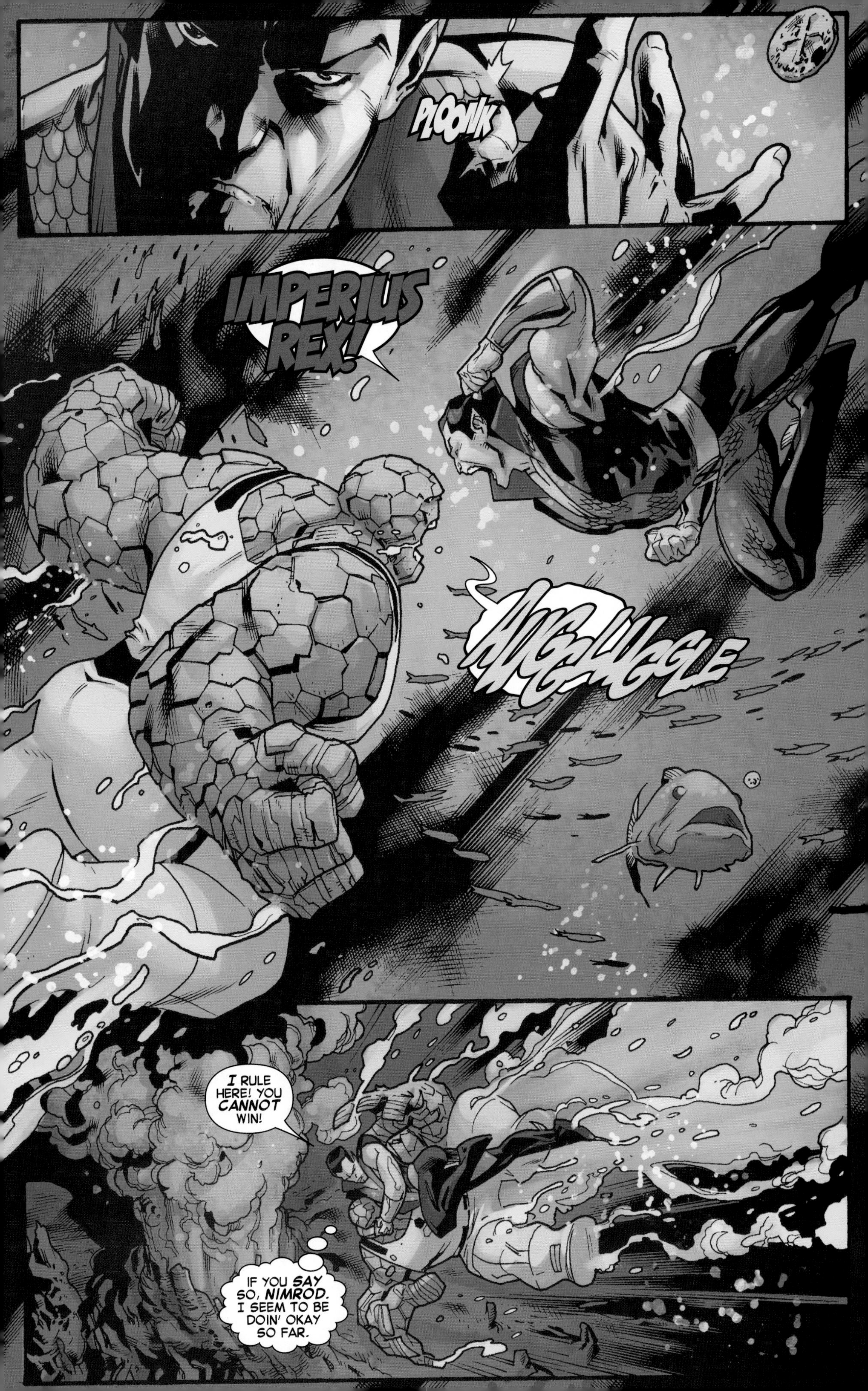
PLOONK
IMPERIUS REX!
HUGGLUGGLE
I RULE HERE! YOU CANNOT WIN!
IF YOU SAY SO, NIMROD. I SEEM TO BE DOIN' OKAY SO FAR.

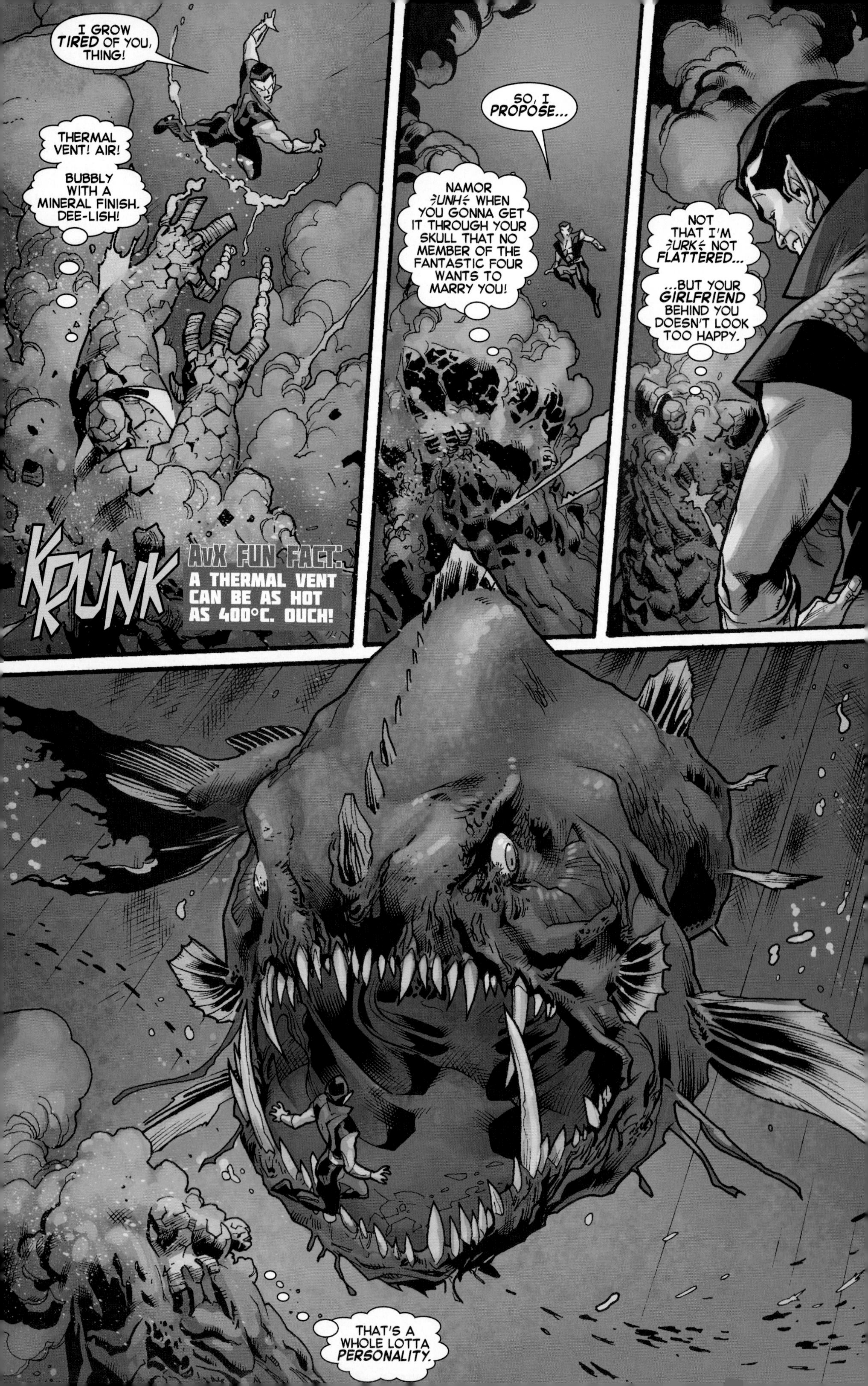
I GROW TIRED OF YOU, THING!
THERMAL VENT! AIR!
BUBBLY WITH A MINERAL FINISH. DEE-LISH!
KRUNK
AvX FUN FACT: A THERMAL VENT CAN BE AS HOT AS 400°C. OUCH!
SO, I PROPOSE...
NAMOR =UNH= WHEN YOU GONNA GET IT THROUGH YOUR SKULL THAT NO MEMBER OF THE FANTASTIC FOUR WANTS TO MARRY YOU!
NOT THAT I'M =URK= NOT FLATTERED...
...BUT YOUR GIRLFRIEND BEHIND YOU DOESN'T LOOK TOO HAPPY.
THAT'S A WHOLE LOTTA PERSONALITY.

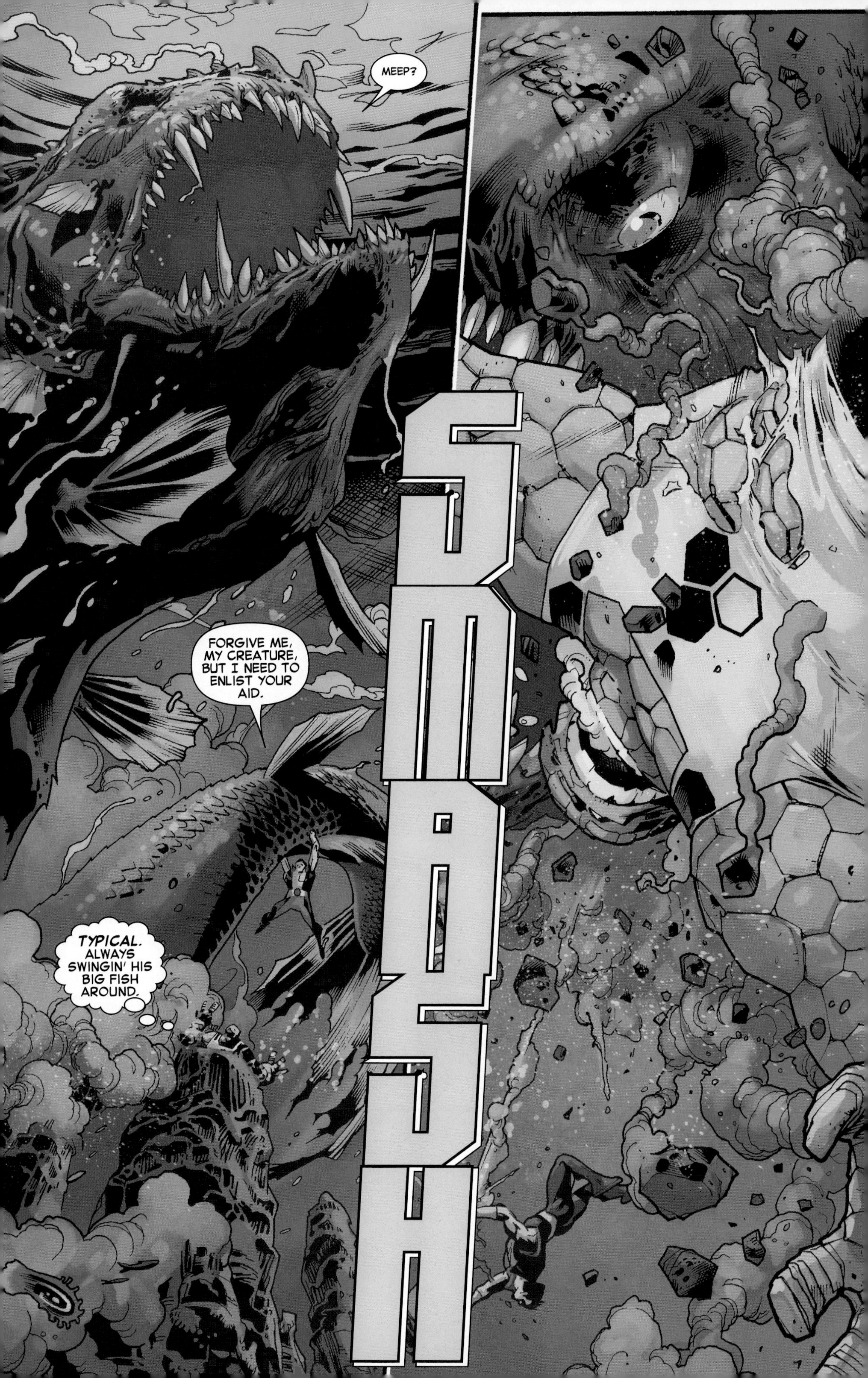
MEEP?
FORGIVE ME, MY CREATURE, BUT I NEED TO ENLIST YOUR AID.
TYPICAL. ALWAYS SWINGIN' HIS BIG FISH AROUND.
SMASH

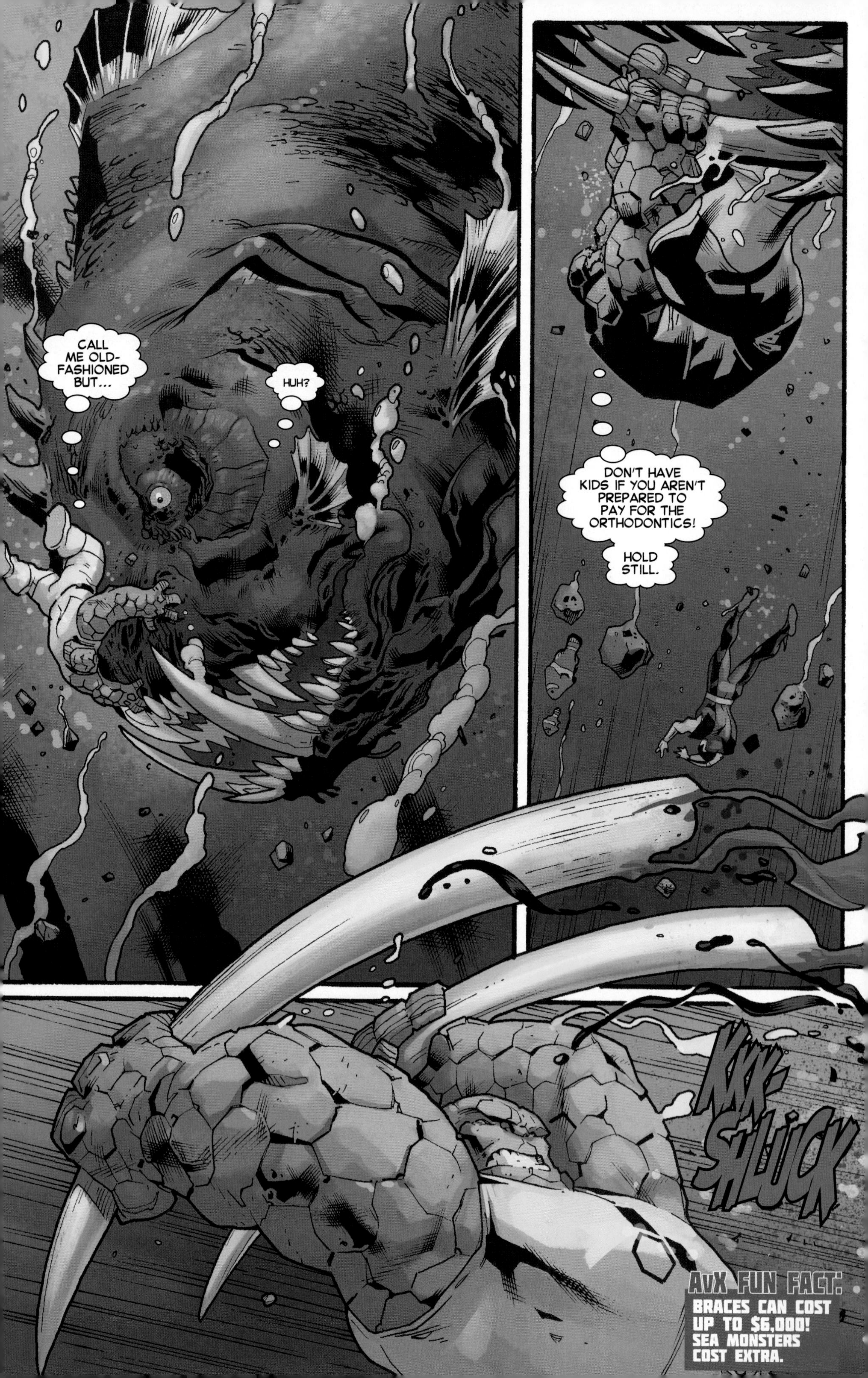

CALL ME OLD-FASHIONED BUT...
HUH?
DON'T HAVE KIDS IF YOU AREN'T PREPARED TO PAY FOR THE ORTHODONTICS!
HOLD STILL.
KKK-SHUCK
AvX FUN FACT:
BRACES CAN COST UP TO $6,000! SEA MONSTERS COST EXTRA.

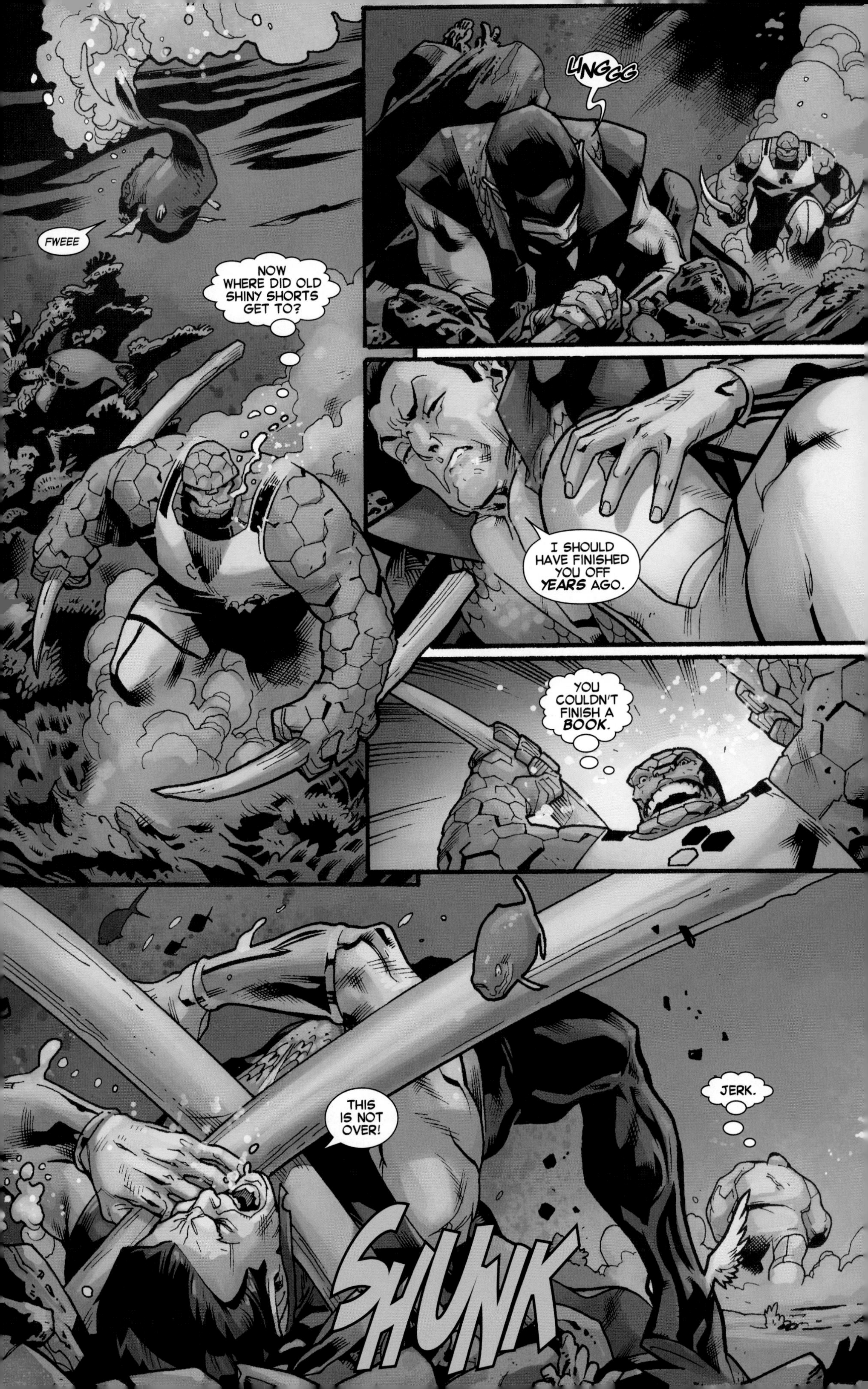

FWEEE
NOW WHERE DID OLD SHINY SHORTS GET TO?
UNGGG
I SHOULD HAVE FINISHED YOU OFF YEARS AGO.
YOU COULDN'T FINISH A BOOK.
THIS IS NOT OVER!
JERK.
SHUNK

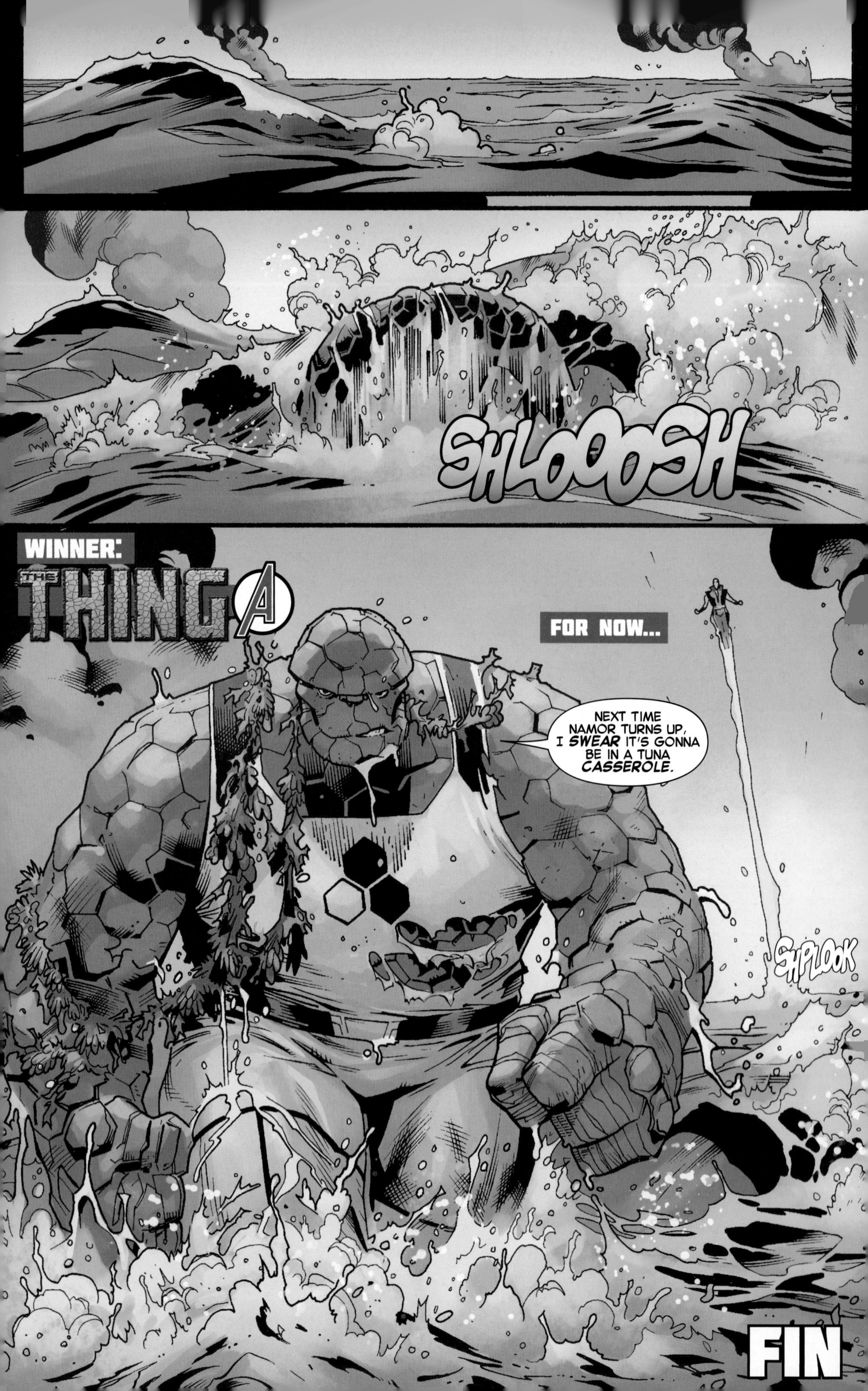

SHLOOOSH
WINNER:
THE THING
FOR NOW...
NEXT TIME NAMOR TURNS UP, I SWEAR IT'S GONNA BE IN A TUNA CASSEROLE.
SHPLOOK
FIN

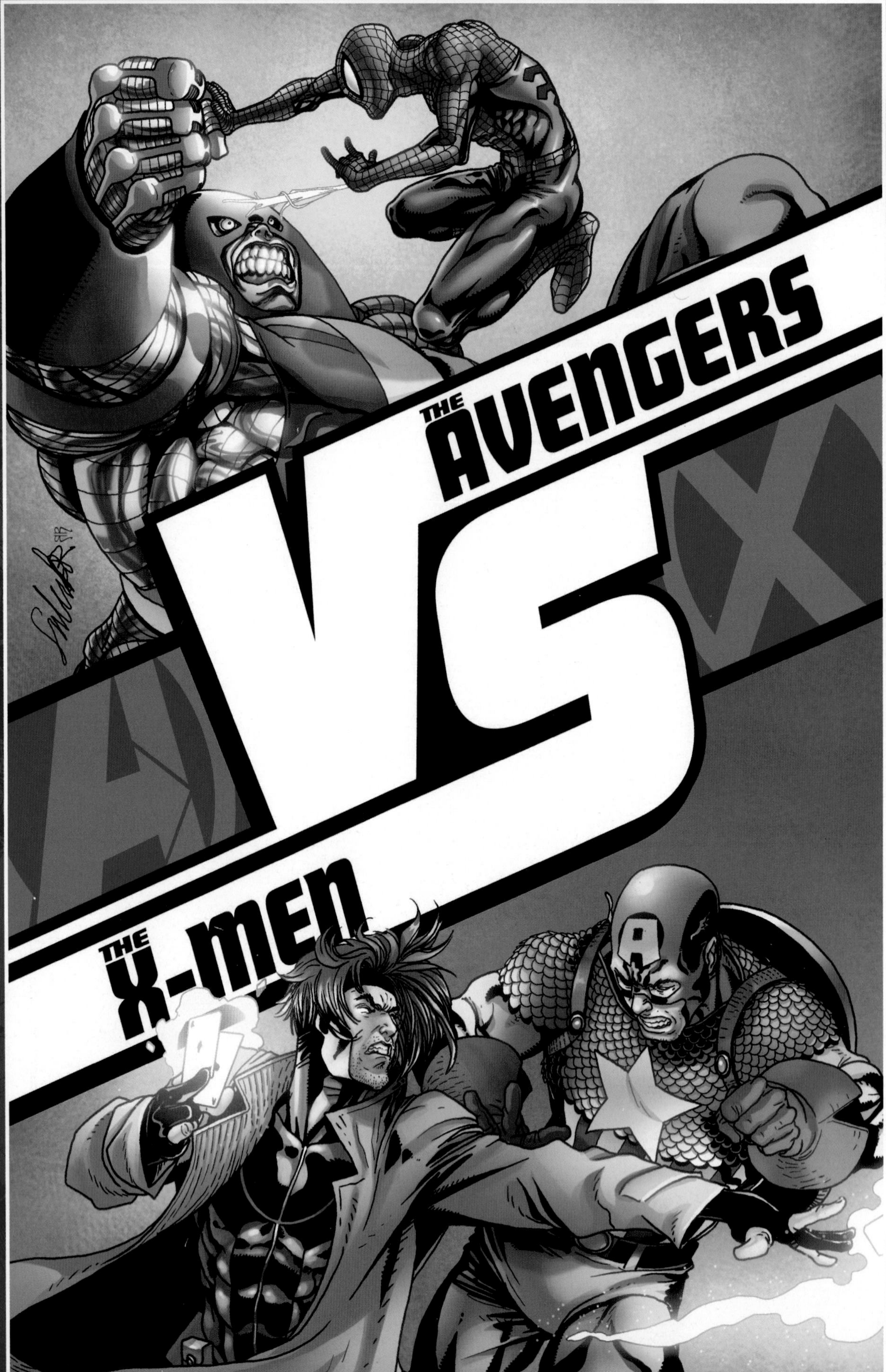
THE AVENGERS
VS
THE X-MEN

ISSUE #2

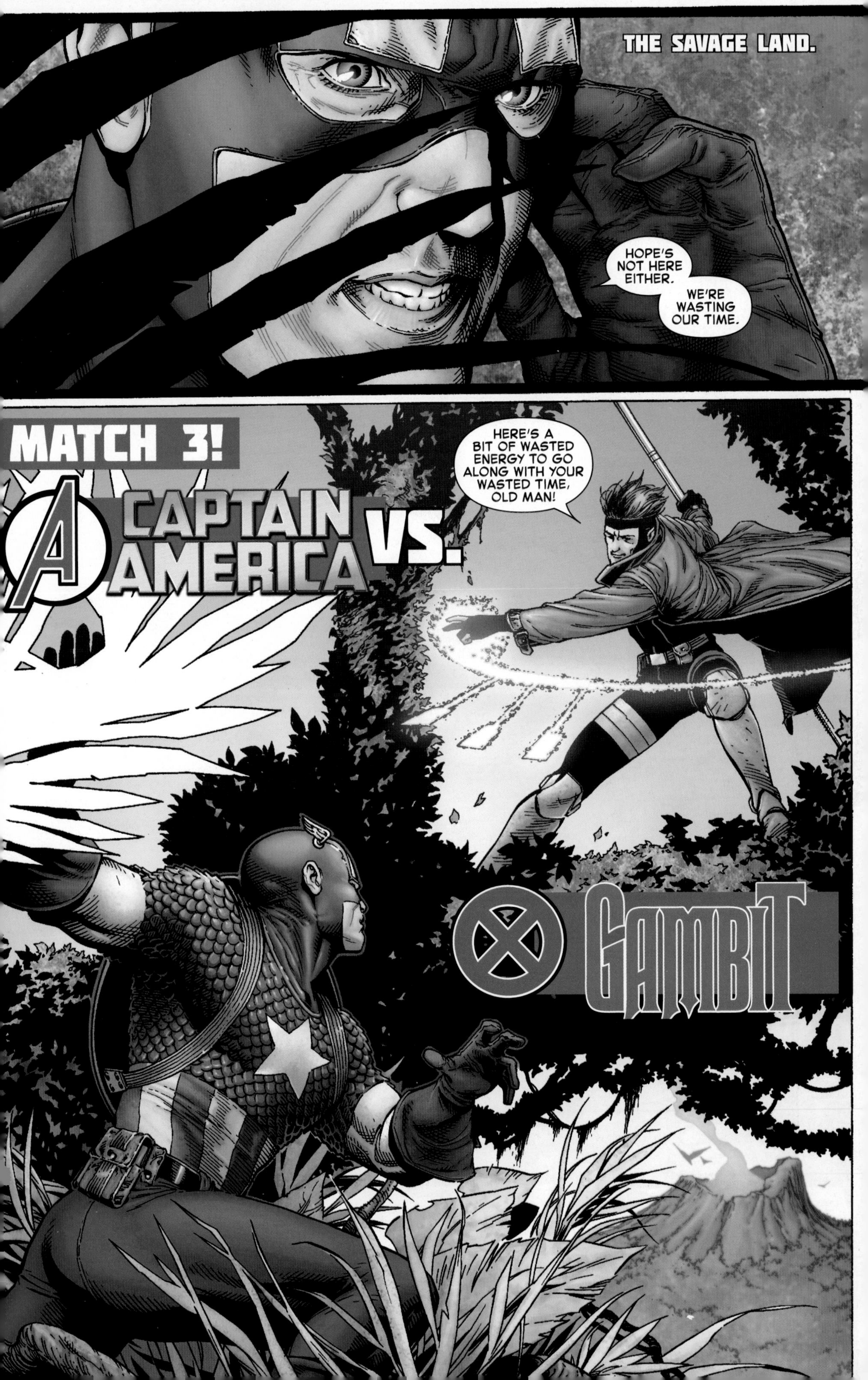
THE SAVAGE LAND.
HOPE'S NOT HERE EITHER.
WE'RE WASTING OUR TIME.
MATCH 3!
CAPTAIN AMERICA VS.
HERE'S A BIT OF WASTED ENERGY TO GO ALONG WITH YOUR WASTED TIME, OLD MAN!
GAMBIT

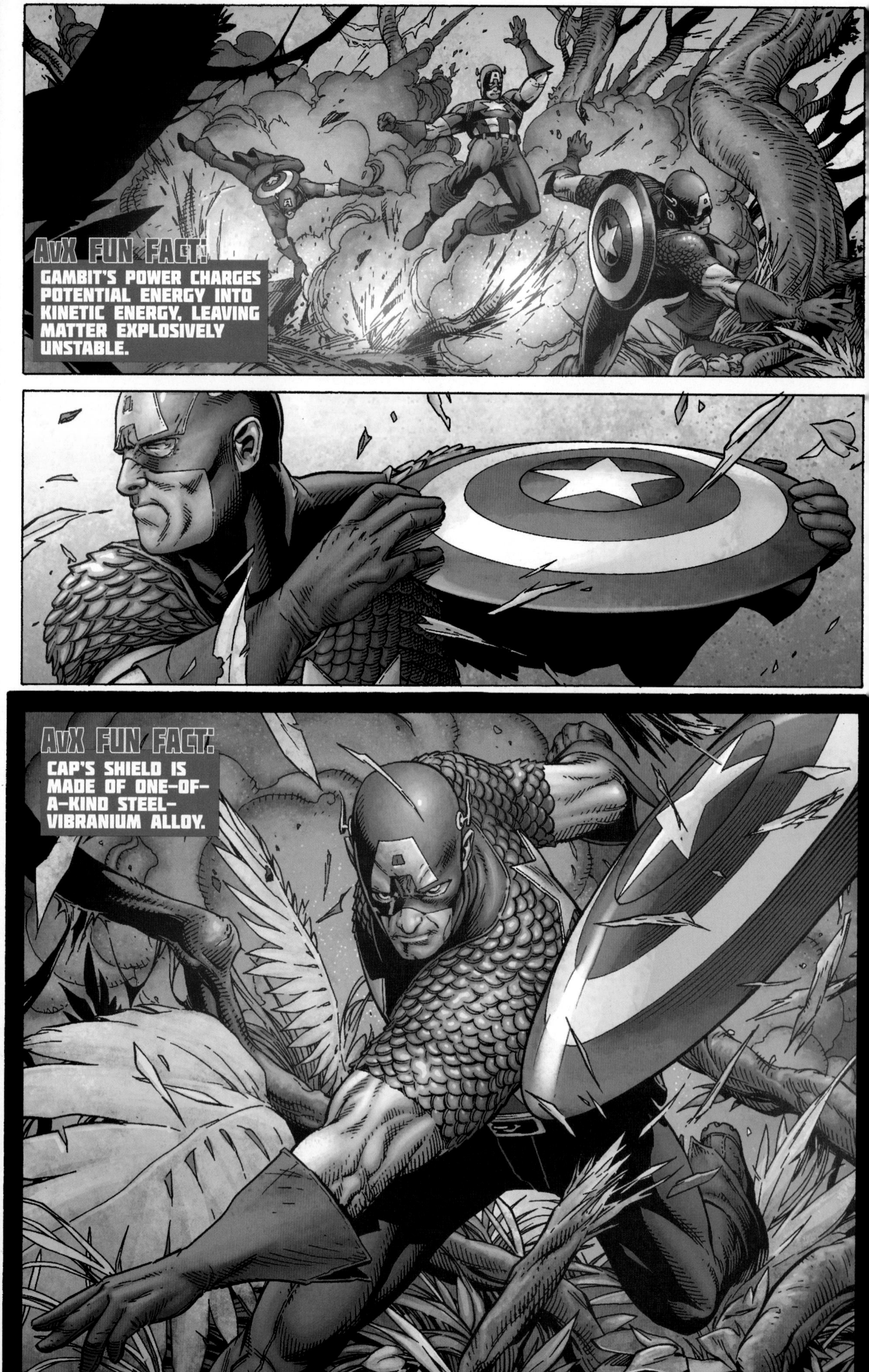
AvX FUN FACT:
GAMBIT'S POWER CHARGES POTENTIAL ENERGY INTO KINETIC ENERGY, LEAVING MATTER EXPLOSIVELY UNSTABLE.
AvX FUN FACT:
CAP'S SHIELD IS MADE OF ONE-OF-A-KIND STEEL-VIBRANIUM ALLOY.

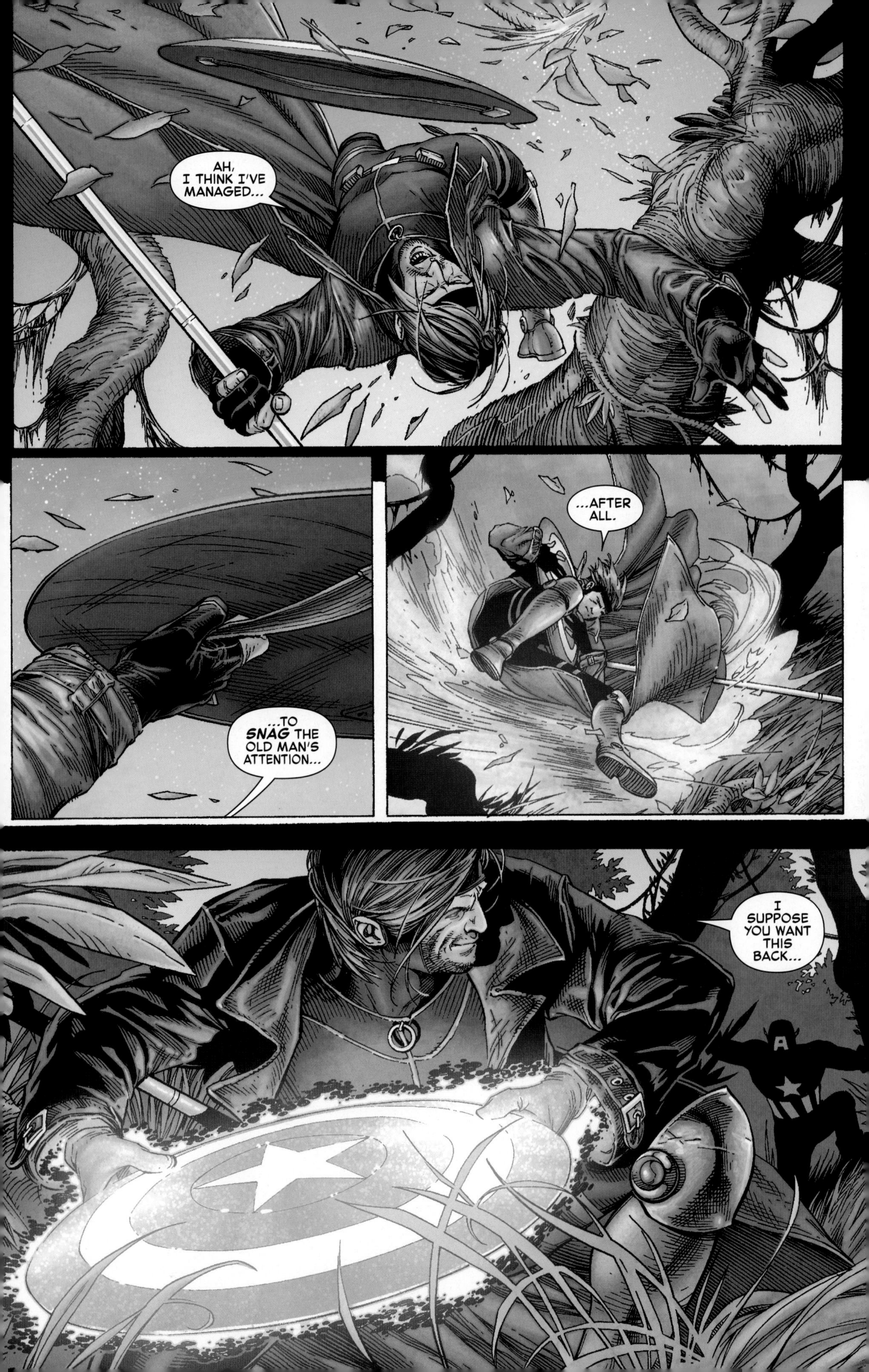
AH, I THINK I'VE MANAGED...
...TO SNAG THE OLD MAN'S ATTENTION...
...AFTER ALL.
I SUPPOSE YOU WANT THIS BACK...

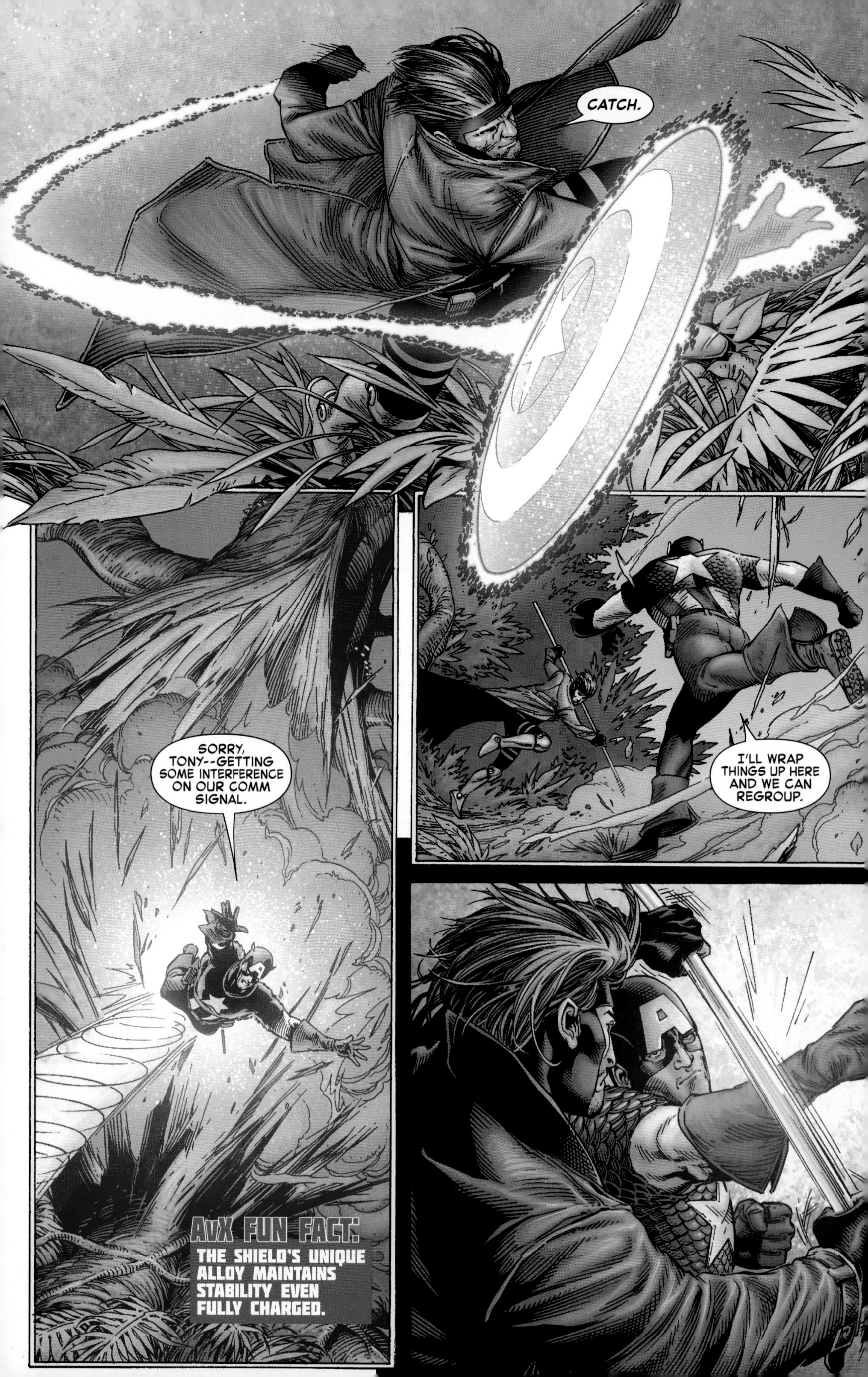
CATCH.
SORRY, TONY--GETTING SOME INTERFERENCE ON OUR COMM SIGNAL.
I'LL WRAP THINGS UP HERE AND WE CAN REGROUP.
AvX FUN FACT:
THE SHIELD'S UNIQUE ALLOY MAINTAINS STABILITY EVEN FULLY CHARGED.

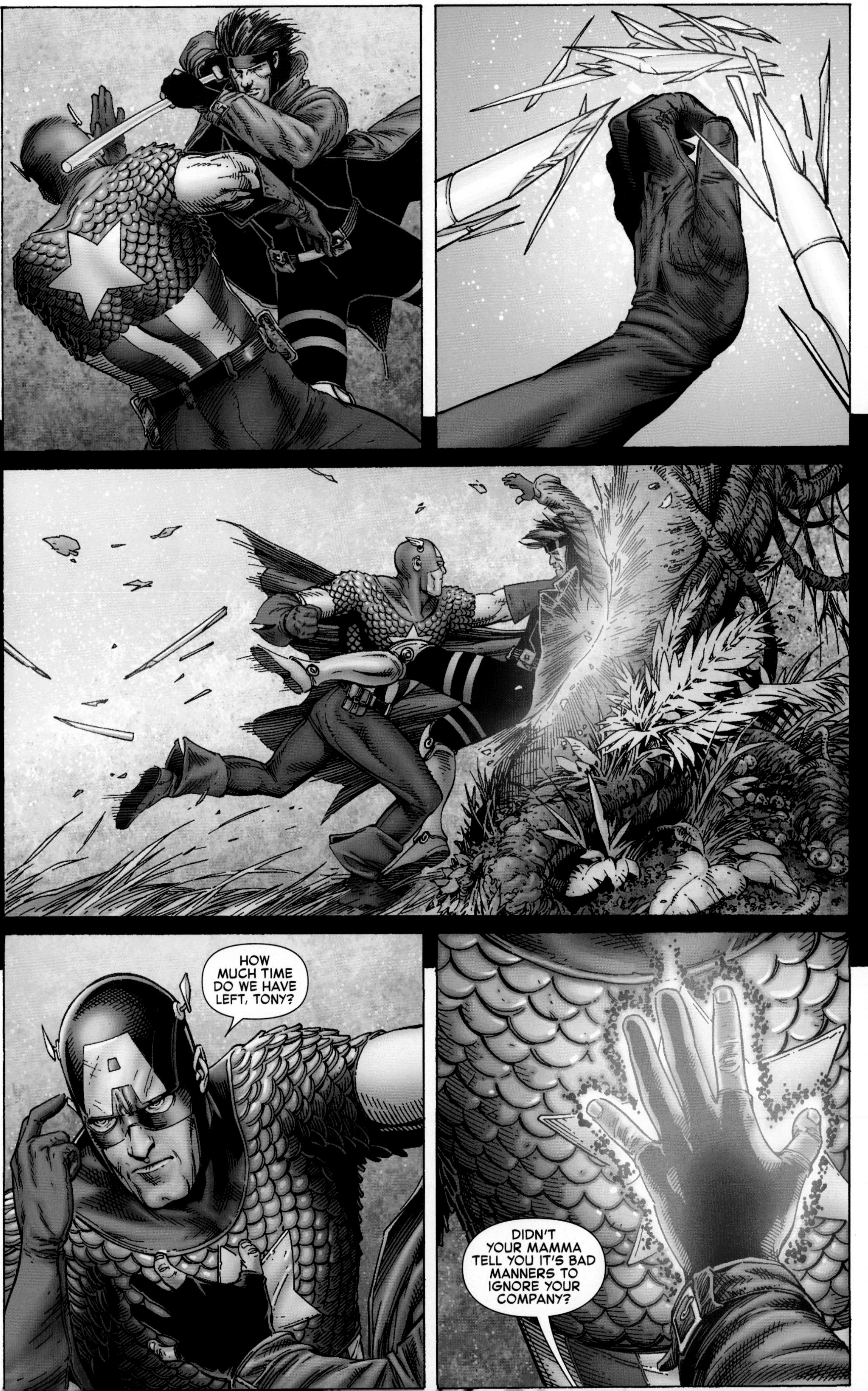
HOW MUCH TIME DO WE HAVE LEFT, TONY?
DIDN'T YOUR MAMMA TELL YOU IT'S BAD MANNERS TO IGNORE YOUR COMPANY?

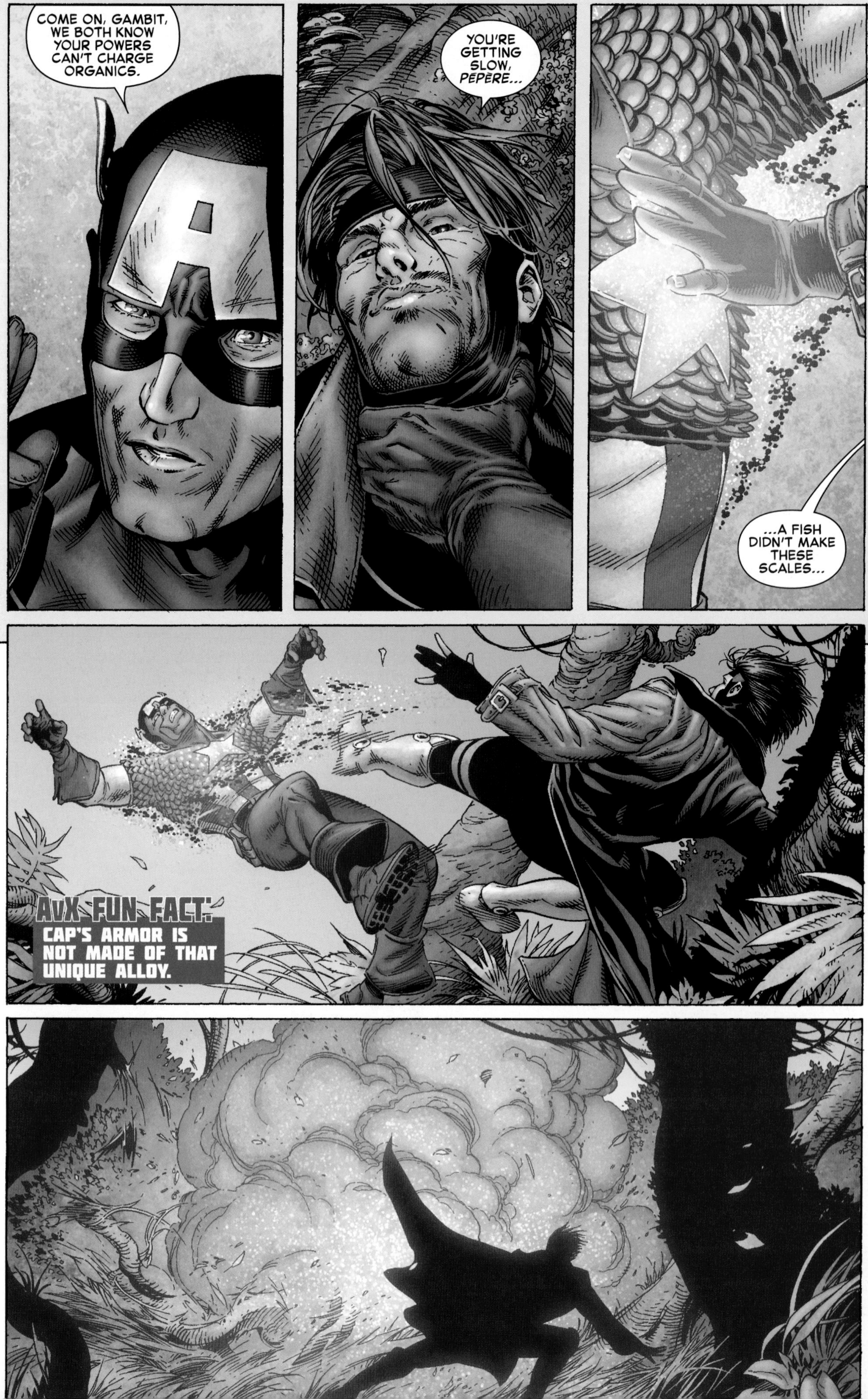
COME ON, GAMBIT, WE BOTH KNOW YOUR POWERS CAN'T CHARGE ORGANICS.
YOU'RE GETTING SLOW, PÈPÈRE...
...A FISH DIDN'T MAKE THESE SCALES...
AvX FUN FACT:
CAP'S ARMOR IS NOT MADE OF THAT UNIQUE ALLOY.

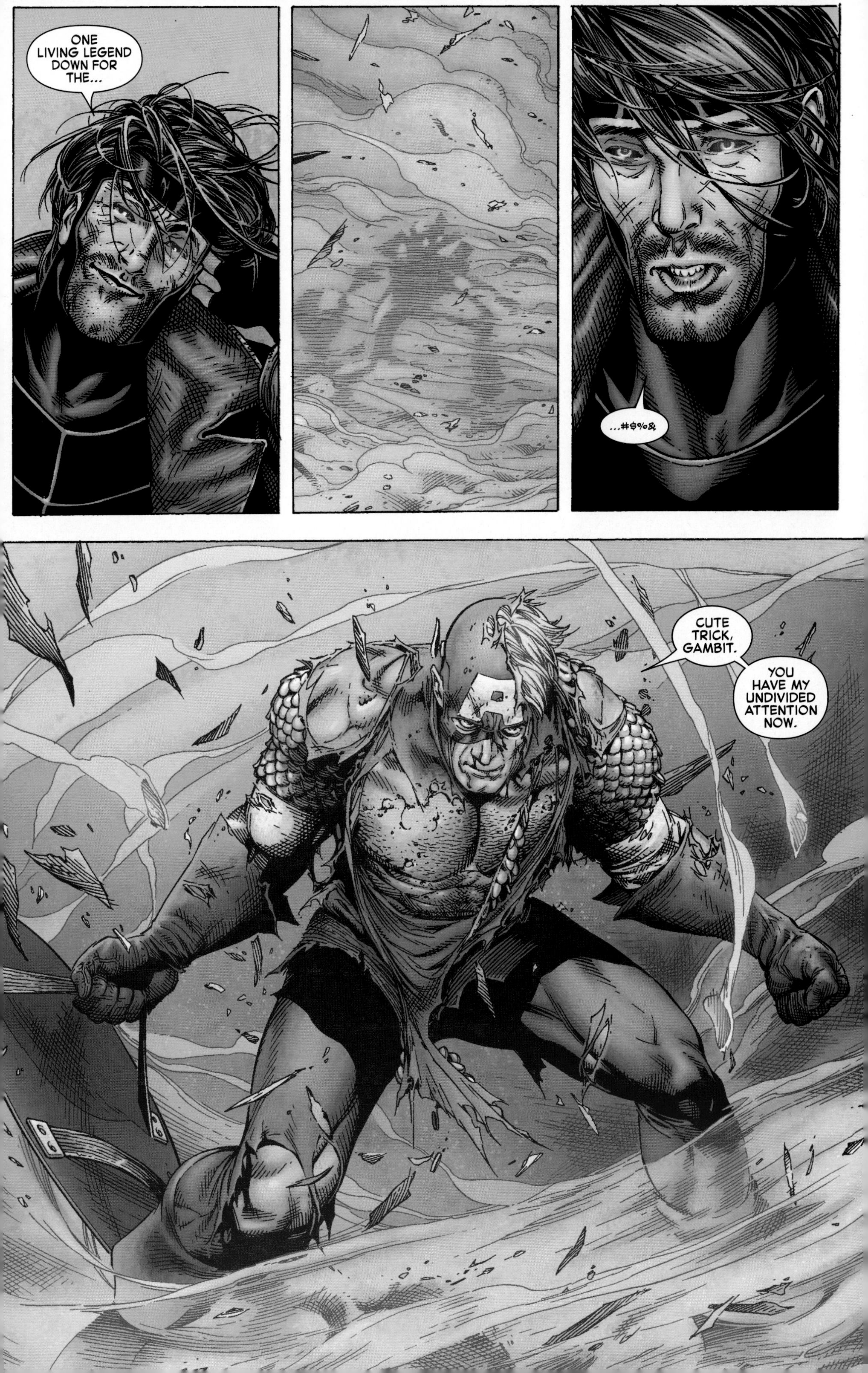
ONE LIVING LEGEND DOWN FOR THE...
...#$%&
CUTE TRICK, GAMBIT.
YOU HAVE MY UNDIVIDED ATTENTION NOW.

AvX FUN FACT: CAPTAIN AMERICA CAN RUN A 40-YARD DASH IN 3.82 SECONDS.

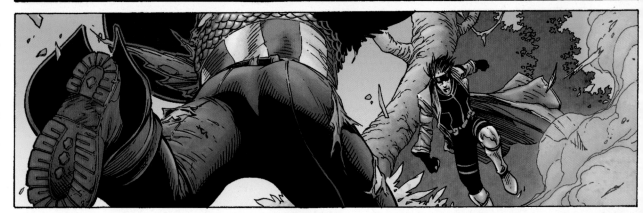

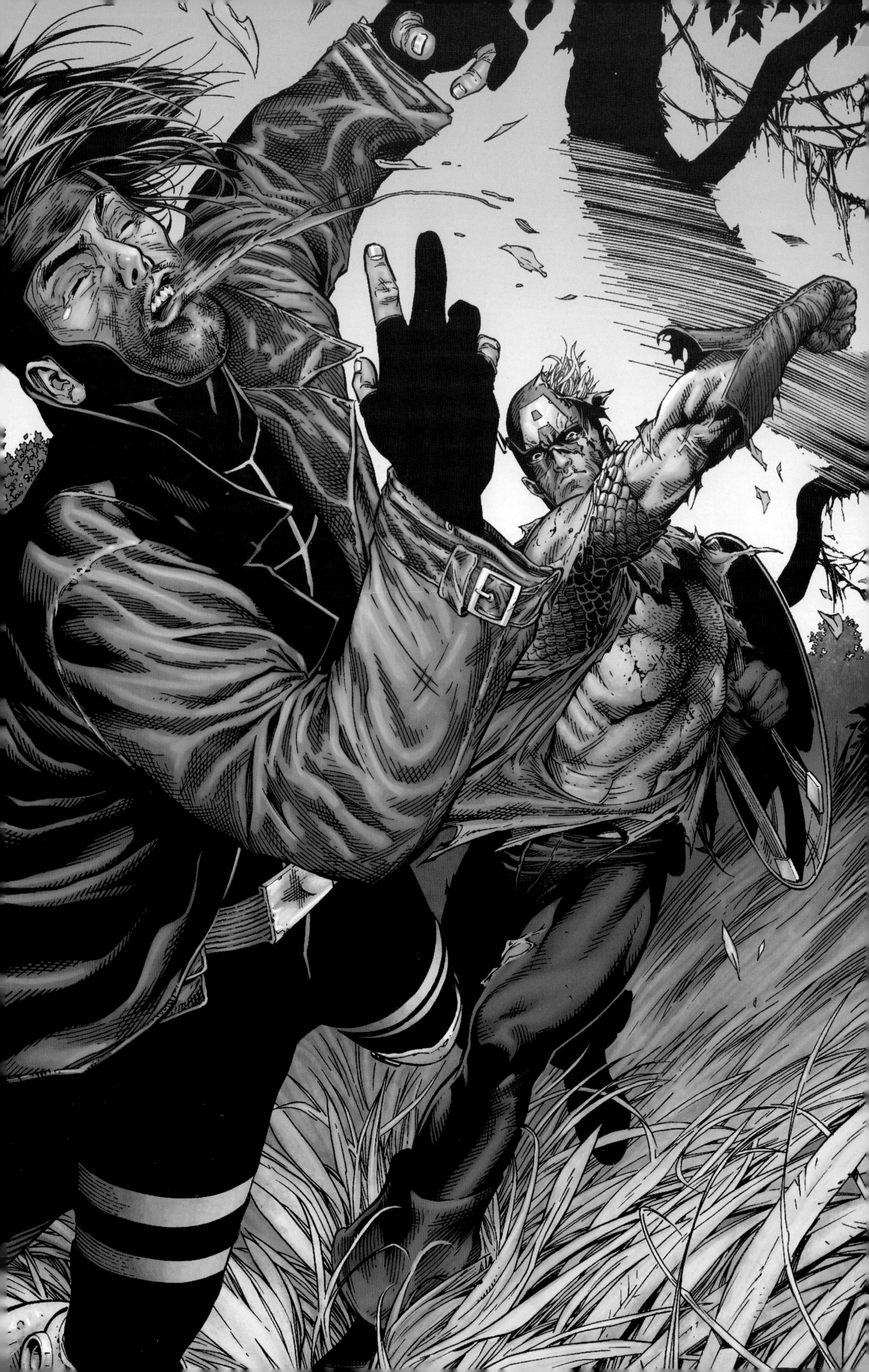

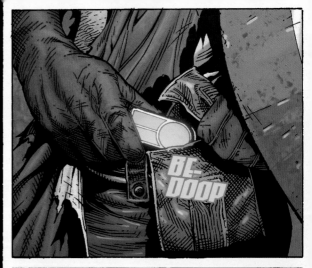

WELL, I'LL BE...

TONY, PLEASE CONTACT ALL THE OTHER TEAMS AND HAVE THEM PULL BACK AND RENDEZVOUS AT THE TOWER.

NEW PLAN. WE DON'T HAVE TO CHASE HOPE ANYMORE.

AND CAN SOMEONE GET IN MY LOCKER AND GRAB MY SPARE UNIFORM?

WINNER:

CAPTAIN AMERICA Ⓐ

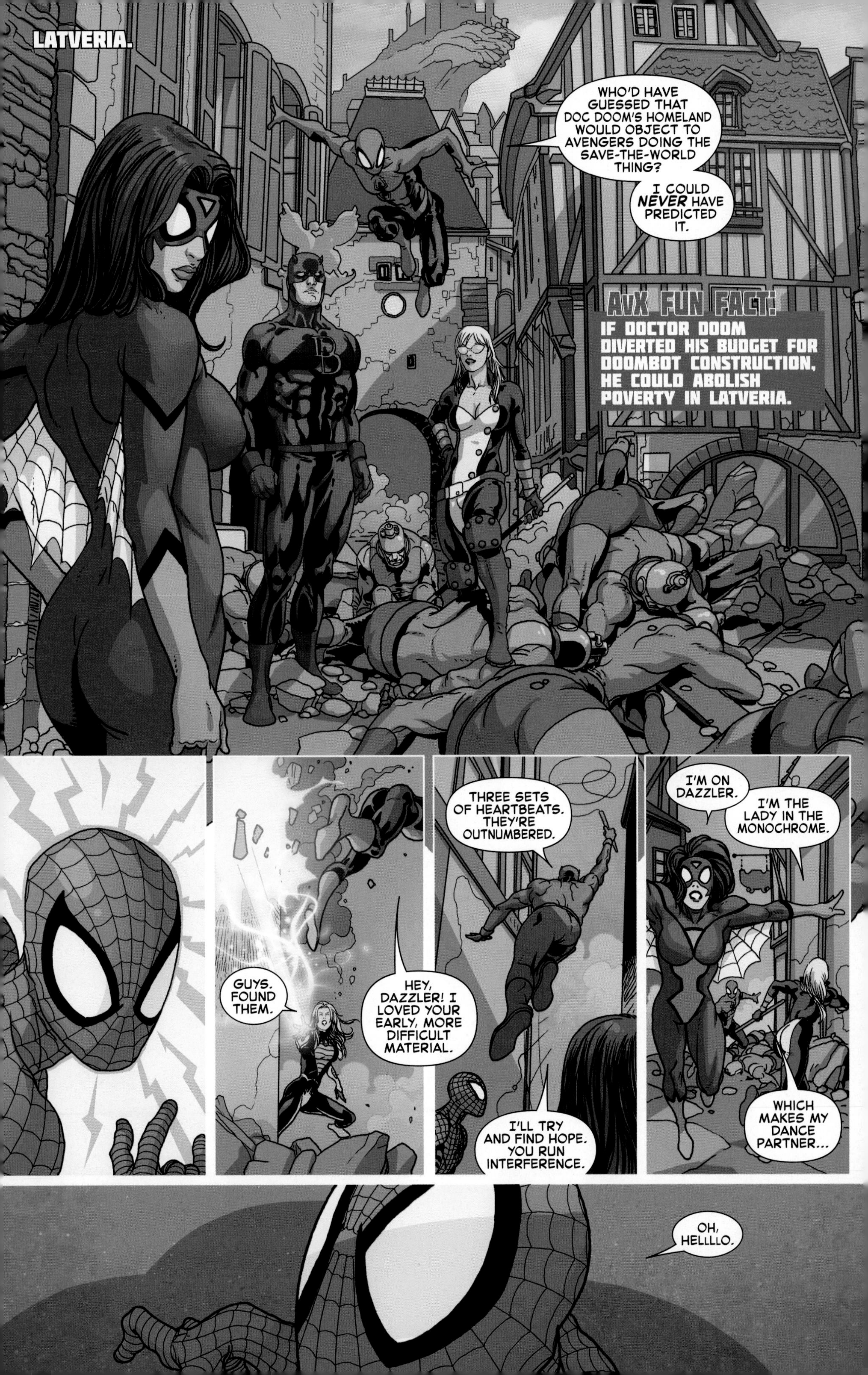
LATVERIA.
WHO'D HAVE GUESSED THAT DOC DOOM'S HOMELAND WOULD OBJECT TO AVENGERS DOING THE SAVE-THE-WORLD THING?
I COULD NEVER HAVE PREDICTED IT.
AvX FUN FACT:
IF DOCTOR DOOM DIVERTED HIS BUDGET FOR DOOMBOT CONSTRUCTION, HE COULD ABOLISH POVERTY IN LATVERIA.
GUYS. FOUND THEM.
HEY, DAZZLER! I LOVED YOUR EARLY, MORE DIFFICULT MATERIAL.
THREE SETS OF HEARTBEATS. THEY'RE OUTNUMBERED.
I'LL TRY AND FIND HOPE. YOU RUN INTERFERENCE.
I'M ON DAZZLER.
I'M THE LADY IN THE MONOCHROME.
WHICH MAKES MY DANCE PARTNER...
OH, HELLLLO.

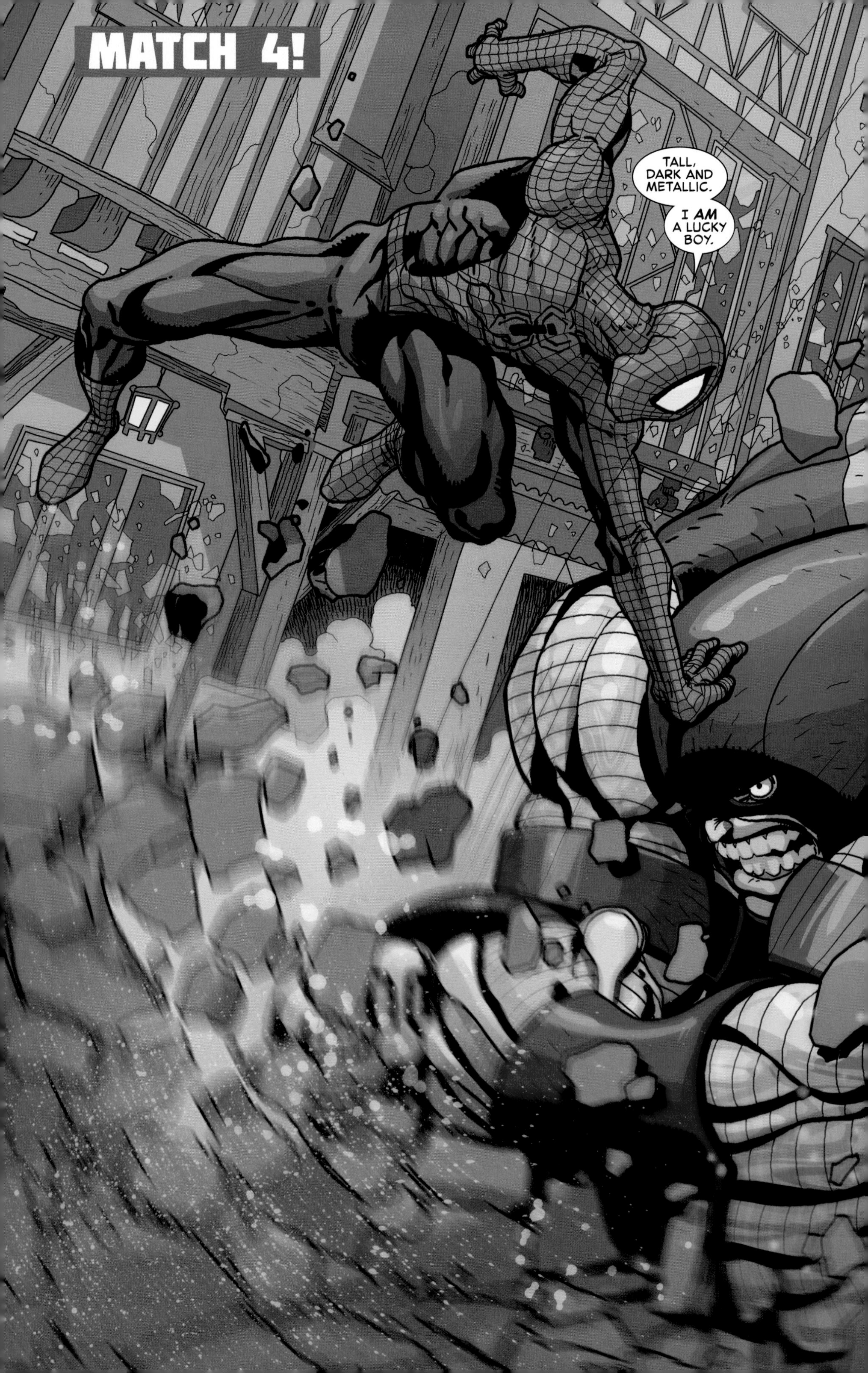
MATCH 4!
TALL, DARK AND METALLIC.
I AM A LUCKY BOY.

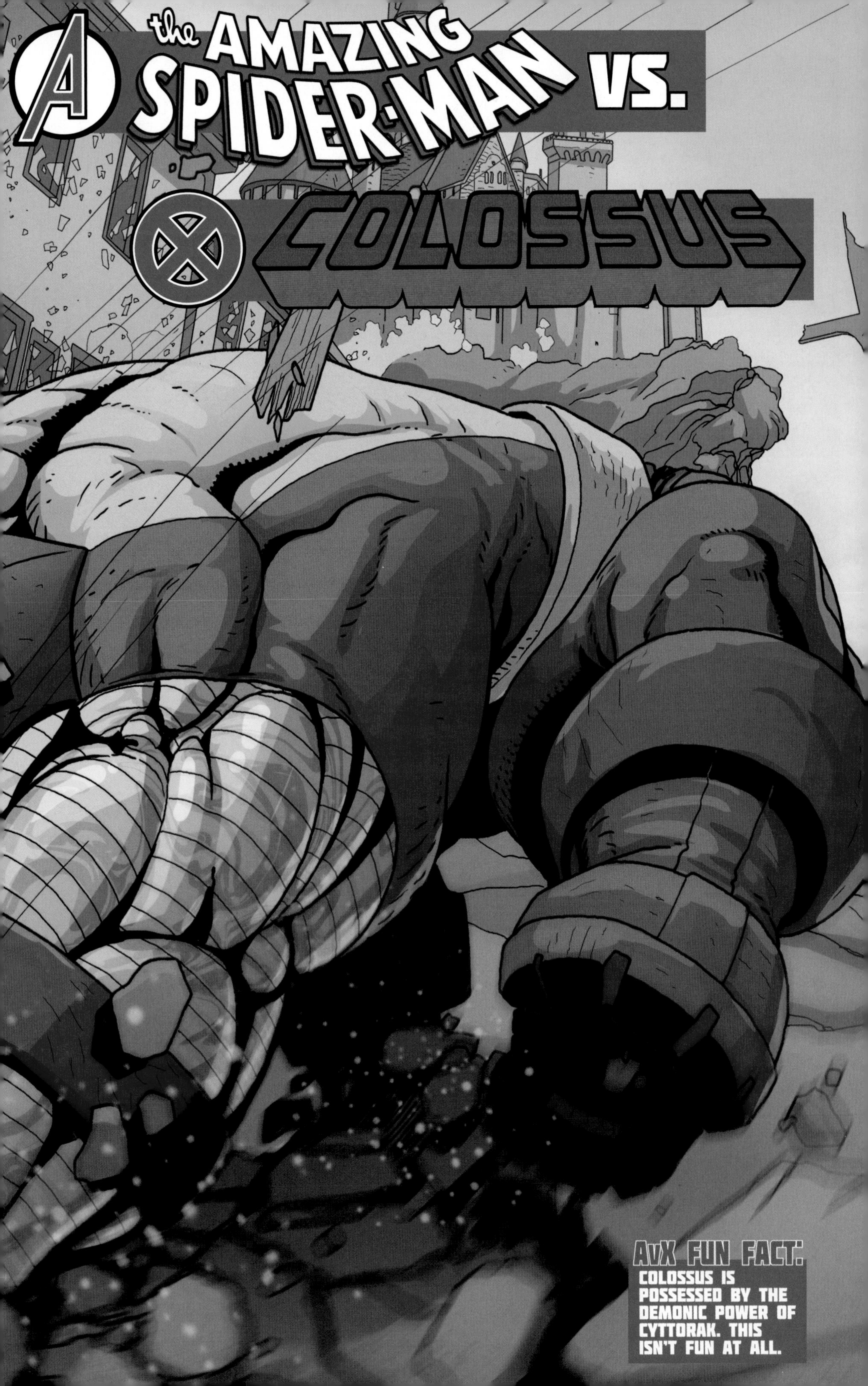

the AMAZING SPIDER-MAN VS.
COLOSSUS
AvX FUN FACT:
COLOSSUS IS POSSESSED BY THE DEMONIC POWER OF CYTTORAK. THIS ISN'T FUN AT ALL.

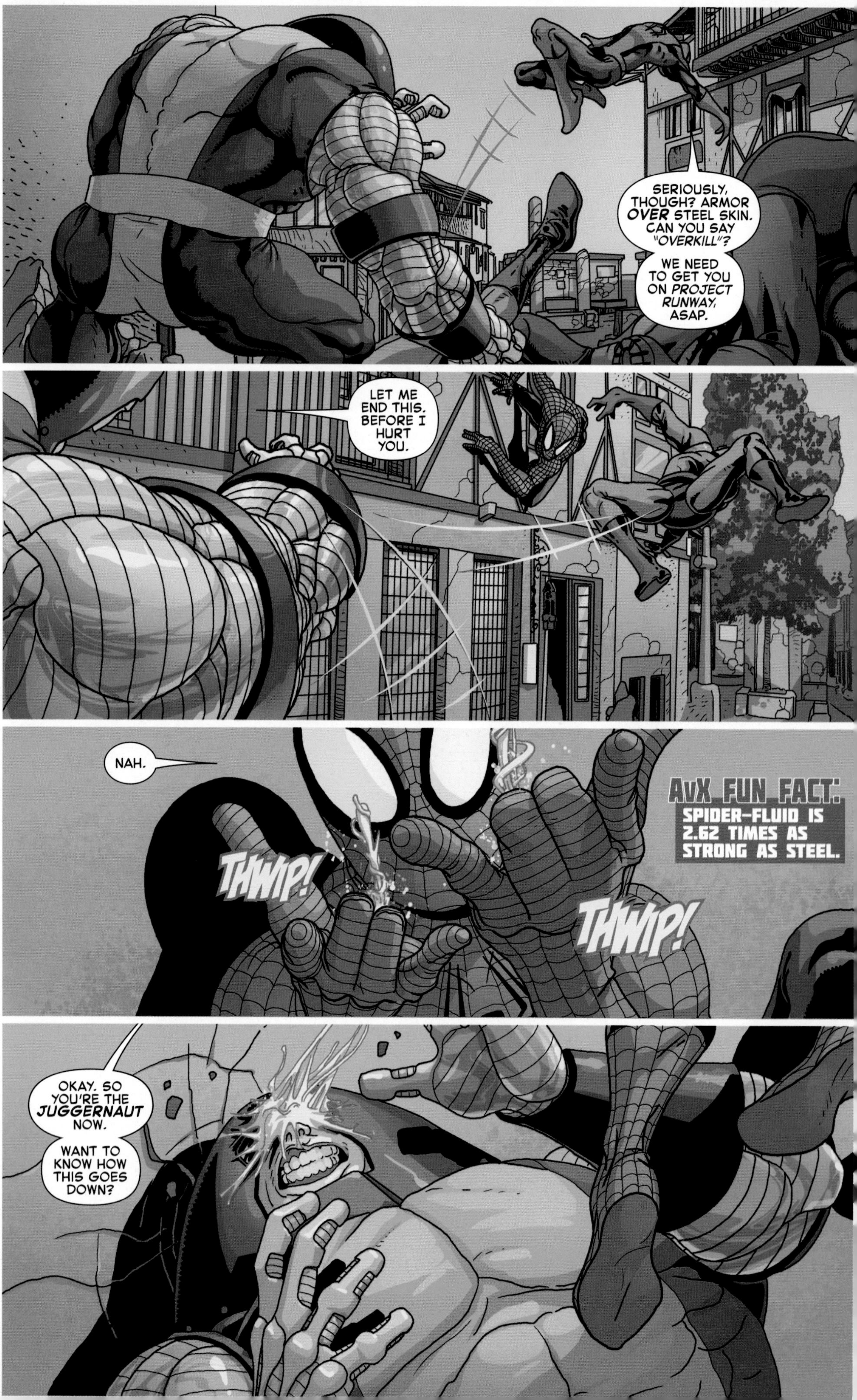

SERIOUSLY, THOUGH? ARMOR OVER STEEL SKIN. CAN YOU SAY "OVERKILL"?
WE NEED TO GET YOU ON PROJECT RUNWAY, ASAP.
LET ME END THIS. BEFORE I HURT YOU.
NAH.
AvX FUN FACT:
SPIDER-FLUID IS 2.62 TIMES AS STRONG AS STEEL.
THWIP!
THWIP!
OKAY. SO YOU'RE THE JUGGERNAUT NOW.
WANT TO KNOW HOW THIS GOES DOWN?

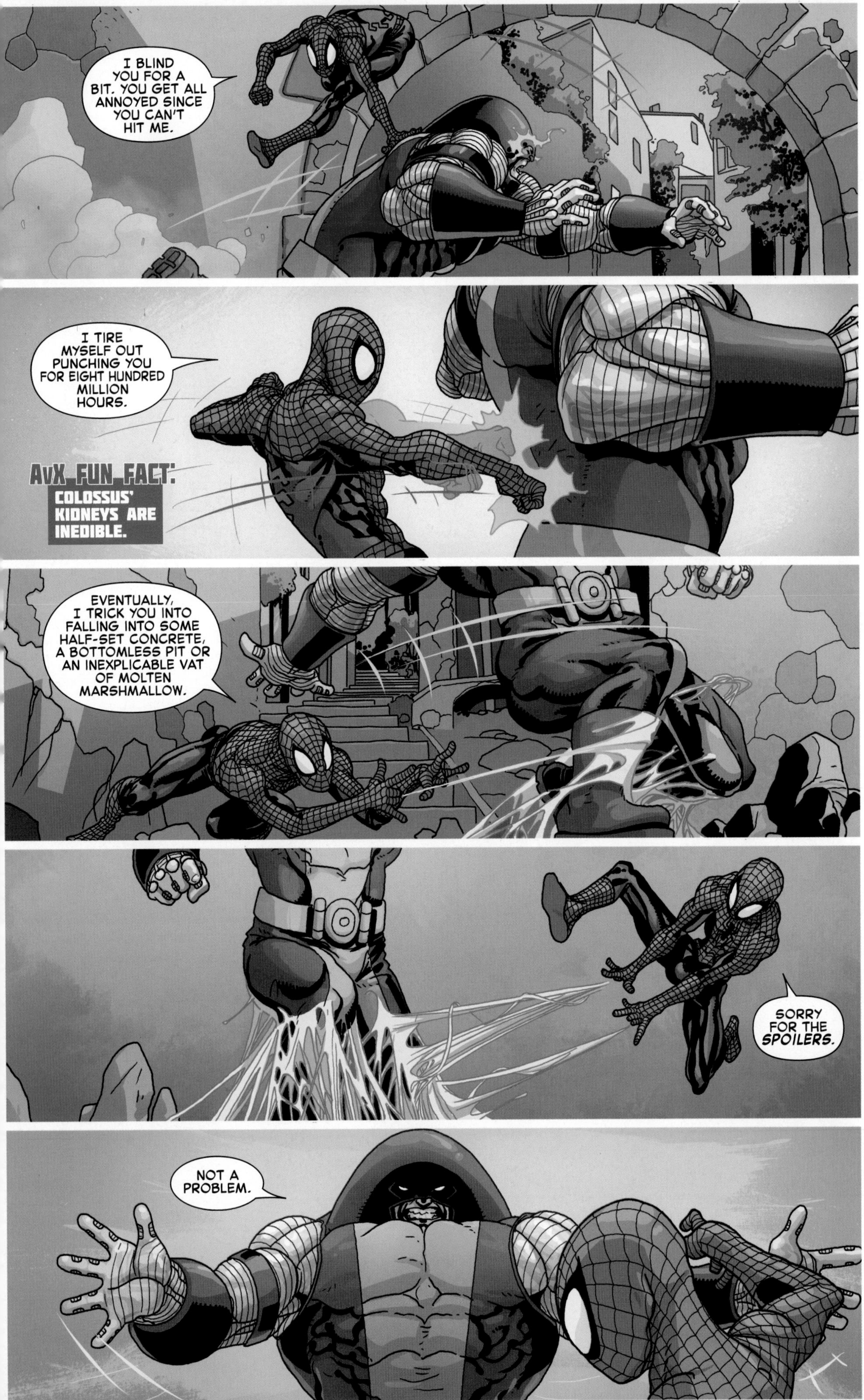
I BLIND YOU FOR A BIT. YOU GET ALL ANNOYED SINCE YOU CAN'T HIT ME.
I TIRE MYSELF OUT PUNCHING YOU FOR EIGHT HUNDRED MILLION HOURS.
AvX FUN FACT:
COLOSSUS' KIDNEYS ARE INEDIBLE.
EVENTUALLY, I TRICK YOU INTO FALLING INTO SOME HALF-SET CONCRETE, A BOTTOMLESS PIT OR AN INEXPLICABLE VAT OF MOLTEN MARSHMALLOW.
SORRY FOR THE *SPOILERS*.
NOT A PROBLEM.

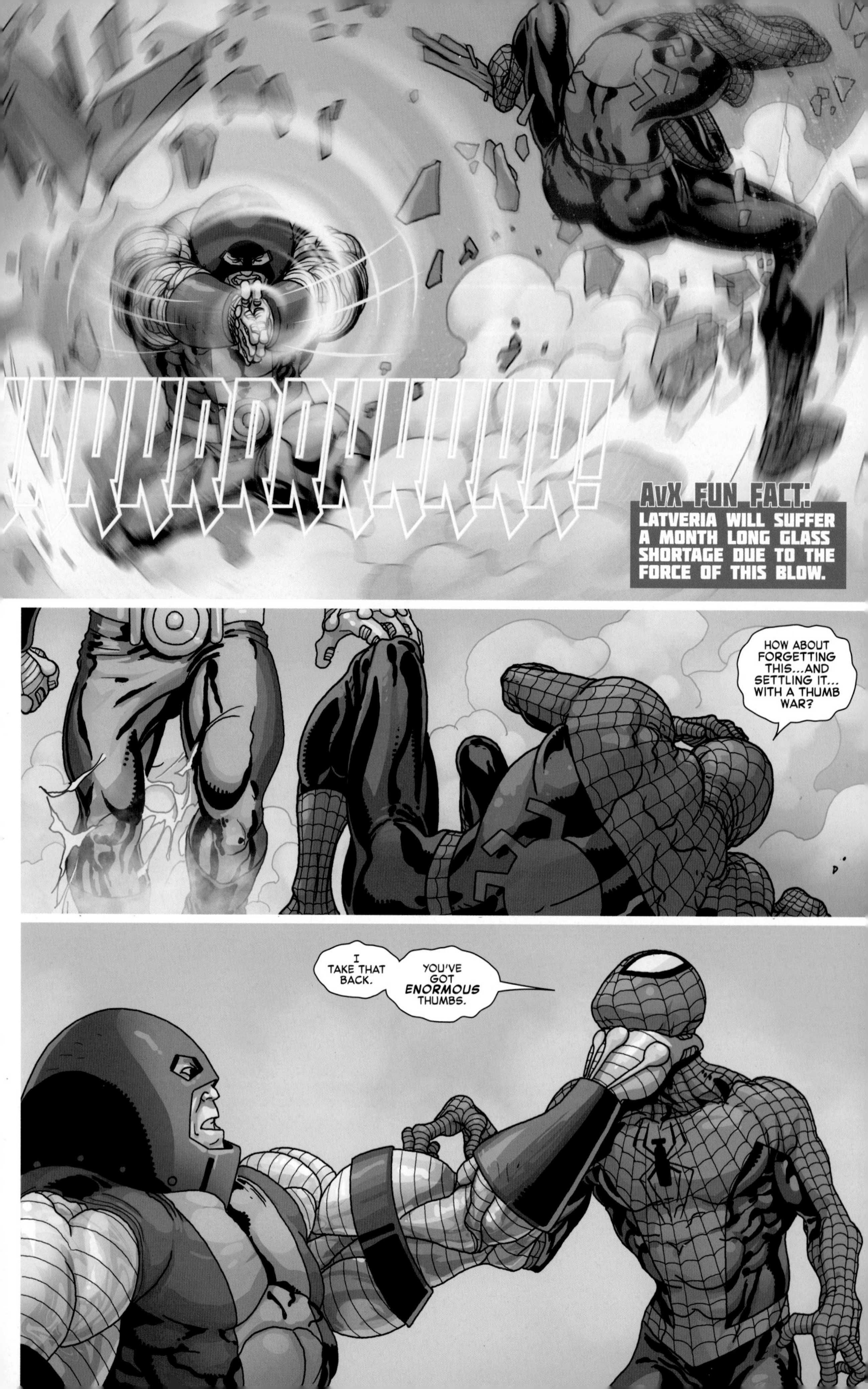
AvX FUN FACT:
LATVERIA WILL SUFFER A MONTH LONG GLASS SHORTAGE DUE TO THE FORCE OF THIS BLOW.
HOW ABOUT FORGETTING THIS...AND SETTLING IT... WITH A THUMB WAR?
I TAKE THAT BACK.
YOU'VE GOT *ENORMOUS* THUMBS.

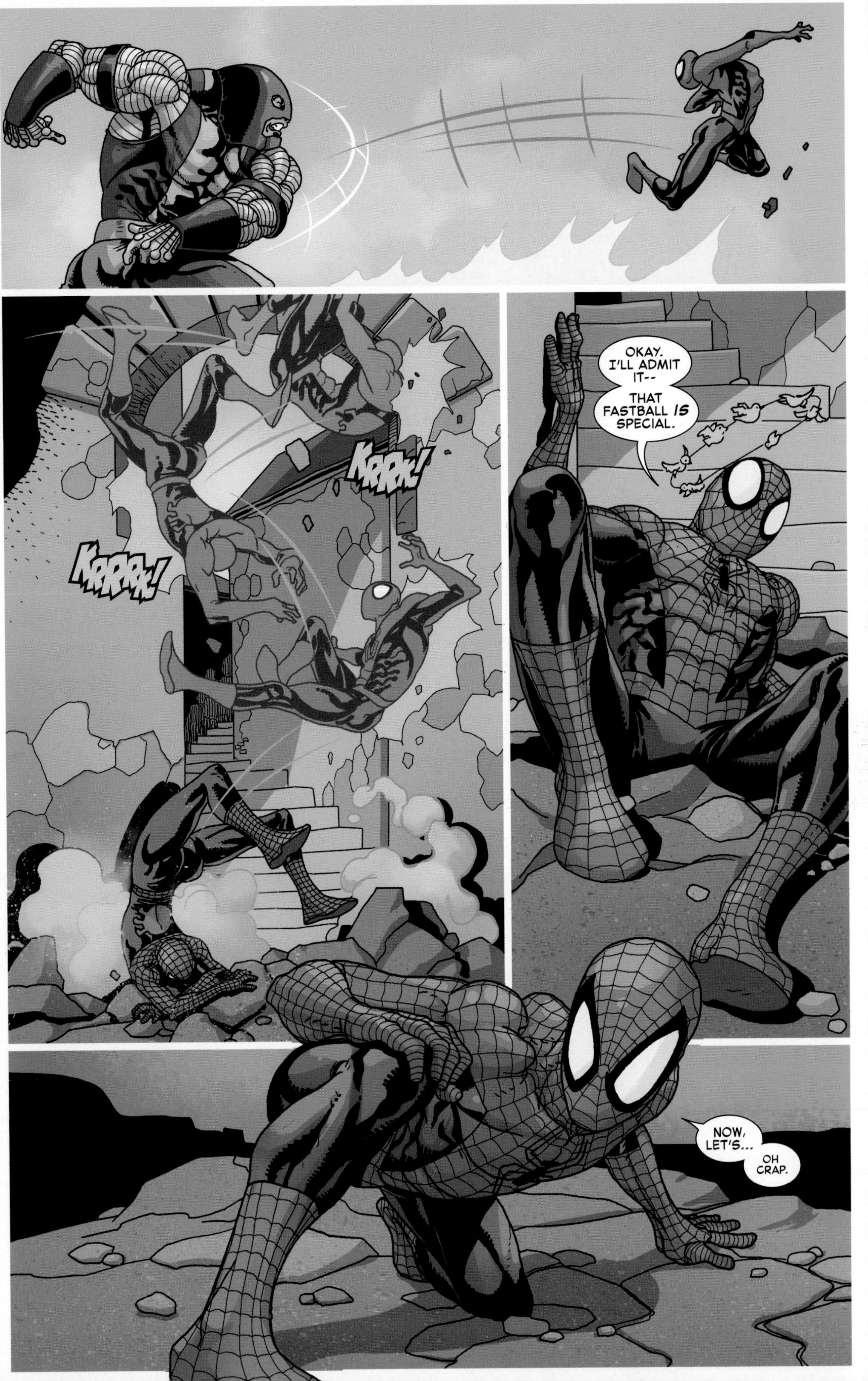
KRRRK!
KRRRK!
OKAY. I'LL ADMIT IT--
THAT FASTBALL IS SPECIAL.
NOW, LET'S...
OH CRAP.

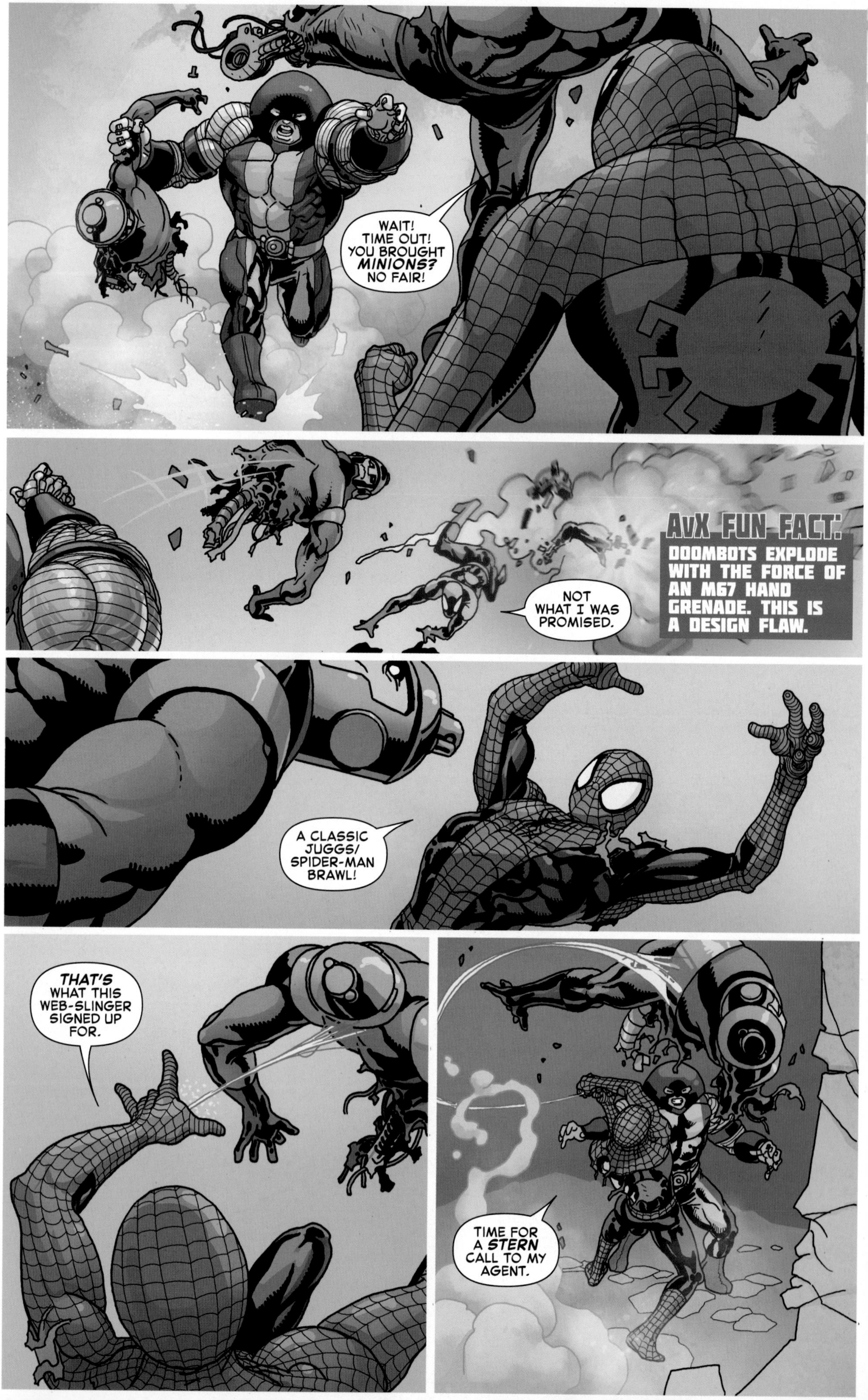
WAIT! TIME OUT! YOU BROUGHT *MINIONS?* NO FAIR!
AvX FUN FACT:
DOOMBOTS EXPLODE WITH THE FORCE OF AN M67 HAND GRENADE. THIS IS A DESIGN FLAW.
NOT WHAT I WAS PROMISED.
A CLASSIC JUGGS/ SPIDER-MAN BRAWL!
THAT'S WHAT THIS WEB-SLINGER SIGNED UP FOR.
TIME FOR A *STERN* CALL TO MY AGENT.

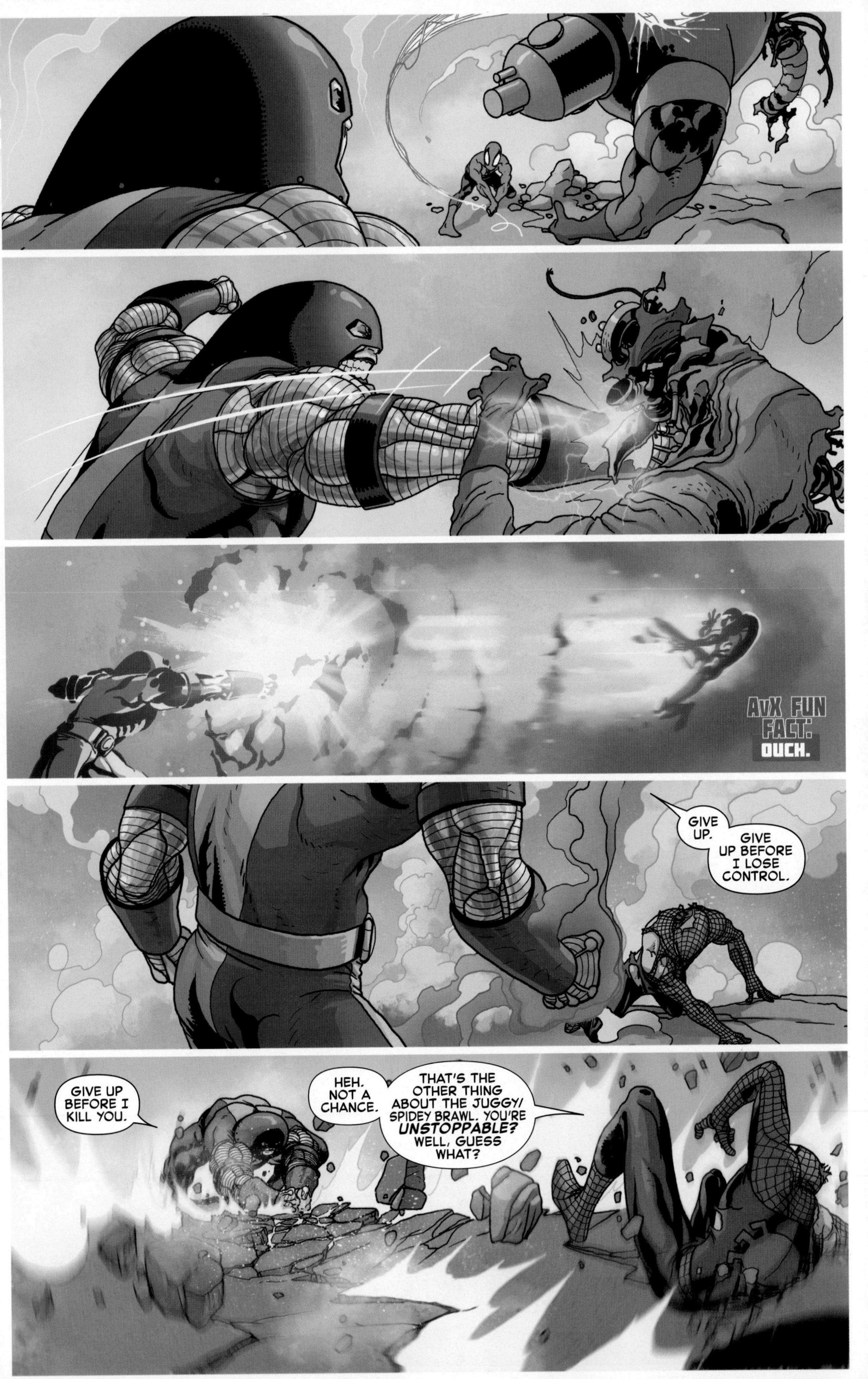
AvX FUN FACT: OUCH.
GIVE UP.
GIVE UP BEFORE I LOSE CONTROL.
GIVE UP BEFORE I KILL YOU.
HEH. NOT A CHANCE.
THAT'S THE OTHER THING ABOUT THE JUGGY/ SPIDEY BRAWL. YOU'RE UNSTOPPABLE? WELL, GUESS WHAT?

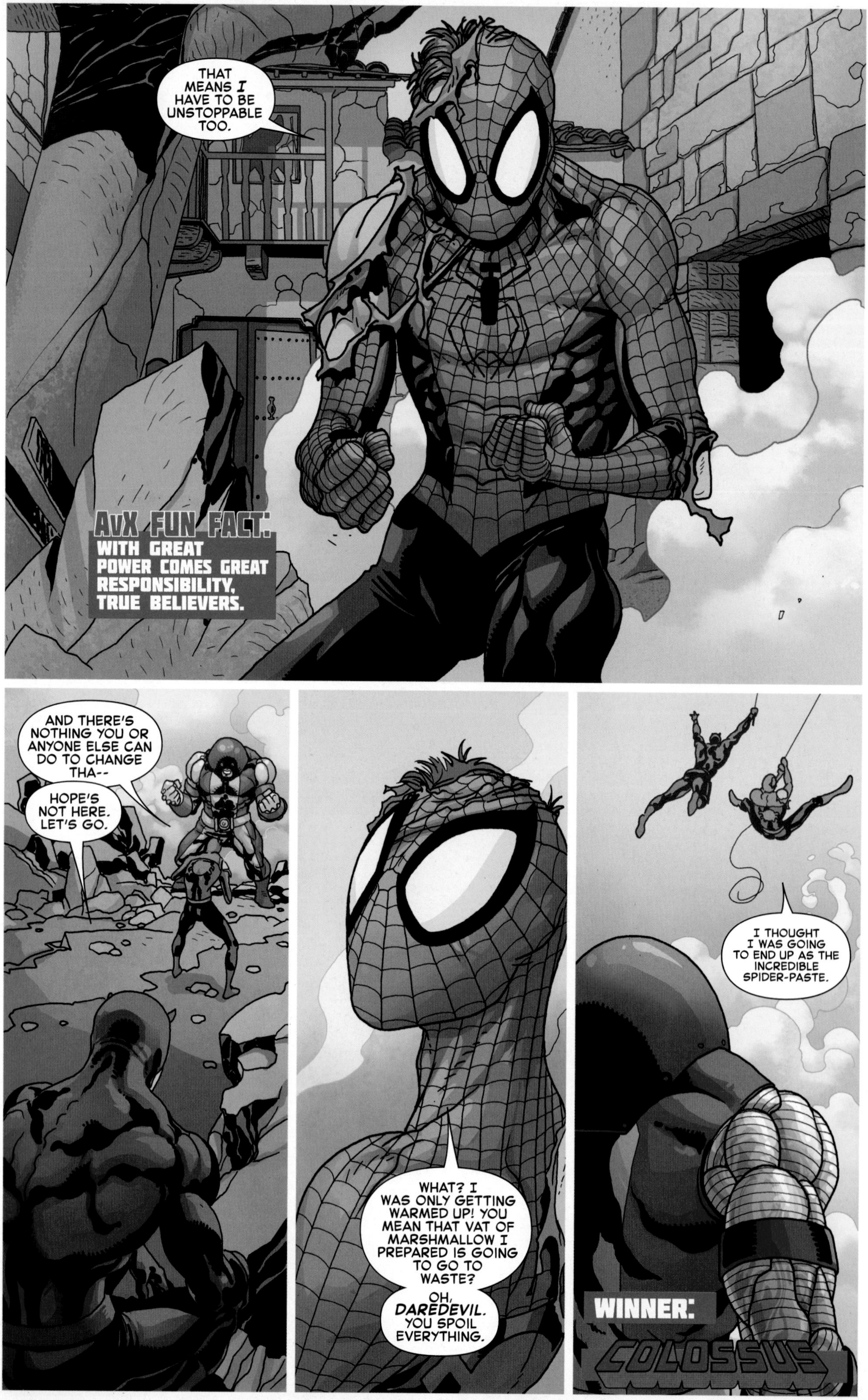
THAT MEANS I HAVE TO BE UNSTOPPABLE TOO.
AvX FUN FACT: WITH GREAT POWER COMES GREAT RESPONSIBILITY, TRUE BELIEVERS.
AND THERE'S NOTHING YOU OR ANYONE ELSE CAN DO TO CHANGE THA--
HOPE'S NOT HERE. LET'S GO.
WHAT? I WAS ONLY GETTING WARMED UP! YOU MEAN THAT VAT OF MARSHMALLOW I PREPARED IS GOING TO GO TO WASTE?
OH, DAREDEVIL. YOU SPOIL EVERYTHING.
I THOUGHT I WAS GOING TO END UP AS THE INCREDIBLE SPIDER-PASTE.
WINNER: COLOSSUS

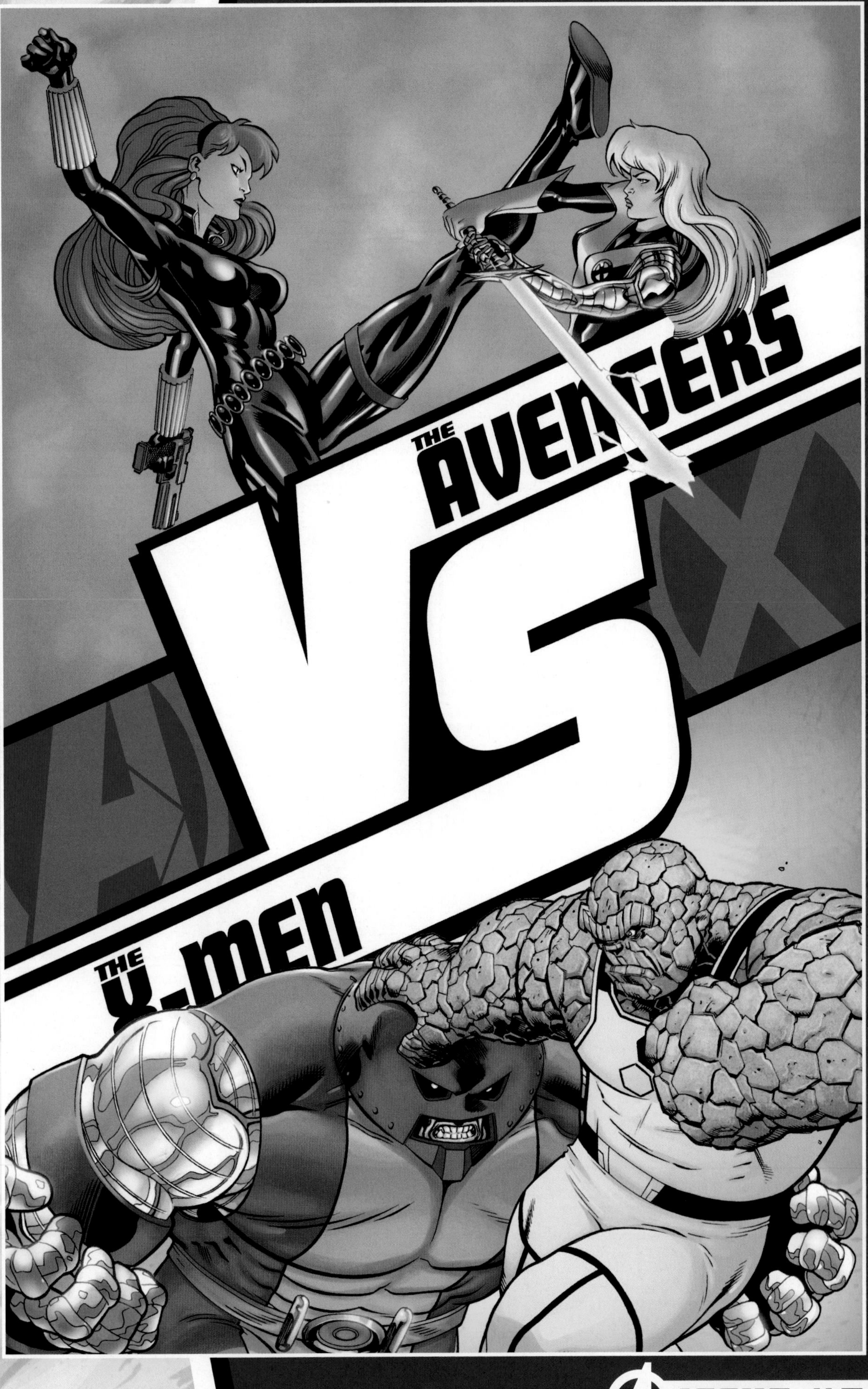

THE AVENGERS
VS
THE X-MEN

ISSUE #3

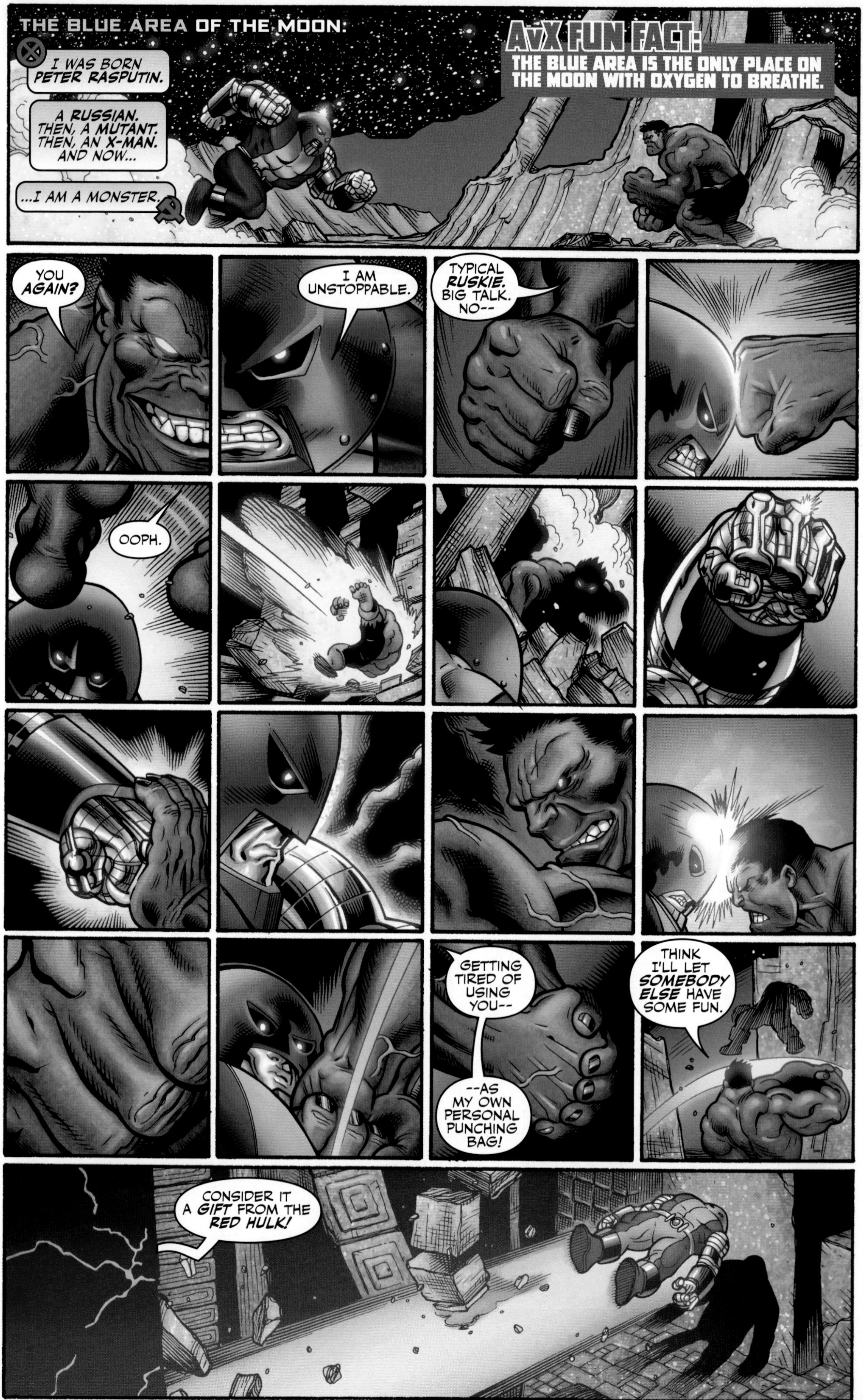
THE BLUE AREA OF THE MOON:
I WAS BORN PETER RASPUTIN.
A RUSSIAN. THEN, A MUTANT. THEN, AN X-MAN. AND NOW...
...I AM A MONSTER.
AvX FUN FACT:
THE BLUE AREA IS THE ONLY PLACE ON THE MOON WITH OXYGEN TO BREATHE.
YOU AGAIN?
I AM UNSTOPPABLE.
TYPICAL RUSKIE. BIG TALK. NO--
OOPH.
GETTING TIRED OF USING YOU--
--AS MY OWN PERSONAL PUNCHING BAG!
THINK I'LL LET SOMEBODY ELSE HAVE SOME FUN.
CONSIDER IT A GIFT FROM THE RED HULK!

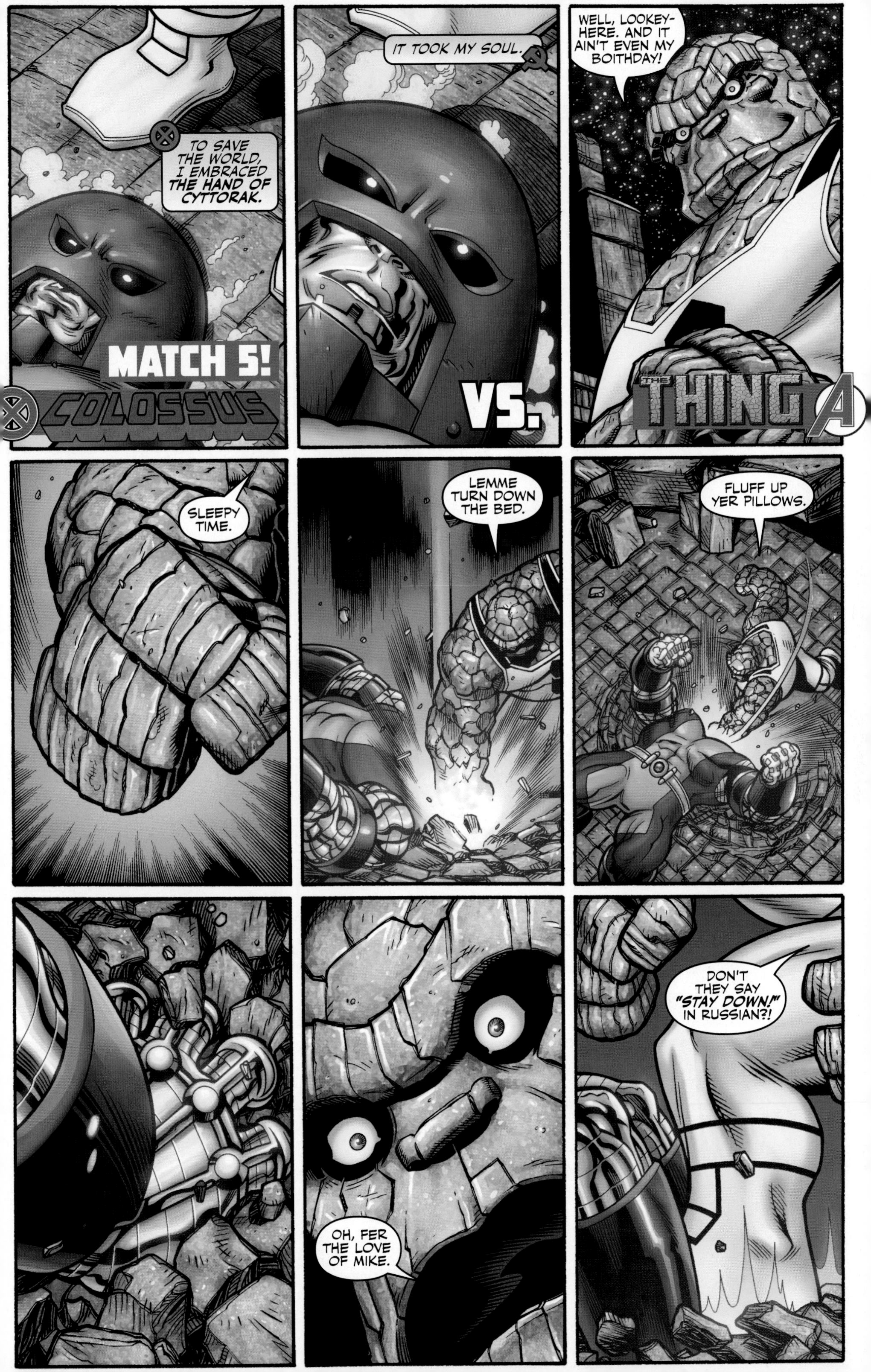
TO SAVE THE WORLD, I EMBRACED THE HAND OF CYTTORAK.
MATCH 5!
COLOSSUS
IT TOOK MY SOUL.
VS.
WELL, LOOKEY-HERE. AND IT AIN'T EVEN MY BOITHDAY!
THE THING
SLEEPY TIME.
LEMME TURN DOWN THE BED.
FLUFF UP YER PILLOWS.
OH, FER THE LOVE OF MIKE.
DON'T THEY SAY "STAY DOWN!" IN RUSSIAN?!

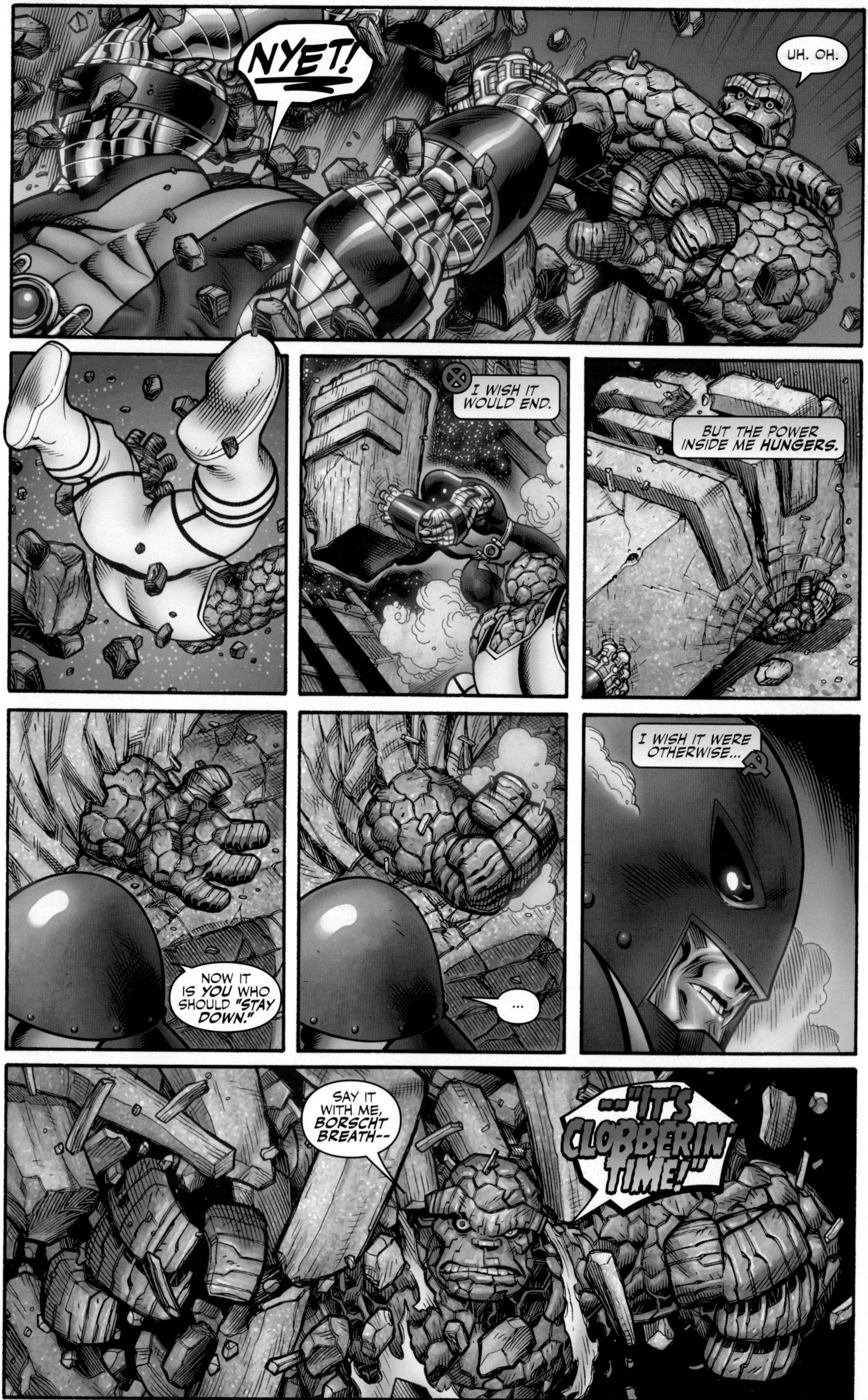
NYET!
UH. OH.
I WISH IT WOULD END.
BUT THE POWER INSIDE ME HUNGERS.
NOW IT IS YOU WHO SHOULD "STAY DOWN."
...
I WISH IT WERE OTHERWISE...
SAY IT WITH ME, BORSCHT BREATH--
..."IT'S CLOBBERIN' TIME!"

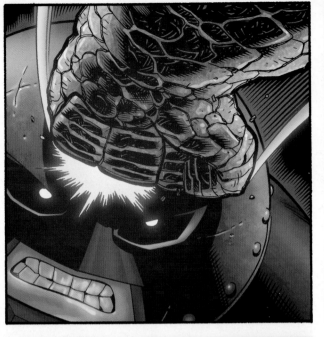

NEVER TRIED THIS BEFORE--

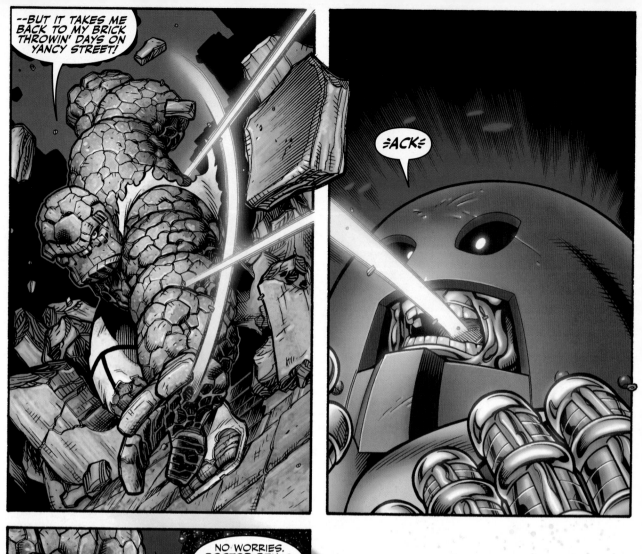

--BUT IT TAKES ME BACK TO MY BRICK THROWIN' DAYS ON YANCY STREET!

≶ACK≶

NO WORRIES. DOCTOR BEN IS HERE TO HEIMLICH THE HECK OUTTA YA.

≶ACK≶
≶CACK≶

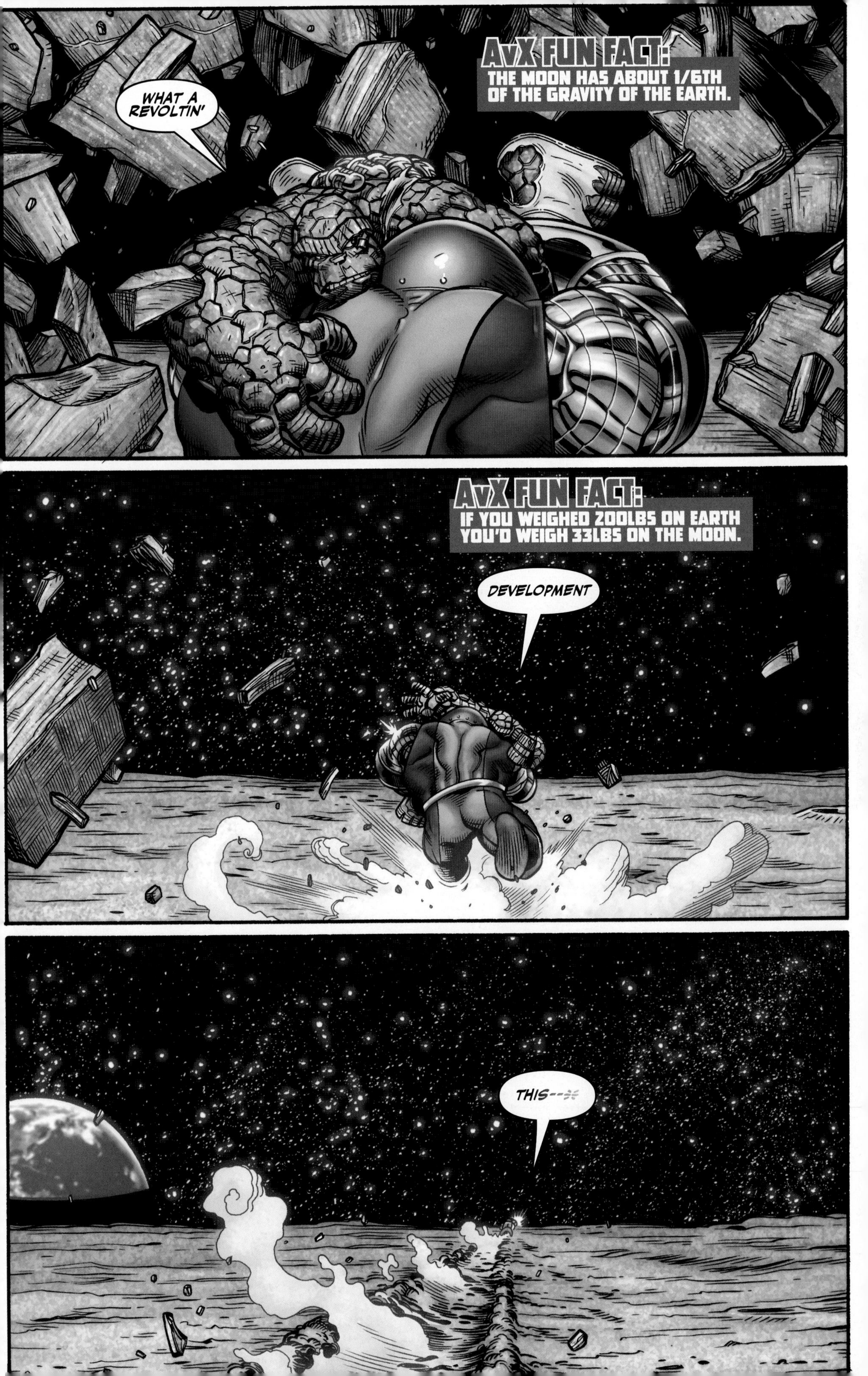

AvX FUN FACT:
THE MOON HAS ABOUT 1/6TH OF THE GRAVITY OF THE EARTH.
WHAT A REVOLTIN'
AvX FUN FACT:
IF YOU WEIGHED 200LBS ON EARTH YOU'D WEIGH 33LBS ON THE MOON.
DEVELOPMENT
THIS--

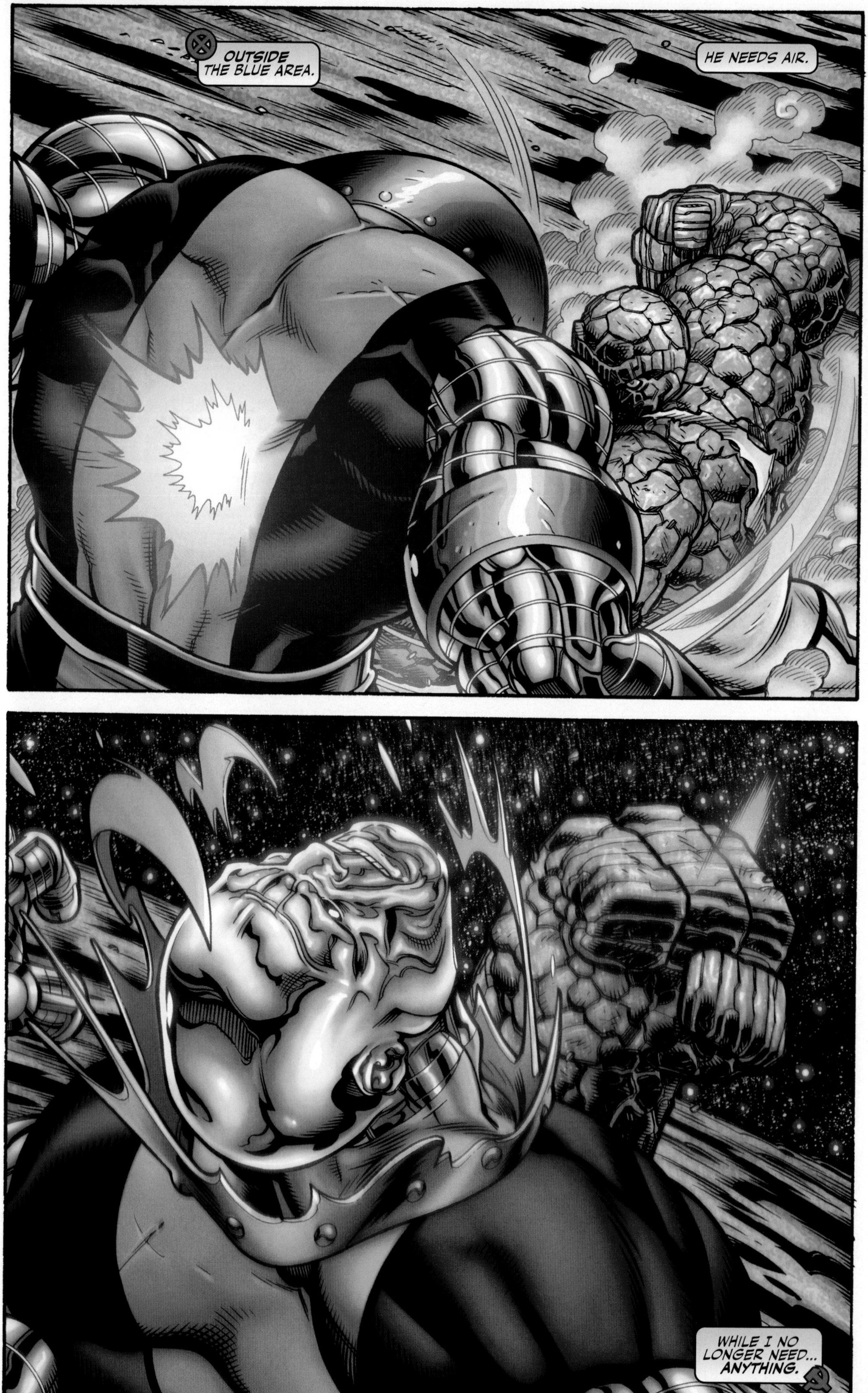
OUTSIDE THE BLUE AREA.
HE NEEDS AIR.
WHILE I NO LONGER NEED... ANYTHING.

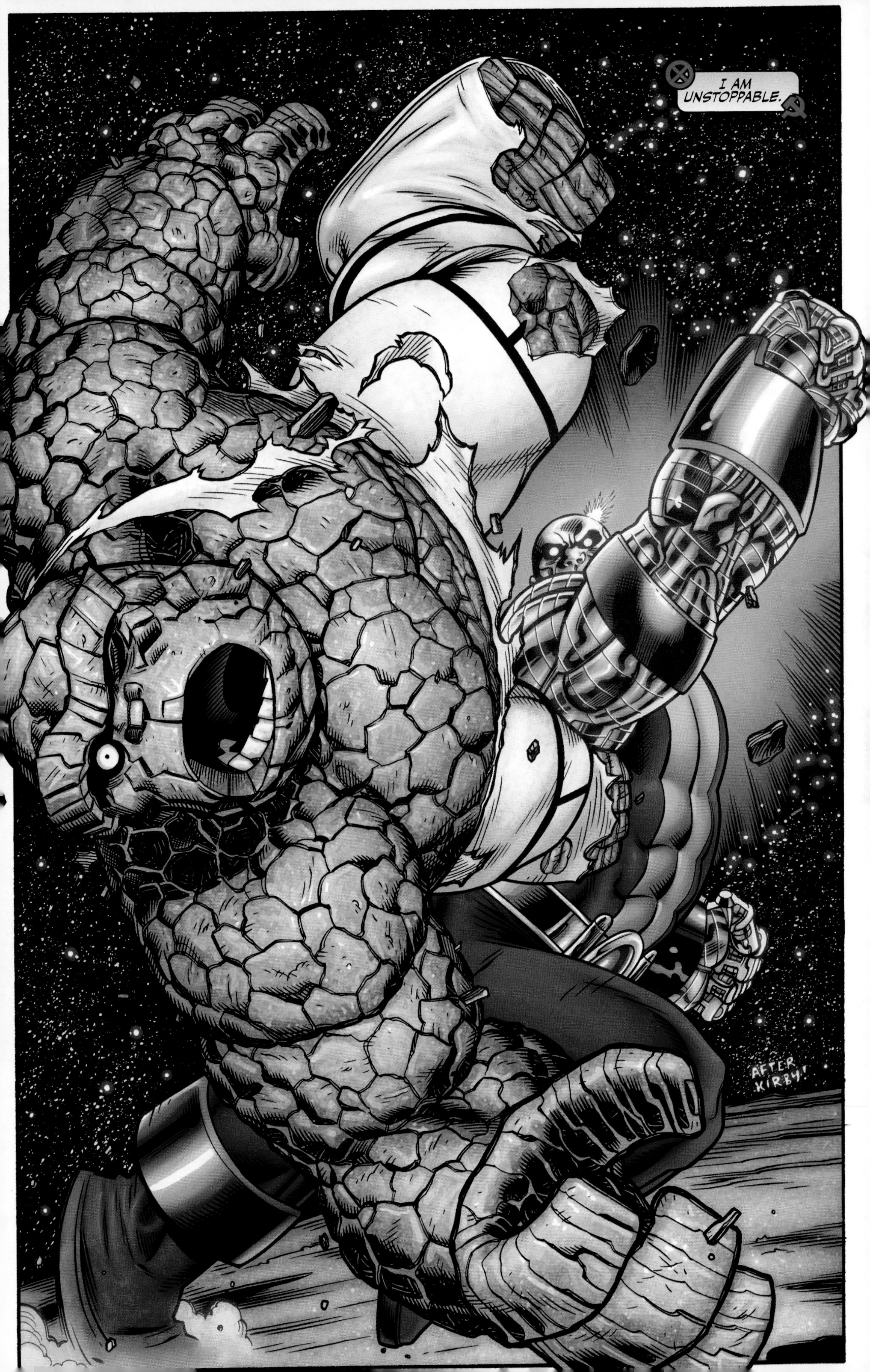
I AM UNSTOPPABLE.
AFTER KIRBY!

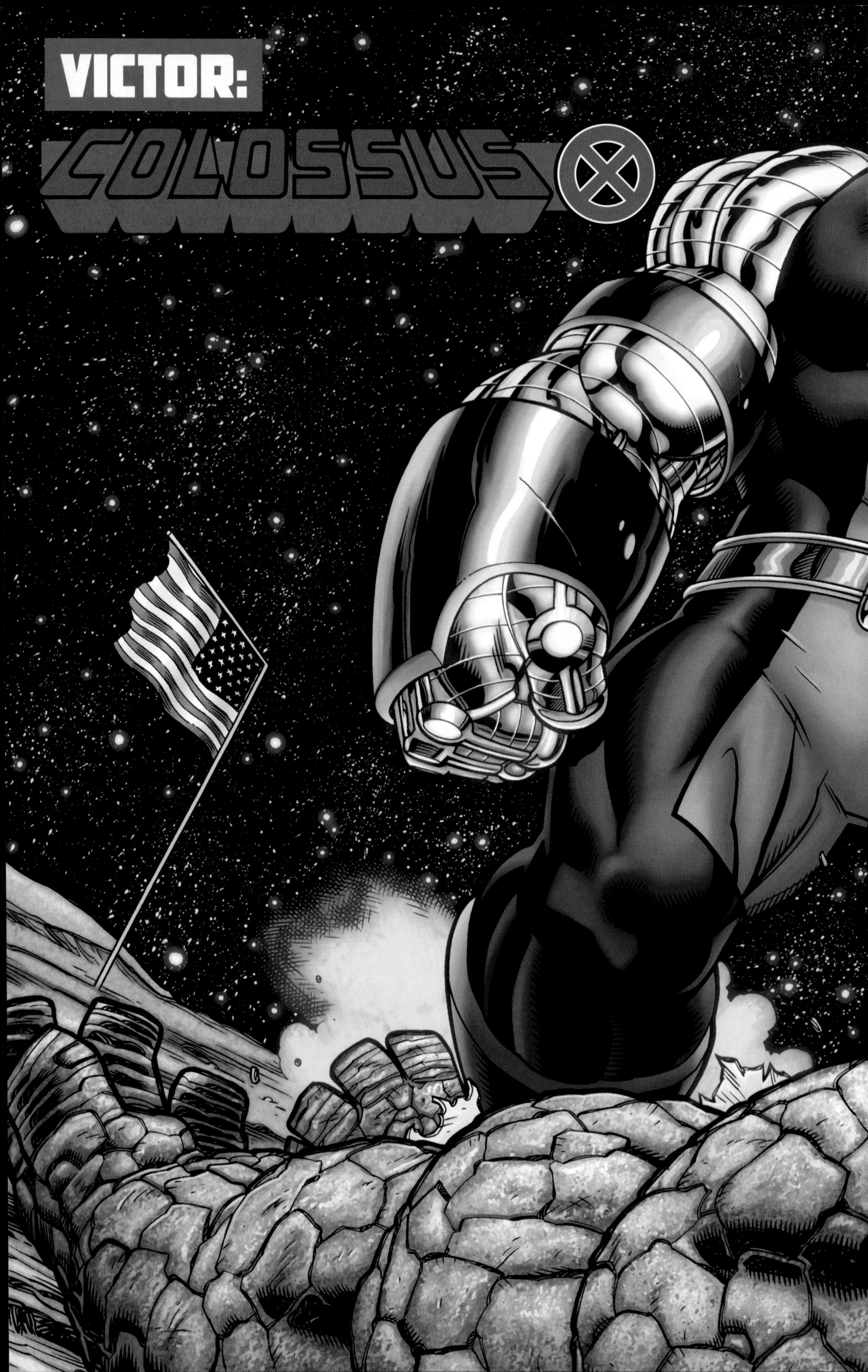

VICTOR:
COLOSSUS

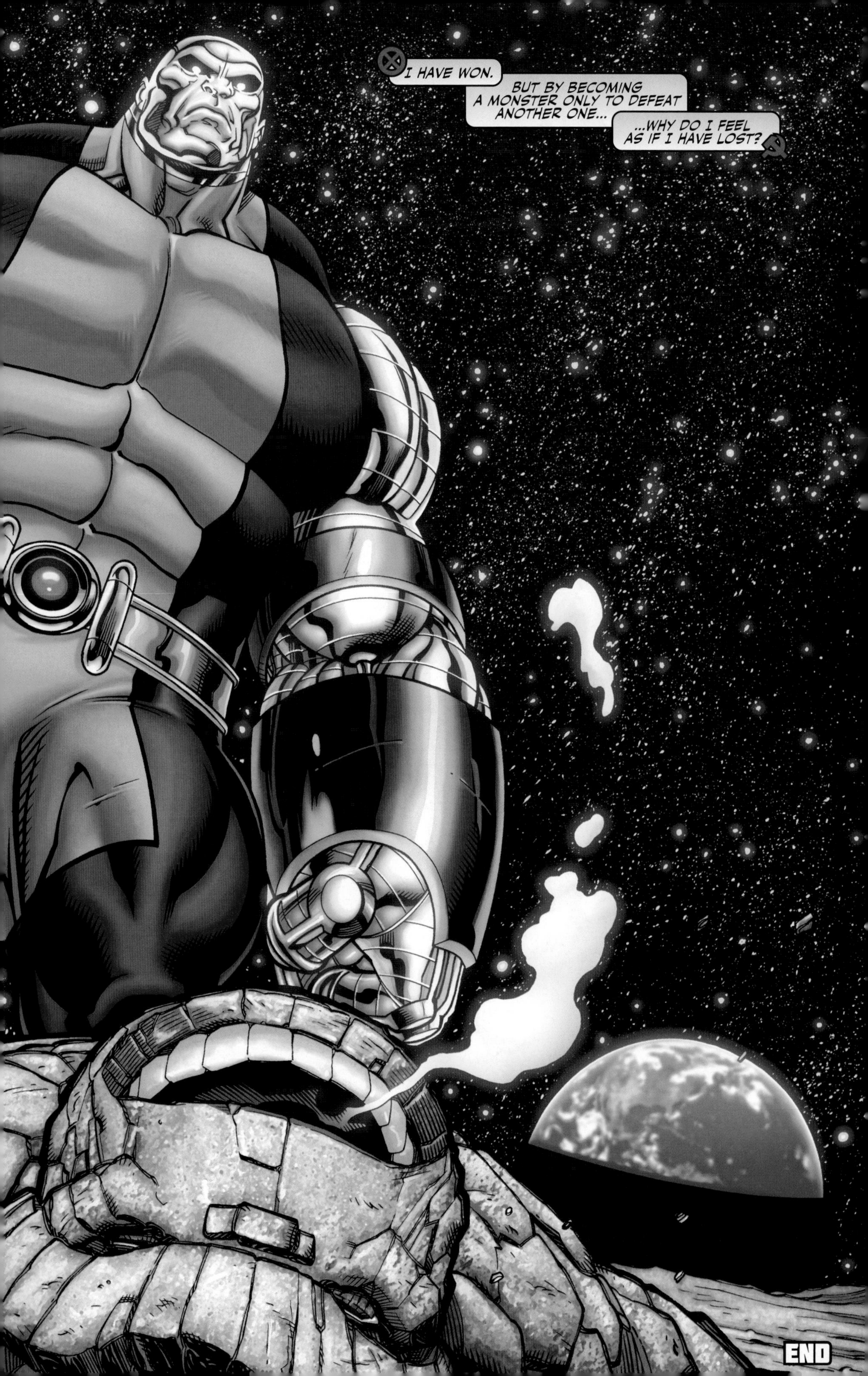
I HAVE WON.
BUT BY BECOMING A MONSTER ONLY TO DEFEAT ANOTHER ONE...
...WHY DO I FEEL AS IF I HAVE LOST?
END

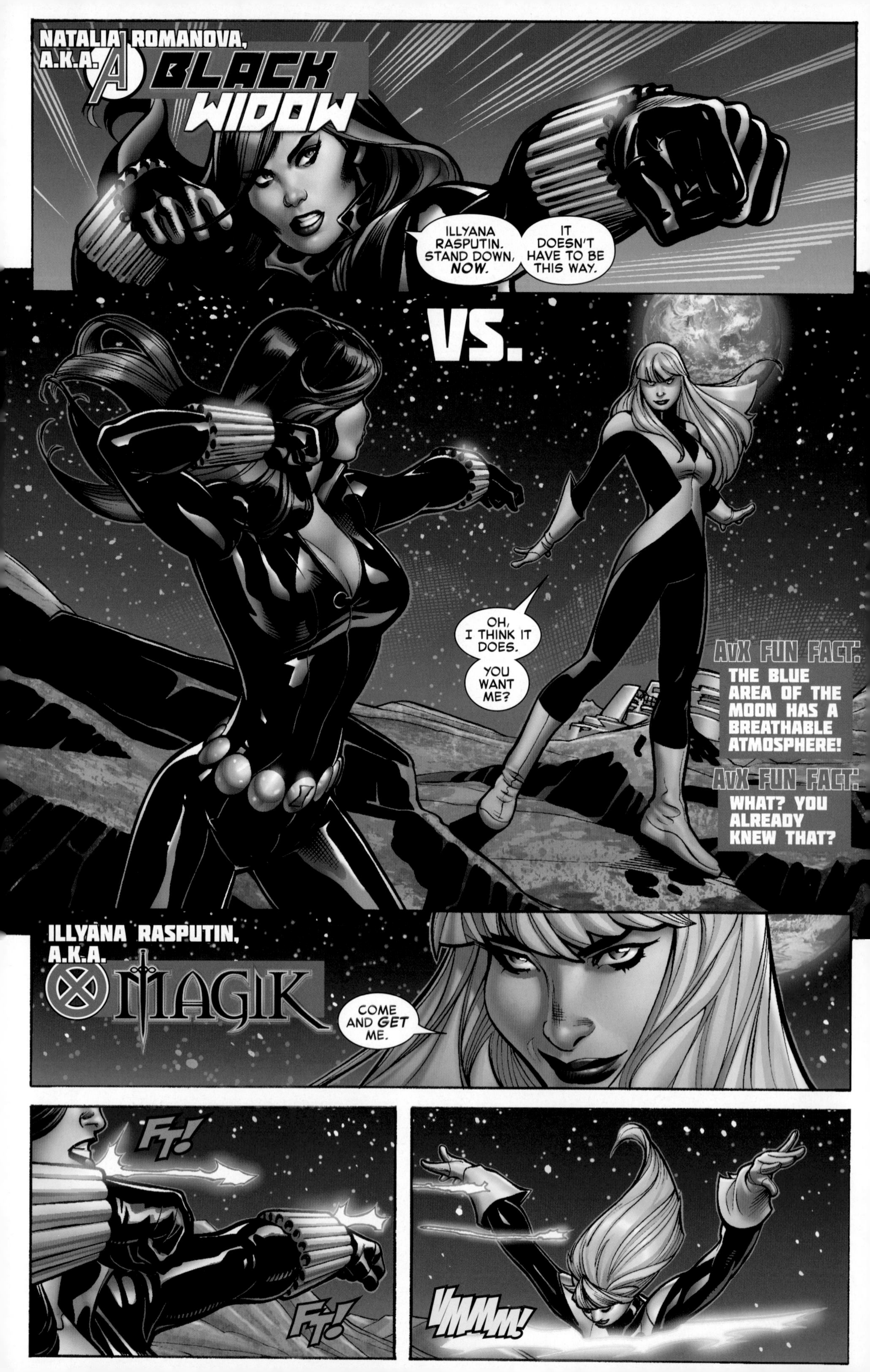
NATALIA ROMANOVA, A.K.A. BLACK WIDOW
ILLYANA RASPUTIN. STAND DOWN, NOW.
IT DOESN'T HAVE TO BE THIS WAY.
VS.
OH, I THINK IT DOES.
YOU WANT ME?
AvX FUN FACT: THE BLUE AREA OF THE MOON HAS A BREATHABLE ATMOSPHERE!
AvX FUN FACT: WHAT? YOU ALREADY KNEW THAT?
ILLYANA RASPUTIN, A.K.A. MAGIK
COME AND GET ME.
FT!
FT!
VMMMM!

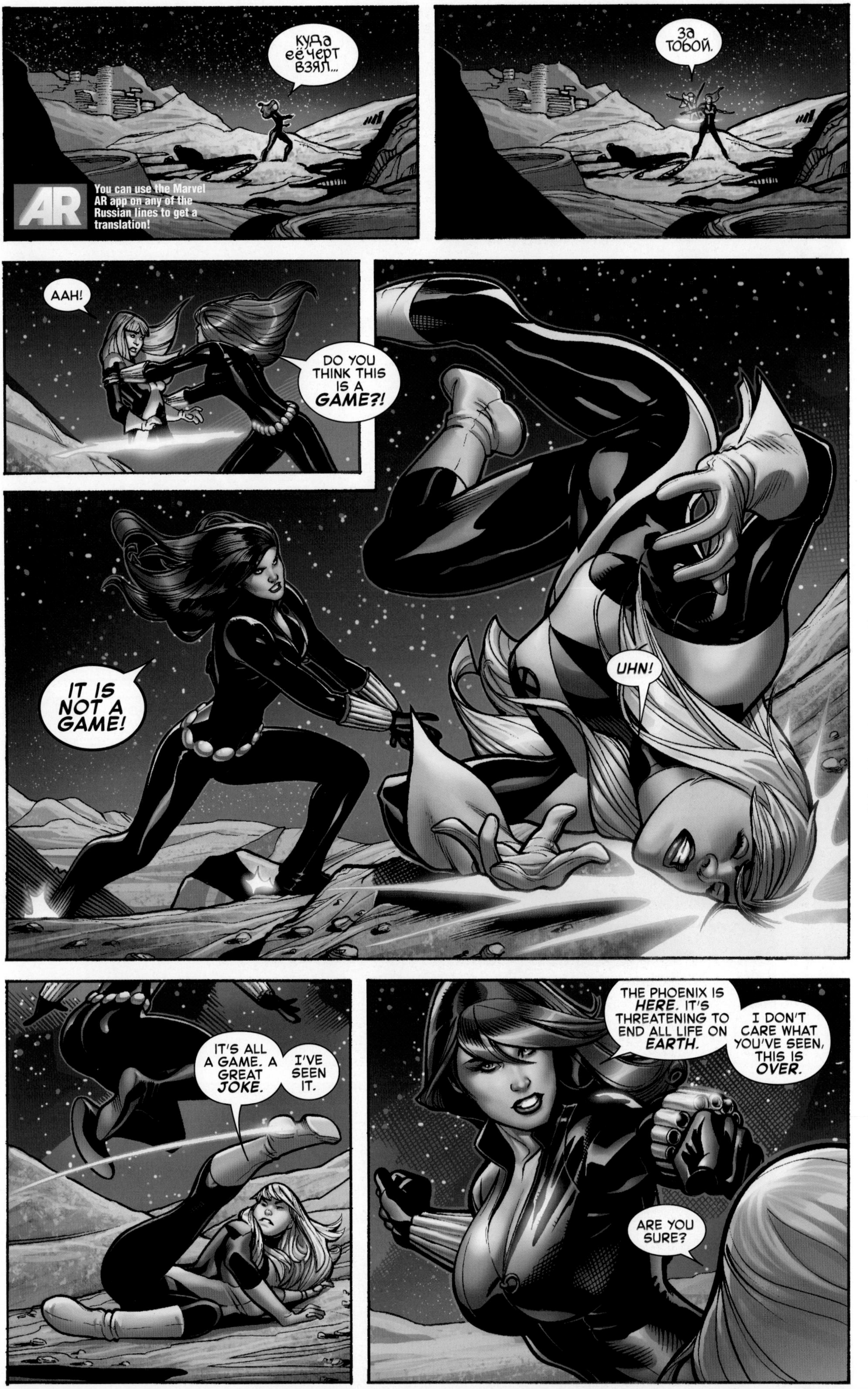

Куда её черт взял...
You can use the Marvel AR app on any of the Russian lines to get a translation!
За тобой.
AAH!
DO YOU THINK THIS IS A GAME?!
IT IS NOT A GAME!
UHN!
IT'S ALL A GAME. A GREAT JOKE.
I'VE SEEN IT.
THE PHOENIX IS HERE. IT'S THREATENING TO END ALL LIFE ON EARTH.
I DON'T CARE WHAT YOU'VE SEEN, THIS IS OVER.
ARE YOU SURE?

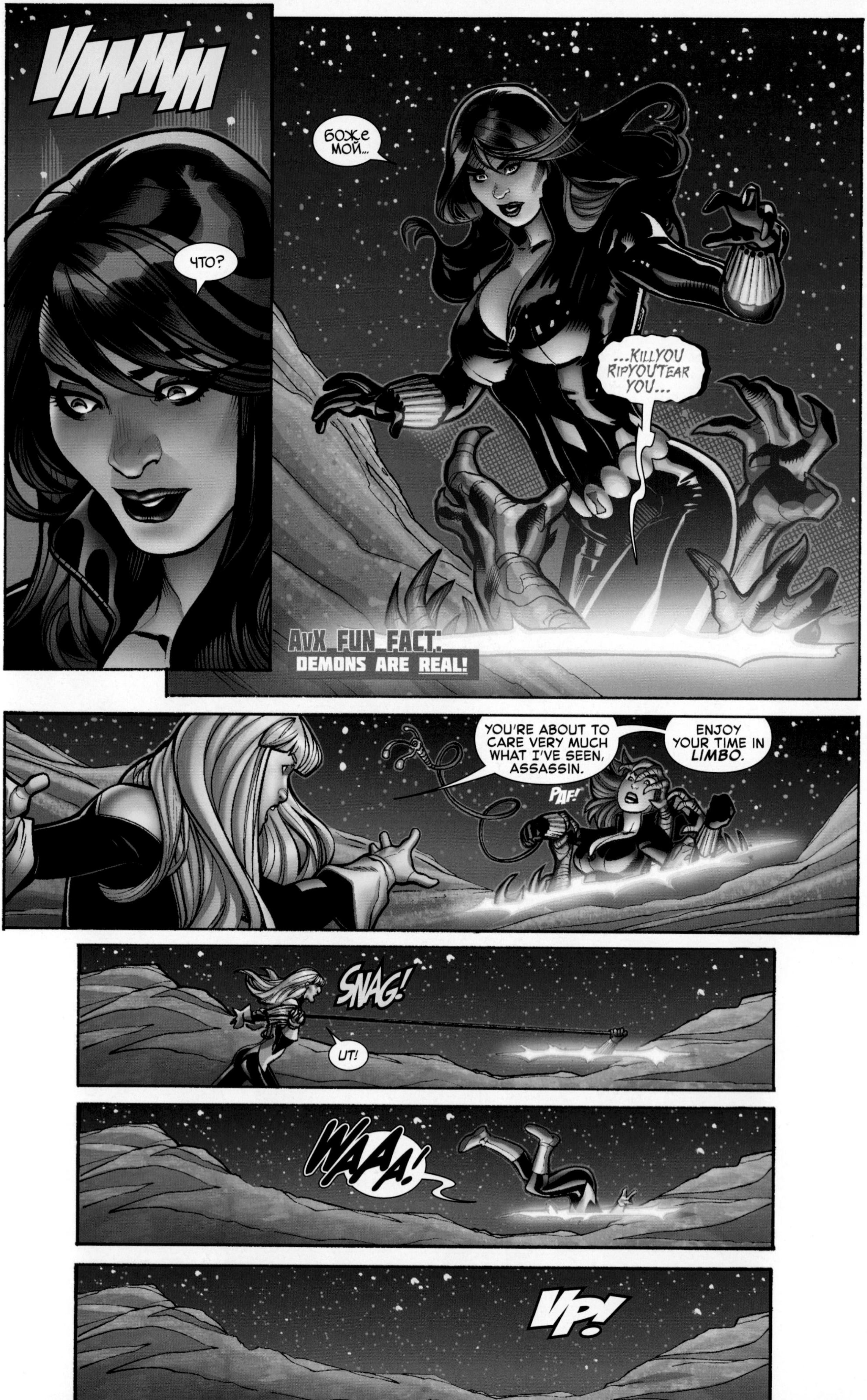
VMMMM
ЧТО?
БОЖЕ МОЙ...
...KILLYOU RIPYOUTEAR YOU...
AvX FUN FACT:
DEMONS ARE REAL!
YOU'RE ABOUT TO CARE VERY MUCH WHAT I'VE SEEN, ASSASSIN.
ENJOY YOUR TIME IN LIMBO.
PAF!
SNAG!
UT!
WAAA!
VP!

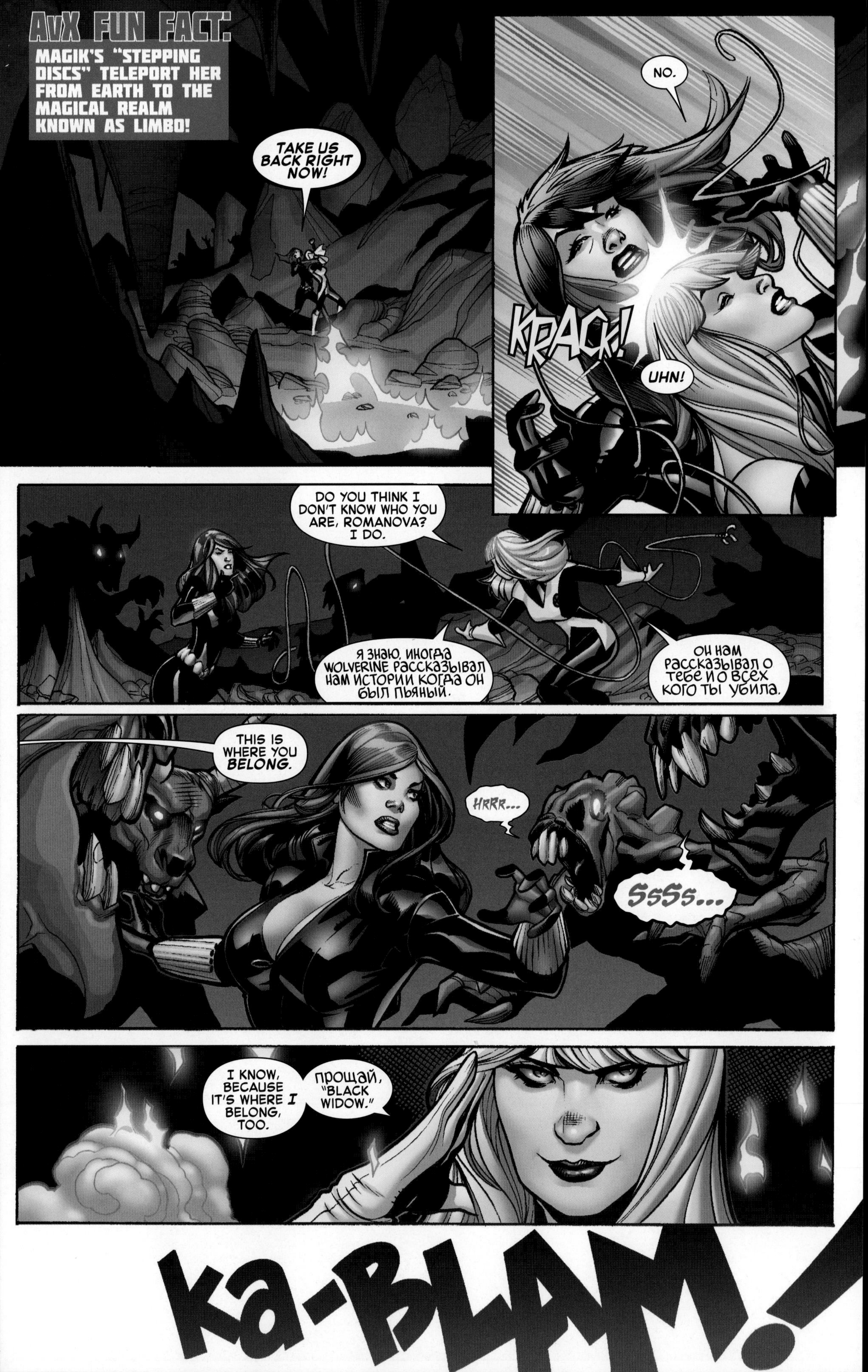
AvX FUN FACT:
MAGIK'S "STEPPING DISCS" TELEPORT HER FROM EARTH TO THE MAGICAL REALM KNOWN AS LIMBO!
TAKE US BACK RIGHT NOW!
NO.
KRACK!
UHN!
DO YOU THINK I DON'T KNOW WHO YOU ARE, ROMANOVA? I DO.
Я ЗНАЮ, ИНОГДА WOLVERINE РАССКАЗЫВАЛ НАМ ИСТОРИИ КОГДА ОН БЫЛ ПЬЯНЫЙ.
ОН НАМ РАССКАЗЫВАЛ О ТЕБЕ И О ВСЕХ КОГО ТЫ УБИЛА.
THIS IS WHERE YOU BELONG.
HRRR...
SSSS...
I KNOW, BECAUSE IT'S WHERE I BELONG, TOO.
ПРОЩАЙ, "BLACK WIDOW."
KA-BLAM!

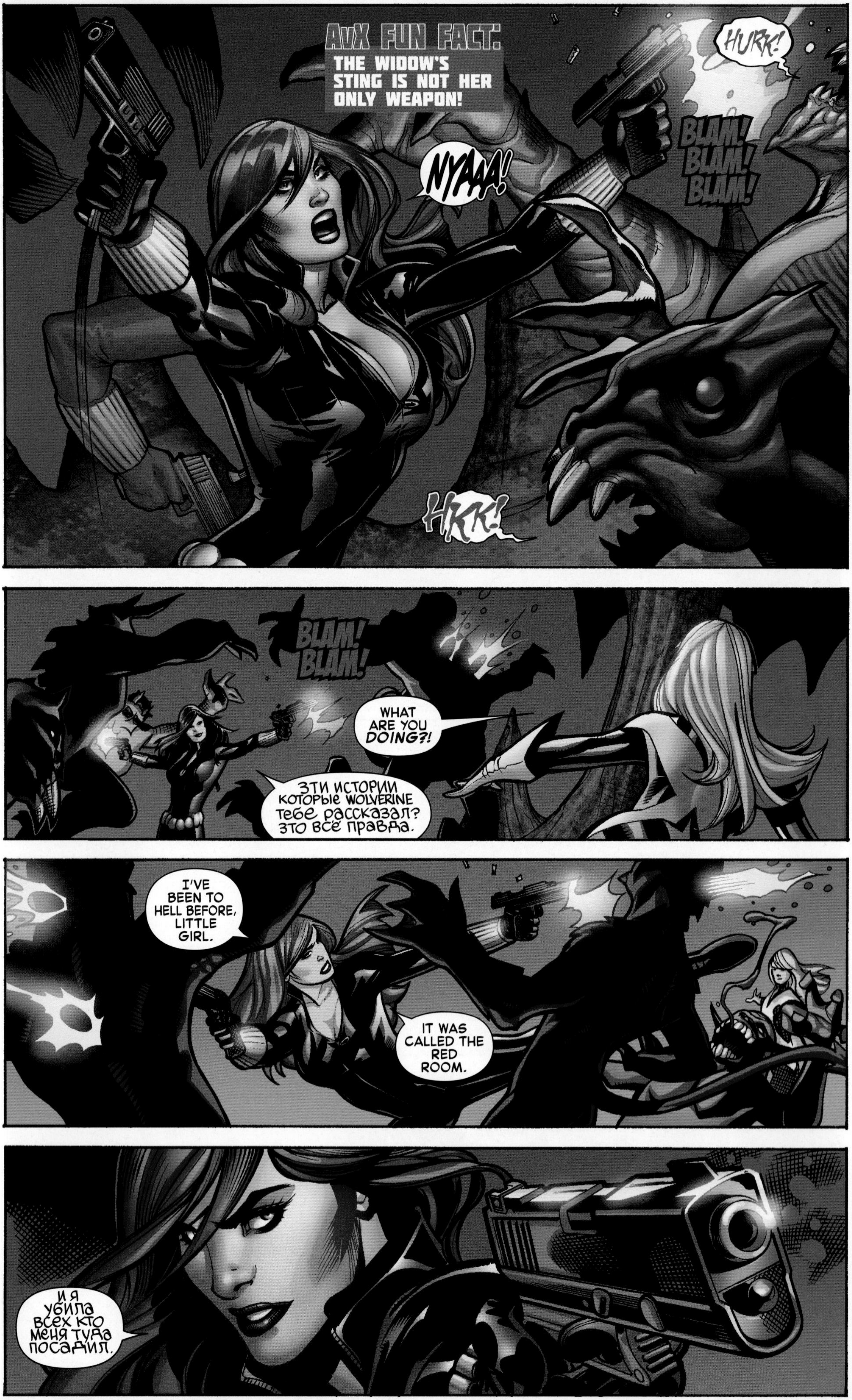

AvX FUN FACT:
THE WIDOW'S STING IS NOT HER ONLY WEAPON!
HURK!
NYAAA!
BLAM! BLAM! BLAM!
HKK!
BLAM! BLAM!
WHAT ARE YOU DOING?!
Эти истории которые WOLVERINE тебе рассказал? Это всё правда.
I'VE BEEN TO HELL BEFORE, LITTLE GIRL.
IT WAS CALLED THE RED ROOM.
И я убила всех кто меня туда посадил.

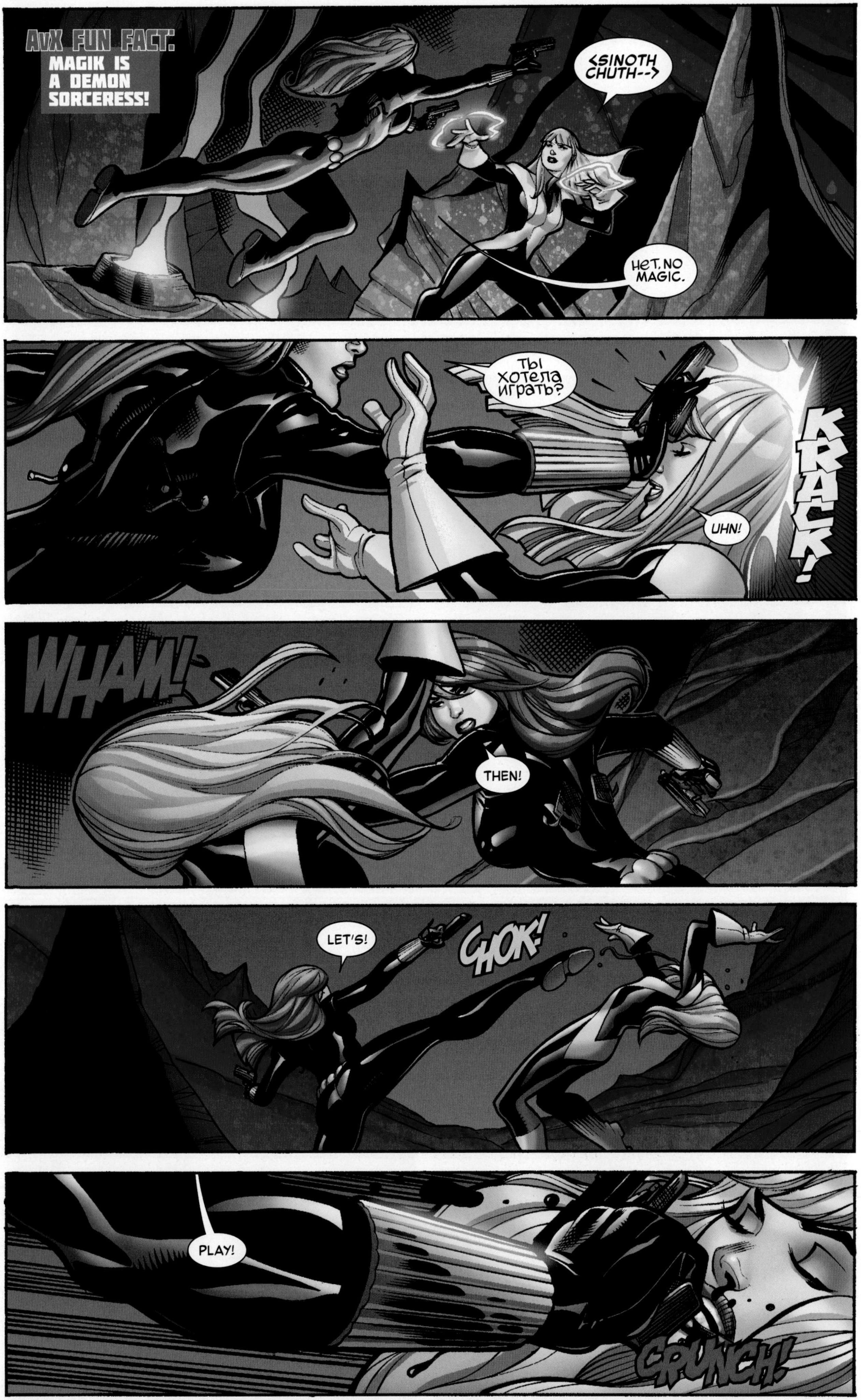

AvX FUN FACT:
MAGIK IS A DEMON SORCERESS!
<SINOTH CHUTH-->
НЕТ. NO MAGIC.
ТЫ ХОТЕЛА ИГРАТЬ?
KRACK!
UHN!
WHAM!
THEN!
LET'S!
CHOK!
PLAY!
CRUNCH!

THOUSAND... THOUSAND DEMONS COMING... FOR YOU...

НЕ МОГУ ИХ ВСЕХ УБИТЬ...

YOU THINK I'M NOT READY TO DIE FOR WHAT I BELIEVE IN?

THINK AGAIN.

THE QUESTION IS, ARE YOU? ARE YOU READY TO DIE, ILLYANA RASPUTIN?

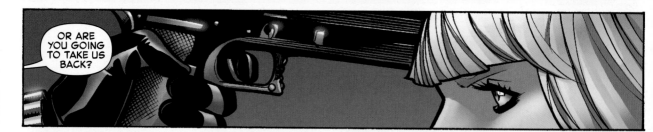

OR ARE YOU GOING TO TAKE US BACK?

УМНИЦА.

VMMM!

VP!

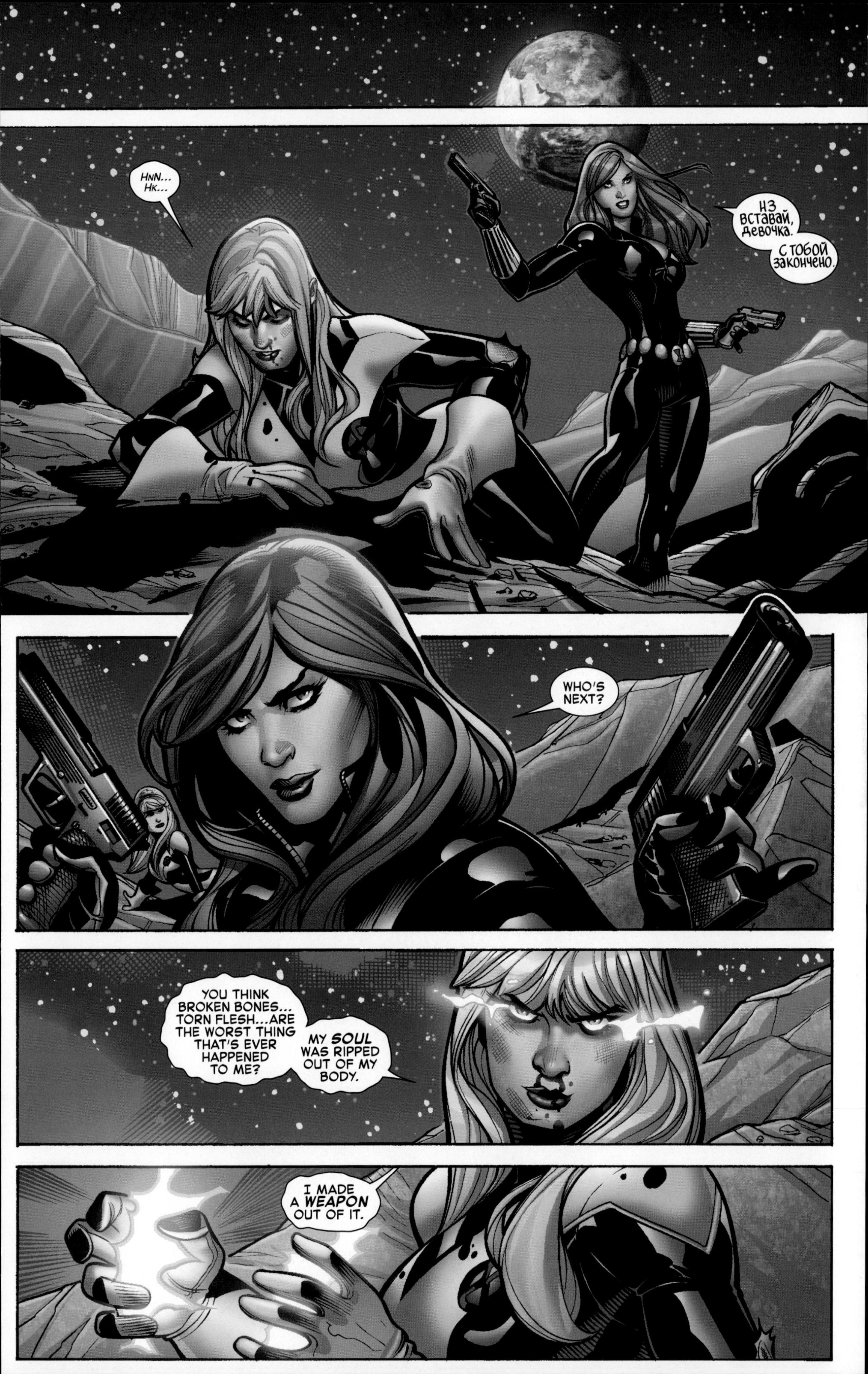
HNN... HK...
НЗ вставай, девочка.
С тобой закончено.
WHO'S NEXT?
YOU THINK BROKEN BONES... TORN FLESH...ARE THE WORST THING THAT'S EVER HAPPENED TO ME?
MY SOUL WAS RIPPED OUT OF MY BODY.
I MADE A WEAPON OUT OF IT.

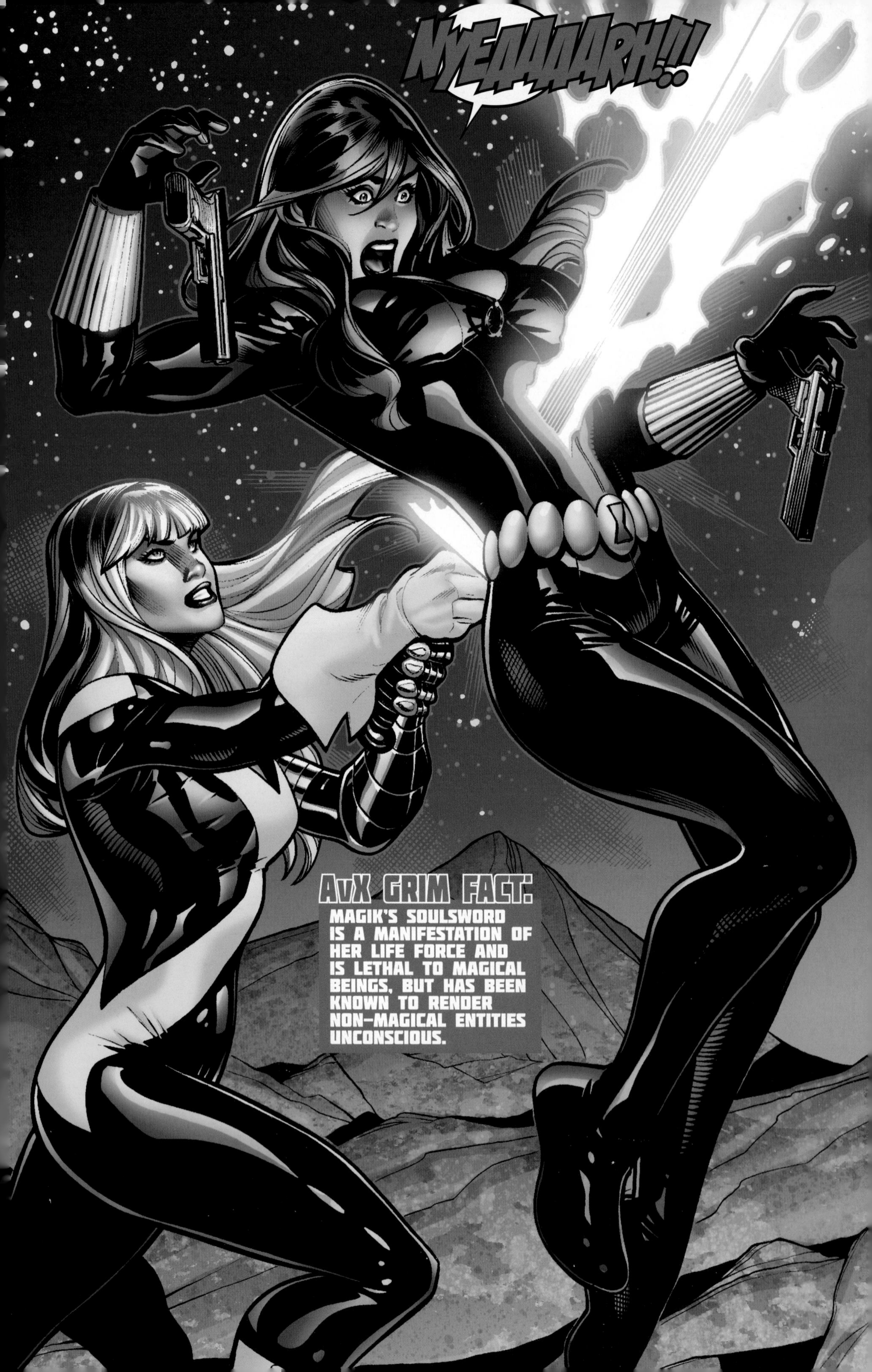
NYEAAAARH!!!
AvX GRIM FACT:
MAGIK'S SOULSWORD IS A MANIFESTATION OF HER LIFE FORCE AND IS LETHAL TO MAGICAL BEINGS, BUT HAS BEEN KNOWN TO RENDER NON-MAGICAL ENTITIES UNCONSCIOUS.

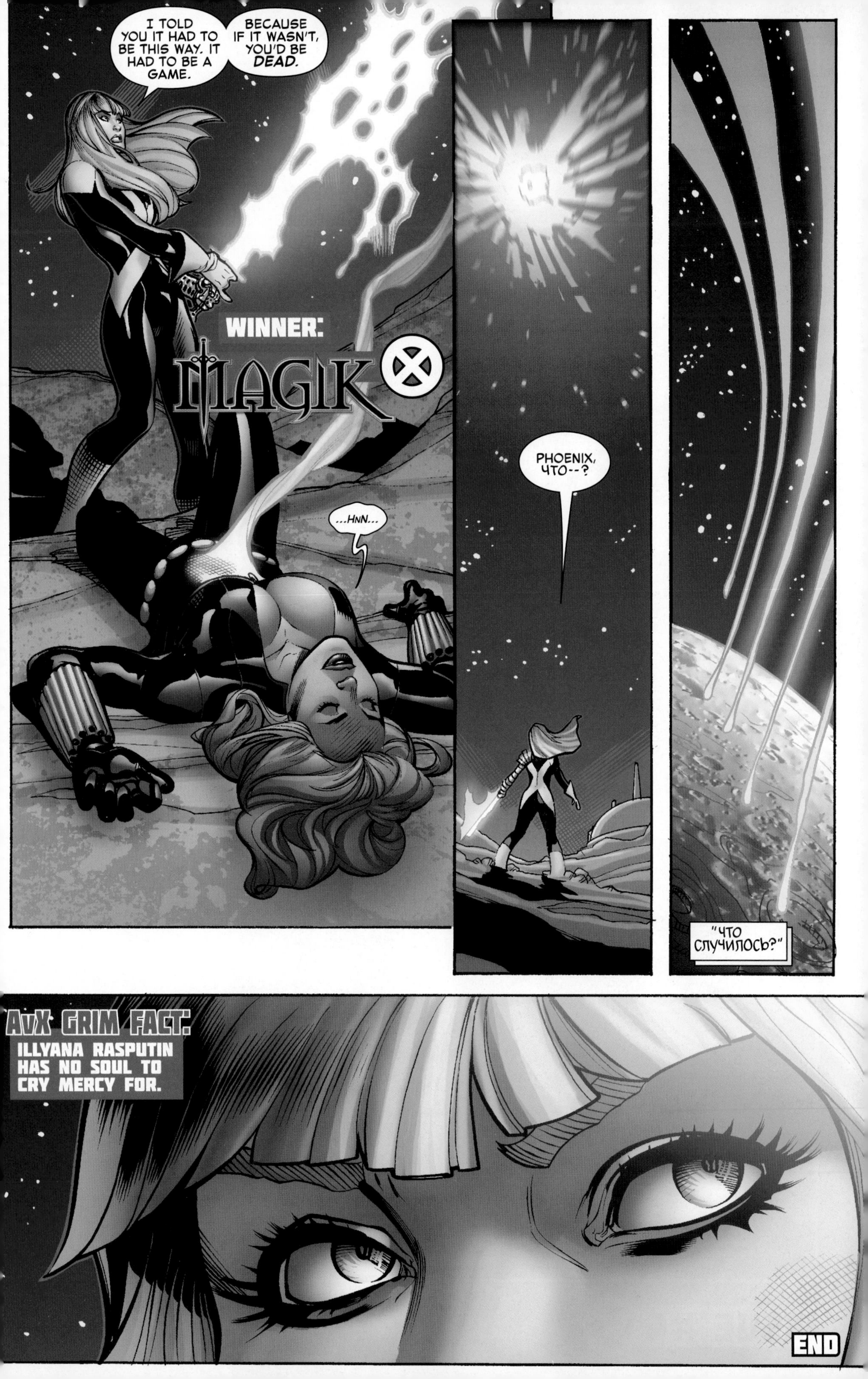
I TOLD YOU IT HAD TO BE THIS WAY. IT HAD TO BE A GAME.
BECAUSE IF IT WASN'T, YOU'D BE DEAD.
WINNER:
MAGIK
...HNN...
PHOENIX, ЧТО--?
"ЧТО СЛУЧИЛОСЬ?"
AvX GRIM FACT:
ILLYANA RASPUTIN HAS NO SOUL TO CRY MERCY FOR.
END

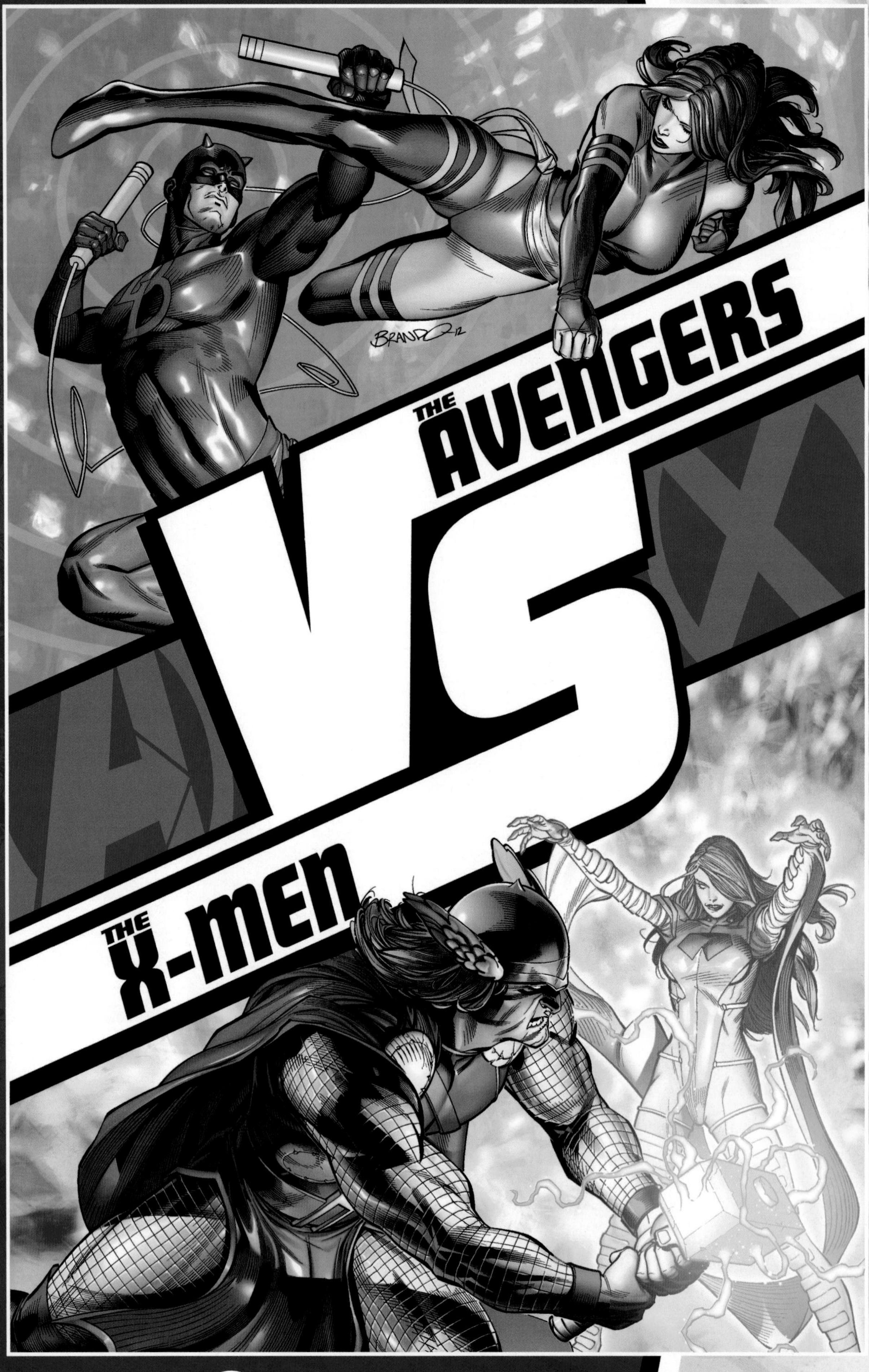
THE AVENGERS
VS
THE X-MEN
BRANDO '12

ISSUE #4

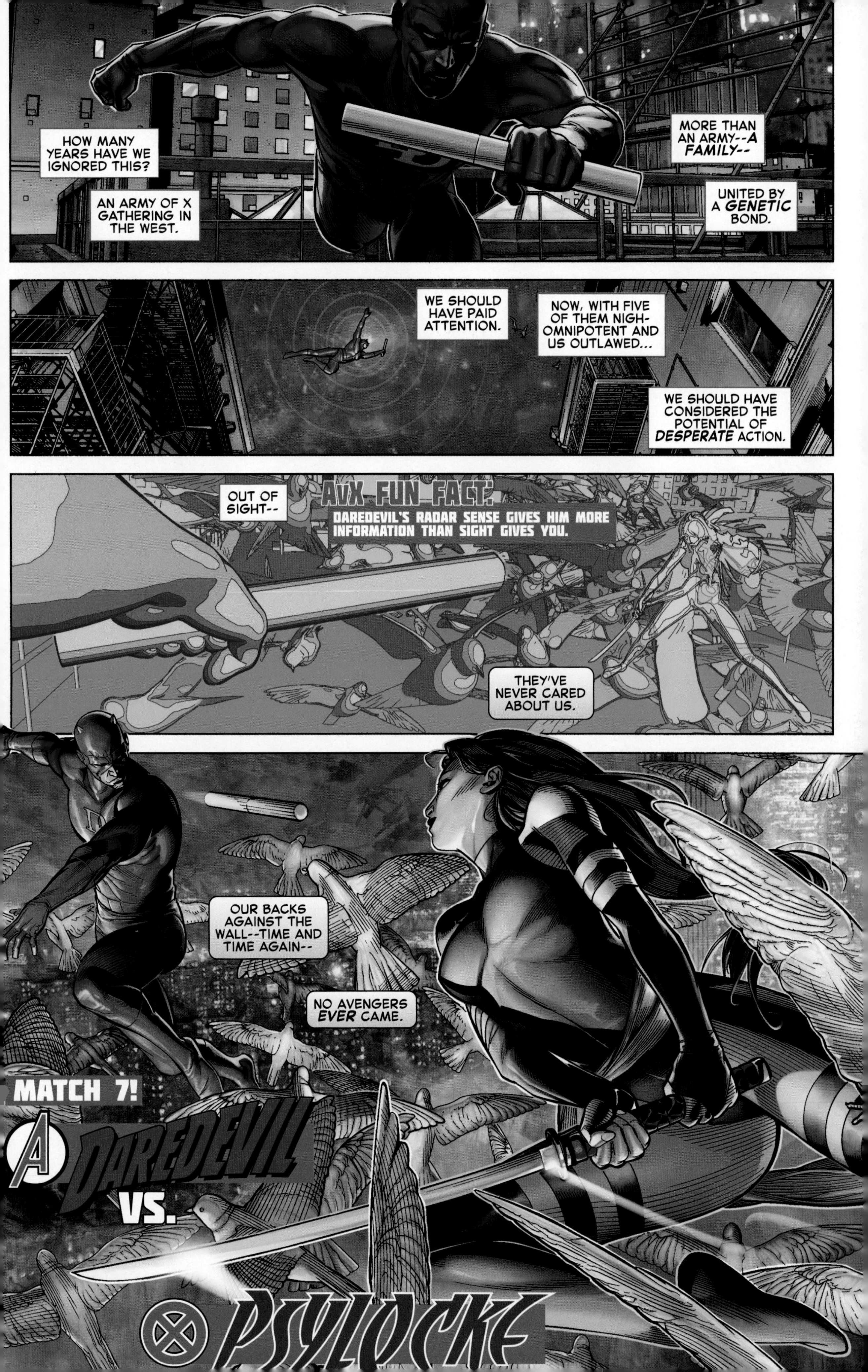
HOW MANY YEARS HAVE WE IGNORED THIS?
AN ARMY OF X GATHERING IN THE WEST.
MORE THAN AN ARMY--A FAMILY--
UNITED BY A GENETIC BOND.
WE SHOULD HAVE PAID ATTENTION.
NOW, WITH FIVE OF THEM NIGH-OMNIPOTENT AND US OUTLAWED...
WE SHOULD HAVE CONSIDERED THE POTENTIAL OF DESPERATE ACTION.
OUT OF SIGHT--
AvX FUN FACT:
DAREDEVIL'S RADAR SENSE GIVES HIM MORE INFORMATION THAN SIGHT GIVES YOU.
THEY'VE NEVER CARED ABOUT US.
OUR BACKS AGAINST THE WALL--TIME AND TIME AGAIN--
NO AVENGERS EVER CAME.
MATCH 7!
DAREDEVIL
VS.
PSYLOCKE

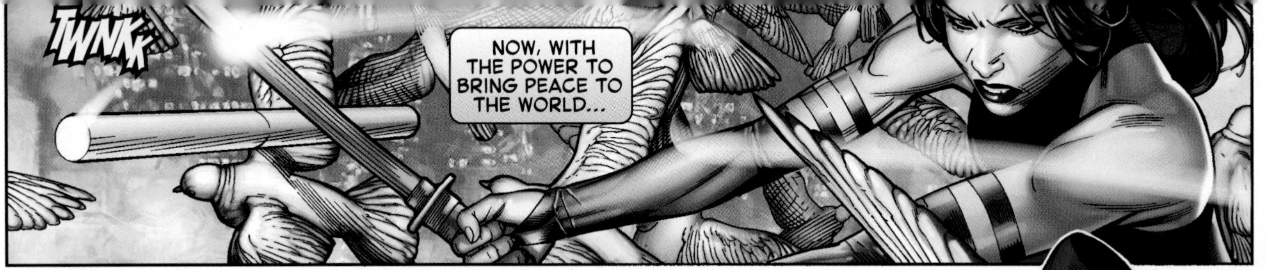
TWNKK
NOW, WITH THE POWER TO BRING PEACE TO THE WORLD...

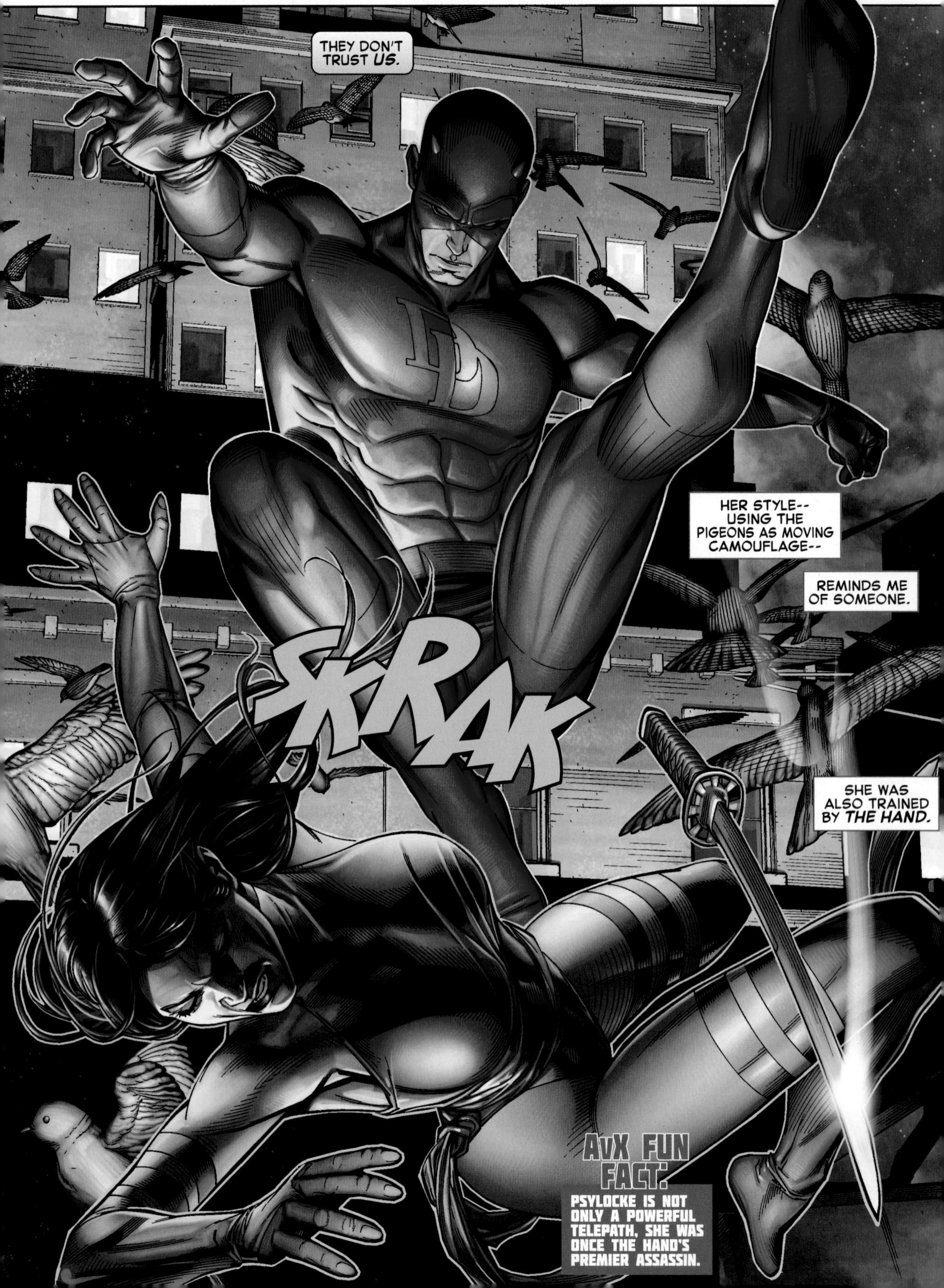
THEY DON'T TRUST US.
HER STYLE-- USING THE PIGEONS AS MOVING CAMOUFLAGE--
REMINDS ME OF SOMEONE.
SKRAK
SHE WAS ALSO TRAINED BY THE HAND.
AvX FUN FACT:
PSYLOCKE IS NOT ONLY A POWERFUL TELEPATH, SHE WAS ONCE THE HAND'S PREMIER ASSASSIN.

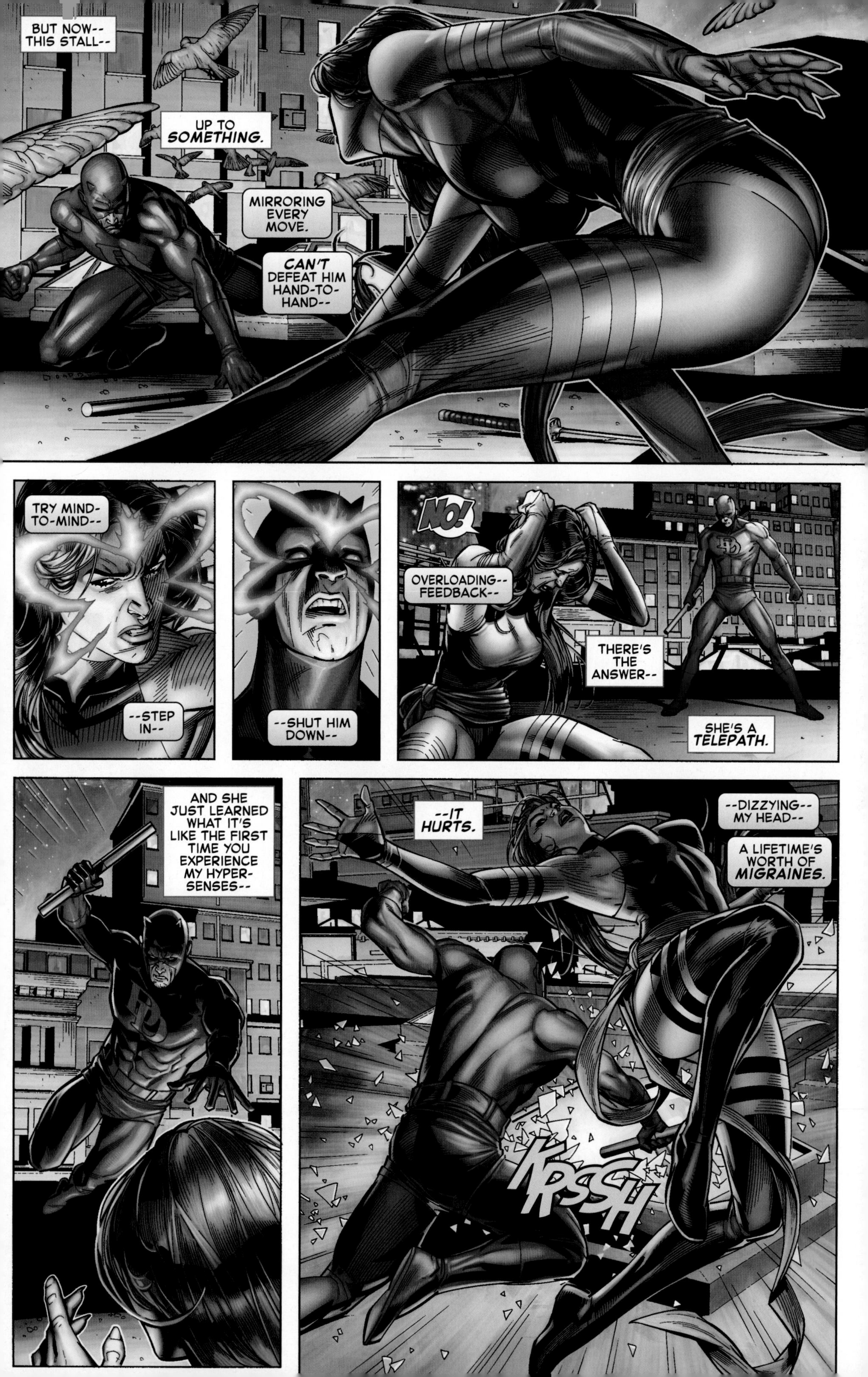
BUT NOW-- THIS STALL--
UP TO SOMETHING.
MIRRORING EVERY MOVE.
CAN'T DEFEAT HIM HAND-TO-HAND--
TRY MIND-TO-MIND--
--STEP IN--
--SHUT HIM DOWN--
NO!
OVERLOADING-- FEEDBACK--
THERE'S THE ANSWER--
SHE'S A TELEPATH.
AND SHE JUST LEARNED WHAT IT'S LIKE THE FIRST TIME YOU EXPERIENCE MY HYPER-SENSES--
--IT HURTS.
--DIZZYING-- MY HEAD--
A LIFETIME'S WORTH OF MIGRAINES.
KRSSH

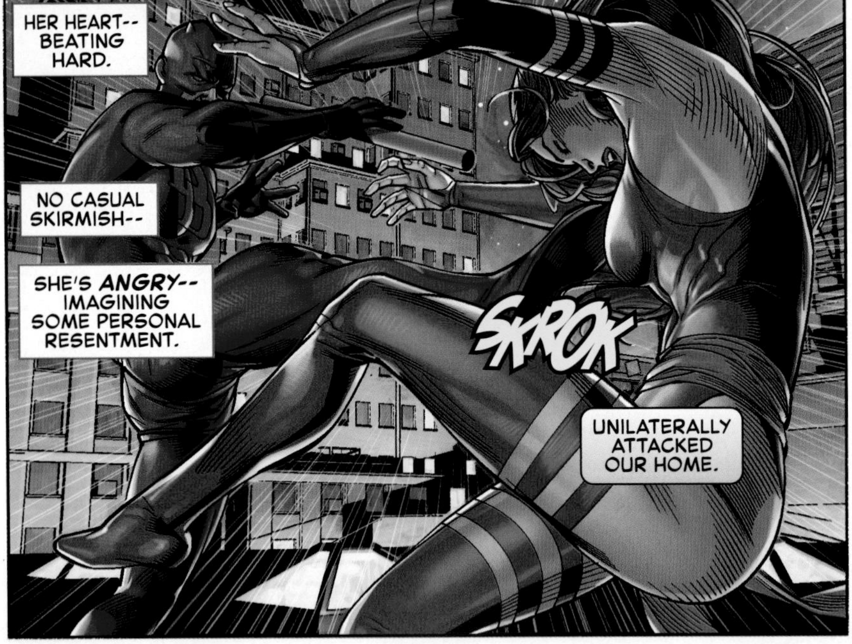
HER HEART--
BEATING HARD.
NO CASUAL SKIRMISH--
SHE'S ANGRY-- IMAGINING SOME PERSONAL RESENTMENT.
SKROK
UNILATERALLY ATTACKED OUR HOME.

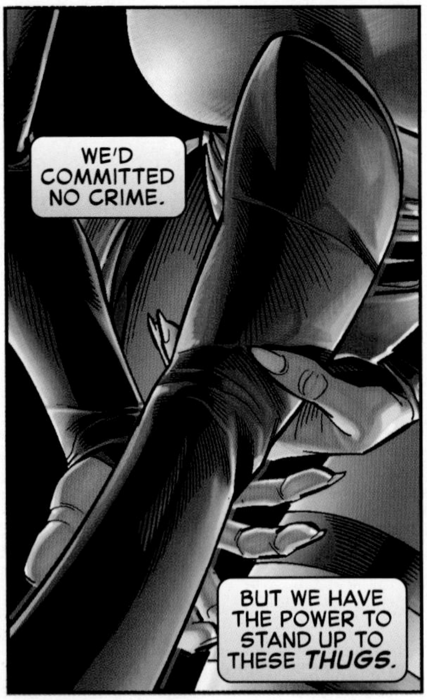
WE'D COMMITTED NO CRIME.
BUT WE HAVE THE POWER TO STAND UP TO THESE THUGS.

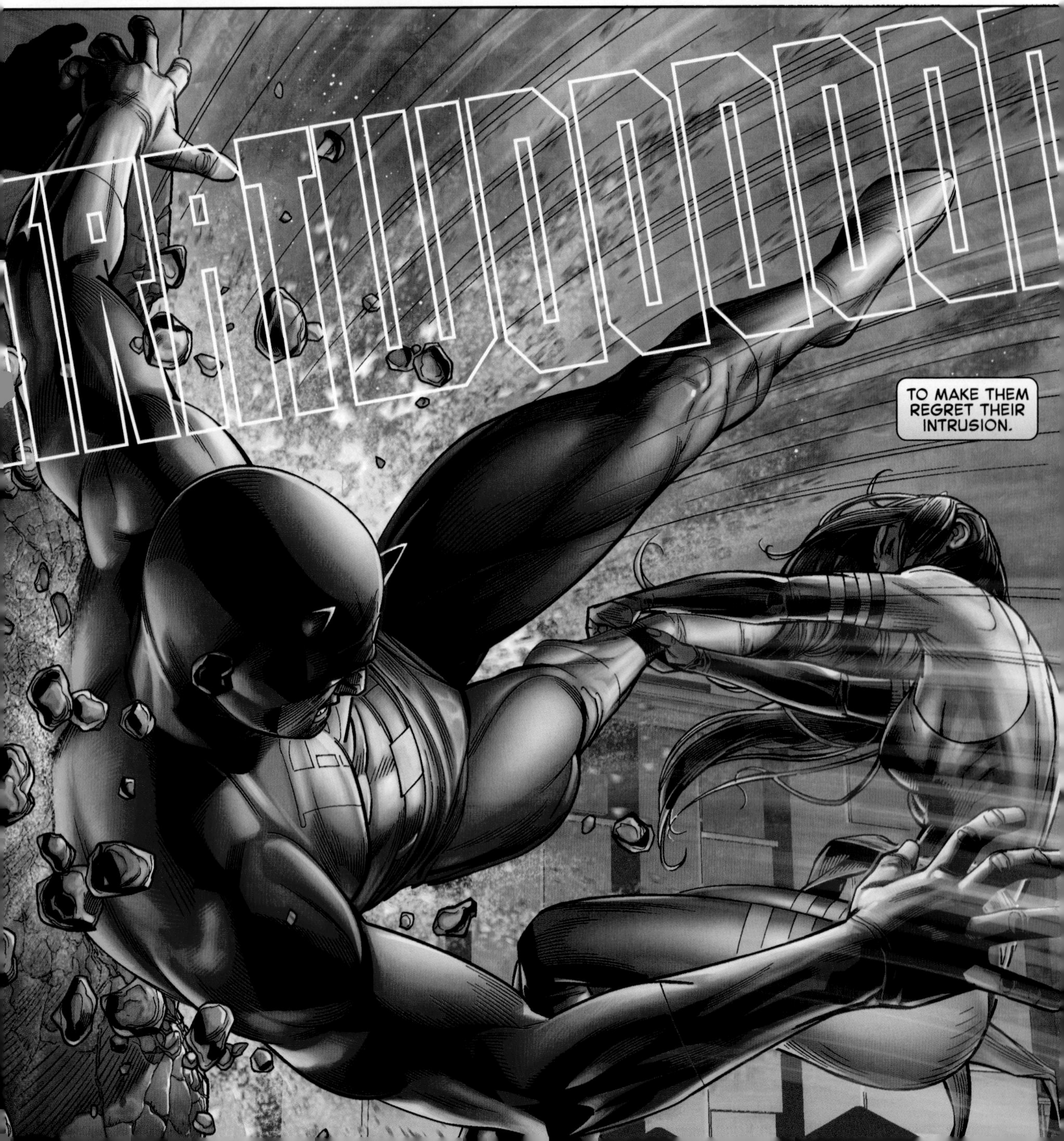
TO MAKE THEM REGRET THEIR INTRUSION.

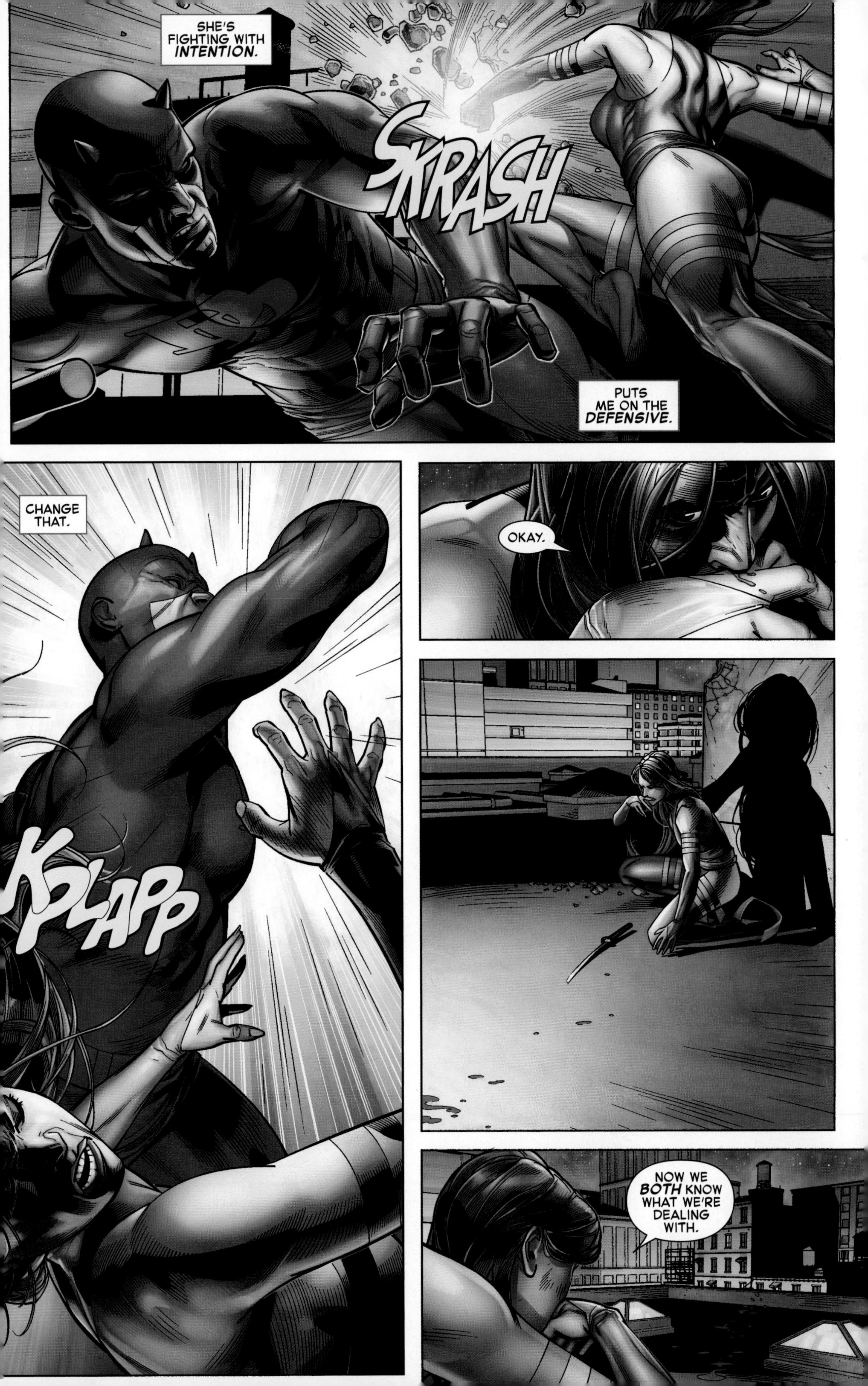
SHE'S FIGHTING WITH INTENTION.
SKRASH
PUTS ME ON THE DEFENSIVE.
CHANGE THAT.
KLAPP
OKAY.
NOW WE BOTH KNOW WHAT WE'RE DEALING WITH.

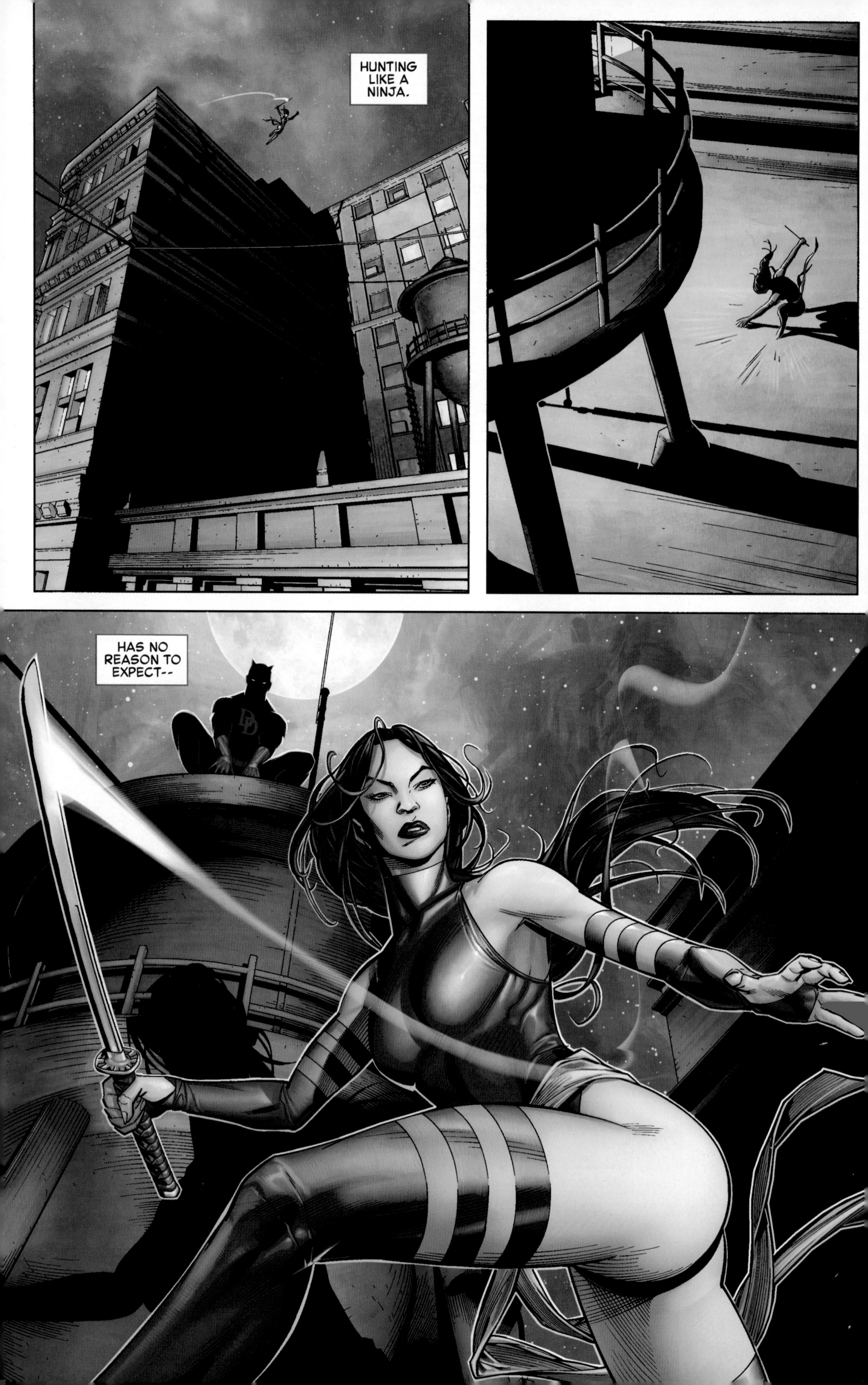
HUNTING LIKE A NINJA.
HAS NO REASON TO EXPECT--

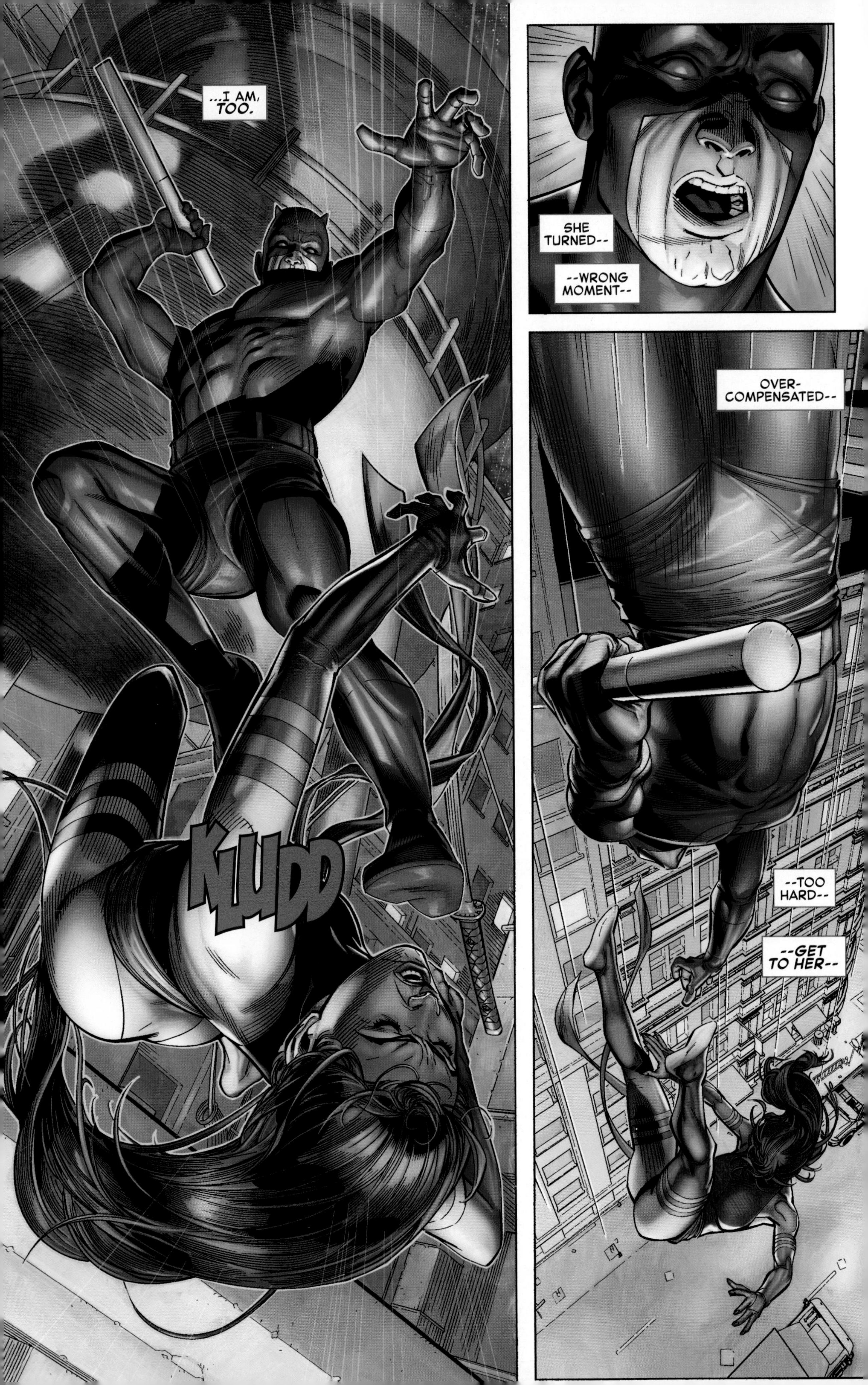
...I AM, TOO.
KLUDD
SHE TURNED--
--WRONG MOMENT--
OVER-COMPENSATED--
--TOO HARD--
--GET TO HER--

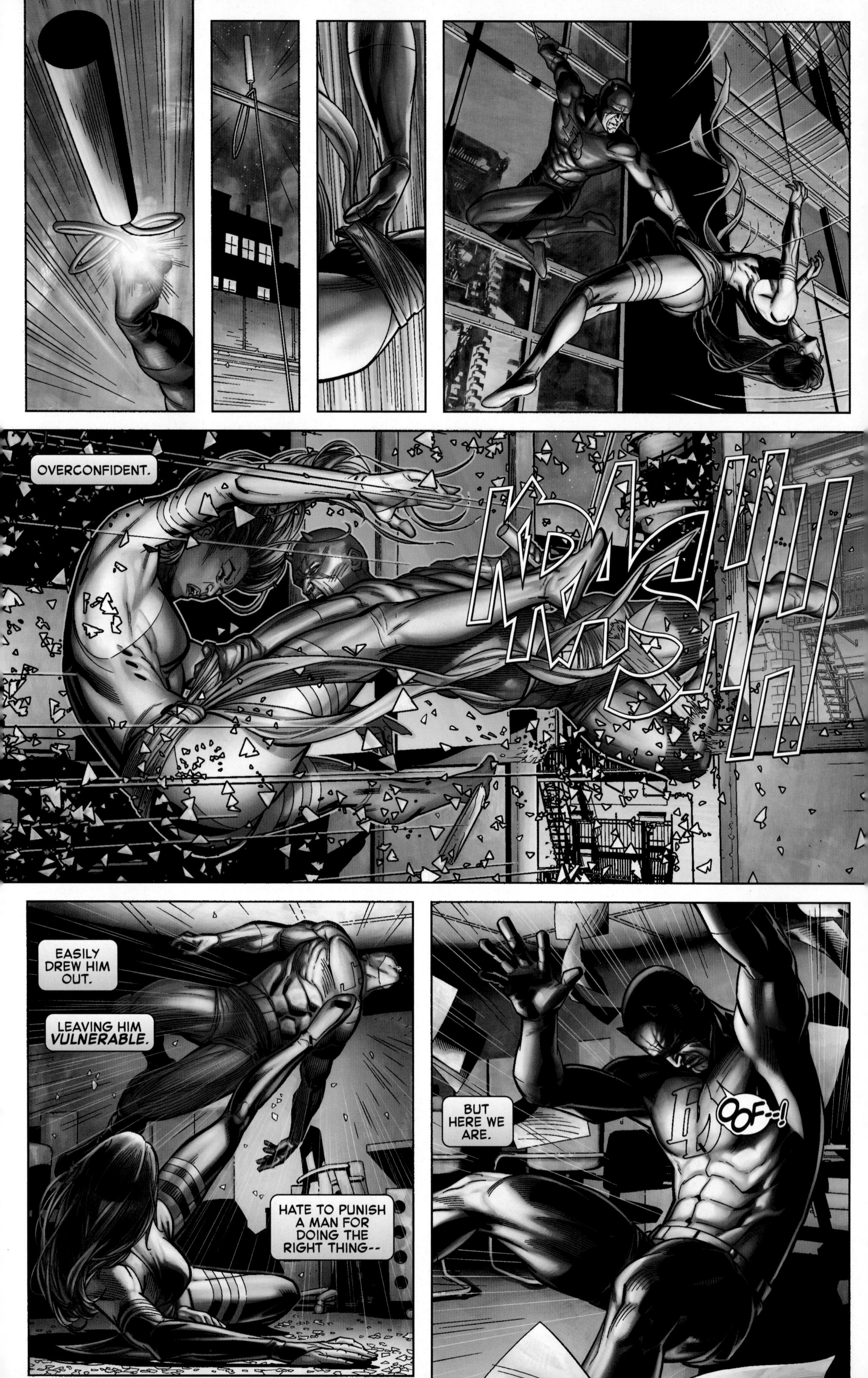
OVERCONFIDENT.
EASILY DREW HIM OUT.
LEAVING HIM VULNERABLE.
HATE TO PUNISH A MAN FOR DOING THE RIGHT THING--
BUT HERE WE ARE.
OOF--!

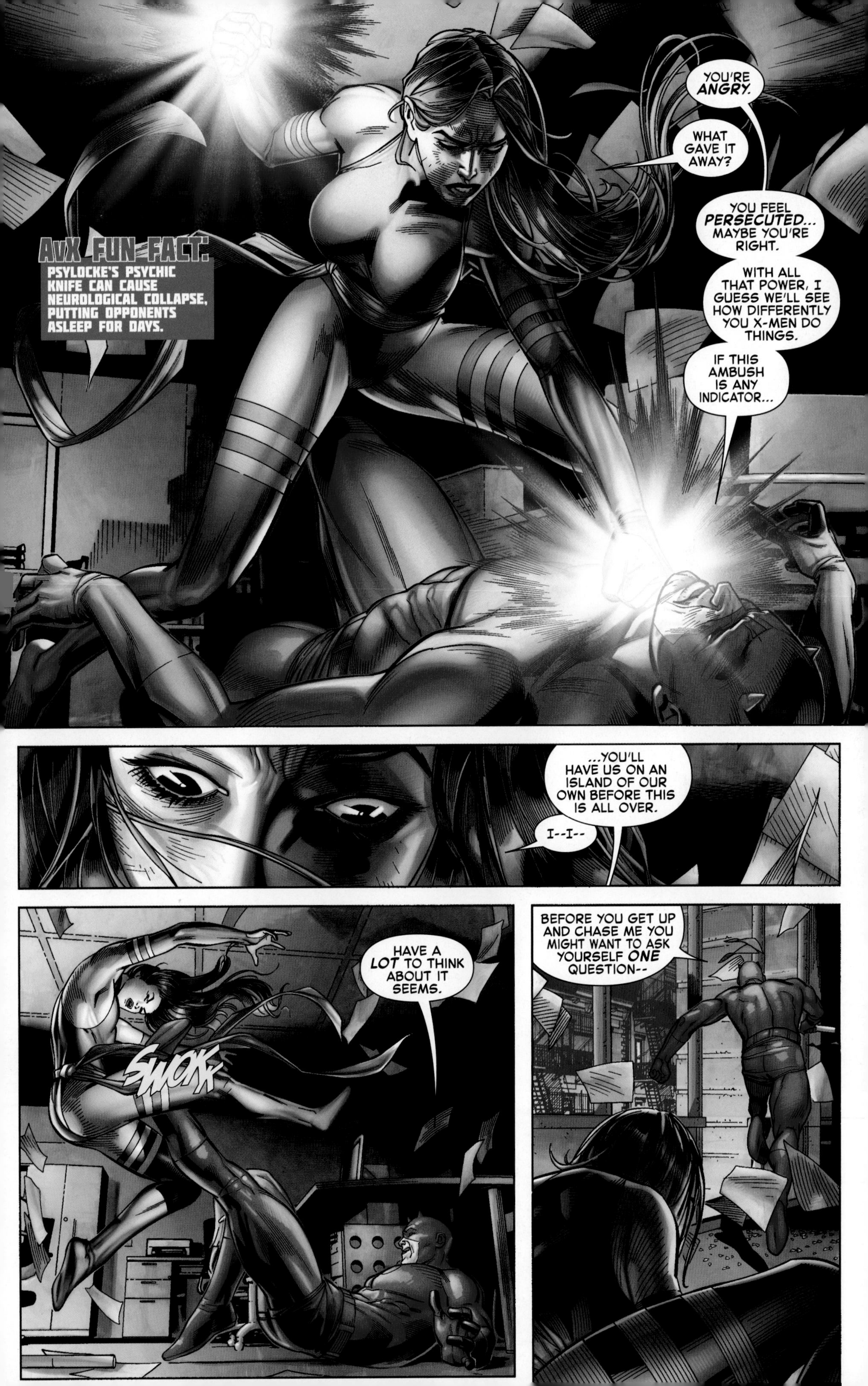
AvX FUN FACT:
PSYLOCKE'S PSYCHIC KNIFE CAN CAUSE NEUROLOGICAL COLLAPSE, PUTTING OPPONENTS ASLEEP FOR DAYS.
YOU'RE ANGRY.
WHAT GAVE IT AWAY?
YOU FEEL PERSECUTED... MAYBE YOU'RE RIGHT.
WITH ALL THAT POWER, I GUESS WE'LL SEE HOW DIFFERENTLY YOU X-MEN DO THINGS.
IF THIS AMBUSH IS ANY INDICATOR...
...YOU'LL HAVE US ON AN ISLAND OF OUR OWN BEFORE THIS IS ALL OVER.
I--I--
HAVE A LOT TO THINK ABOUT IT SEEMS.
SWOKK
BEFORE YOU GET UP AND CHASE ME YOU MIGHT WANT TO ASK YOURSELF ONE QUESTION--

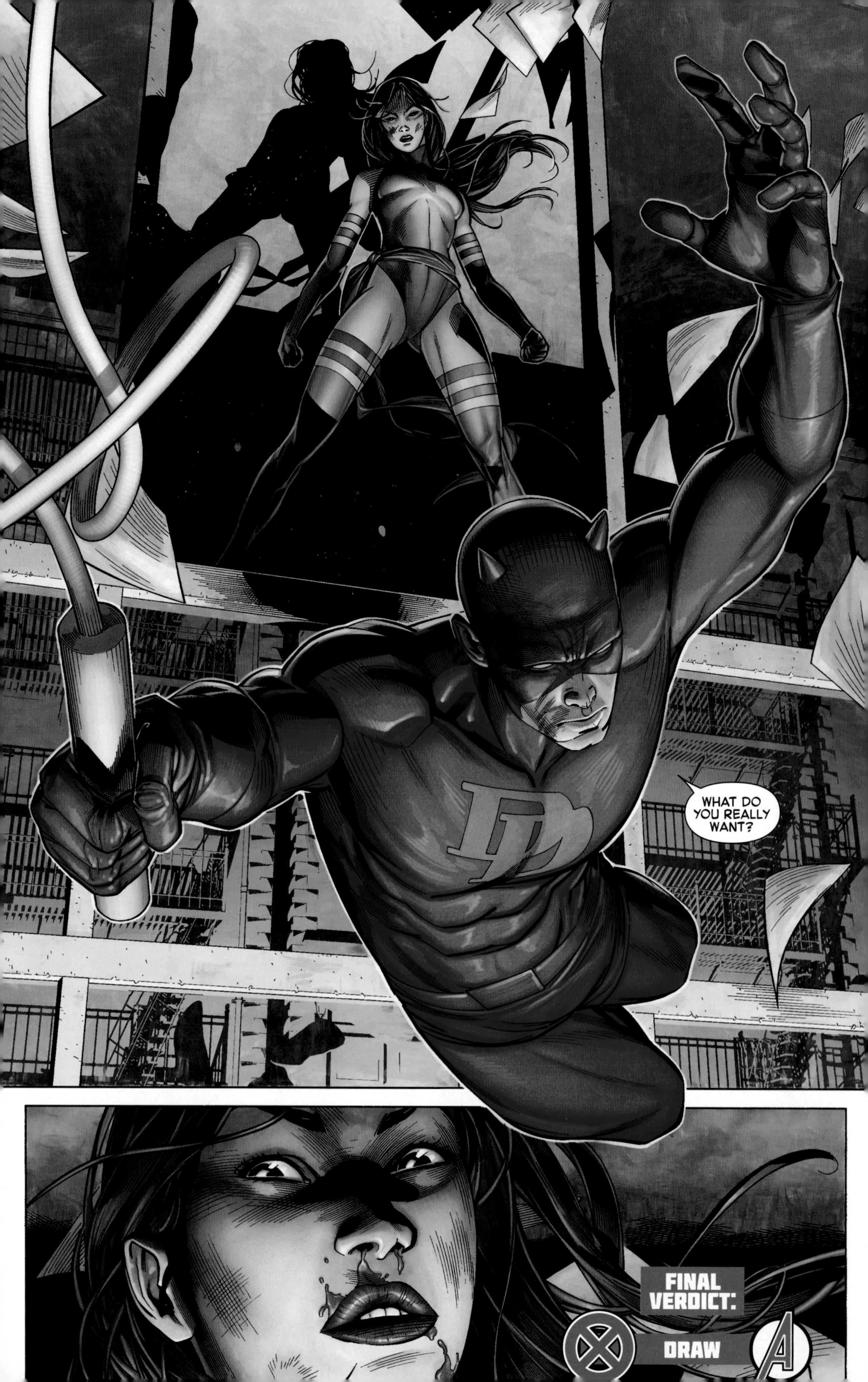
WHAT DO YOU REALLY WANT?
FINAL VERDICT:
DRAW

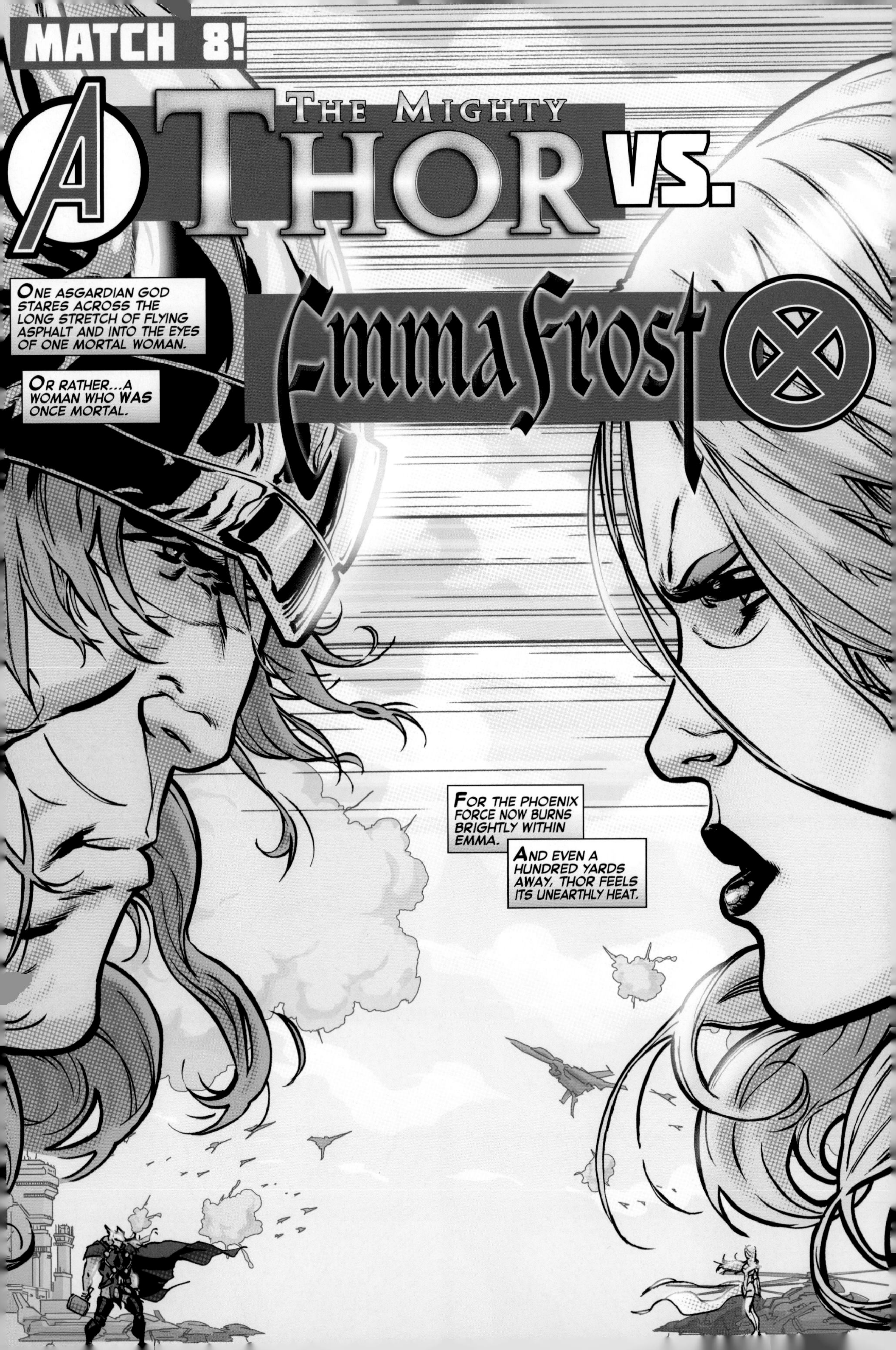
MATCH 8!
THE MIGHTY THOR VS.
EMMA FROST
ONE ASGARDIAN GOD STARES ACROSS THE LONG STRETCH OF FLYING ASPHALT AND INTO THE EYES OF ONE MORTAL WOMAN.
OR RATHER...A WOMAN WHO WAS ONCE MORTAL.
FOR THE PHOENIX FORCE NOW BURNS BRIGHTLY WITHIN EMMA.
AND EVEN A HUNDRED YARDS AWAY, THOR FEELS ITS UNEARTHLY HEAT.

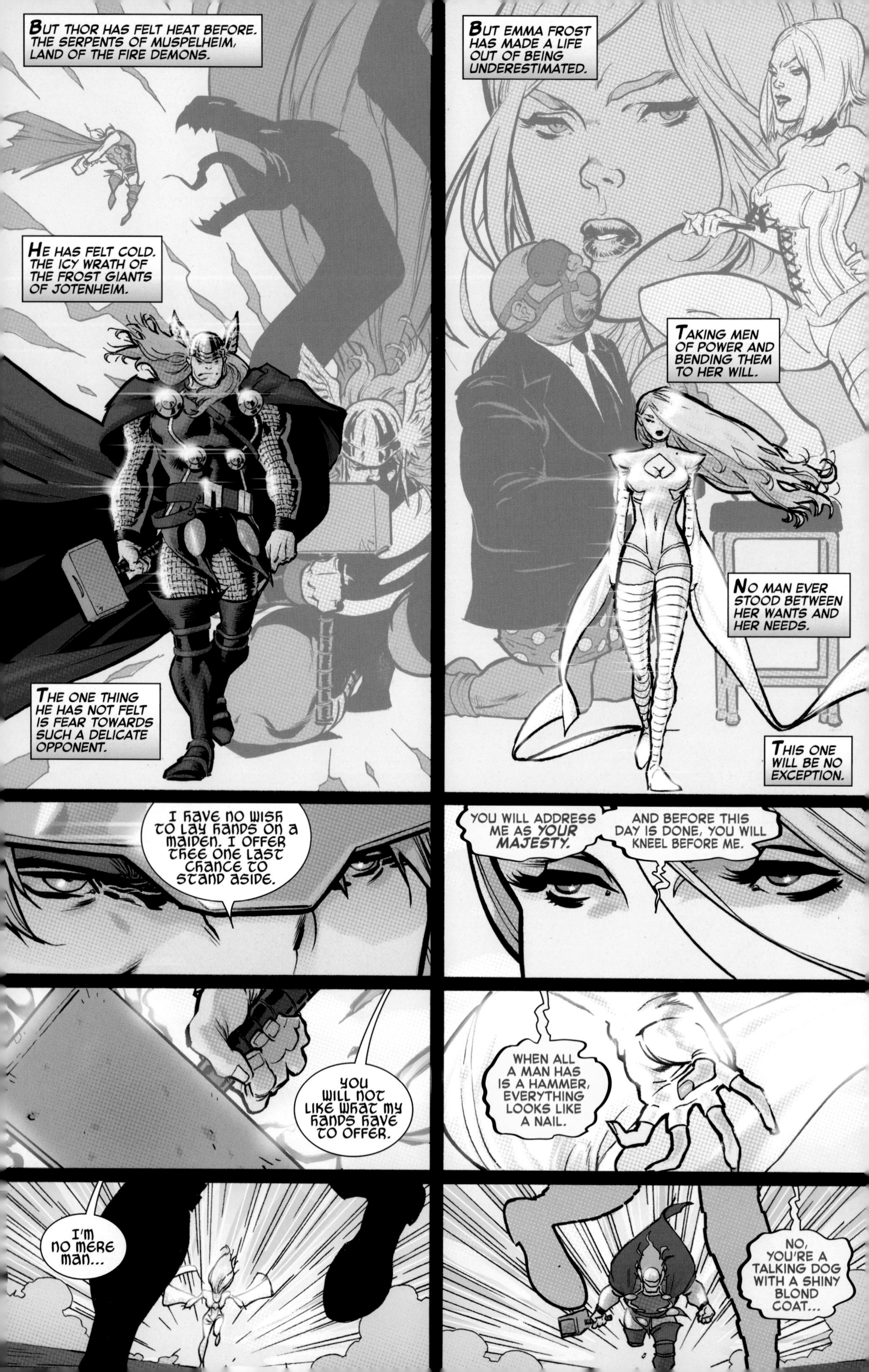

BUT THOR HAS FELT HEAT BEFORE. THE SERPENTS OF MUSPELHEIM, LAND OF THE FIRE DEMONS.
HE HAS FELT COLD. THE ICY WRATH OF THE FROST GIANTS OF JOTENHEIM.
THE ONE THING HE HAS NOT FELT IS FEAR TOWARDS SUCH A DELICATE OPPONENT.
BUT EMMA FROST HAS MADE A LIFE OUT OF BEING UNDERESTIMATED.
TAKING MEN OF POWER AND BENDING THEM TO HER WILL.
NO MAN EVER STOOD BETWEEN HER WANTS AND HER NEEDS.
THIS ONE WILL BE NO EXCEPTION.
I HAVE NO WISH TO LAY HANDS ON A MAIDEN. I OFFER THEE ONE LAST CHANCE TO STAND ASIDE.
YOU WILL ADDRESS ME AS YOUR MAJESTY.
AND BEFORE THIS DAY IS DONE, YOU WILL KNEEL BEFORE ME.
YOU WILL NOT LIKE WHAT MY HANDS HAVE TO OFFER.
WHEN ALL A MAN HAS IS A HAMMER, EVERYTHING LOOKS LIKE A NAIL.
I'M NO MERE MAN...
NO, YOU'RE A TALKING DOG WITH A SHINY BLOND COAT...

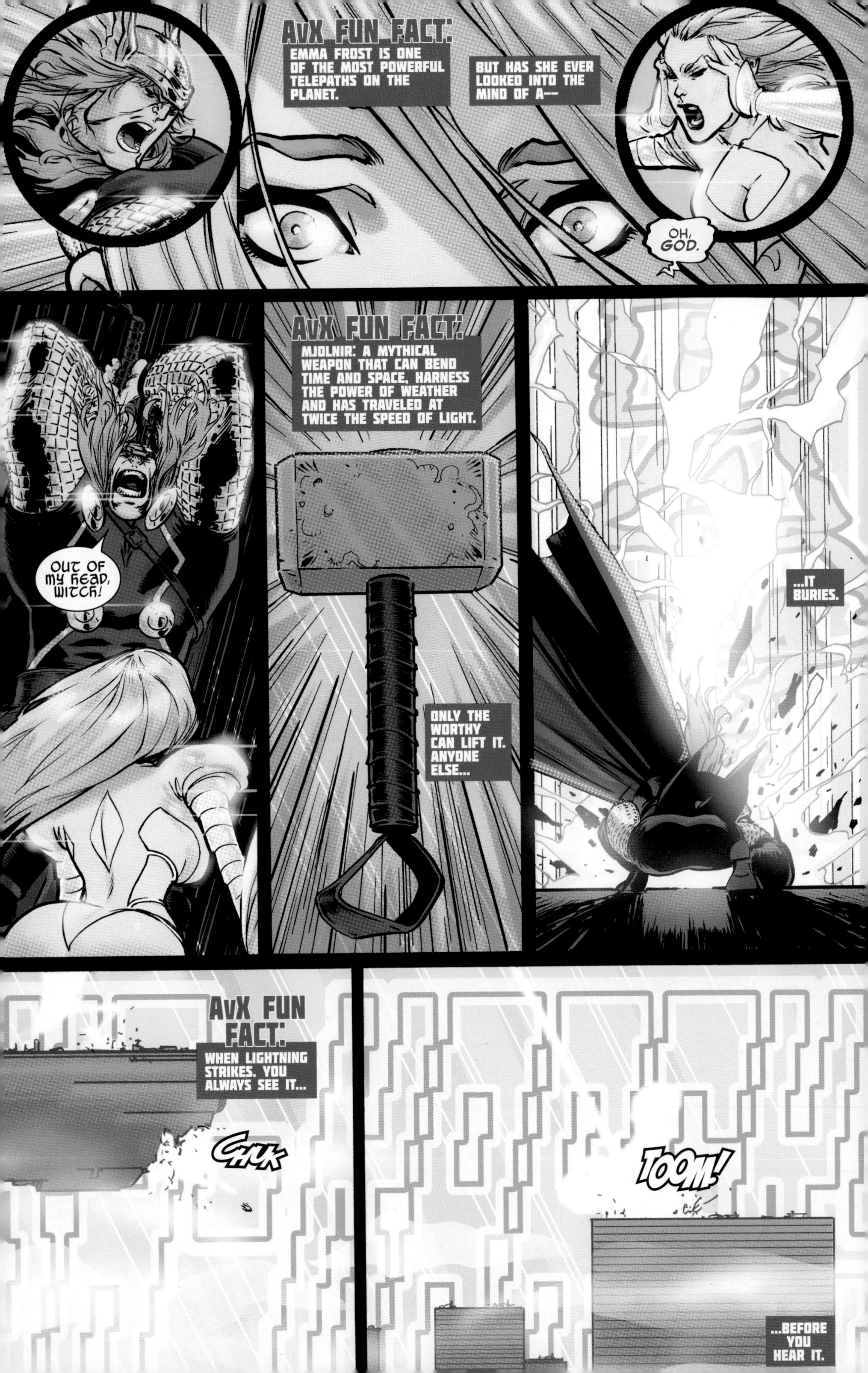
AvX FUN FACT:
EMMA FROST IS ONE OF THE MOST POWERFUL TELEPATHS ON THE PLANET.
BUT HAS SHE EVER LOOKED INTO THE MIND OF A--
OH, GOD.
OUT OF MY HEAD, WITCH!
AvX FUN FACT:
MJOLNIR: A MYTHICAL WEAPON THAT CAN BEND TIME AND SPACE, HARNESS THE POWER OF WEATHER AND HAS TRAVELED AT TWICE THE SPEED OF LIGHT.
ONLY THE WORTHY CAN LIFT IT. ANYONE ELSE...
...IT BURIES.
AvX FUN FACT:
WHEN LIGHTNING STRIKES, YOU ALWAYS SEE IT...
CHUK
TOOM!
...BEFORE YOU HEAR IT.

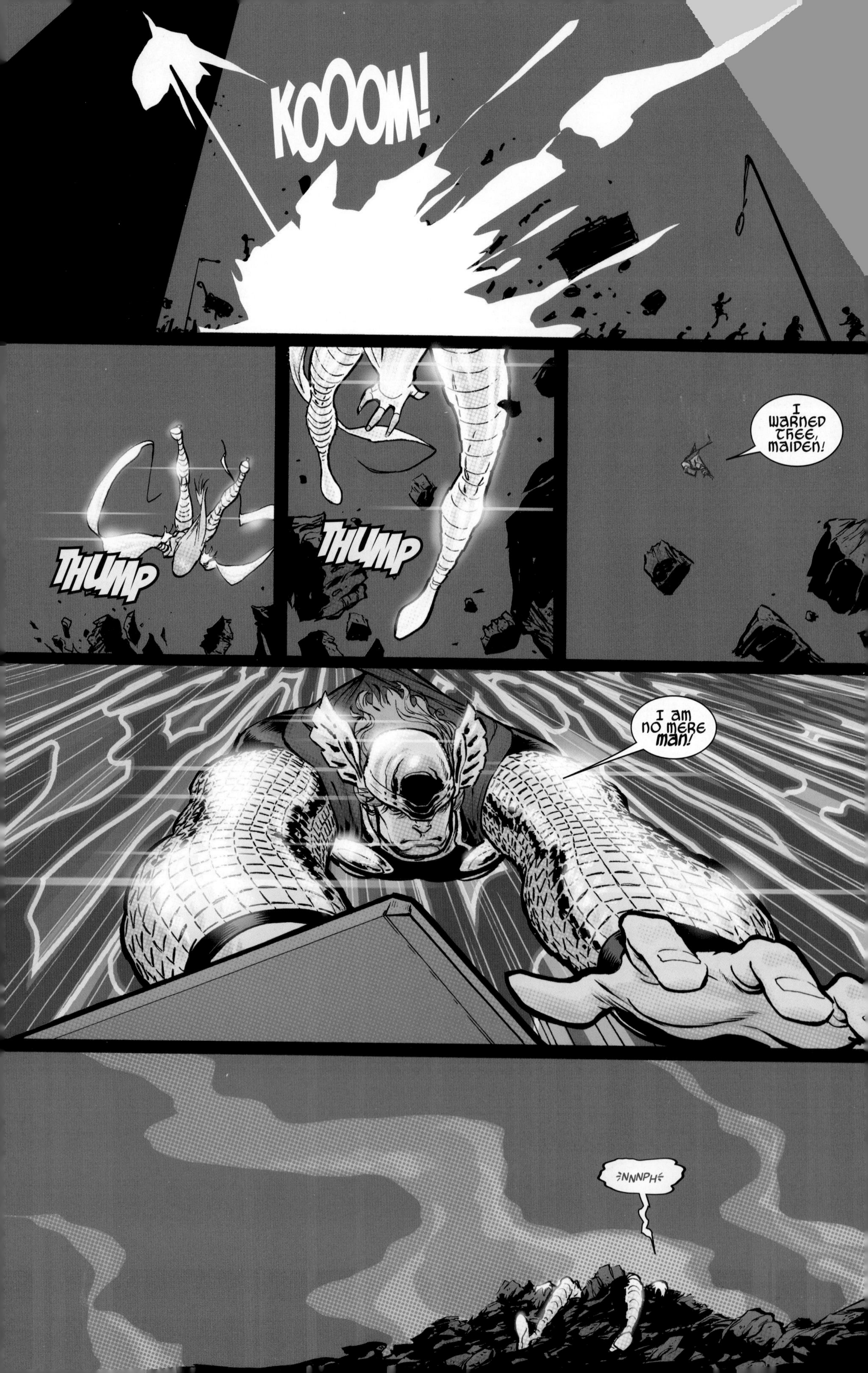
KOOOM!
THUMP
THUMP
I WARNED THEE, MAIDEN!
I am no mere man!
NNNPH

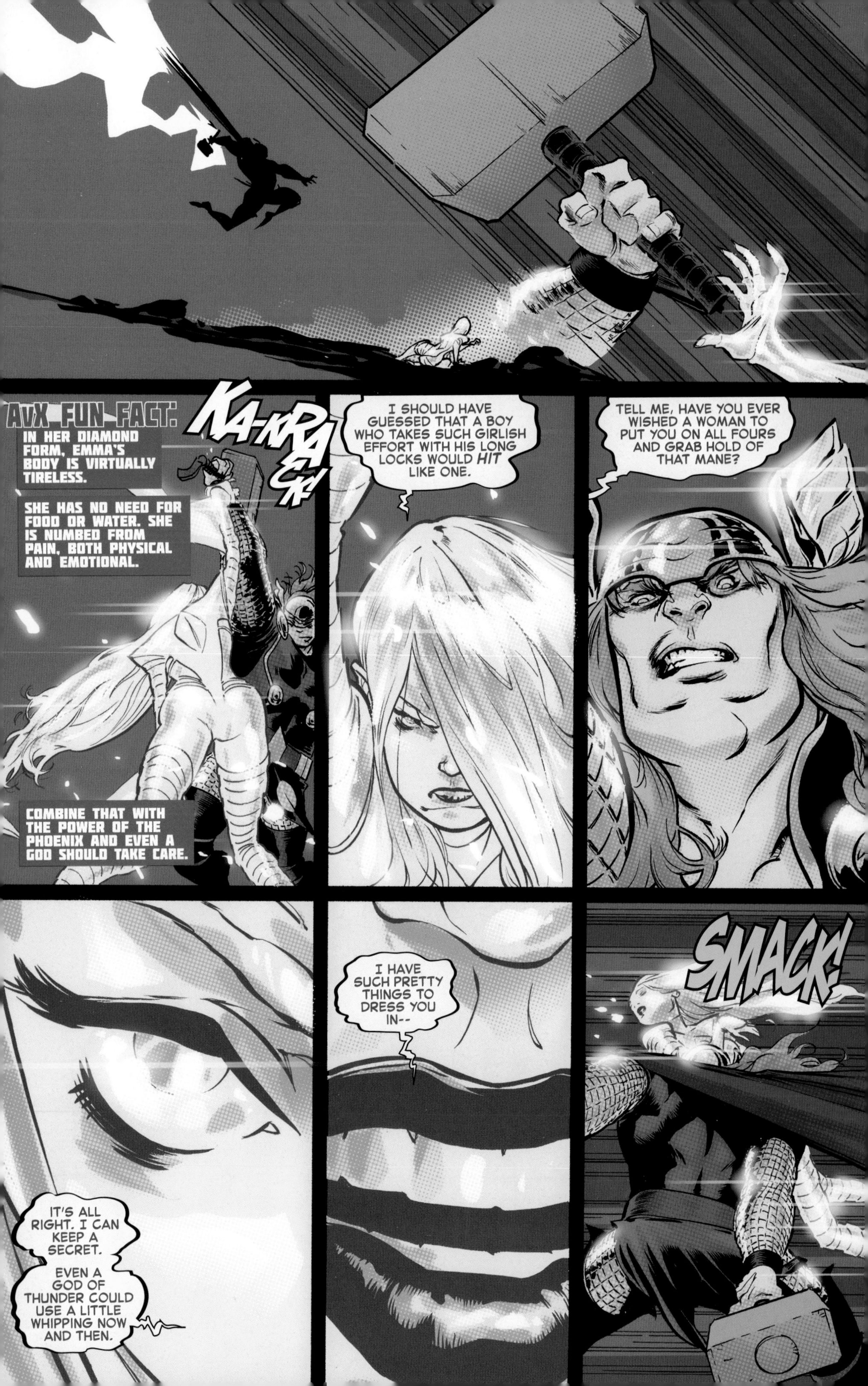
AvX FUN FACT:
IN HER DIAMOND FORM, EMMA'S BODY IS VIRTUALLY TIRELESS.
KA-KRA-ACK!
SHE HAS NO NEED FOR FOOD OR WATER. SHE IS NUMBED FROM PAIN, BOTH PHYSICAL AND EMOTIONAL.
COMBINE THAT WITH THE POWER OF THE PHOENIX AND EVEN A GOD SHOULD TAKE CARE.
I SHOULD HAVE GUESSED THAT A BOY WHO TAKES SUCH GIRLISH EFFORT WITH HIS LONG LOCKS WOULD *HIT* LIKE ONE.
TELL ME, HAVE YOU EVER WISHED A WOMAN TO PUT YOU ON ALL FOURS AND GRAB HOLD OF THAT MANE?
IT'S ALL RIGHT. I CAN KEEP A SECRET.
EVEN A GOD OF THUNDER COULD USE A LITTLE WHIPPING NOW AND THEN.
I HAVE SUCH PRETTY THINGS TO DRESS YOU IN--
SMACK!

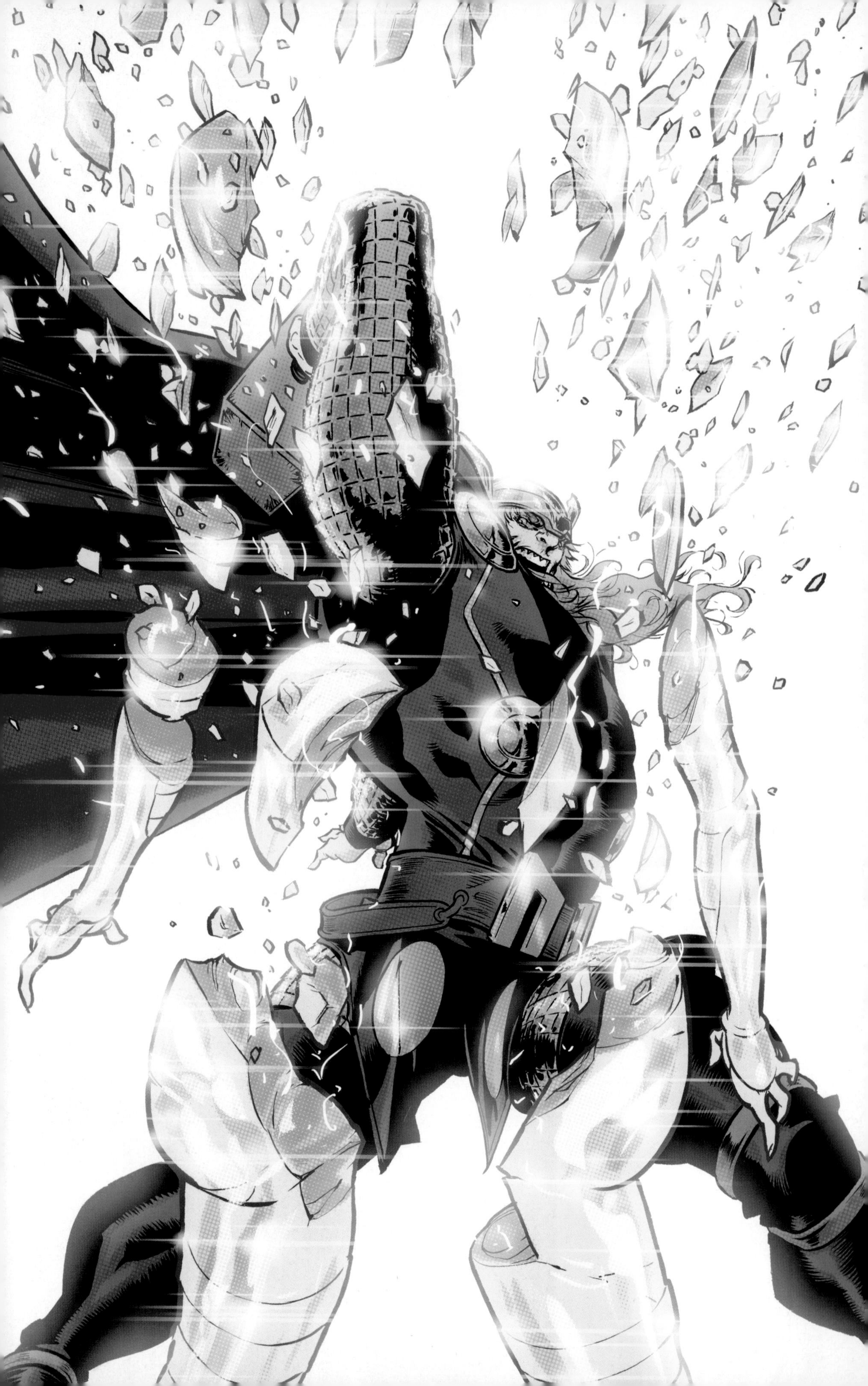

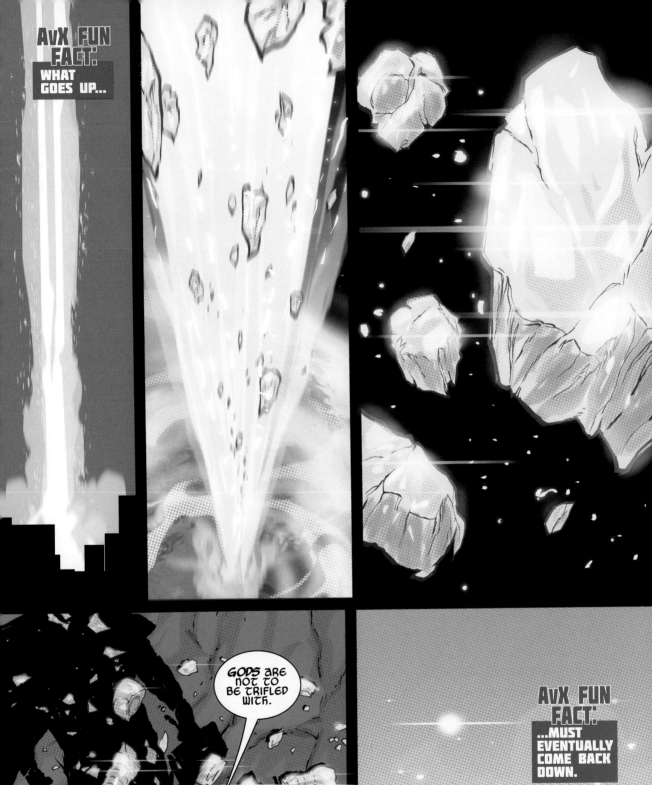

AvX FUN FACT: WHAT GOES UP...

GODS ARE NOT TO BE TRIFLED WITH.

AvX FUN FACT: ...MUST EVENTUALLY COME BACK DOWN.

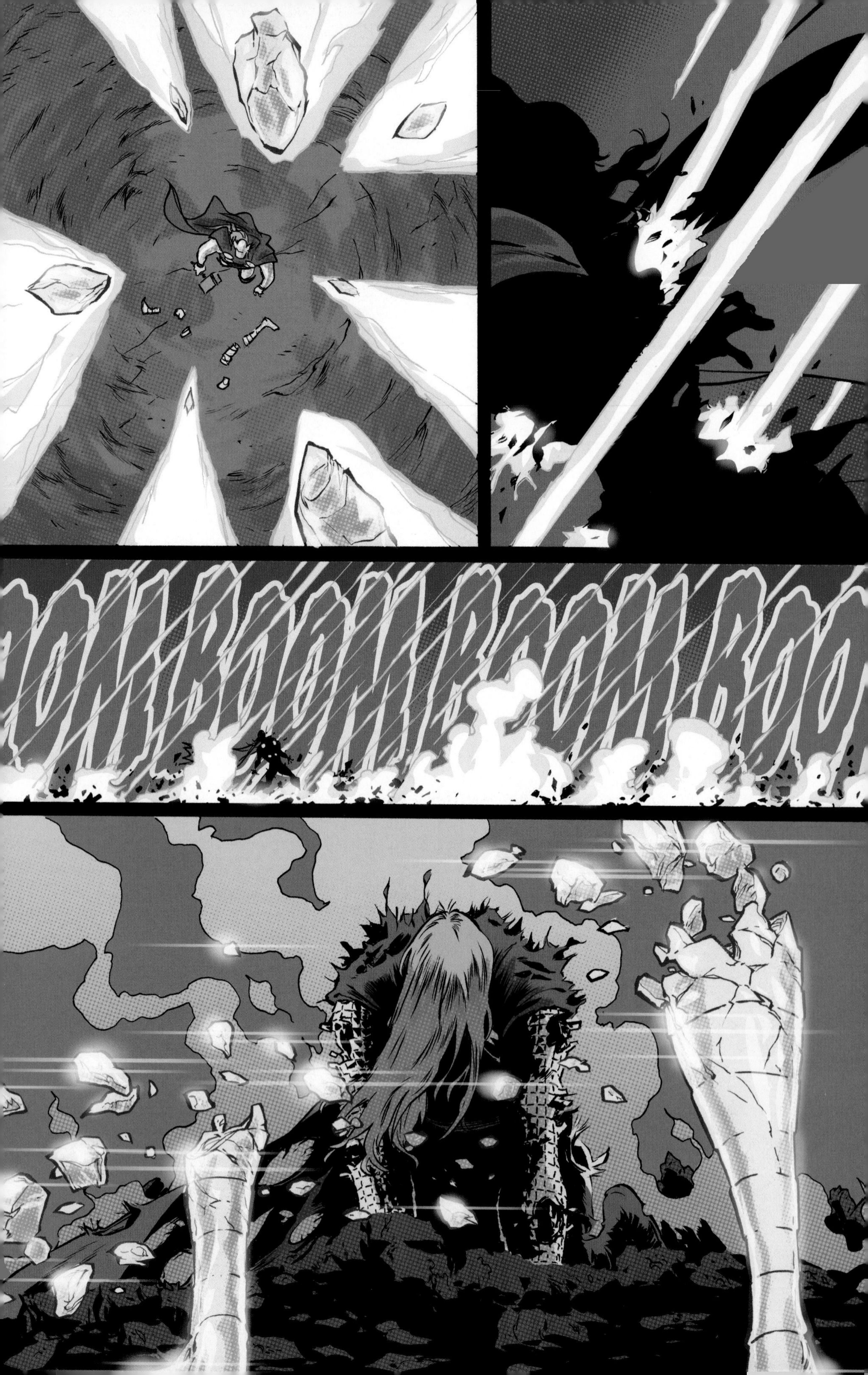
OOMBOOMBOOMBOO

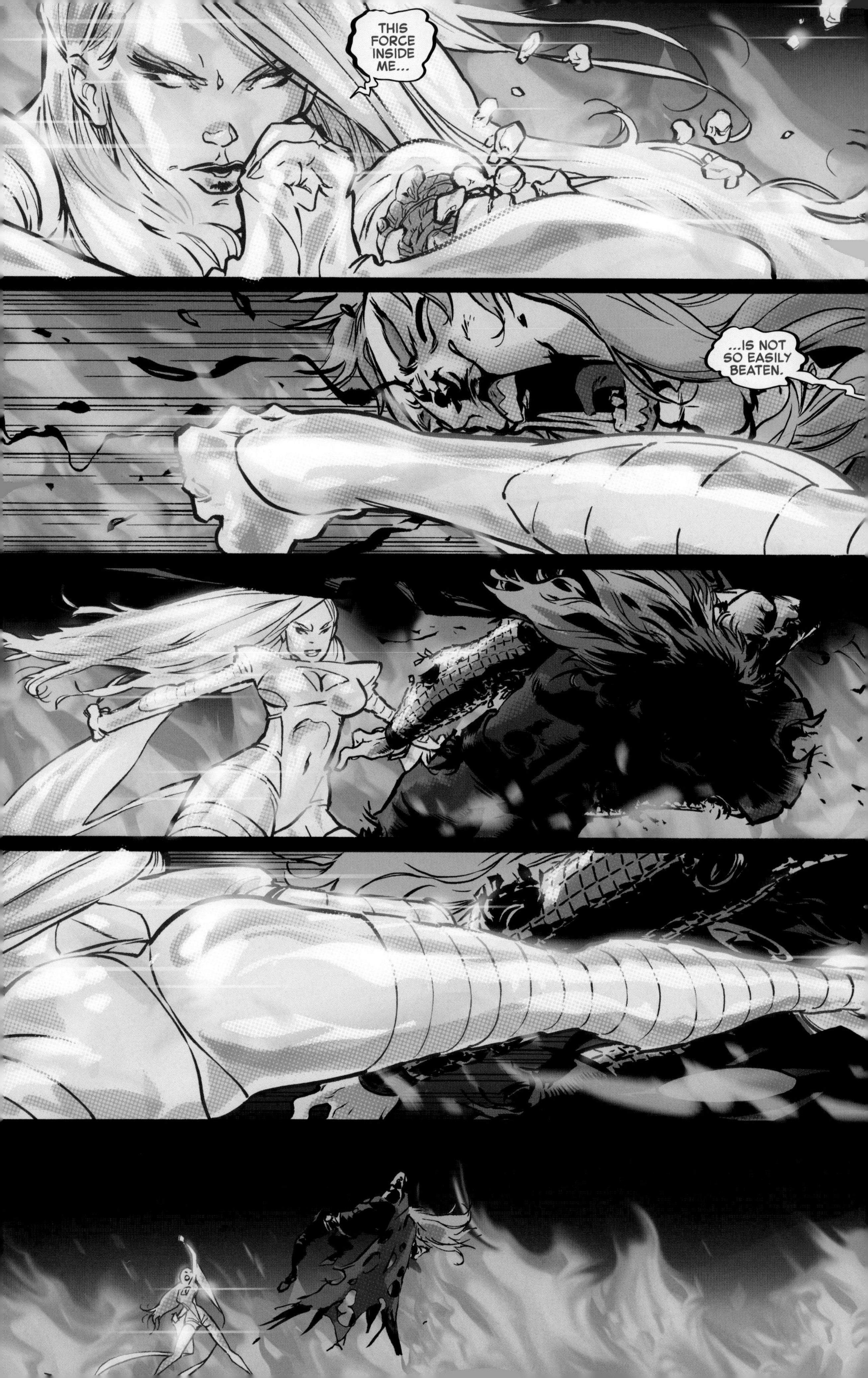
THIS FORCE INSIDE ME...
...IS NOT SO EASILY BEATEN.

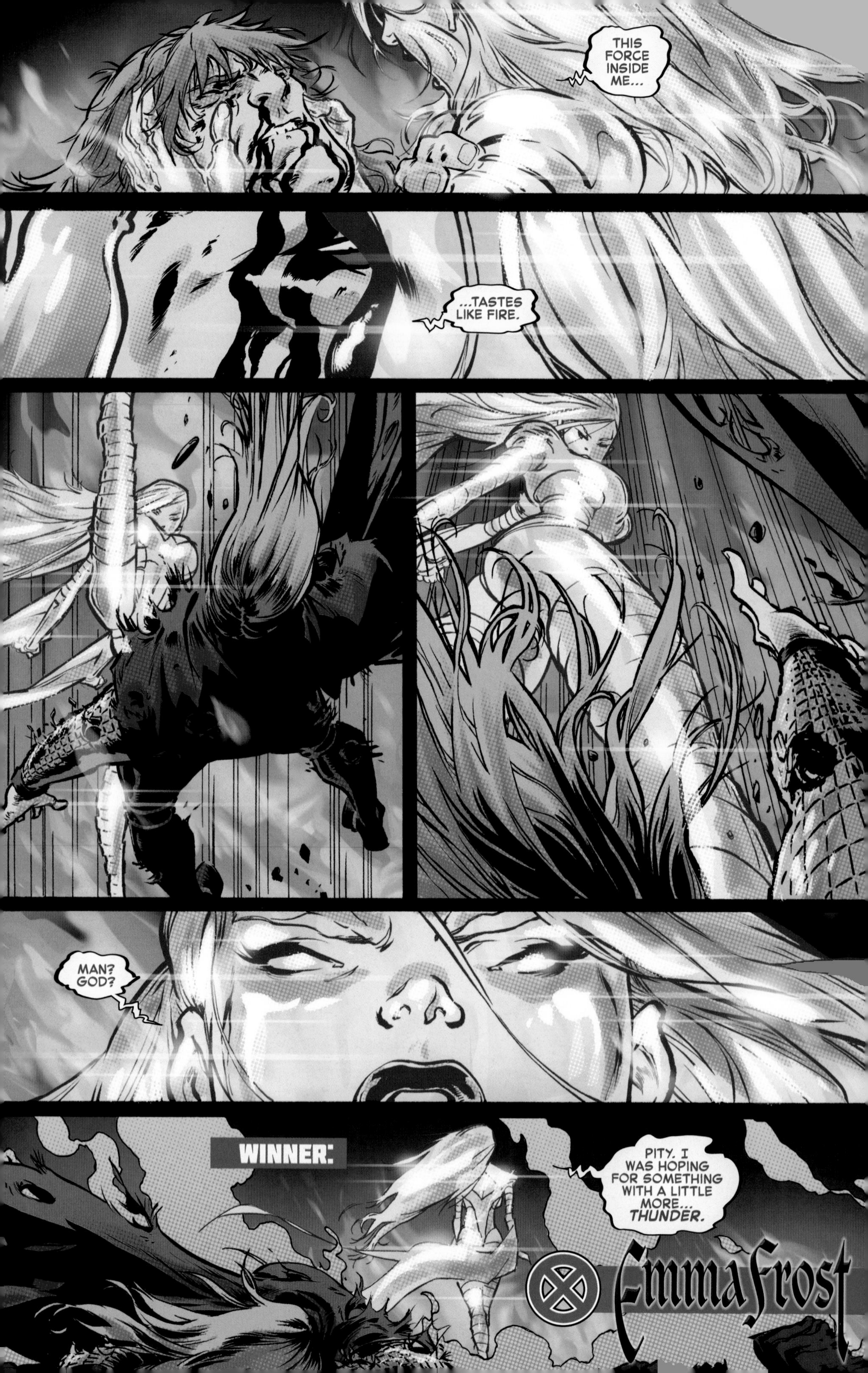
THIS FORCE INSIDE ME...
...TASTES LIKE FIRE.
MAN? GOD?
WINNER:
PITY. I WAS HOPING FOR SOMETHING WITH A LITTLE MORE... *THUNDER.*
Emma Frost

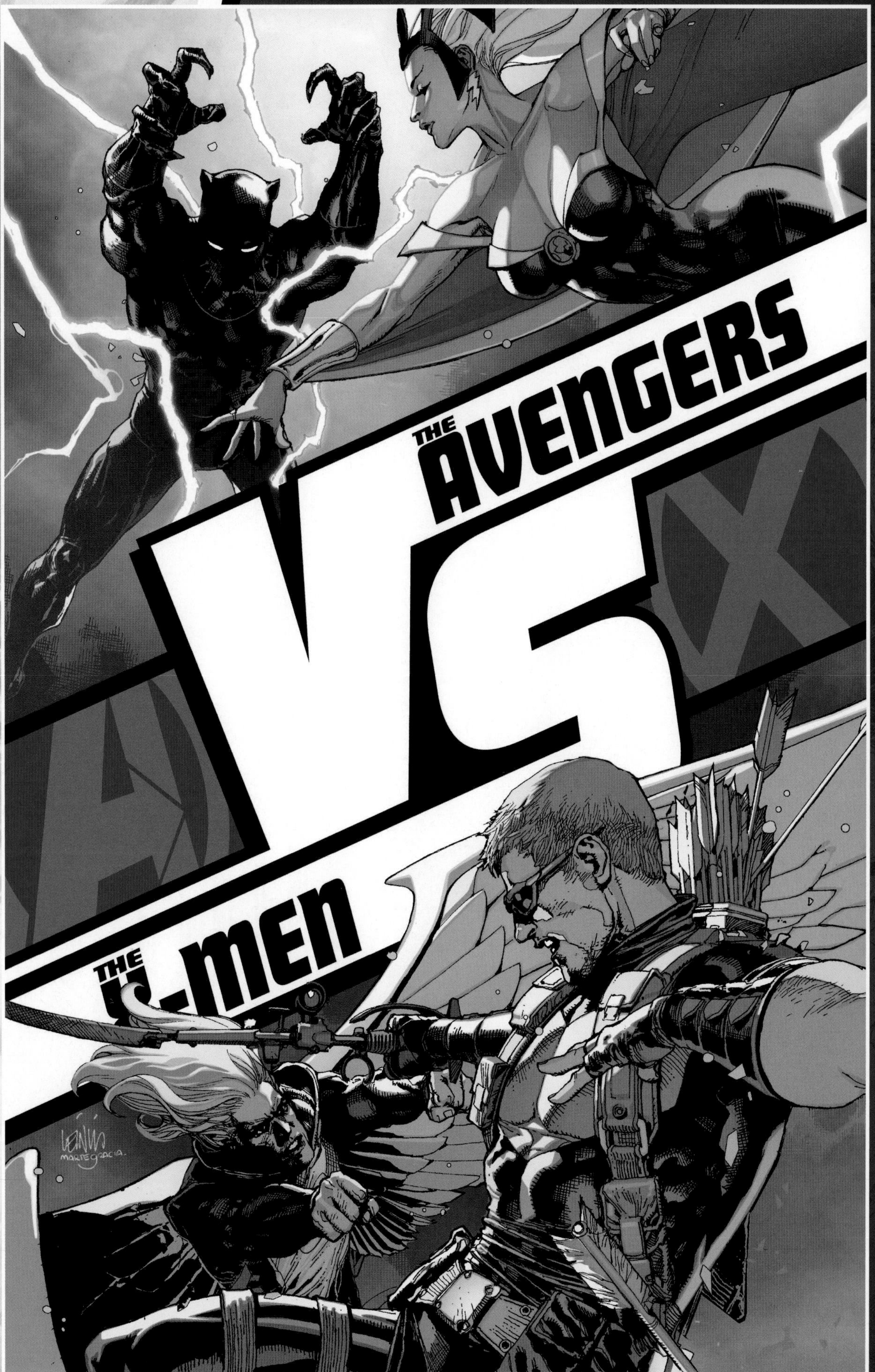
THE AVENGERS
VS
THE X-MEN

ISSUE #5

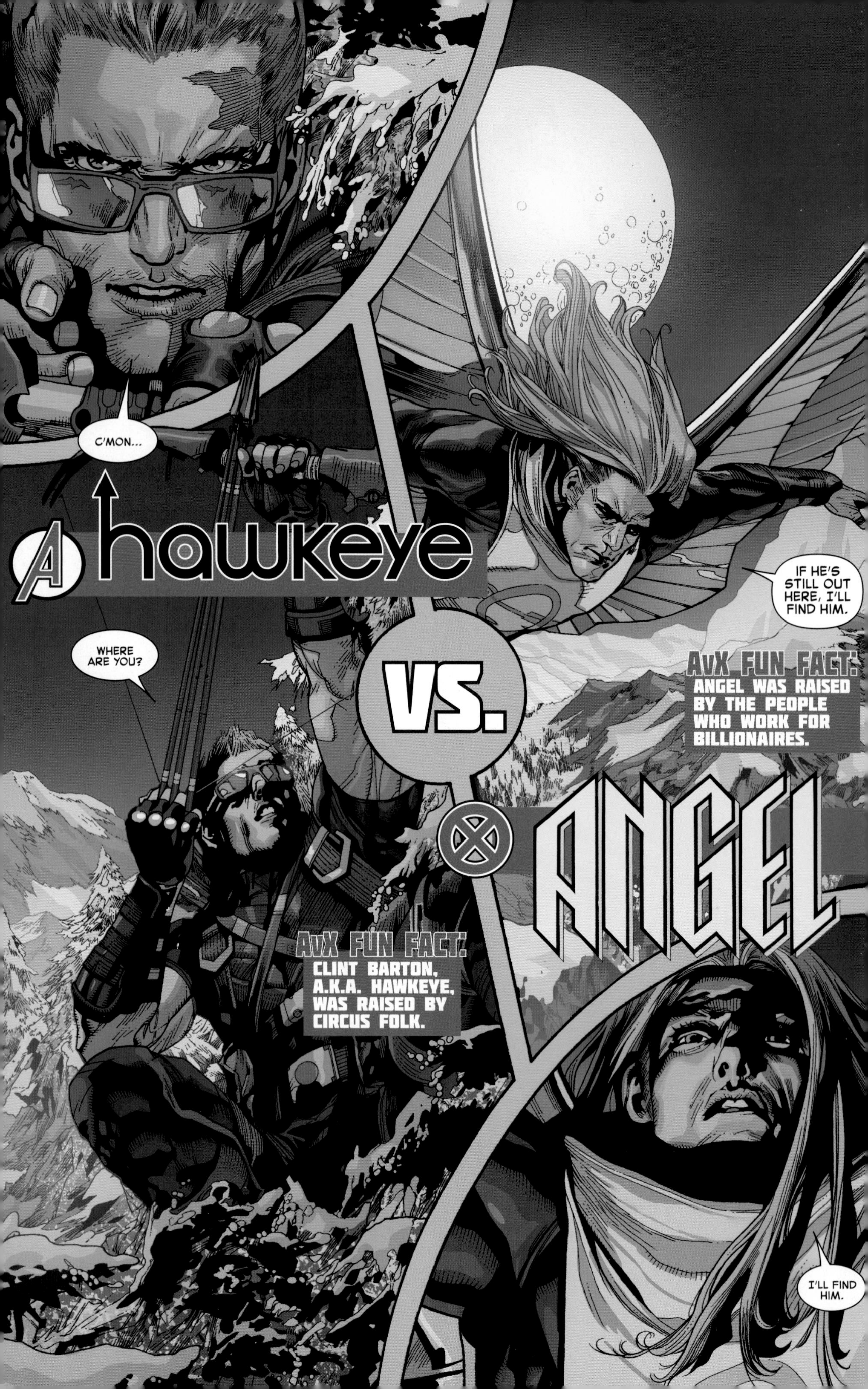
C'MON...
hawkeye
IF HE'S STILL OUT HERE, I'LL FIND HIM.
WHERE ARE YOU?
VS.
AvX FUN FACT:
ANGEL WAS RAISED BY THE PEOPLE WHO WORK FOR BILLIONAIRES.
ANGEL
AvX FUN FACT:
CLINT BARTON, A.K.A. HAWKEYE, WAS RAISED BY CIRCUS FOLK.
I'LL FIND HIM.

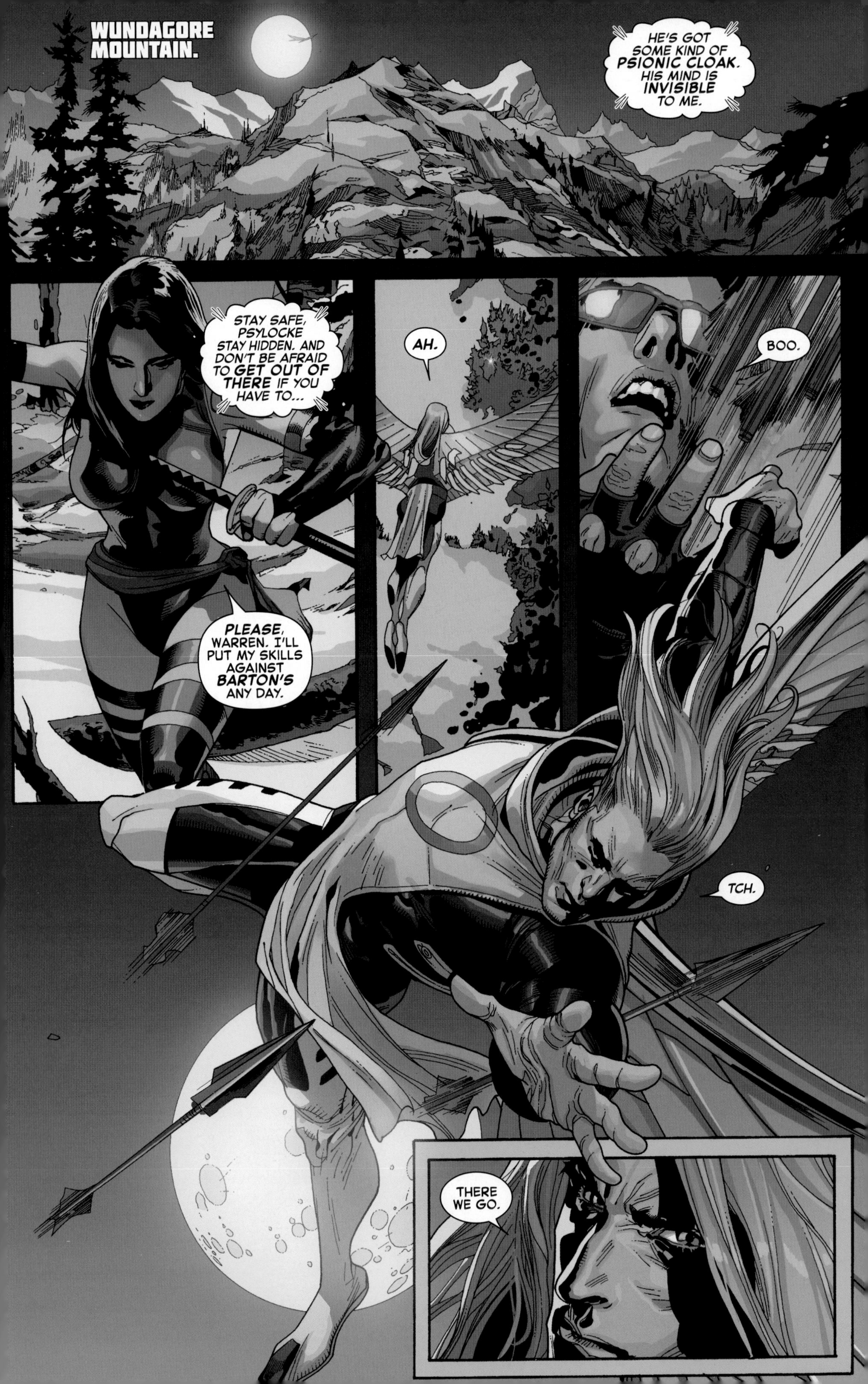
WUNDAGORE MOUNTAIN.
HE'S GOT SOME KIND OF PSIONIC CLOAK. HIS MIND IS INVISIBLE TO ME.
STAY SAFE, PSYLOCKE STAY HIDDEN. AND DON'T BE AFRAID TO GET OUT OF THERE IF YOU HAVE TO...
PLEASE, WARREN. I'LL PUT MY SKILLS AGAINST BARTON'S ANY DAY.
AH.
BOO.
TCH.
THERE WE GO.

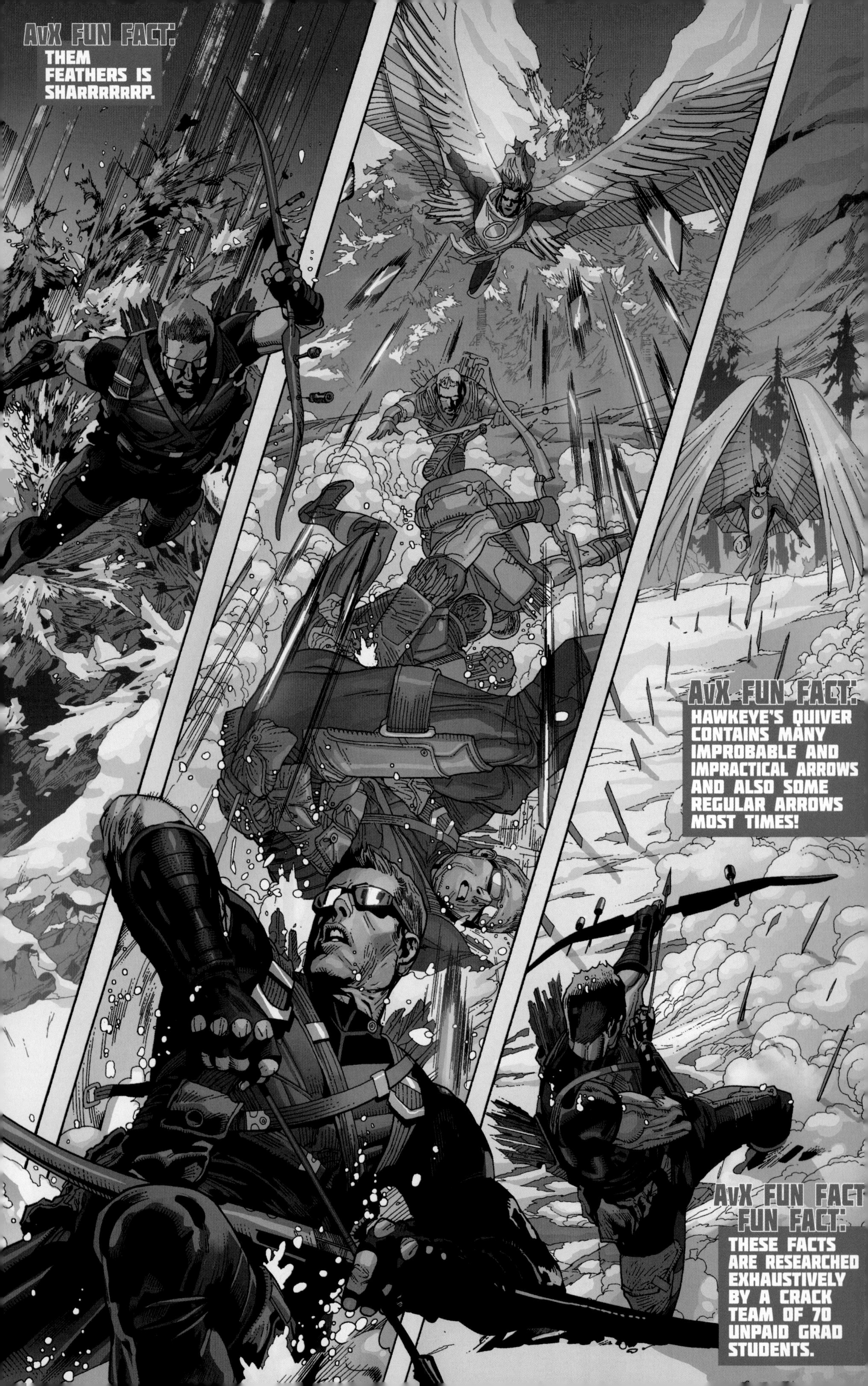
AvX FUN FACT:
THEM FEATHERS IS SHARRRRRRP.
AvX FUN FACT:
HAWKEYE'S QUIVER CONTAINS MANY IMPROBABLE AND IMPRACTICAL ARROWS AND ALSO SOME REGULAR ARROWS MOST TIMES!
AvX FUN FACT FUN FACT:
THESE FACTS ARE RESEARCHED EXHAUSTIVELY BY A CRACK TEAM OF 70 UNPAID GRAD STUDENTS.

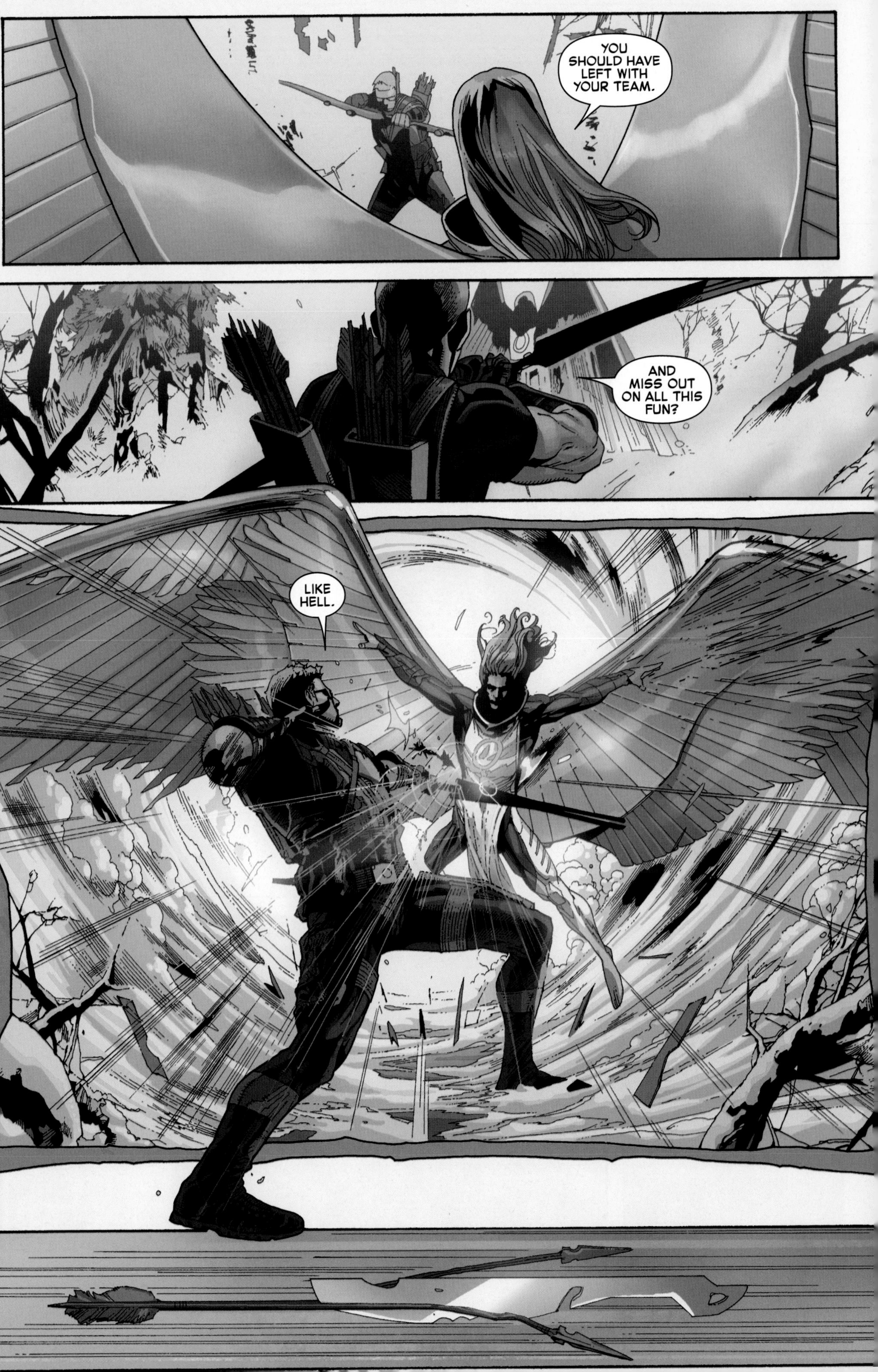
YOU SHOULD HAVE LEFT WITH YOUR TEAM.
AND MISS OUT ON ALL THIS FUN?
LIKE HELL.

UH-OH--

--AAAH!

HA!

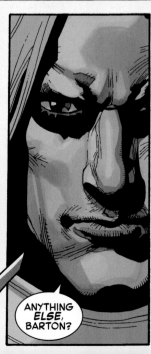

ANYTHING ELSE, BARTON?

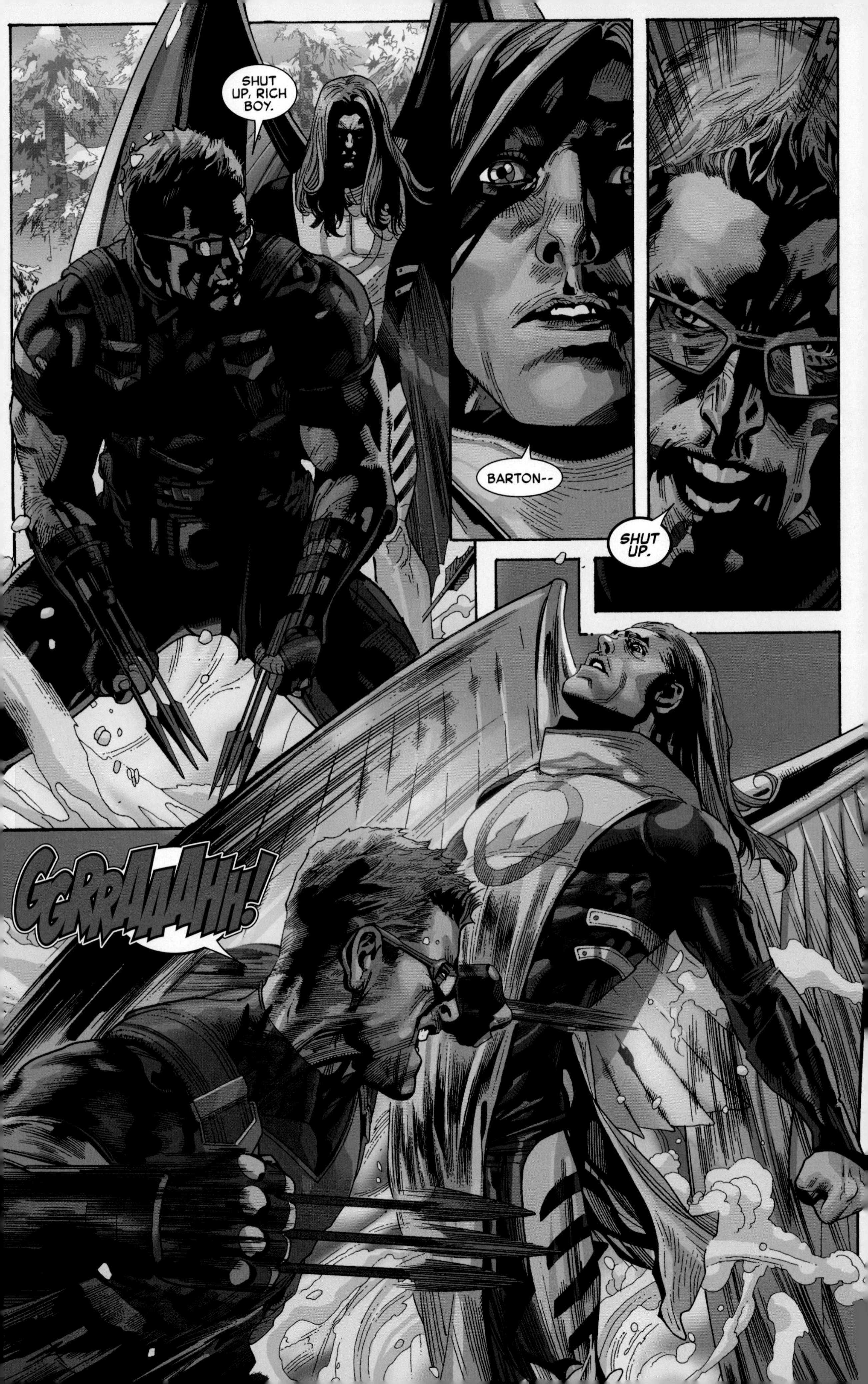
SHUT UP, RICH BOY.
BARTON--
SHUT UP.
GGRRAAAHH!

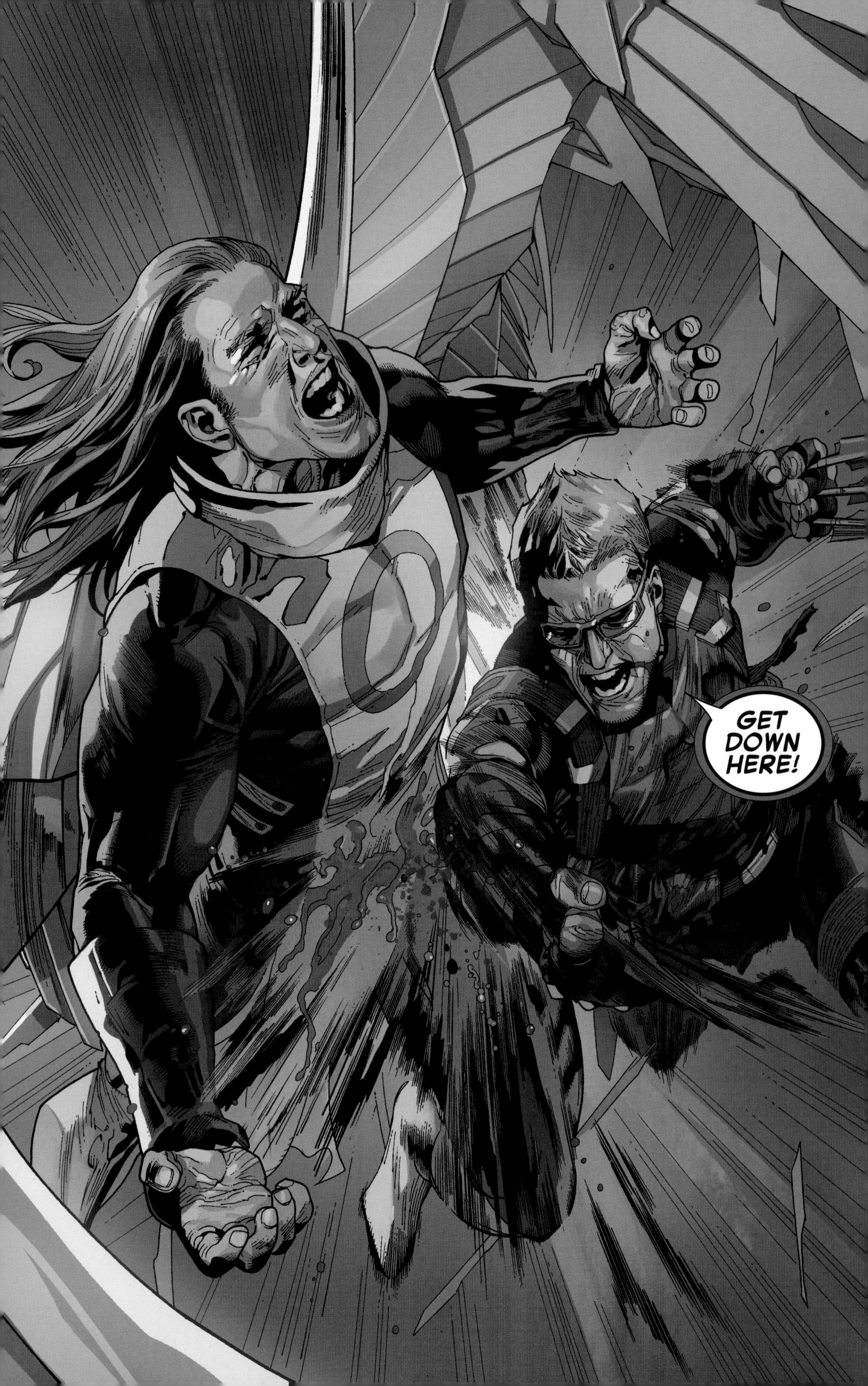
GET DOWN HERE!

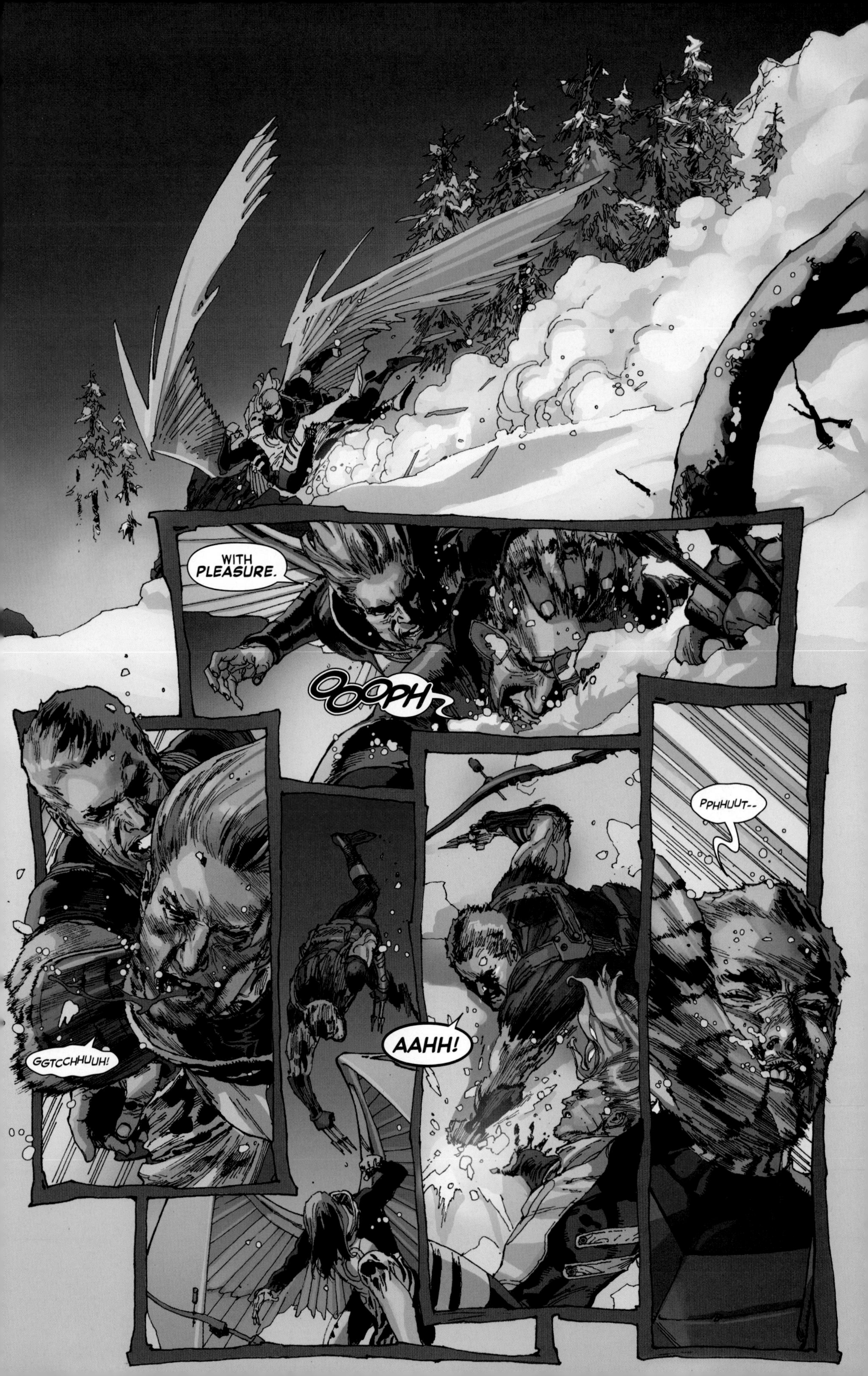
WITH PLEASURE.
OOOPH
GGTCCHHUUH!
AAHH!
PPHHUUT--

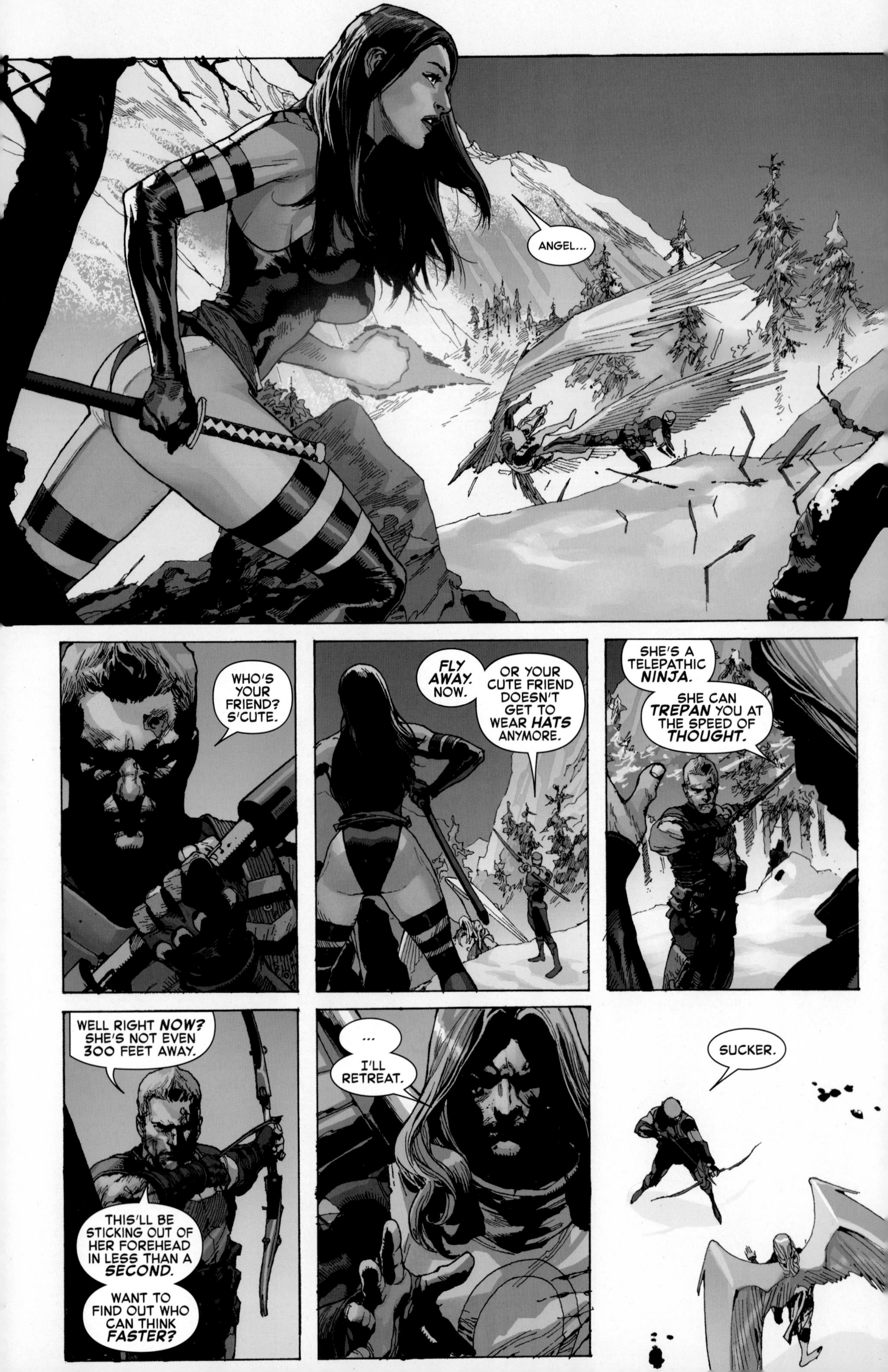
ANGEL...
WHO'S YOUR FRIEND? S'CUTE.
FLY AWAY. NOW.
OR YOUR CUTE FRIEND DOESN'T GET TO WEAR HATS ANYMORE.
SHE'S A TELEPATHIC NINJA.
SHE CAN TREPAN YOU AT THE SPEED OF THOUGHT.
WELL RIGHT NOW? SHE'S NOT EVEN 300 FEET AWAY.
THIS'LL BE STICKING OUT OF HER FOREHEAD IN LESS THAN A SECOND.
WANT TO FIND OUT WHO CAN THINK FASTER?
...
I'LL RETREAT.
SUCKER.

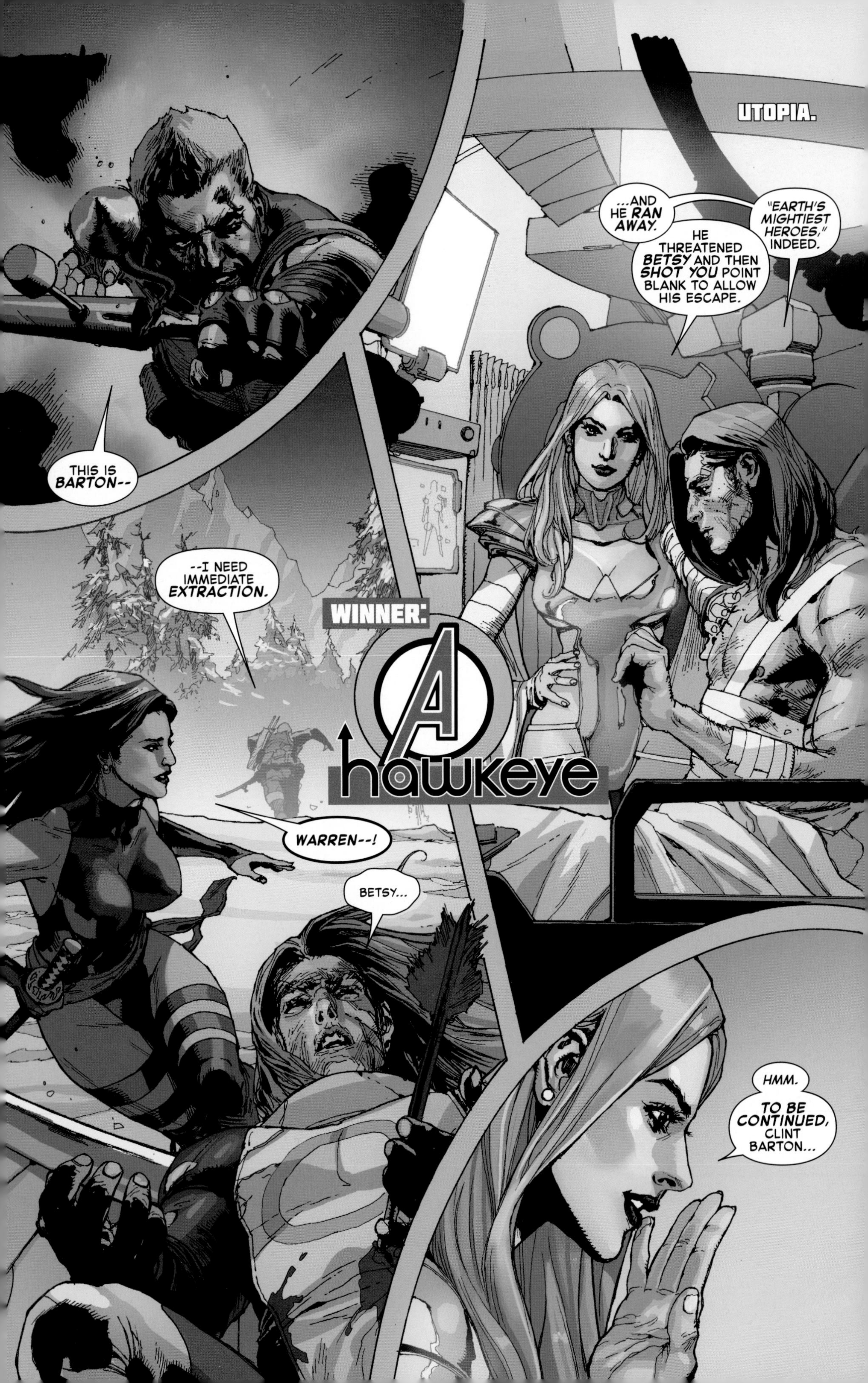
THIS IS BARTON--
--I NEED IMMEDIATE EXTRACTION.
WARREN--!
BETSY...
UTOPIA.
...AND HE RAN AWAY.
HE THREATENED BETSY AND THEN SHOT YOU POINT BLANK TO ALLOW HIS ESCAPE.
"EARTH'S MIGHTIEST HEROES," INDEED.
WINNER:
hawkeye
HMM.
TO BE CONTINUED, CLINT BARTON...

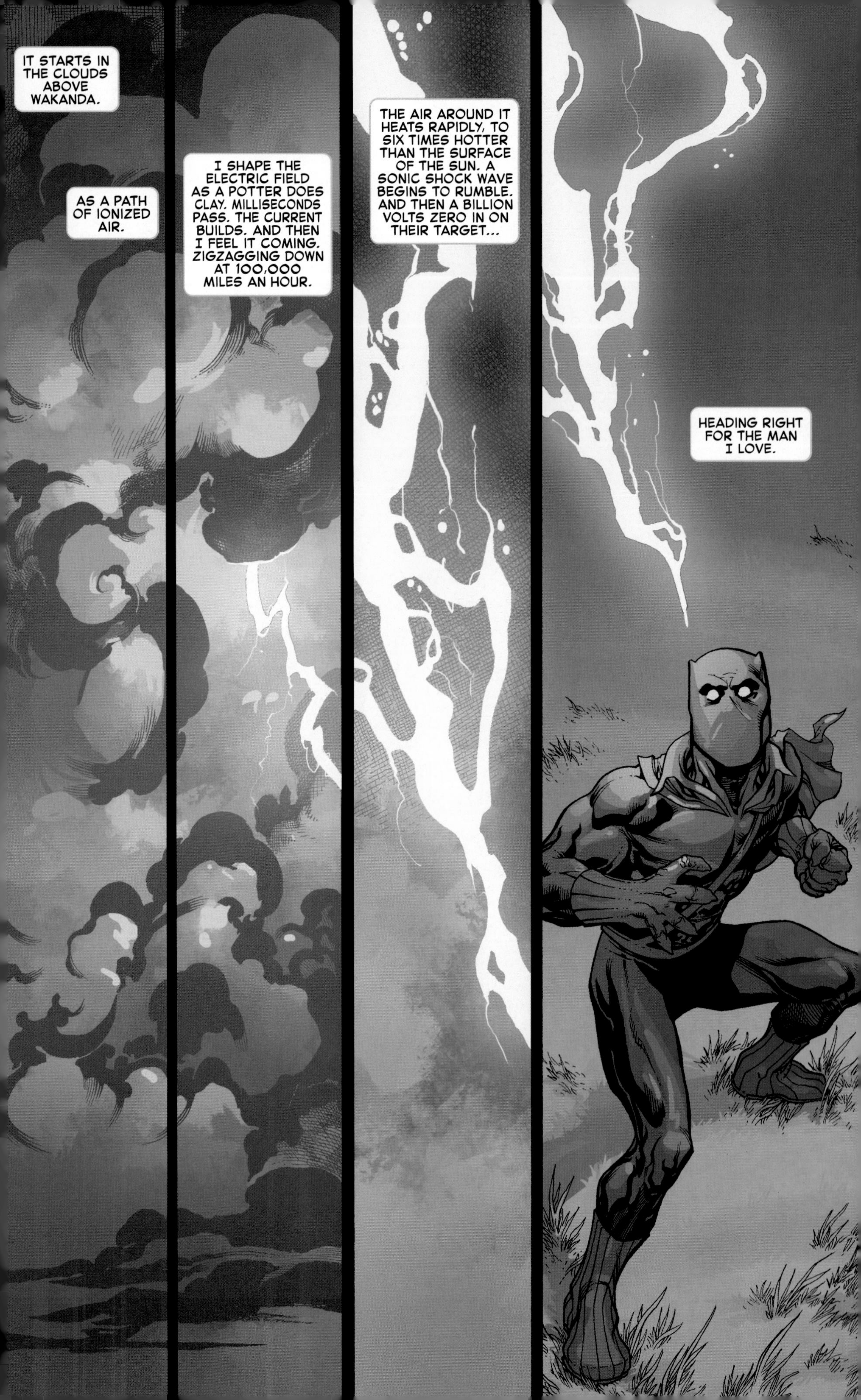
IT STARTS IN THE CLOUDS ABOVE WAKANDA.
AS A PATH OF IONIZED AIR.
I SHAPE THE ELECTRIC FIELD AS A POTTER DOES CLAY. MILLISECONDS PASS. THE CURRENT BUILDS. AND THEN I FEEL IT COMING. ZIGZAGGING DOWN AT 100,000 MILES AN HOUR.
THE AIR AROUND IT HEATS RAPIDLY, TO SIX TIMES HOTTER THAN THE SURFACE OF THE SUN. A SONIC SHOCK WAVE BEGINS TO RUMBLE. AND THEN A BILLION VOLTS ZERO IN ON THEIR TARGET...
HEADING RIGHT FOR THE MAN I LOVE.

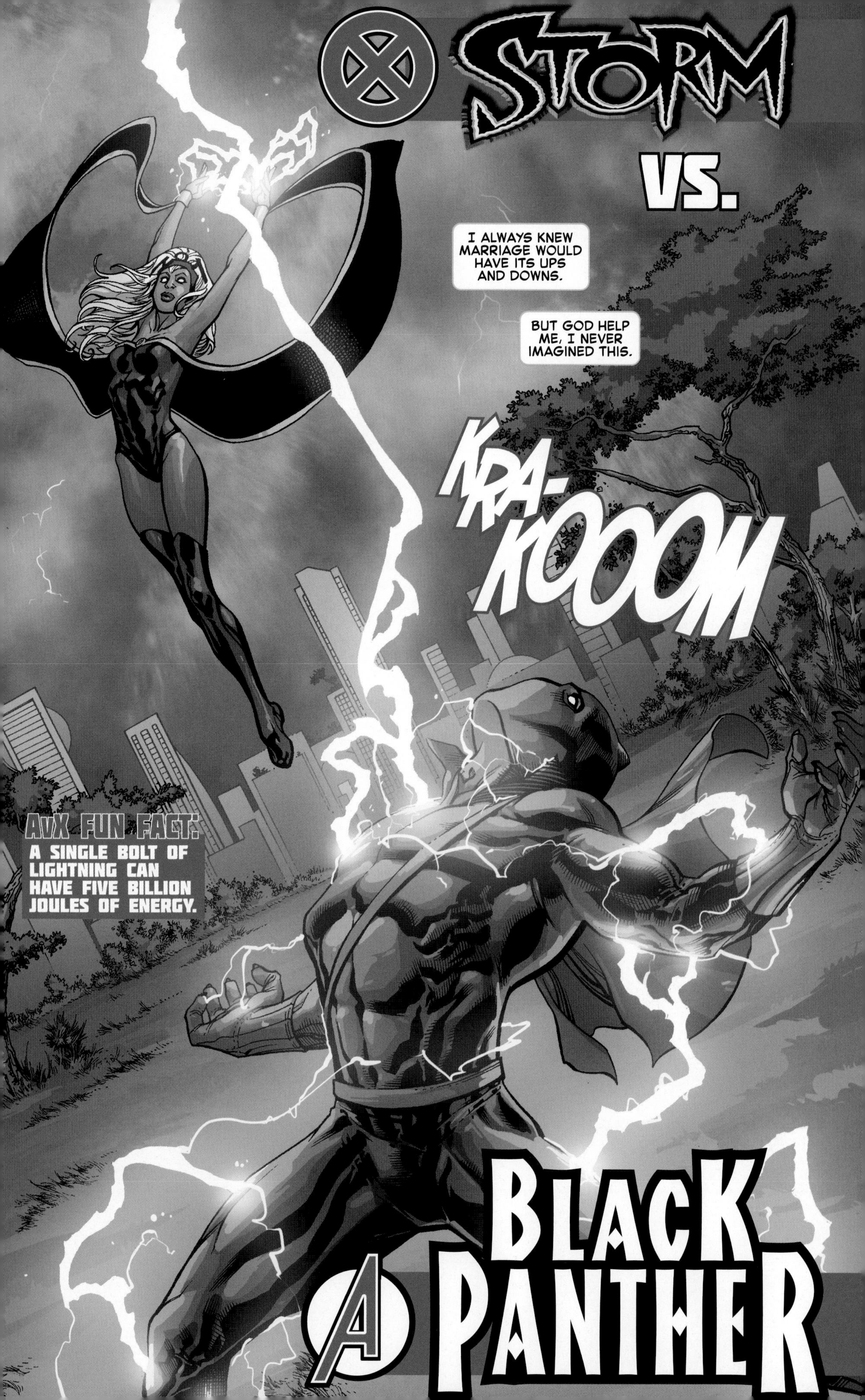
STORM
VS.
I ALWAYS KNEW MARRIAGE WOULD HAVE ITS UPS AND DOWNS.
BUT GOD HELP ME, I NEVER IMAGINED THIS.
KRA-KOOOM
AVX FUN FACT:
A SINGLE BOLT OF LIGHTNING CAN HAVE FIVE BILLION JOULES OF ENERGY.
BLACK PANTHER

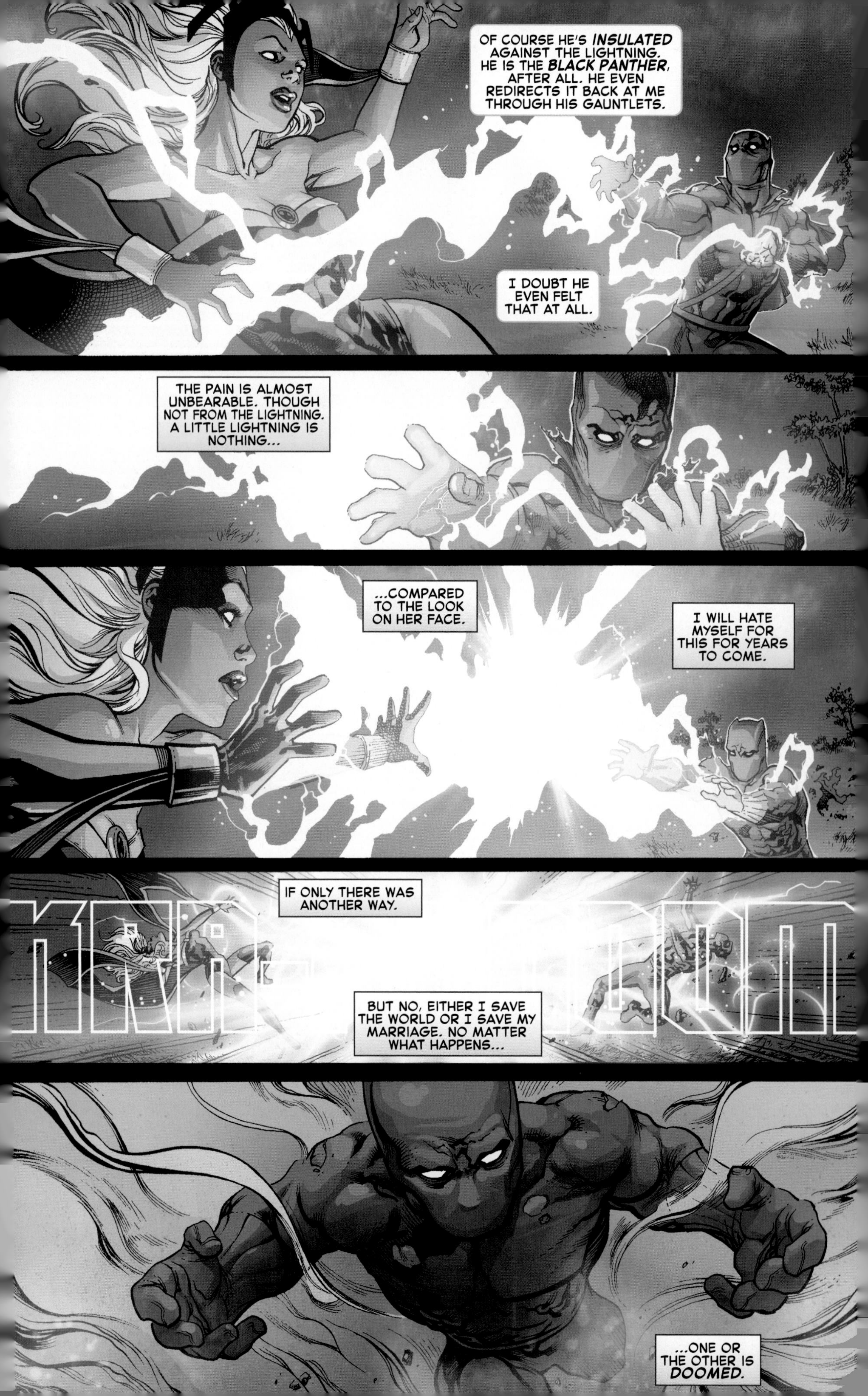
OF COURSE HE'S *INSULATED* AGAINST THE LIGHTNING. HE IS THE *BLACK PANTHER*, AFTER ALL. HE EVEN REDIRECTS IT BACK AT ME THROUGH HIS GAUNTLETS.
I DOUBT HE EVEN FELT THAT AT ALL.
THE PAIN IS ALMOST UNBEARABLE. THOUGH NOT FROM THE LIGHTNING. A LITTLE LIGHTNING IS NOTHING...
...COMPARED TO THE LOOK ON HER FACE.
I WILL HATE MYSELF FOR THIS FOR YEARS TO COME.
IF ONLY THERE WAS ANOTHER WAY.
BUT NO, EITHER I SAVE THE WORLD OR I SAVE MY MARRIAGE. NO MATTER WHAT HAPPENS...
...ONE OR THE OTHER IS *DOOMED*.

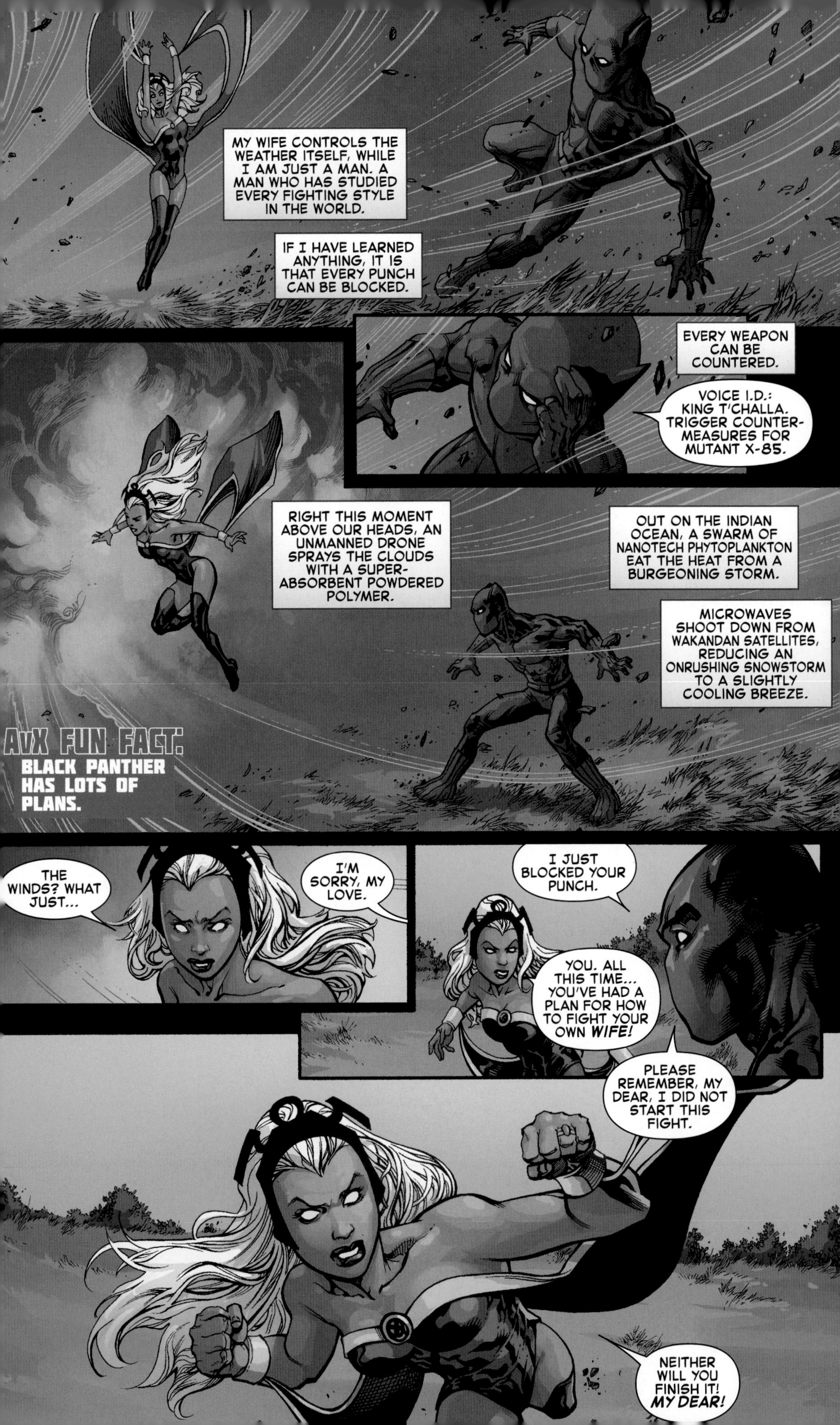

MY WIFE CONTROLS THE WEATHER ITSELF, WHILE I AM JUST A MAN. A MAN WHO HAS STUDIED EVERY FIGHTING STYLE IN THE WORLD.
IF I HAVE LEARNED ANYTHING, IT IS THAT EVERY PUNCH CAN BE BLOCKED.
EVERY WEAPON CAN BE COUNTERED.
VOICE I.D.: KING T'CHALLA. TRIGGER COUNTER-MEASURES FOR MUTANT X-85.
RIGHT THIS MOMENT ABOVE OUR HEADS, AN UNMANNED DRONE SPRAYS THE CLOUDS WITH A SUPER-ABSORBENT POWDERED POLYMER.
OUT ON THE INDIAN OCEAN, A SWARM OF NANOTECH PHYTOPLANKTON EAT THE HEAT FROM A BURGEONING STORM.
MICROWAVES SHOOT DOWN FROM WAKANDAN SATELLITES, REDUCING AN ONRUSHING SNOWSTORM TO A SLIGHTLY COOLING BREEZE.
AvX FUN FACT:
BLACK PANTHER HAS LOTS OF PLANS.
THE WINDS? WHAT JUST...
I'M SORRY, MY LOVE.
I JUST BLOCKED YOUR PUNCH.
YOU. ALL THIS TIME... YOU'VE HAD A PLAN FOR HOW TO FIGHT YOUR OWN *WIFE!*
PLEASE REMEMBER, MY DEAR, I DID NOT START THIS FIGHT.
NEITHER WILL YOU FINISH IT! *MY DEAR!*

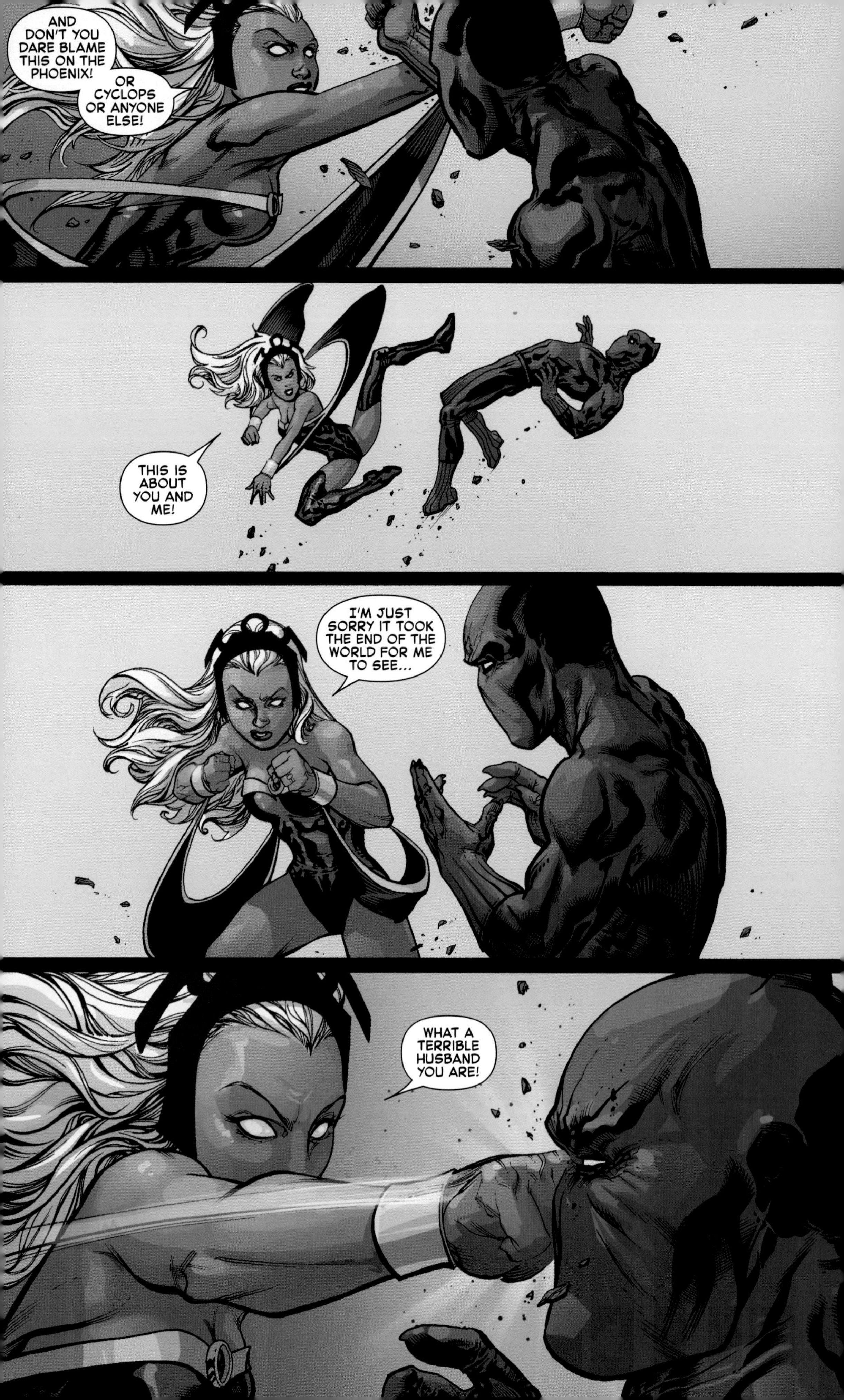
AND DON'T YOU DARE BLAME THIS ON THE PHOENIX!
OR CYCLOPS OR ANYONE ELSE!
THIS IS ABOUT YOU AND ME!
I'M JUST SORRY IT TOOK THE END OF THE WORLD FOR ME TO SEE...
WHAT A TERRIBLE HUSBAND YOU ARE!

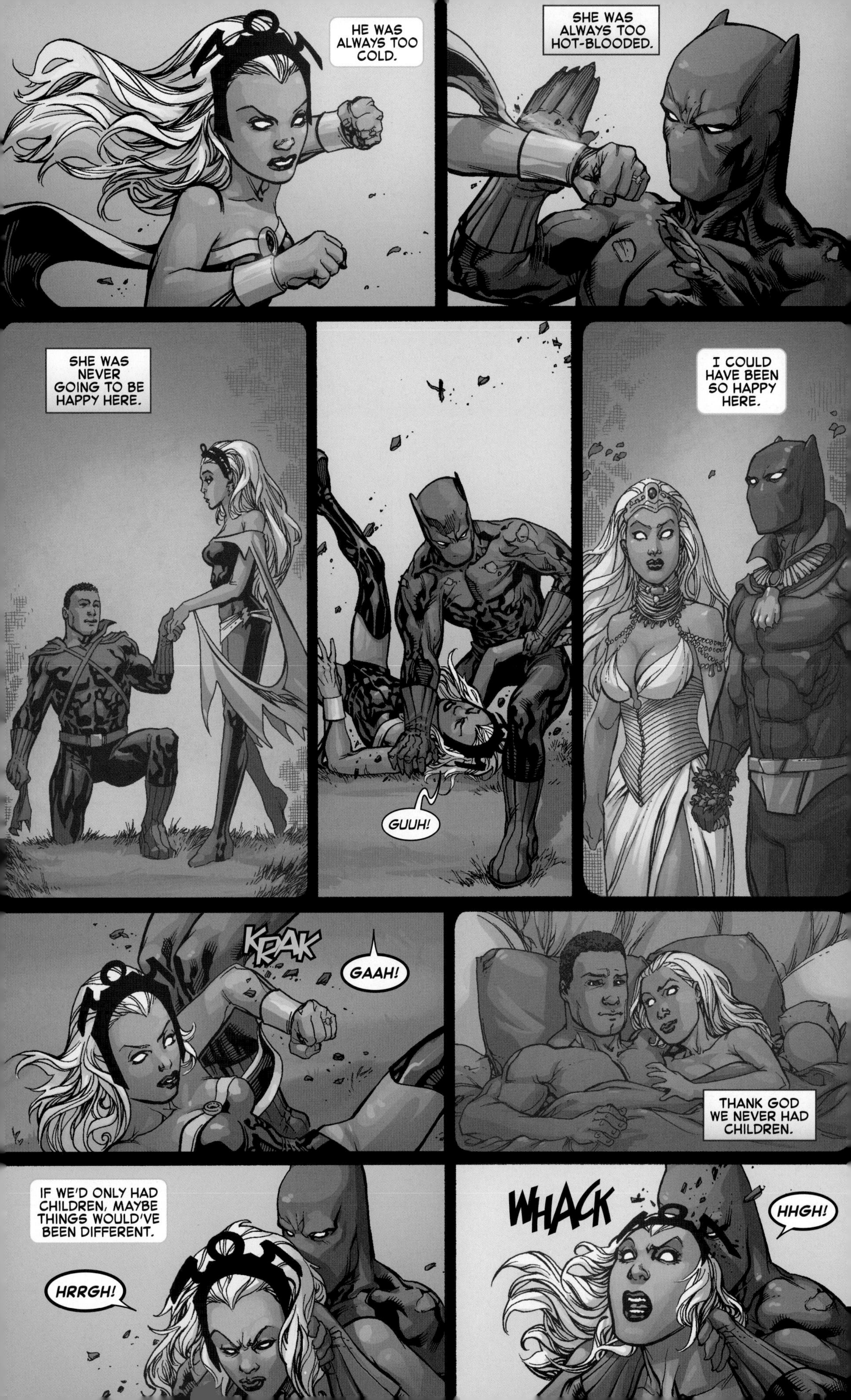
HE WAS ALWAYS TOO COLD.
SHE WAS ALWAYS TOO HOT-BLOODED.
SHE WAS NEVER GOING TO BE HAPPY HERE.
GUUH!
I COULD HAVE BEEN SO HAPPY HERE.
KRAK
GAAH!
THANK GOD WE NEVER HAD CHILDREN.
IF WE'D ONLY HAD CHILDREN, MAYBE THINGS WOULD'VE BEEN DIFFERENT.
HRRGH!
WHACK
HHGH!

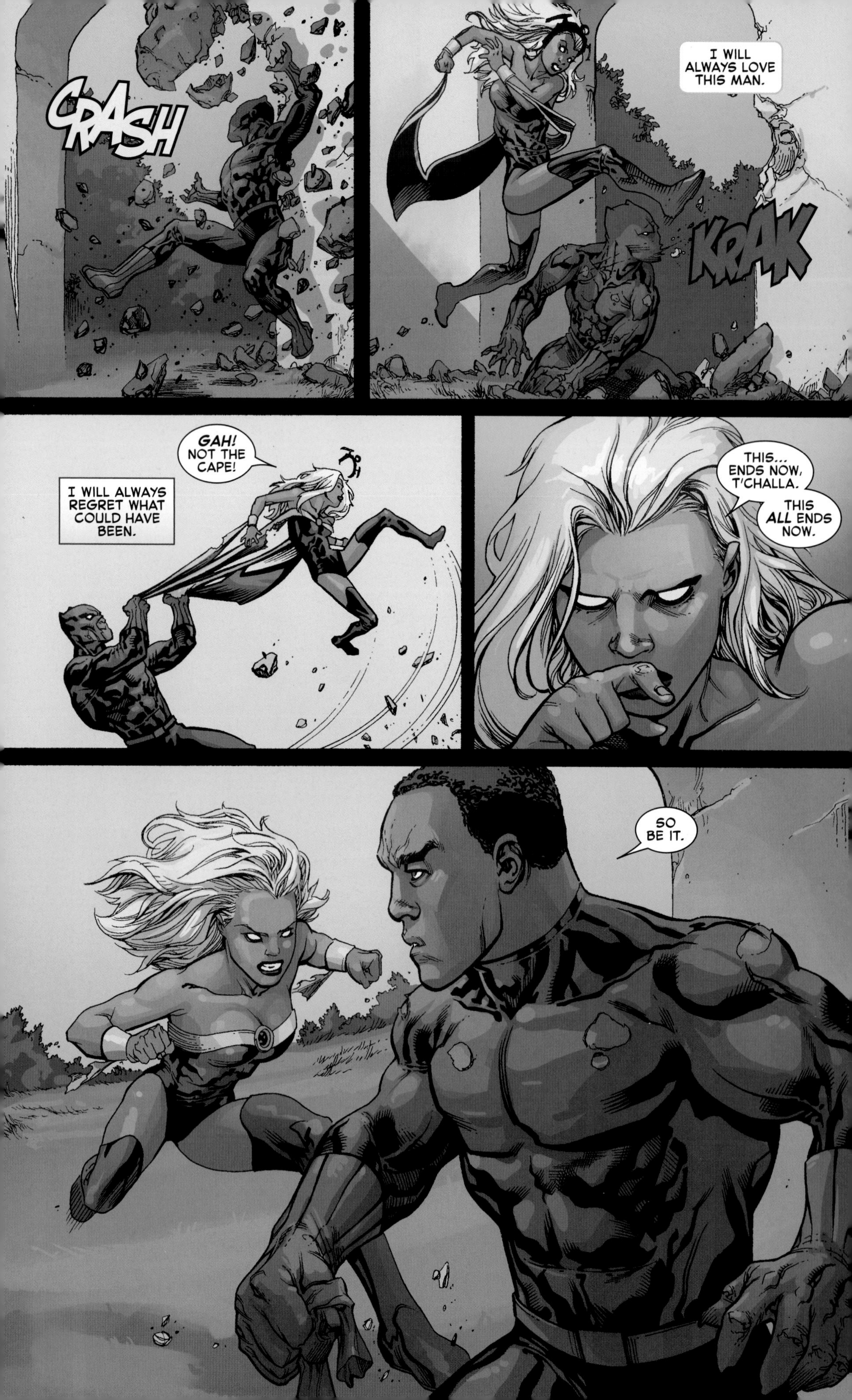
CRASH
I WILL ALWAYS LOVE THIS MAN.
KRAK
GAH! NOT THE CAPE!
I WILL ALWAYS REGRET WHAT COULD HAVE BEEN.
THIS... ENDS NOW, T'CHALLA.
THIS ALL ENDS NOW.
SO BE IT.

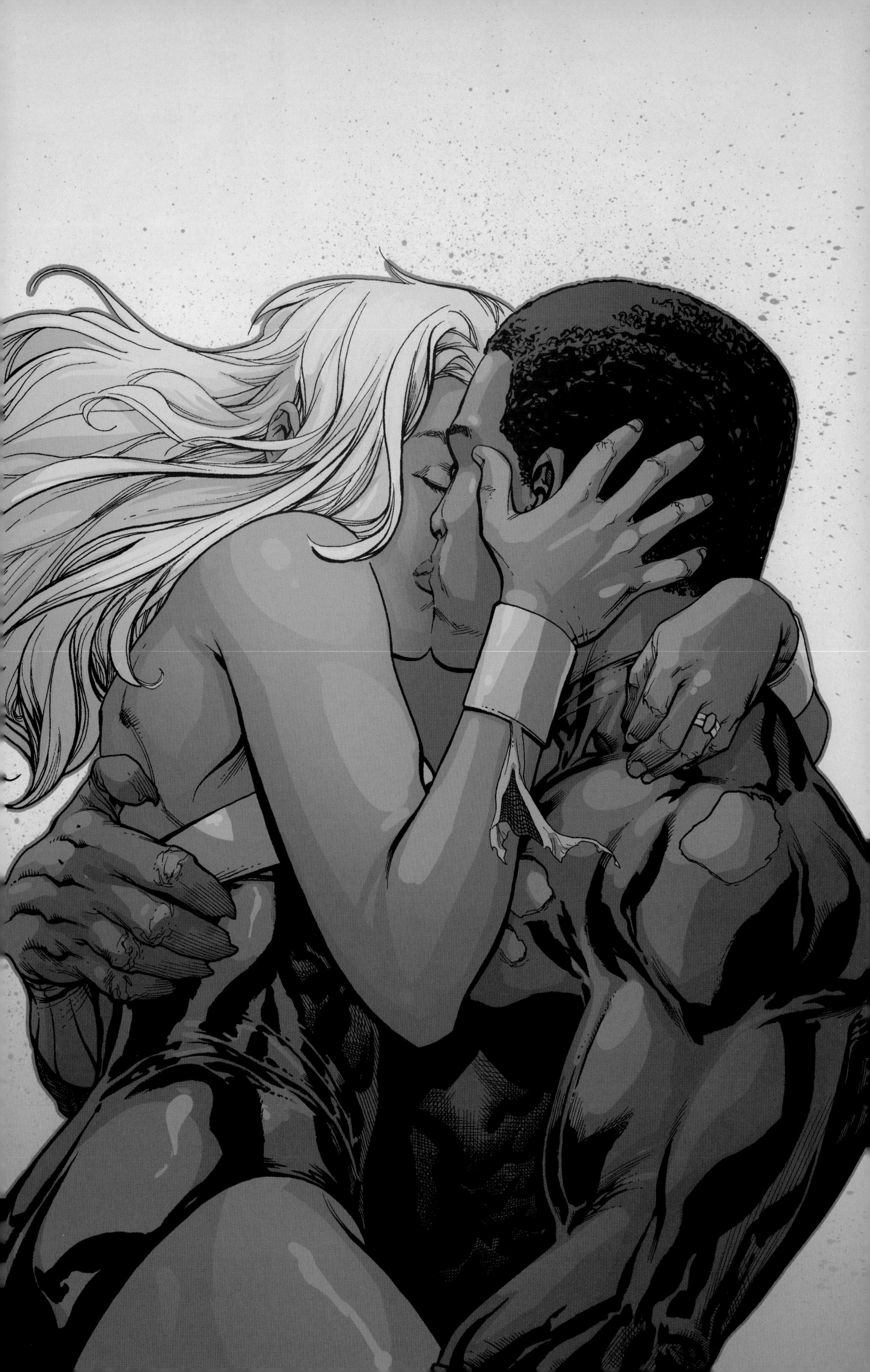

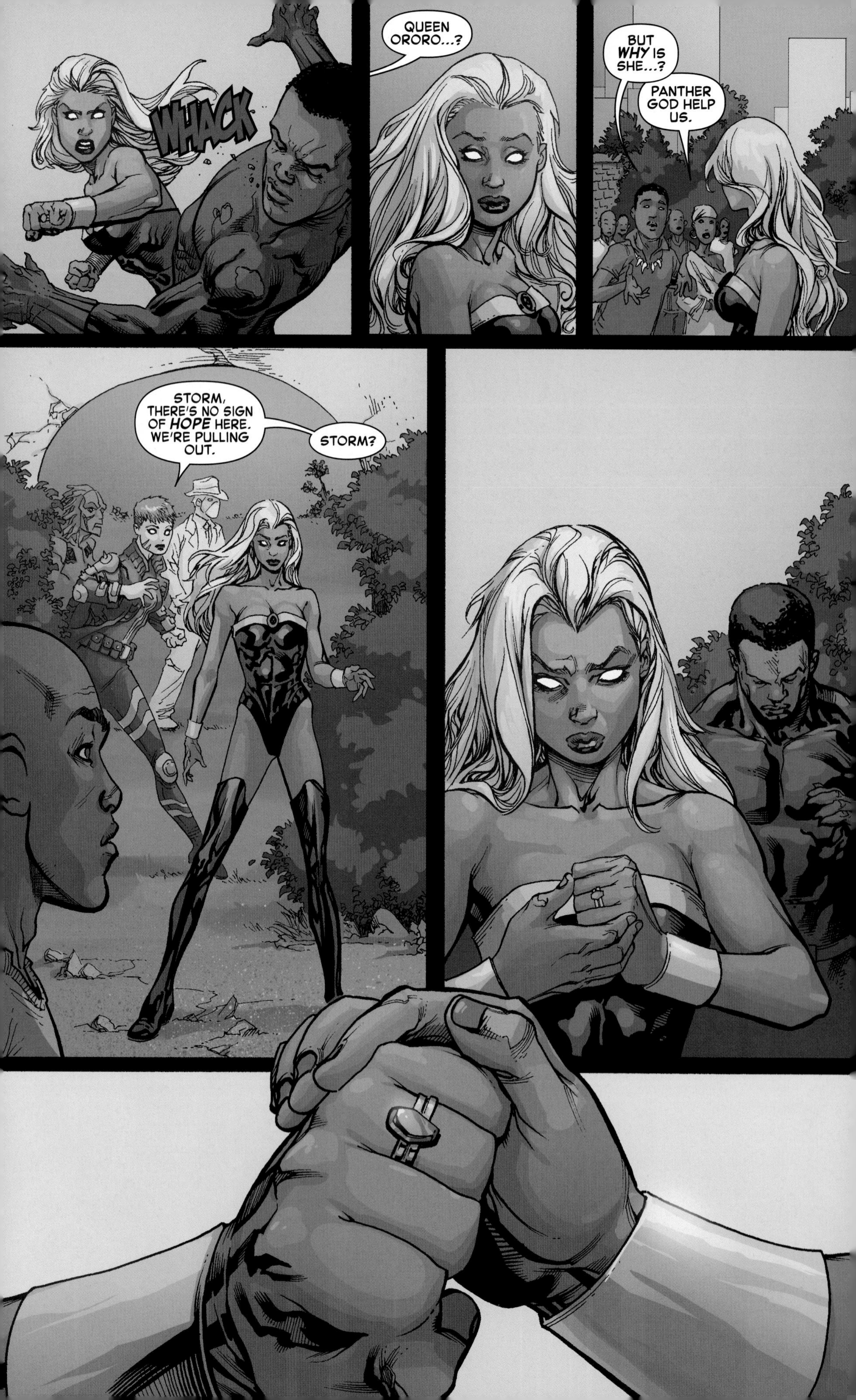
WHACK
QUEEN ORORO...?
BUT WHY IS SHE...?
PANTHER GOD HELP US.
STORM, THERE'S NO SIGN OF HOPE HERE. WE'RE PULLING OUT.
STORM?

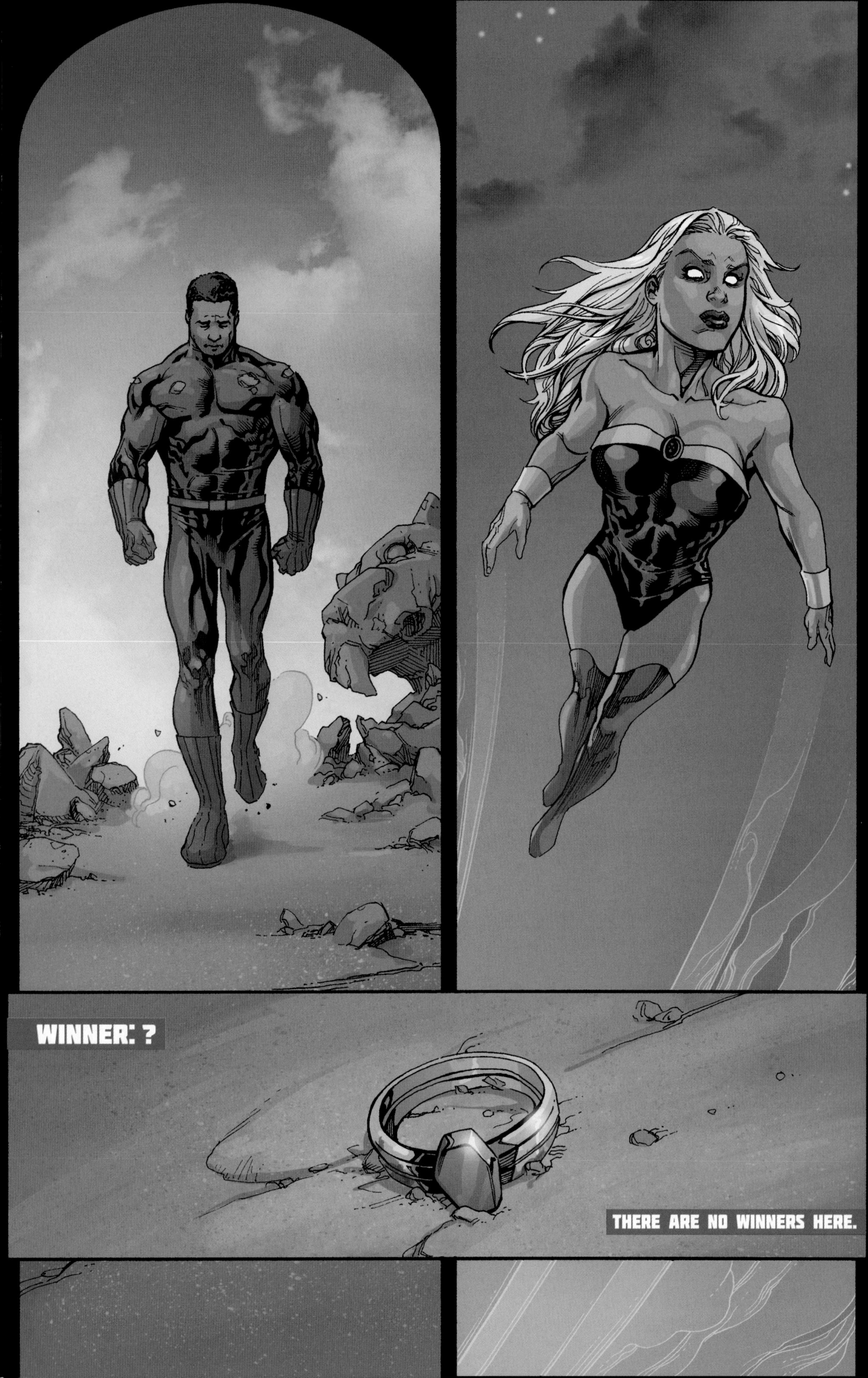
WINNER: ?
THERE ARE NO WINNERS HERE.

THE AVENGERS

VS

THE X-MEN

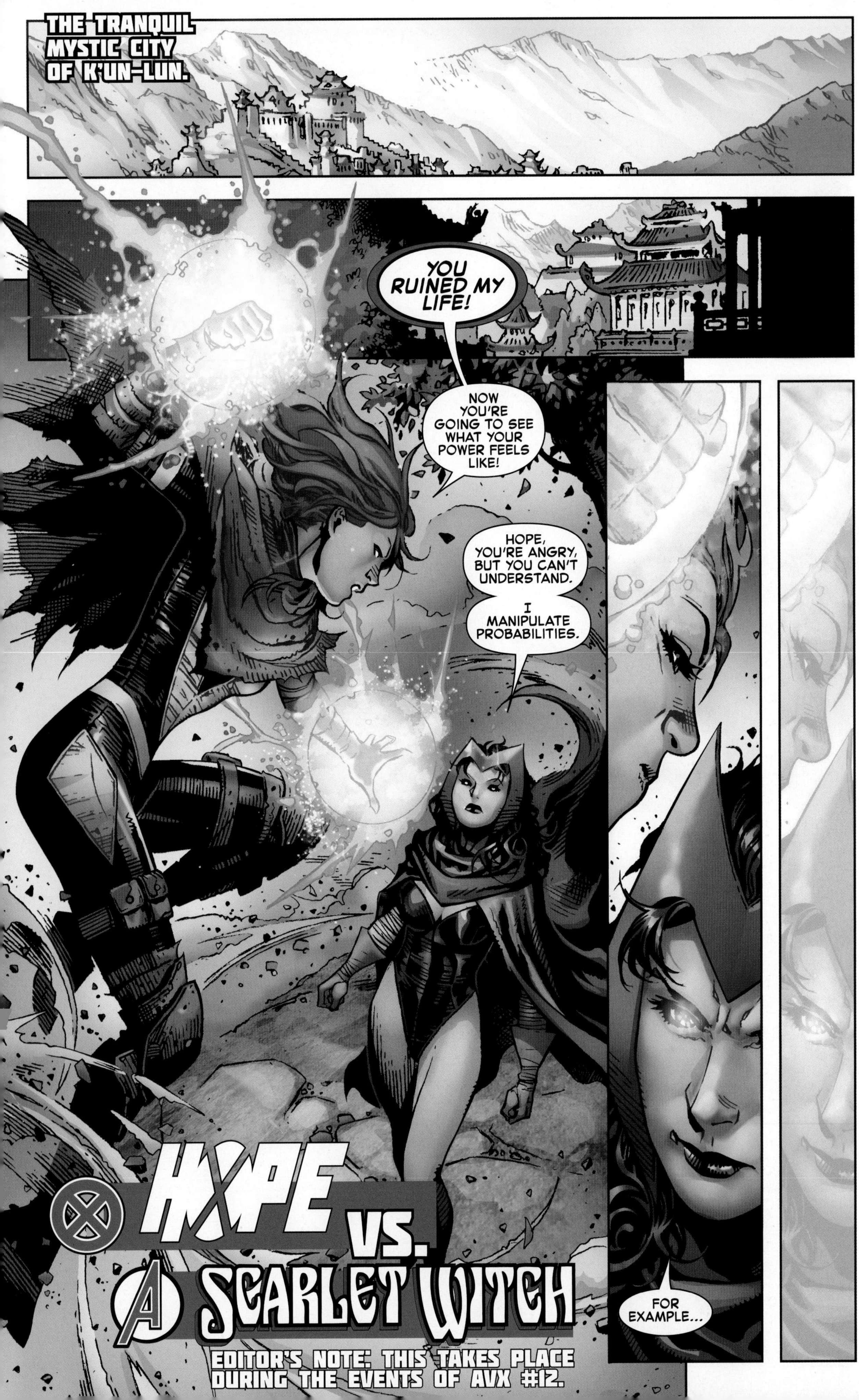
THE TRANQUIL MYSTIC CITY OF K'UN-LUN.
YOU RUINED MY LIFE!
NOW YOU'RE GOING TO SEE WHAT YOUR POWER FEELS LIKE!
HOPE, YOU'RE ANGRY, BUT YOU CAN'T UNDERSTAND.
I MANIPULATE PROBABILITIES.
FOR EXAMPLE...
HOPE VS. SCARLET WITCH
EDITOR'S NOTE: THIS TAKES PLACE DURING THE EVENTS OF AVX #12.

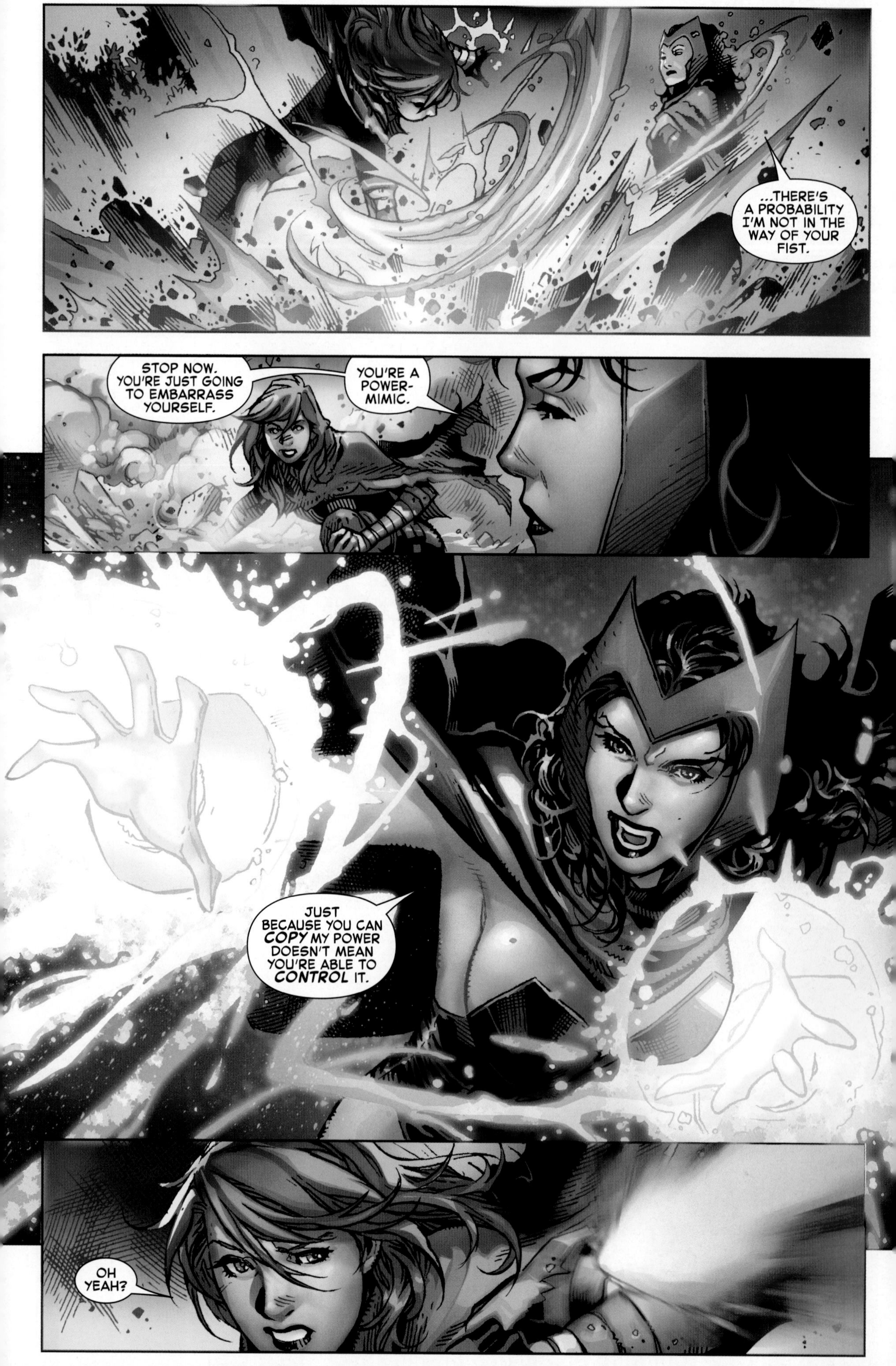
...THERE'S A PROBABILITY I'M NOT IN THE WAY OF YOUR FIST.
STOP NOW. YOU'RE JUST GOING TO EMBARRASS YOURSELF.
YOU'RE A POWER-MIMIC.
JUST BECAUSE YOU CAN COPY MY POWER DOESN'T MEAN YOU'RE ABLE TO CONTROL IT.
OH YEAH?

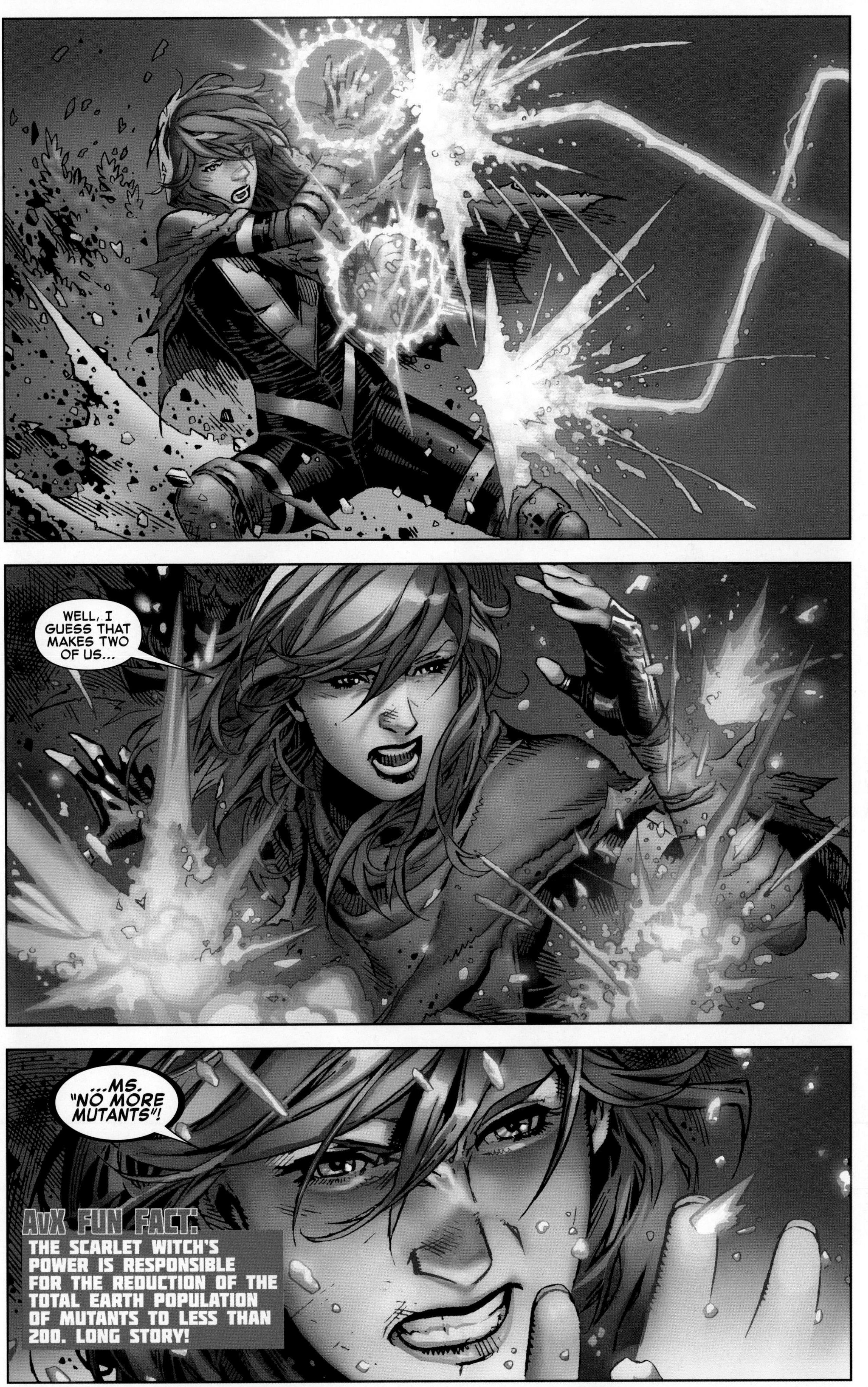
WELL, I GUESS THAT MAKES TWO OF US...
...MS. "NO MORE MUTANTS"!
AvX FUN FACT:
THE SCARLET WITCH'S POWER IS RESPONSIBLE FOR THE REDUCTION OF THE TOTAL EARTH POPULATION OF MUTANTS TO LESS THAN 200. LONG STORY!

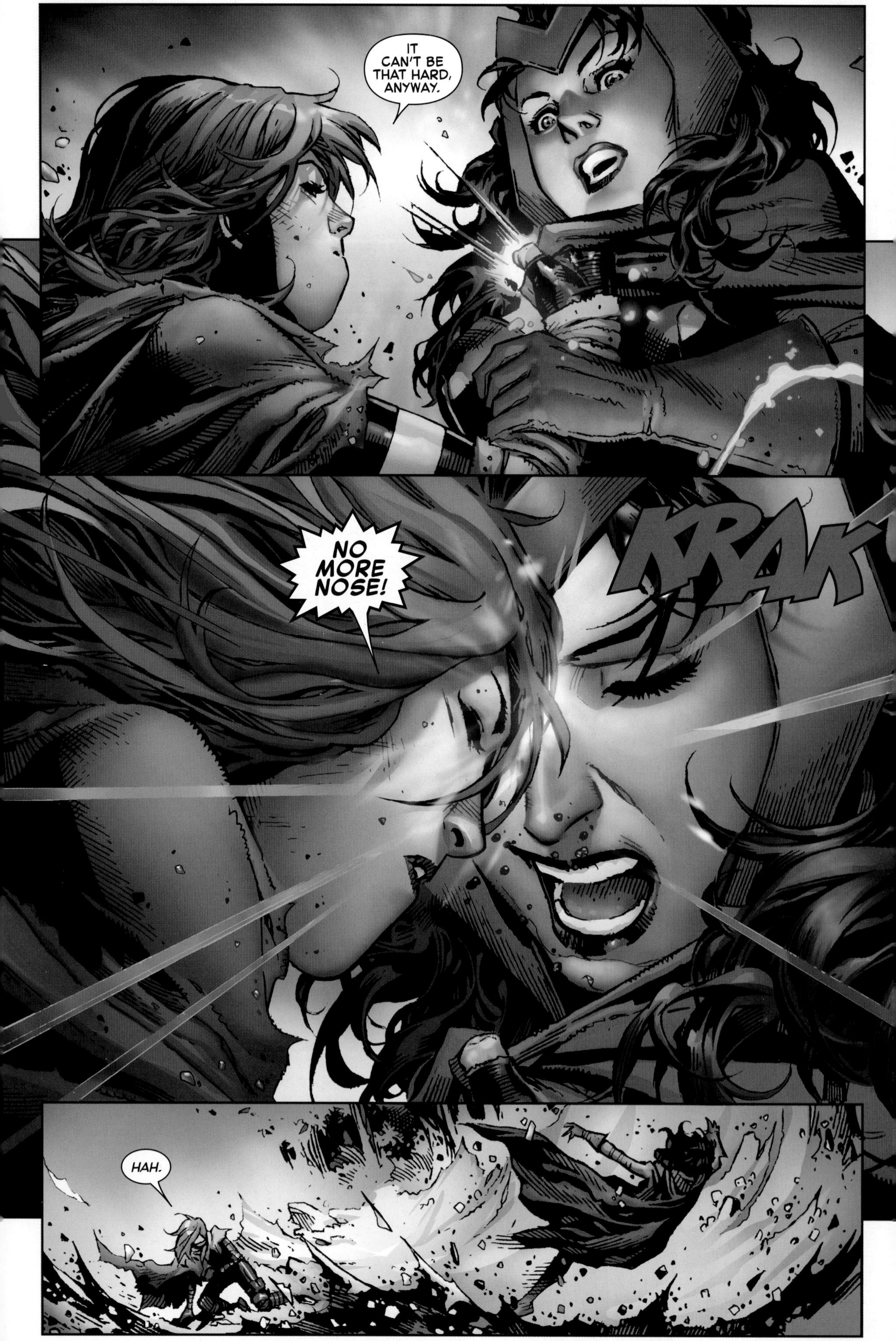
IT CAN'T BE THAT HARD, ANYWAY.
NO MORE NOSE!
KRAK
HAH.

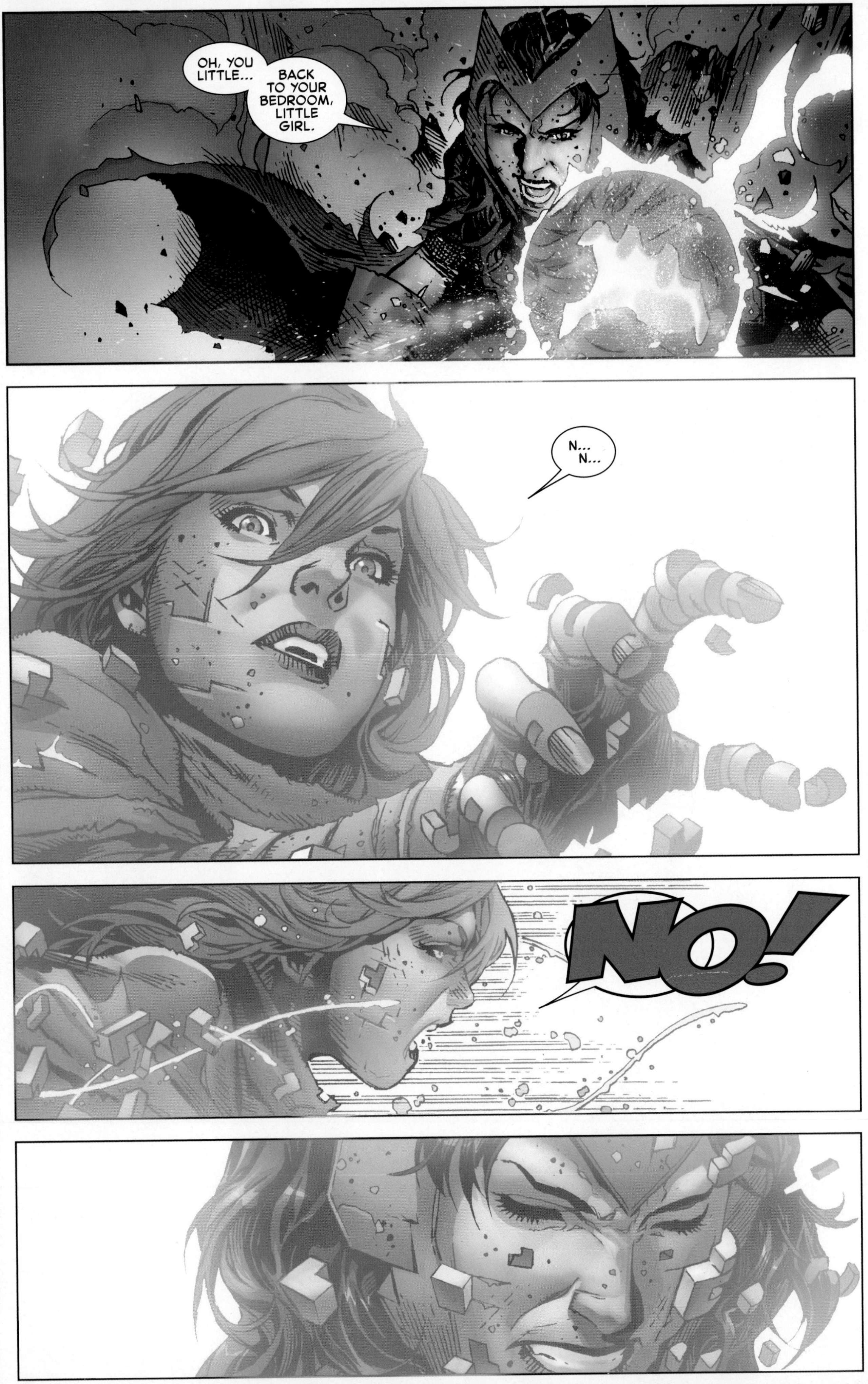
OH, YOU LITTLE...
BACK TO YOUR BEDROOM, LITTLE GIRL.
N... N...
NO!

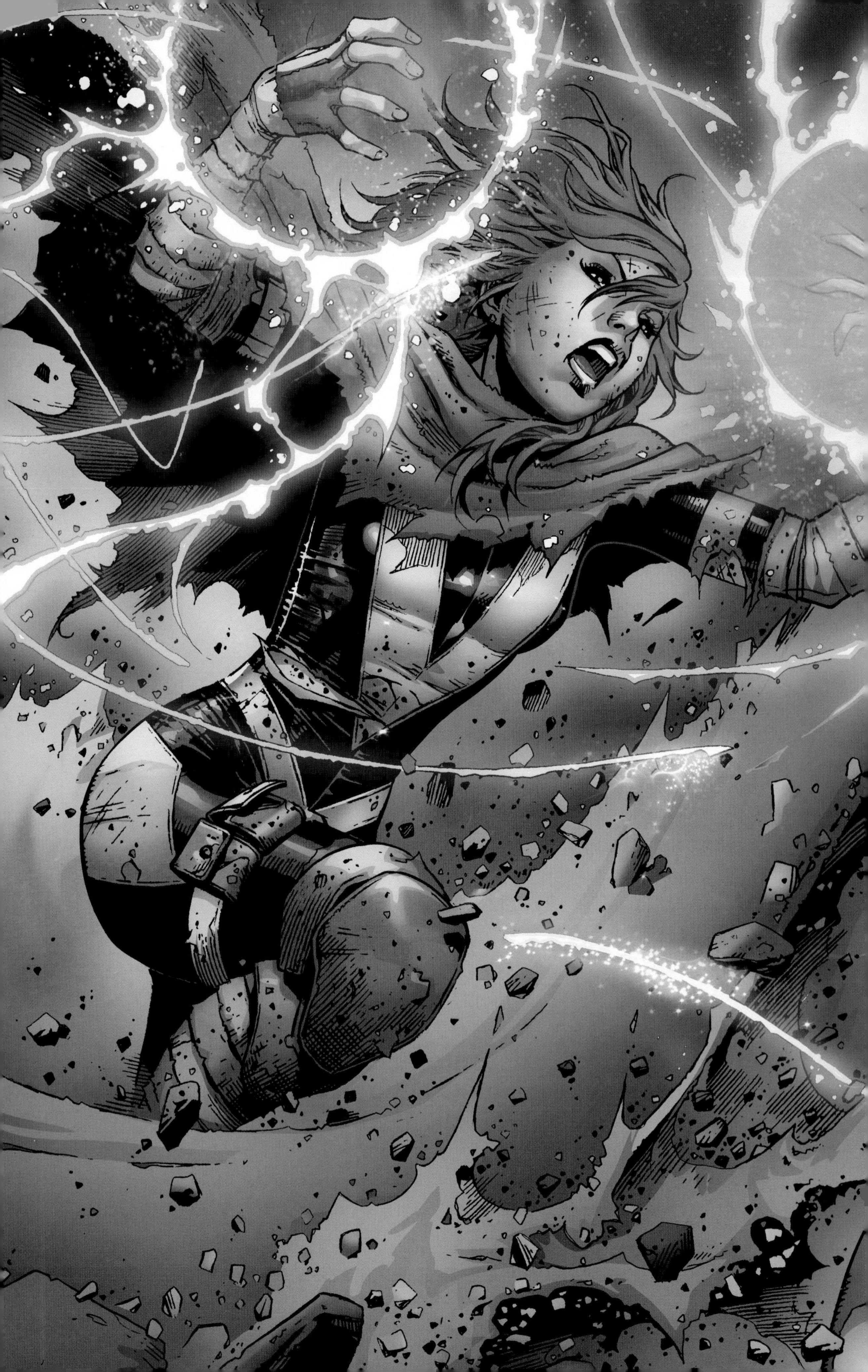

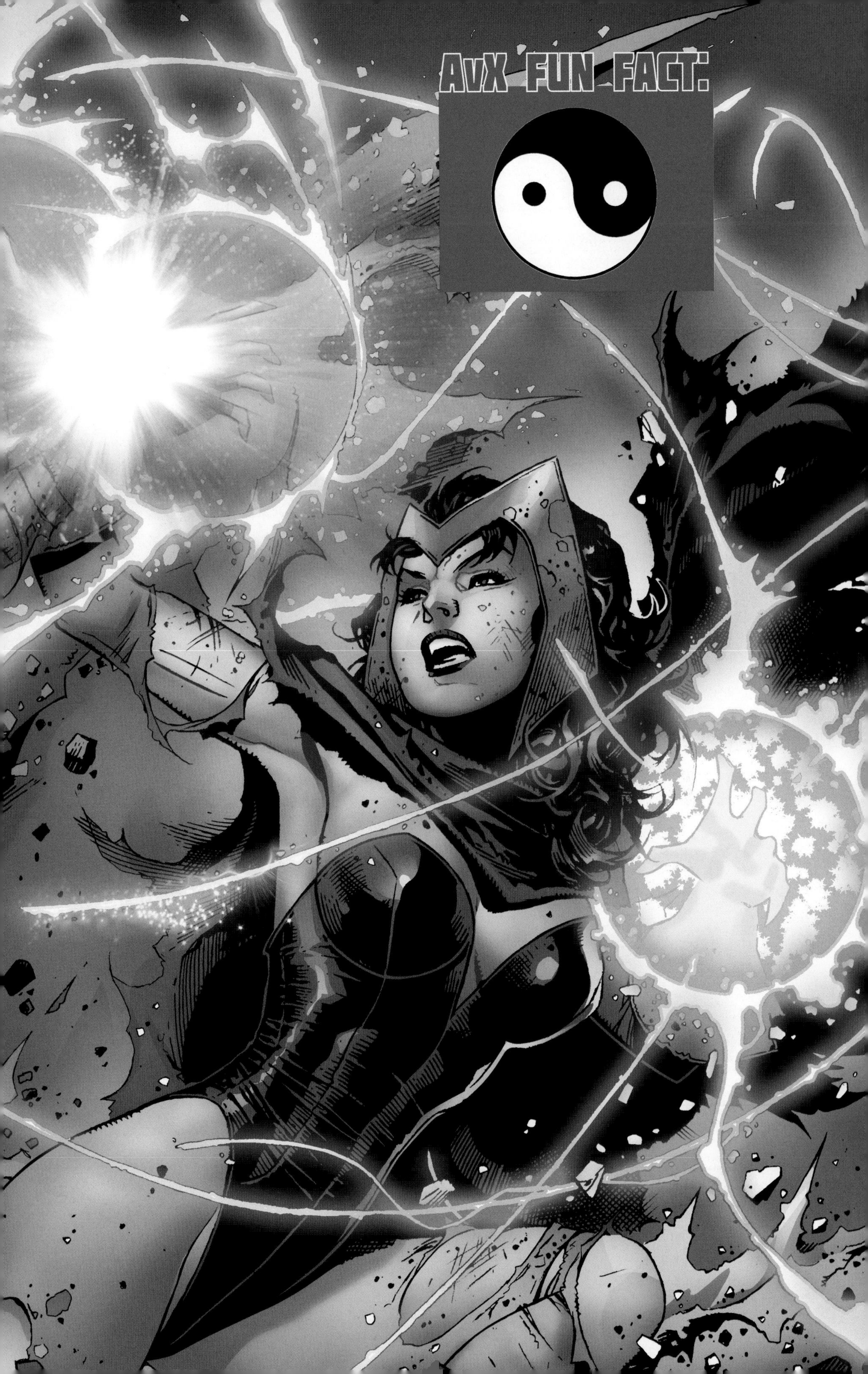
AvX FUN FACT:

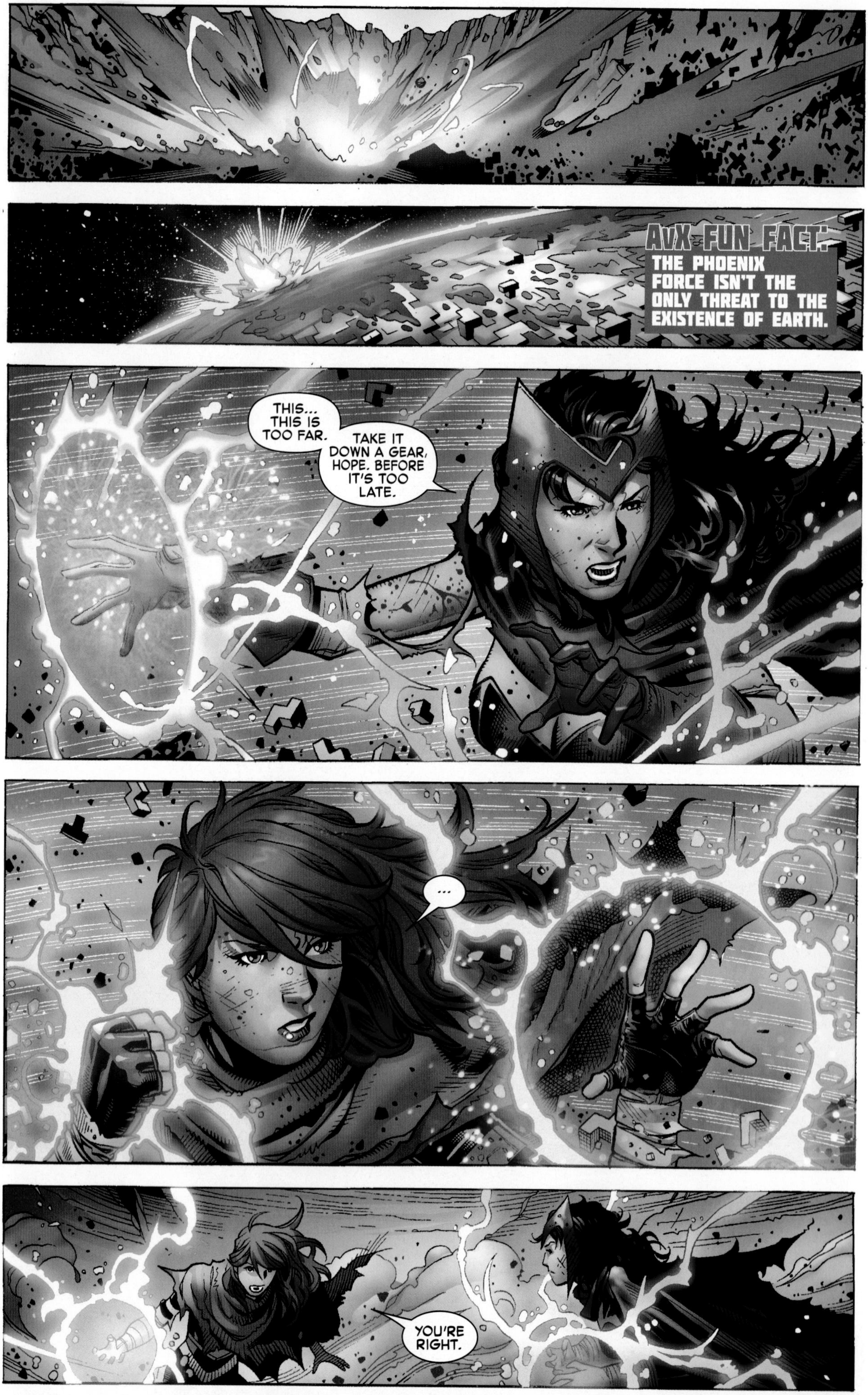
AvX FUN FACT:
THE PHOENIX FORCE ISN'T THE ONLY THREAT TO THE EXISTENCE OF EARTH.
THIS... THIS IS TOO FAR.
TAKE IT DOWN A GEAR, HOPE. BEFORE IT'S TOO LATE.
...
YOU'RE RIGHT.

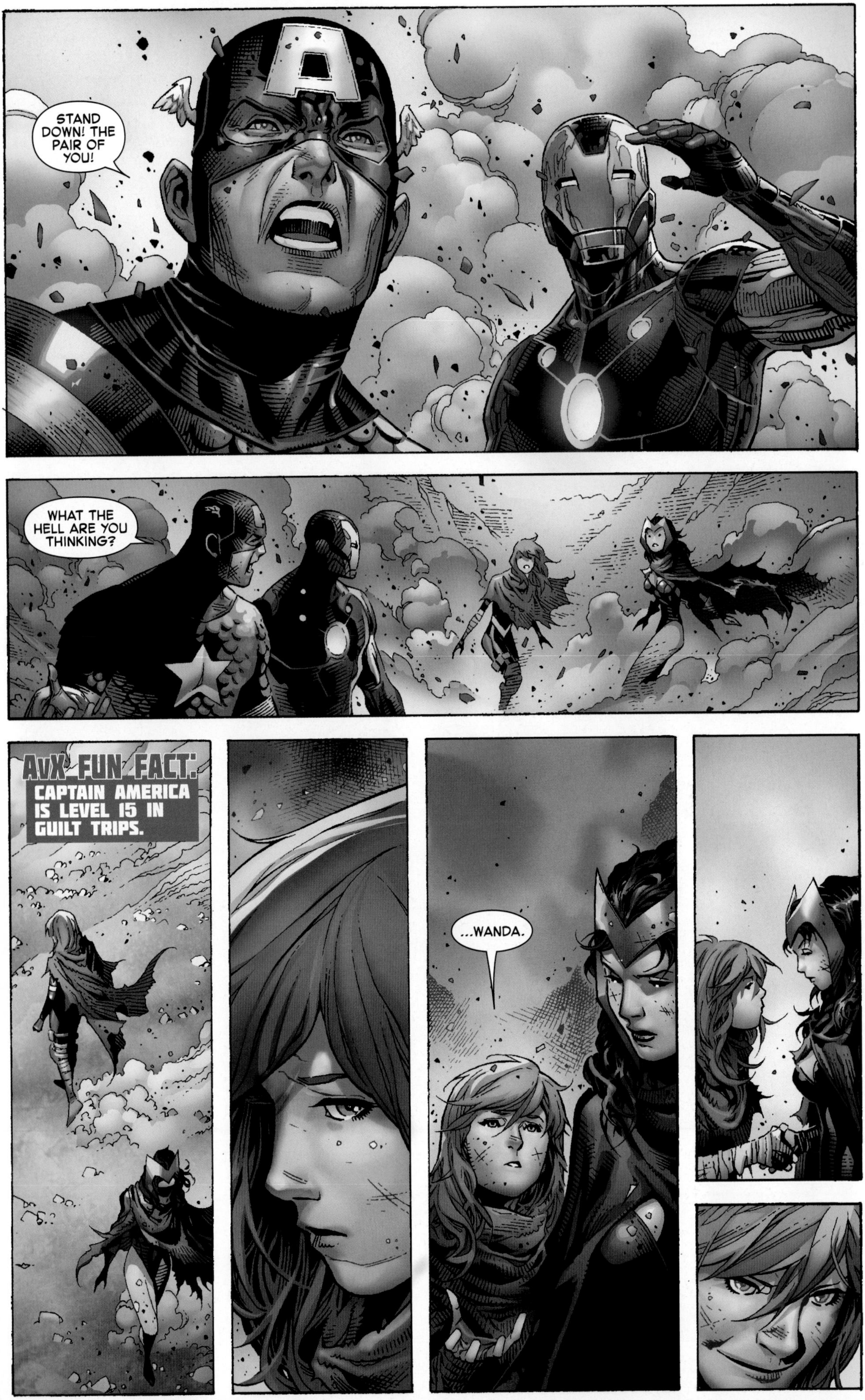
STAND DOWN! THE PAIR OF YOU!
WHAT THE HELL ARE YOU THINKING?
AvX FUN FACT:
CAPTAIN AMERICA IS LEVEL 15 IN GUILT TRIPS.
...WANDA.

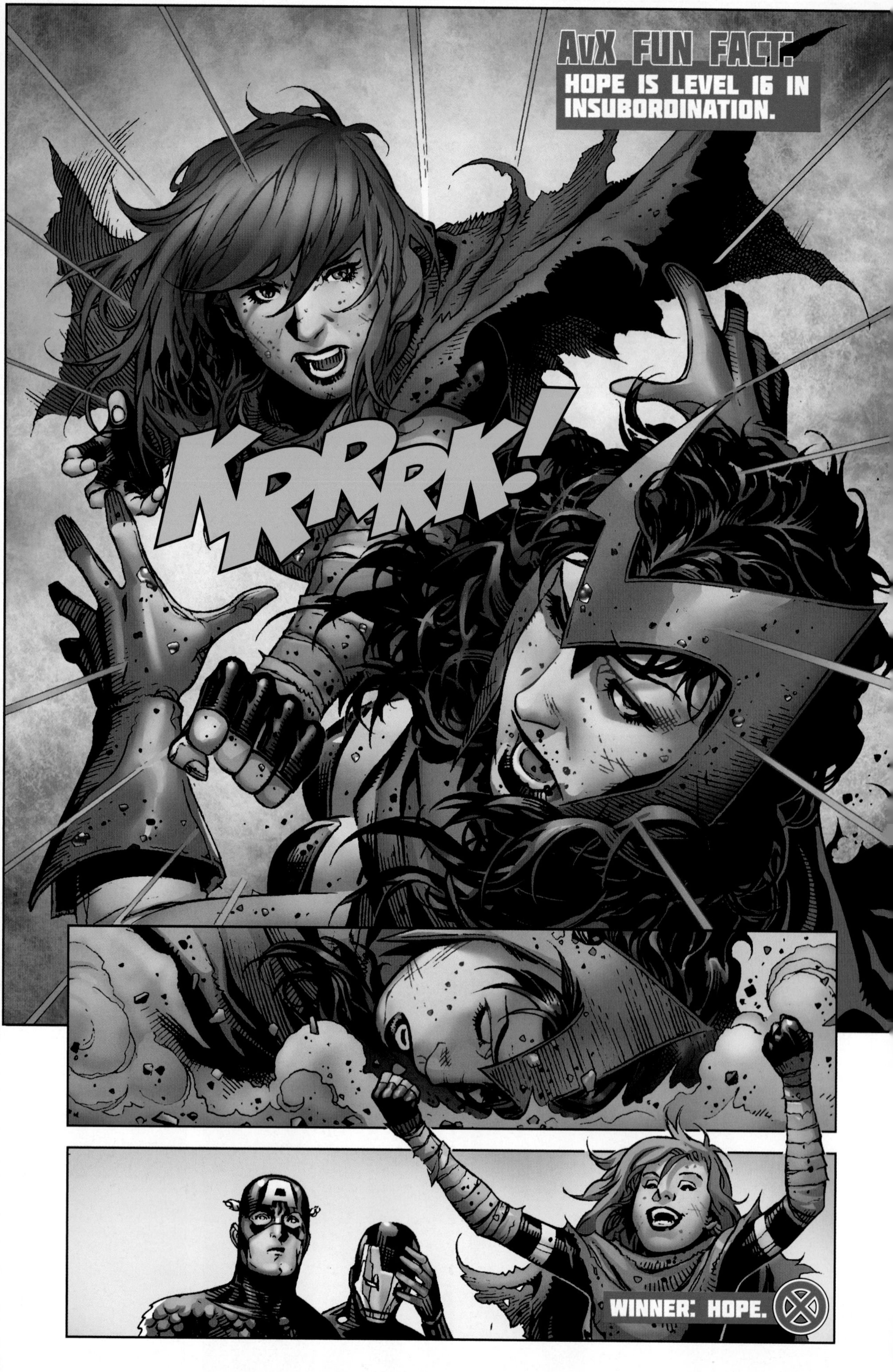
AvX FUN FACT:
HOPE IS LEVEL 16 IN INSUBORDINATION.
KRRRK!
WINNER: HOPE.

CYCLOPS VS. CAPTAIN AMERICA IN VERBAL ABUSE

BY BRIAN MICHAEL BENDIS, JIM MAHFOOD & VC'S JOE CARAMAGNA

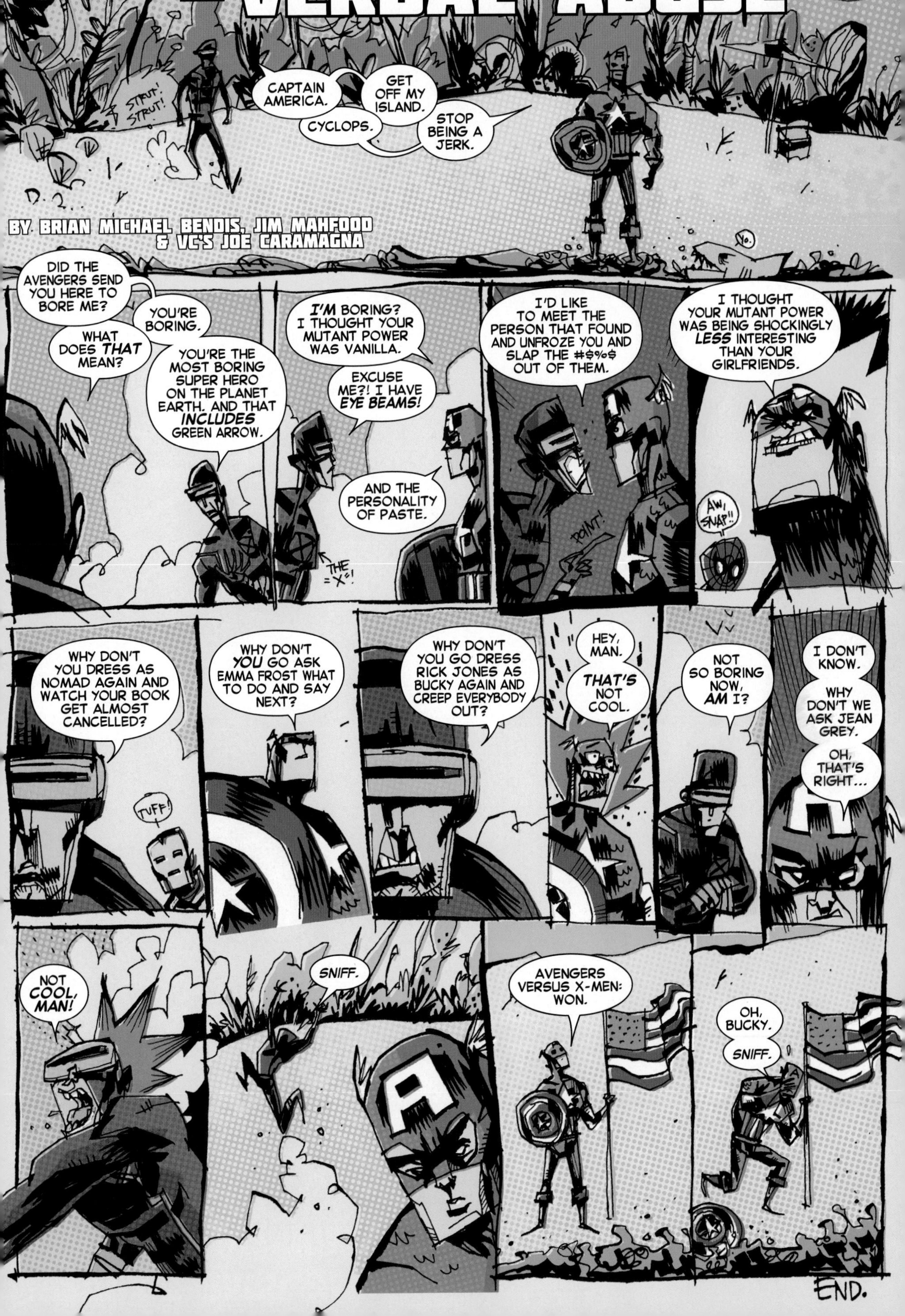
STRUT! STRUT!
CAPTAIN AMERICA.
CYCLOPS.
GET OFF MY ISLAND.
STOP BEING A JERK.
YO.
DID THE AVENGERS SEND YOU HERE TO BORE ME?
YOU'RE BORING.
WHAT DOES THAT MEAN?
YOU'RE THE MOST BORING SUPER HERO ON THE PLANET EARTH. AND THAT INCLUDES GREEN ARROW.
THE "X"!
I'M BORING? I THOUGHT YOUR MUTANT POWER WAS VANILLA.
EXCUSE ME?! I HAVE EYE BEAMS!
AND THE PERSONALITY OF PASTE.
I'D LIKE TO MEET THE PERSON THAT FOUND AND UNFROZE YOU AND SLAP THE #$%$ OUT OF THEM.
POINT!
I THOUGHT YOUR MUTANT POWER WAS BEING SHOCKINGLY LESS INTERESTING THAN YOUR GIRLFRIENDS.
AW, SNAP!!
WHY DON'T YOU DRESS AS NOMAD AGAIN AND WATCH YOUR BOOK GET ALMOST CANCELLED?
TUFF!
WHY DON'T YOU GO ASK EMMA FROST WHAT TO DO AND SAY NEXT?
WHY DON'T YOU GO DRESS RICK JONES AS BUCKY AGAIN AND CREEP EVERYBODY OUT?
HEY, MAN.
THAT'S NOT COOL.
NOT SO BORING NOW, AM I?
I DON'T KNOW.
WHY DON'T WE ASK JEAN GREY.
OH, THAT'S RIGHT...
NOT COOL, MAN!
SNIFF.
AVENGERS VERSUS X-MEN: WON.
OH, BUCKY.
SNIFF.
END.

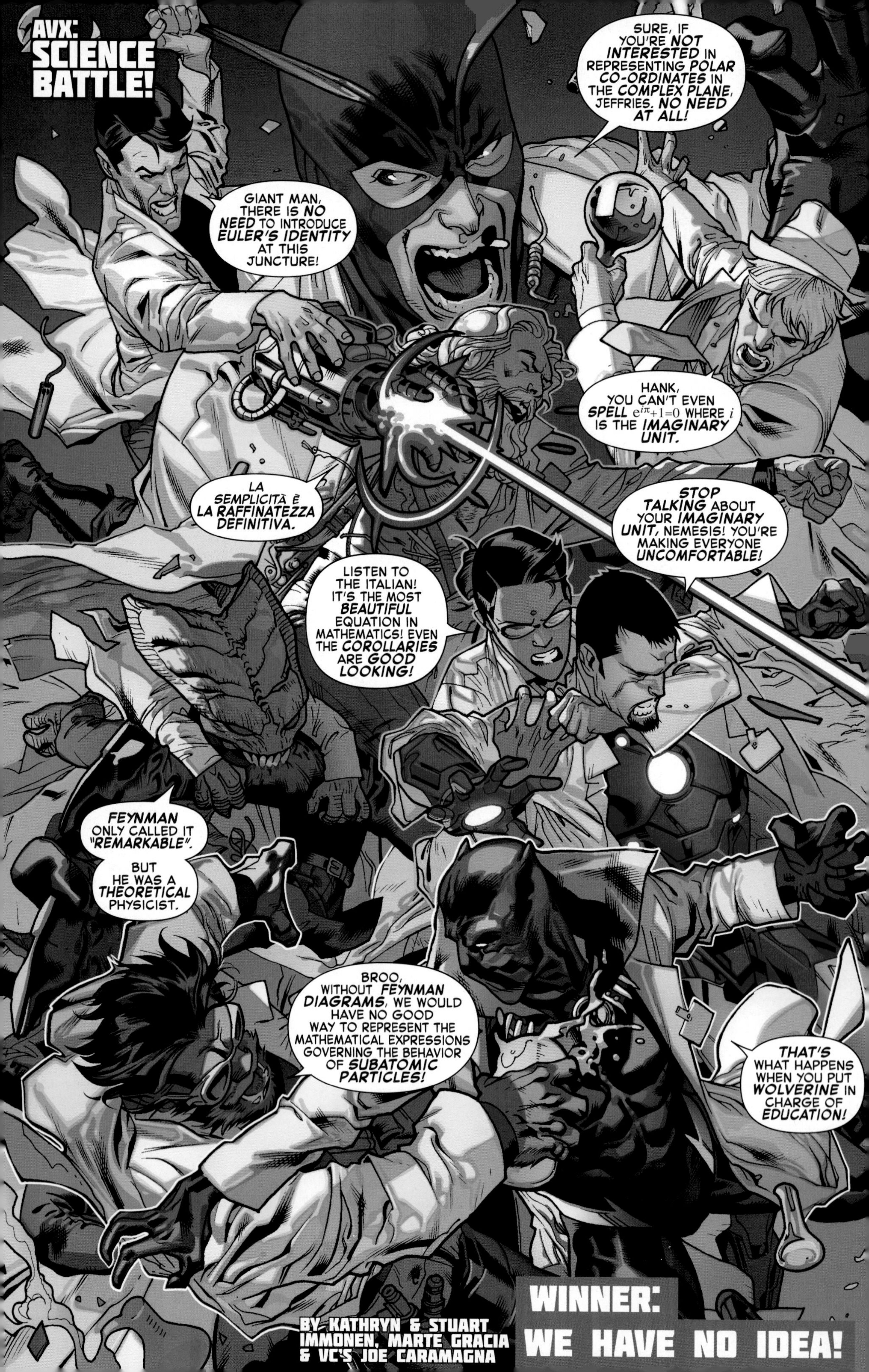
AVX: SCIENCE BATTLE!
GIANT MAN, THERE IS NO NEED TO INTRODUCE EULER'S IDENTITY AT THIS JUNCTURE!
SURE, IF YOU'RE NOT INTERESTED IN REPRESENTING POLAR CO-ORDINATES IN THE COMPLEX PLANE, JEFFRIES. NO NEED AT ALL!
HANK, YOU CAN'T EVEN SPELL $e^{i\pi}+1=0$ WHERE i IS THE IMAGINARY UNIT.
LA SEMPLICITÀ È LA RAFFINATEZZA DEFINITIVA.
STOP TALKING ABOUT YOUR IMAGINARY UNIT, NEMESIS! YOU'RE MAKING EVERYONE UNCOMFORTABLE!
LISTEN TO THE ITALIAN! IT'S THE MOST BEAUTIFUL EQUATION IN MATHEMATICS! EVEN THE COROLLARIES ARE GOOD LOOKING!
FEYNMAN ONLY CALLED IT "REMARKABLE".
BUT HE WAS A THEORETICAL PHYSICIST.
BROO, WITHOUT FEYNMAN DIAGRAMS, WE WOULD HAVE NO GOOD WAY TO REPRESENT THE MATHEMATICAL EXPRESSIONS GOVERNING THE BEHAVIOR OF SUBATOMIC PARTICLES!
THAT'S WHAT HAPPENS WHEN YOU PUT WOLVERINE IN CHARGE OF EDUCATION!
BY KATHRYN & STUART IMMONEN, MARTE GRACIA & VC'S JOE CARAMAGNA
WINNER: WE HAVE NO IDEA!

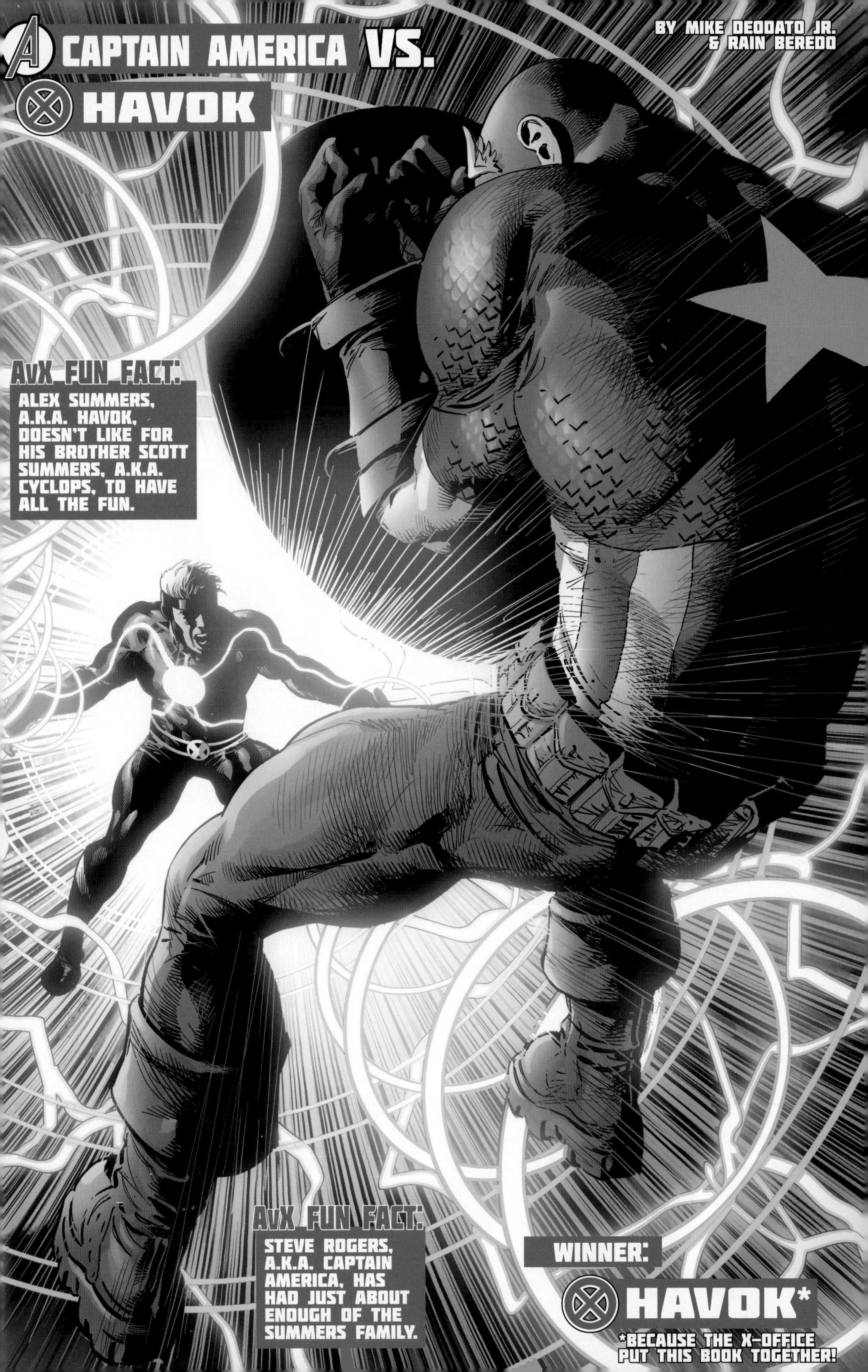
CAPTAIN AMERICA VS.
HAVOK
BY MIKE DEODATO JR. & RAIN BEREDO
AvX FUN FACT:
ALEX SUMMERS, A.K.A. HAVOK, DOESN'T LIKE FOR HIS BROTHER SCOTT SUMMERS, A.K.A. CYCLOPS, TO HAVE ALL THE FUN.
AvX FUN FACT:
STEVE ROGERS, A.K.A. CAPTAIN AMERICA, HAS HAD JUST ABOUT ENOUGH OF THE SUMMERS FAMILY.
WINNER:
HAVOK*
*BECAUSE THE X-OFFICE PUT THIS BOOK TOGETHER!

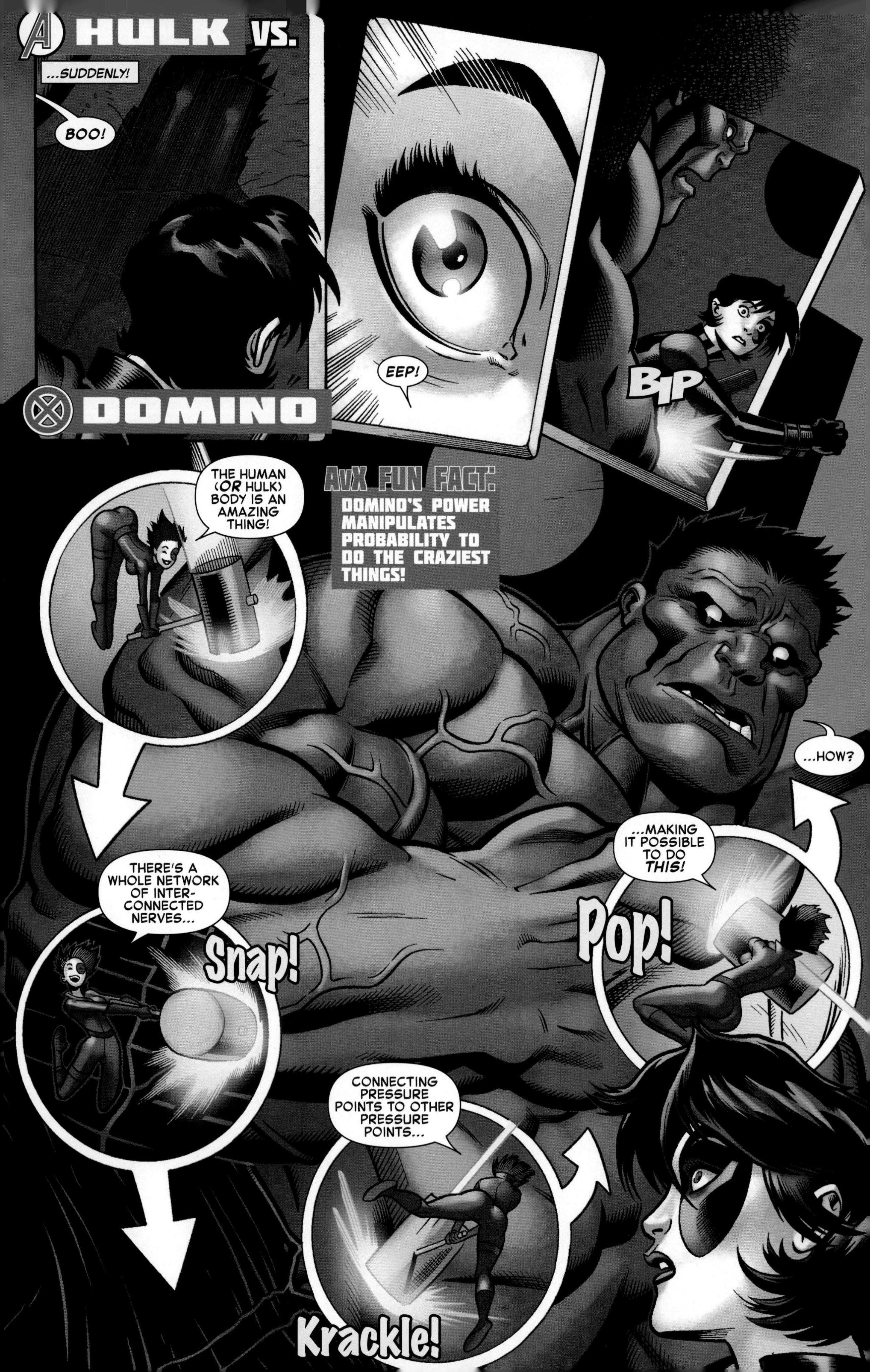
HULK VS.
...SUDDENLY!
BOO!
EEP!
BIP
DOMINO
THE HUMAN (OR HULK) BODY IS AN AMAZING THING!
AvX FUN FACT:
DOMINO'S POWER MANIPULATES PROBABILITY TO DO THE CRAZIEST THINGS!
...HOW?
...MAKING IT POSSIBLE TO DO THIS!
THERE'S A WHOLE NETWORK OF INTER-CONNECTED NERVES...
Snap!
Pop!
CONNECTING PRESSURE POINTS TO OTHER PRESSURE POINTS...
Krackle!

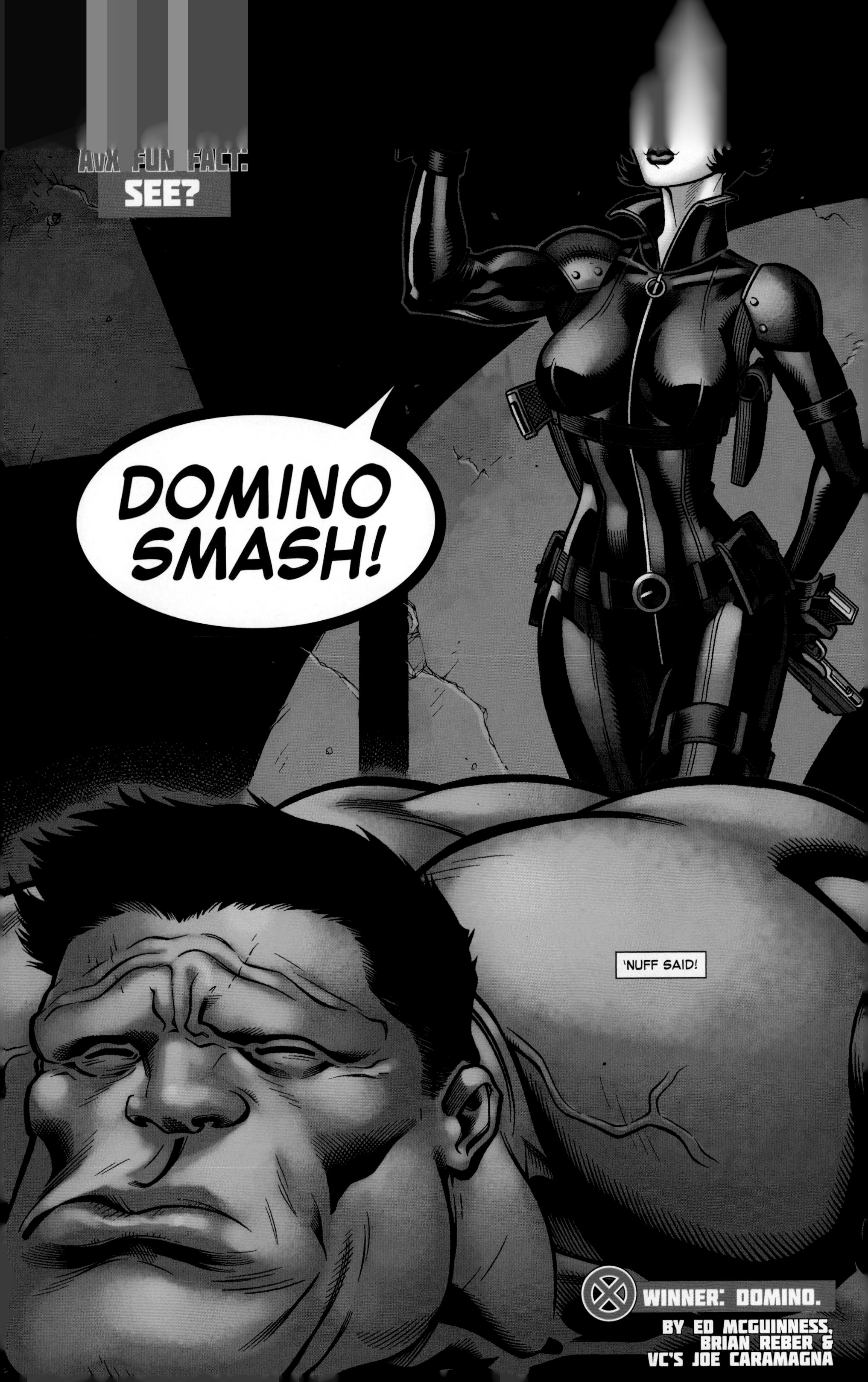

AvX FUN FACT:
SEE?
DOMINO SMASH!
'NUFF SAID!
WINNER: DOMINO.
BY ED MCGUINNESS, BRIAN REBER & VC'S JOE CARAMAGNA

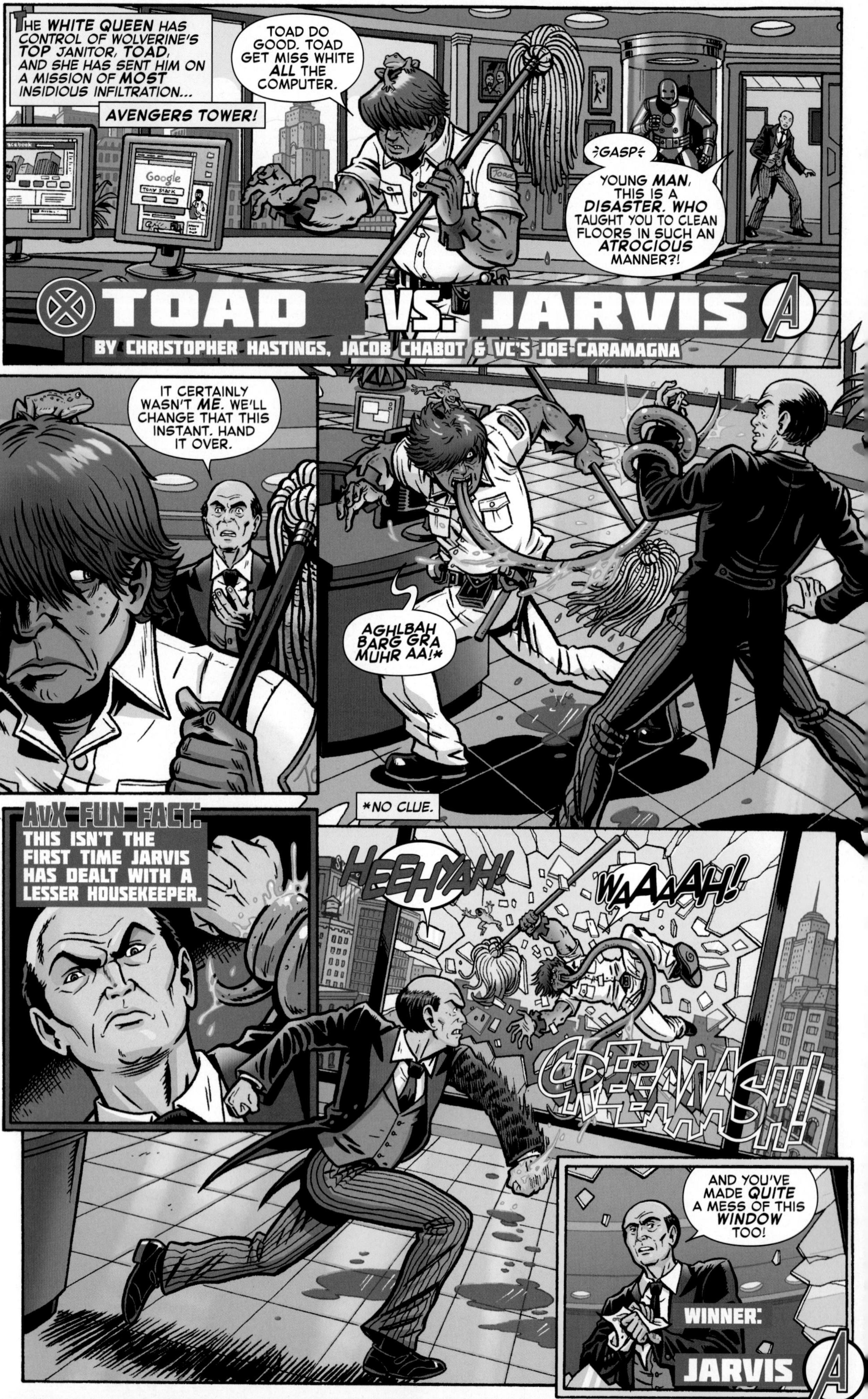
THE WHITE QUEEN HAS CONTROL OF WOLVERINE'S TOP JANITOR, TOAD, AND SHE HAS SENT HIM ON A MISSION OF MOST INSIDIOUS INFILTRATION...
AVENGERS TOWER!
TOAD DO GOOD. TOAD GET MISS WHITE ALL THE COMPUTER.
GASP
YOUNG MAN, THIS IS A DISASTER. WHO TAUGHT YOU TO CLEAN FLOORS IN SUCH AN ATROCIOUS MANNER?!
TOAD VS. JARVIS
BY CHRISTOPHER HASTINGS, JACOB CHABOT & VC'S JOE CARAMAGNA
IT CERTAINLY WASN'T ME. WE'LL CHANGE THAT THIS INSTANT. HAND IT OVER.
AGHLBAH BARG GRA MUHR AA!*
*NO CLUE.
AvX FUN FACT:
THIS ISN'T THE FIRST TIME JARVIS HAS DEALT WITH A LESSER HOUSEKEEPER.
HEEHYAH!
WAAAAH!
CREEMASH!
AND YOU'VE MADE QUITE A MESS OF THIS WINDOW TOO!
WINNER:
JARVIS

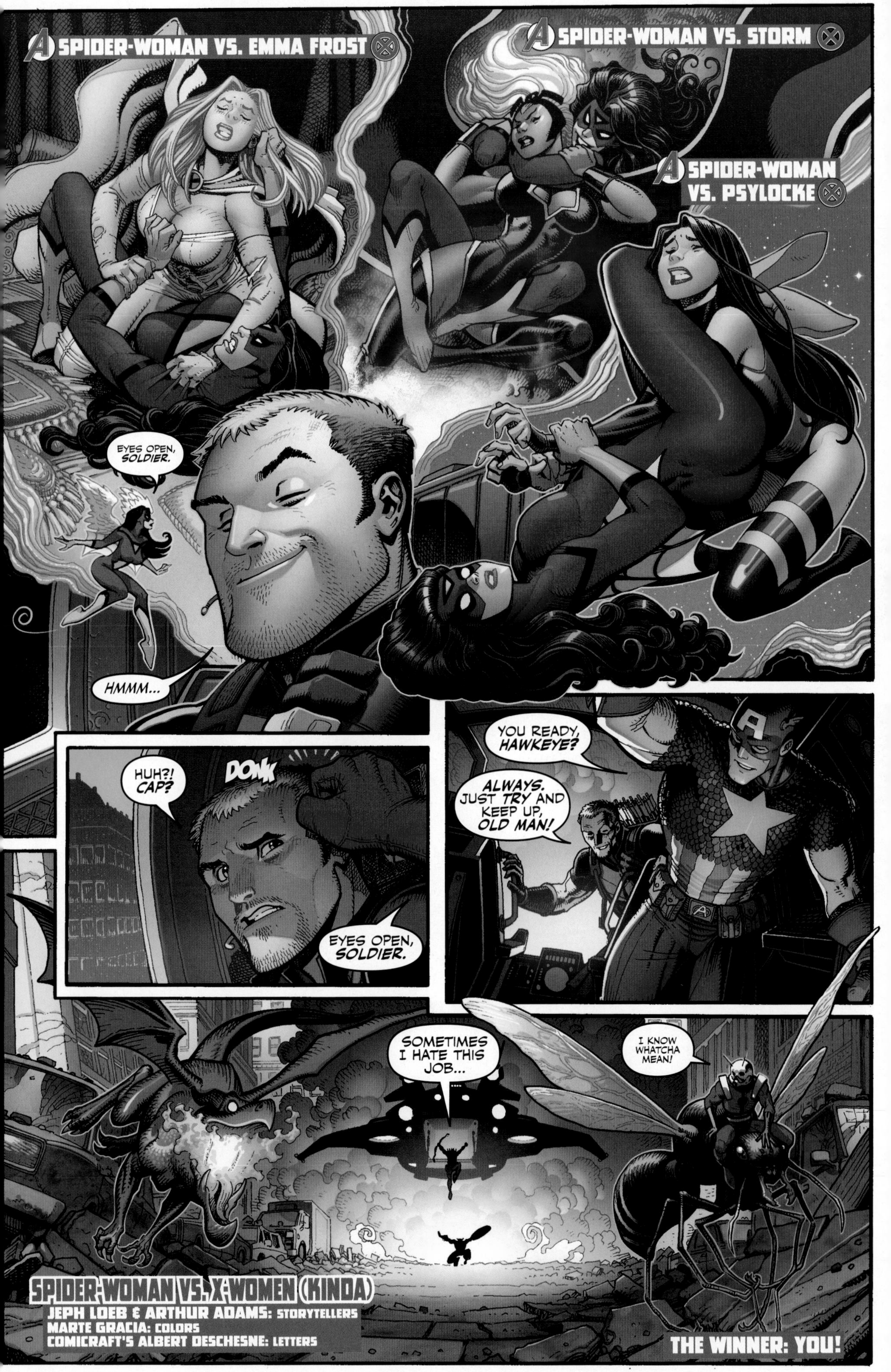
SPIDER-WOMAN VS. EMMA FROST
SPIDER-WOMAN VS. STORM
SPIDER-WOMAN VS. PSYLOCKE
EYES OPEN, SOLDIER.
HMMM...
HUH?! CAP?
DONK
EYES OPEN, SOLDIER.
YOU READY, HAWKEYE?
ALWAYS. JUST TRY AND KEEP UP, OLD MAN!
SOMETIMES I HATE THIS JOB...
I KNOW WHATCHA MEAN!
SPIDER-WOMAN VS. X-WOMEN (KINDA)
JEPH LOEB & ARTHUR ADAMS: STORYTELLERS
MARTE GRACIA: COLORS
COMICRAFT'S ALBERT DESCHESNE: LETTERS
THE WINNER: YOU!

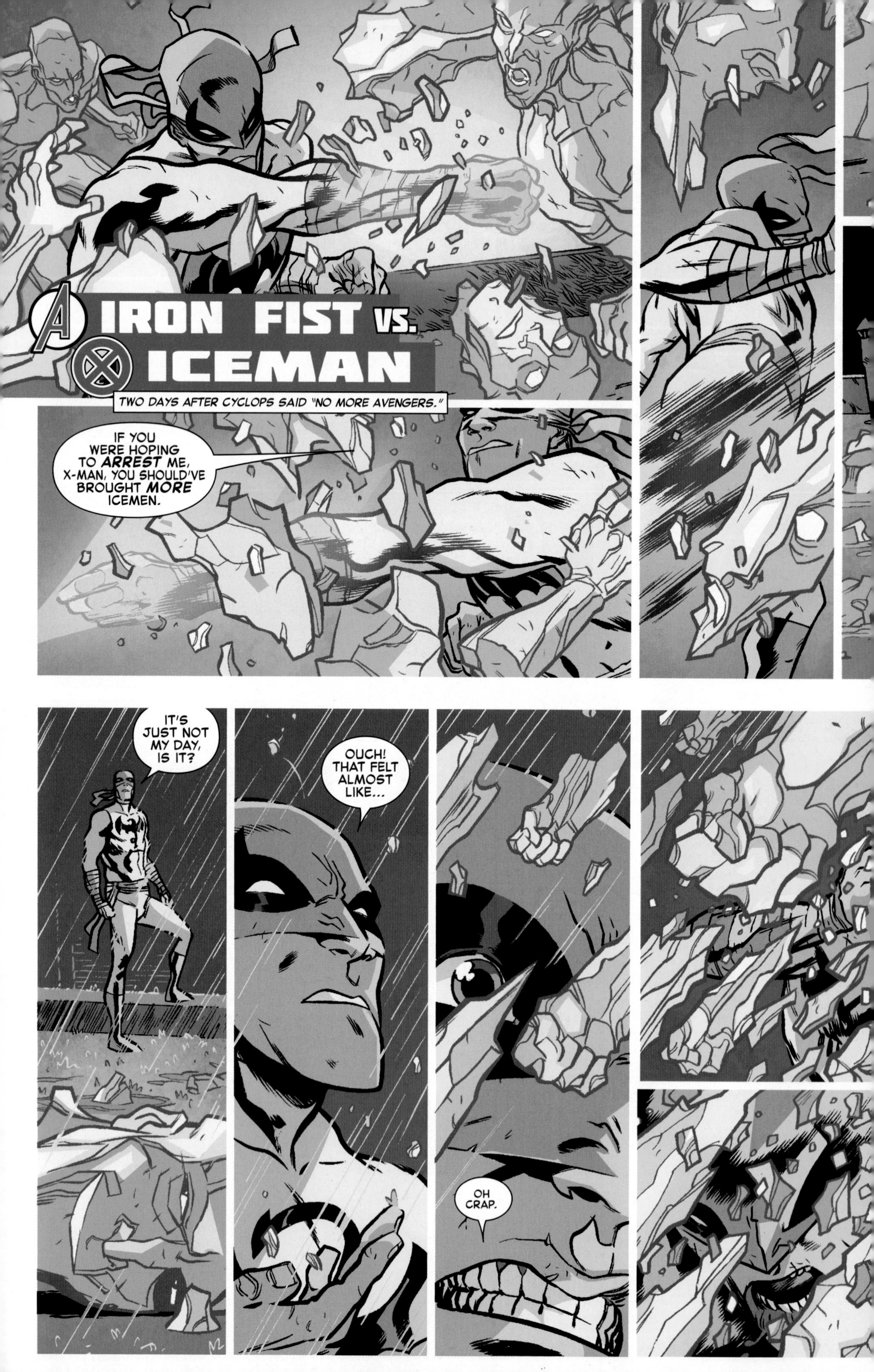
IRON FIST VS. ICEMAN
TWO DAYS AFTER CYCLOPS SAID "NO MORE AVENGERS."
IF YOU WERE HOPING TO ARREST ME, X-MAN, YOU SHOULD'VE BROUGHT MORE ICEMEN.
IT'S JUST NOT MY DAY, IS IT?
OUCH! THAT FELT ALMOST LIKE...
OH CRAP.

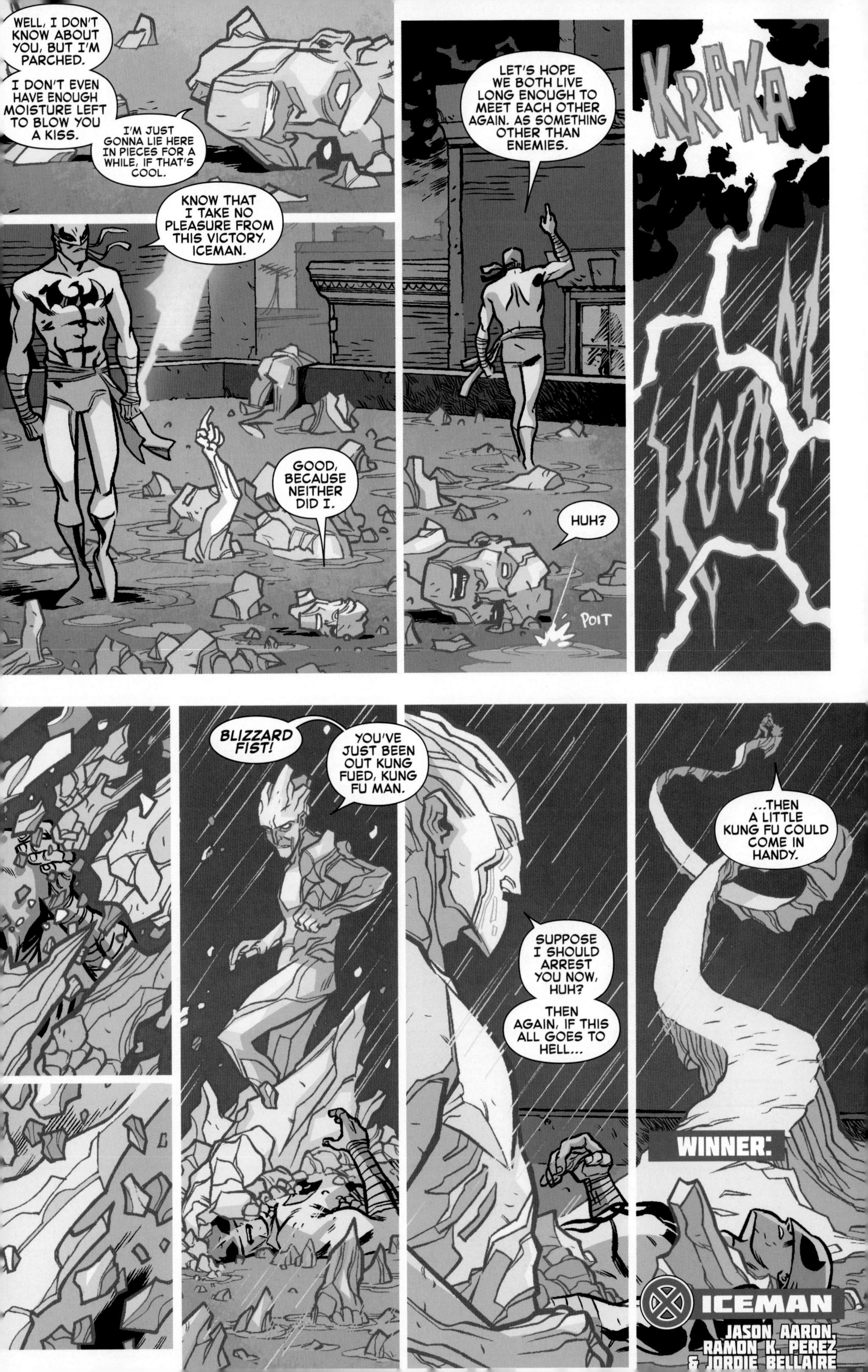
WELL, I DON'T KNOW ABOUT YOU, BUT I'M PARCHED.
I DON'T EVEN HAVE ENOUGH MOISTURE LEFT TO BLOW YOU A KISS.
I'M JUST GONNA LIE HERE IN PIECES FOR A WHILE, IF THAT'S COOL.
KNOW THAT I TAKE NO PLEASURE FROM THIS VICTORY, ICEMAN.
GOOD, BECAUSE NEITHER DID I.
LET'S HOPE WE BOTH LIVE LONG ENOUGH TO MEET EACH OTHER AGAIN. AS SOMETHING OTHER THAN ENEMIES.
HUH?
POIT
KRAKA
VOOM
BLIZZARD FIST!
YOU'VE JUST BEEN OUT KUNG FUED, KUNG FU MAN.
SUPPOSE I SHOULD ARREST YOU NOW, HUH?
THEN AGAIN, IF THIS ALL GOES TO HELL...
...THEN A LITTLE KUNG FU COULD COME IN HANDY.
WINNER:
ICEMAN
JASON AARON,
RAMON K. PEREZ
& JORDIE BELLAIRE

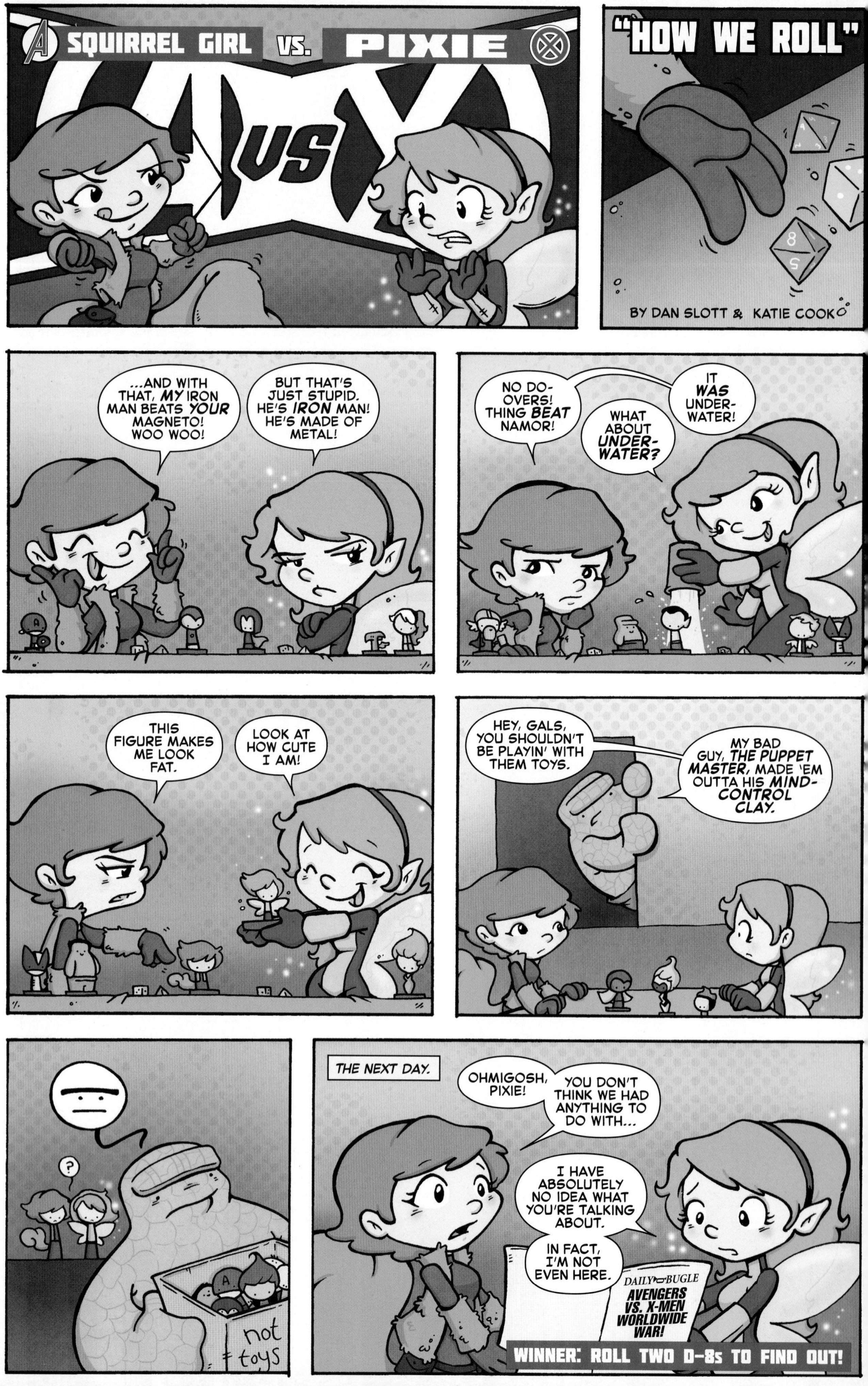
SQUIRREL GIRL VS. PIXIE
VS
"HOW WE ROLL"
8
5
BY DAN SLOTT & KATIE COOK
...AND WITH THAT, MY IRON MAN BEATS YOUR MAGNETO! WOO WOO!
BUT THAT'S JUST STUPID. HE'S IRON MAN! HE'S MADE OF METAL!
NO DO-OVERS! THING BEAT NAMOR!
WHAT ABOUT UNDER-WATER?
IT WAS UNDER-WATER!
THIS FIGURE MAKES ME LOOK FAT.
LOOK AT HOW CUTE I AM!
HEY, GALS, YOU SHOULDN'T BE PLAYIN' WITH THEM TOYS.
MY BAD GUY, THE PUPPET MASTER, MADE 'EM OUTTA HIS MIND-CONTROL CLAY.
?
not toys
THE NEXT DAY.
OHMIGOSH, PIXIE!
YOU DON'T THINK WE HAD ANYTHING TO DO WITH...
I HAVE ABSOLUTELY NO IDEA WHAT YOU'RE TALKING ABOUT.
IN FACT, I'M NOT EVEN HERE.
DAILY BUGLE
AVENGERS VS. X-MEN WORLDWIDE WAR!
WINNER: ROLL TWO D-8s TO FIND OUT!

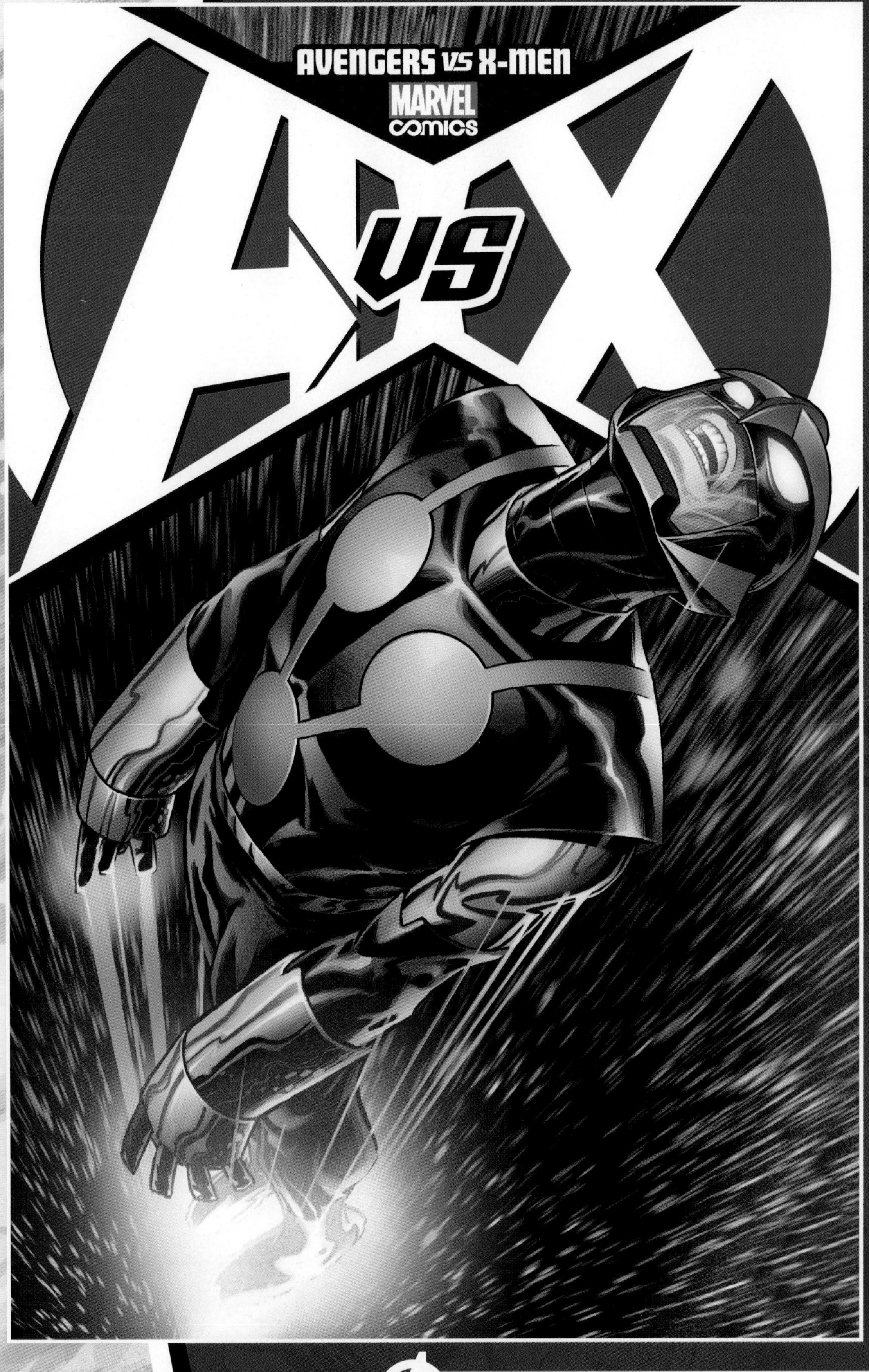
AVENGERS VS X-MEN
MARVEL COMICS
A VS X

INFINITE COMICS #1

Infinite Comics are Marvel's newest and boldest jump into the world of digital comics. Crafted specifically to be read on the Marvel Comics App, Infinite Comics take advantage of new storytelling opportunities the digital realm makes possible. The following stories have been restructured into traditional print comics, but to get the full effect, the original versions can be read on the Marvel Comics App.

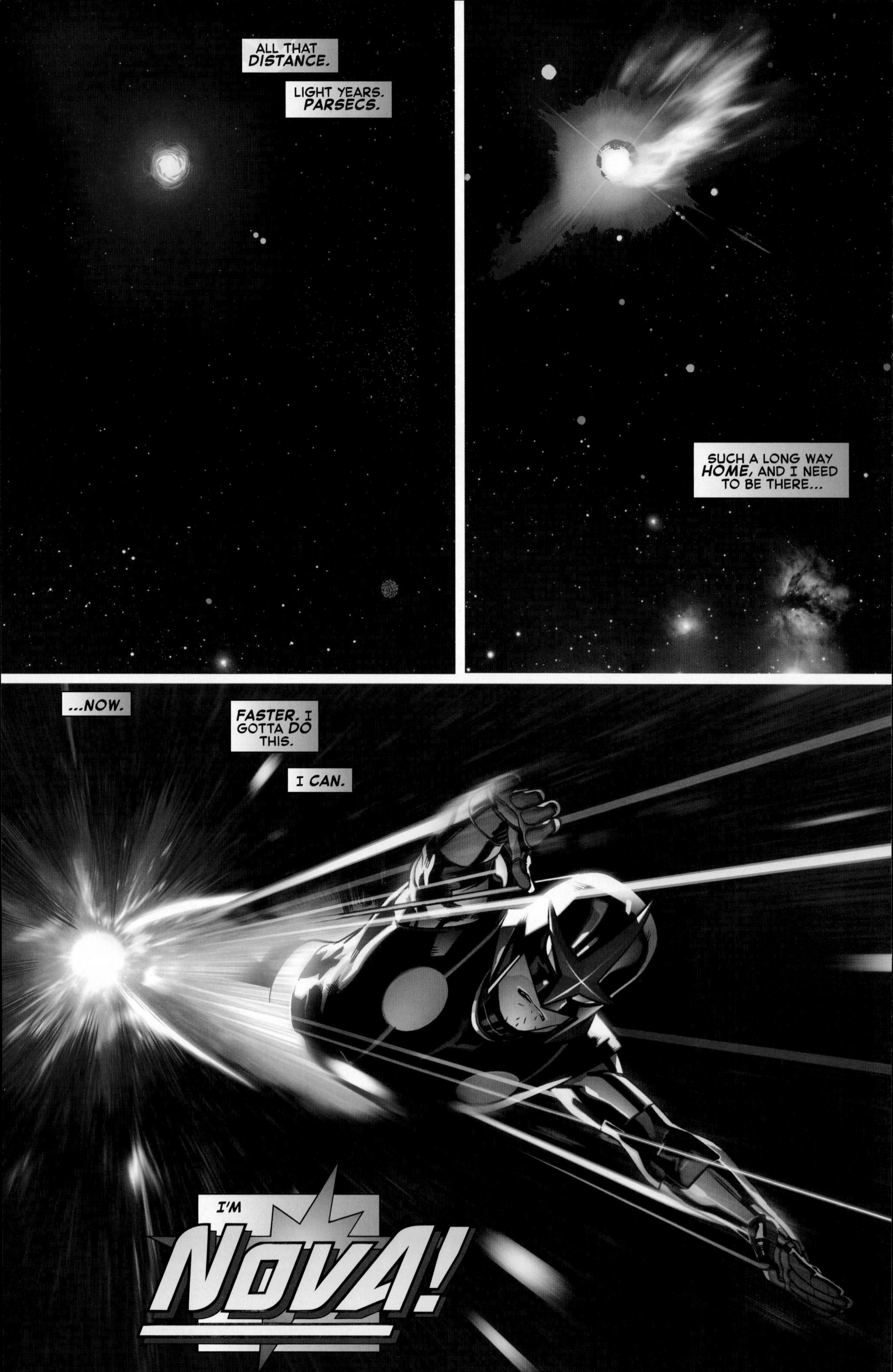
ALL THAT DISTANCE.
LIGHT YEARS. PARSECS.
SUCH A LONG WAY HOME, AND I NEED TO BE THERE...
...NOW.
FASTER. I GOTTA DO THIS.
I CAN.
I'M
NOVA!

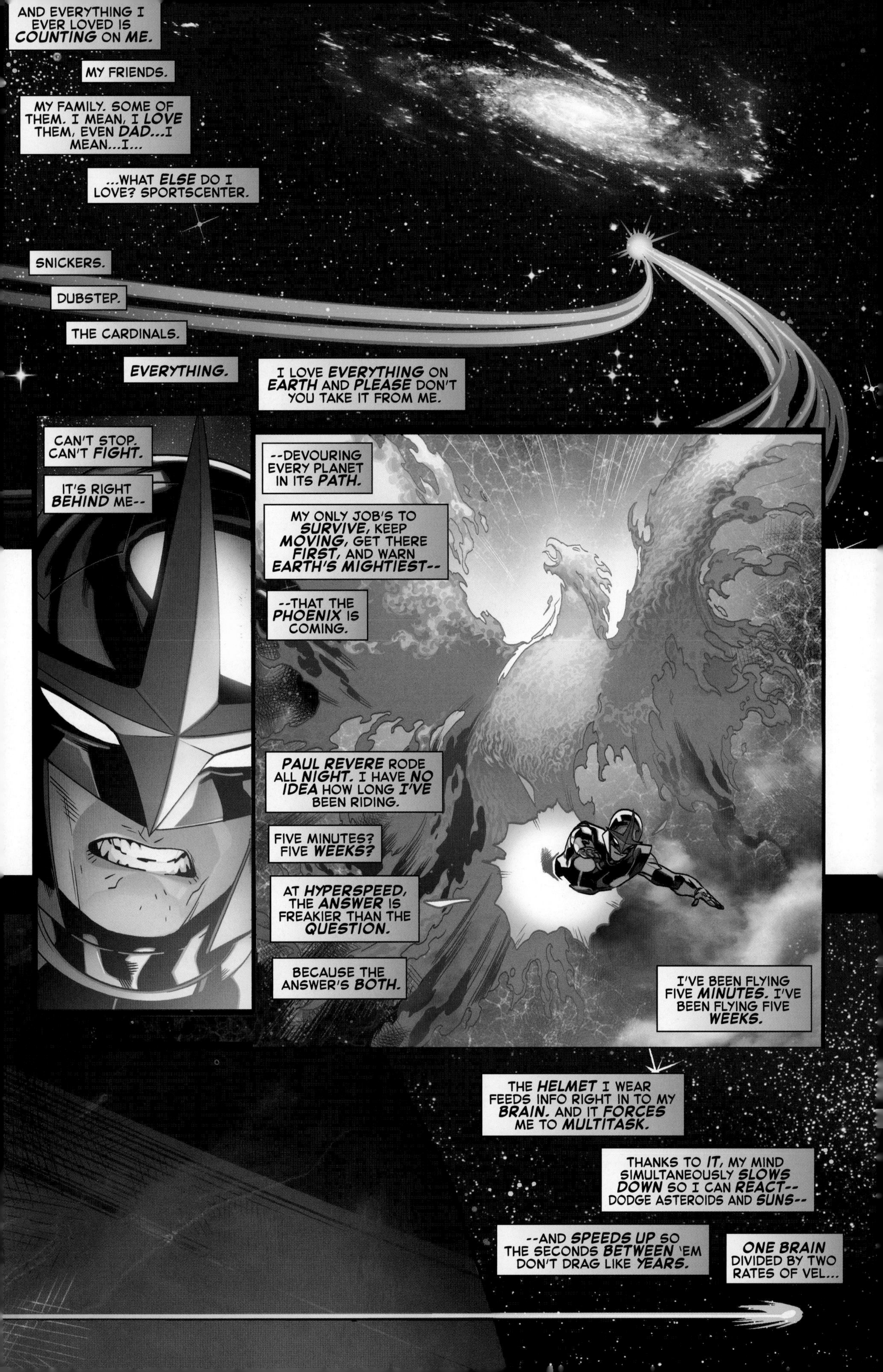
AND EVERYTHING I EVER LOVED IS COUNTING ON ME.
MY FRIENDS.
MY FAMILY. SOME OF THEM. I MEAN, I LOVE THEM, EVEN DAD...I MEAN...I...
...WHAT ELSE DO I LOVE? SPORTSCENTER.
SNICKERS.
DUBSTEP.
THE CARDINALS.
EVERYTHING.
I LOVE EVERYTHING ON EARTH AND PLEASE DON'T YOU TAKE IT FROM ME.
CAN'T STOP. CAN'T FIGHT.
IT'S RIGHT BEHIND ME--
--DEVOURING EVERY PLANET IN ITS PATH.
MY ONLY JOB'S TO SURVIVE, KEEP MOVING, GET THERE FIRST, AND WARN EARTH'S MIGHTIEST--
--THAT THE PHOENIX IS COMING.
PAUL REVERE RODE ALL NIGHT. I HAVE NO IDEA HOW LONG I'VE BEEN RIDING.
FIVE MINUTES? FIVE WEEKS?
AT HYPERSPEED, THE ANSWER IS FREAKIER THAN THE QUESTION.
BECAUSE THE ANSWER'S BOTH.
I'VE BEEN FLYING FIVE MINUTES. I'VE BEEN FLYING FIVE WEEKS.
THE HELMET I WEAR FEEDS INFO RIGHT IN TO MY BRAIN. AND IT FORCES ME TO MULTITASK.
THANKS TO IT, MY MIND SIMULTANEOUSLY SLOWS DOWN SO I CAN REACT--DODGE ASTEROIDS AND SUNS--
--AND SPEEDS UP SO THE SECONDS BETWEEN 'EM DON'T DRAG LIKE YEARS.
ONE BRAIN DIVIDED BY TWO RATES OF VEL...

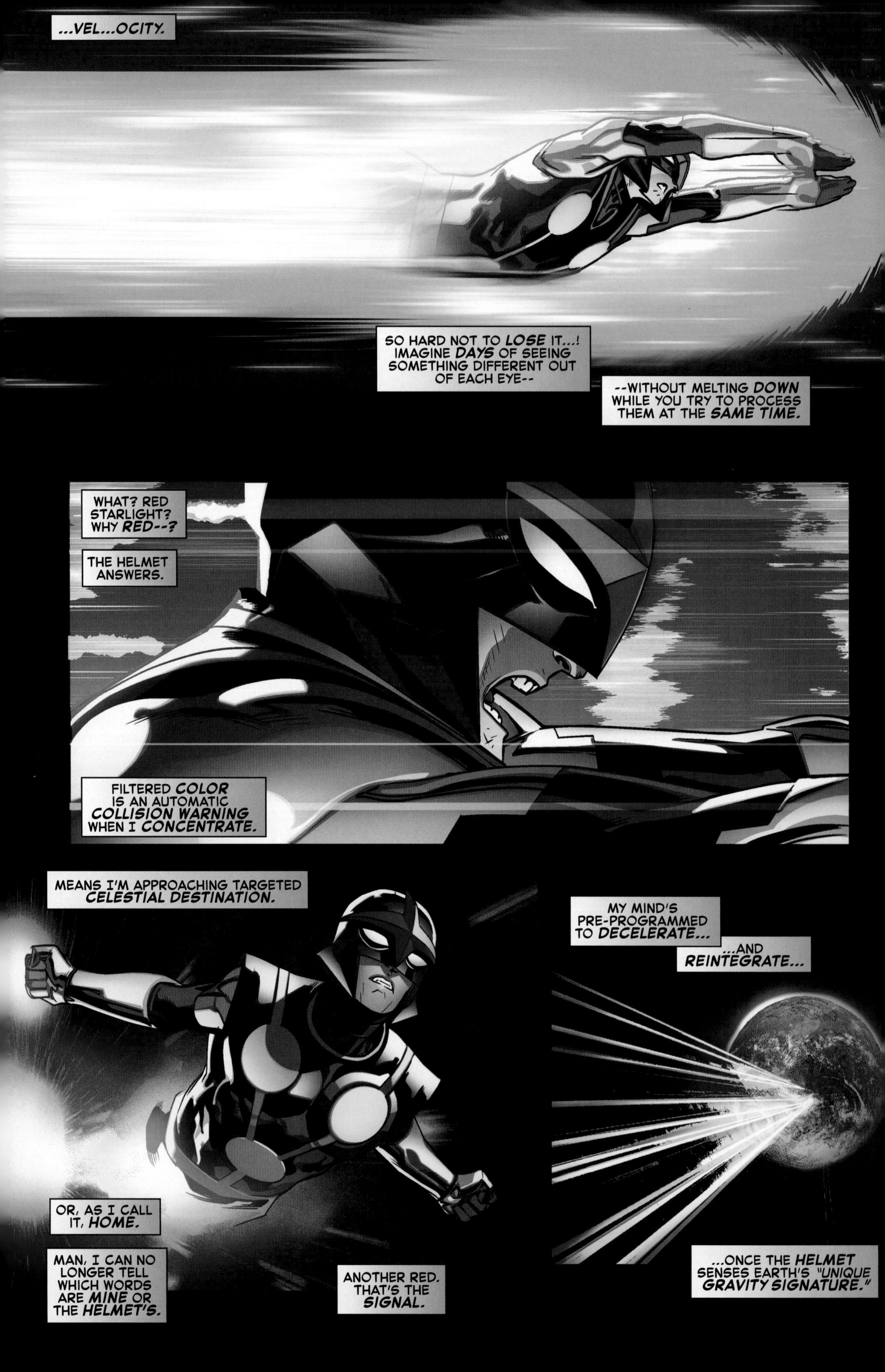
...VEL...OCITY.
SO HARD NOT TO LOSE IT...! IMAGINE DAYS OF SEEING SOMETHING DIFFERENT OUT OF EACH EYE--
--WITHOUT MELTING DOWN WHILE YOU TRY TO PROCESS THEM AT THE SAME TIME.
WHAT? RED STARLIGHT? WHY RED--?
THE HELMET ANSWERS.
FILTERED COLOR IS AN AUTOMATIC COLLISION WARNING WHEN I CONCENTRATE.
MEANS I'M APPROACHING TARGETED CELESTIAL DESTINATION.
OR, AS I CALL IT, HOME.
MAN, I CAN NO LONGER TELL WHICH WORDS ARE MINE OR THE HELMET'S.
ANOTHER RED. THAT'S THE SIGNAL.
MY MIND'S PRE-PROGRAMMED TO DECELERATE...
...AND REINTEGRATE...
...ONCE THE HELMET SENSES EARTH'S "UNIQUE GRAVITY SIGNATURE."

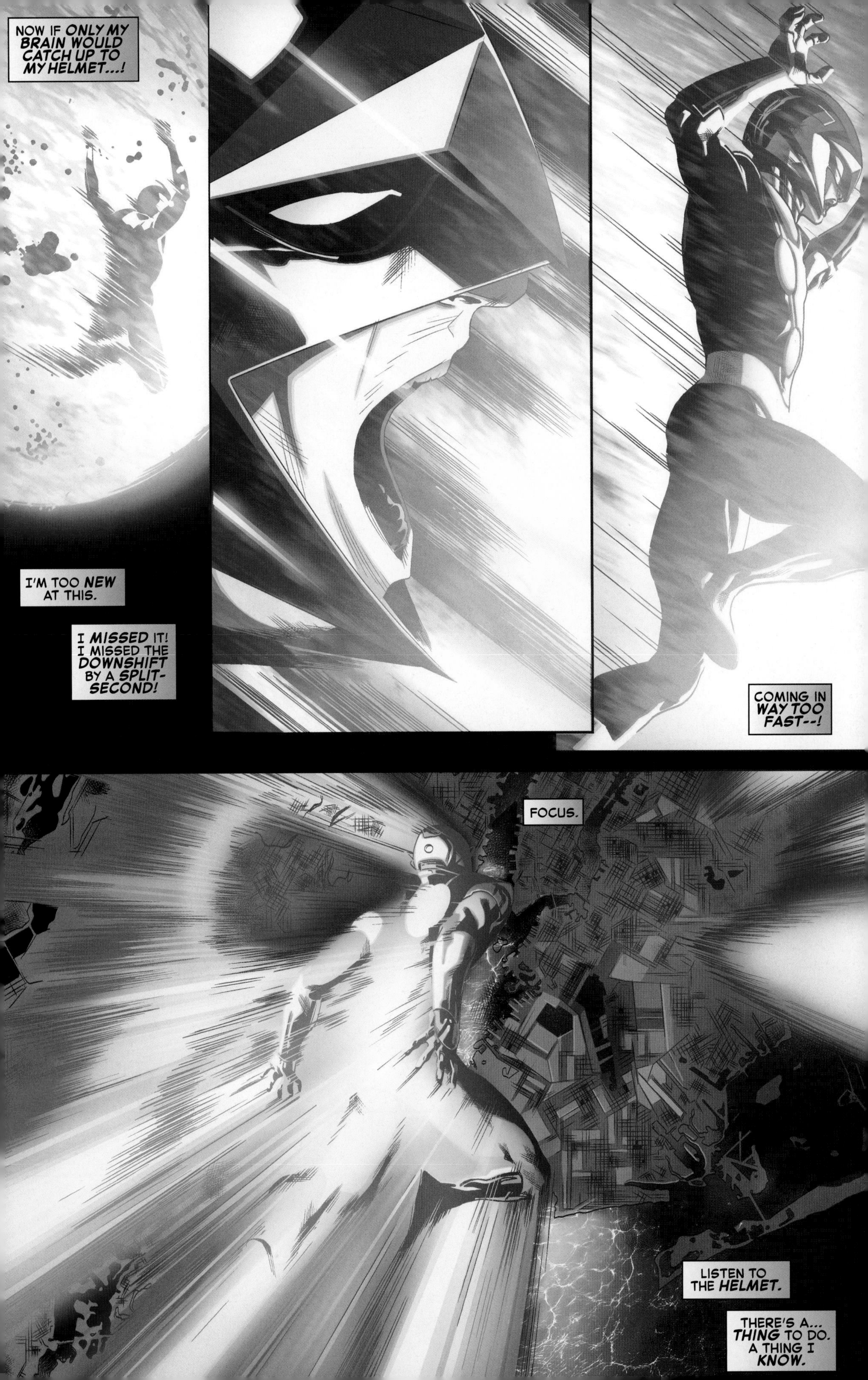

NOW IF ONLY MY BRAIN WOULD CATCH UP TO MY HELMET...!
I'M TOO NEW AT THIS.
I MISSED IT! I MISSED THE DOWNSHIFT BY A SPLIT-SECOND!
COMING IN WAY TOO FAST--!
FOCUS.
LISTEN TO THE HELMET.
THERE'S A... THING TO DO. A THING I KNOW.

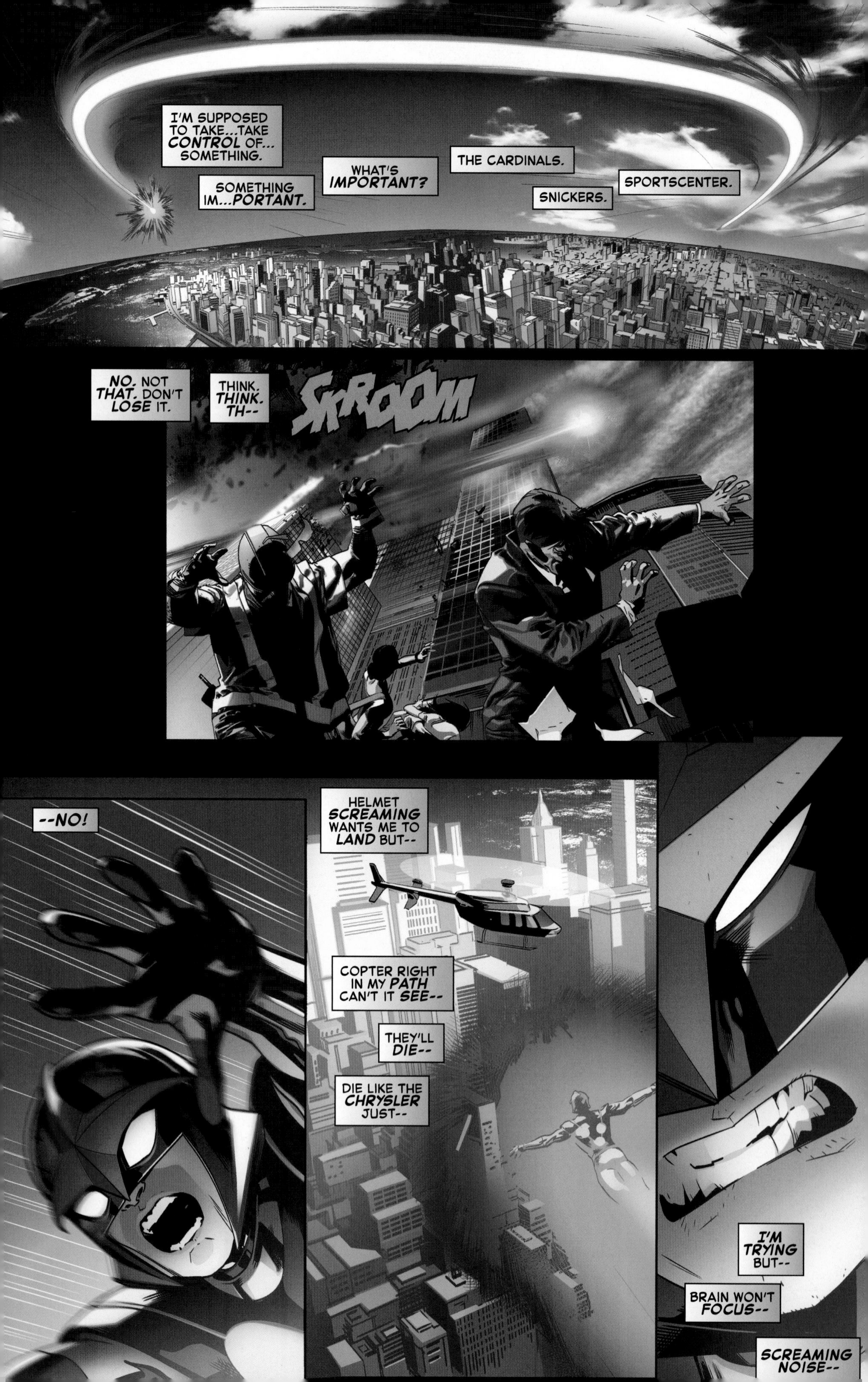
I'M SUPPOSED TO TAKE...TAKE CONTROL OF... SOMETHING.
SOMETHING IM...PORTANT.
WHAT'S IMPORTANT?
THE CARDINALS.
SNICKERS.
SPORTSCENTER.
NO. NOT THAT. DON'T LOSE IT.
THINK. THINK. TH--
SKROOM
--NO!
HELMET SCREAMING WANTS ME TO LAND BUT--
COPTER RIGHT IN MY PATH CAN'T IT SEE--
THEY'LL DIE--
DIE LIKE THE CHRYSLER JUST--
I'M TRYING BUT--
BRAIN WON'T FOCUS--
SCREAMING NOISE--

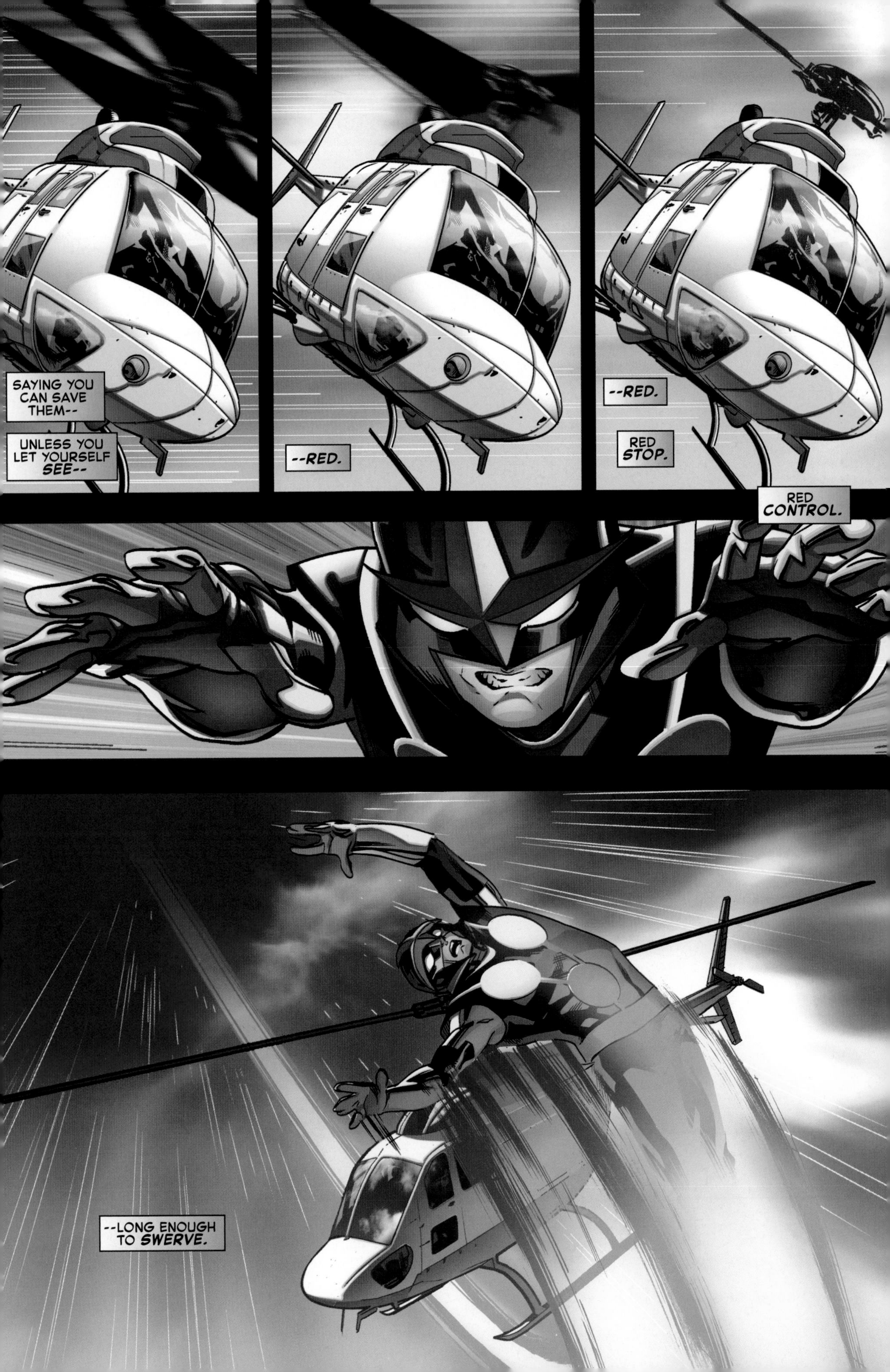
SAYING YOU CAN SAVE THEM--
UNLESS YOU LET YOURSELF SEE--
--RED.
--RED.
RED STOP.
RED CONTROL.
--LONG ENOUGH TO SWERVE.

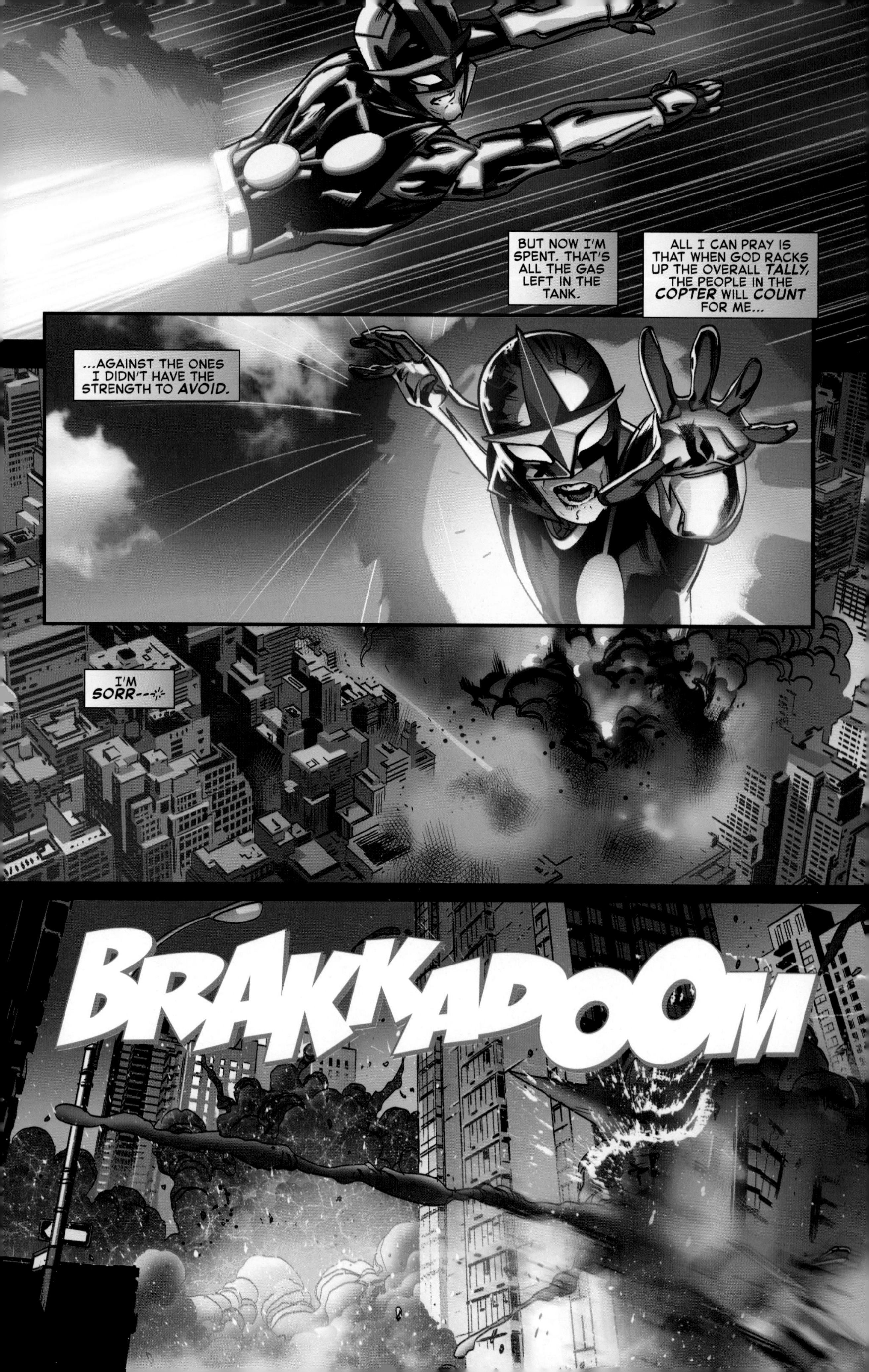
BUT NOW I'M SPENT. THAT'S ALL THE GAS LEFT IN THE TANK.
ALL I CAN PRAY IS THAT WHEN GOD RACKS UP THE OVERALL TALLY, THE PEOPLE IN THE COPTER WILL COUNT FOR ME...
...AGAINST THE ONES I DIDN'T HAVE THE STRENGTH TO AVOID.
I'M SORR---
BRAKKADOOOM

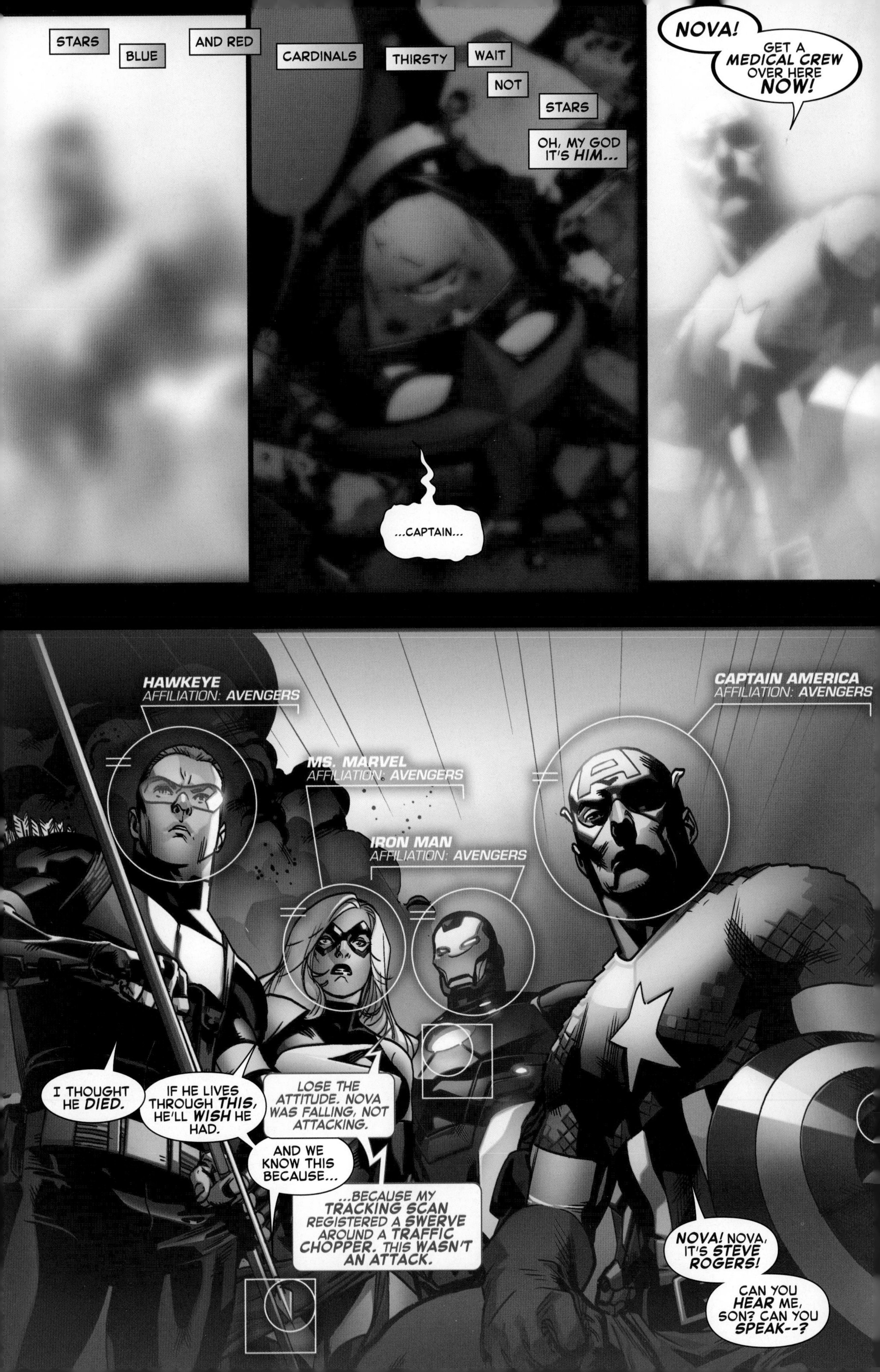

STARS
BLUE
AND RED
CARDINALS
THIRSTY
WAIT
NOT
STARS
OH, MY GOD IT'S HIM...
...CAPTAIN...
NOVA! GET A MEDICAL CREW OVER HERE NOW!
HAWKEYE AFFILIATION: AVENGERS
MS. MARVEL AFFILIATION: AVENGERS
IRON MAN AFFILIATION: AVENGERS
CAPTAIN AMERICA AFFILIATION: AVENGERS
I THOUGHT HE DIED.
IF HE LIVES THROUGH THIS, HE'LL WISH HE HAD.
LOSE THE ATTITUDE. NOVA WAS FALLING, NOT ATTACKING.
AND WE KNOW THIS BECAUSE...
...BECAUSE MY TRACKING SCAN REGISTERED A SWERVE AROUND A TRAFFIC CHOPPER. THIS WASN'T AN ATTACK.
NOVA! NOVA, IT'S STEVE ROGERS!
CAN YOU HEAR ME, SON? CAN YOU SPEAK--?

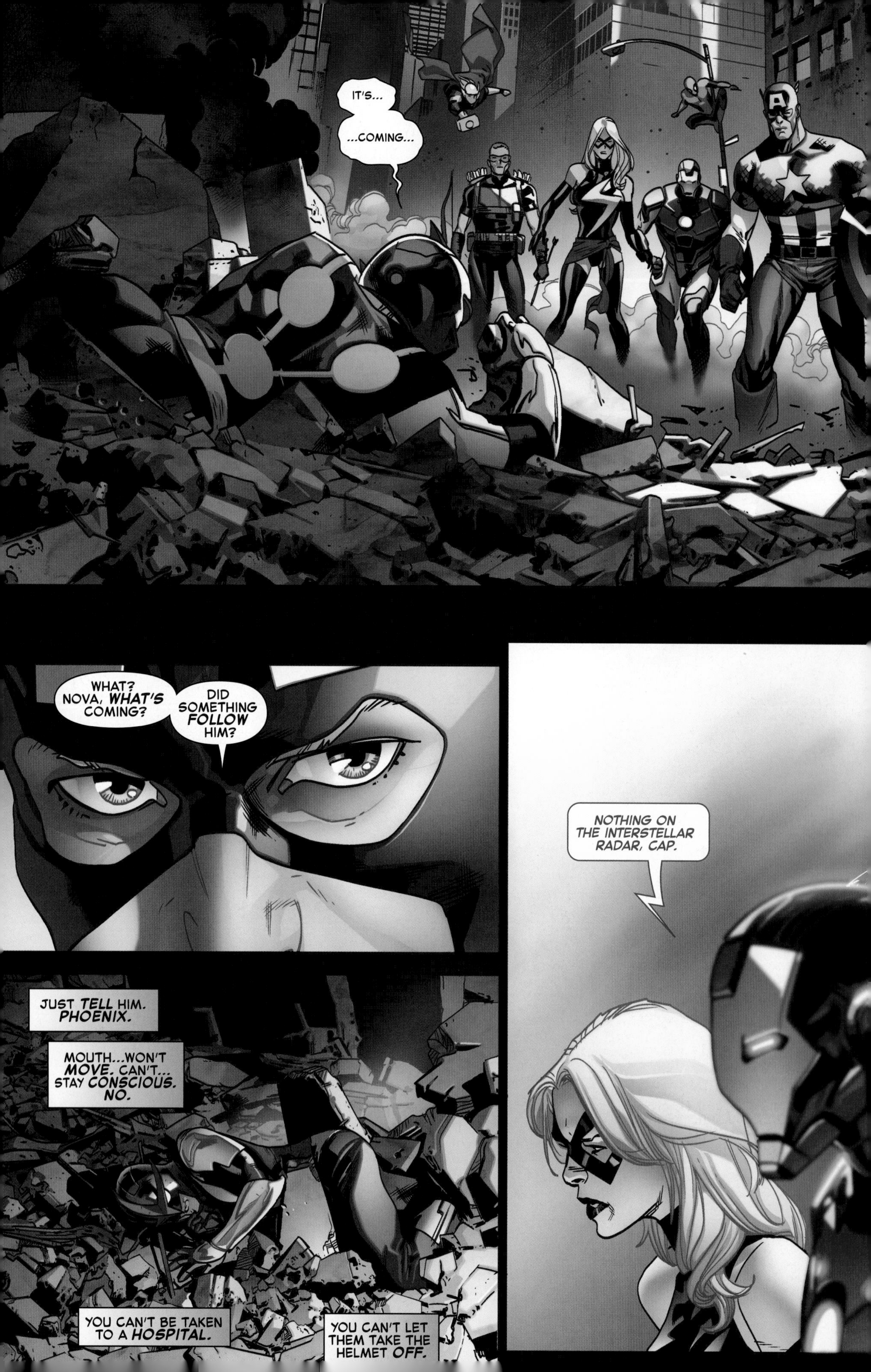
IT'S...
...COMING...
WHAT? NOVA, WHAT'S COMING?
DID SOMETHING FOLLOW HIM?
NOTHING ON THE INTERSTELLAR RADAR, CAP.
JUST TELL HIM. PHOENIX.
MOUTH...WON'T MOVE. CAN'T... STAY CONSCIOUS. NO.
YOU CAN'T BE TAKEN TO A HOSPITAL.
YOU CAN'T LET THEM TAKE THE HELMET OFF.

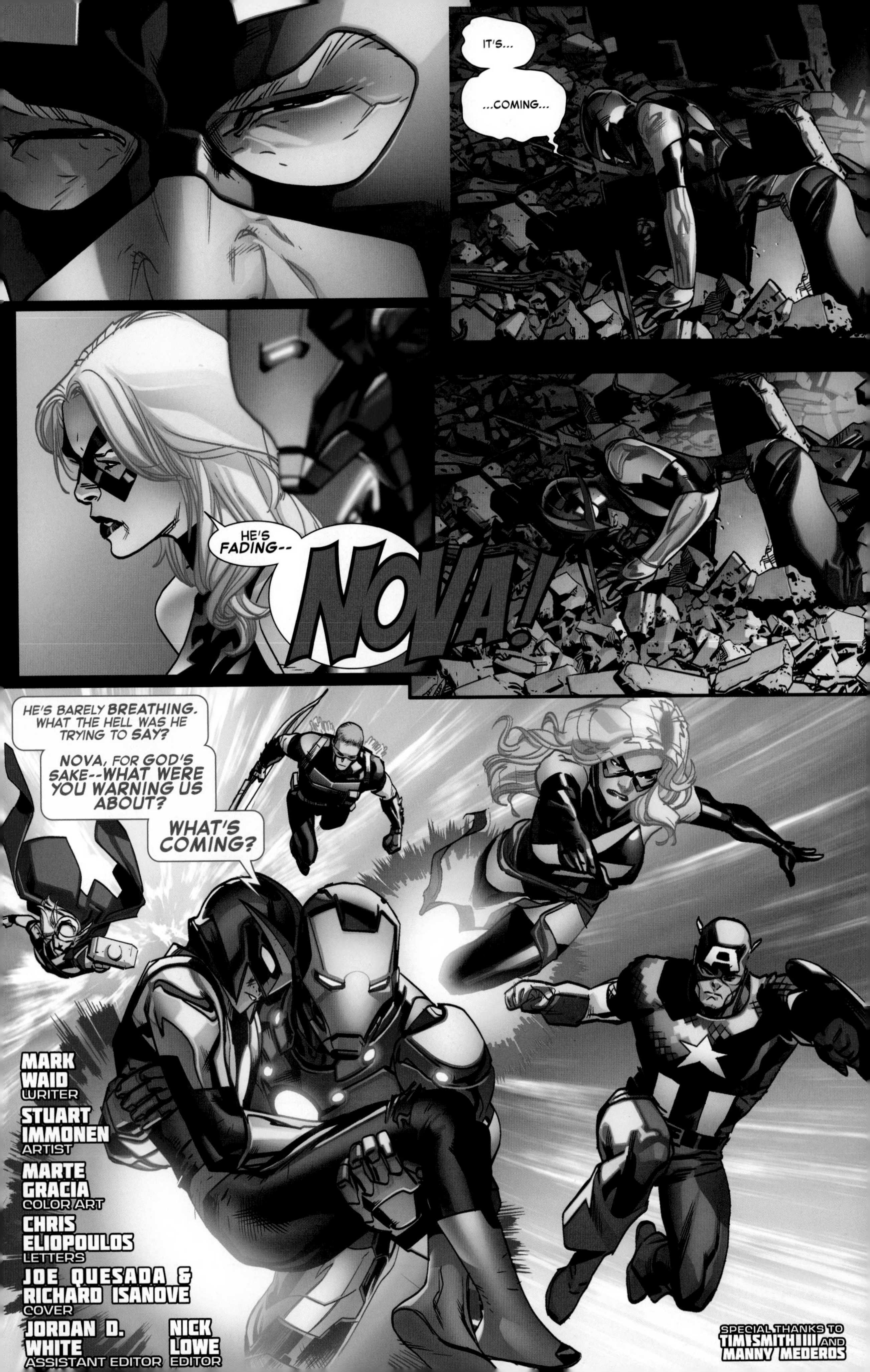
IT'S...
...COMING...
HE'S FADING--
NOVA!
HE'S BARELY BREATHING. WHAT THE HELL WAS HE TRYING TO SAY?
NOVA, FOR GOD'S SAKE--WHAT WERE YOU WARNING US ABOUT?
WHAT'S COMING?
MARK WAID WRITER
STUART IMMONEN ARTIST
MARTE GRACIA COLOR ART
CHRIS ELIOPOULOS LETTERS
JOE QUESADA & RICHARD ISANOVE COVER
JORDAN D. WHITE ASSISTANT EDITOR
NICK LOWE EDITOR
SPECIAL THANKS TO TIM SMITH III AND MANNY MEDEROS

AVENGERS VS X-MEN COMICS #6

"...IN A HANDFUL OF DUST"

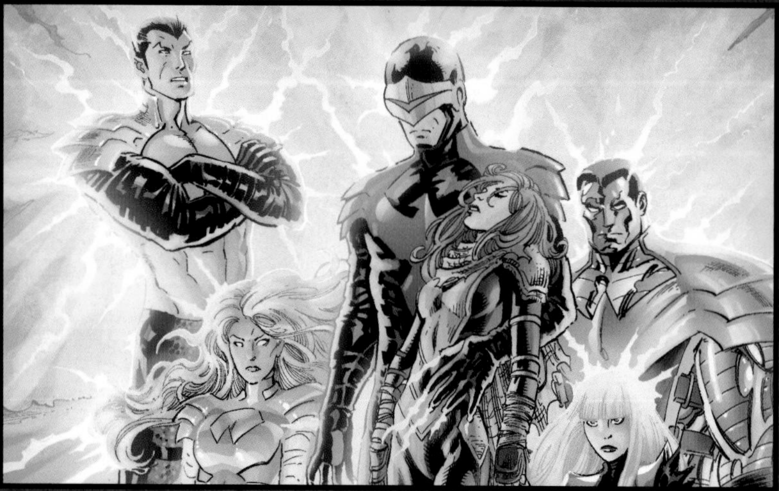

THE PHOENIX FIVE HAVE BEEN FORGED.

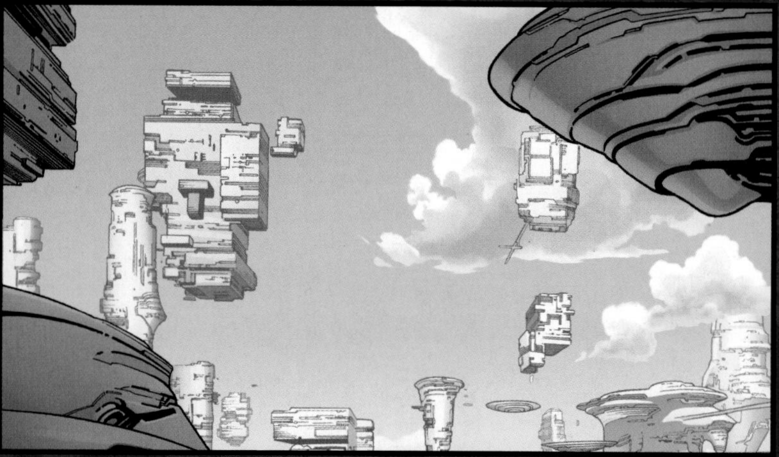

TOGETHER, THEY RECREATE THE WORLD IN THEIR IMAGE, STARTING WITH UTOPIA.

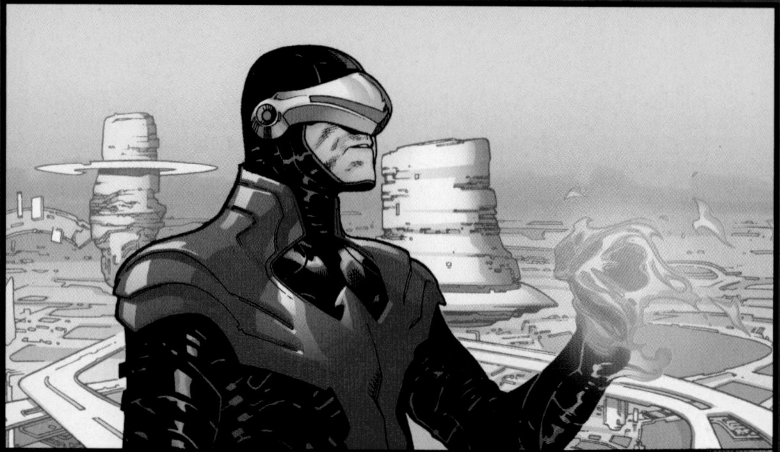

CYCLOPS LOOKS UPON THE NEW KINGDOM BEFORE HIM...

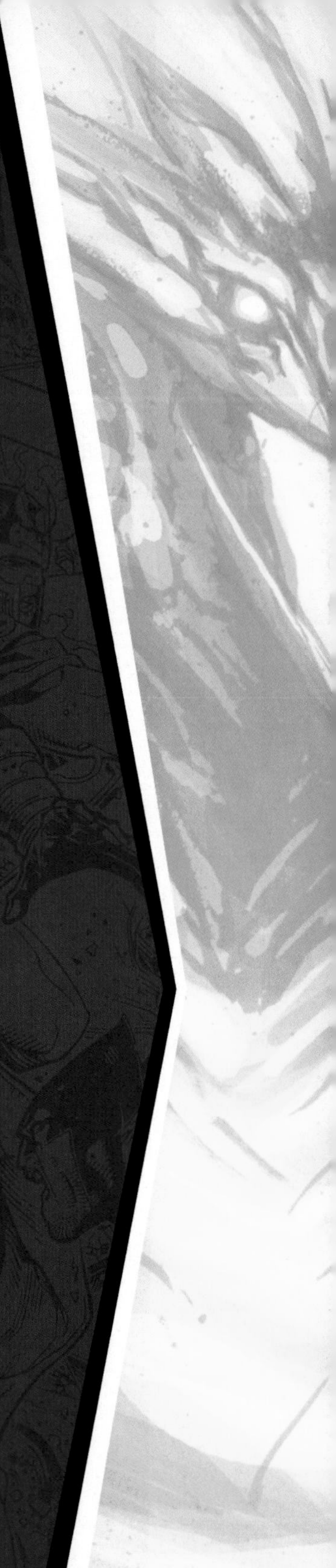

CO-PLOT & SCRIPT:
MARK WAID
CO-PLOT & BREAKDOWNS:
YVES BIGEREL
PENCILS & INKS:
CARLO BARBERI
COLORS: **MARTE GRACIA**
LETTERER:
CHRIS ELIOPOULOS
ASSISTANT EDITOR:
JORDAN D. WHITE
EDITOR: **NICK LOWE**

SPECIAL THANKS TO TIM SMITH III & MANNY MEDEROS

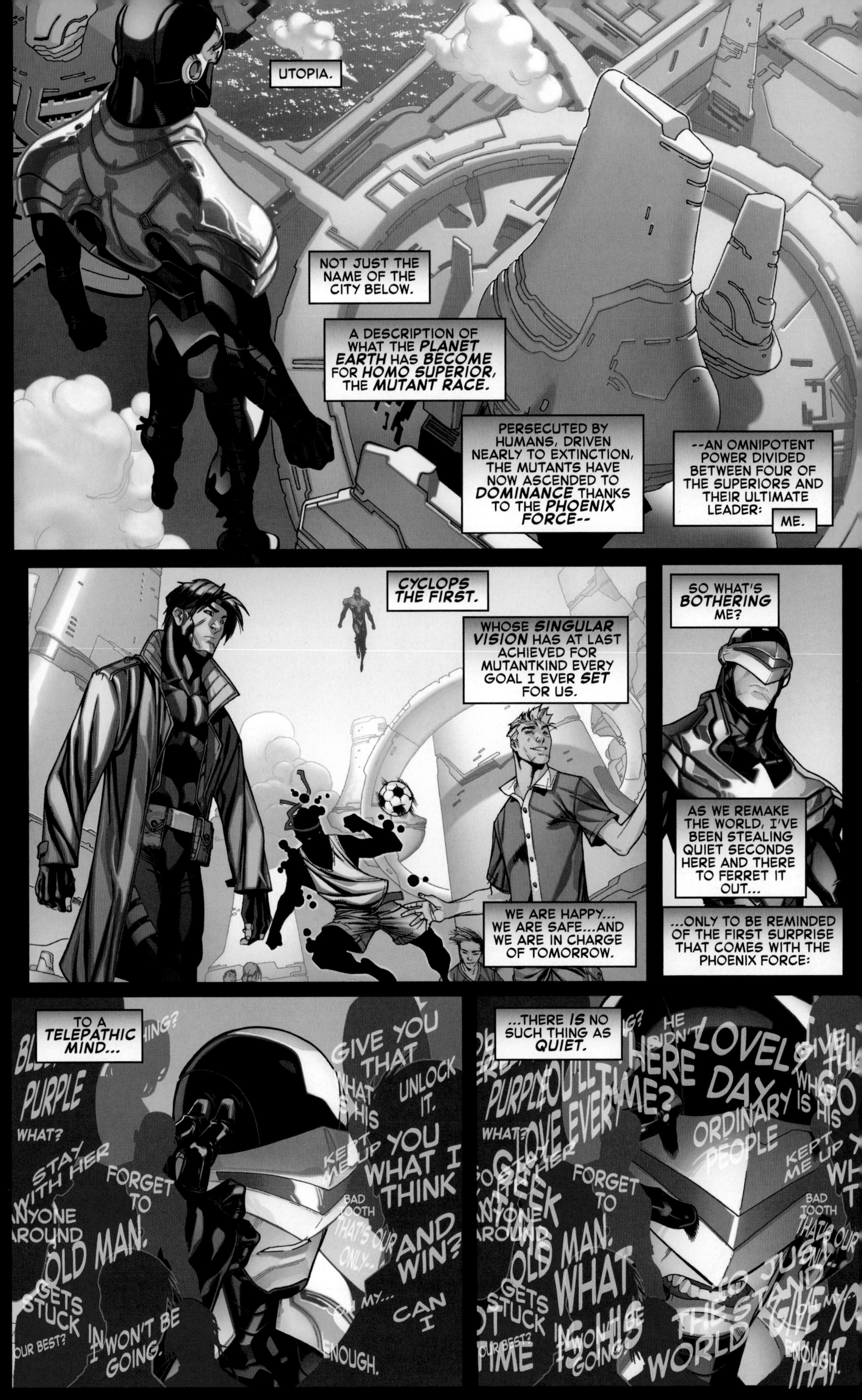
UTOPIA.
NOT JUST THE NAME OF THE CITY BELOW.
A DESCRIPTION OF WHAT THE PLANET EARTH HAS BECOME FOR HOMO SUPERIOR, THE MUTANT RACE.
PERSECUTED BY HUMANS, DRIVEN NEARLY TO EXTINCTION, THE MUTANTS HAVE NOW ASCENDED TO DOMINANCE THANKS TO THE PHOENIX FORCE--
--AN OMNIPOTENT POWER DIVIDED BETWEEN FOUR OF THE SUPERIORS AND THEIR ULTIMATE LEADER:
ME.
CYCLOPS THE FIRST.
WHOSE SINGULAR VISION HAS AT LAST ACHIEVED FOR MUTANTKIND EVERY GOAL I EVER SET FOR US.
WE ARE HAPPY... WE ARE SAFE...AND WE ARE IN CHARGE OF TOMORROW.
SO WHAT'S BOTHERING ME?
AS WE REMAKE THE WORLD, I'VE BEEN STEALING QUIET SECONDS HERE AND THERE TO FERRET IT OUT...
...ONLY TO BE REMINDED OF THE FIRST SURPRISE THAT COMES WITH THE PHOENIX FORCE:
TO A TELEPATHIC MIND...
PURPLE
WHAT?
STAY WITH HER
FORGET TO
ANYONE AROUND
OLD MAN.
GETS STUCK
I WON'T BE GOING.
GIVE YOU THAT
UNLOCK IT.
KEPT ME UP
YOU WHAT I THINK
BAD TOOTH
AND WIN?
CAN I
ENOUGH.
...THERE IS NO SUCH THING AS QUIET.
LOVELY DAY
ORDINARY PEOPLE
WHAT IS HIS
WORLD

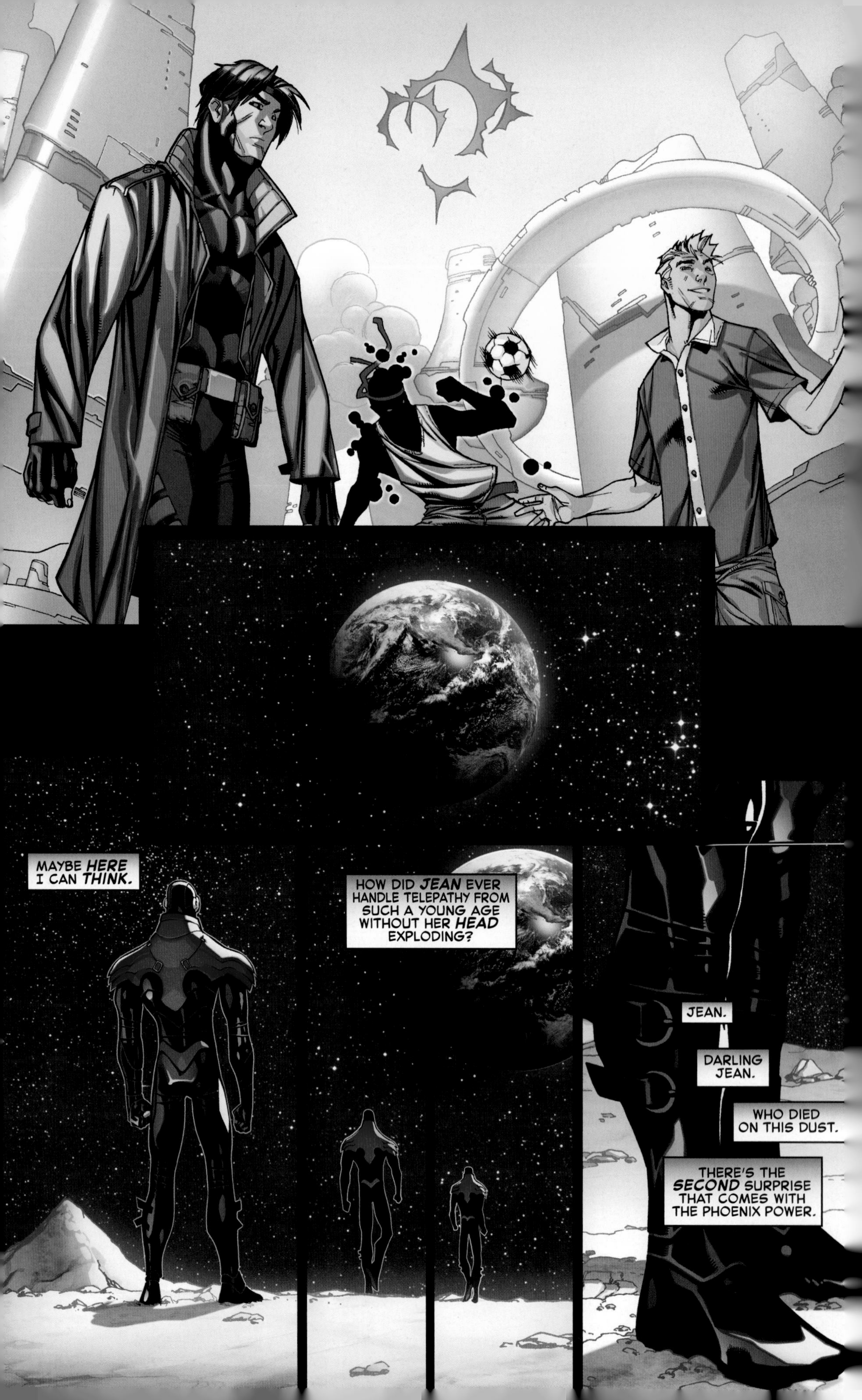
MAYBE HERE I CAN THINK.
HOW DID JEAN EVER HANDLE TELEPATHY FROM SUCH A YOUNG AGE WITHOUT HER HEAD EXPLODING?
JEAN.
DARLING JEAN.
WHO DIED ON THIS DUST.
THERE'S THE SECOND SURPRISE THAT COMES WITH THE PHOENIX POWER.

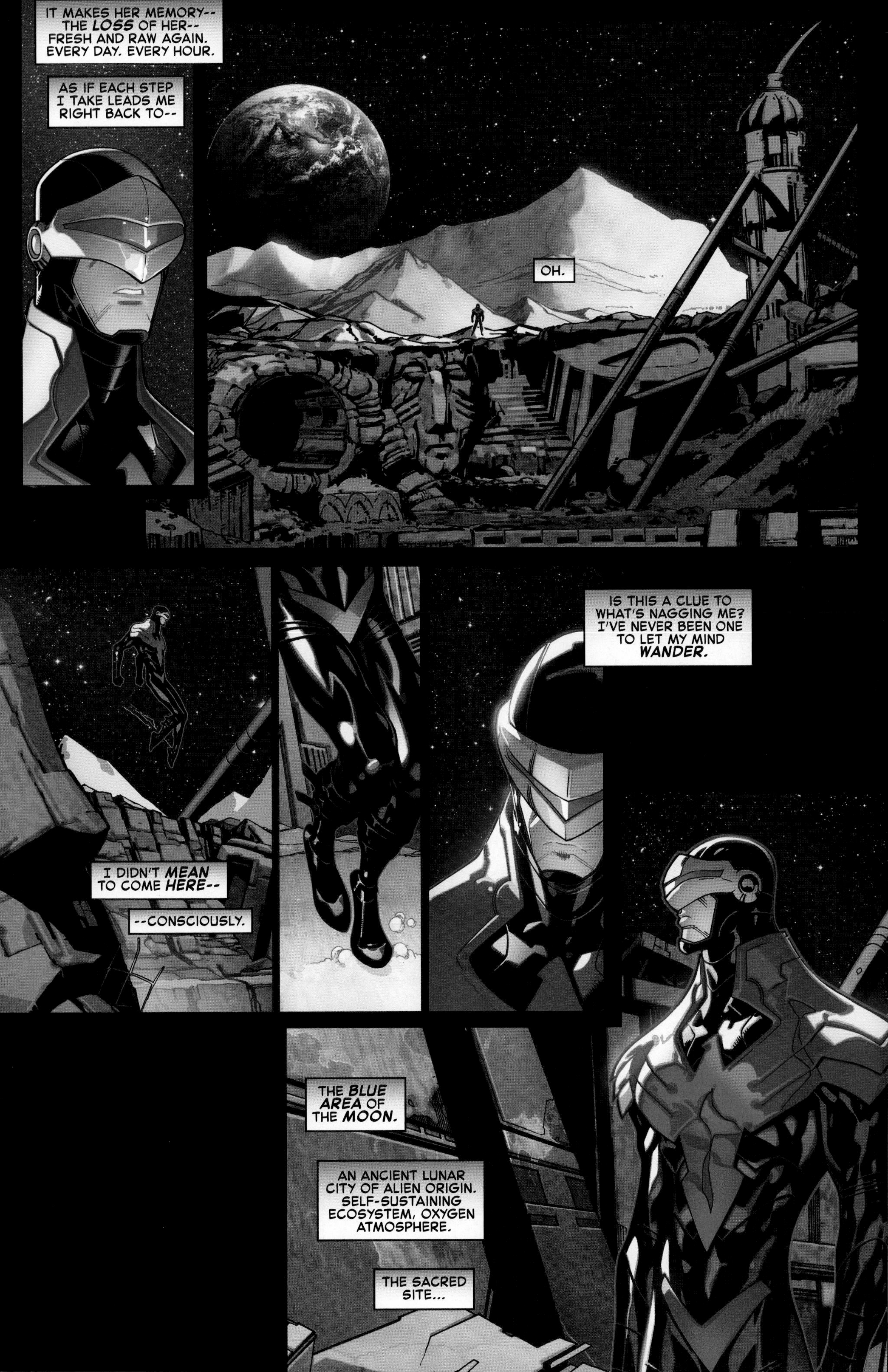
IT MAKES HER MEMORY-- THE LOSS OF HER-- FRESH AND RAW AGAIN. EVERY DAY. EVERY HOUR.
AS IF EACH STEP I TAKE LEADS ME RIGHT BACK TO--
OH.
I DIDN'T MEAN TO COME HERE--
--CONSCIOUSLY.
IS THIS A CLUE TO WHAT'S NAGGING ME? I'VE NEVER BEEN ONE TO LET MY MIND WANDER.
THE BLUE AREA OF THE MOON.
AN ANCIENT LUNAR CITY OF ALIEN ORIGIN. SELF-SUSTAINING ECOSYSTEM, OXYGEN ATMOSPHERE.
THE SACRED SITE...

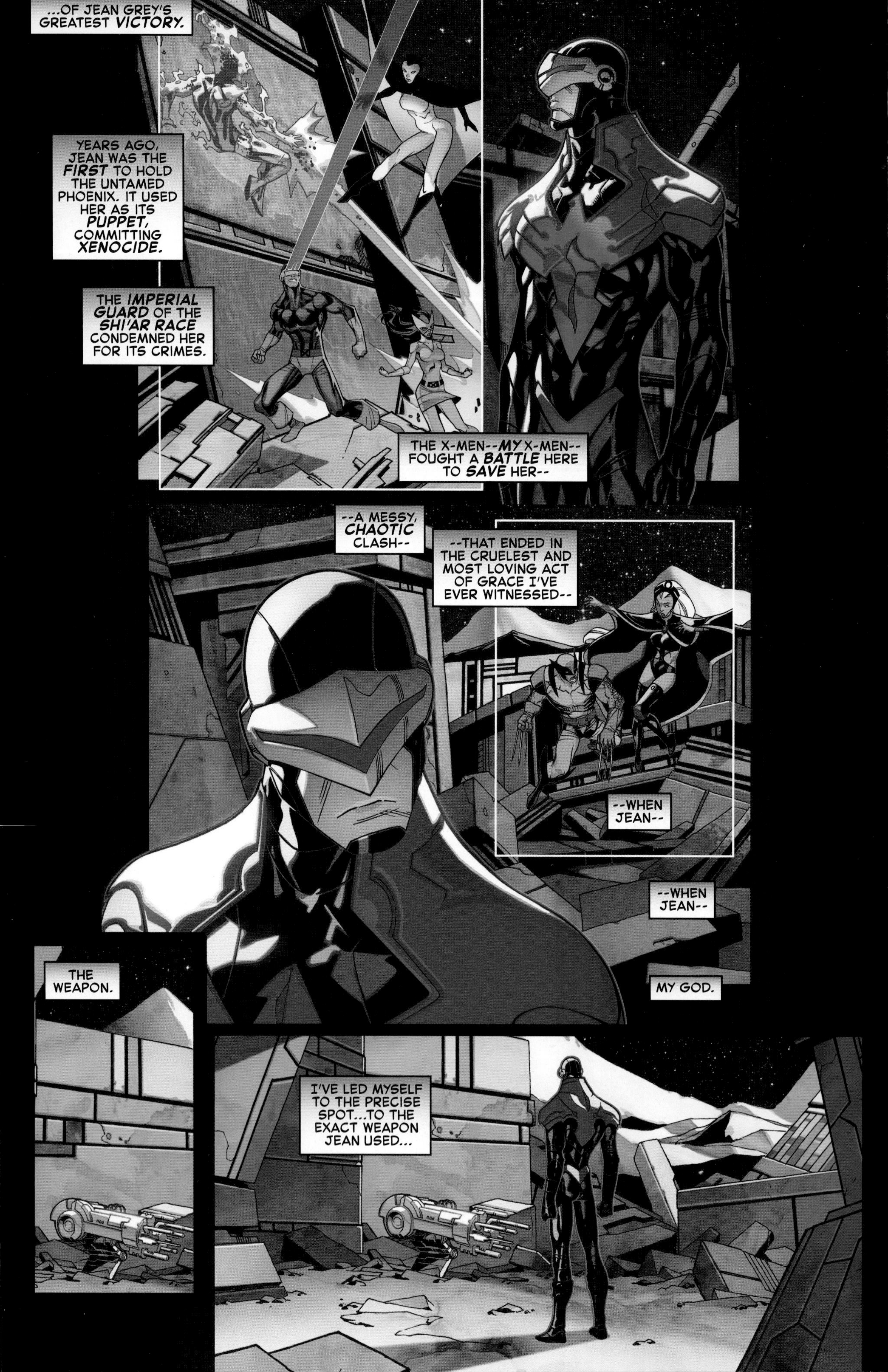

...OF JEAN GREY'S GREATEST VICTORY.
YEARS AGO, JEAN WAS THE FIRST TO HOLD THE UNTAMED PHOENIX. IT USED HER AS ITS PUPPET, COMMITTING XENOCIDE.
THE IMPERIAL GUARD OF THE SHI'AR RACE CONDEMNED HER FOR ITS CRIMES.
THE X-MEN--MY X-MEN--FOUGHT A BATTLE HERE TO SAVE HER--
--A MESSY, CHAOTIC CLASH--
--THAT ENDED IN THE CRUELEST AND MOST LOVING ACT OF GRACE I'VE EVER WITNESSED--
--WHEN JEAN--
--WHEN JEAN--
MY GOD.
THE WEAPON.
I'VE LED MYSELF TO THE PRECISE SPOT...TO THE EXACT WEAPON JEAN USED...

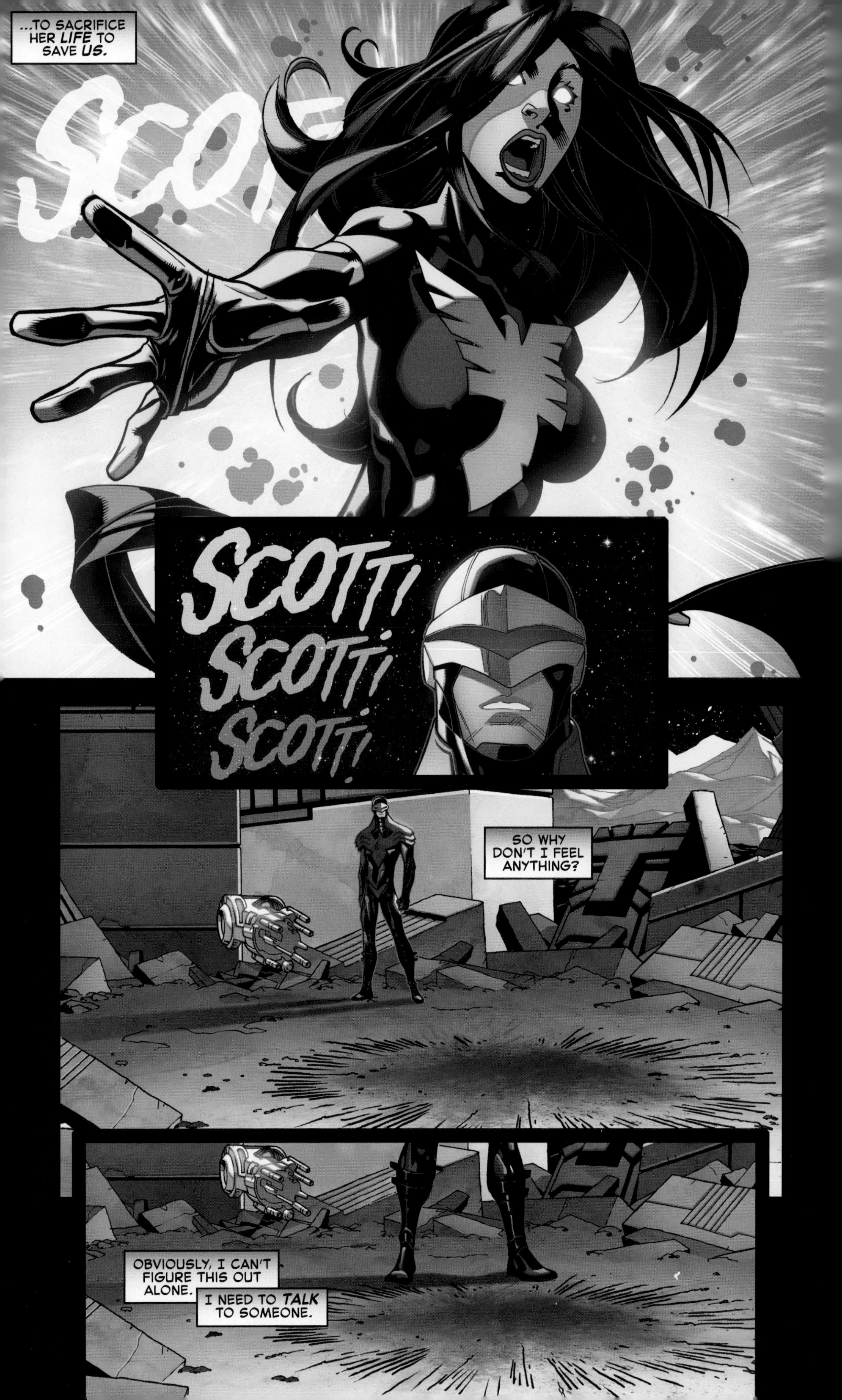

...TO SACRIFICE HER LIFE TO SAVE US.
SCO--
SCOTT! SCOTT! SCOTT!
SO WHY DON'T I FEEL ANYTHING?
OBVIOUSLY, I CAN'T FIGURE THIS OUT ALONE.
I NEED TO TALK TO SOMEONE.

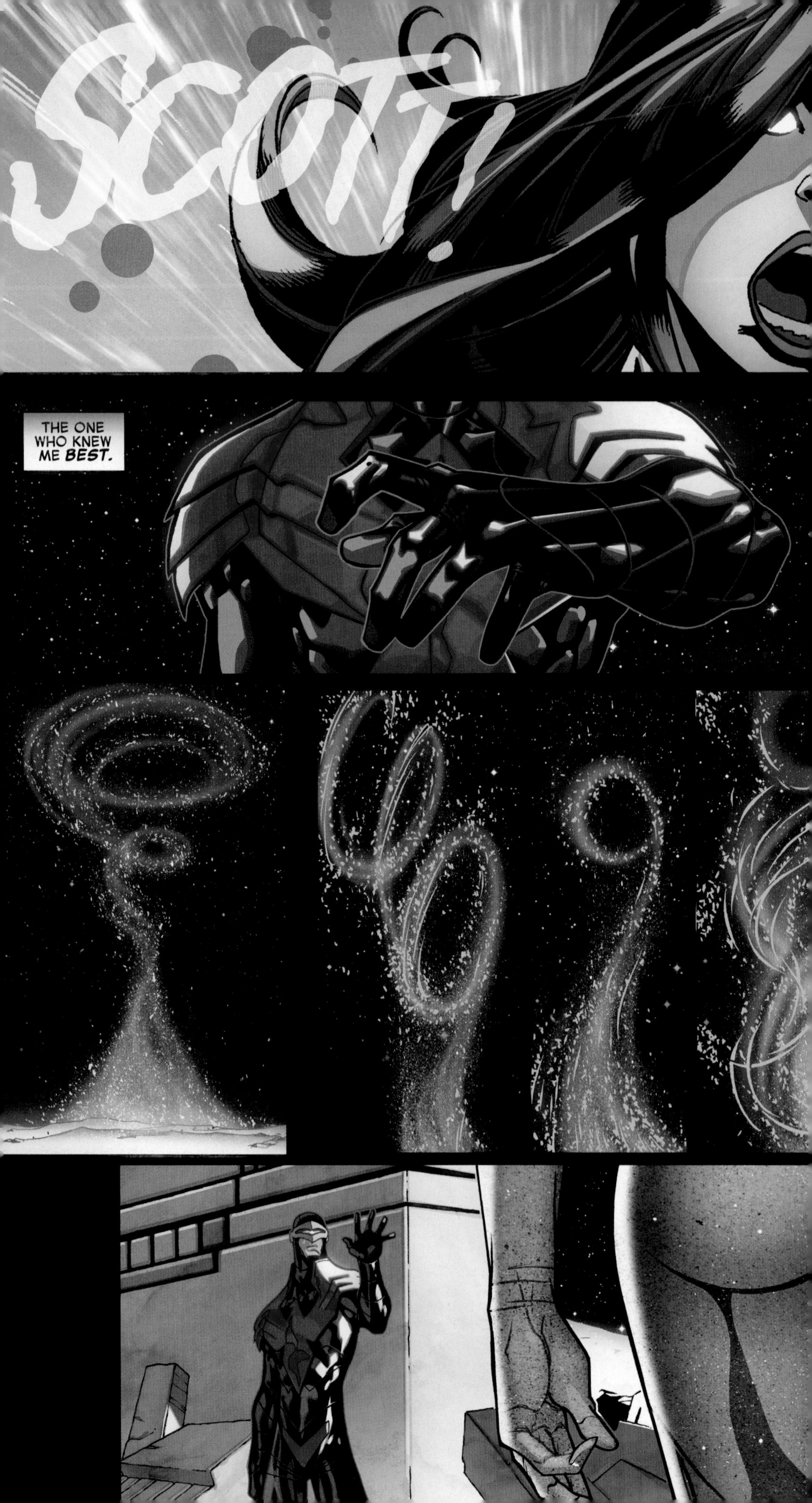
SCOTT!
THE ONE WHO KNEW ME BEST.

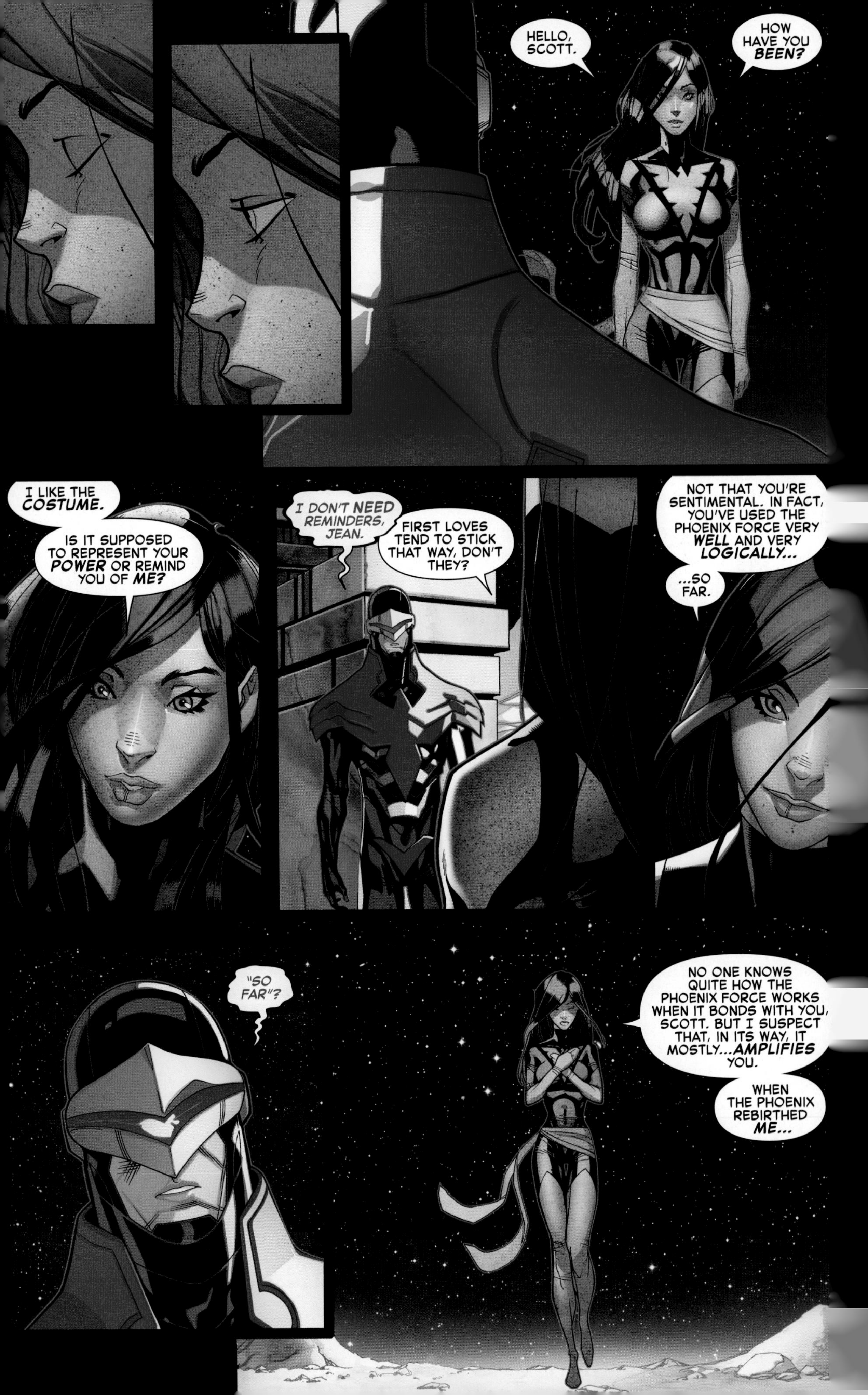

HELLO, SCOTT.
HOW HAVE YOU BEEN?
I LIKE THE COSTUME.
IS IT SUPPOSED TO REPRESENT YOUR POWER OR REMIND YOU OF ME?
I DON'T NEED REMINDERS, JEAN.
FIRST LOVES TEND TO STICK THAT WAY, DON'T THEY?
NOT THAT YOU'RE SENTIMENTAL. IN FACT, YOU'VE USED THE PHOENIX FORCE VERY WELL AND VERY LOGICALLY...
...SO FAR.
"SO FAR"?
NO ONE KNOWS QUITE HOW THE PHOENIX FORCE WORKS WHEN IT BONDS WITH YOU, SCOTT. BUT I SUSPECT THAT, IN ITS WAY, IT MOSTLY...AMPLIFIES YOU.
WHEN THE PHOENIX REBIRTHED ME...

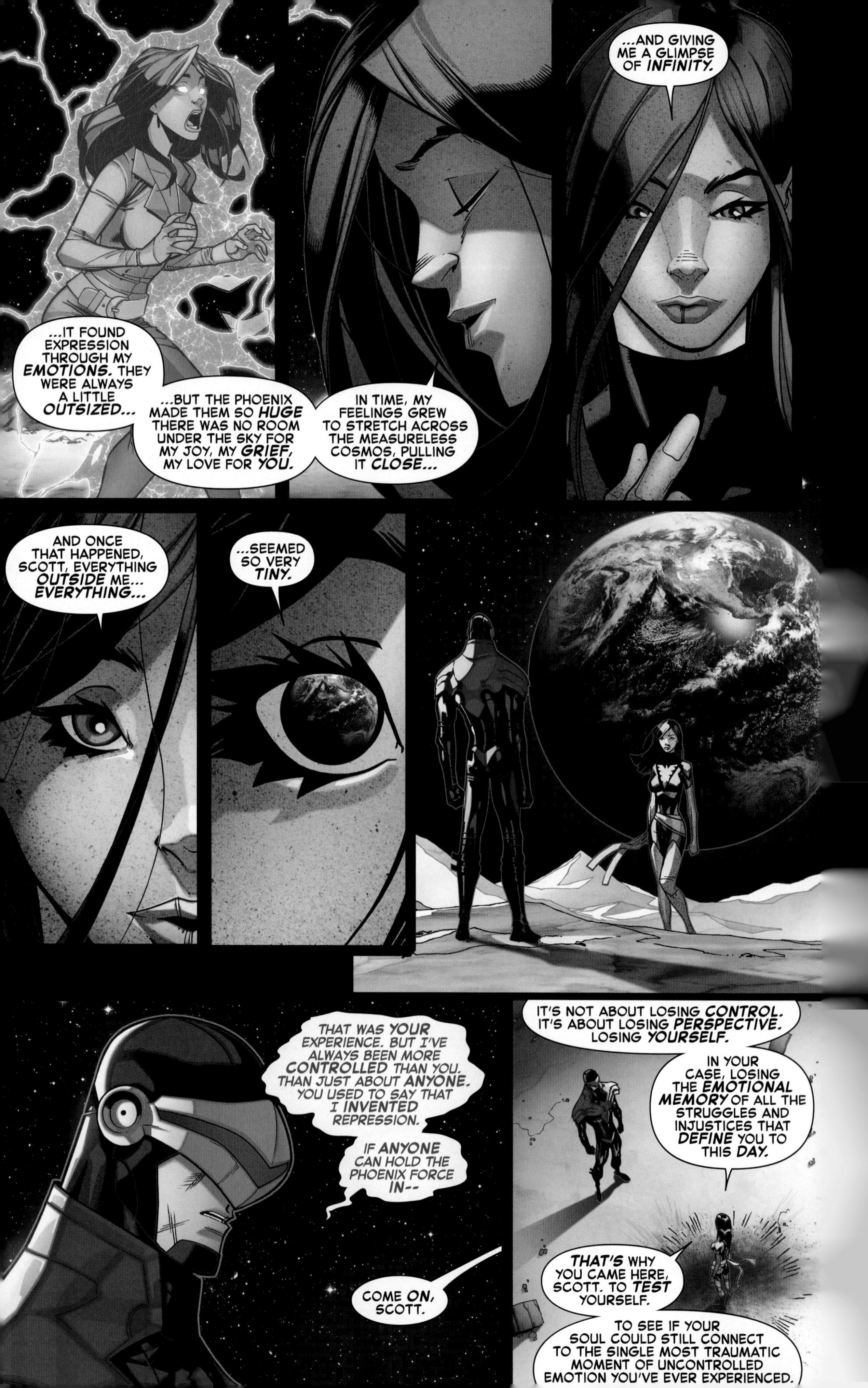
...IT FOUND EXPRESSION THROUGH MY EMOTIONS. THEY WERE ALWAYS A LITTLE OUTSIZED...
...BUT THE PHOENIX MADE THEM SO HUGE THERE WAS NO ROOM UNDER THE SKY FOR MY JOY, MY GRIEF, MY LOVE FOR YOU.
IN TIME, MY FEELINGS GREW TO STRETCH ACROSS THE MEASURELESS COSMOS, PULLING IT CLOSE...
...AND GIVING ME A GLIMPSE OF INFINITY.
AND ONCE THAT HAPPENED, SCOTT, EVERYTHING OUTSIDE ME... EVERYTHING...
...SEEMED SO VERY TINY.
THAT WAS YOUR EXPERIENCE. BUT I'VE ALWAYS BEEN MORE CONTROLLED THAN YOU. THAN JUST ABOUT ANYONE. YOU USED TO SAY THAT I INVENTED REPRESSION.
IF ANYONE CAN HOLD THE PHOENIX FORCE IN--
COME ON, SCOTT.
IT'S NOT ABOUT LOSING CONTROL. IT'S ABOUT LOSING PERSPECTIVE. LOSING YOURSELF.
IN YOUR CASE, LOSING THE EMOTIONAL MEMORY OF ALL THE STRUGGLES AND INJUSTICES THAT DEFINE YOU TO THIS DAY.
THAT'S WHY YOU CAME HERE, SCOTT. TO TEST YOURSELF.
TO SEE IF YOUR SOUL COULD STILL CONNECT TO THE SINGLE MOST TRAUMATIC MOMENT OF UNCONTROLLED EMOTION YOU'VE EVER EXPERIENCED.

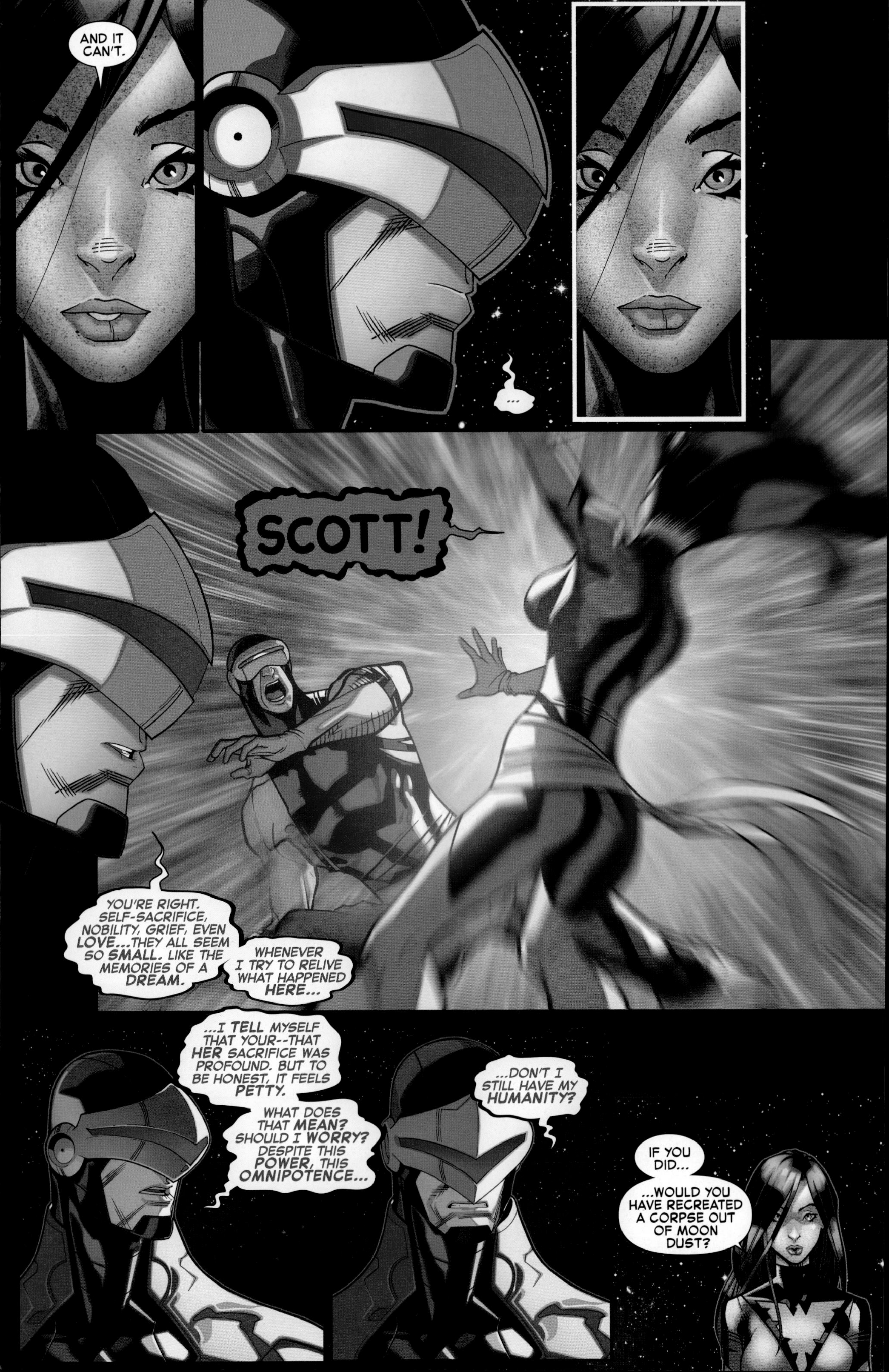
AND IT CAN'T.
...
SCOTT!
YOU'RE RIGHT. SELF-SACRIFICE, NOBILITY, GRIEF, EVEN LOVE...THEY ALL SEEM SO SMALL. LIKE THE MEMORIES OF A DREAM.
WHENEVER I TRY TO RELIVE WHAT HAPPENED HERE...
...I TELL MYSELF THAT YOUR--THAT HER SACRIFICE WAS PROFOUND. BUT TO BE HONEST, IT FEELS PETTY.
WHAT DOES THAT MEAN? SHOULD I WORRY? DESPITE THIS POWER, THIS OMNIPOTENCE...
...DON'T I STILL HAVE MY HUMANITY?
IF YOU DID...
...WOULD YOU HAVE RECREATED A CORPSE OUT OF MOON DUST?

THAT WAS ONE HELL OF A WAKE-UP CALL.

BUT IT DID THE TRICK.

BECAUSE IF I LOSE SIGHT OF *THAT*...

...WHAT'S IT ALL BEEN *FOR?*

I KNOW NOW THAT I HAVE TO BE *VIGILANT.* I *CANNOT*-- I *WILL* NOT--LET THE PHOENIX *CHANGE* ME.

INSIDE ALL THIS POWER, I HAVE TO PRESERVE THE *MAN* I'VE ALWAYS BEEN.

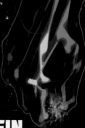

FIN.

AVENGERS VS X-MEN

INFINITE COMICS #10

"HOPELESS"

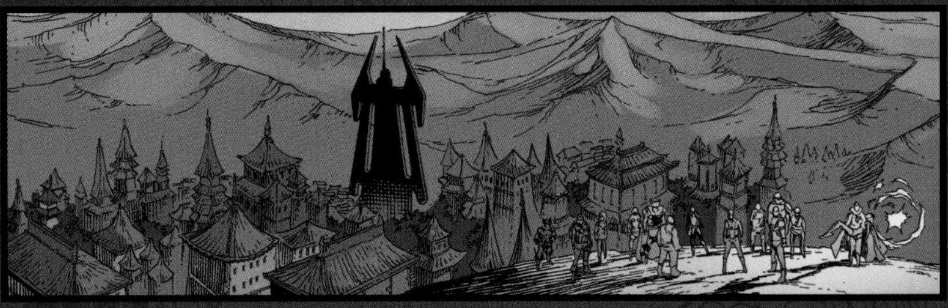

THE AVENGERS HAVE ESCAPED TO K'UN LUN, HIDDEN CITY OF KUNG FU.

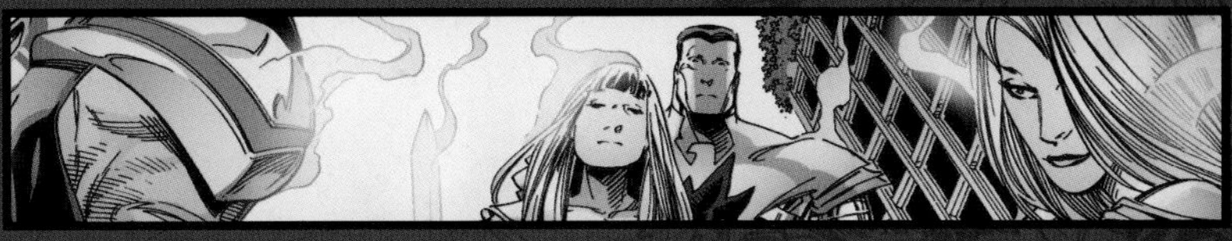

THE PHOENIX POWERED X-MEN WILL NOT REST IN HUNTING THEM DOWN.

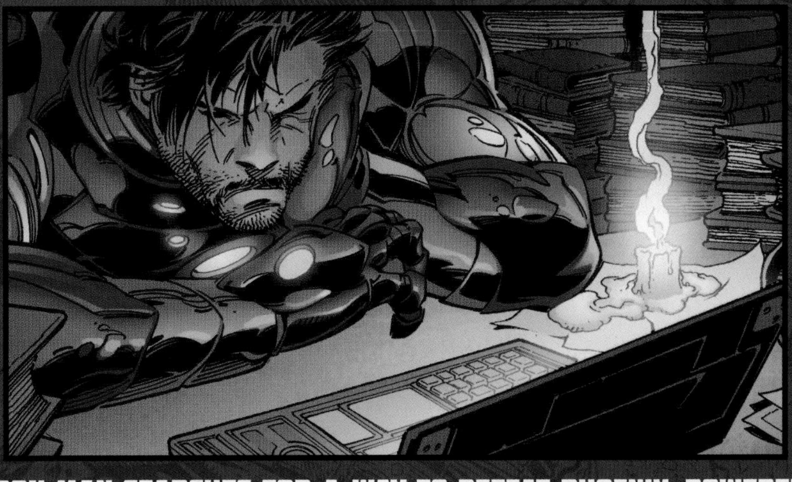

IRON MAN SEARCHES FOR A WAY TO DEFEAT PHOENIX-POWERED CYCLOPS WHEN HE ULTIMATELY REACHES K'UN LUN.

CO-PLOT & SCRIPT:
MARK WAID
CO-PLOT & BREAKDOWNS:
YVES BIGEREL
PENCILS & INKS:
REILLY BROWN
COLORS: **MARTE GRACIA**
& **CHRIS SOTOMAYOR**
LETTERER:
CHRIS ELIOPOULOS
ASSISTANT EDITOR:
JORDAN D. WHITE
EDITOR: **NICK LOWE**
SPECIAL THANKS TO TIM SMITH III
& MANNY MEDEROS

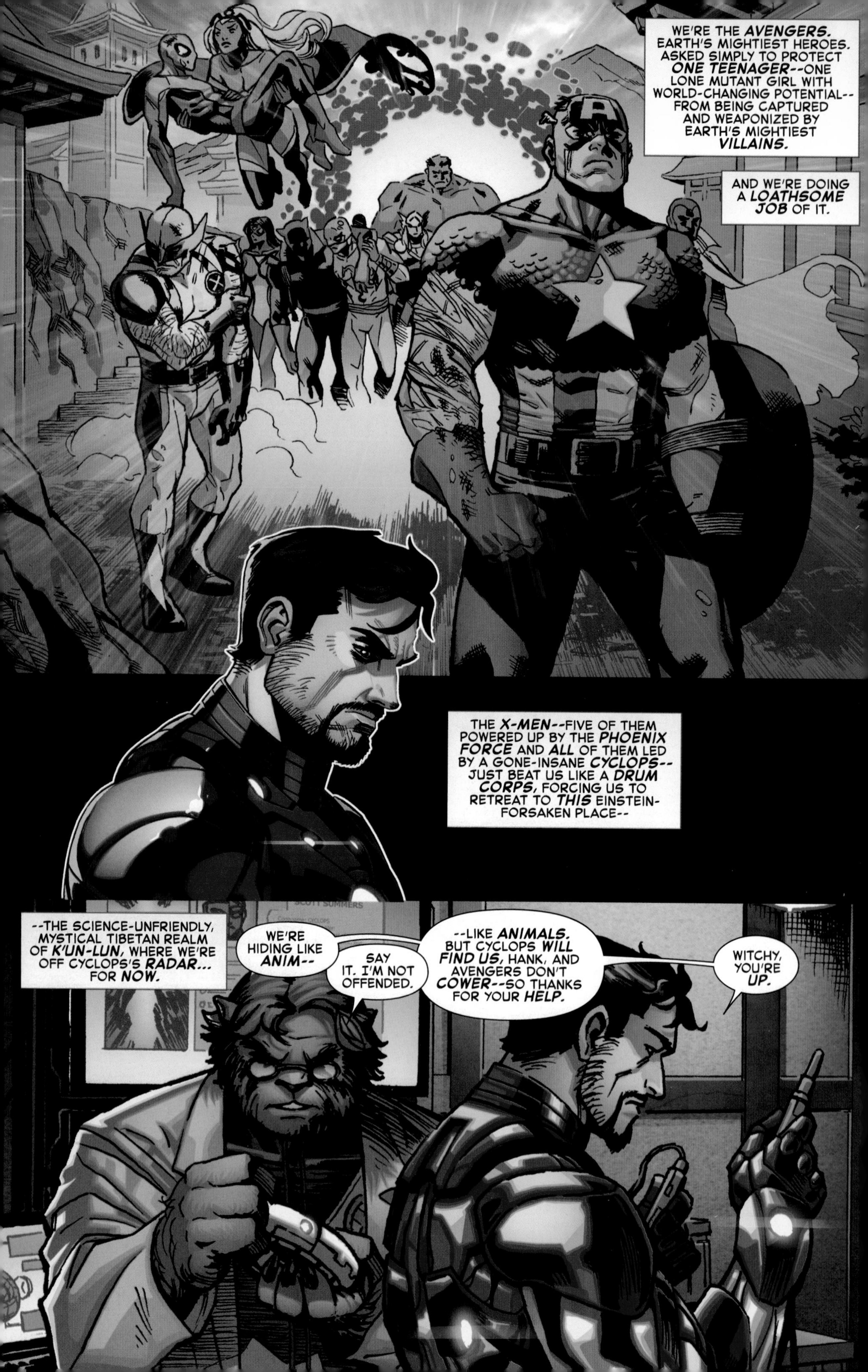
WE'RE THE AVENGERS. EARTH'S MIGHTIEST HEROES. ASKED SIMPLY TO PROTECT ONE TEENAGER--ONE LONE MUTANT GIRL WITH WORLD-CHANGING POTENTIAL--FROM BEING CAPTURED AND WEAPONIZED BY EARTH'S MIGHTIEST VILLAINS.
AND WE'RE DOING A LOATHSOME JOB OF IT.
THE X-MEN--FIVE OF THEM POWERED UP BY THE PHOENIX FORCE AND ALL OF THEM LED BY A GONE-INSANE CYCLOPS--JUST BEAT US LIKE A DRUM CORPS, FORCING US TO RETREAT TO THIS EINSTEIN-FORSAKEN PLACE--
--THE SCIENCE-UNFRIENDLY, MYSTICAL TIBETAN REALM OF K'UN-LUN, WHERE WE'RE OFF CYCLOPS'S RADAR... FOR NOW.
WE'RE HIDING LIKE ANIM--
SAY IT. I'M NOT OFFENDED.
--LIKE ANIMALS. BUT CYCLOPS WILL FIND US, HANK, AND AVENGERS DON'T COWER--SO THANKS FOR YOUR HELP.
WITCHY, YOU'RE UP.

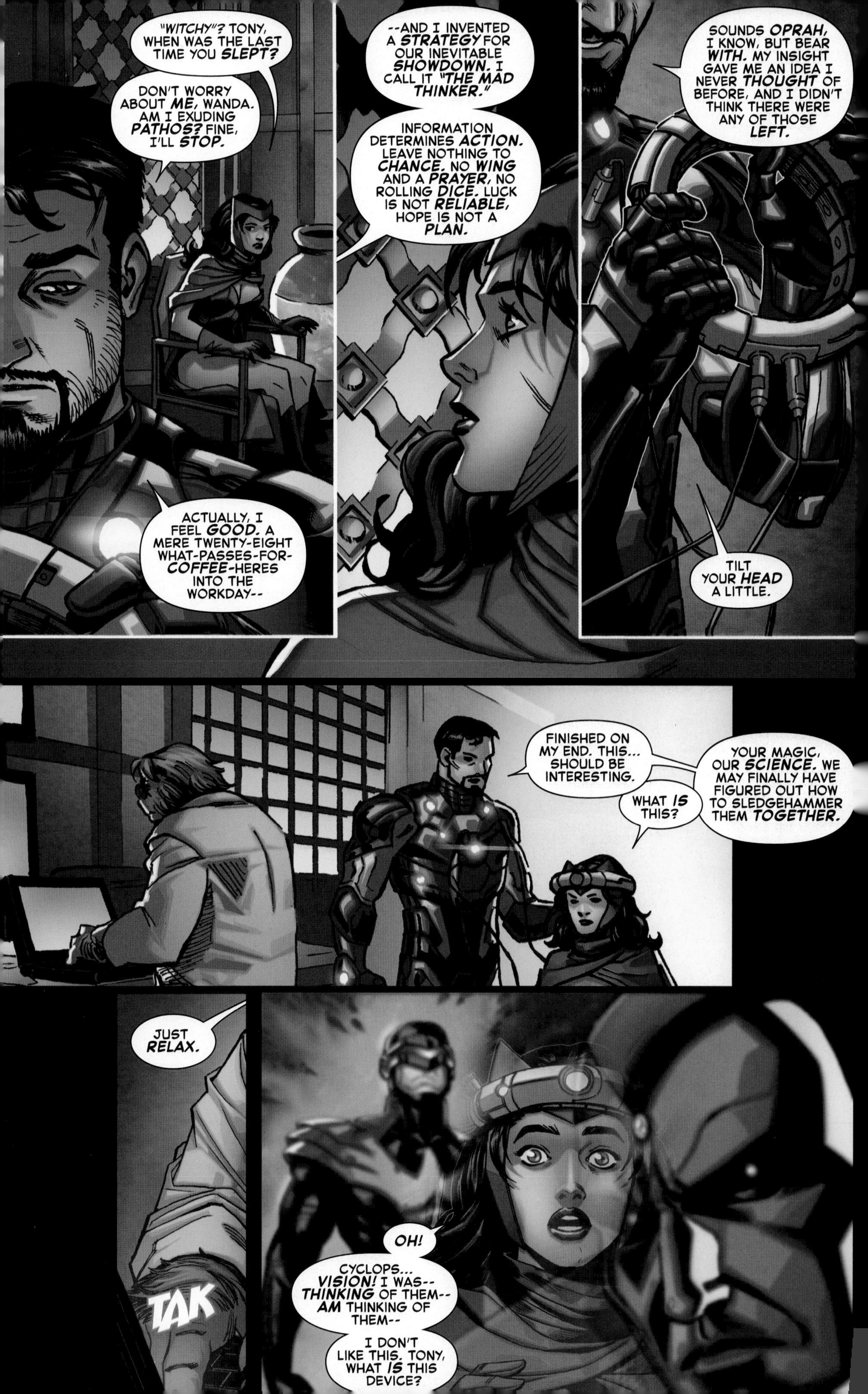
"WITCHY"? TONY, WHEN WAS THE LAST TIME YOU SLEPT?
DON'T WORRY ABOUT ME, WANDA. AM I EXUDING PATHOS? FINE, I'LL STOP.
ACTUALLY, I FEEL GOOD. A MERE TWENTY-EIGHT WHAT-PASSES-FOR-COFFEE-HERES INTO THE WORKDAY--
--AND I INVENTED A STRATEGY FOR OUR INEVITABLE SHOWDOWN. I CALL IT "THE MAD THINKER."
INFORMATION DETERMINES ACTION. LEAVE NOTHING TO CHANCE. NO WING AND A PRAYER, NO ROLLING DICE. LUCK IS NOT RELIABLE, HOPE IS NOT A PLAN.
SOUNDS OPRAH, I KNOW, BUT BEAR WITH. MY INSIGHT GAVE ME AN IDEA I NEVER THOUGHT OF BEFORE, AND I DIDN'T THINK THERE WERE ANY OF THOSE LEFT.
TILT YOUR HEAD A LITTLE.
FINISHED ON MY END. THIS... SHOULD BE INTERESTING.
WHAT IS THIS?
YOUR MAGIC, OUR SCIENCE. WE MAY FINALLY HAVE FIGURED OUT HOW TO SLEDGEHAMMER THEM TOGETHER.
JUST RELAX.
TAK
OH!
CYCLOPS... VISION! I WAS--THINKING OF THEM--AM THINKING OF THEM--
I DON'T LIKE THIS. TONY, WHAT IS THIS DEVICE?

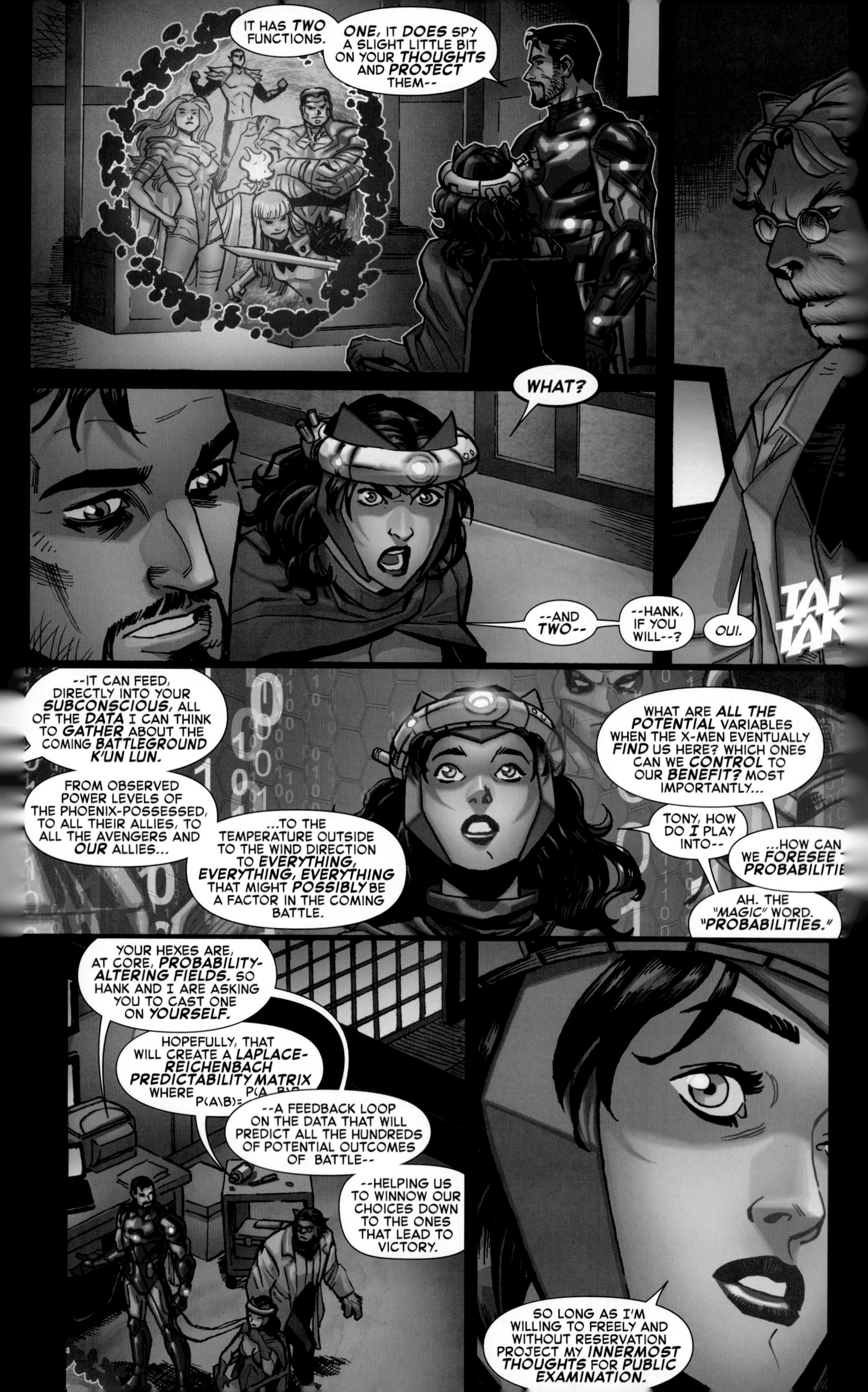
IT HAS TWO FUNCTIONS.
ONE, IT DOES SPY A SLIGHT LITTLE BIT ON YOUR THOUGHTS AND PROJECT THEM--
WHAT?
--AND TWO--
--HANK, IF YOU WILL--?
OUI.
--IT CAN FEED, DIRECTLY INTO YOUR SUBCONSCIOUS, ALL OF THE DATA I CAN THINK TO GATHER ABOUT THE COMING BATTLEGROUND K'UN LUN.
FROM OBSERVED POWER LEVELS OF THE PHOENIX-POSSESSED, TO ALL THEIR ALLIES, TO ALL THE AVENGERS AND OUR ALLIES...
...TO THE TEMPERATURE OUTSIDE TO THE WIND DIRECTION TO EVERYTHING, EVERYTHING, EVERYTHING THAT MIGHT POSSIBLY BE A FACTOR IN THE COMING BATTLE.
WHAT ARE ALL THE POTENTIAL VARIABLES WHEN THE X-MEN EVENTUALLY FIND US HERE? WHICH ONES CAN WE CONTROL TO OUR BENEFIT? MOST IMPORTANTLY...
TONY, HOW DO I PLAY INTO--
AH. THE "MAGIC" WORD. "PROBABILITIES."
YOUR HEXES ARE, AT CORE, PROBABILITY-ALTERING FIELDS. SO HANK AND I ARE ASKING YOU TO CAST ONE ON YOURSELF.
HOPEFULLY, THAT WILL CREATE A LAPLACE-REICHENBACH PREDICTABILITY MATRIX WHERE
--A FEEDBACK LOOP ON THE DATA THAT WILL PREDICT ALL THE HUNDREDS OF POTENTIAL OUTCOMES OF BATTLE--
--HELPING US TO WINNOW OUR CHOICES DOWN TO THE ONES THAT LEAD TO VICTORY.
SO LONG AS I'M WILLING TO FREELY AND WITHOUT RESERVATION PROJECT MY INNERMOST THOUGHTS FOR PUBLIC EXAMINATION.

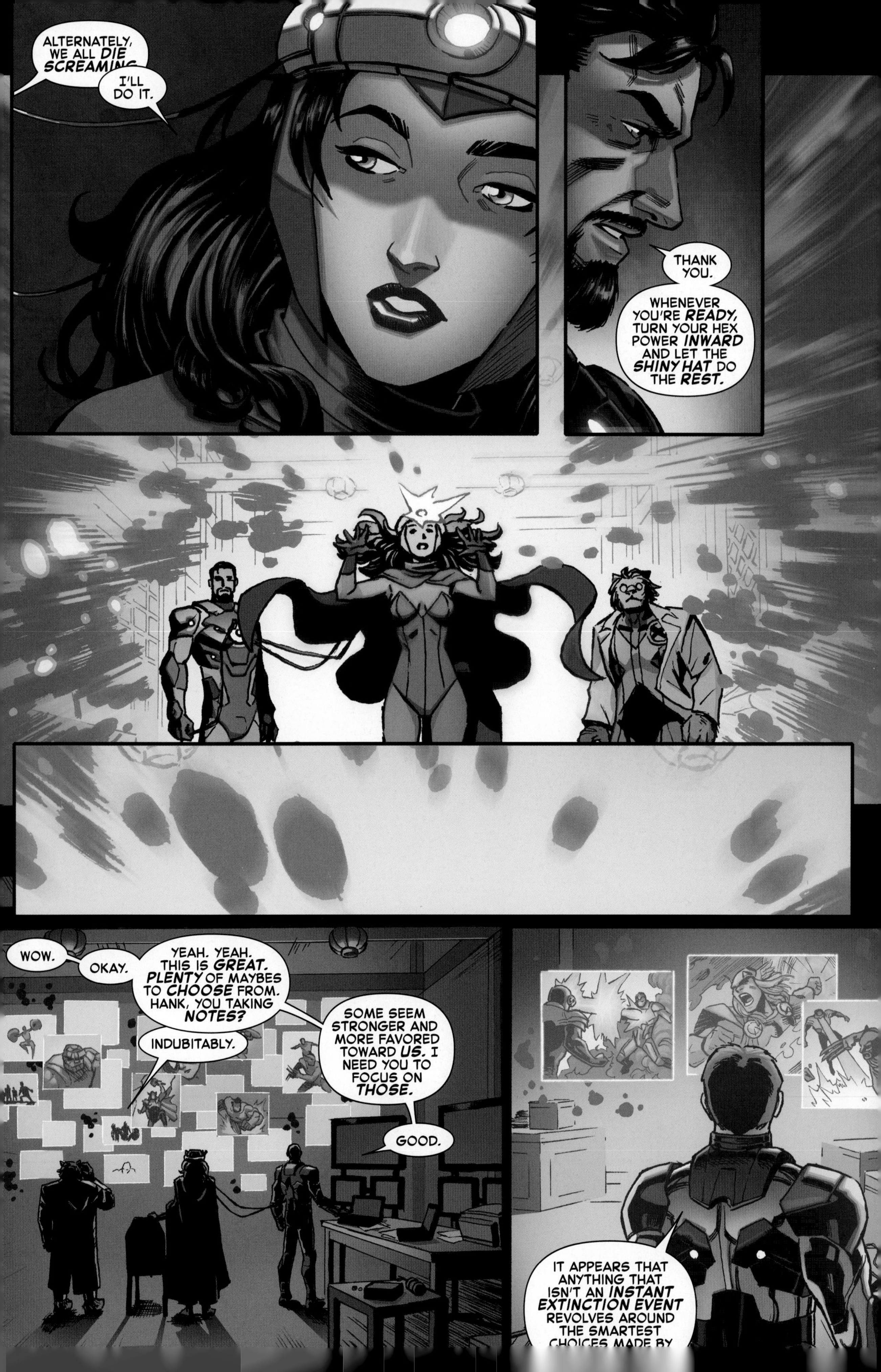

ALTERNATELY, WE ALL DIE SCREAMING.
I'LL DO IT.
THANK YOU.
WHENEVER YOU'RE READY, TURN YOUR HEX POWER INWARD AND LET THE SHINY HAT DO THE REST.
WOW.
OKAY.
YEAH. YEAH. THIS IS GREAT. PLENTY OF MAYBES TO CHOOSE FROM. HANK, YOU TAKING NOTES?
INDUBITABLY.
SOME SEEM STRONGER AND MORE FAVORED TOWARD US. I NEED YOU TO FOCUS ON THOSE.
GOOD.
IT APPEARS THAT ANYTHING THAT ISN'T AN INSTANT EXTINCTION EVENT REVOLVES AROUND THE SMARTEST CHOICES MADE BY

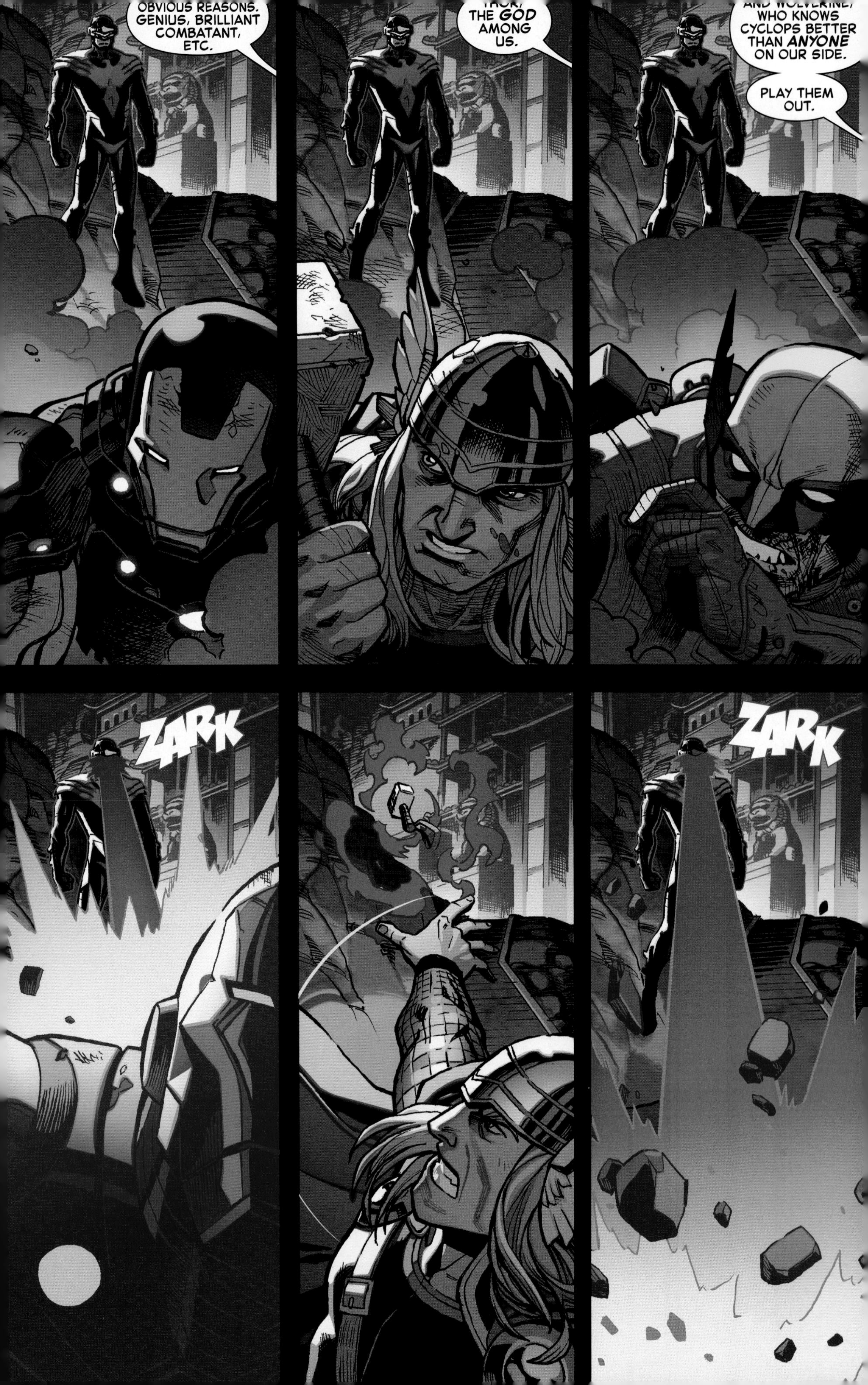
OBVIOUS REASONS. GENIUS, BRILLIANT COMBATANT, ETC.
THE GOD AMONG US.
WHO KNOWS CYCLOPS BETTER THAN ANYONE ON OUR SIDE.
PLAY THEM OUT.
ZARK
ZARK

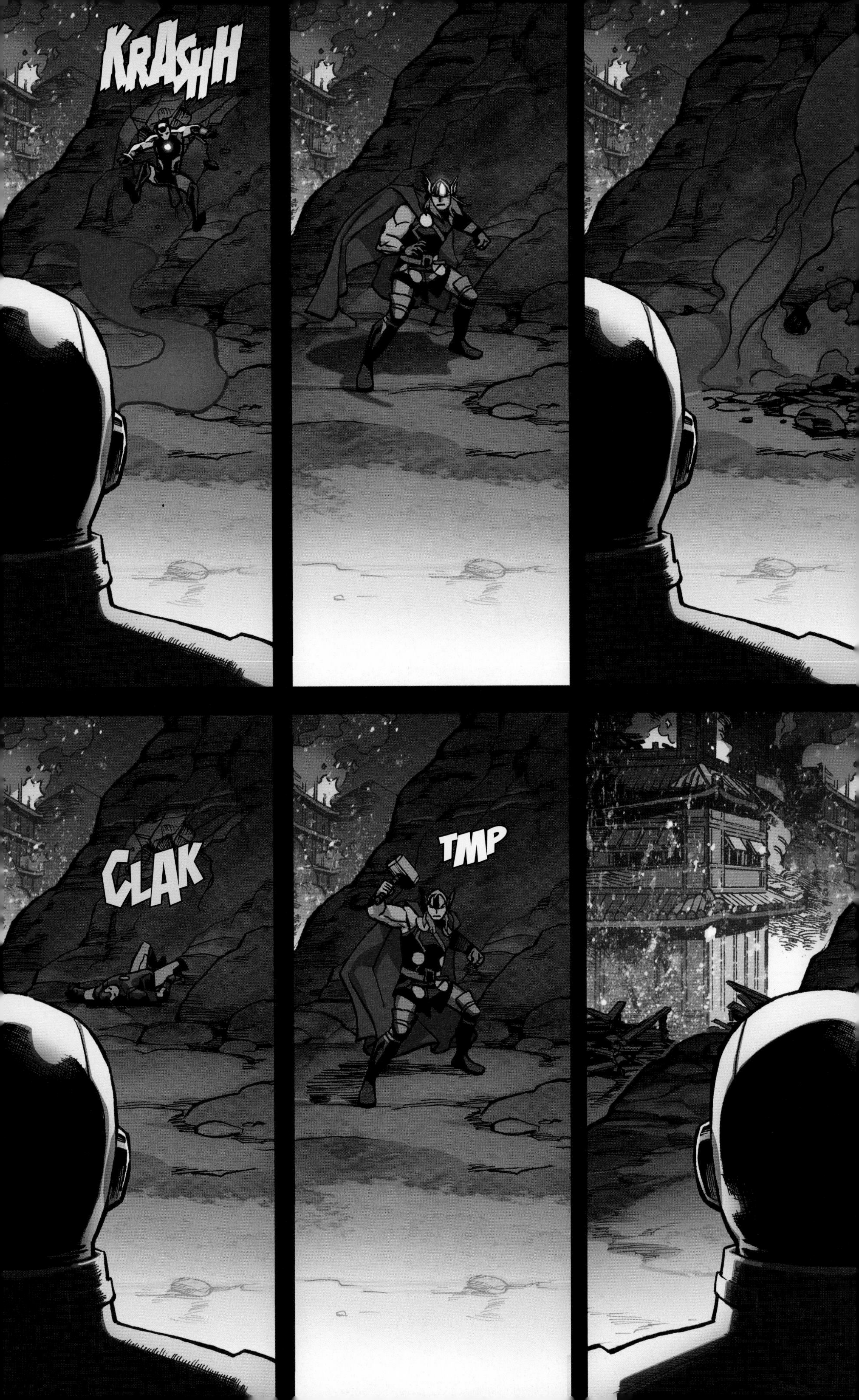
KRASHH
CLAK
TMP

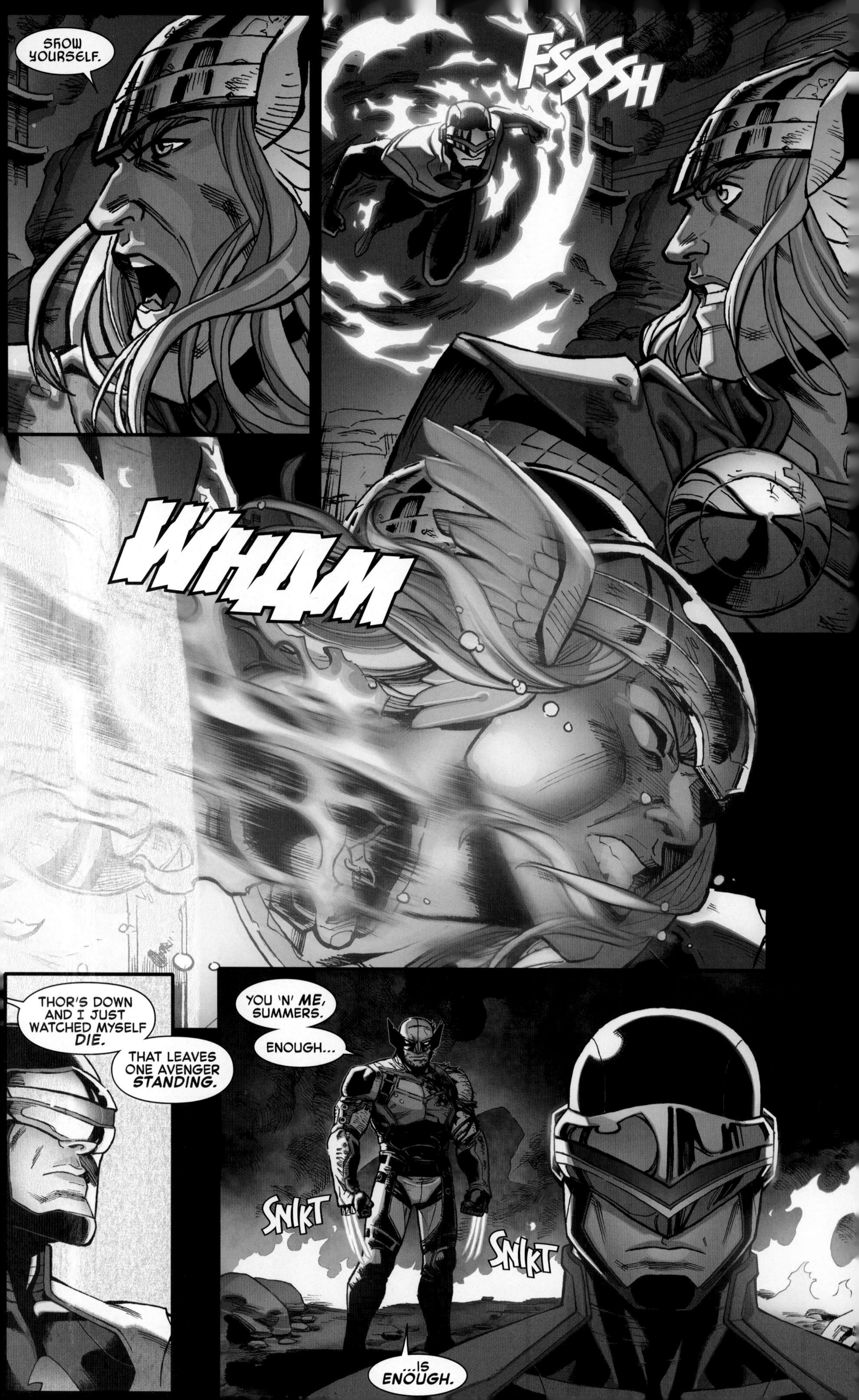
SHOW YOURSELF.
FSSSSH
WHAM
THOR'S DOWN AND I JUST WATCHED MYSELF DIE.
THAT LEAVES ONE AVENGER STANDING.
YOU 'N' ME, SUMMERS.
ENOUGH...
SNIKT
SNIKT
...IS ENOUGH.

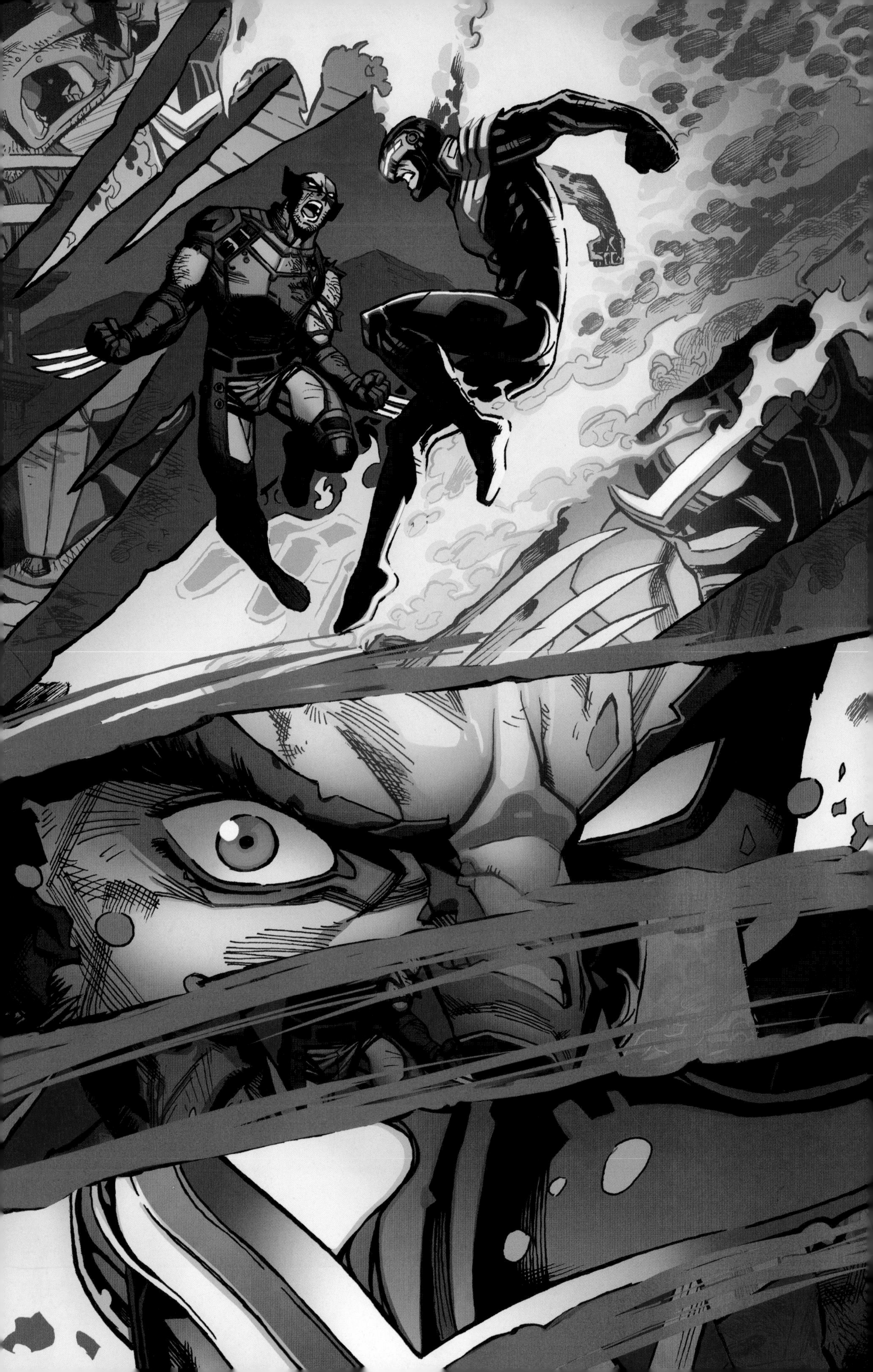

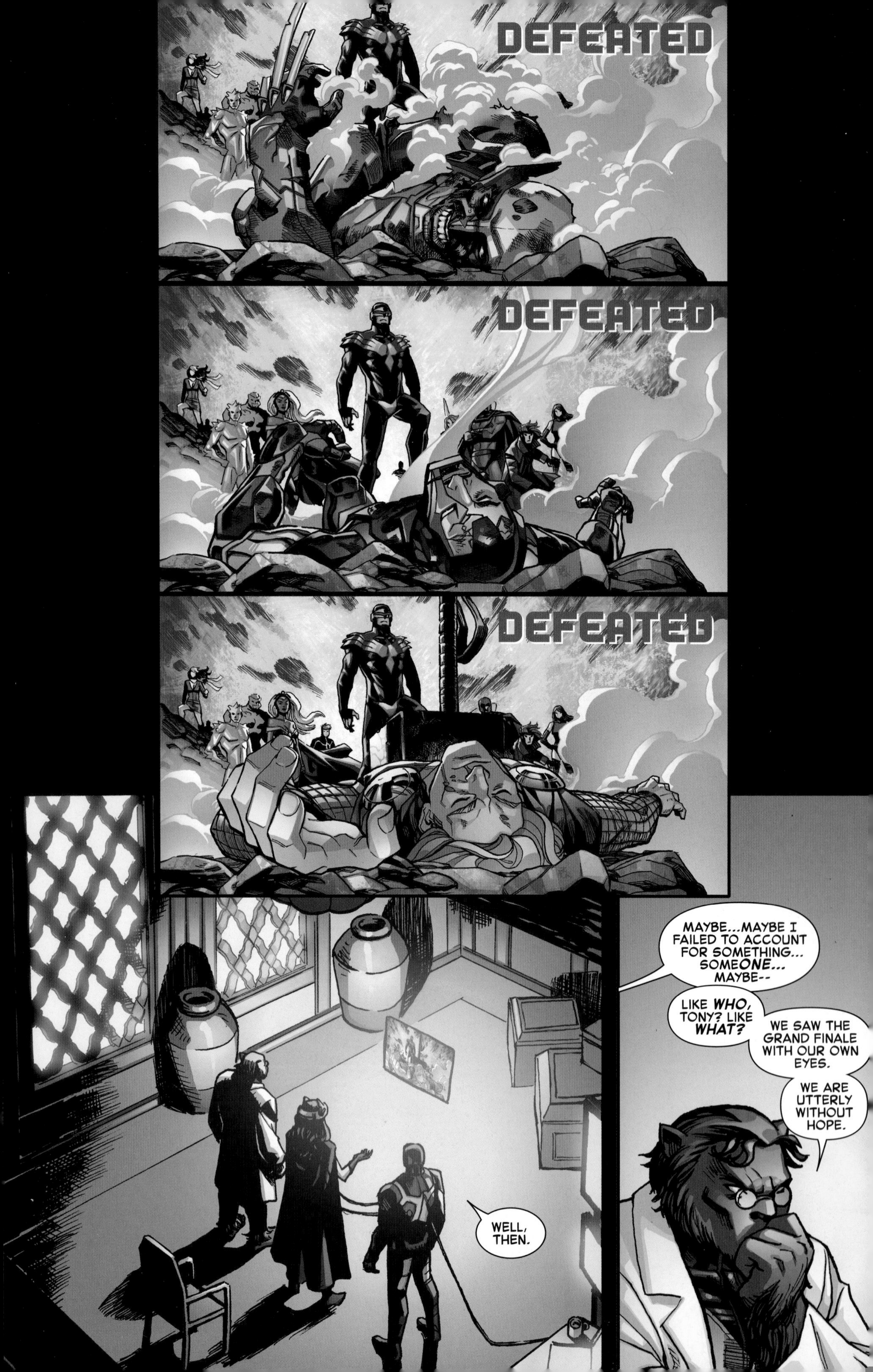
DEFEATED
DEFEATED
DEFEATED
WELL, THEN.
MAYBE...MAYBE I FAILED TO ACCOUNT FOR SOMETHING... SOMEONE... MAYBE--
LIKE WHO, TONY? LIKE WHAT?
WE SAW THE GRAND FINALE WITH OUR OWN EYES.
WE ARE UTTERLY WITHOUT HOPE.

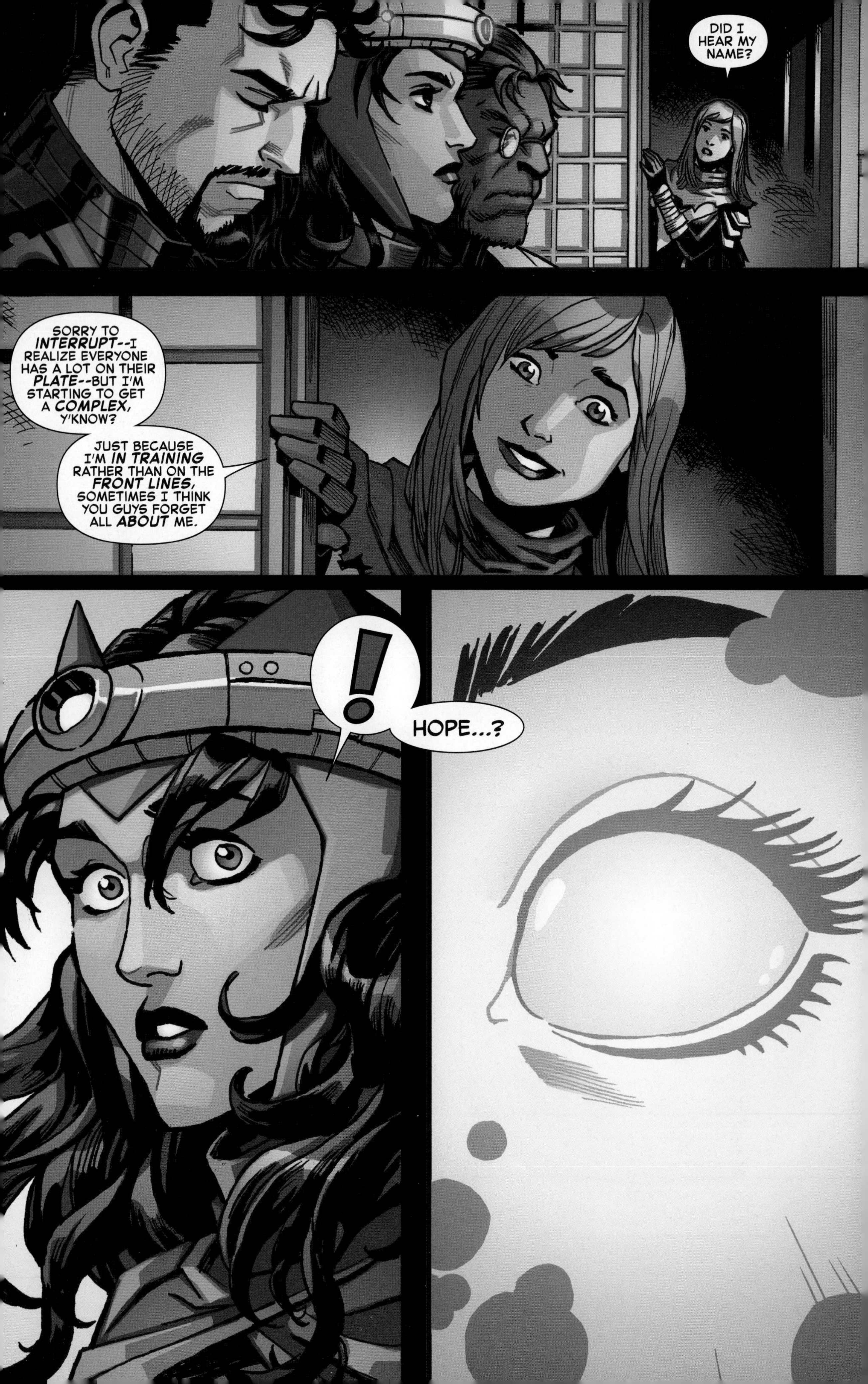
DID I HEAR MY NAME?
SORRY TO INTERRUPT--I REALIZE EVERYONE HAS A LOT ON THEIR PLATE--BUT I'M STARTING TO GET A COMPLEX, Y'KNOW?
JUST BECAUSE I'M IN TRAINING RATHER THAN ON THE FRONT LINES, SOMETIMES I THINK YOU GUYS FORGET ALL ABOUT ME.
!
HOPE...?

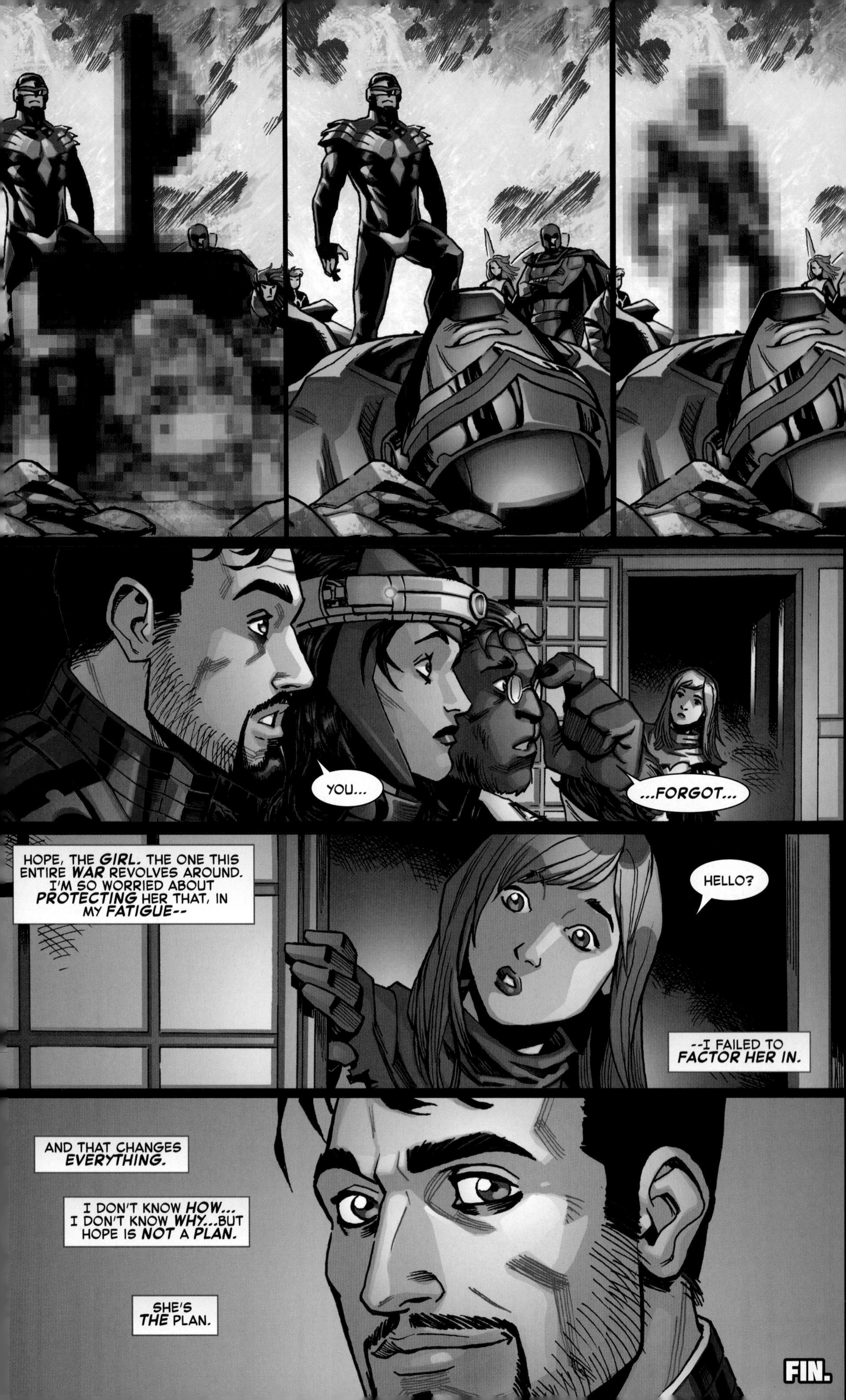
YOU...
...FORGOT...
HOPE, THE GIRL. THE ONE THIS ENTIRE WAR REVOLVES AROUND. I'M SO WORRIED ABOUT PROTECTING HER THAT, IN MY FATIGUE--
HELLO?
--I FAILED TO FACTOR HER IN.
AND THAT CHANGES EVERYTHING.
I DON'T KNOW HOW... I DON'T KNOW WHY...BUT HOPE IS NOT A PLAN.
SHE'S THE PLAN.
FIN.

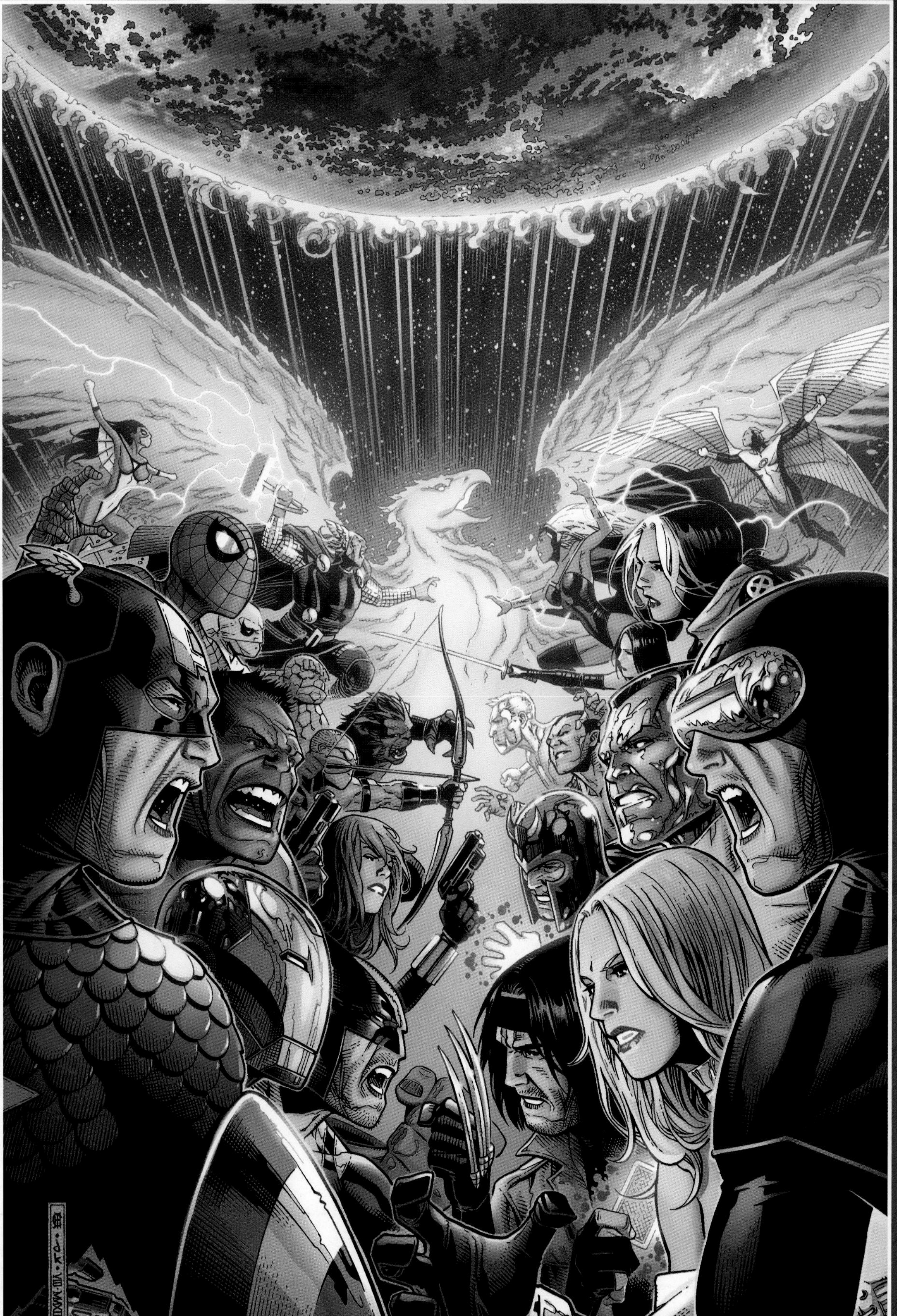

AVENGERS VS. X-MEN COLLECTION COVER

BY **JIM CHEUNG & JASON KEITH**

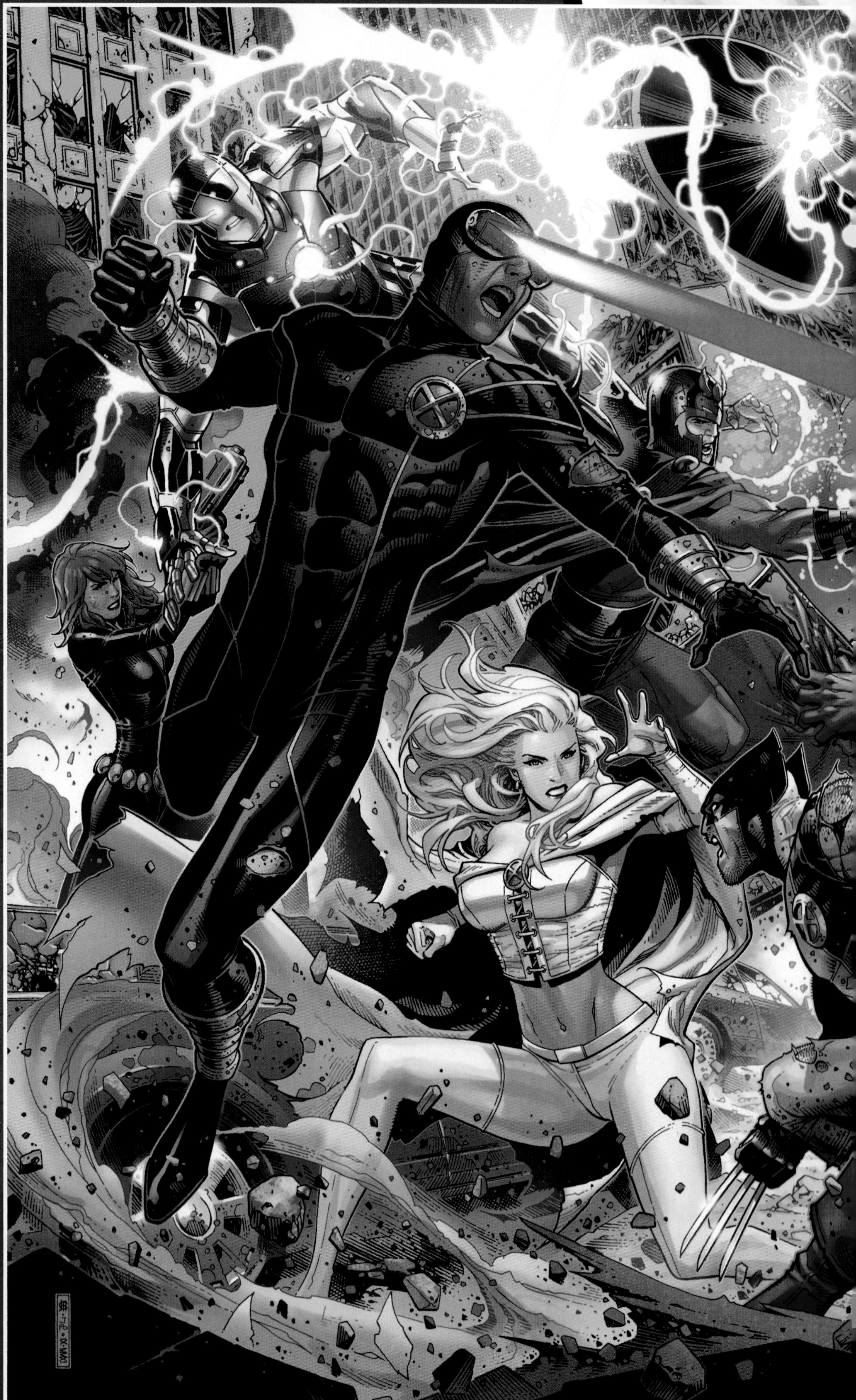

AVX #0 VARIANT

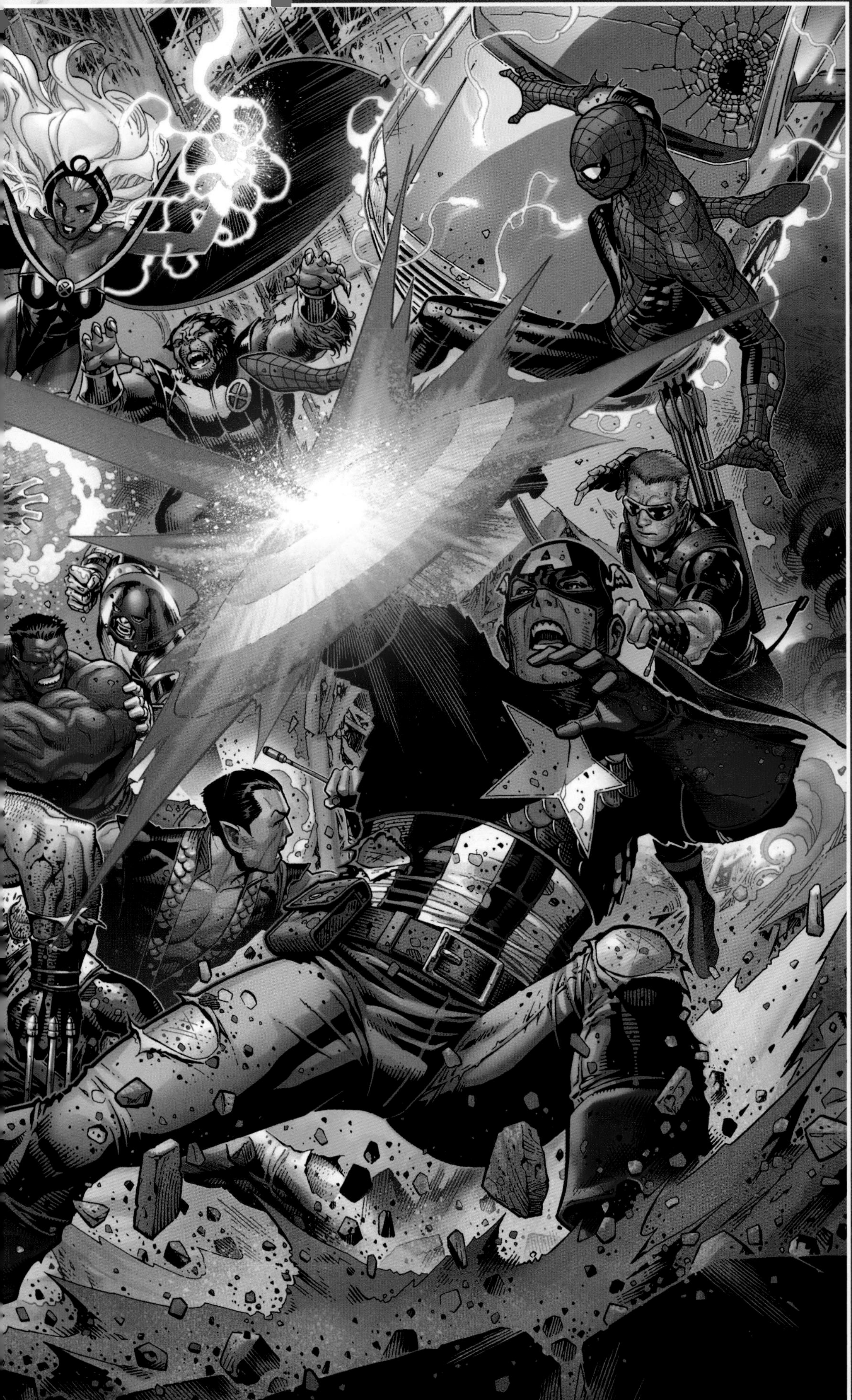

BY JIM CHEUNG & JUSTIN PONSOR

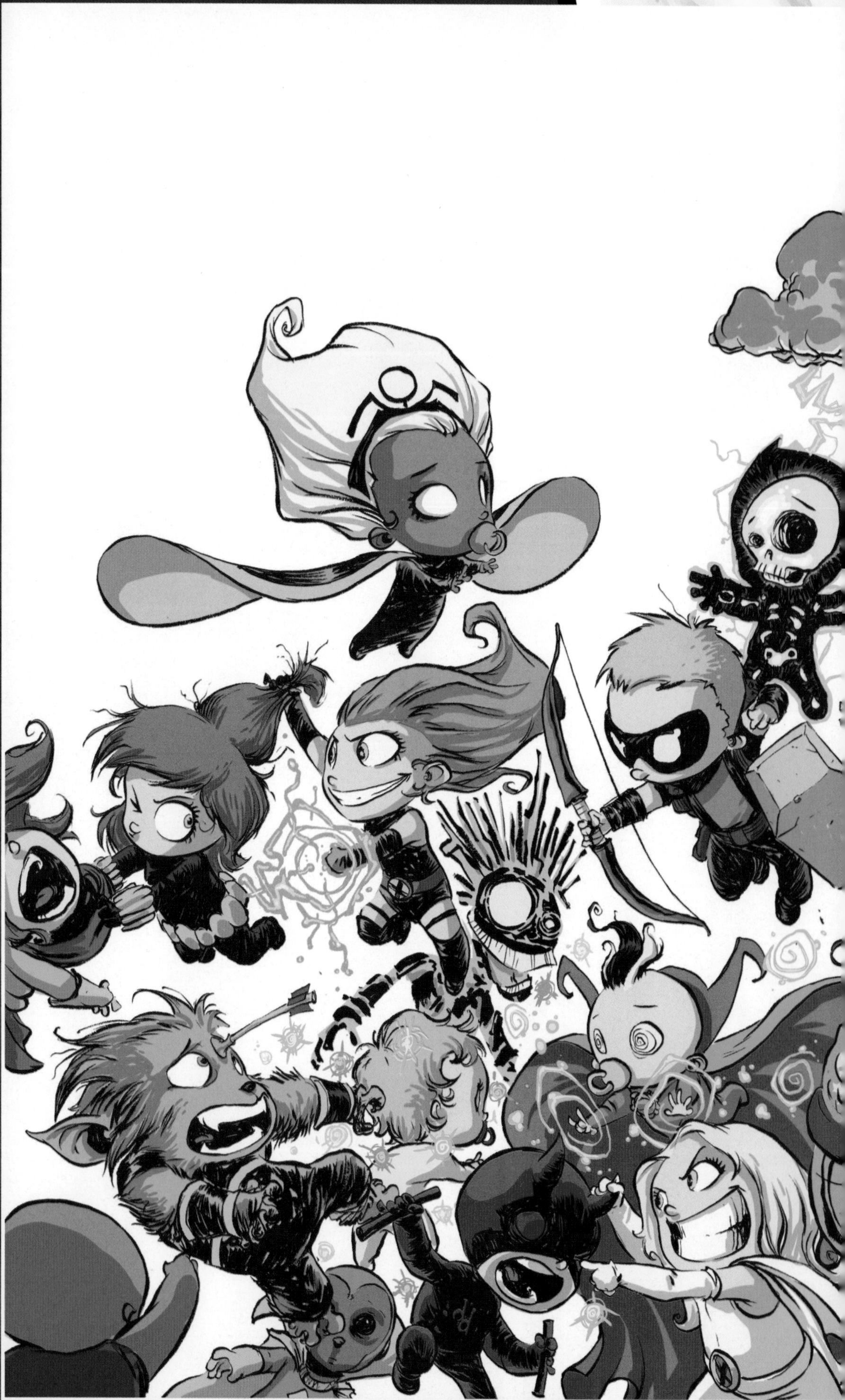

AVX #1 MIDTOWN VARIANT

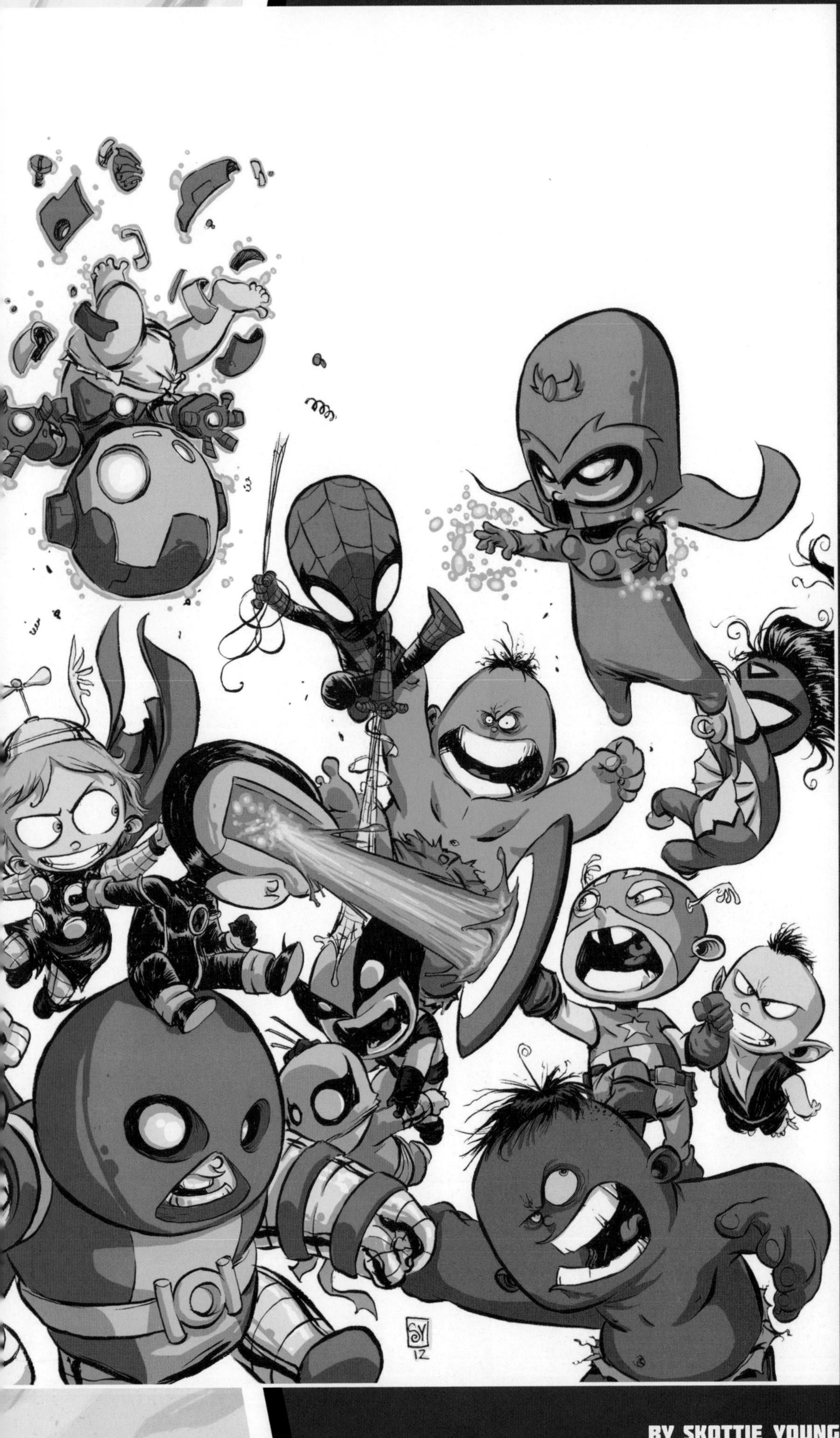

BY SKOTTIE YOUNG

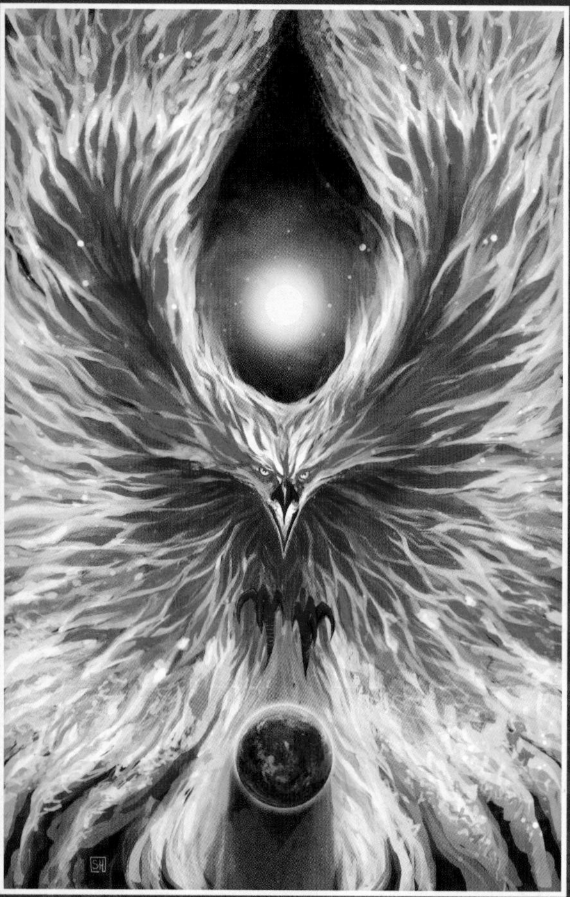

AVX #0 VARIANT
BY **STEPHANIE HANS**

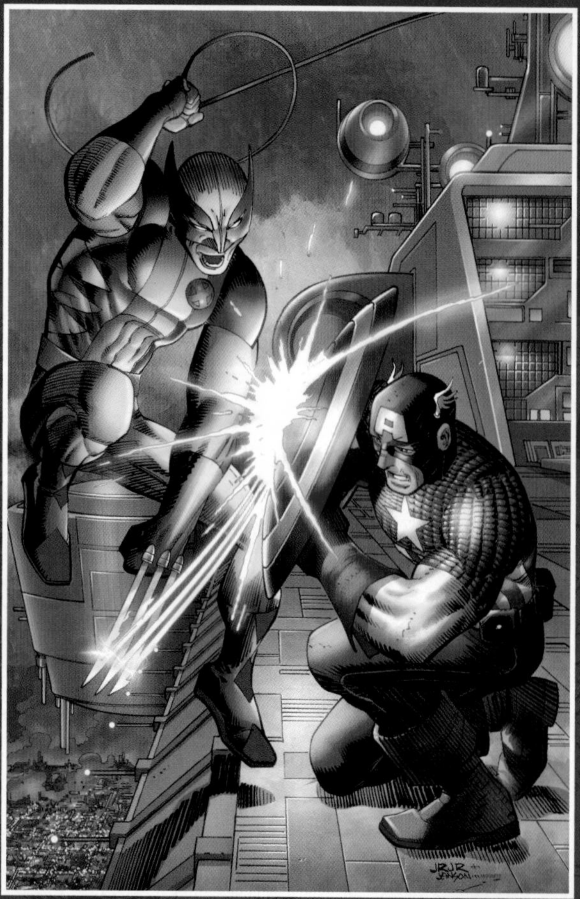

AVX #1 VARIANT
BY **JOHN ROMITA JR., KLAUS JANSON & PAUL MOUNTS**

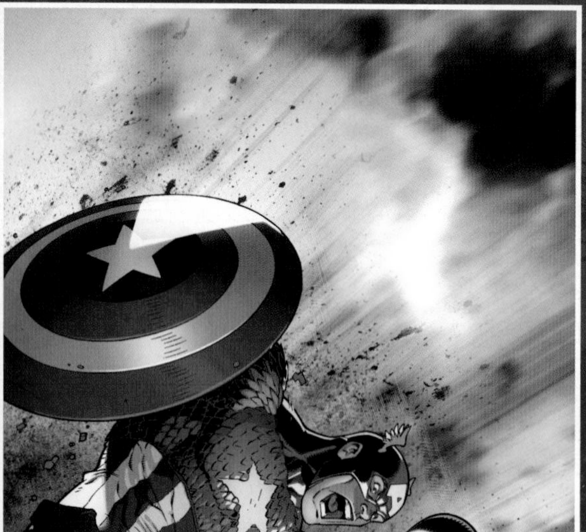

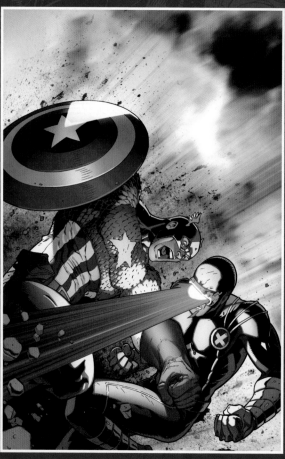

AVX #1 VARIANT
BY **RYAN STEGMAN, MICHAEL BABINSKI & MARTE GRACIA**

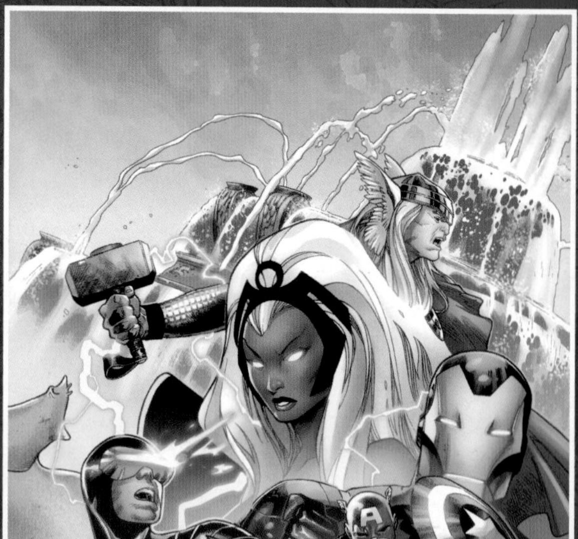

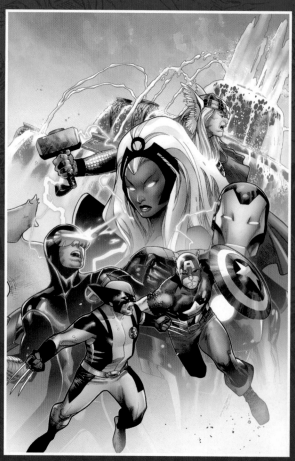

AVX #1 C2E2 VARIANT
BY **OLIVIER COIPEL**

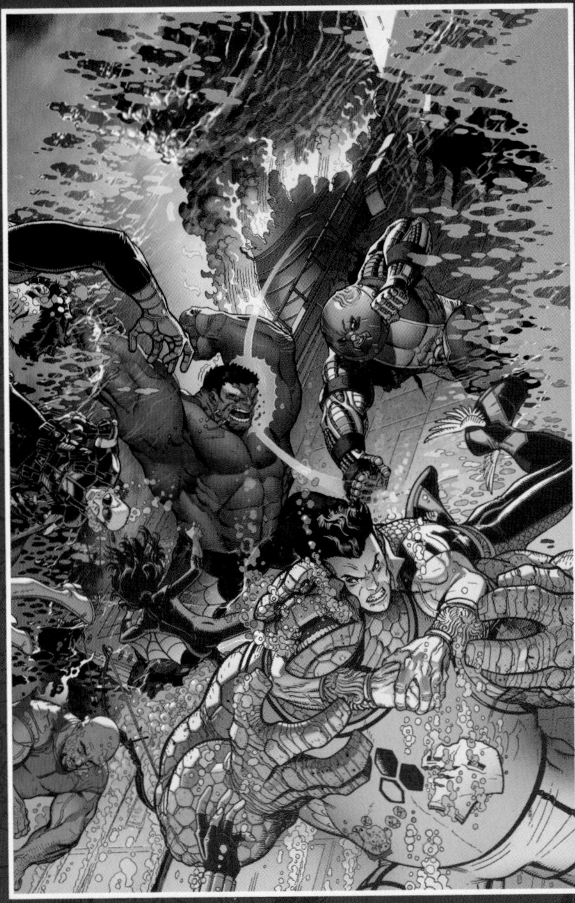

AVX #2 VARIANT
BY **NICK BRADSHAW & MARTE GRACIA**

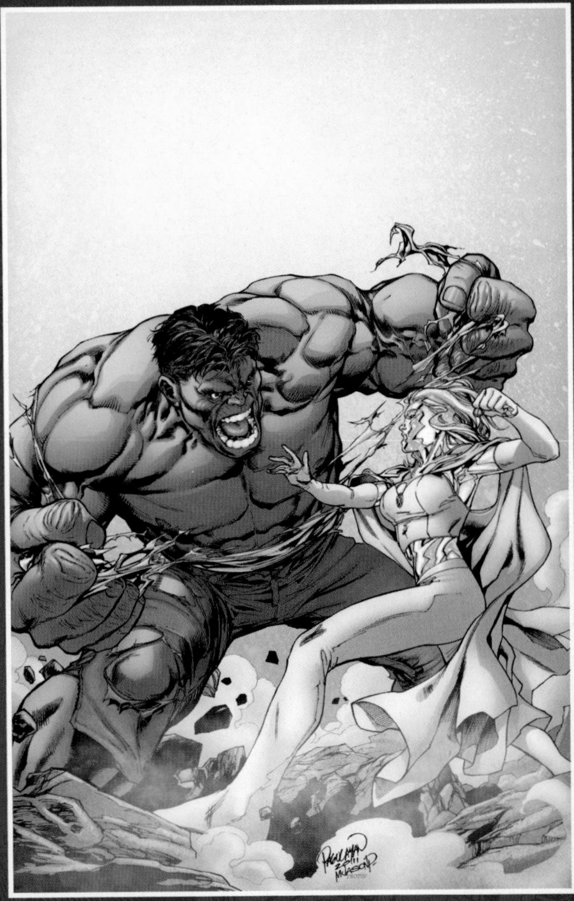

AVX #2 VARIANT
BY **CARLO PAGULAYAN, JASON PAZ & CHRIS SOTOMAYOR**

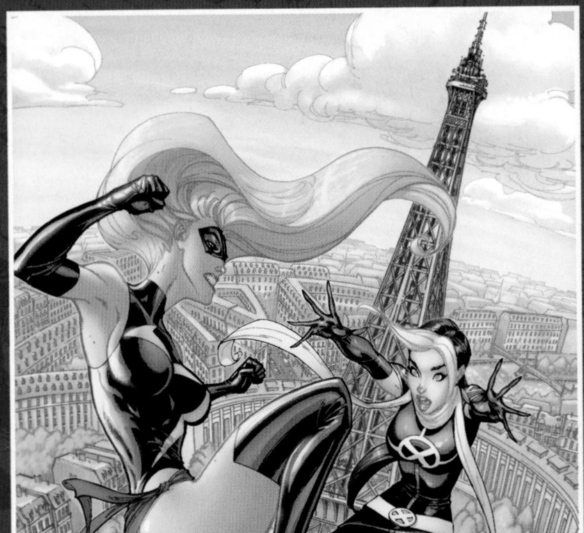

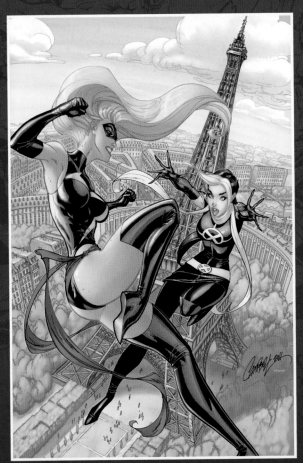

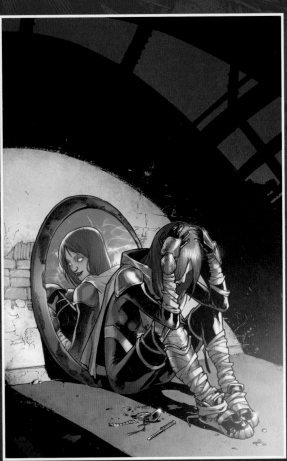

AVX #3 VARIANT
BY **J. SCOTT CAMPBELL & EDGAR DELGADO**

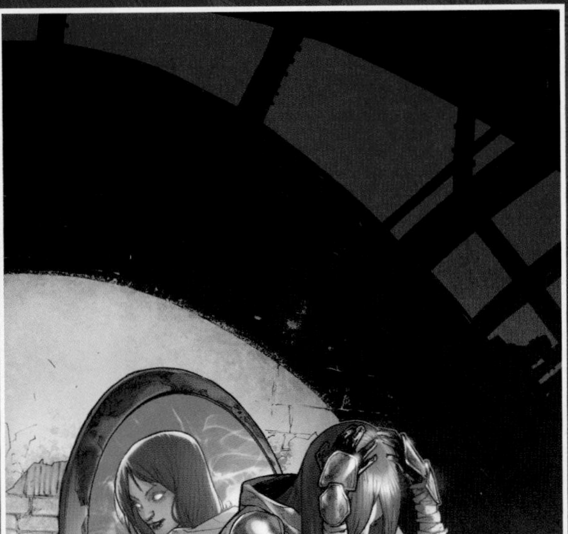

AVX #3 VARIANT
BY **SARA PICHELLI & JUSTIN PONSOR**

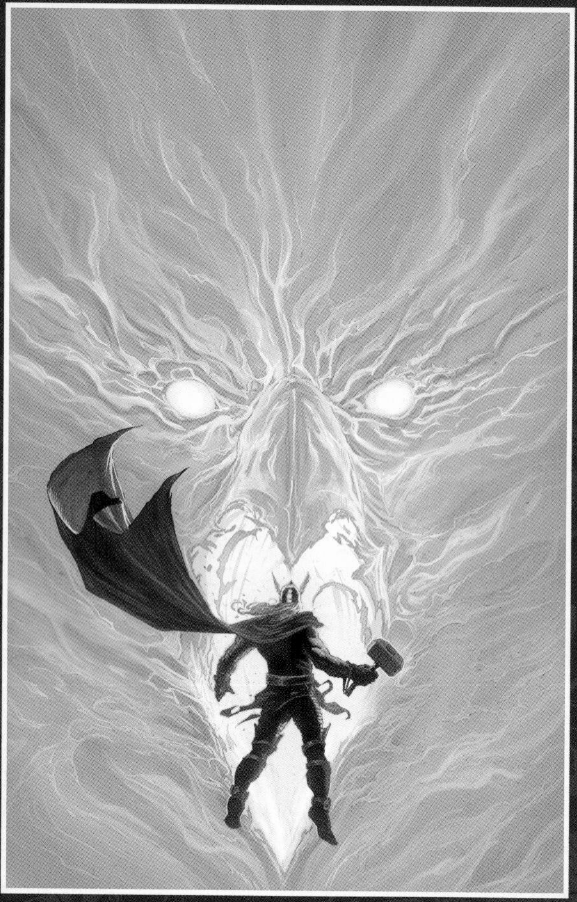

AVX #4 VARIANT
BY **JEROME OPEÑA & DEAN WHITE**

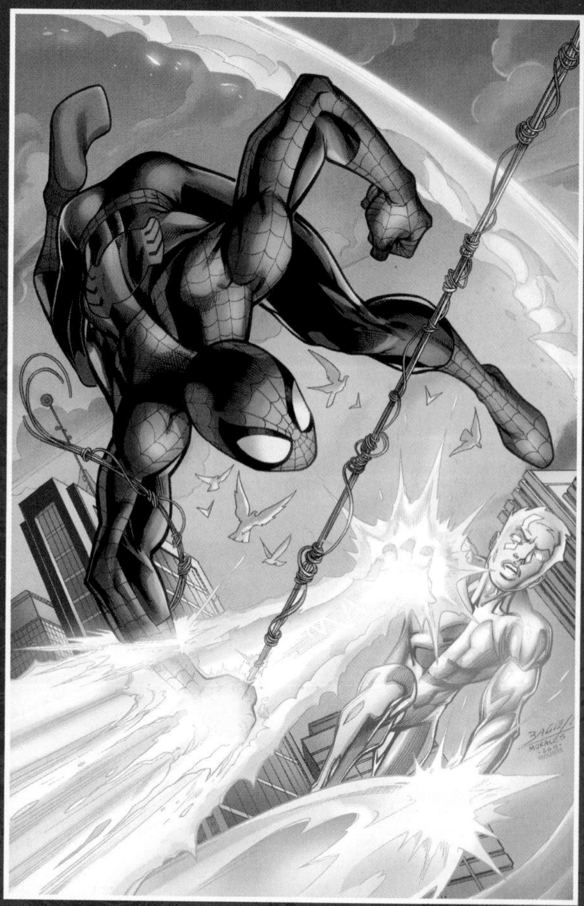

AVX #4 VARIANT
BY **MARK BAGLEY, MARK MORALES & PAUL MOUNTS**

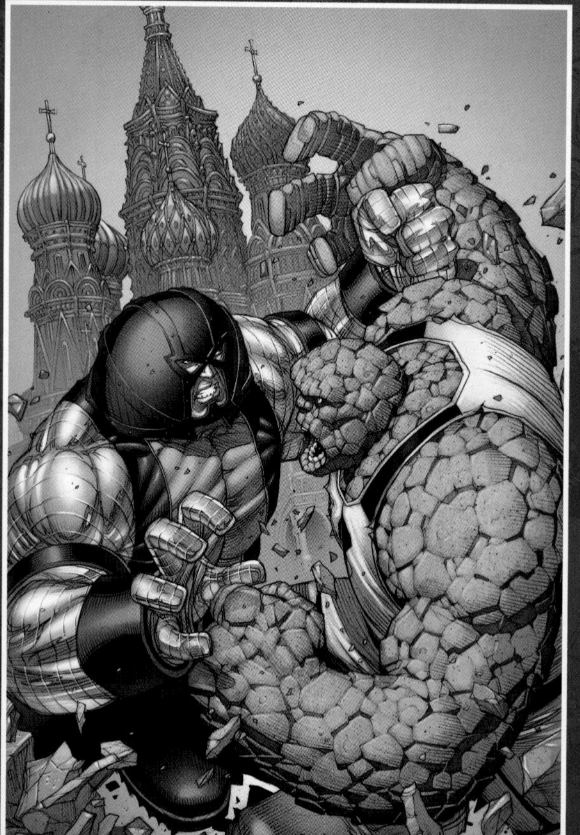

AVX #5 VARIANT
BY **DALE KEOWN & CHRIS SOTOMAYOR**

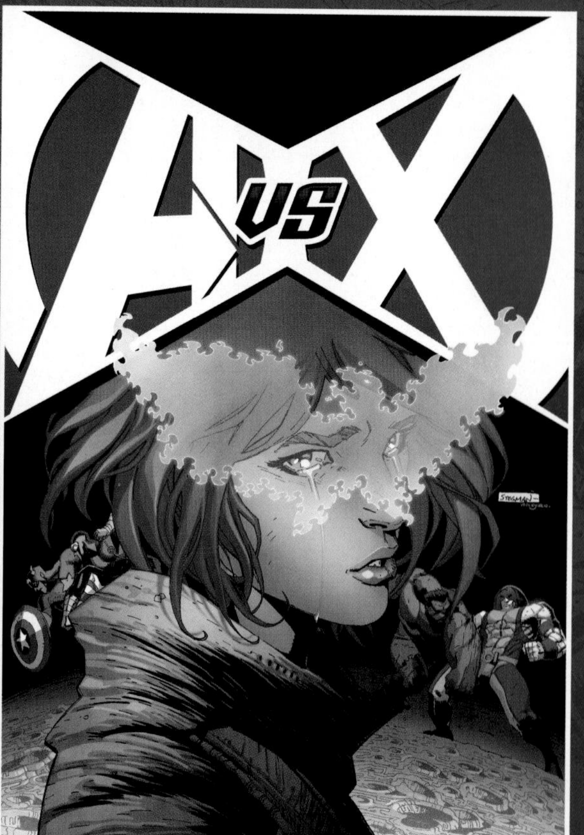
A VS X

AVX #5 VARIANT
BY **RYAN STEGMAN & MARTE GRACIA**

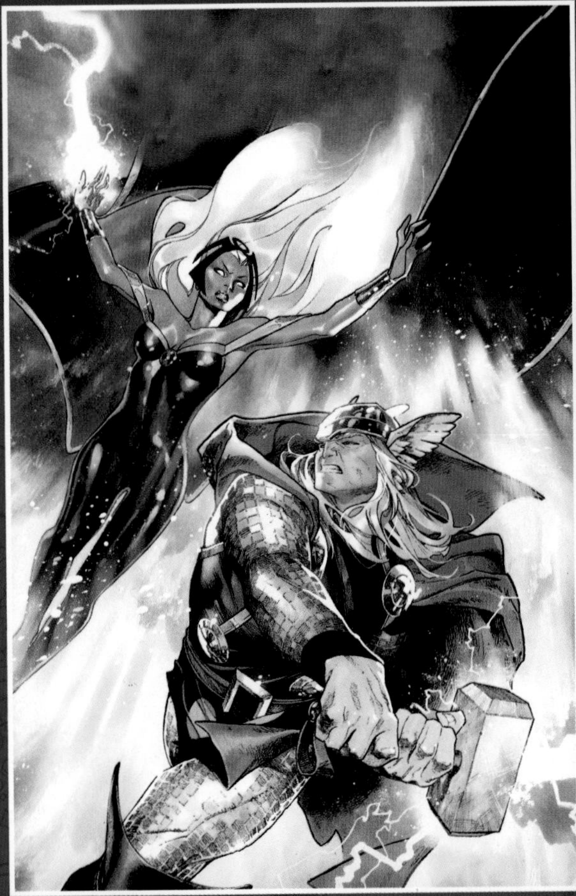

AVX #6 VARIANT
BY OLIVIER COIPEL

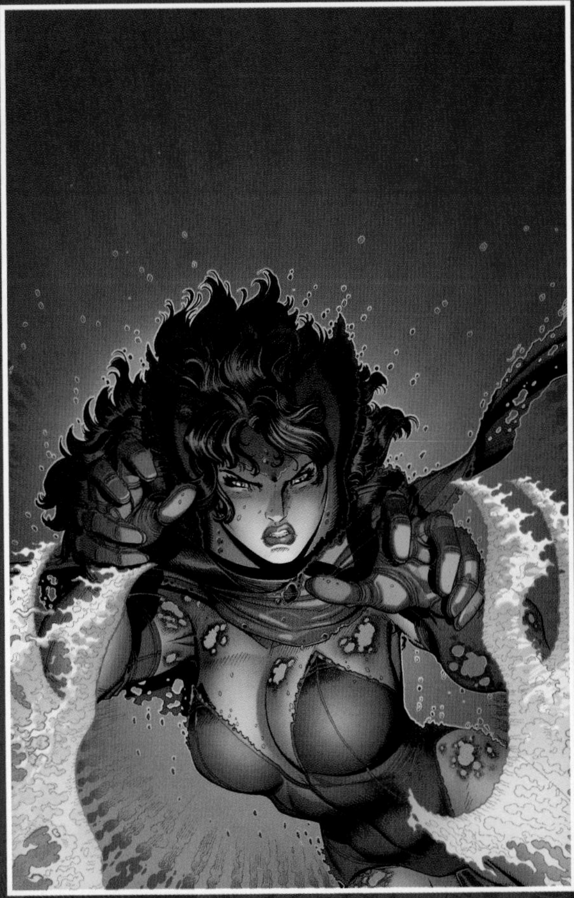

AVX #6 VARIANT
BY NICK BRADSHAW & MARTE GRACIA

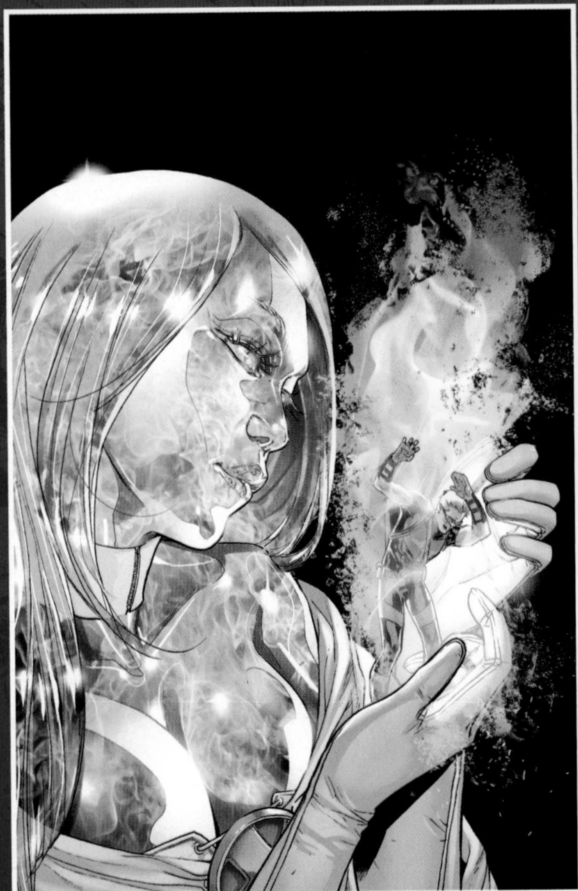

AVX #7 VARIANT
BY SARA PICHELLI & JUSTIN PONSOR

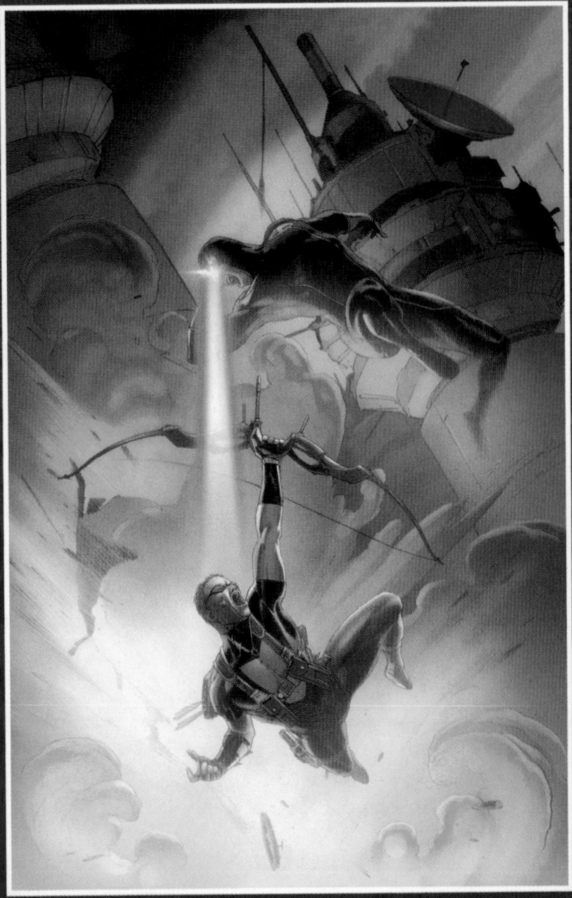

AVX #7 VARIANT
BY ESAD RIBIC

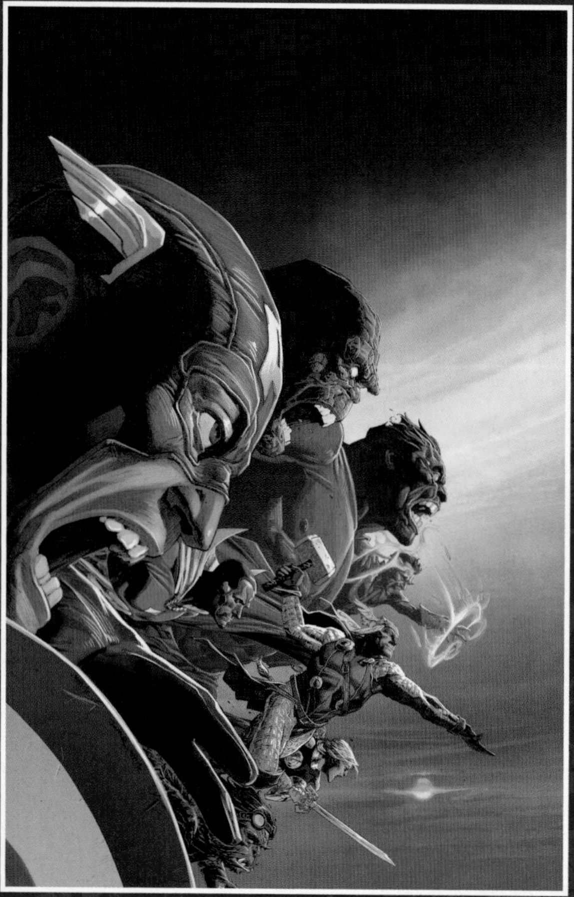

AVX #8 VARIANT
BY **JEROME OPEÑA & DEAN WHITE**

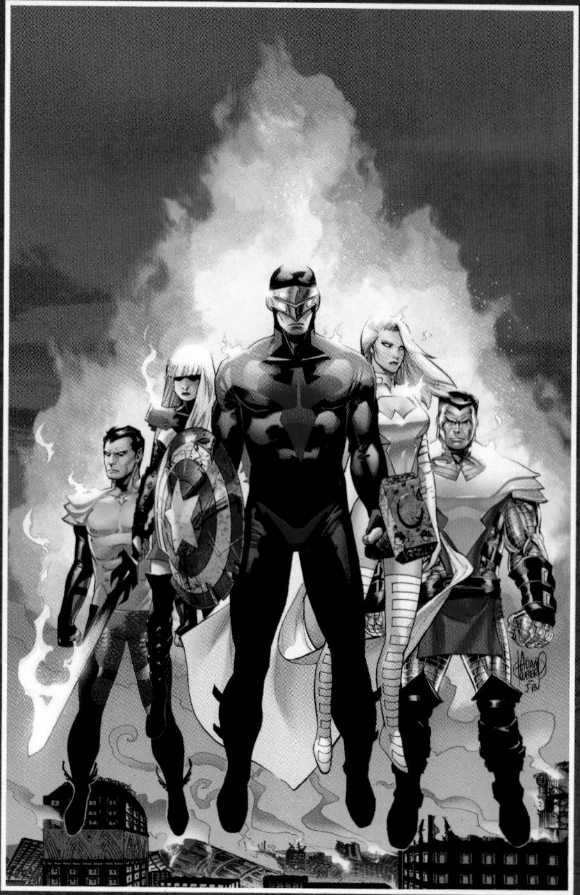

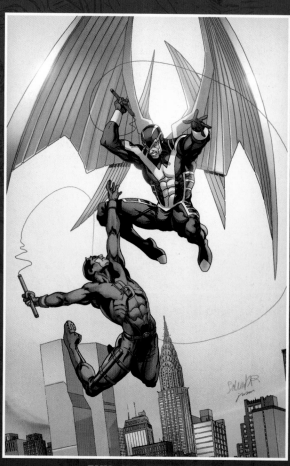

AVX #8 VARIANT
BY **ADAM KUBERT & JUSTIN PONSOR**

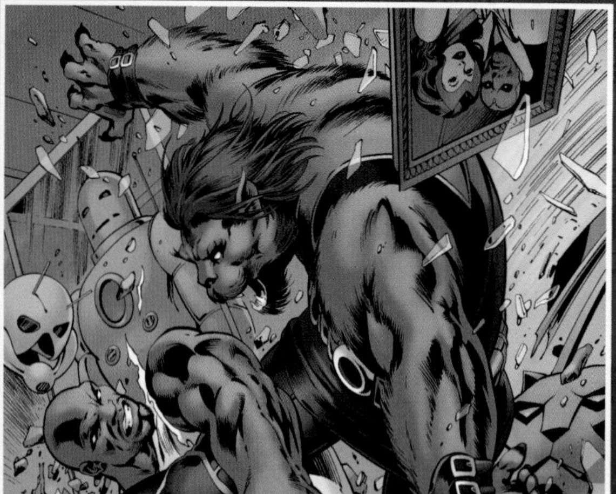

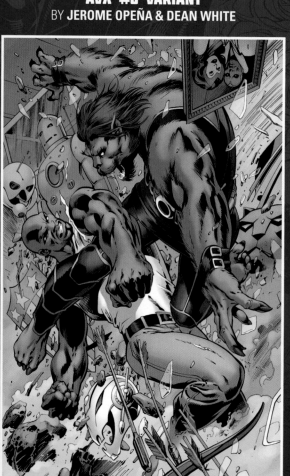

AVX #8 VARIANT
BY **ALAN DAVIS, MARK FARMER & VAL STAPLES**

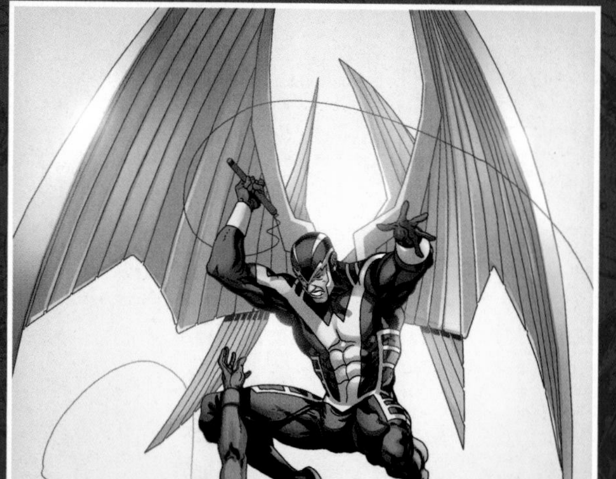

AVX #9 VARIANT
BY **SALVADOR LARROCA & JASON KEITH**

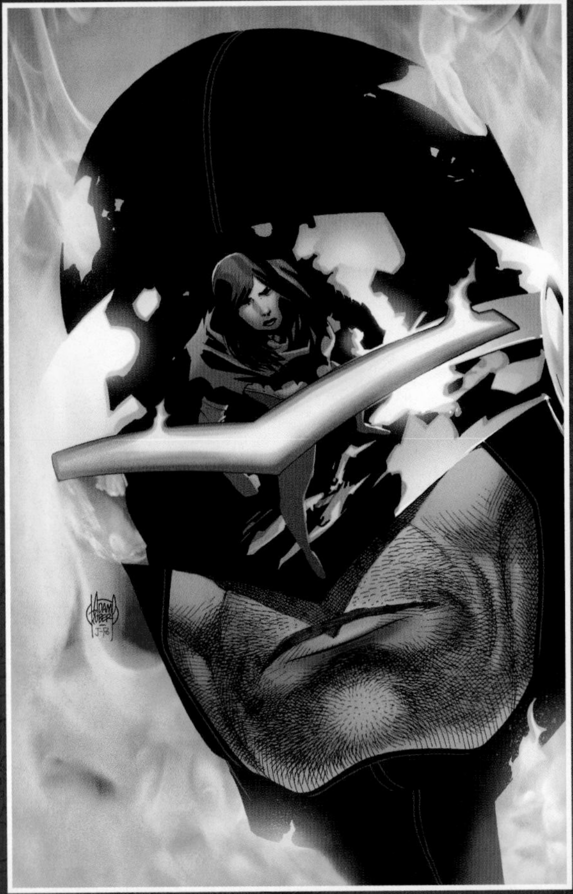

AVX #9 VARIANT
BY **ADAM KUBERT & JUSTIN PONSOR**

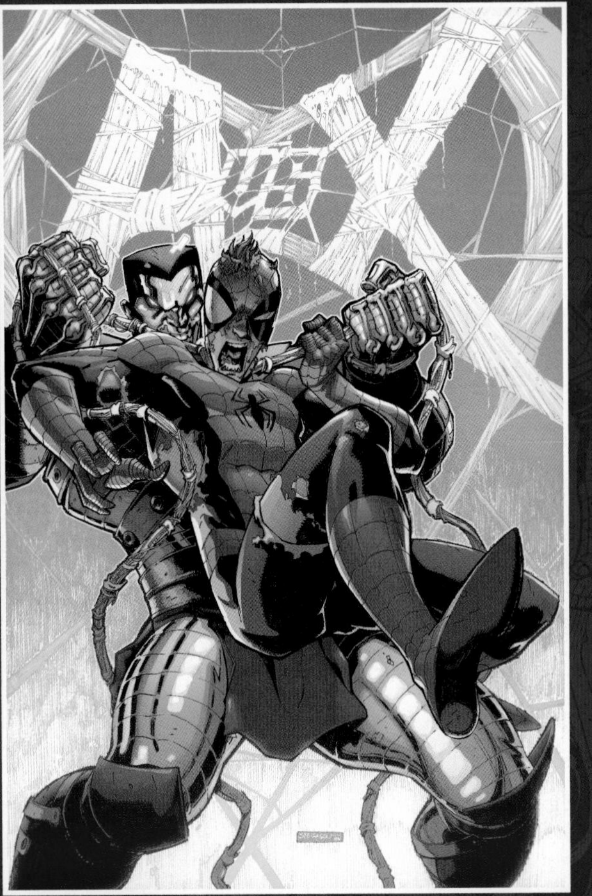
A vs X

AVX #9 VARIANT
BY **RYAN STEGMAN & MATT WILSON**

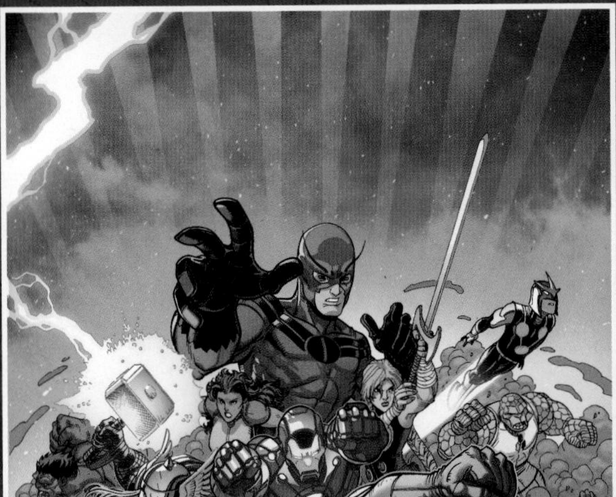

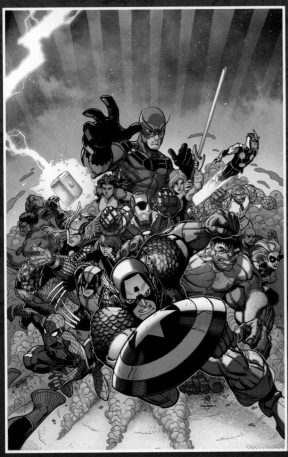

AVX #10 VARIANT
BY **NICK BRADSHAW & MARTE GRACIA**

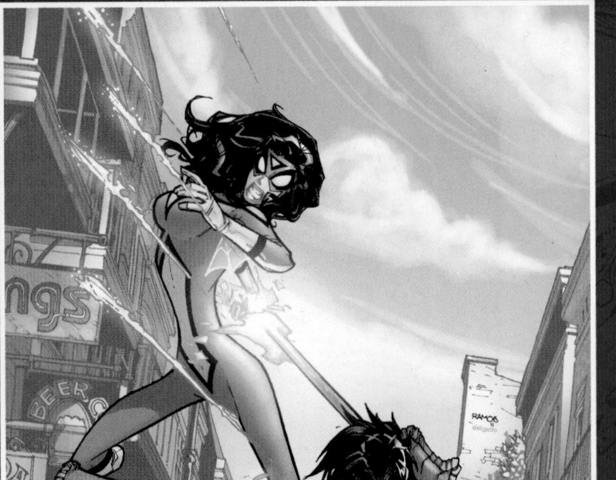

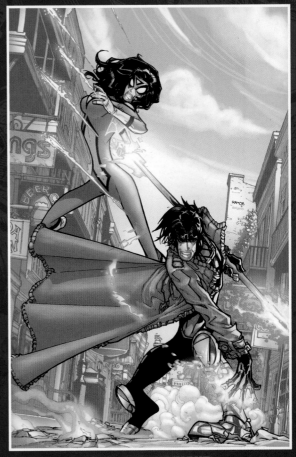

AVX #10 VARIANT
BY **HUMBERTO RAMOS & EDGAR DELGADO**

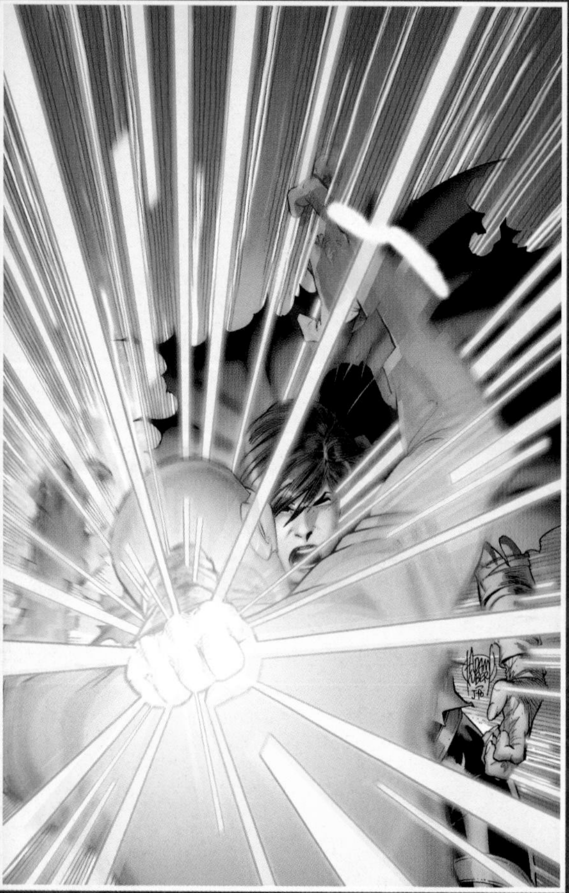

AVX #10 VARIANT
BY **ADAM KUBERT & JUSTIN PONSOR**

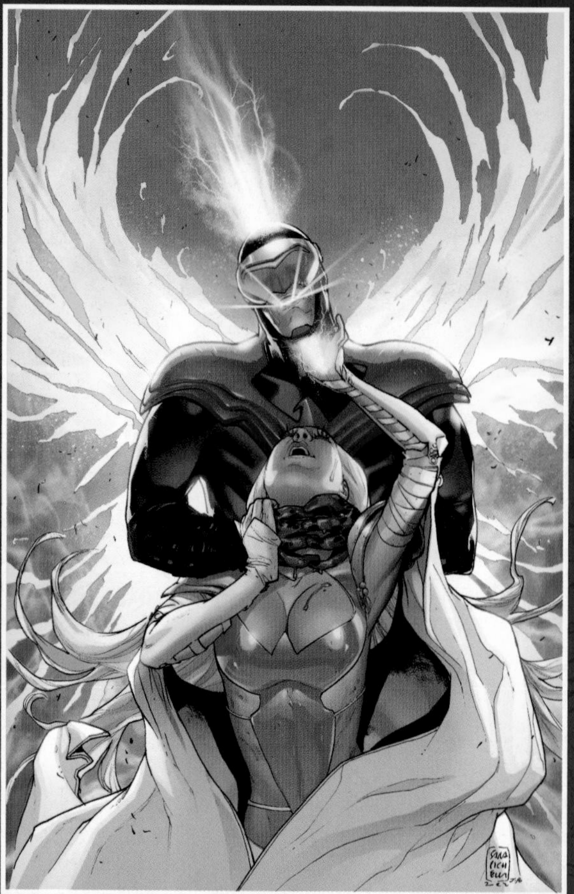

AVX #11 VARIANT
BY **SARA PICHELLI & JUSTIN PONSOR**

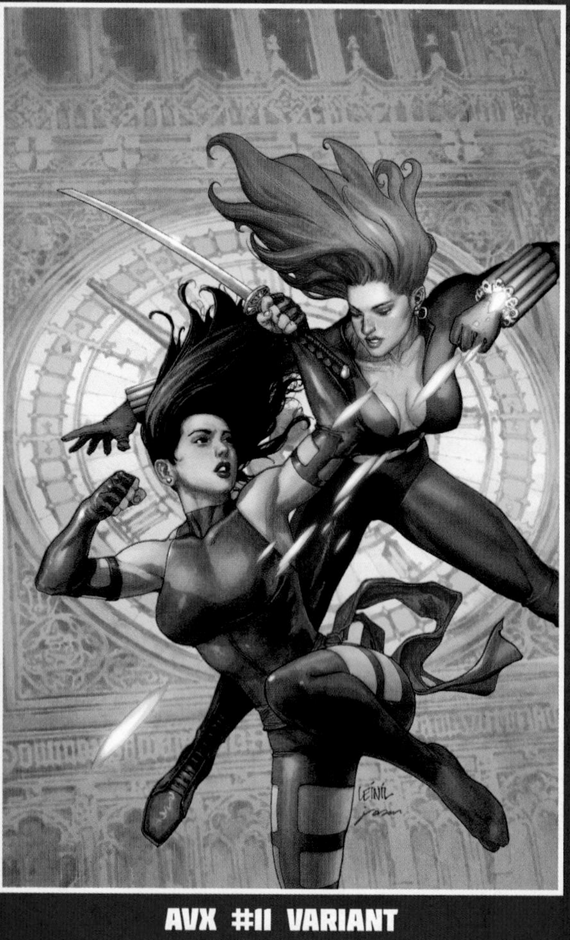

AVX #11 VARIANT
BY **LEINIL YU & JASON KEITH**

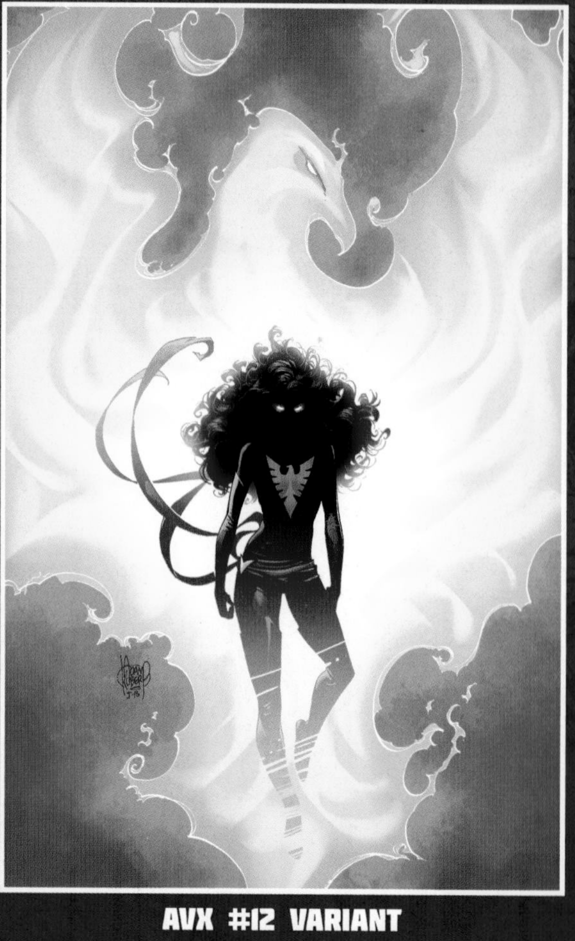

AVX #12 VARIANT
BY **ADAM KUBERT & JUSTIN PONSOR**

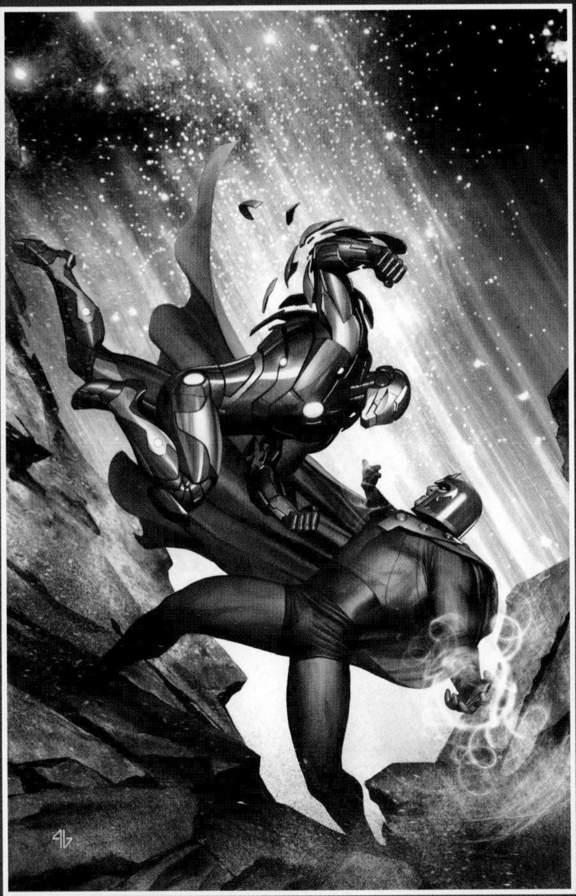

AVX #12 VARIANT
BY **ADI GRANOV**

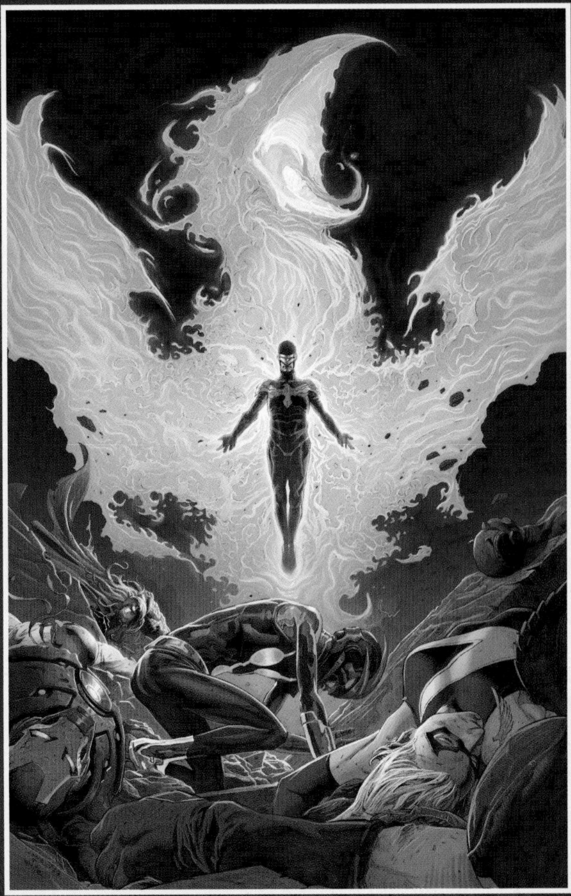

AVX #12 VARIANT
BY **JEROME OPEÑA & DEAN WHITE**

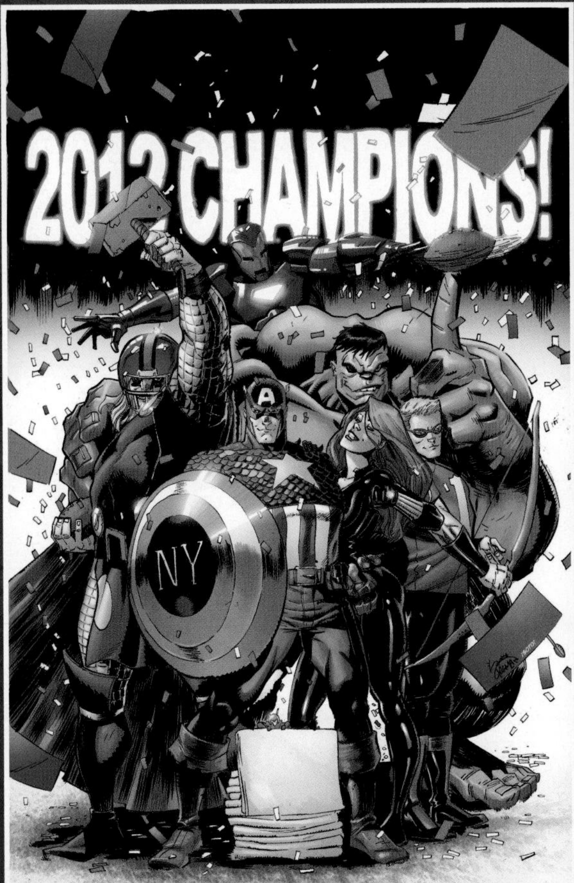
2012 CHAMPIONS!
NY

AVX #12 AVENGERS VARIANT
BY **RYAN STEGMAN & CHRIS SOTOMAYOR**

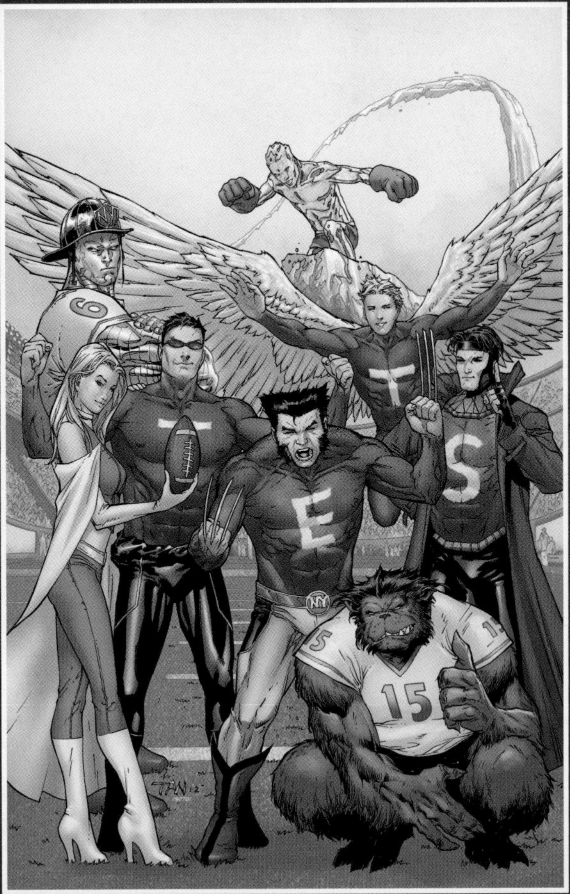
E
S
15

AVX #12 X-MEN VARIANT
BY **BILLY TAN & CHRIS SOTOMAYOR**

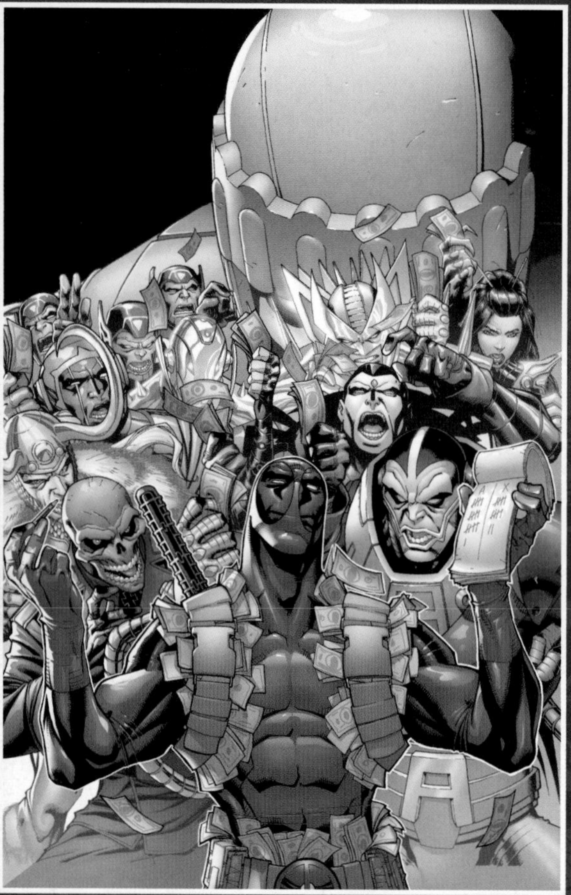

AVX #1 HASTINGS VARIANT
BY CARLO BARBERI & EDGAR DELGADO

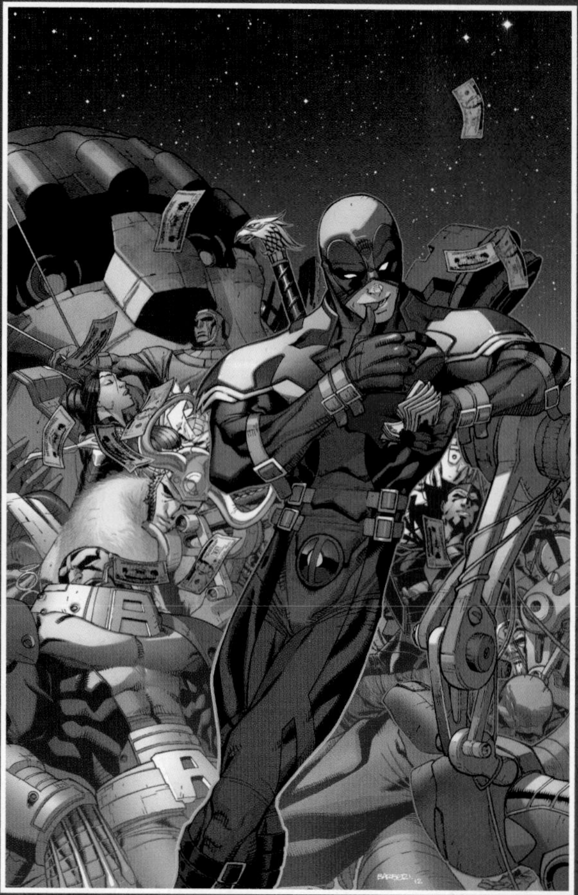

AVX #12 HASTINGS VARIANT
BY CARLO BARBERI & MARTE GRACIA

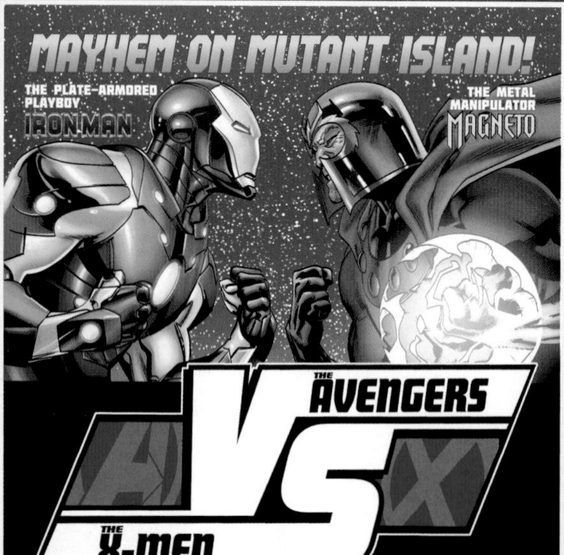

MAYHEM ON MUTANT ISLAND!
THE PLATE-ARMORED PLAYBOY IRON MAN
THE METAL MANIPULATOR MAGNETO
THE AVENGERS VS THE X-MEN
ALSO: A REMATCH FOR THE AGES! THING VS NAMOR

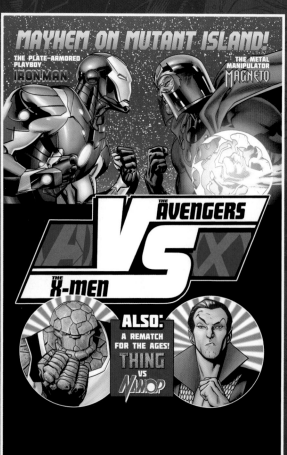

AVX: VS #1 VARIANT
BY STUART IMMONEN & MORRY HOLLOWELL

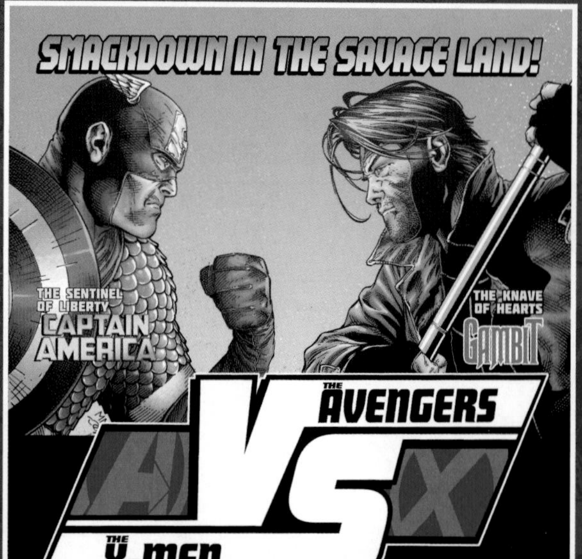

SMACKDOWN IN THE SAVAGE LAND!
THE SENTINEL OF LIBERTY CAPTAIN AMERICA
THE KNAVE OF HEARTS GAMBIT
THE AVENGERS VS THE X-MEN
PLUS: WILL COLOSSUS SQUASH THE AMAZING SPIDER-MAN ?

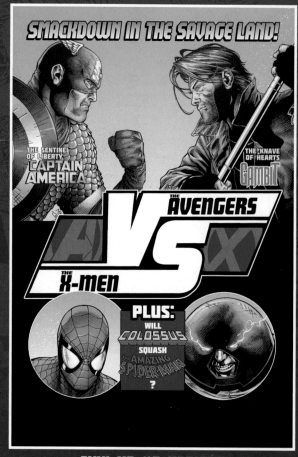

AVX: VS #2 VARIANT
BY STEVE McNIVEN, JOHN DELL & MORRY HOLLOWELL

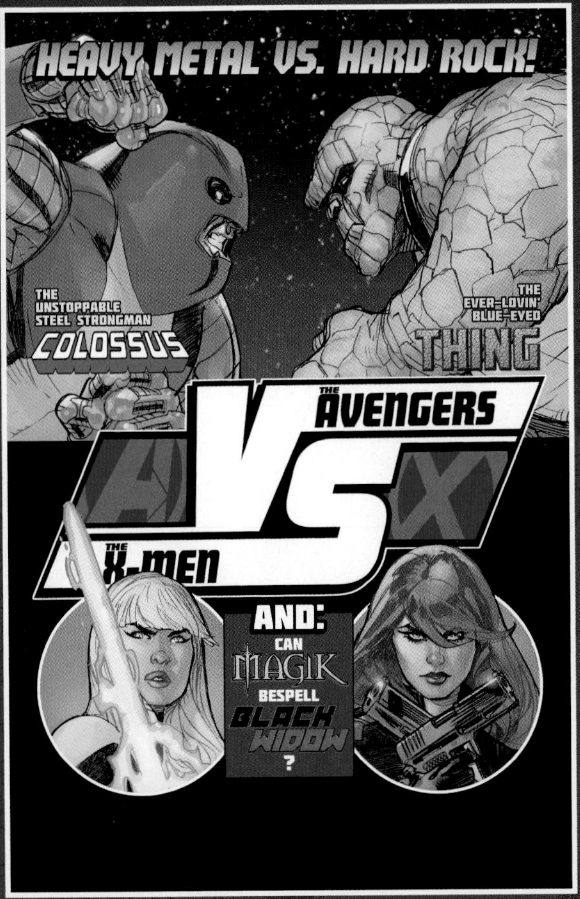
HEAVY METAL VS. HARD ROCK!
THE UNSTOPPABLE STEEL STRONGMAN
COLOSSUS
THE EVER-LOVIN' BLUE-EYED
THING
THE AVENGERS
VS
THE X-MEN
AND:
CAN
MAGIK
BESPELL
BLACK WIDOW
?

AVX: VS #3 VARIANT
BY **TERRY DODSON**

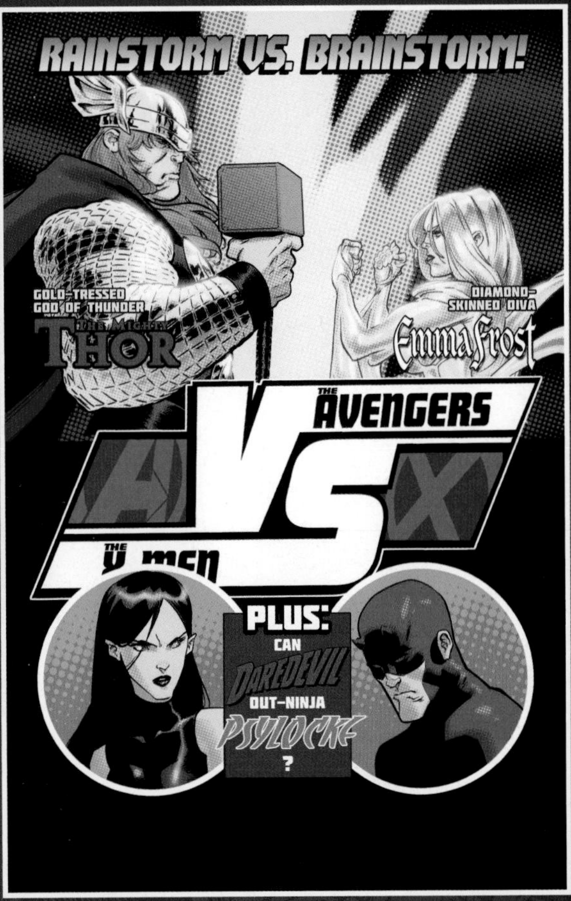
RAINSTORM VS. BRAINSTORM!
GOLD-TRESSED GOD OF THUNDER
THOR
DIAMOND-SKINNED DIVA
Emma Frost
THE AVENGERS
VS
THE X-MEN
PLUS:
CAN
DAREDEVIL
OUT-NINJA
PSYLOCKE
?

AVX: VS #4 VARIANT
BY **KAARE ANDREWS**

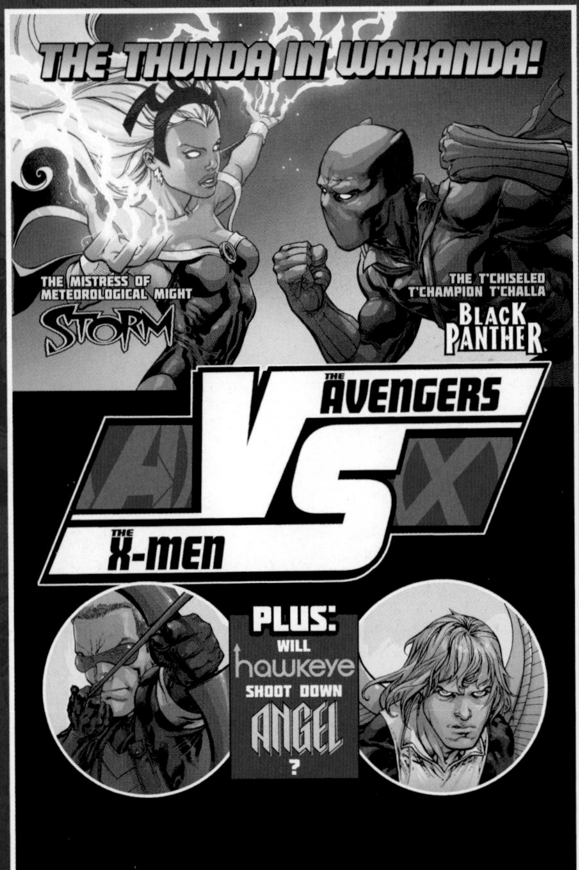
THE THUNDA IN WAKANDA!
THE MISTRESS OF METEOROLOGICAL MIGHT
STORM
THE T'CHISELED T'CHAMPION T'CHALLA
BLACK PANTHER
THE AVENGERS
VS
THE X-MEN
PLUS:
WILL
hawkeye
SHOOT DOWN
ANGEL
?

AVX: VS #5 VARIANT
BY **TOM RANEY & JIM CHARALAMPIDIS**

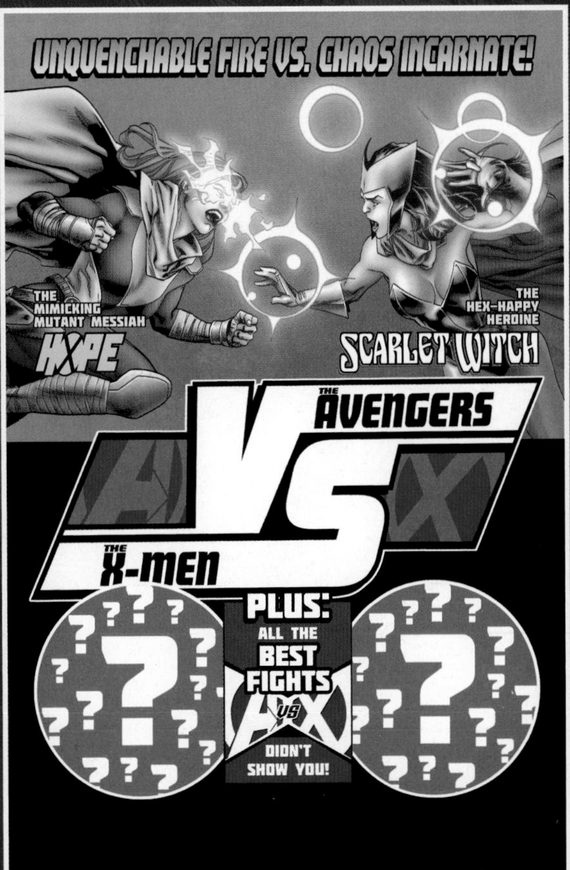
UNQUENCHABLE FIRE VS. CHAOS INCARNATE!
THE MIMICKING MUTANT MESSIAH
HOPE
THE HEX-HAPPY HEROINE
SCARLET WITCH
THE AVENGERS
VS
THE X-MEN
PLUS:
ALL THE
BEST
FIGHTS
AVX
DIDN'T
SHOW YOU!

AVX: VS #6 VARIANT
BY **STUART IMMONEN & MORRY HOLLOWELL**

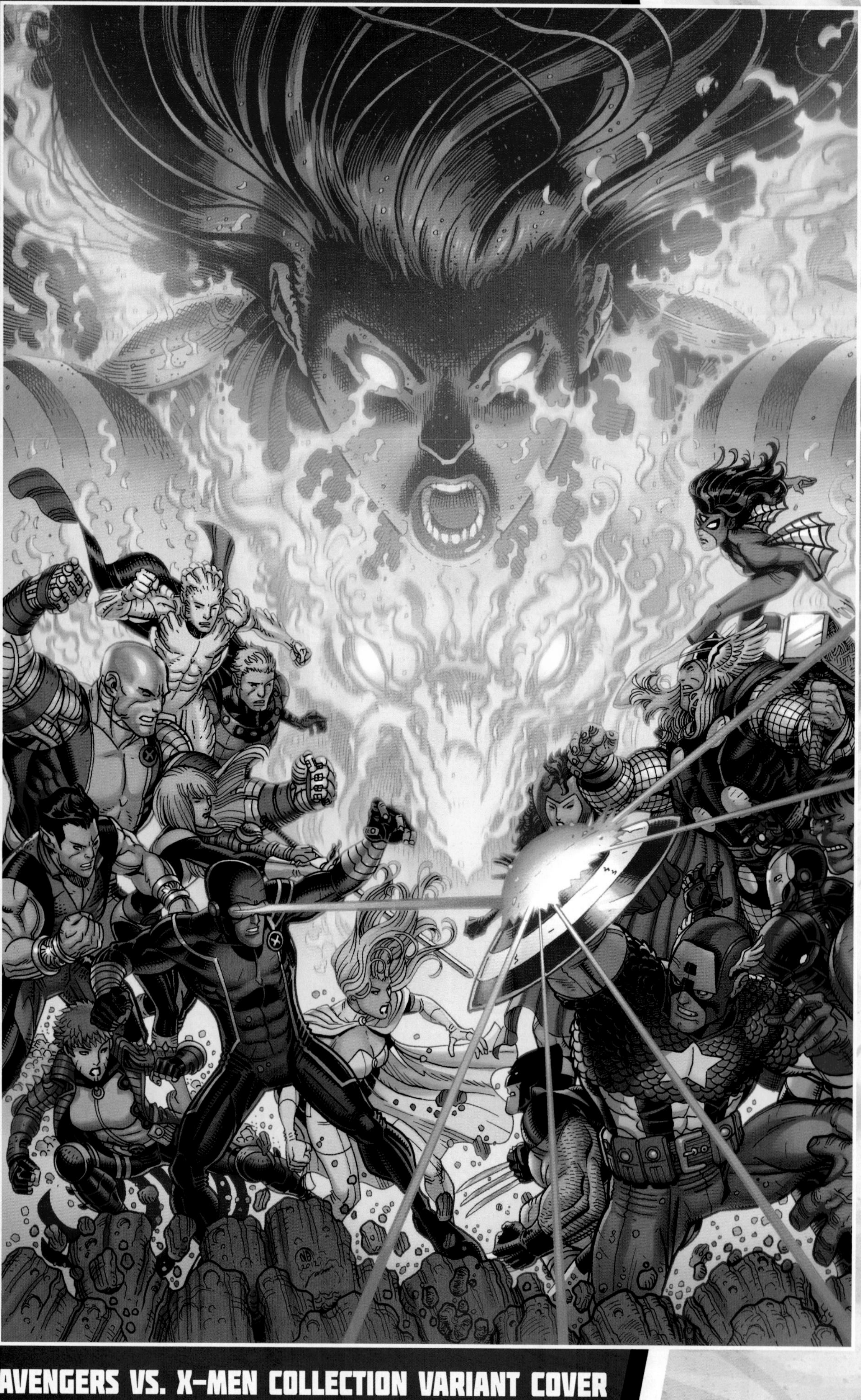

AVENGERS VS. X-MEN COLLECTION VARIANT COVER
BY **NICK BRADSHAW & JASON KEITH**

AvsX

ARTISTS UNITED

BY
JOHN RHETT THOMAS
DESIGN
RODOLFO MURAGUCHI

Avengers vs. X-Men was an event so epic it required more than one artist to bring it home. Enter three aces: John Romita Jr., Olivier Coipel and Adam Kubert — artists whose styles are so different, yet still meshed perfectly during the series' twelve-issue run. Now that the fight between the Avengers and the X-Men is over, John, Olivier and Adam took a moment to share with us what it meant to be part of *Avengers vs. X-Men*!

JOHN ROMITA JR.

What else needs to be said about **John Romita Jr.**? The man's art has spoken for itself for decades, ever since he became a superstar with *Amazing Spider-Man, Uncanny X-Men* and *Daredevil*. His scintillating take on Wolverine in the classic "Enemy of the State" marked him as a favorite for big Marvel events like *World War Hulk* — not to mention creator-owned projects like *Kick-Ass*, which later translated John's visuals to the silver screen. For a guy who broke into the business during the late '70s, his work is fresher and more relevant than ever.

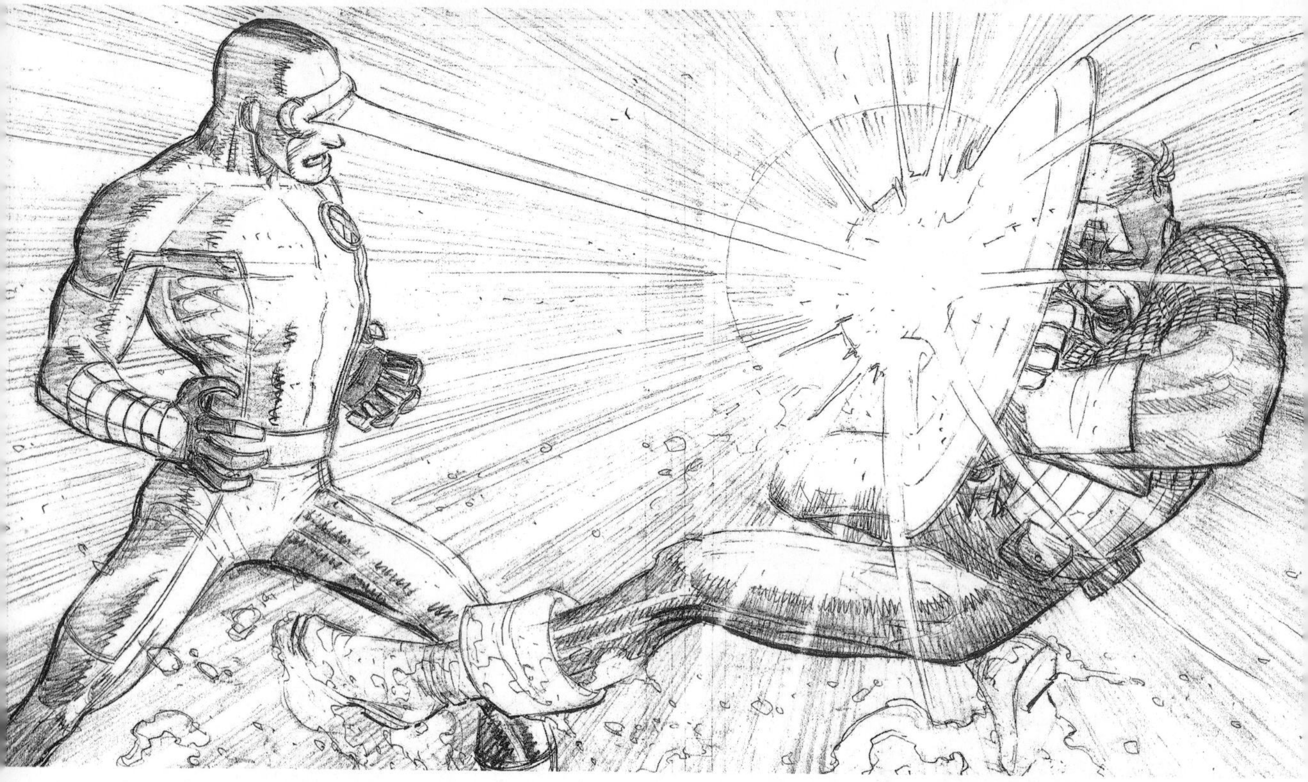

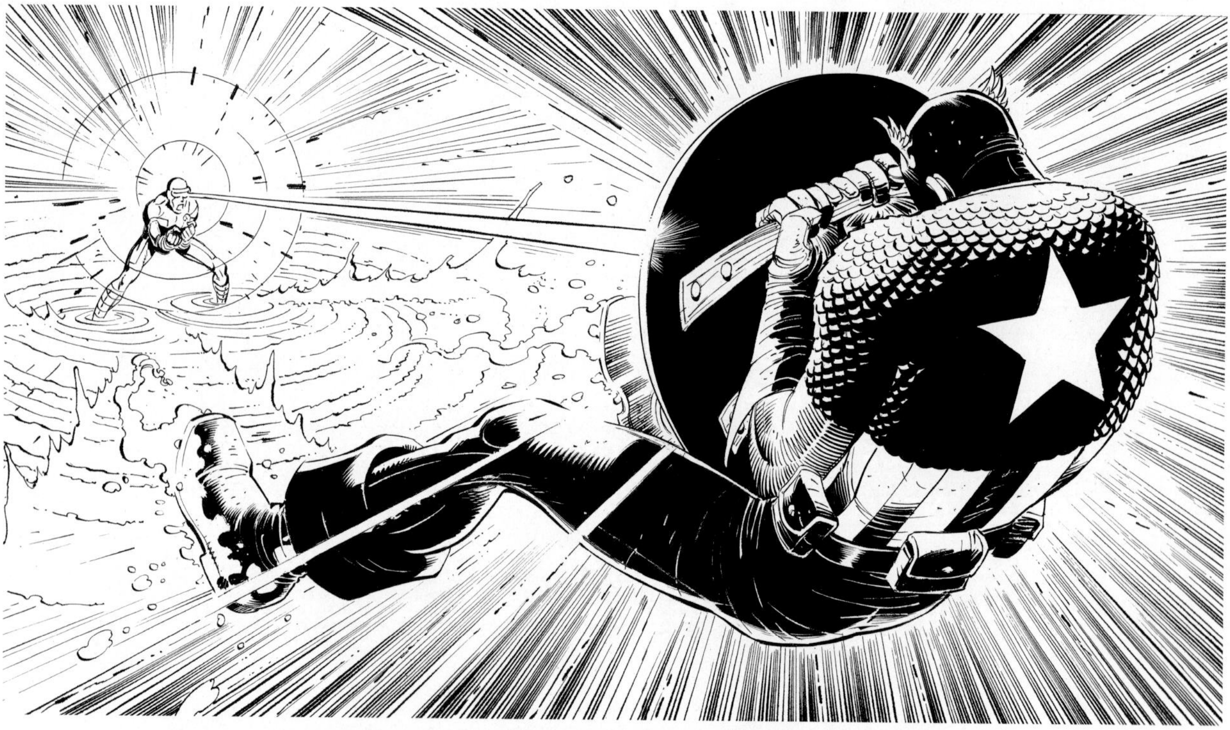

TOP: UNPUBLISHED PENCILS FROM *AVENGERS VS. X-MEN #1* BY JOHN ROMITA JR.
BOTTOM: FINAL ART FROM *AVENGERS VS. X-MEN #1* BY ROMITA JR. AND SCOTT HANNA.

"When a writer proposes a fun scene that works as a pinup shot — especially in a series like this where they are very few and far between — it is, to use a sporting analogy, like an open goal in soccer. Your eyes go wide, and you say 'Please don't let me screw this up!' That's your money shot, you can't screw those up. But with this one, the first time I read the script, in my mind all I read was Scott blasting Cap. I wanted to show the pain and the blast off the shield, and drew a close-up of the two characters. Brian called me up and said, 'Love it, but just would like to see Cap getting blasted into the distance because in the subsequent scene he's far away.' So there it was, I screwed it up and had to redo it! But it worked out very well. The powers of characters like Scott and Hope, which produce long-distance results, are a nice counter-balance to characters like the Red Hulk and Colossus. I love the boxing association when there's two hulking figures beating the snot out of each other, and I love the long-distance blasts. It's a nice juxtaposition."

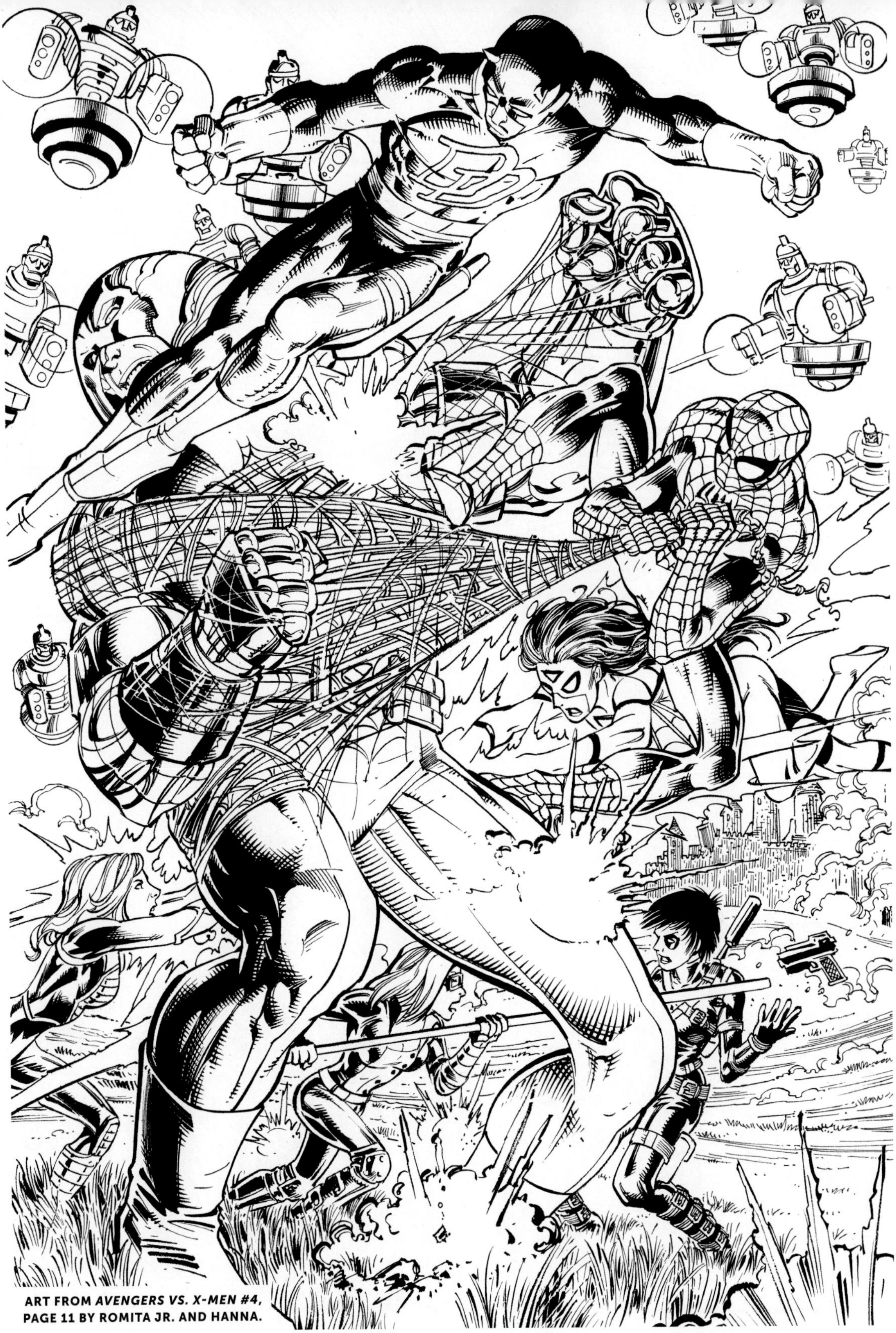

ART FROM *AVENGERS VS. X-MEN #4*, PAGE 11 BY ROMITA JR. AND HANNA.

"Whenever you are asked for a montage like this — a soup, a gigantic cake, a pizza of action, with characters fighting in all different directions — that is a real challenge to an artist. To have it make any sense at all is an accomplishment. If it turns into an iconic image, then you really have hit a home run. I don't know if I reached that point, but I remember thinking let's have this nice imbalance between some of the characters. In a battle like this, guys like Colossus would pick the ones he could conquer quickly, not necessarily going after their immediate equal. The only way guys like Spidey and DD could hold Colossus off would be to use their tools, Spidey trying to web him up and DD with his billy club. It brings back to mind that two-part story I did of Juggernaut vs. Spider-Man way back in the dark ages (*Amazing Spider-Man #229-230*), which I've been told was the point I finally crossed the line from struggling storyteller to a better one!"

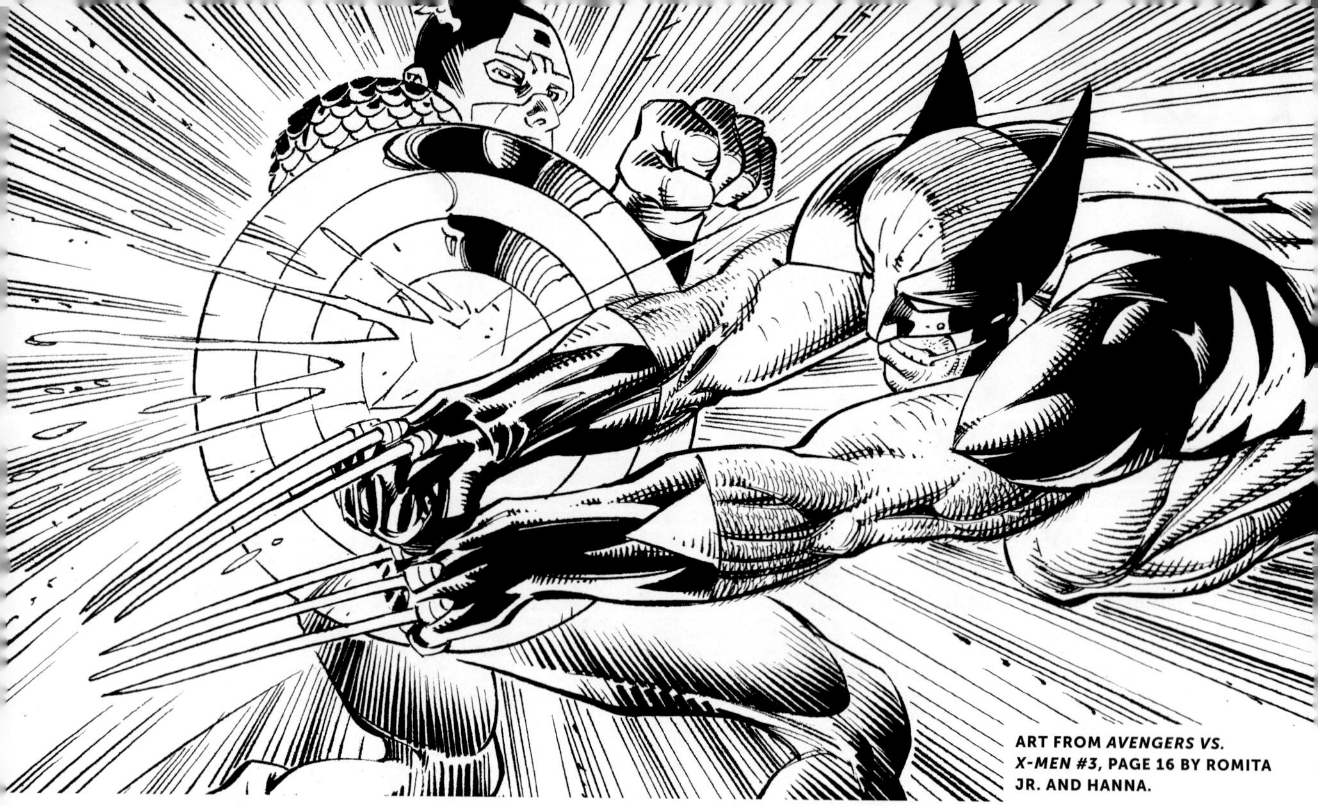

ART FROM *AVENGERS VS. X-MEN* #3, PAGE 16 BY ROMITA JR. AND HANNA.

"I was constantly looking at Olivier and Adam's work and thinking, 'Damn, I have to get better. I have to do better work than these guys, they're so good!' I told Adam that as long as he's in the business, he's my goal line, he's my bar. I think he's one of the best, if not the best in the business. And Olivier — beautiful work. *Beautiful* work. I was constantly trying to climb that greased pole to reach those two!"

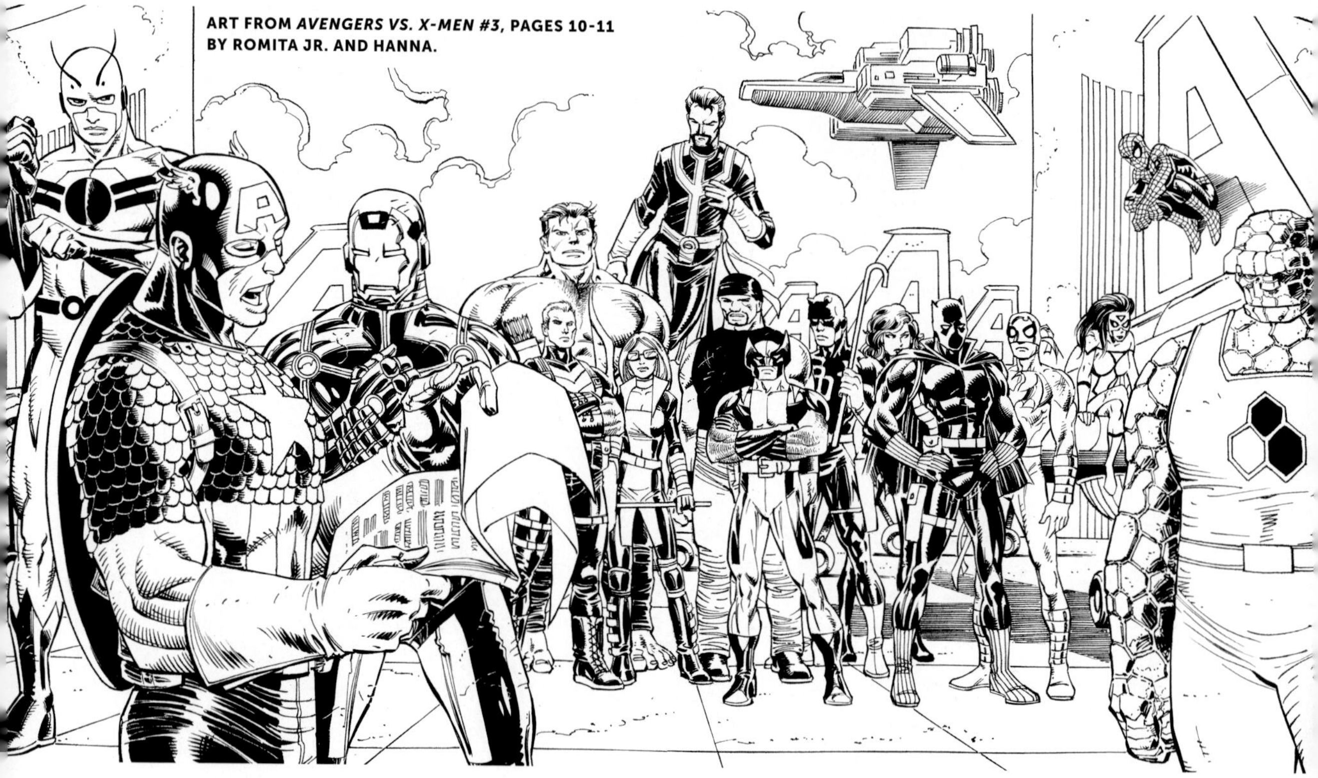

ART FROM *AVENGERS VS. X-MEN* #3, PAGES 10-11 BY ROMITA JR. AND HANNA.

"I enjoyed every minute of *Avengers vs. X-Men*, although it was probably the most grueling job I've ever been on. It was daunting to say the least — many, many characters. I have this bad habit of getting large and Cecil B. Demille-esque projects. I guess I can blame it all on the *Contest of Champions* book I did a million and one years ago! I guess I've got a reputation for being able to do that. I'm very proud of that, although sometimes it makes me want to hide. Writers go, 'I'm working with Romita, so let's bring everybody and his brother into this!' If somebody says to me, '*AvX* was a great series. I loved every minute of it,' as opposed to saying, 'You did a great job on the artwork,' that means I've done my job."

OLIVIER COIPEL

Though he may be the youngest of the bunch, **Olivier Coipel** is no stranger to the big leagues at Marvel: his high-profile projects include Brian Michael Bendis' *House of M*, J. Michael Straczynski's striking relaunch of *Thor* and a reunion with Bendis on *Siege*. His ability to depict human emotion even amid the massive scale of his layouts makes Olivier perfectly suited for events like *AVX*.

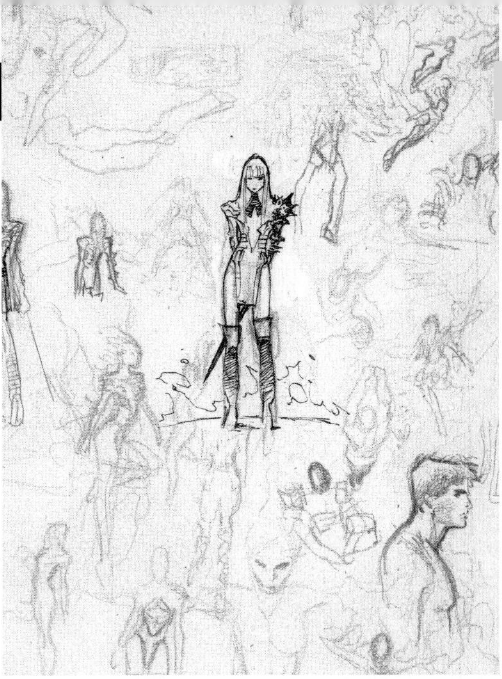

"Finding a design for the Phoenix Five was a bit tricky: Do you play with the classic Jean Grey/Phoenix costume, or do you go with something completely different? I decided to take the second option, since I couldn't picture Cyclops or Colossus in a green-and-gold costume. I chose to keep the bird design on the chest to keep the original theme intact, but then I played around with the rest of it!"

MAGIK AND X-MEN SKETCHES BY OLIVIER COIPEL.

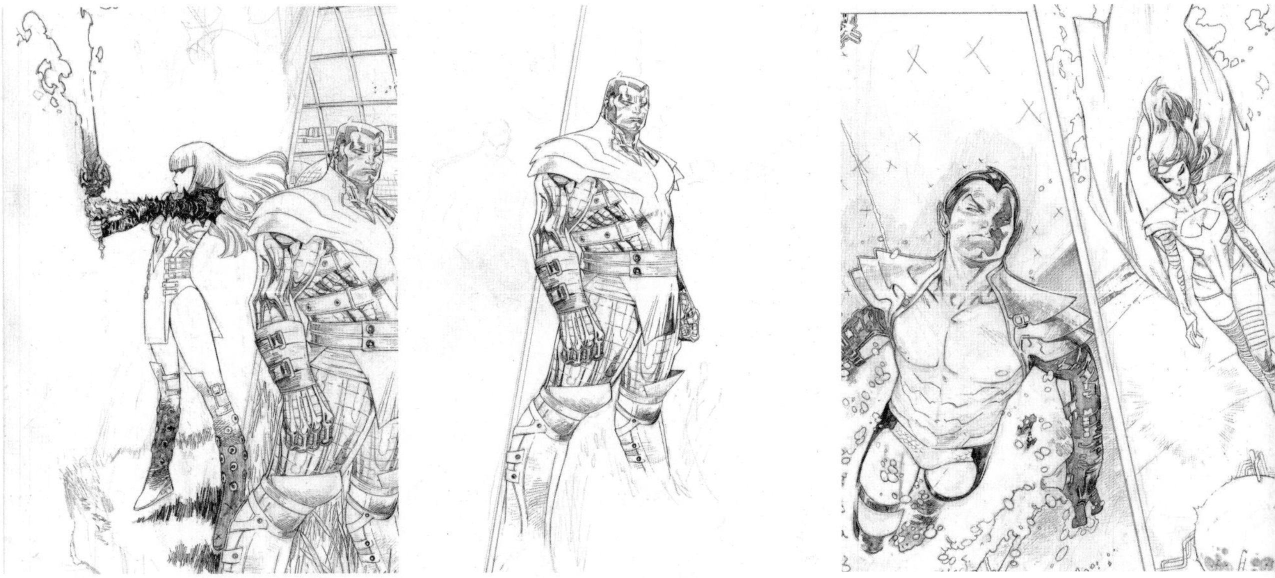

PENCILS OF THE PHOENIX FIVE FROM *AVENGERS VS. X-MEN #6*, PAGES 5-6 BY COIPEL.

"I find the theme of the Phoenix to be somewhat sexy. To achieve that, I combined the bird on the chest (and on the visor for Cyclops). Well, Magik couldn't be too sexy since she's so young, but with Emma I could go pretty far — too far? — since we all know it's part of her personality."

"In the end, I had fun playing with all of them. The only regret I have is that if I knew how the story was to end, (colorist) Laura Martin and I would have chosen yellow and black for Cyclops, and then showed the change of his personality happening slowly throughout the book by slightly fading the yellow to red."

PHOENIX FIVE COLOR GUIDE

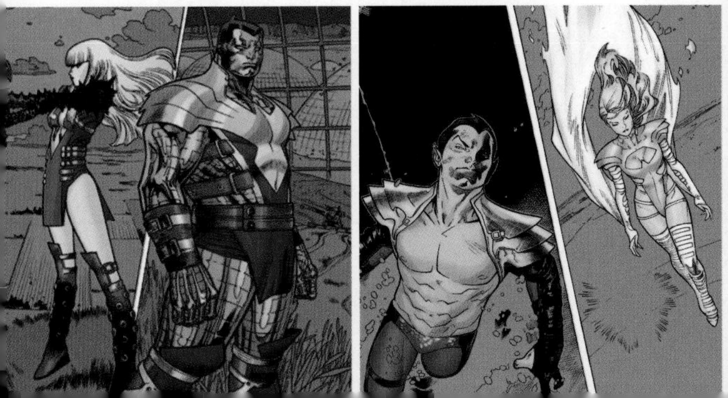

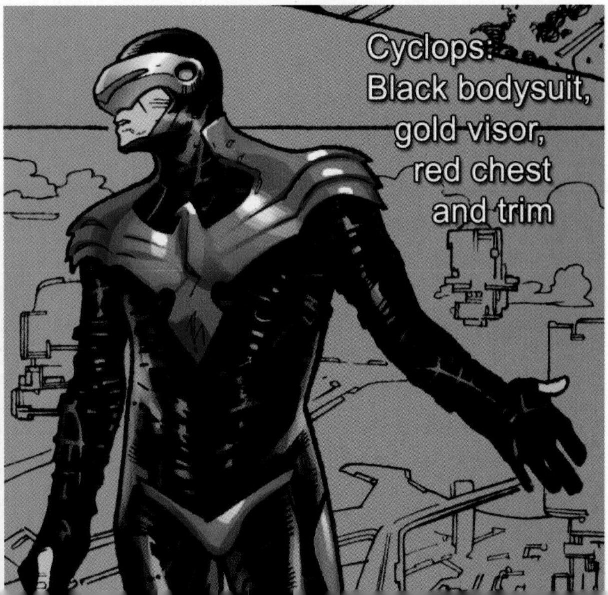
Cyclops:
Black bodysuit,
gold visor,
red chest
and trim

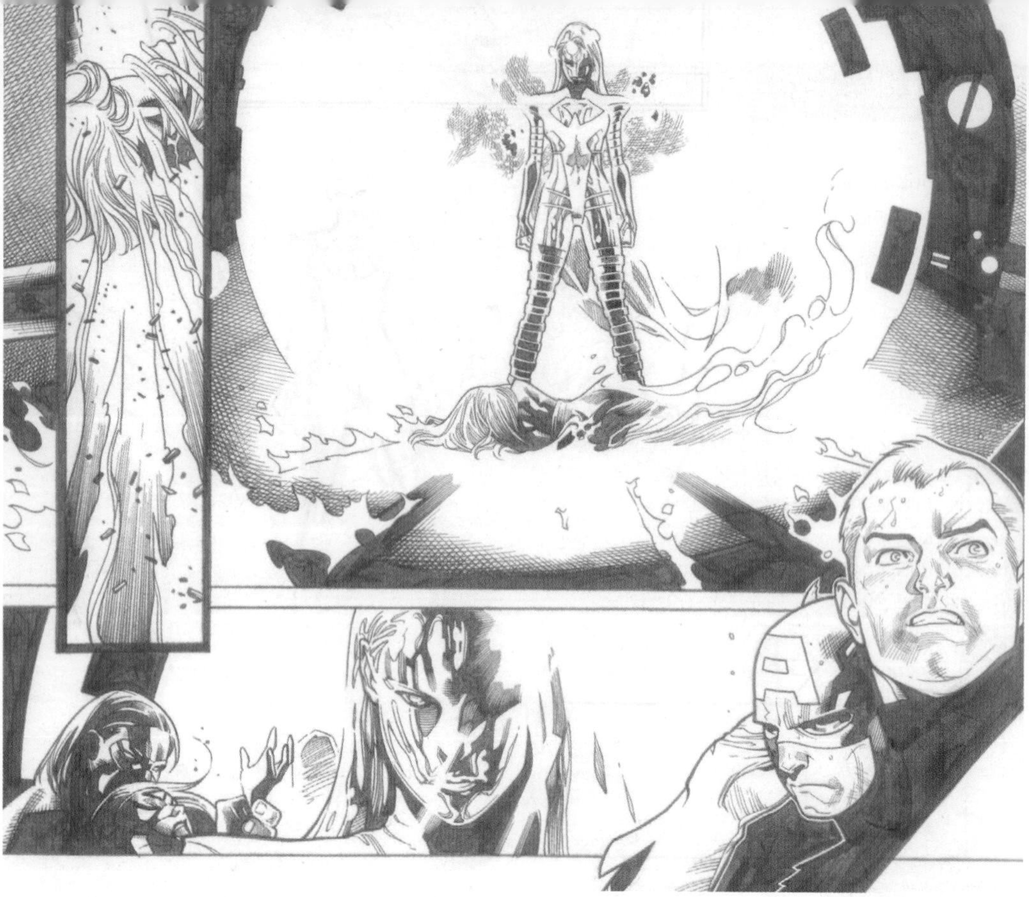

PENCILS FROM *AVENGERS VS. X-MEN #7*, PAGE 6 BY COIPEL.

"The scene in issue #7 where Emma attacks the Avengers to defend Magik was the first time I could visually explore the Phoenix power. I wanted to try something a bit different from the classic firebird in the background and go a bit more 3D, mixing the two entities (Emma and the Phoenix bird)."

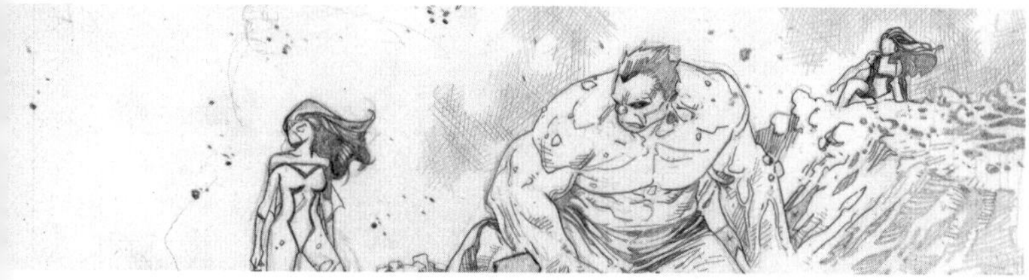

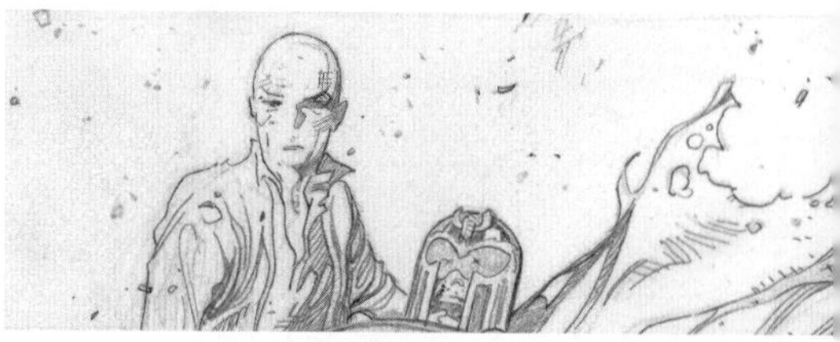

PENCILS FROM *AVENGERS VS. X-MEN #11*, PAGE 24 BY COIPEL.

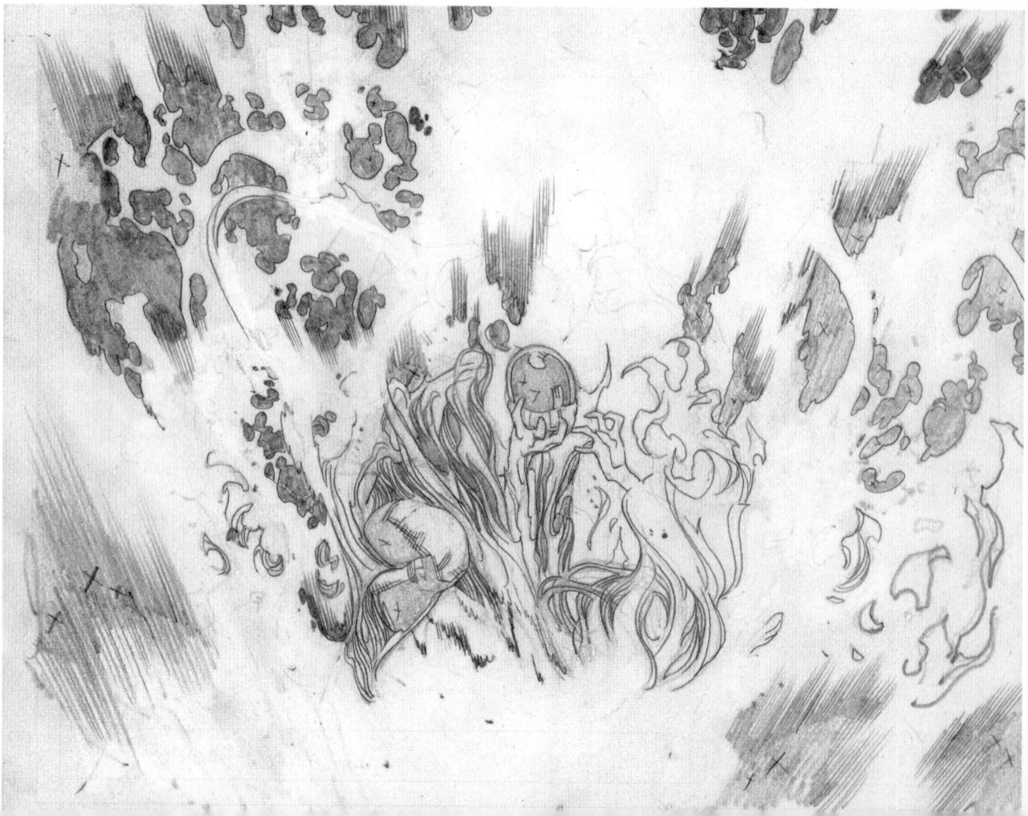

ADAM KUBERT

Alongside brother Andy, **Adam Kubert** is part of a combo that took comics by storm during the early '90s and never let up. Both sons of legendary comic artist Joe Kubert, they've nonetheless created their own indelible identities. Adam's landmark runs on *Incredible Hulk* and *Wolverine* established him as a star capable of showcasing the ferocity of Marvel's premier characters, and his recent return to the House of Ideas with *Astonishing Spider-Man & Wolverine* further reinforced his Marvel bona fides.

PENCILS FROM *AVENGERS VS. X-MEN #8*, PAGES 1-2 BY KUBERT.

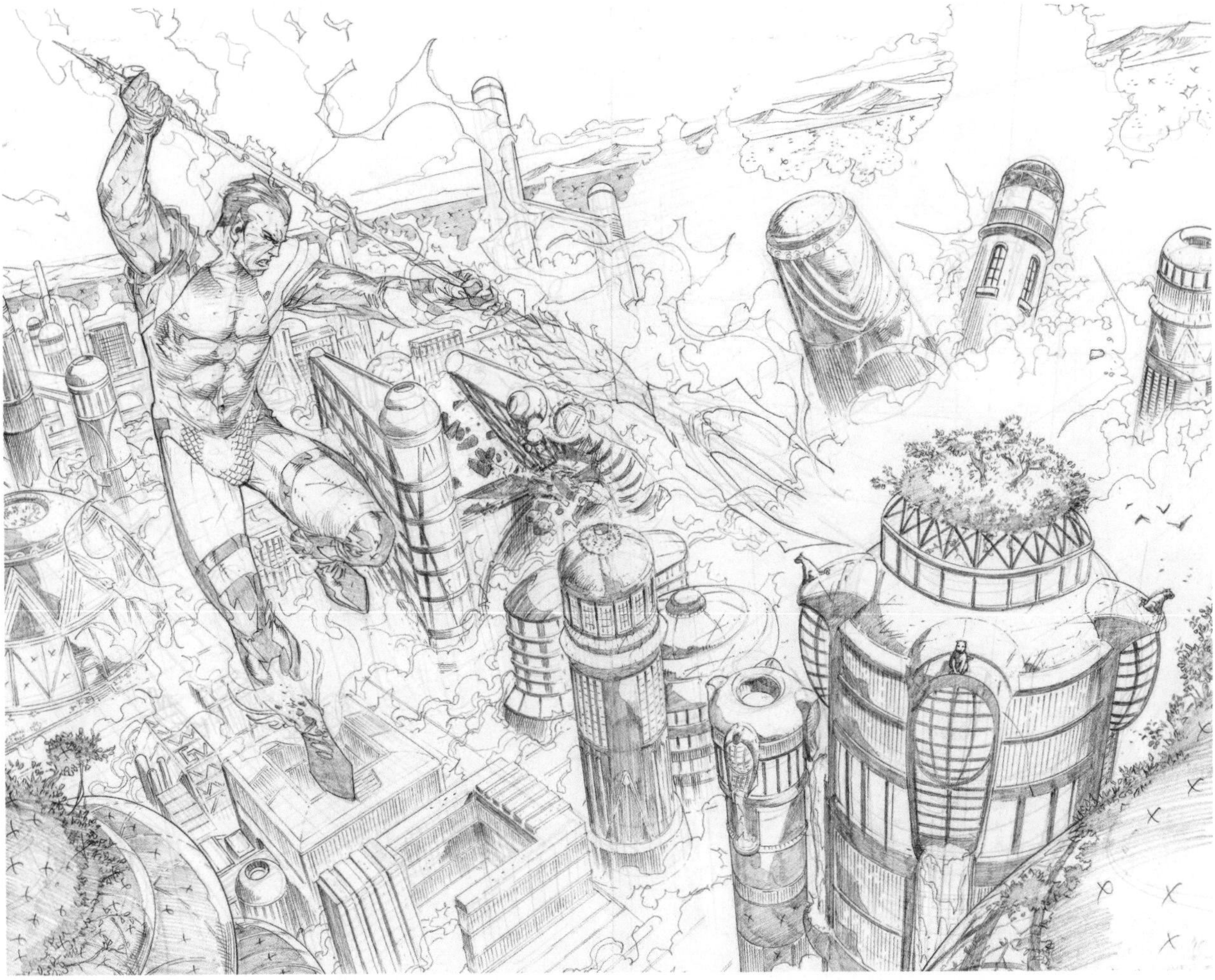

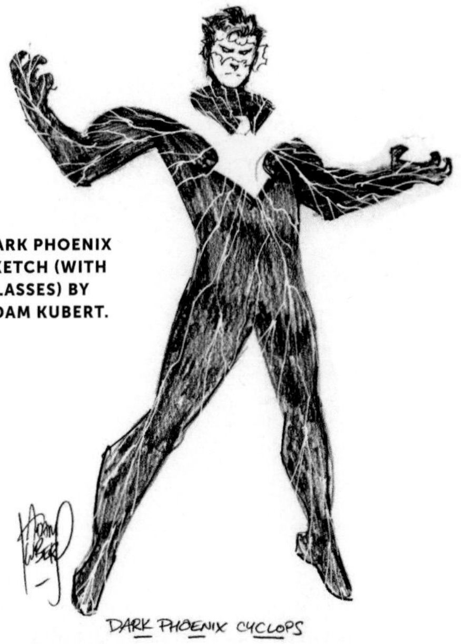
DARK PHOENIX CYCLOPS

DARK PHOENIX SKETCH (WITH GLASSES) BY ADAM KUBERT.

"The Dark Phoenix Cyclops design was a very difficult one, mainly because Olivier had already designed an awesomely dark Cyclops Phoenix as one of his Phoenix Five, which made it that much more difficult for my redesign. Basically, I had to come up with an even *darker* Dark Phoenix!

"Along with editorial, Olivier and I were trying to decide whether or not Cyclops should continue donning his goggles once he evolved into the Dark Phoenix. We decided to keep them. We thought the goggles were too much a part of his character to omit them. But after I did a bunch of sketches with different variations of Cyke with the goggles, I didn't like any of them. Long story short: I removed the goggles, turned his costume completely black, and designed a lightning-type effect emanating from the Phoenix symbol on his chest. Then we gave it to "The Colorista" (Laura Martin) to perform her color magic."

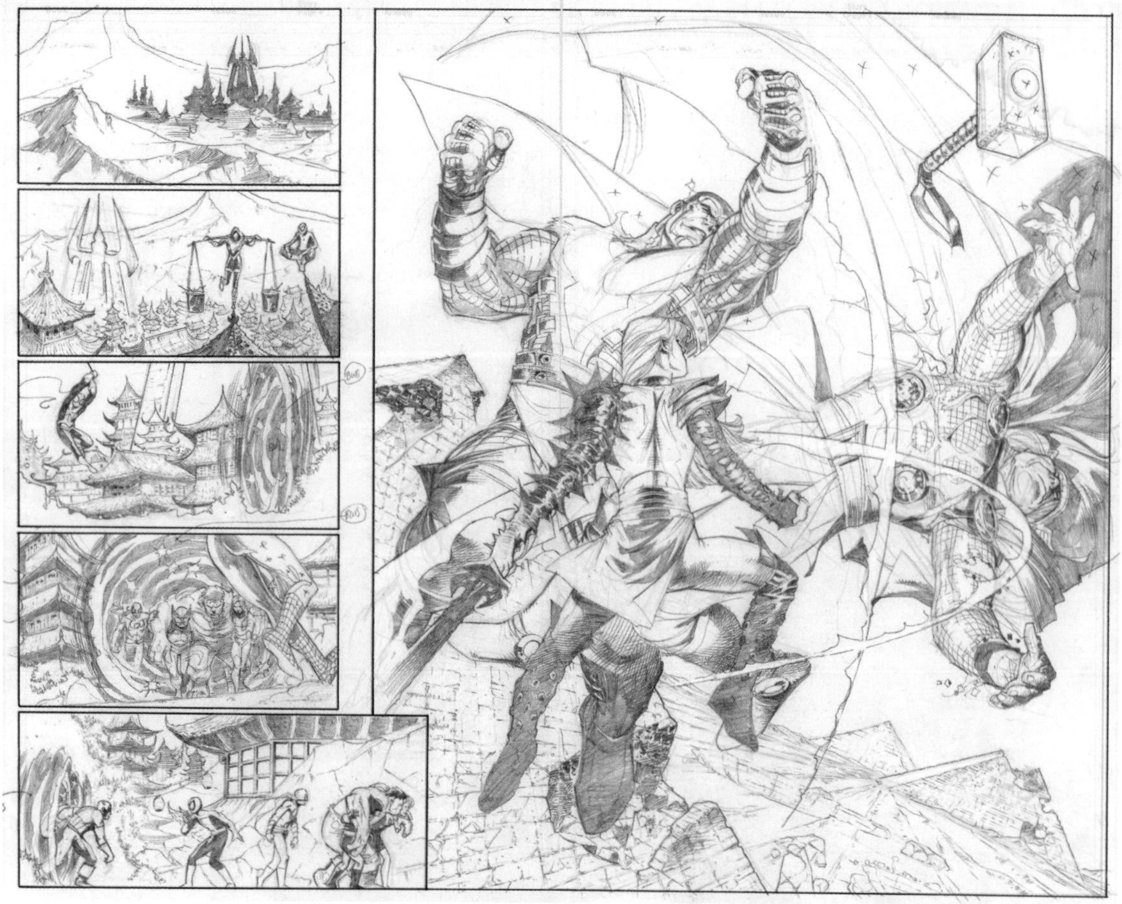

PENCILS FROM *AVENGERS VS. X-MEN #8*, PAGES 1-2 BY KUBERT.

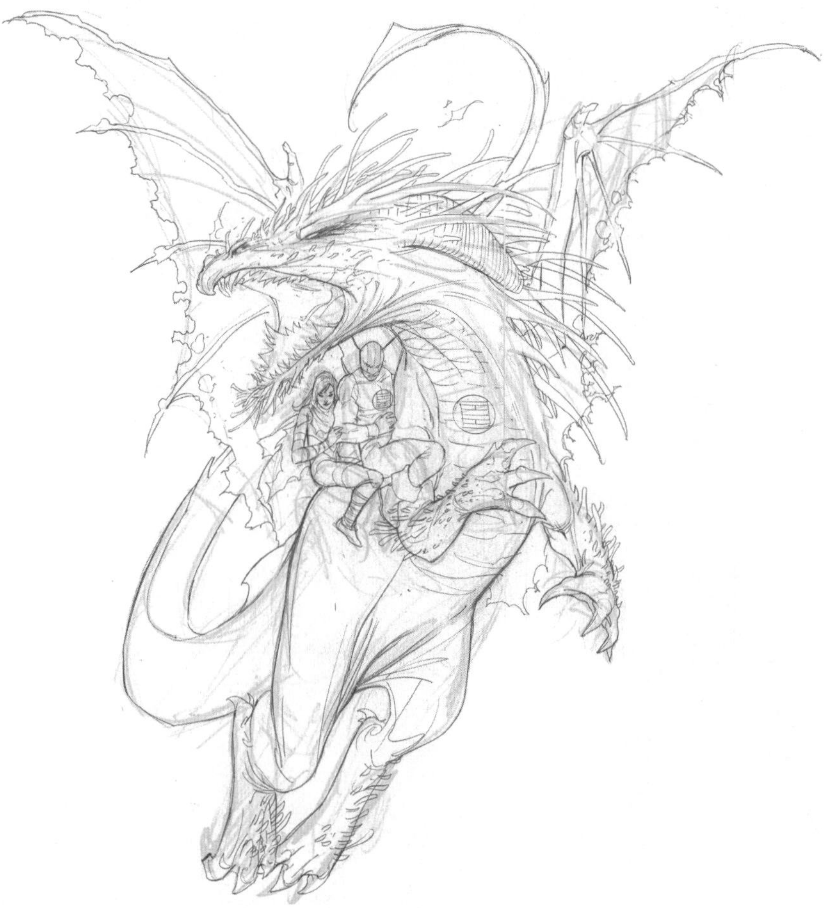

PENCILS FROM *AVENGERS VS. X-MEN #10*, PAGES 12-13 BY KUBERT.

PENCILS FROM *AVENGERS VS. X-MEN #8*, PAGE 5 BY KUBERT.

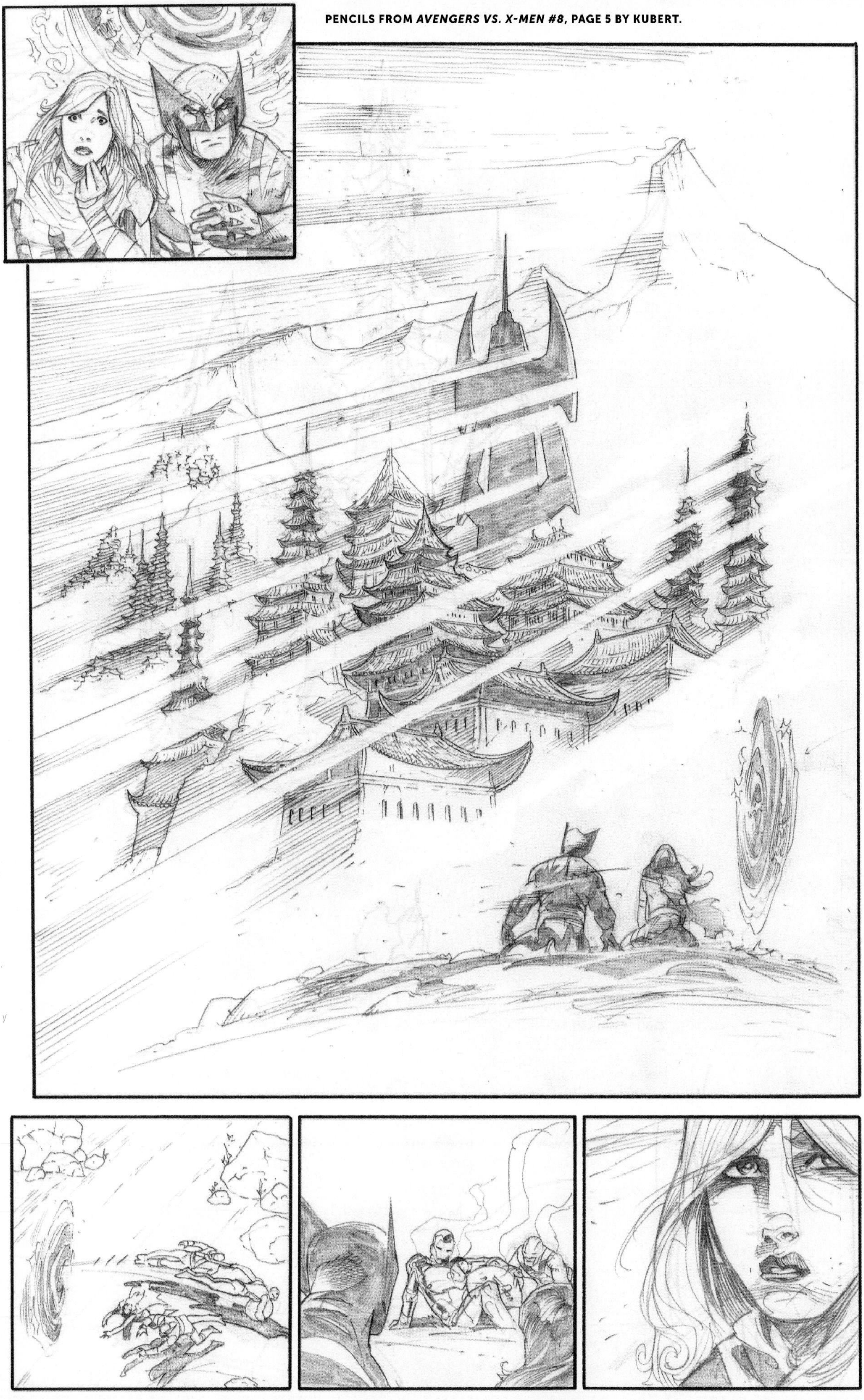

THE SCORECARD!

★ ★ ★ ★

★ ★ ★ ★

WANT TO KNOW WHO BEAT WHOM, WHEN, WHERE AND HOW? FOLLOW OUR PAINSTAKINGLY RESEARCHED GUIDE TO THE FIGHTS OF *AVX!*

THE KEY TO VICTORY:

AVENGERS WIN!	X-MEN WIN!	DISSENSION IN THE RANKS OF THE AVENGERS!	DISSENSION IN THE RANKS OF THE X-MEN!	WILD CARD! A NEUTRAL PARTY TAKES DECISIVE ACTION!

★ ★ ★ **I: UNREST ON UTOPIA!** ★ ★ ★

◄ **KEY BATTLE**
Cyclops strikes the first blow, optic-blasting **Captain America**! But Cap gets in a couple good shield strikes to the head. Honors even! (*AvX #1,2*)

Avengers vs. **Colossus** (*AvX #2*)

Luke Cage vs. **Namor** (*AvX #2*)

Red Hulk vs. **Colossus** (*AvX #2, Uncanny X-Men #11*)	**Quicksilver** vs. **Magneto** (*AvX #2*)	**KEY BATTLE** **Namor** sends **Thing** flying out of the ocean, but Thing splashes back to get the drop on his old foe! (*AvX #2, Vs. #1*)	**Spider-Man** vs. **Warpath** (*AvX #2*)	**Iron Fist** vs. **Domino** (*AvX #2*)
	Iron Man vs **Emma Frost** (*AvX #2*)		**Wolverine** vs. **Magma** and **Sunspot** (*AvX #2*)	**Black Widow** vs. **Jubilee** (*AvX #2*)
Daredevil vs. **Warpath** (*AvX #2*)	**Spider-Woman** vs. **Psylocke** (*AvX #2*)	**Iron Man** vs. **Dr. Nemesis** (*AvX #2*)	**Giant-Man** vs. **Sunspot** (*AvX #2*)	**KEY BATTLE** **Hope Summers** roasts **Wolverine**! (And singes **Spider-Man**!) (*AvX #2, UXM #11*)
KEY BATTLE ▶ After a preliminary skirmish is interrupted, **Iron Man** proves himself too clever for the Master of Magnetism, **Magneto**! (*AvX #2, Vs. #1*)		**KEY BATTLE** **Magik** gives **Dr. Strange** hell in Limbo! (*AvX #2,3*)		**Hope Summers** vs. **Loa**, **Pixie**, **Surge**, **Transonic** and **Velocidad** (*AvX #2*)
		Dr. Strange vs. **Emma Frost** and **Magneto** (*AvX #2*)		

II: AvX GOES GLOBAL!

KEY BATTLE
Captain America (with a little help from **Giant-Man**) kicks insubordinate **Wolverine** out of a plane over the Arctic Circle! (*AvX #3*)

KEY BATTLE ▶
Love hurts for **Black Panther** and **Storm**, as husband and wife face trouble and strife in Wakanda. The only casualty? Their marriage! (*Vs. #5*)

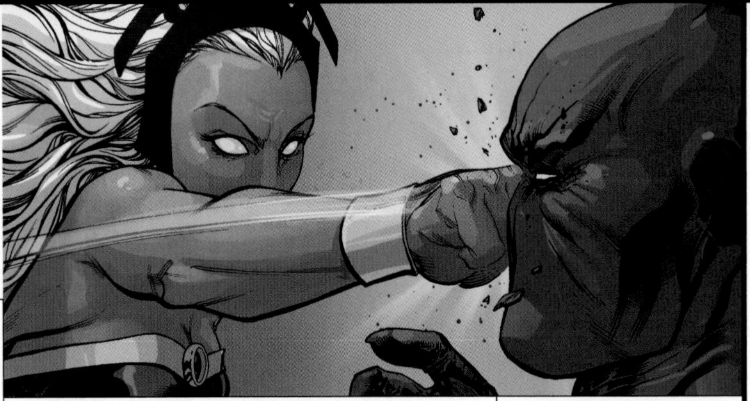

Black Widow, **Black Panther**, **Iron Fist** and **Quicksilver** vs. **Danger**, **Dr. Nemesis**, **Magma**, **Rachel Summers** and **Storm** *— in Wakanda (AvX #4, Wolverine & the X-Men #11)*

Red Hulk vs. **Iceman** and **Kid Gladiator** *— in Wundagore (Wolverine & The X-Men #11)*
Captain America and **Giant-Man** vs. **Gambit**, **Magik**, **Warpath** and **X-Man** *— in the Savage Land (AvX #4)*

Daredevil, **Mockingbird**, **Spider-Man** and **Spider-Woman** vs. **Colossus**, **Dazzler** and **Domino** *— in Latveria (AvX #4)*

Dr. Strange, **Hawkeye** and **Red Hulk** vs. **Angel**, **Iceman**, **Magneto** and **Psylocke** *— in Wundagore (AvX#4)*

KEY BATTLE
A battered **Spider-Man** beats a retreat after a points victory for **Colossus** in Latveria! (*AvX #4, Vs. #2*)

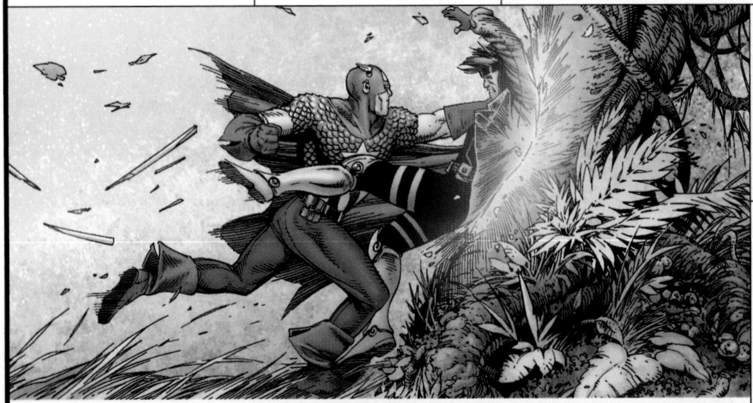

▲KEY BATTLE
Captain America's shield trumps **Gambit**'s playing cards as the ragin' Cajun's face takes a Savage Land beating! (*AvX #4, Vs. #2*)

Luke Cage, **She-Hulk** and **Thing** vs. **Namor**, **Sunspot** and **Hepzibah** *— in Tabula Rasa (AvX #4, UXM #12)*

KEY BATTLE
Hawkeye listens to the devil on his shoulder, suckering a retreating **Angel** with an arrow on snowy Wundagore Mountain! (*Vs. #5*)

Falcon, **Iron Man**, **Moon Knight** and **She-Hulk** vs. **Cannonball**, **Chamber**, **Frenzy**, **Gambit**, **Kitty Pryde** and **Mimic** *— at the Jean Grey School, Westchester (X-Men Legacy #266-267)*

Captain Marvel, **Ms. Marvel** and **Protector** vs. **Beast**, **Captain Britain**, **Ms. Marvel**, **Thor**, **Valkyrie**, **Vision**, **War Machine** *— on Hala (Secret Avengers #27-28)*

Protector vs. **Beast**, **Captain Britain**, **Ms. Marvel**, **Thor**, **Valkyrie**, **Vision**, **War Machine** *— in Space (Avengers #26-27)*

III: LUNAR MADNESS ON THE BLUE AREA OF THE MOON!

KEY BATTLE **Magik** wins her game of Russian Roulette with the **Black Widow**! (*AvX #5, Vs. #3*)

Red Hulk vs. **Colossus** (*AvX #5*)

Wolverine vs. **Cyclops** (*AvX #5*)

Hawkeye vs. **Emma Frost** (*AvX #5*)

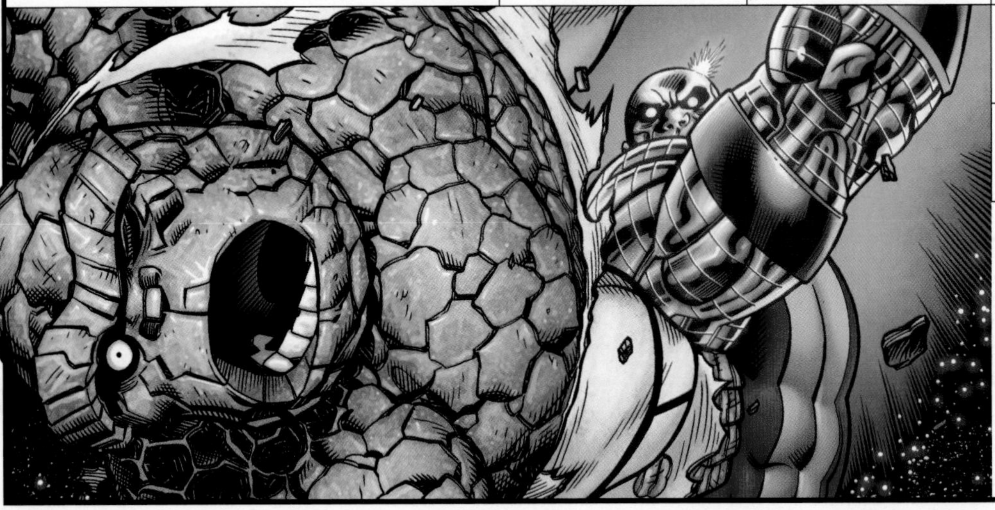

Thing vs. **Namor** (*AvX #5*)

Captain America vs. **Cyclops** (*AvX #5*)

◀KEY BATTLE
Colossus reluctantly embraces the power of the unstoppable Juggernaut to take down the **Thing**! (*AvX #5, Vs. #3*)

IV: REIGN OF THE PHOENIX FIVE!

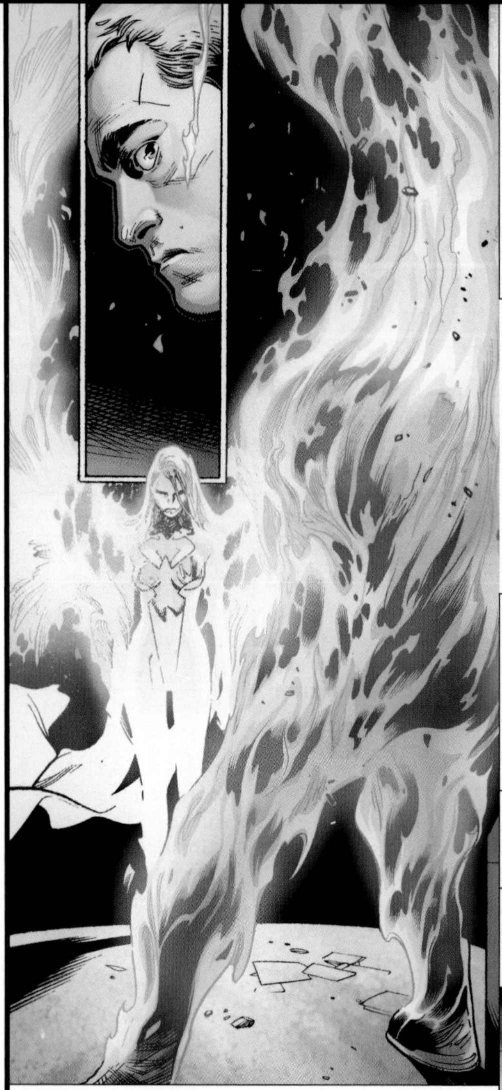

Black Widow, **Captain America**, **Hawkeye**, **Iron Fist**, **Iron Man**, **Spider-Woman**, **Thor** and **Wolverine** vs. **Cyclops** and **Emma Frost** — *on Utopia* (*AvX #6*)

Beast, **Black Widow**, **Captain America**, **Giant-Man**, **Quicksilver**, **Spider-Woman**, **Thor**, **Valkyrie**, **War Machine** and **Wolverine** vs. **Angel**, **Iceman**, **Kid Gladiator**, **Namor** and **Rachel Summers** vs. **Professor X** (*Wolverine & the X-Men #12*, *Avengers #29*)

Captain America, **Hawkeye**, **Iron Fist**, **Scarlet Witch**, **Spider-Woman** and **Vision** vs. **Gambit**, **Havok**, **Magik**, **Polaris**, **Warpath** and **X-Man** (*AvX #7*)

◄ **KEY BATTLE**
Phoenix-powered **Emma Frost** fends off **Scarlet Witch** and burns **Hawkeye** alive, taking the first major prisoner of AvX! (*AvX #7*)

Falcon, **Quicksilver**, **Thor** and **Wolverine** vs. **Boom Boom**, **Domino**, **Emma Frost**, **Surge**, **Velocidad** and **Warpath** — *in Ukraine* (*AvX #7*)

Captain America, **Daredevil**, **Luke Cage**, **Sharon Carter** and **Spider-Man** vs. **Colossus**, **Danger**, **Magma**, **Psylocke** and **Sunspot** — *in New York* (*AvX #7*)

Beast, **Giant-Man**, **Red Hulk**, **She-Hulk** and **Valkyrie** vs. **Armor**, **Cyclops**, **Dr. Nemesis** and **Magneto** — *in the Arctic Circle* (*AvX #7*)

KEY BATTLE
Daredevil is in his element against the deadly ninja skills of **Psylocke** on the rooftops of New York, but it's his line of argument that sows the first seeds of doubt in her mind! (*Vs. #4*)

KEY BATTLE **Scarlet Witch** sends **Namor** reeling back to Utopia with an imperious hex! (*AvX #7*)

Colossus vs. **Deathlok**, **Doop**, **Husk**, **Kitty Pryde**, **Krakoa**, **Lockheed** and **Toad** — *at the Jean Grey School, Westchester* (*Wolverine & the X-Men #14*)

Dr. Strange, **Mockingbird** and **Thing** vs. **Iceman**, **Namor**, **Polaris** and **Transonic** — *in the Pacific Ocean* (*AvX #7*)

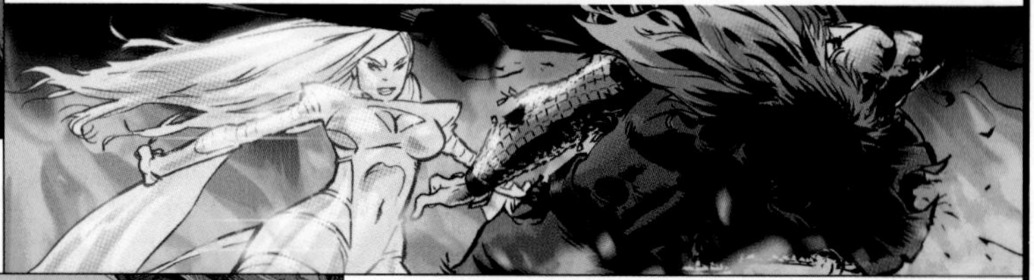

▲ **KEY BATTLE** **Emma Frost** proves herself the ultimate blonde bombshell as she puts down **Thor**! (*Vs. #4*)

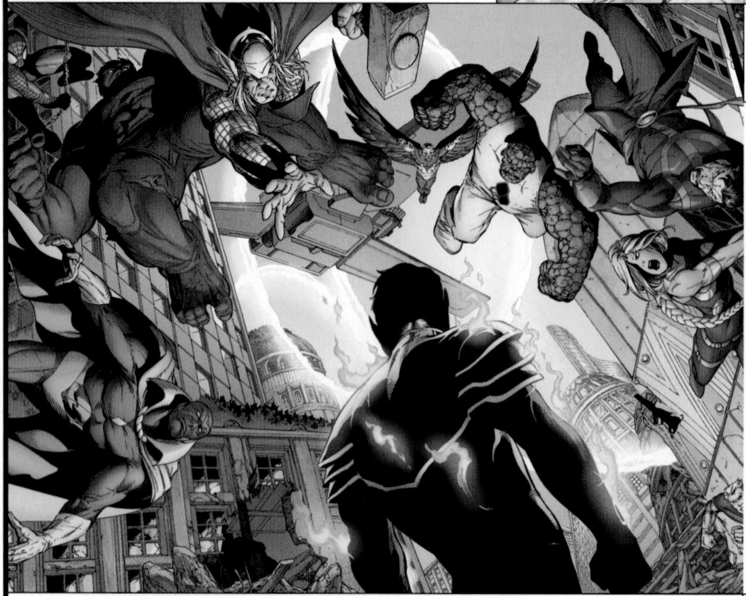

◄ **KEY BATTLE**
It's a rumble in the jungle as **Namor** devastates Wakanda, but then gets taken out of the game by **Scarlet Witch** and an awesome assemblage of Avengers: **Beast**, **Black Panther**, **Captain America**, **Daredevil**, **Dr. Strange**, **Falcon**, **Iron Fist**, **Quicksilver**, **Red-Hulk**, **Spider-Man**, **Thing**, **Thor**, **Vision**

Thing vs. **Angel**, **Iceman** and **Magik** — *in New York* (*Wolverine & the X-Men #13*)

Finesse, **Giant-Man**, **Hazmat**, **Lightspeed**, **Mettle**, **Reptil**, **Striker**, **Tigra**, **White Tiger** and **X-23** vs. **Emma Frost** — *at Avengers Academy, Los Angeles* (*Avengers Academy #32-33*)

Hawkeye, **Luke Cage** and **Spider-Woman** vs. **Danger** (and simulations of **Colossus**, **Cyclops**, **Emma Frost**, **Gambit**, **Havok**, **Polaris**, **Psylocke**, **Sunspot** and **Warpath**) — *in the X-Brig, Utopia* (*New Avengers #28*)

KEY BATTLE The brother-and-sister tag team of **Colossus** and **Magik** capture **Thor** in Egypt! (AvX #9)

KEY BATTLE **Rogue** captures her rival **Ms. Marvel** in New Orleans, but her conscience is pricked — and allegiance altered — by **Magik**'s hellish prison! (*X-Men Legacy #269-270*)

Black Panther, Captain America, Dr. Strange, Iron Fist, Professor X, She-Hulk, Spider-Man, Storm and **Wolverine** vs. **Colossus** and **Magik** — *in Russia* (*AvX #9*)	KEY BATTLE ▶ **Spider-Man** takes the licking of a lifetime from **Colossus** and **Magik**, but keeps on ticking — using his wits to turn them against each other! (*AvX #9*)

 Red Hulk vs. **Colossus, Cyclops, Emma Frost, Magik** and **Magneto** — *on Utopia* (*Avengers #28*)

V: EVERYBODY KUNG FU FIGHTING IN K'UN LUN!

Iron Fist vs. **Cyclops** (*AvX #10*)	KEY BATTLE **Hope Summers** works out her frustrations with **Scarlet Witch**! (*AvX #12, Vs. #6*) 
Iron Man vs. **Cyclops** (*AvX #10*)	
Hawkeye, Thing and **Thor** vs. **Cyclops** (*AvX #10*)	
◀ KEY BATTLE The one-time savior of the X-Men — **Hope Summers**, now siding with the Avengers — uses her K'un-Lun training and the power of a dragon to hit **Cyclops** with the Chaos Fist! (*AvX #10*)	

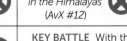
VI: THE FINAL BATTLE!

The combined forces of the **Avengers** and the **X-Men** mount a final attack on Utopia, and the Phoenix-powered **Cyclops** and **Emma Frost**! (*AvX #11*)			**Storm** vs. **Emma Frost** (*AvX #11*)	**Captain America** vs. **Cyclops** (*AvX #11*)
Scarlet Witch vs. **Cyclops** (*AvX #11*)	**Scarlet Witch** vs. **Emma Frost** (*AvX #11*)	**Hulk** vs. **Emma Frost** (*AvX #11*)	**Magneto** and **Scarlet Witch** vs. **Cyclops** (*AvX #11*)	**Thor** vs. **Cyclops** (*AvX #11*)
Hawkeye vs. **Cyclops** (*AvX #11*)	**Iceman** vs. **Cyclops** (*AvX #11*)	KEY BATTLE Needing more firepower, **Cyclops** turns on his lover and only ally, **Emma Frost**, to become Dark Phoenix! (*AvX #11*)		
KEY BATTLE Consumed with rage, **Cyclops** takes the life of his mentor, **Professor X**! (*AvX #11*)	**Wolverine** vs. **Cyclops** (*AvX #11*)	**Thor** vs. **Cyclops** — *in the Himalayas* (*AvX #12*)	**Beast, Captain America, Iron Man, Iron Fist, Storm** and **Wolverine** vs. **Cyclops** — *in the Himalayas* (*AvX#12*)	
	Hulk vs. **Cyclops** — *in Sydney, Australia* (*AvX #12*)	KEY BATTLE With the Avengers reeling, **Nova** enters the fray just in time to bring Cyclops to ground in Tibet — but only **Cyclops** walks away from the landing! (*AvX #12*)		
Havok, Hulk, Iceman, Iron Man, Ms. Marvel, Rachel Summers, Red Hulk, Storm, Thing and **Thor** vs. **Cyclops** — *around the globe* (*AvX #12*)		KEY BATTLE In the climactic showdown, only the combined power of **Scarlet Witch** and **Hope Summers** can tear the Phoenix away from a beaten **Cyclops**! (*AvX #12*)		

Now that the dust has settled, and the scorecards are all in, we make it **20** decisive wins to the **X-Men** and **10** to the **Avengers**. But while the X-Men may have won twice as many battles, only you can decide who — if anyone — won the war!

WRITTEN BY **JESS HARROLD** WITH **JOHN RHETT THOMAS** • DESIGNED BY **RODOLFO MURAGUCHI**